UNIVERSITY CASEBOOK SERIES

CASES AND MATERIALS

INTELLECTUAL PROPERTY

Trademark, Copyright and Patent Law

by

ROCHELLE COOPER DREYFUSS
Professor of Law
New York University

ROBERTA ROSENTHAL KWALL
Professor of Law
DePaul University College of Law

WESTBURY, NEW YORK
THE FOUNDATION PRESS, INC.
1996

 TEXT IS PRINTED ON 10% POST CONSUMER RECYCLED PAPER   Printed with  Environmentally Advanced Water Washable Ink

WE WISH TO DEDICATE THIS BOOK WITH LOVE TO OUR
RESPECTIVE HUSBANDS:

ROBERT M. DREYFUSS

and

JEFFREY L. KWALL

*

ACKNOWLEDGEMENTS

Many people have assisted in the preparation of this book whom we would like to thank. Those legal professionals who have been particularly helpful during various stages of our project include A. Sidney Katz of Welsh & Katz; Frank Vitalos and Bernard Dietz, Heads of the Renewal Section of the Examining Division of the Copyright Office; John Lyhus of Thomson & Thomson; and Kent Dunlap, Principal Legal Advisor for the General Counsel of the U.S. Copyright Office. For teaching from our materials in draft and providing us with helpful suggestions and comments, we gratefully acknowledge A. Samuel Oddi of Northern Illinois University. For providing us with reprints of photographs and other inserts, we wish to add a special thanks to sculptor James Earl Reid, photographer Ron Portee, and Terry Abrahamson. We also wish to thank the Vanderbilt Law Review, the Chicago Sun Times and Wendy Gordon for granting us permission to reprint portions of various articles. To Dean John Roberts of DePaul University, we extend our gratitude for his ongoing support.

Many students also have played an important role in the preparation of this casebook and we would like to thank all of them for their tireless efforts. From DePaul, William Eipert, Melissa Campbell, Joshua Povsner, Anu Gupta and Marko Iglendza. From New York University, David Marsh, Kathleen Jennings, Daniel Barnaby Gibson, and Pierre Hubert. In addition, Professor Dreyfuss acknowledges the contribution that her secretary, Sheryl Jackson, has made to this effort and the financial support of the Filomen D'Agostino and Max E. Greenberg Research Fund, as well as the Alfred B. Engelberg Center on Innovation Law and Policy.

Professor Kwall also would like to say a special thank you to her parents, Millie and Abe Rosenthal, for keeping those intellectual property articles coming, and to her three daughters, Shanna, Rachel, and Nisa, for helping her keep a sense of perspective throughout this project. For her part, Professor Dreyfuss thanks her mother, Dorothy Gartner, for showing her how to juggle a professional career and children. Special gratitude is also owed to the jugglees, Marc and Nicole.

Though this may sound corny and somewhat unorthodox, we would also like to acknowledge one another. Writing a casebook involves a certain amount of drudgery. Our relationship, which combined intense scholarly discussion with many a good giggle, was both professionally satisfying and a great deal of fun.

Finally, we both would like to extend our appreciation to the person who inspired the problem method approach we have adopted in this casebook, Professor Edward H. Rabin of the University of California at Davis School of Law.

ROCHELLE COOPER DREYFUSS
ROBERTA ROSENTHAL KWALL

APRIL, 1996

SUMMARY OF CONTENTS

*

TABLE OF CONTENTS

TABLE OF CASES

Principal cases are in bold type. Non-principal cases are in roman type. References are to pages.

xix

*

INTELLECTUAL PROPERTY

Trademark, Copyright and Patent Law

*

INTRODUCTION TO INTELLECTUAL PROPERTY

Frequently students deciding which upper level courses to pursue in law school are genuinely puzzled by the term "intellectual property." The term seemingly conjures up images of the study of highly complex and esoteric but nonetheless mysterious subject matter. In some respects, this image is not all that far from the truth, since in all candor the study of intellectual property does include a large degree of sophisticated subject matter. We can, however, clarify the mysterious nature of the area at the outset. The "core" subjects of intellectual property are trademarks, copyrights and patents. Each of these areas is governed by a federal statute. In addition, intellectual property encompasses state law analogues such as trade secrets, the right of publicity, moral rights, traditional unfair competition, as well as trademark dilution and misappropriation.

Although some of these topics may seem quite unfamiliar at the outset, it is important to keep in mind that they all define the property rights of owners of intangible assets. Copyrights and patents protect ownership rights with respect to products created through intellectual efforts such as writings and inventions (although this definition of subject matter suffices for this Introduction, you will soon see that it is vastly oversimplified). Trademarks, which indicate the source of a particular product or service, protect the investment businesses make in goodwill. Thus, the intangible nature of intellectual property contrasts with the more tangible nature of realty and personalty, the study of which will be familiar to those of you who have already taken a property course. As we will demonstrate below, the doctrines and theoretical underpinnings of all types of property law are similar. Therefore, before embarking on a specific study of the areas of intellectual property, it will be useful to consider generally both the theoretical similarities as well as the differences between property law and intellectual property.

Nearly all of the doctrines of intellectual property as well as tangible property law reflect a fundamental tension between the desires of property owners versus the desires of other people or entities. Examples of this tension in real property law include a landowner's inability to exclude people from her property in certain circumstances;[1] the doctrines that define the respective rights of landlords and tenants; and zoning laws which attempt to balance a landowner's interests against those of the government.

Similarly, trademark law generally deals with balancing the rights of trademark owners and others who wish to use the same or a similar trademark. Trademark law thus attempts to define not only the appropriate geographic area of trademark use but also the relevant product boundaries in which a particular trademark may be used. In addition, the heart of

---

[1] See, e.g., State v. Shack, 58 N.J. 297, 277 A.2d 369 (N.J.1971), in which the Supreme Court of New Jersey upheld the right of a legal aid attorney and a social worker to visit the living quarters of workers in a migrant labor camp over the objections of the landowner/farmer/employer.

most trademark infringement litigation revolves around the question of the similarity of the trademarks at issue. Trademark owners are only granted the right to prevent other trademark uses that are likely to cause consumer confusion.

A similar tension inheres in copyright law, which seeks to resolve the appropriate balance between protecting creators' rights and insuring the optimal access to copyrighted works. Perhaps the most notable example of this balance is the fair use provision which is codified at 17 U.S.C. § 107. This provision sets forth a balancing test to be used in determining whether a particular unauthorized use of copyrighted property will be allowed. The 1976 Copyright Act is replete with other examples of qualifications of a copyright owner's rights under various circumstances.[2]

Patent law, like copyright law, tries to reward creators for enriching public welfare without unduly sacrificing the interest of the public in enjoying access to their creations. In addition, patent law recognizes that the storehouse of knowledge can grow only if every inventor is allowed to expand upon the insights of earlier creators. As Sir Isaac Newton purportedly stated, "If I have seen farther, it is by standing on the shoulders of giants."[3] Thus, patent law is careful to leave principles and products of nature in the public domain. Protection is available only for applications of these principles and refinements of these products. Even then, only truly significant advances over prior art will merit patents.

The legal concept of ownership also is quite similar for all types of property in that the owner's rights consist of her legal *interests* in the object in which the property is embodied. This conception of property contrasts markedly with the lay person's definition of property which focuses on physical ownership of the thing itself. For example, real property cases refer to these legal interests as a bundle of rights which include the right to exclude, the right to possess, the right to use, the right to dispose, and the right to manage and derive an economic benefit. Ownership of property in the legal sense is not synonymous with ownership of the land itself, but instead constitutes ownership of these legal interests in the land. Thus, although a landlord actually owns a particular piece of land and may have certain legal interests in that property, his tenant also has a legal interest in the property. The tenant's legal interest can be protected in court and thus also constitutes property in the legal sense.

Using copyright law as a relevant comparison, you will see that ownership of the object in which a copyrighted work is embodied is distinct from ownership of the copyright. See 17 U.S.C. § 202 of the 1976 Copyright Act. Moreover, § 106 of the Act secures for copyright owners the sole rights to reproduce, distribute, perform, and display the protected work, as well as the right to prepare derivative works. The copyright owner's exclusive ability to exercise this bundle of rights enables her to safeguard, in large

---

[2] See generally §§ 107–118 of the 1976 Copyright Act. See also Assignments 11 & 12.

[3] See Merton, On the Shoulders of Giants: A Shandrean Postscript (Free Press, 1965).

measure, the pecuniary value of the copyrighted work. These five rights thus represent the judicially protectable interests which render copyright ownership valuable.

Having explored some of the theoretical similarities between intellectual property and tangible property, it is also useful to identify the ways in which intellectual property law differs from tangible property law. Some of the more obvious differences are that tangible property law protection is common law in nature whereas trademark, copyright, and patent protection are statutory. Moreover, a specific duration exists for copyright and patent protection, unlike that for tangible property (you will see that trademark protection can be unlimited in duration, but the trademark owners must actually use the trademark in order to receive continued protection).

The limitations on the duration of protection under copyright and patent law relate to the issue of balancing the optimal degree of public access to intellectual property and the proprietary rights of the owners of the protected material. Although a landowner does not possess an unqualified right to exclude others from his property, the issue of public access to realty generally is less compelling than it is for certain types of intellectual property. For example, part of the reason for the "right versus access" tension in the area of copyright law is that substantial protection for copyrighted works potentially conflicts with the First Amendment which fosters the dissemination of informational and entertainment works. A similar conflict between the need for public dissemination (and use) and the protection of proprietary interests also is manifested in other areas of intellectual property. In the patent law context, keep in mind that Newton could not have seen so far had he been enjoined from standing on his predecessor's shoulders. With respect to trademarks, the law generally attempts to strike a balance between what can be protected by the property owner (i.e., marks which signify source) and what must remain in the public domain (i.e., matter which is generic and therefore belongs in the public domain).

Moreover, from an economics standpoint, tangible property is considered a "private good" because, generally speaking, a possessory interest in tangible property cannot be used by more than one person without each person interfering with the other's enjoyment.[4] In contrast, patents and copyrights can be considered "public goods" in that their possession is "nonrivalrous." That is, it is possible for many people to simultaneously enjoy the benefits of an invention without interfering with one another.[5]

---

[4] An example: two people cannot simultaneously drink the same cup of coffee. At worst, they will consider it unsanitary. At best, each will drink too fast in order to acquire a fair share (although note that different people can occupy different *interests* in the same piece of realty, i.e., a landlord and tenant; and that two or more people actually can own concurrent interests in tangible property in certain instances, i.e., joint tenants). In contrast, two or more people can simultaneously enjoy a picture of a cup of coffee.

[5] An example: two people can use the same discovery of a new flavored coffee brewing technique to make her own cup of coffee without interfering with the other's enjoyment.

Thus, whereas the consequence of private ownership of tangible property is to increase social wealth, private ownership of intangible property decreases social value. A general argument can be made that copyright and patent protection results in too little access to the protected property. The other side of this argument is that without these protections, people may not have the incentive to create works and inventions that will ultimately benefit society.

Finally, the goals of intellectual property and tangible property law are in some critical ways not at all alike. Since the supply of tangible property is essentially fixed, conservation is a vital concern in the law of property. But the supply of ideas is not at all fixed and so there is no need to conserve them. To the contrary, intellectual property law is aimed at encouraging the development of new ideas and facilitating the wide dissemination of those that are already in existence. In addition, people feel differently about their intellectual creations than they do about their land and personalty, and so reputational interests come into play in intellectual property law in a way that they do not in property law. For example, trademarks are protected from tarnishment and copyright protects the integrity of works of fine art.

Now for a few words about our specific approach to intellectual property. Substantively, our book is divided into the three major areas of copyright, trademark, and patent law. Our central insight is that these regimes can, and should, be viewed as a whole. But while each of these regimes faces the same types of problems, the solutions must be tailored specifically to the needs of the industries protected. Thus, we stress the commonalities of the regimes and the reasons underlying the differences.

Insofar as possible, the chapters in each subject area are organized in a parallel manner to reflect their similarities. Common concerns typically are discussed in detail in one of the regimes, and the pertinent discussions in the other regimes will further elaborate upon, and cross reference to, the relevant core discussions.

Furthermore, our approach does not sever state law from its federal counterparts. Our combined teaching experience has convinced us that the applicable doctrines of state law can best be examined in the appropriate chapters of the other three core areas. Essentially these state laws offer similar protections to less concrete types of subject matter. With the exception of the relatively recent moral rights provision of the copyright statute, the state law analogues involve no federal statutes and can easily be juxtaposed with the material covered in the corresponding core sections. Treating state law in this manner complements our integrated approach by illustrating the doctrinal relationship between state law and the other core areas of intellectual property.

We believe that our integrated approach is not only doctrinally sound, but also mirrors the reality of law practice in intellectual property. In many, if not most, of the reported cases, the complaints contain counts grounded in more than one of the major substantive areas of intellectual property. Moreover, in the last several years, several important articles have been published advocating a unified approach to intellectual property.[6]

[6] See, e.g., Dreyfuss, A Wiseguy's Approach to Information Products: Muscling the Copyright and Patent Into a Unitary Theory of Intellectual Property, 1992 S. Ct. Rev. 195; Reichman, Electronic Information Tools—The Outer Edge of World Intellectual Property Law, 17 U. Dayton L. Rev. 797 (1992); Smith, Copyright, Suppression, and the Problem of Unpublished Work: Lessons from the Patent Law, 19 A.I.P.L.A. Q.J. 309 (1991); Wiley, Copyright at the School of Patent, 58 U. Chi. L. Rev. 119 (1991).

TRADEMARK PROTECTION: INTRODUCTION

The three federal intellectual property regimes with which this course deals have much in common, for they all create exclusive rights in informational products. Of the three, copyright and patent law are by far the most similar, both in terms of the needs of the people protected (authors and inventors), and in terms of the goals and substance of the law. Accordingly, these regimes will be considered successively, in Assignments 6–14 and 15–25. This Unit investigates trademark law, which deals with the somewhat different requirements of those who produce and sell goods and services.

In many ways, trademark law is the most curious of the three federal intellectual property regimes. First, of the three, it is the only one that lacks a clear constitutional basis. That is, Article I, Section 8, Clause 8 of the United States Constitution grants Congress the power to "promote the progress of science and useful arts, by securing for limited times to authors and inventors the exclusive right to their respective writings and discoveries." This provision, commonly called the "Copyright Clause," is ample basis for both copyright and patent legislation. However, when Congress attempted, in 1870, to use the same authority to enact a registration system to protect marketing symbols, the Supreme Court balked. According to the *The Trademark Cases*:

"Any attempt . . . to identify the essential characteristics of a trade-mark with inventions and discoveries in the arts and sciences, or with the writings of authors, will show that the effort is surrounded with insurmountable difficulties.

"The ordinary trade-mark has no necessary relation to invention or discovery. The trade-mark recognized by the common law is generally the growth of a considerable period of use, rather than a sudden invention. It is often the result of accident rather than design, and when under the act of Congress it is sought to establish it by registration, neither originality, invention, discovery, science, nor art is in any way essential to the right conferred by that act. If we should endeavor to classify it under the head of writings of authors, the objections are equally strong. In this, as in regard to inventions, originality is required. And while the word *writings* may be liberally construed, as it has been, to include original designs for engravings, prints, & c., it is only such as are *original*, and are founded in the creative powers of the mind. The writings which are to be protected are *the fruits of intellectual labor*, embodied in the form of books, prints, engravings, and the like. The trade-mark may be, and generally is, the adoption of something already in existence as the distinctive symbol of the party using it."[1]

Thus deprived of Copyright Clause authority, Congress shifted gears. When it enacted a new trademark law, it expressly did so under its Commerce Clause powers.[2] This solution has, however, proved to be somewhat problematic. Since this Clause speaks only of commerce "with foreign nations, and among the several states, and with the Indian tribes," it was not originally read to give Congress authority over purely intrastate activity. And although the Clause is now understood to encompass activities affecting interstate commerce,[3] federal trademark law is still used mainly by those who wish to market goods in more than one state.

The second curiosity flows from the first: while it is easy to see why the framers of the Constitution would want to provide exclusive rights in writings and discoveries, it is somewhat more difficult to understand the justification for protecting trademarks. As *The Trademark Cases* noted, patents and copyrights protect works that are original. Producing original works is expensive; exclusive rights in these works provide a mechanism for recouping costs and generating the sort of profit that will encourage others to engage in similar creative efforts. But a trademark can be something as simple as a red triangle.[4] Indeed, trademarks are often symbols, designs, and words that are already a part of the "public domain"—the general storehouse of knowledge. Since the costs of using something already in existence are low, there is no need to devise a vehicle for recouping the costs of creation.

One traditional justification for creating exclusive rights in marks is that it prevents consumer confusion. Consumers are often unable to examine goods (or services)[5] to determine their quality or source. Instead, they must rely on the labels attached to the products offered for sale. The material on these labels is, therefore, a kind of language. Since language is effective only if words have clear and unique meanings, the source of a particular product must have exclusive authority over the marketing symbols it uses. As an example, consider the consumer who wishes to purchase

---

[1] 100 U.S. 82, 93–94 (1879)(emphasis in original).

[2] U.S. Const. art. I, § 8, cl. 3. Congress initially limited trademark registration to marks used in foreign commerce and commerce with the Indians, Act of March 3, 1881, 21 Stat. 502. It added registration for marks in interstate commerce in the Act of Feb. 20, 1905, ch. 592, 33 Stat. 724.

[3] See, e.g., Heart of Atlanta Motel v. United States, 379 U.S. 241, 85 S.Ct. 348, 13 L.Ed.2d 258 (1964).

[4] See, e.g, Bass Ale: according to the label, its red triangle was the first registered trademark in England.

[5] Trademark law protects marketing symbols that are used on goods ("trade marks") and on services ("service marks"). It also protects the marks of collectives, such as the Ladies' Garment Workers Union ("collective marks"), as well as the marks of certification organizations, such as Good Housekeeping's Seal of Approval ("certification marks"), see Assignment 2. Unless otherwise noted, this Unit uses the term "trademark" in a generic sense, to encompass all symbols used for marketing purposes.

a yellow sponge cake surrounding a creamy filling. The cake is likely to come wrapped in plastic; there is no way to test it for freshness, to ascertain the presence of a filling, or to determine its taste. Instead, the consumer must utilize the information on the label. If there is only one producer that can label this cake "Twinkie," then the consumer can rely on the producer's reputation for freshness and the Twinkie's reputation for creamy deliciousness. If, however, other merchants can use the same designation, and other Twinkies are not fresh, or creamy, or delicious, then the consumer could easily wind up dissatisfied.

This justification for trademark law leads directly to the third curiosity: whom does the law protect? The consumer-confusion rationale suggests that the right of action should belong to the consumer—to the consumer who was confused by an ambiguously labeled product into making the wrong purchase. In actual fact, however, consumers generally do not have standing to sue under trademark law. Rather, trademark law gives to the producer who regularly uses a mark the right to prevent others from using the same mark, or a confusingly similar mark, on the same goods, or on related goods.

The reason for vesting the right in the producer rather than the confused consumer could be that the law is trying to reduce the number of lawsuits by concentrating all claims in one litigant (the producer) rather than spreading them out among many (the consumers). The problem with this explanation is that it assumes that the consumers' interests are aligned with the producers'. This is certainly true in the Twinkie example, but it is not universally true. For example, the $5 "Rolex" is a popular street corner purchase. It is not very likely that a person who pays $5 for a watch actually believes she is buying an exquisitely engineered Swiss chronometer. Rather, she probably wants to enjoy the look of a Rolex without sacrificing her bank account. Still, the owner of the Rolex mark ("Rolex") can use trademark law to prevent these vendors from using its mark on watches.

A more producer-centered explanation for trademark rights is therefore needed. Thus, the broad language in *The Trademark Cases* must be taken with a grain of salt. Trademark owners may not be making the same social contribution that authors and inventors make, but they are doing something that requires, and deserves, the protection of exclusivity. That contribution is the production of goodwill: the investment in quality, reputation, and service. That is, without the promise that others can be prevented from utilizing their marks, merchants will not invest their efforts in creating goodwill. Why, for example, would the owner of the Twinkie mark (Continental Baking Co.[6]) use the best ingredients and hire good bakers when another manufacturer could use inferior products and workers, operate at lower costs, and sell Twinkies for less? Not only will

[6] Actually, the picture is more complicated: ITT owns Continental Baking Co., which owns Hostess, which manufactures Twinkies. The complication of the full ownership chain is itself a demonstration of the importance of trademarks in providing a means for consumers to identify the products they wish to purchase.

Continental Baking Co. lose sales, the inferior products will destroy its reputation. For Rolex, exclusivity also gives its mark a certain cachet. The cachet is itself a selling point—and a kind of value—to a certain type of customer.

There are, however, significant downsides to trademark protection. For many people, the drive to own "name brand" products leads them to make purchases they cannot afford. Worse, there have been reports linking robbery and murder to trademarked goods, such as sneakers, that appeal to teenagers.[7] And even without the complication of crime, there is reason for concern. Developing strong marks seems to go hand-in-hand with annoying television commercials, ugly roadway advertisements, and nonbiodegradable packaging. The expense of regulation and clean-up should be counted in the costs imposed by trademark law.

1. FEDERAL TRADEMARK REGISTRATION

The above description implies that the right to enjoin unauthorized uses is at the heart of trademark law. There is a sense in which this is true. Producers want an unambiguous avenue of communication with consumers and a legal right to exclusive use of their marks enables them to have one. Thus, trademark law has its origins in the common law of the states, where it was formulated to prevent a merchant from using a competitor's mark to "pass off" (or "palm off") her goods—that is, to misrepresent them as those of her competitor in order to deceive consumers into buying them by mistake. In most states, the law slowly expanded to prohibit other practices that lead to marketplace confusion, including dilution of the mark's value by overuse, or its tarnishment through unsavory associations.[8]

The development of substantive federal trademark law took a similar course. When Congress enacted the Lanham Act in 1946, 15 U.S.C.A. §§ 1051–1127,[9] it adopted the unfair competition themes of state law, to the point that federal courts (and this casebook) often use state formulations of unfair competition principles to inform their understanding of federal trademark law. Over the years, the Lanham Act has also expanded,

---

[7] Foltz, The Media Business: Addenda; New Nike Commercials Promote Good Conduct, N.Y. Times, July 5, 1990, Sec. D, p. 8, col. 2 (reporting on a $5,000,000 advertising campaign launched by Nike to promote good behavior).

[8] The American Law Institute has recently set out these laws in Restatement of the Law Third, Unfair Competition (1995). (Despite its name, this is the first time this law has been restated as a whole; portions of it were, however, included in the first (but not the second) Restatement of Torts.)

[9] Trademark legislation also embodies one more curiosity. Whereas the patent law is

called the "Patent Act" and the copyright statute is called the "Copyright Act," the trademark law is almost always referred to as the "Lanham Act." Indeed, most practitioners refer to specific provisions of this Act by the numbering system of the bill that led to the final legislation. This casebook, however, uses the numbering system of 15 U.S.C.A. unless otherwise noted. In this Unit, all statutory references are, therefore, to 15 U.S.C.A., unless specifically stated otherwise. (The Lanham Act enumeration is provided in the Statutory Supplement.)

both through judicial and legislative action. Whether it now fully mirrors state law protections is an issue that will be dealt with later in this Unit.[10]

Since federal and state law cover essentially the same practices, what then is the need for federal legislation? The answer lies in recognizing that protecting investments in goodwill requires more than just the substantive right to prevent consumer confusion. To see this, ask how it is that multiple uses of the same trademark can occur. One possibility is that the second (junior) user really is trying to pass off. In such cases, the substantive right to prevent confusion is enough protection: the first (senior) user can obtain an injunction that will protect the integrity of his mark.

However, it is also possible for two perfectly honest merchants to choose the same trademark. After all, entrepreneurs tend to start small and grow. Two merchants could adopt the same mark in different geographical areas and it could take many years for them to run into each other. When, however, their markets do meet, there will be a real problem. If they are both honest merchants, they will want to avoid consumer confusion. But to do so, one will have to abandon his old mark, adopt a new one, design new labels, and then inform customers of the change. This will entail considerable costs: who should bear them? In the passing-off situation, it was clear who acted in bad faith, but in this instance, neither party did. Accordingly, there is no criterion for deciding who keeps the mark and who pays the switching costs.

What trademark law requires is a registration system. First, it needs a list that merchants can consult in order to avoid adopting marks that are already taken. Second, to solve the problem of multiple use, the system needs a priority rule—a way to determine who among multiple-users has the right to keep the mark, and who must pay to switch to a new mark. Of course, states could adopt such systems—and in fact, many of them have. However, since states can solve multiple-user problems only within their own borders, what is really needed is a national system, or, as international trade increases, an international system. Indeed, registration is so much a key to trademark law that early federal law, including the one at issue in *The Trademark Cases*, addressed that issue alone. And although the Lanham Act does contain substantive provisions, its principal significance lies in its Registers and in its priority rules. Both the Registers and the priority rules are described below, in Section 2. The Act also executes the United States' obligations under international trademark treaties. The avenue these create for protecting marks on a global basis is described in Section 3, infra.

2.   THE APPLICATION PROCESS

STATUTORY MATERIALS: §§ 1111, 1051–52, 1057–59, 1062–64, 1066–68, 1070–72, & 1091

The requirements for registration of a trademark—use of the mark as a marketing symbol in commerce, use of the mark interstate, and distinc-

---

[10] See Assignment 3.

tiveness—will be covered in detail in Assignment 2. This section describes the application process for national trademark registration and the priority rules.

The Lanham Act creates three ways to establish an entitlement to registration: 1) use, 2) intent to use, and 3) trademark registration in a foreign country. Domestic applicants (that is, those who begin to utilize their marks first in the United States) generally rely on one of the first two methods (use or intent to use), which are described in this Section. Foreign applicants (that is, those whose marks are utilized abroad before they are used in the United States) usually rely on a foreign registration, which is described in Section 3, infra. The "domestic" routes are, however, available even to foreign applicants.

All registration methods utilize the same initial application form:

APPLICATION

TRADEMARK/SERVICE MARK APPLICATION, PRINCIPAL REGISTER, WITH DECLARATION	MARK (Word(s) and/or Design)	CLASS NO. (If known)

TO THE ASSISTANT SECRETARY AND COMMISSIONER OF PATENTS AND TRADEMARKS:

APPLICANT'S NAME:

APPLICANT'S BUSINESS ADDRESS:
(Display address exactly as it should appear on registration)

APPLICANT'S ENTITY TYPE: (Check one and supply requested information)

Individual - Citizen of (Country):

Partnership - State where organized (Country, if appropriate):
Names and Citizenship (Country) of General Partners:

Corporation - State (Country, if appropriate) of Incorporation:

Other (Specify Nature of Entity and Domicile):

GOODS AND/OR SERVICES:

Applicant requests registration of the trademark/service mark shown in the accompanying drawing in the United States Patent and Trademark Office on the Principal Register established by the Act of July 5, 1946 (15 U.S.C. 1051 et. seq., as amended) for the following goods/services (SPECIFIC GOODS AND/OR SERVICES MUST BE INSERTED HERE):

BASIS FOR APPLICATION: (Check boxes which apply, but never both the first AND second boxes, and supply requested information related to each box checked.)

[ ] Applicant is using the mark in commerce on or in connection with the above identified goods/services. (15 U.S.C. 1051(a), as amended.) Three specimens showing the mark as used in commerce are submitted with this application.
• Date of first use of the mark in commerce which the U.S. Congress may regulate (for example, interstate or between the U.S. and a foreign country):
• Specify the type of commerce:
            (for example, interstate or between the U.S. and a specified foreign country)
• Date of first use anywhere (the same as or before use in commerce date):
• Specify manner or mode of use of mark on or in connection with the goods/services:
(for example, trademark is applied to labels, service mark is used in advertisements)

[ ] Applicant has a bona fide intention to use the mark in commerce on or in connection with the above identified goods/services. (15 U.S.C. 1051(b), as amended.)
• Specify intended manner or mode of use of mark on or in connection with the goods/services:
(for example, trademark will be applied to labels, service mark will be used in advertisements)

[ ] Applicant has a bona fide intention to use the mark in commerce on or in connection with the above identified goods/services, and asserts a claim of priority based upon a foreign application in accordance with 15 U.S.C. 1126(d), as amended.
• Country of foreign filing: • Date of foreign filing:

[ ] Applicant has a bona fide intention to use the mark in commerce on or in connection with the above identified goods/services and, accompanying this application, submits a certification or certified copy of a foreign registration in accordance with 15 U.S.C. 1126(e), as amended.
• Country of registration: • Registration number:

NOTE: Declaration, on Reverse Side, MUST be Signed

PTO Form 1478 (REV. 8/93)   U.S. DEPARTMENT OF COMMERCE/Patent and Trademark Office
OMB No. 0651-0009 (Exp. 6/30/95)

FRONT

If submitted on one page, side two of the form should be "Upside Down" in relation to page 1.

DECLARATION

The undersigned being hereby warned that willful false statements and the like so made are punishable by fine or imprisonment, or both, under 18 U.S.C. 1001, and that such willful false statements may jeopardize the validity of the application or any resulting registration, declares that he/she is properly authorized to execute this application on behalf of the applicant; he/she believes the applicant to be the owner of the trademark/service mark sought to be registered, or, if the application is being filed under 15 U.S.C. 1051(b), he/she believes applicant to be entitled to use such mark in commerce; to the best of his/her knowledge and belief no other person, firm, corporation, or association has the right to use the above identified mark in commerce, either in the identical form thereof or in such near resemblance thereto as to be likely, when used on or in connection with the goods/services of such other person, to cause confusion, or to cause mistake, or to deceive; and that all statements made of his/her own knowledge are true and that all statements made on information and belief are believed to be true.

DATE   SIGNATURE

TELEPHONE NUMBER   PRINT OR TYPE NAME AND POSITION

INSTRUCTIONS AND INFORMATION FOR APPLICANT

TO RECEIVE A FILING DATE, THE APPLICATION <u>MUST</u> BE COMPLETED AND SIGNED BY THE APPLICANT AND SUBMITTED ALONG WITH:

1. The prescribed FEE ($245.00 effective 10/1/93)* for each class of goods/services listed in the application;
2. A DRAWING PAGE displaying the mark in conformance with 37 CFR 2.52;
3. If the application is based on use of the mark in commerce, THREE (3) SPECIMENS (evidence) of the mark as used in commerce for each class of goods/services listed in the application. All three specimens may be in the nature of: (a) labels showing the mark which are placed on the goods; (b) photographs of the mark as it appears on the goods, (c) brochures or advertisements showing the mark as used in connection with the services.
4. An APPLICATION WITH DECLARATION (this form) - The application must be signed in order for the application to receive a filing date. Only the following person may sign the declaration, depending on the applicant's legal entity: (a) the individual applicant; (b) an officer of the corporate applicant; (c) one general partner of a partnership applicant; (d) all joint applicants.

SEND APPLICATION FORM, DRAWING PAGE, FEE, AND SPECIMENS (IF APPROPRIATE) TO:
Commissioner of Patents and Trademarks
Box TRADEMARK
Washington, D.C. 20231

Additional information concerning the requirements for filing an application is available in a booklet entitled Basic Facts About Registering a Trademark, which may be obtained by writing to the above address or by calling: (703) 308-HELP.

*Fees are subject to change; changes usually take effect on October 1. If filing on or after October 1, 1994, please call the PTO to confirm the correct fee.

This form is estimated to take an average of 1 hour to complete, including time required for reading and understanding instructions, gathering necessary information, recordkeeping, and actually providing the information. Any comments on this form, including the amount of time required to complete this form, should be sent to the Office of Management and Organization, U.S. Patent and Trademark Office, U.S. Department of Commerce, Washington, D.C. 20231, and to Paperwork Reduction Project 0651-0009, Office of Information and Regulatory Affairs, Office of Management and Budget, Washington, D.C. 20503. Do NOT send completed forms to either of these addresses.

BACK

The bottom half of the first page of the application poses the choice for the wholly domestic applicant, who may either register under a use-based system,[11] for which she must show that the trademark has been used in commerce, or under intent-to-use provisions, for which she must allege a bona fide intent to use the mark in commerce.[12] The intent-to-use system was introduced for the first time when the Lanham Act was revised in 1988, for reasons that will be discussed below in connection with international applications.[13] Both types of applications are governed by the Rules of Practice in Trademark Cases, 37 C.F.R. §§ 2.2–2.189.

Use-based applications

When an applicant decides to seek trademark protection for a mark presently being used on a product in interstate commerce, she first files an application with the Patent and Trademark Office (PTO). This application, which can be filed with or without the assistance of legal counsel, consists of three elements: the fee, the application form, and a drawing of the mark.

---

[11] § 1051(a).

[12] § 1051(b).

[13] See the Trademark Law Revision Act of 1988, Pub.L. 100–667, 102 Stat. 3935.

The application form asks for the name of the applicant, a detailed description of all of the goods on which she is using the mark,[14] and three specimens of the mark in actual commercial use, such as labels from the actual product depicting the mark.[15] This information determines the scope of the rights the applicant will enjoy once the trademark is registered, for it delineates the words, goods, and services where the applicant wishes to prevent ambiguity.

In addition, the application seeks information that will facilitate the ability of others to search the Register. First, the applicant is asked to help keep the Register indexed by categorizing her goods or services according to a classification system maintained by the PTO.[16] Second, the applicant must furnish a drawing of the mark that complies with strict requirements for size, style, and color notation. The drawing, which must also include the date of the mark's first use and first use in commerce, will be reproduced on the Register and published, so it must be readable.[17] The statement concerning usage, which is also part of the statement on the first page of the application, fulfills the Lanham Act's Commerce Clause limitation. It also establishes the date from which the applicant is considered the owner of the mark. As among two applicants for the same or a similar mark for similar goods, it is the applicant with the earliest use who is entitled to the registration.[18] Further, once a mark is registered, the registered owner acquires the right to prevent others from using a confusingly similar mark for similar goods.[19]

The flip side of the application contains a final, yet important element. It is a verified (i.e. sworn) statement that to the best of the applicant's knowledge, the mark does not so resemble a mark already in use in connection with similar goods that consumers could be confused.[20] This statement forces the applicant to do her part in assuring that the registration system performs its intended function of creating clear lines of communication between consumers and producers.

When the PTO receives all application materials,[21] an examiner from the office studies them to determine whether the mark qualifies under the Lanham Act's general requirements for federal trademark protection.[22] If the application appears to satisfy these requirements, the PTO then publishes the mark in its *Official Gazette*. Those who believe they would be injured if the mark were registered have 30 days from the time of publication in which to oppose registration.[23] If no one opposes the mark, the PTO issues to the applicant a certificate of registration and registers the mark on the *Principal Register*. The owner can then notify others that

---

[14] 37 C.F.R. §§ 2.21–2.47.

[15] 37 C.F.R. §§ 2.56–2.59

[16] 37 C.F.R. §§ 2.21–2.47. See the upper right-hand corner of the application form.

[17] 37 C.F.R. §§ 2.51–2.53.

[18] § 1051–52.

[19] See Assignment 3.

[20] § 1051(a)(1).

[21] This date will be considered the applicant's filing date for the purpose of international filings, see below. 37 C.F.R. § 2.21.

[22] 37 C.F.R. §§ 2.61–2.69.

[23] § 1063.

the mark is registered by displaying it in conjunction with the words "Registered in U.S. Patent and Trademark Office" or, as is more common, with the symbol ®.[24]

Intent-to-use applications

In contrast to the traditional requirement that an applicant be using the mark in commerce before filing to register it, the 1988 amendments allow an applicant to file for trademark protection as soon as she can demonstrate a bona fide intention to use the mark in commerce.

An intent-to-use application substantially mirrors a use-based application in its components. For instance, the applicant must still submit the fee, drawing, and application. However, there are several differences between the two methods of registration. For instance, since the mark has not yet been used, the applicant obviously need not state the first date of use or date of use in commerce. Instead, she must submit a written statement verifying that she believes she is the owner of the mark and that she has a bona fide intention to use the mark in the future on a product in interstate commerce.[25]

Other differences between an intent-to-use application and a use-based application are slight. For instance, because the applicant has not yet used the mark, she is not expected to submit the three specimens of the mark required of a use-based applicant. However, she must still submit a drawing of the mark similar to that required of a use-based applicant. In this case, the drawing is more important than with the use-based application because the PTO will not have a specimen to determine what the mark looks like.

Once the PTO receives the application, it evaluates the proposed trademark, applying the same requirements as for a use-based application. If the mark conforms to the Lanham Act's general provisions, it will be published, as with the use-based application. If no one successfully opposes registration, the applicant receives a Notice of Allowance.[26]

The Notice of Allowance does not, however, constitute federal registration of the mark; the applicant still must submit a verified statement that the mark has been used in commerce before her mark will be placed on the Principal Register. Here, the procedure for an intent-to-use applicant departs from that of the traditional applicant. Within six months of the issuance of a Notice of Allowance, the applicant must file the third form depicted above, a verified written Statement of Use indicating that she has followed through on her bona fide intention to use the mark in commerce.[27] Resembling the use-based application, this written statement must include the date the mark was first used in commerce, the manner of use, three specimens of the mark, and a fee. Once the applicant has filed this Statement of Use and the mark remains published without opposition for

[24] § 1111.

[25] 37 C.F.R. § 2.33(b).

[26] 37 C.F.R. §§ 2.88–2.89.

[27] 37 C.F.R. § 2.88.

the requisite period, the PTO issues a certificate of registration and places the mark on the Principal Register.

ALLEGATION OF USE

STATEMENT OF USE UNDER 37 CFR 2.88, WITH DECLARATION	MARK (Identify the mark)
	SERIAL NO.

TO THE ASSISTANT SECRETARY AND COMMISSIONER OF PATENTS AND TRADEMARKS:

APPLICANT NAME:

NOTICE OF ALLOWANCE ISSUE DATE:

Applicant requests registration of the above-identified trademarks/service mark in the United States Patent and Trademark Office on the Principal Register established by the Act of July 5, 1946 (15 U.S.C. 1051 et. seq., as amended). Three specimens per class showing the mark as used in commerce are submitted with this statement.

☐   Check here if a Request to Divide under 37 C.F.R. 2.87 is being submitted with this statement.

Applicant is using the mark in commerce on or in connection with the following goods/services: (Check One)

☐   Those goods/services identified in the Notice of Allowance in this application.

☐   Those goods/services identified in the Notice of Allowance in this application except: (Identify goods/services to be deleted from application) _____

_____

_____

Date of first use of mark in commerce
which the U.S. Congress may regulate: _____

Specify type of commerce: (e.g., interstate, between the U.S. and a specified foreign country) _____

_____

Date of first use anywhere: _____
(the same as or before use-in-commerce date)

Specify manner or mode of use of mark on or in connection with the goods/services: (e.g., trademark is applied to labels, service mark is used in advertisements) _____

_____

The undersigned being hereby warned that willful false statements and the like so made are punishable by fine or imprisonment, or both, under 18 U.S.C. 1001, and that such willful false statements may jeopardize the validity of the application or any resulting registration, declares that he/she is properly authorized to execute this Statement of Use on behalf of the applicant; he/she believes the applicant to be the owner of the trademark/service mark sought to be registered; the trademark/service mark is now in use in commerce; and all statements made of his/her own knowledge are true and all statements made on information and belief are believed to be true.

_____   _____
Date   Signature

_____   _____
Telephone Number   Print or Type Name and Position

PTO Form 1580 (REV. 8-93)   U.S. Department of Commerce/Patent and Trademark Office
OMB No. 0651-0009
Exp. 6-30-95

If the applicant has not used the mark in commerce by the end of the six month period following the issuance of the Notice of Allowance, she may file for six-month extensions of time to show use of the mark.[28] The first request for an extension consists of a written statement asserting her continuing bona fide intention to use the mark and a fee. However, subsequent requests must be accompanied by a showing of good cause

---

[28] 37 C.F.R. § 2.89.

reasons for needing the extension.[29] "Good cause" statements must cite specific ongoing efforts to use the mark in commerce, such as continued market research about mark selection or promotional activities which will eventually lead to use in commerce. Further, the applicant can use good cause to extend the time for beginning use only for a total of 24 months.

Note that although intent-to-use applications can have the effect of reserving a mark for up to three years, the applicant does not acquire the rights that attach to registration until use begins and the mark is registered. That is, during the interim period between application and registration, the applicant cannot enjoin others from adopting the mark, nor can she prevent prior users from expanding their businesses. After the mark is registered, interim adoptions can be enjoined. It may, however, be that prior user rights are not frozen until actual registration. In other words, it is only when the Notice of Allowance is converted into a registration, that the trademark holder's priority rights come into effect. For the most part, they are then dated from the day the application was filed.

Registration problems

The material above described an application that is ultimately approved. Problems can, however, crop up along the way. First, it is sometimes the case that more than one party applies to use similar marks on similar goods. If so, an interference may be declared.[30] Alternatively, when the mark is published, someone may claim registration will cause ambiguity, in which case, an opposition will be declared.[31] Oppositions and interferences are handled similarly: in an inter partes proceeding, complete with discovery, live-witness testimony, briefs and oral argument, the Trademark Trial and Appeal Board (TTAB), an agency court within the PTO, determines who has the right to the mark, whether the application should be approved, or (in the case of multiple users of similar marks) whether the Commissioner of Trademarks should register both marks with limitations on each of the concurrent uses.[32] Appeals from the Board are generally to the Court of Appeals for the Federal Circuit (CAFC). Alternatively, an action against the Commissioner of Trademarks can be instituted in federal district court.[33]

Of course, it is also possible that the examiner simply does not consider the mark registrable. She may, for example, think the mark is too similar to a mark that is already registered; or that the mark must remain in the public domain because it is the only word for the goods on which it will be used; or that it is merely descriptive of the goods and therefore not distinctive enough to function as a trademark. In such cases, the examiner and applicant enter into correspondence, the applicant will explain why the mark should be registered or make changes to meet the examiner's objec-

---

[29] 37 C.F.R. § 2.89(d).

[30] § 1066.

[31] § 1063.

[32] § 1067–68.

[33] § 1071. Dissatisfied parties can petition the Supreme Court for review of the regional circuit decision or the CAFC decision, but such petitions are rarely granted.

tions. If the two agree on a registrable mark, the course described above will be followed.

If they cannot agree, there are two possibilities. First, the applicant could appeal the disallowance of registration to the TTAB,[34] and then through the federal judicial system in the manner noted above. However, when the problem is lack of distinctiveness, there is sometimes a second choice. If the mark is capable of becoming distinctive—that is, if people could become accustomed to thinking of it as source-indicative, the applicant can register it on the *Supplemental Register*.[35]

Marks on the Supplemental Register do not enjoy the full benefit of federal law. Registration on the Supplemental Register does not, for example, provide constructive notice to subsequent adopters that the mark is in use and so does not confer on the trademark owner the automatic right to enjoin others from using the mark. In addition, this registration does not confer the advantage of certain types of relief, such as the right to stop others from importing infringing goods.[36] The Supplemental Register does, however, offer significant advantages. First, it is a mechanism of actual notice: those who want to avoid ambiguity can use the Supplemental Register as an additional resource for finding marks that have been previously adopted. Marks on the Supplemental Register can even be displayed with the ® that provides actual notice of federal registration.[37] Second, owners of marks on the Supplemental Register can use the federal courts to assert state-based rights and even certain federal rights. Third, marks listed on the Supplemental Register can usually be transferred to the Principal Register after five years' use.[38] Finally, registration on the Supplemental Register meets some of the requirements needed to obtain the benefits of trademark treaties that the United States has entered with foreign countries.

Maintenance

Trademark protection and registration last for however long a mark is in use. However, affirmative steps must be taken to maintain registration. Certificates of registration remain in force for ten years and can be renewed for additional ten-year periods upon payment of fees. In addition, registrants must file periodic affidavits averring continuing use, or setting out special circumstances accounting for nonuse.[39]

These requirements are partly designed to preserve the Commerce Clause limitations of the Lanham Act because they insure that the marks that receive protection are in commerce and thus within Congress's legislative jurisdiction. More important, however, they keep the Register free of deadwood. That way, symbols that are particularly evocative can be utilized even after the original trademark owner has discarded them. The Act also has two other ways to clear the Register of marks that, for one reason or

[34] § 1070.
[35] § 1091.
[36] §§ 1094 & 1096.
[37] § 1111.

[38] § 1052(f).
[39] §§ 1058–59.

another, no longer meet Lanham Act requirements. In certain circumstances, a cancellation proceeding can be instituted in the PTO. These are handled much like interferences and oppositions.[40] In addition, certain types of invalidity can be asserted in infringement actions.[41]

Registration as a solution to the problem of multiple users

This registration system helps to solve the problem of multiple users in a number of ways. First, the Principal and Supplemental Registers, along with the symbols ® next to registered marks, provide newcomers with *actual notice* of what marks have already been taken, thereby allowing them to avoid adopting marks that are likely to confuse consumers.[42] More important, the Principal Register provides *constructive notice* that a mark is in use, thereby conferring on its owner the right to enjoin anyone who, after the mark goes on the Principal Register, adopts the same or a similar mark for similar goods.[43]

Registration does not, however, constitute a complete solution to the multiple-user problem. First, the Registers do not list all marks that are in use. For example, marks protected only under state law do not appear on them. Accordingly, newcomers researching the availability of a particular mark must consult not only the federal Registers, but also state registers, trade journals, catalogues, newspapers, magazines, and the like. Even then, some potential problems will be missed. For instance, marks on which intent-to-use applications have been filed will not appear anywhere until after use has begun. And as the next section will show, neither will the Registers show marks that are entitled to appear by virtue of international filings. These omissions are important because registration on the Principal Register does not necessarily create priority vis á vis these marks. That is, prior users are entitled to continue to use their marks in the geographic areas where they were used prior to the receipt of trademark protection.[44] They are even entitled to a small zone of geographic expansion.

3.   THE INTERNATIONAL STAGE

STATUTORY MATERIALS: § 1126 Paris Convention, Arts. 2, 4, 6[bis], 9, & 10

Trademark *rights* are geographically bounded in that a mark can be enforced only in the jurisdiction in which it is recognized. U.S. marks, for example, are infringed only when there is a likelihood of consumer confu-

---

[40] § 1064.

[41] § 1115(b).

[42] § 1111.

[43] § 1072.

[44] § 1115(b)(5). In theory, of course, there should be no federal registration of a mark already in use: if the applicant knew of the mark, he could not have verified the statement that he had no knowledge that the

mark resembles a mark already in use. Similarly, if the examiner knew of the mark, he would not have approved the application. However, it is sometimes the case that neither the applicant nor the examiner know of a local mark when the federal application is under consideration, and so the mark issues, consumers become accustomed to it, and the trademark holder acquires rights in it.

sion in the United States.[45] Trademark *use* is not, however, territorially constrained. Many producers sell their products in global markets. Moreover, when consumers travel, they encounter foreign advertisements and use foreign goods and services. Even those who stay home learn about foreign products by talking to travelers, watching CNN and foreign films, and reading international publications. Consider, for example, the following marks:

SN 69,873. The Coca-Cola Company, Atlanta, Ga. Filed Mar. 19, 1959.

Ser. No. 254,695. THE COCA COLA COMPANY, Atlanta, Ga. Filed Sept. 13, 1927.

Applicant is the owner of registrations Nos. 22,406, 47,189, and 229,380.
Particular description of goods.—Beverages and Sirups for the Manufacture of Such Beverages.
Claims use since May, 1886.

Ser. No. 254,696. THE COCA COLA COMPANY, Atlanta, Ga. Filed Sept. 13, 1927.

The trademark consists of the distinctively shaped contour, or conformation, and design of the bottle as shown.
Owner of Reg. Nos. 22,406, 415,755, and others.
For Carbonated Soft Drink.
First use July 8, 1916.

Ser. No. 242,569. (CLASS 45. BEVERAGES, NON ALCOHOLIC.) THE COCA-COLA COMPANY, Atlanta, Ga. Filed Jan. 10, 1927.

CLASS 45

BEVERAGES, NONALCOHOLIC

Ser. No. 468,708. THE COCA-COLA COMPANY, Wilmington, Del. Filed Mar. 27, 1944.

Coke

The trade-mark "Coke" is the abbreviation of applicant's registered trade-mark "Coca-Cola."
FOR NON-ALCOHOLIC MALTLESS BEVERAGES AND SYRUPS FOR MAKING SUCH BEVERAGES.
Claims use since Dec. 10, 1941.

Particular description of goods.—Nonalcoholic, Maltless Beverages and Sirups for the Manufacture of Such Beverages.
Claims use since Oct. 22, 1896.

No matter who purchases a beverage labeled with these marks, and no matter where they are purchased, a specific product, taste, and quality are expected. Because these expectations help to sell soda pop, and because its reputational interests are at stake whenever products labeled with these marks are purchased, the owner of the U.S. trademarks would like to own them worldwide.

To achieve worldwide ownership, trademark owners must rely on the law of each nation in which they market their products. Treaties make this

---

[45] See, e.g., American Rice, Inc. v. Arkansas Rice Growers Coop. Ass'n, 701 F.2d 408   (5th Cir.1983).

possible. There are several major international agreements that facilitate worldwide trademark protection. The principal multilateral treaty has, historically, been the International Convention for the Protection of Industrial Property.[46] Commonly called the Paris Convention, it pertains to both patents and trademarks. It was promulgated in 1883, adopted by the United States in 1887, and implemented through domestic legislation in 1903. The Paris Convention is recognized by well over 100 countries.[47]

As it pertains to trademark law, the Convention has four important features. First, under Art. 2 of the Convention:

> "[n]ationals of any country of the Union shall ... enjoy in all the other countries of the Union the advantages that their respective laws now grant, or may hereafter grant, to nationals."

This "national treatment" provision assures trademark holders in each Paris Convention nation that their applications to register marks in other Union countries will receive the same attention these countries accord to domestic applications. Moreover, national treatment means that rights acquired in each Union country will be equivalent to the rights enjoyed by that nation's own trademark holders. In short, Art. 2 insures that all producers operating within a Union country do so on a level playing field: no merchant can use domestic trademark law to acquire a competitive advantage.[48]

Second, Articles 9 and 10 provide manufacturers with a minimum level of substantive protection against products bearing unauthorized trademarks and false designations of source or origin.

Third, under Art. 6[bis], signatories agree to facilitate global marketing by reserving marks that become internationally known for the producers who made them famous. It requires signatories to:

> "refuse ... the registration, and to prohibit the use, of a trademark which constitutes a reproduction, an imitation, or a translation, liable to create confusion, of a mark considered by the competent authority of the country of registration ... to be so well known in that country as already the mark of a person entitled to the benefits of this Convention."

In other words, Art. 6[bis] allows companies like Coca Cola and Rolex to invest in goodwill with the confidence that their marks will be available to them as they expand internationally. They will not be forced to contend with locals who inadvertently adopt similar marks. Nor will they need to deal with opportunists, who register known marks with the hope of passing off their goods as those of the major producer, or with "trademark pirates," who register well known marks for the sole purpose of soliciting payoffs from genuine producers.

---

[46] Other important international treaties that cover trademark rights include the General Agreement on Tariffs and Trade (the GATT Agreement) and the Trademark Law Treaty. Both set minimum standards of trademark protection that a signatory must apply to both its domestic marks and to the marks recognized by other member nations.

[47] A list of signatories is included in McCarthy on Trademarks and Unfair Competition, § 29.08 (4th ed. 1994).

[48] See also Art. 6[quinquies].

The fourth major feature of the Paris Convention is a priority rule. Under Art. 4, an applicant who has filed in one Paris Convention country can use the date of that application as the filing date in every other Union country—provided that the second filing occurs within six months of the first, and the first application eventually matures into a registration. For example, imagine that someone applies to register a mark in France on January 1, 1994 and then applies in the United States on May 1, 1994. Since both the U.S. and France are in the Paris Union, and since May is within six months of January, the filing date of the *U.S.* application will be considered to be January 1, 1994, and not May 1 (so long as the French application results in registration).[49]

Why does this matter? As we saw, it is sometimes the case that two parties apply to register similar marks for similar goods. For wholly domestic applications, the Commissioner will award the trademark to the party who used the mark first, or in the case of intent-to-use applications, who applied first and later met the use requirements. Applications that are filed under the Paris Convention, however, are entitled to use the Paris Convention date for priority purposes. If that date precedes the date on which a domestic applicant first used the mark, the Paris Convention applicant will be awarded the trademark. To continue with the example begun above: if a domestic applicant had applied to register a similar mark for similar goods on February 10, 1994, and based its application on a first-use date of February 1, 1994, that applicant would be out of luck. Although the domestic applicant engaged in activity in the United States before the foreign applicant, the foreign applicant would enjoy the benefit of the Paris Convention date of January 1. Since January 1 precedes February 1, the foreign applicant would win the right to register the mark.

Note that the effect of Art. 4 is to create a third way to acquire trademark rights in the United States, for it allows registration to be based upon a previous filing in a Paris Convention country rather than on use or on intent-to-use. Since many of the Paris Convention countries do not require applicants to have made any use of their mark prior to registration, this back door into the benefits of the Lanham Act has proved troublesome for Americans. After all, designing a mark, making up specimens, attaching the mark to goods, and offering the marked goods for sale is expensive and time consuming. In a race between a domestic applicant who plans to base her application on this burdensome process and a Union applicant, who need do no more than file two applications, the domestic applicant will usually lose.[50]

Indeed, the 1988 Amendments to the Lanham Act were aimed, in part, at solving this problem. The intent-to-use provision was introduced to give wholly domestic applicants an avenue for applying for trademark protection that did not involve the heavy financial investment of the use provision. In addition, the Amendments increased the burden on Paris Union applicants by requiring, for the first time, that these applicants state a bona fide

---

[49] This priority rule is enacted into domestic legislation in § 1126(d).

[50] See, e.g., SCM Corp. v. Langis Foods, Ltd., 539 F.2d 196 (D.C.Cir.1976).

intention to use the mark in commerce.[51] Actual use may not, however, be required prior to the registration of Paris Union marks, the way that it is for intent-to-use marks. Thus, even after the Amendments, a Union applicant may still be in a better position than a domestic applicant.[52]

More recently, international norms of intellectual property protection have come to be set by the General Agreement on Tariffs and Trade (GATT). As initially enacted, GATT was designed to increase international commerce by reducing tariffs and other barriers to trade. When this Agreement went into force in 1948 with the United States as an original signatory, the parties to GATT focused on commerce in products like corn, chickens, lamps, and steel; it was only in 1986, during the so-called Uruguay Round of GATT trade negotiations, that intellectual property was introduced into the discussion. After a slow start in which the propriety of treating intellectual products as equivalent to grain, poultry, and manufactured goods was questioned, the Uruguay Round ended in 1994 with an agreement on Trade–Related Aspects of Intellectual Property Rights (TRIPS). Like the entire GATT, TRIPS is administered by a new body, the World Trade Organization (WTO).

Under TRIPS, the signatory countries agreed to a set of basic principles. The first two mirror the Paris Convention: signatories to TRIPS agree to accord national treatment to foreign patent applicants and to accord priority according to the applicant's national filing date.[53] The third extends the core principle of the GATT to intellectual property: it requires member countries to accord to other member nations most-favored-nation (MFN) treatment.[54] This means that any time one member of the GATT enters into an agreement related to intellectual property with any other member, the advantages of the agreement are generalized to apply to all other signatories.

The fourth significant feature of TRIPS is that it establishes a set of universal minimum standards—similar to those of the Paris Convention—governing the use of intellectual products. Although U.S. law largely complied with these norms before TRIPS, the agreement did require some modifications to all three federal intellectual property regimes. The changes for trademark law, which went into effect on January 1, 1996, were minor and will be discussed in the Assignments to which they pertain.

[51] §§ 1126(c), (d)(2), (e).

[52] Another problem with Art. 4 is that the six-month grace period between the foreign and United States filings creates a blind spot in the registration system—a period when the mark is not in the federal system but is nonetheless entitled to federal registration.

[53] Final Act Embodying the Results of the Uruguay Round of Multilateral Trade Negotiations and Marrakesh Agreement Establishing the World Trade Organization, signed at Marrakesh (Morocco), April 15, 1994, Annex 1C, Agreement on Trade–Related Aspects of Intellectual Property Rights, Arts. 3(1) and 4A(1), reprinted in The Results of the Uruguay Round of Multilateral Trade Negotiations—The Legal Texts (GATT Secretariat ed. 1994)[hereinafter, the TRIPS Agreement].

[54] Id., Art. 4.

Because the Paris Convention and GATT create opportunities to protect marks on a nearly worldwide basis, they represent important benefits to international businesses. They are not, however, a perfect solutions to the problem of international protection because of the expense of filing applications in every country where the mark will be used. Substantive law and filing requirements are not identical and so local counsel must usually be hired and separate applications drawn up. Better would be a unitary system that allowed a producer to obtain worldwide protection with a single filing.

The Madrid Arrangement for the International Registration of Trademarks was developed in 1891 for this purpose. It provides a means to convert a domestic application into an international filing, and ultimately, into an international trademark that each signatory treats as equivalent to a mark registered under its own laws. The Madrid Arrangement is wholly dependent on domestic filings. That is, it imposes no real substantive requirements and does not maintain an examination system. Instead, it accepts on its international register any mark that has been registered in a signatory country.

Although many nations have joined the Madrid Arrangement, the United States has never done so. Prior to 1988, the main problem was the use requirement of the Lanham Act. Since acceptance onto the international register is contingent on national registration, Americans were severely disadvantaged. They had to go through the expense of using the mark in order to achieve the required domestic registration, whereas other Madrid Arrangement registrants only needed to prepare an application and pursue it to registration. In addition, the United States has been concerned with the laxity of the laws of some of the nations whose registrations qualify marks for international protection, with the Madrid Arrangement's treatment of the deadwood problem, and with the methods some nations use for challenging registrations.

In 1989, the Madrid nations supplemented the Agreement with a new "Madrid Protocol," which creates a method for obtaining international trademark protection with a single standardized application and also deals with some of the other issues with which the U.S. has been concerned. With the advent of intent-to-use registrations, most of the United States' objections to international registration have, therefore, been mitigated. However, although the United States signed the Protocol, it has not, as of this writing, been ratified by Congress. The Clinton Administration has asked that accession be postponed until an issue concerning the voting rights of the European Community and its member nations is resolved.

REQUIREMENTS FOR TRADEMARK PROTECTION: USE: AS A SIGNAL, IN COMMERCE, AND INTERSTATE

Laypersons will talk of the "Twinkie trademark" or the "Rolex trademark." Trademark lawyers do not speak this way. They say, "Rolex as a trademark for watches" or "Twinkie for cakes." The difference here is more than rhetorical style; it captures the essence of trademark law. Owning a trademark is not a right to a *word*, rather it is a right to a *signal*—to a particular use of a word. It is control over a message that flows from producer to consumer, a message that is short, but nonetheless rich with information. The trademark for a product, for example, can signal much about its nature, source, and quality. Since the objective of trademark law is to make it possible to send these signals in an unambiguous way, a trademark is protected only when it is being used to communicate.

Use permeates every aspect of federal trademark law. As we saw, marks cannot be registered without either an allegation of use or an allegation of a bona fide intent to use. Trademarks cannot be maintained without filing affidavits of continuing use. Priority depends on use. Indeed, the four types of marks that the Lanham Act protects—trade marks, service marks, collective marks and certification marks—are all defined in terms of their use, § 1127.

This Assignment, which consists of two Principal Problems and associated materials, demonstrates that "use" has both physical and cognitive components. The physical dimensions are first, the word or symbol must have a spatial association with goods or services such that consumers perceive it as a signal conveying information about the trademark owner and its products. Second, the mark must be used in commerce—that is, in connection with marketing activities. Third, to be a *federal* trademark, the signal must come within the jurisdiction of the Lanham Act by being used in interstate commerce. On the cognitive side, the word or symbol must be "distinctive:" intrinsically capable of being understood as a signal rather than as a description of the goods. And, as Part B will demonstrate, certain designations are either disfavored or completely precluded. These include geographic identifications as well as designations that are deceptive, disparaging, or immoral. Finally, the mark that is chosen must not be confusingly similar to a mark that is already in use on similar goods.

PART A: REQUIREMENTS FOR REGISTRATION

1. PRINCIPAL PROBLEM A

Annie Bingaman has come to us for advise on acquiring trademark rights for a new game she has developed. The game uses a board that is similar to the familiar Monopoly board, except that instead of squares designating properties (e.g. Baltic Ave., Reading Railroad, Park Place), her squares represent large companies (e.g. General Electric, Eastman Kodak, U.S. Steel, Alcoa). Instead of the players buying the properties to which the rolling dice take them, and then building houses and hotels there, players of the new game choose whether to institute and prosecute antitrust actions against the companies on which they land. The new game substitutes ANTITRUST DIVISION RULINGS and COURT OPINIONS for CHANCE and COMMUNITY CHEST cards, but retains the square labeled JAIL. For obvious reasons, Bingaman would like to call her new game "Antimonopoly."

Our client has created a mock-up of the game which she has played with friends all over the country, but she needs to line up investors before she can actually go into production, begin distribution, or start advertising. While these efforts are underway, however, Bingaman wants to take whatever steps are necessary to assure her future ability to use "Antimonopoly" as a trademark. In addition, she wants to know whether Parker Brothers, which sells Monopoly, and the companies whose names appear on the board will have any rights under trademark law to interfere with her plans.

2. MATERIALS FOR SOLUTION OF PRINCIPAL PROBLEM A

A. STATUTORY MATERIALS: §§ 1051, 1052(e) and (f), 1053–54, 1056, 1091, & 1127

B. CASES AND OTHER LEGISLATIVE MATERIALS:

In Re Schiapparelli Searle

Trademark Trial and Appeal Board, 1993.
26 U.S.P.Q.2d (BNA) 1520.

■ Opinion by SIMMS, MEMBER

Schiapparelli Searle (applicant), a partnership consisting of a domestic and a foreign corporation, has appealed from a refusal of the Trademark Examining Attorney to register the slogan "THE ACTIVE INGREDIENT IS QUALITY" for pharmaceuticals: namely, laxatives, anti-psychotics, anti-infectives, diuretics, and drugs for the treatment of gastrointestinal maladies, all sold by prescription. In the affixation clause of the amended application, it is indicated that the mark is used on brochures and other documents associated with the goods and their sale.

The Examining Attorney has refused registration because the specimens assertedly do not show trademark use of the slogan sought to be registered. More particularly, the Examining Attorney argues that the specimens of record are brochures describing the goods, which are merely advertising and not displays or point-of-sale materials. The Examining Attorney has also rejected applicant's argument, discussed more fully below, that the nature of applicant's goods makes "traditional" trademark use (affixation to labels, containers, displays, etc.) of the mark "impracticable." Rather, the Examining Attorney argues that it appears to be applicant's practice to affix its other trademarks to the goods, containers or labeling:

> Applicant's brochures show photographs of some of applicant's products . . . These products are packaged in what are traditional looking containers. The photographs show plainly the trademarks "SEARLE" and "SCHIAPPARELLI SEARLE" imprinted on the containers. If these trademarks can be affixed to containers for the goods, then it would seem practicable for the trademark under examination to be affixed in the same manner.

The Examining Attorney states that applicant's pharmaceuticals are not custom-ordered goods or bulk goods whose nature makes them unsuitable for a reasonable method of affixation. Rather, according to the Examining Attorney, applicant's drugs are purchased by pharmacists and are resting on the pharmacist's shelf waiting to be dispensed upon the doctor's prescription. Because applicant's prescription drugs are no less susceptible to trademark affixation than other similar goods, the Examining Attorney argues, his requirement for specimens showing proper trademark use should be sustained.

Applicant, on the other hand, takes the position that under the Trademark Law Revision Act of 1988, its mark is being used on its goods in commerce. The revised definition of "use in commerce" (15 U.S.C.A. § 1127) is:

> *Use in Commerce.* The term "use in commerce" means the bona fide use of a mark in the ordinary course of trade and not made merely to reserve a right in a mark. For purposes of this Act, a mark shall be deemed to be in use in commerce—(1) on goods when—(A) it is placed in any manner on the goods or their containers or the displays associated therewith or on the tags or labels affixed thereto, or if the nature of the goods makes such placement impracticable, then on documents associated with the goods or their sale, and (B) the goods are sold or transported in commerce . . .

Applicant's goods are sold by prescription and their sale is regulated by the Food, Drug and Cosmetic Act, which prohibits them from being dispensed without a doctor's prescription. Because a consumer may not choose the product, any point-of-purchase display, according to applicant, would have no utility as inducement to the sale. Therefore, the practice in the industry, according to applicant, is to promote trademarked goods to doctors in the hope that they will be persuaded to prescribe the product.

The specimen brochures are therefore placed in a doctor's office where the prescription is written. While the doctor's office is not technically the point of sale, it is applicant's position that the specimens constitute documents associated with the goods, that these brochures are designed as an inducement to a sale and that the circumstances make the usual placement of the materials at the actual point of sale impracticable. Applicant argues that, due to FDA restrictions on the nature of the information that may be included on labeling for prescription pharmaceuticals, certain marks such as the mark sought to be registered are often not approved by the government. Since the slogan is assertedly prominently used on documents associated with the goods or their sale and because the placement of the brochures in proximity to the goods is made impracticable by "regulatory restrictions and constraints inherent in the marketing of pharmaceuticals products" (applicant's brief, 7), applicant argues that its current use satisfies the statutory requirements for registration.

We agree with the Examining Attorney that the specimen brochures of record distributed to physicians constitute advertising of applicant's goods and are neither displays associated with applicant's goods nor documents associated with the goods or their sale. The brochure in question is given to doctors in order to convince them of the merits of applicant's pharmaceutical products over those of competing products with the expectation that applicant's products will then be prescribed by the doctor. The brochure is similar in nature to advertising which the physician may see in a trade publication. For this reason and because the physician does not purchase the goods, the specimens cannot be equated with the catalogs (i.e., displays associated with the goods) submitted in Lands' End, Inc. v. Manback, 797 F.Supp. 511 (E.D.Va.1992). In that case, the court held that a mail-order retailer's use of a mark in a catalog together with a picture of the goods, words describing the goods, specifications and options from which a customer might choose, as well as mail-order forms and telephone numbers for phone orders were sufficient use to satisfy the trademark statute. In Lands' End, goods were offered and sales were completed directly from the catalog. No sales are made from applicant's brochures, which bear little resemblance to the mail-order catalog with order forms in Lands' End.

Moreover, while applicant has argued that regulatory restrictions may prohibit use of this slogan on labels or packaging, applicant has not submitted a copy of the pertinent regulation or otherwise persuasively demonstrated that this is the case. In any event, the impracticability of which the revised definition in § 1127 of the statute speaks was not intended to encompass a situation where a mark's affixation may be proscribed by law. Rather, it would appear to apply only to those situations where it is difficult for a mark to be physically affixed to the goods or to displays associated therewith.

Decision: The refusal of registration is affirmed.

■ HANAK, MEMBER, Concurring (omitted).

In Re Remington Products, Inc.

Trademark Trial and Appeal Board, 1987.
3 U.S.P.Q. 2d (BNA) 1714.

■ Opinion by ROONEY, MEMBER

Remington Products, Inc. has appealed the refusal to register the term PROUDLY MADE IN USA (MADE IN USA disclaimed) for electric shavers and parts thereof on the Principal Register under § 1052(f). The ground for refusal is that the term does not function as a trademark within the meaning of § 1127 of the Trademark Act and is therefore unregistrable under §§ 1051 and 1052.

The issue on appeal is stated by both applicant and the Examining Attorney to be whether applicant's slogan functions as a trademark. Specifically the Examining Attorney argues that the term sought to be registered is an unimaginative embellishment of a common informational phrase; that adding the word "proudly" does not change the informational character of the slogan; that applicant has attempted to elevate an informational slogan to the level of a trademark by prominently displaying it on its packages, using the letters "TM" in connection therewith and by attempting to promote the phrase as its own on television and in magazines. It is the Examining Attorney's position that, while the absence of "trademark trappings" may be evidence that the subject matter sought to be registered does not function as a trademark, the reverse does not necessarily follow. In support of her position, the Examining Attorney submitted the results of a Lexis/Nexis search.

Applicant's position is that the word "proudly" adds a new dimension to what is, admittedly, a commonly used expression on numerous products; that that word, appearing before the phrase, changes the impression from purely informational to one of pride. The expression is catchy and is prominent on applicant's packaging, it is asserted, and presents an image separate and apart from other matter thereon. Declarations submitted by applicant indicate that in the three years prior to the date thereof, applicant had sold one hundred twenty million dollars worth of shavers and had expended four hundred fifty thousand dollars in advertising the product, assertedly causing applicant's slogan to become recognized by the purchasing public as indicating the source of applicant's shavers. As further evidence of recognition, applicant has also submitted a letter sent to it by a third party who requested applicant's permission to use the notation PROUDLY MADE IN USA on its own goods.

The term, trademark, means "any word, name, symbol or device or any combination thereof adopted and used by a manufacturer or merchant to identify his goods and distinguish them from those manufactured or sold by others." (§ 1127 of the Trademark Act of 1946). We note that not every word or combination thereof which appears on a party's goods functions as a trademark. See In re Morganroth, 208 U.S.P.Q. 284 (TTAB 1980). Thus, the mere fact that applicant's slogan appears on the specimens, even separate and apart from any other indicia which appear on them, does not make it a trademark. To be a mark, the term, or slogan, must be used in a manner calculated to project to purchasers or potential purchasers a single source or origin for the goods in question. Mere intent that a term function as a trademark is not enough in and of itself, any more than attachment of the trademark symbol would be, to make a term a trademark.

A critical element in determining whether a term is a trademark is the impression the term makes on the relevant public. In this case, the inquiry becomes would the term be perceived as a source indicator or merely an informational slogan?

Applicant concedes the informational function of the phrase "Made in USA" and that it is found on many products. The question then is, what effect does the addition of the adverb PROUDLY have on the relevant public as far as their perception of applicant's slogan is concerned? The Examining Attorney quoted the Board's statement in In re Melville Corporation, 228 U.S.P.Q. 970 (TTAB 1986) to the effect that, "(T)he fact that applicant may convey similar information in a slightly different way than others is not determinative". Applicant's slogan, in addition to informing the public of the product's locale of manufacture, adds further information about the state of mind of the manufacturer and/or its employees in connection with the production of the goods.

It is common knowledge that today's American marketplace has a surplus of foreign-made goods and that American manufacturers are anxious to encourage purchasers to give preference to American products. While the Lexis/Nexis material submitted by the Examining Attorney may not illustrate use of the identical slogan used by applicant, the fact that there is an organization known as The Crafted with Pride in the USA Council is an indication of the extent to which emphasis has been and is being placed on American manufacture. The copy of applicant's ad from the New York Times, December 9, 1984 is in keeping with this trend. For example: We, the employees of Remington Products, Inc. are proud to tell you how our company, manufacturers of superior quality electric shavers, is winning its battle in today's global economic conflict.... Remington shavers, the only shavers manufactured in the United States, are produced by loyal, dedicated American workers who take great pride in producing superior quality shavers ... our workforce has doubled over the last 3 years, providing more jobs for American workers.... These commercials not only promote the quality image of American made Remington shavers but also uplifts the standards world-wide for other quality built American made products.

The text of this ad only impresses upon the public the informational nature of the slogan so that when it is seen on the shaver box, that is the message which comes across. The slogan used by applicant conveys the same information in shorthand form.

Use of the letters "TM" on a product does not make unregistrable matter into a trademark. Nor is recognition by one individual sufficient to do so. While applicant may have had substantial sales and advertising of its product, that does not prove recognition by the public of the subject slogan as a trademark. There is nothing in the record to indicate that purchasers recognize the slogan as a source indicator.

Decision: Accordingly, the refusal to register is affirmed.

Senate Report No. 100–515
P.L. 100–667, Trademark Law Revision Act of 1988
100th Cong., 2d Sess. 4–6 & 23–35.
1988 U.S.C.C.A.N. 5577, 5580–82 & 5585–87.
May 12, 1988.

*   *   *   *   *

INTENT TO USE

Section 1883 will improve the federal trademark registration system by eliminating the requirement that U.S. citizens and businesses, unlike their foreign counterparts, must use a mark in commerce before they can file an application to register it. The Lanham Act currently requires that a U.S. business or individual seeking to register a trademark in the United States first make use of the mark in interstate commerce before it can apply for registration. This requirement unfairly discriminates against U.S. citizens, as compared to foreign citizens, puts significant legal risks on the introduction of new products and services, and gives preference to certain industries over others, frequently disadvantaging small companies and individuals. Today, the United States is the only developed country that requires use of a mark before an application for registration may be filed. This disparity between U.S. law and that of most other countries results in foreign applicants having an advantage over U.S. applicants in obtaining trademark registration rights.

*   *   *   *   *

The Lanham Act's preapplication use requirement also creates unnecessary legal uncertainty for a U.S. business planning to introduce products or services into the marketplace. It simply has no assurance that after selecting and adopting a mark, and possibly making a sizable investment in packaging, advertising and marketing, it will not learn that its use of the mark infringes the rights another acquired through earlier use. In an age of national, if not global, marketing, this has a chilling effect on business investment. This effect is not merely theoretical, but is real. And it can be costly: Marketing a new product domestically often exceeds $30 million for a large company and can consume the life-savings of an individual or small entrepreneur.

*   *   *   *   *

Despite its numerous virtues, a registration system based on intent also carries some potential for abuse. A single business or individual might, for instance, attempt to monopolize a vast number of potential marks on the basis or a mere statement of intent to use the marks in the future. To minimize such risks, S.1883 requires the specified intent to be bona fide.

This bona fide requirement focuses on an objective good-faith test to establish that the intent is genuine.

* * * * *

Subsection (b)(1)(A) [of this Act] specifically requires all applicants who apply to register a trademark on the basis of intended use to state their bona fide intention to use the mark in commerce on or in connection with all the goods identified in the application. The goods must be identified with sufficient specificity to confirm the bona fide nature of the applicant's intent and to permit those searching the trademark records of the Patent and Trademark Office to determine the existence of conflict. Bona fide intent is measured by objective factors. A statement of intent to use a mark on specifically identified products in the future may be sufficient. An applicant may safely make this statement in its original application without having taken concrete steps to create and introduce a new product, provided that in fact it intends to use the mark. However, other circumstances may cast doubt on the bona fide nature of the intent or even disprove it entirely. For example, the applicant may have filed numerous intent-to-use applications to register the same mark for many more new products than are contemplated, numerous intent-to-use applications for a variety of desirable trademarks intended to be used on a single new product, numerous intent-to-use applications to register marks consisting of or incorporating descriptive terms relating to a contemplated new product, numerous intent-to-use applications to replace applications which have lapsed because no timely declaration of use has been filed, an excessive number of intent-to-use applications to register marks which ultimately were not actually used, an excessive number of intent-to-use applications in relation to the number of products the applicant is likely to introduce under the applied-for marks during the pendency of the applications, or applications unreasonably lacking in specificity in describing the proposed goods. Other circumstances may also indicate the absence of genuine bona fide intent to actually use the mark. As the mark proceeds to registration, the goods identified in the application may be narrowed, but they may not be broadened. In addition, subsection (b)(1)(A) expressly provides that use of a mark in commerce will continue to be a prerequisite to registration, unless the mark is applied for registration under § 1126. (Pursuant to present interpretations of U.S. treaty obligations, these applicants are not required to use their marks prior to registration.) This language is included to emphasize the central role that use continues to play in U.S. trademark law. . . . Although "bona fide" is an accepted legal term, it can be read broadly or narrowly, subjectively or objectively, by a court or the Patent and Trademark Office. In connection with this bill, "bona fide" should be read to mean a fair, objective determination of the applicant's intent based on all the circumstances. To avoid abuse of the intent-to-use system, the committee amended the first paragraph of proposed Section 1(b) of the Act to require that applicant's bona fide intention must reflect the good-faith circumstances surrounding the intended use. An applicant's bona fide intention to use a mark must reflect an intention that is firm, though it may be contingent on the outcome of an event (that is, market research or product testing). Thus, an applicant could, under certain circumstances, file more than one intent-to-use application covering the same goods and still have the requisite bona fide intention to use each mark. However, if a product has already been marketed under one mark and an applicant continues to maintain additional applications for marks intended for use on or in connection with the same product, without good cause, this may call into question the bona fide nature of the intent. In addition, and applicant's bona fide intent must reflect an intention to use the mark in the context of the legislation's revised definition of "use in commerce," that is, use "in the ordinary course of trade, commensurate with the circumstances and not [made] merely to reserve a right in a mark." This bona fide intention to use must be present for all the goods or services recited in the application.

G. Heileman Brewing Company, Inc. v. Anheuser–Busch, Inc.

United States Court of Appeals, Seventh Circuit, 1989.
873 F.2d 985.

■ CUDAHY, CIRCUIT JUDGE.

Defendant-appellant Anheuser–Busch, Incorporated ("Busch") appeals a judgment declaring that "LA" is not a protectible trademark for a low alcohol beer introduced by Busch in 1984. The district court found that the initials LA are merely descriptive of low alcohol beer and have not acquired secondary meaning. Accordingly, the district court concluded that the use of LA (or "L.A.") by G. Heileman Brewing Company ("Heileman") and Miller Brewing Company ("Miller") on their own low alcohol beer labels does not constitute trademark infringement or unfair competition. We affirm.

I

While traveling in Australia in 1981, August A. Busch III, the president and chief executive officer of Anheuser–Busch, studied the production and marketing of low alcohol beer, a product that has experienced immense popularity in that country since its introduction in 1979. In Australia, the name "LA" has gained widespread recognition as signifying low or light alcohol beer on labels such as Tooth LA, South Australian LA, Courage LA, and Carling LA. After returning to the United States, Mr. Busch directed his company to commence research and development of a low alcohol beer. [Internal memoranda during this early planning phase reveal that Anheuser–Busch aspired to preempt the low alcohol beer market and emulate the success enjoyed previously by Miller in capturing the low calorie beer segment with its "LITE" beer.] Anheuser–Busch envisaged a new low alcohol product that would appeal to current lifestyle trends, which emphasize physical fitness and moderate drinking habits.

In an effort to select a brand name that could become the "bar call of the 80's," Busch retained the Interbrand Corporation to develop and test

can't use trademark to preempt the market [handwritten margin note] potential names for its new low alcohol beer. After researching the subject, Interbrand advised Busch that using "LA" as a stand-alone brand name "would not, in all likelihood, be protectible since it clearly and obviously stands for low alcohol, and as such is clearly an abbreviation of the generic descriptor." Trial Exhibit 12. Interbrand also warned Busch that low alcohol or LA would probably be referred to as a category descriptor for all low alcohol beers, including those produced by other brewing companies, thereby presenting a significant potential for confusion. Id. Therefore, Interbrand recommended a corporate source approach employing the name "LA from Anheuser–Busch," which Busch ultimately adopted.

On January 20, 1984, Anheuser–Busch issued a press release announcing its new product and informing the industry and the public that "LA from Anheuser–Busch" was a "light alcohol product." Trial Exhibit 22. In its efforts to develop an effective marketing strategy, Busch proceeded warily in pursuit of its dual objectives: to use LA as an arbitrary or suggestive term in order to attain trademark protection and, concurrently, to describe the unique low alcohol quality of its new beer to consumers without violating regulations that proscribed the advertising of reduced alcohol content. Busch orchestrated a publicity campaign in which it tacitly encouraged public relations and advertising agencies, as well as media representatives, to describe LA to consumers as low, less or light in alcohol.[a] Heileman, 676 F.Supp. at 1459. The district court found that, although Anheuser–Busch personnel equated LA with low alcohol in communications within the company and in advertising and point-of-sale materials, Busch subsequently sought to disclaim the initialism in various ways. For example, it deleted the periods from the letters; it claimed that the letters had no meaning; it modified its advertising message from "low alcohol" to "half the alcohol" and promoted the phrase "reduced alcohol" as the category descriptor for the new beer. Id. at 1458.

Meanwhile, the concept of low alcohol beer had been fermenting elsewhere in the beer industry. On March 7, 1984, the Stroh Brewery Company obtained BATF approval for two beer labels: SCHAEFER LA and OLD MILWAUKEE LA. Despite objections from Busch, Stroh then issued a press release announcing its plans to market SCHAEFER LA. Likewise, Heileman had been developing its own version of low alcohol beer since early 1982. Apprised of Busch's new LA product, of Stroh's announced plans to market SCHAEFER LA and of the BATF approval of both brewers' beer labels, Heileman announced on March 29, 1984, its plans to market low alcohol beer under labels containing its own house marks with "L.A." as a category descriptor—for example, CARLING BLACK LABEL L.A. and BLATZ L.A. Heileman, 676 F.Supp. at 1452. Miller was also on the LA campaign trail. In March of 1984, Miller began developing a low alcohol beer and sent its brand manager to Australia to study the estab-

---

[a] By the time of trial, Anheuser–Busch had spent approximately $27,000,000 advertising its LA beer.

lished low alcohol beer market there. After consulting its retained advertising agency, Miller ultimately adopted "SHARP'S LA" as its brand name.

On March 16, 1984, Anheuser–Busch became the first user of the LA label in commerce by sending shipments of low alcohol beer to its wholesalers. After learning of Heileman's plans to begin using the LA label, Anheuser–Busch sent a cease and desist letter to Heileman, dated April 2, 1984, claiming exclusive trademark rights in the initials LA. Heileman responded on April 18 by filing this action to protect its right to use "L.A." with a Heileman house mark on its own low alcohol beer. The following day, Heileman commenced use of the "L.A." mark in commerce.

In its complaint, Heileman seeks a declaratory judgment that LA is descriptive and generic and that, therefore, its use does not constitute trademark infringement or unfair competition. In addition, Heileman requests injunctive relief permanently enjoining Busch from interfering or threatening to interfere with Heileman's use of the term "LA" to denominate low alcohol beer. Miller's complaint requests similar relief.

II

[The court found the case justiciable.]

III

A

The principal argument raised on appeal by Busch is that the district court misapplied the law in holding that the initials LA are merely descriptive and unprotectible. As we delineated in Miller Brewing Co. v. G. Heileman Brewing Co., 561 F.2d 75, 79 (7th Cir.1977), cert. denied, 434 U.S. 1025, 98 S.Ct. 751, 54 L.Ed.2d 772 (1978), a term for which trademark protection is claimed generally fits somewhere in the spectrum of classifications ranging from (1) generic or common descriptive and (2) merely descriptive to (3) suggestive and (4) arbitrary or fanciful. A generic or common descriptive term is one which is commonly used as the name or description of a kind of goods. It cannot become a trademark under any circumstances [, e.g., "light beer," "decaffeinated coffee"].... A merely descriptive term specifically describes a characteristic or ingredient of an article. It can, by acquiring a secondary meaning, i.e., becoming "distinctive of the applicant's goods" (15 U.S.C.A. § 1052(f)), become a valid trademark [, e.g., "bubbly champagne," "Auto Page"]. A suggestive term suggests rather than describes an ingredient or characteristic of the goods and requires the observer or listener to use imagination and perception to determine the nature of the goods. Such a term can be protected without proof of a secondary meaning [, e.g., "Tide," "Coppertone"]. An arbitrary or fanciful term enjoys the same full protection as a suggestive term but is far enough removed from the merely descriptive not to be vulnerable to possible attack as being merely descriptive rather than suggestive [, e.g., "Kodak," "Black & White" scotch]. Id. (citations omitted). In Walt–West Enterprises v. Gannett Co., 695 F.2d 1050 (7th Cir.1982), we provided further clarification:

Properly understood, the so-called trademark spectrum reflects levels of judicial skepticism concerning whether the term actually serves the source denoting function which a mark is supposed to perform. Terms which are arbitrary, fanciful, or suggestive as applied to a given product or service are naturally understood by the consuming public as designations of origin: it is unlikely that such terms would be understood as anything else.... Descriptive terms, on the other hand, are ill-suited to serve as designations of origin, for such terms are naturally understood by the consuming public in their ordinary descriptive sense.

Id. at 1057. Thus, if LA is deemed generic, as Heileman and Miller assert, it is not entitled to trademark protection. Contrariwise, if LA is suggestive, as Busch contends, it is protectible. Finally, if LA is merely descriptive, as the court below determined, it is protectible only upon proof of secondary meaning.

It is unarguable that the phrase "low alcohol" is descriptive and unamenable to trademark protection. But whether the initials for this descriptive phrase should also be deemed descriptive presents a separate, yet related, issue. The law in this circuit is ostensibly incongruous and thus requires some clarification.

Anheuser–Busch argues that the district court misapplied the legal standard in determining the protectibility of initials and that, therefore, we should review the district court's decision de novo. Specifically, Busch adverts to the district court's observation in footnote 48 to its opinion that "initials are merely short forms of the words for which they stand and should be accorded the same degree of protection as those words." Heileman, 676 F.Supp. at 1493 n. 48. This formulation was presumably based on the language in National Conference of Bar Examiners v. Multistate Legal Studies, Inc., 692 F.2d 478, 488 (7th Cir.1982), cert. denied, 464 U.S. 814, 104 S.Ct. 69, 78 L.Ed.2d 83 (1983), that "[a]bbreviations for generic or common descriptive phrases must be treated similarly." In National Conference, this court reversed the district court's decision according trademark protection to the phrase "Multistate Bar Examination" and its initials "MBE." We reasoned that [u]nder settled trademark law if the components of a trade name are common descriptive terms, a combination of such terms retains that quality. We note further that [the fact that] plaintiffs also use the initials "MBE" to designate their test is of no consequence. Abbreviations for generic or common descriptive phrases must be treated similarly. Id. at 488 (citing FS Services, Inc. v. Custom Farm Services, Inc., 471 F.2d 671, 674 (7th Cir.1972)).

Busch argues vigorously against the concept that the initials of descriptive words are inherently descriptive. Instead, Busch contends that the "accepted rule" for determining whether initials are to be treated similarly to the descriptive or generic words that they represent is whether the letters have become generally recognized as descriptive or generic by the general public. According to Busch, National Conference misstates the law in this circuit by misreading the principle of FS Services, Inc. v. Custom Farm Services, Inc., 471 F.2d 671 (7th Cir.1972). In FS Services, we indeed stated that "abbreviations for generic terms where they are generally recognized must be treated similarly." 471 F.2d at 674 (emphasis supplied). There we concluded that the letters "FS have come to signify 'farm service' ... [which] are descriptive or generic terms." Id. Busch cites FS Services and numerous other authorities as support for the principle that initials for descriptive phrases are not ipso facto descriptive; rather, only if initials are generally recognized as signifying the corresponding descriptive phrases are they to be treated similarly for purposes of trademark protection. See, e.g., Modern Optics v. Univis Lens Co., 234 F.2d 504 (C.C.P.A.1956)("CV," initials for "continuous vision," not ipso facto unregistrable; "as a general rule, initials cannot be considered descriptive unless they have become so generally understood as representing descriptive words as to be accepted as substantially synonymous therewith").

Of course, we are aware that Busch's point is valid in principle: the ultimate test of descriptiveness is recognition by the consuming public. But this does not mean that the statement of the district court in footnote 48 is incorrect in any fundamental way. It is possible, although not likely, that the public might become acquainted with initials used in connection with a product without ever being aware that the initials were derived from, and stood for, a descriptive phrase or a generic name. This is conceivable, though rather improbable, because the connection between the initials and the descriptive words is in normal course very likely to become known. The process of identifying initials with the set of descriptive words from which they are derived is, after all, usually fairly simple. Ordinarily, no flight of imagination or keen logical insight is required. There is a natural assumption that initials do generally stand for something. All that needs to be done is to convert the next-to-obvious to the obvious by answering the inevitable question: What do the initials stand for?

As a rule, no very extensive or complicated process of education or indoctrination is required to convey that initials stand for descriptive words. The relatively straightforward answer to an evident question identifies the initials with the descriptive phrase from which they are derived. By contrast, the process whereby the same initials might acquire a secondary meaning pointing to the source of the product is often lengthy and expensive. As a practical matter, there must be a presumption that initials mean, or will soon come to mean, to the public the descriptive phrase from which they are derived. Although the matter is certainly not foreclosed, there is a heavy burden on a trademark claimant seeking to show an independent meaning of initials apart from the descriptive words which are their source. The imposition of such a burden is consistent with the policy of the trademark laws to guard against unjustified appropriation from the public domain of terms needed to perform a descriptive function. Such a burden is also consonant with the general rule that the claimant of trademark law protection bears the burden of establishing by a preponderance of the evidence that an unregistered mark is entitled to trademark status.

Thus, the district court's statement in footnote 48 to the Heileman opinion certainly does not miss the mark so fundamentally as to constitute legal error per se. Rather, it reflects the court's common sense view that, as a practical matter, initials do not usually differ significantly in their trademark role from the descriptive words that they represent.

B

Nor do we think, as Busch suggests, that the court's observation in footnote 48 tainted the district court's factual analysis and ultimate determination that LA is merely descriptive. To the contrary, the court acknowledges throughout its exhaustive opinion that the true test is one of consumer perception—how is LA perceived by the average prospective consumer? Accordingly, the court made specific factual findings that consumers actually understood LA as standing for and descriptive of low alcohol. See Heileman, 676 F.Supp. at 1459, 1460, 1487–88. These factual findings were based upon elaborate consumer surveys as well as Busch's own promotional advertising campaign and extensive media publicity.

Notwithstanding the parties' numerous objections to the consumer survey evidence submitted to the district court, we think the district court carefully and thoroughly sifted through this barrage of statistics and properly ascribed greater weight to those surveys warranting it.

In particular, we agree that the marketing studies conducted by Dr. Yoram Wind, a Professor of Marketing at the Wharton School of the University of Pennsylvania, were not entitled to great weight. In order to determine whether the initialism LA connotes (or denotes) low alcohol when displayed on a can of beer, Dr. Wind isolated the responses of those consumers who had never seen, heard of or tried LA beer. Of this sampling, comprised of those wholly unfamiliar with LA beer, only 4.9% associated LA with light, low or less alcohol, while 76.5% recognized LA as a brand name. When those respondents who had some prior exposure to LA were also taken into account, approximately 80% of the total pool surveyed, after being shown a can of "LA from Anheuser–Busch," identified Anheuser–Busch as the source of the beer. Based on these results, Dr. Wind concluded that LA does not connote low alcohol beer to consumers; rather, consumers perceive LA as a brand name.

We are persuaded by the view of the district court that Dr. Wind's primary focus on a thoroughly uninformed consumer audience renders his conclusions highly suspect. Whether initials stand in the public mind for the descriptive words from which they are derived is a question to be answered by looking at the public as it is—not as it might be in a total and unnatural state of disinformation. Consumer perception should be assessed by examining the average potential consumer in the context of the existing marketplace and exposed to the information currently available in the marketplace. This approach is supported by both law and logic. The opinions of the totally uninformed in an abstract, hypothetical context are of dubious relevance because they do not accurately reflect the perceptions of potential beer purchasers. Typically, someone must first be informed of the existence and nature of a product before he chooses to purchase or consume it. It is the perception of this somewhat informed audience that massive advertising is intended to impact. See Application of Abcor Development Corp., 588 F.2d at 814. In addition, evidence of the context in which a mark is used on labels, packages or in advertising material is probative in assessing the likely reaction of prospective purchasers to the mark. See id. It is normal for the public to learn through advertising, casual exposure or word-of-mouth that the initials of descriptive phrases stand for those descriptive phrases. To disregard these factors and focus on a hypothetical, unenlightened public is illogical and may lead to illusory results.

Further, Dr. Wind's finding that a majority of the total consumer audience perceived LA as a brand name is not determinative of the issue presented. Even though a term is prominently displayed and perceived by poll respondents as a brand name on a beer label, the term may nonetheless be classified as merely descriptive for trademark purposes.

For these reasons, we believe that the district court properly discounted the statistical evidence proffered by Busch and accorded greater weight to the survey results submitted by Heileman and Miller. These results demonstrated that a majority of prospective consumers recognize that LA, as applied to beer, stands for and describes low alcohol. Heileman, 676 F.Supp. at 1487–88. These consumer survey results were buttressed by the evidence of Busch's initial massive advertising campaign and media publicity which were likely to create a public perception that LA means light or low alcohol. See Anheuser–Busch, Inc. v. Stroh Brewery Co., 750 F.2d 631, 649 (Bright, J., dissenting)("I think it crucial to consider the initials 'LA' in the context of the Anheuser–Busch advertising and the probable course of development in the low alcohol beer segment."). Busch has failed to sufficiently counter this evidence and, therefore, has not met the burden of proof entitling it to trademark protection.

[The court goes on to acknowledge that a different conclusion was reached in the Eighth Circuit, which classified LA as suggestive and entitled to protection, Anheuser–Busch, Inc. v. Stroh Brewery Co., 750 F.2d 631 (1984).]

C

Since we do not think that the district court clearly erred in its factual determination that LA is merely descriptive, we further conclude that the district court did not err in denying the requests by Heileman and Miller for a declaratory judgment that LA is generic, as well as for permanent injunctive relief. Heileman and Miller claim that, because LA is generic as a matter of law, they are entitled to an injunction permanently enjoining Busch from interfering with Heileman and Miller's use of the LA name. Presumably, the concern is that the "merely descriptive" designation may allow Busch to later claim secondary meaning and again seek trademark protection. Otherwise we do not understand why the plaintiffs would link a determination of genericness to their request for a permanent injunction. Heileman and Miller contend somewhat cryptically in their briefs that a permanent injunction and a "generic" declaration are necessarily intertwined. If so, our independent conclusion that the district court did not abuse its discretion in denying permanent injunctive relief obviates the need for us to decide the genericness question. In any event, we think LA is probably not generic.

As we recently explained in Henri's Food Products Co., Inc. v. Tasty Snacks, Inc., 817 F.2d 1303, 1305–06 (7th Cir.1987), an adjective can be a generic term when that word is a part of a common descriptive name of a kind of goods. In order to be generic, however (as the word implies), the word in question must serve to denominate a type, a kind, a genus or a subcategory of goods. The dispositive question is whether "LA" was a commonly used and commonly understood term prior to its association with the product or products at issue. And the dictionary, with its continuing catalogue of words arriving in and departing from common speech, is an especially appropriate source of evidence about the meaning attached by a linguistic group to a particular [ ]symbol. Gimix, Inc. v. JS & A Group, Inc., 699 F.2d 901, 905 (7th Cir.1983). With respect to this issue, the district court cited two historical facts which, in its view, precluded a finding of genericness: low alcohol beer was a new arrival on the beer market in this country and, prior to April 27, 1984, BATF regulations prohibited references to low alcohol content in the advertising or labeling of beer. Consequently, consumer surveys illustrated that many consumers evidently were unaware of low alcohol beer at all and, as the district court found, "it was not surprising that the poll takers found that these consumers, as well as those with only recent exposure to the product, had not formed a consensus that 'LA' or 'low alcohol' is the name of a distinctive type of beer." Heileman, 676 F.Supp. at 1490. In addition, the district court noted that there was no evidence that either "LA" or "low alcohol" is defined by any lexicon as a genus of beer. Id. at n. 45. Based upon these findings, it is certainly reasonable to conclude that LA is not generic. Cf. Miller Brewing Co. v. G. Heileman Brewing Co., 561 F.2d 75, 80 ("light" classified as generic where it had been widely used in the beer industry before Miller began using "LITE" and was defined in the dictionary as a characteristic of beer).

* * * * *

In the present case, the initials LA were used descriptively (or possibly generically) in Australia for "low alcohol." They were removed from that context to be brought back by Mr. Busch for use in the United States. Although it is conceivable that they would not fulfill a descriptive function here as well, it is the more plausible assumption that they would.

It would be unusual trademark policy to accord exclusive rights and trademark protection to Anheuser–Busch, which appropriated the LA appellation from Australia and then used it in a descriptive manner to preempt the low alcohol beer market in this country. The trademark laws ... are designed to protect names selected by a company and promoted with the intent of indicating the ownership and source of the goods. It is inconsistent with the objectives of the trademark laws to suggest that the protection of those laws should be extended to cases in which a company attempts to arrogate for business-promotional reasons a mark that is essentially descriptive. Anheuser–Busch, Inc. v. Stroh Brewery Co., 750 F.2d at 651 (Bright, J., dissenting). The determination by the district court that LA is merely descriptive and unprotectible is supported by the record and consistent with sound policy. Therefore, the decision of the district court is affirmed.

NOTES

1. *Categories of marks.* Section 1127 of the Lanham Act defines four categories of marks, which are all made registrable by §§ 1052–1054. A **trademark** (when not used in its generic sense to refer to all kinds of marks protected by the Lanham Act), is a mark that is used with goods (e.g. games, chickens, perfumes). A **service mark** is used in connection with services (e.g. dry cleaners, travel agencies, investment advisors). A **certification mark** is a mark that one entity owns to signal something about goods or services produced or provided by others—for example, that the goods are especially well-made (e.g. the Good Housekeeping Seal of Approval), that they are produced with a particular material (e.g. the Woolmark), that they are made in a specific place (e.g. Champagne), or that they are manufactured by a certain organization (e.g. the Ladies' Garment Workers Union). A **collective mark** is a mark that members of an association use to identify their own goods or services (e.g. the twin pines of cooperative grocery stores or Sebastian for hair-care products sold through salons).

The requirements for trademarks set out in the Principal Cases apply equally to all these marks. There are, however, additional requirements for certification marks. A certification mark is intended to signal that the goods or services in connection with which it is used have met an objective standard. Accordingly, the owner of a certification mark must be neutral and cannot be using the mark for marketing purposes itself. Moreover, a certification mark can be cancelled if the owner fails to exercise control over its use or discriminatorily refuses to certify goods that meet the standard, § 1064(5). Because organizations sometimes try to evade the strict requirements for certification marks by registering their symbols as collective marks, there have been occasional attempts to abolish the collective mark category.[1]

In addition to defining protectable marks, § 1127 also defines a "trade name" and "commercial name" as terms that identify a business or vocation. Because they do not appear in conjunction with goods or services and do not send the appropriate sort of signal to consumers, they do not qualify for protection under the Lanham Act simply by virtue of being trade names. However, there is nothing in the Act that prevents a company from acquiring a trademark right in its trade name by using it on goods or

[1] See, e.g., Breitenfeld, Collective Marks—Should They Be Abolished?, 47 Trademark Rep. 1 (1957). See also Note, The Collective Trademark: Invitation to Abuse, 68 Yale L.J. 528 (1959).

services. For an example, look back at the registrations of Coca Cola for soda pop that were reproduced in the last assignment. The company that is listed as owning these marks is the Coca Cola Company.

2. *Use versus intent to use.* It is difficult to overstate how fundamentally the 1988 Amendment altered U.S. trademark law. Before this change, trademark rights were acquired through *use*, not through *registration*. Federal registration was mainly aimed at enabling producers to transfer the goodwill they had acquired in one location to other locations. It did that by creating a national register that constructively notified every producer in the United States to avoid using the same mark. Without use, there was no right to enter the federal registration system because there was no goodwill to transfer. Or, before use, the producer had not accomplished the socially desirable goal of creating goodwill, and therefore had not paid the price for admission to the federal system. The intent-to-use provisions undermine the core of this rationale. The right to transfer goodwill across the nation is now based on something the PTO has done, not on the applicant's accomplishment of a socially desired activity.

3. *Token uses.* Before 1988, when the Lanham Act did not permit registration without actual use, it often happened that a company invested heavily in bringing a symbol to the point where it could be used, only to find that it was unregistrable; that, for example, another entity fulfilled the requirements for registering the mark sooner. To reduce this risk, courts were inclined to consider some rather flimsy transactions as meeting the use requirement. Examples include single sales, sales internal to the company, soliciting orders from friends, and flying mock-ups cross country.[2] Although the intent-to-use amendment was largely aimed at other concerns, one side benefit is that it removes the need for this so-called "token use" doctrine. Accordingly, another portion of the Senate Report excerpted above implies that the amendment legislatively overrules the token use cases:

> "Token use is a contrived and commercially transparent practice— nothing more than a legal fiction. At the same time, token use is essential under current law because it recognizes present day marketing costs and realities; it reduces some of the legal and economic risks associated with entering the marketplace; and it nominally achieves the threshold 'use' required to apply for federal registration and the creation of trademark rights in advance of commercial use.
>
> Unfortunately, token use is not available to all businesses and industries. For example, it is virtually impossible to make token use of a trademark on a large or expensive product such as an airplane. The same is true for service industries (that is, hotels, restaurants, and banks) prior to opening for business. Similarly, it is difficult for small business and individuals to avail themselves of token use because they frequently lack the resources or the knowledge to engage in the

---

[2] See, e.g., Wallace Computer Services Inc. v. Sun Microsystems Inc., 13 U.S.P.Q.2d (BNA) 1324 (N.D.Ill.1989); Bertolli USA Inc. v. Filippo Bertolli Fine Foods Ltd., 662 F.Supp. 203, 6 U.S.P.Q.2d (BNA) 1043 (S.D.N.Y.1987); Beech Aircraft Corp. v. Lightning Aircraft Co., 1 U.S.P.Q.2d 1290 (T.T.A.B. 1986).

practice. Token use is also troublesome for another reason. It allows companies to obtain registration based on minimal use. Often these companies change their marketing plans and subsequently do not make commercial use. The result is that the trademark register is clogged with unused marks, making the clearance of new marks more difficult and discouraging others from adopting and using marks which should otherwise be available.

* * *

Since token use becomes unnecessary and inappropriate under the intent-to-use application system proposed by S.1883, the definition of 'use in commerce' in § 1127 of the Act is strengthened to reflect this significant change in the law.''[3]

Section 1127 now specifies that "use in commerce" means use "in the ordinary course of trade."

4. *Distinctiveness.* The categorization of meanings used in *Heileman*— generic, descriptive, suggestive, and arbitrary—is generally credited to *Abercrombie & Fitch Co. v. Hunting World, Inc.*[4] They describe a spectrum ranging from marks that can never be registered (generic), to marks that can be placed on the Principal Register upon additional investment (descriptive), to marks that can be placed on the Principal Register immediately (suggestive and arbitrary).

a. *Arbitrary marks.* At first blush, one might think that producers will always adopt arbitrary marks. After all, once such a mark is coined, it can be placed on the Principal Register immediately—no extra investment is required to give it meaning, and no arguments need be had with the examiner about whether it falls on the suggestive rather than descriptive side of the line. In fact, at common law, a coined mark had considerable advantages in litigation. The objective in early cases was usually to prevent passing off—that is, to stop the defendant from marketing his goods in a manner that diverted the plaintiff's consumers to himself. If the plaintiff's mark was at all descriptive of the goods, courts generally took the view that the defendant was using it in its descriptive capacity, and not in order to fool customers. Accordingly, the plaintiff needed to prove that the defendant actually intended to confuse consumers and that he succeeded.[5] If, however, the plaintiff's mark was arbitrary, the use of the very same arbitrary word on defendant's goods gave rise to a presumption that the defendant intended to pass off. Then, the plaintiff only needed to adduce proof that consumers were likely to be confused.

b. *Descriptive marks.* Why, then, would producers ever adopt anything but a coined term? One reason is to save on the costs of consumer education. Choosing an arbitrary word such as Apple for computers is cute, but convincing customers to pay thousands of dollars for something that

---

[3] Sen. Rep. No. 100–515, supra, at 4–6; U.S.C.A.C.A.N. at 5580–5582.

[4] 537 F.2d 4 (2d Cir.1976).

[5] See, e.g., American Washboard Co. v. Saginaw Mfg. Co., 103 F. 281 (6th Cir.1900).

sounds like fruit is not simple. Much better is to call yourself by a name that gives purchasers some sense of what it is that is being sold and some hook on which to hang an association between the mark and the product.

To a certain extent, the best hook is one that actually names the product—INTERNATIONAL BUSINESS MACHINES or PERSONAL COMPUTER, for example. Unfortunately, words like these are so graphic, customers are likely to perceive them as product descriptions, and not as marks. That is why they cannot be registered without proof of secondary meaning. "Secondary meaning" means that consumers have come to see the mark as a signal, not as as a description. Once a mark has secondary meaning, the primary meaning recedes, and so the mark becomes capable of distinguishing the products of the trademark owner from the goods of other producers.

c. *Suggestive marks.* Given that descriptive marks are too informational and arbitrary marks are not informative enough, the obvious conclusion is that suggestive marks are just right. Terms like POWER BOOK and THINK PAD provide hints about the product, but they are only clues: "[a] suggestive mark ... requires imagination to make a connection between the mark and an attribute of the product."[6] Since these words are capable of distinguishing one producer's version of the product category from another's, they can be registered immediately. There is no need to establish secondary meaning because, like arbitrary marks, customers know from their very first encounter with these terms that they are trademarks.

d. *Generic marks.* The previous discussion leaves us with the question of why Anheuser–Busch chose to ignore Interbrand's advice and adopt a mark as descriptive as LA for low alcohol beer. Some companies are attracted to descriptive marks because they hope that in an unconscious way, customers will come to think of their product as the only really genuine version of the goods—a strategy that worked for IBM for many years. However, Anheuser–Busch may have been trying to do more. The court mentioned that "[i]nternal memoranda during this early planning phase reveal that Anheuser–Busch aspired to preempt the low alcohol beer market." In other words, the company was hoping to acquire trademark rights over the *only* way that customers knew to ask for low alcohol beer. That way, every time someone came into a bar and asked for a low alcohol beer, the bartender would be required to fill the order with Anheuser–Busch's product. Heileman, Miller, and other brewers would never make a sale, and so Anheuser–Busch would "preempt" the market.

Trademark law is intended to facilitate competition, not stifle it. Accordingly, trademark rights can never be granted in the only effective means of referring to a product category. This is true whether customers perceive the word as a description or whether they perceive it as a trademark. If a word is generic—if it is the way the public has come to describe the category to which the goods belong—it can never be protected: it cannot be registered under federal law, nor will it be protected by the

[6] Official Airline Guides, Inc. v. Goss, 6 F.3d 1385, 1391 (9th Cir.1993).

unfair competition law of any state. Such words must remain in the public domain for the use of every producer's customers. See also Assignment 4, which describes the loss of trademark protection through genericide.

5. *Foreign words.* The PTO generally translates foreign words into English in order to decide where on the spectrum they fit. Weiss Noodle Co. v. Golden Cracknel and Specialty Co.[7] is an example. In that case, registration of "Ha–Lush–Ka" for egg noodles was refused on the ground that halushka means noodles in Hungarian. The reasons for this practice (which the PTO occasionally forgets to use) are first, goods with foreign names are often aimed initially at ethnic markets. In those markets, the name is as generic as the English translation is to English speakers. Second, when the larger society acquires a taste for foreign goods, it often acquires an interest in the culture as well. Since it will want to use the same word that members of the culture use for the category, the word also becomes generic to English speakers. For example, no one calls a tortilla a corn pancake. Thus, Anheuser–Busch should not have been surprised that America calls its Australian-inspired product by the name Australians attach to the category.

6. *Functionality.* The doctrine of functionality is closely related to the ban on generic marks, as it too prevents producers from stifling competition by asserting trademark rights in an element that is needed to properly market goods within a product category. The best example of functionality comes from a case decided by Learned Hand under state unfair competition law, Crescent Tool Co. v. Kilborn & Bishop Co.[8] Claiming that the public had come to identify the crescent-shaped head of its wrenches as its trademark, the plaintiff argued that the defendant should be enjoined from producing a product of a similar shape. Judge Hand disagreed. He recognized that the plaintiff had a right to prevent passing off, and that it had established a protectable trademark in the name "Crescent Tool Company." However, he refused to enjoin the production of other crescent shape wrenches. In his view, only "nonessential" elements of a product can serve as a trademark. If the crescent shape is essential to the proper operation of a wrench in tight places, it cannot be protected by trademark law.

Part B in this Assignment illustrates how the doctrine of functionality comes into play in deciding whether a mark is registrable.

7. *Secondary meaning.* This term is actually a misnomer. A term acquires secondary meaning when its *primary* meaning in consumers' minds is the trademark meaning. There are, in effect, two ways to demonstrate that a mark has passed from being descriptive and has come to the point where it distinguishes the goods of one particular producer. First, evidence of the type adduced in the Principal Cases can be used to show how consumers actually perceive the mark. Second, the applicant can establish a prima facie case of secondary meaning by proving that the mark has been in substantially exclusive and continuous use for a period of five years,

---

[7] 290 F.2d 845 (C.C.P.A.1961).   [8] 247 Fed. 299 (2d Cir.1917).

§ 1052(f). If the PTO cannot rebut the case, then the mark can be placed on the Principal Register.

What happens to marks that are in the process of acquiring distinctiveness? If all other requirements for registration are met, and the mark is in use in commerce, it can be placed on the Supplemental Register, § 1091. As noted in the previous Assignment, the Supplemental Register does not provide all of the benefits of the Lanham Act. It does, however, provide some of them. Most important, registration on the Supplemental Register creates a record of use. After five years, the mark can be moved almost automatically to the Principal Register.

8. *Evidentiary issues.* Several of the key questions covered in this Assignment turn on factual inquiries about how words are used and what customers think. These questions also arise in connection with other issues, such as cancellation and infringement. The Principal Cases mention what are probably the three most popular methods for shedding light on these issues: dictionary research, Lexis/Nexis searches, and consumer surveys. Sometimes, the testimony of real-life confused consumers is taken as evidence that consumers are likely to be confused by particular marks. A few litigants have even resorted to the testimony of expert linguists.[9]

The admissibility of surveys has been a very controversial issue. Surveys are attacked for problems such as polling the wrong universe of consumers,[10] asking the wrong questions,[11] utilizing the wrong environment,[12] displaying the goods or the mark badly,[13] and poor analytical methodology.[14] Since surveys are, in essence, the comments of out-of-court declarants that are offered for the purpose of proving the truth of the statements declared, they can also be attacked as hearsay. Nonetheless, surveys are to a large extent the only evidence directly probative of what consumers are thinking at the time of the litigation, and so they are widely admitted under a doctrine of necessity.[15] See also Assignment 3.

9. *Disclaimers.* In *Remington*, the TTAB stated the issue as the registrability of the term "PROUDLY MADE IN USA (MADE IN USA disclaimed)." Disclaimer practice is governed by §§ 1056–57 of the Lanham Act. These provisions permit registration of marks that contain unregistrable elements, so long as the trademark owner makes clear that she is not acquiring an exclusive right in the unprotectable parts of her mark. In this case, Remington knew (for reasons that are probably obvious, but will be

---

[9] See, e.g., Quality Inns Int'l. v. McDonald's Corp., 695 F.Supp. 198 (D.Md. 1988)(on the significance of "Mc").

[10] See, e.g. Zippo Mfg. Co. v. Rogers Imports, Inc., 216 F.Supp. 670 (S.D.N.Y.1963).

[11] See, e.g., Sears, Roebuck & Co. v. Allstate Driving School, Inc., 301 F.Supp. 4 (E.D.N.Y.1969).

[12] See, e.g., Scotch Whiskey Assoc. v. Consolidated Distilled Products, Inc., 210 U.S.P.Q. (BNA) 639 (1981).

[13] See, e.g., Carter–Wallace, Inc. v. Procter & Gamble Co., 434 F.2d 794 (9th Cir. 1970).

[14] See, e.g., Sheller–Globe Corp. v. Scott Paper Co., 204 U.S.P.Q. (BNA) 329 (T.T.A.B. 1979).

[15] See, e.g., Zippo Mfg. Co. v. Rogers Imports, Inc. 216 F.Supp. 670 (S.D.N.Y. 1963).

explained in Part B, infra) that it cannot claim rights in the term "MADE IN USA." However, it thought it possible to acquire rights in the entire phrase, PROUDLY MADE IN USA. Accordingly, it tried to register the whole mark, but disclaim that portion of it that was clearly not protectable. Had Remington succeeded in its attempt, it would have been able to enjoin others from using variants of "PROUDLY MADE IN USA" on electric shavers, but not use of the disclaimed portion alone.

10. *Other regulatory regimes.* The *Schiapparelli Searle* case concerned, in part, the interaction between trademark law and the Federal Food, Drug and Cosmetics Act. The Lanham Act is not the only provision of law that regulates labels and trademarks. Trademark holders must thread their way through state trademark law, state and federal consumer protection laws, the Federal Trade Commission Act, and the regulations adopted thereunder. Certain industries also have ethical codes that govern the choice of identifying marks.[16]

11. *State and federal law.* It is worth noting that *Heileman* concerned rights under state unfair competition law rather than federal trademark law. However, because federal and state law generally protect words and symbols in similar fashion, the same spectrum of classification is utilized in analyzing both federal and state claims. Thus, the Seventh Circuit used Lanham Act terminology. Conversely, *Heileman* is cited in cases brought under federal law. And just as *Heileman* was willing to permit the name of a category to function as a trademark when there is only one product in the category, so too § 1127 of the Lanham Act specifically permits the registration of the name of a "unique product." Finally, just as state law refuses to enforce trademark rights in words that become generic, the Lanham Act permits genericity to be used as a defense, § 1065(4), and provides for the cancellation of trademarks that become generic, § 1064(3).

PART B: LIMITS ON REGISTRABILITY

As the Introduction to this Assignment points out, certain designations are completely barred from registration, while others are disfavored. All of these exclusions and qualifications to registration appear in § 1052(a). Principal Problem B and the accompanying materials explore some of these designations. As you read the following materials, think about what policies you believe underlie the treatment in § 1052(a) of the various categories of trademarks.

1. PRINCIPAL PROBLEM B

Graydog Record Co. is a manufacturer of records, cassettes, and CD's. On the side, it also markets T-shirts advertising its records. Your client, the

---

[16] See, e.g., Model Code of Professional Responsibility EC 2–11 (1979); Model Rules of Professional Conduct Rule 7.5 (1980).

Greyhound Corporation, wants to oppose the applications of Graydog to register the following two marks: first, the "1–800" telephone number whose digits correspond on the telephone dial to the phrase "GRAYDOG" for its telephone order business for its music products and T-shirts, and second, the design depicted below, in the color gray exclusively, for its music products and the T-shirts.

Graydog has used both the telephone number and the dog design for about three years, and has advertised them extensively on the radio and in newspapers and magazines. Frequently, the Graydog T-shirts are given away as contest prizes by various radio stations nationally. Both marks have been approved for publication in the Official Gazette.

The running dog is a corporate trademark of Greyhound, under which it and most of its subsidiaries conduct their business. The gray running dog has been used on Greyhound's buses since the early 1920's. Prior to Graydog's adoption and use of its dog design, Greyhound, either itself, or through affiliated companies, had used a design of a running dog, exclusively in the color gray, for various services and goods such as transportation services, toy buses, pillows, and luggage. It owns registrations for this mark in the color gray for such goods and services and the registered version of Greyhound's running dog is depicted below.

Since the early 1930's, Greyhound's bus drivers have purchased and worn uniforms bearing the gray running dog mark on their caps, lapels and shirts. Greyhound has sold items of apparel, bags and jewelry, all bearing the gray running dog design, in bus station restaurants and rest stop shops, and currently uses the design on shoes, shirts, jackets, sweaters, and gloves. A mail order catalog directed to Greyhound's employees and published prior to applicant's claimed date of first use features baseball hats, jackets, sweatshirts and T-shirts, all bearing the gray running dog mark. Greyhound filed an application to register this mark in the color gray for various items of apparel several months ago.

Greyhound's advertising expenditures featuring the symbol of the running dog from 1981 through 1995 amounted to more than $314 million, and the running dog symbol has been referred to in various articles and books on famous American trademarks.

In addition, since 1970, Greyhound has used the telephone number "1–800–GREYHND" for the provision of travel services nationwide. It has also spent large sums of money advertising this number and has an application pending for the registration of this number as a service mark for travel services which was filed a few months ago.

Your senior partner calls your attention to § 1052 of the Lanham Act. She wants you to write a memorandum outlining the grounds applicable in that section for opposing Graydog's application to register its defecating dog and the "1–800" telephone number.

2.   MATERIALS FOR SOLUTION OF PRINCIPAL PROBLEM B

A.   STATUTORY MATERIALS: §§ 1052, 1064, & 1065

B.   CASES:

Dial-A–Mattress Franchise Corp. v. Page

United States Court of Appeals, Second Circuit, 1989.
880 F.2d 675.

■ NEWMAN, CIRCUIT JUDGE.

An increasingly popular marketing technique of some businesses involves the use of telephone numbers whose digits correspond to letters on the telephone dial that spell out an easily remembered word or name. The business then invites telephone customers to dial the word or name. The technique is used extensively as a convenient way to remember the seven digits that follow the "1–800" prefix of toll-free long-distance numbers. Some examples are 1–800–MARINES and 1–800–FLOWERS. The technique is also used for numbers within a local dialing area. As so often happens with new business practices, this one has spawned a new issue for litigation in the field of unfair competition.

This appeal raises the somewhat novel issue of whether it is unfair competition for a business to acquire a telephone number identified by the spelling of a generic term that a competitor is using (with a spelling modification) to identify its telephone number. The issue arises on an appeal from the District Court for the Eastern District of New York (Jack B. Weinstein, Judge), preliminarily enjoining appellant Anthony Page from using the "number" 1–800–MATTRESS within the New York metropolitan area. Page's competitor identifies its local area telephone number by inviting customers to dial the "number" MATTRES. For the reasons stated below, we affirm.

Background

Plaintiff-appellee Dial–A–Mattress Franchise Corp., as its name implies, is a retail mattress dealer that takes orders from customers primarily over the telephone, rather than in person at a retail outlet. Since 1976, Dial–A–Mattress's local phone number in the various area codes of the New York metropolitan area has been 628–8737. These digits correspond to the letters MATTRES on the telephone dial. Dial–A–Mattress has advertised its services and its phone number extensively, using the slogan "DIAL–A–MATTRESS and drop the last 'S' for savings."

In 1981, Dial–A–Mattress sought to obtain the number 1–800–628–8737 from the American Telephone and Telegraph Company so that its customers could make toll-free long-distance calls to the company using the number 1–800–MATTRES. AT & T told Dial–A–Mattress that this 800 number was then unavailable, but that it would be available in January 1989.

Defendant-appellant Anthony Page started in business in 1983 selling an invention of his father's called the EASY BED, a type of sofa bed that opens up vertically into a bunk-bed. Page obtained the phone number 1–800–327–9233, which spells 1–800–EASY–BED, a number he advertised on radio and television. Page then decided to expand into the mattress business. Although aware that Dial–A–Mattress had the local telephone number that spelled "MATTRES" (628–8737) for all the area codes in the New York metropolitan area, Page sought to obtain the same number as a "1–800" number.

Like Dial–A–Mattress, Page was told by AT & T that the number was unavailable. But Page sought to obtain the number more inventively than did Dial–A–Mattress. Page called every number beginning 1–800–MAT until he found the number of a company that had gone out of business. He then bought that number and exchanged the last four digits so that it became 1–800–628–8737, or 1–800–MATTRES.

Page promoted his number as 1–800–MATTRESS. Although the word "mattress" has one letter more than the telephone number, dialing the extra letter does not affect completion of the call.

Dial–A–Mattress filed a complaint in the Eastern District against the Easy Bed Mattress Company, the name under which Page was doing business. The complaint sought an injunction, an accounting, and damages on claims of trademark infringement, unfair competition, and unjust enrichment under federal and New York law. Judge Weinstein issued a temporary restraining order and referred the case to Magistrate A. Simon Chrein for an evidentiary hearing.

The Magistrate recommended that Page be permitted to use the number 1–800–MATTRES(S), but that he be required to answer each telephone call received with the following greeting: "Easy Bed. We are not connected with Dial–A–Mattress which advertises on radio and television." The Magistrate also recommended that Page be required to include a disclaimer of any connection to Dial–A–Mattress in his advertisements.

Judge Weinstein adopted the Magistrate's recommendation that a preliminary injunction should issue but altered the terms of the injunction. The District Judge ordered Page to notify the telephone company not to

connect to Page's telephone any call placed to the number 1–800–MAT–
TRES(S) that originated from area codes 201, 212, 516, 203, and 718, and
to pay any charges required for that purpose. This appeal followed.

Discussion

The issue pressed most vigorously on appeal by Page is whether Dial–
A–Mattress can obtain judicial protection for the call letters of a telephone
number that spell what Dial–A–Mattress concedes is a generic term—
"mattress". It is clear that Dial–A–Mattress could not claim trademark
rights in the word "mattress" used solely to identify its company or its
product. Nor would protection be available if the word was used for these
purposes with a spelling variation, such as "MATTRES", that did not
change the generic significance for the buyer. See Miller Brewing Co. v.
Heileman Brewing Co., 561 F.2d 75 (7th Cir.1977)(LITE used for light
beer), *cert. denied*, 434 U.S. 1025 (1978); American Druggists' Syndicate v.
United States Industrial Alcohol Co., 2 F.2d 942 (D.C.Cir.1924)(AL–KOL
used for rubbing alcohol); 1 J. McCarthy, Trademarks and Unfair Competition § 12:12(B)(2d. ed. 1984). It is equally clear that a second comer,
though entitled to use a generic term already used by its competitor, may
be enjoined from passing itself or its product off as the first user or that
user's product and may be required to take steps to distinguish itself or its
product from the first user or that user's product. See Kellogg Co. v.
National Biscuit Co., 305 U.S. 111 (1938)(shredded wheat).

These general principles concerning generic terms evidently prompted
the Magistrate to recommend that Page be allowed to continue using 1–
800–MATTRES(S) provided he answered calls with a disclaimer distinguishing his company from Dial–A–Mattress. But this case cannot be
decided solely upon the principles applicable to generic terms. Dial–A–
Mattress is not seeking protection against a competitor's use of the word
"mattress" solely to identify the competitor's name or product. What the
plaintiff seeks is protection against a competitor's use of a confusingly
similar telephone number and a confusingly similar means of identifying
that number.

Telephone numbers may be protected as trademarks, and a competitor's use of a confusingly similar telephone number may be enjoined as
both trademark infringement and unfair competition. See Chicago World's
Fair—1992 Corp. v. The 1992 Chicago World's Fair Comm'n, Civ. No. 83 C
3424 (N.D.Ill. Aug. 16, 1983)(LEXIS, Genfed library, Dist file) (protecting
use of telephone number 444–1992 against use of telephone number 434–
1992 in context where "1992" had special significance); see also SODIMA
v. Int'l. Yogurt Co., 662 F.Supp. 839, 852–54 (D.Or.1987) (common law
trademark rights recognized in telephone "number" 800–YO CREAM);
American Airlines, Inc. v. A 1–800–A–M–E–R–I–C–A–N Corp., 622 F.Supp.
673 (N.D.Ill.1985)(granting American Airlines injunction against travel
agency's use of telephone number 1–800–263–7422, which defendant promoted as 1–800–AMERICAN). Companies doing significant business

through telephone orders frequently promote their telephone numbers as a key identification of the source of their products.

In this case, the District Court was clearly entitled to conclude that defendant's use of the telephone number 1–800–628–8737 was confusingly similar to plaintiff's telephone number 628–8737 in those area code regions in which plaintiff solicited telephone orders, especially in view of defendant's identification of its number as 1–800–MATTRESS after plaintiff had promoted identification of its number as (area code)-MATTRES. Plaintiff does not lose the right to protection against defendant's use of a confusingly similar number and a confusingly similar set of letters that correlate with that number on the telephone dial just because the letters spell a generic term. The principles limiting protection for the use of generic terms serve to prevent a marketer from appropriating for its exclusive use words that must remain available to competitors to inform their customers as to the nature of the competitor's business or product. These principles do not require that a competitor remain free to confuse the public with a telephone number or the letters identifying that number that are deceptively similar to those of a first user.

Appellant's remaining contentions are without merit and require no discussion.

The preliminary injunction is affirmed.

Qualitex Co. v. Jacobson Products Co., Inc.

Supreme Court of the United States, 1995.
___ U.S. ___, 115 S.Ct. 1300, 131 L.Ed.2d 248.

■ JUSTICE BREYER delivered the opinion of the Court.

The question in this case is whether the Lanham Trademark Act of 1946 permits the registration of a trademark that consists, purely and simply, of a color. We conclude that, sometimes, a color will meet ordinary legal trademark requirements. And, when it does so, no special legal rule prevents color alone from serving as a trademark.

I

The case before us grows out of petitioner Qualitex Company's use (since the 1950's) of a special shade of green-gold color on the pads that it makes and sells to dry cleaning firms for use on dry cleaning presses. In 1989 respondent Jacobson Products (a Qualitex rival) began to sell its own press pads to dry cleaning firms; and it colored those pads a similar green-gold. In 1991 Qualitex registered the special green-gold color on press pads with the Patent and Trademark Office as a trademark. Registration No. 1,633,711 (Feb. 5, 1991). Qualitex subsequently added a trademark infringement count, 15 U.S.C.A. § 1114(1), to an unfair competition claim, § 1125(a), in a lawsuit it had already filed challenging Jacobson's use of the green-gold color.

Qualitex won the lawsuit in the District Court. 21 U.S.P.Q. 2d (BNA) 1457 (C.D.Cal.1991). But, the Court of Appeals for the Ninth Circuit set aside the judgment in Qualitex's favor on the trademark infringement claim because, in that Circuit's view, the Lanham Act does not permit Qualitex, or anyone else, to register "color alone" as a trademark. 13 F.3d 1297, 1300, 1302 (1994).

The courts of appeals have differed as to whether or not the law recognizes the use of color alone as a trademark. Compare NutraSweet Co. v. Stadt Corp., 917 F.2d 1024, 1028 (C.A.7 1990)(absolute prohibition against protection of color alone), with In re Owens–Corning Fiberglas Corp., 774 F.2d 1116, 1128 (C.A.Fed.1985)(allowing registration of color pink for fiberglass insulation), and Master Distributors, Inc. v. Pako Corp., 986 F.2d 219, 224 (C.A.8 1993)(declining to establish per se prohibition against protecting color alone as a trademark). Therefore, this Court granted certiorari. 512 U.S. (1994). We now hold that there is no rule absolutely barring the use of color alone, and we reverse the judgment of the Ninth Circuit.

II

The Lanham Act gives a seller or producer the exclusive right to "register" a trademark, § 1052, and to prevent his or her competitors from using that trademark, § 1114(1). Both the language of the Act and the basic underlying principles of trademark law would seem to include color within the universe of things that can qualify as a trademark. The language of the Lanham Act describes that universe in the broadest of terms. It says that trademarks "include any word, name, symbol, or device, or any combination thereof." § 1127. Since human beings might use as a "symbol" or "device" almost anything at all that is capable of carrying meaning, this language, read literally, is not restrictive. The courts and the Patent and Trademark Office have authorized for use as a mark a particular shape (of a Coca–Cola bottle), a particular sound (of NBC's three chimes), and even a particular scent (of plumeria blossoms on sewing thread). In re Clarke, 17 U.S.P.Q.2d (BNA) 1238, 1240 (TTAB 1990). If a shape, a sound, and a fragrance can act as symbols why, one might ask, can a color not do the same?

A color is also capable of satisfying the more important part of the statutory definition of a trademark, which requires that a person "use" or "intend to use" the mark

> "to identify and distinguish his or her goods, including a unique product, from those manufactured or sold by others and to indicate the source of the goods, even if that source is unknown." § 1127.

True, a product's color is unlike "fanciful," "arbitrary," or "suggestive" words or designs, which almost automatically tell a customer that they refer to a brand. Abercrombie & Fitch Co. v. Hunting World, Inc., 537 F.2d 4, 9–10 (C.A.2 1976)(Friendly, J.). The imaginary word "Suntost," or the words "Suntost Marmalade," on a jar of orange jam immediately would signal a brand or a product "source"; the jam's orange color does not do so. But, over time, customers may come to treat a particular color on a product or its packaging (say, a color that in context seems unusual, such as pink on a firm's insulating material or red on the head of a large industrial bolt) as signifying a brand. And, if so, that color would have come to identify and distinguish the goods—i.e. to "indicate" their "source"— much in the way that descriptive words on a product (say, "Trim" on nail clippers or "Car–Freshner" on deodorizer) can come to indicate a product's origin. See, e.g., J. Wiss & Sons Co. v. W. E. Bassett Co., 462 F.2d 567, 569 (1972); Car–Freshner Corp. v. Turtle Wax, Inc., 268 F.Supp. 162, 164 (S.D.N.Y.1967). In this circumstance, trademark law says that the word (e.g., "Trim"), although not inherently distinctive, has developed "secondary meaning." See Inwood Laboratories, Inc. v. Ives Laboratories, Inc., 456 U.S. 844, 851, n.11 (1982)("secondary meaning" is acquired when "in the minds of the public, the primary significance of a product feature . . . is to identify the source of the product rather than the product itself."). Again, one might ask, if trademark law permits a descriptive word with secondary meaning to act as a mark, why would it not permit a color, under similar circumstances, to do the same?

We cannot find in the basic objectives of trademark law any obvious theoretical objection to the use of color alone as a trademark, where that color has attained "secondary meaning" and therefore identifies and distinguishes a particular brand (and thus indicates its "source"). In principle, trademark law, by preventing others from copying a source-identifying mark, "reduces the customer's costs of shopping and making purchasing decisions," 1 J. McCarthy, McCarthy on Trademarks and Unfair Competition § 2.01[2], p. 2–3 (3d ed. 1994)(hereinafter McCarthy), for it quickly and easily assures a potential customer that this item—the item with this mark—is made by the same producer as other similarly marked items that he or she liked (or disliked) in the past. At the same time, the law helps assure a producer that it (and not an imitating competitor) will reap the financial, reputation-related rewards associated with a desirable product. The law thereby "encourages the production of quality products," *ibid.*, and simultaneously discourages those who hope to sell inferior products by capitalizing on a consumer's inability quickly to evaluate the quality of an item offered for sale. It is the source-distinguishing ability of a mark—not its ontological status as color, shape, fragrance, word, or sign—that permits it to serve these basic purposes. See Landes & Posner, Trademark Law: An Economic Perspective, 30 J. Law & Econ. 265, 290 (1987). And, for that reason, it is difficult to find, in basic trademark objectives, a reason to disqualify absolutely the use of a color as a mark.

Neither can we find a principled objection to the use of color as a mark in the important "functionality" doctrine of trademark law. The functionality doctrine prevents trademark law, which seeks to promote competition by protecting a firm's reputation, from instead inhibiting legitimate competition by allowing a producer to control a useful product feature. It is the province of patent law, not trademark law, to encourage invention by granting inventors a monopoly over new product designs or functions for a limited time, 35 U.S.C.A. §§ 154, 173, after which competitors are free to use the innovation. If a product's functional features could be used as trademarks, however, a monopoly over such features could be obtained without regard to whether they qualify as patents and could be extended forever (because trademarks may be renewed in perpetuity). See Kellogg Co. v. National Biscuit Co., 305 U.S. 111, 119–120 (1938)(Brandeis, J.); *Inwood Laboratories, Inc., supra*, at 863 (White, J., concurring in result)("A functional characteristic is 'an important ingredient in the commercial success of the product,' and, after expiration of a patent, it is no more the property of the originator than the product itself.")(citation omitted). Functionality doctrine therefore would require, to take an imaginary example, that even if customers have come to identify the special illumination-enhancing shape of a new patented light bulb with a particular manufacturer, the manufacturer may not use that shape as a trademark, for doing so, after the patent had expired, would impede competition—not by protecting the reputation of the original bulb maker, but by frustrating competitors' legitimate efforts to produce an equivalent illumination-enhancing bulb. See, e.g., *Kellogg Co., supra*, at 119–120 (trademark law cannot be used to extend monopoly over "pillow" shape of shredded wheat biscuit after the patent for that shape had expired). This Court consequently has explained that, "in general terms, a product feature is functional," and cannot serve as a trademark, "if it is essential to the use or purpose of the article or if it affects the cost or quality of the article," that is, if exclusive use of the feature would put competitors at a significant non-reputation-related disadvantage. *Inwood Laboratories, Inc.*, 456 U.S. at 850, n.10. Although sometimes color plays an important role (unrelated to source identification) in making a product more desirable, sometimes it does not. And, this latter fact—the fact that sometimes color is not essential to a product's use or purpose and does not affect cost or quality—indicates that the doctrine of "functionality" does not create an absolute bar to the use of color alone as a mark. See *Owens-Corning*, 774 F.2d at 1123 (pink color of insulation in wall "performs no non-trademark function").

It would seem, then, that color alone, at least sometimes, can meet the basic legal requirements for use as a trademark. It can act as a symbol that distinguishes a firm's goods and identifies their source, without serving any other significant function. See U.S. Dept. of Commerce, Patent and Trademark Office, Trademark Manual of Examining Procedure § 1202.04(e), p. 1202–13 (2d ed. May, 1993)(hereinafter PTO Manual) (approving trademark registration of color alone where it "has become distinctive of the applicant's goods in commerce," provided that "there is [no] competitive need for colors to remain available in the industry" and the color is not "functional"); see also 1 McCarthy §§ 3.01[1], 7.26 ("requirements for qualification of a word or symbol as a trademark" are that it be (1) a "symbol," (2) "used ... as a mark," (3) "to identify and distinguish the seller's goods from goods made or sold by others," but that it not be "functional"). Indeed, the District Court, in this case, entered findings (accepted by the Ninth Circuit) that show Qualitex's green-gold press pad color has met these requirements. The green-gold color acts as a symbol. Having developed secondary meaning (for customers identified the green-gold color as Qualitex's), it identifies the press pads' source. And, the green-gold color serves no other function. (Although it is important to use some color on press pads to avoid noticeable stains, the court found "no competitive need in the press pad industry for the green-gold color, since other colors are equally usable." 21 U.S.P.Q.2d (BNA) at 1460.) Accordingly, unless there is some special reason that convincingly militates against the use of color alone as a trademark, trademark law would protect Qualitex's use of the green-gold color on its press pads.

III

Respondent Jacobson Products says that there are four special reasons why the law should forbid the use of color alone as a trademark. We shall explain, in turn, why we, ultimately, find them unpersuasive.

First, Jacobson says that, if the law permits the use of color as a trademark, it will produce uncertainty and unresolvable court disputes about what shades of a color a competitor may lawfully use. Because lighting (morning sun, twilight mist) will affect perceptions of protected color, competitors and courts will suffer from "shade confusion" as they try to decide whether use of a similar color on a similar product does, or does not, confuse customers and thereby infringe a trademark. Jacobson adds that the "shade confusion" problem is "more difficult" and "far different from" the "determination of the similarity of words or symbols."

We do not believe, however, that color, in this respect, is special. Courts traditionally decide quite difficult questions about whether two words or phrases or symbols are sufficiently similar, in context, to confuse buyers. They have had to compare, for example, such words as "Bonamine" and "Dramamine" (motion-sickness remedies); "Huggies" and "Dougies" (diapers); "Cheracol" and "Syrocol" (cough syrup); "Cyclone" and "Tornado" (wire fences); and "Mattres" and "1–800–Mattres" (mattress franchisor telephone numbers). See, e.g., G. D. Searle & Co. v. Chas. Pfizer & Co., 265 F.2d 385, 389 (C.A.7 1959); Kimberly–Clark Corp. v. H. Douglas Enterprises, Ltd., 774 F.2d 1144, 1146–1147 (C.A.Fed.1985); Upjohn Co. v. Schwartz, 246 F.2d 254, 262 (C.A.2 1957); Hancock v. American Steel & Wire Co., 203 F.2d 737, 740–741 (Pat. 1953); Dial–A–Mattress Franchise Corp. v. Page, 880 F.2d 675, 678 (C.A.2 1989). Legal standards exist to guide courts in making such comparisons. See, e.g., 2 McCarthy § 15.08; 1 McCarthy §§ 11.24–11.25 ("Strong" marks, with greater secondary meaning, receive broader protection than "weak" marks). We do not see why courts could not apply those standards to a color, replicating, if necessary, lighting conditions under which a colored product is normally sold. See Ebert, Trademark Protection in Color: Do It By the Numbers!, 84 T. M. Rep. 379, 405 (1994). Indeed, courts already have done so in cases where a trademark consists of a color plus a design, i.e., a colored symbol such as a gold stripe (around a sewer pipe), a yellow strand of wire rope, or a "brilliant yellow" band (on ampules). See, e.g., Youngstown Sheet & Tube Co. v. Tallman Conduit Co., 149 U.S.P.Q. (BNA) 656, 657 (TTAB 1966); Amsted Industries, Inc. v. West Coast Wire Rope & Rigging Inc., 2

U.S.P.Q.2d (BNA) 1755, 1760 (TTAB 1987); In re Hodes–Lange Corp., 167 U.S.P.Q. (BNA) 255, 256 (TTAB 1970).

Second, Jacobson argues, as have others, that colors are in limited supply. See, e.g., *NutraSweet Co.*, 917 F.2d at 1028; Campbell Soup Co. v. Armour & Co., 175 F.2d 795, 798 (C.A.3 1949). Jacobson claims that, if one of many competitors can appropriate a particular color for use as a trademark, and each competitor then tries to do the same, the supply of colors will soon be depleted. Put in its strongest form, this argument would concede that "hundreds of color pigments are manufactured and thousands of colors can be obtained by mixing." L. Cheskin, Colors: What They Can Do For You 47 (1947). But, it would add that, in the context of a particular product, only some colors are usable. By the time one discards colors that, say, for reasons of customer appeal, are not usable, and adds the shades that competitors cannot use lest they risk infringing a similar, registered shade, then one is left with only a handful of possible colors. And, under these circumstances, to permit one, or a few, producers to use colors as trademarks will "deplete" the supply of usable colors to the point where a competitor's inability to find a suitable color will put that competitor at a significant disadvantage.

This argument is unpersuasive, however, largely because it relies on an occasional problem to justify a blanket prohibition. When a color serves as a mark, normally alternative colors will likely be available for similar use by others. See, e.g., *Owens-Corning*, 774 F.2d at 1121 (pink insulation). Moreover, if that is not so—if a "color depletion" or "color scarcity" problem does arise—the trademark doctrine of "functionality" normally would seem available to prevent the anticompetitive consequences that Jacobson's argument posits, thereby minimizing that argument's practical force. The functionality doctrine, as we have said, forbids the use of a product's feature as a trademark where doing so will put a competitor at a significant disadvantage because the feature is "essential to the use or purpose of the article" or "affects [its] cost or quality." *Inwood Laboratories, Inc.*, 456 U.S. at 850, n.10. The functionality doctrine thus protects competitors against a disadvantage (unrelated to recognition or reputation) that trademark protection might otherwise impose, namely their inability reasonably to replicate important non-reputation-related product features. For example, this Court has written that competitors might be free to copy the color of a medical pill where that color serves to identify the kind of medication (e.g., a type of blood medicine) in addition to its source. See *id.*, at 853, 858, n.20 ("Some patients commingle medications in a container and rely on color to differentiate one from another"); see also J. Ginsburg, D. Goldberg, & A. Greenbaum, Trademark and Unfair Competition Law 194–195 (1991)(noting that drug color cases "have more to do with public health policy" regarding generic drug substitution "than with trademark law"). And, the federal courts have demonstrated that they can apply this doctrine in a careful and reasoned manner, with sensitivity to the effect on competition. Although we need not comment on the merits of specific cases, we note that lower courts have permitted competitors to copy the green color of farm machinery (because customers wanted their farm equipment to match) and have barred the use of black as a trademark on outboard boat motors (because black has the special functional attributes of decreasing the apparent size of the motor and ensuring compatibility with many different boat colors). See Deere & Co. v. Farmhand, Inc., 560 F.Supp. 85, 98 (S.D.Iowa 1982), aff'd, 721 F.2d 253 (C.A.8 1983); Brunswick Corp. v. British Seagull Ltd., 35 F.3d 1527, 1532 (C.A.Fed.1994), cert. pending, No. 94–1075; see also Nor–Am Chemical v. O. M. Scott & Sons Co., 4 U.S.P.Q.2d (BNA) 1316, 1320 (E.D.Pa.1987)(blue color of fertilizer held functional because it indicated the presence of nitrogen). The Restatement (Third) of Unfair Competition adds that, if a design's "aesthetic value" lies in its ability to "confer a significant benefit that cannot practically be duplicated by the use of alternative designs," then the design is "functional." Restatement (Third) of Unfair Competition § 17, Comment c, p. 175–176 (1995). The "ultimate test of aesthetic functionality," it explains, "is whether the recognition of trademark rights would significantly hinder competition." *Id.*, at 176.

The upshot is that, where a color serves a significant nontrademark function—whether to distinguish a heart pill from a digestive medicine or to satisfy the "noble instinct for giving the right touch of beauty to common and necessary things," G. K. Chesterton, Simplicity and Tolstoy 61 (1912)—courts will examine whether its use as a mark would permit one competitor (or a group) to interfere with legitimate (nontrademark-related) competition through actual or potential exclusive use of an important product ingredient. That examination should not discourage firms from creating aesthetically pleasing mark designs, for it is open to their competitors to do the same. See, e.g., W. T. Rogers [Co. v. Keene, 778 F.2d 334 (C.A.7 1985)] (Posner, J.). But, ordinarily, it should prevent the anticompetitive consequences of Jacobson's hypothetical "color depletion" argument, when, and if, the circumstances of a particular case threaten "color depletion."

Third, Jacobson points to many older cases—including Supreme Court cases—in support of its position. In 1878, this Court described the common-law definition of trademark rather broadly to "consist of a name, symbol, figure, letter, form, or device, if adopted and used by a manufacturer or merchant in order to designate the goods he manufactures or sells to distinguish the same from those manufactured or sold by another." McLean v. Fleming, 96 U.S. 245, 254 (1877). Yet, in interpreting the Trademark Acts of 1881 and 1905, 21 Stat. 502, 33 Stat. 724, which retained that common-law definition, the Court questioned "whether mere color can constitute a valid trade-mark," A. Leschen & Sons Rope Co. v. Broderick & Bascom Rope Co., 201 U.S. 166, 171 (1906), and suggested that the "product including the coloring matter is free to all who make it." Coca-Cola Co. v. Koke Co. of America, 254 U.S. 143, 147 (1920). Even though these statements amounted to dicta, lower courts interpreted them as forbidding protection for color alone. See, e.g., *Campbell Soup Co.*, 175 F.2d at 798, and n.9; Life Savers Corp. v. Curtiss Candy Co., 182 F.2d 4, 9 (C.A.7 1950)(quoting *Campbell Soup*).

These Supreme Court cases, however, interpreted trademark law as it existed before 1946, when Congress enacted the Lanham Act. The Lanham

Act significantly changed and liberalized the common law to "dispense with mere technical prohibitions," S. Rep. No. 1333, 79th Cong., 2d Sess., 3 (1946), most notably, by permitting trademark registration of descriptive words (say, "U–Build–It" model airplanes) where they had acquired "secondary meaning." See *Abercrombie & Fitch Co.*, 537 F.2d at 9 (Friendly, J.). The Lanham Act extended protection to descriptive marks by making clear that (with certain explicit exceptions not relevant here),

> "nothing ... shall prevent the registration of a mark used by the applicant which has become distinctive of the applicant's goods in commerce."
> § 1052(f).

This language permits an ordinary word, normally used for a nontrademark purpose (e.g., description), to act as a trademark where it has gained "secondary meaning." Its logic would appear to apply to color as well. Indeed, in 1985, the Federal Circuit considered the significance of the Lanham Act's changes as they related to color and held that trademark protection for color was consistent with the

> "jurisprudence under the Lanham Act developed in accordance with the statutory principle that if a mark is capable of being or becoming distinctive of [the] applicant's goods in commerce, then it is capable of serving as a trademark." *Owens-Corning*, 774 F.2d at 1120 .

In 1988 Congress amended the Lanham Act, revising portions of the definitional language, but left unchanged the language here relevant. § 1127. It enacted these amendments against the following background: (1) the Federal Circuit had decided *Owens-Corning*; (2) the Patent and Trademark Office had adopted a clear policy (which it still maintains) permitting registration of color as a trademark, see PTO Manual § 1202.04(e)(at p. 1200–12 of the January 1986 edition and p. 1202–13 of the May 1993 edition); and (3) the Trademark Commission had written a report, which recommended that "the terms 'symbol, or device' ... not be deleted or narrowed to preclude registration of such things as a color, shape, smell, sound, or configuration which functions as a mark," The United States Trademark Association Trademark Review Commission Report and Recommendations to USTA President and Board of Directors, 77 T. M. Rep. 375, 421 (1987)(hereinafter Trademark Commission); see also 133 Cong. Rec. 32812 (1987)(statement of Sen. DeConcini)("The bill I am introducing today is based on the Commission's report and recommendations."). This background strongly suggests that the language, "any word, name, symbol, or device," § 1127, had come to include color. And, when it amended the statute, Congress retained these terms. Indeed, the Senate Report accompanying the Lanham Act revision explicitly referred to this background understanding, in saying that the "revised definition intentionally retains ... the words 'symbol or device' so as not to preclude the registration of colors, shapes, sounds or configurations where they function as trademarks." S. Rep. No. 100–515, at 44. (In addition, the statute retained language providing that "no trademark by which the goods of the applicant may be distinguished from the goods of others shall be refused registration ... on account of its nature") (except for certain specified reasons not relevant here). § 1052.

This history undercuts the authority of the precedent on which Jacobson relies. Much of the pre–1985 case law rested on statements in Supreme Court opinions that interpreted pre-Lanham Act trademark law and were not directly related to the holdings in those cases. Moreover, we believe the Federal Circuit was right in 1985 when it found that the 1946 Lanham Act embodied crucial legal changes that liberalized the law to permit the use of color alone as a trademark (under appropriate circumstances). At a minimum, the Lanham Act's changes left the courts free to reevaluate the pre-existing legal precedent which had absolutely forbidden the use of color alone as a trademark. Finally, when Congress re-enacted the terms "word, name, symbol, or device" in 1988, it did so against a legal background in which those terms had come to include color, and its statutory revision embraced that understanding.

Fourth, Jacobson argues that there is no need to permit color alone to function as a trademark because a firm already may use color as part of a trademark, say, as a colored circle or colored letter or colored word, and may rely upon "trade dress" protection, under § 43(a) of the Lanham Act, if a competitor copies its color and thereby causes consumer confusion regarding the overall appearance of the competing products or their packaging, see § 1125(a). The first part of this argument begs the question. One can understand why a firm might find it difficult to place a usable symbol or word on a product (say, a large industrial bolt that customers normally see from a distance); and, in such instances, a firm might want to use color, pure and simple, instead of color as part of a design. Neither is the second portion of the argument convincing. Trademark law helps the holder of a mark in many ways that "trade dress" protection does not. See § 1124 (ability to prevent importation of confusingly similar goods); § 1072 (constructive notice of ownership); § 1065 (incontestible status); § 1057(b)(prima facie evidence of validity and ownership). Thus, one can easily find reasons why the law might provide trademark protection in addition to trade dress protection.

IV

Having determined that a color may sometimes meet the basic legal requirements for use as a trademark and that respondent Jacobson's arguments do not justify a special legal rule preventing color alone from serving as a trademark (and, in light of the District Court's here undisputed findings that Qualitex's use of the green-gold color on its press pads meets the basic trademark requirements), we conclude that the Ninth Circuit erred in barring Qualitex's use of color as a trademark. For these reasons, the judgment of the Ninth Circuit is

Reversed.

In Re Old Glory Condom Corp.

United States Trademark Trial and Appeal Board, 1993.
26 U.S.P.Q.2d (BNA) 1216.

■ SAMS, CHAIRMAN.

Old Glory Condom Corp. has appealed from the examining attorney's final refusal to register its mark "OLD GLORY CONDOM CORP" (and design), as shown below, for "prophylactics (condoms)." The design feature of applicant's mark consists of a pictorial representation of a condom decorated with stars and stripes in a manner to suggest the American flag.

OLD GLORY CONDOM CORP

The drawing of the mark is lined for the colors red and blue.

The examining attorney refused registration, under Section 2(a) of the Trademark Act, on the grounds that the mark consists of immoral or scandalous matter. In particular, the examining attorney found that the use of the American flag as part of applicant's mark for condoms was scandalous because it was likely to offend "a substantial composite of the general public."

examining attorney

Applicant's Use of Its Mark

The record on appeal shows that applicant corporation was formed after Jay Kritchley, applicant's president, participated in an exhibition at the List Visual Arts Center of the Massachusetts Institute of Technology (M.I.T.) in Cambridge, Massachusetts. The exhibition, held in October 1989, was entitled "Trouble in Paradise" and focused on artists' responses to contemporary social and political issues. Mr. Kritchley's exhibit was an adaptation of the symbols of American patriotism to focus attention on the AIDS epidemic and, in particular, to emphasize that Americans have a patriotic duty to fight the AIDS epidemic and other sexually transmitted diseases. Applicant states that, when the exhibition received widespread critical acclaim, Mr. Kritchley decided to turn his theoretical concepts into a corporate enterprise, which now markets condoms under the mark applicant is seeking to register.

While the American flag design appears as a feature of applicant's trademark for condoms, the flag design is not applied to the condoms themselves. Applicant states that on the back of each condom package is the "Old Glory Pledge":

> We believe it is patriotic to protect and save lives. We offer only the highest quality condoms. Join us in promoting safer sex. Help eliminate AIDS. A portion of Old Glory profits will be donated to AIDS related services.

The Refusal of Registration

In refusing registration of applicant's mark, the examining attorney argues that a majority of the American public would be offended by the use of American flag imagery to promote products associated with sexual activity. She argues that the flag is a sacrosanct symbol whose association with condoms would necessarily give offense.

Applicant characterizes the issue on appeal as one of first impression: whether a trademark may be refused registration as scandalous solely on the basis of its political content. Applicant argues that the Patent and Trademark Office has registered more than a thousand marks for condoms, many of them sexually suggestive and many that might be considered vulgar. Applicant goes on to argue that the Patent and Trademark Office has registered more than one thousand marks in which an image of the American flag appears. Applicant emphasizes that its mark is expressly designed not to offend but to redefine patriotism to include the fight against sexually-transmitted diseases, including AIDS. Applicant points to its exhibit at M.I.T., which employed a frank sense of humor about both condoms and patriotism to encourage people to overcome an aversion to the use of condoms.

prior condom TMs
prior flag TMs

In this record, the only direct evidence of the impact of applicant's mark on the public is that described by applicant in its response to the first office action in this case. Applicant alluded to a "marketing study commissioned by applicant from the Simmons College Graduate School of Management." About this study, applicant noted:

> The study, which was made completely independent of applicant, which took three months to complete, and which was undertaken by Simmons College without cost to applicant (due to the College's recognition of the pressing social need to encourage the use of condoms), found that *there was a negative public reaction of under 5% of those polled* to applicant's use of the subject mark with regard to condoms. [emphasis in original]

We do not know the details of the survey, because applicant did not submit a copy for the record (nor, indeed, did applicant mention the survey in its appeal brief). On the other hand, the examining attorney did not request that applicant submit a copy of the survey, nor did she challenge applicant's summary of the survey results.

"Scandalous" Marks under Section 2(a)

There is relatively little published precedent to guide us in deciding whether a mark is "scandalous" within the meaning of Section 2(a) of the Trademark Act. The examining attorney places principal reliance on In re McGinley, 211 U.S.P.Q. 668 (CCPA 1981), the most recent decision in which the Board's reviewing court has interpreted the section of the Trademark Act here at issue. In *McGinley*, the Court was asked to decide the registrability of a mark comprising a photograph of a man and woman kissing and embracing in a manner appearing to expose the man's genitalia. In deciding whether the mark presented for registration was "scandalous" under Section 2(a), the Court first noted that whether a mark is scandalous is to be determined from the standpoint of a substantial composite of the general public. *Id.*, 211 U.S.P.Q. at 673, citing In re

Riverbank Canning Co., 95 F.2d 327, 37 U.S.P.Q. 268, 270 (CCPA 1938). To define "scandalous," under Section 2(a), the Court looked to the "ordinary and common meaning" of the term, which meaning could be established, according to the Court, by reference to Court and Board decisions and to dictionary definitions. The Court went on to cite dictionary definitions of "scandalous" as "shocking to the sense of ... propriety," "[that which gives] offense to the conscience or moral feelings" and "giving offense to the conscience or moral feelings; exciting reprobation, calling out condemnation ... disgraceful to reputation...." [Webster's New International Dictionary (2d ed. 1942)] and "shocking to the sense of truth, decency, or propriety; disgraceful, offensive; disreputable...." [Funk & Wagnalls New Standard Dictionary (1945)]. In an attempt to put these provisions of Section 2(a) in context, the Court expressed its opinion that this section of the Trademark Act represents not "... an attempt to legislate morality, but, rather a judgment by the Congress that such marks not occupy the time, services, and use of funds of the federal government." Having set forth its opinion as to the underpinnings of this portion of Section 2(a) of the Trademark Act, the Court (one judge dissenting) concluded that the mark for which registration was sought (i. e., the pictorial representation of an embracing nude couple with exposed male genitalia) was scandalous and, therefore, unregistrable.

In the more than ten years since the *McGinley* decision, this Board has decided only [a few] cases involving the issue of whether marks were "scandalous" under Section 2(a). The first of these cases, In re Tinseltown, Inc., 212 U.S.P.Q. 863 (TTAB 1981), involved the mark "BULLSHIT" for attache cases, handbags, purses, belts, and wallets. The Board allowed that the registrability of a profane word was a case of first impression and found that "BULLSHIT," the profane word at issue, was scandalous, within the meaning of Section 2(a), and, therefore, unregistrable. In finding the mark unregistrable, the Board relied on the *McGinley* case and, in particular, two of the dictionary definitions of "scandalous" cited by the Court in that case: "[g]iving offense to the conscience or moral feelings ..." and "shocking to the sense of ... decency or propriety...."

In re Hershey, 6 U.S.P.Q.2d 1470 (TTAB 1988) involved the mark "BIG PECKER BRAND" for T-shirts. The mark had been refused registration, as scandalous, on the grounds that "pecker" was a vulgar expression for "penis" and that the mark as a whole, therefore, was offensive or shocking to a substantial composite of the general public. The Board reversed the refusal of registration, finding the evidence unpersuasive to demonstrate the vulgarity of the word "pecker" and noted that the specimens of record were labels showing a design of a bird in conjunction with the word mark "BIG PECKER BRAND." The Board concluded that, in view of the context of the mark's use, the mark neither offended morality nor raised a scandal.

The most recent case in which the Board considered whether a mark was "scandalous" under Section 2(a) was In re In Over Our Heads Inc., 16 U.S.P.Q.2nd 1653 (TTAB 1990). In that case, the mark involved was

"MOONIES" (and a design feature) for dolls. The particular dolls to which
the mark was applied were novelty items which, upon the squeezing of an
attached collapsible bulb, dropped their pants to reveal buttocks (an action
known as "mooning"). The examining attorney had contended that the
mark was lacking in taste and was an affront to an organized religious
group, namely, the Unification Church, whose members were sometimes
referred to as "Moonies." The Board reversed the refusal of registration,
finding that purchasers were more likely to view the mark as an allusion to
"mooning" than as a reference to members of the Unification Church. In
discussing the Section 2(a) issue presented, the Board noted that the
standards for determining whether a mark is scandalous are somewhat
vague and the determination of the issue necessarily highly subjective. In
view of the subjective nature of the decision, the Board determined that
any doubts about whether a mark was scandalous should be resolved in
favor of allowing the mark to be published, to permit any party who
believes it would be damaged by registration of the mark to file an
opposition to registration.

Although we have concentrated our attention on the more recent cases
arising under Section 2(a), we are aware of several reported cases decided
during the period 1938–1971 by the Court of Customs and Patent Appeals,
the Commissioner of Patents, or this Board, where marks were found
scandalous and, therefore, unregistrable. We find the latter to be of little
precedential value in deciding the case now before us. Most of these older
cases involved a perceived offense to religious sensibilities. Moreover, what
was considered scandalous as a trademark or service mark twenty, thirty or
fifty years ago may no longer be considered so, given the changes in societal
attitudes. Marks once thought scandalous may now be thought merely
humorous (or even quaint), as we suspect is the case with the marks held
scandalous in Ex parte Martha Maid Mfg. Co., 37 U.S.P.Q. 156 (Comr.
Pats. 1938) ["QUEEN MARY" (and design) for women's underwear] and
In re Runsdorf, 171 U.S.P.Q. 443 (TTAB 1971) ["BUBBY TRAP" for
brassieres]. The point to be made here is that, in deciding whether a mark
is scandalous under Section 2(a), we must consider that mark in the
context of contemporary attitudes. See In re Madsen, 180 U.S.P.Q. 335, 336
(TTAB 1973) [where the Board found the mark "WEEKEND SEX" not
scandalous as applied to magazines and noted that ". . . consideration must
be given to the moral values and conduct fashionable at the moment,
rather than that of past decades. . . ."]; In re Thomas Laboratories, Inc.,
189 U.S.P.Q. 50 (TTAB 1975) [where the Board found a design mark,
consisting of "a cartoon-like representation of a melancholy, unclothed
male figure ruefully contemplating an unseen portion of his genitalia," not
scandalous as applied to "a corrective implement for increasing the size of
the human penis" and where the Board, after quoting from the U.S.
Supreme Court's discussion in Roth v. United States, 354 U.S. 476, 477
(1957), concerning what constitutes "obscenity," found that ". . . the
contemporary liberal attitude concerning the question of obscenity as
derived from the present understanding of the meaning of the freedoms
guaranteed under the First Amendment to the Constitution militates

against the narrow interpretation expressed by the Examiner in [refusing registration]...."]

Registrability of Applicant's Mark

Applicant's argument for reversing the refusal to register in this case is essentially two-fold. First, applicant argues that, when viewed in the light of the legal precedent of the Board and the Board's reviewing court, its mark is not scandalous. Second, applicant makes a Constitutional argument that the Board is obligated to apply the provisions of Section 2(a) in a Constitutional manner and that denial of the benefits of registration to applicant's mark because of its political content, even assuming (we presume) the political content of the mark would give offense, would violate the First and Fifth Amendments to the Constitution. Because we are in agreement with applicant's first line of argument, we need not consider the second line of argument in order to allow registration of the mark in this case.

Taking as our starting point the definitions of "scandalous" to which the Board has in previous cases looked for assistance in applying Section 2(a), we have considered whether "OLD GLORY CONDOM CORP" (and flag design) can be characterized as "[g]iving offense to the conscience or moral feelings" or "shocking to the sense of decency or propriety." If any pattern can be discerned from the most recent cases, previously discussed, where the Board or its reviewing court found marks to be scandalous [viz., a mark comprising a photograph of a man and woman kissing and embracing in a manner appearing to expose the man's genitalia, for newsletters (*McGinley, supra*), "BULLSHIT," for handbags, wallets, etc. (*Tinseltown, supra*)], that pattern seems to describe marks that convey, in words or in pictures, vulgar imagery.

As applicant has asserted (and as the examining attorney seems to concede), this Office has registered many trademarks and service marks that include imagery of the American flag. While we realize that there may be citizens of this country who disapprove of any commercial use of the American flag or American flag imagery, such uses have been sufficiently common that there can be no justification for refusing registration of applicant's mark simply on the basis of the presence in that mark of flag imagery. Nor do we find any evidence in this case that convinces us that a mark containing a pictorial representation of a condom should, simply because of that fact, be refused registration as scandalous. The particular pictorial representation featured in applicant's composite mark was not found by the examining attorney to be vulgar, nor do we find it so. The examining attorney's objection to applicant's mark seems to be directed to the mark's linking of flag imagery and a pictorial representation of a condom, each of which, in itself, she apparently finds unobjectionable. Precisely why this combination of images is scandalous the examining attorney fails to articulate.[a]

---

[a] In this case, as in others where the issue has been whether a mark is scandalous, we have detected an undercurrent of concern that the issuance of a trademark registration

Moreover, the examining attorney offers very little evidence in support of her refusal of registration in this case. Her position is supported mainly by an expression of opinion that a substantial composite of the public would be offended by applicant's mark, which opinion is, in turn, supported by her opinion that the American flag is a "sacrosanct" symbol. To bolster the latter opinion, she alluded to an unsuccessful proposed amendment to the U.S. Constitution to prohibit flag burning and to a comment by Chief Justice Rehnquist in his dissent in Texas v. Johnson, 491 U.S. 397, 428 (1989) that many Americans have an "almost mystical reverence" for the American flag. The examining attorney also made of record printouts, from Mead Data's NEXIS data base, of several news stories referring to a video public service announcement promoting voter registration. The video in question showed rock star Madonna, scantily clad and wrapped in an American flag. The news stories made mention of the disapproval in some quarters of the video's use of the American flag. We are not willing, based solely on the examining attorney's opinion, the evidence of the reaction to the Madonna video, and the unsuccessful effort to amend the U.S. Constitution to prohibit the burning of the flag, to presume that the flag imagery of applicant's mark would give offense in a manner that must be deemed "scandalous" under Section 2(a).

Moreover, whether applicant's mark would be likely to offend must be judged not in isolation but in the entire context of the mark's use. The Board has in other cases looked to the entire context of the use in determining whether the mark in question was scandalous. See *In re Hershey, supra* ["BIG PECKER BRAND" applied to T-shirts with labels bearing both the trademark and the design of a bird]; In re Leo Quan Inc., 200 U.S.P.Q. 370 (TTAB 1978) ["BADASS" for bridges for stringed musical instruments found not scandalous, the Board noting that the mark was an acronym derived from the words "Bettencourt Acoustically Designed Audio Sound Systems"]. Here, applicant markets its condoms in packaging which emphasizes applicant's commitment to the sale of high quality condoms as a means of promoting safer sex and eliminating AIDS and its belief that the use of condoms is a patriotic act. Although we know that not everyone would share applicant's view that the use of condoms is a patriotic act, the seriousness of purpose surrounding the use of applicant's mark—a serious-

for applicant's mark amounts to the awarding of the U.S. Government's "imprimatur" to the mark. Such a notion is, of course, erroneous. The duty of this Office under the Trademark Act in reviewing applications for registration is nothing more and nothing less than to register those marks that are functioning to identify and distinguish goods and services in the marketplace, as long as those marks do not run afoul of any statutory provision that would prohibit registration. Moreover, the registration scheme of the Trademark Act is one more inclined to inclusion than exclusion, the obvious idea being to give as comprehensive a notice as possible, to those engaged in commerce, of the trademarks and service marks in which others have claimed rights. Just as the issuance of a trademark registration by this Office does not amount to a government endorsement of the quality of the goods to which the mark is applied, the act of registration is not a government imprimatur or pronouncement that the mark is a "good" one in an aesthetic, or any analogous, sense.

ness of purpose made manifest to purchasers on the packaging for applicant's goods—is a factor to be taken into account in assessing whether the mark is offensive or shocking. When we consider that factor, along with the others we have discussed, we find that applicant's mark can in no way be considered "scandalous" under Section 2(a).

Decision: The refusal to register is reversed.

NOTES

1. *Functional subject matter: colors and numbers. Qualitex* appears to settle the conflict among the circuits regarding the trademark status of color, but the opinion still leaves some important issues unanswered. Does the opinion decide whether color can ever be so inherently distinctive that it should be accorded trademark protection before developing secondary meaning? Do you think many products are likely to qualify for color trademark protection in light of the standard articulated by the Court? Does the opinion indicate whether sounds and fragrances would also qualify as appropriate trademark subject matter? What about product configurations?

Another unresolved issue is the application of the functionality doctrine, which was introduced in Part A of this Assignment. Although the doctrine of functionality is easy to state and explain, it has proved extremely difficult to apply. Consider the functional aspects of color, for example. How satisfactorily does the Court in *Qualitex* apply the functionality doctrine? Does the Court provide sufficient guidance for lower courts to make this determination? If impact on competition is the primary consideration in determining whether to register a particular color as a trademark, how and by whom shall this determination be made? In the context of the Principal Problem, should Graydog be able to trademark the color gray in conjunction with its dog design? What about Greyhound? We return to the concept of functionality in the context of trade dress and product designs in Part A of Assignment 3.

Does the color depletion theory discussed in *Qualitex* have more force when numbers rather than colors are at issue? Do you agree with the ruling in *Dial–A–Mattress* that it is possible to trademark a telephone number that spells out a generic description of the product that the owner of the number sells? The PTO issued an administrative guideline in 1994 requesting that examiners deny registration applications if the mark consists of "a merely descriptive or generic term with numerals in the form of a telephone number."[17] Although this administrative guideline is not binding on courts, it does provide some guidance as to how the PTO believes the Lanham Act should be interpreted. Do you think the result in *Dial–A–Mattress* stems exclusively from the court's belief that the telephone number should be protected as a trademark or might the court be

---

[17] U.S. Patent & Trademark office, Examination Guide No. 1–94, at 3 (issued January 28, 1994).

more concerned with a different policy matter? Should the Principal Problem be decided the same way as *Dial–A–Mattress*? Can you think of any reason why Graydog's telephone number mark presents a more compelling case for trademark protection than the plaintiff's mark in *Dial–A–Mattress*? How successful do you think Greyhound would be in challenging Graydog's telephone mark based on § 2(d)?

2.   *§ 1052(a): immoral, scandalous and disparaging matter; false connections.* In footnote a in *Old Glory*, the court emphasized that the issuance of a registration does not mean the government is endorsing the goods to which the mark is applied. Does § 1052(a) "represent a permissible means toward achieving a valid government purpose"?[18] What is the justification for withholding the benefit of registration from such marks? Can any valid constitutional objections be made regarding the operation of this subsection? Is this subsection consistent with the operation of First Amendment doctrine regarding categorization of speech? In lieu of denying registration, is there a better way to deal with marks that are ostensibly vulgar or in poor taste?

Old Glory notes that the mark's offensiveness should be judged in the context of the mark's entire use (in other words, by also considering the labels and designs accompanying the mark). If a judgment must be made with respect to the immoral or scandalous nature of a particular mark, how should a court go about making this determination? The legislative history of the provision apparently is scarce, and courts therefore have looked to the "ordinary and common meaning" of scandalous.[19] Do you agree? Whose sensibilities should be relevant—only the prospective users or the public at large? How can judges avoid determining the relevant sensibilities without placing undue reliance on their own subjective views?

In In re Mavety Media Group Ltd.,[20] the Federal Circuit held that the T.T.A.B. had erred in its determination that "Black Tail" for an adult entertainment magazine was scandalous. The court objected to the T.T.A.B.'s exclusive reliance on dictionary reference defining "tail" as sexual intercourse, thus ignoring the more fundamental question of whether a substantial composite of the general public would regard the term as a reference to African–American women as sexual objects. The dictionary references relied upon in *Mavety* included not only vulgar, but also non-vulgar definitions of "tail" that would apply in the context of an adult magazine (i.e., rear end). The court noted that "the record is devoid of factual inquiry by the Examiner or the Board concerning the substantial composite of the general public, the context of the relevant marketplace, or contemporary attitudes."[21] It concluded that the mark should be approved for publication and an opposition could perhaps be brought by a group that finds the mark to be scandalous. Who should have standing to bring an

---

[18] See Davis, Registration of Scandalous, Immoral, and Disparaging Matter Under Section 2(a) of the Lanham Act: Can One Man's Vulgarity be Another's Registered Trademark?, 54 Ohio St. L.J. 331, 338 (1993).

[19] In re McGinley, 660 F.2d 481, 485 (C.C.P.A.1981).

[20] 33 F.3d 1367 (Fed.Cir.1994).

[21] Id. at 1372.

opposition based on this subsection? In the Principal Problem, would standing be a problem for Greyhound?

What is the policy underlying § 1052(a)'s preclusion of registration for marks "which may disparage or falsely suggest a connection with persons, ... institutions, beliefs, or national symbols, or bring them into contempt, or disrepute"? The following test is used to determine whether a particular mark is barred from registration based on the "false connection" aspect of § 1052(a): "The mark must be shown to be the same as or a close approximation of the person's previously used name or identity. It must be established that the mark (or part of it) would be recognized as such. It must be shown that the person in question is not connected with the goods or services of the applicant, and finally, the person's name or identity must be of sufficient fame that when it is used as part or all of the mark on applicant's goods, a connection with that person is likely to be made by someone considering purchasing the goods."[22] How should "disparagement" be established? Is this bar to registration relevant to the Principal Problem? Should the test for disparagement differ depending upon whether a person or property is the subject of the disparagement?

Does *Old Glory* provide any guidance for how the Principal Problem should be decided? In determining whether Graydog's mark should be denied on the ground that it is scandalous, how much significance would you attach to the fact that the Board approved the representation depicted below of a urinating dog for commercial paper?[23]

3. *§ 1052(a): deceptive matter vs. § 1052(e): deceptively misdescriptive matter.* Under § 1052(f), marks that are deceptive never can be registered, whereas marks that are deceptively misdescriptive can be registered after they have acquired secondary meaning, see Note 7 in Part A. Thus, it becomes necessary to distinguish between deceptive and deceptively misdescriptive marks. The following inquiries have been developed to aid this analysis. First, does the matter for which registration is desired misdescribe the goods? Second, are consumers likely to believe the misrepresentation? If the answer to both of these questions is yes, the mark is deceptively

---

[22] In re Sauer, 27 U.S.P.Q.2d (BNA) 1073, 1074 (T.T.A.B. 1993)(registration of design of a ball saying BO BALL denied on the ground that the mark falsely suggests a connection with athlete Bo Jackson).

[23] See Davis, supra note 18, at 359, 400.

misdescriptive. If however, the misrepresentation would materially influence the purchasing decision, the mark is considered deceptive rather than merely deceptively misdescriptive.[24] In light of this test, how would you rule on the registrability of the mark SILKEASE for women's blouses and dresses made of polyester crepe de chine? What about CAMEO for jewelry (earrings, necklaces and bracelets) that do not contain cameos or cameo-like elements?

deceptive
deceptively misdescriptive

4.   *§ 1052(b): flag or coat of arms.* This subsection prohibits the registration of a mark which "[c]onsists of or comprises the flag or coat of arms or other insignia of the United States, or of any State or municipality, or of any foreign nation, or any simulation thereof." Does this language preclude the registration of a mark which comprises the coat of arms of a foreign municipality?

5.   *§ 1052(c): identifying matter of a living individual.* This subsection precludes registration of a mark which "consists of or comprises a name, portrait, or signature identifying a particular living individual except by his written consent." It also precludes registration of the same with respect to a deceased President during the life of his widow, except with the written consent of his widow. The key here is whether the use in question identifies the particular individual, and thus it applies not only to full names, but also to surnames, nicknames and shortened names. A name will "identify" a particular individual for purposes of this subsection only if the individual in question will be associated with the mark because "that person is so well known that the public would reasonably assume the connection, or because the individual is publicly connected with the business in which the mark is used."[25] What do you think is the purpose of this provision? Should anybody be able to bring an opposition based on this subsection, or must the opposer have some connection to the person identified by the mark?

6.   *§ 1052(d): matter which resembles another mark so as to be likely to cause confusion.* As will be discussed in Assignment 3, likelihood of consumer confusion is the bottom line determination in trademark infringement actions. Section 1052(d) incorporates this policy into the registration requirements, so that an applicant's mark cannot be registered if it is likely to cause confusion with a registered mark. According to McCarthy, this subsection is the most common basis for rejection of applications for registration.[26] Section 1052(d) does provide, however, that concurrent registrations may be issued in certain circumstances. How does this subsection relate to the analysis in the Principal Problem?

7.   *§ 1052(e): geographical designations.* Geographic marks that are not primarily geographically descriptive are registrable (one example is

[24] See In re Budge Manufacturing Co., 857 F.2d 773, 775 (Fed.Cir.1988).

[25] Ceccato v. Manifattura Lane Gaetano Marzotto & Figli S.p.A., 32 U.S.P.Q.2d (BNA) 1192, 1195 (T.T.A.B. 1994). See also In re Sauer, 27 U.S.P.Q.2d (BNA) 1073, 1074–75 (T.T.A.B. 1993)(registration of design of a

ball saying BO BALL denied on the ground that the mark identifies Bo Jackson).

[26] J. Thomas McCarthy, 2 McCarthy on Trademarks and Unfair Competition § 19.25 (3d ed. 1992).

DUTCHBOY for paint). In contrast, terms which function primarily as indicators of geographical origin are not registrable. Until 1993, marks that were deemed geographically descriptive or geographically deceptively misdescriptive could only be registered after a showing of secondary meaning. Geographically deceptive marks are never registrable. The analysis for making these determinations parallels that for determining misdescriptiveness discussed in Note 3. Specifically, with respect to geographic marks, two questions must initially be asked: First, is the term one which primarily conveys a geographic connotation, and would people believe that the goods come from that place (this is typically referred to as a goods/place association)? Second, do the goods in fact come from that place? If the answer to these questions is affirmative, the mark is geographically descriptive. If the answer to the first question is yes, and the answer to the second is no, the mark is geographically deceptively misdescriptive. In addition, if people would actually buy the goods in reliance on the fact that they come from a particular geographical location, the mark is deceptive.[27]

In 1993, § 1052 was amended in light of our adherence to the North American Free Trade Agreement, so that it now bars registration for terms which are geographically deceptively misdescriptive.[28] Thus, geographically deceptive marks are treated the same as geographically deceptively misdescriptive marks, obviating the need to consider whether consumers actually rely on the misdescription in their purchasing decision. This amendment is applicable to applications filed after December 8, 1993, but a grandfather provision allows registration for such marks which were in use and have become distinctive prior to this date.

Additionally, the TRIPS Agreement (see Assignment 1) contains some provisions which relate to the use of geographical marks. First, TRIPS Article 22 bars the use or registration of "geographic indications" that "identify a good as originating in the territory of a Member, or a region or locality in that territory, where a given quality reputation or other characteristic of the good is essentially attributable to its geographic origin," and that mislead the public regarding the geographic origin of the product. As of this writing, Congress has not amended § 1052(e) to comport with this provision, and the meaning of the term "misleading" is likely to produce some debate.[29] Additionally, § 1052(a) has been amended to comport with Article 23 of TRIPS so that it now bars registration of all wine and spirit trademarks that contain a geographic term which is not representative of the product's origin, even if the designation is not misleading.

Now you be the judge. Here are some trademarks incorporating geographic terms that have been the subject of registration decisions. Based on the brief descriptions that follow, how would you rule?

---

[27] See The Institut National Des Appellations D'Origine v. Vintners International Co., 958 F.2d 1574, 1580 (Fed.Cir.1992); In re Sharky's Drygoods Co., 23 U.S.P.Q.2d (BNA) 1061, 1062 (T.T.A.B. 1992).

[28] See § 1052(e)(3) & (f).

[29] See Seide, Ayala and Szanto, The Impact Upon Intellectual Property Rights by Recent Developments in GATT and Federal Antitrust Guidelines, Brumbaugh Report (Unpublished, on file with Brumbaugh, Graves, Donohue and Raymond, New York, NY) Winter 1995, at pg. 4.

a. PARIS BEACH CLUB for garments, namely T-shirts and sweatshirts which are not made in Paris.

[handwritten: not geo. deceptive]

b. CALIFORNIA PIZZA KITCHEN for restaurant services originating in, and rendered in California (as well as other states).

[handwritten: geo. descriptive]

c. NANTUCKET NECTARS for soft drink products made by a company with its headquarters and research/development center in the Island of Nantucket.

[handwritten: geo. descriptive]

d. HARVEYS BRISTOL CREAM for cakes flavored with sherry wine. The applicant's headquarters are in Bristol, England, but the cakes are not made in Bristol.

[handwritten: not primarily geo. descriptive]

e. SWISS ARMY KNIFE for a pocketknife manufactured in China.

[handwritten: not primarily geo. descriptive]

8. *§ 1052(e): primarily merely surnames.* Section 1052(e)(4) precludes immediate registration for a mark that is "primarily merely a surname," but such marks can be registered after they have acquired secondary meaning. How do you think courts determine whether a mark is source indicative or "primarily merely a surname"?

9. *Incontestability.* As the materials in this part of the Assignment show, there are numerous bars to registration. Even after a mark has been registered, however, it remains vulnerable to cancellation for a period of five years after registration on any ground that would have barred registration in the first place, and at *any* time if the registered mark becomes the generic name for the goods or services with which it is used or the registration was fraudulently obtained.[30] Section 1065 provides, however, that after five years of continuous use, a registered mark becomes incontestable, and it can then no longer be cancelled upon certain grounds. The grounds upon which an incontestable mark cannot be challenged include those based on § 1052(d) & (e): first, that the mark should not have been registered because it was confusingly similar to another mark that was already in use at the time of the application; and second, that the mark is not entitled to protection because it is not inherently distinctive and lacks secondary meaning.

In Park 'N Fly, Inc. v. Dollar Park and Fly, Inc.,[31] the Supreme Court held that the owner of a registered mark can use the incontestable status of a mark to enjoin an infringing use, and the defendant in such an action may not allege that the trademark in question is not valid due to its descriptive nature. This case thus established that incontestability can be used both defensively against the cancellation of a mark, as well as offensively in an infringement action. In *Park 'N Fly*, the dissent objected on the ground that the mark PARK 'N FLY for airport parking services had been registered without any evidence of secondary meaning, and that the record still lacked evidence of secondary meaning for this descriptive

---

[30] § 1064.

[31] 469 U.S. 189, 105 S.Ct. 658, 83 L.Ed.2d 582 (1985).

mark.[32] From a policy standpoint, what objections can be raised with respect to the *Park 'N Fly* decision? We shall return to the topic of incontestability in Part A of Assignment 4.

BIBLIOGRAPHY

General articles on trademark protection include: Kozinski, Essay: Trademarks Unplugged, 68 N.Y.U.L. Rev. 960 (1993); Carter, Comment: The Trouble with Trademark, 99 Yale L.J. 759 (1990); Hughes, The Philosophy of Intellectual Property, 77 Geo. L. Rev. 287 (1988); William M. Landes and Richard A. Posner, Trademark Law: An Economic Perspective, 30 J.L. & Econ. 265, 269 (1987).

Intent to use registrations have spawned a literature of their own: Hellwig, The Trademark Law Revision Act of 1988: The 100th Congress Leaves Its Mark, 79 Trademark Rep. 287 (1989); Leeds, Intent to Use—Its Time Has Come, 79 Trademark Rep. 269 (1989); Vinicombe, The Constitutionality of an Intent to Use Amendment to the Lanham Act, 78 Trademark Rep. 361 (1988).

On the question of secondary meaning, see: McLean, The Birth, Death, and Renaissance of the Doctrine of Secondary Meaning in the Making, 42 Am. U. L. Rev. 737 (1993); Naresh, Incontestability and Rights in Descriptive Trademarks, 53 U. Chi. L. Rev. 953 (1986); Comment, Incontestability: The Park 'N Fly Decision, 33 UCLA L. Rev. 1149 (1986); Comment, Primary Significance: Proving the Consumer's Perception, 14 Seton Hall L. Rev. 315 (1984).

On genericity, see: Comment, Telephone Numbers That Spell Generic Terms: A Protectable Trademark or an Invitation to Monopolize a Market?, 28 U.S.F. L. Rev. 1079 (1994); Folsom & Teply, Surveying "Genericness" in Trademark Litigation, 78 Trademark Rep. 1 (1988); Oddi, Consumer Motivation in Trademark and Unfair Competition Law: On the Importance of Source, 31 Vill. L. Rev. 1 (1986); Note, The Legislative Response to Anti–Monopoly: A Missed Opportunity to Clarify the Genericness Doctrine, 1985 U. Ill. L. Rev. 197 (1985); Comment, Trademarks and Generic Words: An Effect on Competition Test, 51 U. Chi. L. Rev. 868 (1984); Greenbaum, Ginsburg & Weinberg, A Proposal for Evaluating Genericism After 'Anti–Monopoly', 73 Trademark Rep. 101 (1983); Zeisel, The Surveys That Broke Monopoly, 50 U. Chi. L. Rev. 896 (1983); Note, Genericide: Cancellation of a Registered Trademark, 51 Fordham L. Rev 666 (1983); Folsom & Teply, Trademarked Generic Words, 89 Yale L.J. 1323 (1980).

As to trademark rights in non-words: see Summerfield, Color as a Trademark and the Mere Color Rule: The Circuit Split for Color Alone, 68 Chi.-Kent. L. Rev. 973 (1993); Note, Issues in the Federal Registration of Flavors as Trademarks for Pharmaceutical Products, 1993 U. Ill. L. Rev. 105 (1993).

---

[32] Id. at 211.

On disclaimers: Radin, Disclaimers as a Remedy for Trademark Infringement: Inadequacies and Alternatives, 76 Trademark Rep. 59 (1986); Jacoby & Raskopf, Disclaimers in Trademark Infringement Litigation: More Trouble Than They Are Worth?, 76 Trademark Rep. 35 (1986).

Some of the issues discussed in Part B are treated in the following articles: Pace, The Washington Redskins Case and the Doctrine of Disparagement: How Politically Correct Must a Trademark Be?, 22 Pepperdine L. Rev. 7 (1994); Josel, New Wine in Old Bottles: The Protection of Frances's Wine Classification System Beyond its Borders, 12 B.U. Int'l. L.J. 471 (1994)(student work); Clarke, Issues in the Federal Registration of Flavors as Trademarks for Pharmaceutical Products, 1993 U. Ill. L. Rev. 105 (1993)(student work); Davis, Jr., Registration of Scandalous, Immoral, and Disparaging Matter Under Section 2(a) of the Lanham Act: Can One Man's Vulgarity be Another's Registered Trademark?, 54 Ohio St. L.J. 331 (1993); Naresh, Incontestability and Rights in Descriptive Trademarks, 53 U. Chi.L. Rev. 953 (1986).

THE SCOPE OF THE TRADEMARK HOLDER'S RIGHTS: INFRINGEMENT AND CONTRIBUTORY INFRINGEMENT

Because trademark law protects the capacity of suppliers to use their marks to communicate effectively with customers, trademark infringement actions focus on the disruption of the trademark owner's signaling ability by the marketing efforts of others. Such disruption can occur in a variety of ways. The most straightforward kind of infringement is exemplified by the hypothetical used in the Introduction to this Unit: the use of the name "Rolex" for watches that are not manufactured by the famous Swiss watchmaker. These cases, which involve the use of identical signals on the same kind of product, are generally easy to decide because it is evident when this sort of simultaneous usage of a mark interferes with its capacity to indicate source. The harder cases are first, cases in which the products are the same, but the signals are not identical. These cases are examined through Principal Problem A of this Assignment. Even harder are cases that involve the use of the same (or similar) signals on goods that are not the same—in some instances, not even in competition with one another. That situation is examined through Principal Problem B of this Assignment.

There are a variety of legal bases for infringement actions and plaintiffs will usually base their claims on all available theories, citing both federal and state law.[1] Part A of this Assignment examines claims of infringement based on the two available federal theories: trademark infringement under § 1114 of the Lanham Act and violations of § 43(a) of the Lanham Act.[2] As Part A illustrates, the critical difference between a § 43(a) claim and an infringement claim under § 1114 is that § 1114

---

[1] These actions are generally brought in federal courts, which have jurisdiction over both federal trademark claims and also any "claim of unfair competition when joined with a substantial and related claim under the ... trade-mark laws." 28 U.S.C. § 1338(a). Since federal jurisdiction in trademark cases is concurrent with that of the states, § 1338(a), these actions can be heard in state courts as well.

[2] This section's actual cite is 15 U.S.C. § 1125(a), but it is typically referred to as § 43(a), which is the number of this section as it appeared in the bill that resulted in the Lanham Act. In this text, we will follow this general practice of using the § 43(a) designation.

claims are available only for marks that are federally registered and thus they involve infringement of the plaintiff's most distinctive marketing symbol. In contrast, the subject matter at issue in § 43(a) includes trademarks protected only under state law as well as other, less distinctive, aspects of a manufacturer's marketing scheme, such as advertising motifs, business methods, and trade dress. Section 43(a) also provides protection against false advertising.

Putting to one side the false advertising aspect of § 43(a), the operative principles of both federal causes of action are similar. As indicated in Lois Sportswear U.S.A., Inc. v. Levi Strauss & Co. and Ferrari v. Roberts, reprinted in Part A, and McDonald's Corp. v. Druck and Gerner, DDS, reprinted in Part B, the major issue in these cases is likelihood of consumer confusion as to the product's source among "an appreciable number of ordinary prudent purchasers." The existence of likelihood of confusion is determined by considering a set of factors that vary only slightly from court to court. The importance of each factor depends, however, on how closely related the defendant's goods are to the plaintiff's. The issue in the false advertising cases also is consumer confusion, but the focus is on the language of the ads rather than the factor-based analysis used in *Lois Sportswear, Ferrari*, and *McDonald's*.

State-based infringement actions are of two types. The first, usually called "passing off" or "unfair competition," is the predecessor to all of trademark law, see Assignment 1. This cause of action is aimed at preventing someone from using an established trademark to pass off goods—to induce a consumer into buying the second (junior) trademark user's goods under the mistaken assumption that they derive from the first (senior) user. Since these claims are now handled with the same factor-based analytical scheme used in federal law, this cause of action is significant only in states that weigh the factors differently from the way they are assessed under the Lanham Act.[3]

The more significant state causes of action are therefore those that have no clear analogue under federal law: the right to prevent dilution of the trademark, the right to prevent its tarnishment, and the right to prevent its misappropriation. As Part B of this Assignment illustrates, these causes of action focus not so much on the signaling function of trademarks as on their inherent value. Thus, as the law moves from infringement actions under § 1114 of the Lanham Act (and state-law passing off claims), through § 43(a), dilution, tarnishment and misappropriation, it creates a spectrum of coverage. At one end, the mark is regarded only as a signal for its proprietor; at the other, it is seen as having value in its own right—a value that is the property of the trademark holder. This spectrum will be elaborated upon in Note 3 of Part B.

---

[3] For example, some states do not require so strong a mark when there is a showing of bad faith, see, e.g., Laureyssens v. Idea Group, Inc., 964 F.2d 131, 139 (2d Cir.1992).

PART A: COMPETING GOODS

1.   PRINCIPAL PROBLEM A

As a law clerk for Judge Feisty, you are faced with determining the legality of the sale of imitation Coach Leatherware handbags by AnnTaylor, an upscale chain of more than 160 retail women's clothing stores. Coach is alleging that AnnTaylor is producing and selling imitations of its prestigous leather handbags in a manner likely to cause confusion in the marketplace. In addition, Coach is challenging a print ad by AnnTaylor which states, "Come to AnnTaylor and see why women across America believe that our handbags last twice as long as even the designer brands like Coach, Gucci, and Louis Vuitton."

Coach has been designing and selling exclusive handbags for approximately fifty years. Its products are sold exclusively under its own label and are marketed in about fifty stores owned by Coach, in clearly marked Coach display cases in expensive stores, and through Coach mail order catalogues.

Coach initiated this suit after learning that three of its most popular "classic" handbag designs which have been part of its product line for the past fifteen years were being copied and sold by AnnTaylor. Though the various styles of Coach bags do not resemble one another, they do share certain features. All are produced from full-grain cowhide, contain exterior binding at external seams and incorporate brass hardward components. The three AnnTaylor bags at issue also contain these features.

Over the years, Coach has attached to all of its handbags distinctive lozenge-shaped leather tags embossed with the name "Coach Leatherware." The tags, suspended from beaded brass chains, have become distinctive and valuable through Coach's promotional efforts and by virtue of its upscale reputation. The value of these tags is mirrored in Coach's advertising slogan: "It's Not a Coach Bag Without the Coach Tag." In fact, these tags alone often are stolen. Though the designs of Coach bags are themselves not registered, Coach has registered the tag itself on the Principal Register. The three AnnTaylor handbags in question carry a similar leather tag which is, however, embossed with AnnTaylor's name and distinctive typeface.

Coach is suing for trademark infringement under § 1114 of its tags and tradedress infringement of its handbags under § 43(a). In addition, Coach is seeking an injunction of the print ad, based on a claim of false advertising under § 43(a). Judge Feisty wants you to write a memo on the law in this area and advise him as to how he should rule.

2. MATERIALS FOR SOLUTION OF PRINCIPAL PROBLEM A

A. STATUTORY MATERIALS: §§ 1114, 1121, & 1125

B. CASES:

Lois Sportswear v. Levi Strauss & Co.

United States Court of Appeals, Second Circuit, 1986.
799 F.2d 867.

■ TIMBERS, CIRCUIT JUDGE.

I

We summarize only those facts believed necessary to an understanding of the issues raised on appeal.

Appellee [Levi Strauss & Co.] is a world famous clothing manufacturer. One of its most popular products is a line of casual pants known as Levi Jeans. Appellee began manufacturing its denim jeans in the 1850s. Each pair of jeans contains numerous identifying features. One such feature is a distinct back pocket stitching pattern. This pattern consists of two intersecting arcs which roughly bisect both pockets of appellee's jeans. Appellee has an incontestable federal trademark in this stitching pattern. Appellee has used this pattern on all its jeans continuously since 1873. In many ways the back pocket stitching pattern has become the embodiment of Levi Jeans in the minds of jeans buyers. The record is replete with undisputed examples of the intimate association between the stitching pattern and appellee's products in the buying public's mind. Not only has appellee spent considerable sums on promoting the stitching pattern, but various competitors have run nation-wide advertisement campaigns touting the advantages of their jeans' back pockets over appellee's. In addition, one of the largest chains of jeans retailers, the Gap Stores, has run numerous advertisements featuring pictures of appellee's back pocket stitching pattern as the entire visual portion of the ad. The record also contains numerous examples of the public's phenomenal reaction to the stitching pattern and the jeans it epitomizes. These examples range from national magazine cover stories to high school yearbook dedications.

Appellant Lois Sportswear, U.S.A., Inc. ("Lois") imports into the United States jeans manufactured in Spain by [appellant] Textiles Y Confecciones Europeas, S.A. ("Textiles"). The instant litigation was commenced because appellants' jeans bear a back pocket stitching pattern substantially similar to appellee's trademark stitching pattern. On appeal appellants do not challenge the district court's conclusion that the two stitching patterns are substantially similar. Nor could they; the two patterns are virtually identical when viewed from any appreciable distance. In fact, the results from a survey based on showing consumers videotapes of the back pockets of various jeans, including appellants', indicate that

44% of those interviewed mistook appellants' jeans for appellee's jeans.[a] Appellants instead rely on their use of various labels, some permanent and some temporary, to distinguish their jeans and defeat appellee's trademark infringement and unfair competition claims.

The evidence is undisputed that appellants and appellee manufacture and sell a similar product. While stratifying the jeans market with various styles and grades seems to be the current rage, there can be no dispute that the parties before us compete to sell their jeans to the public. The record does indicate that appellants have attempted to target their "designer" jeans at a decidedly upscale market segment. There also was evidence, however, that appellants' jeans were selling at deep discount in cut-rate clothing outlets. Moreover, there was substantial evidence which indicated that appellee's jeans, although originally marketed as work pants, had achieved a certain elan among the fashion conscious. The evidence suggests that appellee's jeans have achieved fad popularity in all sectors of the jeans market. Finally, appellee produced affidavits stating that it was planning to enter the designer jeans market.

[The district court granted appellee's motion for summary judgment, holding that while the labels may prevent confusion as to source at the time of the sale, they do not prevent confusion in the post-sale context.]

II

Appellants' arguments, for the most part, focus only on the likelihood that consumers will buy appellants' jeans thinking they are appellee's jeans due to the similar stitching patterns. Appellants point to their labeling as conclusive proof that no such confusion is likely. We agree with the district court, however, that the two principle [sic] areas of confusion raised by appellants' use of appellee's stitching pattern are: (1) the likelihood that jeans consumers will be confused as to the relationship between appellants and appellee; and (2) the likelihood that consumers will be confused as to the source of appellants' jeans when the jeans are observed in the post-sale context. We hold that the Lanham Act, 15 U.S.C.A. §§ 1051–1127 (1982), as interpreted by our Court, was meant to prevent such likely confusion.

Turning to the principal issues under the Lanham Act, in either a claim of trademark infringement under § 32 or a claim of unfair competition under § 43, a prima facie case is made out by showing the use of one's trademark by another in a way that is likely to confuse consumers as to the source of the product. Compare 15 U.S.C.A. § 1114(1)(a)("use ... of a registered mark ... [that] is likely to cause confusion") with 15 U.S.C.A. § 1125(a)("use in connection with any goods ... [of] a false designation of origin"). See Thompson Medical Co., Inc. v. Pfizer, Inc., 753 F.2d 208, 213 (2d Cir.1985)(quoting Mushroom Makers, Inc. v. R. G. Barry Corp., 580

---

[a] The value of this survey as evidence of actual consumer confusion is disputed by the parties. The district court found that the survey suffered from some methodological shortcomings relating to its simulation of the post-sale environment. The court gave the survey results little weight in determining actual confusion. The survey, however, remains strikingly probative of the similarity of the two stitching patterns.

F.2d 44, 47 (2d Cir.1978), cert. denied, 439 U.S. 1116 (1979)("The ultimate inquiry in most actions for false designation of origin, as with actions for trademark infringement, is whether there exists a 'likelihood that an appreciable number of ordinarily prudent purchasers [will] be misled, or indeed simply confused, as to the source of the goods in question' ")(footnote omitted)).

In deciding the issue of likelihood of confusion in the instant case, the district court relied on the multifactor balancing test set forth by Judge Friendly in Polaroid Corp. v. Polarad Electronics Corp., 287 F.2d 492, 495 (2d Cir.), cert. denied, 368 U.S. 820 (1961).

At the outset, it must be remembered just what the Polaroid factors are designed to test. The factors are designed to help grapple with the "vexing" problem of resolving the likelihood of confusion issue. Polaroid, supra, 287 F.2d at 495. Therefore, each factor must be evaluated in the context of how it bears on the ultimate question of likelihood of confusion as to the source of the product. It also must be emphasized that the ultimate conclusion as to whether a likelihood of confusion exists is not to be determined in accordance with some rigid formula. The Polaroid factors serve as a useful guide through a difficult quagmire. Each case, however, presents its own peculiar circumstances. In the instant case it also is critical first to determine just what type of actionable confusion as to source is presented. Appellants place great reliance on their labeling as a means of preventing any confusion. While such labeling may prevent appellants' use of appellee's stitching pattern from confusing consumers at the point of sale into believing that appellee manufactured and marketed appellants' jeans, the labeling does nothing to alleviate other forms of likely confusion that are equally actionable.

Turning to an application of the Polaroid test, we must stress at the outset that the district court's detailed findings on each of the Polaroid factors are entitled to considerable deference.

The first factor—the strength of the mark—weighs heavily in appellee's favor. We have defined the strength of a mark as "its tendency to identify the goods sold under the mark as emanating from a particular source." McGregor–Doniger, Inc. v. Drizzle, Inc., 599 F.2d 1126, 1131 (2d Cir.1979). As discussed above, appellee's back pocket stitching pattern is a fanciful registered trademark with a very strong secondary meaning. Virtually all jeans consumers associate the stitching pattern with appellee's products. We agree with the district court that the evidence indicates as a matter of law that appellee's stitching pattern is a very strong mark. This factor is crucial to the likelihood of confusion analysis since appellee's intimate association with the trademark makes it much more likely that consumers will assume wrongly that appellee is somehow associated with appellants' jeans or has authorized the use of its mark, or, in the post-sale context, that appellee has manufactured the jeans.

The second factor—the degree of similarity of the marks—also weighs in favor of appellee. As the district court correctly observed, the two stitching patterns are "essentially identical." Both patterns consist of two intersecting arcs placed in the exact same position on the back pockets of the jeans. The only difference—the fact that appellants' arcs extend ¾ inch further down the pocket at their intersection—is imperceptible at any significant distance. In light of the fact that the stitching pattern is in no way dictated by function and an infinite number of patterns are possible, the similarity of the two patterns is striking. When this striking similarity is factored into the likelihood of confusion analysis, its great importance becomes clear. In view of the trademark's strength, this nearly identical reproduction of the stitching pattern no doubt is likely to cause consumers to believe that appellee somehow is associated with appellants or at least has consented to the use of its trademark. In the post-sale context, this striking similarity no doubt will cause consumers to transfer the goodwill they feel for appellee to appellants, at least initially. This misuse of goodwill is at the heart of unfair competition. Appellants' reliance on the effect of their labeling with respect to this factor underscores their misguided focus on only the most obvious form of consumer confusion. Appellants' labeling in no way dispels the likelihood that consumers will conclude that appellants' jeans are somehow connected to appellee by virtue of the nearly identical stitching patterns.

The third factor—the proximity of the products—also weighs in favor of appellee. Both products are jeans. Although appellants argue that their jeans are designer jeans and are sold to a different market segment than appellee's jeans, there is significant evidence in the record of an overlap of market segments. Moreover, even if the two jeans are in different segments of the jeans market, such a finding would not switch this factor to appellants' side of the scale. We are trying to determine if it is likely that consumers mistakenly will assume either that appellants' jeans somehow are associated with appellee or are made by appellee. The fact that appellants' jeans arguably are in a different market segment makes this type of confusion more likely. Certainly a consumer observing appellee's striking stitching pattern on appellants' designer jeans might assume that appellee had chosen to enter that market segment using a subsidiary corporation, or that appellee had allowed appellants' designers to use appellee's trademark as a means of reaping some profits from the designer jeans fad without a full commitment to that market segment. Likewise, in the post-sale context a consumer seeing appellants' jeans on a passer-by might think that the jeans were appellee's long-awaited entry into the designer jeans market segment. Motivated by this mistaken notion— appellee's goodwill—the consumer might then buy appellants' jeans even after discovering his error. After all, the way the jeans look is a primary consideration to most designer jeans buyers.

The fourth factor—bridging the gap—is closely related to the proximity of the products and does not aid appellants' case. Under this factor, if the owner of a trademark can show that it intends to enter the market of the alleged infringer, that showing helps to establish a future likelihood of confusion as to source. We have held that the trademark laws are designed in part to protect "the senior user's interest in being able to enter a related field at some future time." Scarves By Vera, Inc. v. Todo Imports Ltd., 544

F.2d 1167, 1172 (2d Cir.1976). In the instant case, the district court rejected as irrelevant appellee's affidavits which stated that appellee was planning to enter the designer jeans market, since the affidavits did not assert that appellee's designer jeans entry would utilize the stitching pattern.[b] We do not believe, however, that the form appellee's entry into the market segment might take is especially relevant to the likelihood of confusion issue. Appellee's entry into the market, regardless of the form it might take, would increase the chances of consumer confusion as to the source of appellants' jeans because of likely consumer expectations that appellee's designer jeans would bear its famous stitching pattern. If one knew only that appellee had entered the designer jeans market and then saw appellants' jeans in a post-sale context, it is very likely that one could confuse them for appellee's entry. See McGregor–Doniger, supra, 599 F.2d at 1136 ("Because consumer confusion is the key, the assumptions of the typical consumer, whether or not they match reality, must be taken into account."). Also, appellee has an interest in preserving its trademark should it ever wish to produce designer jeans with the stitching pattern. The Lanham Act is meant to protect this interest.

The fifth factor—actual confusion—while not helping appellee, does not really hurt its case. Appellee's only evidence of actual confusion was a consumer survey which the district court discounted due to methodological defects in simulating the post-sale environment. Of course, it is black letter law that actual confusion need not be shown to prevail under the Lanham Act, since actual confusion is very difficult to prove and the Act requires only a likelihood of confusion as to source. While the complete absence of actual confusion evidence after a significant period of competition may weigh in a defendant's favor, such an inference is unjustified in the instant case in view of the survey evidence, even with its methodological defects. While these defects go to the weight of the survey, it is still somewhat probative of actual confusion in the post-sale context. In any event, the record indicates that sales of appellants' jeans have been minimal in the United States thus far and there has been little chance for actual confusion as yet. It would be unfair to penalize appellee for acting to protect its trademark rights before serious damage has occurred.

The sixth factor—the junior user's good faith in adopting the mark—weighs in favor of appellants. The evidence before the district court, when viewed in a light favorable to appellants, indicates that appellants happened on the stitching pattern serendipitously. It must be remembered, however, that intentional copying is not a requirement under the Lanham Act. Also, intent is largely irrelevant in determining if consumers likely will be confused as to source. The history of advertising suggests that consumer reactions usually are unrelated to manufacturer intentions.

The seventh factor—the quality of the respective goods—does add some weight to appellants' position. Appellee has conceded that appellants' jeans are not of an inferior quality, arguably reducing appellee's interest in

[b] This omission no doubt was an oversight on appellee's part since every pair of jeans it has manufactured since 1873 has exhibited the stitching pattern.

protecting its reputation from debasement. It must be noted, however, that under the circumstances of this case the good quality of appellants' product actually may increase the likelihood of confusion as to source. Particularly in the post-sale context, consumers easily could assume that quality jeans bearing what is perceived as appellee's trademark stitching pattern to be a Levi's product. The fact that appellants have produced a quality copy suggests that the possibility of their profiting from appellee's goodwill is still likely.

The eighth and final factor—the sophistication of relevant buyers— does not, under the circumstances of this case, favor appellants. The district court found, and the parties do not dispute, that the typical buyer of "designer" jeans is sophisticated with respect to jeans buying. Appellants argue that this sophistication prevents these consumers from becoming confused by nearly identical back pocket stitching patterns. On the contrary, we believe that it is a sophisticated jeans consumer who is most likely to assume that the presence of appellee's trademark stitching pattern on appellants' jeans indicates some sort of association between the two manufacturers. Presumably it is these sophisticated jeans buyers who pay the most attention to back pocket stitching patterns and their "meanings." Likewise, in the post-sale context, the sophisticated buyer is more likely to be affected by the sight of appellee's stitching pattern on appellants' jeans and, consequently, to transfer goodwill. Finally, to the extent the sophisticated buyer is attracted to appellee's jeans because of the exclusiveness of its stitching pattern, appellee's sales will be affected adversely by these buyers' ultimate realization that the pattern is no longer exclusive.

Our review of the district court's application of the Polaroid factors convinces us that the court correctly concluded that consumers are likely to mistakenly associate appellants' jeans with appellee or will confuse the source of appellants' jeans when the jeans are observed in the post-sale context. This result is eminently reasonable in view of the undisputed evidence of the use by one jeans manufacturer of the trademark back pocket stitching pattern of another jeans manufacturer, coupled with the fact that the trademark stitching pattern is instantly associated with its owner and is important to consumers. There is simply too great a risk that appellants will profit from appellee's hard-earned goodwill to permit the use.

■ MINER, CIRCUIT JUDGE, dissenting (omitted).

Two Pesos, Inc. v. Taco Cabana, Inc.

Supreme Court of the United States.
505 U.S. 763, 112 S.Ct. 2753, 120 L.Ed.2d 615 (1992).

■ JUSTICE WHITE delivered the opinion of the Court.

The issue in this case is whether the trade dress of a restaurant may be protected under § 43(a) of the Trademark Act of 1946 (Lanham Act), 15

U.S.C. § 1125(a), based on a finding of inherent distinctiveness, without proof that the trade dress has secondary meaning.

I

In 1987, Taco Cabana sued Two Pesos in the United States District Court for the Southern District of Texas for trade dress infringement under § 43(a) of the Lanham Act, 15 U.S.C. § 1125(a)(1982 ed.). The case was tried to a jury, which was instructed to return its verdict in the form of answers to five questions propounded by the trial judge. The jury's answers were: Taco Cabana has a trade dress; taken as a whole, the trade dress is nonfunctional; the trade dress is inherently distinctive;[a] the trade dress has not acquired a secondary meaning[b] in the Texas market; and the alleged infringement creates a likelihood of confusion on the part of ordinary customers as to the source or association of the restaurant's goods or services. Because, as the jury was told, Taco Cabana's trade dress was protected if it either was inherently distinctive or had acquired a secondary meaning, judgment was entered awarding damages to Taco Cabana.

The Court of Appeals ruled that the instructions adequately stated the applicable law and that the evidence supported the jury's findings. In particular, the Court of Appeals rejected petitioner's argument that a finding of no secondary meaning contradicted a finding of inherent distinctiveness.

In so holding, the court below followed precedent in the Fifth Circuit. Chevron Chemical Co. v. Voluntary Purchasing Groups, Inc., 659 F.2d 695 (C.A.5 1981). We granted certiorari to resolve the conflict among the Courts of Appeals on the question whether trade dress which is inherently distinctive is protectable under § 43(a) without a showing that it has acquired secondary meaning. 502 U.S. ___ (1992). We find that it is, and we therefore affirm.

II

The Lanham Act[c] was intended to make "actionable the deceptive and misleading use of marks" and "to protect persons engaged in ... commerce against unfair competition." § 45, 15 U.S.C. § 1127. Section 43(a) "prohibits a broader range of practices than does § 32," which applies to registered marks, Inwood Laboratories, Inc. v. Ives Laboratories, Inc., 456 U.S. 844, 858 (1982), but it is common ground that § 43(a) protects qualifying

---

[a] The instructions were that to be found inherently distinctive, the trade dress must not be descriptive.

[b] Secondary meaning is used generally to indicate that a mark or dress "has come through use to be uniquely associated with a specific source." Restatement (Third) of Unfair Competition § 13, Comment e (Tent. Draft No. 2, Mar. 23, 1990). "To establish secondary meaning, a manufacturer must show that, in the minds of the public, the primary significance of a product feature or term is to identify the source of the product rather than the product itself." Inwood Laboratories, Inc. v. Ives Laboratories, Inc., 456 U.S. 844, 851, n. 11 (1982).

[c] The Lanham Act, including the provisions at issue here, has been substantially amended since the present suit was brought. See Trademark Law Revision Act of 1988, 15 U.S.C.A. § 1121.

unregistered trademarks and that the general principles qualifying a mark for registration under § 2 of the Lanham Act are for the most part applicable in determining whether an unregistered mark is entitled to protection under § 43(a).

Marks which are merely descriptive of a product are not inherently distinctive. When used to describe a product, they do not inherently identify a particular source, and hence cannot be protected. However, descriptive marks may acquire the distinctiveness which will allow them to be protected under the Act. Section 2 of the Lanham Act provides that a descriptive mark that otherwise could not be registered under the Act may be registered if it "has become distinctive of the applicant's goods in commerce." §§ 2(e), (f), 15 U.S.C. §§ 1052(e), (f). This acquired distinctiveness is generally called "secondary meaning." The concept of secondary meaning has been applied to actions under § 43(a).

The general rule regarding distinctiveness is clear: an identifying mark is distinctive and capable of being protected if it either (1) is inherently distinctive or (2) has acquired distinctiveness through secondary meaning. Restatement (Third) of Unfair Competition, § 13, pp. 37–38, and Comment a (Tent. Draft No. 2, Mar. 23, 1990). It is also clear that eligibility for protection under § 43(a) depends on nonfunctionality. It is, of course, also undisputed that liability under § 43(a) requires proof of the likelihood of confusion.

Recognizing that a general requirement of secondary meaning imposes "an unfair prospect of theft [or] financial loss" on the developer of fanciful or arbitrary trade dress at the outset of its use, petitioner suggests that such trade dress should receive limited protection without proof of secondary meaning. Petitioner argues that such protection should be only temporary and subject to defeasance when over time the dress has failed to acquire a secondary meaning. This approach is vulnerable for the reasons given by the Court of Appeals. If temporary protection is available from the earliest use of the trade dress, it must be because it is neither functional nor descriptive but an inherently distinctive dress that is capable of identifying a particular source of the product. Such a trade dress, or mark, is not subject to copying by concerns that have an equal opportunity to choose their own inherently distinctive trade dress. To terminate protection for failure to gain secondary meaning over some unspecified time could not be based on the failure of the dress to retain its fanciful, arbitrary, or suggestive nature, but on the failure of the user of the dress to be successful enough in the marketplace. This is not a valid basis to find a dress or mark ineligible for protection. The user of such a trade dress should be able to maintain what competitive position it has and continue to seek wider identification among potential customers.

The Fifth Circuit was quite right in Chevron, and in this case, to inquire whether trade dress for which protection is claimed under § 43(a) is inherently distinctive. If it is, it is capable of identifying products or services as coming from a specific source and secondary meaning is not required. This is the rule generally applicable to trademark, and the protection of trademarks and trade dress under § 43(a) serves the same statutory purpose of preventing deception and unfair competition. There is no persuasive reason to apply different analysis to the two.

It would be a different matter if there were textual basis in § 43(a) for treating inherently distinctive verbal or symbolic trademarks differently from inherently distinctive trade dress. But there is none. The section does not mention trademarks or trade dress, whether they be called generic, descriptive, suggestive, arbitrary, fanciful, or functional. Nor does the concept of secondary meaning appear in the text of § 43(a). Where secondary meaning does appear in the statute, 15 U.S.C.A. § 1052 (1982 ed.), it is a requirement that applies only to merely descriptive marks and not to inherently distinctive ones. We see no basis for requiring secondary meaning for inherently distinctive trade dress protection under § 43(a) but not for other distinctive words, symbols, or devices capable of identifying a producer's product.

Engrafting onto § 43(a) a requirement of secondary meaning for inherently distinctive trade dress also would undermine the purposes of the Lanham Act. Protection of trade dress, no less than of trademarks, serves the Act's purpose to "secure to the owner of the mark the goodwill of his business and to protect the ability of consumers to distinguish among competing producers. National protection of trademarks is desirable, Congress concluded, because trademarks foster competition and the maintenance of quality by securing to the producer the benefits of good reputation." Park' N Fly, 469 U.S. 189, 198 (1985), citing S. Rep. No. 1333, 79th Cong., 2d Sess., 3–5 (1946)(citations omitted). By making more difficult the identification of a producer with its product, a secondary meaning requirement for a nondescriptive trade dress would hinder improving or maintaining the producer's competitive position.

Suggestions that under the Fifth Circuit's law, the initial user of any shape or design would cut off competition from products of like design and shape are not persuasive. Only nonfunctional, distinctive trade dress is protected under § 43(a). The Fifth Circuit holds that a design is legally functional, and thus unprotectable, if it is one of a limited number of equally efficient options available to competitors and free competition would be unduly hindered by according the design trademark protection. This serves to assure that competition will not be stifled by the exhaustion of a limited number of trade dresses.

On the other hand, adding a secondary meaning requirement could have anticompetitive effects, creating particular burdens on the start-up of small companies. It would present special difficulties for a business, such as respondent, that seeks to start a new product in a limited area and then expand into new markets. Denying protection for inherently distinctive nonfunctional trade dress until after secondary meaning has been established would allow a competitor, which has not adopted a distinctive trade dress of its own, to appropriate the originator's dress in other markets and to deter the originator from expanding into and competing in these areas.

As noted above, petitioner concedes that protecting an inherently distinctive trade dress from its inception may be critical to new entrants to the market and that withholding protection until secondary meaning has been established would be contrary to the goals of the Lanham Act. Petitioner specifically suggests, however, that the solution is to dispense with the requirement of secondary meaning for a reasonable, but brief period at the outset of the use of a trade dress. If § 43(a) does not require secondary meaning at the outset of a business' adoption of trade dress, there is no basis in the statute to support the suggestion that such a requirement comes into being after some unspecified time.

■ JUSTICE STEVENS, concurring in the judgment.

[T]he Court interprets [§ 43(a)] as having created a federal cause of action for infringement of an unregistered trademark or trade dress and concludes that such a mark or dress should receive essentially the same protection as those that are registered. Although I agree with the Court's conclusion, I think it is important to recognize that the meaning of the text has been transformed by the federal courts over the past few decades. I agree with this transformation, even though it marks a departure from the original text, because it is consistent with the purposes of the statute and has recently been endorsed by Congress.

I

It is appropriate to begin with the relevant text of § 43(a). Section 43(a) provides a federal remedy for using either "a false designation of origin" or a "false description or representation" in connection with any goods or services. The full text of the section makes it clear that the word "origin" refers to the geographic location in which the goods originated, and in fact, the phrase "false designation of origin" was understood to be limited to false advertising of geographic origin. For example, the "false designation of origin" language contained in the statute makes it unlawful to represent that California oranges came from Florida, or vice versa.[d]

For a number of years after the 1946 enactment of the Lanham Act, a "false description or representation," like "a false designation of origin," was construed narrowly. The phrase encompassed two kinds of wrongs: false advertising and the common-law tort of "passing off."[e] Neither "secondary meaning" nor "inherent distinctiveness" had anything to do with false advertising, but proof of secondary meaning was an element of the common-law passing-off cause of action.

II

Over time, the Circuits have expanded the categories of "false designa-

---

[d] This is clear from the fact that the cause of action created by this section is available only to a person doing business in the locality falsely indicated as that of origin.

[e] The common-law tort of passing off has been described as "a tort consist[ing] of one passing off his goods as the goods of another." 1 J. McCarthy, Trademarks and Unfair Competition § 5.2, p. 133 (2d ed. 1984) (McCarthy).

tion of origin" and "false description or representation." One treatise[f] identified the Court of Appeals for the Sixth Circuit as the first to broaden the meaning of "origin" to include "origin of source or manufacture" in addition to geographic origin.[g] Another early case, described as unique among the Circuit cases because it was so "forward-looking,"[h] interpreted the "false description or representation" language to mean more than mere "palming off." L'Aiglon Apparel, Inc. v. Lana Lobell, Inc., 214 F.2d 649 (C.A.3 1954). The court explained: "We find nothing in the legislative history of the Lanham Act to justify the view that [§ 43(a)] is merely declarative of existing law.... It seems to us that Congress has defined a statutory civil wrong of false representation of goods in commerce and has given a broad class of suitors injured or likely to be injured by such wrong the right to relief in the federal courts." Id., at 651. Judge Clark, writing a concurrence in 1956, presciently observed: "Indeed, there is indication here and elsewhere that the bar has not yet realized the potential impact of this statutory provision [§ 43(a)]." Maternally Yours, Inc. v. Your Maternity Shop, Inc., 234 F.2d 538, 546 (CA2). Although some have criticized the expansion as unwise,[i] it is now "a firmly embedded reality."[j] The United States Trade Association Trademark Review Commission noted this transformation with approval: "Section 43(a) is an enigma, but a very popular one. Narrowly drawn and intended to reach false designations or representations as to the geographical origin of products, the section has been widely interpreted to create, in essence, a federal law of unfair competition.... It has definitely eliminated a gap in unfair competition law, and its vitality is showing no signs of age."[k]

Today, [t]he federal courts are in agreement that § 43(a) creates a federal cause of action for trademark and trade dress infringement claims. 1 J. Gilson, Trademark Protection and Practice § 2.13, p. 2–178 (1991). They are also in agreement that the test for liability is likelihood of confusion. And the Circuits are in general agreement, with perhaps the exception of the Second Circuit,[l] that secondary meaning need not be

[f] 2 id., § 27:3, p. 345.

[g] Federal–Mogul–Bower Bearings, Inc. v. Azoff, 313 F.2d 405, 408 (C.A.6 1963).

[h] Derenberg, 32 N.Y. U. L. Rev., at 1047, 1049.

[i] See, e.g., Germain, Unfair Trade Practices Under § 43(a) of the Lanham Act: You've Come a Long Way Baby—Too Far, Maybe?, 64 Trademark Rep. 193, 194 (1974)("It is submitted that the cases have applied Section 43(a) to situations it was not intended to cover and have used it in ways that it was not designed to function").

[j] 2 McCarthy § 27:3, p. 345.

[k] The United States Trademark Association Trademark Review Commission Report and Recommendations to USTA President and Board of Directors, 77 Trademark Rep. 375, 426 (1987).

[l] Consistent with the common-law background of § 43(a), the Second Circuit has said that proof of secondary meaning is required to establish a claim that the defendant has traded on the plaintiff's good will by falsely representing that his goods are those of the plaintiff. See, e.g., Crescent Tool Co. v. Kilborn & Bishop Co., 247 F. 299 (1917). To my knowledge, however, the Second Circuit has not explained why "inherent distinctiveness" is not an appropriate substitute for proof of secondary meaning in a trade dress case. Most of the cases in which the Second Circuit has said that secondary meaning is required did not involve findings of inherent distinctiveness. For example, in Vibrant Sales, Inc. v. New Body Boutique, Inc., 652

established once there is a finding of inherent distinctiveness in order to establish a trade dress violation under § 43(a).

III

Even though the lower courts' expansion of the categories contained in § 43(a) is unsupported by the text of the Act, I am persuaded that it is consistent with the general purposes of the Act. For example, Congressman Lanham, the bill's sponsor, stated: "The purpose of [the Act] is to protect legitimate business and the consumers of the country." 92 Cong. Rec. 7524 (1946). One way of accomplishing these dual goals was by creating uniform legal rights and remedies that were appropriate for a national economy. Although the protection of trademarks had once been "entirely a State matter," the result of such a piecemeal approach was that there were almost "as many different varieties of common law as there are States" so that a person's right to a trademark "in one State may differ widely from the rights which [that person] enjoys in another." H. R. Rep. No. 944, 76th Cong., 1st Sess., 4 (1939). The House Committee on Trademarks and Patents, recognizing that "trade is no longer local, but ... national," saw the need for "national legislation along national lines [to] secure to the owners of trademarks in interstate commerce definite rights." Ibid.[m]

Congress has revisited this statute from time to time, and has accepted the "judicial legislation" that has created this federal cause of action. Recently, for example, in the Trademark Law Revision Act of 1988, Pub. L. 100–667, 102 Stat. 3935, Congress codified the judicial interpretation of § 43(a), giving its imprimatur to a growing body of case law from the Circuits that had expanded the section beyond its original language.

Although Congress has not specifically addressed the question whether secondary meaning is required under § 43(a), the steps it has taken in this subsequent legislation suggest that secondary meaning is not required if inherent distinctiveness has been established.[n] First, Congress broadened the language of § 43(a) to make explicit that the provision prohibits "any

---

F.2d 299 (1981), cert. denied, 455 U.S. 909 (1982), the product at issue—a velcro belt—was functional and lacked "any distinctive, unique or non-functional mark or feature." 652 F.2d, at 305. Similarly, in Stormy Clime Ltd. v. ProGroup, Inc., 809 F.2d 971, 977 (1987), the court described functionality as a continuum, and placed the contested rainjacket closer to the functional end than to the distinctive end. Although the court described the lightweight bag in Le Sportsac, Inc. v. K Mart Corp., 754 F.2d 71 (1985), as having a distinctive appearance and concluded that the District Court's finding of nonfunctionality was not clearly erroneous, id., at 74, it did not explain why secondary meaning was also required in such a case.

[m] Forty years later, the USTA Trademark Review Commission assessed the state of trademark law. The conclusion that it reached serves as a testimonial to the success of the Act in achieving its goal of uniformity: "The federal courts now decide, under federal law, all but a few trademark disputes. State trademark law and state courts are less influential than ever. Today the Lanham Act is the paramount source of trademark law in the United States, as interpreted almost exclusively by the federal courts." Trademark Review Commission, 77 Trademark Rep., at 377.

[n] "When several acts of Congress are passed touching the same subject-matter, subsequent legislation may be considered to assist in the interpretation of prior legislation upon the same subject." Tiger v. Western Investment Co., 221 U.S. 286, 309 (1911).

word, term, name, symbol, or device, or any combination thereof" that is "likely to cause confusion, or to cause mistake, or to deceive as to the affiliation, connection, or association of such person with another person, or as to the origin, sponsorship, or approval of his or her goods, services, or commercial activities by another person." 15 U.S.C.A. § 1125(a). That language makes clear that a confusingly similar trade dress is actionable under § 43(a), without necessary reference to "falsity." Second, Congress approved and confirmed the extensive judicial development under the provision, including its application to trade dress that the federal courts had come to apply.[o] Third, the legislative history of the 1988 amendments reaffirms Congress' goals of protecting both businesses and consumers with the Lanham Act. And fourth, Congress explicitly extended to any violation of § 43(a) the basic Lanham Act remedial provisions whose text previously covered only registered trademarks.[p] The aim of the amendments was to apply the same protections to unregistered marks as were already afforded to registered marks. See S. Rep. No. 100–515, p. 40 (1988). These steps buttress the conclusion that § 43(a) is properly understood to provide protection in accordance with the standards for registration in § 2. These aspects of the 1988 legislation bolster the claim that an inherently distinctive trade dress may be protected under § 43(a) without proof of secondary meaning.

IV

In light of the general consensus among the Courts of Appeals that have actually addressed the question, and the steps on the part of Congress to codify that consensus, stare decisis concerns persuade me to join the Court's conclusion that secondary meaning is not required to establish a trade dress violation under § 43(a) once inherent distinctiveness has been established. Accordingly, I concur in the judgment, but not in the opinion of the Court.

Ferrari S.P.A. Esercizio Fabriche Automobili E Corse v. Roberts

United States Court of Appeals, Sixth Circuit, 1991.
944 F.2d 1235.

[This case, which was decided before *Two Pesos* removed the necessity of proving secondary meaning in the case of inherently distinctive trade dress,

---

[o] As the Senate Report explained, revision of Section 43(a) is designed "to codify the interpretation it has been given by the courts. Because Section 43(a) of the Act fills an important gap in federal unfair competition law, the committee expects the courts to continue to interpret the section.

"As written, Section 43(a) appears to deal only with false descriptions or representations and false designations of geographic origin. Since its enactment in 1946, however, it has been widely interpreted as creating, in essence, a federal law of unfair competition. For example, it has been applied to cases involving the infringement of unregistered marks, violations of trade dress and certain nonfunctional configurations of goods and actionable false advertising claims." S. Rep. No. 100–515, p. 40 (1988).

[p] See 15 U.S.C.A. §§ 1114, 1116–1118.

provides (among other things) a good demonstration of how to prove secondary meaning when it is required.]

■ RYAN, CIRCUIT JUDGE

I

The Facts

Ferrari is the world famous designer and manufacturer of racing automobiles and upscale sports cars. Between 1969 and 1973, Ferrari produced the 365 GTB/4 Daytona. Because Ferrari intentionally limits production of its cars in order to create an image of exclusivity, only 1400 Daytonas were built; of these, only 100 were originally built as Spyders, soft-top convertibles. Daytona Spyders currently sell for one to two million dollars. Although Ferrari no longer makes Daytona Spyders, they have continuously produced mechanical parts and body panels, and provided repair service for the cars.

Ferrari began producing a car called the Testarossa in 1984. To date, Ferrari has produced approximately 5000 Testarossas. Production of these cars is also intentionally limited to preserve exclusivity: the entire anticipated production is sold out for the next several years and the waiting period to purchase a Testarossa is approximately five years. A new Testarossa sells for approximately $230,000.

Roberts is engaged in a number of business ventures related to the automobile industry. One enterprise is the manufacture of fiberglass kits that replicate the exterior features of Ferrari's Daytona Spyder and Testarossa automobiles. Roberts' copies are called the Miami Spyder and the Miami Coupe, respectively. The kit is a one-piece body shell molded from reinforced fiberglass. It is usually bolted onto the undercarriage of another automobile such as a Chevrolet Corvette or a Pontiac Fiero, called the donor car. Roberts marketed the Miami Spyder primarily through advertising in kit-car magazines. Most of the replicas were sold as kits for about $8,500, although a fully accessorized "turnkey" version was available for about $50,000.

At the time of trial, Roberts had not yet completed a kit-car version of the Miami Coupe, the replica of Ferrari's Testarossa, although he already has two orders for them. He originally built the Miami Coupe for the producers of the television program "Miami Vice" to be used as a stunt car in place of the more expensive Ferrari Testarossa.

The district court found, and it is not disputed, that Ferrari's automobiles and Roberts' replicas are virtually identical in appearance. [T]he case result[ed] in a verdict for Ferrari and a permanent injunction enjoining Roberts from producing the Miami Spyder and the Miami Coupe.

II

"Trade dress" refers to "the image and overall appearance of a product." Allied Mktg. Group, Inc. v. CDL Mktg., Inc., 878 F.2d 806, 812 (5th Cir.1989). It embodies "that arrangement of identifying characteristics or decorations connected with a product, whether by packaging or otherwise, intended to make the source of the product distinguishable from another and to promote its sale." Mr. Gasket Co. v. Travis, 299 N.E.2d 906, 912 n. 13 (1973).

Ferrari's Lanham Act claim in this case is a "trade dress" claim. Ferrari charges, and the district court found, that the unique and distinctive exterior shape and design of the Daytona Spyder and the Testarossa are protected trade dress which Roberts has infringed by copying them and marketing his replicas.

III

To prove a violation of section 43(a), Ferrari's burden is to show, by a preponderance of the evidence:

1) that the trade dress of Ferrari's vehicles has acquired a "secondary meaning,"

2) that there is a likelihood of confusion based on the similarity of the exterior shape and design of Ferrari's vehicles and Roberts' replicas, and

3) that the appropriated features of Ferrari's trade dress are primarily nonfunctional.

See Kwik–Site Corp. v. Clear View Mfg. Co., Inc., 758 F.2d 167, 178 (6th Cir.1985).

A

Secondary Meaning

To acquire a secondary meaning in the minds of the buying public, an article of merchandise when shown to a prospective customer must prompt the affirmation, "That is the article I want because I know its source," and not the negative inquiry as to "Who makes that article?" In other words, the article must proclaim its identification with its source, and not simply stimulate inquiry about it.

West Point Mfg. Co. v. Detroit Stamping Co., 222 F.2d 581, 595 (6th Cir.)(citation omitted), cert. denied, 350 U.S. 840 (1955). Arguably, secondary meaning in this case can be presumed from Roberts' admissions that he intentionally copied Ferrari's designs. Roberts told Vivian Bumgardner, an investigator who recorded her conversations with Roberts, that "we put this whole body right on it and it looks just like a real car, I mean they can't tell by looking.... We build and sell the same car, reproduce it." The intent to copy was also shown by Roberts' use of the distinctive Ferrari prancing horse logo on the front parking lights of the Daytona Spyder and in advertising brochures. The original Miami Coupe brochure even copied the Ferrari name by referring to the Roberts' car as the "Miami Testarossa." The evidence of intentional copying shows the strong secondary meaning of the Ferrari designs because "there is no logical reason for the precise copying save an attempt to realize upon a secondary meaning that is in existence." Audio Fidelity, Inc. v. High Fidelity Recordings, Inc., 283 F.2d 551, 558 (9th Cir.1960).

Ferrari, however, need not rely on a presumption of secondary meaning because the evidence at trial showed that the exterior design of Ferrari's vehicles enjoyed strong secondary meaning. Lawrence Crane, Art Director of Automobile magazine, testified that the shape of a Ferrari "says Ferrari to the general populous (sic)" and that "because it's so instantly recognizable ... we've used even just portions of Ferraris, the Testarossa, for instance, and people recognize it, and our sales are changed." William Moore, Editor of Kit Car Illustrated, and a witness for Roberts, conceded that car replica manufacturers frequently copy Ferraris because the "special image" associated with Ferrari creates a market for cars which look like Ferraris. The testimony of Crane and Moore was supported by survey data which indicated that of survey respondents shown photographs of Ferrari's cars without identifying badges, 73% properly identified a photograph of Daytona Spyder as manufactured by Ferrari and 82% identified the Testarossa as a Ferrari product. Such survey evidence, combined with intentional copying and the widespread publicity surrounding Ferraris, convinced the court in a separate action brought by Ferrari against Roberts' former partner to enjoin him from producing replicas of the Daytona Spyder identical to those produced by Roberts, that the Ferrari vehicle design has a secondary meaning:

> In light of defendants' close intentional copying, their failure to introduce any evidence to show that such copying was for any purpose but to associate themselves with the reputation and marketability of the Ferrari DAYTONA SPYDER, the large amount of recognition of said design with Ferrari shown in continuous magazine articles and books about the DAYTONA SPYDER long after the cessation of its manufacture, the showings of the Ferrari DAYTONA SPYDER at vintage car shows, the highly publicized sales of said car by Ferrari customers, and the percentages of recognition in both the plaintiff's and the defendants' surveys, ... the court finds the evidence thorough and convincing that the Ferrari DAYTONA SPYDER design has achieved a strong secondary meaning.

Ferrari S.p.A. v. McBurnie, 11 U.S.P.Q.2D (BNA) 1843, 1846–47 (S.D.Cal. 1989).

Ferrari's vehicles would not acquire secondary meaning merely because they are unique designs or because they are aesthetically beautiful. The design must be one that is instantly identified in the mind of the informed viewer as a Ferrari design. The district court found, and we agree, that the unique exterior design and shape of the Ferrari vehicles are their "mark" or "trade dress" which distinguish the vehicles' exterior shapes not simply as distinctively attractive designs, but as Ferrari creations.

We also agree with the district court that Roberts' admission that he intentionally copied Ferrari's design, the survey evidence introduced by Ferrari, and the testimony of Crane and Moore amount to abundant evidence that the exterior design features of the Ferrari vehicles are "trade dress" which have acquired secondary meaning.

Roberts argues strongly that section 43(a) provides no trademark infringement protection for the exterior design of a product because "automobile designs are to be protected from copying only pursuant to the design patent statute," and Ferrari, during the period relevant to this case, had not protected the Daytona Spyder or the Testarossa with a design patent. We disagree.

Courts have consistently rejected Roberts' argument that the availability of design patent protection precludes applicability of the Lanham Act for products whose trade dress have acquired strong secondary meaning. Actionable harm results from either infringing a design patent or copying a product with secondary meaning. [T]he distinctive appearance of a Ferrari's exterior shape, as evidenced at trial by surveys and the testimony of car magazine editors and others, entitles Ferrari to Lanham Act protection. This trademark protection does not unduly extend the seventeen-year monopoly guaranteed by the patent laws because the two sources of protection are totally separate:

> Trademark rights, or rights under the law of unfair competition, which happen to continue beyond the expiration of a design patent, do not "extend" the patent monopoly. They exist independently of it, under different law and for different reasons. The termination of either has no legal effect on the continuance of the other.

Application of Mogen David Wine Corp. 328 F.2d 925, 930 (1964). Patent and trademark law are completely distinct fields:

> The protection accorded by the law of trademark and unfair competition is greater than that accorded by the law of patents because each is directed at a different purpose. The latter protects inventive activity which, after a term of years, is dedicated to the public domain. The former protects commercial activity which, in our society, is essentially private.

Truck Equip. Serv. Co. v. Fruehauf Corp., 536 F.2d 1210, 1215 (8th Cir.), cert. denied, 429 U.S. 861 (1976).

The dissent disagrees that patent and trademark law are distinct fields of law. The dissent, citing Bonito Boats, Inc. v. Thunder Craft Boats, Inc., 489 U.S. 141 (1989); Compco Corp. v. Day–Brite Lighting, Inc., 376 U.S. 234 (1964); and Sears, Roebuck & Co. v. Stiffel Co., 376 U.S. 225 (1964), argues that Ferrari's designs are not protected because unpatented goods may be freely copied. In the cases cited in the dissenting opinion, the Supreme Court examined state unfair competition laws to determine whether federal patent law preempted their application. In all three cases, the Court held that a state, through its unfair competition laws, could not extend patent protection to otherwise unprotected designs because such protection conflicted with the federal policy of substantially free trade in unpatented design and utilitarian concepts. See Bonito Boats, 489 U.S. at 152–54.

These cases, however, do not affect the applicability of the Lanham Act in this case. First, the Court in Compco expressly noted that a defendant can copy at will if the design is "not entitled to a design patent *or other federal statutory protection....*" Compco, 376 U.S. at 238 (emphasis added). Thus, Roberts cannot copy at will because "other federal statutory protection," the Lanham Act, applies. Second, these cases involved only the preemption of state unfair competition law by federal patent law, not the scope of federal trademark or unfair competition law. Because trademark law and patent law address different concerns, and because of the narrow focus of the Supreme Court's inquiry in Compco and Sears, courts have explicitly held that these decisions do not preclude Lanham Act protection of designs.

Thus, Lanham Act protection is available to designs which also might have been covered by design patents as long as the designs have acquired secondary meaning. Ferrari's designs have clearly acquired secondary meaning and thus were entitled to protection.

B

Likelihood of Confusion

1

District Court's Findings

This court has held that in determining likelihood of confusion in a Lanham Act case, the court should consider the following factors: strength of the plaintiff's mark; relatedness of the goods; similarity of the marks; evidence of actual confusion; marketing channels used; likely degree of purchaser care; defendant's intent in selecting the mark; and likelihood of expansion of the product lines. Frisch's Restaurants, Inc. v. Elby's Big Boy, 670 F.2d 642, 648 (6th Cir.), cert. denied, 459 U.S. 916 (1982). A party claiming infringement need not show all, or even most, of these factors in order to prevail.

The district court found, based upon an evaluation of the eight Frisch factors, that the similarity of the exterior design of the Ferrari vehicles and the Roberts replicas was likely to confuse the public. The court noted that while no evidence was offered on two of the factors, evidence of actual confusion and likelihood of expansion of the product lines, two others, marketing channels and purchaser care, favored Roberts and the remaining factors "radically favor[ed] Ferrari." Summarized, the district court's findings on the Frisch "likelihood of confusion" factors are as follows:

Factors	Favor
1. Strength of the mark	Ferrari
2. Relatedness of the goods	Ferrari
3. Similarity of the marks	Ferrari
4. Evidence of actual confusion	No evidence
5. Marketing channels used	Roberts
6. Likely degree of purchaser care	Roberts
7. Roberts' intent in selecting "mark"	Ferrari
8. Likelihood of expansion of product lines.	No evidence

Recalling that the claimed mark involved here is the trade dress—the exterior shape and design of the Ferrari vehicles—it is clear that Ferrari's mark is very strong. The strength of the mark is its distinctiveness and Ferrari's designs are unquestionably distinctive. The survey evidence we have discussed, as well as the testimony that the shape of the plaintiff's vehicles "says Ferrari," is evidence of that distinctiveness. Indeed, Roberts' purposeful effort to copy the Ferrari designs is strong circumstantial evidence of the distinctiveness of the originals.

There is no dispute about the relatedness of the goods factor. The products produced by both parties are sports cars.

Likewise, the similarity of the marks—the exterior designs of the vehicles—is indisputable. Ferrari offered survey evidence which showed that 68% of the respondents could not distinguish a photograph of the McBurnie replica, upon which Roberts' Miami Spyder is based, from a photograph of the genuine Ferrari Daytona Spyder. In these photographs, the cars were shown without identifying insignia. Drawings for Roberts' cars show identifying insignia, an "R" on the parking lens and vent window, but the cars produced at the time of trial did not include the "R." Because the survey respondents saw photographs of the McBurnie cars, and because all of the identifying insignia were removed, the survey has limited value in showing the likelihood of confusion between the Roberts and Ferrari vehicles if displayed with identifying emblems. The survey, however, does show that the trade dress of the two car designs, the shapes and exteriors, were quite similar. An examination of the photographs of the cars which are in evidence confirms the striking similarity of the dress of the originals and the replicas. They are virtually indistinguishable.

Finally, Roberts conceded that his intent in replicating the exterior design of Ferrari's vehicles was to market a product that looked as much as possible like a Ferrari original, although Roberts made no claim to his customers that his replicas were Ferraris. " '[The] intent of [a party] in adopting [another's mark] is a critical factor, since if the mark was adopted with the intent of deriving benefit from the reputation of [the plaintiff,] *that fact alone may be sufficient to justify the inference that there is confusing similarity.' "* Frisch's Restaurants, 670 F.2d at 648 (emphasis in original)(quoting Amstar Corp. v. Domino's Pizza, Inc., 615 F.2d 252, 263 (5th Cir.), cert. denied, 449 U.S. 899 (1980)). This is especially true in cases, such as this one, where the defendant sold a comparatively cheap imitation of an expensive, exclusive item. Intentional copying, however, is not actionable under the Lanham Act "absent evidence that the copying was done with the intent to derive a benefit from the reputation of another." Zin–Plas Corp. v. Plumbing Quality AGF Co., 622 F.Supp. 415, 420 (W.D.Mich.1985). "Where the copying by one party of another's product is not done to deceive purchasers and thus derive a benefit from another's name and reputation, but rather to avail oneself of a design which is attractive and desirable, a case of unfair competition is not made out." West Point Mfg., 222 F.2d at 586. In this case, where Ferrari's design enjoyed strong secondary meaning and Roberts admitted that he designed his cars to look like Ferrari's, the intent to copy was clear.

We conclude that aside from the presumption of likelihood of confusion that follows from intentional copying, Ferrari produced strong evidence that the public is likely to be confused by the similarity of the exterior design of Ferrari's vehicles and Roberts' replicas.

2

Roberts' Objections

Roberts disagrees with the legal significance of the district court's findings of likelihood of confusion. He argues that for purposes of the Lanham Act, the requisite likelihood of confusion must be confusion at the point of sale—purchaser confusion—and not the confusion of nonpurchasing, casual observers. The evidence is clear that Roberts assured purchasers of his replicas that they were not purchasing Ferraris and that his customers were not confused about what they were buying.

Roberts also argues that actionable confusion may not be inferred from intentional copying when the intentional copying involves the design of a product as opposed to the copying of a trademark, trade name or trade dress. Implicit, of course, is Roberts' related argument that the exterior shape and design of the Ferrari cars is not, and cannot be, a trademark or trade dress. We disagree with these contentions.

a

Confusion as to Source

Roberts is correct that, for the most part, similarity of products alone is not actionable; there must also be confusion as to the origin of the product. Similarity of products, however, does become actionable when the similarity leads to confusion as to source and the public cares who the source of the product is.

Because consumers care that they are purchasing a Ferrari as opposed to a car that looks like a Ferrari, and because Roberts' replicas look like Ferraris, Ferrari presented an actionable claim as to confusion of source.

b

Confusion at Point of Sale

Roberts argues that his replicas do not violate the Lanham Act because he informed his purchasers that his significantly cheaper cars and kits were not genuine Ferraris and thus there was no confusion at the point of sale. The Lanham Act, however, was intended to do more than protect consumers at the point of sale. When the Lanham Act was enacted in 1946, its protection was limited to the use of marks "likely to cause confusion or mistake or to deceive purchasers as to the source of origin of such goods or services." In 1967, Congress deleted this language and broadened the Act's protection to include the use of marks "likely to cause confusion or mistake or to deceive." Thus, Congress intended "to regulate commerce within [its control] by making actionable the deceptive and misleading use of marks in such commerce; [and] ... to protect persons engaged in such commerce against unfair competition...." 15 U.S.C.A. § 1127. Although, as the dissent points out, Congress rejected an anti-dilution provision when recently amending the Lanham Act, it made no effort to amend or delete this language clearly protecting the confusion of goods *in commerce*. The Rolex Watch court noted that this interpretation was necessary to protect against the cheapening and dilution of the genuine product, and to protect the manufacturer's reputation. Rolex Watch, U.S.A., Inc. v. Canner, 645 F.Supp. 484, 495 (S.D.Fla.1986).

Such is the damage which could occur here. As the district court explained when deciding whether Roberts' former partner's Ferrari replicas would be confused with Ferrari's cars:

> Ferrari has gained a well-earned reputation for making uniquely designed automobiles of quality and rarity. The DAYTONA SPYDER design is well-known among the relevant public and exclusively and positively associated with Ferrari. If the country is populated with hundreds, if not thousands, of replicas of rare, distinct, and unique vintage cars, obviously they are no longer unique. Even if a person seeing one of these replicas driving down the road is not confused, Ferrari's exclusive association with this design has been diluted and eroded. If the replica Daytona looks cheap or in disrepair, Ferrari's reputation for rarity and quality could be damaged....

Ferrari, 11 U.S.P.Q.2d at 1848. The dissent argues that the Lanham Act requires proof of confusion at the point of sale because the eight factor test used to determine likelihood of confusion focuses on the confusion of the purchaser, not the public. The dissent submits that three of the factors, marketing channels used, likely degree of purchaser care and sophistication, and evidence of actual confusion, specifically relate to purchasers. However, evidence of actual confusion is not limited to purchasers. The survey evidence in this case showed that members of the public, but not necessarily purchasers, were actually confused by the similarity of the products. Moreover, the other five factors, strength of the mark, relatedness of the goods, similarity of the marks, defendant's intent in selecting the mark, and likelihood of product expansion, do not limit the likelihood of confusion test to purchasers.

Since Congress intended to protect the reputation of the manufacturer as well as to protect purchasers, the Act's protection is not limited to confusion at the point of sale. Because Ferrari's reputation in the field could be damaged by the marketing of Roberts' replicas, the district court did not err in permitting recovery despite the absence of point of sale confusion.

3

Product Confusion

Roberts argues that the exterior design features of the Ferrari vehicles are not entitled to Lanham Act protection because only packages in which products are marketed, not products themselves, are covered as protected trade dress. In many cases, the policy of fulfilling consumer demand mandates that trade dress, including packaging and labeling, but not products, are protected from imitation.

In this case, where the exterior shape and design of the car is a "form of dress . . . primarily adopted for purposes of identification and individuality," the interest in free competition of cars would not be impeded by protecting the product itself. We are fortified in this conclusion by the large number of cases extending trademark protection to product designs. Ferrari, 11 U.S.P.Q.2D (BNA) 1843 (Ferrari design); see also Vuitton Et Fils S.A. v. J. Young Enterprises, Inc., 644 F.2d 769, 772 (9th Cir.1981)(purse design); Dallas Cowboys Cheerleaders Inc. v. Pussycat Cinema, Ltd., 604 F.2d 200 (2d Cir.1979)(configuration of color and pattern on uniform); Truck Equip. Serv., 536 F.2d 1210 (trapezoidal shape of semi-trailer truck); Pagliero v. Wallace China Co., 198 F.2d 339 (9th Cir.1952)(china patterns); Rolex Watch, 645 F.Supp. 484 (Rolex watch design); Zin–Plas, 622 F.Supp. at 419 (shape of tub spouts and shower heads).

Even if a product cannot be protected, Ferrari is correct in asserting that its exteriors qualify as a trade dress. As the court explained in a replication case involving expensive silver patterns, "A product's trade dress ordinarily consists of its packaging. However, the design given a product by its manufacturer also may serve to distinguish it from the products of other manufacturers and hence be protectible trade dress." Wallace Int'l Silversmiths, Inc. v. Godinger Silver Art Co., 916 F.2d 76, 78–79 (2d Cir.1990), cert. denied, 499 U.S. 976 (1991). In this case, the exterior design is the "packaging" that is the distinctiveness of a Ferrari automobile. The evidence is that Ferraris need no labeling; the shape of the vehicles "says Ferrari."

C

Nonfunctionality of Appropriated Features

Trademark law does not protect the functional features of products because such protection would provide a perpetual monopoly of features which could not be patented. Keene Corp. v. Paraflex Indus., Inc., 653 F.2d 822, 825 (3d Cir.1981). A product feature is functional "if it is essential to the use or purpose of the article or if it affects the cost or quality of the article." Inwood Laboratories, Inc. v. Ives Laboratories, Inc., 456 U.S. 844, 850 n. 10 (1982). Functionality is a factual determination reviewed only for clear error.

The district court found that Ferrari proved, by a preponderance of the evidence, that the exterior shapes and features of the Daytona Spyder and Testarossa were nonfunctional. The court based this conclusion on the uncontroverted testimony of Angelo Bellei, who developed Ferrari's grand touring cars from 1964–75, that the company chose the exterior designs for beauty and distinctiveness, not utility. Roberts disagrees that Ferrari established nonfunctionality because he believes that the designs are excluded from protection by the "aesthetic functionality doctrine."

The aesthetic functionality test was developed by the Ninth Circuit in Pagliero, 198 F.2d 339. In Pagliero, the court found that the defendant's copying of the plaintiff's designs for hotel china was not actionable because the designs were functional as "an important ingredient in the commercial success of the product" as opposed to "a mere arbitrary embellishment, a form of dress for the goods primarily adopted for purposes of identification and individuality and, hence, unrelated to basic consumer demands in connection with the product...." Id. at 343. As the court explained:

> One of the essential selling features of hotel china, if, indeed, not the primary, is the design. The attractiveness and eye-appeal of the design sells the china. Moreover, from the standpoint of the purchaser china satisfies a demand for the aesthetic as well as for the utilitarian, and the design on china is, at least in part, the response to such demand. The granting of relief in this type of situation would render Wallace immune from the most direct and effective competition with regard to these lines of china.

Id. at 343–44.

The broad scope of aesthetic functionality defined in Pagliero has been subsequently criticized and limited. Relating functionality to the commercial desirability of the feature regardless of its utilitarian function discourages the development of appealing designs because such designs would be entitled to less protection. Keene Corp., 653 F.2d at 825. Moreover, Pagliero's "important ingredient" formula has been rejected because "trade dress associated with a product that has accumulated goodwill ... will almost always be 'an important ingredient' in the 'salability' of the product." LeSportsac, Inc. v. K Mart Corp., 754 F.2d 71, 77 (2d Cir.1985). In part because of these concerns, the Ninth Circuit itself later rejected the view that "any feature of a product which contributes to the consumer appeal and salability of the product is, as a matter of law, a functional element of that product." Vuitton, 644 F.2d at 773.

Our own circuit seems to have implicitly rejected Pagliero's aesthetic functionality test. In WSM, Inc. v. Tennessee Sales Co., 709 F.2d 1084 (6th Cir.1983), the defendant, who copied plaintiff's amusement park souvenir T-shirts, argued that the design was not protected because of its aesthetic functionality. The court rejected this argument. Thus, the precedent in this circuit suggests that aesthetic functionality will not preclude a finding of nonfunctionality where the design also indicates source.

Other circuits also emphasize identification of source in limiting Pagliero. In Keene Corp., the Third Circuit suggested that "the inquiry should focus on the extent to which the design feature is related to the utilitarian function of the product or feature." Keene Corp., 653 F.2d at 825. Thus, trademark law would protect designs not significantly related to a product's utilitarian function which had achieved secondary meaning. Id. The court noted that this view had already received acceptance in cases holding that distinctive features used for identification were entitled to protection where such features were only incidentally functional. The Ninth Circuit also seemed to accept this formulation as a legitimate reading of Pagliero. In Vuitton, the court noted that the designs in Pagliero were adopted because of their aesthetic features and only after extensive advertising later became associated with the manufacturer. Vuitton, 644 F.2d at 773. That situation differs greatly from this case in which the Ferrari designs were selected for their distinctiveness.

■ KENNEDY, CIRCUIT JUDGE, dissenting.

I respectfully dissent because the majority opinion does more than protect consumers against a likelihood of confusion as to the source of goods; it protects the source of the goods, Ferrari, against plaintiff's copying of its design even if the replication is accompanied by adequate labelling so as to prevent consumer confusion. I believe the majority commits two errors in reaching this result. The majority first misconstrues the scope of protection afforded by the Lanham Act by misapplying the "likelihood of confusion" test and reading an anti-dilution provision into the language of section 43(a). The majority then affirms an injunction that is overbroad. The product of these errors is a remedy that provides defendant with absolute protection in perpetuity against copying its unpatented design. This remedy is contrary to the language and purpose of the Lanham Act and runs afoul of Supreme Court precedent. Bonito Boats, Inc. v. Thunder Craft Boats, Inc., 489 U.S. 141 (1989); Compco Corp. v. Day–Brite Lighting, Inc., 376 U.S. 234 (1964); Sears, Roebuck & Co. v. Stiffel Co., 376 U.S. 225 (1964).

I.   Section 43(a) and Trade Dress Protection

The majority invokes the appropriate test to determine whether protection is available for an unregistered trademark pursuant to section 43(a) of the Lanham Act. Kwik–Site Corp. v. Clear View Mfg. Co., 758 F.2d 167 (6th Cir.1985)(secondary meaning; likelihood of confusion; and nonfunctionality of trade dress). While I agree that Ferrari's designs have acquired secondary meaning and are primarily non-functional, I disagree with the majority's construction and application of the likelihood of confusion test and their conclusion that the Lanham Act protects against dilution of a manufacturer's goods.

This Circuit applies an eight-factor test to determine whether relevant consumers in the marketplace will confuse one item with another item. The majority correctly points out one purpose this test is not designed to accomplish: "Where the copying by one party of another's product is not done to *deceive purchasers* and thus derive a benefit from another's name and reputation, but rather to avail oneself of a design which is attractive and desirable, a case of unfair competition is not made out." West Point Mfg. v. Detroit Stamping Co., 222 F.2d 581, 586 (6th Cir.) (emphasis added), cert. denied, 350 U.S. 840 (1955). This passage properly notes that the statute is triggered when a copier attempts to "palm off" his replica as an original. In other words, the protection afforded by the Lanham Act is primarily to potential purchasers. The protection accruing to a producer is derivative of and only incidental to this primary protection: a producer can market his goods with the assurance that another may not market a replica in a manner that will allow potential purchasers to associate the replica with the producer of the original. Unfortunately, the majority merely pays lip service to this fundamental tenet in its application of the eight-factor test.

The majority never clearly defines the target group that is likely to be confused. Although West Point counsels that purchasers must be deceived, the majority concludes that the target group is the "public." The majority errs to the extent that its analysis shifts from potential purchasers to the broader more indefinite group of the "public."

The eight-factor test contemplates that the target group is comprised of potential purchasers. For example, the importance of one factor—evidence of actual confusion—is determined by the kinds of persons confused and degree of confusion. "Short-lived confusion or confusion of individuals casually acquainted with a business is worthy of little weight...." Homeowners Group, Inc. v. Home Marketing Specialists, Inc., 931 F.2d 1100, 1110 (6th Cir.1991)(quoting Safeway Stores, Inc. v. Safeway Discount Drugs, Inc., 675 F.2d 1160, 1167 (11th Cir.1982)). Two other factors obviously refer to potential purchasers: the marketing channels used and the likely degree of purchaser care and sophistication. Thus, three of the eight factors expressly focus on the likelihood of confusion as to potential purchasers.

[Roberts'] replicas are not likely to confuse potential purchasers. Plaintiff's vehicles display an "R" on the parking lenses and vent windows. No symbols or logos affiliated with Ferrari are displayed. Roberts informs all purchasers that his product is not affiliated with Ferrari. In light of these distinctions, and the high degree of customer care and sophistication that normally accompanies such a purchase—defendant's vehicles at issue sell for a minimum of $230,000, as well as the distinctly different marketing channels employed by the parties, I find the evidence insufficient to prove a likelihood of confusion by potential purchasers in the marketplace.

To be sure, some courts have expanded the application of the likelihood of confusion test to include individuals other than point-of-sale purchasers. These courts have included potential purchasers who may contemplate a purchase in the future, reasoning that in the pre-sale context an "observer would identify the [product] with the [original manufacturer], and the [original manufacturer]'s reputation would suffer damage if the [product] appeared to be of poor quality." Polo Fashions, Inc. v. Craftex, Inc., 816 F.2d 145, 148 (4th Cir.1987); see Mastercrafters Clock & Radio Co. v. Vacheron & Constantin–Le Coultre Watches, Inc., 221 F.2d 464 (2d Cir.), cert. denied, 350 U.S. 832 (1955); Rolex Watch, U.S.A., Inc. v. Canner, 645 F.Supp. 484 (S.D.Fla.1986).

In applying the test in this manner, these courts appear to recognize that the deception of a consumer under these circumstances could dissuade such a consumer from choosing to buy a particular product, thereby foreclosing the possibility of point-of-sale confusion but nevertheless injuring the consumer based on this confusion. The injury stems from the consumer's erroneous conclusion that the "original" product is poor quality based on his perception of a replica that he thinks is the original. These cases protect a potential purchaser against confusion as to the source of a particular product. Hence, even when expanding the scope of this test, these courts did not lose sight of the focus of section 43(a): the potential purchaser. The majority applies the likelihood of confusion test in a manner which departs from this focus.

The cases which have expanded the scope of the target group are distinguishable from the instant case, however. In Rolex, the counterfeit watches were labelled "ROLEX" on their face. Similarly, the Mastercrafters court found that the clock was labelled in a manner that was not likely to come to the attention of an individual. It is also noteworthy that the Second Circuit has limited Mastercrafters "by pointing out that 'in that case there was abundant evidence of actual confusion, palming off and an intent to deceive.'" Bose Corp. v. Linear Design Labs, Inc., 467 F.2d 304, 310 n. 8 (2d Cir.1972)(quoting Norwich Pharmacal Co. v. Sterling Drug, Inc., 271 F.2d 569 (2d Cir.1959), cert. denied, 362 U.S. 919 (1960)). No evidence was introduced in the instant case to show actual confusion, palming off or an intent to deceive and, as previously noted, plaintiff does not use any name or logo affiliated with Ferrari on its replicas.

Further, these cases conclude that the proper remedy is to require identification of the source of the replica, not prohibit copying of the product. See West Point, 222 F.2d at 589 (stating that under such circumstances "the only obligation of the copier is to identify its product lest the public be mistaken into believing that it was made by the prior patentee"). Accordingly, even if I were to conclude that plaintiff's copies created confusion in the pre-sale context, I would tailor the remedy to protect only against such confusion; this would best be accomplished through adequate labelling. The majority's remedy goes well beyond protection of consumers against confusion as to a product's source. It protects the design itself from being copied.

II.   The Sears–Compco–Bonito Boats Trilogy

The majority does not address this line of cases because it determines that federal trademark laws and federal patent laws are premised upon entirely different and mutually exclusive interests and objectives. It holds that no interrelationship exists between these laws; the availability of design patent protection does not preclude availability of Lanham Act protection. Thus, the majority concludes that this line of cases—Sears, Compco and Bonito Boats—has no relevance to federal trademark laws.

I conclude that these cases are directly relevant to the issue at hand. While the purposes of the Lanham Act and federal patent laws are not identical, I nonetheless find some overlap and congruity of purpose among these laws. Both the Lanham Act and federal patent laws affect commercial activity, particularly in the area of design patents. Patent laws confer a monopoly of limited duration upon the holder of the patent; this directly affects the marketplace. Similarly, the Lanham Act protects against certain unfair trade practices including a likelihood of confusion among potential purchasers. It is simply inaccurate to say that trademark law affects commercial activity and patent law affects private activity.

Moreover, the Supreme Court in Sears, Compco and Bonito Boats states unequivocally that an interrelationship exists between unfair competition laws and federal patent laws. The statutes at issue in Sears, Compco, and Bonito Boats were state unfair competition statutes similar to the Lanham Act in their purpose and objectives. By holding that these statutes conflicted with federal patent laws, the Supreme Court implicitly rejected the distinction urged by the majority. Hence, the rationale applied in this trilogy of cases to state unfair competition laws applies with equal force to federal trademark laws.

Avon Products v. S.C. Johnson & Son

United States District Court, S.D.N.Y., 1994.
32 U.S.P.Q.2D (BNA) 1001.

■ SCHWARTZ, J.

BACKGROUND

Avon and Skin–So–Soft Bath Oil

Avon is a New York corporation that sells a wide variety of personal care products. Among the products that Avon markets through its Sales Representatives (independent contractors who purchase Avon products for resale to customers) is a family of bath and skin products sold under the federally registered trade name Skin–So–Soft. The Skin–So–Soft line constitutes Avon's second largest selling brand, and has yielded hundreds of millions of dollars in retail sales over the past five years. The Skin–So–Soft line includes a bath oil product that is packaged in the form of lotion ("Skin–So–Soft Bath Oil") and spray ("Skin–So–Soft Bath Oil Spray"). Avon, although not encouraging such use, is aware that many consumers have used Skin–So–Soft bath oil products as an insect repellent. In 1993, the United States Environmental Protection Agency ("EPA") requested that Avon take steps to avoid the promotion of its Skin–So–Soft bath oil products as an insect repellent. In response, Avon communicated to its Sales Representatives that Skin–So–Soft products could not be promoted for insect repellent purposes. Avon did not, however, run any newspaper, magazine, or television commercials which communicated this point directly to consumers.

At some time prior to December 1993, Avon made the decision to add to its Skin–So–Soft product family a suncare product that would also be an E.P.A-registered insect repellent. On December 17, 1993, Avon reached an agreement with Primavera Laboratories, Inc. ("Primavera") that, permitted Avon to distribute Treo SPF 15[a] under the name Avon Herbal Fresh Skin–So–Soft Moisturizing Suncare Mosquito, Flea, & Deer Tick Repellent SPF 15 PABA–Free Sunscreen Lotion ("Skin–So–Soft Insect Repellent Lotion").

Avon has invested significant amounts of time and several millions of dollars in launching the Skin–So–Soft Insect Repellent Lotion. Avon's

---

[a] Primavera holds an E.P.A. pesticide registration for TREO SPF 15 insect repellent and sunscreen lotion (EPA registration number 65233–1, registered May 7, 1992).

actions in this regard during recent months include: (1) providing both advance notice of the launch and gifts of Skin–So–Soft Insect Repellent Lotion to Sales Representatives who sell a high volume of Avon products; (2) retaining the advertising agency FCB/Leber Katz ("FCB") in January 1994 to conduct consumer research and plan an advertising campaign for the new product; and (3) announcing, on March 31, 1994, the launch to the editors of eighty five national women's magazines.

Johnson and Off! Skintastic

Johnson is a Wisconsin corporation which markets many consumer products, including the popular RAID line of insecticides and OFF! line of insect repellent. OFF!, which is sold in a variety of forms (e.g., aerosol, lotion, and towelettes) is the leading insect repellent sold through retail outlets in the United States. Johnson began marketing the lotion form of Off!, under the mark Off! Skintastic ("Skintastic"), in 1991, prompted largely as a competitive response to the widespread use among consumers of Skin–So–Soft Bath Oil as an insect repellent. From 1991 until the advertising campaign at issue here, Johnson has compared Skintastic to Skin–So–Soft Bath Oil as insect repellents in both print and television advertising without objection from Avon. The advertising campaign challenged here relates to such comparisons.

The Challenged Advertisements

Avon's motion concerns two advertisements. The first is a two-page print advertisement ("the print ad"), the content of which came to the attention of Avon on May 20, 1994. The print ad includes the headline "Is OFF! Skintastic better than Avon Skin–So–Soft?". The ad includes a footnote which reads "Avon SKIN–SO–SOFT . . . is not EPA-registered for use as an insect repellent." The second challenged advertisement is a television commercial, the original version of which Avon learned of on May 18, 1994. The commercial opens with a road sign that reads "Jacksonville," then depicts a picnic scene. The accompanying verbal text is as follows (" "enclose lines delivered by actors on screen):

> Welcome to bug heaven . . . "We have bigger bugs . . . Prehistoric" . . . Pterodactyl skeeters . . . A funny thing happened when we threw a party for Avon Skin–So–Soft Bath Oil users but gave them OFF! Skintastic instead . . . "I used to use Avon Skin–So–Soft . . . but Off! Skintastic is just a hundred times better" . . . "It's not greasy" . . . That's why 4 out of 5 Avon users prefer the feel of Off! Skintastic . . . "Smells very, very nice . . ." "Love it" . . . "Need it" . . . From S.C. Johnson Wax.

One footnote, appearing simultaneous to the dialogue "4 out of 5 Avon users . . ." states "Based on skin feel preference of consumers surveyed." Another footnote follows, which reads "Avon Skin–So–Soft Bath Oil is not E.P.A. registered as an insect repellent."

Avon's Allegations

Avon alleges that the Johnson print ad falsely represents that no product in Avon's Skin–So–Soft line is E.P.A. registered as an insect repellent. In addition, Avon alleges that the television commercial contains the following false messages:

(1) "4 out of 5 users prefer the feel of Off! Skintastic" to Skin–So–Soft Bath Oil (the "4 out of 5" claim); and

(2) Skintastic is "100 times better" than Skin–So–Soft Bath Oil (the "100 times better" claim).

Finally, Avon alleges that because the commercial is ambiguous as to which Skin–So–Soft product (Bath Oil vs. Insect Repellent Lotion) Skintastic is compared, consumers will be misled to believe that the "4 out of 5 claim" and the "100 times better" claim apply to both Skin–So–Soft products, thus tainting the brand image/integrity of the bath oil and undermining the launch of Avon's new insect repellent. For the reasons set forth below, we preliminarily enjoin the distribution of the print ad, but decline to issue a preliminary injunction with respect to the television commercial.

DISCUSSION

Standard for Preliminary Injunction Under § 43(a)

A plaintiff who brings a claim against a competitor for false advertising under 43(a) of the Lanham Act must demonstrate that "an advertisement is either literally false or that the advertisement, though literally true, is likely to mislead and confuse consumers . . ." Id. (emphasis added). Thus, the threshold analytical differentiation in a Lanham Act § 43(a) false advertising claim lies between allegations of literal falsity and likelihood that consumers will be misled or confused.

LITERAL FALSITY

The Print Ad

As noted, we issued a temporary restraining order dated May 31, 1994, enjoining the distribution of the print ad pending the hearing, on the ground that Avon had demonstrated a likelihood of success on the merits of its claim that the statement "Avon Skin–So–Soft . . . is not registered with the E.P.A. as an insect repellent," is literally false.[b] After reviewing the submissions of both parties and the evidence offered at the June 7 hearing, we once again conclude that Avon has satisfied this burden, and is thus entitled to preliminary injunctive relief.

The "4 out of 5" Claim

Avon relies on R.J. Reynolds Tobacco Co. v. Loew's Theatres, Inc., 511 F.Supp. 867, 875–76 (1980) to support the proposition that the television commercial is literally false because the "4 out of 5 . . . based on preference

[b] Injunctive relief is appropriate under the Lanham Act § 43(a) where plaintiff establishes a likelihood of success on the merits of a literal falsity claim, because a court may "may presume irreparable harm where plaintiff demonstrates a likelihood of success in showing literally false defendant's comparative advertisement which mentions plaintiff's product by name." Castrol, 977 F.2d at 61. Here, it is undeniable that the print ad mentions the Avon Skin–So–Soft product line in the disputed footnote.

for skin feel" claim is supported by only one measurement of skin feel ("oiliness/greasiness"). Such reliance is misplaced. In Reynolds, the court enjoined a cigarette manufacturer that claimed general superiority in taste, based on consumers' response to one question measuring taste, but failed to disclose or account for other questions directed at taste. The court noted, however, that defendant in that action "failed to establish a basis upon which the answers to Questions 3 and 4 relating to those two brands could be disregarded or considered less controlling than the answers to Question 2." Id, at 876.

Here, by contrast Johnson avers that in the insect repellent industry, "oiliness/greasiness" has for forty years been regarded as the primary and defining component of skin feel, and that the other factors appearing in the study (e.g., residue or lack of stickiness) are of "substantially less importance." Avon has submitted no evidence of the saliency of other factors in consumers' evaluation of "skin feel." Accordingly, in the absence of evidence in the record to controvert Johnson's position, we find that the failure to address all of the literal components of "skin feel" in the commercial does not establish a likelihood of Avon's ultimate success in demonstrating that Johnson's claim is literally false.

no evidence

"100 Times Better"

Avon suggests that the "100 times better" claim in the commercial is not mere "puffery," which is not actionable under Lanham Act § 43(a). See, e.g., Nikkal Industries, Ltd. v. Salton, Inc., 735 F.Supp. 1227, 1235 n.3 (S.D.N.Y.1990)(statements that defendant's ice cream maker was "better" than that of plaintiff "constitute mere puffing [and] are not actionable as false advertising"); American Express, 776 F.Supp. at 791 ("'A claim in general terms of superiority of one's product over that of a competitor is mere "puffing" and is not actionable.'")(internal citations omitted). Rather, according to Avon, "a representation of superiority crosses the line between puffing and an actionable claim when it becomes quantified numerically." Plaintiff's Reply Mem. at n.6. We find Avon's application of this proposition to the facts in this action to be flawed. The Court acknowledges that Cook, Perkiss & Liehe v. N. Cal. Collection Serv., 911 F.2d 242, 246 (9th Cir.1990) does stand for the proposition cited by Avon, "(common theme in cases involving assertions of puffery is that customer reliance is induced by specific assertions such as superiority claims quantified numerically)," as does W.L. Gore & Associates, Inc. v. Totes Inc., 788 F.Supp. 800, 809 (D.Del.1992) ("numerical comparison [seven times more breathable] gives the impression that the claim is based upon independent testing" and "is not a claim of general superiority or mere puffing.")

mere "puffery" not actionable

It does not follow, however, from the foregoing decisions, as Avon appears to urge in its papers, that a bright-line rule should apply to the effect that whenever a number appears in a claim, its presence should be deemed to preclude a defense of puffery or a finding that the challenged language merely constitutes an advertiser's general claim of product superiority. At most, Cook, Perkiss and Totes admonish courts to examine closely "puffery" defenses that involve challenged claims which refer to numbers. In particular, Totes—in which the multiplier of breathability was 7— suggests that such caution in granting a puffery defense is particularly significant where the numeral chosen is both low and not the type of "round" number one advertiser might select at random for the purpose of exaggerating its product's general superiority (e.g. , 100 or 1000). Thus, our conclusion might differ if the consumer in the Johnson commercial had stated "Skintastic is three times better than Skin–So–Soft." She does not. While there clearly exists a slippery slope on the continuum between numerical claims that imply independent corroboration and numerical claims involving mere puffery, we conclude that the "100 times" claim falls into the latter category.

Avon's counsel argued a somewhat different position at the hearing, suggesting that an inquiry into the defense of "puffing" should focus not on the number in front of the claimed "puffery," but rather on whether there is an underlying claim of superior performance. This reasoning ignores the fact that nearly every "puffery" defense involves a claim of superior performance,—the critical point is whether the claim is exaggerated to such an extent that it simply cannot be deemed to suggest to consumers the existence of quantitative or other substantial support. Here, the "100 times better" claim reaches such a level of exaggeration.[c]

The Commercial As a Whole

In the alternative, Avon urges us to subject the commercial to a facial falsity analysis because a challenged representation may be subjected to such evaluation even if the advertisement does not explicitly state the representation, but, instead, necessarily implies the challenged claim. Avon suggests that "the necessary implication of Johnson's revised commercial, viewed as a whole, is that Skintastic is a better insect repellent than Avon's product." Plaintiff's Reply Mem. 9. We disagree. Johnson does not shy from connecting its data (i.e, the Skintastic Lotion/greasiness test result) to the actual function and performance of Skintastic. Rather, Johnson readily acknowledges that the test result is meant to communicate to the consumer the notion that Skintastic performs well—better than Avon Skin–So–Soft Bath Oil—on one of the measures of performance for an insect repellent (i.e., skin feel). There exist, however, other components of overall performance or general superiority as to which Johnson makes no claims relative to Skin–So–Soft Bath Oil (e.g., fragrance and safety) or engages in mere

[c] We note that even were we to assume arguendo that the "100 times" better claim represents "an endorsement claiming substantial superiority," Plaintiff Reply Mem. at 11, it would strain credulity for us to infer that the "100 times" figure implies the existence of a particular scientific test supporting the challenged claim. Avon's alternative grounds for inferring such a test, the reference to a picnic at which Johnson had picnic goers use Skintastic rather than Skin–So– Soft Bath Oil, requires an equally tortured (and naive) interpretation of the commercial. Given the foregoing, the Second Circuit's decision in Castrol makes clear that, where a competitor merely asserts product superiority over a named product, without any explicit or implicit reference to scientific tests, plaintiff bears the burden to "adduce evidence" that "affirmatively proves defendant's product equal or inferior." 977 F.2d at 62. Avon concedes that it has submitted no such evidence.

puffery (e.g., efficacy at repelling insects). As a matter of law, then, we cannot conclude that the commercial necessarily implies that Skintastic is a more efficacious, or, more generally, a superior overall insect repellent than Skin–So–Soft Bath Oil, such that the commercial is subject to a literal falsity analysis as to the implied claims.

LIKELIHOOD OF MISLEADING CONSUMERS

Avon also alleges that the commercial is misleading because it "remains vague as to which Skin–So–Soft product is being compared," Plaintiff's Reply Mem. at 13, and this "ambiguity is highly likely to cause consumers viewing this commercial to assume that Skintastic is being compared with Avon's Skin–So–Soft Insect Repellent Lotion." Id. Avon emphasizes that the commercial mentions Skin–So–Soft Bath Oil by name only once, and never depicts the product on screen. Id. We analyze this claim below.

In a false advertising case in which the plaintiff alleges that an advertisement is misleading rather than, or as well as, literally false, the Second Circuit requires the plaintiff to introduce evidence as to what the public found to be the implicit message of the commercial. This requirement derives from the concern that, in analyzing an advertisement's potential to mislead,

> the court's reaction is at best not determinative and at worst irrelevant. The question in such cases is—what does the person to whom the advertisement is addressed find to be the message?

American Home Products Corp. v. Johnson & Johnson, 577 F.2d 160, 166, quoting American Brands, Inc. v. R.J. Reynolds Tobacco Co., 413 F.Supp. 1352, 1357 (S.D.N.Y.1976); see also Coca–Cola Company v. Tropicana Products, Inc., 690 F.2d 312, 317 (2d Cir.1982)(where a plaintiff contends that a "challenged advertisement is implicitly rather than explicitly false, its tendency to violate the Lanham Act by misleading, confusing or deceiving should be tested by public reaction")(citations omitted). In fact, "if plaintiff fails to introduce a consumer reaction survey, plaintiff cannot prevail on the theory of implicit falsity." American Exp. Travel Related Serv. v. Mastercard, 776 F.Supp. 787, 792 (S.D.N.Y.1991), citing Avis Rent A Car System, Inc. v. Hertz Corp., 782 F.2d 381, 386 (2d Cir.1986). Accordingly, we hold Avon to its burden of proof, and must therefore find that plaintiff has not demonstrated a likelihood of success on the merits of its claim that the commercial is likely to mislead or confuse consumers.

CONCLUSION

Thus, we grant that part of Avon's motion for a preliminary injunction that seeks to enjoin distribution of Johnson's print advertisement, and deny that part of Avon's motion for a preliminary injunction that is directed toward Johnson's television commercial.

SO ORDERED.

NOTES

1. *The likelihood of confusion test.* The test for likelihood of confusion differs somewhat in its articulation in the various circuits, but essentially all of the tests focus on the same type of factors. The *Polaroid* test used in *Lois Sportswear* is representative. Note that the tests used in *Lois Sportswear* and *Ferrari* are essentially similar, except that the *Lois Sportswear* formulation considers the quality of the respective goods whereas *Ferrari* calls for a consideration of the respective marketing channels. Courts often consider additional factors aside from those mentioned in the precedents.[4] In addition to those factors mentioned in the cases, what other factors would you deem relevant to a consideration of likelihood of confusion?

In terms of the test's operation, no single factor is determinative and courts typically perform a balancing test in weighing the various factors.[5] Should the balancing process differ depending upon whether the action is one for trademark infringement or trade dress infringement under § 43(a)? Keep in mind that registered trademarks are entitled to a prima facie presumption of validity.[6] Can you think of any circumstances in which the likelihood of confusion test should be reduced to a "possibility of confusion" standard?

There is disagreement among the circuits as to the standard of appellate review regarding likelihood of confusion. Although the majority of circuits treat this issue purely as a question of fact, subject to a clearly erroneous standard, a few circuits treat it as a mixed question of law and fact. These courts hold that although likelihood of confusion is a question of law subject to de novo review, the specific findings supporting this conclusion are questions of fact subject to the clearly erroneous standard.[7]

a. *Strength of the mark.* Courts often determine strength with reference to the generic-descriptive-suggestive-arbitrary spectrum utilized at the registration stage, see Part A of Assignment 2. The cases almost universally say that the stronger the mark, the more protection it should receive. Is the reason for this view that consumers are more likely to be confused when a strong mark is infringed, or is there some other theory at work here? Couldn't an argument be made that confusion is more likely to be mitigated with a strong mark?

In assessing the strength of a plaintiff's mark, a court must evaluate the impact of certain factual scenarios. For example, what should be the relevance of third parties owning registrations for similar marks that are used on similar goods? Other such scenarios include the plaintiff's owner-

---

[4] See, e.g., Payless Shoesource, Inc. v. Reebok International Ltd., 998 F.2d 985, 988 (Fed.Cir.1993); Centaur Communications v. A/S/M Communications, 830 F.2d 1217, 1228 n.2 (2d Cir.1987).

[5] Id.

[6] See §§ 1057(b) & 1115(a).

[7] The Ninth Circuit, in contrast, treats the issue as a mixed question of law and fact, but accords the clearly erroneous standard of review to the entire issue. A student work exploring this topic generally is Kaeding, Clearly Erroneous Review of Mixed Questions of Law and Fact: The Likelihood of Confusion Determination in Trademark Law, 59 U. Chi. L. Rev. 1291 (1992).

ship of a family of marks, see Part B of this Assignment, and the incontestable status of the plaintiff's mark[8] (see Part B of Assignment 2).

b. *Similarity of marks.* In evaluating this factor, should only the marks themselves be considered, or should courts also consider the logo surrounding the marks? Should the answer to this question depend on whether a registered trademark is at issue as opposed to subject matter under § 43(a)?

c. *Similarity of goods/bridging the gap.* These two factors are somewhat related in that the more proximate the products, "the shorter the gap is to bridge."[9] Likelihood of confusion can be decreased where the two marks in question are used before separate groups of consumers or where the distinct nature of the products clearly suggests that the two users are unrelated. Factors determinative of the competitive proximity of the products "include appearance, style, function, fashion appeal, advertising orientation and price."[10] *Lois Sportswear*, by emphasizing the difference between designer and regular jeans, endorsed a rather narrow view regarding the similarity of the goods factor. Part B will demonstrate the broader view taken in cases involving noncompeting goods.

d. *Consumer sophistication.* The concept of consumer sophistication encompasses a variety of factors including the price of the product, the potential for impulse purchasing, and the nature of the product itself. In general, courts take the view that the more sophisticated the consumer, the less the likelihood of confusion.[11] In contrast, in *Lois Sportswear*, the court found that in the post-sale context, sophisticated consumers are "more likely to be affected by the sight of appellee's stitching pattern on appellants' jeans and, consequently, to transfer goodwill." Do you agree with the analysis of *Lois Sportswear* on this point? How should this factor be evaluated in the context of the Principal Problem?

e. *Actual confusion.* Although proof of actual confusion need not be demonstrated, such proof can be extremely probative of likelihood of confusion. Sometimes actual confusion is demonstrated by direct evidence such as testimonial or anecdotal evidence, but frequently proof of actual confusion stems from market research surveys. The following summarizes the governing principles regarding the admissibility of survey evidence:

> "The trustworthiness of surveys depends upon foundation evidence that (1) the 'universe' was properly defined, (2) a representative sample of that universe was selected, (3) the questions to be asked of interviewees were framed in a clear, concise and nonleading manner, (4) sound interview procedures were followed by competent interview-

---

[8] See Times Newspapers Ltd. v. Times Publishing Co., 25 U.S.P.Q.2d (BNA) 1835, 1840 (M.D.Fla.1993)(suggesting that although incontestable status is a factor in the likelihood of confusion analysis, it is not necessarily determinative of infringement).

[9] Jordache Enterprises Inc. v. Levi Strauss & Co., 841 F.Supp. 506, 517 (S.D.N.Y.1993).

[10] Id.

[11] Private Eyes Sunglass Corp. v. Private Eye Vision Center, 25 U.S.P.Q.2d (BNA) 1709, 1718 (D.Conn.1992).

ers who had no knowledge of the litigation or the purpose for which the survey was conducted, (5) the data gathered was accurately reported, (6) the data was analyzed in accordance with accepted statistical principles and (7) objectivity of the entire process was assured."[12]

The term "universe" represents the portion of the population which possesses the characteristics required for making the critical mental association.[13] Frequently, the validity of the survey's universe is at issue.[14]

The issue of post-sale confusion is at issue in *Lois Sportswear* and discussed extensively in *Ferrari*, where the majority notes that when the Lanham Act was amended in 1967, Congress specifically deleted the statute's reference to confusion among *purchasers*, thus broadening the scope of the statute. This issue is also raised in the Principal Problem.

f. *Good faith.* The role of good faith in the likelihood of confusion analysis is, in and of itself, rather confusing. As *Ferrari* illustrates, some courts have held that intentional copying gives rise to a presumption of secondary meaning, while other courts treat a showing of intentional copying only as evidence of secondary meaning.[15] *Ferrari* also discusses the presumption of likelihood of confusion that some courts apply in cases involving intentional copying.[16] Although some courts refuse to apply such a presumption and instead treat intentional copying as just one of the factors that must be considered in a likelihood of confusion analysis,[17] the Second Circuit has long indulged in this presumption.[18] Is *Lois Sportswear* inconsistent with the application of this presumption? Should intentional copying give rise to either a presumption of secondary meaning or likeli-

---

[12] Schieffelin & Co. v. The Jack Company of Boca, 850 F.Supp. 232, 245 (S.D.N.Y. 1994).

[13] Id.

[14] See, e.g., Sterling Drug, Inc. v. Bayer AG, USA, 14 F.3d 733, 741 (2d Cir.1994)(in case where "the relevant issue is whether consumers mistakenly believe that the senior user's products actually originate with the junior user, it is appropriate to survey the senior user's customers" rather than the junior user's consumer base); Jordache Enterprises, Inc. v. Levi Strauss & Co., 841 F.Supp. 506, 518–19 (S.D.N.Y.1993)(universe defective because it included only those who had worn jeans within the past six months, but failed to include potential purchasers of jeans).

[15] Compare Maryland Stadium Authority v. Becker, 806 F.Supp. 1236, 1241 (D.Md. 1992)(in the Fourth Circuit, evidence of intentional copying gives rise to a "*prima facie* case of secondary meaning sufficient to shift the burden of persuasion to the defendant")

with Brooks Shoe Mfg. Co. v. Suave Shoe Corp., 716 F.2d 854, 860 (11th Cir.1983)(although intentional copying is "probative evidence" of secondary meaning, the defendant may have had motivations other than capitalizing on the plaintiff's goodwill). See also Perfect Fit Industries, Inc. v. Acme Quilting Co., 618 F.2d 950 (2d Cir.1980)(under New York law, intentional copying can substitute for secondary meaning).

[16] See, e.g., Anheuser–Busch, Inc. v. L & L Wings, Inc., 962 F.2d 316, 321 (4th Cir.1992)(appearing to limit presumption to cases involving an intent to confuse); Academy of Motion Picture Arts and Sciences v. Creative House Promotions, Inc., 944 F.2d 1446, 1456 (9th Cir.1991); Chevron Chemical Co. v. Voluntary Purchasing Groups, 659 F.2d 695, 704 (5th Cir.1981); Maryland Stadium Authority v. Becker, 806 F.Supp. 1236, 1241 (D.Md.1992).

[17] Schwinn Bicycle Co. v. Ross Bicycles, Inc., 870 F.2d 1176, 1184–85 (7th Cir.1989).

[18] See Perfect Fit Industries, Inc. v. Acme Quilting Co., 618 F.2d 950, 954 (2d Cir.1980).

hood of confusion? Do the facts of the Principal Problem or *Ferrari* present a stronger case of intentional copying?

Sometimes the good faith analysis can become intertwined with a discussion of asserted defenses. This issue is touched on in *John Deere*, infra, Part B, and discussed in greater detail in Assignment 4. Can you think of any other measures a defendant can take to show its good faith?

g. *Quality of the products/marketing channels.* Unlike *Lois Sportswear*, *Ferrari* does not invoke "quality of the products" as a specific factor in the likelihood of confusion analysis, but it does consider the respective marketing channels used. As *Ferrari* illustrates, instances can arise in which the quality factor may favor the plaintiff because the defendant is producing a cheap imitation, but the marketing channels factor will favor the defendant because cheaper imitations often are sold in different trade channels.

2. *Parameters of § 43(a).* As *Two Pesos* illustrates, a wide variety of conduct now is actionable under § 43(a), even though the original scope of this provision was quite narrow. Some of the more frequent types of actions under and issues surrounding § 43(a) are discussed below.

a. *Trade dress and functionality.* Many actions under § 43(a) involve trade dress infringement. *Ferrari* demonstrates that trade dress protection can extend not only to a product's packaging, but also to the design of the product itself. One of the most difficult issues in these cases is the application of the functionality doctrine. Although *Ferrari* places the burden of proof regarding nonfunctionality on the plaintiff,[19] other courts take the view that proving functionality is the defendant's responsibility.[20] Even more complicated, however, are the various tests for functionality that have been articulated by courts. The test used by the Fifth Circuit, which is discussed in *Two Pesos*, asks whether the design is "one of a limited number of equally efficient options available to competitors." Is this test essentially the same as the one articulated in *Ferrari* which posits that a product feature is functional "if it is essential to the use or purpose of the article or if it affects the cost or quality of the article" (recall that this was the test invoked in *Qualitex*, reprinted in Assignment 2)? Should the test for functionality instead protect against the use of a feature which is superior or optimal with respect to manufacture or accommodation of utilitarian performance? Which test is better and why?

Ferrari also discusses, and rejects, yet another functionality test. According to the Ninth Circuit's aesthetic functionality test, something is functional if it is "an important ingredient in the commercial success of the product" as opposed to something that primarily indicates source identification. Was the *Ferrari* court correct in discrediting the aesthetic function-

---

[19] See also Aromatique, Inc. v. Gold Seal, Inc., 28 F.3d 863, 869 (8th Cir.1994); Truck Equipment Service Co. v. Fruehauf Corp., 536 F.2d 1210 (8th, Cir.1976); Deere & Co. v. Farmhand, Inc., 560 F.Supp. 85 (S.D.Iowa 1982).

[20] See Schwinn Bicycle Co. v. Ross Bicycles, Inc., 870 F.2d 1176, 1188 (7th Cir.1989)(stating that the copier has the burden of proving functionality).

ality test? If this test were applied to the facts of the Principal Problem, in whose favor would it apply?

The case law also illustrates that combinations of functional features nevertheless can constitute protectable trade dress,[21] and that secondary meaning can be established from a combination of both functional and nonfunctional features.[22] In this respect, the law of trademark infringement parallels that of copyright infringement, which sometimes extends copyright protection to combinations of uncopyrightable elements. See Assignment 7. Another parallel between the functionality doctrine of trademark law and copyright law is the latter's general refusal to protect useful articles such as clothing even if they also contain artistic or ornamental components. See Assignment 8.

One way to deal with the problem of marginally functional trade dress is by tailoring relief. For example, the dissent in the *Ferrari* case would have preserved competition in the market for cars shaped like the Daytona and Spyder by limiting relief to a labelling requirement. Do the facts of the Principal Problem present a compelling case for injunctive relief?

b. *Inherent distinctiveness.* In *Two Pesos*, the Supreme Court deferred to the lower court's determination that the decor of the Mexican restaurant was "inherently distinctive." Accordingly, it did not approve specific guidelines for deciding when trade dress is inherently distinctive. In making this determination, many courts apply the test used by the district court, which was developed for trade names in Abercrombie & Fitch Co. v. Hunting World, Inc., see Note 4 of Part A of Assignment 2, and utilized in G. Heileman Brewing Company, Inc. v. Anheuser–Busch, Inc., also in Assignment 2. Thus, these courts classify trade dress as: 1) generic; 2) descriptive; 3) suggestive; or 4) arbitrary or fanciful. Arbitrary and suggestive trade dress are considered "inherently distinctive," whereas descriptive trade dress requires secondary meaning to be protected. For an example, see Chevron Chemical Co. v. Voluntary Purchasing Groups, Inc., 659 F.2d 695 (5th Cir.1981), cert. denied, 457 U.S. 1126, 102 S.Ct. 2947, 73 L.Ed.2d 1342 (1982).

c. *False designation of origin.* As the concurrence in *Two Pesos* notes, originally false designation of origin was understood to encompass only false designations of geographic origins. Over time, however, the interpretation of origin has expanded to include "origin of source or manufacture." Currently, the facts of cases in which plaintiffs allege false designations of origin illustrate the varied conduct that can be actionable under this phrase. Several recent cases have involved the application of § 43(a) to commercial advertisements invoking an individual's persona without au-

---

[21] See Aromatique, Inc. v. Gold Seal, Inc., 28 F.3d 863, 883–84 (8th Cir.1994)(Gibson, dissenting); Hartford House, Ltd. v. Hallmark Cards, Inc., 846 F.2d 1268, 1272 (10th Cir.), cert. denied, 488 U.S. 908, 109 S.Ct. 260, 102 L.Ed.2d 248 (1988).

[22] See, e.g., American Greetings Corp. v. Dan–Dee Imports, Inc., 807 F.2d 1136, 1143 (3d Cir.1986).

thorization. These cases typically involve implicit false endorsements.[23] Other cases involve the use of § 43(a) as a surrogate for prohibiting conduct that would be actionable in other countries under the moral rights of integrity and paternity.[24] One case even held that copying the design of a square clear glass nail polish bottle "with a simple cylindrical white cap" is a false designation of origin under § 43(a) where the bottle design's simplicity reveals its origin even absent explicit attribution.[25]

Currently before Congress is an amendment to § 43(a) that will require labelling of a materially altered film if the artistic author, as defined in the statute, objects to the alterations. This bill, the Film Disclosure Act, was initially introduced before the House in 1993, and has been assigned to the Judiciary Committee.

d. *False description or representation.* The concurrence in *Two Pesos* also notes the original narrow construction of the phrase "false description or representation," encompassing only the common law tort of passing off and false advertising. Passing off, the representation of the defendant's goods as those of the plaintiff, historically was essential for proving common law unfair competition,[26] and the early interpretations of § 43(a)

---

[23] See, e.g., Waits v. Frito–Lay, Inc., 978 F.2d 1093 (9th Cir.1992), cert. denied, 506 U.S. 1080, 113 S.Ct. 1047, 122 L.Ed.2d 355 (1993)(singer prevailed in a § 43(a) action against an advertising agency for using a sound-alike imitating his distinctive voice in a commercial for chips); White v. Samsung Electronics America, Inc., 971 F.2d 1395 (9th Cir.1992), cert. denied, ___ U.S. ___, 113 S.Ct. 2443, 124 L.Ed.2d 660 (1993)(holding actress Vanna White raised a genuine issue of material fact regarding likelihood of confusion stemming from defendant's advertisement for VCRs featuring a robot dressed in a wig, gown and jewelry suggestive of White and posed next to the Wheel of Fortune game board); Allen v. National Video, Inc., 610 F.Supp. 612 (S.D.N.Y.1985)(actor Woody Allen obtained summary judgment on § 43(a) claim in case where defendant hired a look-alike to pose in an advertisement for its national video rental chain). But see Advanced Resources Int'l, Inc. v. Tri–Star Petroleum Co., 4 F.3d 327, 335 (4th Cir.1993)(refusing to extend the rationale of "courts that have found protectable interests in voices, likenesses and images, and to interpret § 43(a) to prohibit the use of a commissioned, signed, unaltered report when that use implies an unauthorized and false endorsement").

[24] See, e.g., King v. Innovation Books, 976 F.2d 824 (2d Cir.1992)(court affirmed preliminary injunction of use of possessory credit in § 43(a) action where the plaintiff writer was neither involved in nor approved of a movie that was loosely based on his short story); Smith v. Montoro, 648 F.2d 602 (9th Cir.1981)(sustaining plaintiff actor's § 43(a) claim where defendant film distributor removed plaintiff's name from the film credits and advertising materials and substituted the name of another actor); Gilliam v. American Broadcasting Companies, Inc., 538 F.2d 14 (2d Cir.1976)(plaintiff group of writers and performers stated a § 43(a) claim based on the defendant network's broadcasting of a program truthfully designated as having been written and performed by the plaintiffs but which had been edited, without plaintiffs' consent, into a mutilated and distorted form that substantially departed from the original work). See also Cleary v. News Corp., 30 F.3d 1255, 1260–61 (9th Cir.1994)(raising, but not deciding, whether "the Lanham Act protects an author against an inaccurate designation of authorship despite the fact that the author expressly contracted away the right to attribution").

[25] Essie Cosmetics Ltd. v. Dae Do Int'l, Ltd., 808 F.Supp. 952, 954 (E.D.N.Y.1992).

[26] See American Washboard Co. v. Saginaw Mfg. Co., 103 F. 281 (6th Cir.1900).

simply continued this theme. In L'Aiglon Apparel v. Lana Lobell, Inc.,[27] the Third Circuit allowed a plaintiff to recover under § 43(a) where the defendant used a picture of the plaintiff's dress to market its dress of alleged poorer quality. Today, § 43(a) covers both not only passing off, but also reverse passing off, which occurs when the plaintiff's goods are represented as the defendant's.[28]

False advertising, the defendant's representation that his goods or services have characteristics or qualities they do not have, always has been actionable under § 43(a). In 1988, Congress amended § 43(a) to expressly include trade disparagement, the defendant's misrepresentation of the quality of the plaintiff's goods. As *Avon Products* indicates, to recover for false advertising, a plaintiff must demonstrate either that the defendant's advertising is literally false, or that, while literally true, it is nevertheless likely to mislead and confuse consumers. With respect to advertising that is literally false, the plaintiff's burden varies according to whether the defendant's advertising includes tests that purport to prove the superiority of the defendant's product: "Where the defendant's advertisement claims that its product is superior plaintiff must affirmatively prove defendant's product equal or inferior. Where ... the defendant's ad explicitly or implicitly represents that tests or studies prove its product superior, plaintiff satisfies its burden by showing that the tests did not establish the proposition for which they were cited."[29] If a plaintiff satisfies this burden, a court will enjoin the advertisement without evaluating the advertisement's impact on the public.[30]

Avon Products also shows that where the plaintiff is attempting to prove that the advertisement is implicitly false, the plaintiff must introduce extrinsic evidence, usually in the form of consumer surveys, showing that the advertisement tends to mislead or confuse consumers.[31] For advertisements that are alleged to be literally false but which do not rely upon tests, how can a plaintiff prove the literal falsity? Is this issue raised in the Principal Problem? In reality, how easy is it to make distinctions between advertisements that are literally false and those that are implicitly false?

e. *Consumer standing.* The issue of whether consumers and non-competitors have standing to sue in false endorsement and false advertising cases currently is quite problematic. Many courts take the position that

[27] 214 F.2d 649 (3d Cir.1954).

[28] See, e.g., Smith v. Montoro, 648 F.2d 602 (9th Cir.1981)(see footnote 24). In Cleary v. News Corp., 30 F.3d 1255, 1261–62 (9th Cir.1994), the court noted that the test for reverse passing off differs among the circuits. The Ninth Circuit uses a demanding standard which requires a reverse passing off plaintiff to show that the material in question was "bodily appropriated," whereas in the Second Circuit, the less rigorous "consumer confusion" standard is invoked.

[29] Castrol, Inc. v. Quaker State Corp., 977 F.2d 57, 62–63 (2d Cir.1992).

[30] Id. at 62.

[31] See Tyco Industries, Inc. v. Lego Systems, Inc., 5 U.S.P.Q.2d (BNA) 1023, 1035–36 (D.N.J.1987)(court found misleading toy company's claim that its pre-school and standard-size blocks "connect" to each other accompanied by illustration of blocks directly connecting because the need to use an adapter block was not disclosed).

§ 43(a) only applies to commercial parties, and thus exclude consumers.[32] At least one court allowed consumers standing.[33] Recently, the Ninth Circuit reconciled conflicting authority there by holding that competition in the traditional sense is not required for a plaintiff to bring a false endorsement action under § 43(a), although a discernible competitive interest is required in false advertising actions.[34] The 1988 amendments to the Lanham Act left this difficult issue unresolved. Should consumers be allowed to bring a § 43(a) action for either false endorsement or false advertising?

3. *Reverse confusion.* The typical type of confusion that can support a claim of trademark infringement or unfair competition under § 43(a) occurs when consumers have the misimpression that the senior user is the source of the junior's product. Another form of confusion, called reverse confusion, exists when consumers have the misimpression that the junior user is the source of the senior user's product.

Reverse confusion cases typically involve a smaller senior user and a larger junior user. For example, in Banff, Ltd. v. Federated Department Stores, Inc.,[35] the owner of the unregistered trademark "Bee Wear" for clothing brought suit against the renowned department store Bloomingdale's for the use of "B Wear" in various typestyles for a line of women's clothing. In recognizing a cause of action for reverse confusion, the Second Circuit stated: "The objectives of [the Lanham Act]—to protect an owner's interest in its trademark by keeping the public free from confusion as to the source of goods and ensuring fair competition—are as important in a case of reverse confusion as in typical trademark infringement. Were reverse confusion not a sufficient basis to obtain Lanham Act protection, a larger company could with impunity infringe the senior mark of a smaller one."[36]

Absent the doctrine of reverse confusion, a junior user would be able to overwhelm the senior user by saturating the market with a similar trademark, so that the public would eventually believe that the senior user's products are really the junior user's, or that the senior user has become connected to or associated with, the junior user. The result of this unchecked saturation could be the senior user's loss of the value of its trademark, its product and corporate identity, the control over its goodwill,

---

[32] See, e.g., Serbin v. Ziebart International Corp., 11 F.3d 1163 (3d Cir.1993); Colligan v. Activities Club of New York, Ltd., 442 F.2d 686, 692 (2d Cir.), cert. denied, 404 U.S. 1004, 92 S.Ct. 559, 30 L.Ed.2d 557 (1971); Ortho Pharmaceutical Corp. v. Cosprophar Inc., 828 F.Supp. 1114, 1124 (S.D.N.Y.1993)(commercial plaintiff need not be in competition with defendant, but must have a "reasonable interest to be protected" against the false advertising).

[33] Arnesen v. The Raymond Lee Organization, Inc., 333 F.Supp. 116 (C.D.Cal.1971).

[34] Waits v. Frito–Lay Inc., 978 F.2d 1093, 1107–10 (9th Cir.1992), cert. denied, 506 U.S. 1080, 113 S.Ct. 1047, 122 L.Ed.2d 355 (1993). See also American Ventures Inc. v. Post Buckley, Schuh & Jernigan Inc., 27 U.S.P.Q.2d (BNA) 1587, 1590–91 (W.D.Wash. 1993).

[35] 841 F.2d 486 (2d Cir.1988).

[36] Id. at 490–491.

and reputation, and the ability to move into new markets.[37] Should the test for infringement be applied differently in reverse confusion cases?

4. *Contributory infringement.* The Supreme Court had occasion to deal with the subject of contributory trademark infringement in Inwood Laboratories, Inc. v. Ives Laboratories, Inc.[38] In that case, the manufacturer of a drug marketed under a registered trademark sued the manufacturers of a generic version of that drug on the theory that the defendants should be vicariously liable for trademark infringement by the pharmacists who dispensed the generic drug. The district court in that case had ruled in favor of the generic drug manufacturers because it found that they had not suggested, or even implied, that pharmacists should dispense the generic drugs incorrectly identified with the plaintiff's trademark.[39] The Second Circuit reversed,[40] and the Supreme Court reversed the Second Circuit on the ground that it had set aside factual findings by the district court that were not clearly erroneous. In the course of its opinion, the Court articulated the following standard for contributory trademark infringement: "[I]f a manufacturer or distributor intentionally induces another to infringe a trademark, or if it continues to supply its product to one whom it knows or has reason to know is engaging in trademark infringement, the manufacturer or distributor is contributorially responsible for any harm done as a result of the deceit."[41] This standard is a more narrow one than that which is applied for copyright infringement. See Sony Corp. of America v. Universal City Studios, Inc., reprinted in Assignment 12.

PART B: NONCOMPETING GOODS

This section deals with the use of the same or similar marks on goods that are not necessarily in competition with one another. In one sense, the issues in this Part mirror those in Part A, for noncompeting usages can give rise to consumer confusion. Consumers, after all, cannot assume that every trademark holder makes, sells, or furnishes only one kind of good or only one kind of service. But as Deere & Co. v. MTD Products and Chicago Board of Trade v. Dow Jones, reprinted infra illustrate, trademark holders sometimes feel their interests are harmed whether or not consumers are confused. In dilution cases, the claim is that the distinctive quality of the mark is eroded when it is used broadly; in tarnishment, the fear is that its value will decrease if it is utilized in unwholesome or unsavory contexts. Finally, misappropriation allows the the trademark holder to capture the value that consumers attach to the mark, as distinct from the goods on which the mark is used.

---

[37] See Fisons Horticulture, Inc. v. Vigoro Industries, Inc., 30 F.3d 466, 474–475 (3d Cir.1994)(quoting Ameritech, Inc. v. American Information Technologies, Corp., 811 F.2d 960, 964 (6th Cir.1987)).

[38] 456 U.S. 844, 102 S.Ct. 2182, 72 L.Ed.2d 606 (1982).

[39] See Ives Laboratories, Inc. v. Darby Drug Co., 488 F.Supp. 394 (1980).

[40] See Ives Laboratories, Inc. v. Darby Drug Co., 638 F.2d 538 (2d Cir.1981).

[41] 456 U.S. at 854.

1. PRINCIPAL PROBLEM B

Our client, Lester Stern is a resident of New York and the inventor of a water soluble multi-purpose plant food which he sells under the federally-registered trademark "Miracle–Gro." Invented in 1951, this product was an immediate marketing success. Since it is completely water-soluble, gardeners can produce a gallon of liquid plant food by simply dissolving a tablespoon of bright turquoise Miracle–Gro crystals in a gallon of water. Plants regularly watered with this solution receive all the nutrients they need to grow. Indeed, according to Stern, the product starts to work within minutes of application and leads almost immediately to spectacular results—bigger flowers, more color, more fruits and vegetables.

Miracle–Gro has always been heavily promoted. Stern distributes advertising, promotional and informational materials, and advertises regularly in print and on national television. In total, he has spent over $100,000,-000 making his product known across the nation. In 1992 alone, he spent $14,000,000. As a result, Miracle–Gro is probably the best known plant food in the United States. It is sold in more than 40,000 retail stores and is used regularly by a large percentage of home gardeners.

Stern has come to see us because he recently saw an ad for a hair treatment product that is also called Miracle Gro. This product is sold in the form of turquoise crystals which, when dissolved in water, create a kind of conditioner. According to the ad, daily use of this conditioner nourishes the scalp and leads almost immediately to a spectacular head of hair, with fabulous sheen and texture—even on heads where hair has ceased to grow.

Stern already called Shark Products, the manufacturer of the "other" Miracle–Gro, and asked it to stop using this mark on its hair treatment product. The company refused, and he has now come to find out what we can do to stop it. Somewhat hirsutely-challenged himself, Stern has tried every hair treatment product on the market and believes that none of them deliver as promised. He hasn't tried Shark Products' treatment yet, but he doubts it is any better than the others. In addition, he feels that it is his product that led consumers to value turquoise crystals. If there is a market in this form that is ripe for commercialization, he wants it for himself. Can we help him?

2. MATERIALS FOR SOLUTION OF PRINCIPAL PROBLEM B

A. STATUTORY MATERIALS: §§ 1114, 1121, & 1125

B. CASES:

McDonald's Corporation v. Druck and Gerner, DDS., P.C.

United States District Court, N.D. New York, 1993.
814 F.Supp. 1127.

■ SCULLIN, DISTRICT JUDGE.

BACKGROUND

Plaintiff McDonald's Corporation ("Plaintiff" or "McDonald's") is a

Delaware corporation whose principal place of business is in Oak Brook, Illinois. McDonald's and its franchisees operate over 8,000 restaurants in the United States, over 400 of which are located in New York State. McDonald's maintains a regional office in Latham, New York (the "Latham office"), located approximately 150 miles from Plattsburgh, New York.

Defendant Druck and Gerner, D.D.S., P.C., d/b/a McDental ("McDental" or "Defendant") is a New York professional corporation located in Plattsburgh, New York that provides dental services under the name "McDental." Drs. Druck and Gerner named their corporation "McDental," and have operated under this name since the business opened on March 20, 1981 in the Pyramid Mall in Plattsburgh. At the time that they opened, Drs. Druck and Gerner placed an orange illuminated sign with the name "McDental" above the front of the office, and placed a fee schedule sign in the window. Shortly after opening in 1981, Defendant obtained a state service mark for the name "McDental" from the State of New York.

McDonald's alleges that it first learned of McDental in 1987, and that it quickly communicated its concern of Defendant's use of its name by way of protest letters sent to Defendant. The parties communicated via correspondence regarding the use of the name McDental, and engaged in settlement discussions, but were unable to reach an agreement.

Having been unsuccessful in its attempts to persuade Defendant to cease using the name "McDental," McDonald's initiated this lawsuit on August 30, 1990, alleging trademark infringement pursuant to 15 U.S.C.A. §§ 1114, 1121 and 1125, dilution of business pursuant to N.Y.Gen.Bus.Law § 368–d and unfair competition under New York common law. Plaintiff seeks a permanent injunction against all further use of "McDental," all costs associated with this action (including the cost of its consumer survey), and reasonable attorney's fees.

DISCUSSION

I.   TRADEMARK INFRINGEMENT CLAIMS

The first step in resolving [the claims under §§ 1114 and 1125] is determining whether Plaintiff possesses a trademark entitled to protection; if this is established, the court must then determine the "likelihood of confusion" with Plaintiff's marks that will result from Defendant's use of its mark. See McDonald's Corporation v. McBagel's, Inc., 649 F.Supp. 1268, 1272 (S.D.N.Y.1986).

A.   FAMILY OF MARKS

McDonald's has used in commerce, and obtained federal registrations for, a number of marks distinguished by the "Mc" formative and is the exclusive owner of numerous registrations issued by the USPTO. These registrations encompass both food-related (e.g., "McDonuts") and non-food/generic ("generic")(e.g., "McD", an all-purpose cleaner) items. Underlying its trademark infringement claims is Plaintiff's contention that it possessed at the time of McDental's inception, and continues to possess, a family of "Mc" marks such that Defendant's use of "McDental" is likely to cause confusion among consumers. This contention has been addressed by other courts in litigation involving this plaintiff. See, e.g., J & J Snack Foods Corp. v. McDonald's Corporation, 932 F.2d 1460 (Fed.Cir.1991)(in affirming USPTO ruling that denied trademark registration to snacks food company, court held that McDonald's possesses a family of marks wherein the prefix "Mc" is used with generic food names); McDonald's Corp. v. McBagel's Inc., 649 F.Supp. 1268, 1272 (S.D.N.Y.1986)(court held that McDonald's owned a family of marks using "Mc" in combination with a generic food item).

The McBagel's court, which granted McDonald's request to enjoin the defendant's use of the name "McBagel's" for its restaurant, stated that, "[w]hile it does not hold a registered mark in 'Mc', plaintiff may claim protection for this prefix as a common component of a 'family of marks.' " Id. at 1272 (reference omitted). And, the McBagel's court noted that, "[t]he existence vel non of a family of marks is a question of fact based on the distinctiveness of the common formative component and other factors, including the extent of the family's use, advertising, promotion, and its inclusion in a number of registered and unregistered marks owned by a single party." Id. On an appeal from the USPTO, the Federal Circuit Court of Appeals defined a "family of marks" as a group of marks having a recognizable common characteristic, wherein the marks are composed and used in such a way that the public associates not only the individual marks, but the common characteristic of the family, with the trademark owner. Simply using a series of similar marks does not of itself establish the existence of a family. There must be a recognition among the purchasing public that the common characteristic is indicative of a common origin of the goods. J & J Snack Foods at 1462.

Evidence produced at trial and recent caselaw clearly establish that Plaintiff possesses a family of marks comprised of the prefix "Mc" combined with food items. However, in the present case, Plaintiff must show that it has a protectable family of marks using the "Mc" prefix such that the use of "McDental" would be confused with Plaintiff's family of marks. As the McBagel's court explained: Under the Lanham Act, Section 32(1)(a), 15 USC § 1114(1)(a); as well as Section 43(a), 15 USC § 1125(a), defendants are liable for infringement if their use of the name [McDental] is likely "to cause confusion, or to cause mistake or to deceive" typical consumers into believing some sponsorship, association, affiliation, connection or endorsement exists between McDonald's and defendants. McBagel's, 649 F.Supp. at 1273.

Whether the family of marks possessed by Plaintiff is entitled to protection from Defendant's use of "McDental" turns on "whether there exists a 'likelihood that an appreciable number of ordinarily prudent purchasers [will] be misled, or indeed simply confused, as to the source of the goods in question.' " Thompson Medical Co., Inc. v. Pfizer, Inc., 753

F.2d 208, 213 (2d Cir.1985)(citation omitted). The Second Circuit has held that "such an assessment properly turns on the examination of many factors," and that this list is not exhaustive—the court may consider others. Id. at 213–214 (citation omitted). The factors are: [The] strength of the mark, the degree of similarity between the marks, the proximity of the products, the likelihood that the prior owner will bridge the gap, actual confusion, and the reciprocal of defendant's good faith in adopting its own mark, the quality of defendant's product, and the sophistication of the buyers. Id. at 213 (citing Polaroid Corp. v. Polarad Elects. Corp., 287 F.2d 492, 495 (2d Cir.), cert. denied, 368 U.S. 820, 82 S.Ct. 36, 7 L.Ed.2d 25 (1961)).

Applying the Polaroid factors, the court finds that, as in Quality Inns [International, Inc. v. McDonald's Corp.], 695 F.Supp. 198 (D.Md.1988)(enjoining use of the mark "McSleep Inn" for a chain of economy hotels), the following factors are of particular importance in assessing the likelihood of confusion in this case: the strength of the mark; the evidence of confusion; the similarity between the marks (including signage and advertising); the proximity of the markets for the products and services identified for the marks, and the likelihood that Plaintiff will bridge the gap; and the intent of Defendant in choosing its mark and its good faith in doing so. See Quality Inns, 695 F.Supp. at 217. The court will discuss each of these seriatim.

a.   Strength of the mark

Although the strength of Plaintiff's family of marks has already been discussed at some length, it should be noted that Plaintiff offered at trial numerous exhibits and testimony attesting to the widespread familiarity of the public with Plaintiff's use of the "Mc" language. Based on all of the evidence this court concludes, as others have, that Plaintiff's family of marks is a strong one. See, e.g., id. at 211–212; McBagel's, 649 F.Supp. at 1274–1275.

b.   Evidence of confusion

Plaintiff also presented survey evidence through its witness, Philip Johnson. Johnson conducted two surveys, in 1988 and 1991, both of which evidenced a likelihood of confusion resulting from Defendant's name. Among the conclusions drawn from the surveys was a finding that some 30% of the population surveyed associated Defendant's name with Plaintiff, the same percentage that another court found to be "substantial." Quality Inns at 218.

In addition to the survey evidence, Plaintiff introduced into evidence deposition testimony including that of former employees of Defendant. See Deps. of Kari Hathaway; William Miller; Holly Lamar. This testimony supports a finding that Defendant's name caused confusion among the public as to whether Defendant was somehow associated with Plaintiff. The court finds simply incredible Dr. Druck's testimony that he never heard anyone, even in a joking manner, associate McDental with McDonald's prior to the commencement of this lawsuit, nor did he himself ever associate the name with that of the Plaintiff.

c. Similarity between the two marks

The Quality Inns court stated that, "it is not the logo or the word 'sleep' that causes the [infringement] problem; it is the use of the fancifully coined word 'McSleep'." Id. at 220. Likewise, the similarity between Defendant's name and Plaintiff's various "Mc" marks is obvious, and Defendant cannot hope to distinguish the two on the basis that it is the "Dental" and not the "Mc" that makes the name "instantly recognized." See id.

d. Proximity of the products and the likelihood that Plaintiff will bridge the gap

This factor involves the likelihood "that customers mistakenly will assume either that [the defendant's goods] are somehow associated with [the plaintiff's] or are made by [the plaintiff]." Centaur Communications, Ltd. v. A/S/M Communications, Inc., 830 F.2d 1217, 1226 (2d Cir.1987)(citation omitted). Initially, it would appear that dental services and fast food have nothing in common, except for the obvious connection between eating and dentistry, and that this factor should thus be weighed in Defendant's favor.

There was no showing at trial that the Plaintiff planned to enter the dental business per se. However, Dr. Cromie, who works with the Ronald McDonald charity houses, testified that since 1985, Plaintiff has included toothbrushes and other similar products in certain of its "Happy Meals" (a product for children). Dr. Cromie also testified that Plaintiff has sponsored dental cleaning via a mobile van that has travelled to different parts of the country, including parts of northern New York. Finally, Dr. Cromie added that the University of Mississippi, through a grant from Plaintiff, has been devising a dental machine for children. Although Dr. Cromie testified that Plaintiff provided the money for this machine, he could not say for certain whether the Plaintiff's name is on the machine.

The Quality Inns court found a connection between fast food and lodging, as one is logically associated with the other. See Quality Inns, 695 F.Supp. at 220–221. However, notwithstanding the fact that oral hygiene normally follows the ingestion of fast (or any other) food, this court is disinclined to find that Plaintiff, even if it begins providing dental floss with its french fries, is likely to "bridge the gap" in any appreciable manner in this case. The evidence presented by Plaintiff did not convince the court that the proximity of the products in this case, or the likelihood that Plaintiff will "bridge the gap," i.e., enter the field of dental service, weighs in Plaintiff's favor.

e. Intent of Drs. Druck and Gerner and good faith in choosing the name "McDental"

When asked at trial why the name "McDental" was chosen for the business, Dr. Druck testified that the name was chosen because it had a "cute" sound to it, and a "quality of retentiveness." Dr. Druck disavowed any attempt to capitalize on the Plaintiff's well-recognized name and its association with family service and quality. He claimed, in essence, that the name was chosen because a friend of his and Dr. Gerner's, Mr. Josh Patrick, thought it was a name that they could remember—more so than other type names—that he never perceived any association with the two names, nor did he perceive anyone else having any association between the two, even in a social or humorous context.

The court need not deliberate long on the question of intent here. In short, the court finds that the explanations and statements of Drs. Druck and Gerner regarding the choice of the name "McDental" defy common sense and credibility; that they were fully cognizant of the name's similarity to McDonald's and chose to capitalize on Plaintiff's popularity. Consequently, the court easily finds that the good faith factor weighs in Plaintiff's favor.

Summarizing the relevant Polaroid factors, the court concludes that the strength of Plaintiff's mark, evidence of confusion, similarity of the marks and lack of good faith on the part of the individual defendants in choosing their name together support a finding of trademark infringement that warrants the issuance of an injunction in this case.

Deere & Company v. MTD Products, Inc.

United States Court of Appeals, Second Circuit, 1994.
41 F.3d 39.

■ JON O. NEWMAN, CHIEF JUDGE:

This appeal in a trademark case presents a rarely litigated issue likely to recur with increasing frequency in this era of head-to-head comparative advertising. The precise issue, arising under the New York anti-dilution statute, N.Y.Gen.Bus.Law § 368–d (McKinney 1984), is whether an advertiser may depict an altered form of a competitor's trademark to identify the competitor's product in a comparative ad.

Although a number of dilution cases in this Circuit have involved use of a trademark by a competitor to identify a competitor's products in comparative advertising,[a] as well as use by a noncompetitor in a humorous variation of a trademark,[b] we have not yet considered whether the use of an altered version of a distinctive trademark to identify a competitor's product and achieve a humorous effect can constitute trademark dilution.

[a] See, e.g., Diversified Marketing, Inc. v. Estee Lauder, Inc., 705 F.Supp. 128 (S.D.N.Y. 1988)(no dilution under section 368–d where defendant used name for comparison purposes with advertising slogan, "If You Like Estee Lauder ... You'll Love Beauty USA").

[b] See, e.g., McDonald's Corp. v. McBagel's, Inc., 649 F.Supp. 1268 (S.D.N.Y. 1986)(take-off on McDonald's trade-name); Universal City Studios, Inc. v. T–Shirt Gallery, Ltd., 634 F.Supp. 1468 (S.D.N.Y.1986) (T-shirt picturing "Miami Mice" poked fun at plaintiff's "Miami Vice" trademark); Coca–Cola Co. v. Gemini Rising, Inc., 346 F.Supp. 1183 (E.D.N.Y.1972)("Enjoy Cocaine" poster making fun of Coca–Cola trademark).

Though we find MTD's animated version of Deere's deer amusing, we agree with Judge McKenna that the television commercial is a likely violation of the anti-dilution statute. We therefore affirm the preliminary injunction.

Background

Deere, a Delaware corporation with its principal place of business in Illinois, is the world's largest supplier of agricultural equipment. For over one hundred years, Deere has used a deer design ("Deere Logo") as a trademark for identifying its products and services. Deere owns numerous trademark registrations for different versions of the Deere Logo. Although these versions vary slightly, all depict a static, two-dimensional silhouette of a leaping male deer in profile. The Deere Logo is widely recognizable and a valuable business asset.

MTD, an Ohio company with its principal place of business in Ohio, manufactures and sells lawn tractors. In 1993, W.B. Doner & Company ("Doner"), MTD's advertising agency, decided to create and produce a commercial—the subject of this litigation—that would use the Deere Logo, without Deere's authorization, for the purpose of comparing Deere's line of lawn tractors to MTD's "Yard–Man" tractor. The intent was to identify Deere as the market leader and convey the message that Yard–Man was of comparable quality but less costly than a Deere lawn tractor.

Doner altered the Deere Logo in several respects. For example, as Judge McKenna found, the deer in the MTD version of the logo ("Commercial Logo") is "somewhat differently proportioned, particularly with respect to its width, than the deer in the Deere Logo." Doner also removed the name "John Deere" from the version of the logo used by Deere on the front of its lawn tractors, and made the logo frame more sharply rectangular.

More significantly, the deer in the Commercial Logo is animated and assumes various poses. Specifically, the MTD deer looks over its shoulder, jumps through the logo frame (which breaks into pieces and tumbles to the ground), hops to a pinging noise, and, as a two-dimensional cartoon, runs, in apparent fear, as it is pursued by the Yard–Man lawn tractor and a barking dog. Judge McKenna described the dog as "recognizable as a breed that is short in stature," and in the commercial the fleeing deer appears to be even smaller than the dog. Doner's interoffice documents reflect that the animated deer in the commercial was intended to appear "more playful and/or confused than distressed."

MTD submitted the commercial to ABC, NBC, and CBS for clearance prior to airing, together with substantiation of the various claims made regarding the Yard–Man lawn tractor's quality and cost relative to the corresponding Deere model. Each network ultimately approved the commercial, though ABC reserved the right to re-evaluate it "should there be [a] responsible complaint," and CBS demanded and received a letter of indemnity from Doner. The commercial ran from the week of March 7, 1994, through the week of May 23, 1994.

Deere filed a complaint, along with an order to show cause seeking a preliminary injunction and a temporary restraining order, alleging violations of the New York anti-dilution statute and section 43(a) of the Lanham Act, 15 U.S.C.A. § 1125(a)(1988), as well as common law claims of unfair competition and unjust enrichment. Following a hearing, the District Court denied Deere's application for a temporary restraining order, but subsequently found that Deere had demonstrated a likelihood of prevailing on its dilution claim and granted preliminary injunctive relief limited to activities within New York State. In its August 11, 1994, Supplemental Findings of Fact, Conclusions of Law, and Order ("Supplemental Order"), the Court concluded that Deere had not shown a likelihood of success on the merits of its Lanham Act claim.

On appeal, MTD argues that the anti-dilution statute does not prohibit commercial uses of a trademark that do not confuse consumers or result in a loss of the trademark's ability to identify a single manufacturer, or tarnish the trademark's positive connotations. Deere cross-appeals, contending that injunctive relief should not have been limited to New York State. We affirm both the finding of likely dilution and the scope of the injunction.

Discussion

Section 368–d, which has counterparts in more than twenty states, reads as follows:

> Likelihood of injury to business reputation or of dilution of the distinctive quality of a mark or trade name shall be a ground for injunctive relief in cases of infringement of a mark registered or not registered or in cases of unfair competition, notwithstanding the absence of competition between the parties or the absence of confusion as to the source of goods or services.

N.Y.Gen.Bus.Law § 368–d (McKinney 1984). The anti-dilution statute applies to competitors as well as noncompetitors, see Nikon Inc. v. Ikon Corp., 987 F.2d 91, 96 (2d Cir.1993), and explicitly does not require a plaintiff to demonstrate a likelihood of consumer confusion, see Sally Gee, Inc. v. Myra Hogan, Inc., 699 F.2d 621, 624 (2d Cir.1983).

In order to prevail on a section 368–d dilution claim, a plaintiff must prove, first, that its trademark either is of truly distinctive quality or has acquired secondary meaning, and, second, that there is a "likelihood of dilution." Sally Gee, 699 F.2d at 625. A third consideration, the predatory intent of the defendant, may not be precisely an element of the violation, but, as we discuss below, is of significance, especially in a case such as this, which involves poking fun at a competitor's trademark.

MTD does not dispute that the Deere Logo is a distinctive trademark that is capable of dilution and has acquired the requisite secondary meaning in the marketplace. See Allied Maintenance Corp. v. Allied Mechanical Trades, Inc., 42 N.Y.2d 538, 545, 399 N.Y.S.2d 628, 632, 369 N.E.2d 1162, 1166 (1977). Therefore, the primary question on appeal is whether Deere can establish a likelihood of dilution of this distinctive mark under section 368–d.

Likelihood of Dilution. Traditionally, this Court has defined dilution under section 368–d "as either the blurring of a mark's product identification or the tarnishment of the affirmative associations a mark has come to convey." See Mead Data Central, Inc. v. Toyota Motor Sales, U.S.A., Inc., 875 F.2d 1026, 1031 (2d Cir.1989).

In previous cases, "blurring" has typically involved "the whittling away of an established trademark's selling power through its unauthorized use by others upon dissimilar products." Mead Data, 875 F.2d at 1031 (describing such "'hypothetical anomalies' as 'DuPont shoes, Buick aspirin tablets, Schlitz varnish, Kodak pianos, Bulova gowns, and so forth' ")(quoting legislative history of section 368–d)(citation omitted). Thus, dilution by "blurring" may occur where the defendant uses or modifies the plaintiff's trademark to identify the defendant's goods and services, raising the possibility that the mark will lose its ability to serve as a unique identifier of the plaintiff's product.[c]

"Tarnishment" generally arises when the plaintiff's trademark is linked to products of shoddy quality, or is portrayed in an unwholesome or unsavory context likely to evoke unflattering thoughts about the owner's product.[d] In such situations, the trademark's reputation and commercial value might be diminished because the public will associate the lack of quality or lack of prestige in the defendant's goods with the plaintiff's unrelated goods, or because the defendant's use reduces the trademark's reputation and standing in the eyes of consumers as a wholesome identifier of the owner's products or services.

At the hearing on Deere's application for a temporary restraining order, the District Court initially suggested that there was neither blurring nor tarnishment as those terms have been used, and consequently no dilution of the Deere Logo. The Court observed that MTD's commercial "makes it clear that Deere is a distinct product coming from a different source than Yard–Man," and does not "bring the plaintiff's mark into disrepute." However, in its preliminary injunction ruling, the Court found that Deere would probably be able to establish a likelihood of dilution by blurring under section 368–d; tarnishment was not discussed.

The District Court noted that "the instant case [wa]s one of first impression" because it involved a defendant's use of a competitor's trade-

---

[c] See, e.g., Jordache Enterprises, Inc. v. Levi Strauss & Co., 841 F.Supp. 506 (S.D.N.Y.1993)(Jordache used Levi's mark to identify Jordache's product); Dreyfus Fund, Inc. v. Royal Bank of Canada, 525 F.Supp. 1108 (S.D.N.Y.1981)(defendant used version of plaintiff's lion trademark to advertise defendant's products).

[d] See, e.g., Coca–Cola Co., 346 F.Supp. at 1183 (defendant sold posters reading "Enjoy Cocaine" in script and color identical to that used for Coca–Cola trademark); Academy of Motion Picture Arts and Sciences v. Creative House Promotions, Inc., 944 F.2d 1446, 1457 (9th Cir.1991)(finding dilution because "[i]f the Star Award looks cheap or shoddy, ... the Oscar's distinctive quality as a coveted symbol of excellence ... is threatened"); Chemical Corp. of America v. Anheuser-Busch, Inc., 306 F.2d 433 (5th Cir.1962)(defendant adapted plaintiff's slogan, "Where there's life ... there's Bud," for its insecticide slogan, "Where there's life ... there's bugs"), cert. denied, 372 U.S. 965, 83 S.Ct. 1089, 10 L.Ed.2d 129 (1963).

mark to refer to the competitor's products rather than to identify the defendant's products. For this reason, the traditional six-factor test for determining whether there has been dilution through blurring of a trademark's product identification was not fully applicable.[e] Focusing only on the alteration of the static Deere Logo resulting from MTD's animation, the Court concluded that MTD's version constituted dilution because it was likely to diminish the strength of identification between the original Deere symbol and Deere products, and to blur the distinction between the Deere Logo and other deer logos in the marketplace, including those in the insurance and financial markets. Although we agree with the District Court's finding of a likelihood of dilution, we believe that MTD's commercial does not fit within the concept of "blurring," but, as we explain below, nonetheless constitutes dilution.

The District Court's analysis endeavored to fit the MTD commercial into one of the two categories we have recognized for a section 368–d claim. However, the MTD commercial is not really a typical instance of blurring, see, e.g., Toys "R" US, Inc. v. Canarsie Kiddie Shop, Inc., 559 F.Supp. 1189, 1208 (E.D.N.Y.1983)(finding blurring of "Toys 'R' Us" mark by "Kids 'r' Us" mark), because it poses slight if any risk of impairing the identification of Deere's mark with its products. Nor is there tarnishment, which is usually found where a distinctive mark is depicted in a context of sexual activity, obscenity, or illegal activity. See, e.g., Coca–Cola, 346 F.Supp. at 1191 (relying on dilution by tarnishment as alternative basis for issuance of preliminary injunction against defendant's "Enjoy Cocaine" poster); Pillsbury Co. v. Milky Way Productions, Inc., 215 U.S.P.Q. 124, 135 (N.D.Ga.1981)(concluding that defendant's sexually-oriented variation tarnished plaintiff's mark). But the blurring/tarnishment dichotomy does not necessarily represent the full range of uses that can dilute a mark under New York law.

In giving content to dilution beyond the categories of blurring or tarnishment, however, we must be careful not to broaden section 368–d to prohibit all uses of a distinctive mark that the owner prefers not be made. Several different contexts may conveniently be identified. Sellers of commercial products may wish to use a competitor's mark to identify the competitor's product in comparative advertisements. See, e.g., R.G. Smith v. Chanel, Inc., 402 F.2d 562, 567 (9th Cir.1968)(perfume manufacturer used competitor's mark in comparative advertisements; injunction denied). As long as the mark is not altered, such use serves the beneficial purpose of imparting factual information about the relative merits of competing products and poses no risk of diluting the selling power of the competitor's mark. Satirists, selling no product other than the publication that contains their expression, may wish to parody a mark to make a point of social commentary, see, e.g., Stop the Olympic Prison v. United States Olympic

---

[e] See Mead Data, 875 F.2d at 1035 (Sweet, J., concurring)(suggesting that courts evaluating blurring claims look at (1) similarity of the marks, (2) similarity of the products covered by the marks, (3) sophistication of consumers, (4) predatory intent, (5) renown of the senior mark, and (6) renown of the junior mark).

Committee, 489 F.Supp. 1112, 1123 (S.D.N.Y.1980) (poster used defendant's trademark to criticize trademark owner's involvement with proposed prison; injunction denied), to entertain, see, e.g., L.L. Bean v. Drake Publishers, Inc., 811 F.2d 26 (1st Cir.)(satiric magazine parodying L.L. Bean catalogue; injunction denied), cert. denied, 483 U.S. 1013, 107 S.Ct. 3254, 97 L.Ed.2d 753 (1987), or perhaps both to comment and entertain, see, e.g., Girl Scouts of USA v. Personality Posters Manufacturing Co., 304 F.Supp. 1228, 1233 (S.D.N.Y.1969)(poster depicting pregnant Girl Scout to suggest humorously that trademark owner's traditional image of chastity and wholesomeness was somewhat illusory; injunction denied). Such uses risk some dilution of the identifying or selling power of the mark, but that risk is generally tolerated in the interest of maintaining broad opportunities for expression.

Sellers of commercial products who wish to attract attention to their commercials or products and thereby increase sales by poking fun at widely recognized marks of noncompeting products, see, e.g., Eveready Battery Co., Inc. v. Adolph Coors Co., 765 F.Supp. 440 (N.D.Ill.1991)(beer manufacturer spoofed Energizer Bunny trademark; preliminary injunction under Lanham Act and state dilution statute denied), risk diluting the selling power of the mark that is made fun of. When this occurs, not for worthy purposes of expression, but simply to sell products, that purpose can easily be achieved in other ways. The potentially diluting effect is even less deserving of protection when the object of the joke is the mark of a directly competing product.

Whether the use of the mark is to identify a competing product in an informative comparative ad, to make a comment, or to spoof the mark to enliven the advertisement for a noncompeting or a competing product, the scope of protection under a dilution statute must take into account the degree to which the mark is altered and the nature of the alteration. Not every alteration will constitute dilution, and more leeway for alterations is appropriate in the context of satiric expression and humorous ads for noncompeting products. But some alterations have the potential to so lessen the selling power of a distinctive mark that they are appropriately proscribed by a dilution statute. Dilution of this sort is more likely to be found when the alterations are made by a competitor with both an incentive to diminish the favorable attributes of the mark and an ample opportunity to promote its products in ways that make no significant alteration.

We need not attempt to predict how New York will delineate the scope of its dilution statute in all of the various contexts in which an accurate depiction of a distinctive mark might be used, nor need we decide how variations of such a mark should be treated in different contexts. Some variations might well be de minimis, and the context in which even substantial variations occur may well have such meritorious purposes that any diminution in the identifying and selling power of the mark need not be condemned as dilution.

Wherever New York will ultimately draw the line, we can be reasonably confident that the MTD commercial challenged in this case crosses it. The commercial takes a static image of a graceful, full-size deer—symbolizing Deere's substance and strength—and portrays, in an animated version, a deer that appears smaller than a small dog and scampers away from the dog and a lawn tractor, looking over its shoulder in apparent fear. Alterations of that sort, accomplished for the sole purpose of promoting a competing product, are properly found to be within New York's concept of dilution because they risk the possibility that consumers will come to attribute unfavorable characteristics to a mark and ultimately associate the mark with inferior goods and services. See Sally Gee, 699 F.2d at 624–25 ("The interest protected by § 368–d is not simply commercial goodwill, but the selling power that a distinctive mark or name with favorable associations has engendered for a product in the mind of the consuming public.").

Significantly, the District Court did not enjoin accurate reproduction of the Deere Logo to identify Deere products in comparative advertisements. MTD remains free to deliver its message of alleged product superiority without altering and thereby diluting Deere's trademarks. The Court's order imposes no restriction on truthful advertising properly comparing specific products and their "objectively measurable attributes." FTC Policy Statement on Comparative Advertising, 16 C.F.R. § 14.15 n. 1 (1993). In view of this, the District Court's finding of a likelihood of dilution was entirely appropriate, notwithstanding the fact that MTD's humorous depiction of the deer occurred in the context of a comparative advertisement.

Predatory Intent. The District Court recognized that we have not been authoritatively advised by New York courts nor have we made a clear-cut prediction as to whether "a showing of predatory intent is required for, or merely relevant to, a finding that the anti-dilution statute has been violated."

Until New York courts clarify the relevance of intent under section 368–d, we prefer to proceed cautiously, eschewing definitive statements that endeavor to characterize a subjective element appropriate for all contexts. In the context of trademark parody or alteration, a modest version of subjective intent can helpfully distinguish uses of trademarks that endeavor to sell products from uses that seek to make a social or political commentary or an artistic expression. To serve this purpose, all that is needed is an intent to promote one's product. As the District Court found, at least such intent was clearly present in this case.

Scope of Injunction. Finally, turning to Deere's objection to the geographic scope of the injunction, we conclude that the District Court did not exceed its discretion in limiting the scope of relief to New York State. See Nikon, 987 F.2d at 94 (scope of injunction reviewed for abuse of discretion).

Although the record does not clearly reflect the reasons for the limitation, the District Court observed that "the same considerations that led [it] to limit the injunctive relief for the violation of the New York anti-dilution statute to activities originating or having an effect within the boundaries of the State of New York likewise would apply to injunctive relief granted pursuant to Deere's common law claims of unfair competition and unjust enrichment."

It is thus clear that the District Court believed it had the power to grant broader injunctive relief but declined to exercise it. In view of the novelty of the issues raised, we cannot say that limiting interim relief to conduct in New York State was beyond "the range of [the District Court's] decision-making authority," Stormy Clime Ltd. v. ProGroup, Inc., 809 F.2d 971, 974 (2d Cir.1987), notwithstanding the fact that district courts have in other circumstances granted nationwide injunctive relief on trademark dilution claims.

Conclusion

The order of the District Court granting a preliminary injunction as to activities within New York State is affirmed.

Board of Trade of the City of Chicago v. Dow Jones & Co., Inc.

Supreme Court of Illinois, 1983.
98 Ill.2d 109, 456 N.E.2d 84, 74 Ill.Dec. 582.

■ GOLDENHERSH, JUSTICE:

Defendant, a Delaware corporation with its principal office in New York City, publishes the Wall Street Journal, Barrons, a weekly business magazine, and the Asian Wall Street Journal. It also maintains the Dow Jones News Service, through which it distributes financial news to subscribers. It produces several stock market indexes, the Dow Jones Industrial Average, Transportation Average, and Utilities Average, which are computed on the basis of the current prices of stocks of certain companies selected by defendant's editorial board.

Plaintiff is the oldest and largest commodities exchange market in the United States. It was organized in 1848, and in 1859 the General Assembly granted plaintiff a special charter which incorporated it as a not-for-pecuniary-profit organization. Over the years plaintiff has added different types of futures contracts and now offers these contracts in a variety of fields, including agricultural products, precious metals and financial instruments. All commodities exchanges in the United States are regulated by the Commodities Futures Trading Commission (CFTC), and no exchange may trade a futures contract until the CFTC approves the futures contract and designates the exchange as a contract market for that contract.

A futures contract is a contract traded on a commodities exchange which binds the parties to a particular transaction at a specified future date. A stock index futures contract is a futures contract based upon the value of a particular stock market index. Dr. James H. Lorie, stipulated by the parties to be an expert, called by plaintiff, testified that these contracts have been traded since February 1982. He stated that their "overriding purpose is the management of risk." Unlike other futures contracts, no underlying commodity exists to be delivered at the future date, but rather the transaction is settled by the delivery of a certified promissory note in lieu of cash. He explained that the total risks of investing in the stock market are divided into two parts. One part is the "nonsystematic risk," which occurs when an individual company encounters problems such as strikes, changing consumer attitudes or other problems which would devalue that company's stock. "Nonsystematic risk" can be controlled by an investor through the use of a diversified portfolio. The other type of risk is "systematic risk," which is the risk associated with the broad general movements of the stock market as a whole. Diversification of one's stock portfolio will not provide protection against sharp declines in the stock market. He explained that there are only two ways to protect against systematic risk. The most direct way is for an investor to sell his stocks. This method is rather costly because of the transactional costs in selling and buying stocks, such as brokerage fees. Additionally, if capital gains are realized, the transaction becomes even more costly. The second method of protecting against systematic risk is to deal in stock market futures contracts. This method is more efficient, Professor Lorie explained, since an investor holding a hypothetical $100,000 portfolio could purchase two futures contracts in the Chicago Mercantile Exchange for one-fifteenth the cost of selling his stocks.

An investor who holds a diversified stock portfolio may "hedge" against systematic risk by entering into a stock index futures contract predicting that the market index would decline. Dr. Lorie testified that this was the most effective method of "hedging" of which he was aware.

Plaintiff, desiring to be designated as a contract market for stock index futures contracts, devoted more than two years to developing its own index to be used as the basis for its stock index futures contract.

On February 26, 1982, plaintiff submitted an application to the CFTC asking that it be designated as a contract market for Chicago Board of Trade Portfolio Futures Contracts. The application proposed the use of three indexes, the stock market index, transport index, and the electric index portfolio contracts. It was explained:

> "Each index covers a significant portion of the overall stock market. The stock market index covers industrial firms, the Transport Index covers air, rail, and trucking firms, and the Gas and Electric Index covers utility companies. This division is similar to the way other major market indices divide the stock market."

No mention of the Dow Jones name appeared in the application, but the stocks used in each of the indexes were identical to those used in the Dow Jones averages. In a draft proposal to the CFTC for trading "CBT indexes," the Dow Jones averages stock lists were cut out of the Wall Street Journal and pasted into the proposals. The CFTC advised plaintiff that the CBT indexes were not just similar to, but were identical to the Dow Jones averages and that this should be explicitly stated in its application. On May 7, 1982, plaintiff amended its application to state that the CBT indexes were identical to Dow Jones averages and that when Dow Jones changed a component stock or revised the divisor, plaintiff would make the same change so that the CBT indexes would remain identical to the Dow Jones averages. Plaintiff also added a disclaimer to the application disclaiming any association with Dow Jones. On May 13, the CFTC approved plaintiff's use of the stock market index portfolio contract, but did not rule concerning the use of the transportation or utility index portfolio contracts.

The circuit court held that the burden of producing evidence and the burden of persuading the trier of fact fell upon defendant, and found that defendant had a "property right and valuable interest in the Dow Jones averages" but that plaintiff's use of the averages in the manner proposed did not violate those rights. The order, however, required that there be imprinted upon the CBT index contract a disclaimer disavowing any association with or sponsorship by defendant, Dow Jones. The appellate court reversed, holding that plaintiff had the burden of production and persuasion, and that plaintiff's use of the averages constituted commercial misappropriation "of the Dow Jones index and averages."

Plaintiff argues that the appellate court's holding erroneously expands the tort of misappropriation and that its decision contravenes public policy. [P]laintiff argues that competitive injury is a fundamental prerequisite essential to a finding of misappropriation. It argues that the facts of this case are analogous to National Football League v. Governor of Delaware (D.Del.1977), 435 F.Supp. 1372, and Loeb v. Turner (Tex.Civ.App.1953), 257 S.W.2d 800, in which the courts refused to find misappropriation because, inter alia, the parties were not in competition with each other. It argues that it has done nothing immoral or unethical but has merely created a "new product" which is "outside the primary market which the producer of the original product originally set out to satisfy * * *." (See J. Rahl, The Right to "Appropriate" Trade Values, 23 Ohio St. L.J. 56, 62–63 (1962).) Finally, plaintiff argues that the appellate court's decision is against public policy in that it grants what amounts to a common law patent monopoly to defendant which permits it to exclude others from using its product for any purpose "regardless of whether the producer is being injured or intends to exploit the product itself."

The doctrine of misappropriation as a form of unfair competition was first enunciated by the Supreme Court in International News Service v. Associated Press (1918), 248 U.S. 215, 39 S.Ct. 68, 63 L.Ed. 211. In that case, INS was copying news stories from bulletin boards of members of AP and transmitting the fresh news contained on those bulletin boards to its own members. Thus, INS could obtain information collected by AP at great expense and transmit this information to its midwestern and west coast members, who could then print the news at the same time as the competing AP members or, in some instances, earlier. In affirming the decree enjoining the practice the majority opinion suggested that without the revenues derived from this exclusive, timely presentation of the news, AP or other news services would not have sufficient incentive to continue performing their services. 248 U.S. 215, 235, 39 S.Ct. 68, 71, 63 L.Ed. 211, 219; see

Developments In The Law: Competitive Torts, 77 Harv.L.Rev. 888, 934 (1964).

Competing with the policy that protection should be afforded one who expends labor and money to develop products is the concept that freedom to imitate and duplicate is vital to our free market economy. Indeed, when the doctrine of misappropriation was first enunciated, Justice Brandeis recognized this competing policy: "He who follows the pioneer into a new market, or who engages in the manufacture of an article newly introduced by another, seeks profits due largely to the labor and expense of the first adventurer; but the law sanctions, indeed encourages, the pursuit." (International News Service v. Associated Press (1918), 248 U.S. 215, 259, 39 S.Ct. 68, 79, 63 L.Ed. 211, 229 (Brandeis, J., dissenting).) Similarly, Professor Rahl reasons: "Substantial similarity of alternatives can come about in only one of two ways—by independent development or by imitation. While there are many instances of simultaneous independent innovation, our economy would still be in the Dark Ages if this were the only circumstance under which competing alternatives could be offered. Imitation is inherent in any system of competition and it is imperative for an economy in which there is rapid technological advance." Rahl, The Right to "Appropriate" Trade Values, 23 Ohio St. L.J. 56, 72 (1962).

In balancing the factors that should determine which of the competing concepts should prevail, it appears unlikely that an adverse decision will cause defendant to cease to produce its averages or that the revenue it currently receives for the distribution of those averages will be materially affected. Defendant correctly asserts that it will lose its right to prospective licensing revenues in the event that in the future it elects to have its name associated with stock index futures contracts, but reliance upon the existence of a property right based upon the ability to license the product to prospective markets which were not originally contemplated by the creator of the product is somewhat "circular." Williams & Wilkins Co. v. United States (1973) 203 Ct.Cl. 74, 487 F.2d 1345, 1357 n. 19; see Metropolitan Opera Association v. Wagner–Nichols Recorder Corp. (N.Y.S.Ct.1950) 199 Misc. 786, 101 N.Y.S.2d 483, 493; Developments In the Law: Competitive Torts, 77 Harv.L.Rev. 888, 935 (1964).

Alternatively, holding that plaintiff's use of defendant's indexes in the manner proposed is a misappropriation may stimulate the creation of new indexes perhaps better suited to the purpose of "hedging" against the "systematic" risk present in the stock market.

Whether protection against appropriation is necessary to foster creativity depends in part upon the expectations of that sector of the business community which deals with the particular intangible. If the creator of an intangible product expects to be able to control the licensing or distribution of the intangible in order to profit from his effort, and similarly those who would purchase the product expect and are willing to pay for the use of the intangible, a better argument can be made in favor of granting protection. (See generally Rahl, The Right to "Appropriate" Trade Values, 23 Ohio St. L.J. 56, 61–69 (1962).) The record shows that the plaintiff sought to develop its own index prior to the CFTC's requirement that the contracts be based on well-known, well-established indexes. It then offered defendant 10 cents per transaction, which it estimated would be somewhere between $1 million and $2 million per year, for the use of its name and averages. While there appears to be some dispute as to whether this offer of payment was primarily for the use of defendant's name or for the use of the averages, the offer of money is relevant to the extent that it acknowledges the value of the association of defendant's name and good will with the averages it produces.

To hold that defendant has a proprietary interest in its indexes and averages which vests it with the exclusive right to license their use for trading in stock index futures contracts would not preclude plaintiff and others from marketing stock index futures contracts. The extent of defendant's monopoly would be limited, for as defendant points out, there are an infinite number of stock market indexes which could be devised. As one commentator notes, the effect of granting a "monopoly" at the base of the production pyramid is much less objectionable than granting a monopoly at the top of the pyramid: "Social cost assumes more manageable size and so less significance near the base of the pyramid. Exclusive rights in a special kind of typewriter key are far less objectionable than a monopoly in the lever, because far less is swept into the monopolist's control." Developments In the Law: Competitive Torts, 77 Harv.L.Rev. 888, 938 (1964).

We conclude that the possibility of any detriment to the public which might result from our holding that defendant's indexes and averages may not be used without its consent in the manner proposed by plaintiff are outweighed by the resultant encouragement to develop new indexes specifically designed for the purpose of hedging against the "systematic" risk present in the stock market.

We have considered plaintiff's contention that defendant has failed to prove that the proposed use of the averages would cause it injury. The publication of the indexes involves valuable assets of defendant, its good will and its reputation for integrity and accuracy. Despite the fact that plaintiff's proposed use is not in competition with the use defendant presently makes of them, defendant is entitled to protection against their misappropriation.

■ SIMON, JUSTICE, dissenting [omitted]. WARD and THOMAS J. MORAN, JJ., join in this dissent.

NOTES

1. *Trademark infringement versus trademark registration.* The ability of trademark holders to successfully assert rights against those with whom they do not compete creates a curious anomaly. Recall that one of the requirements for federal registration is use—or at least, the intent to use. At the registration stage, "use" is not measured in the abstract. Rather, the applicant is required to designate the goods on which the mark is or will be used; the validity of the mark is determined by its appropriateness for particular goods; and the issue whether the mark is likely to be confused with a previously registered mark is also determined with reference to the registered owner's and applicant's actual usage, see Assignment 2. Yet, despite this careful attention paid to use at the registration stage, cases like *McDonald's* allow mark holders to expand the reach of their marks to products that they do not sell or intend to sell. When a plaintiff is successful in such a case, what she has managed to do is create a right to a mark that she has not "used" within the meaning of the Lanham Act.

What is the justification for treating the registration and infringement contexts so differently? One possibility is that the law is being used to give trademark holders a zone of expansion. That is, the law is construed so that once a merchant develops a successful business in one kind of goods, she can use the goodwill that the mark has developed to enter into a new field. This construction is socially desirable from the customer's point of view. A consumer who liked the first product can use the mark on the new one as an indication that he is likely to be satisfied with it as well.[42] From the merchant's perspective, the ability to use the mark to expand provides added incentives to create goodwill in the first place.

This justification cannot, however, explain all of the cases. As *McDonald's* and the cases cited therein indicate, McDonald's has managed to prevent use of its mark in the dentistry, bagel, and motel fields—even though it is not too likely that the company would consider entering all (or any) of these businesses. Thus, it is likely that the law is doing something more than simply protecting the trademark holder's ability to expand into new fields. See Note 3, infra.

2. *The family-of-marks doctrine.* Merchants who sell a variety of products often try to transfer goodwill in one good to others by using a common element in all of their marks, thereby creating a "family." To fully protect the family's goodwill, other merchants must be prevented from using the common element—this was the issue in the *McDonald's* case. Others must also be prevented from registering marks using the common element. Accordingly, the family-of-marks doctrine often arises in opposition proceedings.

As a general matter, when the applicant is not planning to use the mark on goods similar to those of the registered trademark holder, the Patent and Trademark Office will not permit the trademark holder to successfully oppose registration. The justification is related to the discussion in Note 1: the PTO reasons that permitting these oppositions would allow trademark holders to own their rights "in gross"—that is, unconnected with the mark's use as a signal on particular goods or services.[43] However, there are cases where particular features of marks take on such a strong association for consumers that the PTO is willing to protect the

---

[42] For example, it is said that Coca Cola did not use the Coke trademark in connection with its first entry into the diet soda business because it did not think its first soda (Tab) was good enough for the mark. When Diet Coke was finally introduced, customers were especially eager to try it.

[43] See, e.g., Bissell, Inc. v. Easy Day Mfg. Co., 130 U.S.P.Q. (BNA) 485 (T.T.A.B. 1961).

trademark holder. Examples include the "Mc" prefix for food items,[44] and the "to" suffix for snacks.[45] Recently the Federal Circuit, the court that reviews the registration decisions of the PTO, clarified the circumstances where a family-of-marks argument should succeed. According to the court, the issue is whether the group of goods for which the common element is registered has a recognizable common characteristic that is associated by the public with the common element and is considered indicative of the common origin of the goods.[46]

3. *The unfair competition spectrum: trademarks as signals vs. trademarks as property.* Another way to look at the noncompeting-goods line of cases is as a departure from the idea that trademark law protects only the signaling function of marks. Rather, as these cases move from protecting the most distinctive signals (§ 1114 claims), to protecting marks' less clear signaling elements (§ 43(a) claims), to protecting aspects of the marks themselves, the law moves from encouraging the merchant to produce goodwill to allowing her to maintain it and capture its inherent value.

a. *Dilution.* Even a trademark holder who has no interest in using a mark in a new field may fear that too broad a usage of the mark will lead to a deterioration of its impact as a signal. One way to appreciate this problem is to consider the hypotheticals offered by the *Deere & Co.* court: DuPont shoes, Buick aspirin, Schlitz varnish, Kodak pianos, and Bulova gowns. DuPont, Buick, Schlitz, Kodak, and Bulova are effective signals because they unambiguously refer to sources that are extremely well known. Allowing other producers to use these marks would blur their identity, thereby making them less powerful constituents of the marketing vocabulary.

Another way to see the dilution problem is to consider marks that have a certain cachet—Chanel No. 5 for perfume, Rolex for watches, or Ferrari for cars. If other producers could use these marks on their products, the pizzazz of owning a bottle of Chanel No. 5, receiving a Rolex, or driving a Ferrari would diminish. If the products were very different, simultaneous usage of the marks might not be confusing. Nonetheless, a little bit of fun would have gone out of life. Anti-dilution statutes protect the cachet of these marks by preventing their use even in the absence of consumer confusion.

b. *Tarnishment.* In many jurisdictions, only very strong marks are eligible for protection against dilution. This is because only very strong marks have the significant impact, cachet, or pizzazz that is the concern of the anti-dilution statutes. But closely related to the loss-of-cachet idea is the notion of tarnishment. An example of such a case is Dallas Cowboys

---

[44] J & J Snack Foods Corp. v. McDonald's Corporation, 932 F.2d 1460 (Fed.Cir.1991)(upholding refusal to register "McPretzel" for pretzels).

[45] The Frito Co. v. Buckeye Foods, 130 U.S.P.Q. (BNA) 347 (T.T.A.B. 1991).

[46] J & J Snack Foods Corp. v. McDonald's Corporation, 932 F.2d 1460, 1462 (Fed.Cir.1991).

Cheerleaders, Inc. v. Pussycat Cinema, Ltd.,[47] which dealt with a film, "Debbie Does Dallas." In the court's words:

"[The] plot, to the extent there is one, involves a cheerleader at a fictional high school, Debbie, who has been selected to become a 'Texas Cowgirl.' In order to raise enough money to send Debbie, and eventually the entire squad to Dallas, the cheerleaders perform sexual services for a fee. The movie consists largely of a series of scenes graphically depicting the sexual escapades of the 'actors.' In the movie's final scene, Debbie dons a uniform strikingly similar to that worn by the Dallas Cowboy Cheerleaders and for approximately twelve minutes of film footage engages in various sex acts while clad or partially clad in the uniform."[48]

Claiming the Cheerleader uniform as a state-law trademark, the Dallas Cowboys moved to preliminarily enjoin exhibition and distribution of the movie. Although the court was uncertain whether, at trial, the plaintiff would be able to establish consumer confusion, it nonetheless granted preliminary relief, reasoning that trademark laws are also designed to protect a product's reputation. Association of the Cowboys with this salacious material was, in short, a form of tarnishment.

c. *Misappropriation.* Misappropriation takes the protection of the mark one step further. Trademark infringement, dilution, and tarnishment insure a merchant's ability to use the mark to profit from his *product;* misappropriation gives the merchant the ability to profit from the *trademark.* In the *Chicago Board of Trade* case, for example, the publisher of the Wall Street Journal was not in the business of putting together investment vehicles: the only thing that belonged to the Journal that the Board of Trade sold was its mark. The court reasoned that since the mark has a value that derived from the efforts of the Journal, it is the Journal that should be allowed to capture that benefit.

A good way to appreciate the rise in the vitality of the misappropriation theory is to consider the licensing programs of universities and major league sports teams. Under a traditional consumer confusion/trademark-assignal regime, it is unlikely that these entities could prevent clothing companies from using their logos. For example, no one is likely to be confused into thinking that a Wolverine tee shirt is manufactured by the University of Michigan: the University of Michigan is in the education business and not the clothing business. At the same time, however, it is apparent that consumers attach value to the Wolverine mark in that they are willing to pay more for a Wolverine tee shirt than for a plain tee shirt. The misappropriation theory creates a way for the University to enjoy this consumer value (or, as economists call it, consumer surplus), for it permits the University to enjoin anyone who uses the mark without its authorization. The royalties produced by granting authority to clothing companies

[47] 604 F.2d 200 (2d Cir.1979).

[48] 604 F.2d at 202–03 (footnote omitted).

represent an increasingly important element of university funding and sports team profits.[49]

In fact, there is some circular reasoning going on here. If consumers think that courts stop all unauthorized uses of marks (even on noncompeting goods), then they will come to believe that every use of a mark can be attributed to the mark holder. Accordingly, as the doctrine of misappropriation is utilized more, traditional trademark doctrine becomes increasingly applicable, for consumers are indeed likely to begin to be confused. For instance, even a consumer who understands that the University of Michigan does not manufacture Wolverine tee-shirts may come to believe that the mark could not have been used unless the University sponsored or approved the shirts. As a result, any dissatisfaction the consumer experiences with the shirt will, in fact, be attributed to the University. As Part A illustrated, confusion as to association, sponsorship, or approval is, in fact, actionable under § 43(a).

4. *Preemption.* Does this expanded form of trademark protection make sense? Consider, first, the normative perspective. The *Chicago Board of Trade* court reasoned that as between the Chicago Board of Trade and the Wall Street Journal, the Journal should reap the value of the Dow Jones mark because it was the Journal that turned it into a valuable asset. But is this the right choice? If there were no misappropriation doctrine, the *public* would capture the value of the mark, not the *defendant*.

For instance, in the Wolverine example, if no one could prevent the use of the Wolverine mark on tee shirts, the price of marked shirts should, theoretically, fall: the premium the public was paying would attract the interest of other tee-shirt manufacturers. That is, when these producers saw that extra sales could be made if they put a Wolverine on their shirts, they would go into competition with the first manufacturer by undercutting its prices. The cost of Wolverine tee shirts would be competed down so that in the end, the consumer surplus in the shirts would go into the pockets of consumers. Isn't this where the surplus belongs? Certainly, it is easy to agree with the *Chicago Board of Trade* court that it does not belong to the tee-shirt manufacturer. But why should it belong to the University? After all, so long as the University has an unambiguous signal for its sports teams, it receives the benefit that trademark law intended it to enjoy: why give it any more than the law intended?

Another way to look at this is to ask how well these causes of action square with federal copyright and patent law. These two regimes do create rights to the values inherent in the fruits of creativity; they are not meant merely to protect writers' and inventors' ability to communicate with customers. Both regimes differ from trademark law in significant ways. First, they protect only material that the right holder created herself. Second, copyrights do not protect facts and patents protect only works that

---

[49] See, e.g., Eskenazi, Sports Logos Now Symbols of Big Profits, N.Y. Times, Sept. 27, 1989, at A1, col. 1.

are so novel that a person with ordinary skill could not have thought them up. Third, copyrights and patents subsist for only a limited number of years (20 for patents, about 75 for copyrights). In contrast, there is no requirement that a trademark owner invent her mark; within limits, a mark can be plucked straight out of the public domain. Moreover, trademark rights endure for however long the trademark holder continues to use the mark.

Does it make sense to give a trademark holder unlimited rights to the inherent value of something she may not have created herself when authors and inventors have only a circumscribed period in which to capture the value of truly innovative efforts? Should the fact that Testarossas and Daytonas are not innovative enough to patent have informed the *Ferrari* court's decision, as the dissent suggested? Should the fact that the Dow Jones Industrial Average is not copyrightable have influenced the *Chicago Board of Trade* court? The question whether the state claims analyzed in this Part are preempted by federal law will be reconsidered in connection with Copyright Law, see Assignment 14, and Patent Law, see Assignment 25. Federal trademark law is not, of course, subject to preemption analysis. Nonetheless, does it make sense to interpret the Lanham Act in a manner that circumvents the limitations that Congress established in the Copyright and Patent Acts, or that the Copyright Clause imposes on Congress's authority to enact copyright and patent legislation?[50]

It is also worth considering that in 1988, Congress considered, but rejected, adding an anti-dilution provision to the Lanham Act.[51] Should this affect the way that the courts in the Principal Cases interpreted federal and state law? Should the reasons Congress rejected the revision matter? Some witnesses stressed that states have traditionally safeguarded the anti-dilution right. If deference to the states was the basis for Congress's decision, was not the *Ferrari* dissent right to argue that § 43(a) should not be interpreted to protect against dilution? Other witnesses were concerned with laws that protect words in gross, apart from their source-indicative function, on the theory that such laws seriously burden small businesses that do not have the resources to search numerous marks before getting clearance. If that was Congress's principal justification, should state laws that create the same problems be considered preempted?

Finally, it should be noted that as this casebook went to press, Congress passed a bill amending § 43 to protect famous marks from dilution of their distinctive qualities.[52]   To determine whether a mark is distinctive and famous, courts are instructed to consider a variety of

---

[50] At least one court has recently decided that this does not make sense and has withheld Lanham Act protection to a product that was the subject of an expired utility patent, see Vornado Air Circulation Systems Inc. v. Duracraft Corp., 58 F.3d 1498, 35 U.S.P.Q.2d (BNA) 1332 (10th Cir.1995).

[51] See Trademark Law Revision Act of 1988: Hearings on H.R.4156.2 Before the Subcomm. on Courts, Civil Liberties & the Administration of Justice of the House Comm. on the Judiciary, 100th Cong., 2nd Sess. (1988). It is worth noting that in an unreproduced section of the Ferrari dissent, Judge Kennedy made precisely this point, Ferrari v. Roberts, 944 F.2d at 1251.

[52] See, e.g., H.R. 1295, 104th Cong., 1st Sess.

factors, including the inherent or acquired distinctiveness of the mark, the duration and extent of its use on goods and in advertising, the size of the trading area and channels of trade in which it is used, the degree to which the owner's and the user's marks are recognized, the use made of the same or similar marks by third parties, and whether the mark is federally registered. Dilution is defined to mean "the lessening of the capacity of a famous mark to identify and distinguish goods or services, regardless of the presence or absence of (1) competition between the owner of the famous mark and other parties, or (2) likelihood of confusion, mistake, or deception." Only injunctive relief is available under this provision, unless the owner proves that the junior user "willfully intended to trade on the owner's reputation or to cause dilution of the famous mark." Three defenses are provided: fair use, noncommercial use, and use in all forms of news reporting and news commentary.

Should states be permitted to protect marks against dilution when this bill becomes law? For example, should states be permitted to protect against dilution a marketing device that is not famous enough to qualify for federal protection?

5. *You be the judge.* Here are a list of trademarks that have been the subject of litigation on the likelihood of confusion issue. Based on the brief descriptions that follow, how would you rule?

a. PRIVATE EYES for upscale non-prescription eyeglasses, sunglasses and optical frames v. PRIVATE EYE VISION CENTER for an eyecare center selling mostly prescription products.

b. PINK PANTHER for a cartoon and a series of comic films v. THE PINK PANTHER PATROL for a gay rights organization.

c. CURVEE DOM PERIGNON for champagne v. DOM POPINGON for gourmet popcorn sold in a bottle with a similar shield label.

d. SAKO for shoes and footwear v. SEIKO for watches.

e. SAKS FIFTH AVENUE for an elite department store v. SACKS THRIFT AVENUE for a secondhand clothing store.

BIBLIOGRAPHY

Articles on various aspects of trademark infringement include: Allen, The Role of Actual Confusion Evidence in Federal Trademark Infringement Litigation, 16 Campbell L. Rev. 19 (1994); Pasquarella, Trademark Law—Confusion Over the Likelihood of Confusion? Dranoff–Perlstein Associates v. Sklar, 38 Vill. L. Rev. 1317 (1993); Allen, The Scope of Confusion Actionable Under Federal Trademark Law: Who Must be Confusesd and When?, 26 Wake Forest L. Rev. 321 (1991); Kirkpatrick, Area Summary, Likelihood of Confusion Issues: The Federal Circuit's Standard of Review, 40 Am. U.L. Rev. 1221 (1991); Jones, Developing and Using Survey Evidence in Trademark Litigation, 19 Memphis St. U. L. Rev. 471 (1989); Lipton, A New Look at the Use of Social Science Evidence in Trademark Litigation, 78 Trademark Rep. 32 (1988);

Articles on contributory infringement include, Cross, Contributory Infringment and Related Theories of Secondary Liability for Trademark Infringement, 80 Iowa L. Rev. 101 (1994).

Articles specifically treating § 43(a) include: Evans & Hoover, Protection of Product Configurations Under the Lanham Act, 1 U.Balt. Intell. Prop. L.J. 126 (1993); Langvardt, Section 43(a), Commercial Falsehood, and the First Amendment: A Proposed Framework, 78 Minn. L. Rev. 309 (1993); McLean, The Birth, Death, and Renaissance of the Doctrine of Secondary Meaning in the Making, 42 Am. U. L. Rev. 737 (1993); Verbit, Moral Rights and Section 43 (a) of the Lanham Act: Oasis or Illusion?, 9 Hastings Comm./Ent. L.J. 383 (1987); Bauer, A Federal Law of Unfair Competition: What Should be the Reach of Section 43(a) of the Lanham Act?, 31 U.C.L.A. L. Rev. 671 (1984).

Recent articles on false advertising include: Burns, The Paradox of Antitrust and Lanham Act Standing, 42 U.C.L.A. L. Rev. 47 (1994); Morrison, Corrective Advertising as a Remedy for the False Advertising of Prescription Drugs and Other Professionally–Promoted Medical Products, 49 Food & Drug L.J. 385 (1994); Goldman, The World's Best Article on Competitor Suits for False Advertising, 45 Fla. L. Rev. 487 (1993); BeVier, Competitor Suits for False Advertising Under § 43(a) of the Lanham Act: A Puzzle in the Law of Deception, 78 Va. L. Rev. 1 (1992); McChesney, Deception, Trademark Infringement, and the Lanham Act: A Property–Rights Reconciliation, 78 Va. L. Rev. 49 (1992); Schechter, Additional Pieces of the Deception Puzzle: Some Reactions to Professor Bevier, 78 Va. L. Rev. 57 (1992); Walsh & Klein, From Dog Food to Prescription Drug Advertising: Litigating False Scientific Establishment Claims Under the Lanham Act, 22 Seton Hall L. Rev. 389 (1992); Frederickson, Recovery for False Advertising Under the Revised Lanham Act; A Methodology for the Computation of Damages, 29 Am. Bus. L.J. 585 (1991); Petty, Supplanting Government Regulation with Competitor Lawsuits: The Case of Controlling False Advertising, 25 Ind. L. Rev. 351 (1991); Petty, Competitor Suits Against False Advertising: Is Section 43(a) of the Lanham Act a Proconsumer Rule or an Anticompetitive Tool?, 20 Balt. L. Rev. 381 (1991).

Materials on the protection of product design include: Reese, Defining the Elements of Trade Dress Infringment Under Section 43(a) of the Lanham Act, 2 Tex. Intell. Prop. L.J. 103 (1994); Davis, Of "Ugly Stiks" and Uglier Case Law: A Comment on the Federal Registration of Functional Designs After Shakespeare Co. v. Silstar Corp. of America, 51 Wash. & Lee L. Rev. 1257 (1994); Horta, Without Secondary Meaning, Do Product Design Trade Dress Protections Function as Infinite Patents?, 27 Suffolk U. L. Rev. 113 (1993); Gifford, The Interplay of Product Definition, Design and Trade Dress, 75 Minn. L. Rev. 769 (1991); Dratler, Trademark Protection for Industrial Designs, 1988 U. Ill. L. Rev. 887 (1988); Schuman, Trademark Protection of Container and Package Configurations—A Primer, 59 Chi.-Kent. L. Rev. 779 (1983).

Articles on infringement actions under state law and preemption include: Welkowitz, Preemption, Extraterratoriality, and the Problem of

State Antidilution Laws, 67 Tulane L. Rev. 1 (1992); Heald, Federal Intellectual Property Law and the Economics of Preemption, 76 Iowa L. Rev. 959 (1991); Welkowitz, Reexamining Trademark Dilution, 44 Vand. L. Rev. 531 (1991); Handler, Are the State Antidilution Laws Compatible with the National Protection of Trademarks?, 75 Trademark Rep. 269 (1985); Callmann, Unfair Competition Without Competition? 95 U. Pa. L. Rev. 443 (1947).

A germinal piece on dilution is Schechter, The Rational Basis of Trademark Protection, 40 Harvard L. Rev. 813 (1927). Other dilution pieces include Swann & Davis, Dilution, An Idea Whose Time Has Gone; Brand Equity As Protectable Property, The New/Old Paradigm, 1 J. Intell. Prop. L. 219 (1994); Raman, Ferrari—Can Dilution be the Standard for Likelihood of Confusion?, 1 Tex. Intell. Prop. L.J. 1 (1992); Welkowitz, Reexamining Trademark Dilution, 44 Vand. L. Rev. 531 (1991); Casenote, In Search of a Consistent Trademark Dilution Test: Mead Data Central, Inc. v. Toyota Motor Sales, U.S.A., Inc., 58 U. Cin. L. Rev. 1449 (1990).

Articles on misappropriation can be found after Assignment 14.

ASSIGNMENT 4

THE INTEREST IN PUBLIC ACCESS

The last Assignment demonstrated the usages of a trademark that its owner can control through actions for trademark infringement and unfair competition. This Assignment looks at the other side of the coin: the uses of the trademark that remain within the control of the public.

At the core of the defenses to infringement lie two sorts of issues: "when" questions and "what" questions. Both carry forward the themes introduced in earlier parts of this Unit. The "when" questions—the defenses based on timing—echo the concerns discussed in connection with use. As *Dawn Donut*, infra, illustrates, the ability to enjoin other uses of the mark is not automatic once it is registered. That is, even though registration gives others constructive (if not actual) notice of the registered owner's right to the mark, the ability to actually stop unauthorized use may accrue only when the registered owner enters—or plans to enter—the unauthorized user's trading region. By the same token, trademark rights continue to be enforceable only for so long as the holder continues to use the mark and to protect the goodwill it represents. In markets that the trademark holder has not reached, and after he has abandoned the mark, the public enjoys free access to it.

Similarly, the "what" questions—questions about what the use of the trademark means—mirror the same interest in the vocabulary that supported the substantive requirements for trademark registration. For example, recall that certain terms—surnames, geographic designations, descriptions—have primary meanings that are so important to the marketplace, they can be registered only if consumers come to see them as conveying mainly a trademark-type message. *The New Kids on the Block* and *L.L. Bean*, infra, demonstrate that at the enforcement stage, courts remain sensitive to the perceived meaning of the mark. Through defenses like the fair use defense of § 1115(b)(4), the Lanham Act ensures that the public can continue to enjoy the ordinary language dimensions of registered marks.

The law, in short, has two ways to protect the public's interest in access to the words and symbols of discourse and commerce. The first line is drawn at registration, where access is assured by withholding exclusivity from terms and symbols whose usage is of critical importance. Free speech is, however, a concern of constitutional magnitude and competitive markets are a cornerstone of a capitalist economy. Accordingly, a strong secondary line of defense is also necessary. The materials for the solution of Problem A demonstrate the main principles that protect the public's interest in language, in having a vehicle with which to discuss and compete with the trademark holder and her products, and in utilizing references that, by dint of heavy advertising, have become a part of the cultural heritage. Part B illustrates the special problem of abandonment.

PART A: TRADEMARKS AS LANGUAGE

1. PRINCIPAL PROBLEM A

Our client, Kathleen Boddie, has been a masseuse since October, 1988, when she opened a small massage parlor, "Boddie Workers," in Greenwich Village, New York City. Kathleen uses all her own massage oils, which are made of plants, herbs, fruits, flowers, and seeds. Because she cares about nature, she has carefully avoided ingredients that have been tested on animals. When massage became popular, Kathleen decided to expand her business to the greater New York area. In January, 1990, she opened a second parlor in Westport, Connecticut, which is a very wealthy community about 50 miles from the Greenwich Village location.

Both parlors are managed from Kathleen's tiny headquarters in Greenwich Village and are staffed by masseuses and masseurs that she has personally trained. Ads run in New York Magazine (which also did a small feature on her parlors), The Connecticut Shopper, and The National Body Builder Newsletter.

Kathleen's problems began in March 1990, when The Body Works, Ltd., an English company that manufactures and sells soaps, perfumes, bath oils, and cosmetics, opened its first American store, Body Works, in Deerfield, Illinois. Since that time, the company has expanded across the Midwest and the West Coast. It has recently opened a store in New York City and is looking for sites in Boston, Massachusetts and in Westport, Connecticut.

Kathleen's operation came to the English company's attention in an unusual way. The Body Works, Ltd. advertises extensively in national papers such as the Chicago Tribune, the New York Times and the Wall Street Journal. The ads, which feature a cute little bunny rabbit, claim that the products sold are made of natural ingredients and that no animals have been used to test them. As soon as she saw the first ad, Kathleen's professional interest was piqued. On a trip to Chicago, she stopped in Deerfield, purchased a bottle of bath oil, and then had it analyzed. When it turned out to contain a synthetic color that Kathleen knew had been tested on rabbits, she changed her ads to include a cartoon strongly resembling the Body Works' bunny. Enfeebled and dressed in a hospital gown, the bunny has a word balloon overhead with the words, "WHAT'S UP **NOW**, DOC?" Underneath, the ad says:

BODDIE WORKERS: FOR PEOPLE WHO CARE
BODY WORKS: FOR PEOPLE WHO DON'T

The ads then list the addresses of Kathleen's parlors. The enfeebled version of the Body Works bunny has proved popular with animal-rights advocates. To publicize the issue further, Kathleen now sells mugs and tee shirts featuring the same cartoon as her ads.

The Body Works, Ltd. has sued Kathleen under the Lanham Act, seeking to enjoin her from using the name "Boddie Workers" for her parlors and from using the words "Body Works" and the sickly bunny in her ads and on her mugs and tee-shirts. In thinking about how to defend this suit, keep in mind that Body Works applied to federally register the term "Body Works" and the bunny in November 1988 based on its own prior registration in the United Kingdom. The marks were placed on the Principal Register in December 1989. Kathleen has never registered "Boddie Workers."

2.   MATERIALS FOR SOLUTION OF PRINCIPAL PROBLEM A

A.   STATUTORY MATERIALS: §§ 1057, 1064–1065, 1072, 1114–1115, & 1126–1127

B.   CASES:

Dawn Donut Company, Inc. v. Hart's Food Stores, Inc.

United States Court of Appeals, Second Circuit, 1959.
267 F.2d 358.

■ LUMBARD, CIRCUIT JUDGE.

The principal question is whether the plaintiff, a wholesale distributor of doughnuts and other baked goods under its federally registered trademarks "Dawn" and "Dawn Donut," is entitled under the provisions of the Lanham Trade–Mark Act to enjoin the defendant from using the mark "Dawn" in connection with the retail sale of doughnuts and baked goods entirely within a six county area of New York State surrounding the city of Rochester. The primary difficulty arises from the fact that although plaintiff licenses purchasers of its mixes to use its trademarks in connection with the retail sales of food products made from the mixes, it has not licensed or otherwise exploited the mark at the retail level in defendant's market area for some thirty years.

We hold that because no likelihood of public confusion arises from the concurrent use of the mark in connection with retail sales of doughnuts and other baked goods in separate trading areas, and because there is no present likelihood that plaintiff will expand its retail use of the mark into defendant's market area, plaintiff is not now entitled to any relief under the Lanham Act, 15 U.S.C.A. § 1114. Accordingly, we affirm the district court's dismissal of plaintiff's complaint.

This is not to say that the defendant has acquired any permanent right to use the mark in its trading area. On the contrary, we hold that because of the effect of the constructive notice provision of the Lanham Act, should the plaintiff expand its retail activities into the six county area, upon a proper application and showing to the district court, it may enjoin defendant's use of the mark.

Plaintiff, Dawn Donut Co., Inc., of Jackson, Michigan since June 1, 1922 has continuously used the trademark 'Dawn' upon 25 to 100 pound bags of doughnut mix which it sells to bakers in various states, including New York, and since 1935 it has similarly marketed a line of sweet dough mixes for use in the baking of coffee cakes, cinnamon rolls and oven goods in general under that mark. In 1950 cake mixes were added to the company's line of products. Dawn's sales representatives call upon bakers to solicit orders for mixes and the orders obtained are filled by shipment to the purchaser either directly from plaintiff's Jackson, Michigan plant, where the mixes are manufactured, or from a local warehouse within the customer's state. For some years plaintiff maintained a warehouse in Jamestown, New York, from which shipments were made, but sometime prior to the commencement of this suit in 1954 it discontinued this warehouse and has since then shipped its mixes to its New York customers directly from Michigan.

Plaintiff furnishes certain buyers of its mixes, principally those who agree to become exclusive Dawn Donut Shops, with advertising and packaging material bearing the trademark 'Dawn' and permits these bakers to sell goods made from the mixes to the consuming public under that trademark. These display materials are supplied either as a courtesy or at a moderate price apparently to stimulate and promote the sale of plaintiff's mixes.

The district court found that with the exception of one Dawn Donut Shop operated in the city of Rochester, New York during 1926–27, plaintiff's licensing of its mark in connection with the retail sale of doughnuts in the state of New York has been confined to areas not less than 60 miles from defendant's trading area. The court also found that for the past eighteen years plaintiff's present New York state representative has, without interruption, made regular calls upon bakers in the city of Rochester, N.Y., and in neighboring towns and cities, soliciting orders for plaintiff's mixes and that throughout this period orders have been filled and shipments made of plaintiff's mixes from Jackson, Michigan into the city of Rochester. But it does not appear that any of these purchasers of plaintiff's mixes employed the plaintiff's mark in connection with retail sales.

The defendant, Hart Food Stores, Inc., owns and operates a retail grocery chain within the New York counties of Monroe, Wayne, Livingston, Genesee, Ontario and Wyoming. The products of defendant's bakery, Starhart Bakeries, Inc., are distributed through these stores, thus confining the distribution of defendant's product to an area within a 45 mile radius of Rochester. Its advertising of doughnuts and other baked products over television and radio and in newspapers is also limited to this area. Defendant's bakery corporation was formed on April 13, 1951 and first used the imprint "Dawn" in packaging its products on August 30, 1951. The district court found that the defendant adopted the mark "Dawn" without any actual knowledge of plaintiff's use or federal registration of the mark, selecting it largely because of a slogan "Baked at midnight, delivered at Dawn" which was originated by defendant's president and used by defendant in its bakery operations from 1929 to 1935. Defendant's president testified, however, that no investigation was made prior to the adoption of the mark to see if anyone else was employing it. Plaintiff's marks were registered federally in 1927, and their registration was renewed in 1947. Therefore by virtue of the Lanham Act, 15 U.S.C.A. § 1072, the defendant had constructive notice of plaintiff's marks as of July 5, 1947, the effective date of the Act.

Defendant's principal contention is that because plaintiff has failed to exploit the mark "Dawn" for some thirty years at the retail level in the Rochester trading area, plaintiff should not be accorded the exclusive right to use the mark in this area.

We reject this contention as inconsistent with the scope of protection afforded a federal registrant by the Lanham Act.

Prior to the passage of the Lanham Act courts generally held that the owner of a registered trademark could not sustain an action for infringement against another who, without knowledge of the registration, used the mark in a different trading area from that exploited by the registrant so that public confusion was unlikely. By being the first to adopt a mark in an area without knowledge of its prior registration, a junior user of a mark could gain the right to exploit the mark exclusively in that market.

But the Lanham Act, 15 U.S.C.A. § 1072, provides that registration of a trademark on the principal register is constructive notice of the registrant's claim of ownership. Thus, by eliminating the defense of good faith and lack of knowledge, § 1072 affords nationwide protection to registered marks, regardless of the areas in which the registrant actually uses the mark.

That such is the purpose of Congress is further evidenced by 15 U.S.C.A. § 1115(a) and (b) which make the certificate of registration evidence of the registrant's "exclusive right to use the * * * mark in commerce." "Commerce" is defined in 15 U.S.C.A. 1127 to include all the commerce which may lawfully be regulated by Congress. These two provisions of the Lanham Act make it plain that the fact that the defendant employed the mark "Dawn," without actual knowledge of plaintiff's registration, at the retail level in a limited geographical area of New York state before the plaintiff used the mark in that market, does not entitle it either to exclude the plaintiff from using the mark in that area or to use the mark concurrently once the plaintiff licenses the mark or otherwise exploits it in connection with retail sales in the area.

Accordingly, we turn to the question of whether on this record plaintiff has made a sufficient showing to warrant the issuance of an injunction against defendant's use of the mark "Dawn" in a trading area in which the plaintiff has for thirty years failed to employ its registered mark.

The Lanham Act, 15 U.S.C.A. § 1114, sets out the standard for awarding a registrant relief against the unauthorized use of his mark by another. It provides that the registrant may enjoin only that concurrent use which creates a likelihood of public confusion as to the origin of the products in connection with which the marks are used. Therefore if the use of the marks by the registrant and the unauthorized user are confined to two sufficiently distinct and geographically separate markets, with no likelihood that the registrant will expand his use into defendant's market, so that no public confusion is possible, then the registrant is not entitled to enjoin the junior user's use of the mark.

As long as plaintiff and defendant confine their use of the mark "Dawn" in connection with the retail sale of baked goods to their present separate trading areas it is clear that no public confusion is likely.

The district court took note of what it deemed common knowledge, that "retail purchasers of baked goods, because of the perishable nature of such goods, usually make such purchases reasonably close to their homes, say within about 25 miles, and retail purchases of such goods beyond that distance are for all practical considerations negligible." No objection is made to this finding and nothing appears in the record which contradicts it as applied to this case.

Moreover, we note that it took plaintiff three years to learn of defendant's use of the mark and bring this suit, even though the plaintiff was doing some wholesale business in the Rochester area. This is a strong indication that no confusion arose or is likely to arise either from concurrent use of the marks at the retail level in geographically separate trading areas or from its concurrent use at different market levels, viz. retail and wholesale in the same area.

The decisive question then is whether plaintiff's use of the mark "Dawn" at the retail level is likely to be confined to its current area of use or whether in the normal course of its business, it is likely to expand the retail use of the mark into defendant's trading area. If such expansion were probable, then the concurrent use of the marks would give rise to the conclusion that there was a likelihood of confusion.

The district court found that in view of the plaintiff's inactivity for about thirty years in exploiting its trademarks in defendant's trading area at the retail level either by advertising directed at retail purchasers or by retail sales through authorized licensed users, there was no reasonable expectation that plaintiff would extend its retail operations into defendant's trading area. There is ample evidence in the record to support this conclusion and we cannot say that it is clearly erroneous.

However, because of the effect we have attributed to the constructive notice provision of the Lanham Act, the plaintiff may later, upon a proper showing of an intent to use the mark at the retail level in defendant's market area, be entitled to enjoin defendant's use of the mark.

[The remainder of this opinion, which deals with abandonment, appears in Part B of the Assignment.]

The New Kids on the Block v. News America Publishing, Inc.

United States Court of Appeals, Ninth Circuit, 1992.
971 F.2d 302.

■ KOZINSKI, CIRCUIT JUDGE.

The individual plaintiffs perform professionally as The New Kids on the Block, reputedly one of today's hottest musical acts. This case requires us to weigh their rights in that name against the rights of others to use it in identifying the New Kids as the subjects of public opinion polls.

Background

No longer are entertainers limited to their craft in marketing themselves to the public. This is the age of the multi-media publicity blitzkrieg: Trading on their popularity, many entertainers hawk posters, T-shirts, badges, coffee mugs and the like—handsomely supplementing their incomes while boosting their public images. The New Kids are no exception; the record in this case indicates there are more than 500 products or services bearing the New Kids trademark. Among these are services taking advantage of a recent development in telecommunications: 900 area code numbers, where the caller is charged a fee, a portion of which is paid to the call recipient. Fans can call various New Kids 900 numbers to listen to the New Kids talk about themselves, to listen to other fans talk about the New Kids, or to leave messages for the New Kids and other fans.

The defendants, two newspapers of national circulation, conducted separate polls of their readers seeking an answer to a pressing question: Which one of the New Kids is the most popular? USA Today's announcement contained a picture of the New Kids and asked, "Who's the best on the block?" The announcement listed a 900 number for voting, noted that "any USA Today profits from this phone line will go to charity," and closed with the following: "New Kids on the Block are pop's hottest group. Which of the five is your fave? Or are they a turn off? . . . Each call costs 50 cents. Results in Friday's Life section." The Star's announcement, under a picture of the New Kids, went to the heart of the matter: "Now which kid is the sexiest?" The announcement, which appeared in the middle of a page containing a story on a New Kids concert, also stated: Which of the New Kids on the Block would you most like to move next door? STAR wants to know which cool New Kid is the hottest with our readers. Readers were directed to a 900 number to register their votes; each call cost 95 cents per minute.

Fearing that the two newspapers were undermining their hegemony over their fans, the New Kids filed a shotgun complaint in federal court raising no fewer than ten claims [under the common law of unfair competition and the Lanham Act.] The two papers raised the First Amendment as a defense, on the theory that the polls were part and parcel of their "newsgathering activities." The district court granted summary judgment for defendants. 745 F.Supp. 1540 (C.D.Cal.1990).

Discussion

I

A. Throughout the development of trademark law, the purpose of trademarks remained constant and limited: Identification of the manufacturer or sponsor of a good or the provider of a service. And the wrong protected against was traditionally equally limited: Preventing producers from free-riding on their rivals' marks. Justice Story outlined the classic scenario a century and a half ago when he described a case of "unmitigated and designed infringement of the rights of the plaintiffs, for the purpose of defrauding the public and taking from the plaintiffs the fair earnings of their skill, labor and enterprise." Taylor v. Carpenter, 23 F.Cas. 742, 744 (C.C.D.Mass.1844). The core protection of the Lanham Act remains faithful to this conception. See 15 U.S.C.A. § 1114 (prohibiting unauthorized use in commerce of registered marks). Indeed, this area of the law is generally referred to as "unfair competition"—unfair because, by using a rival's mark, the infringer capitalizes on the investment of time, money and resources of his competitor; unfair also because, by doing so, he obtains the consumer's hard-earned dollar through something akin to fraud. See Paul Heald, Federal Intellectual Property Law and the Economics of Preemption, 76 Iowa L.Rev. 959, 1002–03 (1991).

A trademark is a limited property right in a particular word, phrase or symbol. And although English is a language rich in imagery, we need not belabor the point that some words, phrases or symbols better convey their intended meanings than others. See San Francisco Arts & Athletics, Inc. v. U.S.O.C., 483 U.S. 522, 569, 107 S.Ct. 2971, 2998, 97 L.Ed.2d 427 (1987)(Brennan, J., dissenting)("[A] jacket reading 'I Strongly Resent the Draft' would not have conveyed Cohen's message."). Indeed, the primary cost of recognizing property rights in trademarks is the removal of words from (or perhaps non-entrance into) our language. Thus, the holder of a trademark will be denied protection if it is (or becomes) generic, i.e., if it does not relate exclusively to the trademark owner's product. See, e.g., Kellogg Co. v. National Biscuit Co., 305 U.S. 111, 59 S.Ct. 109, 83 L.Ed. 73 (1938)("shredded wheat"); Eastern Air Lines, Inc. v. New York Air Lines, Inc., 559 F.Supp. 1270 (S.D.N.Y.1983) ("air-shuttle" to describe hourly plane service). This requirement allays fears that producers will deplete the stock of useful words by asserting exclusive rights in them.[a] When a trademark comes to describe a class of goods rather than an individual product, the courts will hold as a matter of law that use of that mark does not imply sponsorship or endorsement of the product by the original holder.

A related problem arises when a trademark also describes a person, a place or an attribute of a product. If the trademark holder were allowed exclusive rights in such use, the language would be depleted in much the same way as if generic words were protectable. Thus trademark law recognizes a defense where the mark is used only "to describe the goods or services of [a] party, or their geographic origin." 15 U.S.C.A. § 1115(b)(4).

---

[a] It's far more convenient, for example, to ask your local pharmacist for "aspirin"—once a trademark—than to remember or pronounce "salicylic acid." An interesting question is whether a word, although once generic, may become protectable. For example, the word "Jeep," which originally meant a general purpose military vehicle and, later, any rugged sport-utility vehicle, is now being used as a trademark by Chrysler. Cf. Crescent Tool Co. v. Kilborn & Bishop Co., 247 F. 299 (2d Cir.1917) (protecting plaintiff's use of the trademark "Crescent," which originally described a certain kind of wrench).

"The 'fair-use' defense, in essence, forbids a trademark registrant to appropriate a descriptive term for his exclusive use and so prevent others from accurately describing a characteristic of their goods." Soweco, Inc. v. Shell Oil Co., 617 F.2d 1178, 1185 (5th Cir.1980). Once again, the courts will hold as a matter of law that the original producer does not sponsor or endorse another product that uses his mark in a descriptive manner. See, e.g., Schmid Laboratories v. Youngs Drug Products Corp., 482 F.Supp. 14 (D.N.J.1979)("ribbed" condoms).

With many well-known trademarks, such as Jell–O, Scotch tape and Kleenex, there are equally informative non-trademark words describing the products (gelatin, cellophane tape and facial tissue). But sometimes there is no descriptive substitute, and a problem closely related to genericity and descriptiveness is presented when many goods and services are effectively identifiable only by their trademarks. For example, one might refer to "the two-time world champions" or "the professional basketball team from Chicago," but it's far simpler (and more likely to be understood) to refer to the Chicago Bulls. In such cases, use of the trademark does not imply sponsorship or endorsement of the product because the mark is used only to describe the thing, rather than to identify its source.

Indeed, it is often virtually impossible to refer to a particular product for purposes of comparison, criticism, point of reference or any other such purpose without using the mark. For example, reference to a large automobile manufacturer based in Michigan would not differentiate among the Big Three; reference to a large Japanese manufacturer of home electronics would narrow the field to a dozen or more companies. Much useful social and commercial discourse would be all but impossible if speakers were under threat of an infringement lawsuit every time they made reference to a person, company or product by using its trademark.

A good example of this is Volkswagenwerk Aktiengesellschaft v. Church, 411 F.2d 350 (9th Cir.1969), where we held that Volkswagen could not prevent an automobile repair shop from using its mark. We recognized that in "advertising [the repair of Volkswagens, it] would be difficult, if not impossible, for [Church] to avoid altogether the use of the word 'Volkswagen' or its abbreviation 'VW,' which are the normal terms which, to the public at large, signify appellant's cars." Id. at 352. Church did not suggest to customers that he was part of the Volkswagen organization or that his repair shop was sponsored or authorized by VW; he merely used the words "Volkswagen" and "VW" to convey information about the types of cars he repaired. Therefore, his use of the Volkswagen trademark was not an infringing use.

The First Circuit confronted a similar problem when the holder of the trademark "Boston Marathon" tried to stop a television station from using the name: "[T]he words 'Boston Marathon' . . . do more than call attention to Channel 5's program; they also describe the event that Channel 5 will broadcast. Common sense suggests (consistent with the record here) that a viewer who sees those words flash upon the screen will believe simply that Channel 5 will show, or is showing, or has shown, the marathon, not that

Channel 5 has some special approval from the [trademark holder] to do so. In technical trademark jargon, the use of words for descriptive purposes is called a 'fair use,' and the law usually permits it even if the words themselves also constitute a trademark." WCVB–TV v. Boston Athletic Ass'n, 926 F.2d 42, 46 (1st Cir.1991). Similarly, competitors may use a rival's trademark in advertising and other channels of communication if the use is not false or misleading. See, e.g., Smith v. Chanel, Inc., 402 F.2d 562 (9th Cir.1968)(maker of imitation perfume may use original's trademark in promoting product).

Cases like these are best understood as involving a non-trademark use of a mark—a use to which the infringement laws simply do not apply, just as videotaping television shows for private home use does not implicate the copyright holder's exclusive right to reproduction.[b] Indeed, we may generalize a class of cases where the use of the trademark does not attempt to capitalize on consumer confusion or to appropriate the cachet of one product for a different one. Such nominative use of a mark—where the only word reasonably available to describe a particular thing is pressed into service—lies outside the strictures of trademark law: Because it does not implicate the source-identification function that is the purpose of trademark, it does not constitute unfair competition; such use is fair because it does not imply sponsorship or endorsement by the trademark holder. "When the mark is used in a way that does not deceive the public we see no such sanctity in the word as to prevent its being used to tell the truth." Prestonettes, Inc. v. Coty, 264 U.S. 359, 368, 44 S.Ct. 350, 351, 68 L.Ed. 731 (1924)(Holmes, J.).

To be sure, this is not the classic fair use case where the defendant has used the plaintiff's mark to describe the defendant's own product. Here, the New Kids trademark is used to refer to the New Kids themselves. We therefore do not purport to alter the test applicable in the paradigmatic fair use case. If the defendant's use of the plaintiff's trademark refers to something other than the plaintiff's product, the traditional fair use inquiry will continue to govern. But, where the defendant uses a trademark to describe the plaintiff's product, rather than its own, we hold that a commercial user is entitled to a nominative fair use defense provided he meets the following three requirements: First, the product or service in question must be one not readily identifiable without use of the trademark; second, only so much of the mark or marks may be used as is reasonably

[b] The common law has recognized a fair use defense to claims of copyright infringement involving relatively harmless violations for centuries. [It is now codified in 17 U.S.C.A. § 107.] Sound policies underlie the fair use defense. The copyright holder has a property interest in preventing others from reaping the fruits of his labor, not in preventing the authors and thinkers of the future from making use of, or building upon, his advances. The process of creation is often an incremental one, and advances building on past developments are far more common than radical new concepts. Where the infringement is small in relation to the new work created, the fair user is profiting largely from his own creative efforts rather than free-riding on another's work. A prohibition on all copying whatsoever would stifle the free flow of ideas without serving any legitimate interest of the copyright holder.

necessary to identify the product or service;[c] and third, the user must do nothing that would, in conjunction with the mark, suggest sponsorship or endorsement by the trademark holder.

B. The New Kids do not claim there was anything false or misleading about the newspapers' use of their mark. Rather, the first seven causes of action, while purporting to state different claims, all hinge on one key factual allegation: that the newspapers' use of the New Kids name in conducting the unauthorized polls somehow implied that the New Kids were sponsoring the polls. It is no more reasonably possible, however, to refer to the New Kids as an entity than it is to refer to the Chicago Bulls, Volkswagens or the Boston Marathon without using the trademark. Indeed, how could someone not conversant with the proper names of the individual New Kids talk about the group at all? While plaintiffs' trademark certainly deserves protection against copycats and those who falsely claim that the New Kids have endorsed or sponsored them, such protection does not extend to rendering newspaper articles, conversations, polls and comparative advertising impossible. The first nominative use requirement is therefore met.

Also met are the second and third requirements. Both The Star and USA Today reference the New Kids only to the extent necessary to identify them as the subject of the polls; they do not use the New Kids' distinctive logo or anything else that isn't needed to make the announcements intelligible to readers. Finally, nothing in the announcements suggests joint sponsorship or endorsement by the New Kids. The USA Today announcement implies quite the contrary by asking whether the New Kids might be "a turn off." The Star's poll is more effusive but says nothing that expressly or by fair implication connotes endorsement or joint sponsorship on the part of the New Kids.

The New Kids argue that, even if the newspapers are entitled to a nominative fair use defense for the announcements, they are not entitled to it for the polls themselves, which were money-making enterprises separate and apart from the newspapers' reporting businesses. According to plaintiffs, defendants could have minimized the intrusion into their rights by using an 800 number or asking readers to call in on normal telephone lines which would not have resulted in a profit to the newspapers based on the conduct of the polls themselves.

The New Kids see this as a crucial difference, distinguishing this case from Volkswagenwerk, WCBV–TV and other nominative use cases. The New Kids' argument in support of this distinction is not entirely implausible: They point out that their fans, like everyone else, have limited resources. Thus a dollar spent calling the newspapers' 900 lines to express loyalty to the New Kids may well be a dollar not spent on New Kids products and services, including the New Kids' own 900 numbers. In short,

---

[c] Thus, a soft drink competitor would be entitled to compare its product to Coca-Cola or Coke, but would not be entitled to use Coca-Cola's distinctive lettering.

plaintiffs argue that a nominative fair use defense is inapplicable where the use in question competes directly with that of the trademark holder.

We reject this argument. While the New Kids have a limited property right in their name, that right does not entitle them to control their fans' use of their own money. Where, as here, the use does not imply sponsorship or endorsement, the fact that it is carried on for profit and in competition with the trademark holder's business is beside the point. Voting for their favorite New Kid may be, as plaintiffs point out, a way for fans to articulate their loyalty to the group, and this may diminish the resources available for products and services they sponsor. But the trademark laws do not give the New Kids the right to channel their fans' enthusiasm (and dollars) only into items licensed or authorized by them. The New Kids could not use the trademark laws to prevent the publication of an unauthorized group biography or to censor all parodies or satires which use their name. We fail to see a material difference between these examples and the use here.

II

The New Kids raise three additional claims that merit brief attention.

A. The New Kids claim that USA Today's and The Star's use of their name amounted to both commercial and common law misappropriation under California law. Although there are subtle differences between these two causes of action, all that's material here is a key similarity between them: The papers have a complete defense to both claims if they used the New Kids name "in connection with any news, public affairs, or sports broadcast or account" which was true in all material respects. See Cal.Civ. Code § 3344(d).

B. The New Kids' remaining claim is for intentional interference with prospective economic advantage, but they ignore the maxim that all's fair in love, war and the free market. Plaintiffs' case rests on the assumption that the polls operated to siphon off the New Kids' fans or divert their resources away from "official" New Kids products. Even were we to accept this premise, no tort claim has been made out: "So long as the plaintiff's contractual relations are merely contemplated or potential, it is considered to be in the interest of the public that any competitor should be free to divert them to himself by all fair and reasonable means. . . . In short, it is no tort to beat a business rival to prospective customers." A–Mark Coin Co. v. General Mills, Inc., 148 Cal.App.3d 312, 323, 195 Cal.Rptr. 859 (1983).

L.L. Bean, Inc. v. Drake Publishers, Inc.

United States Court of Appeals, First Circuit, 1987.
811 F.2d 26.

■ BOWNES, CIRCUIT JUDGE.

Imitation may be the highest form of flattery, but plaintiff-appellee L.L. Bean, Inc., was neither flattered nor amused when High Society magazine published a prurient parody of Bean's famous catalog. Defendant-appellant Drake Publishers, Inc., owns High Society, a monthly periodical featuring adult erotic entertainment. Its October 1984 issue contained a two-page article entitled "L.L. Beam's Back–To–School–Sex–Catalog." The article was labelled on the magazine's contents page as "humor" and "parody." The article displayed a facsimile of Bean's trademark and featured pictures of nude models in sexually explicit positions using "products" that were described in a crudely humorous fashion.

L.L. Bean sought a temporary restraining order to remove the October 1984 issue from circulation. The complaint alleged trademark infringement, unfair competition, trademark dilution, deceptive trade practices, interference with prospective business advantage and trade libel. [Among other things, the district court granted] Bean summary judgment with respect to the trademark dilution claim raised under Maine law. Me.Rev. Stat.Ann. tit. 10, § 1530 (1981). It ruled that the article had tarnished Bean's trademark by undermining the goodwill and reputation associated with the mark. The court also held that enjoining the publication of a parody to prevent trademark dilution did not offend the first amendment. An injunction issued prohibiting further publication or distribution of the "L.L. Beam Sex Catalog." [Drake appealed.]

I

A trademark is a word, name or symbol adopted and used by a manufacturer or merchant to identify goods and distinguish them from those manufactured by others. 15 U.S.C.A. § 1127 (1985 Supp.). One need only open a magazine or turn on television to witness the pervasive influence of trademarks in advertising and commerce. Designer labels appear on goods ranging from handbags to chocolates to every possible form of clothing. Commercial advertising slogans, which can be registered as trademarks, have become part of national political campaigns. "Thus, trademarks have become a natural target of satirists who seek to comment on this integral part of the national culture." Dorsen, Satiric Appropriation and the Law of Libel, Trademark and Copyright: Remedies Without Wrongs, 65 B.U.L.Rev. 923, 939 (1986); Note, Trademark Parody: A Fair Use and First Amendment Analysis, 72 Va.L.Rev. 1079 (1986).

The ridicule conveyed by parody inevitably conflicts with one of the underlying purposes of the Maine anti-dilution statute, which is to protect against the tarnishment of the goodwill and reputation associated with a particular trademark. The court below invoked this purpose as the basis for its decision to issue an injunction. The issue before us is whether enjoining the publication of appellant's parody violates the first amendment guarantees of freedom of expression.

II

The district court disposed of the first amendment concerns raised in this matter by relying on the approach taken in Dallas Cowboys Cheerleaders, Inc. v. Pussycat Cinema, Ltd., 604 F.2d 200 (2d Cir.1979). In rejecting Drake's claim that the first amendment protects the unauthorized use of another's trademark in the process of conveying a message, the district court cited the following language from Dallas Cowboys Cheerleaders: "Plaintiff's trademark is in the nature of a property right, ... and as such it need not 'yield to the exercise of First Amendment rights under circumstances where adequate alternative avenues of communication exist.' Lloyd Corp. v. Tanner, 407 U.S. 551 [92 S.Ct. 2219, 33 L.Ed.2d 131] (1972)."

We do not believe that the first amendment concerns raised here can be resolved as easily as was done in Dallas Cowboys Cheerleaders. Aside from our doubts about whether there are alternative means of parodying plaintiff's catalog, we do not think the court fully assessed the nature of a trademark owner's property rights.

The limits on the scope of a trademark owner's property rights was considered recently in Lucasfilm Ltd. v. High Frontier, 622 F.Supp. 931 (D.D.C.1985). In that case, the owners of the trademark "Star Wars" alleged injury from public interest groups that used the term in commercial advertisements presenting their views on President Reagan's Strategic Defense Initiative. Judge Gesell stressed that the sweep of a trademark owner's rights extends only to injurious, unauthorized commercial uses of the mark by another. 622 F.Supp. at 933–35. Trademark rights do not entitle the owner to quash an unauthorized use of the mark by another who is communicating ideas or expressing points of view. Id.

III

The district court's opinion suggests that tarnishment may be found when a trademark is used without authorization in a context which diminishes the positive associations with the mark. Neither the strictures of the first amendment nor the history and theory of anti-dilution law permit a finding of tarnishment based solely on the presence of an unwholesome or negative context in which a trademark is used without authorization. Such a reading of the anti-dilution statute unhinges it from its origins in the marketplace. A trademark is tarnished when consumer capacity to associate it with the appropriate products or services has been diminished. The threat of tarnishment arises when the goodwill and reputation of a plaintiff's trademark is linked to products which are of shoddy quality or which conjure associations that clash with the associations generated by the owner's lawful use of the mark: "[T]he risk may be that of detracting from the plaintiff's good will by the possibility that a defendant's use of plaintiff's unique mark will tarnish plaintiff's trade name by reason of public dissatisfaction with defendant's product and a resultant holding of this dissatisfaction against plaintiff. An alternative to this ... risk is the danger of public identification of plaintiff's trade name or mark with a product or service of a type incompatible with the quality and prestige previously attached by the public to the plaintiff's product." Tiffany & Co. v. Boston Club, Inc., 231 F.Supp. 836, 844 (D.Mass.1964).

As indicated by Judge Caffrey in Tiffany, the dilution injury stems from an unauthorized effort to market incompatible products or services by trading on another's trademark. The Constitution is not offended when the anti-dilution statute is applied to prevent a defendant from using a trademark without permission in order to merchandise dissimilar products or services. Any residual effect on first amendment freedoms should be balanced against the need to fulfill the legitimate purpose of the anti-dilution statute. The law of trademark dilution has developed to combat an unauthorized and harmful appropriation of a trademark by another for the purpose of identifying, manufacturing, merchandising or promoting dissimilar products or services. The harm occurs when a trademark's identity and integrity—its capacity to command respect in the market—is undermined due to its inappropriate and unauthorized use by other market actors. When presented with such circumstances, courts have found that trademark owners have suffered harm despite the fact that redressing such harm entailed some residual impact on the rights of expression of commercial actors. See, e.g., Chemical Corp. of America v. Anheuser–Busch, Inc., 306 F.2d 433 (5th Cir.1962), cert. denied, 372 U.S. 965, 83 S.Ct. 1089, 10 L.Ed.2d 129 (1963)(floor wax and insecticide maker's slogan, "Where there's life, there's bugs," harmed strength of defendant's slogan, "Where there's life, there's Bud."); Original Appalachian Artworks, Inc. v. Topps Chewing Gum, 642 F.Supp. 1031 (N.D.Ga.1986)(merchandiser of "Garbage Pail Kids" stickers and products injured owner of Cabbage Patch Kids mark); General Electric Co. v. Alumpa Coal Co., 205 U.S.P.Q. (BNA) 1036 (D.Mass.1979)("Genital Electric" monogram on underpants and T-shirts harmful to plaintiff's trademark).

While the cases cited above might appear at first glance to be factually analogous to the instant one, they are distinguishable for two reasons. First, they all involved unauthorized commercial uses of another's trademark. Second, none of those cases involved a defendant using a plaintiff's trademark as a vehicle for an editorial or artistic parody. In contrast to the cases cited, the instant defendant used plaintiff's mark solely for noncommercial purposes. Appellant's parody constitutes an editorial or artistic, rather than a commercial, use of plaintiff's mark. The article was labelled as "humor" and "parody" in the magazine's table of contents section; it took up two pages in a one-hundred-page issue; neither the article nor appellant's trademark was featured on the front or back cover of the magazine. Drake did not use Bean's mark to identify or promote goods or services to consumers; it never intended to market the "products" displayed in the parody.

We think the Constitution tolerates an incidental impact on rights of expression of commercial actors in order to prevent a defendant from unauthorizedly merchandising his products with another's trademark.[a] In

a We have no occasion to consider the constitutional limits which might be imposed on the application of anti-dilution statutes to unauthorized uses of trademarks on products whose principal purpose is to convey a message. Mutual of Omaha Ins. Co. v. Novak, 775 F.2d 247 (8th Cir.1985) (plaintiff entitled to preliminary injunction against peace activist protesting nuclear weapons proliferation by marketing "Mutant of Omaha" T-shirts). Such a situation undoubtedly would require a balancing of the harm suffered by the trademark owner against the benefit derived by the parodist and the public from the unau-

such circumstances, application of the anti-dilution statute constitutes a legitimate regulation of commercial speech, which the Supreme Court has defined as "expression related solely to the economic interests of the speaker and its audience." Central Hudson Gas & Elec. v. Public Serv. Comm'n, 447 U.S. 557, 561, 100 S.Ct. 2343, 2348, 65 L.Ed.2d 341 (1980). It offends the Constitution, however, to invoke the anti-dilution statute as a basis for enjoining the noncommercial use of a trademark by a defendant engaged in a protected form of expression.

Our reluctance to apply the anti-dilution statute to the instant case also stems from a recognition of the vital importance of parody. Although, as we have noted, parody is often offensive, it is nevertheless "deserving of substantial freedom—both as entertainment and as a form of social and literary criticism." Berlin v. E.C. Publications, Inc., 329 F.2d 541 (2d Cir.), cert. denied, 379 U.S. 822, 85 S.Ct. 46, 13 L.Ed.2d 33 (1964). It would be anomalous to diminish the protection afforded parody solely because a parodist chooses a famous trade name, rather than a famous personality, author or creative work, as its object.[b]

The district court's injunction falls not only because it trammels upon a protected form of expression, but also because it depends upon an untoward judicial evaluation of the offensiveness or unwholesomeness of the appellant's materials. The Supreme Court has recognized the threat to free speech inherent in sanctioning such evaluations. Cohen v. California, 403 U.S. 15, 25, 91 S.Ct. 1780, 1788, 29 L.Ed.2d 284 (1971).

Reversed and remanded.

■ LEVIN H. CAMPBELL, CHIEF JUDGE (dissenting)[omitted].

Mutual of Omaha Insurance Company v. Novak

United States Court of Appeals, Eighth Circuit, 1987.
836 F.2d 397.

■ BOWMAN, CIRCUIT JUDGE.

Beginning in 1952, Mutual of Omaha Insurance Company (Mutual) acquired trademark registrations for marks used in connection with its

thorized use of a trademark on a product designed to convey a message.

b We recognize that the plaintiffs in Pillsbury Co. v. Milky Way Productions, Inc., 215 U.S.P.Q. (BNA) 124 (N.D.Ga.1981), obtained injunctive relief against Screw magazine, which had published pictures of facsimiles of Pillsbury's trade characters, "Poppin Fresh" and "Poppie Fresh," engaged in sexual intercourse and fellatio. The pictorial also featured plaintiff's trademark and the refrain of its jingle, "The Pillsbury Baking Song." While the district court granted relief under Georgia's anti-dilution statute, 215 U.S.P.Q.

at 135, it did so only after specifically declining to consider whether defendants' presentation constituted a parody. Id. at 129–30. The defendants in Pillsbury had tried to proffer parody as a defense to plaintiff's copyright infringement claim; they did not assert it as a defense to the dilution claim. Pillsbury, therefore, does not stand for the proposition that the publication of a parody properly may be enjoined under an anti-dilution statute, since the court never considered whether defendants had presented a parody, and defendants never asserted parody as a defense to the dilution claim.

insurance services and a television program it sponsors. These marks include the familiar "Indian head" logo and the designations "Mutual of Omaha" and "Mutual of Omaha's Wild Kingdom."

In 1983 Franklyn Novak (Novak) produced a design reminiscent of the Mutual marks. It uses the words "Mutant of Omaha" and depicts a side view of a feather-bonneted, emaciated human head. Novak initially put the design on T-shirts along with the words "Nuclear Holocaust Insurance." Novak marketed approximately 4000 of these shirts before Mutual obtained a preliminary injunction. He also had the design placed on sweatshirts, caps, buttons, and coffee mugs, which he has offered for sale at retail shops, exhibitions, and fairs. Novak also has advertised such merchandise on television and in newspapers and magazines.

[Mutual sued for trademark infringement under §§ 1114(1) and 43(a). Upon finding that Novak's use of the design created a likelihood of confusion as to Mutual's sponsorship of or affiliation with Novak's merchandise, the District Court permanently enjoined Novak from advertising or marketing T-shirts, coffee mugs, and other products featuring the designations "Mutant of Omaha," "Mutant Kingdom," and "Mutant of Omaha's Mutant Kingdom," or confusingly similar designations, and also permanently enjoined Novak from using as a logo a design confusingly similar to Mutual's "Indian head" logo. Novak appealed. After reviewing the record, including survey evidence demonstrating a likelihood of confusion, the Eighth Circuit stated:]

The record contains ample support for the District Court's finding of a likelihood of confusion. We therefore cannot say that this pivotal finding is clearly erroneous.

The cases Novak relies upon to support his view that there is no likelihood of confusion here, but merely obvious parody, lack persuasiveness in relation to the situation before us. Those cases either did not involve surveys demonstrating confusion or involved surveys of doubtful validity. For example, in Carson v. Here's Johnny Portable Toilets, Inc., 698 F.2d 831 (6th Cir.1983), the plaintiffs presented no surveys demonstrating confusion, and in Tetley, Inc. v. Topps Chewing Gum, Inc., 556 F.Supp. 785, 793 (E.D.N.Y.1983), the court noted that the plaintiff presented no evidence at all of either the likelihood of or actual confusion.

Novak argues that his use of the design in question is an exercise of his right of free speech and is protected by the First Amendment. We believe, however, that the protection afforded by the First Amendment does not give Novak license to infringe the rights of Mutual. Mutual's trademarks are a form of property, Hanover Star Milling Co. v. Metcalf, 240 U.S. 403, 413, 36 S.Ct. 357, 360, 60 L.Ed. 713 (1916), and Mutual's rights therein need not "yield to the exercise of First Amendment rights under circumstances where adequate alternative avenues of communication exist." Lloyd Corp. v. Tanner, 407 U.S. 551, 567, 92 S.Ct. 2219, 2228, 33 L.Ed.2d 131 (1972). Given the circumstances of this case, Mutual's property rights should not yield. The injunction our decision upholds prohibits Novak's conduct only insofar as Novak uses Mutual's marks as logos or "to market, advertise, or identify [his] services or products." Designated Record (D.R.) at 76–77. Other avenues for Novak to express his views exist and are unrestricted by the injunction; for example, it in no way infringes upon the constitutional protection the First Amendment would provide were Novak to present an editorial parody in a book, magazine, or film. Because the injunction leaves open many such avenues of expression, it deprives neither Novak nor the public of the benefits of his ideas. It follows that the District Court did not violate Novak's First Amendment rights by issuing the injunction.[a]

We conclude that the District Court's finding of a likelihood of confusion between Mutual's valid trademarks and Novak's design is not clearly erroneous. That finding warrants the District Court's issuance of a permanent injunction restricting Novak's further use of his infringing design.[b]

■ HEANEY, CIRCUIT JUDGE, dissenting.

I respectfully dissent. In my view, the trial court's finding that there exists a likelihood of confusion is clearly erroneous. Moreover, the majority's holding sanctions a violation of Novak's first amendment rights. The T-shirts simply expressed a political message which irritated the officers of Mutual, who decided to swat this pesky fly buzzing around in their backyard with a sledge hammer (a federal court injunction). We should not be a party to this effort. [The remainder of the dissent is omitted.]

Quality Inns International, Inc. v. McDonald's Corp.

United States District Court for the District of Maryland, 1988.
695 F.Supp. 198.

■ NIEMEYER, DISTRICT JUDGE.

On September 21, 1987, Quality Inns International, Inc. announced a new chain of economy hotels to be marketed under the name "McSleep Inn." The response of McDonald's Corporation was immediate. It demanded by letter sent three days later that Quality International not use the name "McSleep" because it infringed on McDonald's family of marks that

---

[a] Our analysis is not at odds with L.L. Bean, Inc. v. Drake Publishers, Inc., 811 F.2d 26 (1st Cir.), appeal dismissed, 483 U.S. 1013, 107 S.Ct. 3254, 97 L.Ed.2d 753 (1987). L.L. Bean involved "editorial or artistic" use of a mark "solely for noncommercial purposes," id. at 32, and the holding did not encompass the likelihood of confusion issue. Id. at 32 n. 3 (court notes in dictum that "a parody which engenders consumer confusion would be entitled to less protection than is granted by our decision today"). By contrast, our case centers on Novak's commercial use of Mutual's marks in a way that causes consumer confusion.

[b] The dissent suggests that we are imposing liability for "satiric appropriation," post at 405, and in support of this assertion cites Dorsen, Satiric Appropriation and the Law of Libel, Trademark, and Copyright: Remedies Without Wrongs, 65 B.U.L.Rev. 923, 964 (1985). But, according to Dorsen, courts do this in trademark cases only when they abandon "the traditional trademark infringement test—likelihood of confusion." Id. at 951. We, of course, have not abandoned this test but use it as the foundation for our decision. Consonant with our holding, Dorsen writes that where likelihood of consumer confusion can be shown, the law should and does provide remedies. Dorsen, supra, at 952, 964.

are characterized by the use of the prefix "Mc" combined with a generic word. [Quality Inns then filed this declaratory judgment action.]

QUALITY INTERNATIONAL

Quality International is a Delaware corporation with its principal offices in Silver Spring, Maryland. It is engaged in the lodging business, particularly in inns, hotels, suites, and resorts.

Having no product to compete in the economy segment, Quality International designed a concept for a hotel with a smaller basic room which would rent for between $20 and $29 per night. Each room would have a queen size bed, plush carpeting, color TV, and a contiguous bathroom. There would be no conference rooms, food or other amenities on the premises, except a swimming pool in certain geographical areas. These economy hotels would all be of new construction and a consistent architecture. The name selected by Mr. Hazard for this product was "McSleep Inn." The first McSleep Inn is scheduled to open in December, 1988.

MCDONALD'S CORPORATION

McDonald's Corporation is a Delaware corporation with its principal offices in Oak Brook, Illinois. Founded by Ray A. Kroc, it opened its first restaurant in April, 1955, in Des Plaines, Illinois. It is now the largest fast food business in the world, with over 10,000 restaurants in 45 countries and over $14 billion in sales annually.

In recent years, McDonald's began to focus on a long distance travel market, defined by customers traveling on the road who are more than 30 miles from home when they use the service. Pursuing this market, McDonald's took over numerous tollway restaurants and converted them to McDonald's restaurants. After the first year of conversion, the increased sales at all of the restaurants that were converted averaged over three times the previous year's sales, and indeed the sale of gas at the neighboring gas station increased significantly, although not as much. McDonald's attributes these successes to its recognition.

The attribution to McDonald's, however, has not been totally under its control. Journalists have created their own words by adding "Mc" to a generic word. The Court was presented with literally hundreds of such uses, such as McLaw, McTax, McNews, McPaper, McSurgery, McArt, even McGod. Since the issue is raised in this action that "Mc" words have become generic, the Court will address the scope of this usage more fully below.

As part of its promotion, McDonald's created a language that it called "McLanguage" from which it developed a family of marks for its products such as McChicken, McNugget, McPizza, as well as marks outside the food area related to its business such as McStop, McKids, and McShuttle. There is no evidence that this language or these marks existed before McDonald's created them or that, outside of McDonald's sphere of promotion and presence, anyone would understand these words to mean anything. "Mc" obviously is a Scottish or Irish surname used in proper names. The use to form words, however, was unique at the time. The marks that are owned by McDonald's and that were formulated by combining "Mc" and a generic word are fanciful and enjoy a meaning that associates the product immediately with McDonald's and its products and service.

They also constitute a family of marks that is enforceable against infringing uses, and since they are fanciful they will be given the strongest protection. McDonald's Corp. v. McBagel's, Inc., 649 F.Supp. 1268 (S.D.N.Y.1986).

THIRD–PARTY USES OF "MC"

Quality International has pointed out that there are a substantial number of third-party uses of "Mc" with a generic word that would give rise to infringement to the same extent as would the mark McSleep Inn. Quality International urges that these uses by third parties are so pervasive that McDonald's should now be denied the right to enforce its marks against McSleep Inn.

The evidence established that there are many third-party uses. McHappy and McDonuts are used for baked goods and doughnuts in Ohio and the midwest area. McMaid is used for maid service franchising in various midwestern states. McDivots is used for golf accessories in the Colorado area. McFranchise is used for management consulting in the northeast. McMoose is used in Heritage Park on the east coast. McWest is used for contracting. McSports is used for a sports store in a strip shopping center. McPrint is used for franchised printing in the New York area. McQuick is used for quick change lubrications in the midwest area, mostly Indiana. McBud is a florist in the midwest. [The court went on to provide many other examples of third-party uses, both present and past.]

Permitting the use by third parties of infringing marks can be relevant to three specific issues in a trademark case. If a trademark owner has expressly or impliedly given an assurance to another user that he will not assert his trademark rights, he may be barred from enforcing his mark against that user, by reason of estoppel by acquiescence. Sweetheart Plastics, Inc. v. Detroit Forming, Inc., 743 F.2d 1039 (4th Cir.1984).

Acquiescence may be inferred from conduct as well. Thus, delay in enforcement of a mark against a defendant may become relevant to the question of estoppel by acquiescence. Whether a trademark owner delayed in enforcing its trademark rights against others, however, is not relevant to establishing an estoppel defense, since estoppel by acquiescence focuses on a plaintiff's acts toward the defendant, not toward others. Acquiescence is a personal defense that merely results in a loss of rights against the defendant.

Third-party uses permitted by the owner of a mark may also be probative of the abandonment of a mark by the owner. A mark is abandoned when any course of conduct of the owner, including acts of omission as well as commission, causes the mark to lose its significance as an indication of origin. See 15 U.S.C.A. § 1127(b). Failing to take action against an infringer has been held to be such an "act of omission." Once a mark has been held abandoned, it is free for all to use and falls into the public domain. It may be seized by another, and the person doing so gains rights against the whole world. 15 U.S.C.A. § 1115. However, as the court in Sweetheart Plastics emphasized, "[t]he issue is hardly ever 'abandonment,' because that requires proof that the mark has lost all significance as an indication of origin" and is "completely without signs of life." 743 F.2d at 1047–48.

So long as there is no abandonment or estoppel by acquiescence, a trademark owner's tolerance of third-party uses of his marks will not bar enforcement of his rights against an infringing user. It may, however, bear on the issue of the strength of his mark. The damage that third-party users of a mark can cause an owner who seeks to enforce his mark is the weakening of the mark's strength. Failure to take reasonable steps to prevent third-party uses of the mark may weaken a mark to the point where it is entitled to only a narrow scope of enforcement, and ultimately the question may become one of abandonment. However, where the owner of the mark has been reasonably diligent in protecting his rights, even though infringements exist, no intent to abandon will be inferred.

In this case Quality International does not contend that McDonald's has abandoned its family of marks or that McDonald's has acquiesced in Quality International's use of McSleep Inn. The Court likewise reaches those same conclusions based on the evidence presented. McDonald's gave no assurances, expressly or impliedly, to Quality International that it could use McSleep Inn, and McDonald's did not delay in pursuing enforcement of its marks. The evidence of third-party uses introduced by Quality Inns therefore is probative only of the strength and scope of McDonald's family of marks. These uses will not preclude the enforcement of those marks against Quality International.

The Court can point to no evidence that public awareness of McDonald's family of marks and their attribution of source to McDonald's has been lessened by the third-party uses. The more important question, and probably the only relevant one, is whether third-party uses are so prevalent that the public would not likely confuse McSleep Inn with McDonald's. The Court found no evidence to suggest impact by third-party uses on this question of confusion. Although the question is more fully encompassed in the answer to the issue whether McSleep Inn is likely to cause confusion, which is discussed below, suffice it to conclude at this point that third-party uses do not preclude McDonald's enforcement of its family of marks.

GENERIC DEFENSE

Both Mr. Hazard, Quality International's CEO, and Mr. Mosser, its vice president in charge of franchising, urged at trial that "Mc" has become a generic prefix meaning thrifty, consistent, and perhaps convenient. They urge that the notion of thriftiness comes from the association with the Scots and the perception that the Scots are thrifty. The Court was directed to the writings of H.L. Mencken, the famous Baltimore journalist and writer, who said: Nearly all the English words and phrases based on Scotch embody references to the traditional penuriousness of the Scots, for example Scotch coffee, hot water flavored with burnt biscuit; to play the Scotch organ, to put money in a cash register; Scotch pint, a two-quart bottle; Scotch sixpence, a threepence; and the Scotchman's cinema, Piccadilly Circus, because it offers many free attractions. The American Language by H.L. Mencken (4th Ed. Abridged with Annotations and Material by Raven I. [appropriately] McDavid, Jr.), at pages 388–89.

Both Mr. Hazard and Mr. Mosser acknowledge that the aspect of "Mc" that includes consistency and convenience derives from McDonald's and its extensive promotional efforts. They urge, however, that any such association with McDonald's is now lost to the public domain by common usage.

In support of the contention that "Mc" as a prefix has derived a singular meaning and become part of the language, Dr. Roger W. Shuy, a linguist from Georgetown University, reviewed hundreds of journalistic uses of the prefix "Mc" for purposes of deriving its meaning and to evidence it common usage. Several examples will give a sampling of the broad range of his findings.

The term "McFood" has been used as follows: "It's a push-button, do-it-yourself, convenience-oriented world.... Why cook when we can zap a Lean Cuisine in the micro, or order McFood from a drive-in McSpeaker." Similarly, the word McLunch has been used for what kids are eating in school.

In the area of clothes, McFashion has been used in connection with smaller, specialized express stores for kids, imitating the concept of a fast food outlet.

McMedicine has been used to refer to prompt, inexpensive medical care centers, and McSurgery becomes surgery without overnight hospital stays.

McLaw has been used to describe the legal franchise phenomenon, suggesting that legal advice is dispensed through drive-in windows. Describing franchising in other areas have been McFuneral for funeral operations; McLube or McOil Change for the fast, little drive-in shops offering ten-minute oil changes; and McMiz for franchising of the Broadway musical "Les Miserables." Even the franchising of local post office branches has been suggested to become McMail, and franchised tax preparation as McTax.

In the news and media area, USA Today has been characterized as McPaper, "fast news for the fast-food generation." There was even a book called The Making of McPaper. The distillation of books or books without substance has been referred to as McBook, and similar characterizations have been made about digested news stories, McNews.

Even culture that has been subjected to mass marketing has been characterized with the prefix "Mc." The proliferation of low-cost mass-produced art is McArt. One article even referred to McMozart.

Movies that are analogized to fast food which satisfy the appetite and taste good have been called McMovies or McCinemas. Similarly, there is McTelevision, McTelecast, and McVideo.

No subject seems to have been excluded. In connection with religion there has been a reference to McGod: "It was a difficult year for the McGod family network. [Jimmy Baker, Jimmy Swaggart, and Jerry Falwell] fought a major turf battle over control of the PTL McTelevangelism."

One article perhaps summarized it all, "This is the era of instant gratification, of poptops, quick wash, fast fix, frozen foods, McEverything."

A news report placed into evidence referred to the trial before this Court as taking place in the McCourt, which, of course, would make the judge the McJudge. While the Court understood that association with the Courthouse in Baltimore, it could not come to grips with the suggestion that the trial was before a McJudge. The Court could find few, if any, of the attributes of "Mc" used by McDonald's or by the journalists otherwise to fit. Perhaps this McPinion will fulfill that prophecy.

After reviewing these articles and numerous others, Dr. Shuy reviewed the context of the "Mc" word and derived a list of 27 definitions for the prefix "Mc": highly advertised; franchise; easy access; inexpensive; high volume; lacks prestige, comfort, cost; everyday; prepackaged; specialty chain; quick; convenient; reduces choices; self-service; mass merchandising; standardized; state of the art marketing; low brow; assembly line precision; uniform; market dominance formula; handy location; positive attitude; simple; comfortable; honest; looks okay; and working man. He reduced these to four terms which he characterizes as the definition of "Mc," that is, "basic, convenient, inexpensive, and standardized."

McDonald's retained an outside firm to do its own internal marketing research into the public perception of the meaning of "Mc" and the conclusions reached were similar to those reached by Dr. Shuy. McDonald's list, which was much shorter, distilled the following definitions: (1) "reliable at a good price," (2) "prepackaged, consistent, fast, and easy" (3) "a prefix McDonald's adds to everything it does," and (4) "processed, simplified, has the punch taken out of it."

Dr. David W. Lightfoot, a linguist from the University of Maryland, testified at trial on behalf of McDonald's. He took no issue with the meanings derived by Dr. Shuy and by McDonald's own internal survey. However, he disputed vigorously any notion that "Mc" is a generic word. He pointed out that "Mc" does not have a single easy identifiable meaning. For instance, of the 27 or so definitions derived by Dr. Shuy from the journalistic uses, many were not incorporated into Dr. Shuy's condensed definition. Dr. Lightfoot concluded that all the meanings derived by Dr. Shuy, by McDonald's and by him were essentially descriptive of McDonald's Corporation and the reputation it has earned over the years. He concluded that whether or not there was a specific reference to McDonald's Corporation in each article, in every case the allusion was to McDonald's and its family of marks in a manner that was intended to be cute and playful.

The Court concludes that indeed the uses in the press of "Mc" plus a generic word are coined and novel to each article for the playful use by the author. In each case the allusion, whether express or implied, was to McDonald's, sometimes flattering and sometimes pejorative. There was no single independent meaning of "Mc" understood in the language and its uses have been created to convey any one of several attributes that the author makes to McDonald's.

This is not analogous to a circumstance where a product is referred to so frequently by brand name that even competitive brands are called by the one name and the brand identity is lost. On the contrary, the attribution of source to McDonald's in the use of "Mc" is strong and persists. The Court notes that while most of the articles used by Dr. Shuy did not contain express allusions to McDonald's, a very similar group of articles that he did not use in his analysis, but which conveyed the same meanings, made express allusions to McDonald's. The Court therefore rejects any contention that McDonald's has lost its right to enforce its marks because "Mc" has become a prefix with a single meaning that has become part of the English language and beyond McDonald's control.

[Finding that there is sufficient likelihood that consumers will be confused, the court declared that McSleep would infringe McDonald's trademarks and permanently enjoined Quality Inns from utilizing that term.]

NOTES

1. *Cancellation.* The Introduction to this Assignment speaks of two lines for defending the public's interest in freely using words and symbols: the requirements for registration and the defenses to infringement actions. In fact, there is a third line as well, for under § 1064, any party "who believes that he is or will be damaged" by a mark on the Principal Register can petition for its cancellation. Cancellation proceedings, which are akin to the interferences described in Assignment 1, can be used to air any of the defenses to infringement that are based on the mark's suitability for registration. A mark can also be cancelled if it has been abandoned, see Part B, infra, or if it has become generic. In addition, certification marks can be cancelled if they are used discriminatorily, or for purposes other than to certify.

Cancellation proceedings have several advantages over litigation. The administrative procedure is cheaper and usually quicker than adjudication. Moreover, in most cases, cancellation is the clearest way to put a mark back into the public domain. This procedure is not, however, an appropriate vehicle for making the sorts of claims involved in *New Kids on the Block* or *L.L.Bean*. That is, it is not the place for a challenger to argue that she is using a registered mark in a manner that is not infringing.

2. *Defenses to infringement and incontestability.* Because the trademark owner has a right, after five years of continuous use, to file an affidavit rendering her mark incontestable, see § 1065 and Part B of Assignment 2, defenses to trademark infringement—and grounds for cancellation—must be divided into two categories: those that can be raised only before the mark becomes incontestable and those that can be raised at any time. Reading the statute, it can be difficult to sort the two categories out. In fact, the best way to do so is to read § 1115(b) in conjunction with § 1064. Putting these provisions together, it becomes clear that "incontestability" is something of a misnomer in that only two major defenses are lost once a mark achieves that status. These are the challenges based on §§ 1052(d) and (e): first, that the mark should not have been registered because it was confusingly similar to mark that was already in use at the time of application and second, that the mark is not entitled to protection because it is not inherently distinctive and lacks secondary meaning.

also functionality: shakespeare

This leaves more than 20 defenses that are good at any time.[1] The category includes defenses based on the geographic limits of trademarks, see Note 3, infra; the problems listed in § 1052(a)-(c); and the genericity of the mark for the goods on which it is used, see Note 6. It also encompasses the statutory defenses listed in § 1115(b): fraud in procuring registration, abandonment, use of the mark to misrepresent source, fair use, pre-registration use by the defendant, prior registration by the defendant, use of the mark to violate the antitrust laws, and the equitable defenses of laches, estoppel, and acquiescence.

3. *Geographic limitations.* The timing problems to which the Introduction referred can, alternatively, be conceptualized as geographic boundary problems. There are two variations:

a. *Market entry by the registered owner.* Under the geographic approach, *Dawn Donut*'s holding is that the enforcement of trademark rights is geographically bounded by the territory in which the mark is in actual use. The theory is that before a trademark holder enters a particular marketing region, it is unlikely that consumers within the market would be confused by use of the mark by another. Accordingly, prior to entry into a territory, there is no basis for bringing an infringement action.

This view of trademark protection is rather close to the common law of unfair competition that existed prior to the adoption of registration systems. Under the so-called *Rectanus* doctrine, named after United Drug Co. v. Theodore Rectanus Co.,[2] the first merchant to use a mark in any particular marketing region earned the exclusive right to use the mark in that location on similar goods—irrespective of who, on an absolute basis, was the first to adopt the mark for those goods.[3] Priority was, in short,

---

[1] Thomas McCarthy puts the number at 21, 4 J. Thomas McCarthy, Trademarks and Unfair Competition § 32.44 (3d ed. 1992).

[2] 248 U.S. 90, 39 S.Ct. 48, 63 L.Ed. 141 (1918).

[3] An example: A is the first merchant in the United States to adopt the mark "Willie" for widgets. A operates exclusively in New York State. B later adopts the same mark for widgets and operates in Illinois. B then expands her business to Ohio. If A later enters Ohio, who has the right to use Willie for widgets in the state? Under the Rectanus doctrine, the answer is B. Although A was first on an absolute basis (the first in the United States), B was the first to use Willie for widgets in Ohio, and so has priority in that location.

determined by who was first in a particular geographic locality, not by who was first to adopt a particular mark.

So long as most commerce was local, the *Rectanus* doctrine was acceptable. However, as it became more common for merchants to market in more than one region, the inability to reserve marks on a nationwide basis became problematic. The solution to this problem is what national registration systems are all about, see Assignment 1 (which also discusses this same problem in relation to international marketing). Under the Lanham Act, a merchant who plans to market nationwide can register her mark, thereby giving constructive notice to future merchants that the mark is taken. Anyone who adopts a similar mark for similar goods after registration can be ousted under § 1114(1).

Given that the intent of federal registration is to reduce consumer confusion and to give registered owners the ability to use their marks to expand geographically, is *Dawn Donut* rightly decided? Why require a registered owner to wait until she enters a marketing region before she can enforce her rights? Won't consumers who travel across marketing regions be confused during the period of dual use? Won't local consumers who are acquainted with the local producer become confused when use of the mark shifts to the registered owner? Furthermore, how should a court determine when a registered owner has made the expansion efforts required to trigger the right to sue? These difficult problems have led some courts to allow trademark owners to enjoin junior users as soon as their marks are registered.[4] Many courts do, however, follow *Dawn Donut*.[5] Indeed, a similar principle is used in connection with intent-to-use registrations. A merchant who has received a Notice of Allowance is not been permitted to enjoin junior users until after her own use has begun and the mark has been registered.[6]

b. *Section 1115(b)(5): market retention by an unregistered senior user.* Geography and timing combine to create another way for members of the public to utilize a mark without the authority of its registered owner—and to foster yet another source of confusion. Since notice (constructive or otherwise) can operate only against those who adopt a mark *after* the notice

---

[4] See, e.g., Sterling Brewing Inc. v. Cold Spring Brewing Corp., 100 F.Supp. 412 (D.Mass.1951). An alternative approach confines Dawn Donut to cases involving products, like donuts, that are consumed close to their source, see, e.g., Gastown, Inc. of Delaware v. Gastown, Inc., 331 F.Supp. 626, 632 (D.Conn.1971)("The American motorist is no longer subject to the limitations of provincial or state line horizons. Transportation, advertising, and communication have regionalized or in some instances nationalized the general public's exposure to tradenames, especially in the field of gasoline products.").

[5] See, e.g., Minnesota Pet Breeders Inc. v. Schell & Kampeter Inc., 41 F.3d 1242, 33

U.S.P.Q.2d (BNA) 1140 (8th Cir.1994); Armand's Subway, Inc. v. Doctor's Assocs., Inc., 604 F.2d 849 (4th Cir.1979); Mister Donut of America, Inc. v. Mr. Donut, Inc., 418 F.2d 838 (9th Cir.1969).

[6] See, e.g., Talk To Me Products, Inc. v. Larami Corp., 804 F.Supp. 555, 559 (S.D.N.Y. 1992), aff'd, 992 F.2d 469 (2d Cir.1993). Cf. Fila Sport S.p.A v. Diadora America Inc., 141 F.R.D. 74 (N.D.Ill.1991)(finding no basis for federal jurisdiction without actual registration). See also Report of the Trademark Review Comm'n, 77 Trademark Rep. 375, 403 (1987).

is given, a trademark holder cannot acquire rights over merchants who used the mark before it was registered. In such cases, all that registration can do is freeze the prior-user's rights—that is, confine the prior user to the geographic location where he was using the mark at the time it was registered, § 1115(b)(5). Some courts will, in addition, provide a modest zone of expansion.[7]

Section 1115(b)(5) may be the most equitable way to deal with those who used a mark prior to its registration. However, it has the side-effect of creating localities where a registered mark is in the exclusive possession of someone other than its registered owner. Consider, for example, Thrifty Rent–A–Car System, Inc. v. Thrift Cars Inc.,[8] which involved the service mark, "Thrifty Rent-a-Car System." The predecessor of the registered owner (Thrifty) began using the mark in Tulsa, Oklahoma in March, 1958. The mark was registered in July, 1964. Thrifty's national expansion efforts led it to enter the car rental market in Massachusetts in December, 1967.

The defendant (Thrift) was a much smaller company. Its main operations, which began in October 1962, were limited to East Taunton, Cape Cod, Massachusetts. However, it advertised all over the Cape Cod region: in the Taunton yellow pages, in the Taunton Daily Gazette, in The Cape Cod Times, in The Anchor (the newspaper of the local Roman Catholic Diocese), and in The Inquirer and Mirror (a Nantucket newspaper). These uses of the mark were initially tolerated by Thrifty. However, when Thrift tried to open a car rental facility at the Nantucket airport, where Thrifty had a facility of its own, Thrifty sued. It sought to limit Thrift to car rentals in East Taunton, and to prevent it from doing business in Taunton or to directly advertise to the Cape Cod community.

The district court enjoined Thrift Cars from using "Thrift" in conducting a car rental business outside of Taunton and from from advertising in media directed outside of East Taunton. However, the court allowed Thrift to continue to advertise in publications where it had placed ads prior to Thrifty's registration. In addition, it ordered the *plaintiff*, Thrifty, to refrain from operating in East Taunton and from advertising in any media principally intended to target the East Taunton area. Both sides appealed. In affirming, the First Circuit held that the "limited area" defense of § 1115(b)(5) required Thrift to demonstrate "(1) that it adopted its mark before Thrifty's 1964 registration under the Lanham Act, and without knowledge of Thrifty's prior use; (2) the extent of the trade area in which Thrift Cars used the mark prior to Thrifty's registration; and (3) that Thrift Cars has continuously used the mark in the pre-registration trade area." Since Thrift could make this showing with respect to East Taunton, it was permitted to continue to use the mark there. However, it was not permitted to expand:

---

[7] See, e.g., Wiener King, Inc. v. The Wiener King Corp., 407 F.Supp. 1274 (D.N.J. 1976). Indeed, some courts give junior users not only a modest right to expand geographically, but also a margin in which to expand from one category of goods to another, see, e.g., Rodeo Collection, Ltd. v. West Seventh, 812 F.2d 1215, 1219 (9th Cir.1987).

[8] 831 F.2d 1177 (1st Cir.1987).

"The limited advertising Thrift Cars had done was not deemed sufficient to establish a presence outside East Taunton; nor were Thrift Cars' sporadic rentals in Nantucket and elsewhere in southeastern Massachusetts enough to sustain Thrift Cars' claim that it had already expanded out of East Taunton prior to Thrifty's federal registration.

"We also note that the fact that Thrift Cars had desired to expand into the Nantucket market prior to July 1964 by unsuccessfully applying for a license to operate at the airport is not sufficient to meet the requirements of § 1115(b)(5). A mere desire, without more, will not confer upon Thrift Cars the ability to exclude Thrifty from Nantucket."

As to the advertising issue, the First Circuit said:

"Thrifty now urges that the court allowed Thrift Cars too broad an advertising distribution base, because it extended outside East Taunton to Cape Cod and Nantucket. Thrifty says that by permitting both parties to advertise in the major resort area publications, the court abused its discretion because substantial consumer confusion is likely to result.

"We reject Thrifty's arguments and agree with the district court that to contract Thrift Cars' advertising base would be a punitive move. The district court did not allow Thrift Cars to advertise in any publications that it had not used prior to Thrifty's registration. On the contrary, the court simply authorized Thrift Cars to use only the same newspapers it had used prior to that critical date. While we recognize that some consumer confusion may result because there will be some overlap in advertising, the Lanham Act does not require the complete elimination of all confusion. We think, moreover, that the confusion spawned as a result of Thrift Cars' advertising will be minimal and should not significantly interfere with Thrifty's proprietary rights in its mark. See Burger King of Florida, Inc. v. Hoots, 403 F.2d 904, 908–09 (7th Cir.1968)."

4. *Geographic expansion and product expansion.* Compare *Dawn Donut* to *Lois Sportswear* and the other cases in Assignment 3. Allowing a merchant to control the use of his mark on noncompeting goods facilitates product expansion. The product category is "reserved" in the sense that consumers do not build an association between the mark for that category and another producer. When the trademark holder eventually enters the field, consumers automatically draw a connection between the goodwill he has built up in his old line and the new goods. (For instance, the consumer who liked her Sony TV will be more willing to buy a Sony VCR if she is sure it is manufactured by the same producer).

Why is geographic expansion not treated in the same way as product expansion? Why was Dawn Donut required to wait until it penetrated northern New York before it could reserve its mark for baked goods? Why was its opportunity to transfer the goodwill it developed in one region of the country to another region hampered? Or, if the *Dawn Donut* rule is right, why not require trademark owners to enter a product category before they are permitted to enjoin other competitors in that category from using their marks?

5. *The expressive dimension of trademarks.* Consider this quotation from a biography of Senator Edward (Ted) Kennedy's first wife, Joan:

> "When I campaign alone I'm approachable. Women talk to me, complain, but when I'm with Ted I'm a Barbie doll."[9]

Is this use of the term "Barbie" the same as the use made of the trademark in *L.L. Bean, New Kids on the Block,* or *Mutual of Omaha*? Is it similar to the uses involved in the cases of Assignment 3, such as *Deere & Co.* and *Lois Sportswear*? Trademark usages can be arranged on a spectrum. At one end, are cases like *Lois Sportswear,* where the defendant is using the mark purely in its signaling sense, to communicate with customers about the defendant's own goods. At the other end are expressive uses such as the one in the quotation, where the trademark "Barbie" was not used to sell dolls, but rather to convey an image that readers understand because of their familiarity with the product with which the mark is associated. Between the polls, are hybrid uses of the types exemplified by the cases in this and the previous Assignment.

Should the difference in the way a mark is used influence the outcome of infringement actions? Because every successful infringement action limits someone's ability to utilize communicative symbols, trademark law always implicates expressive concerns. However, a strong argument can be made that when the defendant is using the mark as a signal, interference with free speech does not rise to the level of a constitutional violation. The signaling function is purely commercial, and commercial speech receives limited First Amendment protection.[10] Accordingly, when courts balance the value in giving merchants an unambiguous avenue with which to communicate with customers against the interest in free expression, trademark interests win.

What about nonsignaling uses? Pure expression is entitled to the highest level of constitutional scrutiny. Accordingly, it can be argued that purely expressive uses of trademarks should never be enjoined. In fact, most courts do side with purely-expressive users. However, most manage to avoid constitutional adjudication by considering these nonsignaling usages as outside the purview of trademark law,[11] or as unlikely to give rise to a

[9] Marcia Chellis, The Joan Kennedy Story: Living With the Kennedys 191 (Jove ed. 1986). Along the same lines: "Betsy McCaughey, Lieutenant Governor of New York, once described herself as Barbie and Gov. George Pataki as Ken." N.Y. Times Magazine, June 4, 1995 at 18, col. 1.

[10] See, e.g., Posadas de Puerto Rico Assoc. v. Tourism Company of Puerto Rico, 478 U.S. 328, 340, 106 S.Ct. 2968, 2976, 92 L.Ed.2d 266 (1986); Central Hudson Gas & Electric Corp. v. Public Service Comm'n of New York, 447 U.S. 557, 562–563, 100 S.Ct. 2343, 2349–2350, 65 L.Ed.2d 341 (1980).

[11] See, e.g., Restatement Third Unfair Competition, § 25(2) and Comment i.

consumer confusion.[12] For Lanham Act claims, these uses are sometimes found to be within the "fair use" defense of § 1115(b)(4).

But this leaves some problem cases. First, there are the hybrid usages, where the mark is used as a marketing signal, but the defendant's intent is expressive. Second are state claims for antidilution, misappropriation, and tarnishment, where the defenses of the Lanham Act are not available. As this Assignment and the previous one indicate, the lower courts have gone both ways. The Supreme Court has done likewise. For example, in Prestonettes, Inc. v. Coty,[13] the Court allowed the defendant, a manufacturer of scented face powders, to use on its labels the trademarks of the perfumes used as ingredients. According to Justice Holmes:

"A trade mark only gives the right to prohibit the use of it so far as to protect the owner's good will against the sale of another's product as his.... When the mark is used in a way that does not deceive the public we see no such sanctity in the word as to prevent its being used to tell the truth. It is not taboo."[14]

More recently, however, the Court has shown less sympathy for the expressive dimension of a defendant's usage. In San Francisco Arts & Athletics Inc. (SFAA) v. United States Olympic Committee (USOC),[15] a gay-rights group sponsored a series of international athletic competitions. To evoke the tenets of ancient Greece, including its spirit of cooperation, mutual acceptance and international friendship, and to make the point that sexual preference is unrelated to athleticism, the group called its events the "Gay Olympic Games" and used that title on its letterheads and promotional materials, including advertising, tee shirts, buttons, and bumper stickers. The USOC sued, claiming infringement of its trademark rights and its right under 36 U.S.C.A. § 380(a), which provides special protection for the words "Olympic," "Olympiad," "Citius Altius Fortius," and for the five interlocking olympic rings. The Supreme Court agreed with the USOC. After noting that § 380 did not require a showing of consumer confusion,[16] the Court stated:

"One reason for Congress to grant the USOC exclusive control of the word 'Olympic,' as with other trademarks, is to ensure that the USOC receives the benefit of its own efforts so that the USOC will have an

---

[12] An example here is Reddy Communications, Inc. v. Environmental Action Foundation, 477 F.Supp. 936 (D.D.C.1979), where plaintiffs, investor-owned public utilities, had sued the defendant under traditional trademark law for caricaturing their cartoon-figure trademark, Reddy Kilowatt, on brochures criticizing the electric power industry. On a finding that the text surrounding the caricature eliminated any likelihood of consumer confusion, the court held for defendant.

[13] 264 U.S. 359, 44 S.Ct. 350, 68 L.Ed. 731 (1924).

[14] Id. at 368. Another oft-cited example is Champion Plug Co. v. Sanders, 331 U.S. 125, 67 S.Ct. 1136, 91 L.Ed. 1386 (1947), allowing a spark plug reconditioner to use the trademark of the reconditioned spark plug on its products, so long as the word "repaired" or "used" was stamped on the plug in a visible fashion.

[15] 483 U.S. 522, 107 S.Ct. 2971, 97 L.Ed.2d 427 (1987).

[16] Id. at 530–31.

incentive to continue to produce a 'quality product' that, in turn, benefits the public."[17]

This part of the Court's rationale seems to be that if there is a benefit to using the trademark, it should flow to its holder. Should this rationale be extended to prohibit the hybrid usages in all of the cases in this and the previous Assignment? Was the problem that the SFAA was earning too much through the sale of shirts, buttons, and such, thereby making untenable their claim to be using the mark expressively?

6. *Genericity.* As *Quality Inns* demonstrates, the meaning of words is a function of their use. As the public becomes acquainted with a mark, the mark can become so closely associated with a category of goods that everyone who markets goods in the category needs to use the word to compete. At that point, the word becomes unprotectable. Aspirin, thermos, cellophane, shredded wheat, and escalator are all examples of trademarks that were lost in this way.

A finding that a mark is generic is a calamity to its owner. The entire investment in the old mark is lost and new efforts must be undertaken to educate the public about a new one. In fact, many companies work hard to make sure their marks do not become generic. Xerox sends requests to its shareholders to use the word "photocopy" in their workplaces. It has also published advertisements depicting graveyards of generic marks and asking the public to use the word "photocopy" rather than "xerox." Sanka began calling itself "Sanka *brand* decaffeinated coffee" after it became clear that customers were ordering "sanka" when they meant decaf. And no one does more to establish the term "plastic strips" than Johnson & Johnson, which is trying to protect its trademark rights in "Band-aid."

These efforts are not, however, determinative of the genericity of a mark. In Judge Learned Hand's words, the test for genericity is:

> "What do the buyers understand by the word for whose use the parties are contending? If they understand by it only the kind of goods sold, then, I take it, it makes no difference whatever what efforts the plaintiff has made to get them to understand more."[18]

Note, however, that the category—"the kind of goods sold"—must be defined with care. Every merchant tries to create a unique niche for her goods. If each niche were considered a category, then success in creating a niche would divest the merchant of trademark protection.[19] To counter this

---

[17] Id. at 537.

[18] Bayer v. United Drug Co., 272 Fed. 505, 509 (2d Cir.1921). See also Kellogg Co. v. National Biscuit Co., 305 U.S. 111, 59 S.Ct. 109, 83 L.Ed. 73 (1938)("shredded wheat"), King–Seeley Thermos Co. v. Aladdin Industries, Inc., 321 F.2d 577 (2d Cir.1963).

[19] See, for example, Anti–Monopoly, Inc. v. General Mills Fun Group, 684 F.2d 1316

(9th Cir.1982), cert. denied, 459 U.S. 1227 (1983), where the court defined the category in which plaintiff was marketing monopoly-type games rather than board games, and proceeded to hold the word "Monopoly" generic for the category. (This is the case on which Problem A of Assignment 2 was based).

problem, the Trademark Clarification Act of 1984[20] amended the Lanham Act to specify that genericity is determined by the "primary significance of the registered mark to the relevant public" and not by "purchaser motivation" to buy goods within the niche.[21]

Review G. Heileman Brewing Company, Inc. v. Anheuser–Busch, Inc. in Assignment 2. Given that "LA" became generic for low alcohol beer in Australia, was Anheuser–Busch wise to try to acquire trademark rights for it in the United States?

7. *Functionality.* Recall that at the registration stage, genericity and functionality were treated similarly. Just as certain words were considered too important to communication to be made anyone's exclusive property, certain shapes were considered too utilitarian to be registered. If words that were once registrable can become unprotectable, can shapes also become too functional to protect? At least one circuit has held that after a mark becomes incontestable, the functionality defense is not available.[22] Given that the genericity defense survives incontestability, does this holding make sense? Review Assignment 3.

8. *The first sale doctrine.* The *Prestonettes* case discussed in Note 5 illustrates yet another vehicle for expanding public access to trademarks. Under a common law principle called the "first sale doctrine," a trademark owner's right to control the distribution of a marked good is limited to the first sale of the good. That is, once an embodiment of the trademark holder's product is sold under the trademark owner's authority, the trademark rights are exhausted; subsequent sellers of the embodiment can use the trademark without authorization, so long as no consumer confusion results. In *Prestonettes,* for example, the first sale occurred when Coty sold its fragrances to the face powder manufacturer. The manufacturer could then use the trademark to sell the powder that incorporated the perfume without being liable under either trademark or unfair competition law. However, the manufacturer was required to make clear to consumers that Coty was not associated in any way with the powder.

The first sale doctrine is also applicable in copyright and patent law, see Assignments 11 and 23.

PART B: ABANDONMENT

As pointed out in the Introduction to Part A, once a trademark is abandoned, the public has free access to the mark. Trademark abandonment usually is raised as an affirmative defense in an infringement suit, but it can also be the basis for a petition to cancel a trademark.[23] There

---

[20] P.L. 98–620, 98 Stat. 3335 (1984).

[21] § 1064(c).

[22] Shakespeare Company v. Silstar Corporation of America, Inc., 9 F.3d 1091 (4th Cir.1993), cert. denied, ___ U.S. ___, 114 S.Ct. 2134, 128 L.Ed.2d 864 (1994).

[23] §§ 1064 (cancellation of registration permissible at any time if the mark has been

are two types of abandonment: commissive or omissive conduct on the part of the owner that causes the mark to lose its distinctiveness; and discontinuation of the mark with intent not to resume use.[24] The following problem and cases demonstrate some of the issues that arise in conjunction with the operation of trademark abandonment.

1. PRINCIPAL PROBLEM B

In the ~~1970~~ 1950's, a musical group called the Diamonds became a smash hit with songs such as "Why Do Fools Fall in Love" and "Little Darlin'." The group's manager was Nathan Goodman. During the course of time, as is sometimes typical of singing groups, the composition of the group changed. Still, through 1987, Goodman served as their manager. His successive contracts with the group gave him the responsibility of managing the group and acting as the representative for the band in all business duties. Moreover, his contracts provided that the individual singers would not, "without the written consent of Goodman, use, nor cause to be used, nor in any way exploit the trade or professional name the Diamonds." The group sang in very glittery, distinctive-looking outfits which attracted much interest nationwide. Therefore, in addition to getting bookings and managing the group, Goodman launched a line of similar-looking sportswear using the name "the Diamonds" in 1985 and registered the trademark. Goodman shared this venture with his brother John and the line continued until 1987.

In 1987, Goodman and the individual members of the group entered into an agreement, pursuant to which the Diamonds' name became Goodman's exclusive property. The individuals composing the Diamonds at that time continued to perform as the Diamonds pursuant to a license granted them by Goodman, with Goodman still acting as manager. Shortly after the execution of this agreement, however, Goodman began having difficulties collecting royalties due him from the singers, who also began to refuse to agree to Goodman's bookings and other managerial decisions. Goodman sued the individual members of the group in 1988, and in 1993, obtained a declaration that he possessed sole ownership of the Diamonds' trade name and an injunction against future use of the trade name by the individual singers without his authorization.

During the period of this lawsuit, one of the former members of the group continued to lead a group called the Diamonds, which performed around the country without Goodman's authorization. Plaintiff Glenn Stetson first joined this group on a permanent basis in 1991. In 1992, Stetson became the leader of this band.

In 1993, shortly after the termination of the lawsuit, Goodman licensed to John the right to use the name the Diamonds for a new line of sportswear. The agreement between Goodman and his brother did not provide for strict inspection and quality control formalities. Subsequently,

---

abandoned); 1115(b)(incontestable status subject to abandonment defense).

[24] See § 1127 (defining when a mark is considered "abandoned").

Goodman got together two of the former members of the group, who resumed touring under the name the Diamonds. Thus, as of 1994, two competing groups were using the name the Diamonds.

Stetson filed this suit in January, 1995 for damages for the alleged infringing use by Goodman. Goodman denied Stetson's ownership and counterclaimed for an injunction and damages. The main issue is whether Goodman abandoned his interest in the trademark the Diamonds on the grounds that Goodman licensed the use of the Diamonds without adequate quality control and also failed to use the trade name between 1988 and 1993, the time of the lawsuit, lacking the requisite intent to resume use in the foreseeable future.

wrong standard:
Silverman

The district court found that Goodman "never intended to abandon his right" to the Diamonds' trademark and trade name. You are the law clerk of one of the appellate court judges before whom the case is pending. Advise her.

2.   Materials for Solution of Principal Problem B

A.   STATUTORY MATERIALS: §§ 1060, 1064, 1115(b), & 1127

B.   CASES:

Taco Cabana International, Inc. v. Two Pesos, Inc.

Court of Appeals, Fifth Circuit, 1991.
932 F.2d 1113, aff'd, 505 U.S. 763, 112 S.Ct. 2753, 120 L.Ed.2d 615 (1992).

[The Supreme Court opinion appears in Part A of Assignment 3.]

■ REAVLEY, CIRCUIT JUDGE.

Taco Cabana complained of the imitation of the appearance and motif of its Mexican restaurants by Two Pesos. Taco Cabana won a judgment for trade dress infringement under the Lanham Act and misappropriation of trade secrets under Texas law. Two Pesos appeals, claiming that Taco Cabana's trade dress is not protectable because the Mexican motif is not protectable, and that Taco Cabana surrendered any claim it had to Lanham Act protection by cross-licensing with another restaurant and retaining the same trade dress for two different restaurant names. We affirm.

Background

Two brothers, Felix and Mike Stehling, opened the first Taco Cabana restaurant in San Antonio in September 1978, and opened five more restaurants in San Antonio by 1985. In December 1985, Marno McDermott and Jim Blacketer opened Two Pesos in Houston. Two Pesos adopted a motif essentially consistent with Taco Cabana's trade dress, and expanded rapidly in Houston and other markets in and out of Texas,[a] but did not enter San Antonio. In 1987, Taco Cabana sued Two Pesos for trade dress

[a] Between December 1985 and August 1988, Two Pesos opened 29 restaurants.

infringement under section 43(a) of the Lanham Act and for theft of trade secrets under Texas common law.

Six days before filing suit against Two Pesos, the Stehling brothers entered into a series of agreements dividing the Taco Cabana restaurants between themselves and going their separate ways. Felix Stehling retained the "Taco Cabana" name, and Michael Stehling adopted the name "TaCasita." The agreements allowed the two groups to use the same trade dress, though one provision required "reasonable efforts to modify their trade dress for their respective future restaurants sufficiently to distinguish the restaurants of each Group from the restaurants of the other Group in the public's mind." The Stehlings have not altered their respective trade dresses. After filing suit, Taco Cabana expanded into several cities, including Houston and Dallas where Two Pesos was already doing business.

Discussion

I. Trade Dress Infringement
[The court found that Taco Cabana's trade dress could be deemed nonfunctional and inherently distinctive.]

The Legal Effect of the Cross–License

Prior to this litigation, the Stehling brothers divided the Taco Cabana restaurants. Felix Stehling retained the name "Taco Cabana," and Michael Stehling adopted the name "TaCasita." The agreement allowed the two groups to use the same trade dress, which Two Pesos calls a "naked license." But Two Pesos faces a stringent standard because finding a "naked license" signals involuntary trademark abandonment and forfeits protection. See American Foods, Inc. v. Golden Flake, Inc., 312 F.2d 619, 624–25 (5th Cir.1963). While this cross-license arrangement is not governed closely by any precedent, we find no basis for an involuntary abandonment.

An owner may license its trademark or trade dress and retain proprietary rights if the owner maintains adequate control over the quality of goods and services that the licensee sells with the mark or dress. See Kentucky Fried Chicken Corp. v. Diversified Packaging Corp., 549 F.2d 368, 387 (5th Cir.1977)(quality-control rationale is that public has right to expect consistent quality of goods or services associated with trademark or trade dress). Two Pesos argues that the cross-license creates two separate sources of good will and thus cannot indicate a single origin. This argument ignores the emergence of the "quality theory," which broadens the older source theory "to include not only manufacturing source but also the source of the standards of quality of goods bearing the mark" or dress. 1 J. McCarthy, Trademark and Unfair Competition, § 1 3:4 at 112 (2d ed. 1984). So long as customers entering a Taco Cabana or a TaCasita can expect a consistent level of quality, the trade dress retains its "utility as an informational device." *Kentucky Fried*, 549 F.2d at 387.

While the parties dispute the actual level of quality control, the jury's finding—that Taco Cabana exercises adequate supervision and control over TaCasita to ensure that the quality of TaCasita's goods and services are not inferior to Taco Cabana's—enjoys adequate record support. We also reject Two Pesos' argument that the district court erred in refusing to instruct the jury that TaCasita must also exercise quality control over Taco Cabana. Ignoring the record evidence of at least some bilateral quality monitoring, the law requires consistent quality, not equivalent policing. The jury found the requisite quality consistency; we need not demand rigorous bilateral regulation.

The purpose of the quality-control requirement is to prevent the public deception that would ensue from variant quality standards under the same mark or dress. Where the particular circumstances of the licensing arrangement persuade us that the public will not be deceived, we need not elevate form over substance and require the same policing rigor appropriate to more formal licensing and franchising transactions. Where the license parties have engaged in a close working relationship, and may justifiably rely on each parties' intimacy with standards and procedures to ensure consistent quality, and no actual decline in quality standards is demonstrated, we would depart from the purpose of the law to find an abandonment simply for want of all the inspection and control formalities. See Embedded Moments, Inc. v. International Silver Co., 648 F.Supp. 187, 194 (E.D.N.Y.1986)(license agreement without explicit provision for supervisory control and absence of actual inspection nevertheless no basis for abandonment where prior working relationship established basis for reliance on licensee's integrity and history of manufacture was "trouble-free").

The history of the Stehling brothers' relationship warrants this relaxation of formalities. Prior to the licensing agreement at issue, the Stehling brothers operated Taco Cabana together for approximately eight years. Taco Cabana and TaCasita do not use significantly different procedures or products, and the brothers may be expected to draw on their mutual experience to maintain the requisite quality consistency. They cannot protect their trade dress if they operate their separate restaurants in ignorance of each other's operations, but they need not maintain the careful policing appropriate to more formal license arrangements. Two Pesos adduces no evidence to indicate any decline in the level of quality at Taco Cabana or TaCasita, and we find nothing in the record to substantiate Two Pesos' claim that the licensing arrangement diminishes any proprietary rights in the trade dress.

Dawn Donut Company, Inc. v. Hart's Food Stores, Inc.

United States Court of Appeals, Second Circuit, 1959.
267 F.2d 358.

[In this continuation of the first Principal Case from Part A, the court deals with the question whether any of Dawn Donut's activities worked an abandonment.]

■ Lumbard, Circuit Judge.

Plaintiff's failure to license its trademarks in defendant's trading area during the thirty odd years that have elapsed since it licensed them to a

Rochester baker does not work an abandonment of the rights in that area. We hold that 15 U.S.C.A. § 1127, which provides for abandonment in certain cases of non-use, applies only when the registrant fails to use his mark, within the meaning of § 1127, anywhere in the nation. Since the Lanham Act affords a registrant nationwide protection, a contrary holding would create an insoluble problem of measuring the geographical extent of the abandonment.

Accordingly, since plaintiff has used its trademark continuously at the retail level, it has not abandoned its federal registration rights even in defendant's trading area.

The final issue presented is raised by defendant's appeal from the dismissal of its counterclaim for cancellation of plaintiff's registration on the ground that the plaintiff failed to exercise the control required by the Lanham Act over the nature and quality of the goods sold by its licensees.

We are all agreed that the Lanham Act places an affirmative duty upon a licensor of a registered trademark to take reasonable measures to detect and prevent misleading uses of his mark by his licensees or suffer cancellation of his federal registration. § 1064, provides that a trademark registration may be canceled because the trademark has been "abandoned." And "abandoned" is defined in § 1127 to include any act or omission by the registrant which causes the trademark to lose its significance as an indication of origin.

Prior to the passage of the Lanham Act many courts took the position that the licensing of a trademark separately from the business in connection with which it had been used worked an abandonment. The theory of these cases was that:

> "A trade-mark is intended to identify the goods of the owner and to safeguard his good will. The designation if employed by a person other than the one whose business it serves to identify would be misleading. Consequently, a right to the use of a trade-mark or a trade-name cannot be transferred in gross." American Broadcasting Co. v. Wahl Co., 121 F.2d 412, 413 (2d Cir.1941).

Other courts were somewhat more liberal and held that a trademark could be licensed separately from the business in connection with which it had been used provided that the licensor retained control over the quality of the goods produced by the licensee. E. I. duPont De Nemours & Co. v. Celanese Corporation of America, 167 F.2d 484 (1948). But even in the *duPont* case the court was careful to point out that naked licensing, viz. the grant of licenses without the retention of control, was invalid. E. I. DuPont de Nemours & Co. v. Celanese Corporation of America, *supra*, 167 F.2d, at 489.

The Lanham Act clearly carries forward the view of these latter cases that controlled licensing does not work an abandonment of the licensor's registration, while a system of naked licensing does. § 1055 provides:

"Where a registered mark or a mark sought to be registered is or may be used legitimately by related companies, such use shall inure to the benefit of the registrant or applicant for registration, and such use shall not affect the validity of such mark or of its registration, provided such mark is not used in such manner as to deceive the public."

And § 1127 defines "related company" to mean "any person who legitimately controls or is controlled by the registrant or applicant for registration in respect to the nature and quality of the goods or services in connection with which the mark is used."

Without the requirement of control, the right of a trademark owner to license his mark separately from the business in connection with which it has been used would create the danger that products bearing the same trademark might be of diverse qualities. If the licensor is not compelled to take some reasonable steps to prevent misuses of his trademark in the hands of others the public will be deprived of its most effective protection against misleading uses of a trademark. The public is hardly in a position to uncover deceptive uses of a trademark before they occur and will be at best slow to detect them after they happen. Thus, unless the licensor exercises supervision and control over the operations of its licensees the risk that the public will be unwittingly deceived will be increased and this is precisely what the Act is in part designed to prevent. See Sen. Report No. 1333, 79th Cong., 2d Sess. (1946). Clearly the only effective way to protect the public where a trademark is used by licensees is to place on the licensor the affirmative duty of policing in a reasonable manner the activities of his licensees.

The critical question on these facts therefore is whether the plaintiff sufficiently policed and inspected its licensees' operations to guarantee the quality of the products they sold under its trademarks to the public. The trial court found that: "By reason of its contacts with its licensees, plaintiff exercised legitimate control over the nature and quality of the food products on which plaintiff's licensees used the trademark 'Dawn.' Plaintiff and its licensees are related companies within the meaning of Section 45 of the Trademark Act of 1946." It is the position of the majority of this court that the trial judge has the same leeway in determining what constitutes a reasonable degree of supervision and control over licensees under the facts and circumstances of the particular case as he has on other questions of fact; and particularly because it is the defendant who has the burden of proof on this issue they hold the lower court's finding not clearly erroneous.

I dissent from the conclusion of the majority that the district court's findings are not clearly erroneous because while it is true that the trial judge must be given some discretion in determining what constitutes reasonable supervision of licensees under the Lanham Act, it is also true that an appellate court ought not to accept the conclusions of the district court unless they are supported by findings of sufficient facts. It seems to me that the only findings of the district judge regarding supervision are in such general and conclusory terms as to be meaningless. In the absence of supporting findings or of undisputed evidence in the record indicating the kind of supervision and inspection the plaintiff actually made of its licensees, it is impossible for us to pass upon whether there was such supervision as to satisfy the statute. There was evidence before the district court in the matter of supervision, and more detailed findings thereon should have been made.

Plaintiff's licensees fall into two classes: (1) those bakers with whom it made written contracts providing that the baker purchase exclusively plaintiff's mixes and requiring him to adhere to plaintiff's directions in using the mixes; and (2) those bakers whom plaintiff permitted to sell at retail under the "Dawn" label doughnuts and other baked goods made from its mixes although there was no written agreement governing the quality of the food sold under the Dawn mark.[a]

The contracts that plaintiff did conclude, although they provided that the purchaser use the mix as directed and without adulteration, failed to provide for any system of inspection and control. Without such a system plaintiff could not know whether these bakers were adhering to its standards in using the mix or indeed whether they were selling only products made from Dawn mixes under the trademark "Dawn".

The absence, however, of an express contract right to inspect and supervise a licensee's operations does not mean that the plaintiff's method of licensing failed to comply with the requirements of the Lanham Act. Plaintiff may in fact have exercised control in spite of the absence of any express grant by licensees of the right to inspect and supervise.

The question then, with respect to both plaintiff's contract and non-contract licensees, is whether the plaintiff in fact exercised sufficient control.

Here the only evidence in the record relating to the actual supervision of licensees by plaintiff consists of the testimony of two of plaintiff's local sales representatives that they regularly visited their particular customers and the further testimony of one of them, Jesse Cohn, the plaintiff's New York representative, that "in many cases" he did have an opportunity to inspect and observe the operations of his customers. The record does not

---

[a] On cross-examination plaintiff's president conceded that during 1949 and 1950 the company in some instances, the number of which is not made clear by his testimony, distributed its advertising and packaging material to bakers with whom it had not reached any agreement relating to the quality of the goods sold in packages bearing the name "Dawn". It also appears from plaintiff's list of the 16 bakers who were operating as exclusive Dawn shops at the time of the trial that plaintiff's contract with 3 of these shops had expired and had not been renewed and that in the case of 2 other such shops the contract had been renewed only after a sub-stantial period of time had elapsed since the expiration of the original agreement. The record indicates that these latter 2 bakers continued to operate under the name "Dawn" and purchase "Dawn" mixes during the period following the expiration of their respective franchise agreements with the plaintiff. Particularly damaging to plaintiff is the fact that one of the 2 bakers whose franchise contracts plaintiff allowed to lapse for a substantial period of time has also been permitted by plaintiff to sell doughnuts made from a mix other than plaintiff's in packaging labeled with plaintiff's trademark.

indicate whether plaintiff's other sales representatives made any similar efforts to observe the operations of licensees.

Moreover, Cohn's testimony fails to make clear the nature of the inspection he made or how often he made one. His testimony indicates that his opportunity to observe a licensee's operations was limited to "those cases where I am able to get into the shop" and even casts some doubt on whether he actually had sufficient technical knowledge in the use of plaintiff's mix to make an adequate inspection of a licensee's operations.

The fact that it was Cohn who failed to report the defendant's use of the mark "Dawn" to the plaintiff casts still further doubt about the extent of the supervision Cohn exercised over the operations of plaintiff's New York licensees.

Thus I do not believe that we can fairly determine on this record whether plaintiff subjected its licensees to periodic and thorough inspections by trained personnel or whether its policing consisted only of chance, cursory examinations of licensees' operations by technically untrained salesmen. The latter system of inspection hardly constitutes a sufficient program of supervision to satisfy the requirements of the Act.

Therefore it is appropriate to remand the counterclaim for more extensive findings on the relevant issues rather than hazard a determination on this incomplete and uncertain record. I would direct the district court to order the cancellation of plaintiff's registrations if it should find that the plaintiff did not adequately police the operations of its licensees.

But unless the district court finds some evidence of misuse of the mark by plaintiff in its sales of mixes to bakers at the wholesale level, the cancellation of plaintiff's registration should be limited to the use of the mark in connection with sale of the finished food products to the consuming public. Such a limited cancellation is within the power of the court. Section 1119 specifically provides that "In any action involving a registered mark the court may * * * order the cancellation of registrations, in whole or in part, * * *". Moreover, partial cancellation is consistent with § 1051(a)(1), governing the initial registration of trademarks which requires the applicant to specify "the goods in connection with which the mark is used and the mode or manner in which the mark is used in connection with such goods * * *".

The district court's denial of an injunction restraining defendant's use of the mark "Dawn" on baked and fried goods and its dismissal of defendant's counterclaim are affirmed.

Silverman v. CBS, Inc.

Court of Appeals, Second Circuit, 1989.
870 F.2d 40.

■ NEWMAN, CIRCUIT JUDGE.

Facts

The "Amos 'n' Andy" characters were created in 1928 by Freeman F. Gosden and Charles J. Correll, who wrote and produced for radio broadcasting "The Amos 'n' Andy Show." The show became one of the country's most popular radio programs. The characters in the Amos 'n' Andy programs were Black. Gosden and Correll, who were White, portrayed Amos and Andy on radio. The authors appeared in blackface in publicity photos. Black actors played the parts in the subsequent television programs.

Gosden and Correll assigned all of their rights in the "Amos 'n' Andy Show" scripts and radio programs to CBS Inc. in 1948. Gosden and Correll continued to create new "Amos 'n' Andy" scripts, which formed the basis for CBS radio programs. The radio programs continued until 1955. Beginning in 1951 CBS also broadcast an "Amos 'n' Andy" television series. The television series was aired on CBS affiliate stations until 1953 and continued in reruns and non-network syndication until 1966. CBS has not aired or licensed for airing any of the radio or television programs since 1966.

In 1981, Silverman began writing a script for a Broadway musical based on the "Amos 'n' Andy" characters. The title of this work was originally "Amos 'n' Andy Go To The Movies." A revision was titled "Amos 'n' Andy In Hollywood," and a more extensive revision was titled "Fresh Air Taxi." Silverman sought a license to use the "Amos 'n' Andy" characters, but CBS refused.

Silverman filed this lawsuit seeking a declaration that the "Amos 'n' Andy" radio programs broadcast from March 1928 through March 1948 (the "pre–1948 radio programs") are in the public domain and that he is therefore free to make use of the content of the programs, including the characters, character names, and plots. He also sought a declaration that CBS has no rights in these programs under any body of law, including trademark law.

On the trademark side of the case, Judge Goettel ruled that the name "Amos 'n' Andy," as well as the names and appearances of "Amos 'n' Andy" characters and "other distinctive features of the . . . radio and television shows" are protectable marks. Silverman v. CBS, 632 F.Supp. 1344 at 1356 (S.D.N.Y.1986). He then set down for trial the issue of whether CBS's non-use of the marks constituted abandonment.

After a bench trial on the issue of abandonment, Judge Goettel concluded that CBS had not abandoned its trademarks. Silverman v. CBS, 666 F.Supp. 575 (S.D.N.Y.1987).

Discussion

1. Trademark Issues

Silverman challenges the District Court's rulings that CBS has protectable trademarks in the "Amos 'n' Andy" names, characters, and other features of the radio and television programs, including phrases of dialogue, and that CBS has not abandoned these marks. We find it unnecessary to decide which features of the programs might give rise to protectable marks because we agree with Silverman that CBS has abandoned the marks. Section 45 of the Lanham Act provides:

> A mark shall be deemed to be "abandoned"—
>
> (a) When its use has been discontinued with intent not to resume. Intent not to resume may be inferred from circumstances. Nonuse for two consecutive years shall be prima facie abandonment.

15 U.S.C.A. § 1127 (1982). There are thus two elements for abandonment: (1) non-use and (2) intent not to resume use. Two years of non-use creates a rebuttable presumption of abandonment.

On the undisputed facts of this case, CBS made a considered decision to take the "Amos 'n' Andy" television programs off the air. It took this action in response of complaints by civil rights organizations, including the NAACP, that the programs were demeaning to Blacks. By the time the abandonment issue came before the District Court, non-use of the AMOS 'N' ANDY marks had continued for 21 years. Although CBS has no current plans to use the marks within the foreseeable future, CBS asserts that it has always intended to resume using them at some point in the future, should the social climate become more hospitable.

Ordinarily, 21 years of non-use would easily surpass the non-use requirement for finding abandonment. See, e.g., I.H.T. Corp. v. Saffir Publishing Corp., 444 F.Supp. 185 (S.D.N.Y.1978)(denying preliminary injunction to protect trademark after 12 years of non-use). The District Court concluded, however, that CBS had successfully rebutted the presumption of abandonment arising from its prolonged non-use by offering a reasonable explanation for its decision to keep the programs off the air and by asserting its intention to resume use at some indefinite point in the future. This conclusion raises a question as to the proper interpretation of the statutory phrase "intent not to resume": Does the phrase mean intent never to resume use or does it merely mean intent not to resume use within the reasonably foreseeable future?

We conclude that the latter must be the case. The statute provides that intent not to resume may be inferred from circumstances, and two consecutive years of non-use is prima facie abandonment. Time is thereby made relevant. Indeed, if the relevant intent were intent never to resume use, it would be virtually impossible to establish such intent circumstantially. Even after prolonged non-use, and without any concrete plans to resume use, a company could almost always assert truthfully that at some point, should conditions change, it would resume use of its mark.

We do not think Congress contemplated such an unworkable standard. More likely, Congress wanted a mark to be deemed abandoned once use has been discontinued with an intent not to resume within the reasonably foreseeable future. This standard is sufficient to protect against the forfeiture of marks by proprietors who are temporarily unable to continue using them, while it also prevents warehousing of marks, which impedes commerce and competition.

We are buttressed in this conclusion by the fact that the statute requires proof of "intent not to resume," rather than "intent to abandon." The statute thus creates no state of mind element concerning the ultimate issue of abandonment. On the contrary, it avoids a subjective inquiry on this ultimate question by setting forth the circumstances under which a mark shall be "deemed" to be abandoned. Of course, one of those circumstances is intent not to resume use, which is a matter of subjective inquiry. But we think the provision, by introducing the two concepts of "deemed" abandonment and intent not to resume use, contemplates a distinction, and it is a distinction that turns at least in part on duration of the contemplated non-use.

Congress's choice of wording appears to have been deliberate. One early version of what became section 45 of the Lanham Act had provided that "intent to *abandon* may be inferred from the circumstances." H.R. Rep. 4744, 76th Cong., 1st Sess. (1939)(emphasis added). However, shortly thereafter a new bill modified this phrase by substituting "intent not to resume" for "intent to abandon." H.R. Rep. 6618, 76th Cong., 1st Sess. (1939). Though it has been suggested that the phrases are interchangeable, see Note, 56 Fordham L. Rev. 1003, 1020 n.113 (1988), we agree with the Fifth Circuit that the phrases are better understood as having distinct meanings. See Exxon Corp. v. Humble Exploration Co., 695 F.2d 96, 102, 103 n.7 (5th Cir.1983). "Abandonment" connotes permanent relinquishment. See Webster's Third New International Dictionary 2 (1981)(defining "abandon" to mean "to cease to assert ... an interest ... esp. with the intent of *never* again resuming or reasserting it")(emphasis added). We think that Congress, by speaking of "intent not to resume" rather than "intent to abandon" in this section of the Act meant to avoid the implication that intent never to resume use must be shown.[a]

This approach is consistent with our recent decisions concerning trademark abandonment. In *Saratoga Vichy* we rejected a claim of abandonment based on seven years of non-use where the initial decision to cease use resulted from a decision of the state legislature and the state, which was the trademark owner, continuously sought to sell the mark along with the mineral water business to which it applied. Similarly, in Defiance Button Machine Co. v. C & C Metal Products Corp., 759 F.2d 1053 (2d Cir.), *cert. denied*, 474 U.S. 844 (1985), we rejected an abandonment claim where, during a brief period of non-use, the proprietor tried to sell the mark, its associated goodwill, and some other assets and, upon failing to find a buyer, became a subsidiary of a company in its original line of trade and prepared

---

[a] An early Supreme Court case involving abandonment under pre-Lanham Act, common law trademark said that proof of abandonment must include proof of an "intent to abandon." Saxlehner v. Eisner & Mendelson Co., 179 U.S. 19, 31 (1900). In cases applying the Act, we have also on occasion used the phrase "intent to abandon," see Saratoga Vichy Spring Co. v. Lehman, [625 F.2d 1037] at 1044 (C.A.2 1980), but decisions using the phrase have not faced the issue whether the requisite intent is never to resume use or not to resume in the reasonably foreseeable future. Where that choice matters, as in this case, the statutory phrase "intent not to resume" better describes the requisite mental element.

to resume its business. In both cases, the proprietor of the mark had an intention to exploit the mark in the reasonably foreseeable future by resuming its use or permitting its use by others.

The undisputed facts of the pending case are entirely different. Unlike the proprietors in *Saratoga Vichy* and *Defiance Button*, CBS has not been endeavoring to exploit the value of its marks, failing to do so only because of lack of business opportunities. Instead, it has decided, albeit for socially commendable motives, to forgo whatever business opportunities may currently exist in the hope that greater opportunities, unaccompanied by adverse public reaction, will exist at some undefined time in the future.

A proprietor who temporarily suspends use of a mark can rebut the presumption of abandonment by showing reasonable grounds for the suspension and plans to resume use in the reasonably foreseeable future when the conditions requiring suspension abate. But a proprietor may not protect a mark if he discontinues using it for more than 20 years and has no plans to use or permit its use in the reasonably foreseeable future. A bare assertion of possible future use is not enough.

We recognize the point, forcefully made by Judge Goettel, when he wrote:

> It would be offensive to basic precepts of fairness and justice to penalize CBS, by stripping it of its trademark rights, merely because it succumbed to societal pressures and pursued a course of conduct that it reasonably believes to be in the best interests of the community.

Silverman, 666 F.Supp. at 581. Nonetheless, we believe that however laudable one might think CBS's motives to be, such motives cannot overcome the undisputed facts that CBS has not used its marks for more than 20 years and that, even now, it has no plans to resume their use in the reasonably foreseeable future. Though we agree with Judge Goettel that CBS should not be penalized for its worthy motive, we cannot adjust the statutory test of abandonment to reward CBS for such motive by according it protection where its own voluntary actions demonstrate that statutory protection has ceased. Moreover, we see nothing in the statute that makes the consequence of an intent not to resume use turn on the worthiness of the motive for holding such intent.

We are also mindful of the facts, relied on by the District Court, that show some minor activities by CBS regarding its properties, allegedly sufficient to rebut abandonment of the marks. These are CBS's actions in licensing the programs for limited use in connection with documentary and educational programs, challenging infringing uses brought to its attention, renewing its copyrights, and periodically reconsidering whether to resume use of the programs. But challenging infringing uses is not use, and sporadic licensing for essentially non-commercial uses of a mark is not sufficient use to forestall abandonment. Cf. Exxon Corp. v. Humble Exploration Co., *supra*, 695 F.2d at 102 (use must be "commercial use" to avoid abandonment). Such uses do not sufficiently rekindle the public's identification of the mark with the proprietor, which is the essential condition for trademark protection, nor do they establish an intent to resume commercial use. CBS's minor activities, like worthy motives for non-use, cannot dispel the legal consequence of prolonged non-use coupled with an intent not to resume use in the reasonably foreseeable future.

An adjudication of trademark rights often involves a balancing of competing interests. In weighing the competing interests and reaching our conclusion concerning abandonment, we are influenced in part by the context in which this dispute arises—one in which the allegedly infringing use is in connection with a work of artistic expression. Just as First Amendment values inform application of the idea/expression dichotomy in copyright law, in similar fashion such values have some bearing upon the extent of protection accorded a trademark proprietor against use of the mark in works of artistic expression.

Ordinarily, the use of a trademark to identify a commodity or a business "is a form of commercial speech and nothing more." Friedman v. Rogers, 440 U.S. 1, 11 (1979). Requiring a commercial speaker to choose words and labels that do not confuse or deceive protects the public and does not impair expression.

In the area of artistic speech, however, enforcement of trademark rights carries a risk of inhibiting free expression, not only in the case at hand but in other situations where authors might contemplate use of trademarks in connection with works of artistic expression. These risks add some weight to Silverman's claims.

From the standpoint of the proprietor of a mark in a work of artistic expression, there is also an interest in expression, along with the traditional trademark interest in avoiding public confusion as to source. Trademark law can contribute to a favorable climate for expression by complementing the economic incentive that copyright law provides to create and disseminate artistic works. In this case, however, the expression interest on CBS's side is markedly diminished by its decision to withhold dissemination of the works with which its marks are associated.

The interest of CBS, and the public, in avoiding public confusion, an interest obviously entitled to weight in every trademark case, is also somewhat diminished in the context of this case. This interest is not as weighty as in a case involving a non-artistic product whose trademark is associated with high quality or other consumer benefits. Though Silverman undoubtedly hopes that some of his audience will be drawn from those who favorably recall the "Amos 'n' Andy" programs, we doubt if many who attend Broadway musicals are motivated to purchase tickets because of a belief that the musical is produced by the same entity responsible for the movie, book, or radio or television series on which it is based. That is not to say that the musical is in a sufficiently distinct line of commerce to preclude all protection; the holder of a mark associated with a television series would normally be entitled to "bridge the gap" and secure some protection against an infringing use of the mark in connection with a Broadway musical. It is to say, however, that most theater-goers have sufficient awareness that the quality of a musical depends so heavily on a combination of circumstances, including script, score, lyrics, cast, and direction, that they are not likely to be significantly influenced in their ticket-purchasing decision by an erroneous belief that the musical emanated from the same production source as the underlying work.

The point must not be overstated. Trademark protection is not lost simply because the allegedly infringing use is in connection with a work of artistic expression. But in determining the outer limits of trademark protection—here, concerning the concept of abandonment—the balance of risks just noted is relevant and in some cases may tip the scales against trademark protection. These considerations are especially pertinent in the pending case where some aspects of the material claimed to be protected by trademark are in the public domain as far as copyright law is concerned.

For all of these reasons, we conclude that the undisputed facts establish abandonment of the AMOS 'N' ANDY marks.

NOTES

1. *Abandonment based on non-use.* Prior to GATT, § 1127 provided that two years of non-use resulted in prima facie evidence of abandonment. This period has been increased to three years pursuant to GATT, which amendment became effective on January 1, 1996. Of course, even if there is non-use for less than three years, abandonment still can be established if it can be proven that a trademark owner has no intent to resume use of a particular trademark.

How is "intent to abandon" different from "intent to resume use"? Which standard is stricter from the standpoint of the trademark challenger? Was *Silverman* correct in adopting "intent to resume use" as the appropriate standard?

With respect to the "non-use" standard resulting in prima facie evidence of abandonment, courts have split on whether a showing of non-use for two (now three) consecutive years should shift only the burden of production to the trademark owner (thus requiring the trademark owner to go forward and produce evidence of intent to resume), or whether it should shift the ultimate burden of proof.[25] Which standard is better?

Silverman raises the issue of what type of use is sufficient to preserve an owner's rights in a mark. Was the reason for the non-use in *Silverman*

[25] The Second, Ninth, and Federal Circuits have held that a showing of prima facie abandonment based on non-use for the requisite period of time establishes a rebuttable presumption of abandonment that the plaintiff can counter by showing intent to resume. Thus, these circuits hold that this showing shifts the burden of production to the trademark owner. Once the trademark owner produces evidence rebutting the presumption of abandonment, the final burden of proof returns to the challenger. See, e.g., Cerveceria Centroamericana, S.A. v. Cerveceria India, Inc., 892 F.2d 1021, 1026 (Fed.Cir.1989); Star–Kist Foods, Inc. v. P.J. Rhodes & Co., 769 F.2d 1393, 1396 (9th Cir.1985); Saratoga Vichy Spring Co. v. Lehman, 625 F.2d 1037, 1043–44 (2d Cir.1980). In contrast, the Fifth and Eleventh Circuits hold that a showing of prima facie abandonment shifts the ultimate burden of proof to the trademark owner. See, e.g., E. Remy Martin & Co. v. Shaw–Ross International Imports, Inc., 756 F.2d 1525, 1532 (11th Cir.1985); Exxon Corp. v. Humble Exploration Co., 695 F.2d 96, 99 (5th Cir.1983).

involuntary? Should this matter? Is the Principal Problem distinguishable from *Silverman* in any significant respects?

A finding of abandonment in a given situation is very much a factual issue. For example, one court held that summary judgment for the defendants on plaintiff's claim for trade dress infringement of its car body style (the Ferrari) was not warranted even though the plaintiff had not manufactured cars with that body style for over thirteen years and had no intention of resuming production of such cars since the plaintiff presented evidence of goodwill associated with its vehicle and "evidence of ongoing parts support for the vehicle."[26] Is a finding of abandonment warranted if a trademark owner modifies its trademark? Once a mark has been abandoned, what should be the result if the trademark owner resumes use?

2. *Abandonment through loss of distinctiveness.* Trademarks are unlike copyrights and patents in that they require an ongoing business enterprise. Section 1060 codifies the common law rule that a trademark cannot be assigned apart from "the goodwill of the business in which the mark is used." This also is true with respect to the trademark of an insolvent or bankrupt. Thus, if the buyer of the bankrupt's assets fails to continue the business, abandonment of the mark will result and anyone, including the bankrupt, is free to use the trademark.[27]

As *Dawn Donut* and *Two Pesos* indicate, the uncontrolled licensing of a trademark also can result in abandonment because the mark will fail to represent a symbol of consistency and thus will no longer have the necessary source indicative function.[28] Why does trademark law impose a quality control requirement through the doctrine of abandonment? How much supervision should be required? Note that this is the crux of the split between Judge Lumbard and the majority in *Dawn Donut*. Should the courts be involved in making determinations regarding the adequacy of supervision? Absent a quality control requirement, would licensees or franchisees fail to exercise quality control?

With respect to national and international restaurant chains, it is possible that the precise ingredients and suppliers of certain products differ both within the United States as well as abroad. Some differences may even be intentional as a response to varying consumer preferences in different regions. See the Principal Problem in Assignment 5. Are large companies in danger of losing their trademark rights as a result of such variations?

In *Silverman*, the court noted that CBS's challenging infringing uses was not "use," and thus could not preclude a finding of abandonment. What should be the relationship between challenging infringing uses, or *failing* to challenge such uses, and abandonment? Is this issue relevant to the Principal Problem?

[26] Ferrari S.p.A. Esercizio Fabbriche Automobili E Corse v. McBurnie Coachcraft Inc., 10 U.S.P.Q.2d (BNA) 1278, 1282 (S.D.Cal.1988).

[27] See J. Thomas McCarthy, 2 McCarthy on Trademarks and Unfair Competition § 18.09 [1] (3d ed. 1992).

[28] See also Restatement (Third) of Unfair Competition § 33, comment b (1994).

BIBLIOGRAPHY

As to defenses to infringement, see Pollack, Unconstitutional Incontestability? The Intersection of the Intellectual Property and Commerce Clauses of the Constitution: Beyond a Critique of Shakespeare Co. v. Silstar Corp., 18 Seattle U. L. Rev. 45 (1995); Casenote, New Kids on the Block v. News America Publishing, Inc.: New Nominative Use Defense Increases the Likelihood of Confusion Surrounding the Fair Use Defense to Trademark Infringement, 24 Golden Gate U. L. Rev. 685 (1994); Dreyfuss, Expressive Genericity: Trademarks as Language in the Pepsi Generation, 65 Notre Dame L. Rev. 397 (1990); Kravitz, Trademarks, Speech and the Gay Olympics Case, 69 B.U. L. Rev. 131 (1989); Oddi, Consumer Motivation in Trademark and Unfair Competition Law: On the Importance of Source, 31 Vill. L. Rev. 1 (1986); Dorsen, Satiric Appropriation and the Law of Libel, Trademark and Copyright: Remedies Without Wrongs, 65 B.U. L. Rev. 923, 939 (1986); Denicola, Trademarks As Speech: Constitutional Implications of the Emerging Rationales for the Protection of Trade Symbols, 1982 Wis.L.Rev. 158.

Parodies have attracted many student authors: Note, Trademark Infringement, Likelihood of Confusion, and Trademark Parody: Anheuser–Busch, Inc. v. L & L Wings, Inc. 28 Wake Forest L. Rev. 705 (1993); Comment, Trademark Parodies and Free Speech: An Expansion of Parodists' First Amendment Rights in L.L. Bean, Inc. v. Drake Publishers, Inc., 73 Iowa L. Rev. 961 (1988); Note, Trademark Parody: A Fair Use and First Amendment Analysis, 72 Va. L. Rev. 1079 (1986); Comment, Trademark Parody Litigation and the Lanham Act: Fitting a Square Peg Into a Round Hole, 54 U. Cin. L. Rev. 1311 (1986).

The topic of trademark abandonment has not fostered a wealth of scholarship, but the following student note may be of interest: The Song is Over but the Melody Lingers on: Persistence of Goodwill and the Intent Factor in Trademark Abandonment, 56 Fordham L. Rev. 1003 (1988).

ASSIGNMENT 5

REMEDIES

1. INTRODUCTION

Remedies for trademark infringement, as is true of copyright and patent infringement, are statutorily based and include injunctive relief as well as various forms of monetary relief. The remedial provisions of the Lanham Act apply not only to trademark infringement under § 1114(1) but also to violations of § 43(a).[1] Section 1116(a) of the Lanham Act provides that courts can grant injunctions "according to the principles of equity."[2] This means that successful plaintiffs must show that they lack an adequate remedy at law or that they will be irreparably harmed absent an injunction. With respect to the availability of preliminary injunctions, a plaintiff also must establish a likelihood of success on the merits.[3] Sometimes courts also will order a freezing of the defendant's assets in conjunction with the entry of preliminary injunctive relief if such is believed to be necessary to insure the availability of permanent relief.[4]

Section 1117(a) of the Lanham Act, which provides for monetary relief, states that successful plaintiffs can obtain the specified monetary relief of defendant's profits, damages sustained by the plaintiff, and costs "subject to the principles of equity."[5] Thus, equitable considerations play a pivotal role in awarding these monetary remedies under trademark law.[6] Section 1122 of the Lanham Act expressly nullifies the states' sovereign immunity

---

[1] See §§ 1116, 1117, 1118, & 1125(b)(prohibiting the importation of goods violating § 43(a)). Of course, § 1119, which grants courts the authority to take certain actions with respect to registrations, is limited in application to registered trademarks.

[2] § 1116(a).

[3] See, e.g., Dial–A–Mattress Operating Corp. v. Mattress Madness, Inc., 841 F.Supp. 1339, 1345, reconsideration denied 847 F.Supp. 18 (E.D.N.Y.1994).

[4] See, e.g., Levi Strauss & Co. v. Sunrise International Trading Inc., 51 F.3d 982, 987 (11th Cir.1995); Reebok International Ltd. v. Marnatech, 970 F.2d 552, 560 (9th Cir.1992).

[5] § 1117(a). Monetary recovery by the plaintiff generally is viewed as cumulative, so that a plaintiff may receive both damages and defendant's profits as long as there is no double recovery. See, e.g., Babbit Electronics Inc. v. Dynascan Corp., 38 F.3d 1161, 1183 (11th Cir.1994); J. Thomas McCarthy, 4 McCarthy on Trademarks and Unfair Competition § 30:27[1][a] (3rd ed. 1992)(both damages and profits "will be appropriate in a case where the parties do not compete, since in that case defendant's profits are granted under the theory of unjust enrichment, which does not attempt to measure plaintiff's actual loss"). But see Nintendo of America, Inc. v. Dragon Pacific International, 40 F.3d 1007, 1010 (9th Cir.1994) cert. denied, Sheng v. Nintendo of America, ___ U.S. ___, 115 S.Ct. 2256, 132 L.Ed.2d 263 (1995)(recovery of both damages and defendant's profits is generally considered double recovery).

[6] See Brown, Civil Remedies for Intellectual Property Invasions: Themes and Variations, 55 L. & Contemp. Probs. 45, 65 (1992).

under the Eleventh Amendment, and so the same remedies are available against states and state officials as against private parties.[7] In some instances, recovery of monetary remedies is precluded by the Lanham Act. For example, a registrant's failure to provide the appropriate notice of registration will preclude an award of profits and damages "unless the defendant had actual notice of the registration."[8] Moreover, § 1114(1) provides that infringers who merely reproduce a registered mark on labels or packaging "intended to be used in commerce," as opposed to those who infringe by using the marks in commerce, are not liable for profits or damages "unless the acts have been committed with knowledge that such imitation is intended to be used to cause confusion. . . ."[9] Additionally, § 1114(2) specifies that printers and publishers who qualify as innocent infringers are subject only to injunctive relief.

Other remedies provided in the Lanham Act include treble damages and attorney's fees,[10] cancellation and restoration of registrations,[11] the destruction of infringing articles,[12] and the prohibition of importation of goods that "copy or simulate" a registered trademark.[13] One issue that arises in conjunction with the prohibition on importation is whether the Lanham Act is violated by the importation of grey market goods (goods that are manufactured and sold abroad under a valid license but imported into the United States without the permission of the owner of the United States' trademark rights in the identical mark[14]). This issue is explored further in the Principal Problem and the accompanying materials, which also treat some of the other interesting issues that arise in connection with the imposition of trademark remedies.

2. PRINCIPAL PROBLEM

Plaintiffs Nestle, S.A., the registered owner of the trademark PERUGINA for chocolate candy in the United States and Puerto Rico, and its wholly owned subsidiary Nestlé Puerto Rico, Inc., the exclusive distributor in Puerto Rico, are suing Casa Helvetia based on the defendant's unauthorized importation and distribution of PERUGINA chocolates in Puerto Rico. Plaintiffs' chocolates are made in Italy, and the defendant's choco-

---

[7] The statute does not provide that the federal government can be sued for trademark infringement. See also U.S. Gold & Silver Inv., Inc. v. United States, 885 F.2d 620, 621 (9th Cir.1989), cert. denied, 497 U.S. 1004, 110 S.Ct. 3239, 111 L.Ed.2d 750 (1990)(court expressly declined to express an opinion as to whether the United States can be sued directly under the Lanham Act). The federal government can, however, be sued under the Federal Tort Claims Act for trademark infringement resulting from state, but not federal, claims. As a point of comparison, the federal government can be liable for copyright infringement, but damages are the only available relief. See Note 3 in Assignment 13.

[8] § 1111.

[9] § 1114(1).

[10] § 1117(a).

[11] § 1119.

[12] § 1118.

[13] § 1124.

[14] See Vivitar Corp. v. United States, 761 F.2d 1552, 1555 (Fed.Cir.1985), cert. denied 474 U.S. 1055, 106 S.Ct. 791, 88 L.Ed.2d 769 (1986). Where the United States' trademark owner also imports goods into this country, the grey market goods are called "parallel importations." Id. at 1555.

lates are made in Venezuela but are nonetheless genuine PERUGINA candies that have been purchased by defendant from Nestle's official licensee and authorized distributor in Venezuela of the PERUGINA candies. Plaintiffs are suing for trademark infringement under § 1114(1), unfair competition under § 43(a), and violating § 1124 for importing a materially different product.

The respective candies are similar in color and have an identical appearance, both inside and out. Both come in boxes that display the PERUGINA logo and the same logo type; both have Pegasus symbols and a picture of the product on the back of the box. Still, certain differences exist between the Italian and Venezuelan chocolates and their packaging. First, the Venezuelan chocolate is made from domestic beans, and the Italian chocolate is made from Ecuadorian and African beans. The Italian chocolate is produced from cane sugar while the Venezuelan chocolate is sweetened with corn syrup. The Italian chocolate contains five per cent more milk fat to prolong shelf life. The Venezuelan chocolate contains imported hazelnuts and the Italian chocolate has fresh hazelnuts. The Italian candies come in a wider variety of shapes than the Venezuelan products.

With respect to the packaging of the two products, the Italian candies come in a box that has a glossy wax finish with a silver tray, whereas the Venezuelan candy comes in a more ordinary-looking box with a transparent tray. The Italian product is described on the box in English and French, whereas the Venezuelan product displays Spanish and English. Both products clearly identify the different places of manufacture of the respective products. Moreover, the Italian chocolates cost over $5.00 more per box than the Venezuelan chocolates.

There is no dispute that the Venezuelan products are genuine PERUGINA products that are manufactured under Nestle's authorization, and there is no evidence as to whether the Venezuelan products fail to satisfy any required quality control standards. The shipping and handling procedures of the two products are, however, markedly different. Moreover, the testimony of the plaintiffs' witnesses at the trial conveyed the impression that the plaintiffs were inferring that the Venezuelan product is an inferior chocolate in commonplace packaging.

The district court dismissed the plaintiffs' complaint and held that the defendant's unauthorized distribution of the Venezuelan chocolates in Puerto Rico did not violate the Lanham Act. Plaintiffs have hired you as their attorney for the appeal, and have offered to provide you with as many free samples of both products as you can consume. Now comes the not-so-fun part. Your clients want to know your opinion as to the merits of their case and the likelihood that the appellate court will reverse. They also want to know what remedies they can obtain under the Lanham Act, and if you foresee any difficulties with obtaining any particular remedies in the event they prevail on appeal.

3. MATERIALS FOR SOLUTION OF PRINCIPAL PROBLEM

A. STATUTORY MATERIALS: §§ 1114, 1116, 1117, 1118, 1119, 1120, 1122, 1124, & 1125(b)

B. CASES:

George Basch Co. v. Blue Coral, Inc.

United States Court of Appeals, Second Circuit, 1992.
968 F.2d 1532.

■ WALKER, CIRCUIT JUDGE.

Along with several issues regarding the particulars of injunctive relief, this case presents the general question of whether, in an action for trade dress infringement, a plaintiff may recover a defendant's profits without establishing that the defendant engaged in deliberately deceptive conduct. The district court concluded that bad faith was not a necessary predicate for an accounting. We disagree. Accordingly, we hold that in order to justify an award of profits, a plaintiff must establish that the defendant engaged in willful deception.

Background

The George Basch Co., Inc., ("Basch") manufactures and distributes NEVR–DULL, a cotton wadding metal polish. NEVR–DULL is packaged in a five ounce cylindrical metal can, about 3½ inches high by 3½ inches in diameter, and navy blue in color. Along with a product description and directions, the product's name is printed on the can in white block lettering. On either side of the product's name there are two red and white icons that depict what the product may be used for: the radiator grill of a car, silverware, a brass lamp, and a motor boat on a trailer.

Appellants, Blue Coral, Inc., its subsidiary Simoniz Canada Ltd., and their mutual president, Michael Moshontz (hereafter collectively referred to as "Blue Coral") manufacture and distribute a line of automotive wheel cleaning and polishing products. In both the United States and Canada, Blue Coral markets these products under the trademark ESPREE. In 1987, Blue Coral approached Basch with respect to becoming Basch's exclusive NEVR–DULL distributor in Canada. By agreement of the parties, effective July 28, 1987, Blue Coral became NEVR–DULL's exclusive Canadian distributor. NEVR–DULL was not sold under the ESPREE mark, and its Canadian trade dress remained substantially the same as the United States' version, with the exception that the French language was employed on the front of the can.

In April 1988, Blue Coral asked Basch to produce a wadding metal polish for Blue Coral to market in the United States. Blue Coral intended to add the polish to its line of ESPREE products. The parties negotiated through August of that year, at which time they ended their talks unsuccessfully due to an impasse regarding price. Blue Coral ultimately contracted with another manufacturer of metal polish.

On July 25, 1988, Blue Coral introduced EVER BRITE—the new ESPREE wadding metal polish—into the United States market. EVER BRITE was packaged in the same size cylindrical metal can used by Basch to package NEVR–DULL. The base color of the EVER BRITE can was black. On its front appeared an angled silver grid-like background. Superimposed over the center of the grid, also on an angle, were large white block letters which read "EVER BRITE." Five different types of wheel faces were depicted in the upper right hand corner of the grid. To the right of the wheel faces appeared six red and white icons that represented silverware, chrome wheels, brassware, brass beds, copperware, and car bumpers and trim.

Relations between Basch and Blue Coral turned bleak. In March 1989, Basch terminated Blue Coral's Canadian distributorship. Approximately one year later, Blue Coral introduced EVER BRITE into the Canadian market. Blue Coral's Canadian trade dress was also substantially the same as its United States' version—merely substituting French print in some places on the can where English had been used, and placing a hyphen between EVER and BRITE where none had been before.

On March 7, 1989, Basch brought this action in the United States District Court for the Eastern District of New York. In its complaint, Basch alleged trade dress infringement in violation of § 43(a) of the Lanham Act. Blue Coral moved for summary judgment [which the district court] denied.

The action was tried to a jury in July 1991. The district court ruled that, as a matter of law, Basch was precluded from receiving damages on its trade dress infringement claim because it had failed to produce any evidence regarding actual consumer confusion or that Blue Coral acted with intent to deceive the public.

The district court concluded, however, that despite Basch's failure to introduce evidence on either of these points, Basch could recover Blue Coral's profits if it succeeded on its trade dress infringement claim. The case was submitted to the jury by special verdict. The jury found against [Blue Coral] on Basch's trade dress infringement claim. Accordingly, it awarded Basch $200,000 in Blue Coral's profits, allegedly stemming from Blue Coral's wrongful use of its EVER BRITE trade dress.

Blue Coral timely moved for judgment n.o.v. In its motion, Blue Coral argued that: (1) Basch had failed to prove that its NEVR–DULL trade dress enjoyed secondary meaning; (2) since Basch had not shown actual consumer confusion, or deceptive conduct on Blue Coral's part, Basch could not recover any of Blue Coral's profits; (3) it was for the district judge sitting as a court in equity, and not the jury, to make an award of profits; and (4) in any event, the $200,000 award was grossly in excess of its actual profits.

The district court denied Blue Coral's motion, and entered its judgment which included the $200,000 jury award. The judgment also contained an injunction allowing Blue Coral to sell off its remaining inventory of infringing cans, but prohibiting any future use of the existing trade dress in the United States market. The district court also denied Basch's application for attorney fees. This appeal followed.

Discussion

[W]e affirm the district court's judgment that Basch sufficiently established the necessary elements to support the jury's finding of liability.

Grounds for Awarding Profits

We turn now to the issue of whether the district court correctly authorized an award of Blue Coral's profits. Section 35(a) of the Lanham Act generally provides that a successful plaintiff under the act shall be entitled, "subject to the principles of equity, to recover (1) defendant's profits, (2) any damages sustained by the plaintiff, and (3) costs of the action." 15 U.S.C.A. § 1117(a). Clearly, the statute's invocation of equitable principles as guideposts in the assessment of monetary relief vests the district court with some degree of discretion in shaping that relief. See *id.*, (both damage and profit awards may be assessed "according to the circumstances of the case"). Nevertheless, that discretion must operate within legally defined parameters.

For example, it is well settled that in order for a Lanham Act plaintiff to receive an award of damages the plaintiff must prove either "actual consumer confusion or deception resulting from the violation," Getty Petroleum Corp. v. Island Transportation Corp., 878 F.2d 650, 655 (2d Cir.1989)(quoting PPX Enterprises, Inc. v. Audiofidelity Enterprises, Inc., 818 F.2d 266, 271 (2d Cir.1987)), or that the defendant's actions were intentionally deceptive thus giving rise to a rebuttable presumption of consumer confusion. See Resource Developers, Inc. v. Statue of Liberty–Ellis Island Foundation, Inc., 926 F.2d 134, 140 (2d Cir.1991); *PPX Enterprises*, 818 F.2d at 273. Here, Basch failed to present any evidence regarding consumer confusion or intentional deception. Accordingly, prior to the jury's deliberation, the district court correctly decided that damages were not an available form of relief. Basch does not appeal from this ruling.

However, with respect to authorizing an award of Blue Coral's profits, the district judge concluded that § 35(a) affords a wider degree of equitable latitude. In denying its j.n.o.v. motion, the district court rejected Blue Coral's position that, absent a finding of defendant's willfully deceptive conduct, a court may not award profits. Rather, it relied upon contrary dictum in Louis Vuitton S.A. v. Lee, 875 F.2d 584, 588–89 (7th Cir.1989), in determining that a Lanham Act plaintiff may be entitled to the profits of an innocent infringer, i.e., one who inadvertently misappropriates the plaintiff's trade dress. To the extent that the cases are ambiguous as to whether deceptive conduct is a necessary basis for an accounting, we take this opportunity to clarify the law.

The rule in this circuit has been that an accounting for profits is normally available "only if the 'defendant is unjustly enriched, if the plaintiff sustained damages from the infringement, or if the accounting is necessary to deter a willful infringer from doing so again.' " Burndy Corp. v. Teledyne Industries, Inc., 748 F.2d 767, 772 (2d Cir.1984) (quoting W. E. Bassett Co. v. Revlon, Inc., 435 F.2d 656, 664 (2d Cir.1970)). Courts have interpreted the rule to describe three categorically distinct rationales. See e.g., Cuisinarts, Inc. v. Robot–Coupe Intern. Corp., 580 F.Supp. 634, 637 (S.D.N.Y.1984)("These justifications are stated in the disjunctive. Any one will do.").

Thus, the fact that willfulness expressly defines the third rationale (deterrence) may suggest that the element of intentional misconduct is unnecessary in order to require an accounting based upon a theory of unjust enrichment or damages. However, the broad language contained in *Burndy Corp.* and *W. E. Bassett Co.* is in no way dispositive on this point. Indeed, a closer investigation into the law's historical development strongly supports our present conclusion that, under any theory, a finding of defendant's willful deceptiveness is a prerequisite for awarding profits.

Unjust Enrichment: The fact that an accounting may proceed on a theory of unjust enrichment is largely a result of legal institutional evolution. Prior to the fusion of law and equity under the Federal Rules of Civil Procedure, see Fed.R.Civ.P. 2., courts of law were the sole dispensary of damages, while the chancellor issued specific relief. However, in order to avoid piecemeal litigation, once a court of equity took jurisdiction over a case it would do complete justice—even if that entailed granting a monetary award. This resulted in the development of parallel remedial schemes.

Long ago, the Supreme Court explained the origin of profit awards in trademark infringement suits:

> The infringer is required in equity to account for and yield up his gains to the true owner [of the mark], upon a principle analogous to that which charges a trustee with the profits acquired by the wrongful use of the property of the *cestui que trust*. Not that equity assumes jurisdiction upon the ground that a trust exists.... The jurisdiction must be rested upon some other equitable ground—in ordinary cases, as in the present, the right to an injunction—but the court of equity, having acquired jurisdiction upon such a ground, retains it for the purpose of administering complete relief, rather than send the injured party to a court of law for his damages. And profits are then allowed as an equitable measure of compensation, on the theory of a trust *ex maleficio*.

Hamilton–Brown Shoe Co. v. Wolf Brothers & Co., 240 U.S. 251, 259 (1916).

Thus, a defendant who is liable in a trademark or trade dress infringement action may be deemed to hold its profits in constructive trust for the injured plaintiff. However, this results only "when the defendant's sales 'were attributable to its infringing use' of the plaintiff's" mark, *Burndy Corp.*, 748 F.2d at 772 (quoting *W. E. Bassett Co.*, 435 F.2d at 664), and when the infringing use was at the plaintiff's expense. *Id.* at 773. In other words, a defendant becomes accountable for its profits when the plaintiff can show that, were it not for defendant's infringement, the defendant's sales would otherwise have gone to the plaintiff. *Id.* at 772.

At bottom, this is simply another way of formulating the element of consumer confusion required to justify a damage award under the Lanham Act. As such, it follows that a profits award, premised upon a theory of unjust enrichment, requires a showing of actual consumer confusion—or at least proof of deceptive intent so as to raise the rebuttable presumption of consumer confusion. See *Resource Developers*, 926 F.2d at 140; *PPX Enterprises*, 818 F.2d at 273.

Moreover, the doctrine of constructive trust has traditionally been invoked to defeat those gains accrued by wrongdoers as a result of fraud. See Latham v. Father Divine, 85 N.E.2d 168, 170 (1949)("A constructive trust will be erected whenever necessary to satisfy the demands of justice.... Its applicability is limited only by the inventiveness of men who find new ways to enrich themselves by grasping what should not belong to them."); Restatement of Restitution, § 160 cmt.d (1937); cf. Robert Stigwood Group Ltd. v. O'Reilly, 530 F.2d 1096, 1100–1101 & n.9 (2d Cir.), *cert. denied*, 429 U.S. 848 (1976)(recognizing that imposition of a constructive trust over defendant's profits may be an available remedy for willful copyright infringement).

The rationale underlying the Supreme Court's holding in *Hamilton Shoe Co.* reflects this purpose. There, the Court upheld a profits award for trademark infringement where the "imitation of complainant's mark was fraudulent, [and] the profits included in the decree [were] confined to such as accrued to the defendant through its persistence in the unlawful simulation...." 240 U.S. at 261. Thus, it would seem that for the defendant's enrichment to be "unjust" in terms of warranting an accounting, it must be the fruit of willful deception. See El Greco Leather Products Co. v. Shoe World Inc., 726 F.Supp. 25, 29–30 (E.D.N.Y.1989).

Where Plaintiff Sustains Damages: Historically, an award of defendant's profits has also served as a rough proxy measure of plaintiff's damages. Champion Plug Co. v. Sanders, 331 U.S. 125, 131 (1947); Mishawaka Mfg. Co. v. S.S. Kresge Co., 316 U.S. 203, 206 (1942); *Hamilton Shoe Co.*, 240 U.S. at 261–62; see also, Restatement (Third) of Unfair Competition § 37 cmt.b (Tent. Draft No.3, 1991) ("Restatement"). Due to the inherent difficulty in isolating the causation behind diverted sales and injured reputation, damages from trademark or trade dress infringement are often hard to establish. Recognizing this, the Supreme Court has stated that, "infringement and damage having been found, the Act requires the trademark owner to prove only the sales of articles bearing the infringing mark." *Mishawaka Mfg. Co.*, 316 U.S. at 206.

Under this rule, profits from defendant's proven sales are awarded to the plaintiff unless the defendant can show "that the infringement had no relationship" to those earnings. *Id.* This shifts the burden of proving economic injury off the innocent party, and places the hardship of disproving economic gain onto the infringer. Of course, this "does not stand for the proposition that an accounting will be ordered merely because there has been an infringement." *Champion Plug Co.*, 331 U.S. at 131. Rather, in order to award profits there must first be "a basis for finding damage." *id.*; *Mishawaka Mfg. Co.*, 316 U.S. at 206. While a plaintiff who seeks the defendant's profits may be relieved of certain evidentiary requirements otherwise carried by those trying to prove damages, a plaintiff must nevertheless establish its general right to damages before defendant's profits are recoverable.

Thus, under the "damage" theory of profits, a plaintiff typically has been required to show consumer confusion resulting from the infringement. Cf. Perfect Fit Indus., Inc. v. Acme Quilting Co., 618 F.2d 950, 955 (2d Cir.), cert. denied, 459 U.S. 832 (1980)(New York law of unfair competition); G.H. Mumm Champagne v. Eastern Wine Corp., 142 F.2d 499, 501 (2d Cir.), cert. denied, 323 U.S. 715 (1944)(L. Hand, J.). Whether a plaintiff also had to show willfully deceptive conduct on the part of the defendant is not so clear. While some courts "rejected good faith as a defense to an accounting for profits," Burger King Corp. v. Mason, 855 F.2d 779, 781 (11th Cir.1988)(citing Wolfe v. National Lead Co., 272 F.2d 867, 871 (9th Cir.1959), cert. denied, 362 U.S. 950 (1960)), others have concluded that a defendant's bad faith is the touchstone of accounting liability. Cf. *Champion Plug Co.*, 331 U.S. at 131 (accounting was unavailable where "there had been no showing of fraud or palming off"); Carl Zeiss Stiftung v. VEB Carl Zeiss Jena, 433 F.2d 686, 706–08 (2d Cir.1970)(discussing monetary awards which are inclusive of both damages and profits).

Deterrence: Finally, we have held that a court may award a defendant's profits solely upon a finding that the defendant fraudulently used the plaintiff's mark. See Monsanto Chemical Co. v. Perfect Fit Mfg. Co., 349 F.2d 389, 396 (2d Cir.1965), cert. denied, 383 U.S. 942 (1966). The rationale underlying this holding is not compensatory in nature, but rather seeks to protect the public at large. By awarding the profits of a bad faith infringer to the rightful owner of a mark, we promote the secondary effect of deterring public fraud regarding the source and quality of consumer goods and services. *id.*; *W. E. Bassett Co.*, 435 F.2d at 664.

* * *

Although these three theories address slightly different concerns, they do share common ground. In varying degrees, a finding of defendant's intentional deceptiveness has always been an important consideration in determining whether an accounting was an appropriate remedy. In view of this, the American Law Institute has recently concluded that a finding of willful infringement is the necessary catalyst for the disgorgement of ill-gotten profits. See Restatement, § 37(1)(a)("One ... is liable for the net profits earned on profitable transactions resulting from [the infringement], if, but only if, the actor engaged in conduct with the intention of causing confusion or deception ... ").

We agree with the position set forth in § 37 of the Restatement and therefore hold that, under § 35(a) of the Lanham Act, a plaintiff must prove that an infringer acted with willful deception before the infringer's profits are recoverable by way of an accounting. Along with the Restatement's drafters, we believe that this requirement is necessary to avoid the conceivably draconian impact that a profits remedy might have in some cases. While damages directly measure the plaintiff's loss, defendant's profits measure the defendant's gain. Thus, an accounting may overcompensate for a plaintiff's actual injury and create a windfall judgment at the defendant's expense. See Restatement, § 37 at cmt.e. Of course, this is not to be confused with plaintiff's lost profits, which have been traditionally compensable as an element of plaintiff's damages.

So as to limit what may be an undue windfall to the plaintiff, and prevent the potentially inequitable treatment of an "innocent" or "good faith" infringer, most courts require proof of intentional misconduct before allowing a plaintiff to recover the defendant's profits. *id.*; see also ALPO Petfoods, Inc. v. Ralston Purina Co., 913 F.2d 958, 968 (D.C.Cir.1990); Frisch's Restaurants, Inc. v. Elby's Big Boy, 849 F.2d 1012, 1015 (6th Cir.1988); Schroeder v. Lotito, 747 F.2d 801, 802 (1st Cir.1984)(per curiam)(applying Rhode Island law). We underscore that in the absence of such a showing, a plaintiff is not foreclosed from receiving monetary relief. Upon proof of actual consumer confusion, a plaintiff may still obtain damages—which, in turn, may be inclusive of plaintiff's own lost profits. See *Getty Petroleum Corp.*, 878 F.2d at 655.

Neither *Burndy Corp.* or *W. E. Bassett Co.* rejects the notion that willful deceptiveness is a necessary predicate for an award of defendant's profits. See *El Greco Leather Products Co.*, 726 F.Supp. at 29. To the contrary, both cases reflect the centrality of this factor. For example, defendant's profits were denied in *Burndy Corp.* because the plaintiff failed to establish that its own sales were diverted as a result of the infringement and that the defendant acted willfully. This finding precluded both unjust enrichment and deterrence as available grounds for relief. See 748 F.2d at 773. On the other hand, an accounting was ordered in *W. E. Bassett Co.* solely because the defendant had "deliberately and fraudulently infringed Bassett's mark." 435 F.2d at 664. Finally, to the extent that these cases suggest that a defendant's profits are recoverable whenever a plaintiff may obtain damages, we conclude that the language of *Burndy Corp.* and *W. E. Bassett Co.* was simply imprecise on this point, and we reject such a reading. Cf. *Carl Zeiss Stiftung*, 433 F.2d at 706–08.

Having stated that a finding of willful deceptiveness is necessary in order to warrant an accounting for profits, we note that it may not be sufficient. While under certain circumstances, the egregiousness of the fraud may, of its own, justify an accounting, see *W. E. Bassett Co.*, 435 F.2d at 664, generally, there are other factors to be considered. Among these are such familiar concerns as: (1) the degree of certainty that the defendant benefited from the unlawful conduct; (2) availability and adequacy of other remedies; (3) the role of a particular defendant in effectuating the infringement; (4) plaintiff's laches; and (5) plaintiff's unclean hands. See generally Restatement, § 37(2) at cmt.f & cases cited in the reporter's notes. The district court's discretion lies in assessing the relative importance of these factors and determining whether, on the whole, the equities weigh in favor of an accounting. As the Lanham Act dictates, every award is "subject to equitable principles" and should be determined "according to the circumstances of the case." § 1117.

In light of the foregoing legal analysis, the district court's error becomes apparent. To begin with, the district judge concluded that an accounting was warranted in order to prevent Blue Coral's unjust enrichment. However, as stated earlier, Basch produced no evidence to suggest that the infringement caused any sales diversion. As a result, there is nothing to suggest that Blue Coral's EVER BRITE sales were at Basch's expense. It follows that "an accounting based on unjust enrichment is precluded." *Burndy Corp.*, 748 F.2d at 773.

Secondly, even if Basch had shown loss of sales, it still would not have been entitled to an accounting for profits under a theory of unjust enrichment—or any other theory. The jury made no finding to the effect that Blue Coral was a bad faith infringer. Indeed, one reason why the judge refused to let the jury assess damages was the fact that Basch failed to present any evidence regarding bad faith infringement. Nevertheless, Basch argues that the court's jury instruction on liability—which suggested that the jury consider whether Blue Coral intended "to benefit" from Basch's NEVR–DULL trade dress—taken in conjunction with the special verdict finding that Blue Coral "intended to imitate Basch's NEVR–DULL trade dress," results in a constructive finding that Blue Coral engaged in intentionally deceptive conduct. We disagree.

There is an "essential distinction ... between a deliberate attempt to deceive and a deliberate attempt to compete. Absent confusion, imitation of certain successful features in another's product is not unlawful and to that extent a 'free ride' is permitted." Norwich Pharmacal Co. v. Sterling Drug, Inc., 271 F.2d 569, 572 (2d Cir.1959) (citation omitted). Of course, even when a likelihood of confusion does arise, that does not inexorably lead to the conclusion that the defendant acted with deliberate deceit. Depending upon the circumstances, consumer confusion might as easily result from an innocent competitor who inadvertently crosses the line between a "free ride" and liability, as it could from a defendant's intentionally fraudulent conduct.

In this regard, we note that the jury specifically found that "the acts of [Blue Coral] in violation of Basch's rights [were not] done wantonly and maliciously and in reckless disregard of Basch's rights." This conclusion is buttressed by the fact this is not a case of a counterfeit trade dress from which a jury might infer that Blue Coral "intended to deceive the public concerning the origin of the goods." WSM, Inc. v. Tennessee Sales Co., 709 F.2d 1084, 1087 (6th Cir.1983). Thus, we find no merit in Basch's contention that the jury effectively concluded that Blue Coral acted with wrongful intent.

Accordingly, we reverse the district court's denial of Blue Coral's j.n.o.v. motion, insofar as it related to the availability of an accounting in this case, and we vacate the jury's profits award. Because we hold that an accounting was not available in this case, we need not reach the issue of whether it was appropriate for the jury to calculate profits.

II.   Basch's Cross–Appeal

A.   The District Court's Injunction

The district court's injunction restrained Blue Coral from using the present EVER BRITE trade dress in the United States, but authorized the defendant

> to manufacture, sell and distribute metal polishing cleaners in the same shape and size containers as previously used in the infringing trade dress if the color of the can is either silver or red . . . with leave granted to plaintiff for additional relief based upon a showing of actual confusion.

The court's order also permitted Blue Coral to continue using its present trade dress outside of the United States, and to sell off its remaining inventory of infringing cans.

In its cross-appeal, Basch argues that this relief was insufficient. Specifically, Basch contends that: the substantive breadth of the injunction is too narrow—i.e., a can by any other color is likely to confuse; and, the court erred in allowing Blue Coral to sell off its remaining inventory without ordering the defendant to account for the profits obtained from those sales. We find no merit in any of these arguments.

It is axiomatic that the contours of an injunction are shaped by the sound discretion of the trial judge and, barring an abuse of that discretion, they will not be altered on appeal. Springs Mills, Inc. [v. Ultracashmere House, Ltd.], 724 F.2d [352], 355 [(2d Cir.1983)]. Moreover, "a finding of likelihood of confusion in an infringement action does not automatically compel the issuance of an injunction. . . ." Jim Beam Brands Co. v. Beamish & Crawford Ltd., 937 F.2d 729, 737 (2d Cir.1991), *cert. denied*, 112 S.Ct. 1169 (1992). If the trial judge ultimately determines that injunctive relief is warranted, "the relief granted should be no broader than necessary to cure the effects of the harm caused." Soltex Polymer Corp. [v. Fortex Industries, Inc.], 832 F.2d [1325], 1329 [(2d Cir.1987)].

The instant injunction is consistent with these principles. First, given the fact that the EVER BRITE trade dress is, at best, only moderately similar to the overall appearance of the NEVR–DULL can, we agree with the district court that there was no need for Blue Coral to make major aesthetic changes. Basch was unable to produce any evidence of actual consumer confusion between NEVR–DULL and EVER BRITE during the approximately three years that EVER BRITE used the infringing trade dress. This suggests to us that the likelihood of confusion created by Blue Coral was minimal, thereby requiring only minimal correction. The district court's assessment that a change of can color would supply the needed distinction between products seems reasonable. In any event, the district court granted Basch leave to apply for additional relief upon a future showing of actual confusion.

Finally, we cannot fault the district court for allowing Blue Coral to liquidate its remaining inventory of infringing cans without requiring the defendant to account for the profits on those sales. Our approval stems largely from the fact that Basch never moved for a preliminary injunction to restrain Blue Coral's use of the trade dress in question. Actions speak louder than words, and motions speak loudest of all. Since Basch itself apparently concluded that the economic loss it was suffering, if any, did not warrant a remedy from the outset of this action, we cannot say that the district court abused its discretion in allowing Blue Coral to sell off its remaining cans and retain the profits. Cf. E.I. Dupont De Nemours & Co. v. Yoshida Int'l, Inc., 393 F.Supp. 502, 528 (E.D.N.Y.1975)(in minimizing injury to good faith infringer, injunction may provide for a grace period before use of infringing mark is permanently restrained); Carling Brewing Co. v. L. Fatato, Inc., 305 F.Supp. 1070, 1071 (E.D.N.Y.1969)(use grace period incorporated into permanent injunction).

B. Attorney Fees

The Lanham Act provides that "the court in exceptional cases may award reasonable attorney fees to the prevailing party." § 1117(a). The decision whether or not to award such fees also rests within the broad discretion of the district judge. Getty Petroleum Corp. v. Bartco Petroleum Corp., 858 F.2d 103, 114 (2d Cir.1988), *cert. denied*, 490 U.S. 1006 (1989). Basch argues that the district judge abused his discretion in denying its application for reasonable attorney fees. We disagree. In view of the fact that there was no finding of bad faith infringement in this case, indeed the jury specifically found that Blue Coral's actions in fashioning its EVER BRITE trade dress were not egregious, we find no abuse of discretion here. Orient Express Trading Co., Ltd. v. Federated Dep't Stores, Inc., 842 F.2d 650, 655 (2d Cir.1988).

Conclusion

Having reviewed the development of the relevant case law under §§ 43(a) and 35(a) of the Lanham Act, and having considered the underlying policies that the law seeks to implement, we conclude that before a defendant may be held to account for profits received in conjunction with a trade dress infringement, a plaintiff must first prove that the defendant acted with willful intent to deceive the public. Since the plaintiff in this case failed to establish this vital element, we partially reverse the district court's denial of Blue Coral's motion for judgment n.o.v., and vacate the jury award. We affirm the district court's grant of injunctive relief and denial of attorney fees.

Affirmed in part; reversed in part; and jury award vacated.

■ KEARSE, CIRCUIT JUDGE, dissenting in part.

I respectfully dissent from so much of the majority decision as reverses the monetary award to plaintiff George Basch Co. ("Basch") on account of the infringement by defendant Blue Coral, Inc. ("Blue Coral"), of the trade dress for Basch's product, NEVR–DULL. The district court, though finding that damages were unavailable because there was no proof of actual consumer confusion, determined that an award to Basch of Blue Coral's profits was appropriate because Blue Coral had been unjustly enriched by its infringement. The court had noted that if the question of profits was a matter to be decided by the court rather than the jury, the court would accept the jury's findings as advisory. See Fed.R.Civ.P. 39(c). Whether the final judgment reflects findings and conclusions by the court or a refusal to set aside the jury's verdict, I think the award of profits was a remedy permitted by law and was supported by the findings of a properly instructed jury.

The Lanham Act, § 1051 et seq. (1988), provides, in pertinent part, that when the plaintiff has established a violation of § 1125(a), which prohibits, *inter alia*, trade practices that falsely indicate a product's origin, the plaintiff is generally entitled, "subject to the principles of equity, to recover (1) defendant's profits, [and] (2) any damages sustained by the plaintiff." § 1117(a). The term "profits" is not coextensive with the term "damages," see, e.g., Monsanto Chemical Co. v. Perfect Fit Products Manufacturing Co., 349 F.2d 389 (2d Cir.1965) (affirming denial of damages, reversing denial of profits), *cert. denied*, 383 U.S. 942 (1966), and even where the plaintiff has not proven any loss of its own sales, and hence has not proven damages, an award of profits may be justified as an equitable remedy where the defendant has been unjustly enriched by his infringement, see *Id.* at 395; W. E. Bassett Co. v. Revlon, Inc., 435 F.2d 656, 664 (2d Cir.1970)("An accounting should be granted if the defendant is unjustly enriched. . . .").

In the present case, the evidence was that Blue Coral, having been the exclusive distributor of Basch's NEVR–DULL in Canada, asked Basch to produce a Blue Coral version of the product that Blue Coral could distribute in the United States under its own trademark. When negotiations failed to achieve agreement, Blue Coral set out to copy Basch's NEVR–DULL. (See, e.g., Plaintiff's Exhibit 34, a Blue Coral document dated March 28, 1988, entitled "LABORATORY MEMORANDUM NO. 19 [-] DUPLICATION OF NEVR–DULL," discussing "the feasibility of duplicating Nevr–Dull for manufacturing by Blue Coral.")

The jury was instructed, *inter alia*, that it could not find infringement of the NEVR–DULL trade dress simply on the basis that Blue Coral had intentionally copied it. Rather, it was told that if it found that Blue Coral had intentionally copied the NEVR–DULL trade dress, it could find infringement only if it also found a likelihood of confusion, which it might infer if it found "there was an intent to benefit from Basch's protectable right in its NEVR–DULL trade dress." The court also told the jury that the amount of monetary damages it could award for trade-dress infringement was "limited to what you find the defendant Blue Coral made as a result of the violation of Nevr–Dull trade dress." The court explained that the jury could properly award to Basch only the amount Blue Coral made that it would not be fair or equitable for Blue Coral to retain.

Having been thus instructed, the jury was asked the following questions and gave the following answers:

> "Was Basch's trade dress for its NEVR–DULL product inherently distinctive? Yes."

"Did the trade dress for Basch's NEVR–DULL product acquire secondary meaning? Yes."

"Did defendants intend to imitate Basch's NEVR–DULL trade dress? Yes."

"Did defendants' use of its trade dress in marketing EVER BRITE create a likelihood of confusion among a substantial number of members of the consuming public as to the source of EVER BRITE, i.e., as to whether EVER BRITE was manufactured by the maker of NEVR–DULL? Yes."

"Did the violation of Basch's rights proximately cause damage to Basch? Yes."

The jury found that the "profits earned by Blue Coral due to trade dress infringement" totaled "$200,000."

These findings of Blue Coral's intentional copying of a distinctive trade dress that had acquired secondary meaning, thereby creating a likelihood of consumer confusion, in order to benefit from the breach of Basch's rights, and culminating in the unfair receipt by Blue Coral of $200,000 in profits due to the infringement, suffice, in my view, to support the conclusion that Blue Coral was unjustly enriched. I would affirm the district court's judgment that an award of profits was justified.

Sands, Taylor & Wood Co. v. Quaker Oats Co.

United States Court of Appeals, Seventh Circuit, 1992.
978 F.2d 947, cert. denied ___ U.S. ___, 113 S.Ct. 1879, 123 L.Ed.2d 497 (1993).

■ CUDAHY, CIRCUIT JUDGE.

Sands, Taylor & Wood Company (STW) brought this action against The Quaker Oats Company (Quaker) for federal trademark infringement and related state-law claims, alleging that Quaker's use of the words "Thirst Aid" in its advertising slogan "Gatorade is Thirst Aid" infringed STW's registered trademark for THIRST–AID. The district court agreed, and entered judgment for STW in the amount of $42,629,399.09, including prejudgment interest and attorney's fees. The court also permanently enjoined Quaker from using the words "Thirst Aid." Not surprisingly, Quaker appeals.

The district court awarded STW ten percent of Quaker's profits on sales of Gatorade for the period during which the "Thirst Aid" campaign ran—$24,730,000—based on its finding that Quaker had acted in bad faith. The court also ordered Quaker to pay STW's attorney's fees, again based on the finding of bad faith, as well as prejudgment interest on the award of profits beginning from May 12, 1984. Quaker challenges all three of these rulings.

A. Profits

Quaker argues that an award of its profits was inappropriate here because there was no evidence that Quaker intended to trade on STW's good will or reputation; indeed, such an intent is necessarily absent in a reverse confusion case. According to Quaker, an award of the defendant's profits is justified only where the defendant has been unjustly enriched by appropriating the plaintiff's good will. There is some support for this position in the case law. "To obtain an accounting of profits, the courts usually require that defendant's infringement infer some connotation of 'intent,' or a knowing act denoting an intent, to infringe or reap the harvest of another's mark and advertising." [2 J. Thomas McCarthy, Trademarks and Unfair Competition § 30:25, at 498 (2d ed. 1984)]. The law of this circuit is not, however, so limited. As we stated in Roulo [v. Russ Berrie & Co., Inc.]:

> The Lanham Act specifically provides for the awarding of profits in the discretion of the judge subject only to principles of equity. As stated by this Court, "The trial court's primary function is to make violations of the Lanham Act unprofitable to the infringing party." [citation omitted] Other than general equitable considerations, there is no express requirement that the parties be in direct competition or that the infringer wilfully infringe the trade dress to justify an award of profits. [citation omitted] Profits are awarded under different rationales including unjust enrichment, deterrence, and compensation.

886 F.2d [931], 941 [(7th Cir.1989)]. This broader view seems to be more consistent with the language of the Lanham Act than is the narrower (though perhaps more logical) rule espoused by Quaker. 2 McCarthy, *supra* § 30:28, at 514–15. We decline to adopt Quaker's restrictive interpretation in light of Seventh Circuit precedent.

Nevertheless, we are mindful of the fact that awards of profits are to be limited by "equitable considerations." The district court justified the award of profits based on its finding that Quaker acted in bad faith. The evidence of bad faith in this case, however, is pretty slim. The court based its finding on (1) Quaker's "failure to conduct a basic trademark search until days before the airing of the Thirst Aid commercial," and its "anonymous, cursory investigations" of Karp's[a] use of the mark once it obtained such a search; (2) Quaker's decision to continue with the "Thirst Aid" campaign after it discovered Karp's registrations; (3) the fact that Quaker did not seek a formal legal opinion regarding potential trademark issues until after the first "Thirst Aid" commercials were aired; and (4) Quaker's failure to take "reasonable precautions" to avoid the likelihood of confusion. Sands, Taylor & Wood [v. The Quaker Oats Co.], 18 U.S.P.Q.2d [(BNA) 1457], 1472–73 [(N.D.Ill.1990)].

None of these facts is particularly good evidence of bad faith. For example, Quaker's in-house counsel, Lannin, testified at trial that his review of the "Thirst Aid" campaign in February or March of 1984 did not include a trademark search because he concluded that the proposed advertisements used the words "Thirst Aid" descriptively, and not as a trademark, and therefore did not raise any trademark issues. The district court apparently accepted this testimony, but nonetheless found Quaker's failure

---

[a] [Karp was the assignee of STW's registrations for THIRST–AID, but it entered into a licenseback agreement with STW, resulting in STW's ownership of the trademark registrations.]—eds.

to investigate indicative of bad faith. Further, the court stated that it is a "close question" whether "Thirst Aid" is a descriptive term. Indeed, this court has found that the district court erred in concluding that "Thirst Aid" was not descriptive as a matter of law. A party who acts in reasonable reliance on the advice of counsel regarding a close question of trademark law generally does not act in bad faith. Cuisinarts, Inc. v. Robot–Coupe Int'l Corp., 580 F.Supp. 634, 637 (S.D.N.Y.1984).

Nor does Quaker's decision to proceed with the "Thirst Aid" campaign once it learned of Karp's registrations necessarily show bad faith. Based both on his earlier conclusion that "Thirst Aid" was descriptive and on his investigation into Karp's use of the term, which revealed that Karp was not currently using the THIRST–AID mark on any products sold at retail, Lannin concluded that Quaker's ads did not infringe Karp's rights in its marks. That conclusion was confirmed by the opinion Quaker obtained a few weeks later from its outside counsel, which concluded that Quaker was making a fair use of "Thirst Aid" because "Thirst–Aid" [sic] is not used as a trademark on the product but rather clearly as a positioning statement or claim in advertising. It is used descriptively to inform the purchaser that the product will aid your thirst, and as a play on the words "First Aid." "The fact that one believes he has a right to adopt a mark already in use because in his view no conflict exists since the products are separate and distinct cannot, by itself, stamp his conduct as in bad faith." Nalpac, Ltd. v. Corning Glass Works, 784 F.2d 752, 755 (6th Cir.1986)(quoting Mushroom Makers, Inc. v. R.G. Barry Corp., 441 F.Supp. 1220, 1230 (S.D.N.Y.1977), aff'd, 580 F.2d 44 (2d Cir.1978)). Even the defendant's refusal to cease using the mark upon demand is not necessarily indicative of bad faith. Absent more, courts should "not make an inference of bad faith from evidence of conduct that is compatible with a good faith business judgment." Munters Corp. v. Matsui America, Inc., 730 F.Supp. 790, 799–800 (N.D.Ill.1989), aff'd, 909 F.2d 250 (7th Cir.1990).

Quaker's failure to obtain a formal legal opinion from outside counsel until after the "Thirst Aid" campaign began is similarly weak evidence of bad faith. Given Lannin's sincere, reasonable conclusion that Quaker's ads used "Thirst Aid" descriptively, so that no trademark issue was raised, Quaker had no reason to seek the opinion of outside trademark counsel. Similarly, Quaker had no reason to take any precautions to avoid likelihood of confusion; Quaker's research had revealed that there was no product about which people were likely to be confused.[b]

A determination of bad faith is a finding of fact subject to the clearly erroneous standard of review. Web Printing Controls Co. v. Oxy–Dry Corp.,

---

[b] The district court finds it indicative of bad faith that Quaker did not contact STW after receiving its trademark search, even though STW's name was "referenced on the trademark report." Sands, Taylor & Wood, 18 U.S.P.Q.2d at 1472. The reference to STW appears in a list of "Thirst Aid" uses found by searching various directories—in the case of STW, the Thomas Grocer Register. STW's name does not appear on any of the federal registrations that the search turned up, nor does it appear anywhere in conjunction with Karp's name. Quaker's failure to contact STW based on the reference in the trademark report is at best weak evidence of bad faith.

906 F.2d 1202, 1205 n.3 (7th Cir.1990). We cannot say on this record that the district court's conclusion was clearly erroneous. We do think, however, that the evidence of bad faith here is marginal at best. Further, this is not a case where the senior user's trademark is so well-known that the junior user's choice of a confusingly similar mark, out of the infinite number of marks in the world, itself supports an inference that the junior user acted in bad faith. 2 McCarthy, *supra* § 23:33, at 147. There is no question that Quaker developed the "Thirst Aid" campaign entirely independently, with no knowledge of STW's marks. In such a case, an award of $24 million in profits is not "equitable"; rather, it is a windfall to the plaintiff. Quaker may have been unjustly enriched by using STW's mark without paying for it, but the award of profits bears no relationship to that enrichment. A reasonable royalty, perhaps related in some way to the fee STW was paid by Pet, would more accurately reflect both the extent of Quaker's unjust enrichment and the interest of STW that has been infringed. We therefore reverse the district court's award of profits and remand for a redetermination of damages. A generous approximation of the royalties Quaker would have had to pay STW for the use of the THIRST–AID mark had it recognized the validity of STW's claims seems to us an appropriate measure of damages, although perhaps not the only one. In any event, we can conceive of no rational measure of damages that would yield $24 million.[c]

B.   Attorney's Fees

The Lanham Act provides for recovery of attorney's fees by the prevailing party in "exceptional cases." § 1117(a). The district court concluded that this was such an exceptional case based on its finding that Quaker acted in bad faith. Because we affirm that finding, we also affirm the award of attorney's fees. The "equitable considerations" which lead us to reverse the award of profits do not apply to this issue.

C.   Prejudgment Interest

As the district court noted, the Lanham Act is silent with respect to prejudgment interest. The court nevertheless decided to award such interest, relying on this Circuit's rule that "prejudgment interest should be presumptively available to victims of federal law violations. Without it, compensation is incomplete and the defendant has an incentive to delay." Gorenstein Enterprises, Inc. v. Quality Care–USA, Inc., 874 F.2d 431, 436 (7th Cir.1989). Quaker argues that the Lanham Act's silence means that

---

[c] Because neither Judge Ripple nor Judge Fairchild joins this part of the court's opinion, it expresses the individual views of Judge Cudahy. To enable this issue to be decided by majority vote, however, Judge Cudahy has no difficulty with deferring to Judge Ripple's view, expressed in his separate opinion, that the district court's award of damages should be reversed and remanded for "a more precise determination" not limited to a reasonable royalty. Thus, Judges Cudahy and Ripple agree that, in recalculating the award of damages, the district court should be guided by the following principles: (1) the court may not simply award STW a percentage of Quaker's profits; (2) the court should use a reasonable royalty as a baseline or sorting point for determining the appropriate award; (3) in determining the appropriate award, the court may take into account the possible need for deterrence, which may involve consideration of the amount of Quaker's profits.

prejudgment interest is not available in an action for infringement under the Act. No court of appeals has accepted this argument, and we decline to do so here. We do, however, vacate the award of prejudgment interest and remand for recalculation based on the redetermination of damages we have ordered.

For the foregoing reasons, the decision of the district court is AFFIRMED in part, REVERSED in part and REMANDED for further proceedings.

■ RIPPLE, CIRCUIT JUDGE, concurring.

In my view, Quaker's corporate conduct in this matter deserves a somewhat less charitable appraisal than that presented. Therefore, in assessing damages, I believe the district court, in the exercise of its discretion, might well place substantial emphasis on deterrence. See Roulo v. Russ Berrie & Co., Inc., 886 F.2d 931, 941 (7th Cir.1989). Therefore, I doubt very much that damages measured by a "reasonable royalty"—a speculative approximation itself—necessarily would suffice in this case. Nevertheless, I agree with Judge Cudahy that the district court's use of a "percentage of profits" benchmark for the award of damages is difficult to sustain. I therefore concur in his conclusion that a more precise determination is appropriate.

■ FAIRCHILD, SENIOR CIRCUIT JUDGE, dissenting in part.

Twenty-four million dollars ($24 million) is, indeed, a big number. It is, however, only 10% of the profit realized by Quaker out of the product it marketed by using STW's mark. We are affirming the finding that Quaker used the mark in bad faith. The real question, it seems to me, is one of causation. What portion of Quaker's profit resulted from its use of THIRST AID, and therefore constituted unjust enrichment? I am unable to say that the district court's estimate of 10% was unreasonable or clearly erroneous. Quaker made no showing that it should have been a different number. The 90% ($216 million) of profit which Quaker retains is no paltry reward for everything it contributed to the success of the venture.

Therefore, I respectfully dissent from the decision to reverse the award.

Texas Pig Stands, Inc. v. Hard Rock Cafe International, Inc.

United States Court of Appeals, Fifth Circuit, 1992.
951 F.2d 684.

■ BROWN, CIRCUIT JUDGE.

We traverse the barbecue heartland of the South to resolve this trademark dispute between Texas Pig Stands, Inc. (TPS), and Hard Rock Cafe International, Inc. ("Hard Rock" or "Hard Rock Cafe"). The controversy centers around the two restaurant chains' use of the term "pig sandwich" to describe a Tennessee dish of barbecued pig meat on wheat or white bun. TPS owns a registration on the term and brought suit contending that Hard Rock's use of it in its Dallas restaurant constituted an infringement on TPS' rights to the two-word title. TPS sought equitable relief and attorney's fees.

At the trial below, the jury agreed with TPS that Hard Rock was guilty of deliberate infringement on TPS' mark, which it determined was capable of registration, and concluded also that TPS could recover for Hard Rock's unjust enrichment. The trial court accepted the jury finding of infringement but reversed its finding of unjust enrichment, essentially granting a j.n.o.v. Consequently, the court refused to award TPS the profits Hard Rock gained from pushing the porcine fare under the "pig sandwich" moniker. Finally, the trial court awarded TPS attorney's fees. Both parties appealed to this Court.

We affirm the trial court's holding that the term "pig sandwich" is protectable and capable of registration. We also affirm the court's reversal of the jury finding of unjust enrichment. Finally, we conclude that the court abused its discretion in awarding TPS attorney's fees for bringing this litigation.

This Little Piggy Went to Market

The pig sandwich's long and illustrious career has its origins in the hills of western Tennessee. The porcine delicacy has endeared itself to the hearts and stomachs of the citizenry there since the turn of the century. The founder of the Hard Rock Cafe, Isaac Tigrett, grew up in this area, and Jesse Kirby, one of the founders of the predecessor company to TPS, traveled extensively in the heartland of pig sandwiches in the early 1920's. Both men were apparently inspired by the dish's popularity and eventually included the garnished barbecued pork sandwich in their menus.

TPS' predecessor, Pig Stands Company, Inc. (Pig Stands), opened its very first "Pig Stand" in Dallas on September 15, 1921, which quickly enjoyed great success. In the early years of its operation, Pig Stands was in veritable hog-heaven, with over one hundred Pig Stands opening up from California to New York. The entire time, the term "pig sandwich" was used to describe its barbecued pork sandwich. The term had also become part of its distinctive sign, menus, and promotional advertising items.

Alas, however, the nation's love affair with pig sandwiches eventually chilled, resulting in the widespread closing of most Pig Stands. The last Pig Stand in Dallas closed in September, 1985, and currently less than ten Pig Stands still operate in Texas.

Tigrett first offered a barbecued pork sandwich with the name "pig sandwich" at the Hard Rock Cafe restaurant he opened in Jackson, Tennessee, in 1982. Tigrett later introduced the pig sandwich to New York and Stockholm, Sweden, when he opened Hard Rock Cafe restaurants in those cities. Then, in November 1986, just over a year after TPS closed its last Stand in Dallas, Tigrett opened up a Hard Rock Cafe restaurant there, featuring the pig sandwich on its menu.

This Little Piggy Went to See His Lawyer

TPS notified Hard Rock in writing on October 20, 1987, of TPS' claim to rights to the term "pig sandwich" and demanded that Hard Rock cease its infringement. Hard Rock contends that at the time it did not know that TPS even existed, much less that it claimed any rights to the term "pig sandwich." Believing that it had the right to use the term "pig sandwich" as the generic name for its barbecued pork sandwich, Hard Rock refused to cease using it and instead chose to stay in its house and let TPS try to blow it down. Whether Hard Rock's legal edifice is made of brick, twigs, or straw remains to be seen.

TPS commenced this action against Hard Rock in 1989 claiming trademark and service mark infringement and unfair competition under the Lanham Act. In its complaint, TPS requested a permanent injunction against Hard Rock's use of the term "pig sandwich," as well as an award of Hard Rock's profits, reasonable attorney's fees, prejudgment interest, and costs. The case was tried to a jury on nine special issues. The jury found in favor of TPS on each issue, concluding both that Hard Rock's infringement was willful and that Hard Rock was unjustly enriched by its infringement.

The trial court conducted a post-trial hearing to consider the amount of Hard Rock's profits and the question whether TPS should be awarded attorney's fees. While the trial court found that Hard Rock profited from its sale of pig sandwiches, it refused to award any profits to TPS, stating that it was "convinced that [Hard Rock] would have sold just as many pig sandwiches by any other name." Further, the trial court asserted that "the jury's finding of unjust enrichment is not supported by the record and cannot stand." The trial court then granted the sought-for injunction and, in a subsequent damages hearing, awarded attorney's fees and costs in excess of $400,000.

Neither party was pleased with this decision, and a flurry of appeals and cross appeals ensued. TPS contests the trial court's refusal to award profits in accordance with the jury's finding of unjust enrichment. Hard Rock returns the volley, contending that there was insufficient evidence to support the jury finding that "pig sandwich," standing alone, is a protectable mark and that the trial court erred in not cancelling TPS' registration for "pig sandwich," and in awarding attorney's fees to TPS.

[The Court affirmed the jury's conclusion that "pig sandwich" was not generic and had acquired secondary meaning; cancellation therefore was not warranted.]

Unjust Enrichment—Did Hard Rock Bring Home the Bacon?

With the underlying determination of the protectability of "pig sandwich" intact, we move on to the trial court's rejection of the jury's unjust enrichment finding. As TPS argues, the trial court's order vitiates the jury findings, effectively granting partial j.n.o.v. against TPS. During the post-trial damages hearing, the trial court stated: "having heard all the evidence in the case, [the court] is of the opinion that monetary relief is not warranted in this case." Later in its holding, however, the court specifically rejected the jury finding of unjust enrichment.

Had the court gone no further than its first statement, and not overturned the jury finding, we would review this issue under a much different standard. Under § 1117(a) the trial court has wide discretion to increase or reduce the amount of profits recoverable by the plaintiff "if the court shall find that the amount of the recovery based on profits is either inadequate or excessive ... according to the circumstances of the case." Under an abuse of discretion standard, we would have little difficulty upholding the trial court's determination that monetary relief is not warranted. See [Dixiepig Corp. v. Pig Stand Co., 31 S.W.2d 325 (Tex.Civ. App.1930)]. However, because the court did not merely adjust the amount of the recovery, but rather threw out the jury finding for recovery altogether, we must apply the *Boeing* standard. [Boeing Co. v. Shipman, 411 F.2d 365 (5th Cir., 1969)]. See e.g., Oxford Indus. Inc. v. Hartmarx Corp., 15 U.S.P.Q.2d (BNA) 1648, 1655 (N.D.Ill.1990)(while the origins of unjust enrichment are both legal and equitable, a jury finding of fact in favor of unjust enrichment may be overturned "only under the standards for granting a motion for judgment notwithstanding the verdict")(citing Hussein v. Oshkosh Motor Truck Co., 816 F.2d 348, 355 (7th Cir.1987)).

The definition of unjust enrichment provided to the jury accurately frames the questions that must be answered here: (i) Would Hard Rock's retention of its profits for pig sandwich sales be unjust and inequitable? and (ii) Did Hard Rock use the reputation and good will of TPS to sell its own pig sandwiches? In assessing the evidence presented, while no single evidentiary fact carries the day, from the totality of the circumstances present we conclude that the jury did not have before it sufficient competent evidence "of such quality and weight that reasonable and fairminded men in the exercise of impartial judgment," *Boeing*, 411 F.2d at 374, might arrive at a finding of unjust enrichment.

On a review of the evidence, we conclude that there is simply no indication that Hard Rock attempted to "palm off" its pig sandwiches as those of TPS, nor did they attempt to associate their operation with TPS. TPS acknowledges that it did not lose a single sale due to Hard Rock's use of "pig sandwich." While the diversion of sales is not a prerequisite to an award of profits, Maltina Corp. v. Cawy Bottling Co., 613 F.2d 582, 585 (5th Cir.1980), it is one of the factors to be considered. Bandag, Inc. v. Al Bolser's Tire Stores, Inc., 750 F.2d 903, 919 (Fed.Cir.1984). The same is true of palming off—while it is not a prerequisite to finding unjust enrichment, it is an important circumstance bearing on the determination. Champion Spark Plug Co. v. Sanders, 331 U.S. 125, 130 (1947). Here, the total absence of all of these factors fatally undercuts the jury's conclusion. See *Bandag*, 750 F.2d at 917–19 (no equitable recovery without showing of fraud or palming off; examination of the record did not reveal any evidence showing that plaintiff had lost substantial business and profits as a result of defendant's unfair competition).

In sum, we hold that the evidence before the jury simply was not of the quality and weight necessary to support a finding of unjust enrichment. See *Boeing*, 411 F.2d at 374. The granted permanent injunction adequately remedies the complained-of infringement, and awarding TPS any of Hard Rock's profits would be far from equitable—it would be a windfall. See *Bandag*, 750 F.2d at 917–18 (plaintiff is not entitled to a windfall of profits if an injunction alone will satisfy the equities of the case).

Award of Attorney Fees—Did the Trial Court Go Hog Wild?

After throwing out the jury's unjust enrichment finding at the post-trial damages hearing, the trial court also determined that this case was "exceptional" under § 1117(a), and awarded attorney's fees to TPS accordingly. Under this section of the Lanham Act, the trial court judge may, in his discretion, award attorney's fees in "exceptional" cases to the prevailing party. Hard Rock contests this determination, arguing that this case fell far short of the interpretation the courts have uniformly given to the term "exceptional."

We emphasize that here we are not dealing with the *Boeing* sanctity of the jury verdict. Imposition of attorney's fees on the unsuccessful infringer is not a matter for the jury. In the first place, the unique situation of this case and its trial reflects that no monetary awards were before the jury on the infringer's substantive liability. More than that, the imposition of attorney's fees by nature and statute, see § 1117(a), is reserved to the trial judge. This means that, unlike a jury verdict or a finding of fact as such, the standard or review is whether the court abused its discretion. For the reasons set forth, we hold that it did.

In support of the award, the trial court determined that Hard Rock acted "in simple disregard of plaintiff's rights." This disregard, the trial court held, made the case "exceptional." The trial court then justified this holding by making a notable observation which reveals its true conception of "exceptional":

> The large, prosperous company was unwilling to show any respect to the smaller, struggling business.... The larger, guilty company can more easily absorb the loss than the smaller, innocent one. If plaintiff had to pay its own fees, it would suffer for having to protect its trademark and service mark rights.

This noble sentiment does not meet the congressional standard of "exceptional." The legislative history of § 1117 suggests that an "exceptional case" is one in which the defendant's trademark infringement "can be characterized as 'malicious,' 'fraudulent,' 'deliberate,' or 'willful.'" S.Rep. No. 93–1400, 93rd Cong., 2d Sess., reprinted in 1974 U.S.Code Cong. & Ad.News 7132, 7133. The statutory provision has been interpreted by courts to require a showing of a high degree of culpability on the part of the infringer, for example, bad faith or fraud. See Baskin–Robbins Ice Cream v. Pillsbury Co., 1 U.S.P.Q.2d (BNA) 1223, 1224 (N.D.Tex.1986); see also Joy Mfg. Co. v. CGM Valve & Gauge Co., Inc., 730 F.Supp. 1387, 1395 (S.D.Tex.1989)(attorney's fees awarded where defendant reconditioned and painted valves and affixed unauthorized new name plates to make valves look like new); compare *V.I.P. Foods, Inc. v. Vulcan Pet, Inc.*, 675 F.2d 1106, 1107 (10th Cir.1982)(refusing to award attorney's fees where the court found that defendant had no intent to deceive or confuse the public). On the other hand, the parties' relative economic positions should not enter into the determination, even when an award of punitive damages would serve as an example to deter other infringers. As one court has stated:

> [Plaintiff] gives a persuasive argument as to the sound reason for allowing attorney's fees, that is to seek to prevent by example others from pirating trademarks belonging to those who have them registered and who will properly and legally be using them and that argument has great merit and perhaps should be the law, but as I read the statute it is not the law.

Plough, Inc. v. Sun Fun Prods., Inc., 200 U.S.P.Q. (BNA) 236, 237 (M.D.Fla.1977).[a]

The trial court pointed to the jury determination that Hard Rock's infringement was willful in an attempt to bring its determination in line with this established precedent, but this attempt is unavailing. A jury finding of willfulness does not bind the trial court in determining whether this case is "exceptional";[b] it may, however, serve as a guide. Here, the guide is a poor one due to the definition of "willful" provided in the special interrogatories: "An act is done 'willfully' if it is done voluntarily and intentionally and not because of accident or other innocent reason." This standard falls far short of the kind of culpability required to render a case "exceptional." While we do not condone Hard Rock's infringement, its actions do not approach "deliberate pirating" or "egregious conduct."[c]

The trial court's own conclusions built Hard Rock's house, brick by brick, that neither the court nor TPS could blow down—one wall, the absence of palming off; the second wall, the lack of any intent to deceive or

---

[a] Some cases have also recognized the plaintiff's loss of profits or the suffering of economic damage as important factors. See *V.I.P. Foods*, 675 F.2d at 1107 ("the court also found that plaintiff had suffered no ascertainable damage or loss of profits because of defendant's use of the V.I.P. mark"); *Burger King Corp. v. Metro Club, Inc.*, 208 U.S.P.Q. 293, 306 (E.D.Mich.1980)(an "exceptional case" almost invariably involves "a situation where the infringer is either hurting the protected mark holder financially or has it within his power by his wrongful conduct to do so"). While the lack of such damage does not prohibit a trial court from finding the case to be "exceptional," *The Post Office v. Portec, Inc.*, 913 F.2d 802, 812 (10th Cir.1990), such a finding is an important circumstance to consider.

[b] The Department of Commerce, in requesting the insertion of the provision for attorney's fees in the Lanham Act, stated

that the decision "whether to award treble damages, attorney fees, or both, or neither" would be within the trial court's discretion. S.Rep. No. 1400, 93rd Cong.2d Sess., reprinted in 1974 U.S.Code Cong. & Admin.News 7132, 7136.

[c] A few cases have gone as far as to require "very egregious conduct" to constitute an "exceptional" case. See e.g., *Burger King*, 208 U.S.P.Q. at 306; *Kayser–Roth Corp. v. Fruit of the Loom, Inc.*, 219 U.S.P.Q. 736, 752 (S.D.N.Y.1983)(holding that infringer's conduct must be egregious, as "the intentional infringement of a trademark has been held insufficient to justify an award under the statute"). We do not attempt to draw a bright line determination for what conduct constitutes an "exceptional" case for all circumstances and situations; we hold only that the facts before us today do not reach the "exceptional" level.

confuse; the third wall, the lack of any attempt to profit from such infringement; and to complete the structure, the finding of a total lack of any damage or hardship to TPS' business and good will. Hard Rock's financial success and size do not undermine this construction; these facts do not even enter into it. This being an "unexceptional" case, we hold that the trial court abused its discretion in awarding attorney's fees to TPS under § 1117(a).

D–D–Dt D–D–Dt That's All, Folks!

TPS now leaves this legal barnyard with its mark intact, but we cannot allow it to attain a windfall on account of Hard Rock's infringement. While the jury had sufficient evidence to find "pig sandwich" to be a descriptive mark that had acquired secondary meaning, Hard Rock's infringement merits only the grant of a permanent injunction, and not an award of profits. Furthermore, though not entirely kosher, Hard Rock's actions were not sufficiently swinish to bring this case to the "exceptional" level required for an award of attorney's fees. Thus, the trial court order granting a permanent injunction for trademark infringement and denying the award of profits is AFFIRMED, and the order awarding attorney's fees is REVERSED.

AFFIRMED IN PART, REVERSED IN PART.

■ JOHNSON, CIRCUIT JUDGE, dissenting.

Despite the majority's attempt to diminish the jury's finding of a knowing, deliberate infringement, the majority quotes with seeming approval the district court's assessment of the evidence that the "defendant sold pig sandwiches knowing of plaintiff's mark ... in simple disregard of plaintiff's rights." There can be no question that Hard Rock deliberately infringed on Texas Pig Stands' trademark. It knew of that mark and openly refused to honor it. In such a case, trademark law demands that the infringer be penalized, lest such infringement be encouraged and the valuable protections of the trademark laws vitiated. Mistakenly, in this writer's opinion, the majority today goes to great lengths to avoid imposing any penalty whatsoever on an admittedly willful and deliberate infringer.

Upon a finding of a knowing trademark violation, the victim of the violation is entitled to both injunctive and monetary relief. §§ 1114, 1117. There is no question here that it was appropriate to enjoin Hard Rock from further use of Texas Pig Stands' mark in the future. The question here is whether Texas Pig Stands should have been afforded any monetary recovery for previous violations. The prior cases of this Court and the purposes of the trademark laws demand that Hard Rock be required to pay a monetary penalty, in order to render its deliberate infringement unprofitable.

The possible monetary remedies for trademark infringement include

(a) the profits acquired by the defendant as a result of its infringement,

(b) the damages sustained by the trademark owner,

(c) the costs of the action, *and*

(d) in an "exceptional case," reasonable attorneys' fees.

§ 1117(a)(emphasis added). See also Bandag, Inc. v. Al Bolser's Tire Stores, 750 F.2d 903, 917 (Fed.Cir.1984). The district court is given great discretion to fashion an equitable remedy. § 1117(a); *Bandag*, 750 F.2d at 917.

This is not the first time this Court has addressed the issue of whether a plaintiff should have any monetary recovery if it has not itself suffered any lost sales or other damages as a result of a defendant's willful infringement. Just over a decade ago, this Court was faced with a similar case—one in which the infringer acted knowingly and deliberately, yet did not cause the victim to lose any sales. We there noted initially that the Lanham Act, and in particular § 1117, "entitles a markholder to recover, subject to the principles of equity, the profits earned by a defendant from infringement of the mark." Maltina Corp. v. Cawy Bottling Co., Inc., 613 F.2d 582, 584 (5th Cir.1980). The question, though, was whether the plaintiff should recover those profits even if it had not itself lost any profits or sales as a result of the infringement.

> The courts have expressed two views of the circumstances in which an accounting is proper under Section 1117. Some courts view the award of an accounting as simply a means of compensating a markholder for loss or diverted sales. Other courts view an accounting not as compensation for lost or diverted sales, but as redress for the defendant's unjust enrichment and as a deterrent to further infringement. See Maier Brewing Co. v. Fleischmann Distilling Corp., 390 F.2d 117, 121 (9th Cir.), *cert. denied*, 391 U.S. 966 (1968).... Accordingly, we must decide whether diversion of sales is a prerequisite to an award of an accounting. We hold that it is not.

> In *Maier Brewing* the Ninth Circuit awarded an accounting to a plaintiff who was not in direct competition with a defendant and who, accordingly, had not suffered any diversion of sales from the defendant's infringement. The court noted that the defendant had wilfully and deliberately infringed. It reasoned that awarding an accounting would further Congress' purpose in enacting Section 1117 of making infringement unprofitable. *This Court is in accord with this reasoning.*

Id. at 584–85 (emphasis added). This Court observed that an accounting "serves two purposes: remedying unjust enrichment and deterring future infringement." Furthermore, the Court recognized that because an accounting alone does not render infringement unprofitable, it "will not adequately deter future infringement." *Id.*

In this case there were two potential penalties which might, in equity, have been imposed on Hard Rock for its deliberate violation of federal law. Either would have rendered Hard Rock's infringement unprofitable and provided an appropriate deterrent. Based on the facts found by the jury, the district court in this case could have either 1) forced Hard Rock to disgorge the profits it made selling food under Texas Pig Stands' trademark, or 2) compelled Hard Rock to pay Texas Pig Stands' attorneys' fees. The district court, exercising its discretion to fashion an equitable result, chose the second of these options. The majority of this panel, substituting its judgment for that of the district court, now refuses to allow the imposition of any penalty and allows Hard Rock to keep whatever profits accrued from Hard Rock's willful and deliberate infringement.

There should be no question that the district court could have either awarded Texas Pig Stands the profits earned by Hard Rock or could have awarded Texas Pig Stands its attorneys' fees. Section 1117 plainly allows an award of the infringer's profits upon a showing of a knowing violation, and the majority acknowledges that Texas Pig Stands need not have proved that it lost any sales in order to recover Hard Rock's profits. Thus, while the district court was not required to do so, it certainly had the authority to award Hard Rock's profits to Texas Pig Stands. In the judgment of the district court, however, such an award was not required to reach an equitable result, and the district court thus exercised its discretion to deny such an award.

At the same time, however—and as part of its equitable resolution of this matter—the district court determined that it would be inequitable and unjust to require Texas Pig Stands to bear the expense and burden of defending its mark, when the only result would be an injunction forbidding *continued* infringement. After all, while the injunction might restore the *status quo ante*, the victim of the infringement, Texas Pig Stands, has had to bear the entire burden of the past infringement. Refusing to inflict such a Pyrrhic victory on Texas Pig Stands, the district court required Hard Rock to pay Texas Pig Stands' attorneys' fees. The majority now sets aside the judgment of the district court, makes its own determination of the equities of this fact sensitive case, and decrees a new and different result. The majority's proffered reason is that this is not an "exceptional" case and Texas Pig Stands therefore does not qualify for attorneys' fees. The short answer to this assertion is that, as the majority seemingly acknowledges, the legislative history of section 1117 makes plain that an exceptional case is one in which the infringement is "deliberate" or "willful." Here the jury made a specific finding that the infringement was willful. Furthermore, the majority admits that the infringement was knowing and deliberate. Clearly, this case not only qualifies as one in which attorneys' fees are available but also calls out for such a result.

The majority's oft-expressed concern about a "windfall" for the plaintiffs has led it to an unjust and unwarranted result. For one thing, there would be no windfall here. Awarding attorneys' fees to Texas Pig Stands would not in any way constitute a windfall—such fees would do no more than provide appropriate compensation to Texas Pig Stands for its efforts to vindicate its protected economic rights. Moreover, even if there were a windfall, certainly it is far better to allow a windfall to the innocent victim than to place the entire burden of the litigation on that victim and allow the culpable party to profit from its infringement.

The message conveyed by the majority's determination here is that despite what this Court has heretofore written, it may now be permissible and profitable to infringe on the trademark of another. While the Fifth Circuit might eventually put a stop to that illegal infringement, that infringement nonetheless still could be profitable. The trademark laws generally, and section 1117 in particular, do not countenance such a result. The message this Court should send is that infringement—and particularly the knowing, deliberate, and willful infringement—will have two consequences. It will be enjoined and it will be made unprofitable.

As the majority does not send that message, I must respectfully dissent.

Lever Bros. Co. v. United States

United States Court of Appeals, District of Columbia, 1993.
981 F.2d 1330.

■ SENTELLE, CIRCUIT JUDGE.

The District Court entered a judgment invalidating the "affiliate exception" of 19 C.F.R. § 133.21(c)(2)(1988) as inconsistent with the statutory mandate of the Lanham Act of 1946, 15 U.S.C.A. § 1124 (1988), prohibiting importation of goods which copy or simulate the mark of a domestic manufacturer, and issued a nationwide injunction barring enforcement of the regulation with respect to any foreign goods bearing a valid United States trademark but materially and physically differing from the United States version of the goods. The United States appeals. We conclude that the District Court, obedient to our limited remand in a prior decision in this same cause, properly determined that the regulation is inconsistent with the statute. However, because we conclude that the remedy the District Court provided is overbroad, we vacate the judgment and remand for entry of an injunction against allowing the importation of the foreign-produced Lever Brothers brand products at issue in this case.

I. Background[a]

Lever Brothers Company ("Lever US" or "Lever"), an American company, and its British affiliate, Lever Brothers Limited ("Lever UK"), both manufacture deodorant soap under the "Shield" trademark and hand dishwashing liquid under the "Sunlight" trademark. The trademarks are registered in each country. The products have evidently been formulated differently to suit local tastes and circumstances. The U.S. version lathers more, the soaps smell different, the colorants used in American "Shield" have been certified by the FDA whereas the colorants in British "Shield" have not, and the U.S. version contains a bacteriostat that enhances the deodorant properties of the soap. The British version of "Sunlight" dishwashing soap produces less suds, and the American version is formulated to work best in the "soft water" available in most American cities, whereas the British version is designed for "hard water" common in Britain.

The packaging of the U.S. and U.K. products is also somewhat different. The British "Shield" logo is written in script form and is packaged in

[a] We present an abbreviated background as we have already provided some detail in our prior opinion. Lever Bros. Co. v. United States, 877 F.2d 101 (D.C.Cir.1989)("Lever I").

foil wrapping and contains a wave motif, whereas the American "Shield" logo is written in block form, does not come in foil wrapping and contains a grid pattern. There is small print on the packages indicating where they were manufactured. The British "Sunlight" comes in a cylindrical bottle labeled "Sunlight Washing Up Liquid." The American "Sunlight" comes in a yellow, hourglass-shaped bottle labeled "Sunlight Dishwashing Liquid."

Lever asserts that the unauthorized influx of these foreign products has created substantial consumer confusion and deception in the United States about the nature and origin of this merchandise, and that it has received numerous consumer complaints from American consumers who unknowingly bought the British products and were disappointed.

Lever argues that the importation of the British products was in violation of section 42 of the Lanham Act, which provides that with the exception of goods imported for personal use:

> [N]o article of imported merchandise which shall copy or simulate the name of the [sic] any domestic manufacture, or manufacturer ... or which shall copy or simulate a trademark registered in accordance with the provisions of this chapter ... shall be admitted to entry at any customhouse of the United States.

Id. The United States Customs Service ("Customs"), however, was allowing importation of the British goods under the "affiliate exception" created by 19 C.F.R. § 133.21(c)(2), which provides that foreign goods bearing United States trademarks are not forbidden when "the foreign and domestic trademark or tradename owners are parent and subsidiary companies or are otherwise subject to common ownership or control."[b]

In *Lever I*, we concluded that "the natural, virtually inevitable reading of section 42 is that it bars foreign goods bearing a trademark identical to the valid U.S. trademark but physically different," without regard to affiliation between the producing firms or the genuine character of the trademark abroad. 877 F.2d 101, 111 (D.C.Cir.1989). In so concluding, we applied the teachings of Chevron U.S.A. Inc. v. NRDC, 467 U.S. 837 (1984). Under the *Chevron* analysis, if Congress has clearly expressed an intent on a matter, we give that intent full effect (Step One of *Chevron*). If there is any ambiguity, we accept Customs' interpretation, provided only that it is reasonable (Step Two of *Chevron*). See *Lever I*, 877 F.2d at 105 (citing *Chevron* 467 U.S. at 842–43). The *Lever I* panel found the present controversy to survive barely *Chevron* Step One and "provisionally" concluded that the affiliate exception is inconsistent with section 42 with respect to physically different goods.[c] The "provisional" qualifier on our determina-

---

[b] This case does not involve a dispute between corporate affiliates. Neither Lever US nor Lever UK has authorized the importation which is being conducted by third parties. See *Lever I*, 877 F.2d at 103.

[c] In *Lever I*, we expressly recognized that our decision was not in conflict with the Supreme Court's decision in K Mart Corp. v.

Cartier Inc., 486 U.S. 281 (1988), which upheld the affiliate exception against a challenge based on section 526 of the Tariff Act of 1930, 19 U.S.C.A. § 1526 (1988), but "did not reach the question of the exception's validity under section 42 of the Lanham Act." *Lever I*, 877 F.2d at 108 & n.8.

tion of the invalidity of the exception was a very limited one. Noting that "neither party has briefed the legislative history nor administrative practice in any detail," we adopted the apparently controlling reading of section 42 only "tentatively" and remanded the case to the District Court to allow the parties to "join issue on those points." *Lever I*, 877 F.2d at 111. The panel in *Lever I* thus created a very small window of opportunity for the government to establish that the affiliate exception regulation was consistent with section 42 of the Lanham Act. At that time we said, "subject to some persuasive evidence running against our tentative conclusion, we must say that Lever's probability of success on its legal argument is quite high." *Id.*

Our task today is clearly circumscribed. Under the "law of the case" doctrine, any determination as to an issue in the case which has previously been determined is ordinarily binding upon us. Because no reason exists in this case to avoid application of the general rule, we are bound by this Court's prior determinations concerning the application of the *Chevron* doctrine.

After reviewing the submissions of the parties, the District Court found that Customs' administrative practice was "at best inconsistent" and, in any event, had "never addressed the specific question of physically different goods that bear identical trademarks." Lever Bros. Co. v. United States, 796 F.Supp. 1, 5 (D.D.C.1992). The District Court concluded that "section 42 ... prohibits the importation of foreign goods that ... are physically different, regardless of the validity of the foreign trademark or the existence of an affiliation between the U.S. and foreign markholders." *Id.* The court accordingly concluded that "neither the legislative history of the statute nor the administrative practice of the Customs Service clearly contradicts the plain meaning of section 42" and granted summary judgment against the government. *Id.* at 13.

By way of remedy, the District Court enjoined Customs "from enforcing 19 C.F.R. § 133.21(c)(2) as to foreign goods that bear a trademark identical to a valid United States trademark but which are materially, physically different." *Lever Bros. Co.*, 796 F.Supp. at 6.

II. Analysis

Here the specific question at Step Two of *Chevron* is whether the intended prohibition of section 42 admits of an exception for materially different goods manufactured by foreign affiliates. We apply a very limited Step Two *Chevron* analysis, see *Chevron*, 467 U.S. at 842–43, because we previously concluded that the intent of Congress is virtually plain. *Lever I*, 877 F.2d 101 at 104–05. The government bears a heavy burden in attempting to overcome the apparent meaning of the statute. A presumption in favor of reasonably clear statutory language will be disrupted only if there is a "'clearly expressed legislative intention' contrary to that language." INS v. Cardoza–Fonseca, 480 U.S. 421, 432 n.12 (1987)(quoting United States v. James, 478 U.S. 597, 606 (1986)). When we remanded this case, we indicated that the Government could not prevail unless it produced "persuasive evidence" rebutting our tentative reading of the statute, *Lever I*, 877 F.2d at 111, because the affiliate exception appears to contradict the clear implication of the language of section 42. The legislative history and administrative practice before us, as before the District Court, will not perform that onerous task.

A. Legislative History and Administrative Practice Prior to Enactment of Lanham Act

The first federal statute regulating the importation of trademarked merchandise was enacted in 1871. It prohibited the importation of "watches, watch cases, watch movements, or parts of watch movements, of foreign manufacture, which shall copy or simulate the name or trade-mark of any domestic manufacturer," unless the domestic manufacturer was the importer. Act of March 3, 1871, ch.125, § 1, 16 Stat. 580. Little legislative history accompanied the 1871 Act as the final legislation was adopted without debate in either house of Congress. See Cong. Globe, 41st Cong., 3d Sess. 1926, 1994 (1871). The administrative record is also sparse, but it does make clear that the domestic manufacturer was to have complete control over the importation of watches bearing its trademark.

In 1883, Congress amended the law to extend trademark protection to all kinds of domestic merchandise. The amended statute provided that "no watches, watch-cases, watch-movements, or parts of watch-movements, or any other articles of foreign manufacture" that simulated or copied the trademark of a domestic manufacturer would be allowed entry. 22 Stat. 488, 490 (1883). Although the phrase "any other articles of foreign manufacture" was added at conference, the conference report does not explain the addition. See 14 Cong. Rec. 3713 (1883). The Treasury Department ("Treasury") interpreted the 1883 statute to prohibit foreign manufacturers from importing goods that an American manufacturer had requested to be manufactured abroad on its behalf and stamped with its trademark.

Section 7 of the Tariff Act of 1890 revised the protection accorded to domestic merchandise, providing in relevant part, that "no article of imported merchandise which shall copy or simulate the name or trademark of any domestic manufacture or manufacturer, shall be admitted to entry at any custom-house of the United States." 26 Stat. 567, 613 (1890). Unlike the earlier provisions, this statute did not include an exception for foreign merchandise imported by the domestic trademark owner, nor was any provision made for entry with the domestic trademark owner's consent. It is unclear from the legislative history why Congress did not include special language allowing importations by the domestic trademark owner. It is clear, however, that the domestic trademark owner still retained effective control over the importation of goods bearing its trademark since all foreign merchandise bearing its mark was barred from entry.

The 1890 trademark importation provision was reenacted with almost identical language in 1894. Tariff Act of 1894, § 6, 28 Stat. 547. An 1897 reenactment expanded the sweep of the provision to prohibit the entry of articles marked in a manner "calculated to induce the public to believe that the article is manufactured in the United States." Tariff Act of 1897, § 11, 30 Stat. 207. Although the legislative history is again sparse, it appears the language was added to provide further protection to the public against deceptive marks. See 4 Treas. Dec. 506, 508 (1901) (ruling that even if Customs found a recorded trademark to be invalid, foreign merchandise must nevertheless be excluded if bottled or labeled so as to lead public to believe it was manufactured in United States).

Section 27 of the Trade–Mark Act of 1905, 33 Stat. 724, 730 (1905), amplified governmental protection of trademarks against imports. Trademark protection was extended to all trademarks registered with the then Patent Office. Certain foreign interests were allowed to register their trademarks in the United States, and "traders" as well as manufacturers were given import protection. Again, however, there was no mention of anything akin to the affiliate exception.

In Fred Gretsch Manufacturing Co. v. Schoening, 238 F. 780 (2d Cir.1916), the Second Circuit held that section 27 did not prohibit a third party from importing violin strings manufactured in Germany that bore a trademark registered in the United States by an American who had contracted to be the exclusive agent for the sale of the strings in the United States. The Treasury Department interpreted this decision narrowly and instructed local customs officers that this opinion was "to be applied only to cases where the mark covered by the United States registration is one which was adopted and is used by a foreign manufacturer upon merchandise manufactured by him, and the registration of which in the United States is to protect and cover the foreign article when sold in this country." Treas. Dec. Int. Rev. 37021, 32 Treas. Dec. 203, 204 (1917).

The Supreme Court interpreted section 27 more broadly. In A. Bourjois & Co. v. Katzel, 260 U.S. 689 (1923), the Court held that a third party could not import a face powder manufactured in France when the plaintiff owned the United States trademarks for the product, even though the product sold was "the genuine product of the French concern...." *Id.* at 691. The Supreme Court concluded that even an authentic foreign trademark on "genuine" merchandise may infringe a registered United States trademark. In another case that year involving the same Bourjois company, the Supreme Court held in a per curiam memorandum that third-party importation of goods bearing an authentic identical foreign trademark infringed the United States trademark owner's rights under section 27 and must be excluded from entry by Customs. A. Bourjois Co. v. Aldridge, 263 U.S. 675 (1923)(answering questions certified to it by the Second Circuit at 292 Fed. 1013 (2d Cir.1922)).

Until 1936, the regulations implementing section 27 quoted the statute, then provided for an absolute ban on imports bearing trademarks that copied or simulated United States marks. In 1936 the Treasury Department adopted new regulations implementing section 27 in light of *Aldridge.* See T.D. 48537, 70 Treas. Dec. 336 (1936). Section 518(b) of the regulations stated that a foreign mark, even if a "genuine trade-mark ... in a foreign country," shall be deemed to "copy or simulate" a United States mark if the foreign mark is "identical with a trade-mark ... protected by the laws of the United States." *Id.*

Section 518(b) of the 1936 regulations also included a "same person" exception, the first precursor of the affiliate exception:

> However, merchandise manufactured or sold in a foreign country under a trade-mark or trade name, which trade-mark is registered and recorded, shall not be deemed for the purpose of these regulations to copy or simulate such United States trade-mark or trade name if such foreign trade-mark or trade name and such United States trade-mark or trade name are owned by the same person, partnership, association, or corporation.

Id. The regulation did not explain the source of this exception, and there is no evidence that Customs considered the issue of physically different imports.

Several conclusions can be drawn from the pre-Lanham Act legislative history and administrative practice. First, at least until 1936, protection from unauthorized importation was consistently based upon ownership of a United States trademark, not upon the nature of the relationship between the trademark owner and the foreign producer. Second, as trademark law became more international, the trend was toward greater protection from foreign importation. Third, although the 1936 regulations implemented the first version of the affiliate exception, the specific question of materially different goods is nowhere addressed.

B. Legislative History of Section 42 of Lanham Act

In the late 1930s and early 1940s, Congress considered a wholesale revision and codification of the United States trade-mark laws, resulting in the Lanham Trade–Mark Act of 1946. In 1944, the Tariff Commission submitted a memorandum to the Senate Subcommittee on Patents which, after discussing the legislative and administrative history of section 27, stated that "in the light of the Supreme Court's decision in the *Bourjois* case, ... Section 27 of the Trade–Mark Act of 1905 prohibits the entry of all articles bearing marks which infringe registered trade-marks." Hearings on H.R. 82 Before the Subcomm. of the Senate Comm. on Patents, 78th Cong., 2d Sess. 86 (1944)(hereinafter "1944 Hearings"). The memorandum explicitly stated that the 1905 Act's phrase "all articles" included "articles identical with those sold by the registrant under his mark and bearing identical trade-marks." *Id.* The memorandum then added: "However, section 27 does not apply to the registrant's own merchandise, i.e., merchandise of the registrant bearing the registrant's mark, which mark has been applied by or for the account of the registrant." *Id.*

In *Lever I*, we concluded that the Tariff Commission's memorandum "falls far short of ratification of the affiliate exception, at least in the broad form applied by Customs here." 877 F.2d at 106. We noted two shortcomings with reliance on this memorandum. First, the memorandum refers to "articles identical to those sold by the registrant," but "makes no mention of the situation presented here, where a third party imports foreign goods bearing a valid foreign trademark identical to a US trademark but covering physically different goods." *Id*. Customs failed to respond to this point on remand, and for good reason: the 1944 memorandum does not address the distinction between identical and materially different merchandise.

Second, we stated that "we can find no indication that a single member of Congress, much less the committee, much less members speaking on the floor of either house, ever excavated these paragraphs from the mass in which they lay embedded." *Id*. The United States responds to this by noting that Senator Pepper, Chairman of the Subcommittee, requested the memorandum to be made part of the record, 1944 Hearings at 83, from which it infers congressional awareness of Customs' policy. We conclude that this evidence is insufficient to meet our earlier stated objection. The routine insertion into the record of an agency's prepared hearing testimony is at best minuscule evidence that this testimony reflected shared congressional intent at the time of enactment.

It is also noteworthy that the 1944 memorandum does not refer to "affiliates" or "closely affiliated" companies, but only to the importation of one's "own" merchandise. In short, there is nothing in the record concerning the Lanham Act indicating that Congress contemplated—much less intended to allow—an affiliate exception. More to the point, there is no evidence that Congress intended to allow third parties to import physically different trademarked goods that are manufactured and sold abroad by a foreign affiliate of the American trademark holder.

C. Legislative History and Developments Since Passage of Lanham Act

The Treasury Department's administrative practice after passage of the Lanham Act has been inconsistent. The 1936 regulations remained in effect until 1953, when the Department briefly adopted a "related companies" exception. See T.D. 53399, 88 Treas. Dec. 376, 384 (1953). There was no indication that this regulation took cognizance of physically different goods. In any event, Treasury abandoned the related-companies exception in 1959 because it was inconsistent with section 42. Treas. Dec. Int. Rev. 54932, 94 Treas. Dec. 433 (1959), 24 FR 7522 (Sept. 18, 1959). There is some evidence that Customs continued to apply the related-companies exception, even after the Customs regulations were returned to their earlier formulation, although apparently only to identical "gray market" goods. See K Mart Corp. v. Cartier, Inc., 486 U.S. 281, 311 (1988).

In the 1950s, several attempts were made to enact the affiliate exception into law. None of these bills were passed; furthermore, none of them suggest that physically different infringing imports would be permitted.

After Congress repeatedly considered and failed to enact the affiliate exception, the Treasury Department revived the exception. In 1972 the affiliate exception was adopted in the form at issue here. See 37 FR 20677 (1972). Under the 1972 regulations, section 42's protections were rendered inapplicable where:

(1) Both the foreign and the U.S. trademark or trade name are owned by the same person or business entity;

(2) The foreign and domestic trademark or trade name owners are parent and subsidiary companies or are otherwise subject to common ownership or control;

(3) The articles of foreign manufacture bear a recorded trademark or trade name applied under authorization of the U.S. owner.

19 C.F.R. § 133.21(c)(citations omitted).[d]

Neither the notice proposing the regulations, 35 FR 19269 (1970), nor the final notice adopting them, Treas. Dec. Int. Rev. 72–266, 6 Cust. B. & Dec. 538 (1972), explained their rationale. The statement accompanying the final rule contained no response to objections raised by several companies and associations.

Customs has not even adhered consistently to its own 1972 regulations. In Bell & Howell: Mamiya Co. v. Masel Supply Co., 719 F.2d 42 (2d Cir.1983), the Department of Justice and Customs filed an amicus curiae brief urging that import protection be provided to exclude parallel imports of identical foreign goods made by a company affiliated with the U.S. trademark owner. At that time, Customs took the position that "neither the legislative reports nor the congressional debate contain any clear evidence of a legislative intent to deny trademark protection where the owner of the U.S. mark is owned or controlled by the foreign manufacturer of the trademarked goods." Brief of the United States as Amicus Curiae at 8, Bell & Howell: Mamiya Co. v. Masel Supply Co., 719 F.2d 42 (2d Cir.1983).

The United States denounces its *Bell & Howell* brief now on the grounds that Customs signed the brief without the knowledge or approval of the Treasury Department, and deems it irrelevant because it never resulted in a change to the regulations at issue in this case. We stress that monumental inferences cannot be drawn from inconsistent litigating positions taken by a large agency, but the Customs Service's position in favor of excluding imports in *Bell & Howell* is evidence of Lever's claim that Customs' administrative policy has been inconsistent. And Customs' assertion in the *Bell & Howell* brief that the legislative history of the Lanham Act contains no clear evidence in support of the affiliate exception is undeniably relevant given that Customs defends the opposite position here.

In 1978, Congress added an exception to section 42 for goods imported for personal consumption. Customs Procedural Reform and Simplification

---

[d] In K Mart Corp. v. Cartier, Inc., 486 U.S. 281 (1988), the Supreme Court struck down 19 C.F.R. § 133.21(c)(3), which allowed the importation of foreign-made goods where the United States trademark owner has authorized the use of the mark, as in conflict with the unequivocal language of section 526 of the Tariff Act. Section 526 prohibits the importation of "any merchandise of foreign manufacture" bearing a trademark "owned by" a citizen of, or by a "corporation . . . organized within, the United States" unless written consent of the trademark owner is produced at the time of entry. 19 U.S.C.A. § 1526. By a different majority, the Supreme Court upheld 19 C.F.R. § 133.21(c)(2), the regulation at issue here, as consistent with section 526. As we noted above, the *K Mart* case did not address the validity of these regulations under the Lanham Act. See *supra* n.c.

Act of 1978, 19 U.S.C.A. § 1526(d)(1978). However, neither the 1978 amendment nor the accompanying legislative history sheds any light on the application of section 42 in general, or the affiliate exception in particular.

In 1984, Congress enacted the Trademark Counterfeiting Act of 1984, 18 U.S.C.A. § 2320 (1984). That statute, however, was a criminal statute and did not take the form of an amendment to section 42. Thus, any views expressed in the legislative history of that statute "form a hazardous basis for inferring the intent" of the Congress that enacted section 42. Consumer Prod. Safety Comm'n v. GTE Sylvania, Inc., 447 U.S. 102, 117 (1980). In any event, the legislative history accompanying the 1984 Act does not address the question of the importation of physically different trademarked goods manufactured by affiliated companies.

Customs' main argument from the legislative history is that section 42 of the Lanham Act applies only to imports of goods bearing trademarks that "copy or simulate" a registered mark. Customs thus draws a distinction between "genuine" marks and marks that "copy or simulate." A mark applied by a foreign firm subject to ownership and control common to that of the domestic trademark owner is by definition "genuine," Customs urges, regardless of whether or not the goods are identical. Thus, any importation of goods manufactured by an affiliate of a U.S. trademark owner cannot "copy or simulate" a registered mark because those goods are *ipso facto* "genuine."

This argument is fatally flawed. It rests on the false premise that foreign trademarks applied to foreign goods are "genuine" in the United States. Trademarks applied to physically different foreign goods are not genuine from the viewpoint of the American consumer. As we stated in *Lever I*:

> On its face ... section [42] appears to aim at deceit and consumer confusion; when identical trademarks have acquired different meanings in different countries, one who imports the foreign version to sell it under that trademark will (in the absence of some specially differentiating feature) cause the confusion Congress sought to avoid. The fact of affiliation between the producers in no way reduces the probability of that confusion; it is certainly not a constructive consent to importation.

877 F.2d at 111.

There is a larger, more fundamental and ultimately fatal weakness in Customs' position in this case. Section 42 on its face appears to forbid importation of goods that "copy or simulate" a United States trademark. Customs has the burden of adducing evidence from the legislative history of section 42 and its administrative practice of an exception for materially different goods whose similar foreign and domestic trademarks are owned by affiliated companies. At a minimum, this requires that the specific question be addressed in the legislative history and administrative practice. The bottom line, however, is that the issue of materially different goods was not addressed either in the legislative history or the administrative record. It is not enough to posit that silence implies authorization, when the authorization sought runs counter to the evident meaning of the governing statute. Therefore, we conclude that section 42 of the Lanham Act precludes the application of Customs' affiliate exception with respect to physically, materially different goods.

IV. Scope of Injunction

The United States alternatively argues that this Court should vacate the District Court's injunction that applies to materially different goods other than those directly at issue in this case. The District Court's injunction provides that the Customs Service is "enjoined from enforcing [the common ownership or control provision] as to foreign goods that bear a trademark identical to a valid United States trademark but which are materially, physically different." Lever Bros. Co. v. United States, 796 F.Supp. 1, 5 (D.D.C.1992).

The United States points out that this suit was brought by a single company, proceeding solely on its own behalf, to protect two specific trademarks. Lever never asked the District Court to enjoin Customs from applying the affiliate exception to other trademarks or other companies, nor did Lever seek to certify this suit as a class action. In its prayer for relief, Lever asked only that the Customs Service be permanently enjoined "from enforcing said regulations with respect to plaintiff's 'Shield' and 'Sunlight' trademarks, and directing defendants to exclude from entry into the United States any foreign-manufactured merchandise and material bearing said trademarks." To be sure, Lever did include boilerplate language requesting that the court award "such other and further relief as the Court may deem just and proper," *id.* at 8, but this is too slender a reed upon which to rest a nationwide injunction under the facts of this case. We therefore conclude that Lever is entitled only to that relief specifically sought in its complaint, namely, that Customs be enjoined from allowing the importation of Lever's "Shield" and "Sunlight" trademarks.

V. Conclusion

For the foregoing reasons, we affirm the District Court's ruling that section 42 of the Lanham Act, § 1124, bars the importation of physically different foreign goods bearing a trademark identical to a valid U.S. trademark, regardless of the trademark's genuine character abroad or affiliation between the producing firms. Injunctive relief, however, is limited to the two products which were the subject of this action. We therefore vacate the District Court's prior order to the extent that it renders global relief and remand for the entry of an injunction consistent with this opinion.

So ordered.

NOTES

1. *Injunctive relief.* Injunctive relief is the standard remedy in trademark cases and a plaintiff need only prove likelihood of confusion in order to obtain this remedy.[15] Still, courts do consider equitable defenses such as laches and estoppel in determining the propriety of injunctive relief.[16] Because likelihood of confusion is the touchstone in trademark litigation, an objectionable use may be infringing in some contexts, but not in others. Therefore, frequently injunctions are qualified so that they clearly specify the nature of the prohibited conduct. Another issue that arises in conjunction with the imposition of injunctive relief in trademark infringement actions was explored in Part A of Assignment 4. Recall the *Dawn Donut* case which held that the plaintiff could not obtain injunctive relief in a region that it had not yet physically entered. Courts which follow *Dawn Donut* hold that "the nationwide right conferred by registration does not entitle the owner to injunctive relief unless there is a present likelihood of confusion."[17]

2. *Compensatory damages.* Due to the ease with which injunctive relief is obtained in trademark infringement actions, damages are of secondary importance.[18] This is illustrated by the more restrictive requirements of actual confusion or bad faith which are imposed by some circuits. For example, *Basch* indicated that, to recover damages, a plaintiff must prove actual consumer confusion or that the defendant acted in an intentionally deceptive manner. As *Sands* observed, sometimes the reasonable royalty approach popular in patent law is invoked as a means of determining damages in trademark cases.[19] One form of monetary relief unique to trademark and unfair competition cases is the imposition on the defendants of the costs for corrective advertising.[20]

3. *Defendant's profits.* *Basch* highlights the distinction between an award of damages and profits by stating that "[w]hile damages directly measure the plaintiff's loss, defendant's profits measure the defendant's gain" and "[t]hus, an accounting may overcompensate for a plaintiff's actual injury and create a windfall judgment at the defendant's expense." *Sands* and *Basch* illustrate that courts are split over whether to award the defendant's profits in the absence of bad faith. If Nestle relies on *Sands* for an award of profits in the Principal Problem, what do you think the defendant would argue in response? Professor McCarthy has stated that "[t]he courts appear not willing to grant an accounting of profits unless the judge 'gets mad' at the defendant."[21] When an award of profits is made, the plaintiff must only establish the defendant's sales, and the "defendant must prove all elements of cost or deduction."[22] Moreover, apportionment is appropriate with respect to those profits that are not attributable to the infringement.

---

[15] See Brown, supra note 6, at 51, 65.

[16] See, e.g., Dial–A–Mattress Operating Corp. v. Mattress Madness, Inc., 841 F.Supp. 1339, 1355 (E.D.N.Y.1994)(laches and estoppel together will bar injunctive relief); Death Tobacco Inc. v. Black Death USA, 31 U.S.P.Q.2d 1899, 1907 (C.D.Cal.1993)(court considering whether to grant injunctive relief "sits in equity and must take all equitable considerations into account").

[17] Minnesota Pet Breeders Inc. v. Schell & Kampeter Inc., 41 F.3d 1242, 1246 (8th Cir.1994).

[18] Brown, supra note 6, at 65.

[19] Id.

[20] Id.

[21] 4 McCarthy § 30:25[3].

[22] § 1117(a).

The Lanham Act is unique in that it provides that the award of defendant's profits can be increased or decreased at the court's discretion. The statute also provides that such a sum "shall constitute compensation and not a penalty."[23] Still, the statute does not provide a ceiling on the increase of profits.[24] How is an increased profit award different from punitive damages (see Note 6)? The profits adjustment clause has been used infrequently, and therefore its scope has not been defined.[25]

4. *Attorney's fees.* Section 1117(a) also provides that reasonable attorney's fees may be awarded to the prevailing party in "exceptional cases." As *Hard Rock Cafe* illustrates, determining what constitutes an exceptional case often is difficult. Some cases require a showing of bad faith, fraud, malice, or knowing infringement on the part of the losing party in order for an award of attorney's fees to be imposed. Some courts also will refrain from awarding attorney's fees if the plaintiff fails to show any damages.[26] One court has stated that "[t]ypically attorneys' fee cases involve deliberate attempts by the defendant to pass off its goods as those of the plaintiff by applying plaintiff's trademark to defendant's goods."[27] What do you think of Judge Cudahy's resolution of the attorney's fees issue in *Sands*? Should a distinction be drawn between the awarding of attorney's fees to prevailing plaintiffs and to prevailing defendants? When attorney's fees are awarded, how shall they be calculated? Should attorney's fees be awarded in cases involving the importation of grey market goods?

5. *Treble damages.* Section 1117(a) provides that "[i]n assessing damages, the court may enter judgment, according to the circumstances of the case, for any sum above the amount found as actual damages, not exceeding three times such amount."[28] How are treble damages different from punitive damages? Note that an award of treble damages is mandatory when the infringement is intentional and the use of a counterfeit trademark is involved. See Note 9 infra.

6. *Punitive damages.* Following the *Sands* opinion reprinted in the casebook, the district court recalculated the plaintiff's damages in the amount of $20,656,822, which represented a doubling of the hypothetical base royalty of $10,328,411. This award was based on a deterrence rationale. On appeal, *Quaker* maintained that the doubling of the base royalty was a penalty which is prohibited by § 1117(a) of the Lanham Act. The court's opinion contains an excellent discussion of the tension between the provisions for enhancement of profits and treble damages, on the one hand, and the prohibition of punitive damages on the other.[29] It emphasized that the final remedy must "provide a sufficient deterrent to ensure that the guilty party will not return to its former ways and once again pollute the

[23] Id.

[24] Id.

[25] Brown, supra note 6, at 74.

[26] See CJC Holdings, Inc. v. Wright & Lato, Inc., 979 F.2d 60, 66 (5th Cir.1992); Ferrero U.S.A., Inc. v. Ozak Trading, Inc., 952 F.2d 44, 47 (3d Cir.1991).

[27] *Ferrero,* 952 F.2d at 48.

[28] § 1117(a).

[29] Sands, Taylor & Wood v. Quaker Oats Co., 34 F.3d 1340, 1346–50 (7th Cir.1994).

marketplace.''[30] Royalty payments, without more, do not promote deterrence and therefore enhancement is appropriate. Ultimately, the court approved the base royalty rate but remanded the case so that the district court could state the basis of the award with more precision.[31]

7. *Prejudgment interest. Sands* affirms the availability of prejudgment interest in trademark infringement actions, even though the Lanham Act does not expressly provide for this remedy. The availability of this remedy is completely within the court's discretion.

8. *Grey market goods.* In *Lever,* the court prohibited the importation of goods made by a foreign affiliate of a U.S. corporation where the foreign goods differed materially from the goods made by the U.S. company. Can you articulate an appropriate legal standard for determining materiality? Should physical differences in the products be the only type of differences that matter in determining materiality?

In footnotes c and d of *Lever,* the court notes that the Supreme Court had upheld the affiliate exception against a challenge based on § 526 of the Tariff Act in K Mart Corp. v. Cartier Inc.[32] Section 526 bars the importation of ''any merchandise of foreign manufacture if such merchandise ... bears a trademark owned by a citizen of, or by a corporation or association created or organized within, the United States, and registered ... by a person domiciled in the United States ..., unless written consent of the owner of such trademark is produced at the time of making entry.''[33] Thus, *K Mart* approved ''Customs' decision to permit third-party purchasers to buy goods produced abroad by a foreign subsidiary of a US firm and import them over the US firm's opposition.''[34] In light of *Lever*'s holding, what would be the result if *K Mart* were extended to allow importation under the affiliate exception where a U.S. firm's ''*domestically* manufactured goods are identical to the imports?''[35] The court in *K Mart* did not reach, however, the validity of the affiliate exception under § 1124 of the Lanham Act.

9. *Trademark Counterfeiting Act of 1984.* Counterfeit goods are ''made so as to imitate a well-known product in all details of construction and appearance so as to deceive customers into thinking that they are getting genuine merchandise.''[36] The Trademark Counterfeiting Act provides criminal penalties and enhanced civil remedies for anyone who ''intentionally traffics or attempts to traffic in goods or services and knowingly uses a counterfeit mark on or in connection with such goods or services.''[37] Thus, the dual mental-state of intention and knowing trafficking must be satisfied before liability can be imposed. The term ''counterfeit'' is defined in the statute as ''a spurious mark'' that is likely to cause confusion or to

---

[30] Id. at 1348.

[31] Id. at 1352.

[32] 486 U.S. 281, 108 S.Ct. 1811, 100 L.Ed.2d 313 (1988).

[33] 19 U.S.C.A. § 1526(a).

[34] Lever Brothers Co. v. U.S., 877 F.2d 101, 110–111 (D.C.Cir.1989)(Lever I).

[35] Id. at 111 (emphasis in original).

[36] 3 McCarthy § 25.01[5][a].

[37] 18 U.S.C. § 2320(a).

deceive and "(i) that is used in connection with trafficking in goods or services; [and] (ii) that is identical with, or substantially indistinguishable from, a mark registered for those goods or services on the principal register," regardless of whether the defendant knew of such registration.[38] The criminal penalties under the Act include maximum fines and/or prison terms for individuals, and even higher fines for corporations.[39] The civil remedies include the seizure of goods and counterfeit marks upon an ex parte application,[40] and a mandatory award of reasonable attorney's fees plus the greater of three times the defendant's profits or treble damages, absent "extenuating circumstances."[41]

BIBLIOGRAPHY

Davis, "Lever Bros. v. United States" and the Legality of Gray Market Imports: A New Shield for United States Trademark Owners in Transnational Markets, 28 Wake Forest L. Rev. 571 (1993); Inman, Gray Marketing of Imported Trademarked Goods: Tariffs and Trademark Issues, 31 Am. Bus. L.J. 59 (1993); Pollack, Your Image is My Image: When Advertising Dedicates Trademarks to the Public Domain—With an Example from the Trademark Counterfeiting Act of 1984, 14 Cardozo L. Rev. 1391 (1993); Brown, Civil Remedies for Intellectual Property Invasions: Themes and Variations, 55 L. & Contemp. Probs. 45 (1992); Frederickson, Recovery for False Advertising Under the Revised Lanham Act: A Methodology for the Computation of Damages, 29 Am. Bus. L.J. 585 (1991); Lipner, Trademarked Goods and Their Gray Market Equivalents: Should Product Differences Result in the Barring of Unauthorized Goods from the U.S. Markets?, 18 Hofstra L. Rev. 1029 (1990); Koelemay, Monetary Relief for Trademark Infringement under the Lanham Act, 72 Trademark Rep. 458 (1982).

---

[38] 18 U.S.C. § 2320(d)(1).

[39] 18 U.S.C. § 2320(a).

[40] 15 U.S.C. § 1116(d)(1)(A).

[41] 15 U.S.C. § 17(b).

ASSIGNMENT 6

COPYRIGHT PROTECTION: INTRODUCTION

STATUTORY MATERIALS: §§ 104A, 401–412 & 701–710

The authority for the law discussed in this Copyright Unit and the Patent Unit which follows derives from the federal constitution, and in this respect copyright and patent law differs from trademark law which lacks a similar explicit constitutional foundation. In the United States, the need for a uniform federal law governing copyrights and patents is recognized in the Copyright Clause, Article I, Section 8, Clause 8 of the United States Constitution. Clause 8 grants Congress the power "to promote the progress of science and useful arts, by securing for limited times to authors and inventors the exclusive right to their respective writings and discoveries."[1] Pursuant to this constitutional authority, Congress enacted the first United States' copyright statute in 1790. Several revisions of and amendments to the statute subsequently ensued. The current copyright statute, the 1976 Copyright Act, became effective on January 1, 1978 and is codified at §§ 101 et seq.[2] The 1976 Act embodies a major substantive revision of its immediate predecessor, the 1909 Copyright Act, more about which will be said below.

Before delving into an exploration of copyright law, it is important to consider the underlying policies that have shaped the doctrines in this area. To realize the objective of the Copyright Clause, Congress has authorized limited monopolies for creators of copyrighted works. These monopolies contain limits on both the duration of the rights and their substantive exercise. After the period of copyright protection has expired, the property becomes part of the public domain, to be enjoyed freely by all. The copyright law also sanctions certain types of unauthorized uses of copyrighted property.[3] On numerous occasions, the Supreme Court has observed that the promotion of the arts and sciences is the primary purpose of the monopoly granted to copyright owners, with financial rewards to creators as a secondary concern.[4] This analysis of the Copyright Clause

---

[1] U.S. Const. art. I, § 8, cl. 8.

[2] Unless otherwise noted, all statutory citations in the Copyright Unit are to 17 U.S.C.

[3] See Assignments 11 & 12 infra.

[4] See Fogerty v. Fantasy, Inc., ___ U.S. ___, ___–___, 114 S.Ct. 1023, 1029, 127 L.Ed.2d 455 (1994); Feist Publications, Inc. v. Rural Telephone Service Co., 499 U.S. 340, 349–50, 111 S.Ct. 1282, 1289–1290, 113 L.Ed.2d 358 (1991); Mazer v. Stein, 347 U.S. 201, 74 S.Ct. 460, 98 L.Ed. 630 (1954). See also H.R. Rep. No. 2222, 60th Cong., 2d Sess. 7 (1909).

suggests that the sovereign's duty to promote the public welfare must take precedence over the specific property rights enjoyed by copyright proprietors. Nevertheless, rewards to individuals under copyright law are essential to effectuating copyright law's major objective of enhancing societal progress, because an absence of monetary protections might well result in diminished creativity. Thus, copyright law represents a delicate balance between society's optimal use of resources and the optimal impetus for individual creativity.

The focus of our attention in the following Assignments will be on the provisions of the 1976 Act and the interpretative doctrines. Before you conclude that you can forget completely about the 1909 Act, however, you should know that its provisions still govern works created *prior* to January 1, 1978, the effective date of the 1976 Act. Therefore, students must be familiar with certain key aspects of the 1909 Act. Although the 1909 Act and the 1976 Act share certain features and frequently the case law decided under the 1909 Act bears some relevance to judicial interpretations of the 1976 Act, the two statutes also differ from one another in several critical respects. Two of the most important differences are the degree to which formalities are emphasized in these respective statutes and the duration of copyright protection.

Under the 1909 Act, federal copyright protection was available for works from the time of publication, and the state common law regime protected unpublished works. Prior to the 1909 Act, copyright protection was available only upon registration. Therefore, to receive federal copyright protection under the 1909 Act, an author had to publish her work. Also, if the work was published without the proper notice, copyright protection was forfeited (more on this below). The length of protection under the 1909 Act was an initial 28–year term, with an optional renewal term of an additional 28 years.

The 1976 Act reduced the significance of formalities such as publication with the requisite notice. In fact, under the 1976 Act, a work receives protection as soon as it is created, regardless of whether it bears a copyright notice. Effectively, this aspect of the 1976 Act abolished the notion of state common law copyright, although we should add that state common law protections still are available for some types of works.[5] Part of the reason why Congress felt the need for de-emphasizing certain formalities for copyright protection stemmed from a prevalent sentiment that the United States should become a member of the Berne Convention. As will be discussed below, Berne is an international copyright treaty which espouses the view that copyright formalities should not be required in order to receive protection. Many of the provisions of the 1909 Act were inconsistent with Berne, and precluded our potential adherence to the treaty. The other reason for the declining focus on formalities undoubtedly was a response to certain real-world consequences. Compliance with formalities as a prerequisite for protection is far more problematic for copyright owners than for

[5] See Assignment 14.

trademark owners and inventors. Unlike trademark holders who are in business and therefore have attorneys, or inventors who already have invested considerable resources in their inventions (and for whom attorney or agent fees are not so momentous), authors and artists often work in garrets with no money at all (hence the term "starving artist"). Uncounselled, they frequently lost their rights inadvertently. By providing protection for authors and artists from the moment of creation rather than upon publication with notice, the 1976 Act reduces this risk of loss. The declining importance of copyright formalities is even more apparent in certain amendments to the 1976 Act following our ultimate adherence to Berne in 1988. These amendments will be discussed below.

In addition to dispensing with certain formalities, the 1976 Act also abandoned the dual period of protection in favor of a single term of protection lasting generally for the duration of the author's life plus fifty years.[6] This duration also complies with the Berne Convention, although it was adopted prior to our formal adherence to Berne.

Although compliance with copyright formalities is certainly not essential under the current copyright regime, we should nonetheless emphasize that such compliance is highly desirable for reasons that will be discussed below. Therefore, the following section examines the mechanics of the three significant copyright formalities: registration, deposit and notice. It also details briefly the application and judicial process.

1.   FEDERAL COPYRIGHT FORMALITIES

There is a government office for registering copyrights similar to that for trademarks and patents. The Copyright Office, part of the Library of Congress, is the principle source for copyright information and services. The primary functions of the Copyright Office include: 1) registering copyrights; 2) maintaining records pertinent to copyrights such as assignments and transfers of copyright ownership; 3) acquiring works for the Library of Congress; 4) furnishing information on copyright searches; and 5) advising Congress on proposed amendments to copyright law.[7]

A.   REGISTRATION

The process of registering for a copyright involves depositing material with the Copyright Office to be reviewed by an examiner who decides whether to issue a registration certificate. Section 410 provides that "the Register [of Copyrights] shall register the claim and issue to the applicant a certificate of registration" where "the material deposited constitutes copyrightable subject matter and . . . the other legal and formal requirements

---

[6] § 302(a). The European Union has voted to increase the term of protection to life plus seventy years. This increased term of protection currently is being considered in the United States.

[7] See Peters, The Copyright Office and the Formal Requirements of Registration of Claims to Copyright, 17 U. Dayton L. Rev. 737, 737–38 (1992).

... have been met."[8] The material reviewed by the Copyright Office includes a completed application form (see Appendix infra for a sample application),[9] the appropriate deposit material,[10] and the filing fee.[11]

Registration, while not mandatory, affords the copyright claimant certain advantages. Most importantly, § 411 of the 1976 Act provides that registration is a prerequisite for instituting an infringement action for works originating in the United States, and § 412 provides that registration is a prerequisite for recovering statutory damages and attorney's fees (an exception is made for infringements occurring during the first three months after a work is published if registration is made before the end of the three months).[12] In addition, a registration certificate made before or within five years after first publication constitutes prima facie evidence of the validity of the copyright and of the facts stated in the certificate;[13] and registration is required before a document recorded with the Copyright Office provides constructive notice of the facts contained therein.[14]

B. DEPOSIT

The deposit requirement is treated in § 407 of the 1976 Act. Although a copyright claimant is required to deposit two copies of her work in the Copyright Office, the statute provides that such deposit is not a condition of copyright protection. However, failure to satisfy the deposit requirement will result in a fine.[15] One court has held that the mandatory deposit requirement is not a "taking" requiring just compensation since Congress, in enacting the copyright law, is permitted to condition its protections upon satisfying certain requirements.[16]

C. NOTICE

As discussed above, under the 1976 Act a creator receives copyright protection immediately upon the fixation of her work. Although publication with a copyright notice therefore is not currently required to obtain copyright protection, providing a copyright notice can be beneficial. For one thing, it provides psychological comfort to the creator who simply may not believe that copyright protection is automatic. Other reasons for providing a copyright notice will be explored in our subsequent discussion of the Berne Convention.[17] In order to receive the benefits of notice, the proper

---

[8] § 410(a).

[9] The requirements for this are detailed at § 409. Application forms are also available from the Copyright Office and may be ordered by telephoning the Forms and Circulars Hotline at (212) 707–9100. There are different application forms for different types of works. The application form reprinted infra is for nondramatic literary works, serials and periodicals.

[10] See § 408(b).

[11] The filing fee is currently twenty dollars as provided in 37 C.F.R. § 202.3(b)(4)(ii)(1991).

[12] § 412.

[13] § 410(c).

[14] § 205(c).

[15] See § 407(d).

[16] Ladd v. Law & Technology Press, 762 F.2d 809 (9th Cir.1985), cert. denied, 475 U.S. 1045, 106 S.Ct. 1260, 89 L.Ed.2d 570 (1986).

[17] See note 42 and accompanying text.

statutory form of notice must be used.[18] There are three general components to proper notice: 1) the term "Copyright" or "Copr." or the symbol for copyright which is the letter "c" enclosed in a circle; 2) the copyright owner's name or a recognized designation or abbreviation thereof; and 3) the date of publication.[19]

D. THE APPLICATION AND JUDICIAL PROCESS

The legislative history of the 1976 Copyright Act established "originality and fixation in a tangible form" as the fundamental criteria for copyright protection.[20] Once all the required materials are deposited, an examiner studies the record and determines whether the material falls within the subject matter of copyright and if it is an original work of authorship.[21] These two questions are asked regardless of the type of work for which a copyright is being sought. The subject matter question involves determining whether the work before the examiner falls within the categories listed in § 102(a) which include literary works; musical works; dramatic works; pantomimes and choreographic works; pictorial, graphic, and sculptural works; motion pictures and other audiovisual works; sound recordings; and architectural works.[22] The concept of originality is treated in the Originality Assignment infra. In making these decisions, examiners follow various guidelines. The first of these guidelines is found at 37 C.F.R. § 202 (1991) (Code of Federal Regulations). Another set of guidelines is found in the Compendium of Copyright Office Practices. Both of these are promulgated by the Copyright Office. Additionally, there are examining divisions which adhere to detailed practices and the Copyright Office also submits "Circulars" applicable to different categories of works.[23] Perhaps the most important rule examiners follow is the "rule of doubt," which provides that the Copyright Office should register the work if "a court could reasonably find that this work might be subject to copyright."[24]

If an author has completed the registration process and her work is infringed,[25] the next issue is determining what course of action the author should take to have the infringement rectified. For civil actions "arising under any Act of Congress relating to ... copyrights," the federal district

---

[18] § 401(b).

[19] Id. In some cases, "(c)" has been allowed as a valid substitute for the copyright symbol. See Videotronics, Inc. v. Bend Elec., 586 F.Supp. 478, 481 (D.Nev.1984). Additionally, the date may be omitted for certain works including some pictorial, graphic and sculptural works. § 401(b)(2).

[20] H.R. Rep. No. 1476, 94th Cong., 2d Sess. 51 (1976), reprinted in 1976 U.S.C.C.A.N. 5659, 5664. See § 102.

[21] See Peters, supra note 7, at 737–38.

[22] § 102(a).

[23] See Peters, supra note 7, at 739.

[24] Id. at 758. But see Tanenbaum, An Analysis and Guide to the Berne Convention Implementation Act: Amendments to the United States Copyright Act, 13 Hamline L. Rev. 253, 269 (1990)("Some observers have concluded that the standards used by the Copyright Office to determine registrability may be more restrictive than those used by the courts to determine copyrightability.").

[25] Section 106 identifies the exclusive rights the copyright owner has in her work. These rights are subject to §§ 107–120.

courts have original jurisdiction which is exclusive of the state courts.[26] Even if a copyright claimant has been refused registration, she can maintain an infringement action under § 411(a), which allows an applicant to institute an action if "deposit, application and fee have been delivered to the Copyright Office in proper form and registration has been refused."[27] In these circumstances, the copyright claimant must notify the Register and serve a copy of the complaint on the Register. The Register of Copyrights has the option of intervening in the action with respect to the registrability of the work. At least one court has held that during the interim period between the filing of an application and a final decision respecting registration, no infringement action can be maintained by the copyright claimant in federal district court.[28]

2. THE INTERNATIONAL STAGE

United States' copyright law provides protection only against infringement in the United States, but American books, films, and television shows are enjoyed internationally, so authors want protection all over the world. To ensure rights for Americans in foreign markets, the United States has entered into two multilateral treaties. The central thrust of these treaties is the principle of "national treatment": "A work of an American national first generated in America will receive the same protection in a foreign nation as that country accords to the works of its own nationals."[29]

The first of these treaties, the Universal Copyright Convention ("UCC"), took effect in 1955. It was originally conceived as a temporary measure to protect the interests of United States' copyright proprietors internationally until our copyright law could be revised to conform with the requirements of the Berne Convention, the second multilateral treaty. As

---

[26] 28 U.S.C. § 1338(a). An important issue is determining what "arising under" entails. See Cohen, "Arising Under" Jurisdiction and the Copyright Laws, 44 Hastings L.J. 337, 337 (1993).

Inconsistencies occur in cases involving contractual relations between authors and their assignees. The issue is whether suit should be brought in state court under state contract law or whether the appropriate forum is federal court as an action arising under copyright law. Id. at 340. Although the Supreme Court has not addressed this issue in the context of copyright law, lower courts have developed two different approaches to the question. Id. at 341. The first approach is to decide jurisdiction by determining what is the "principle and controlling issue." This requires the court to decide whether the case is really a contract dispute or rather a "genuine" copyright issue. Id. at 362. Professor Cohen identifies the problem with this ap-

proach as the lack of clear guidelines and inability to predict what the court will decide. Id. at 374. The second approach is to look "only to the language of the plaintiff's complaint." Id. at 341. Professor Cohen recognizes the advantages of this approach as "clarity and relative predictability" but thinks the disadvantage of deferring to the plaintiff's choice outweighs these attributes. Id. at 372–73. She endorses the approach of identifying the relative weight of the federal and state interests involved and granting jurisdiction to the court with the outweighing interest. Id.

[27] § 411(a).

[28] Hudson's Bay Co. of New York, Inc. v. Seattle Fur Exch., 15 U.S.P.Q.2d 1316 (S.D.N.Y.1990).

[29] Subafilms, Ltd. v. MGM–Pathe Communications Co., 24 F.3d 1088, 1097 (9th Cir.1994).

discussed earlier, the emphasis on formalities in the 1909 Act precluded our membership in the Berne Convention while that statute was in effect.

The United States joined the Berne Convention in 1988 via the Berne Convention Implementation Act of 1988 which became effective on March 1, 1989.[30] The Berne Convention, which is considered "the oldest and most comprehensive copyright treaty,"[31] binds approximately ninety countries to a unitary copyright law system which is administered by the World Intellectual Property Organization (WIPO).[32] The primary motivation for the United States' adherence to Berne was to make an "international statement about our moral posture in adhering to the world's foremost multilateral copyright treaty."[33] While Berne was originally "an attempt to create a universal international copyright law,"[34] it has become a "minimum protection instrument with an emphasis on national treatment and independent protection."[35] Adherence to the Berne Convention is not self-executing in the United States which means copyright protection is still vindicated by bringing suit under the Copyright Act and not directly under the provisions of the Berne Convention.[36] Since the United States is one of the most influential world powers and is a major exporter of intellectual property, its adherence strengthens the Berne Convention.[37] The United States' membership in the Berne Convention means any work first published in the United States will automatically be protected in other Berne countries.[38]

As discussed above, one of the primary doctrines endorsed by Berne is the lack of formalities required in order to receive copyright protection.[39] One especially important aspect of Berne is that it has reduced significantly the importance of the notice requirement. Historically, a work would fall into the public domain unless a copyright notice appeared on publicly distributed copies of the work. Even before the adoption of Berne, however, the importance of notice had declined. Under the 1909 Act, publication with notice was still essentially a prerequisite for copyright protection.

---

[30] Berne Convention Implementation Act of 1988, Pub. L. No. 100–568, 102 Stat. 2853 (1988). See also D. Nimmer, Nation, Duration, Violation, Harmonization: An International Copyright Proposal for the United States, 55 Law & Contemp. Probs. 211, 217 (1992).

[31] See D. Nimmer, The Impact of Berne on United States Copyright Law, 8 Cardozo Arts & Ent. L.J. 27, 27–28 (1989).

[32] See Ricketson, The 1992 Horace S. Manges Lecture—People or Machines: The Berne Convention and the Changing Concept of Authorship, 16 Colum.-VLA J.L. & Arts 1, 2 (1991). Our adherence to the Berne Convention does not affect our membership in the UCC, which is administered by the United Nations Educational Scientific and Cultural Organization (UNESCO). See Arden, The Questionable Utility of Copyright Notice: Statutory and Nonlegal Incentives in the Post–Berne Era, 24 Loy. U. Chi. L.J. 259, 277 (1993); Tanenbaum, supra note 24, at 253.

[33] See Nimmer, supra note 31, at 29.

[34] Stanton, Comment, Development of the Berne International Copyright Convention and Implications of United States Adherence, 13 Hous. J. Int'l L. 149 (1990).

[35] Id.

[36] Berne Convention Implementation Act of 1988, § 2(1).

[37] See Stanton, supra note 34, at 177.

[38] See 37 Pat. Trademark & Copyright J. (BNA) 462 (1989).

[39] See 134 Cong. Rec. H3082 (daily ed. May 10, 1988) ("The central feature of Berne is its prohibition of formalities.") (statement of Rep. Robert Kastenmeier); Tanenbaum, supra note 24, at 256–57.

Under the 1976 Act, the notice requirements were liberalized, especially with respect to the measures a creator could take to rescue her copyright even after publication without notice.[40] Now, with the adoption of Berne, copyright notice is permissive rather than mandatory for works published after the effective date of Berne.[41] Nevertheless, Berne still provides an incentive to use notice by specifying that in the case of defendants who have access to copies bearing the proper notice, courts shall not give any weight to a claim of innocent infringement in mitigation of actual or statutory damages.[42]

Berne modified the existing law on registration by providing for a dual system under which registration is a prerequisite for bringing an infringement suit for works originating in the United States but not for Berne Convention works whose country of origin is *not* the United States. This dual system arguably is not unfair to American creators because presumably they are more familiar with American Copyright Office procedures. Moreover, all creators are treated equally regarding the need to register in order to obtain the benefits of the presumptive validity of the copyright deriving from registration,[43] and awards of statutory damages and attorney's fees.

Additionally, Berne modified § 407(a) of the 1976 Act by making the mandatory deposit provisions applicable to all works, not just those works that display a copyright notice. This modification parallels the new optional nature of notice under Berne, and also was intended to expand the Library of Congress' collection.

Another change under Berne is the elimination of the requirement of recording assignments and other transactions prior to bringing an infringement suit.[44] This applies to both works of United States' origin and foreign works. However, like other post-Berne provisions, there are incentives for recording. Recording a transfer provides actual notice to persons who search the Copyright Office records and provides constructive notice even if

---

[40] See § 405(a)(2)(i.e., registration for work within 5 years and a reasonable effort to add notice to all copyrights distributed after the omission is discovered).

[41] See §§ 401(a) and 402(a) (providing that copyright notice *may* be placed on protected works) (emphasis added).

[42] See §§ 401(d) and 402(d) of the 1976 Act as amended by Berne.

In addition to providing benefits in the United States, notice confers copyright protection in countries that adhere to the UCC rather than Berne. Complying with the UCC notice requirements (which are virtually the same as the 1976 Act except that the copyright symbol must be used rather than the term "copyright" or abbreviation "copr.") ex-

empts the copyright owner from meeting the requirements of the individual country adhering to the UCC. See Tanenbaum, supra note 24, at 263. Another way to receive protection in countries not adhering to Berne or the UCC is to include the phrase "All Rights Reserved." This phrase confers copyright protection in some South American and Latin American countries. Id. at 263 (referring to the hemispheric treaty known as the Copyright Convention Between the United States and Other American Republics).

[43] See § 410(c).

[44] § 205(a)(1988)("[a]ny transfer of copyright ownership or other document pertaining to a copyright *may* be recorded....") (emphasis added).

the records are not searched.[45] Additionally, recording a transfer with the Copyright Office protects an assignee against subsequent transfers to third parties by creating statutory priority for the party who first records.[46]

Finally, the 1994 legislation implementing the General Agreement on Tariffs and Trade (GATT) made some critical changes in the copyright law (as well as in the patent and trademark laws) which became effective as of January 1, 1996. Although several of the changes regarding the copyright law are noted in the subsequent chapters of this unit, one in particular should be mentioned at this point. Section 104A now provides that copyright protection is automatically restored to certain foreign works that are still under foreign copyright protection but which have fallen into the public domain in the United States due to a lack of compliance with our formalities or for other specified reasons. The duration of United States' protection for these restored works is equivalent to what they would have received had the United States' copyright remained in effect. Section 104A has significant ramifications for reliance parties currently using the restored works. Such parties are immunized for activities prior to the copyright restoration date, but are precluded from reproducing any restored work as of the date they have effective notice that an owner intends to enforce the restored work. See also Assignment 9.

---

[45] § 205(c).   [46] § 205(d).

APPENDIX

FORM TX
UNITED STATES COPYRIGHT OFFICE

REGISTRATION NUMBER

	TX	TXU

EFFECTIVE DATE OF REGISTRATION

Month	Day	Year

DO NOT WRITE ABOVE THIS LINE. IF YOU NEED MORE SPACE, USE A SEPARATE CONTINUATION SHEET.

1

TITLE OF THIS WORK ▼

PREVIOUS OR ALTERNATIVE TITLES ▼

PUBLICATION AS A CONTRIBUTION   If this work was published as a contribution to a periodical, serial, or collection, give information about the collective work in which the contribution appeared.   **Title of Collective Work ▼**

If published in a periodical or serial give: **Volume ▼**   Number ▼   Issue Date ▼   On Pages ▼

2

a

NAME OF AUTHOR ▼   DATES OF BIRTH AND DEATH
Year Born ▼   Year Died ▼

Was this contribution to the work a "work made for hire"?
☐ Yes
☐ No

AUTHOR'S NATIONALITY OR DOMICILE
Name of Country
OR { Citizen of ▶_____
Domiciled in ▶_____

WAS THIS AUTHOR'S CONTRIBUTION TO THE WORK
Anonymous?   ☐ Yes ☐ No
Pseudonymous?   ☐ Yes ☐ No
If the answer to either of these questions is "Yes," see detailed instructions

NATURE OF AUTHORSHIP   Briefly describe nature of the material created by this author in which copyright is claimed. ▼

NOTE
Under the law, the "author" of a "work made for hire" is generally the employer, not the employee (see instructions) For any part of this work that was "made for hire" check "Yes" in the space provided, give the employer (or other person for whom the work was prepared) as "Author" of that part, and leave the space for dates of birth and death blank.

b

NAME OF AUTHOR ▼   DATES OF BIRTH AND DEATH
Year Born ▼   Year Died ▼

Was this contribution to the work a "work made for hire"?
☐ Yes
☐ No

AUTHOR'S NATIONALITY OR DOMICILE
Name of country
OR { Citizen of ▶_____
Domiciled in ▶_____

WAS THIS AUTHOR'S CONTRIBUTION TO THE WORK
Anonymous?   ☐ Yes ☐ No
Pseudonymous?   ☐ Yes ☐ No
If the answer to either of these questions is "Yes," see detailed instructions

NATURE OF AUTHORSHIP   Briefly describe nature of the material created by this author in which copyright is claimed. ▼

c

NAME OF AUTHOR ▼   DATES OF BIRTH AND DEATH
Year Born ▼   Year Died ▼

Was this contribution to the work a "work made for hire"?
☐ Yes
☐ No

AUTHOR'S NATIONALITY OR DOMICILE
Name of Country
OR { Citizen of ▶_____
Domiciled in ▶_____

WAS THIS AUTHOR'S CONTRIBUTION TO THE WORK
Anonymous?   ☐ Yes ☐ No
Pseudonymous?   ☐ Yes ☐ No
If the answer to either of these questions is "Yes," see detailed instructions

NATURE OF AUTHORSHIP   Briefly describe nature of the material created by this author in which copyright is claimed. ▼

3

a YEAR IN WHICH CREATION OF THIS WORK WAS COMPLETED   This information must be given in all cases.   ◀ Year

b DATE AND NATION OF FIRST PUBLICATION OF THIS PARTICULAR WORK
Complete this information ONLY if this work has been published.   Month ▶_____ Day ▶_____ Year ▶_____ ◀ Nation

4

COPYRIGHT CLAIMANT(S) Name and address must be given even if the claimant is the same as the author given in space 2.▼

See instructions before completing this space

TRANSFER If the claimant(s) named here in space 4 are different from the author(s) named in space 2, give a brief statement of how the claimant(s) obtained ownership of the copyright.▼

APPLICATION RECEIVED

ONE DEPOSIT RECEIVED

TWO DEPOSITS RECEIVED

REMITTANCE NUMBER AND DATE

DO NOT WRITE HERE   OFFICE USE ONLY

MORE ON BACK ▶   • Complete all applicable spaces (numbers 5-11) on the reverse side of this page.
• See detailed instructions.   • Sign the form at line 10.

DO NOT WRITE HERE

Page 1 of_____ pages

EXAMINED BY	FORM TX
CHECKED BY	
☐ CORRESPONDENCE Yes	FOR COPYRIGHT OFFICE USE ONLY

DO NOT WRITE ABOVE THIS LINE. IF YOU NEED MORE SPACE, USE A SEPARATE CONTINUATION SHEET.

PREVIOUS REGISTRATION Has registration for this work, or for an earlier version of this work, already been made in the Copyright Office?

☐ **Yes** ☐ **No** If your answer is "Yes," why is another registration being sought? (Check appropriate box) ▼

a. ☐ This is the first published edition of a work previously registered in unpublished form.

b. ☐ This is the first application submitted by this author as copyright claimant.

c. ☐ This is a changed version of the work, as shown by space 6 on this application.

If your answer is "Yes," give: **Previous Registration Number** ▼   **Year of Registration** ▼

5

DERIVATIVE WORK OR COMPILATION Complete both space 6a & 6b for a derivative work; complete only 6b for a compilation.

a. Preexisting Material Identify any preexisting work or works that this work is based on or incorporates. ▼

b. Material Added to This Work Give a brief, general statement of the material that has been added to this work and in which copyright is claimed. ▼

See instructions before completing this space

6

—space deleted—

7

REPRODUCTION FOR USE OF BLIND OR PHYSICALLY HANDICAPPED INDIVIDUALS   A signature on this form at space 10, and a check in one of the boxes here in space 8, constitutes a non-exclusive grant of permission to the Library of Congress to reproduce and distribute solely for the blind and physically handicapped and under the conditions and limitations prescribed by the regulations of the Copyright Office: (1) copies of the work identified in space 1 of this application in Braille (or similar tactile symbols); or (2) phonorecords embodying a fixation of a reading of that work; or (3) both.

a ☐ Copies and Phonorecords   b ☐ Copies Only   c ☐ Phonorecords Only

See instructions

8

DEPOSIT ACCOUNT If the registration fee is to be charged to a Deposit Account established in the Copyright Office, give name and number of Account.

Name ▼   **Account Number** ▼

CORRESPONDENCE Give name and address to which correspondence about this application should be sent. Name/Address/Apt/City/State/Zip ▼

Area Code & Telephone Number ▶

Be sure to give your daytime phone ◀ number

9

CERTIFICATION* I, the undersigned, hereby certify that I am the

Check one ▶

☐ author
☐ other copyright claimant
☐ owner of exclusive right(s)
☐ authorized agent of _____

of the work identified in this application and that the statements made by me in this application are correct to the best of my knowledge.

Name of author or other copyright claimant, or owner of exclusive right(s) ▲

Typed or printed name and date ▼ If this application gives a date of publication in space 3, do not sign and submit it before that date.

_____ date ▶ _____

Handwritten signature (X) ▼

10

MAIL CERTIFI- CATE TO	Name ▼	• Complete all necessary spaces • Sign your application in space 10
Certificate will be mailed in window envelope	Number Street/Apartment Number ▼	SEND ALL 3 ELEMENTS IN THE SAME PACKAGE 1. Application form 2. Nonrefundable $20 filing fee in check or money order payable to *Register of Copyrights* 3. Deposit material
	City State ZIP ▼	MAIL TO Register of Copyrights Library of Congress Washington, D.C. 20559

11

* 17 U.S.C. § 506(e) Any person who knowingly makes a false representation of a material fact in the application for copyright registration provided for by section 409, or in any written statement filed in connection with the application, shall be fined not more than $2,500.

September 1991—100,000   ☆U.S. GOVERNMENT PRINTING OFFICE: 1991-282-170-40,005

THE REQUIREMENTS OF ORIGINALITY AND AUTHORSHIP

1. INTRODUCTION

Under the 1976 Copyright Act, copyright protection is accorded to "original works of authorship fixed in any tangible medium of expression."[1] This phrase encompasses three requirements: 1) originality; 2) authorship; and 3) fixation. This Assignment explores the parameters of originality and authorship (the statutory concept of fixation is discussed in Note 9, infra). One easily stated rule is that a work is original if it is not copied from another work.[2] According to the legislative history accompanying the 1976 Act, the standard for original works of authorship, which was already established by the courts under the 1909 Copyright Act, "does not include requirements of novelty, ingenuity, or aesthetic merit."[3] Therefore, because material capable of copyright protection does not have to be new, just original, it is much easier to obtain copyright protection, as opposed to patent protection, which requires that the materials protected be both new and original (see Assignments 18 & 19).

The application of the originality standard in copyright law has given rise to much litigation, and, as the following materials suggest, can be extremely problematic. The originality requirement is especially difficult to apply with respect to two specific areas of works protected under copyright law, compilations and derivative works, because these works are, by definition, based on material already in existence. Section 101 of the statute defines a derivative work as "a work based upon one or more preexisting works" in any "form in which a work may be recast, transformed, or adapted." Section 101 defines a compilation as "a work formed by the collection and assembling of preexisting materials or of data that are selected, coordinated, or arranged in such a way that the resulting work as a whole constitutes an original work of authorship." Compilations also can include "collective works" which consist of an assembly of "separate and independent works in themselves."[4] Thus, the "compilation" category is broader than the "collective work" category because the component parts of a compilation, unlike a collective work, do not necessarily have to be

---

[1] § 102.

[2] See Sheldon v. Metro–Goldwyn Pictures Corp., 81 F.2d 49 (2d Cir.), cert. denied, 298 U.S. 669, 56 S.Ct. 835, 80 L.Ed. 1392 (1936).

[3] H.R. Rep. No. 1476, 94th Cong., 2d Sess. 51 (1976), reprinted in 1976 U.S.C.C.A.N. 5659, 5664.

[4] See § 101 (defining "collective work" and "compilation").

independently copyrightable. Section 103 of the statute is clear that although copyright protection does extend to compilations and derivative works, such protection only applies to the material "contributed by the author of such work."[5] Thus, cases involving these works require a determination as to whether the author has made any contributions that can be deemed sufficiently original to merit copyright protection.

2. PRINCIPAL PROBLEM

Atwell Corporation has created and marketed a ball and paddle video game called STRYKER. The game's visual display consists of a wall formed by pink, purple, gold, and blue layers of rectangles representing bricks. A player works with a control knob that causes a triangular-shaped representation of a paddle to hit a circle-shaped image of a ball against the brick wall. When the ball hits a brick, that brick disappears from its row, the player scores points, and a brick on a higher row becomes visible. A "Stryker" occurs when the ball passes through all rows of bricks and moves into the space between the wall and the top of the screen. The ball then ricochets in a zig-zag pattern off the sides of the screen and the top layer of the wall, removing bricks upon contact and further augmenting the player's score. Various tones are audible as the ball hits different objects on the screen. The paddle becomes smaller and the ball's speed becomes faster as the game is played.

When Atwell applied to the Copyright Office to register STRYKER as an audiovisual work, its application was denied under § 410(b) of the statute on the grounds that the game "does not contain sufficient original visual or musical authorship to warrant registration." Although stating that the Register of Copyrights views the work "as a whole" to determine registrability, the Examiner explained her denial of registration by treating the game's component parts. Specifically, the Examiner determined that STRYKER did not qualify for copyright protection since neither the common geometric shapes contained in the work nor the coloring of those shapes constitute copyrightable subject matter. Her letter stated: "The use of a symbol for a wall drawn in a familiar tile type design is not copyrightable. The same is true of the image of a triangle used in place of a paddle, a circle for a ball, and a common four-colored stripe embellishing the wall." The Examiner also determined that "the three tones used before the ball hits, and the string of double tones used after it hits do not constitute any copyrightable audio authorship." Further, the Examiner concluded that the images created by playing the video game are not registrable since they are created randomly by the player and not by the author of the video game. Finally, the Examiner stated that the arrangement of the "stationary screen display" contains no copyrightable authorship because "so few items" appear on the screen and "the arrangement is basically dictated by the functional requirements of this or similar backboard type games."

[5] § 103(b).

Atwell has retained your firm to challenge the Register's decision in federal district court under the Administrative Procedure Act[6] (see § 701(d)). Before reaching an opinion, consider the following materials.

3. MATERIALS FOR SOLUTION OF PRINCIPAL PROBLEM

A. STATUTORY MATERIALS: §§ 101 (all definitions), 102, & 103

B. CASES:

Feist Publications, Inc. v. Rural Telephone Service Co.

Supreme Court of the United States, 1991.
499 U.S. 340, 111 S.Ct. 1282, 113 L.Ed.2d 358.

■ JUSTICE O'CONNOR delivered the opinion of the Court.

This case requires us to clarify the extent of copyright protection available to telephone directory white pages.

I

Rural Telephone Service Company is a certified public utility that provides telephone service to several communities in northwest Kansas. It is subject to a state regulation that requires all telephone companies operating in Kansas to issue annually an updated telephone directory. Accordingly, as a condition of its monopoly franchise, Rural publishes a typical telephone directory, consisting of white pages and yellow pages. The white pages list in alphabetical order the names of Rural's subscribers, together with their towns and telephone numbers. The yellow pages list Rural's business subscribers alphabetically by category and feature classified advertisements of various sizes. Rural distributes its directory free of charge to its subscribers, but earns revenue by selling yellow pages advertisements.

Feist Publications, Inc., is a publishing company that specializes in area-wide telephone directories. Unlike a typical directory, which covers only a particular calling area, Feist's area-wide directories cover a much larger geographical range, reducing the need to call directory assistance or consult multiple directories. The Feist directory that is the subject of this litigation covers 11 different telephone service areas in 15 counties and contains 46,878 white pages listings—compared to Rural's approximately 7,700 listings. Like Rural's directory, Feist's is distributed free of charge and includes both white pages and yellow pages. Feist and Rural compete vigorously for yellow pages advertising.

As the sole provider of telephone service in its service area, Rural obtains subscriber information quite easily. Persons desiring telephone service must apply to Rural and provide their names and addresses; Rural then assigns them a telephone number. Feist is not a telephone company,

[6] 5 U.S.C. §§ 701–706.

let alone one with monopoly status, and therefore lacks independent access to any subscriber information. To obtain white pages listings for its area-wide directory, Feist approached each of the 11 telephone companies operating in northwest Kansas and offered to pay for the right to use its white pages listings.

Of the 11 telephone companies, only Rural refused to license its listings to Feist. Rural's refusal created a problem for Feist, as omitting listings would have left a gaping hole in its area-wide directory, rendering it less attractive to potential yellow pages advertisers. In a decision subsequent to that which we review here, the District Court determined that this was precisely the reason Rural refused to license its listings. The refusal was motivated by an unlawful purpose "to extend its monopoly in telephone service to a monopoly in yellow pages advertising." Rural Telephone Service Co. v. Feist Publications, Inc., 737 F.Supp. 610, 622 (D.Kan.1990).

Unable to license Rural's white pages listings, Feist used them without Rural's consent. Feist began by removing several thousand listings that fell outside the geographic range of its area-wide directory, then hired personnel to investigate the 4,935 that remained. These employees verified the data reported by Rural and sought to obtain additional information. As a result, a typical Feist listing includes the individual's street address; most of Rural's listings do not. Notwithstanding these additions, however, 1,309 of the 46,878 listings in Feist's 1983 directory were identical to listings in Rural's 1982–1983 white pages. Four of these were fictitious listings that Rural had inserted into its directory to detect copying.

Rural sued for copyright infringement in the District Court for the District of Kansas taking the position that Feist, in compiling its own directory, could not use the information contained in Rural's white pages. Rural asserted that Feist's employees were obliged to travel door-to-door or conduct a telephone survey to discover the same information for themselves. Feist responded that such efforts were economically impractical and, in any event, unnecessary because the information copied was beyond the scope of copyright protection. The District Court granted summary judgment to Rural, explaining that "courts have consistently held that telephone directories are copyrightable" and citing a string of lower court decisions. 663 F.Supp. 214, 218 (1987). In an unpublished opinion, the Court of Appeals for the Tenth Circuit affirmed "for substantially the reasons given by the district court." [J]udgt. order reported at 916 F.2d 718 (1990). We granted certiorari, 498 U.S. 808 (1990), to determine whether the copyright in Rural's directory protects the names, towns, and telephone numbers copied by Feist.

II

A

This case concerns the interaction of two well-established propositions. The first is that facts are not copyrightable; the other, that compilations of facts generally are. Each of these propositions possesses an impeccable pedigree. That there can be no valid copyright in facts is universally understood. The most fundamental axiom of copyright law is that "no author may copyright his ideas or the facts he narrates." Harper & Row, Publishers, Inc. v. Nation Enterprises, 471 U.S. 539, 556 (1985). Rural wisely concedes this point, noting in its brief that "facts and discoveries, of course, are not themselves subject to copyright protection." At the same time, however, it is beyond dispute that compilations of facts are within the subject matter of copyright. Compilations were expressly mentioned in the Copyright Act of 1909, and again in the Copyright Act of 1976.

There is an undeniable tension between these two propositions. Many compilations consist of nothing but raw data—i.e., wholly factual information not accompanied by any original written expression. On what basis may one claim a copyright in such a work? Common sense tells us that 100 uncopyrightable facts do not magically change their status when gathered together in one place. Yet copyright law seems to contemplate that compilations that consist exclusively of facts are potentially within its scope.

The key to resolving the tension lies in understanding why facts are not copyrightable. The sine qua non of copyright is originality. To qualify for copyright protection, a work must be original to the author. See *Harper & Row, supra,* at 547–549. Original, as the term is used in copyright, means only that the work was independently created by the author (as opposed to copied from other works), and that it possesses at least some minimal degree of creativity. 1 M. Nimmer & D. Nimmer, Copyright §§ 2.01[A], [B] (1990)(hereinafter Nimmer). To be sure, the requisite level of creativity is extremely low; even a slight amount will suffice. The vast majority of works make the grade quite easily, as they possess some creative spark, "no matter how crude, humble or obvious" it might be. *id.,* § 1.08[C][1]. Originality does not signify novelty; a work may be original even though it closely resembles other works so long as the similarity is fortuitous, not the result of copying. To illustrate, assume that two poets, each ignorant of the other, compose identical poems. Neither work is novel, yet both are original and, hence, copyrightable. See Sheldon v. Metro–Goldwyn Pictures Corp., 81 F.2d 49, 54 (C.A.2 1936).

Originality is a constitutional requirement. The source of Congress' power to enact copyright laws is Article I, § 8, cl.8, of the Constitution, which authorizes Congress to "secure for limited Times to Authors . . . the exclusive Right to their respective writings." In two decisions from the late 19th century—The Trade–Mark Cases, 100 U.S. 82 (1879); and Burrow–Giles Lithographic Co. v. Sarony, 111 U.S. 53 (1884)—this Court defined the crucial terms "authors" and "writings." In so doing, the Court made it unmistakably clear that these terms presuppose a degree of originality.

In the *Trade-Mark Cases,* the Court addressed the constitutional scope of "writings." For a particular work to be classified "under the head of writings of authors," the Court determined, "originality is required." 100 U.S., at 94. The Court explained that originality requires independent creation plus a modicum of creativity. In *Burrow-Giles,* the Court distilled the same requirement from the Constitution's use of the word "authors." The Court defined "author," in a constitutional sense, to mean "he to whom anything owes its origin; originator; maker." 111 U.S., at 58 (internal quotation marks omitted).

The originality requirement articulated in *The Trade–Mark Cases* and *Burrow-Giles* remains the touchstone of copyright protection today. See Goldstein v. California, 412 U.S. 546, 561–562 (1973). It is the very "premise of copyright law." Miller v. Universal City Studios, Inc., 650 F.2d 1365, 1368 (C.A.5 1981).

It is this bedrock principle of copyright that mandates the law's seemingly disparate treatment of facts and factual compilations. "No one may claim originality as to facts." [Nimmer] § 2.11[A], p. 2–157. This is because facts do not owe their origin to an act of authorship. The distinction is one between creation and discovery: The first person to find and report a particular fact has not created the fact; he or she has merely discovered its existence. Census takers, for example, do not "create" the population figures that emerge from their efforts; in a sense, they copy these figures from the world around them. Denicola, Copyright in Collections of Facts: A Theory for the Protection of Nonfiction Literary Works, 81 Colum. L. Rev. 516, 525 (1981)(hereinafter Denicola). Census data therefore do not trigger copyright because these data are not "original" in the constitutional sense. Nimmer § 2.03[E]. The same is true of all facts— scientific, historical, biographical, and news of the day. "They may not be copyrighted and are part of the public domain available to every person." *Miller*, supra, at 1369.

Factual compilations, on the other hand, may possess the requisite originality. The compilation author typically chooses which facts to include, in what order to place them, and how to arrange the collected data so that they may be used effectively by readers. These choices as to selection and arrangement, so long as they are made independently by the compiler and entail a minimal degree of creativity, are sufficiently original that Congress may protect such compilations through the copyright laws. Nimmer §§ 2.11[D], 3.03; Denicola 523, n.38. Thus, even a directory that contains absolutely no protectible written expression, only facts, meets the constitutional minimum for copyright protection if it features an original selection or arrangement. See *Harper & Row*, 471 U.S., at 547. Accord, Nimmer § 3.03.

This protection is subject to an important limitation. The mere fact that a work is copyrighted does not mean that every element of the work may be protected. Originality remains the sine qua non of copyright; accordingly, copyright protection may extend only to those components of a work that are original to the author. Patterson & Joyce, Monopolizing the Law: The Scope of Copyright Protection for Law Reports and Statutory Compilations, 36 UCLA L. Rev. 719, 800–802 (1989)(hereinafter Patterson and Joyce); Ginsburg, Creation and Commercial Value: Copyright Protection of Works of Information, 90 Colum. L. Rev. 1865, 1868, and n.12 (1990)(hereinafter Ginsburg). Thus, if the compilation author clothes facts with an original collocation of words, he or she may be able to claim a copyright in this written expression. Others may copy the underlying facts from the publication, but not the precise words used to present them. Where the compilation author adds no written expression but rather lets the facts speak for themselves, the expressive element is more elusive. The only conceivable expression is the manner in which the compiler has selected and arranged the facts. Thus, if the selection and arrangement are original, these elements of the work are eligible for copyright protection. No matter how original the format, however, the facts themselves do not become original through association.

This inevitably means that the copyright in a factual compilation is thin. Notwithstanding a valid copyright, a subsequent compiler remains free to use the facts contained in another's publication to aid in preparing a competing work, so long as the competing work does not feature the same selection and arrangement.

It may seem unfair that much of the fruit of the compiler's labor may be used by others without compensation. As Justice Brennan has correctly observed, however, this is not "some unforeseen byproduct of a statutory scheme." *Harper & Row*, 471 U.S., at 589 (dissenting opinion). It is, rather, "the essence of copyright," *ibid.*, and a constitutional requirement. The primary objective of copyright is not to reward the labor of authors, but "to promote the Progress of Science and useful Arts." Art. I, § 8, cl.8. To this end, copyright assures authors the right to their original expression, but encourages others to build freely upon the ideas and information conveyed by a work. *Harper & Row, supra*, at 556–557. This principle, known as the idea/expression or fact/expression dichotomy, applies to all works of authorship. As applied to a factual compilation, assuming the absence of original written expression, only the compiler's selection and arrangement may be protected; the raw facts may be copied at will. This result is neither unfair nor unfortunate. It is the means by which copyright advances the progress of science and art.

This, then, resolves the doctrinal tension: Copyright treats facts and factual compilations in a wholly consistent manner. Facts, whether alone or as part of a compilation, are not original and therefore may not be copyrighted. A factual compilation is eligible for copyright if it features an original selection or arrangement of facts, but the copyright is limited to the particular selection or arrangement. In no event may copyright extend to the facts themselves.

B

As we have explained, originality is a constitutionally mandated prerequisite for copyright protection. The Court's decisions announcing this rule predate the Copyright Act of 1909, but ambiguous language in the 1909 Act caused some lower courts temporarily to lose sight of this requirement.

The 1909 Act embodied the originality requirement, but not as clearly as it might have. See Nimmer § 2.01. The subject matter of copyright was set out in §§ 3 and 4 of the Act. Section 4 stated that copyright was available to "all the writings of an author." 35 Stat. 1076. By using the words "writings" and "author"—the same words used in Article I, § 8, of the Constitution and defined by the Court in The *Trade–Mark Cases* and *Burrow–Giles*—the statute necessarily incorporated the originality requirement articulated in the Court's decisions. It did so implicitly, however, thereby leaving room for error.

Section 3 was similarly ambiguous. It stated that the copyright in a work protected only "the copyrightable component parts of the work." It thus stated an important copyright principle, but failed to identify the specific characteristic—originality—that determined which component parts of a work were copyrightable and which were not. Most courts construed the 1909 Act correctly, notwithstanding the less-than-perfect statutory language. They understood from this Court's decisions that there could be no copyright without originality. See Patterson & Joyce 760–761. But some courts misunderstood the statute. See, e. g., Leon v. Pacific Telephone & Telegraph Co., 91 F.2d 484 (C.A.9 1937); Jeweler's Circular Publishing Co. v. Keystone Publishing Co., 281 F. 83 (C.A.2 1922). These courts ignored §§ 3 and 4, focusing their attention instead on § 5 of the Act. Section 5, however, was purely technical in nature: It provided that a person seeking to register a work should indicate on the application the type of work, and it listed 14 categories under which the work might fall. One of these categories was "books, including composite and cyclopaedic works, directories, gazetteers, and other compilations." § 5(a). Section 5 did not purport to say that all compilations were automatically copyrightable. Indeed, it expressly disclaimed any such function, pointing out that "the subject-matter of copyright is defined in section four." Nevertheless, the fact that factual compilations were mentioned specifically in § 5 led some courts to infer erroneously that directories and the like were copyrightable per se, "without any further or precise showing of original—personal—authorship." Ginsburg 1895.

Making matters worse, these courts developed a new theory to justify the protection of factual compilations. Known alternatively as "sweat of the brow" or "industrious collection," the underlying notion was that copyright was a reward for the hard work that went into compiling facts. The classic formulation of the doctrine appeared in *Jeweler's Circular Publishing Co.*, 281 F. at 88:

> "The right to copyright a book upon which one has expended labor in its preparation does not depend upon whether the materials which he has collected consist or not of matters which are publici juris, or whether such materials show literary skill *or originality*, either in thought or in language, or anything more than industrious collection. The man who goes through the streets of a town and puts down the names of each of the inhabitants, with their occupations and their street number, acquires material of which he is the author" (emphasis added).

The "sweat of the brow" doctrine had numerous flaws, the most glaring being that it extended copyright protection in a compilation beyond selection and arrangement—the compiler's original contributions—to the facts themselves. Under the doctrine, the only defense to infringement was independent creation. A subsequent compiler was "not entitled to take one word of information previously published," but rather had to "independently work out the matter for himself, so as to arrive at the same result from the same common sources of information." *id.* at 88–89 (internal quotations omitted). "Sweat of the brow" courts thereby eschewed the most fundamental axiom of copyright law—that no one may copyright facts or ideas.

C

"Sweat of the brow" decisions did not escape the attention of the Copyright Office. When Congress decided to overhaul the copyright statute and asked the Copyright Office to study existing problems, the Copyright Office promptly recommended that Congress clear up the confusion in the lower courts as to the basic standards of copyrightability. The Register of Copyrights explained in his first report to Congress that "originality" was a "basic requisite" of copyright under the 1909 Act, but that "the absence of any reference to [originality] in the statute seems to have led to misconceptions as to what is copyrightable matter." Report of the Register of Copyrights on the General Revision of the U.S. Copyright Law, 87th Cong., 1st Sess., p.9 (H. Judiciary Comm. Print 1961). The Register suggested making the originality requirement explicit. *ibid.*

Congress took the Register's advice. In enacting the Copyright Act of 1976, Congress dropped the reference to "all the writings of an author" and replaced it with the phrase "original works of authorship." § 102(a). In making explicit the originality requirement, Congress announced that it was merely clarifying existing law: "The two fundamental criteria of copyright protection [are] originality and fixation in tangible form.... The phrase 'original works of authorship,' which is purposely left undefined, is intended to incorporate without change *the standard of originality established by the courts under the present [1909] copyright statute.*" H.R. Rep. No. 94–1476, p.51 (1976)(emphasis added)(hereinafter H. R. Rep.); S. Rep. No. 94–473, p.50 (1975)(emphasis added)(hereinafter S. Rep.). This sentiment was echoed by the Copyright Office: "Our intention here is to maintain the established standards of originality...." Supplementary Report of the Register of Copyrights on the General Revision of U.S. Copyright Law, 89th Cong., 1st Sess., pt.6, p.3 (H. Judiciary Comm. Print 1965) (emphasis added).

To ensure that the mistakes of the "sweat of the brow" courts would not be repeated, Congress took additional measures. For example, § 3 of the 1909 Act had stated that copyright protected only the "copyrightable component parts" of a work, but had not identified originality as the basis for distinguishing those component parts that were copyrightable from those that were not. The 1976 Act deleted this section and replaced it with § 102(b), which identifies specifically those elements of a work for which copyright is not available: "In no case does copyright protection for an original work of authorship extend to any idea, procedure, process, system, method of operation, concept, principle, or discovery, regardless of the form in which it is described, explained, illustrated, or embodied in such work."

Section 102(b) is universally understood to prohibit any copyright in facts. As with § 102(a), Congress emphasized that § 102(b) did not change the law, but merely clarified it: "Section 102(b) in no way enlarges or contracts the scope of copyright protection under the present law. Its purpose is to restate ... that the basic dichotomy between expression and idea remains unchanged." H.R. Rep., at 57; S. Rep., at 54.

Congress took another step to minimize confusion by deleting the specific mention of "directories ... and other compilations" in § 5 of the 1909 Act. As mentioned, this section had led some courts to conclude that directories were copyrightable per se and that every element of a directory was protected. In its place, Congress enacted two new provisions. First, to make clear that compilations were not copyrightable per se, Congress provided a definition of the term "compilation." Second, to make clear that the copyright in a compilation did not extend to the facts themselves, Congress enacted § 103.

The definition of "compilation" is found in § 101 of the 1976 Act. It defines a "compilation" in the copyright sense as "a work formed by the collection and assembling of preexisting materials or of data that are selected, coordinated, or arranged *in such a way that* the resulting work as a whole constitutes an original work of authorship" (emphasis added).

The purpose of the statutory definition is to emphasize that collections of facts are not copyrightable per se. It conveys this message through its tripartite structure, as emphasized above by the italics. The statute identifies three distinct elements and requires each to be met for a work to qualify as a copyrightable compilation: (1) the collection and assembly of pre-existing material, facts, or data; (2) the selection, coordination, or arrangement of those materials; and (3) the creation, by virtue of the particular selection, coordination, or arrangement, of an "original" work of authorship.

At first glance, the first requirement does not seem to tell us much. It merely describes what one normally thinks of as a compilation—a collection of pre-existing material, facts, or data. What makes it significant is that it is not the sole requirement. It is not enough for copyright purposes that an author collects and assembles facts. To satisfy the statutory definition, the work must get over two additional hurdles. In this way, the plain language indicates that not every collection of facts receives copyright protection. Otherwise, there would be a period after "data."

The third requirement is also illuminating. It emphasizes that a compilation, like any other work, is copyrightable only if it satisfies the originality requirement ("an original work of authorship"). Although § 102 states plainly that the originality requirement applies to all works, the point was emphasized with regard to compilations to ensure that courts would not repeat the mistake of the "sweat of the brow" courts by concluding that fact-based works are treated differently and measured by some other standard. As Congress explained it, the goal was to "make plain that the criteria of copyrightable subject matter stated in section 102 apply with full force to works ... containing preexisting material." H.R. Rep., at 57; S. Rep., at 55.

The key to the statutory definition is the second requirement. It instructs courts that, in determining whether a fact-based work is an original work of authorship, they should focus on the manner in which the collected facts have been selected, coordinated, and arranged. This is a straight-forward application of the originality requirement. Facts are never original, so the compilation author can claim originality, if at all, only in the way the facts are presented. To that end, the statute dictates that the principal focus should be on whether the selection, coordination, and arrangement are sufficiently original to merit protection.

Not every selection, coordination, or arrangement will pass muster. This is plain from the statute. It states that, to merit protection, the facts must be selected, coordinated, or arranged "in such a way" as to render the work as a whole original. This implies that some "ways" will trigger copyright, but that others will not. Otherwise, the phrase "in such a way" is meaningless and Congress should have defined "compilation" simply as "a work formed by the collection and assembly of preexisting materials or data that are selected, coordinated, or arranged." That Congress did not do so is dispositive. In accordance with "the established principle that a court should give effect, if possible, to every clause and word of a statute," Moskal v. United States, 498 U.S. 103, 109–110 (1990)(internal quotation marks omitted), we conclude that the statute envisions that there will be some fact-based works in which the selection, coordination, and arrangement are not sufficiently original to trigger copyright protection.

As discussed earlier, however, the originality requirement is not particularly stringent. A compiler may settle upon a selection or arrangement that others have used; novelty is not required. Originality requires only that the author make the selection or arrangement independently (i.e., without copying that selection or arrangement from another work), and that it display some minimal level of creativity. Presumably, the vast majority of compilations will pass this test, but not all will. There remains a narrow category of works in which the creative spark is utterly lacking or so trivial as to be virtually nonexistent. Such works are incapable of sustaining a valid copyright.

Even if a work qualifies as a copyrightable compilation, it receives only limited protection. This is the point of § 103 of the Act. Section 103 explains that "the subject matter of copyright ... includes compilations," § 103(a), but that copyright protects only the author's original contributions—not the facts or information conveyed:

> "The copyright in a compilation ... extends only to the material contributed by the author of such work, as distinguished from the preexisting material employed in the work, and does not imply any exclusive right in the preexisting material." § 103(b).

As § 103 makes clear, copyright is not a tool by which a compilation author may keep others from using the facts or data he or she has collected. "The most important point here is one that is commonly misunderstood today: copyright . . . has no effect one way or the other on the copyright or public domain status of the preexisting material." H.R. Rep., at 57; S. Rep., at 55. The 1909 Act did not require, as "sweat of the brow" courts mistakenly assumed, that each subsequent compiler must start from scratch and is precluded from relying on research undertaken by another. Rather, the facts contained in existing works may be freely copied because copyright protects only the elements that owe their origin to the compiler— the selection, coordination, and arrangement of facts.

In summary, the 1976 revisions to the Copyright Act leave no doubt that originality, not "sweat of the brow," is the touchstone of copyright protection in directories and other fact-based works. Nor is there any doubt that the same was true under the 1909 Act. The 1976 revisions were a direct response to the Copyright Office's concern that many lower courts had misconstrued this basic principle, and Congress emphasized repeatedly that the purpose of the revisions was to clarify, not change, existing law. The revisions explain with painstaking clarity that copyright requires originality, § 102(a); that facts are never original, § 102(b); that the copyright in a compilation does not extend to the facts it contains, § 103(b); and that a compilation is copyrightable only to the extent that it features an original selection, coordination, or arrangement, § 101.

III

There is no doubt that Feist took from the white pages of Rural's directory a substantial amount of factual information. At a minimum, Feist copied the names, towns, and telephone numbers of 1,309 of Rural's subscribers. Not all copying, however, is copyright infringement. To establish infringement, two elements must be proven: (1) ownership of a valid copyright, and (2) copying of constituent elements of the work that are original. The first element is not at issue here; Feist appears to concede that Rural's directory, considered as a whole, is subject to a valid copyright because it contains some foreword text, as well as original material in its yellow pages advertisements.

The question is whether Rural has proved the second element. In other words, did Feist, by taking 1,309 names, towns, and telephone numbers from Rural's white pages, copy anything that was "original" to Rural? Certainly, the raw data does not satisfy the originality requirement. Rural may have been the first to discover and report the names, towns, and telephone numbers of its subscribers, but this data does not "owe its origin" to Rural. *Burrow-Giles*, 111 U.S., at 58. Rather, these bits of information are uncopyrightable facts; they existed before Rural reported them and would have continued to exist if Rural had never published a telephone directory. The originality requirement "rules out protecting . . . names, addresses, and telephone numbers of which the plaintiff by no stretch of the imagination could be called the author." Patterson & Joyce 776.

Rural essentially concedes the point by referring to the names, towns, and telephone numbers as "preexisting material." Section 103(b) states explicitly that the copyright in a compilation does not extend to "the preexisting material employed in the work."

The question that remains is whether Rural selected, coordinated, or arranged these uncopyrightable facts in an original way. As mentioned, originality is not a stringent standard; it does not require that facts be presented in an innovative or surprising way. It is equally true, however, that the selection and arrangement of facts cannot be so mechanical or routine as to require no creativity whatsoever. The standard of originality is low, but it does exist. As this Court has explained, the Constitution mandates some minimal degree of creativity, see *The Trade–Mark Cases*, 100 U.S., at 94; and an author who claims infringement must prove "the existence of . . . intellectual production, of thought, and conception." *Burrow-Giles*, *supra*, at 59–60.

The selection, coordination, and arrangement of Rural's white pages do not satisfy the minimum constitutional standards for copyright protection. As mentioned at the outset, Rural's white pages are entirely typical. Persons desiring telephone service in Rural's service area fill out an application and Rural issues them a telephone number. In preparing its white pages, Rural simply takes the data provided by its subscribers and lists it alphabetically by surname. The end product is a garden-variety white pages directory, devoid of even the slightest trace of creativity.

Rural's selection of listings could not be more obvious: It publishes the most basic information—name, town, and telephone number—about each person who applies to it for telephone service. This is "selection" of a sort, but it lacks the modicum of creativity necessary to transform mere selection into copyrightable expression. Rural expended sufficient effort to make the white pages directory useful, but insufficient creativity to make it original.

We note in passing that the selection featured in Rural's white pages may also fail the originality requirement for another reason. Feist points out that Rural did not truly "select" to publish the names and telephone numbers of its subscribers; rather, it was required to do so by the Kansas Corporation Commission as part of its monopoly franchise. See 737 F.Supp., at 612. Accordingly, one could plausibly conclude that this selection was dictated by state law, not by Rural.

Nor can Rural claim originality in its coordination and arrangement of facts. The white pages do nothing more than list Rural's subscribers in alphabetical order. This arrangement may, technically speaking, owe its origin to Rural; no one disputes that Rural undertook the task of alphabetizing the names itself. But there is nothing remotely creative about arranging names alphabetically in a white pages directory. It is an age-old practice, firmly rooted in tradition and so commonplace that it has come to be expected as a matter of course. It is not only unoriginal, it is practically inevitable. This time-honored tradition does not possess the minimal creative spark required by the Copyright Act and the Constitution.

We conclude that the names, towns, and telephone numbers copied by Feist were not original to Rural and therefore were not protected by the copyright in Rural's combined white and yellow pages directory. As a constitutional matter, copyright protects only those constituent elements of a work that possess more than a de minimis quantum of creativity. Rural's white pages, limited to basic subscriber information and arranged alphabetically, fall short of the mark. As a statutory matter, § 101 does not afford protection from copying to a collection of facts that are selected, coordinated, and arranged in a way that utterly lacks originality. Given that some works must fail, we cannot imagine a more likely candidate. Indeed, were we to hold that Rural's white pages pass muster, it is hard to believe that any collection of facts could fail.

Because Rural's white pages lack the requisite originality, Feist's use of the listings cannot constitute infringement. This decision should not be construed as demeaning Rural's efforts in compiling its directory, but rather as making clear that copyright rewards originality, not effort. As this Court noted more than a century ago, "great praise may be due to the plaintiffs for their industry and enterprise in publishing this paper, yet the law does not contemplate their being rewarded in this way." Baker v. Selden, 101 U.S. 99, 105 (1880).

The judgment of the Court of Appeals is Reversed.

Kregos v. Associated Press

United States Court of Appeals, Second Circuit, 1991.
937 F.2d 700, cert. denied, ___ U.S. ___, 114 S.Ct. 1056, 127 L.Ed.2d 376 (1994).

■ Newman, Circuit Judge.

The primary issue on this appeal is whether the creator of a baseball pitching form is entitled to a copyright. The appeal requires us to consider the extent to which the copyright law protects a compiler of information. George L. Kregos appeals from the April 30, 1990, judgment of the District Court for the Southern District of New York (Gerard L. Goettel, Judge) dismissing on motion for summary judgment his copyright and trademark claims against the Associated Press ("AP") and Sports Features Syndicate, Inc. ("Sports Features"). We affirm dismissal of the trademark claims, but conclude that Kregos is entitled to a trial on his copyright claim, though the available relief may be extremely limited.

Facts

The facts are fully set forth in Judge Goettel's thorough opinion, 731 F.Supp. 113 (S.D.N.Y.1990). The reader's attention is particularly called to the appendices to that opinion, which set forth Kregos' pitching form and the allegedly infringing forms. *Id.* at 122–24. Kregos distributes to newspapers a pitching form, discussed in detail below, that displays information concerning the past performances of the opposing pitchers scheduled to start each day's baseball games. The form at issue in this case, first distributed in 1983, is a redesign of an earlier form developed by Kregos in the 1970's. Kregos registered his form with the Copyright Office and obtained a copyright. Though the form, as distributed to subscribing newspapers, includes statistics, the controversy in this case concerns only Kregos' rights to the form without each day's data, in other words, his rights to the particular selection of categories of statistics appearing on his form.

In 1984, AP began publishing a pitching form provided by Sports Features. The AP's 1984 form was virtually identical to Kregos' 1983 form. AP and Sports Features changed their form in 1986 in certain respects, which are discussed in part I(D) below.

Kregos' 1983 form lists four items of information about each day's games—the teams, the starting pitchers, the game time, and the betting odds, and then lists nine items of information about each pitcher's past performance, grouped into three categories. Since there can be no claim of a protectable interest in the categories of information concerning each day's game, we confine our attention to the categories of information concerning the pitchers' past performances. For convenience, we will identify each performance item by a number from 1 to 9 and use that number whenever referring to the same item in someone else's form.

The first category in Kregos' 1983 form, performance during the entire season, comprises two items—won/lost record (1) and earned run average (2). The second category, performance during the entire season against the opposing team at the site of the game, comprises three items—won/lost record (3), innings pitched (4), and earned run average (5). The third category, performance in the last three starts, comprises four items—won/lost record (6), innings pitched (7), earned run average (8), and men on base average (9). This last item is the average total of hits and walks given up by a pitcher per nine innings of pitching.

It is undisputed that prior to Kregos' 1983 form, no form had listed the same nine items collected in his form. It is also undisputed that some but not all of the nine items of information had previously appeared in other forms. In the earlier forms, however, the few items common to Kregos' form were grouped with items different from those in Kregos' form.

The District Court granted summary judgment for the defendants on both Kregos' copyright and trademark claims. On the copyright side of the case, the Court ruled that Kregos lacked a copyrightable interest in his pitching form on three grounds. First, the Court concluded that Kregos' pitching form was insufficiently original in its selection of statistics to warrant a copyright as a compilation. Second, the Court concluded that, in view of the limited space available for displaying pitching forms in newspapers, the possible variations in selections of pitching statistics were so limited that the idea of a pitching form had merged into its expression. Third, the Court ruled that Kregos' pitching form was not entitled to a copyright because of the so-called "blank form" doctrine.

Discussion

I. Copyright Claim

A. Copyright for a Compilation of Facts

The basic principles concerning copyright protection for compilations of facts are clear and have recently been authoritatively restated in the Supreme Court's decision rejecting copyright protection for telephone book white pages. Feist Publications, Inc. v. Rural Telephone Service Co., Inc., 499 U.S. 340 (1991)("*Feist*"). Thus, as to compilations of facts, independent creation as to selection and arrangement will not assure copyright protection; the requirement of minimal creativity becomes an important ingredient of the test for copyright entitlement.

Prior to *Feist*, we had applied these principles to require some minimal level of creativity in two fairly recent cases that illustrate compilations of facts one of which is and one of which is not entitled to a copyright, Eckes v. Card Prices Update, 736 F.2d 859 (2d Cir.1984), and Financial Information, Inc. v. Moody's Investors Service, 808 F.2d 204 (2d Cir.1986)("*FFI*"), *cert. denied*, 484 U.S. 820 (1987). In *Eckes* we upheld a District Court's finding, made after trial, that a selection of 5,000 out of 18,000 baseball cards to be considered "premium" was entitled to a copyright. *Eckes*, 736 F.2d, at 863. In *FFI* we upheld a District Court's finding, also made after trial, that the listing of five items of information concerning municipal bond calls lacked sufficient selection to warrant a copyright; in almost all instances, the five items for the various bond issues had all appeared in "tombstone" ads, and only "minor additional research" was needed to complete the listings. *FFI*, 808 F.2d, at 208.

Kregos' pitching form presents a compilation of facts that falls between the extremes illustrated by *Eckes* and *FFI*. Kregos has selected nine items of information concerning a pitcher's performance. The universe of known facts available only from inspection of box scores of prior games is considerably greater than nine, though perhaps not as great as the quantity of 18,000 cards in *Eckes*. For example, Kregos could have selected past performances from any number of recent starts, instead of using the three most recent starts. And he could have chosen to include strikeouts, walks, balks, or hit batters. In short, there are at least scores of available statistics about pitching performance available to be calculated from the underlying data and therefore thousands of combinations of data that a selector can choose to include in a pitching form.[a]

It cannot be said as a matter of law that in selecting the nine items for his pitching form out of the universe of available data, Kregos has failed to display enough selectivity to satisfy the requirement of originality. Whether in selecting his combination of nine items he has displayed the requisite degree of creativity is a somewhat closer question. Plainly he has done better than the compiler in *FFI* who "selected" only the five facts about

---

[a] If the universe of available data included even 20 items and a selector was limited to 9 items, there would be 167,960 combinations of items available.

bond calls already grouped together in nearly all tombstone ads. Judge Goettel was persuaded to rule against Kregos, at least in part, because "most of the statistics ... had been established in previously existing forms." 731 F.Supp., at 118. But that observation is largely irrelevant to the issue of whether Kregos' selection of statistics displays sufficient creativity to warrant a copyright. Nearly all copyrighted compilations of facts convey facts that have been published elsewhere. Each of the cards selected for the "premium" category in *Eckes* had previously been published. To hold a valid copyright, a compiler of facts need not be a discoverer of facts. Indeed, any discovered fact, or, in Kregos' case, any newly devised statistic, would not, in and of itself, be eligible for copyright protection.

[T]he record discloses no prior pitching form with more than three of the pitching performance statistics that are included in Kregos' selection of nine statistics. There is no prior form that is identical to his nor one from which his varies in only a trivial degree. The validity of his copyright in a compilation of facts cannot be rejected as a matter of law for lack of the requisite originality and creativity.

B. Idea/Expression Merger

The fundamental copyright principle that only the expression of an idea and not the idea itself is protectable, see Mazer v. Stein, 347 U.S. 201, 217 (1954), has produced a corollary maxim that even expression is not protected in those instances where there is only one or so few ways of expressing an idea that protection of the expression would effectively accord protection to the idea itself. Our Circuit has considered this so-called "merger" doctrine in determining whether actionable infringement has occurred, rather than whether a copyright is valid, see Durham Industries, Inc. v. Tomy Corp., 630 F.2d 905, 916 (2d Cir.1980), an approach the Nimmer treatise regards as the "better view." See 3 Nimmer on Copyright § 13.03[B][3] at 13–58 (1990). Assessing merger in the context of alleged infringement will normally provide a more detailed and realistic basis for evaluating the claim that protection of expression would inevitably accord protection to an idea.

In this case, Judge Goettel understood Kregos' idea to be "to publish an outcome predictive pitching form." 731 F.Supp., at 119. In dissent, Judge Sweet contends that Kregos' idea is that the nine statistics he has selected are the most significant ones to consider when attempting to predict the outcome of a baseball game. Unquestionably, if that is the idea for purposes of merger analysis, then merger of that idea and its expression has occurred—by definition.

Though there is room for fair debate as to the identification of the pertinent idea whenever merger analysis is applied to a compilation of facts, we think the "idea" in this case is the one as formulated by Judge Goettel. Kregos has not devised a system that he seeks to withdraw from the public domain by virtue of copyright. He does not present his selection of nine statistics as a method of predicting the outcome of baseball games. His idea is that of "an outcome predictive pitching form" in the general sense that it selects the facts that he thinks newspaper readers should consider in making their own predictions of outcomes. He does not purport to weight the nine statistics, much less provide a method for comparing the aggregate value of one pitcher's statistics against that of the opposing pitcher in order to predict an outcome or even its probability of occurring. He has not devised a system, as had the deviser of a bookkeeping system in Baker v. Selden, 101 U.S. 99 (1879). He has compiled facts, or at least categories of facts.

Though formulating the idea as "an outcome predictive pitching form," Judge Goettel applied the merger doctrine, concluding that the idea of selecting outcome predictive statistics to rate pitching performance was capable of expression in only a very limited number of ways.

As the various pitching forms in the record indicate, the past performances of baseball pitchers can be measured by a variety of statistics. Kregos' selection of categories includes three statistics for the pitcher's current season performance against the day's opponent at the site of the day's game; other charts select "at site" performance against the opponent during the prior season, and some select performance against the opponent over the pitcher's career, both home and away. Some charts include average men on base per nine innings; others do not. The data for most recent starts could include whatever number of games the compiler thought pertinent. These variations alone (and there are others) abundantly indicate that there are a sufficient number of ways of expressing the idea of rating pitchers' performances to preclude a ruling that the idea has merged into its expression.

In reaching this conclusion, we confess to some unease because of the risk that protection of selections of data, or, as in this case, categories of data, have the potential for according protection to ideas. Our concern may be illustrated by an example of a doctor who publishes a list of symptoms that he believes provides a helpful diagnosis of a disease. There might be many combinations of symptoms that others could select for the same purpose, but a substantial question would nonetheless arise as to whether that doctor could obtain a copyright in his list, based on the originality of his selection. If the idea that the doctor is deemed to be expressing is the general idea that the disease in question can be identified by observable symptoms, then the idea might not merge into the doctor's particular expression of that idea by his selection of symptoms. That general idea might remain capable of many other expressions. But it is arguable that the doctor has conceived a more precise idea—namely, the idea that his selection of symptoms is a useful identifier of the disease. That more limited idea can be expressed only by his selection of symptoms, and therefore might be said to have merged into his expression.

As long as selections of facts involve matters of taste and personal opinion, there is no serious risk that withholding the merger doctrine will extend protection to an idea. That was surely the case with the selection of premium baseball cards in *Eckes*. It is also true of a selection of prominent families for inclusion in a social directory. See Social Register Ass'n v.

Murphy, 128 F. 116 (C.C.R.I. 1904). However, where a selection of data is the first step in an analysis that yields a precise result or even a better-than-average probability of some result, protecting the "expression" of the selection would clearly risk protecting the idea of the analysis.

Kregos' pitching form is part way along the continuum spanning matters of pure taste to matters of predictive analysis. He is doing more than simply saying that he holds the opinion that his nine performance characteristics are the most pertinent. He implies that his selections have some utility in predicting outcomes. On the other hand, he has not gone so far as to provide a system for weighing the combined value of the nine characteristics for each of two opposing pitchers and determining a probability as to which is more likely to win. Like the compilers of horse racing statistics, Kregos has been content to select categories of data that he obviously believes have some predictive power, but has left it to all sports page readers to make their own judgments as to the likely outcomes from the sets of data he has selected. His "idea," for purposes of the merger doctrine, remains the general idea that statistics can be used to assess pitching performance rather than the precise idea that his selection yields a determinable probability of outcome. Since there are various ways of expressing that general idea, the merger doctrine need not be applied to assure that the idea will remain in the public domain.

C.   "Blank Form" Doctrine

The District Court also ruled that Kregos could not obtain a valid copyright in his pitching form because of the so-called "blank form" doctrine. The doctrine derives from the Supreme Court's decision in Baker v. Selden, *supra*. The Court there denied copyright protection to blank forms contained in a book explaining a system of double-entry bookkeeping. The forms displayed an arrangement of columns and headings that permitted entries for a day, a week, or a month to be recorded on one page or two facing pages. The Court made clear that the author could not obtain copyright protection for an "art" that "might or might not have been patented" and reasoned that since the "art" was available to the public, "the ruled lines and headings of accounts must necessarily be used as incident to it." *Id*. at 104. Then, in a concluding statement that is susceptible to overreading, the Court said that "blank account-books are not the subject of copyright." *Id*. at 107.

Though there are some statements suggesting broadly that no blank forms are copyrightable, many courts have recognized that there can be protectable elements of forms that include considerable blank space.[b]

The regulations of the Copyright Office are careful to preclude copyright registration to:

[b] We are concerned with protectable elements in the selection (and perhaps arrangement) of the categories of information to be recorded on the forms. There is widespread agreement that a work containing a blank form may be copyrightable because of the protectable elements of the textual matter accompanying the form.

> Blank forms, such as ... account books, diaries, bank checks, scorecards, address books, report forms, order forms and the like, which are designed for recording information *and do not in themselves convey information*.

37 C.F.R. § 202.1(c)(1990)(emphasis added).

Of course, a form that conveys no information and serves only to provide blank space for recording information contains no expression or selection of information that could possibly warrant copyright protection. See, e.g., John H. Harland Co. v. Clarke Checks, Inc., 711 F.2d 966, 971–72 (11th Cir.1983)(check stubs). At the same time, it should be equally obvious that a writing that does contain a selection of categories of information worth recording, sufficiently original and creative to deserve a copyright as a compilation of facts, cannot lose that protection simply because the work also contains blank space for recording the information. When the Copyright Office denies a copyright to scorecards or diaries that "do not in themselves convey information," it must be contemplating works with headings so obvious that their selection cannot be said to satisfy even minimal creativity (a baseball scorecard with columns headed "innings" and lines headed "players"; a travel diary with headings for "cities" "hotels," and "restaurants"). Such a work conveys no information, not just because it contains blanks, but because its selection of headings is totally uninformative. On the other hand, if a scorecard or diary contained a group of headings whose selection (or possibly arrangement) displayed cognizable creativity, the author's choice of those headings would convey to users the information that this group of categories was something out of the ordinary. See 1 Nimmer on Copyright § 2.18[C][1] at 2–201 (1990)("Thus books intended to record the events of baby's first year, or a record of a European trip, or any one of a number of other subjects, *may* evince considerable originality in suggestions of specific items of information which are to be recorded, and in the arrangement of such items.")(emphasis added; footnote omitted).

The Ninth Circuit has rejected this approach. With deference, we suggest that this critique of cases recognizing a copyright in the selection of categories of information for forms is not well taken. All forms may convey that the information called for is important (or at least worth recording), but the form-maker does not necessarily display even minimal creativity by selecting categories of "important" information. [C]ourts are obliged to determine as to forms, as with all compilations of information, whether the author's selection of categories of data to be recorded displays at least minimal creativity. The check stub in Clarke Checks was plainly deficient in this regard. But all forms need not be denied protection simply because many of them fail to display sufficient creativity.

In the pending case, once it is determined that Kregos' selection of categories of statistics displays sufficient creativity to preclude a ruling as a matter of law that it is not a copyrightable compilation of information, that same conclusion precludes rejecting his copyright as a "blank form."

D. Extent of Protection

Our ruling that Kregos' copyright claim survives defendants' motion for summary judgment does not, of course, mean that he will necessarily obtain much of a victory. If Kregos prevails at trial on the factual issues of originality and creativity, he will be entitled to protection only against infringement of the protectable features of his form. Only the selection of statistics might be entitled to protection. We agree entirely with Judge Goettel that nothing in Kregos' arrangement of the selected statistics displays the requisite creativity. As to the arrangement, Kregos' form is surely a "garden-variety" pitching form. The statistics are organized into the "obvious" arrangement of columns, and the form follows the pattern of most other forms: the statistics are organized into three groups, first the statistics about each pitcher's performance for the season, then the statistics about the pitcher's performance against the day's opponent, and finally the statistics concerning the pitcher's recent starts.

Even as to the selection of statistics, if Kregos establishes entitlement to protection, he will prevail only against other forms that can be said to copy his selection. That would appear to be true of the AP's 1984 form, which, as Judge Goettel noted, is "identical in virtually every sense to plaintiff's form." 731 F.Supp., at 115. Whether it is also true of the AP's current form, revised in 1986, is far less certain. That form contains six of Kregos' nine items (1, 2, 6, 7, 8, 9). It also includes four items that Kregos does not have. Three of these items concern performance against the day's opposing team—won-lost record, innings pitched, and earned run average; though these three statistics appear on Kregos' form, the AP's 1986 form shows data for the current season both home and away, whereas Kregos' form shows data for the pitcher's current season at the site of that day's game. The fourth item on the AP's 1986 form and not on Kregos' form shows the team's record in games started by that day's pitcher during the season.

The reason for doubting that the AP's 1986 form infringes Kregos' form arises from the same consideration that supports Kregos' claim to a copyright. Kregos can obtain a copyright by displaying the requisite creativity in his selection of statistics. But if someone else displays the requisite creativity by making a selection that differs in more than a trivial degree, Kregos cannot complain. Kregos contends that the AP's 1986 form makes insignificant changes from its 1984 form. But Kregos cannot have it both ways. If his decision to select, in the category of performance against the opposing team, statistics for the pitcher's current season at the site of today's game displays, in combination with his other selections, enough creativity to merit copyright protection, then a competitor's decision to select in that same category performance statistics for the pitcher's season performance both home and away may well insulate the competitor from a claim of infringement. Thus, though issues remain to be explored before any determination can be made, it may well be that Kregos will have a valid claim only as to the AP's 1984 form.

[In part II of the opinion, the court affirmed the district court's grant of summary judgment for the defendants on the trademark claims because the plaintiff did not demonstrate secondary meaning in his form.]

APPENDIX 1

(Kregos' 1983 Pitching Fora)

THE HARTFORD COURANT: Sunday, May 6, 1984

SCOREBOARD

Today's Games

				1984		vs. team at site			Last 3 starts			
Team	**Probable Pitcher (H)**	**Time**	**Odds**	**W/L**	**ERA**	**W/L**	**IP**	**ERA**	**W/L**	**IP**	**ERA**	**MBA**
				AMERICAN LEAGUE								
DET	Wilcox (R)		Even–6	3–0	3.34	0–2	10	9.00	2–0	22	2.05	11.05
CLEV	Blyleven (R)	1:35	*	3–2	3.14	0–0	6	3.00	1–1	22	3.68	12.68
K.C.	Gura (L)		*	4–0	2.55	0–2	9⅔	9.31	2–0	21⅓	1.69	9.28
TORN	Alexander (R)	1:35	5½–6½	1–1	3.82	*	*	*	1–1	21⅔	2.91	9.97
CHIC	Bannister (L)		Even–6	2–2	5.12	0–1	8	2.25	1–1	19⅔	5.03	15.10
BOST	Hurst (L)	2:05	*	3–3	2.02	1–1	13⅓	4.73	2–1	18	1.50	15.00
OAK	Warren (R)		Even–6	3–3	3.82	*	*	*	2–1	18	5.00	15.50
MINN	Hodge (L)	2:15	*	0–0	7.20	*	*	*	0–0	5	7.20	23.40
N.Y.	Fontenot (L)		*	0–4	4.88	1–0	7	5.14	0–2	16⅓	2.76	13.22
MIL	Cocanower (R)	2:30	5½–6½	0–4	3.00	*	*	*	0–3	23⅔	1.90	12.55
BALT	Boddicker (R)		6–7	1–3	3.19	1–0	6	4.50	1–1	23	1.57	10.17
TEX	Darwin (R)	3:05	*	3–0	2.40	1–0	6⅔	0.00	2–0	25	1.08	7.54
CAL	John (L)		5½–6½	2–2	2.04	*	*	*	1–1	21⅓	2.11	11.39
SEAT	Young (L)	4:35	*	2–2	6.52	1–0	11⅔	0.77	0–1	11⅔	8.49	20.83
				NATIONAL LEAGUE								
ATL	McMurtry (R)		*	2–3	3.58	1–0	7	3.86	1–1	20⅓	3.10	13.28
MONT	Lea (R)	1:05	6–7	4–1	2.61	0–1	7	6.43	2–0	20	2.70	13.05
ATL	Camp (R)		*	2–0	2.31	0–1	4	4.50	2–0	11⅔	2.31	10.03
MONT	Palmer (R)		6–7	2–0	2.29	*	*	*	1–0	14⅔	2.45	5.52
L.A.	Pena (R)		*	4–1	1.41	0–0	7⅔	2.35	3–0	24⅔	1.11	7.40
PITT	McWilliams (L)	1:35	Pick 'em	0–3	3.24	0–0	8	2.25	0–2	17	3.18	12.18
L.A.	Valenzuela (L)		5½–6½	3–2	2.93	0–0	7⅓	3.68	3–0	27	0.67	6.33
PITT	Tudor (L)		*	1–1	2.91	*	*	*	0–1	19⅓	4.19	14.43
CINN	Russell (R)		*	1–3	3.14	*	*	*	0–2	22	1.23	11.45
PHIL	Carlton (L)	1:35	7½–8½	1–1	2.50	1–0	8	4.50	0–1	21	2.14	11.57
HOUS	Ryan (R)		*	1–2	3.65	2–0	15⅓	2.30	0–1	16	5.06	12.94
METS	Gooden (R)	1:35	Pick 'em	2–1	2.63	*	*	*	1–0	19	0.47	9.95
S.F.	Laskey (R)		*	0–3	2.20	*	*	*	0–2	19⅔	2.29	10.98
STL	Andujar (R)	2:15	6½–7½	4–2	3.09	0–1	15⅔	2.87	2–1	25	3.24	10.08
S.D.	Show (R)		*	4–1	1.89	2–0	14	1.93	2–1	17⅓	1.56	10.90
CUBS	Ruthven (R)	2:20	Even–6	2–2	5.35	*	*	*	0–2	17⅓	7.79	12.98

Bottom team is home team. Favored team is designated by odds beside pitcher's name. All pitching data reflects the pitcher's past performance as a "starter." 1984—Pitcher's 1984 record as "starter." Vs Team at site—Pitcher's past performance vs. today's opponent at the site of today's game. Last 3 Starts—Reflects how pitcher is currently going. Details his performance over his last three starts. W/L—Won/lost record as a "starter". IP—Innings pitched. ERA—Earned run average. MBA—Men on base average. (Average number of men allowed to reach base via hits and walks per nine innings pitched.) The odds are estimated lines. Time is Eastern Daylight Time

APPENDIX 2

(AP's 1984 Pitching Fora)

FRIDAY'S PITCHERS
American

Away Home	Probable Pitcher	Time	Line	1983 W–L	1983 ERA	vs. opp. at site W–L	IP	ERA	last 3 starts W–L	IP	ERA	AHWG
DET	Matt Wilcox (R)		EV–6	11–10	.397	0–0	90	0.00	0–0	00.0	0.00	0.0
at CHI	Rich Dotson (R)	1:30		22–7	3.22	1–0	80	2.25	0–0	00.0	0.00	0.0
NY	John Montefusco (R)		5.5–6.5	14–4	3.31	0–0	00	00	000	00.0	0.00	0.0
at TEX	Frank Tanana (L)	7:35		7–9	3.05	0–1	71	6.14	0–0	00.0	0.00	0.0
CLE	Bert Blyleven (R)			7–10	3.91	0–0	00	00	00.0	0.00	0.00	0.0
at KC	Mark Gubicza (R)	7:35	PK	0–0	0–0	0.0	00	00.0	0.00	0.00	0.00	0.0
BALT	Mike Boddiker (R)		5.5–6.5	16–8	2.77	1–0	70	0.0	0–0	00.0	0.00	0.0
at MINN	Mike Smithson (R)	7:35		10–11	3.91	0–0	00	0–0	00.0	00.0	0.00	0.0
TOR	Doyle Alexander (R)		5.5–6.5	7–8	4.41	1–0	111	1.59	0–0	00	0.00	0.0
at CAL	Steve Brown (R)	9:30		3–4	4.50	1–1	32	7.36	0.0	00.0	0.00	0.0
BOST	Dennis Boyd (R)			4–8	3.34	0–0	00	0–0	00.0	00.0	0.00	0.0
at OAK	Larry Sorensen (R)	9:35	EV–6	12–11	4.24	0–0	00	0–0	0.00	00.0	0.00	0.0
MILW	Moose Haas (R)		7.5–8.5	13–3	3.27	0–0	70	129	0–0	00.0	0.00	0.0
at SEA	Matt Young (L)	9:35		11–15	3.27	0–0	00	0–0	00.0	00.0	0.00	0.0

National

Away Home	Probable Pitcher	Time	Line	1983 W–L	1983 ERA	vs. opp. at site W–L	IP	ERA	last 3 starts W–L	IP	ERA	AHWG
PHIL	Charles Hudson (R)		EV–6	8–8	3.35	0–0	52	9.53	0–0	00.0	0.00	0.0
at CINN	Joe Price (L)	6:35		10–6	3.38	1–0	81	1.08	0–0	0.00	00.0	0.0
MONT	Bryn Smith (R)			6–11	.349	0–0	12	5.40	0–0	00.0	0.00	0.0
at ATL	Ken Dayley (L)	6:40	6–7	5–8	4.30	0–1	61	2.84	0–0	00.0	0.00	0.0
NY	Walt Terrell (R)			8–8	3.50	1–0	60	1.50	0–0	00.0	0.00	0.0
at HOU	Tony Scott (L)	7:35	7.5–8.5	10–6	3.72	1–1	161	2.20	0–0	00.0	0.00	0.0
CHI	Scott Sanderson (R)		6.5–7.5	6–7	.445	0–0	10	27.00	0–0	00.0	0.00	0.0
at SD	Tim Lollar (L)	9:05		7–12	4.58	1–1	131	3.38	0–0	00.0	0.00	0.0
PITT	John Tudor (L)		6.5–7.5	13–12	4.05	0–3	00	0–0	00.0	0.00	0.00	0.0
at LA	Bob Welch (R)	9:35		15–12	2.65	0–0	70	2.57	0–0	00.0	0.00	0.0
ST L	Joaquin Andujar (R)		EV–6	7–16	4.00	0–1	80	5.63	0–0	00.0	0.00	0.0
at SF	Bill Laskey (R)	10:05		13–10	4.19	1–0	90	1.00	0–0	00.0	0.00	0.0

Legend W–L Won–Lost IP Innings pitched ERA Earned run average AHWG Average hits and walks per nine innings

APPENDIX 3

(AP's 1984 Pitching Fora)

	PITCHERS	LINE	1987 W–L	ERA	TEAM REC	1987 VS W–L	OPP IP	ERA	LAST 3 STARTS W–L	IP	ERA	AHWG
Minnesota	Niekro (R)	2:35p	7–12	5.00	6–11	1–1	10.0	3.60	1–1	17.2	4.58	13.2
Kansas City	Gubicza (R)	6–7	12–18	4.10	14–20	0–1	6.0	7.50	1–2	23.0	2.35	12.1
Seattle	Langston (L)	3:05p	18–13	3.86	20–14	2–0	18.0	1.00	1–2	21.0	3.00	15.4
Texas	Hough (R)	5½–6½	18–12	3.78	22–17	1–0	12.0	4.50	1–1	25.0	2.88	9.7
Cleveland	Farrell (R)	3:10p	4–1	3.21	3–5	No Record			0–1	21.0	4.71	14.1
California	Witt (R)	6–7	16–13	3.85	18–17	No Record			1–1	23.0	3.91	11.3

KEY =

TEAM REC—Team's record in games started by today's pitcher.
AHWG—Average hits and walks allowed per 9 innings.
VS OPP—Pitcher's record versus this opponent, 1987 statistics.
Copyright 1987 Sports Features Syndicate, Inc. and Computer Sports World.
AP–NY–01–25–89 1635 EST <

■ SWEET, DISTRICT JUDGE, concurring in part and dissenting in part.

While I concur in the majority's conclusion that Kregos has displayed sufficient creativity to satisfy the *Feist Publications* standard for copyrightability, I would affirm the district court's grant of summary judgment because I conclude that Kregos' idea here has merged into his expression.

1. Kregos' Idea

I respectfully disagree with the majority's statement that Kregos' idea was the abstract "general idea that statistics can be used to assess pitching performance," because I do not believe that the majority has set forth convincing grounds for its determination as to the idea at issue here.

In my opinion, Kregos' form constitutes an explanation of his preferred system of handicapping baseball games, and he seeks to use his copyright here to prevent others from practicing that system.

The majority characterizes Kregos' work as dealing with "matters of taste and opinion," and therefore compares it to the list of baseball card prices in Eckes v. Card Prices Update, 736 F.2d 859 (2d Cir.1984) or to a listing of socially prominent families rather than to the hypothetical doctor's diagnostic chart. In my view, both the pitching form and the diagnostic chart are expressions intended to assist in predicting particular outcomes, with the data intended to be used as a basis for that prediction. In contrast, neither the card price list nor the social register is associated with any defined event or result, and the information reported—the card prices, the names of the families—is itself the primary feature or attraction.

Finally, in light of the majority's agreement with the district court that Kregos' arrangement of the statistics was not itself creative or original, and therefore that his particular ordering is not protected, it is difficult to grasp exactly what "expression" the majority intends to protect, if not the fundamental expression that these nine items are valuable in predicting games. This difficulty becomes apparent as the majority speculates about the extent of protection to be given to Kregos' form.

2. The Application of the Merger Doctrine

As a secondary matter, I disagree with the majority's characterization of how the merger doctrine is applied in this Circuit.

I believe the proper approach requires the court first to decide whether the copyrighted work satisfies the primary requirement of creativity, then to determine whether there is merger before extending copyright protection. This is based on the wording of § 102(b) of the Copyright Act, which provides

> In no case does copyright protection for an original work of authorship extend to any idea, procedure, process, system, method of operation, concept, principle, or discovery, regardless of the form in which it is described, explained, illustrated, or embodied in such work.

I interpret this language as indicating that protection cannot be given to a work which is inseparable from its underlying idea.

The Nimmer treatise supports the majority's approach, suggesting that merger must be considered in the context of determining whether infringement has occurred rather than in deciding the issue of copyrightability. Under this approach, a court which finds that merger exists should hold that the two works in question are not "substantially similar," even where they are in fact identical, a result which I view as a not useful variety of doublespeak.

Nimmer notwithstanding, the majority of cases have rejected this approach and instead followed the method in which merger becomes an issue only when the two works in question—the copyrighted one and the alleged infringement—appear on the surface to be similar, and under which merger is used as a reason for denying all copyright protection to the plaintiff and thereby excusing the defendant's use of a similar or even identical expression.

The difference in applying these two approaches is not insignificant. Nimmer's method lends itself much more readily to the erroneous conclusion that merger is only available where the defendant has independently created an expression which happens coincidentally to be similar to the plaintiff's work. Merger is then viewed as a means of explaining the unintentional similarity between the two works—thus Nimmer's characterization of it as a means of negating substantial similarity. In other words, if a defendant has actually copied the plaintiff's work, it is unlikely to be allowed to rely on merger to avoid liability. This approach owes little if anything to the strictures of § 102(b), and instead depends on the fundamental principle of copyright law that independent creation is never infringement.

The more common approach, in which merger is considered as part of the determination of copyrightability, absolves even a defendant who has directly copied the plaintiff's work if the idea of that work is merged into the expression. I believe this approach accords more fully with both the language and the purpose of § 102(b), and serves to focus consideration on the proper definition of the idea at the outset of the inquiry.

Oddzon Products, Inc. v. Oman

United States District Court, District of Columbia, 1989.
16 U.S.P.Q.2d (BNA) 1225.

■ GREENE, JUDGE.

This is an action under the Administrative Procedure Act (APA) claiming that the defendant's refusal to register the plaintiff's product was arbitrary, capricious, and an abuse of discretion. Presently before the Court is the defendant's motion for summary judgment. The issues have been fully briefed, and the Court has heard oral argument.

I

The plaintiff initially filed an application for a copyright in its product, called a KOOSH ball, on May 3, 1988. As described by the plaintiff, the KOOSH ball is formed "of many hundreds of floppy, wiggly, elastomeric, spaghetti-like filaments radiating in three dimensions." When this object is free-standing it approximates a sphere, but unlike a regular ball, it has a discontinuous surface which is defined by the distal ends of the radiating filaments. Additionally, because the ball is made largely of soft filaments, the object changes shape or flattens when held or set down. The plaintiff sought to register the KOOSH BALL as a sculptural work.[a]

On May 13, 1988, the Copyright Office informed the plaintiff that the work is not copyrightable because the work basically constituted a sphere and that "familiar shapes and symbols are not copyrightable . . . nor are simple variations or combinations of basic geometric designs capable of supporting a copyright registration." The plaintiff responded to this denial on July 1, 1988 by arguing that the KOOSH ball was not a familiar shape and additionally that the ball's unique feel merited copyright protection. These arguments were rejected, and after a further unsuccessful appeal exhausted the plaintiff's administrative remedies, it filed suit in this Court.

II

Under copyright regulations, "familiar symbols or designs" are examples of works not subject to copyright. 37 C.F.R. § 202.1(a). The defendant argues that such shapes or designs are precluded from copyright protection because they do not originate with the putative author. If such shapes were given copyrights, the public would be deprived of the right to use common shapes and designs that have been in the public domain for centuries. In the words of the Second Circuit, "to extend copyrightability to minuscule variations [of familiar symbols] would simply put a weapon for harassment in the hands of mischievous copiers intent on appropriating and monopolizing public domain work." L. Batlin & Son Inc. v. Snyder, 536 F.2d 486, 492 (2d Cir.1976).

The plaintiff contends that there is a genuine issue of material fact as to whether the KOOSH ball is a familiar object and that, therefore, the defendant's summary judgment motion must be denied. Plaintiff argues on this point that the Register's determination that the KOOSH ball is a familiar design was conclusory, and that the agency's factfinding procedures were inadequate, thus permitting this Court to conduct a de novo review of that finding. Alternatively, plaintiff argues that if the Court adopts an abuse of discretion standard, plaintiff should be allowed discovery into the basis for defendant's definition and criteria for determining whether the KOOSH ball is a familiar design.

The Court need not directly address these issues for, although the defendant rests primarily on its determination that the KOOSH ball is a familiar design, the outcome of this litigation does not turn on such a finding. To the extent that the Register of the Copyright Office argues that the KOOSH ball is not copyrightable simply because its shape approximates a sphere, the argument is not well taken.

Certainly an object's shape cannot be the sine quo non of the copyright determination. The defendant presumably would not argue that a painting

---

[a] The plaintiff seeks a copyright in order to prevent imports of less expensive "knock-offs."

of a spherical shape by Pablo Picasso is per se not copyrightable. Moreover, the Register has granted protection to other objects that have familiar shapes, and some such objects were produced in this Court.[b]

Rather, the test is whether a work contains certain "minimal levels of creativity and originality." John Muller & Co. Inc. v. N.Y. Arrows Soccer Team, 802 F.2d 989, 990 (8th Cir.1986).[c] Where, as here, the applicant seeks to register an item as a sculptural work, it must "embody some creative authorship in its delineation or form." *Id*. Presumably, the Register's incantation of the regulation barring registration of familiar designs is a short hand method of expressing the conclusion that the KOOSH ball does not embody a sufficient degree of creative authorship. In other words, it is not merely that the KOOSH ball approximates a sphere, it is also that there is not enough additional creative work beyond the object's basic shape to warrant a copyright.

The Court finds that there was no abuse of discretion in the Register's refusal to copyright the KOOSH ball. That object was carefully examined on three different occasions at different levels in the Copyright Office. In each instance, the examiners concluded that there was insufficient creative authorship to merit copyright protection. The arguments and authority

A KOOSH BALL

[b] One such was a Christmas tree ornament in the shape and coloring of a soccer ball.

[c] There appears to be no issue as to the work's originality. Rather, the focus is on creative authorship.

forwarded by the plaintiff were carefully considered. Moreover, the conclusion reached by the Register is certainly within the bounds of prior case law which has refused to find sufficient creative authorship in works involving familiar symbols and designs. See, e.g., *John Muller, supra,* 802 F.2d, at 990 (upholding Register's decision to refuse copyright in chevron-shaped logo); Bailie v. Fisher, 258 F.2d 425, 426 (D.C.Cir.1958)(per curiam)(upholding Register's refusal to copyright cardboard star with folded flaps).

Hearn v. Meyer

United States District Court, S.D. New York, 1987.
664 F.Supp. 832.

■ Leisure, District Judge.

The complaint in this action seeks monetary damages, recovery of printing plates and other printing materials, and other relief for alleged copyright infringement in connection with a book authored by defendant Susan Meyer and published in 1983 by co-defendant Harry N. Abrams, Inc., entitled "A Treasury of the Great Children's Illustrators" ("Treasury"). In particular, plaintiff Michael Patrick Hearn, the author of several books and a number of articles concerning children's illustrators, contends that certain reproductions in "Treasury" of original illustrations by W.W. Denslow which were also reproduced in plaintiff's book, entitled "The Annotated Wizard of Oz", infringe plaintiff's copyright on his reproductions.

Defendants now move for summary judgment seeking the dismissal of plaintiff's claims. Defendants contend that their reproductions of plaintiff's reproductions of the originally published illustrations of W.W. Denslow do not constitute violations of the law of copyright because plaintiff's reproductions of Denslow's illustrations are not original and, therefore, are not copyrightable. For the purposes of this motion, defendants concede access to plaintiff's work. Plaintiff cross-moves for summary judgment on his claims regarding the reproductions of the illustrations.

Discussion

The legal principles governing defendants' motion are well-settled. "[A] court may determine non-infringement as a matter of law on a motion for summary judgment, either because the similarity between two works concerns only '*non*-copyrightable elements of the plaintiff's work,' or because no reasonable jury, properly instructed, could find that the two works are substantially similar." Warner Bros. Inc. v. American Broadcasting Cos., Inc., 720 F.2d 231, 240 (2d Cir.1983)(citations omitted)(emphasis in original).

A.   Copyrightable Elements

When copyright infringement is alleged, "the analysis must first be to determine exactly what the [plaintiff's] copyright covers, and then to see if there has been an infringement thereof." Axelbank v. Rony, 277 F.2d 314, 317 (9th Cir.1960). The general rule is that "[a] copyright does not give to the owner thereof an exclusive right to use the basic material, but only the exclusive right to reproduce his individual presentation of the material." Rochelle Asparagus Co. v. Princeville Canning Co., 170 F.Supp. 809, 812 (S.D.Ill.1959). Accordingly, "the fact that the same subject matter may be present in two paintings does not prove copying or infringement." Franklin Mint Corp. v. National Wildlife Art Exchange, Inc., 575 F.2d 62, 65 (3d Cir.), *cert. denied*, 439 U.S. 880 (1978). As Justice Holmes stated: "Others are free to copy the original [subject matter]. They are not free to copy the copy." *Id.* (quoting Bleistein v. Donaldson Lithographing Co., 188 U.S. 239, 249 (1903)).

B. Plaintiff Owns No Copyright in Copies of Public Domain Reproductions of Original Illustrations

Plaintiff is the author of a book which contains reproductions, Color Plates XXII, XXVII and XLI, of three illustrations drawn by W.W. Denslow which were reproduced originally in the famous children's book, "The Wonderful World of Oz." Plaintiff concedes that the reproductions of the original illustrations appearing in "The Wonderful World of Oz" are in the public domain, having been published originally in 1900. Plaintiff argues, however, that the reproductions of these illustrations appearing in his book "The Annotated Wizard of Oz" are entitled to their own copyrights as reproductions of works of art. Plaintiff alleges that defendants violated his purported copyright by making copies of his reproductions of the 1900 reproductions of the original illustrations. Defendants move for dismissal of this claim arguing that "[n]one of the illustrations ... upon which plaintiff sues are protected by copyright." In particular, defendants argue that plaintiff's work fails to satisfy " 'the one pervading element prerequisite to copyright protection regardless of the form of the work' ... the requirement of originality—that the work be the original product of the claimant." L. Batlin & Son, Inc. v. Snyder, 536 F.2d 486, 489–90 (2d Cir.), *cert. denied*, 429 U.S. 857 (1976)(quoting 1 M. Nimmer, The Law of Copyright § 10, at 32 (1975)).

The requirement of "originality" stems "from the fact that, constitutionally, copyright protection may be claimed only by 'authors.' " *L. Batlin*, *supra*, 536 F.2d, at 490 (quoting U.S.Const., art. I, § 8; Burrow–Giles Lithographic Co. v. Sarony, 111 U.S. 53, 58 (1884)). "Thus, '[o]ne who has slavishly or mechanically copied from others may not claim to be an author.' " *L. Batlin*, *supra*, 536 F.2d, at 490 (quoting 1 M. Nimmer, *supra*, § 6, at 10.2). Moreover, "[s]ince the constitutional requirement must be read into the Copyright Act, the requirement of originality is also a statutory one." *L. Batlin*, *supra*, 536 F.2d, at 490 (citing Chamberlin v. Uris Sales Corp., 150 F.2d 512 (2d Cir.1945)). "It has been the law of this circuit for at least 30 years that in order to obtain a copyright upon a reproduction of a work of art ... that the work 'contain[s] some substantial, not merely trivial originality....' " *L. Batlin*, *supra*, 536 F.2d, at 490 (quoting *Chamberlin*, *supra*, 150 F.2d, at 513).

It is clear, therefore, that to rule upon any claim for infringement of copyright, the Court must explore the concept of originality. The Second

Circuit has noted that "[t]he test of originality is concededly one with a low threshold in that '[a]ll that is needed ... is that the "author" contributed something more than a "merely trivial" variation, something recognizably "his own." ' " *id.* (quoting Alfred Bell & Co. v. Catalda Fine Arts, Inc., 191 F.2d 99, 102–03 (2d Cir.1951)). However, as the Second Circuit has stated "[w]hile a copy of something in the public domain will not, if it be merely a copy, support a copyright, a distinguishable variation will ..." Gerlach–Barklow Co. v. Morris & Bendien, Inc., 23 F.2d 159, 161 (2d Cir.1927)(cited in *L. Batlin, supra,* 536 F.2d, at 490). Finally, it is well settled that the foregoing principles are applicable to both reproductions of a work of art and works of art themselves. "The requirement of substantial as opposed to trivial variation and the prohibition of mechanical copying, both of which are inherent in and subsumed by the concept of originality, apply to both statutory categories." *L. Batlin, supra,* 536 F.2d, at 490.

The Second Circuit has applied this standard in a wide variety of cases. It has held that "mass-produced commercial objects with a minimal element of artistic craftsmanship may satisfy the statutory requirement of such a work." *id.* at 491 (citation omitted). Nevertheless, the Second Circuit has held that "the mere reproduction of a work of art in a different medium should not constitute the required originality...." *id.* (quoting 1 M. Nimmer, *supra,* § 20.2 at 94). Moreover, the Court of Appeals has stated that "the requirement of originality [cannot] be satisfied simply by the demonstration of 'physical skill' or 'special training'.... A considerably higher degree of skill is required, true artistic skill, to make the reproduction copyrightable." *L. Batlin, supra,* 536 F.2d, at 491 (emphasis in original). Finally, the Second Circuit has recognized that although "the test of 'originality' may leave a lot to be desired, ... it is the only one we have...." *id.* at 492.

Mindful of the foregoing principles, the Court turns to the reproductions here in dispute. The Court examined the appearance of the reproductions contained in "The Annotated Wizard of Oz" and compared them to the original reproductions of the illustrations contained in "The Wonderful World of Oz." The Court agrees with plaintiff that:

> The "Witch of the North" plate in the Annotated Wizard is greener than the original and the witch's face has a deeper yellow. The colors in the "China" plate are lighter than the original which has a bluer sky and a deeper brown in Dorothy's dress. The cowardly lion is more brown in the reproduction than the original.

The Court, however, does not share plaintiff's conclusion that "[t]hese variations enhance the copyrightability of the reproductions."

The Court notes that plaintiff does not claim that these insignificant variations were created intentionally. Moreover, plaintiff fails to argue—and this Court fails to see—how these minor variations express the plaintiff's own artistic viewpoint. In short, the Court finds that, at least with respect to the works' appearance, plaintiff's reproductions are mere slavish copies of W.W. Denslow's illustrations, as reproduced originally in "The Wonderful World of Oz." Accordingly, the Court concludes that the appearance of plaintiff's reproductions is clearly insufficient to vest them with copyright protection.

Deprived of the assistance of the appearance of his reproductions, plaintiff turns, as he must, to the alleged difficulty of the copying process itself, as a way to satisfy the requirement of originality. Plaintiff claims that "the process by which he arranged for the reproduction of the five items at issue here involved a difficult, time-consuming and concentrated artistic effort to recreate the precise colors originally employed by Denslow in the first edition of the 'Wizard of Oz.' " Plaintiff noted the specific steps he took in order to produce the illustrations:

1. Photograph the key block from the original illustration, dropping all of the other colors.

2. Have each of the secondary colors hand-drawn on acetate which would require the tracing of the original plates in India ink or with coated mylar.

3. Then each secondary color had to be photographed individually, and each printed in one color only.

4. Then all the plates would be printed one on top of the other to give a variety of hue and color.

"sweat of brow"

Plaintiff also described the process as follows:

The work done by the various participants was long, time-consuming, and artistic in every sense of the word. The original drawings had to be retraced by hand in three separate stages to correspond to the three separate colors, red, yellow, and blue. Every bit of grass, every check on Dorothy's dress, every bit of shine on the Tin Woodman's body had to be redrawn with pen and ink on acetate and sometimes twice or more if it involved a secondary color, green, orange or brown, because these colors were created only by the printing of two primary colors on top of one another.... This was time consuming, exacting work because no overlapping of colors could be accepted; any overlapping would result in peculiar rather than pure secondary colors. These errors could only be seen when the proofs of the separations were made, and if any errors were discovered, again retracing by hand was required to align all carelessnesses.

In support of his attempt to cast the above described effort in a manner which would satisfy the originality requirement, plaintiff relies heavily on Alfred Bell & Co., Ltd. v. Catalda Fine Arts, Inc., 74 F.Supp. 973 (S.D.N.Y.1947), aff'd 191 F.2d 99 (2d Cir.1951); Millworth Converting Corp. v. Slifka, 276 F.2d 443 (2d Cir.1960); and Alva Studios, Inc. v. Winninger, 177 F.Supp. 265 (S.D.N.Y.1959).

In *Alfred Bell*, plaintiff, "a British print producer and dealer, ... copyrighted in the United States eight mezzotint engravings of old masters produced at its order by three mezzotint engravers." 74 F.Supp., at 974–75. Plaintiff brought the action against "a color lithographer, a dealer in lithographs and the dealer's president, [who] produced and sold color lithographs of the eight mezzotints." *Id.* at 975. It was undisputed that the subjects of the eight engravings were all well known works of art all in the public domain. *Id.* [The District Court found] that defendants had violated plaintiff's copyright. The Second Circuit affirmed. The Court of Appeals noted that the mezzotints " 'originated' with those who made them, and ... amply met the standards imposed by the Constitution and the statute." 191 F.2d, at 104. The Second Circuit then noted:

"Again, an engraver is almost invariably a copyist, but although his work may infringe copyright in the original painting if made without the consent of the owner of the copyright therein, his work may still be original in the sense that he has employed skill and judgment in its production. He produces the resemblance he is desirous of obtaining by means very different from those employed by the painter or draughtsman from whom he copies: means which require great labour and talent. The engraver produces his effects by the management of light and shade, or as the term of his art expresses it, the *chiarooscuro* [sic]. The due degrees of light and shade are produced by different lines and dots; he who is the engraver must decide on the choice of the different lines or dots for himself, and on his choice depends the success of his print."

id. at 104–05 n.22.

Plaintiff contends that:

The description of the mezzotint process matches precisely what was done in this case. Instead of working on copper, the modern artisan works with pen and ink on acetate. But he must hand-draw each and every mark that must be reproduced in a single color. Indeed in this case it had to be done two or three times. Every color had to be traced or redrawn individually on acetate. Primary colors were printed on top of each other to make secondary colors. Proofs had to be pulled at every stage to check the register and density of color. There was constant redrawing and reapplication of mylar—the gummed plastic that indicates the color. The process took over a year.

Plaintiff also seeks support from *Millworth Converting* in which Judge Friendly held that plaintiff was entitled to copyright a three-dimensional embroidered effect based on a public domain two-dimensional fabric design. Judge Friendly, relying on *Alfred Bell*, noted that the plaintiff "offered substantial evidence that its creation of a three-dimensional effect, giving something of the impression of embroidery on a flat fabric, required effort and skill." 276 F.2d, at 445. Accordingly, the Second Circuit found that "plaintiff's contribution to its reproduction of this design sufficed to meet the modest requirement of a copyright proprietor 'that his work contains some substantial, not merely trivial, originality . . . .' " *Id.* (quoting *Chamberlin, supra,* 150 F.2d, at 513).

Finally, plaintiff cites *Alva Studios* as support for his claim of originality. In *Alva Studios,* plaintiff was engaged in the business of reproducing "three-dimensional works of art, the originals of which [were] owned by various museums throughout the United States and several foreign countries." 177 F.Supp., at 266. The subject of the dispute in *Alva Studios* was plaintiff's reproduction of Auguste Rodin's sculpture, "Hand of God." Plaintiff copyrighted its reproduction; it then sued defendant for infringement because defendant was copying plaintiff's Rodin replica and marketing products embodying this copying through retail operation. It was undisputed that the original sculpture was in the public domain.

The District Court first examined whether plaintiff satisfied the requirement of originality. The Court found that plaintiff had done so because:

[Plaintiff's] copyrighted work embodies and resulted from its skill and originality in producing an accurate scale reproduction of the original. In a work of sculpture, this reduction requires far more than an abridgment of a written classic; great skill and originality is called for when one seeks to produce a scale reduction of a great work with exactitude.

* * *

The originality and distinction between the plaintiff's work and the original also lies in the treatment of the rear side of the base. The rear side of the original base is open; that of the plaintiff's work is closed. We find that this difference when coupled with the skilled scaled sculpture is itself creative.

177 F.Supp., at 267. In addition, the Court found "that the granting of approval by the Carnegie Institute's department of Fine Arts, experts in the field, to be extremely persuasive that the plaintiff's copyrighted work is in itself a work of art which bears the stamp of originality and of skill." *Id.* at 267. Accordingly, the Court found that plaintiff's work was original.

The Court has examined the aforementioned cases and finds that although, at first blush, they appear to support plaintiff's position, careful scrutiny and analysis reveals them to be inapposite. In *Alfred Bell* the District Court's finding of originality was based primarily on plaintiff's conversion of the original art work, oil paintings done on canvas, to mezzotint engravings. The District Court emphasized that "[w]hat is original ... is the handling of the painting in another medium.... It is only this treatment in another medium which is original...." 74 F.Supp., at 976. Moreover, in *Millworth Converting* the Court based its finding of originality on plaintiff's conversion of a two-dimensional fabric design into a three-dimensional embroidered effect. Finally, in *Alva Studios*, the District Court based its finding of originality on more than just the skill of the artisan doing the reproduction; the District Court noted that it took great creativity, as well as skill, to interpret, project and transpose the original Rodin work in order to create a scale model thereof. In addition, the Court relied on substantial differences in the appearance between the reproduction and the original. Finally, the District Court based its finding of originality on the accrediting of the reproduction by an expert.

In the instant action, plaintiff has not reproduced W.W. Denslow's illustrations in another medium or form. It is undisputed that the original illustrations were previously reproduced in the first edition of "The Wonderful World of Oz" and a scrapbook of the "Wizard of Oz" musical. The publisher of "The Wonderful World of Oz" was the first to reproduce W.W. Denslow's illustrations for a book. Plaintiff's contribution is merely the reproduction of the original reproductions.[a] Moreover, although it is undisputed that plaintiff expended great effort and time in reproducing the reproductions of W.W. Denslow's illustrations, such effort and time alone are not sufficient for a finding of originality. Accordingly, the Court finds

---

[a] There is no evidence in the record regarding the skill and effort exercised by the original publisher in reproducing W. W. Denslow's illustrations for "The Wonderful

that, as a matter of law, plaintiff's reproductions of the 1900 reproductions of W.W. Denslow's illustrations are not original and are therefore, not copyrightable.

Plaintiff's last claim for the copyrightability of his reproductions of the reproductions of W.W. Denslow's original illustrations stems from the alleged public benefit he has provided by making available to the public reproductions of rarely seen reproductions of original illustrations. It is undisputed that the original W.W. Denslow drawings are unavailable. It is also agreed that the original edition of "The Wonderful World of Oz" is a "rare work" and difficult to find in libraries. Therefore, plaintiff argues that his reproductions should be protected under the copyright law. Plaintiff also suggests that "defendants could have avoided the entire problem if they had bothered to find original illustrations by Denslow, as plaintiff Hearn did.... All they have to do is find the originals themselves, rather than appropriating the work of plaintiff here."

Although the Court agrees with plaintiff that, to some extent, defendants and the public have benefited from plaintiff's work, this, in and of itself, does not mandate copyright protection for the work. There are equally sound policy reasons—regarding these concededly rare and public domain reproductions of original illustrations—which militate against plaintiff's position. Plaintiff must not be permitted to "monopolize rights to reproduce what are concededly rare and public domain illustrations, and hence restrict public access to them." As the Second Circuit noted:

> Absent a genuine difference between the underlying work of art and the copy of it for which protection is sought, the public interest in promoting progress in the arts—indeed, the constitutional demand, could hardly be served. To extend copyrightability to minuscule variations would simply put a weapon for harassment in the hands of mischievous copiers intent on appropriating and monopolizing public domain work.

L. Batlin, supra, 536 F.2d, at 492. Thus, the alleged public benefit conferred by plaintiff is not dispositive of this question.

Accordingly, the Court finds that plaintiff's reproductions of the reproductions of W.W. Denslow's illustrations do not satisfy the originality requirement under copyright law. Plaintiff's reproductions, therefore, are not protected, as a matter of law, by copyright. Plaintiff's claims in connection with said reproductions are thus dismissed.

Registration of Colorized Black and White Motion Pictures As Derivative Works

Vol. 52 Federal Register No. 119, (1987).

1. Background

The Copyright Act, title 17 of the U.S. Code, defines a derivative work as "a work based upon one or more preexisting works such as a translation,

World of Oz." Presumably, such effort and skill was equal to that allegedly displayed by plaintiff.

musical arrangement, dramatization, fictionalization, motion picture version, sound recording, art reproduction, abridgement, condensation, or any other form in which a work may be recast, transformed, or adapted. A work consisting of editorial revisions, annotations, elaborations, or other *modifications, which, as a whole, represent an original work of authorship*, is a 'derivative work'." § 101 (emphasis added).

The Copyright Act also spells out that copyright protection in a derivative work "extends only to the material contributed by the author of such work, as distinguished from the preexisting material employed in the work, and does *not imply any exclusive right in the preexisting material. The copyright in such work is independent of, and does not affect or enlarge the scope, duration, ownership, or subsistence of, any copyright protection in the preexisting material*." § 103(b)(emphasis added).

An existing Copyright Office regulation provides that "mere variations of . . . coloring" are not subject to copyright. 37 CFR 202.1(a). This does not preclude registration where the work contains some other elements of originality such as an original arrangement or combination of colors. Courts have held that while color per se is uncopyrightable and unregistrable, arrangements or combinations of colors may warrant copyright protection.[a]

Between 1985 and 1986, several parties submitted the colorized versions of ten motion pictures and one television program to the Copyright Office for registration of the colorized version as a derivative work. The Copyright Office did not register any of these works. Because of the unusual nature of the claimed authorship and to obtain information about the process of creating the colorized versions from persons other than the claimants, on September 15, 1986, the Copyright Office published a Notice of Inquiry in the Federal Register (51 FR 32665) asking for comments in four specific areas:

1. Which steps, if any, in the colorization processes involve individual creative human authorship?

2. Who are the authors of the copyrightable elements, if any, in colorized film?

3. With specific reference to the role of computer programs in colorization processes:

(a) How are colors selected? How are colors made available for selection? What factors influence color selection? How wide is the range of choice?

(b) In addition to coloring in the strict sense, are other cinematographic contributions, such as animation or other hand or computer assisted effects, utilized in colorizing?

4. Are all colorization processes intended solely to create videotapes in color? Are any methods now available or under development that would permit the commercially feasible colorization of 35mm prints of a quality that would permit theatrical distribution?

[a] See also 1 Nimmer on Copyright § 2.14 (1985).

The Copyright Office explained that it was interested in this information in order to come to a determination of whether the coloring of black and white motion pictures is subject to copyright registration; furthermore, the Copyright Office specified that aesthetic or moral arguments about the propriety of coloring black and white film did not, and could not, form any part of its inquiry.[b]

2. Summary of the Comments

In all 46 comments (43 original and three reply) were filed with the Copyright Office. Despite the Copyright Office's caveat against arguments regarding aesthetic considerations, many of the comments filed related simply to the question of whether or not the commentator found the colorized motion picture aesthetically pleasing. And most did not. Other comments attempted to respond to the four question areas set out in the Notice of Inquiry.

a. The colorization processes

The Copyright Office noted the existence of two different types of processes in which color is added to a black and white film. One ("chromoloid") involves a color-retrieval process and the other ("colorization") adds color to individual scenes and then the entire film. The second system is the one used by both the Color Systems Technology, Inc. of Hollywood, and Colorization, Inc. of Toronto, Canada.

(1) The chromoloid process

In this process a fine grained black and white positive print is first reproduced by an optical printer in three distinct prints: red, blue, and green. Then a subsequent printing process combines the three prints into a single full color film. This process was not described in any of the comments, and no films colored by this process have been submitted to the Copyright Office for registration.

(2) The colorization process

Both the Canadian firm, Colorization, Inc. that is associated with Hal Roach Studios, and Color Systems Technology use separately developed processes that basically involve colorization of one frame by a computer operator and then colorization of each succeeding frame in the entire scene by the computer.

The first step of the colorization process is to transform a pristine black and white print to a videotape. This videotape is then broken down into discrete scenes and sequences. A color plan is developed for each scene as well as the entire videotape. The spectrum of colors initially available is

---

[b] Copyright registration determinations cannot be made on aesthetic grounds. Original works of authorship that meet the legal and formal requirements of the Copyright Act are entitled to registration, irrespective of their artistic worth. Moreover, the present federal Copyright law does not extend protection to the so-called "moral right" of an author to prevent the distortion or mutilation of the work, after transfer of the Copyright.

virtually unlimited,[c] but colors are generally selected to convey a particular time period, to create a certain mood, and to be faithful where possible to the coloring of the actors and actresses involved.

Next an artist uses a computer controlled graphics tablet and an electronic palette to hand-color key frames. Then a high-speed computer is directed to color the intervening frames, gearing adjustments to variations in the luminosity of the black and white original.

Each color converted scene is reviewed and revisions are made where necessitated, e.g., where dictated by a change in one of the intervening frames not consistent with the hand-colored key frame.

b.   Original authorship

Although the general public response was against copyright registration on aesthetic grounds, the consensus of those who responded regarding the legal issue of original authorship was that colorized versions of black and white motion pictures satisfied the copyright law's standard for copyright subject matter. They based this argument on the position that the creation of a computer color version is a process that involves individual creative human authorship and requires an amount of technical or artistic judgment that meets copyright law standards of original, creative expression. One justification was that all of the steps involved in colorization involve human authorship since the process is directed by human operators who follow the dictates of a human art director. The more prevalent justification is that the selection, coordination and application of color, and the review of the final product amount to "individual creative human authorship."

Those opposed to copyright registration asserted that colorizing is a technical process that does not have sufficient *human* authorship to merit copyright protection. This commentator examined three steps involved in the process: color selection, the data base, and the computer program and argued that none justify registration of colorized films under the following tests for derivative works claims:

(1) Are they based on more than ideas or mere facts, and

(2) If so, are they based on more than trivial variations in the actual expression of an underlying work, these being both

   (a) Attributable to original authorship, and

   (b) Representing a modicum of creativity.

As to color selection the opponents claimed that an artist's selection of palette is an idea that has not as yet produced any copyrightable expression. As to the "data base," this party noted that copyright does not cover the factual content of a work and contended that it is the color facts in the data base which are integrated into a preexisting visual pattern of the black

---

[c] The comment of Colorization, Inc. alleges that selections are made from a palette of 16 million colors, from which 4,096 colors are selected for each movie and 64 colors for each scene.

and white film that is being reprocessed. These patterns, it was argued, serve as the actual expression in the new video product, which merely organizes the facts previously compiled in a different order. Furthermore, the opponents argued that "the protectible forms in which the facts were once compiled, that is, expressed and organized, say, as a computer-readable data base, will, in the final video product, be quite simply left behind...." Finally, the opponents asserted that copyright in a computer program cannot also support a claim in the product or output of the program—in this case the color-recoded film.

Several commentators raised the issue of whether only the handcolored scenes and not those done by computer are copyrightable. Another related issue is even if sufficient human authorship exists given today's colorization technology, what happens to a copyright claim when the complete coloring process is done by a computer program?

3. Appropriate Judicial Standard

Proponents and opponents would probably agree that whether or not a derivative work will support a copyright depends upon whether it is a distinguishable variation or merely a trivial variation. See L. Batlin and Son v. Snyder, 536 F.2d 486 (2d Cir.1976), *cert. denied*, 429 U.S. 857 (1976). The disagreement between the two sides centers on what makes a variation distinguishable and also on whether a higher standard is required for a derivative work, especially if it is based on a work that is already in the public domain.

The [S]econd [C]ircuit held in the *Batlin* case that a higher standard exists for determining copyrightability of contributions to public domain works. Later this same court said that copyright for derivative works is subject to two related and important limitations:

1. To support a copyright the original aspects of a derivative work must be more than trivial.

2. The scope of protection afforded a derivative work must reflect the degree to which it relies on the preexisting material and must not in any way affect the scope of any copyright in this preexisting material.

Durham Industries, Inc. v. Tomy Corporation, 630 F.2d 905, 909 (2d Cir.1980).

The [S]eventh [C]ircuit has also indicated that a higher standard of originality is required in derivative works in order to prevent the first creator of a derivative work from interfering with the right of subsequent authors to depict the underlying work without fear of copyright problems. Gracen v. Bradford Exchange, 698 F.2d 300 (7th Cir.1983).

Proponents of copyright for computer-colorized films assert that the *Gracen* case is a misreading of *Batlin*, that *Batlin* grapples with the problem of substantial similarity in the case of works grounded in common antecedents, and that the ruling does not deny copyright registrability to colorized motion pictures which meet the tests of original authorship as set out in *Batlin* and other cases.

Opponents of copyright in computer-colorized films argue that colorizing a film does not meet the *Batlin* test for authorship in derivative works. They interpret *Batlin* as distinguishing between human contributions that require sustained "artistic skill and effort" and those that exhibit only "physical skill" or technical competence. The former could be copyrightable; the latter would not.

Before the *Batlin* case was decided, a district court upheld the copyrightability of a compilation of colors on the basis of color selection which the court found to require "careful consideration of numerous artistic factors including the aesthetic attributes of each shade and its use in the commercial art field." Pantone Inc. v. A. J. Friedman Inc., 294 F.Supp. 545, 547 (S.D.N.Y.1968).

4. Registration Decision

After studying the comments responsive to the questions listed above, the Copyright Act, and the case law, the Copyright Office has concluded that certain colorized versions of black and white motion pictures are eligible for copyright registration as derivative works. The Office will register as derivative works those color versions that reveal a certain minimum amount of individual creative human authorship. This decision is restricted to the colorized films prepared through the computer-colorization process described above. No comments were received regarding the chromoloid process, and no claims are pending before the Copyright Office. The record before us does not contain sufficient information to make a decision regarding chromoloid films.

The Copyright Office finds that the issue of copyright in computer-colorized films requires a difficult determination of the presence of original authorship. The policy of the existing regulation prohibiting registration for "mere variations ... of coloring" is sound and fully supported by case law. The regulation is applied by the Copyright Office to deny registration when the only authorship claimed consists of the addition of a relatively few number of colors to an existing design or work. The regulation also prohibits registration of multiple colored versions of the same basic design or work. Registration is not precluded, however, where the work consists of original selection, arrangement, or combinations of a large number of colors, or where the lines of an original design are fired by gradations of numerous colors. The Copyright Office finds that these registration practices are consistent with the standards of original authorship set by the Copyright Act, and we affirm the validity of the existing regulation.

The Office concludes that some computer-colorized films may contain sufficient original authorship to justify registration, but our decision is a close, narrow one based on the allegations that the typical colorized film is the result of the selection of as many as 4000 colors, drawn from a palette of 16 million colors. The Office does not consider registration would be justified based on a claimed "arrangement" or "combination" of the colors because the original black and white film predetermines the arrangement of colors. The Office is concerned about implications of registering a claim to copyright in public domain films based on colorizing, and we address that point below. Our decision is also limited to existing computer-coloring technology. We will monitor technological developments, and may reconsider the issue if the role of the computer in selecting the colors becomes more dominant.

The general standard for determining whether the color added to a black and white motion picture is sufficient to merit copyright protection is the statutory standard that already applies to all derivative works, i.e. "modifications" to a preexisting work "which, as a whole, represent an original work of authorship." § 101. In determining whether the coloring of a particular black and white film is a modification that satisfies the above standard, the Office will apply the following criteria:

(1) Numerous color selections must be made by human beings from an extensive color inventory.

(2) The range and extent of colors added to the black and white work must represent more than a trivial variation.

(3) The overall appearance of the motion picture must be modified; registration will not be made for the coloring of a few frames or the enhancement of color in a previously colored film.

(4) Removal of color from a motion picture or other work will not justify registration.

(5) The existing regulatory prohibition on copyright registration based on mere variations of color is confirmed.

When registration is warranted, the copyright will cover only the new material, that is, the numerous selections of color that are added to the original black and white film. The copyright status of the underlying work is unaffected. The black and white film version will remain in the public domain or enter the public domain as dictated by its own copyright term. When an underlying work is in the public domain, another party is free to use that work to make a different color version which may also be eligible for copyright protection.

Dated: June 11, 1987.
Ralph Oman,
Register of Copyrights.
Approved by:
Daniel J. Boorstin,
The Librarian of Congress.

NOTES

1. *Policies underlying the originality requirement.* Why do you suppose the originality requirement under copyright law is not more rigorous? Can the originality requirement as it is applied by the court in *Feist* be criticized for being too rigorous? What is the practical effect of the originality requirement as it is currently applied? Doesn't it call for difficult line-drawing on the part of the Register that might otherwise be unnecessary? Moreover, as *Feist* suggests, the level of originality present in a given work will determine the scope of protection for that work. Thus, during the course of an infringement suit, a court will be called upon to determine the appropriate scope of protection for a copyrighted work. If such is the case, why not allow all works to be registered, regardless of their originality, and have the courts determine the appropriate scope of copyright protection?

Subsequent to *Feist,* a federal appellate court held that a plaintiff's coordination and arrangement of its yellow pages listings were not sufficiently original to merit copyright protection. In BellSouth Advertising & Publishing Corp. v. Donnelley Information Publishing, Inc.,[7] the court explained that the plaintiff's alphabetized listing of business categories, together with the individual businesses listed in alphabetical order under the relevant headings was "entirely typical" and "practically inevitable" for a business telephone directory, and that "[b]ecause this is the one way to construct a useful business directory, the arrangement has 'merged' with the idea of a business directory, and thus is uncopyrightable."[8]

2. *The essence of "authorship": idea vs. expression.* The line between idea and expression often is extremely difficult to draw, as the major cases suggest. In fact, this inquiry really is the bottom line in many of the originality cases. Consider this hypothetical. Plaintiff is the organizer of McDonald's Charity Christmas Parade in Chicago. Plaintiff sold exclusive Chicago broadcast rights to ABC. Defendant is WGN, a local television station, which intends to telecast the parade using its own personnel and equipment, simultaneously with ABC's telecast. Plaintiff argues that the production of the parade and the parade itself is a "compilation" of creative works under §§ 101 & 103(a) under the 1976 Act. How should the Court rule?

3. *Protection for star pagination.* In West Publishing Co. v. Mead Data Central,[9] West was seeking to enjoin Lexis' star pagination feature which inserts page numbers from West's reporters into the body of Lexis reports, providing "jump" citations to the location in West's reporters of the material viewed on Lexis. Through the use of star pagination, Lexis users would be able to obtain the exact West reporter page number of the material viewed on Lexis without having to open up a West volume. In granting West preliminary injunctive relief, the Federal Court of Appeals for the Eighth Circuit viewed the pagination of West's volumes as an expression of its case arrangements. According to the court in *West,* there is no per se rule excluding case arrangements from protection. Instead, the inquiry centers on whether the particular arrangement meets the "origi-

[7] 999 F.2d 1436 (11th Cir.1993), cert. denied, ___ U.S. ___, 114 S.Ct. 943, 127 L.Ed.2d 323 (1994).

[8] Id. at 1442. But see Warren Publishing, Inc. v. Microdos Data Corp., 52 F.3d 950 (11th Cir.1995)(distinguishing *Feist* and *Bell-South,* and holding that a publisher's system of selecting communities geographically by "principal" communities served for listing cable television systems was a copyrightable compilation).

[9] 799 F.2d 1219 (8th Cir.1986), cert. denied, 479 U.S. 1070, 107 S.Ct. 962, 93 L.Ed.2d 1010 (1987).

nality and intellectual-creation standards."[10] The following is an excerpt from the opinion which discusses West's arrangement process:

> [W]est separates the decisions of state courts from federal-court decisions. West further divides the federal opinions and the state opinions and then assigns them to the appropriate West reporter series. State court decisions are divided by geographic region and assigned to West's corresponding regional reporter. Federal decisions are first divided by the level of the court they come from into district court decisions, court of appeals decisions, and Supreme Court decisions.... Before being assigned to a reporter, district court decisions are subdivided according to subject matter into bankruptcy decisions, federal rules decisions, and decisions on other topics. After an opinion is assigned to a reporter, it is assigned to a volume of the reporter and then arranged within the volume. Federal court of appeals decisions, for example, are arranged according to circuit within each volume of West's Federal Reporter, Second Series, though there may be more than one group of each circuit's opinions in each volume.[11]

The court concluded that West's arrangement process is the result of "considerable labor, talent, and judgment."[12] Do you agree? How different are West's arrangements from the alphabetical listings involved in *Feist*?

On July 21, 1988, Mead and West announced a settlement of the copyright and other pending suits under which all suits were to be dismissed and Mead would pay West an undisclosed licensing fee in exchange for both the use of West's page numbers in a star-pagination system and the use of West's numbering systems in various state code compilations. Thus, Mead has effectively recognized West's copyright in those items. In addition, at the level of state legislatures in at least two states (Texas and Illinois), West has succeeded in claiming ownership of the chapter and section numbers of the state statutory compilations which it publishes.[13]

4. *Arrangement vs. research.* Although arrangements of facts are copyrightable, it seems to be fairly well settled that the research involved in obtaining facts is not protectable under copyright law. There used to be a split in the circuits on the question of research, with Hoehling v. Universal City Studios, Inc.[14] holding that research is not protectable, and Miller v. Universal City Studios, Inc., at the lower court level,[15] holding that the expense and labor of research are distinct from the facts and make research more similar to expression of facts. The Fifth Circuit, however, ultimately reversed,[16] and explicitly held that research is not copyrightable.

[10] Id. at 1225.

[11] Id. at 1226.

[12] Id.

[13] See Patterson & Joyce, Monopolizing the Law: The Scope of Copyright Protection for Law Reports and Statutory Compilations, 36 UCLA L. Rev. 719, 720, 725–26 (1989).

[14] 618 F.2d 972 (2d Cir.), cert. denied, 449 U.S. 841, 101 S.Ct. 121, 66 L.Ed.2d 49 (1980).

[15] 460 F.Supp. 984 (S.D.Fla.1978).

[16] 650 F.2d 1365 (5th Cir.1981).

What about interpretative theories based on historical fact? In this regard, consider the following facts: Plaintiff wrote books of historical non-fiction in which he developed the thesis that John Dillinger, the notorious bank robber, was not shot outside Chicago's Biograph Theater in 1934. According to the plaintiff's thesis, FBI agents instead mistakenly shot and killed a small-time hoodlum named Jimmy Lawrence. In his books, the plaintiff constructs an elaborate theory showing that other criminals set up Lawrence and that FBI agents, afraid of embarrassment, covered up their killing of the wrong man and that shortly after the incident, Dillinger moved to the west coast where he lived until 1979. Defendant, CBS, aired an episode of the television program Simon and Simon with the following plot: A retired FBI agent, who believes that Dillinger was not killed in 1934, is mysteriously murdered with Dillinger's old pistol. An investigation reveals that the gun bears the fresh fingerprints of Dillinger. The daughter of the murdered FBI agent hires the Simon detectives to track down the killer. The Simons discover various discrepancies surrounding Dillinger's death, including some of the discrepancies detailed in the plaintiff's books. In the end, the Simons prove that another person, not Dillinger, murdered the FBI agent, but the final scene of the episode is a "teaser" suggesting that Dillinger may still be living. Is the material which the defendants allegedly infringed copyrightable?

5. *Different standards for different types of works.* Sometimes courts invoke a higher originality standard for derivative works. The court in *Hearn* quotes from a Second Circuit opinion suggesting that with respect to reproductions of artistic works, a higher degree of skill, "true artistic skill", may be required to make a reproduction copyrightable (see Section B of case where the *L. Batlin* case is quoted). The Copyright Office regulation on colorized films discusses Gracen v. Bradford Exchange,[17] which also endorsed a higher standard of originality for derivative works. Should the originality requirement be applied differently to derivative works? What does the Copyright Office's regulation suggest should be the appropriate standard for derivative works? Is *Hearn* inconsistent with the Copyright Office regulation regarding what types of efforts are required to satisfy the originality requirement?

Although STRYKER is not a derivative work, should a higher standard of originality also be applied specifically to video games, and if so, why? How does this inquiry bear on the Principal Problem?

6. *The parts vs. the whole.* The 1976 Copyright Act defines audiovisual works as "works that consist of a series of related images which are intrinsically intended to be shown by the use of machines or devices such as projectors, viewers, or electronic equipment, together with accompanying sounds...."[18] Did the Register of Copyrights in the Principal Problem properly apply this definition? Should shapes be copyrightable when they are combined in some sort of a design?

---

[17] 698 F.2d 300 (7th Cir.1983). [18] See § 101.

7. *Originality vs. creativity.* In order to receive protection, the 1976 Act states that a work must be an "original work of authorship." Is there a difference between originality and a "work of authorship"? Does the work of authorship requirement mandate that the creator infuse some of her own personality into the work? Can a work be original (i.e., not copied from another source) but lack the necessary degree of creative authorship for copyright protection? How would you analyze the Principal Problem in this respect?

Section 102(b) of the Copyright Act provides that "[i]n no case does copyright protection for an original work of authorship extend to any idea, procedure, process, system, method of operation, concept, principle, or discovery, regardless of the form in which it is described, explained, illustrated, or embodied in such work."[19] Interestingly, despite the fact that the Patent Act does not specifically exclude principles, discoveries, etc., the courts have uniformly interpreted it as not extending to these things. See Assignment 16. However, many of the issues decided under the guise of "originality" and "authorship" in copyright law are decided as questions about "subject matter" in patent law.

8. *Genetic sequences.* The human genome consists of 23 pairs of chromosomes that contain the complete set of instructions for all inherited attributes. Every chromosome's inherited information is recorded by the chemical DNA. Each molecule contains two strands of material wrapped around each other and connected by rungs of chemicals called bases. Four different bases are present in DNA—adenine (A), thymine (T), cytosine (C), and guanine (G); it is the sequence in which they appear (e.g., ATTCCT-GAGG) that is important because it is through this ordering that the molecules transmit information to new generations of cells. Only parts of the strands carry the information required for other chemicals found in the cell. These parts, called genes, are the basic physical and functional units of heredity. Sequencing each gene will permit scientists to develop treatments for hereditary disorders; locating the genes on chromosomes—that is, mapping the human genome—will ultimately enable scientists to develop the tools to predict genetic diseases.

Since there are over 3 billion base pairs and at least 100,000 genes in the human genome, sequencing and mapping will be long and expensive tasks, to which Congress has committed over $3,000,000.[20] Universities, other research institutes, and commercial entities around the country are participating in this project. Should these sequences be copyrightable? Is a genetic map different from any other "pictorial, graphic, and sculptural work"? If the sequences and/or map are copyrightable, who should own the copyrights—the United States, which funded the research,[21] the institute

---

[19] § 102(b).

[20] U.S. Dep't of Health and Human Services & U.S. Dep't of Energy, Understanding Our Genetic Inheritance; The Human Genome Project (1990).

[21] But see § 105 ("Copyright protection . . . is not available for any work of the United States Government, but the United States Government is not precluded from receiving and holding copyrights transferred to it by assignment, bequest, or otherwise.")

where it was conducted, or the individual researcher? Does it make a difference in your answer that the United States has begun to apply for patents on pieces of DNA as they are sequenced (but before they are mapped)? Does your answer depend on whether these patents are granted? See Assignments 9 (discussing work for hire) and 16 (patents on sequences), infra.

9. *The "fixation" requirement.* The fixation requirement also derives from § 102 of the 1976 Act, which provides that "copyright protection subsists . . . in original works of authorship fixed in any tangible medium of expression, now known or later developed, from which they can be perceived, reproduced, or otherwise communicated, either directly or with the aid of a machine or device."[22] According to the definitions section of the 1976 Act, a work is " 'fixed' in a tangible medium of expression" when, "by or under the authority of the author," it is embodied in a copy or phonorecord that is "sufficiently permanent or stable to permit it to be perceived, reproduced, or otherwise communicated for a period of more than transitory duration."[23] That section also provides: "A work consisting of sounds, images, or both, that are being transmitted, is 'fixed' for purposes of this title if a fixation of the work is being made simultaneously with its transmission."[24]

Recently, a genre of visual art has evolved that is not confined by the canvas and instead interacts directly with the viewer and the exhibition space. Two interesting works illustrative of this category are "Crucifixion," by Chris Burden, in which the artist is crucified onto a Volkswagen, and "Seedbed," by Vito Acconci, in which the artist sits under a wooden ramp covering the gallery floor and masturbates for eight hours a day for a two week period during which time he voices his sexual fantasies about the audience through a loudspeaker. Obviously, neither of these works is fixed within the meaning of the 1976 Act.[25] What other types of works would not be considered "fixed" within the meaning of the statute? What about choreography? Consider also the McDonald's parade discussed in Note 2. Does a telecast of the parade satisfy the fixation requirement? Should WGN be prevented from telecasting the parade under the circumstances described in the Note?

GATT altered the application of the fixation requirement in one limited respect. Regarding live musical performances, the GATT amendments to the copyright statute have resulted in civil and criminal liability for fixations, reproductions, transmissions, and distributions of such performances without the consent of the performers.[26] Thus, even if such a performance is not fixed by or under the authority of the copyright owner, the remedial provisions of the copyright statute will be applied regarding the prohibited activities. See also Note 6 of Assignment 11.

[22] § 102(a).

[23] § 101.

[24] Id.

[25] See Kwall, Copyright and the Moral Right: Is an American Marriage Possible?, 38 Vand. L. Rev. 1, 75 (1985).

[26] § 1101. See also 18 U.S.C. § 2319A (providing for criminal penalties).

10. *Film colorization.* Subsequent to the Copyright Office Regulation reprinted in the text, the Copyright Office issued a new rule on the copyright registration for colorized films which requires the deposit of a copy of the colorized version as well as a copy of the original black and white version.[27] This regulation will result in the preservation of copies of black and white films that are colorized and registered. In addition, the National Film Preservation Act of 1988[28] provided for the establishment of a Film Preservation Board that is empowered to nominate up to twenty-five classic films annually for inclusion in the National Film Registry in the Library of Congress.[29] The 1988 Act also provided that the designated films were subject to certain labelling requirements in the event they were materially altered, but these labelling requirements were eliminated by the National Film Preservation Act of 1991.[30] Thus, the 1991 Act continues the 1988 Act's focus on film preservation activities, but veers away from a concern with moral rights and labelling. If the United States had a more cohesive and defined moral rights doctrine which would safeguard a creator's right to prevent unauthorized alterations of her work, filmmakers would have a powerful doctrinal basis for banning colorized versions of black and white films. As demonstrated in Assignment 9, however, very limited protection for moral rights exists in this country.

BIBLIOGRAPHY

The following is a sampling of some of the literature on originality: Samuelson, The Originality Standard for Literary Works Under U.S. Copyright Law, 42 Am. J. Comp. L. 393 (1994); VerSteeg, Rethinking Originality, 34 Wm. & Mary L. Rev. 801 (1993); Abrams, Originality and Creativity in Copyright Law, 55 Law & Contemp. Probs. 3 (1992); Ginsburg, No "Sweat"? Copyright and Other Protection of Works of Information After "Feist v. Rural Telephone", 92 Colum. L. Rev. 338 (1992); Gordon, Reality as Artifact: From "Feist" to Fair Use, 55 Law & Contemp. Probs. 93 (1992); Litman, After "Feist", 17 U. Dayton L. Rev. 607 (1992); Litman, Copyright and Information Policy, 55 Law & Contemp. Probs. 185 (1992); Jaszi, Toward a Theory of Copyright: The Metamorphoses of "Authorship", 1991 Duke L.J. 455; Yen, The Legacy of "Feist": Consequences of the Weak Connection Between Copyright and the Economics of Public Goods, 52 Ohio St. L.J. 1343 (1991); Patterson & Joyce, Monopolizing the Law: The Scope of Copyright Protection for Law Reports and Statutory

---

[27] Copyright Registration for Colorized Versions of Black and White Motion Pictures; Final Rule, 53 Fed. Reg. 29,887 (1988).

[28] 2 U.S.C. § 178.

[29] For a detailed discussion on the relationship of the National Film Preservation Act of 1988 and the preservation of black and white films, see Comment, The Colorization Dispute: Moral Rights Theory as a Means of Judicial and Legislative Reform, 38 Emory L.J. 237, 266–269 (1989).

[30] 2 U.S.C. § 179 (1992). The legislative history reveals that although the labelling requirements were able to be administered relatively easily for colorized films, the labelling requirements for films that had been subject to other types of material alterations were far more controversial due to the difficulty of achieving a consensus for the definition of "material alteration", the term upon which the requirements were based. H.R. Rep. No. 379, 102d Cong., 1st Sess. 15 (1991), reprinted in 1992 U.S.C.C.A.N. 166, 175.

Compilations, 36 UCLA L. Rev. 719 (1989); Samuels, The Idea–Expression Dichotomy in Copyright Law, 56 Tenn. L. Rev. 321 (1989); Denicola, Copyright in Collections of Facts: A Theory for the Protection of Nonfiction Literary Works, 81 Colum. L. Rev. 516 (1981); Gorman, Copyright Protection for the Collection and Representation of Facts, 76 Harv. L. Rev. 1569 (1963). See also the following student work: The Adaptation of Copyright Law to Video Games, 131 U. Pa. L. Rev. 171 (1982). See also the following symposiums treating the concept of originality: Intellectual Property and the Construction of Authorship, 10 Cardozo Arts & Ent. L.J. 277–720 (1992); Copyright Symposium Parts I & II: Copyright Protection for Computer Databases, CD–ROMs and Factual Compilations, 17 U. Dayton L. Rev. 323–629, 731–1018 (1992).

SUBJECT MATTER: USEFUL ARTICLES AND PROTECTION FOR CHARACTERS

1. INTRODUCTION

Sections 102–105 of the 1976 Act deal with copyrightable subject matter. We saw in the prior Assignment that § 103 provides copyright protection for two particular categories of works—compilations and derivative works. Section 102(a) specifically lists the following general categories of works of authorship that are eligible for copyright protection: literary works; musical works; dramatic works; pantomimes and choreographic works; pictorial, graphic, and sculptural works; motion pictures and other audiovisual works; sound recordings; and architectural works.[1]

Section 102(b), by precluding copyright protection for "any idea, procedure, process, system, method of operation, concept, principle, or discovery," excludes from copyright protection matter which is functional and must remain free for all to use. Of all the categories of "works of authorship" enumerated in § 102(a), the "pictorial, graphic, and sculptural works" category has spawned the most litigation involving the extent to which functional or "useful articles" should be protected. The 1976 Act defines a "useful article" as one with "an intrinsic utilitarian function that is not merely to portray the appearance of the article or to convey information."[2] This "useful article" definition is intended to provide an exception to the protection that otherwise would extend to "pictorial, graphic, and sculptural works."[3] Further, the definition of "pictorial, graphic, and sculptural works" in § 101 provides that "the design of a useful article ... shall be considered a pictorial, graphic, or sculptural work only if, and only to the extent that, such design incorporates pictorial, graphic, or sculptural features that can be identified separately from, and are capable of existing independently of, the utilitarian aspects of the article."[4]

---

[1] Section 102 provides that "[w]orks of authorship *include* the following categories" (emphasis added). Under the definitions provided in § 101, the term "including" is "illustrative and not limitative." Thus, it is conceivable that other categories of "works of authorship" also could be protected by copyright law in addition to those specified in § 102.

[2] § 101.

[3] See Harper House, Inc. v. Thomas Nelson, Inc., 889 F.2d 197, 202 (9th Cir.1989).

[4] § 101.

Presumably, Congress' decision to allow three-dimensional works of art to be protected by copyright law but to disallow such protection for three-dimensional works of utility stems from a concern with restraining competition.[5] Although we might question whether it is more important for works of utility to remain freely available than works of art, this judgment is reflected not only in copyright law, but also in patent and trademark law.[6] Still, although the decision to disallow protection for functional or useful subject matter may be clear, the determination as to what constitutes such subject matter often is difficult. This is one of the themes explored in the materials which follow.

The second theme of this Assignment concerns the scope of copyright protection for fictional characters. Although fictional characters are not expressly protected in the 1976 Act under an independent subject matter category, they have received varying degrees of protection by the courts as components of the underlying works in which they appear. Some commentators have argued that express copyright protection for characters is necessary,[7] while others dispute this approach.[8] The question of copyright protection for fictional characters is not only a colorful, but also an increasingly important issue in light of the increased commercial value these characters possess as a result of the burgeoning entertainment industry. After reading the following materials, decide what degree of protection for characters you believe is most appropriate.

2. PRINCIPAL PROBLEM

Barney Smith seeks a copyright registration for a children's Superman costume. Warner Brothers and D.C. Comics own the copyrights in various works embodying the character Superman. Since the creation of Superman in comics in 1938, Warner and D.C. have successfully exploited their rights to Superman in various media and have licensed the character in connection with a variety of merchandising efforts. Superman's familiar attire consists of a skin-tight blue leotard with red briefs, boots, a cape, and a large "S" emblazoned in red and gold upon the chest and cape.

Barney's costume consists of a very form-fitting blue leotard, the chest of which contains a large "S" emblazoned in red and gold. Although the leotard is not particularly comfortable to wear for long periods of time,

---

[5] See House Comm. On The Judiciary, 87th Cong., 1st Sess., Copyright Law Revision, Report of the Register of Copyrights of the General Revision on the U.S. Copyright Law 13 (Comm. Print 1961).

[6] Patent law, which typically protects useful subject matter, has a far shorter duration of protection than copyright law and the standards for patent law protection are far more rigorous. See Assignment 16 (discussing standards for design patent law protection). Moreover, under trademark law, protection for the functional features of an object's trade dress is disallowed. See Assignment 3. See also Lynch, Copyright in Utilitarian Objects: Beneath Metaphysics, 16 U. Dayton L. Rev. 647, 655–657 (1991).

[7] See, e.g., Comment, Finding a Home for Fictional Characters: A Proposal for Change in Copyright Protection, 78 Cal. L. Rev. 687 (1990).

[8] See, e.g., Nevins, Copyright + Character = Catastrophe, 39 J. Copyright Soc'y 303 (1992).

many children have become extremely attached to the costume and want to use the leotard as either sleepwear or as long underwear. The costume also comes with red briefs, boots, a cape displaying the same "S" as the leotard, and an ornate mask of Superman's face. Children who wear the costume outside do not need to wear regular clothes underneath the costume since the leotard is designed to cover all the necessary parts and to keep a child sufficiently warm even on chilly October Halloween days. The costume is rather expensive, selling for $60.00.

Barney wants to obtain copyright protection for the exterior appearance of the entire costume as an integrated ensemble of its component parts, which results in the portrayal of Superman. The Copyright Register, quoting its 1991 ruling on the Registrability of Costume Designs, has denied registration based on its position that "[f]anciful costumes will be registered only upon a finding of separately identifiable pictorial and/or sculptural authorship."[9] Warner and D.C. got wind of Barney's application and want to sue him for copyright infringement. Barney retains your services in dealing with Warner and D.C. and in appealing the registration decision to the federal district court. He wants you to explain to him all of the legal issues involved in this situation and wants your opinion as to how a court is likely to rule with respect to both the registration application and a potential infringement lawsuit.

3.   MATERIALS FOR SOLUTION OF PRINCIPAL PROBLEM

A.   STATUTORY MATERIALS: §§ 102–104, 105, 113 (a)-(c), & 120

B.   CASES:

Baker v. Selden

Supreme Court of the United States, 1879.
101 U.S. (11 Otto) 99, 25 L.Ed. 841.

■ MR. JUSTICE BRADLEY delivered the opinion of the Court.

Charles Selden, the testator of the complainant in this case, in the year 1859 took the requisite steps for obtaining the copyright of a book, entitled "Selden's Condensed Ledger, or Book-keeping Simplified," the object of which was to exhibit and explain a peculiar system of book-keeping. In 1860 and 1861, he took the copyright of several other books, containing additions to and improvements upon the said system. The bill of complaint was filed against the defendant, Baker, for an alleged infringement of these copyrights. The latter, in his answer, denied that Selden was the author or designer of the books, and denied the infringement charged, and contends on the argument that the matter alleged to be infringed is not a lawful subject of copyright.

A decree was rendered for the complainant, and the defendant appealed.

[9] Vol. 56 Fed. Register, No 214, 56531 (November 5, 1991).

The book or series of books of which the complainant claims the copyright consists of an introductory essay explaining the system of book-keeping referred to, to which are annexed certain forms or blanks, consisting of ruled lines, and headings, illustrating the system and showing how it is to be used and carried out in practice. This system effects the same results as book-keeping by double entry; but, by a peculiar arrangement of columns and headings, presents the entire operation, of a day, a week, or a month, on a single page, or on two pages facing each other, in an account-book. The defendant uses a similar plan so far as results are concerned; but makes a different arrangement of the columns, and uses different headings. If the complainant's testator had the exclusive right to the use of the system explained in his book, it would be difficult to contend that the defendant does not infringe it, notwithstanding the difference in his form of arrangement; but if it be assumed that the system is open to public use, it seems to be equally difficult to contend that the books made and sold by the defendant are a violation of the copyright of the complainant's book considered merely as a book explanatory of the system. Where the truths of a science or the methods of an art are the common property of the whole world, any author has the right to express the one, or explain and use the other, in his own way. As an author, Selden explained the system in a particular way. It may be conceded that Baker makes and uses account-books arranged on substantially the same system; but the proof fails to show that he has violated the copyright of Selden's book, or that he has infringed Selden's right in any way, unless the latter became entitled to an exclusive right in the system.

The evidence of the complainant is principally directed to the object of showing that Baker uses the same system as that which is explained and illustrated in Selden's books. It becomes important, therefore, to determine whether, in obtaining the copyright of his books, he secured the exclusive right to the use of the system or method of book-keeping which the said books are intended to illustrate and explain. It is contended that he has secured such exclusive right, because no one can use the system without using substantially the same ruled lines and headings which he has appended to his books in illustration of it. In other words, it is contended that the ruled lines and headings, given to illustrate the system, are a part of the book, and, as such, are secured by the copyright; and that no one can make or use similar ruled lines and headings, or ruled lines and headings made and arranged on substantially the same system, without violating the copyright. And this is really the question to be decided in this case. Stated in another form, the question is, whether the exclusive property in a system of book-keeping can be claimed, under the law of copyright, by means of a book in which that system is explained? The complainant's bill, and the case made under it, are based on the hypothesis that it can be.

It cannot be pretended, and indeed it is not seriously urged, that the ruled lines of the complainant's account-book can be claimed under any special class of objects, other than books, named in the law of copyright existing in 1859. The law then in force was that of 1831, and specified only books, maps, charts, musical compositions, prints, and engravings. An account-book, consisting of ruled lines and blank columns, cannot be called by any of these names unless by that of a book.

There is no doubt that a work on the subject of book-keeping, though only explanatory of well-known systems, may be the subject of a copyright; but, then, it is claimed only as a book. Such a book may be explanatory either of old systems, or of an entirely new system; and, considered as a book, as the work of an author, conveying information on the subject of book-keeping, and containing detailed explanations of the art, it may be a very valuable acquisition to the practical knowledge of the community. But there is a clear distinction between the book, as such, and the art which it is intended to illustrate. The mere statement of the proposition is so evident, that it requires hardly any argument to support it. The same distinction may be predicated of every other art as well as that of book-keeping. A treatise on the composition and use of medicines, be they old or new; on the construction and use of ploughs or watches would be the subject of copyright; but no one would contend that the copyright of the treatise would give the exclusive right to the art or manufacture described therein. The copyright of the book, if not pirated from other works, would be valid without regard to the novelty, or want of novelty, of its subject-matter. The novelty of the art or thing described or explained has nothing to do with the validity of the copyright. To give to the author of the book an exclusive property in the art described therein, when no examination of its novelty has ever been officially made, would be a surprise and a fraud upon the public. That is the province of letters-patent, not of copyright. The claim to an invention or discovery of an art or manufacture must be subjected to the examination of the Patent Office before an exclusive right therein can be obtained; and it can only be secured by a patent from the government.

The difference between the two things, letters-patent and copyright, may be illustrated by reference to the subjects just enumerated. Take the case of medicines. Certain mixtures are found to be of great value in the healing art. If the discoverer writes and publishes a book on the subject (as regular physicians generally do), he gains no exclusive right to the manufacture and sale of the medicine; he gives that to the public. If he desires to acquire such exclusive right, he must obtain a patent for the mixture as a new art, manufacture, or composition of matter. He may copyright his book, if he pleases; but that only secures to him the exclusive right of printing and publishing his book. So of all other inventions or discoveries.

The copyright of a work on mathematical science cannot give to the author an exclusive right to the methods of operation which he propounds, or to the diagrams which he employs to explain them, so as to prevent an engineer from using them whenever occasion requires. The very object of publishing a book on science or the useful arts is to communicate to the world the useful knowledge which it contains. But this object would be frustrated if the knowledge could not be used without incurring the guilt of piracy of the book. And where the art it teaches cannot be used without employing the methods and diagrams used to illustrate the book, or such as are similar to them, such methods and diagrams are to be considered as necessary incidents to the art, and given therewith to the public; not given for the purpose of publication in other works explanatory of the art, but for the purpose of practical application.

Of course, these observations are not intended to apply to ornamental designs, or pictorial illustrations addressed to the taste. Of these it may be said, that their form is their essence, and their object, the production of pleasure in their contemplation. This is their final end. They are as much the product of genius and the result of composition, as are the lines of the poet or the historian's periods. On the other hand, the teachings of science and the rules and methods of useful art have their final end in application and use; and this application and use are what the public derive from the publication of a book which teaches them. But as embodied and taught in a literary composition or book, their essence consists only in their statement. This alone is what is secured by the copyright. The use by another of the same methods of statement, whether in words or illustrations, in a book published for teaching the art, would undoubtedly be an infringement of the copyright.

Recurring to the case before us, we observe that Charles Selden, by his books, explained and described a peculiar system of book-keeping, and illustrated his method by means of ruled lines and blank columns, with proper headings on a page, or on successive pages. Now, whilst no one has a right to print or publish his book, or any material part thereof, as a book intended to convey instruction in the art, any person may practice and use the art itself which he has described and illustrated therein. The use of the art is a totally different thing from a publication of the book explaining it. The copyright of a book on book-keeping cannot secure the exclusive right to make, sell, and use account-books prepared upon the plan set forth in such book. Whether the art might or might not have been patented, is a question which is not before us. It was not patented, and is open and free to the use of the public. And, of course, in using the art, the ruled lines and headings of accounts must necessarily be used as incident to it.

The plausibility of the claim put forward by the complainant in this case arises from a confusion of ideas produced by the peculiar nature of the art described in the books which have been made the subject of copyright. In describing the art, the illustrations and diagrams employed happen to correspond more closely than usual with the actual work performed by the operator who uses the art. Those illustrations and diagrams consist of ruled lines and headings of accounts; and it is similar ruled lines and headings of accounts which, in the application of the art, the book-keeper makes with his pen, or the stationer with his press; whilst in most other cases the diagrams and illustrations can only be represented in concrete forms of wood, metal, stone, or some other physical embodiment. But the principle is the same in all. The description of the art in a book, though entitled to the benefit of copyright, lays no foundation for an exclusive claim to the art itself. The object of the one is explanation; the object of the other is use.

The former may be secured by copyright. The latter can only be secured, if it can be secured at all, by letters-patent.

Another case, that of Page v. Wisden (20 L.T.N.S. 435), which came before Vice–Chancellor Malins in 1869, has some resemblance to the present. There a copyright was claimed in a cricket scoring-sheet, and the Vice–Chancellor held that it was not a fit subject for copyright, partly because it was not new, but also because "to say that a particular mode of ruling a book constituted an object for a copyright is absurd."

The conclusion to which we have come is, that blank account-books are not the subject of copyright; and that the mere copyright of Selden's book did not confer upon him the exclusive right to make and use account-books, ruled and arranged as designated by him and described and illustrated in said book.

The decree of the Circuit Court must be reversed, and the cause remanded with instructions to dismiss the complainant's bill; and it is

So ordered.

Brandir International, Inc. v. Cascade Pacific Lumber Co.

United States Court of Appeals, Second Circuit, 1987.
834 F.2d 1142.

■ OAKES, CIRCUIT JUDGE.

In passing the Copyright Act of 1976 Congress attempted to distinguish between protectable "works of applied art" and "industrial designs not subject to copyright protection." See H.R. Rep. No. 1476, 94th Cong., 2d Sess. 54, reprinted in 1976 U.S. Code Cong. & Admin. News 5659, 5667 (hereinafter H.R. Rep. No. 1476). The courts, however, have had difficulty framing tests by which the fine line establishing what is and what is not copyrightable can be drawn. Once again we are called upon to draw such a line, this time in a case involving the "RIBBON Rack," a bicycle rack made of bent tubing that is said to have originated from a wire sculpture. (A photograph of the rack is contained in the appendix to this opinion.) The Register of Copyright, named as a third-party defendant under the statute, 17 U.S.C. § 411, but electing not to appear, denied copyrightability. In the subsequent suit, the district court granted summary judgment on the copyright claim to defendant Cascade Pacific Lumber Co., d/b/a Columbia Cascade Co., manufacturer of a similar bicycle rack. We affirm as to the copyright claim.

Against the history of copyright protection well set out in the majority opinion in Carol Barnhart Inc. v. Economy Cover Corp., 773 F.2d 411, 415–18 (2d Cir.1985), and in Denicola, Applied Art and Industrial Design: A Suggested Approach to Copyright in Useful Articles, 67 Minn. L. Rev. 707, 709–17 (1983), Congress adopted the Copyright Act of 1976. The "works of art" classification of the Copyright Act of 1909 was omitted and replaced by reference to "pictorial, graphic, and sculptural works," § 102(a)(5). According to the House Report, the new category was intended to supply "as clear a line as possible between copyrightable works of applied art and uncopyrighted works of industrial design." H.R. Rep. No. 1476, at 55. The statutory definition of "pictorial, graphic, and sculptural works" states that "the design of a useful article, as defined in this section, shall be considered a pictorial, graphic, or sculptural work only if, and only to the extent that, such design incorporates pictorial, graphic, or sculptural features that can be identified separately from, and are capable of existing independently of, the utilitarian aspects of the article." § 101.[a] The legislative history added gloss on the criteria of separate identity and independent existence in saying:

> On the other hand, although the shape of an industrial product may be aesthetically satisfying and valuable, the Committee's intention is not to offer it copyright protection under the bill. Unless the shape of an automobile, airplane, ladies' dress, food processor, television set, or any other industrial product contains some element that, physically or conceptually, can be identified as separable from the utilitarian aspects of that article, the design would not be copyrighted under the bill.

H.R. Rep. No. 1476, at 55.

As courts and commentators have come to realize, however, the line Congress attempted to draw between copyrightable art and noncopyrightable design "was neither clear nor new." Denicola, *supra*, 67 Minn. L. Rev. at 720. One aspect of the distinction that has drawn considerable attention is the reference in the House Report to "physically *or conceptually*" (emphasis added) separable elements. The District of Columbia Circuit in Esquire, Inc. v. Ringer, 591 F.2d 796, 803–04 (D.C.Cir.1978)(holding outdoor lighting fixtures ineligible for copyright), *cert. denied*, 440 U.S. 908 (1979), called this an "isolated reference" and gave it no significance. Professor Nimmer, however, seemed to favor the observations of Judge Harold Leventhal in his concurrence in *Esquire*, who stated that "the overall legislative policy ... sustains the Copyright Office in its efforts to distinguish between the instances where the aesthetic element is conceptually severable and the instances where the aesthetic element is inextricably interwoven with the utilitarian aspect of the article." 591 F.2d at 807; see 1 Nimmer on Copyright § 2.08[B] at 2–93 to 2–96.2 (1986). But see Gerber, Book Review, 26 U.C.L.A. L. Rev. 925, 938–43 (1979)(criticizing Professor Nimmer's view on conceptual separability). Looking to the section 101 definition of works of artistic craftsmanship requiring that artistic features be "capable of existing independently of the utilitarian aspects," Professor Nimmer queries whether that requires *physical* as distinguished from *conceptual* separability, but answers his query by saying "[t]here is reason to conclude that it does not." See 1 Nimmer on Copyright § 2.08[B] at 2–96.1. In any event, in Kieselstein–Cord v. Accessories by Pearl, Inc., 632

---

[a] The statute also defines "useful article" as one "having an intrinsic utilitarian function that is not merely to portray the appearance of the article or to convey information. An article that is normally a part of a useful article is considered a 'useful article.'" § 101.

F.2d 989, 993 (2d Cir.1980), this court accepted the idea that copyrightability can adhere in the "conceptual" separation of an artistic element. Indeed, the court went on to find such conceptual separation in reference to ornate belt buckles that could be and were worn separately as jewelry. *Kieselstein-Cord* was followed in Norris Industries, Inc. v. International Telephone & Telegraph Corp., 696 F.2d 918, 923–24 (11th Cir.), *cert. denied*, 464 U.S. 818 (1983), although there the court upheld the Register's refusal to register automobile wire wheel covers, finding no "conceptually separable" work of art. See also Trans–World Mfg. Corp. v. Al Nyman & Sons, Inc., 95 F.R.D. 95 (D.Del.1982)(finding conceptual separability sufficient to support copyright in denying summary judgment on copyrightability of eyeglass display cases).

In Carol Barnhart Inc. v. Economy Cover Corp., 773 F.2d 411 (2d Cir.1985), a divided panel of this circuit affirmed a district court grant of summary judgment of noncopyrightability of four life-sized, anatomically correct human torso forms. *Carol Barnhart* distinguished *Kieselstein-Cord*, but it surely did not overrule it. The distinction made was that the ornamented surfaces of the *Kieselstein-Cord* belt buckles "were not in any respect required by their utilitarian functions," but the features claimed to be aesthetic or artistic in the *Carol Barnhart* forms were "inextricably intertwined with the utilitarian feature, the display of clothes." 773 F.2d at 419. But cf. Animal Fair, Inc. v. Amfesco Indus., Inc., 620 F.Supp. 175, 186–88 (D.Minn.1985)(holding bear-paw design conceptually separable from the utilitarian features of a slipper), aff'd mem., 794 F.2d 678 (8th Cir. 1986). As Judge Newman's dissent made clear, the *Carol Barnhart* majority did not dispute "that 'conceptual separability' is distinct from 'physical separability' and, when present, entitles the creator of a useful article to a copyright on its design." 773 F.2d at 420.

"Conceptual separability" is thus alive and well, at least in this circuit. The problem, however, is determining exactly what it is and how it is to be applied. Judge Newman's illuminating discussion in dissent in *Carol Barnhart*, see 773 F.2d at 419–24, proposed a test that aesthetic features are conceptually separable if "the article . . . stimulate[s] in the mind of the beholder a concept that is separate from the concept evoked by its utilitarian function." *Id.* at 422. This approach has received favorable endorsement by at least one commentator, W. Patry, Latman's The Copyright Law 43–45 (6th ed. 1986), who calls Judge Newman's test the "temporal displacement" test. It is to be distinguished from other possible ways in which conceptual separability can be tested, including whether the primary use is as a utilitarian article as opposed to an artistic work, and whether the article is marketable as art, [neither] of which is very satisfactory. But Judge Newman's test was rejected outright by the majority as "a standard so ethereal as to amount to a 'nontest' that would be extremely difficult, if not impossible, to administer or apply." 773 F.2d at 419 n.5.

Perhaps the differences between the majority and the dissent in *Carol Barnhart* might have been resolved had they had before them the Denicola article on Applied Art and Industrial Design: A Suggested Approach to

Copyright in Useful Articles, *supra*. There, Professor Denicola points out that although the Copyright Act of 1976 was an effort "to draw as clear a line as possible," in truth "there is no line, but merely a spectrum of forms and shapes responsive in varying degrees to utilitarian concerns." 67 Minn. L. Rev. at 741. He suggests that "the dominant characteristic of industrial design is the influence of nonaesthetic, utilitarian concerns" and hence concludes that copyrightability "ultimately should depend on the extent to which the work reflects artistic expression uninhibited by functional considerations."[b] *Id.* To state the Denicola test in the language of conceptual separability, if design elements reflect a merger of aesthetic and functional considerations, the artistic aspects of a work cannot be said to be conceptually separable from the utilitarian elements. Conversely, where design elements can be identified as reflecting the designer's artistic judgment exercised independently of functional influences, conceptual separability exists.

We believe that Professor Denicola's approach provides the best test for conceptual separability and, accordingly, adopt it here for several reasons. First, the approach is consistent with the holdings of our previous cases. In *Kieselstein-Cord*, for example, the artistic aspects of the belt buckles reflected purely aesthetic choices, independent of the buckles' function, while in *Carol Barnhart* the distinctive features of the torsos—the accurate anatomical design and the sculpted shirts and collars—showed clearly the influence of functional concerns. Though the torsos bore artistic features, it was evident that the designer incorporated those features to further the usefulness of the torsos as mannequins. Second, the test's emphasis on the influence of utilitarian concerns in the design process may help, as Denicola notes, to "alleviate the de facto discrimination against nonrepresentational art that has regrettably accompanied much of the current analysis." *Id.* at 745.[c] Finally, and perhaps most importantly, we think Denicola's test will not be too difficult to administer in practice. The work itself will continue to give "mute testimony" of its origins. In addition, the parties will be required to present evidence relating to the design process and the nature of the work, with the trier of fact making the

---

[b] Professor Denicola rejects the exclusion of all works created with some utilitarian application in view, for that would not only overturn Mazer v. Stein, 347 U.S. 201 (1954), on which much of the legislation is based, but also "a host of other eminently sensible decisions, in favor of an intractable factual inquiry of questionable relevance." 67 Minn. L. Rev. at 741. He adds that "any such categorical approach would also undermine the legislative determination to preserve an artist's ability to exploit utilitarian markets." *Id.* (citing § 113(a)(1976)).

[c] We are reminded not only by Judge Gesell in the district court in *Esquire*, 414

F.Supp. 939, 941 (D.D.C.1976), but by Holmes in Bleistein v. Donaldson Lithographing Co., 188 U.S. 239, 251–52 (1903), by Mazer v. Stein, 347 U.S. at 214, and by numerous other opinions, that we judges should not let our own view of styles of art interfere with the decisionmaking process in this area. Denicola suggests that the shape of a Mickey Mouse telephone is copyrightable because its form is independent of function, and "[a] telephone shape owing more to Arp, Brancusi, or Moore than Disney may be equally divorced from utilitarian influence." 67 Minn. L. Rev. at 746.

determination whether the aesthetic design elements are significantly influenced by functional considerations.

Turning now to the facts of this case, we note first that Brandir contends, and its chief owner David Levine testified, that the original design of the RIBBON Rack stemmed from wire sculptures that Levine had created, each formed from one continuous undulating piece of wire. These sculptures were, he said, created and displayed in his home as a means of personal expression, but apparently were never sold or displayed elsewhere. He also created a wire sculpture in the shape of a bicycle and states that he did not give any thought to the utilitarian application of any of his sculptures until he accidentally juxtaposed the bicycle sculpture with one of the selfstanding wire sculptures. It was not until November 1978 that Levine seriously began pursuing the utilitarian application of his sculptures, when a friend, G. Duff Bailey, a bicycle buff and author of numerous articles about urban cycling, was at Levine's home and informed him that the sculptures would make excellent bicycle racks, permitting bicycles to be parked under the overloops as well as on top of the underloops. Following this meeting, Levine met several times with Bailey and others, completing the designs for the RIBBON Rack by the use of a vacuum cleaner hose, and submitting his drawings to a fabricator complete with dimensions. The Brandir RIBBON Rack began being nationally advertised and promoted for sale in September 1979.

In November 1982 Levine discovered that another company, Cascade Pacific Lumber Co., was selling a similar product. Thereafter, beginning in December 1982, a copyright notice was placed on all RIBBON Racks before shipment and on December 10, 1982, five copyright applications for registration were submitted to the Copyright Office. The Copyright Office refused registration by letter, stating that the RIBBON Rack did not contain any element that was "capable of independent existence as a copyrightable pictorial, graphic or sculptural work apart from the shape of the useful article." An appeal to the Copyright Office was denied by letter dated March 23, 1983, refusing registration on the above ground and alternatively on the ground that the design lacked originality, consisting of "nothing more than a familiar public domain symbol." In February 1984, after the denial of the second appeal of the examiner's decision, Brandir sent letters to customers enclosing copyright notices to be placed on racks sold prior to December 1982.

Between September 1979 and August 1982 Brandir spent some $38,500 for advertising and promoting the RIBBON Rack, including some 85,000 pieces of promotional literature to architects and landscape architects. Additionally, since October 1982 Brandir has spent some $66,000, including full-, half-, and quarter-page advertisements in architectural magazines such as Landscape Architecture, Progressive Architecture, and Architectural Record, indeed winning an advertising award from Progressive Architecture in January 1983. The RIBBON Rack has been featured in Popular Science, Art and Architecture, and Design 384 magazines, and it won an Industrial Designers Society of America design award in the spring of 1980.

In the spring of 1984 the RIBBON Rack was selected from 200 designs to be included among 77 of the designs exhibited at the Katonah Gallery in an exhibition entitled "The Product of Design: An Exploration of the Industrial Design Process," an exhibition that was written up in the New York Times.

Sales of the RIBBON Rack from September 1979 through January 1985 were in excess of $1,367,000. Prior to the time Cascade Pacific began offering for sale its bicycle rack in August 1982, Brandir's sales were $436,000. The price of the RIBBON Rack ranges from $395 up to $2,025 for a stainless steel model and generally depends on the size of the rack, one of the most popular being the RB–7, selling for $485.

Applying Professor Denicola's test to the RIBBON Rack, we find that the rack is not copyrightable. It seems clear that the form of the rack is influenced in significant measure by utilitarian concerns and thus any aesthetic elements cannot be said to be conceptually separable from the utilitarian elements. This is true even though the sculptures which inspired the RIBBON Rack may well have been—the issue of originality aside—copyrightable.

Brandir argues correctly that a copyrighted work of art does not lose its protected status merely because it subsequently is put to a functional use. The Supreme Court so held in Mazer v. Stein, 347 U.S. 201 (1954), and Congress specifically intended to accept and codify *Mazer* in section 101 of the Copyright Act of 1976. See H.R. Rep. No. 1476 at 54–55. The district court thus erred in ruling that, whatever the RIBBON Rack's origins, Brandir's commercialization of the rack disposed of the issue of its copyrightability.

Had Brandir merely adopted one of the existing sculptures as a bicycle rack, neither the application to a utilitarian end nor commercialization of that use would have caused the object to forfeit its copyrighted status. Comparison of the RIBBON Rack with the earlier sculptures, however, reveals that while the rack may have been derived in part from one of more "works of art," it is in its final form essentially a product of industrial design. In creating the RIBBON Rack, the designer has clearly adapted the original aesthetic elements to accommodate and further a utilitarian purpose. These altered design features of the RIBBON Rack, including the spacesaving, open design achieved by widening the upper loops to permit parking under as well as over the rack's curves, the straightened vertical elements that allow in-and above-ground installation of the rack, the ability to fit all types of bicycles and mopeds, and the heavy-gauged tubular construction of rustproof galvanized steel, are all features that combine to make for a safe, secure, and maintenance-free system of parking bicycles and mopeds. Its undulating shape is said in Progressive Architecture, January 1982, to permit double the storage of conventional bicycle racks. Moreover, the rack is manufactured from 2 3/8–inch standard steam pipe that is bent into form, the six-inch radius of the bends evidently resulting from bending the pipe according to a standard formula that yields bends having a radius equal to three times the nominal internal diameter of the pipe.

Brandir argues that its RIBBON Rack can and should be characterized as a sculptural work of art within the minimalist art movement. Minimalist sculpture's most outstanding feature is said to be its clarity and simplicity, in that it often takes the form of geometric shapes, lines, and forms that are pure and free of ornamentation and void of association. As Brandir's expert put it, "The meaning is to be found in, within, around and outside the work of art, allowing the artistic sensation to be experienced as well as intellectualized." People who use Foley Square in New York City see in the form of minimalist art the "Tilted Arc," which is on the plaza at 26 Federal Plaza. Numerous museums have had exhibitions of such art, and the school of minimalist art has many admirers.

It is unnecessary to determine whether to the art world the RIBBON Rack properly would be considered an example of minimalist sculpture. The result under the copyright statute is not changed. Using the test we have adopted, it is not enough that, to paraphrase Judge Newman, the rack may stimulate in the mind of the reasonable observer a concept separate from the bicycle rack concept. While the RIBBON Rack may be worthy of admiration for its aesthetic qualities alone, it remains nonetheless the product of industrial design. Form and function are inextricably intertwined in the rack, its ultimate design being as much the result of utilitarian pressures as aesthetic choices. Indeed, the visually pleasing proportions and symmetricalness of the rack represent design changes made in response to functional concerns. Judging from the awards the rack has received, it would seem in fact that Brandir has achieved with the RIBBON Rack the highest goal of modern industrial design, that is, the harmonious fusion of function and aesthetics. Thus there remains no

APPENDIX 1

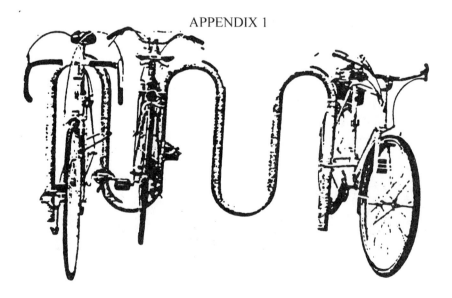

artistic element of the RIBBON Rack that can be identified as separate and "capable of existing independently of the utilitarian aspects of the article." Accordingly, we must affirm on the copyright claim.

APPENDIX 2

Brandir Ribbon Bicycle Rack
1979

Steven Levine worked in wire to develop the basic form

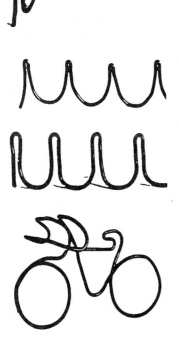

The Design Problem   To translate a sculpture into a working product design

Steven Levine started his career as an industrial engineer and computer analyst. Working with doodles, and then wire, he formed a sculptural piece. As he refined this form, he discovered that it could have a useful purpose as a bicycle and moped parking device. Aesthetics were the main concern how the size would relate to open spaces.

The rack is made of one piece of tubular construction 140 Steel Pipe and can be mounted below grace. Levine is both designer and manufacturer of the Ribbon Rack. He has stated that "the form was an inspiration that found a function."

■ Winter, Circuit Judge, concurring in part and dissenting in part.

I respectfully dissent from the majority's discussion and disposition of the copyright claim.

My colleagues, applying an adaptation of Professor Denicola's test, hold that the aesthetic elements of the design of a useful article are not conceptually separable from its utilitarian aspects if "[f]orm and function are inextricably intertwined" in the article, and "its ultimate design [is] as much the result of utilitarian pressures as aesthetic choices." Applying the test to the instant matter, they observe that the dispositive fact is that "in creating the Ribbon Rack, [Levine] has clearly adapted the *original* aesthetic elements to accommodate and further a utilitarian purpose" (emphasis added). The grounds of my disagreement are that: (1) my colleagues' adaptation of Professor Denicola's test diminishes the statutory concept of "conceptual separability" to the vanishing point; and (2) their focus on the process or sequence followed by the particular designer makes copyright protection depend upon largely fortuitous circumstances concerning the creation of the design in issue.

With regard to "conceptual separability," my colleagues deserve considerable credit for their efforts to reconcile Carol Barnhart Inc. v. Economy Cover Corp., 773 F.2d 411 (2d Cir.1985) with Kieselstein–Cord v. Accessories by Pearl, Inc., 632 F.2d 989 (2d Cir.1980). In my view, these cases are not reconcilable. *Carol Barnhart* paid only lip service to the fact that the "conceptual separability" of an article's aesthetic utilitarian aspects may render the design of a "useful article" a copyrightable "sculptural work." § 101 (1982). Actually, the *Carol Barnhart* majority applied a test of physical separability. They thus stated:

> What distinguishes [the *Kieselstein-Cord*] buckles from the Barnhart forms is that the ornamented surfaces of the buckles were not in any respect required by their utilitarian functions; the artistic and aesthetic features could thus be conceived of as having been *added to, or superimposed upon,* an otherwise utilitarian article. The unique artistic design was wholly unnecessary to performance of the utilitarian function. In the case of the Barnhart forms, on the other hand, the features claimed to be aesthetic or artistic, e.g., the life-size configuration of the breasts and the width of the shoulders are inextricably intertwined with the utilitarian feature, the display of clothes.

773 F.2d at 419 (emphasis added). In contrast, *Kieselstein-Cord* focused on the fact that the belt buckles at issue could be perceived as objects other than belt buckles:

> We see in appellant's belt buckles conceptually separable sculptural elements, as apparently have the buckles' wearers who have used them as ornamentation for parts of the body other than the waist.

632 F.2d at 993.

My colleagues' adaptation of the Denicola test tracks the *Carol Barnhart* approach, whereas I would adopt that taken in *Kieselstein-Cord*, which allows for the copyrightability of the aesthetic elements of useful articles even if those elements simultaneously perform utilitarian functions. The latter approach received its fullest elaboration in Judge Newman's dissent in *Carol Barnhart*, where he explained that "[f]or the [artistic] design features to be 'conceptually separate' from the utilitarian aspects of the useful article that embodies the design, the article must stimulate in the mind of the beholder a concept that is separate from the concept evoked by its utilitarian function." 773 F.2d at 422 (Newman, J., dissenting).

In other words, the relevant question is whether the design of a useful article, however intertwined with the article's utilitarian aspects, causes an ordinary reasonable observer to perceive an aesthetic concept not related to the article's use. The answer to this question is clear in the instant case because any reasonable observer would easily view the Ribbon Rack as an ornamental sculpture.[a] Indeed, there is evidence of actual confusion over whether it is strictly ornamental in the refusal of a building manager to accept delivery until assured by the buyer that the Ribbon Rack was in fact a bicycle rack. Moreover, Brandir has received a request to use the Ribbon Rack as environmental sculpture, and has offered testimony of art experts who claim that the Ribbon Rack may be valued solely for its artistic features. As one of those experts observed: "If one were to place a Ribbon Rack on an island without access, or in a park and surround the work with a barrier, ... its status as a work of art would be beyond dispute."[b]

My colleagues also allow too much to turn upon the process or sequence of design followed by the designer of the Ribbon Rack. They thus suggest that copyright protection would have been accorded "had Brandir merely adopted ... as a bicycle rack" an enlarged version of one of David Levine's original sculptures rather than one that had wider upper loops and straightened vertical elements. I cannot agree that copyright protection for the Ribbon Rack turns on whether Levine serendipitously chose the final design of the Ribbon Rack during his initial sculptural musings or whether the original design had to be slightly modified to accommodate bicycles. Copyright protection, which is intended to generate incentives for designers by according property rights in their creations, should not turn on purely fortuitous events. For that reason, the Copyright Act expressly states that the legal test is how the final article is perceived, not how it was developed through various stages. It thus states in pertinent part:

> the design of a useful article ... shall be considered a ... sculptural work only if, and only to the extent that, such design incorporates ... *sculptural features that can be identified separately from, and are capable of existing independently of, the utilitarian aspects of the article.*

§ 101 (1982)(emphasis added).

[a] The reasonable observer may be forgiven, however, if he or she does not recognize the Ribbon Rack as an example of minimalist art.

[b] The Copyright Office held that the Ribbon Rack was not copyrightable because it lacked originality. There may be some merit in that view in light of the Ribbon Rack's use of standard radii. This issue, however, was not raised in defendant's motion for summary judgment, was not addressed by the district court, and is not implicated here.

I therefore dissent from the decision so far as it relates to copyrightability.

Anderson v. Stallone

United States District Court, C.D. California, 1989.
11 U.S.P.Q.2D (BNA) 1161.

■ KELLER, JUDGE.

This matter came before the Court on the Motion for Summary Judgment of defendants Sylvester Stallone, Freddie Fields, Dean Stolber and MGM/UA Communications Co. Having reviewed the materials submitted and the arguments of counsel, the Court hereby orders the Motion granted in part and denied in part.

Factual Background

The movies Rocky I, II, and III were extremely successful motion pictures. Sylvester Stallone wrote each script and played the role of Rocky Balboa, the dominant character in each of the movies. In May of 1982, while on a promotional tour for the movie Rocky III, Stallone informed members of the press of his ideas for Rocky IV. Although Stallone's description of his ideas would vary slightly in each of the press conferences, he would generally describe his ideas as follows:

> I'd do it [Rocky IV] if Rocky himself could step out a bit. Maybe tackle world problems.... So what would happen, say, if Russia allowed her boxers to enter the professional ranks? Say Rocky is the United States' representative and the White House wants him to fight with the Russians before the Olympics. It's in Russia with everything against him. It's a giant stadium in Moscow and everything is Russian Red. It's a fight of astounding proportions with 50 monitors sent to 50 countries. It's the World Cup—a war between 2 countries.

Waco Tribune Herald, May 28, 1982; Section D, p. 1.

In June of 1982, after viewing the movie Rocky III, Timothy Anderson wrote a thirty-one page treatment entitled "Rocky IV" that he hoped would be used by Stallone and MGM[R] UA Communications Co. (hereinafter "MGM") as a sequel to Rocky III. The treatment incorporated the characters created by Stallone in his prior movies and cited Stallone as a co-author.

In October of 1982, Mr. Anderson met with Art Linkletter, who was a member of MGM's board of directors. Mr. Linkletter set up a meeting on October 11, 1982, between Mr. Anderson and Mr. Fields, who was president of MGM at the time. Mr. Linkletter was also present at this October 11, 1982 meeting. During the meeting, the parties discussed the possibility that plaintiff's treatment would be used by defendants as the script for Rocky IV. At the suggestion of Mr. Fields, the plaintiff, who is a <u>lawyer</u> and was accompanied by a lawyer at the meeting, signed a release that purported to relieve MGM from liability stemming from use of the treatment. Plaintiff alleges that Mr. Fields told him and his attorney that "if they [MGM &

Stallone] use his stuff [Anderson's treatment] it will be big money, big bucks for Tim."

On April 22, 1984, Anderson's attorney wrote MGM requesting compensation for the alleged use of his treatment in the forthcoming Rocky IV movie. On July 12, 1984, Stallone described his plans for the Rocky IV script on the Today Show before a national television audience. Anderson, in his deposition, states that his parents and friends called him to tell him that Stallone was telling "his story" on television. In a diary entry of July 12, 1984, Anderson noted that Stallone "explained my story" on national television.

Stallone completed his Rocky IV script in October of 1984. Rocky IV was released in November of 1985. The complaint in this action was filed on January 29, 1987.

Defendants Are Entitled To Summary Judgment On Anderson's Copyright Infringement Claims

This Court finds that the defendants are entitled to summary judgment on plaintiff's copyright infringement claims on two separate grounds. First, Anderson's treatment is an infringing work that is not entitled to copyright protection. Second, Rocky IV is not substantially similar to Anderson's treatment, and no reasonable jury could find that Rocky IV is a picturization of Anderson's script.

A. Defendants Are Entitled To Summary Judgment Because Anderson's Treatment Is An Infringing Work That Is Not Entitled To Copyright Protection

The Court finds that Anderson's treatment is not entitled to copyright protection. This finding is based upon the following determinations that will be delineated further below: (a) the Rocky characters developed in Rocky I, II and III constitute expression protected by copyright independent from the story in which they are contained; (b) Anderson's treatment appropriated these characters and created a derivative work based upon these characters without Stallone's permission in violation of Section 106(2); (c) no part of Anderson's treatment is entitled to copyright protection as his work is pervaded by the characters of the first three Rocky movies that are afforded copyright protection.

1. Visually Depicted Characters Can Be Granted Copyright Protection

The precise legal standard this Court should apply in determining when a character may be afforded copyright protection is fraught with uncertainty. The Second Circuit has followed Judge Learned Hand's opinion in Nichols v. Universal Pictures, 45 F.2d 119 (2d. Cir.1930), *cert. denied*, 282 U.S. 902 (1931). Judge Hand set forth a test, simple in theory but elusive in application, to determine when a character should be granted copyright protection. Essentially, under this test, copyright protection is granted to a character if it is developed with enough specificity so as to constitute protectable expression. *Id.* at 121.

This circuit originally created a more rigorous test for granting copyright protection to characters. In Warner Bros. Pictures, Inc. v. Columbia Broadcasting System, Inc., (hereinafter the *"Sam Spade"* opinion) this circuit held that the literary character Sam Spade was not copyrightable, opining that a character could not be granted copyright protection unless it "constituted the story being told." 216 F.2d 945, 950 (9th Cir.1954). The *Sam Spade* case has not been explicitly overruled by this circuit and its requirement that a character "constitute the story being told" appears to greatly circumscribe the protection of characters in this circuit.

Subsequent decisions in the Ninth Circuit cast doubt on the reasoning and implicitly limit the holding of the *Sam Spade* case. In Walt Disney Productions v. Air Pirates, this circuit held that several Disney comic characters were protected by copyright. 581 F.2d 751, 755 (9th Cir.1978). In doing so the Court of Appeals reasoned that because "comic book characters . . . are distinguishable from literary characters, the *Warner Bros.* language does not preclude protection of Disney's characters." *Id. Air Pirates* can be interpreted as either attempting to harmonize granting copyright protection to graphic characters with the "story being told" test enunciated in the *Sam Spade* case or narrowing the "story being told" test to characters in literary works. If *Air Pirates* is construed as holding that the graphic characters in question constituted the story being told, it does little to alter the *Sam Spade* opinion. However, it is equally as plausible to interpret *Air Pirates* as applying a less stringent test for protectability of graphic characters. Professor Nimmer has adopted the latter reading as he interprets *Air Pirates* as limiting the story being told requirement to word portraits. 1 M. Nimmer, THE LAW OF COPYRIGHT, § 2.12, p. 2–176 (1988).

This circuit's most recent decision on the issue of copyrightability of characters, Olson v. National Broadcasting Corporation, 855 F.2d 1446 (9th Cir.1988) does little to clarify the uncertainties in this circuit as to how the *Air Pirates* decision effects the continued viability of the *Sam Spade* test. In *Olson,* the Court of Appeals cited with approval the *Sam Spade* "story being told test" and declined to characterize this language as dicta. *Id.* at 1451–52 n.6. The Court then cited *Air Pirates* along with Second Circuit precedent and "recognize[d] that cases subsequent to *Warner Bros.* [*Sam Spade*] have allowed copyright protection for characters who are especially distinctive." *Id.* at 1452. *Olson* also stated definitively that "copyright protection may be afforded to characters visually depicted in a television series or in a movie." *Id.* But later in the opinion, the court in *Olson* distanced itself from the character delineation test that these cases employed, referring to it as "the more lenient standards adopted elsewhere". *Id.*

In an implicit acknowledgment of the unsettled state of the law, in considering the characters at issue in *Olson,* the circuit court evaluates the characters in the suit under *both tests. Id.* at 1452–53.

2. The Rocky Characters Are Entitled To Copyright Protection As A Matter Of Law

Olson's evaluation of literary characters is clearly distinguishable from the visually depicted characters of the first three Rocky movies for which the defendant seeks protection here. Thus, the more restrictive "story being told test" is inapplicable to the facts of this case. *Air Pirates*, 581 F.2d at 755, 1 M. Nimmer, § 2.12, p. 2–176. However, out of an abundance of caution this Court will determine the protectability of the Rocky characters under both tests. As shown below, the Rocky characters are protected from bodily appropriation under either standard.

The Rocky characters are one of the most highly delineated group of characters in modern American cinema. The physical and emotional characteristics of Rocky Balboa and the other characters were set forth in tremendous detail in the three Rocky movies before Anderson appropriated the characters for his treatment. The interrelationships and development of Rocky, Adrian, Apollo Creed, Clubber Lang, and Paulie are central to all three movies. Rocky Balboa is such a highly delineated character that his name is the title of all four of the Rocky movies and his character has become identified with specific character traits ranging from his speaking mannerisms to his physical characteristics. This Court has no difficulty ruling as a matter of law that the Rocky characters are delineated so extensively that they are protected from bodily appropriation when taken as a group and transposed into a sequel by another author. Plaintiff has not and cannot put before this Court any evidence to rebut the defendants' showing that Rocky characters are so highly delineated that they warrant copyright protection.

Plaintiff's unsupported assertions that Rocky is merely a stock character, made in the face of voluminous evidence that the Rocky characters are copyrightable, do not bar this Court from granting summary judgment on this issue. See Anderson v. Liberty Lobby, 477 U.S. 242, 247–48 (1986) ("the mere existence of *some* alleged factual dispute between the parties will not defeat an otherwise properly supported motion for summary judgment; the requirement is that there be no *genuine* issue of *material* fact")(emphasis in original). If any group of movie characters is protected by copyright, surely the Rocky characters are protected from bodily appropriation into a sequel which merely builds on the relationships and characteristics which these characters developed in the first three Rocky movies. No reasonable jury could find otherwise.

This Court need not and does not reach the issue of whether any single character alone, apart from Rocky, is delineated with enough specificity so as to garner copyright protection. Nor does the Court reach the issue of whether these characters are protected from less than bodily appropriation. See 1 M. Nimmer, § 2.12, p. 2–171 (copyrightability of characters is "more properly framed as relating to the degree of substantial similarity required to constitute infringement rather than in terms of copyrightability per se").

This Court also finds that the Rocky characters were so highly developed and central to the three movies made before Anderson's treatment that they "constituted the story being told." All three Rocky movies focused on the development and relationships of the various characters. The movies did not revolve around intricate plots or story lines. Instead, the focus of these movies was the development of the Rocky characters. The same evidence which supports the finding of delineation above is so extensive that it also warrants a finding that the Rocky characters—Rocky, Adrian, Apollo Creed, Clubber Lang, and Paulie—"constituted the story being told" in the first three Rocky movies.

3.   Anderson's Work Is An Unauthorized Derivative Work

Under Section 106(2), the holder of a copyright has the exclusive right to prepare derivative works based upon his copyrighted work. In this circuit a work is derivative *"only if it would be considered an infringing work if the material which it had derived from a prior work had been taken without the consent of the copyright proprietor of the prior work."* Litchfield v. Spielberg, 736 F.2d 1352, 1354 (9th Cir.1984)(emphasis in original), citing United States v. Taxe, 540 F.2d 961, 965 n.2 (9th Cir.1976). This Court must now examine whether Anderson's treatment is an unauthorized derivative work under this standard.

Usually a court would be required to undertake the extensive comparisons under the *Krofft* substantial similarity test to determine whether Anderson's work is a derivative work. [Sid and Marty Krofft Television Productions, Inc. v. McDonald's Corp., 562 F.2d 1157 (9th Cir.1977)]. See 1 M. Nimmer, § 3.01 at 3–3; p. 25–28 *supra*. However, in this case, Anderson has bodily appropriated the Rocky characters in his treatment. This Court need not determine whether the characters in Anderson's treatment are substantially similar to Stallone's characters, as it is uncontroverted that the characters were lifted lock, stock, and barrel from the prior Rocky movies. Anderson retained the names, relationships and built on the experiences of these characters from the three prior Rocky movies. 1 M. Nimmer, § 2.12 at 2–177 (copying names of characters is highly probative evidence of infringement). His characters are not merely substantially similar to Stallone's, they *are* Stallone's characters. Anderson's bodily appropriation of these characters infringes upon the protected expression in the Rocky characters and renders his work an unauthorized derivative work. 1 Nimmer, § 2.12 at 2–171. By bodily appropriating the significant elements of protected expression in the Rocky characters, Anderson has copied protected expression and his treatment infringes on Stallone's copyrighted work.

4.   Since Anderson's Work Is An Unauthorized Derivative Work, No Part Of The Treatment Can Be Granted Copyright Protection

Stallone owns the copyrights for the first three Rocky movies. Under section 106(2), he has the exclusive right to prepare derivative works based on these copyrighted works. This Court has determined that Anderson's treatment is an unauthorized derivative work. Thus, Anderson has infringed upon Stallone's copyright. See section 501(a).

Nevertheless, plaintiff contends that his infringing work is entitled to copyright protection and he can sue Stallone for infringing upon his treatment. Plaintiff relies upon section 103(a) as support for his position that he is entitled to copyright protection for the non-infringing portions of his treatment. Section 103(a) reads:

> The subject matter of copyright as specified by section 102 includes compilations and derivative works, but protection for a work employing preexisting material in which copyright subsists does not extend to any part of the work in which the material has been used unlawfully.

Plaintiff has not argued that section 103(a), on its face, requires that an infringer be granted copyright protection for the non-infringing portions of his work. He has not and cannot provide this Court with a single case that has held that an infringer of a copyright is entitled to sue a third party for infringing the original portions of his work. Nor can he provide a single case that stands for the extraordinary proposition he proposes here, namely, allowing a plaintiff to sue the party whose work he has infringed upon for infringement of his infringing derivative work.

Instead, Anderson alleges that the House Report on section 103(a) indicates that Congress intended protection for the non-infringing portions of derivative works such as his treatment. The House Report for section 103(a) first delineates the difference between compilations and derivative works. H.R. Rep. No. 1476, 94th Cong., 2d Sess. at 57–58 (1976). The House Report then reads as follows:

> The second part of the sentence that makes up section 103(a) deals with the status of a compilation or derivative work unlawfully employing preexisting copyrighted material. In providing that protection does not extend to "any part of the work in which such material has been used unlawfully," the bill prevents an infringer from benefiting, through copyright protection, from committing an unlawful act, but preserves protection for those parts of the work that do not employ the preexisting work. Thus, an unauthorized translation of a novel could not be copyrighted at all, but the owner of copyright in an anthology of poetry could sue someone who infringed the whole anthology, even though the infringer proves that publication of one of the poems was unauthorized.

The Court recognizes that the House Report language is muddled. It makes a general statement that non-infringing portions of a work should be granted protection if these portions do not employ the pre-existing work. The report then provides two examples: one involving a compilation where the noninfringing portion was deemed protected, and another involving a derivative work where no part of the work could be protected. The general statement, when taken in the context of the comparison of compilations and derivative works in the section and the two examples given, is best understood as applying only to compilations. Although it is not crystal clear, it appears that the Committee assumed that in a derivative work the underlying work is "employed" throughout.

Professor Nimmer also interprets the House Report language as generally denying copyright protection to any portion of an unauthorized derivative work. After setting forth some of the language from the House Report regarding section 103(a) he states,

> the effect [of section 103(a)] generally would be to deny copyright to derivative works, in which the preexisting work tends to pervade the entire derivative work, but not to collective works, where the infringement arises from the copying of the selection and arrangement of a number of preexisting works, and not per se from the reproduction of any particular prior work.

1 M. Nimmer, § 3.06, p. 3–22.3 thru 3–22.4.

Like the House Report, Nimmer also preceded his conclusion that no part of [a] derivative work unlawfully employing preexisting material should be copyrightable with a general statement that "only that portion of a derivative or collective work which employs the preexisting work would be denied copyright." 1 M. Nimmer, § 3.06, p. 3–22.3. At first blush, both Nimmer's and the Committee's language are internally inconsistent. Both start with a general proposition that only the portion of a work which unlawfully employs the prior work should be denied copyright protection. Both then appear to conclude that no part of an infringing derivative work should be granted copyright protection. Only if a derivative work is assumed to employ the infringing work throughout do these passages read coherently.

The case law interpreting section 103(a) also supports the conclusion that generally no part of an infringing derivative work should be granted copyright protection. In Eden Toys, Inc. v. Florelee Undergarment Co., the circuit court dealt primarily with the question of whether an authorized derivative work contained sufficient originality to gain copyright protection. 697 F.2d 27, 34–35 (2d. Cir.1982). However, in dicta the court opined on what result would be warranted if the derivative work had been made without the permission of the original author. The Court cited to the aforementioned passages from Professor Nimmer's treatise and the House Report and *assumed* without discussion that the "derivative copyrights would be invalid, since the preexisting illustration used without permission would tend to pervade the entire work." *Id.* at 34 n.6. In Gracen v. Bradford, the Seventh Circuit also dealt primarily with whether plaintiff's derivative work had sufficient originality to comply with [the] requirements of section 103. 698 F.2d 300, 302–303 (7th Cir.1983). *Gracen* also discussed the issue of the copyrightability of an unauthorized derivative work. The Court stated "if Miss Gracen had no authority to make derivative works from the movie, she could not copyright the painting and drawings, and she infringed MGM's copyright by displaying them publicly." *Id.* at 303. Once again, the Circuit court *assumed* that no part of an unlawful derivative work could be copyrighted.

Plaintiff has written a treatment which is an unauthorized derivative work. This treatment infringes upon Stallone's copyrights and his exclusive right to prepare derivative works which are based upon these movies. § 106(2). Section 103(a) was not intended to arm an infringer and limit the applicability of section 106(2) on unified derivative works. As the House

Report and Professor Nimmer's treatise explain, 103(a) was not intended to apply to derivative works and most certainly was not an attempt to modify section 106(2). Section 103(a) allows an author whose authorship essentially is the arrangement or ordering of several independent works to keep the copyright for his arrangement even if one of the underlying works he arranged is found to be used unlawfully. The infringing portion would be easily severable and the scope of the compilation author's own work would be easily ascertainable. Even if this Court were to interpret section 103(a) as allowing an author of an infringing derivative work to sue third parties based on the non-infringing portions of his work, section 106(2) most certainly precludes the author of an unauthorized infringing derivative work from suing the author of the work which he has already infringed. Thus, the Court holds that the defendants are entitled to summary judgment on plaintiff's copyright claims as the plaintiff cannot gain copyright protection for any portion of his work under section 103(a). In addition, Anderson is precluded by section 106(2) from bringing an action for copyright infringement against Stallone and the other defendants.

NOTES

1. *Functional subject matter.* *Baker* is the core of the separability doctrine and its application will be revisited in Assignment 10, which treats the copyrightability of computer programs. What is the relevance of Baker v. Selden to the Principal Problem?

Although many proposals have been introduced in Congress to provide a form of protection analogous to copyright law for the designs of useful articles, none of these legislative attempts have ever fared successfully. The Principal Problem involves a costume. Should the analysis differ if a dress design, historical period piece, or theatrical costume were involved? The Copyright Register's 1991 ruling on the Registrability of Costume Designs,[10] concludes that although "fanciful costumes will be registered [only] if they contain separable pictorial or sculptural authorship", "[g]arment designs (excluding separately identifiable pictorial representations of designs imposed upon the garment) will not be registered even if they contain ornamental features, or are intended to be used as historical or period dress."[11] The ruling also states that this "general policy of nonregistrability of garment designs will be applied not only to ordinary wearing apparel, but also to period and historical dress, and uniforms."[12] Moreover, "[w]earing apparel incorporated into theatrical productions will likewise be treated under the standards applying to garment designs in general."[13]

2. *Conceptual separability.* Which test for conceptual separability discussed in *Brandir* is the most theoretically satisfying? The majority in *Brandir* adopts Professor Denicola's test whereas the dissent endorses Judge Newman's "temporal displacement" test. Which of these tests allows

[10] Vol. 56 Fed. Register, No. 214, 56531 (November 5, 1991).

[11] Id. at 56531–56532.

[12] Id. at 56532.

[13] Id.

greater latitude for registrability? The *Brandir* majority also notes that its application will require the parties to present evidence relating to the "design process and the nature of the work." According to the majority, such a test would not be difficult to apply since "the work itself will continue to give 'mute testimony' of its origins." The dissent disagrees with this approach because, in his view, copyrightability should not be made to depend upon the fortuitous design process. Should *Brandir* have relied upon the sequences of actions or decisions in the design process? Is the majority or the dissent more persuasive? Why should a creator's intent be relevant? What if a creator does not fulfill her actual intent? Who should have the ultimate responsibility for determining whether a particular work possesses the requisite degree of artistic merit to qualify for copyright protection? This concern is evident in footnote c of *Brandir* which mentions Bleistein v. Donaldson Lithographing Co.[14] In that case, Justice Holmes made the now famous observation that "[i]t would be a dangerous undertaking for persons trained only to the law to constitute themselves final judges of the worth of pictorial illustrations, outside of the narrowest and most obvious limits."[15]

3. *Compilations vs. derivative works.* In *Anderson,* the court draws a distinction between compilations and derivative works, concluding that although protection can be obtained for the noninfringing portions of a compilation, similar protection is inappropriate for such portions of a derivative work. How persuasive is this part of the court's discussion? Note that the court was apparently outraged by the defendant's attempt to sue the author of the work which the defendant had infringed.

4. *Protection for characters.* One of the germinal cases discussing whether characters should receive copyright protection is Warner Bros. v. Columbia Broadcasting System, a 1954 opinion from the Ninth Circuit.[16] In that case, the plaintiff was Warner Brothers, who had entered into an agreement with the defendant, Dashiel Hammett, author of "The Maltese Falcon." The agreement granted the plaintiff the right to use the "The Maltese Falcon" in movies, radio and television. Plaintiff claimed that this grant also entitled it to use the individual characters in "The Maltese Falcon" and their names. The defendant argued that the plaintiff's rights were limited to those contained in the agreement, which failed to grant any rights to the use of the characters and their names. Thus, the defendant was free to use these characters in his other works and could license the rights in the characters to third parties. The court found for the defendant as a matter of contract law. As noted in *Anderson,* however, the *Warner Brothers* court also indicated that a character is not copyrightable unless it "constitute[s] the story being told." When does a character constitute "the story being told?" Should comic book characters be treated differently from literary characters? If so, where do characters in movies or television fit in?

---

[14] 188 U.S. 239, 23 S.Ct. 298, 47 L.Ed. 460 (1903).

[15] Id. at 251.

[16] 216 F.2d 945 (9th Cir.1954), cert. denied, 348 U.S. 971, 75 S.Ct. 532, 99 L.Ed. 756 (1955).

What does the *Anderson* court ultimately conclude regarding the protectability of the Rocky characters? Should it make a difference whether the creator is trying to protect his own character (essentially this is *Anderson*) or whether someone other than the creator is trying to prevent the creator from using his own creation (as in *Warner Brothers*)? The Anderson court quotes Nimmer for the proposition that the question whether characters are copyrightable is "more properly framed [in terms of] . . . the degree of substantial similarity required to constitute infringement rather than in terms of copyrightability per se."[17] What does this quote mean?

In addition to determining the appropriate test for copyright protection of fictional characters, courts wanting to protect characters under copyright law must confront additional difficult questions. For example, what aspects of a character should be protected by copyright? With respect to comic book characters specifically, should the protection be limited to graphic depictions or should additional aspects of the character be considered? Should Barney be allowed to manufacture the costume without a license from Warner and D.C.? What would you tell a client who wanted to market a superhero costume? What if your client wanted to market a video game featuring a graphical depiction of a superhero, or a television program featuring a superhero? Attorneys desiring assistance in determining the copyright status of particular characters can order a Copyright Character Search & Report from an independent research company. These reports search a number of sources such as the records of the U.S. Copyright Office, the U.S. Patent and Trademark Office, state trademark registrations, newspaper and trade notices, an international licensing directory, and the case law.

Another difficult issue involves the appropriate degree of protection for series characters. The problem in this regard is that some of the works in which a character appears may have fallen into the public domain, while others remain protected under copyright law. In Silverman v. CBS, Inc.,[18] an excerpt from which appears in Part B of Assignment 4, the Second Circuit held that a producer of a Broadway musical based on the series characters "Amos 'n' Andy" could use any aspects of the characters that were sufficiently delineated in radio scripts currently in the public domain, but that any aspects of these characters that were further delineated in subsequent works still protected by copyright could not be used.[19] Is this a viable solution? Can you think of any other resolutions to this problem?

Frequently, a license involving the right to use a character is merely the right to make new works deriving from the original, underlying work in which the character first appears. To the extent these derivative rights in characters involve use of the characters on clothing, games, toys, and even food, merchandising rights typically covered by unfair competition or trademark law are being implicated as well copyright law. From the

---

[17] See Section IV(A)(2) of *Anderson*, quoting 1 M. Nimmer, § 2.12, p. 2–171.

[18] 870 F.2d 40 (2d Cir.1989).

[19] Id. at 49–50.

standpoint of copyright law, how significant is the appropriation of the character's name as well as its appearance?

Query. Does your local grocery store commit copyright infringement under § 106(2) if it markets a cake in the shape and appearance of Mickey Mouse without a license from Disney? Can the cake be considered a "derivative work" within the meaning of the statute?

5. *Architectural works.* As of 1990, copyright law specifically protects architectural works. The Architectural Works Copyright Protection Act ("AWCPA"), which applies to works created on or after December 1, 1990, and to unconstructed works embodied in unpublished plans created before this date,[20] amended the copyright statute by adding architectural works as a specific subject matter category in § 102. Other additions to the statute include a definition of "architectural work" in § 101 and certain limitations on the scope of protection for such works in § 120. The definition of "architectural work" covers the "design of a building as embodied in any tangible medium of expression, including a building, architectural plans, or drawings." How should the term "building" be interpreted?

Prior to the AWCPA, only the plans could be protected as "pictorial, graphic, and sculptural works" under § 102(a)(5). Thus, the construction of a building from copyrighted plans was not considered infringement.[21] Now it appears as though the plans enjoy a dual form of protection, as do nonfunctional monuments that qualify as "sculptures."[22] What are the consequences of this dual protection? What caveat does § 120(a) impose on architectural works? What do you think is the purpose of this provision? What limitations does § 120(b) provide? Why do you think the AWCPA crafted relatively narrow protections for architectural works?

BIBLIOGRAPHY

The following works explore themes relating to copyrightable subject matter in general: Ward, Copyrighting Context: Law for Plumbing's Sake, 17 Colum.-VLA J.L. & Arts 159 (1993); LoBello, The Dichotomy Between Artistic Expression and Industrial Design: To Protect or Not to Protect, 13 Whittier L. Rev. 107 (1992); Aoki, Contradiction and Context in American Copyright Law, 9 Cardozo Arts & Ent. L.J. 303 (1991); Lynch, Copyright in Utilitarian Objects: Beneath Metaphysics, 16 U. Dayton L. Rev. 647 (1991); Burgunder, Product Design Protection After "Bonito Boats": Where it Belongs and How it Should Get There, 28 Am. Bus. L.J. 1 (1990); Perlmutter, Conceptual Separability and Copyright in the Designs of Useful

---

[20] Architectural Works Copyright Protection Act, Pub. L. No. 101–650, tit. 7, § 706(1) & (2), 104 Stat. 5133, 5134 (1990). Under the Act, the protection afforded to works in unpublished plans not constructed as of 1990 will expire on December 31, 2002, unless the work has been constructed by this date.

[21] See, e.g., Imperial Homes Corp. v. Lamont, 458 F.2d 895, 899 (5th Cir.1972).

[22] See H.R. Rep. No. 735, 101st Cong., 2d Sess. 18, 20 n.43 (1990), reprinted in 1990 U.S.C.C.A.N. 6935, 6951 n.43 ("Monumental, nonfunctional works of architecture are currently protected under section 102(a)(5) of title 17 as sculptural works. These works are, nevertheless, architectural works, and as such, will not be protected exclusively under section 102(a)(8).").

Articles, 37 J. Copyright Soc'y 339 (1990); Samuels, The Idea-Expression Dichotomy in Copyright Law, 56 Tenn. L. Rev. 321 (1989); Brown, Design Protection: An Overview, 34 UCLA L. Rev. 1341 (1987); Milch, Protection for Utilitarian Works of Art: The Design Patent/Copyright Conundrum, 10 Colum.-VLA J.L. & Arts 211 (1986); Reichman, Design Protection After the Copyright Act of 1976: A Comparative View of the Emerging Models, 31 J. Copyright Soc'y 267 (1984); Denicola, Applied Art and Industrial Design: A Suggested Approach to Copyright in Useful Articles, 67 Minn. L. Rev. 707 (1983); Reichman, Design Protection in Domestic and Foreign Copyright Law: From the Berne Revision of 1948 to the Copyright Act of 1976, 1983 Duke L.J. 1143 (1983). See also Symposium on Industrial Design Law & Practice, 19 U. Balt. L. Rev. 160 (1989).

These works discuss protection for fictional characters: Symposium, Licensing and Merchandising of Characters: Art Law Topic for AALS 1994, 11 U. Miami Ent. & Sports L. Rev. 421 (1995); Niro, Protecting Characters Through Copyright Law: Paving a New Road Upon Which Literary, Graphic, and Motion Picture Characters Can All Travel, 41 DePaul L. Rev. 359 (1992); Nevins, Copyright + Character = Catastrophe, 39 J. Copyright Soc'y 303 (1992); Kurtz, The Independent Legal Lives of Fictional Characters, 1986 Wis. L. Rev. 429 (1986); Zissu, Whither Character Rights: Some Observations, 29 J. Copyright Soc'y 121 (1981); Brylawski, Protection of Characters—Sam Spade Revisited, 22 Bull. Copyright Soc'y 77 (1974).

THE RECIPIENTS OF COPYRIGHT'S INCENTIVES: OWNERSHIP, THE WORK FOR HIRE DOCTRINE, RENEWAL AND TERMINATION RIGHTS, AND MORAL RIGHTS

1. INTRODUCTION

Section 201(a) of the 1976 Copyright Act provides that the copyright in a protected work "vests initially in the author or authors of the work." The authors of a "joint work," which is defined in § 101 as "a work prepared by two or more authors with the intention that their contributions be merged into inseparable or interdependent parts of a unitary whole," are considered co-owners of the copyright, and essentially are viewed as tenants in common with respect to the work. Each co-owner has the unilateral right to use or license the work, as long as an accounting of profits is made to the other co-owners. Section 201(b) of the Act provides that "[i]n the case of a work made for hire, the employer or other person for whom the work was prepared is considered the author ... unless the parties have expressly agreed otherwise in a written instrument signed by them...." Thus, the work for hire doctrine is an exception to the rule that copyright ownership vests initially in the work's creator, and in recognizing this doctrine, the United States probably is the only country that allows the employer of a work's creator to obtain "authorship" status.[1]

The importance of determining whether a particular work is a work for hire is manifest, as this determination dictates who is the initial owner of the copyright. Other consequences also attach to a determination that a work is a work made for hire. For example, when a work for hire has been licensed, that license is not subject to termination under § 203 of the Act. See infra Note 3 following major cases. Also, the employer of a work for hire can exercise the renewal right under § 304(a), as opposed to the actual creator or her statutory successors. See infra Note 4. Moreover, the recently enacted moral rights protections for visual art discussed below do not apply to works made for hire (see § 106A and the definition of "work of visual art" in § 101). The duration of copyright protection also is different

---

[1] See Childress v. Taylor, infra, at footnote d of the opinion.

for works for hire, since with respect to works for hire, "the copyright endures for a term of seventy-five years from the year of its first publication, or a term of one hundred years from the year of its creation, whichever expires first" (see § 302(c)). Copyright protection in regular works currently extends for the life of the author plus fifty years (see § 302(a)), and in the case of joint works, the period of protection lasts for fifty years after the last surviving author's death (see § 302(b)).

Section 201(d) of the Act also provides that the copyright owner can transfer any or all of the rights safeguarded by the 1976 Act. Section 106 of the statute assures the copyright owner the exclusive rights to reproduce and distribute the original work, to prepare derivative works, and to perform and display publicly certain types of copyrighted works. Each of these rights can be transferred by the copyright owner and separately owned. As the list of rights provided in § 106 suggests, the 1976 Act continued the United States' tradition of protecting only the pecuniary rights of a copyright owner. Since the 1976 Act generally does not purport to protect the creator, but rather the copyright owner, if the original creator of a work assigned all of her rights under § 106 to another party, traditionally the creator no longer retained any rights with respect to her work. One exception to this general rule appears in the termination provisions in § 203 of the statute, which allow a creator to terminate transfers and licenses after a period of time, but the creator must wait a minimum of thirty-five years after the execution of the grant to exercise this right (see Note 3, infra).

Another exception to the general rule that creators who assign their copyrights retain no rights with respect to their works appears in § 106A, which was added to the 1976 Copyright Act in 1990. As will be explained more fully below, Section 106A provides the creators of "visual art," as that term is defined in § 101, limited protection against unauthorized modifications to their works that will prejudice their honor or reputation. Section 106A thus provides limited recognition of what is known as moral rights, a doctrine that protects a creator's personal, as opposed to economic, interests in her work. Absent the application of § 106A, creators in the United States are unable to invoke moral rights protection. In contrast to the United States, many European and Third World nations have well-developed moral right doctrines. In those countries that have moral rights protection, the doctrine essentially is said to encompass three major components: the right of disclosure, the right of attribution, and the right of integrity. Underlying the right of disclosure is the idea that the creator, as the sole judge of when a work is ready for public dissemination, is the only one who can possess any rights in an uncompleted work. The right of attribution, as its name suggests, safeguards a creator's right to compel recognition for her work and to prevent others from naming anyone else as the creator. It also protects a creator's negative rights of anonymity and pseudonymity. The right of integrity lies at the heart of the moral right doctrine, as it prohibits any alterations of a creator's work that will destroy the spirit and character of the creator's work. Although adaptations of a work from one medium to another present the most obvious potential for violations of a creator's right of integrity, in reality any modification of a work can be problematic from an integrity standpoint.[2]

In 1988, the United States joined the Berne Convention for the Protection of Literary and Artistic Works, the oldest multilateral treaty governing copyright protection. As a result, American creators can now obtain increased copyright protection internationally (see generally Assignment 6, supra). Section 6bis of the Berne Convention recognizes a right of attribution and a right of integrity, but the treaty contemplates that the specific legislation of the respective Union members will govern substantive applications of these rights within each member country. When the United States joined the Convention, Congress believed that no additional moral rights protections were needed in this country given federal protections such as § 43(a) of the Lanham Act (see Assignment 3) and § 106(2) of the 1976 Copyright Act (governing the right to prepare derivative works), as well as the existing common law doctrines such as unfair competition, breach of contract, defamation and invasion of privacy law that had been used to redress moral rights violations.[3] In addition, several states provided specific statutory moral rights protections for certain types of works, notably visual art.[4] Still, in 1990 Congress amended the 1976 Copyright Act by adding the Visual Artists Rights Act ("VARA"), which provides creators of visual art, as that term is defined in the statute, with relatively limited rights of attribution and integrity when modifications to their works are

[2] Some formulations of the moral right doctrine also include the right to withdraw one's work from the public, the right to prevent excessive criticism, and the right to prevent assaults upon one's personality. See generally Kwall, Copyright and the Moral Right: Is an American Marriage Possible?, 38 Vand. L. Rev. 1, 5–16 (1985).

[3] See Final Report of Ad Hoc Working Group on U.S. Adherence to the Berne Convention, 10 Colum.-VLA J.L. & Arts 513, 555 (1986); H.R. Rep. No. 609, 100th Cong., 2d Sess. 38 (1988).

[4] See, e.g., Cal. Civ. Code §§ 987–90 (West 1982 & Supp. 1993); Conn. Gen. Stat. Ann. §§ 42–116s to 42–116t (West 1992); La. Rev. Stat. Ann. §§ 2151–56 (West 1987); Me. Rev. Stat. Ann. tit. 27, § 303 (West 1988); Mass. Gen. Laws Ann. ch. 231, § 85S (West Supp. 1993); Nev. Rev. Stat. §§ 598.970–.978 (1987); N.J. Stat. Ann. §§ 2A:24A–1 to 2A:24A–8 (West 1987); N.M. Stat. Ann. §§ 13–4B–1 to 13–4B–3 (Michie 1992); N.Y. Arts & Cult. Aff. Law §§ 14.01–.08 (McKinney 1984 & Supp. 1993); Pa. Stat. Ann. tit. 73, §§ 2101–10 (Supp. 1993); R.I. Gen. Laws §§ 5–62–2 to 5–62–6 (1987). The specific con-

tent of these statutes varies. Some statutes such as those in California, Connecticut, Massachusetts, and Pennsylvania provide relief for the actual commission of an alteration, while other statutes such as those in Louisiana, Maine, Nevada, New Jersey, New York, and Rhode Island provide relief for the display or publication of an altered work. The definitions of protected works also vary among the states. Compare California's definition of protected "fine art" ("an original painting, sculpture, or drawing . . . of recognized quality," § 987(b)(2)) with the extremely detailed and broad definition of "fine art" in the Connecticut statute (see § 42–116s(2)). Some of the state statutes offer more extensive protections than VARA. For example, California, Massachusetts, and New Mexico apparently presume that any alteration will harm a creator's honor or reputation. Massachusetts and New Mexico allow relief for alterations resulting from gross negligence. The provisions in Louisiana, Maine, New Jersey, New York, and Rhode Island extend to reproductions of protected works. These differences are significant with respect to the issue of preemption. See Note 5, infra in the text.

made that will prejudice their honor or reputation.[5] The statute also contains special provisions for works of visual art that have become part of buildings (see § 113(d)).

Although VARA certainly is a step in the right direction, numerous problems exist with respect to its scope and implementation. For example, VARA only applies to a very narrow category of visual art which includes "a painting, drawing, print, or sculpture, . . . or a still photographic image produced for exhibition purposes only existing in a single copy . . ., or in a limited edition of 200 copies or fewer that are signed and consecutively numbered by the author."[6] Moreover, the right of integrity is limited to intentional modifications and fails to include rights in reproductions of the protected work. The statute also fails to define or provide any guidance with respect to how a determination of "prejudice" should be made. In addition, the right of attribution in VARA, while unlike the right of integrity in that it is not limited to intentional alterations, does not include the negative rights of anonymity or pseudonymity.[7] Other problems with VARA are discussed in Note 5, infra.

As the following materials demonstrate, the issues surrounding who are the recipients of copyright's incentives present some difficult issues. Some of these issues revolve around identifying the original copyright owners. In general, these questions involve application of the work for hire and joint authorship doctrines. Other questions involve the rights of both the original creators and subsequent grantees of the copyright. For example, when the original creator assigns some or all of the copyrights in her work to another party, issues can arise regarding the respective parties' rights upon termination of the grant. The doctrine of moral rights also illustrates the tension between the rights of the creator and subsequent assignees of the copyright who may also have made significant investments in the work. These issues are explored in the following Principal Problem.

2. PRINCIPAL PROBLEM

David writes dual-language dictionaries of street slang English words that are intended to be used by people who are learning English. He is very well known for this endeavor and enjoys an international reputation, since he has written such dictionaries for people who speak Spanish, German, French, and Russian. All of his dictionaries contain groupings by categories of expressions (i.e., expressions relating to eating and food, expressions relating to recreational activities, etc.). He now wants to do an English–Hebrew dictionary. To assist him with this project, he enters into agreements with Sam and Rivkah. Rivkah was an art major in college and did

---

[5] See § 106A.

[6] See § 101 (definition of a "work of visual art"). Compare the statutes in Louisiana, Maine, Nevada, New Jersey, and Rhode Island which define the protected works as including limited editions of no more than three hundred copies.

[7] See generally Damich, The Visual Artists Rights Act of 1990: Toward a Federal System of Moral Rights Protection for Visual Art, 39 Cath. U. L. Rev. 945 (1990).

the illustrations for all of David's other dictionaries. For this dictionary, David wants her to draw illustrations of famous Israeli and American scenes and sights. Since Rivkah has never been to Israel, David sends her to Israel for two weeks so that she can make preliminary sketches of the sights to be included in the book. David pays for all of her travel and living expenses while Rivkah is in Israel, including the medical bills she incurred when she injured her ankle and had to be taken to a hospital emergency room. After Rivkah returned from Israel, she did most of the work on the illustrations at her own home, using her own art supplies.

Sam is an Israeli living in America who currently is looking for a job teaching Hebrew at an American university. He has never before worked with David, and his job is to provide assistance with translating the English expressions into Hebrew. David gave Sam an office to use in his office suite and they had daily contact during the period of time the dictionary was being prepared. David did all of the groupings and generally decided which English expressions should be included in the dictionary. Sam did all of the actual translations.

The agreement that David entered into with both Sam and Rivkah provided that they agreed to work "with and for" David on the street slang English–Hebrew dictionary. Both were paid in cash, based on an hourly wage.

While they were in the process of writing the dictionary, David entered into an agreement with Chaim Corp., who agreed to publish the dictionary on the condition that Chaim can also create and market an audio cassette of the dictionary so that people can play it in their cars. Without consulting Sam or Rivkah, David granted Chaim the right to publish the dictionary and the right to make a derivative work of the dictionary. Unfortunately, when David hears the completed cassette, he is shocked by the strange background music, the annoying tone of the announcer, the re-ordering of the categories of his expressions, and the inclusion of a category of sex-related expressions. The cover of the cassette states that it is "based upon" David's English–Hebrew dictionary.

David retains you as his counsel. Believing that the cassette is a perversion of his artistic integrity and his original creative vision, David wants to sue Chaim. He wants your advice with respect to what causes of action he can bring against Chaim for mutilating his work. David also wants to terminate Chaim's license immediately, and if this is not possible, David wants to know when he can and if such a termination of Chaim's rights also will terminate Chaim's right to produce and market the cassette. Moreover, David has just learned that Rivkah and Sam have filed for a declaratory judgment that they are joint authors of the copyright in the dictionary. They want to join in David's lawsuit against Chaim, and also sue David for failing to get their permission to license the work to Chaim. David is vigorously disputing their joint authorship claim.

What are the legal issues raised by the foregoing set of circumstances and how do you think all of these issues are likely to be resolved? Before giving your answers, consider the following materials.

3. MATERIALS FOR SOLUTION OF PRINCIPAL PROBLEM

A. STATUTORY MATERIALS: §§ 101 (definitions of "work made for hire", "joint work" & "work of visual art"), 106, 106A, 201–205, 301(f), & 302–305

B. CASES:

Community for Creative Non–Violence v. Reid

Supreme Court of the United States, 1989.
490 U.S. 730, 109 S.Ct. 2166, 104 L.Ed.2d 811.

■ JUSTICE MARSHALL delivered the opinion of the Court.

In this case, an artist and the organization that hired him to produce a sculpture contest the ownership of the copyright in that work. To resolve this dispute, we must construe the "work made for hire" provisions of the Copyright Act of 1976 (Act or 1976 Act), 17 U.S.C. §§ 101 and 201(b), and in particular, the provision in § 101, which defines as a "work made for hire" a "work prepared by an employee within the scope of his or her employment" (hereinafter § 101(1)).

I

Petitioners are the Community for Creative Non–Violence (CCNV), a nonprofit unincorporated association dedicated to eliminating homelessness in America, and Mitch Snyder, a member and trustee of CCNV. In the fall of 1985, CCNV decided to participate in the annual Christmastime Pageant of Peace in Washington, D.C., by sponsoring a display to dramatize the plight of the homeless. As the District Court recounted:

> "Snyder and fellow CCNV members conceived the idea for the nature of the display: a sculpture of a modern Nativity scene in which, in lieu of the traditional Holy Family, the two adult figures and the infant would appear as contemporary homeless people huddled on a streetside steam grate. The family was to be black (most of the homeless in Washington being black); the figures were to be life-sized, and the steam grate would be positioned atop a platform 'pedestal,' or base, within which special-effects equipment would be enclosed to emit simulated 'steam' through the grid to swirl about the figures. They also settled upon a title for the work—'Third World America'—and a legend for the pedestal: 'and still there is no room at the inn.' " 652 F.Supp. 1453, 1454 (D.C.1987).

Snyder made inquiries to locate an artist to produce the sculpture. He was referred to respondent James Earl Reid, a Baltimore, Maryland, sculptor. In the course of two telephone calls, Reid agreed to sculpt the three human figures. CCNV agreed to make the steam grate and pedestal for the statue. Reid proposed that the work be cast in bronze, at a total cost of approximately $100,000 and taking six to eight months to complete. Snyder rejected that proposal because CCNV did not have sufficient funds, and because the statue had to be completed by December 12 to be included in the pageant. Reid then suggested, and Snyder agreed, that the sculpture would be made of a material known as "Design Cast 62," a synthetic substance that could meet CCNV's monetary and time constraints, could be tinted to resemble bronze, and could withstand the elements. The parties agreed that the project would cost no more than $15,000, not including Reid's services, which he offered to donate. The parties did not sign a written agreement. Neither party mentioned copyright.

After Reid received an advance of $3,000, he made several sketches of figures in various poses. At Snyder's request, Reid sent CCNV a sketch of a proposed sculpture showing the family in a crechelike setting: the mother seated, cradling a baby in her lap; the father standing behind her, bending over her shoulder to touch the baby's foot. Reid testified that Snyder asked for the sketch to use in raising funds for the sculpture. Snyder testified that it was also for his approval. Reid sought a black family to serve as a model for the sculpture. Upon Snyder's suggestion, Reid visited a family living at CCNV's Washington shelter but decided that only their newly born child was a suitable model. While Reid was in Washington, Snyder took him to see homeless people living on the streets. Snyder pointed out that they tended to recline on steam grates, rather than sit or stand, in order to warm their bodies. From that time on, Reid's sketches contained only reclining figures.

Throughout November and the first two weeks of December 1985, Reid worked exclusively on the statue, assisted at various times by a dozen different people who were paid with funds provided in installments by CCNV. On a number of occasions, CCNV members visited Reid to check on his progress and to coordinate CCNV's construction of the base. CCNV rejected Reid's proposal to use suitcases or shopping bags to hold the family's personal belongings, insisting instead on a shopping cart. Reid and CCNV members did not discuss copyright ownership on any of these visits.

On December 24, 1985, 12 days after the agreed-upon date, Reid delivered the completed statue to Washington. There it was joined to the steam grate and pedestal prepared by CCNV and placed on display near the site of the pageant. Snyder paid Reid the final installment of the $15,000. The statue remained on display for a month. In late January 1986, CCNV members returned it to Reid's studio in Baltimore for minor repairs. Several weeks later, Snyder began making plans to take the statue on a tour of several cities to raise money for the homeless. Reid objected, contending that the Design Cast 62 material was not strong enough to withstand the ambitious itinerary. He urged CCNV to cast the statue in bronze at a cost of $35,000, or to create a master mold at a cost of $5,000. Snyder declined to spend more of CCNV's money on the project.

In March 1986, Snyder asked Reid to return the sculpture. Reid refused. He then filed a certificate of copyright registration for "Third World America" in his name and announced plans to take the sculpture on a more modest tour than the one CCNV had proposed. Snyder, acting in his capacity as CCNV's trustee, immediately filed a competing certificate of copyright registration.

Snyder and CCNV then commenced this action against Reid, seeking return of the sculpture and a determination of copyright ownership. The

District Court granted a preliminary injunction, ordering the sculpture's return. After a 2–day bench trial, the District Court declared that "Third World America" was a "work made for hire" under § 101 of the Copyright Act and that Snyder, as trustee for CCNV, was the exclusive owner of the copyright in the sculpture. 652 F.Supp., at 1457. The court reasoned that Reid had been an "employee" of CCNV within the meaning of § 101(1) because CCNV was the motivating force in the statue's production. Snyder and other CCNV members, the court explained, "conceived the idea of a contemporary Nativity scene to contrast with the national celebration of the season," and "directed enough of [Reid's] effort to assure that, in the end, he had produced what they, not he, wanted." *Id.* at 1456.

The Court of Appeals for the District of Columbia Circuit reversed and remanded, holding that Reid owned the copyright because "Third World America" was not a work for hire. 846 F.2d 1485, 1494 (1988). Adopting what it termed the "literal interpretation" of the Act as articulated by the Fifth Circuit in Easter Seal Society for Crippled Children and Adults of Louisiana, Inc. v. Playboy Enterprises, 815 F.2d 323, 329 (1987), *cert. denied*, 485 U.S. 981 (1988), the court read § 101 as creating "a simple dichotomy in fact between employees and independent contractors." 846 F.2d, at 1492. Because, under agency law, Reid was an independent contractor, the court concluded that the work was not "prepared by an employee" under § 101(1). *Id.* at 1494. Nor was the sculpture a "work made for hire" under the second subsection of § 101 (hereinafter § 101(2)): sculpture is not one of the nine categories of works enumerated in that subsection, and the parties had not agreed in writing that the sculpture would be a work for hire. *Ibid.* The court suggested that the sculpture nevertheless may have been jointly authored by CCNV and Reid, *id.* at 1495, and remanded for a determination whether the sculpture is indeed a joint work under the Act, *id.*, 1498–1499.

We granted certiorari to resolve a conflict among the Courts of Appeals over the proper construction of the "work made for hire" provisions of the Act.[a] 488 U.S. 940 (1988). We now affirm.

II

A

The Copyright Act of 1976 provides that copyright ownership "vests initially in the author or authors of the work." § 201(a). As a general rule, the author is the party who actually creates the work, that is, the person who translates an idea into a fixed, tangible expression entitled to copy-

[a] Compare Easter Seal Society for Crippled Children and Adults of Louisiana, Inc. v. Playboy Enterprises, 815 F.2d 323 (C.A.5 1987), *cert. denied*, 485 U.S. 981 (1988)(agency law determines who is an employee under § 101), with Brunswick Beacon, Inc. v. Schock-Hopchas Publishing Co., 810 F.2d 410 (C.A.4 1987)(supervision and control standard determines who is an employee under § 101); Evans Newton, Inc. v. Chicago Systems Software, 793 F.2d 889 (CA7), *cert. denied*, 479 U.S. 949 (1986) (same); and Aldon Accessories Ltd. v. Spiegel, Inc., 738 F.2d 548 (CA2), *cert. denied*, 469 U.S. 982 (1984)(a multifactor formal, salaried employee test determines who is an employee under § 101).

[handwritten margin note: Reid sole author → 1991 WL 415523]

right protection. § 102. The Act carves out an important exception, however, for "works made for hire."[b] If the work is for hire, "the employer or other person for whom the work was prepared is considered the author" and owns the copyright, unless there is a written agreement to the contrary. § 201(b). Classifying a work as "made for hire" determines not only the initial ownership of its copyright, but also the copyright's duration, § 302(c), and the owners' renewal rights, § 304(a), termination rights, § 203(a), and right to import certain goods bearing the copyright, § 601(b)(1). The contours of the work for hire doctrine therefore carry profound significance for freelance creators—including artists, writers, photographers, designers, composers, and computer programmers—and for the publishing, advertising, music, and other industries which commission their works.

Section 101 of the 1976 Act provides that a work is "for hire" under two sets of circumstances:

> "(1) a work prepared by an employee within the scope of his or her employment; or
>
> (2) a work specially ordered or commissioned for use as a contribution to a collective work, as a part of a motion picture or other audiovisual work, as a translation, as a supplementary work, as a compilation, as an instructional text, as a test, as answer material for a test, or as an atlas, if the parties expressly agree in a written instrument signed by them that the work shall be considered a work made for hire."[c]

Petitioners do not claim that the statue satisfies the terms of § 101(2). Quite clearly, it does not. Sculpture does not fit within any of the nine categories of "specially ordered or commissioned" works enumerated in that subsection, and no written agreement between the parties establishes "Third World America" as a work for hire.

The dispositive inquiry in this case therefore is whether "Third World America" is "a work prepared by an employee within the scope of his or her employment" under § 101(1). The Act does not define these terms. In the absence of such guidance, four interpretations have emerged. The first holds that a work is prepared by an employee whenever the hiring party[d] retains the right to control the product. See Peregrine v. Lauren Corp., 601 F.Supp. 828, 829 (D.Colo.1985); Clarkstown v. Reeder, 566 F.Supp. 137, 142 (S.D.N.Y.1983). Petitioners take this view. A second, and closely related, view is that a work is prepared by an employee under § 101(1) when the hiring party has actually wielded control with respect to the creation of a particular work. This approach was formulated by the Court of Appeals for the Second Circuit, Aldon Accessories Ltd. v. Spiegel, Inc., 738 F.2d 548, *cert. denied*, 469 U.S. 982 (1984), and adopted by the Fourth

---

[b] We use the phrase "work for hire" interchangeably with the more cumbersome statutory phrase "work made for hire."

[c] Section 101 of the Act defines each of the nine categories of "specially ordered or commissioned" works.

[d] By "hiring party," we mean to refer to the party who claims ownership of the copyright by virtue of the work for hire doctrine.

Circuit, Brunswick Beacon, Inc. v. Schock–Hopchas Publishing Co., 810 F.2d 410 (1987), the Seventh Circuit, Evans Newton, Inc. v. Chicago Systems Software, 793 F.2d 889, *cert. denied*, 479 U.S. 949 (1986), and, at times, by petitioners. A third view is that the term "employee" within § 101(1) carries its common-law agency law meaning. This view was endorsed by the Fifth Circuit in Easter Seal Society for Crippled Children and Adults of Louisiana, Inc. v. Playboy Enterprises, 815 F.2d 323 (1987), and by the Court of Appeals below. Finally, respondent and numerous amici curiae contend that the term "employee" only refers to "formal, salaried" employees. The Court of Appeals for the Ninth Circuit recently adopted this view. See Dumas v. Gommerman, 865 F.2d 1093 (1989).

The starting point for our interpretation of a statute is always its language. The Act nowhere defines the terms "employee" or "scope of employment." It is, however, well established that "where Congress uses terms that have accumulated settled meaning under ... the common law, a court must infer, unless the statute otherwise dictates, that Congress means to incorporate the established meaning of these terms." NLRB v. Amax Coal Co., 453 U.S. 322, 329 (1981). In the past, when Congress has used the term "employee" without defining it, we have concluded that Congress intended to describe the conventional master-servant relationship as understood by common-law agency doctrine. [Citations omitted.] Nothing in the text of the work for hire provisions indicates that Congress used the words "employee" and "employment" to describe anything other than "the conventional relation of employer and employe[e]." [Citation omitted.] [C]ompare NLRB v. Hearst Publications, 322 U.S. 111, 124–132 (1944)(rejecting agency law conception of employee for purposes of the National Labor Relations Act where structure and context of statute indicated broader definition). On the contrary, Congress' intent to incorporate the agency law definition is suggested by § 101(1)'s use of the term, "scope of employment," a widely used term of art in agency law. See Restatement (Second) of Agency § 228 (1958)(hereinafter Restatement).

In past cases of statutory interpretation, when we have concluded that Congress intended terms such as "employee," "employer," and "scope of employment" to be understood in light of agency law, we have relied on the general common law of agency, rather than on the law of any particular State, to give meaning to these terms. [Citations omitted.] This practice reflects the fact that "federal statutes are generally intended to have uniform nationwide application." Mississippi Band of Choctaw Indians v. Holyfield, 490 U.S. 30, 43 (1989). Establishment of a federal rule of agency, rather than reliance on state agency law, is particularly appropriate here given the Act's express objective of creating national, uniform copyright law by broadly pre-empting state statutory and common-law copyright regulation. See § 301(a). We thus agree with the Court of Appeals that the term "employee" should be understood in light of the general common law of agency.

In contrast, neither test proposed by petitioners is consistent with the text of the Act. The exclusive focus of the right to control the product test on the relationship between the hiring party and the product clashes with the language of § 101(1), which focuses on the relationship between the hired and hiring parties. The right to control the product test also would distort the meaning of the ensuing subsection, § 101(2). Section 101 plainly creates two distinct ways in which a work can be deemed for hire: one for works prepared by employees, the other for those specially ordered or commissioned works which fall within one of the nine enumerated catego- ries and are the subject of a written agreement. The right to control the product test ignores this dichotomy by transforming into a work for hire under § 101(1) any "specially ordered or commissioned" work that is subject to the supervision and control of the hiring party. Because a party who hires a "specially ordered or commissioned" work by definition has a right to specify the characteristics of the product desired, at the time the commission is accepted, and frequently until it is completed, the right to control the product test would mean that many works that could satisfy § 101(2) would already have been deemed works for hire under § 101(1). Petitioners' interpretation is particularly hard to square with § 101(2)'s enumeration of the nine specific categories of specially ordered or commis- sioned works eligible to be works for hire, e.g., "a contribution to a collective work," "a part of a motion picture," and "answer material for a test." The unifying feature of these works is that they are usually prepared at the instance, direction, and risk of a publisher or producer. By their very nature, therefore, these types of works would be works by an employee under petitioners' right to control the product test.

The actual control test, articulated by the Second Circuit in *Aldon Accessories*, fares only marginally better when measured against the lan- guage and structure of § 101. Under this test, independent contractors who are so controlled and supervised in the creation of a particular work are deemed "employees" under § 101(1). Thus work for hire status under § 101(1) depends on a hiring party's *actual* control of, rather than *right to* control, the product. *Aldon Accessories*, 738 F.2d, at 552. Under the actual control test, a work for hire could arise under § 101(2), but not under § 101(1), where a party commissions, but does not actually control, a product which falls into one of the nine enumerated categories. Nonethe- less, we agree with the Fifth Circuit Court of Appeals that "[t]here is simply no way to milk the 'actual control' test of *Aldon Accessories* from the language of the statute." *Easter Seal Society*, 815 F.2d, at 334. Section 101 clearly delineates between works prepared by an employee and commis- sioned works. Sound though other distinctions might be as a matter of copyright policy, there is no statutory support for an additional dichotomy between commissioned works that are actually controlled and supervised by the hiring party and those that are not.

We therefore conclude that the language and structure of § 101 of the Act do not support either the right to control the product or the actual control approaches.[e] The structure of § 101 indicates that a work for hire

---

[e] We also reject the suggestion of respon- dent and amici that the § 101(1) term "em- ployee" refers only to formal, salaried em- ployees. While there is some support for such

can arise through one of two mutually exclusive means, one for employees and one for independent contractors, and ordinary canons of statutory interpretation indicate that the classification of a particular hired party should be made with reference to agency law.

This reading of the undefined statutory terms finds considerable support in the Act's legislative history. The Act, which almost completely revised existing copyright law, was the product of two decades of negotiation by representatives of creators and copyright-using industries, supervised by the Copyright Office and, to a lesser extent, by Congress. Despite the lengthy history of negotiation and compromise which ultimately produced the Act, two things remained constant. First, interested parties and Congress at all times viewed works by employees and commissioned works by independent contractors as separate entities. Second, in using the term "employee," the parties and Congress meant to refer to a hired party in a conventional employment relationship. These factors militate in favor of the reading we have found appropriate.

In 1955, when Congress decided to overhaul copyright law, the existing work for hire provision was § 62 of the 1909 Copyright Act. It provided that "the word 'author' shall include an employer in the case of works made for hire." Because the 1909 Act did not define "employer" or "works made for hire," the task of shaping these terms fell to the courts. They concluded that the work for hire doctrine codified in § 62 referred only to works made by employees in the regular course of their employment. As for commissioned works, the courts generally presumed that the commissioned party had impliedly agreed to convey the copyright, along with the work itself, to the hiring party. [Citations omitted.]

In 1961, the Copyright Office's first legislative proposal retained the distinction between works by employees and works by independent contractors. See Report of the Register of Copyrights on the General Revision of the U.S. Copyright Law, 87th Cong., 1st Sess., Copyright Law Revision 86–87 (H. Judiciary Comm. Print 1961). After numerous meetings with representatives of the affected parties, the Copyright Office issued a preliminary draft bill in 1963. Adopting the Register's recommendation, it defined "work made for hire" as "a work prepared by an employee within the scope of the duties of his employment, but not including a work made on special

a definition in the legislative history, the language of § 101(1) cannot support it. The Act does not say "formal" or "salaried" employee, but simply "employee." Moreover, respondent and those amici who endorse a formal, salaried employee test do not agree upon the content of this test. Compare, e.g., Brief for Respondent 37 (hired party who is on payroll is an employee within § 101(1)) with Tr. of Oral Arg. 31 (hired party who receives a salary or commissions regularly is an employee within § 101(1)); and Brief for Volunteer Lawyers for the Arts Inc. et al. as Amici Curiae 4 (hired party who receives a salary *and* is treated as an employee for Social Security and tax purposes is an employee within § 101(1)). Even the one Court of Appeals to adopt what it termed a formal, salaried employee test in fact embraced an approach incorporating numerous factors drawn from the agency law definition of employee which we endorse. See *Dumas*, 865 F.2d at 1104.

order or commission." Preliminary Draft for Revised U.S. Copyright Law and Discussions and Comments on the Draft, 88th Cong., 2d Sess., Copyright Law Revision, Part 3, p.15, n.11 (H. Judiciary Comm. Print 1964)(hereinafter Preliminary Draft).

In response to objections by book publishers that the preliminary draft bill limited the work for hire doctrine to "employees," the 1964 revision bill expanded the scope of the work for hire classification to reach, for the first time, commissioned works. The bill's language, proposed initially by representatives of the publishing industry, retained the definition of work for hire insofar as it referred to "employees," but added a separate clause covering commissioned works, without regard to the subject matter, "if the parties so agree in writing." S. 3008, H.R. 11947, H.R. 12354, 88th Cong., 2d Sess., § 54 (1964), reproduced in 1964 Revision Bill with Discussions and Comments, 89th Cong., 1st Sess., Copyright Law Revision, pt.5, p.31 (H. R. Judiciary Comm. Print 1965). Those representing authors objected that the added provision would allow publishers to use their superior bargaining position to force authors to sign work for hire agreements, thereby relinquishing all copyright rights as a condition of getting their books published. See Supplementary Report, at 67.

In 1965, the competing interests reached an historic compromise, which was embodied in a joint memorandum submitted to Congress and the Copyright Office,[f] incorporated into the 1965 revision bill, and ultimately enacted in the same form and nearly the same terms 11 years later, as § 101 of the 1976 Act. The compromise retained as subsection (1) the language referring to "a work prepared by an employee within the scope of his employment." However, in exchange for concessions from publishers on provisions relating to the termination of transfer rights, the authors consented to a second subsection which classified four categories of commissioned works as works for hire if the parties expressly so agreed in writing: works for use "as a contribution to a collective work, as a part of a motion picture, as a translation, or as supplementary work." S. 1006, H.R. 4347, H.R. 5680, H.R. 6835, 89th Cong., 1st Sess., § 101 (1965). The interested parties selected these categories because they concluded that these commissioned works, although not prepared by employees and thus not covered by the first subsection, nevertheless should be treated as works for hire because they were ordinarily prepared "at the instance, direction, and risk of a publisher or producer." Supplementary Report of the Register of Copyrights on the General Revision of the U.S. Copyright Law: 1965 Revision Bill, 89th Cong., 1st Sess., Copyright Law Revision, 67 (H.R. Judiciary Comm. Print 1965)(hereinafter Supplementary Report). The Supplementary Report emphasized that only the "four special cases specifically mentioned" could qualify as works made for hire; "other works made on

---

[f] The parties to the joint memorandum included representatives of the major competing interests involved in the copyright revision process: publishers and authors, composers, and lyricists. See Copyright Law Revision: Hearings on H.R. 4347, 5680, 6831, 6835 before Subcommittee No. 3 of the House Committee on the Judiciary, 89th Cong., 1st Sess., pt.1, p.134 (1965).

special order or commission would not come within the definition." *Id.* at 67–68.

In 1966, the House Committee on the Judiciary endorsed this compromise in the first legislative report on the revision bills. See H.R. Rep. No. 2237, 89th Cong., 2d Sess., 114, 116 (1966). Retaining the distinction between works by employees and commissioned works, the House Committee focused instead on "how to draw a statutory line between those works written on special order or commission that should be considered as works made for hire, and those that should not." *Id.* at 115. The House Committee added four other enumerated categories of commissioned works that could be treated as works for hire: compilations, instructional texts, tests, and atlases. *Id.* at 116. With the single addition of "answer material for a test," the 1976 Act, as enacted, contained the same definition of works made for hire as did the 1966 revision bill, and had the same structure and nearly the same terms as the 1966 bill.[g] Indeed, much of the language of the 1976 House and Senate Reports was borrowed from the Reports accompanying the earlier drafts.

Thus, the legislative history of the Act is significant for several reasons. First, the enactment of the 1965 compromise with only minor modifications demonstrates that Congress intended to provide two mutually exclusive ways for works to acquire work for hire status: one for employees and the other for independent contractors. Second, the legislative history underscores the clear import of the statutory language: only enumerated categories of commissioned works may be accorded work for hire status. The hiring party's right to control the product simply is not determinative. Indeed, importing a test based on a hiring party's right to control, or actual control of, a product would unravel the "carefully worked out compromise aimed at balancing legitimate interests on both sides." H.R. Rep. No. 2237, *supra*, at 114, quoting Supplemental Report, at 66.[h]

[P]etitioners' construction of the work for hire provisions would impede Congress' paramount goal in revising the 1976 Act of enhancing predictability and certainty of copyright ownership. See H.R. Rep. No. 94–1476, *supra*, at 129. In a "copyright marketplace," the parties negotiate with an expectation that one of them will own the copyright in the completed work. *Dumas*, 865 F.2d, at 1104–1105, n.18. With that expecta-

---

[g] An attempt to add "photographic or other portrait[s]," S. Rep. No. 94–473, p. 4 (1975), to the list of commissioned works eligible for work for hire status failed after the Register of Copyrights objected:

"The addition of portraits to the list of commissioned works that can be made into 'works made for hire' by agreement of the parties is difficult to justify. Artists and photographers are among the most vulnerable and poorly protected of all the beneficiaries of the copyright law, and it seems clear that, like serious composers and choreographers, they were not intended to be treated as 'employees' under the carefully negotiated definition in section 101."

Second Supplementary Report of the Register of Copyrights on the General Revision of the U.S. Copyright Law: 1975 Revision Bill, Chapter XI, p. 12–13.

[h] Strict adherence to the language and structure of the Act is particularly appropriate where, as here, a statute is the result of a series of carefully crafted compromises.

tion, the parties at the outset can settle on relevant contractual terms, such as the price for the work and the ownership of reproduction rights.

To the extent that petitioners endorse an actual control test,[i] CCNV's construction of the work for hire provisions prevents such planning. Because that test turns on whether the hiring party has closely monitored the production process, the parties would not know until late in the process, if not until the work is completed, whether a work will ultimately fall within § 101(1). Under petitioners' approach, therefore, parties would have to predict in advance whether the hiring party will sufficiently control a given work to make it the author. "If they guess incorrectly, their reliance on 'work for hire' or an assignment may give them a copyright interest that they did not bargain for." *Easter Seal Society*, 815 F.2d, at 333; accord, *Dumas*, 865 F.2d, at 1103. This understanding of the work for hire provisions clearly thwarts Congress' goal of ensuring predictability through advance planning. Moreover, petitioners' interpretation "leaves the door open for hiring parties, who have failed to get a full assignment of copyright rights from independent contractors falling outside the subdivision (2) guidelines, to unilaterally obtain work-made-for-hire rights years after the work has been completed as long as they directed or supervised the work, a standard that is hard not to meet when one is a hiring party." Hamilton, Commissioned Works as Works Made for Hire Under the 1976 Copyright Act: Misinterpretation and Injustice, 135 U. Pa. L. Rev. 1281, 1304 (1987).

In sum, we must reject petitioners' argument. Transforming a commissioned work into a work by an employee on the basis of the hiring party's right to control, or actual control of, the work is inconsistent with the language, structure, and legislative history of the work for hire provisions. To determine whether a work is for hire under the Act, a court first should ascertain, using principles of general common law of agency, whether the work was prepared by an employee or an independent contractor. After making this determination, the court can apply the appropriate subsection of § 101.

B

We turn, finally, to an application of § 101 to Reid's production of "Third World America." In determining whether a hired party is an employee under the general common law of agency, we consider the hiring party's right to control the manner and means by which the product is accomplished. Among the other factors relevant to this inquiry are the skill required; the source of the instrumentalities and tools; the location of the work; the duration of the relationship between the parties; whether the hiring party has the right to assign additional projects to the hired party; the extent of the hired party's discretion over when and how long to work; the method of payment; the hired party's role in hiring and paying assistants; whether the work is part of the regular business of the hiring

---

[i] Petitioners concede that, as a practical matter, it is often difficult to demonstrate the existence of a right to control without evidence of the actual exercise of that right.

party; whether the hiring party is in business; the provision of employee benefits; and the tax treatment of the hired party. See Restatement § 220(2)(setting forth a nonexhaustive list of factors relevant to determining whether a hired party is an employee).[j] No one of these factors is determinative.

Examining the circumstances of this case in light of these factors, we agree with the Court of Appeals that Reid was not an employee of CCNV but an independent contractor. 846 F.2d, at 1494, n.11. True, CCNV members directed enough of Reid's work to ensure that he produced a sculpture that met their specifications. 652 F.Supp., at 1456. But the extent of control the hiring party exercises over the details of the product is not dispositive. Indeed, all the other circumstances weigh heavily against finding an employment relationship. Reid is a sculptor, a skilled occupation. Reid supplied his own tools. He worked in his own studio in Baltimore, making daily supervision of his activities from Washington practicably impossible. Reid was retained for less than two months, a relatively short period of time. During and after this time, CCNV had no right to assign additional projects to Reid. Apart from the deadline for completing the sculpture, Reid had absolute freedom to decide when and how long to work. CCNV paid Reid $15,000, a sum dependent on "completion of a specific job, a method by which independent contractors are often compensated." Holt v. Winpisinger, 811 F.2d 1532, 1540 (1987). Reid had total discretion in hiring and paying assistants. "Creating sculptures was hardly 'regular business' for CCNV." 846 F.2d, at 1494, n.11. Indeed, CCNV is not a business at all. Finally, CCNV did not pay payroll or Social Security taxes, provide any employee benefits, or contribute to unemployment insurance or workers' compensation funds.

Because Reid was an independent contractor, whether "Third World America" is a work for hire depends on whether it satisfies the terms of § 101(2). This petitioners concede it cannot do. Thus, CCNV is not the author of "Third World America" by virtue of the work for hire provisions of the Act. However, as the Court of Appeals made clear, CCNV nevertheless may be a joint author of the sculpture if, on remand, the District Court determines that CCNV and Reid prepared the work "with the intention that their contributions be merged into inseparable or interdependent parts of a unitary whole." § 101.[k] In that case, CCNV and Reid would be co-owners of the copyright in the work. See § 201(a).

For the aforestated reasons, we affirm the judgment of the Court of Appeals for the District of Columbia Circuit.

It is so ordered.

[j] In determining whether a hired party is an employee under the general common law of agency, we have traditionally looked for guidance to the Restatement of Agency.

[k] Neither CCNV nor Reid sought review of the Court of Appeals' remand order. We therefore have no occasion to pass judgment on the applicability of the Act's joint authorship provisions to this case.

"Third World America." Reprinted with the permission of James Earl Reid, sculptor and Community for Creative Non-Violence. Photography by Ron Portee. Print supplied by James Earl Reid and Ron Portee.

AND STILL THERE IS NO ROOM AT THE INN

Childress v. Taylor

United States Court of Appeals, Second Circuit, 1991.
945 F.2d 500.

■ NEWMAN, CIRCUIT JUDGE.

This appeal requires consideration of the standards for determining when a contributor to a copyrighted work is entitled to be regarded as a joint author. The work in question is a play about the legendary Black comedienne Jackie "Moms" Mabley. The plaintiff-appellee Alice Childress claims to be the sole author of the play. Her claim is disputed by defendant-appellant Clarice Taylor, who asserts that she is a joint author of the play. Taylor, Paul B. Berkowsky, Ben Caldwell, and the "Moms" Company appeal from the February 21, 1991, judgment of the District Court for the Southern District of New York (Charles S. Haight, Jr., Judge) determining, on motion for summary judgment, that Childress is the sole author. We affirm.

Facts

Defendant Clarice Taylor has been an actress for over forty years, performing on stage, radio, television, and in film. After portraying

"Moms" Mabley in a skit in an off-off-Broadway production ten years ago, Taylor became interested in developing a play based on Mabley's life. Taylor began to assemble material about "Moms" Mabley, interviewing her friends and family, collecting her jokes, and reviewing library resources.

In 1985, Taylor contacted the plaintiff, playwright Alice Childress, about writing a play based on "Moms" Mabley. Childress had written many plays, for one of which she won an "Obie" award. Taylor had known Childress since the 1940s when they were both associated with the American Negro Theatre in Harlem and had previously acted in a number of Childress's plays.

When Taylor first mentioned the "Moms" Mabley project to Childress in 1985, Childress stated she was not interested in writing the script because she was too occupied with other works. However, when Taylor approached Childress again in 1986, Childress agreed, though she was reluctant due to the time constraints involved. Taylor had interested the Green Plays Theatre in producing the as yet unwritten play, but the theatre had only one slot left on its summer 1986 schedule, and in order to use that slot, the play had to be written in six weeks.

Taylor turned over all of her research material to Childress, and later did further research at Childress's request. It is undisputed that Childress wrote the play, entitled "Moms: A Praise Play for a Black Comedienne." However, Taylor, in addition to providing the research material, which according to her involved a process of sifting through facts and selecting pivotal and key elements to include in a play on "Moms" Mabley's life, also discussed with Childress the inclusion of certain general scenes and characters in the play. Additionally, Childress and Taylor spoke on a regular basis about the progress of the play.

Taylor identifies the following as her major contributions to the play: (1) she learned through interviews that "Moms" Mabley called all of her piano players "Luther," so Taylor suggested that the play include such a character; (2) Taylor and Childress together interviewed Carey Jordan, "Moms" Mabley's housekeeper, and upon leaving the interview they came to the conclusion that she would be a good character for the play, but Taylor could not recall whether she or Childress suggested it; (3) Taylor informed Childress that "Moms" Mabley made a weekly trip to Harlem to do ethnic food shopping; (4) Taylor suggested a street scene in Harlem with speakers because she recalled having seen or listened to such a scene many times; (5) the idea of using a minstrel scene came out of Taylor's research; (6) the idea of a card game scene also came out of Taylor's research, although Taylor could not recall who specifically suggested the scene; (7) some of the jokes used in the play came from Taylor's research; and (8) the characteristics of "Moms" Mabley's personality portrayed in the play emerged from Taylor's research. Essentially, Taylor contributed facts and details about "Moms" Mabley's life and discussed some of them with Childress. However, Childress was responsible for the actual structure of the play and the dialogue.

Childress completed the script within the six-week time frame. Childress filed for and received a copyright for the play in her name. Taylor produced the play at the Green Plays Theatre in Lexington, New York, during the 1986 summer season and played the title role. After the play's run at the Green Plays Theatre, Taylor planned a second production of the play at the Hudson Guild Theatre in New York City.

At the time Childress agreed to the project, she did not have any firm arrangements with Taylor, although Taylor had paid her $2,500 before the play was produced. On May 9, 1986, Taylor's agent, Scott Yoselow, wrote to Childress's agent, Flora Roberts, stating:

> Per our telephone conversation, this letter will bring us up-to-date on the current status of our negotiation for the above mentioned project:
>
> 1) CLARICE TAYLOR will pay ALICE CHILDRESS for her playwriting services on the MOMS MABLEY PROJECT the sum of $5,000.00, which will also serve as an advance against any future royalties.
>
> 2) The finished play shall be equally owned and be the property of both CLARICE TAYLOR and ALICE CHILDRESS. It is my understanding that Alice has commenced writing the project. I am awaiting a response from you regarding any additional points we have yet to discuss.

Flora Roberts responded to Yoselow in a letter dated June 16, 1986:

> As per our recent telephone conversation, I have told Alice Childress that we are using your letter to me of May 9, 1986 as a partial memo preparatory to our future good faith negotiations for a contract. There are two points which I include herewith to complete your two points in the May 9th letter, i.e.:
>
> 1) The $5,000 advance against any future royalties being paid by Clarice Taylor to Alice Childress shall be paid as follows. Since $1,000 has already been paid, $1,500 upon your receipt of this letter and the final $2,500 to be paid upon submission of the First Draft, but in no event later than July 7, 1986.
>
> 2) It is to be understood that pending the proper warranty clauses to be included in the contract, Miss Childress is claiming originality for her words only in said script.

After the Green Plays Theatre production, Taylor and Childress attempted to formalize their relationship. Draft contracts were exchanged between Taylor's attorney, Jay Kramer, and Childress's agent, Roberts. During this period, early 1987, the play was produced at the Hudson Guild Theatre with the consent of both Taylor and Childress. Childress filed for and received a copyright for the new material added to the play produced at the Hudson Guild Theatre.

In March 1987, Childress rejected the draft agreement proposed by Taylor,[a] and the parties' relationship deteriorated. Taylor decided to mount

---

[a] The preamble to this draft agreement stated:

The Producer [Taylor] wishes to acquire from the Author [Childress] the rights to produce and present a dramatic play written by Author and heretofore presented at the Hudson Guild Theatre

another production of the play without Childress. Taylor hired Ben Caldwell to write another play featuring "Moms" Mabley; Taylor gave Caldwell a copy of the Childress script and advised him of elements that should be changed.

The "Moms" Mabley play that Caldwell wrote was produced at the Astor Place Theatre in August 1987.[b] No reference to Childress was made with respect to this production. However, a casting notice in the trade paper "Back Stage" reported the production of Caldwell's play and noted that it had been "presented earlier this season under an Equity LOA at the Hudson Guild Theatre."

Flora Roberts contacted Jay Kramer to determine whether this notice was correct. Kramer responded:

> Ben Caldwell has written the play which I will furnish to you when a final draft is available. We have tried in every way to distinguish the new version of the play from what was presented at the Hudson Guild, both by way of content and billing.
>
> Undoubtedly, because of the prevalence of public domain material in both versions of the play, there may be unavoidable similarities. Please also remember that Alice was paid by Clarice for rights to her material which we have never resolved.

Kramer never sent a copy of Caldwell's play. Childress's attorney, Alvin Deutsch, sent Kramer a letter advising him of Childress's rights in the play as produced at the Hudson Guild and of her concerns about the advertising connecting Caldwell's play to hers. For example, one advertisement for Caldwell's play at the Astor Place Theatre quoted reviews referring to Childress's play. Other advertisements made reference to the fact that the play had been performed earlier that season at the Hudson Guild Theatre.

Childress sued Taylor and other defendants alleging violations of the Copyright Act. Taylor contended that she was a joint author with Childress, and therefore shared the rights to the play. Childress moved for summary judgment, which the District Court granted. The Court concluded that Taylor was not a joint author of Childress's play and that Caldwell's play was substantially similar to and infringed Childress's play. In rejecting Taylor's claim of joint authorship, Judge Haight ruled (a) that a work qualifies as a "joint work" under the definition section of the Copyright Act, § 101, only when *both* authors intended, at the time the work was created, "that their contributions be merged into inseparable or interdependent parts of a unitary whole," *id.*, and (b) that there was insufficient evidence to permit a reasonable trier to find that Childress had the requisite intent. The Court further ruled that copyright law requires the contributions of both authors to be independently copyrightable, and that Taylor's contributions, which consisted of ideas and research, were not copyrightable.

based on the life and career of Moms Mabley....

[b] The Caldwell play was billed as being "based on a concept by Clarice Taylor." Taylor was not listed as an author of that play.

Discussion

In common with many issues arising in the domain of copyrights, the determination of whether to recognize joint authorship in a particular case requires a sensitive accommodation of competing demands advanced by at least two persons, both of whom have normally contributed in some way to the creation of a work of value. Care must be taken to ensure that true collaborators in the creative process are accorded the perquisites of co-authorship and to guard against the risk that a sole author is denied exclusive authorship status simply because another person rendered some form of assistance. Copyright law best serves the interests of creativity when it carefully draws the bounds of "joint authorship" so as to protect the legitimate claims of both sole authors and co-authors.

Co-authorship was well known to the common law. An early formulation, thought by Learned Hand to be the first definition of "joint authorship," see Edward B. Marks Music Corp. v. Jerry Vogel Music Co., 140 F.2d 266, 267 (2d Cir.1944)("Marks"), is set out in Levy v. Rutley, L.R., 6 C.P. 523, 529 (Keating, J.)(1871): "a joint laboring in furtherance of a common design." Three decades later, he adopted the formulation of this Circuit in *Marks,* determining that the words and music of a song ("December and May") formed a work of joint authorship even though the lyricist wrote the words before he knew the identity of the composer who would later write the music.

Though the early case law is illuminating, our task is to apply the standards of the Copyright Act of 1976 and endeavor to achieve the results that Congress likely intended.

The Copyright Act defines a "joint work" as:

> a work prepared by two or more authors with the intention that their contributions be merged into inseparable or interdependent parts of a unitary whole.

§ 101. The definition concerns the *creation* of the work by the joint authors, not the circumstances, in addition to joint authorship, under which a work may be *jointly owned,* for example, by assignment of an undivided interest. The distinction affects the rights that are acquired. Joint authors hold undivided interests in a work, like all joint owners of a work, but joint authors, unlike other joint owners, also enjoy all the rights of authorship, including the renewal rights applicable to works in which a statutory copyright subsisted prior to January 1, 1978. See § 304.

Some aspects of the statutory definition of joint authorship are fairly straightforward. Parts of a unitary whole are "inseparable" when they have little or no independent meaning standing alone. That would often be true of a work of written text, such as the play that is the subject of the pending litigation. By contrast, parts of a unitary whole are "interdependent" when they have some meaning standing alone but achieve their primary significance because of their combined effect, as in the case of the words and music of a song. Indeed, a novel and a song are among the examples offered by the legislative committee reports on the 1976 Copyright Act to illustrate the difference between "inseparable" and "interdependent" parts. See H.R. Rep. No. 1476, 94th Cong., 2d Sess. 120 (1976)("House Report"), reprinted in 1976 U.S.C.C.A.N. 5659, 5736; S. Rep. No. 473, 94th Cong., 2d Sess. 103–04 (1975)("Senate Report").

The legislative history also clarifies other aspects of the statutory definition, but leaves some matters in doubt. Endeavoring to flesh out the definition, the committee reports state:

> [A] work is "joint" if the authors collaborated with each other, or if *each* of the authors prepared his or her contribution with the knowledge and *intention* that it would be merged with the contributions of other authors as "inseparable or interdependent parts of a unitary whole." The touchstone here is the *intention, at the time the writing is done*, that the parts be absorbed or combined into an integrated unit. . . .

House Report at 120; Senate Report at 103 (emphasis added). This passage appears to state two alternative criteria—one focusing on the act of collaboration and the other on the parties' intent. However, it is hard to imagine activity that would constitute meaningful "collaboration" unaccompanied by the requisite intent on the part of both participants that their contributions be merged into a unitary whole, and the case law has read the statutory language literally so that the intent requirement applies to all works of joint authorship. See, e.g., Weissmann v. Freeman, 868 F.2d 1313, 1317–19 (2d Cir.1989); Eckert v. Hurley Chicago Co., Inc., 638 F.Supp. 699, 702–03 (N.D.Ill.1986).

A more substantial issue arising under the statutory definition of "joint work" is whether the contribution of each joint author must be copyrightable or only the combined result of their joint efforts must be copyrightable. The Nimmer treatise argues against a requirement of copyrightability of each author's contribution, see 1 Nimmer on Copyright § 6.07; Professor Goldstein takes the contrary view, see 1 Paul Goldstein, Copyright: Principles, Law and Practice § 4.2.1.2 (1989), with the apparent agreement of the Latman treatise, see William F. Patry, Latman's The Copyright Law 116 (6th ed. 1986)(hereinafter "Latman"). The case law supports a requirement of copyrightability of each contribution. [Citations omitted.] The Register of Copyrights strongly supports this view, arguing that it is required by the statutory standard of "authorship" and perhaps by the Constitution. See Moral Rights in Our Copyright Laws: Hearings on S. 1198 and S. 1253 Before the Subcomm. on Patents, Copyrights and Trademarks of the Senate Comm. on the Judiciary, 101st Cong., 1st Sess. 210–11 (1989)(statement of Ralph Oman).

The issue, apparently open in this Circuit, is troublesome. If the focus is solely on the objective of copyright law to encourage the production of creative works, it is difficult to see why the contributions of all joint authors need be copyrightable. An individual creates a copyrightable work by combining a non-copyrightable idea with a copyrightable form of expression; the resulting work is no less a valuable result of the creative process simply because the idea and the expression came from two different individuals. Indeed, it is not unimaginable that there exists a skilled writer who might never have produced a significant work until some other person supplied the idea. The textual argument from the statute is not convincing. The Act surely does not say that each contribution to a joint work must be copyrightable, and the specification that there be "authors" does not necessarily require a copyrightable contribution. "Author" is not defined in the Act and appears to be used only in its ordinary sense of an originator. The "author" of an uncopyrightable idea is nonetheless its author even though, for entirely valid reasons, the law properly denies him a copyright on the result of his creativity. And the Register's tentative constitutional argument seems questionable. It has not been supposed that the statutory grant of "authorship" status to the employer of a work made for hire exceeds the Constitution, though the employer has shown skill only in selecting employees, not in creating protectable expression.[c]

Nevertheless, we are persuaded to side with the position taken by the case law and endorsed by the agency administering the Copyright Act. The insistence on copyrightable contributions by all putative joint authors might serve to prevent some spurious claims by those who might otherwise try to share the fruits of the efforts of a sole author of a copyrightable work. More important, the prevailing view strikes an appropriate balance in the domains of both copyright and contract law. In the absence of contract, the copyright remains with the one or more persons who created copyrightable material. Contract law enables a person to hire another to create a copyrightable work, and the copyright law will recognize the employer as "author." § 201(b). Similarly, the person with non-copyrightable material who proposes to join forces with a skilled writer to produce a copyrightable work is free to make a contract to disclose his or her material in return for assignment of part ownership of the resulting copyright. *Id.* § 201(d). And, as with all contract matters, the parties may minimize subsequent disputes by formalizing their agreement in a written contract. It seems more consistent with the spirit of copyright law to oblige all joint authors to make copyrightable contributions, leaving those with non-copyrightable contributions to protect their rights through contract.

There remains for consideration the crucial aspect of joint authorship—the nature of the intent that must be entertained by each putative joint author at the time the contribution of each was created. The wording of the statutory definition appears to make relevant only the state of mind

[c] Judge Friendly has suggested that the concept of authorship in the constitutional grant implies some limitations. "It would thus be quite doubtful that Congress could grant employers the exclusive right to the writings of employees regardless of the circumstances." Scherr v. Universal Match Corp., 417 F.2d 497, 502 (2d Cir.1969) (Friendly, J., dissenting), *cert. denied*, 397 U.S. 936 (1970). He suggested that the "work for hire" doctrine, whether applied to employees or independent contractors (commissioned works) squares with the constitutional concept because vesting rights of authorship in the employer is what the parties "contemplated at the time of the contracting, or at least what they probably would have contemplated if they had thought about it." *Id.* However, this seems more like a justification for transfer of ownership than for recognition of authorship. Though the United States is perhaps the only country that confers "authorship" status on the employer of the creator of a work made for hire, see Latman at 114 n.2, its decision to do so is not constitutionally suspect.

regarding the unitary nature of the finished work—an intention "that their contributions be merged into inseparable or interdependent parts of a unitary whole." However, an inquiry so limited would extend joint author status to many persons who are not likely to have been within the contemplation of Congress. For example, a writer frequently works with an editor who makes numerous useful revisions to the first draft, some of which will consist of additions of copyrightable expression. Both intend their contributions to be merged into inseparable parts of a unitary whole, yet very few editors and even fewer writers would expect the editor to be accorded the status of joint author, enjoying an undivided half interest in the copyright in the published work. Similarly, research assistants may on occasion contribute to an author some protectable expression or merely a sufficiently original selection of factual material as would be entitled to a copyright, yet not be entitled to be regarded as a joint author of the work in which the contributed material appears. What distinguishes the writer-editor relationship and the writer-researcher relationship from the true joint author relationship is the lack of intent of both participants in the venture to regard themselves as joint authors.[d]

Focusing on whether the putative joint authors regarded themselves as joint authors is especially important in circumstances, such as the instant case, where one person (Childress) is indisputably the dominant author of the work and the only issue is whether that person is the sole author or she and another (Taylor) are joint authors. This concern requires less exacting consideration in the context of traditional forms of collaboration, such as between the creators of the words and music of a song.

In this case, appellant contends that Judge Haight's observation that "Childress never shared Taylor's notion that they were co-authors of the play" misapplies the statutory standard by focusing on whether Childress "intended the legal consequences which flowed from her prior acts." We do not think Judge Haight went so far. He did not inquire whether Childress intended that she and Taylor would hold equal undivided interests in the play. But he properly insisted that they entertain in their minds the concept of joint authorship, whether or not they understood precisely the legal consequences of that relationship. Though joint authorship does not require an understanding by the co-authors of the legal consequences of their relationship, obviously some distinguishing characteristic of the relationship must be understood in order for it to be the subject of their intent. In many instances, a useful test will be whether, in the absence of contractual agreements concerning listed authorship, each participant intended that all would be identified as co-authors. Though "billing" or "credit" is not decisive in all cases and joint authorship can exist without

[d] In some situations, the editor or researcher will be the employee of the primary author, in which event the copyright in the contributions of the editor or researcher would belong to the author, under the "work made for hire" doctrine. But in many situations the editor or researcher will be an independent contractor or an employee of some person or entity other than the primary author, in which event a claim of joint authorship would not be defeated by the "work made for hire" doctrine.

any explicit discussion of this topic by the parties,[e] consideration of the topic helpfully serves to focus the fact-finder's attention on how the parties implicitly regarded their undertaking.

An inquiry into how the putative joint authors regarded themselves in relation to the work has previously been part of our approach in ascertaining the existence of joint authorship. In Gilliam v. American Broadcasting Companies, Inc., 538 F.2d 14 (2d Cir.1976), we examined the parties' written agreements and noted that their provisions indicated "that the parties *did not consider themselves joint authors* of a single work." *Id.* at 22 (emphasis added). This same thought is evident in Judge Leval's observation that "[i]t is only where the dominant author *intends to be sharing authorship* that joint authorship will result." Fisher v. Klein, 16 U.S.P.Q.2d (BNA) 1795 at 1798 (S.D.N.Y.1990)(emphasis added). See also Weissmann v. Freeman, 868 F.2d at 1318 (each of those claiming to be joint authors "must intend to contribute to a joint work."). Judge Haight was entirely correct to inquire whether Childress ever shared Taylor's "notion that they were co-authors of the Play."

Examination of whether the putative co-authors ever shared an intent to be co-authors serves the valuable purpose of appropriately confining the bounds of joint authorship arising by operation of copyright law, while leaving those not in a true joint authorship relationship with an author free to bargain for an arrangement that will be recognized as a matter of both copyright and contract law. Joint authorship entitles the co-authors to equal undivided interests in the work, see § 201(a). That equal sharing of rights should be reserved for relationships in which all participants fully intend to be joint authors. The sharing of benefits in other relationships involving assistance in the creation of a copyrightable work can be more precisely calibrated by the participants in their contract negotiations regarding division of royalties or assignment of shares of ownership of the copyright, see § 201(d).

In this case, the issue is not only whether Judge Haight applied the correct standard for determining joint authorship but also whether he was entitled to conclude that the record warranted a summary judgment in favor of Childress. We are satisfied that Judge Haight was correct as to both issues. We need not determine whether we agree with his conclusion that Taylor's contributions were not independently copyrightable since, even if they were protectable as expression or as an original selection of facts, we agree that there is no evidence from which a trier could infer that Childress had the state of mind required for joint authorship. As Judge Haight observed, whatever thought of co-authorship might have existed in Taylor's mind "was emphatically not shared by the purported co-author." There is no evidence that Childress ever contemplated, much less would

---

[e] Obviously, consideration of whether the parties contemplated listed co-authorship (or would have accepted such billing had they though about it) is not a helpful inquiry for works written by an uncredited "ghost writer," either as a sole author, as a joint author, or as an employee preparing a work for hire.

have accepted, crediting the play as "written by Alice Childress and Clarice Taylor."

Childress was asked to write a play about "Moms" Mabley and did so. To facilitate her writing task she accepted the assistance that Taylor provided, which consisted largely of furnishing the results of research concerning the life of "Moms" Mabley. As the actress expected to portray the leading role, Taylor also made some incidental suggestions, contributing ideas about the presentation of the play's subject and possibly some minor bits of expression. But there is no evidence that these aspects of Taylor's role ever evolved into more than the helpful advice that might come from the cast, the directors, or the producers of any play. A playwright does not so easily acquire a co-author.

Judge Haight was fully entitled to bolster his decision by reliance on the contract negotiations that followed completion of the script. Though his primary basis for summary judgment was the absence of any evidence supporting an inference that Childress shared "Taylor's notion that they were co-authors," he properly pointed to the emphatic rejection by Childress of the attempts by Taylor's agent to negotiate a co-ownership agreement and Taylor's acquiescence in that rejection. Intent "at the time the writing is done" remains the "touchstone," House Report at 120; Senate Report at 103, but subsequent conduct is normally probative of a prior state of mind.

Taylor's claim of co-authorship was properly rejected, and with the rejection of that claim, summary judgment for Childress was properly entered. The judgment of the District Court is affirmed.

Stewart v. Abend

Supreme Court of the United States, 1990.
495 U.S. 207, 110 S.Ct. 1750, 109 L.Ed.2d 184.

■ JUSTICE O'CONNOR delivered the opinion of the Court.

The author of a pre-existing work may assign to another the right to use it in a derivative work. In this case the author of a pre-existing work agreed to assign the rights in his renewal copyright term to the owner of a derivative work, but died before the commencement of the renewal period. The question presented is whether the owner of the derivative work infringed the rights of the successor owner of the pre-existing work by continued distribution and publication of the derivative work during the renewal term of the pre-existing work.

I

Cornell Woolrich authored the story "It Had to Be Murder," which was first published in February 1942 in Dime Detective Magazine. The magazine's publisher, Popular Publications, Inc., obtained the rights to magazine publication of the story and Woolrich retained all other rights. Popular

Publications obtained a blanket copyright for the issue of Dime Detective Magazine in which "It Had to Be Murder" was published.

The Copyright Act of 1909 (1909 Act) provided authors a 28–year initial term of copyright protection plus a 28–year renewal term. In 1945, Woolrich agreed to assign the rights to make motion picture versions of six of his stories, including "It Had to Be Murder," to B. G. DeSylva Productions for $9,250. He also agreed to renew the copyrights in the stories at the appropriate time and to assign the same motion picture rights to DeSylva Productions for the 28–year renewal term. In 1953, actor Jimmy Stewart and director Alfred Hitchcock formed a production company, Patron, Inc., which obtained the motion picture rights in "It Had to Be Murder" from DeSylva's successors in interest for $10,000.

In 1954, Patron, Inc., along with Paramount Pictures, produced and distributed "Rear Window," the motion picture version of Woolrich's story "It Had to Be Murder." Woolrich died in 1968 before he could obtain the rights in the renewal term for petitioners as promised and without a surviving spouse or child. He left his property to a trust administered by his executor, Chase Manhattan Bank, for the benefit of Columbia University. On December 29, 1969, Chase Manhattan Bank renewed the copyright in the "It Had to Be Murder" story. Chase Manhattan assigned the renewal rights to respondent Abend for $650 plus 10% of all proceeds from exploitation of the story.

"Rear Window" was broadcast on the ABC television network in 1971. Respondent then notified petitioners Hitchcock (now represented by cotrustees of his will), Stewart, and MCA Inc., the owners of the "Rear Window" motion picture and renewal rights in the motion picture, that he owned the renewal rights in the copyright and that their distribution of the motion picture without his permission infringed his copyright in the story. Hitchcock, Stewart, and MCA nonetheless entered into a second license with ABC to rebroadcast the motion picture. In 1974, respondent filed suit against these same petitioners, and others, in the United States District Court for the Southern District of New York, alleging copyright infringement. Respondent dismissed his complaint in return for $25,000.

Three years later, the United States Court of Appeals for the Second Circuit decided Rohauer v. Killiam Shows, Inc., 551 F.2d 484, *cert. denied*, 431 U.S. 949 (1977), in which it held that the owner of the copyright in a derivative work may continue to use the existing derivative work according to the original grant from the author of the pre-existing work even if the grant of rights in the pre-existing work lapsed. 551 F.2d, at 494. Several years later, apparently in reliance on *Rohauer*, petitioners re-released the motion picture in a variety of media, including new 35 and 16 millimeter prints for theatrical exhibition in the United States, videocassettes, and videodiscs. They also publicly exhibited the motion picture in theaters, over cable television, and through videodisc and videocassette rentals and sales.

Respondent then brought the instant suit in the United States District Court for the Central District of California against Hitchcock, Stewart, MCA, and Universal Film Exchanges, a subsidiary of MCA and the distributor of the motion picture. Respondent's complaint alleges that the release of the motion picture infringes his copyright in the story because petitioners' right to use the story during the renewal term lapsed when Woolrich died before he could register for the renewal term and transfer his renewal rights to them. Respondent also contends that petitioners have interfered with his rights in the renewal term of the story in other ways. He alleges that he sought to contract with Home Box Office (HBO) to produce a play and television version of the story, but that petitioners wrote to him and HBO stating that neither he nor HBO could use either the title, "Rear Window" or "It Had to Be Murder." Respondent also alleges that petitioners further interfered with the renewal copyright in the story by attempting to sell the right to make a television sequel and that the re-release of the original motion picture itself interfered with his ability to produce other derivative works.

Petitioners filed motions for summary judgment based on the decision in *Rohauer*. Respondent moved for summary judgment on the ground that petitioners' use of the motion picture constituted copyright infringement. The District Court granted petitioners' motions for summary judgment based on *Rohauer*. Respondent appealed to the United States Court of Appeals for the Ninth Circuit.

The Court of Appeals reversed. 863 F.2d 1465 (1988). The issue before the court was whether petitioners were entitled to distribute and exhibit the motion picture without respondent's permission despite respondent's valid copyright in the pre-existing story. Relying on the renewal provision of the 1909 Act, § 24 (1976 ed.), respondent argued before the Court of Appeals that because he obtained from Chase Manhattan Bank, the statutory successor, the renewal right free and clear of any purported assignments of any interest in the renewal copyright, petitioners' distribution and publication of "Rear Window" without authorization infringed his renewal copyright. Petitioners responded that they had the right to continue to exploit "Rear Window" during the 28–year renewal period because Woolrich had agreed to assign to petitioners' predecessor in interest the motion picture rights in the story for the renewal period.

Petitioners also relied, as did the District Court, on the decision in Rohauer v. Killiam Shows, Inc., *supra*. In *Rohauer*, the Court of Appeals for the Second Circuit held that statutory successors to the renewal copyright in a pre-existing work under § 24 could not "depriv[e] the proprietor of the derivative copyright of a right ... to use so much of the underlying copyrighted work as already has been embodied in the copyrighted derivative work, as a matter of copyright law." *Id.* at 492. The Court of Appeals in the instant case rejected this reasoning, concluding that even if the pre-existing work had been incorporated into a derivative work, use of the pre-existing work was infringing unless the owner of the derivative work held a valid grant of rights in the renewal term.

The court relied on Miller Music Corp. v. Charles N. Daniels, Inc., 362 U.S. 373 (1960), in which we held that assignment of renewal rights by an author before the time for renewal arrives cannot defeat the right of the author's statutory successor to the renewal rights if the author dies before the right to renewal accrues. An assignee of the renewal rights takes only an expectancy. The Court of Appeals reasoned that "[i]f *Miller Music* makes assignment of the full renewal rights in the underlying copyright unenforceable when the author dies before effecting renewal of the copyright, then a fortiori, an assignment of part of the rights in the underlying work, the right to produce a movie version, must also be unenforceable if the author dies before effecting renewal of the underlying copyright." 863 F.2d, at 1476. Finding further support in the legislative history of the 1909 Act and rejecting the *Rohauer* court's reliance on the equities and the termination provisions of the 1976 Act, §§ 203(b)(1), 304(c)(6)(A)(1988 ed.), the Court of Appeals concluded that petitioners received from Woolrich only an expectancy in the renewal rights that never matured; upon Woolrich's death, Woolrich's statutory successor, Chase Manhattan Bank, became "entitled to a renewal and extension of the copyright," which Chase Manhattan secured "within one year prior to the expiration of the original term of copyright." § 24 (1976 ed.). Chase Manhattan then assigned the existing rights in the copyright to respondent.

We granted certiorari to resolve the conflict between the decision in *Rohauer, supra,* and the decision below. 493 U.S. 807 (1989).

II

A

Petitioners would have us read into the Copyright Act a limitation on the statutorily created rights of the owner of an underlying work. They argue in essence that the rights of the owner of the copyright in the derivative use of the pre-existing work are extinguished once it is incorporated into the derivative work, assuming the author of the pre-existing work has agreed to assign his renewal rights. Because we find no support for such a curtailment of rights in either the 1909 Act or the 1976 Act, or in the legislative history of either, we affirm the judgment of the Court of Appeals.

Petitioners and amicus Register of Copyrights assert, as the Court of Appeals assumed, that § 23 of the 1909 Act, § 24 (1976 ed.), and the case law interpreting that provision, directly control the disposition of this case. Respondent counters that the provisions of the 1976 Act control, but that the 1976 Act re-enacted § 24 in § 304 and, therefore, the language and judicial interpretation of § 24 are relevant to our consideration of this case. Under either theory, we must look to the language of and case law interpreting § 24.

The right of renewal found in § 24 provides authors a second opportunity to obtain remuneration for their works. Section 24 provides:

> "[T]he author of [a copyrighted] work, if still living, or the widow, widower, or children of the author, if the author be not living, or if such author, widow, widower, or children be not living, then the author's executors, or in the absence of a will, his next of kin shall be entitled to a renewal and extension of the copyright in such work for a further term of

twenty-eight years when application for such renewal and extension shall have been made to the copyright office and duly registered therein within one year prior to the expiration of the original term of copyright." § 24 (1976 ed.).

Since the earliest copyright statute in this country, the copyright term of ownership has been split between an original term and a renewal term. Originally, the renewal was intended merely to serve as an extension of the original term; at the end of the original term, the renewal could be effected and claimed by the author, if living, or by the author's executors, administrators, or assigns. In 1831, Congress altered the provision so that the author could assign his contingent interest in the renewal term, but could not, through his assignment, divest the rights of his widow or children in the renewal term. "The evident purpose of [the renewal provision] is to provide for the family of the author after his death. Since the author cannot assign his family's renewal rights, [it] takes the form of a compulsory bequest of the copyright to the designated persons." DeSylva v. Ballentine, 351 U.S. 570, 582 (1956).

In its debates leading up to the Copyright Act of 1909, Congress elaborated upon the policy underlying a system comprised of an original term and a completely separate renewal term. The renewal term permits the author, originally in a poor bargaining position, to renegotiate the terms of the grant once the value of the work has been tested. With these purposes in mind, Congress enacted the renewal provision of the Copyright Act of 1909, § 24 (1976 ed.). With respect to works in their original or renewal term as of January 1, 1978, Congress retained the two-term system of copyright protection in the 1976 Act. See §§ 304(a) and (b)(1988 ed.) (incorporating language of § 24 (1976 ed.)).

Applying these principles in Miller Music Corp. v. Charles N. Daniels, Inc., 362 U.S. 373 (1960), this Court held that when an author dies before the renewal period arrives, his executor is entitled to the renewal rights, even though the author previously assigned his renewal rights to another party. Thus, the renewal provisions were intended to give the author a second chance to obtain fair remuneration for his creative efforts and to provide the author's family a "new estate" if the author died before the renewal period arrived.

An author holds a bundle of exclusive rights in the copyrighted work, among them the right to copy and the right to incorporate the work into derivative works. By assigning the renewal copyright in the work without limitation, as in *Miller Music*, the author assigns all of these rights. After *Miller Music*, if the author dies before the commencement of the renewal period, the assignee holds nothing. If the assignee of all of the renewal rights holds nothing upon the death of the assignor before arrival of the renewal period, then, a fortiori, the assignee of a portion of the renewal rights, e.g., the right to produce a derivative work, must also hold nothing. Therefore, if the author dies before the renewal period, then the assignee may continue to use the original work only if the author's successor transfers the renewal rights to the assignee. This is the rule adopted by the

Court of Appeals below and advocated by the Register of Copyrights. Application of this rule to this case should end the inquiry. Woolrich died before the commencement of the renewal period in the story, and, therefore, petitioners hold only an unfulfilled expectancy. Petitioners have been "deprived of nothing. Like all purchasers of contingent interests, [they took] subject to the possibility that the contingency may not occur." *Miller Music, supra*, at 378.

B

The reason that our inquiry does not end here, and that we granted certiorari, is that the Court of Appeals for the Second Circuit reached a contrary result in Rohauer v. Killiam Shows, Inc., 551 F.2d 484 (1977). Petitioners' theory is drawn largely from *Rohauer*. The Court of Appeals in *Rohauer* attempted to craft a "proper reconciliation" between the owner of the pre-existing work, who held the right to the work pursuant to *Miller Music*, and the owner of the derivative work, who had a great deal to lose if the work could not be published or distributed. 551 F.2d, at 490. Addressing a case factually similar to this case, the court concluded that even if the death of the author caused the renewal rights in the pre-existing work to revert to the statutory successor, the owner of the derivative work could continue to exploit that work. The court reasoned that the 1976 Act and the relevant precedents did not preclude such a result and that it was necessitated by a balancing of the equities:

> "[T]he equities lie preponderantly in favor of the proprietor of the derivative copyright. In contrast to the situation where an assignee or licensee has done nothing more than print, publicize and distribute a copyrighted story or novel, a person who with the consent of the author has created an opera or a motion picture film will often have made contributions literary, musical and economic, as great as or greater than the original author.... [T]he purchaser of derivative rights has no truly effective way to protect himself against the eventuality of the author's death before the renewal period since there is no way of telling who will be the surviving widow, children or next of kin or the executor until that date arrives." *Id.* at 493.

The Court of Appeals for the Second Circuit thereby shifted the focus from the right to use the pre-existing work in a derivative work to a right inhering in the created derivative work itself. By rendering the renewal right to use the original work irrelevant, the court created an exception to our ruling in *Miller Music* and, as petitioners concede, created an "intrusion" on the statutorily created rights of the owner of the pre-existing work in the renewal term.

Though petitioners do not, indeed could not, argue that its language expressly supports the theory they draw from *Rohauer*, they implicitly rely on § 6 of the 1909 Act, § 7 (1976 ed.), which states that "dramatizations ... of copyrighted works when produced with the consent of the proprietor of the copyright in such works ... shall be regarded as new works subject to copyright under the provisions of this title." Petitioners maintain that the creation of the "new," i.e., derivative, work extinguishes any right the owner of rights in the pre-existing work might have had to sue for infringement that occurs during the renewal term.

We think that ... aspects of a derivative work added by the derivative author are that author's property, but the element drawn from the pre-existing work remains on grant from the owner of the pre-existing work. So long as the pre-existing work remains out of the public domain, its use is infringing if one who employs the work does not have a valid license or assignment for use of the pre-existing work. It is irrelevant whether the pre-existing work is inseparably intertwined with the derivative work. Indeed, the plain language of § 7 supports the view that the full force of the copyright in the pre-existing work is preserved despite incorporation into the derivative work. See § 7 (1976 ed.) (publication of the derivative work "shall not affect the force or validity of any subsisting copyright upon the matter employed"). This well-settled rule also was made explicit in the 1976 Act:

> "The copyright in a compilation or derivative work extends only to the material contributed by the author of such work, as distinguished from the pre-existing material employed in the work, and does not imply any exclusive right in the pre-existing material. The copyright in such work is independent of, and does not affect or enlarge the scope, duration, ownership, or subsistence of, any copyright protection in the pre-existing material." § 103(b)(1988 ed.).

Properly conceding there is no explicit support for their theory in the 1909 Act, its legislative history, or the case law, petitioners contend, as did the court in *Rohauer*, that the termination provisions of the 1976 Act, while not controlling, support their theory of the case. For works existing in their original or renewal terms as of January 1, 1978, the 1976 Act added 19 years to the 1909 Act's provision of 28 years of initial copyright protection and 28 years of renewal protection. See §§ 304(a) and (b)(1988 ed.). For those works, the author has the power to terminate the grant of rights at the end of the renewal term and, therefore, to gain the benefit of that additional 19 years of protection. See § 304(c). In effect, the 1976 Act provides a third opportunity for the author to benefit from a work in its original or renewal term as of January 1, 1978. Congress, however, created one exception to the author's right to terminate: The author may not, at the end of the renewal term, terminate the right to use a derivative work for which the owner of the derivative work has held valid rights in the original and renewal terms. See § 304(c)(6)(A). The author, however, may terminate the right to create new derivative works. *Ibid.* For example, if petitioners held a valid copyright in the story throughout the original and renewal terms, and the renewal term in "Rear Window" were about to expire, petitioners could continue to distribute the motion picture even if respondent terminated the grant of rights, but could not create a new motion picture version of the story. Both the court in *Rohauer* and petitioners infer from this exception to the right to terminate an intent by Congress to prevent authors of pre-existing works from blocking distribution of derivative works. In other words, because Congress decided not to permit authors to exercise a third opportunity to benefit from a work incorporated into a derivative work, the Act expresses a general policy of undermining the author's second opportunity. We disagree.

The process of compromise between competing special interests leading to the enactment of the 1976 Act undermines any such attempt to draw an overarching policy out of § 304(c)(6)(A), which only prevents termination with respect to works in their original or renewal copyright terms as of January 1, 1978, and only at the end of the renewal period.

In fact, if the 1976 Act's termination provisions provide any guidance at all in this case, they tilt against petitioners' theory. The plain language of the termination provision itself indicates that Congress assumed that the owner of the pre-existing work possessed the right to sue for infringement even after incorporation of the pre-existing work in the derivative work.

> "A derivative work *prepared* under authority of the grant before its termination may continue to be utilized under the terms of the grant after its termination, but this privilege does not extend to the preparation after the termination of other derivative works based upon the copyrighted work covered by the terminated grant." § 304(c)(6)(A)(emphasis added).

Congress would not have stated explicitly in § 304(c)(6)(A) that, at the end of the renewal term, the owner of the rights in the pre-existing work may not terminate use rights in existing derivative works unless Congress had assumed that the owner continued to hold the right to sue for infringement even after incorporation of the pre-existing work into the derivative work. Cf. Mills Music, Inc. v. Snyder, 469 U.S. 153, 164 (1985) (§ 304(c)(6)(A) "carves out an exception from the reversion of rights that takes place when an author exercises his right to termination").

Accordingly, we conclude that neither the 1909 Act nor the 1976 Act provides support for the theory set forth in *Rohauer*. And even if the theory found some support in the statute or the legislative history, the approach set forth in *Rohauer* is problematic. While the result in *Rohauer* might make some sense in some contexts, it makes no sense in others. In the case of a condensed book, for example, the contribution by the derivative author may be little, while the contribution by the original author is great. Yet, under the *Rohauer* "rule," publication of the condensed book would not infringe the pre-existing work even though the derivative author has no license or valid grant of rights in the pre-existing work. Thus, even if the *Rohauer* "rule" made sense in terms of policy in that case, it makes little sense when it is applied across the derivative works spectrum.

Finally, petitioners urge us to consider the policies underlying the Copyright Act. They argue that the rule announced by the Court of Appeals will undermine one of the policies of the Act—the dissemination of creative works—by leading to many fewer works reaching the public. These arguments are better addressed by Congress than the courts.

In any event, the complaint that respondent's monetary request in this case is so high as to preclude agreement fails to acknowledge that an initially high asking price does not preclude bargaining. Presumably, respondent is asking for a share in the proceeds because he wants to profit from the distribution of the work, not because he seeks suppression of it.

Moreover, although dissemination of creative works is a goal of the Copyright Act, the Act creates a balance between the artist's right to control the work during the term of the copyright protection and the public's need for access to creative works. The copyright term is limited so that the public will not be permanently deprived of the fruits of an artist's labors. But nothing in the copyright statutes would prevent an author from hoarding all of his works during the term of the copyright. In fact, this Court has held that a copyright owner has the capacity arbitrarily to refuse to license one who seeks to exploit the work. See Fox Film Corp. v. Doyal, 286 U.S. 123, 127 (1932).

The limited monopoly granted to the artist is intended to provide the necessary bargaining capital to garner a fair price for the value of the works passing into public use. When an author produces a work which later commands a higher price in the market than the original bargain provided, the copyright statute is designed to provide the author the power to negotiate for the realized value of the work. That is how the separate renewal term was intended to operate. At heart, petitioners' true complaint is that they will have to pay more for the use of works they have employed in creating their own works. But such a result was contemplated by Congress and is consistent with the goals of the Copyright Act.

With the Copyright Act of 1790, Congress provided an initial term of protection plus a renewal term that did not survive the author. In the Copyright Act of 1831, Congress devised a completely separate renewal term that survived the death of the author so as to create a "new estate" and to benefit the author's family, and, with the passage of the 1909 Act, his executors. The 1976 Copyright Act provides a single, fixed term, but provides an inalienable termination right. See §§ 203, 302. This evolution of the duration of copyright protection tellingly illustrates the difficulties Congress faces in attempting to "secur[e] for limited Times to Authors ... the exclusive Right to their respective Writings." U.S. Const., Art. I, § 8, cl.8. Absent an explicit statement of congressional intent that the rights in the renewal term of an owner of a pre-existing work are extinguished upon incorporation of his work into another work, it is not our role to alter the delicate balance Congress has labored to achieve.

[Affirmed.]

Excerpts From Kwall, Copyright and the Moral Right: Is an American Marriage Possible?

38 Vanderbilt L. Rev. 1 (1985).

* * *

III.   The Copyright—Moral Right Interface

A.   Copyright Law as a Limited Substitute for the Moral Right

Courts and commentators have posited copyright law as a substitute theory for the moral right doctrine, but traditional copyright law is of limited utility in vindicating all of the interests protected by moral rights. The court in Gilliam v. American Broadcasting Companies, Inc., [538 F.2d 14 (2d Cir.1976)] applied the 1909 Copyright Act in a novel fashion to grant relief to the plaintiffs, a group of British writers and performers whose scripts had been edited extensively after they were produced into British television programs but prior to their broadcast on defendant's American television network. The court ultimately concluded that the defendant, a remote sublicensee of the British Broadcasting Corporation (BBC), committed copyright infringement as a result of the extensive editing because the contract between the plaintiffs and BBC did not grant specifically to BBC the right to edit the programs once they had been recorded. BBC, therefore, could not grant rights that it did not possess to benefit its sublicensee. Critical to the court's ruling was its finding that the group had retained a common-law copyright in their original, unpublished scripts upon which BBC based the recorded television programs. Analogizing the situation to one in which a user licensed to create certain derivative works from a copyrighted script exceeds the media or time restrictions of his license in the production of a derivative work, the court held that the extensive editing exceeded the scope of any license that BBC was entitled to grant.

The peculiar fact situation in *Gilliam* arguably militates against the decision's application in a broad range of copyright cases concerning aspects of the moral right. In *Gilliam* the court relied heavily upon the agreement between the plaintiffs and BBC which provided that all rights which were not granted to BBC were retained by the plaintiffs. Thus, *Gilliam*'s ultimate moral right significance may be that in the face of a silent contract, an artist will not be held to have granted his licensee the right to perform extensive editing.

* * *

The economic interests protected by the copyright laws are intertwined substantially with the personal interests that are the focus of the moral right doctrine. Indeed, if the moral right doctrine were to become a part of our jurisprudence in the future, its scope would be influenced significantly by the 1976 Act. The relationship between the 1976 Act and the moral right doctrine must be examined, therefore, to assess any future development of the doctrine in the United States.

B.   The 1976 Copyright Act

* * *

1.   The Act's Potential for Safeguarding Moral Rights

The 1976 Act does contain several provisions that could have a significant effect upon the scope of a moral right doctrine in this country. As the following discussion demonstrates, some of these provisions have a sizable potential for vindicating the personal rights of creators. One of the most important provisions in this regard is section 106(2), which grants to the copyright owner the exclusive right to prepare and to authorize the preparation of "derivative works based upon the copyrighted work." Section 101 defines a "derivative work" as one that "represent[s] an original work of authorship" but is "based upon one or more preexisting works."

A creator can prevent unauthorized alterations and modifications of his work by invoking section 106(2), for such actions presumably would result in an unauthorized derivative work. In this situation the effect of section 106(2) is most obvious because there is no dispositive contractual arrangement between the creator and the entity making the unauthorized alterations. In addition, however, the copyright proprietor's exclusive rights relating to the preparation of derivative works raises a fascinating issue concerning a creator's paternity and integrity interests in authorized derivative works. For purposes of illustration, [consider a] playwright [who] authorizes a motion picture company to produce a movie based on her work, but has retained all other rights in her play. In the playwright's opinion, however, the motion picture company's final product, which is publicized as "based upon" her play, is a substantial distortion of her original theme and story line. Does the playwright have any recourse in this situation under section 106(2) of the 1976 Act?

The playwright could rely upon the *Gilliam* rationale by asserting that the movie company has violated the scope of their agreement. Specifically, she could argue that in the agreement, she assigned to the company her right under section 106(2) to prepare a derivative work based upon her play, and to use her name in connection therewith, but that the company violated this agreement because the movie ultimately produced was so extensively altered that it was not "based upon" her play within the meaning of section 106(2). Of course, the situations in *Gilliam* and our hypothetical case are not identical. In *Gilliam* a licensee of the creators authorized the defendants to reproduce the work, but due to the contractual agreement between the licensee and the creators, the licensee could not have authorized the defendants to perform the type of editing at issue. In our hypothetical case, the playwright authorized the movie company to prepare a derivative work, which authorization in itself necessitates a certain number of changes. Although *Gilliam* does not hold explicitly that copyright ownership includes the right to prohibit mutilating changes in a work, the *Gilliam* opinion relied upon the existence of an implied condition of assignment that would preclude the defendants from exercising the reproduction and performance rights which they were granted if they made material changes in the work. Similarly, when the right to prepare a derivative work is at issue, the *Gilliam* rationale supports an inferred condition that the right cannot be exercised if the changes which are made constitute mutilation and the derivative work is billed as "based upon" the creator's underlying work. Hence, the performance of such alterations and resulting false attribution constitute an infringement under section 106(2), just as the performance of the unauthorized editing in *Gilliam* violated the rights granted to the defendants in that case.

The ultimate success of the *Gilliam* argument depends upon the interpretation of the phrase "derivative works *based upon* the copyrighted work" as it is used in section 106(2). Although the phrase "based upon" may, at first glance, appear self-explanatory, application of the phrase in this context is difficult because it requires a determination of the degree of creative liberty that is properly exercisable by one who transforms a preexisting work into another medium. No court has had occasion to interpret section 106(2) in this particular context, but decisions exist in which the import of the phrase "based upon" was explored in analogous circumstances. At least one court, in determining whether a defendant's movie was "based upon" a particular book in the context of plaintiffs' allegation that the movie infringed the book, invoked the "substantial similarity" test used by the courts in deciding copyright infringement actions. The court ultimately concluded, as a matter of law, that the film was not "based upon" the book because a reasonable jury could not find that the two works were "substantially similar beyond the level of generalized ideas or themes." [See Burroughs v. Metro–Goldwyn–Meyer, Inc., 683 F.2d 610, 623–24 (2d Cir.1982).]

On balance, the "substantial similarity" test is the appropriate standard to judge whether a derivative work is "based upon" a preexisting work within the meaning of section 106(2). In providing that the copyright owner has the exclusive right to prepare or authorize the preparation of any derivative works based upon the copyrighted work, Congress, in section 106(2), contemplated that the preparation of an unauthorized derivative work constitutes copyright infringement. Although the legislative history discloses no specific guidelines for determining when an unauthorized derivative work infringes the original work, most courts would invoke the "substantial similarity" test to determine infringement. Therefore, if our playwright had never entered into an agreement with the movie company, the playwright would have an action for copyright infringement under section 106(2), perhaps with a corresponding right to compel recognition for her work, assuming she could prove that the movie company's product was substantially similar to her own. Logically, courts should apply the same standard in the converse situation presented by the hypothetical case. If the movie company's product can satisfy the "substantial similarity" test, the playwright should not be able to rely successfully on *Gilliam* to support her claim under section 106(2). The alterations of the play would not be sufficiently extreme to warrant a holding that the movie company had exceeded its derivative rights assignment. If, however, the movie is not substantially similar to the play, the playwright should prevail.

Application of the "substantial similarity" test, however, is extremely problematic, particularly in the context of adaptations. One popular method for determining substantial similarity is the "ordinary observation or impression" test. This test requires the ordinary observer to perceive a substantial similarity between the two works in question, "so that the alleged copy comes so near to the original as to give the audience the idea created by the original." The use of this test with respect to derivative and preexisting works requires caution, however, because the technical requirements of a different medium usually necessitate certain changes, which could lull an ordinary observer into believing that no substantial similarity exists. In commenting on this problem, one court noted the importance of educating the trier of fact with respect to any differences that are mandated by the adaptation process so as to preserve the creator's valuable rights under section 106(2).

Although section 106(2) does not mention moral rights, the foregoing analysis illustrates how section 106(2) can be utilized by a creator to protect certain aspects of his moral rights, assuming that he has retained some copyright in his work. In our hypothetical situation, if the movie company had exceeded the scope of its rights under section 106(2) by virtue of its distorted use of the playwright's underlying work, the company would be liable to the playwright assuming she had retained all of her other rights under the copyright laws. Suppose, however, that the playwright had transferred to the movie company her other rights in her work, including her right to authorize all derivative works. In this situation would the playwright be able to safeguard her personal interest in preventing an unwarranted mutilation of her work by the movie company?

Section 501(b) of the 1976 Act provides that the "legal or beneficial owner of an exclusive right under a copyright is entitled ... to institute an action for any infringement of that particular right committed while he or she is the owner of it." Although section 501(b) does not define the term "beneficial owner," the legislative history states that a " 'beneficial owner' for this purpose would include, for example, an author who had parted with legal title to the copyright in exchange for percentage royalties based on sales or license fees." Consistent with this interpretation, courts have allowed creators, who have assigned copyrights in their works in exchange for royalties, to maintain infringement actions, regardless of whether the legal owners of the copyrights also are parties to the actions.

This analysis of section 501(b) suggests that even creators who no longer own the copyrights in their works can maintain infringement actions to protect aspects of their moral rights by using section 106(2), assuming they have transferred their copyright interests in exchange for a share of royalties. Most creators presumably would not transfer these valuable rights absent some type of royalty arrangement. Nevertheless, a strong argument can be made that all creators who have transferred their copyrights should be deemed beneficial owners within the meaning of section 501(b), regardless of whether their transfer agreements contemplate royalties. Although no court has had the opportunity to review this issue, a grant of standing to all creators is consistent with the legislative history, which speaks of an author who parts with legal title in exchange for royalties merely *as an example* of a "beneficial owner."

On the other hand, one can argue that a creator who retains no economic ties to his copyrighted work should not receive the protections afforded by the statute, which exist to safeguard economic rights. This argument, however, ignores the application of the termination provisions of the 1976 Act, under which all creators retain a potential economic interest in their works. In fact, the termination provisions codified in section 203, which govern all copyrights executed on or after the effective date of the 1976 Act, and section 304(c), the comparable provision for subsisting copyrights, have been hailed as a departure from our copyright tradition of subordinating the author's interests to those of the publisher. Section 203 provides that an author, except an author of a work made for hire, may terminate any grant of a copyright or any right under a copyright "at any time during a period of five years beginning at the end of thirty-five years from the date of execution of the grant," provided he complies with the stipulated notice requirements. If an author is dead, his termination interest may be exercised by his spouse and his children or grandchildren in accordance with the terms of the termination statute. The legislative history for this provision discloses an intent to safeguard authors against unremunerative transfers. Similarly, section 304(c) details the circumstances in which a transfer or license of a 1909 Act copyright may be terminated by the author or those entitled to exercise his interest if he is dead. Section 304(c) closely tracks section 203. According to the legislative history, the arguments for granting rights of termination under section 304 are even stronger than they are under section 203 because section 304(b) also creates a new property right by adding nineteen years "to the duration of any renewed copyright whose second term started during the twenty-eight years immediately preceding the effective date of the Act." Thus, the author, as "the fundamental beneficiary of copyright under the Constitution," should have an opportunity to share in this new property right.

The foregoing analysis suggests that even an author who has transferred his copyright interest without a royalty arrangement retains some economic and beneficial interest in the copyright. One commentator has suggested that section 203 might allow an author to terminate his copyright grant if the transferee has violated any of the creator's moral rights. Although this position is consistent with the legislative history's emphasis on the creator's economic needs, no court yet has linked personal rights with the additional economic safeguards offered to creators by these provisions. Courts easily could make this correlation in an appropriate case, however, given that a creator's economic interests in his work can be threatened by violations of his personal rights that impair the work's marketability.

NOTES

1. *Ownership vs. authorship.* Should the sculpture at issue in *Community for Creative Non-Violence* be considered a joint work? Note that the Court of Appeals remanded on this issue, although neither CCNV nor Reid requested the Supreme Court to review this remand order. If the sculpture was determined to be a joint work, could Reid object to CCNV's proposed tour? Could Reid stop the tour if Reid were declared the sole owner of the

copyright (see §§ 109(a) & (c) of the 1976 Copyright Act)? Who would have the right to any profits from the tour if Reid was the sole copyright owner? Should Reid have to give the sculpture back to CCNV regardless of the determination of copyright ownership (see § 202)? If the sculpture had been protected under VARA (§ 106A), could CCNV destroy the sculpture if Reid were declared the sole owner of the copyright?

Childress notes the distinction between joint authorship and joint ownership of a copyrighted work, and observes that only joint authors can invoke the rights of authorship such as exercise of the renewal rights pursuant to § 304. Can you think of any other rights that a joint author, but not co-owner, of a copyrighted work can exercise? Given these distinctions, how persuasive is the court's conclusion that parties who make non-copyrightable contributions to works should resort to contract law to protect their interests? Will reliance on contract law always be a feasible option?

2. *Work for hire.* How well does the Supreme Court's decision in *Community for Creative Non–Violence* accomplish "Congress' paramount goal in revising the 1976 Act of enhancing predictability and certainty of copyright ownership" (see Section II(A) of case)? Are there any other approaches which the Court could have adopted that would have been more consistent with this goal? Does Chaim have a stronger work for hire argument with respect to Rivkah or Sam under the second subpart of the work for hire definition dealing with specifically commissioned works? How would you analyze whether their respective works should be considered works for hire under both subparts of the statutory definition?

3. *Termination provisions.* Section 304(c) provides a mechanism whereby an author, or her statutory successors, can terminate transfers and licenses covering the extended renewal term for copyrights in works created before the effective date of the 1976 Act. According to § 304(c)(3), "[t]ermination of the grant may be effected at any time during a period of five years beginning at the end of fifty-six years from the date copyright was originally secured, or beginning on January 1, 1978, whichever is later." Section 304(c)(6)(D) provides that after the copyright owner terminates a grant pursuant to § 304(c), any further grant of any rights covered under the terminated grant can only be made after the effective date of the termination, although an agreement of a further grant between the author (or her successors) and the original grantee (or its successors) can be made after a notice of termination has been served. This provision gives the original grantee a bit of an advantage from a negotiation standpoint.

Section 203 incorporates the termination provisions for works created after the effective date of the 1976 Act. Since the 1976 Act eliminated the two successive 28–year periods of protection in favor of a single term consisting of the life of the author plus 50 years (see § 302(a)), the period in which a notice of termination can be served was modified so that it could "be effected at any time during a period of five years beginning at the end of thirty-five years from the date of execution of the grant; or, if the grant covers the right of publication of the work, the period begins at the end of thirty-five years from the date of publication of the work under the grant or at the end of forty years from the date of execution of the grant, whichever term ends earlier" (see § 203(a)(3)). Why do you think the statute draws a distinction between grants covering the right of publication and all other works?

Section 203(b)(1) mirrors § 304(C)(6)(A), which was discussed in *Stewart,* in that it provides that upon termination, the owner of a derivative work prepared under a grant of the underlying work may continue to utilize the derivative work after termination, but the owner of the derivative work cannot prepare new derivative works of the underlying work once the initial grant has been terminated. See also Note 4, infra. How do the provisions in § 203 relate to the Principal Problem? What issues in the Problem are left unanswered by § 203?

In Mills Music, Inc. v. Snyder,[8] the Supreme Court had occasion to consider another novel question concerning the application of the derivative works exception in § 304(c)(6)(A). In *Mills,* the author of a copyrighted song assigned to a music publishing company the rights to the renewal term for the song in exchange for a share of royalties from mechanical reproductions of the song (i.e., records as opposed to sheet music). The music publishing company then issued licenses to record companies pursuant to this renewal right authorizing the use of the song by the record companies in mechanical reproductions. These agreements required the record companies to pay royalties to the music publishing company, who in turn was contractually required to pay royalties to the song's author. After the author's death, the widow and son of the song's author terminated the grant to the music publishing company of rights in the renewal copyright, pursuant to § 304(c). Termination did not, however, affect rights to sell recordings prepared under the original grant, nor did it affect the grantees' obligation to pay royalties. Thus, the issue in *Mills* was to whom should the royalties be paid: to the middleman music publishing company, as the grantee of the original creator, or to the heirs of the author. In reversing the Second Circuit, the Supreme Court recognized that although § 304 was enacted to benefit authors, the derivative works exception contained in § 304(c)(6)(A) was nonetheless sufficiently broad to support the music publisher's right to royalties. In what respect is the rationale of *Mills* inconsistent with *Stewart?*

4. *Renewal rights. Stewart* deals with one of the sticky issues pertaining to renewal rights in that it focuses on a grantee's continued right to use a derivative work that is based on the copyrighted work subject to the renewal right. *Stewart* was decided in 1990, and as of that year, the ramifications of the opinion were confined to underlying works published between 1962 and January 1, 1978 (the latter being the effective date of the 1976 Act). The renewal right is inapplicable to any work created after the effective date of the 1976 Act. Moreover, any work published before 1962

---

[8] 469 U.S. 153, 105 S.Ct. 638, 83 L.Ed.2d 556 (1985).

would have already entered its renewal period before 1990. Is *Stewart* a good decision from a policy standpoint? Why or why not?

Under the pre-amended § 304(a), the author, if living, or her statutory renewal successors had to apply for and register the renewal right in the year prior to the expiration of the first 28–year period of protection, and, in the absence of this application for renewal, the copyright terminated at the end of the first 28–year period of protection. Section § 304(a) was amended in 1992 to provide that registration of the renewal interest is no longer required. This section now provides that the copyright is automatically extended for a 47–year renewal period at the end of the original 28–year term, and technically there is no need to register an application to extend the term. Still, if an author survives into the 28th year of the first term of copyright protection and files a renewal registration before dying, the renewal right will vest in the author rather than the statutory renewal successors. If the author has filed such a renewal registration, any assignments made by the author of the renewal term will continue to be honored. On the other hand, if the author does not survive into the 28th year or dies in the 28th year but fails to file a renewal before dying, the renewal right vests automatically in the statutory renewal successors of the author (i.e., those who would have been entitled to claim renewal as of the last day of the original 28–year copyright term). The new provision does not change the identity of the statutory renewal successors (the specific order of the statutory renewal successors is discussed below).

Nevertheless, incentives exist for filing an application to renew during the 28th year of the original term. For example, registration for renewal made during the 28th year of the original term will affect the right to utilize a derivative work prepared under authority of a grant in the first copyright term. If a statutory renewal claimant (including the author) registers a renewal within the 28th year, the claimant can terminate an assignment made by the author that authorizes the exploitation of a derivative work in the renewal term. If the renewal is not made by the statutory claimant in the 28th year, then the statutory claimant cannot prevent the continued exploitation, in the renewal term, of a derivative work created during the first 28–year term (note that since the author is considered a statutory claimant, an author who fails to register the renewal will lose the right to prevent the exploitation of the derivative work in the renewal term just like all other statutory claimants). However, there still is no authorization to create or prepare new derivative works based on the copyrighted work subject to the grant. This amendment does not affect the operation of § 203. It is intended to parallel the derivative works clauses of § 203(b)(1) and § 304(c)(6)(A) (see Note 3, supra). The new amendment also leaves undisturbed the *Stewart* decision, since in that case the copyright owner's successor renewed in the 28th year of the original term.

The Court's opinion in *Stewart* also explores the rationale underlying the renewal right in general as a means of safeguarding the economic interests of an author and her family. Section 304(a) mandates the following order of statutory successors of the renewal right, in the event the author is deceased: the author's widow, widower, or children; the author's executor; or in the absence of a will, the author's next of kin. In Saroyan v. William Saroyan Foundation,[9] a district court held that the allegedly estranged children of the writer William Saroyan were able to exercise the statutory renewal right over the objections of the foundation to whom Saroyan had bequeathed all of his copyrights. According to the court, Saroyan died before the renewal rights vested and therefore, the renewal rights never became part of Saroyan's estate and he could not bequeath them. Should the government have the right to mandate the recipients of an author's renewal rights in "the form of a compulsory bequest of the copyright to the designated persons" (see Section II(A) of *Stewart*)? Can you think of any other instances where the government mandates the recipient of an individual's property upon death, notwithstanding contrary provisions in a will?

5. *Moral rights under VARA and otherwise.* The duration of the rights specified in § 106A varies, depending on when the work was created with respect to the effective date of VARA (June 1, 1991). Section 106A(d) provides that the moral rights safeguarded by the statute expire with the death of the author for works created on or after the effective date of VARA. For works created before the effective date of VARA, but title to which has not been transferred at the time of the effective date, the duration of rights under § 106A is co-extensive with those under copyright law. Neither the statute nor the legislative history offers any explanation for this strange dichotomy, but in its original form VARA provided a duration equal to that of copyright law. The current duration for works created on or after the effective date of VARA was a result of a last-minute amendment by the Senate. VARA also provides that the rights in joint works last until the death of the last surviving author.

Other countries that recognize the moral right doctrine can be divided into two groups with respect to the question of the right's duration. The first group, which includes the former West Germany and the Netherlands, follows the approach advocated by the Berne Convention and simultaneously terminates a creator's moral rights and copyright. The second group adheres to the French view that moral rights are perpetual.[10] What arguments support limiting the existence of moral rights to the creator's life and what arguments support their survival beyond the creator's death? If they do survive the author's death, who should be able to exercise them?

Professor Kwall's excerpt discusses the compatibility between the moral right doctrine and the 1976 Copyright Act. Her analysis is especially relevant for evaluating how works not covered by VARA can be afforded some type of moral rights protection in this country. How can David attempt to safeguard his right of integrity in the book? Although Professor Kwall suggests that certain provisions of the 1976 Act have the potential for assisting creators seeking to vindicate aspects of their moral rights, the

[9] 675 F.Supp. 843 (S.D.N.Y.1987), aff'd, 862 F.2d 304 (2d Cir.1988).

[10] See Kwall, Copyright and the Moral Right: Is an American Marriage Possible?, 38 Vand. L. Rev. 1, 15 (1985).

statute contains other provisions that pose both impediments to and limitations upon the enforcement of a creator's personal interests. Can you think of specific provisions of the 1976 Copyright Act which directly circumscribe moral rights protection in this country for works not covered by VARA? Keep this question in mind as you study the provisions in the 1976 Copyright Act which are treated in the subsequent assignments.

One particularly complicated problem raised by VARA is the preemptive effect of the statute with respect to state moral rights statutes such as those detailed in footnote 4, supra. VARA provides that state law actions are not preempted if they 1) arise "from undertakings commenced before the effective date" of VARA; or 2) stem from activities violating rights that are not equivalent to those provided in § 106A; or 3) arise from "activities violating ... rights which extend beyond the life of the author."[11] Note that by virtue of this last preemption exemption, states are free to protect a creator's moral rights posthumously. Many state moral rights statutes do, in fact, provide protection for the life of the author plus fifty years.[12] In light of these preemption exemptions, how should we analyze whether the state moral rights statutes such as those discussed in footnote 4, supra, should be preempted under VARA? The subject of preemption under the 1976 Act in general is treated in Assignment 14.

BIBLIOGRAPHY

The following is a sampling of some recent literature on renewal and termination rights: Hart & Kaufman, An Overview of the Copyright Renewal Amendment and its Impact on Renewal Practices Under U.S. Law, 17 Colum.-VLA J.L. & Arts 311 (1994); Frisch & Fortnow, Termination of Copyrights in Sound Recordings: Is There a Leak in the Record Company Vaults?, 17 Colum.-VLA J.L. & Arts 211 (1993); Kreiss, Abandoning Copyrights to Try to Cut Off Termination Rights, 58 Mo. L. Rev. 85 (1993); Diliberto, Looking Through the "Rear Window": A Review of the United States Supreme Court Decision in Stewart v. Abend, 12 Loy. L.A. Ent. L.J. 299 (1992); D. Nimmer, Refracting the Window's Light: Stewart v. Abend in Myth and in Fact, 39 J. Copyright Soc'y 18 (1991); Allen & Swift, Shattering Copyright Law: Will James Stewart's Rear Window Become a Pane in the Glass?, 22 Pac. L.J. 1 (1990); Abrams, Who's Sorry Now? Termination Rights and the Derivative Works Exception, 62 U. Det. L. Rev. 181 (1985); Jaszi, When Works Collide: Derivative Motion Pictures, Underlying Rights, and the Public Interest, 28 UCLA L. Rev. 715 (1981);

---

[11] See § 301(f)(2).

[12] California, Connecticut, Massachusetts, New Mexico, and Pennsylvania provide protection for the life of the author plus fifty years. Louisiana's statute says that "[t]he provisions of this Chapter apply to any works of fine art regardless of when created." La. Rev. Stat. Ann. § 2155G (West 1987). This language suggests that protection may be perpetual in that state. California also provides that a public interest organization can obtain injunctive relief to preserve the integrity of a covered work, see Cal. Civ. Code § 989(c)(West Supp. 1993), and at least one commentator has suggested that this public enforcement right should be perpetual. See Zuber, The Visual Artists Rights Act of 1990—What it Does, and What it Preempts, 23 Pac. L.J. 445, 456–57 (1992).

Ellingson, The Copyright Exception for Derivative Works and the Scope of Utilization, 56 Ind. L.J. 1 (1980); M. Nimmer, Termination of Transfers Under the Copyright Act of 1976, 125 U. Pa. L. Rev. 947 (1977).

Articles discussing joint works and the work for hire doctrine include: Brophy, Joint Authorship under the Copyright Law, 16 Hastings Comm. & Ent. L.J. 451 (1994); Spyke, The Joint Works Dilemma: The Separately Copyrightable Contribution Requirement and Co–Ownership Principles, 40 J. Copyright Soc'y 463 (1993); Jaszi, Toward a Theory of Copyright: The Metamorphoses of "Authorship," 91 Duke L.J. 455 (1991); Kreiss, Scope of Employment and Being an Employee Under the Work–Made–For–Hire Provision of the Copyright Law: Applying the Common–Law Agency Tests, 40 Kan. L. Rev. 119 (1991); Landau, "Works Made for Hire" After Community for Creative Non–Violence v. Reid: The Need For Statutory Reform and the Importance of Contract, 9 Cardozo Arts & Ent. L.J. 107 (1990); Burr, A Critical Assessment of *Reid*'s Work for Hire Framework and its Potential Impact on the Marketplace for Scholarly Works, 24 J. Marshall L. Rev. 119 (1990); Dreyfuss, The Creative Employee and the Copyright Act of 1976, 54 U. Chi. L. Rev. 590 (1987). See also Symposium, Works–Made–For–Hire—Practical Perspectives: A Roundtable Discussion, 14 Colum.-VLA J.L. & Arts 507 (1990).

Works addressing moral rights and VARA include: Kelly, Moral Rights and the First Amendment: Putting Honor Before Free Speech?, 11 U. Miami Ent. & Sports L. Rev. 211 (1995); Yonover, The "Dissing" of Da Vinci: The Imaginary Case of Leonardo v. Duchamp: Moral Rights, Parody, and Fair Use, 29 Val. U. L. Rev. 935 (1995); Netanel, Alienability Restrictions and the Enhancement of Author Autonomy in United States and Continental Copyright Law, 12 Cardozo Arts & Ent. L.J. 1 (1994); Netanel, Copyright Alienability Restrictions and Enhancement of Author Autonomy: A Normative Evaluation, 24 Rutgers L.J. 347 (1993); VerSteeg, Federal Moral Rights for Visual Artists: Contract Theory and Analysis, 67 Wash. L. Rev. 827 (1992); Zuber, The Visual Artists Rights Act of 1990– What it Does, and What it Preempts, 23 Pac. L.J. 445 (1992); Damich, The Visual Artists Rights Act of 1990: Toward a Federal System of Moral Rights Protection for Visual Art, 39 Cath. U. L. Rev. 945 (1990); Gorman, Visual Artists Rights Act of 1990, 38 J. Copyright Soc'y 233 (1990); Karlen, Joint Ownership of Moral Rights, 38 J. Copyright Soc'y 242 (1990); Damich, The Right of Personality: A Common—Law Basis for the Protection of the Moral Rights of Authors, 23 Ga. L. Rev. 1 (1988); Kwall, Copyright and the Moral Right: Is an American Marriage Possible?, 38 Vand. L. Rev. 1 (1985). See also California Art Legislation Goes Federal: American Association of Law Schools Art Law Section Symposium, 15 Hastings Comm. & Ent. L.J. 893 (1993).

THE SCOPE OF THE COPYRIGHT HOLDER'S RIGHTS: INFRINGEMENT

1. INTRODUCTION

The essential predicate of copyright protection is that the copyright proprietor has the exclusive right to engage in certain activities with respect to the copyrighted work. Section 106 of the 1976 Act provides the copyright owner with the exclusive rights to reproduce, distribute, perform, and display the protected work, as well as the right to prepare derivative works based on the underlying protected work.[1] The copyright owner's exclusive ability to exercise and to authorize the exercise of this bundle of rights enables her to safeguard, in large measure, the pecuniary value of the copyrighted work. As such, copyright law promotes the creative process by providing financial incentives to creators.

This assignment will explore the unauthorized uses of copyrighted property in different contexts such as literature, music, art, and even computer programs. It illustrates that the application of the test for copyright infringement presents some troublesome issues. It is not always easy to decide when one work is based so heavily upon another that the substantial similarity between them should be infringement. Moreover, it is difficult to implement the idea/expression and fact/expression dichotomies that are at the core of the protectability requirements. Finally, one of the most important issues that must be addressed is whether the test for copyright infringement should vary according to the type of work at issue. The Principal cases offer several different approaches to these issues.

2. PRINCIPAL PROBLEM

Your client, William Dawson, is the copyright owner of an arrangement of the spiritual "Ezekiel Saw De Wheel," many copies of which have been sold over the years in the form of sheet music. In 1987, Gilbert M. Martin composed an arrangement of the spiritual, and subsequently granted Hinshaw Music, Inc. the exclusive rights to publish, distribute, and sell his arrangement in the form of sheet music. Dawson sued Martin and Hinshaw for copyright infringement. The district court held for the defendants after a bench trial.

The court found that reasonable minds might conclude that the idea of the defendants' work was substantially similar to the idea of the plaintiff's

---

[1] § 106.

work. According to the court, the pattern, theme and organization of the plaintiff's arrangement is unique among any other arrangement of this spiritual, and substantial similarities could be found to exist between the plaintiff's and defendants' arrangements with respect to this unique pattern. Still, the court ruled against the plaintiff because it felt that no reasonable jury could find that, in comparing the "total concept and feel" of the two works, the expression of ideas in defendants' work was substantially similar to the expression of ideas in plaintiff's work. In applying this test, the court relied only on the sheet music of the two arrangements since the plaintiff did not present recordings of performances of the two arrangements.

Dawson wants you to appeal the district court's ruling. He wants to know what the test for copyright infringement is and whether the district court applied the correct test. Before advising him, consider the following materials.

3. Materials for Solution of Principal Problem

A. STATUTORY MATERIALS: § 501(a) & (b)

B. CASES:

Nichols v. Universal Pictures Corporation

United States Court of Appeals, Second Circuit, 1930.
45 F.2d 119.

■ L. Hand, Circuit Judge.

The plaintiff is the author of a play, "Abie's Irish Rose", which it may be assumed was properly copyrighted under section five, subdivision (d), of the Copyright Act, 17 USCA § 5(d). The defendant produced publicly a motion picture play, "The Cohens and The Kellys", which the plaintiff alleges was taken from it. As we think the defendant's play too unlike the plaintiff's to be an infringement, we may assume, arguendo, that in some details the defendant used the plaintiff's play, as will subsequently appear, though we do not so decide. It therefore becomes necessary to give an outline of the two plays.

"Abie's Irish Rose" presents a Jewish family living in prosperous circumstances in New York. The father, a widower, is in business as a merchant, in which his son and only child helps him. The boy has philandered with young women, who to his father's great disgust have always been Gentiles, for he is obsessed with a passion that his daughter-in-law shall be an orthodox Jewess. When the play opens the son, who has been courting a young Irish Catholic girl, has already married her secretly before a Protestant minister, and is concerned to soften the blow for his father, by securing a favorable impression of his bride, while concealing her faith and race. To accomplish this he introduces her to his father at his home as a Jewess, and lets it appear that he is interested in her, though he conceals the marriage. The girl somewhat reluctantly falls in with the plan; the father takes the bait, becomes infatuated with the girl, concludes that they must marry, and assumes that of course they will, if he so decides. He calls in a rabbi, and prepares for the wedding according to the Jewish rite.

Meanwhile the girl's father, also a widower, who lives in California, and is as intense in his own religious antagonism as the Jew, has been called to New York, supposing that his daughter is to marry an Irishman and a Catholic. Accompanied by a priest, he arrives at the house at the moment when the marriage is being celebrated, but too late to prevent it, and the two fathers, each infuriated by the proposed union of his child to a heretic, fall into unseemly and grotesque antics. The priest and the rabbi become friendly, exchange trite sentiments about religion, and agree that the match is good. Apparently out of abundant caution, the priest celebrates the marriage for a third time, while the girl's father is inveigled away. The second act closes with each father, still outraged, seeking to find some way by which the union, thus trebly insured, may be dissolved.

The last act takes place about a year later, the young couple having meanwhile been abjured by each father, and left to their own resources. They have had twins, a boy and a girl, but their fathers know no more than that a child has been born. At Christmas each, led by his craving to see his grandchild, goes separately to the young folks' home, where they encounter each other, each laden with gifts, one for a boy, the other for a girl. After some slapstick comedy, depending upon the insistence of each that he is right about the sex of the grandchild, they become reconciled when they learn the truth, and that each child is to bear the given name of a grandparent. The curtain falls as the fathers are exchanging amenities, and the Jew giving evidence of an abatement in the strictness of his orthodoxy.

"The Cohens and The Kellys" presents two families, Jewish and Irish, living side by side in the poorer quarters of New York in a state of perpetual enmity. The wives in both cases are still living, and share in the mutual animosity, as do two small sons, and even the respective dogs. The Jews have a daughter, the Irish a son; the Jewish father is in the clothing business; the Irishman is a policeman. The children are in love with each other, and secretly marry, apparently after the play opens. The Jew, being in great financial straits, learns from a lawyer that he has fallen heir to a large fortune from a great-aunt, and moves into a great house, fitted luxuriously. Here he and his family live in vulgar ostentation, and here the Irish boy seeks out his Jewish bride, and is chased away by the angry father. The Jew then abuses the Irishman over the telephone, and both become hysterically excited. The extremity of his feelings makes the Jew sick, so that he must go to Florida for a rest, just before which the daughter discloses her marriage to her mother.

On his return the Jew finds that his daughter has borne a child; at first he suspects the lawyer, but eventually learns the truth and is overcome with anger at such a low alliance. Meanwhile, the Irish family who have been forbidden to see the grandchild, go to the Jew's house, and after a violent scene between the two fathers in which the Jew disowns his daughter, who decides to go back with her husband, the Irishman takes her back with her baby to his own poor lodgings. The lawyer, who had hoped to marry the Jew's daughter, seeing his plan foiled, tells the Jew that his fortune really belongs to the Irishman, who was also related to the dead woman, but offers to conceal his knowledge, if the Jew will share the loot. This the Jew repudiates, and, leaving the astonished lawyer, walks through the rain to his enemy's house to surrender the property. He arrives in great dejection, tells the truth, and abjectly turns to leave. A reconciliation ensues, the Irishman agreeing to share with him equally. The Jew shows some interest in his grandchild, though this is at most a minor motive in the reconciliation, and the curtain falls while the two are in their cups, the Jew insisting that in the firm name for the business, which they are to carry on jointly, his name shall stand first.

It is of course essential to any protection of literary property, whether at common-law or under the statute, that the right cannot be limited literally to the text, else a plagiarist would escape by immaterial variations. That has never been the law, but, as soon as literal appropriation ceases to be the test, the whole matter is necessarily at large, so that, as was recently well said by a distinguished judge, the decisions cannot help much in a new case. When plays are concerned, the plagiarist may excise a separate scene, or he may appropriate part of the dialogue. Then the question is whether the part so taken is "substantial"; it is the same question as arises in the case of any other copyrighted work. But when the plagiarist does not take out a block in situ, but an abstract of the whole, decision is more troublesome. Upon any work, and especially upon a play, a great number of patterns of increasing generality will fit equally well, as more and more of the incident is left out. The last may perhaps be no more than the most general statement of what the play is about, and at times might consist only of its title; but there is a point in this series of abstractions where they are no longer protected, since otherwise the playwright could prevent the use of his "ideas", to which, apart from their expression, his property is never extended. Nobody has ever been able to fix that boundary, and nobody ever can. In some cases the question has been treated as though it were analogous to lifting a portion out of the copyrighted work, but the analogy is not a good one, because, though the skeleton is a part of the body, it pervades and supports the whole. In such cases we are rather concerned with the line between expression and what is expressed. As respects plays, the controversy chiefly centers upon the characters and sequence of incident, these being the substance.

We did not in Dymow v. Bolton, 11 F.2d 690 (1926), hold that a plagiarist was never liable for stealing a plot. We found the plot of the second play was too different to infringe, because the most detailed pattern, common to both, eliminated so much from each that its content went into the public domain; and for this reason we said, "this mere subsection of a plot was not susceptible of copyright". But we do not doubt that two plays may correspond in plot closely enough for infringement. How far that correspondence must go is another matter. Nor need we hold that the same may not be true as to the characters, quite independently of the "plot" proper, though, as far as we know, such a case has never arisen. If Twelfth Night were copyrighted, it is quite possible that a second comer might so closely imitate Sir Toby Belch or Malvolio as to infringe, but it would not be enough that for one of his characters he cast a riotous knight who kept wassail to the discomfort of the household, or a vain and foppish steward who became amorous of his mistress. These would be no more than Shakespeare's "ideas" in the play, as little capable of monopoly as Einstein's Doctrine of Relativity, or Darwin's theory of the Origin of Species. It follows that the less developed the characters, the less they can be copyrighted; that is the penalty an author must bear for marking them too indistinctly.

In the two plays at bar we think both as to incident and character, the defendant took no more—assuming that it took anything at all—than the law allowed. The stories are quite different. One is of a religious zealot who insists upon his child's marrying no one outside his faith; opposed by another who is in this respect just like him, and is his foil. Their difference in race is merely an obbligato to the main theme, religion. They sink their differences through grandparental pride and affection. In the other, zealotry is wholly absent; religion does not even appear. It is true that the parents are hostile to each other in part because they differ in race; but the marriage of their son to a Jew does not apparently offend the Irish family at all, and it exacerbates the existing animosity of the Jew, principally because he has become rich, when he learns it. They are reconciled through the honesty of the Jew and the generosity of the Irishman; the grandchild has nothing whatever to do with it. The only matter common to the two is a quarrel between a Jewish and an Irish father, the marriage of their children, the birth of grandchildren and a reconciliation.

If the defendant took so much from the plaintiff, it may well have been because her amazing success seemed to prove that this was a subject of enduring popularity. Even so, granting that the plaintiff's play was wholly original, and assuming that novelty is not essential to a copyright, there is no monopoly in such a background. Though the plaintiff discovered the vein, she could not keep it to herself; so defined, the theme was too generalized an abstraction from what she wrote. It was only a part of her "ideas".

Nor does she fare better as to her characters. It is indeed scarcely credible that she should not have been aware of those stock figures, the low comedy Jew and Irishman. The defendant has not taken from her more than their prototypes have contained for many decades. If so, obviously so to generalize her copyright, would allow her to cover what was not original with her. But we need not hold this as matter of fact, much as we might be justified. Even though we take it that she devised her figures out of her brain de novo, still the defendant was within its rights.

There are but four characters common to both plays, the lovers and the fathers. The lovers are so faintly indicated as to be no more than stage properties. They are loving and fertile; that is really all that can be said of them, and anyone else is quite within his rights if he puts loving and fertile lovers in a play of his own, wherever he gets the cue. The plaintiff's Jew is quite unlike the defendant's. His obsession is his religion, on which depends such racial animosity as he has. He is affectionate, warm and patriarchal. None of these fit the defendant's Jew, who shows affection for his daughter only once, and who has none but the most superficial interest in his grandchild. He is tricky, ostentatious and vulgar, only by misfortune redeemed into honesty. Both are grotesque, extravagant and quarrelsome; both are fond of display; but these common qualities make up only a small part of their simple pictures, no more than any one might lift if he chose. The Irish fathers are even more unlike; the plaintiff's a mere symbol for religious fanaticism and patriarchal pride, scarcely a character at all. Neither quality appears in the defendant's, for while he goes to get his grandchild, it is rather out of a truculent determination not to be forbidden, than from pride in his progeny. For the rest he is only a grotesque hobbledehoy, used for low comedy of the most conventional sort, which any one might borrow, if he chanced not to know the exemplar.

We assume that the plaintiff's play is altogether original, even to an extent that in fact it is hard to believe. We assume further that, so far as it has been anticipated by earlier plays of which she knew nothing, that fact is immaterial. Still, as we have already said, her copyright did not cover everything that might be drawn from her play; its content went to some extent into the public domain. We have to decide how much, and while we are as aware as any one that the line, wherever it is drawn, will seem arbitrary, that is no excuse for not drawing it; it is a question such as courts must answer in nearly all cases. Whatever may be the difficulties a priori, we have no question on which side of the line this case falls. A comedy based upon conflicts between Irish and Jews, into which the marriage of their children enters, is no more susceptible of copyright than the outline of Romeo and Juliet.

The plaintiff has prepared an elaborate analysis of the two plays, showing a "quadrangle" of the common characters, in which each is represented by the emotions which he discovers. She presents the resulting parallelism as proof of infringement, but the adjectives employed are so general as to be quite useless. Take for example the attribute of "love" ascribed to both Jews. The plaintiff has depicted her father as deeply attached to his son, who is his hope and joy; not so, the defendant, whose father's conduct is throughout not actuated by any affection for his daughter, and who is merely once overcome for the moment by her distress when he has violently dismissed her lover. "Anger" covers emotions aroused by quite different occasions in each case; so do "anxiety", "despondency" and "disgust". It is unnecessary to go through the catalogue for emotions are too much colored by their causes to be a test when used so broadly. This is not the proper approach to a solution; it must be more ingenuous, more like that of a spectator, who would rely upon the complex of his impressions of each character.

We cannot approve the length of the record, which was due chiefly to the use of expert witnesses. Argument is argument whether in the box or at the bar, and its proper place is the last. The testimony of an expert upon such issues, especially his cross-examination, greatly extends the trial and contributes nothing which cannot be better heard after the evidence is all submitted. It ought not to be allowed at all; and while its admission is not a ground for reversal, it cumbers the case and tends to confusion, for the more the court is led into the intricacies of dramatic craftsmanship, the less likely it is to stand upon the firmer, if more naive, ground of its considered impressions upon its own perusal. We hope that in this class of cases such evidence may in the future be entirely excluded, and the case confined to the actual issues; that is, whether the copyrighted work was original, and whether the defendant copied it, so far as the supposed infringement is identical.

Decree affirmed.

Computer Associates International, Inc. v. Altai, Inc.

United States Court of Appeals, Second Circuit, 1992.
982 F.2d 693.

■ WALKER, CIRCUIT JUDGE.

In recent years, the growth of computer science has spawned a number of challenging legal questions, particularly in the field of copyright law. As scientific knowledge advances, courts endeavor to keep pace, and some-times—as in the area of computer technology—they are required to venture into less than familiar waters. This is not a new development, though. "From its beginning, the law of copyright has developed in response to significant changes in technology." Sony Corp. v. Universal City Studios, Inc., 464 U.S. 417, 430 (1984).

[T]he copyright law seeks to establish a delicate equilibrium. On the one hand, it affords protection to authors as an incentive to create, and, on the other, it must appropriately limit the extent of that protection so as to avoid the effects of monopolistic stagnation. In applying the federal act to new types of cases, courts must always keep this symmetry in mind.

Among other things, this case deals with the challenging question of whether and to what extent the "non-literal" aspects of a computer program, that is, those aspects that are not reduced to written code, are protected by copyright. While a few other courts have already grappled with this issue, this case is one of first impression in this circuit. As we shall discuss, we find the results reached by other courts to be less than satisfactory. Drawing upon long-standing doctrines of copyright law, we take an approach that we think better addresses the practical difficulties embedded in these types of cases. In so doing, we have kept in mind the necessary balance between creative incentive and industrial competition.

This appeal comes to us from the United States District Court for the Eastern District of New York, the Honorable George C. Pratt, Circuit Judge, sitting by designation. By Memorandum and Order, Judge Pratt found that defendant Altai, Inc.'s ("Altai"), OSCAR 3.4 computer program had infringed plaintiff Computer Associates' ("CA"), copyrighted computer program entitled CA–SCHEDULER. Accordingly, the district court awarded CA $364,444 in actual damages and apportioned profits. Altai has abandoned its appeal from this award. With respect to CA's second claim for copyright infringement, Judge Pratt found that Altai's OSCAR 3.5 program was not substantially similar to a portion of CA–SCHEDULER called ADAPTER, and thus denied relief.

Because we are in full agreement with Judge Pratt's decision and in substantial agreement with his careful reasoning, we affirm the judgment of the district court in its entirety.

Background

I. Computer Program Design

Certain elementary facts concerning the nature of computer programs are vital to the following discussion. The Copyright Act defines a computer program as "a set of statements or instructions to be used directly or indirectly in a computer in order to bring about a certain result". 17 U.S.C. § 101. In writing these directions, the programmer works "from the general to the specific". Whelan Associates, Inc. v. Jaslow Dental Laboratory, Inc., 797 F.2d 1222, 1229 (3d Cir.1986), *cert. denied*, 479 U.S. 1031 (1987). See generally, Steven R. Englund, Note, Idea, Process, or Protected Expression? : Determining the Scope of Copyright Protection of the Structure of Computer Programs, 88 Mich.L.Rev. 866, 867–73 (1990) (hereinafter "Englund"); Peter S. Menell, An Analysis of the Scope of Copyright Protection for Application Programs, 41 Stan.L.Rev. 1045, 1051–57 (1989)(hereinafter "Menell"); Mark T. Kretschmer, Note, Copyright Protection For Software Architecture: Just Say No!, 1988 Colum.Bus.L.Rev. 823, 824–27 (1988)(hereinafter "Kretschmer"); Peter G. Spivack, Comment, Does Form Follow Function? The Idea/Expression Dichotomy In Copyright Protection of Computer Software, 35 U.C.L.A. L.Rev. 723, 729–31 (1988)(hereinafter "Spivack").

The first step in this procedure is to identify a program's ultimate function or purpose. An example of such an ultimate purpose might be the creation and maintenance of a business ledger. Once this goal has been achieved, a programmer breaks down or "decomposes" the program's ultimate function into "simpler constituent problems or 'subtasks,' " Englund, at 870, which are also known as subroutines or modules. See Spivack, at 729. In the context of a business ledger program, a module or subroutine might be responsible for the task of updating a list of outstanding accounts receivable. Sometimes, depending upon the complexity of its task, a subroutine may be broken down further into sub-subroutines.

Having sufficiently decomposed the program's ultimate function into its component elements, a programmer will then arrange the subroutines or modules into what are known as organizational or flow charts. Flow charts map the interactions between modules that achieve the program's end goal. See Kretschmer, at 826.

In order to accomplish these intra-program interactions, a programmer must carefully design each module's parameter list. A parameter list, according to the expert appointed and fully credited by the district court, Dr. Randall Davis, is "the information sent to and received from a subroutine". The term "parameter list" refers to the form in which information is passed between modules (e.g. for accounts receivable, the designated time frame and particular customer identifying number) and the information's actual content (e.g. 8/91–7/92; customer No. 3). With respect to form, interacting modules must share similar parameter lists so that they are capable of exchanging information.

"The functions of the modules in a program together with each module's relationships to other modules constitute the 'structure' of the program". Englund, at 871. Additionally, the term structure may include the category of modules referred to as "macros". A macro is a single instruction that initiates a sequence of operations or module interactions within the program. Very often the user will accompany a macro with an instruction from the parameter list to refine the instruction (e.g. current total of accounts receivable (macro), but limited to those for 8/91 to 7/92 from customer No. 3 (parameters)).

In fashioning the structure, a programmer will normally attempt to maximize the program's speed, efficiency, as well as simplicity for user operation, while taking into consideration certain externalities such as the memory constraints of the computer upon which the program will be run. See *id.*; Kretschmer, at 826; Menell, at 1052. "This stage of program design often requires the most time and investment". Kretschmer, at 826.

Once each necessary module has been identified, designed, and its relationship to the other modules has been laid out conceptually, the resulting program structure must be embodied in a written language that the computer can read. This process is called "coding", and requires two steps. *Whelan*, 797 F.2d at 1230. First, the programmer must transpose the program's structural blue-print into a source code. This step has been described as "comparable to the novelist fleshing out the broad outline of his plot by crafting from words and sentences the paragraphs that convey the ideas". Kretschmer, at 826. The source code may be written in any one of several computer languages, such as COBAL, FORTRAN, BASIC, EDL, etc., depending upon the type of computer for which the program is intended. *Whelan*, 797 F.2d at 1230. Once the source code has been completed, the second step is to translate or "compile" it into object code. Object code is the binary language comprised of zeros and ones through which the computer directly receives its instructions. *Id.*, at 1230–31; Englund, at 868 & n.13.

After the coding is finished, the programmer will run the program on the computer in order to find and correct any logical and syntactical errors. This is known as "debugging" and, once done, the program is complete. See Kretschmer, at 826–27.

II. Facts

CA is a Delaware corporation, with its principal place of business in Garden City, New York. Altai is a Texas corporation, doing business primarily in Arlington, Texas. Both companies are in the computer software industry—designing, developing and marketing various types of computer programs.

The subject of this litigation originates with one of CA's marketed programs entitled CA–SCHEDULER. CA–SCHEDULER is a job scheduling program designed for IBM mainframe computers. Its primary functions are straightforward: to create a schedule specifying when the computer should run various tasks, and then to control the computer as it executes the schedule. CA–SCHEDULER contains a sub-program entitled ADAPTER, also developed by CA. ADAPTER is not an independently marketed product of CA; it is a wholly integrated component of CA–SCHEDULER and has no capacity for independent use.

Nevertheless, ADAPTER plays an extremely important role. It is an "operating system compatibility component", which means, roughly speaking, it serves as a translator. An "operating system" is itself a program that manages the resources of the computer, allocating those resources to other programs as needed. The IBM's System 370 family of computers, for which CA–SCHEDULER was created, is, depending upon the computer's size, designed to contain one of three operating systems: DOS/VSE, MVS, or CMS. As the district court noted, the general rule is that "a program written for one operating system, e.g., DOS/VSE, will not, without modification, run under another operating system such as MVS". Computer Associates Int'l, Inc. v. Altai, Inc., 775 F.Supp. 544, 550 (E.D.N.Y.1991). ADAPTER's function is to translate the language of a given program into the particular language that the computer's own operating system can understand.

The district court succinctly outlined the manner in which ADAPTER works within the context of the larger program. In order to enable CA–SCHEDULER to function on different operating systems, CA divided the CA–SCHEDULER into two components:

> — a first component that contains only the task-specific portions of the program, independent of all operating system issues, and

> — a second component that contains all the interconnections between the first component and the operating system.

> In a program constructed in this way, whenever the first, task-specific, component needs to ask the operating system for some resource through a "system call", it calls the second component instead of calling the operating system directly.

> The second component serves as an "interface" or "compatibility component" between the task-specific portion of the program and the operating system. It receives the request from the first component and translates it into the appropriate system call that will be recognized by whatever operating system is installed on the computer, e.g., DOS/VSE, MVS, or CMS. Since the first, task-specific component calls the adapter

component rather than the operating system, the first component need not be customized to use any specific operating system. The second interface component insures that all the system calls are performed properly for the particular operating system in use.

Id. at 551. ADAPTER serves as the second, "common system interface" component referred to above.

A program like ADAPTER, which allows a computer user to change or use multiple operating systems while maintaining the same software, is highly desirable. It saves the user the costs, both in time and money, that otherwise would be expended in purchasing new programs, modifying existing systems to run them, and gaining familiarity with their operation. The benefits run both ways. The increased compatibility afforded by an ADAPTER-like component, and its resulting popularity among consumers, makes whatever software in which it is incorporated significantly more marketable.

Starting in 1982, Altai began marketing its own job scheduling program entitled ZEKE. The original version of ZEKE was designed for use in conjunction with a VSE operating system. By late 1983, in response to customer demand, Altai decided to rewrite ZEKE so that it could be run in conjunction with an MVS operating system.

At that time, James P. Williams ("Williams"), then an employee of Altai and now its President, approached Claude F. Arney, III ("Arney"), a computer programmer who worked for CA. Williams and Arney were longstanding friends, and had in fact been co-workers at CA for some time before Williams left CA to work for Altai's predecessor. Williams wanted to recruit Arney to assist Altai in designing an MVS version of ZEKE.

At the time he first spoke with Arney, Williams was aware of both the CA–SCHEDULER and ADAPTER programs. However, Williams was not involved in their development and had never seen the codes of either program. When he asked Arney to come work for Altai, Williams did not know that ADAPTER was a component of CA–SCHEDULER.

Arney, on the other hand, was intimately familiar with various aspects of ADAPTER. While working for CA, he helped improve the VSE version of ADAPTER, and was permitted to take home a copy of ADAPTER's source code. This apparently developed into an irresistible habit, for when Arney left CA to work for Altai in January, 1984, he took with him copies of the source code for both the VSE and MVS versions of ADAPTER. He did this in knowing violation of the CA employee agreements that he had signed.

Once at Altai, Arney and Williams discussed design possibilities for adapting ZEKE to run on MVS operating systems. Williams, who had created the VSE version of ZEKE, thought that approximately 30% of his original program would have to be modified in order to accommodate MVS. Arney persuaded Williams that the best way to make the needed modifications was to introduce a "common system interface" component into ZEKE. He did not tell Williams that his idea stemmed from his familiarity with ADAPTER. They decided to name this new component-program OSCAR.

Arney went to work creating OSCAR. No one at Altai, including Williams, knew that he had the ADAPTER code, and no one knew that he was using it to design OSCAR/VSE. In three months, Arney successfully completed the OSCAR/VSE project. In an additional month he developed an OSCAR/MVS version. When the dust finally settled, Arney had copied approximately 30% of OSCAR's code from CA's ADAPTER program.

The first generation of OSCAR programs was known as OSCAR 3.4. From 1985 to August 1988, Altai used OSCAR 3.4 in its ZEKE product, as well as in programs entitled ZACK and ZEBB. In late July 1988, CA first learned that Altai may have appropriated parts of ADAPTER. After confirming its suspicions, CA secured copyrights on its 2.1 and 7.0 versions of CA–SCHEDULER. CA then brought this copyright action against Altai.

Apparently, it was upon receipt of the summons and complaint that Altai first learned that Arney had copied much of the OSCAR code from ADAPTER. After Arney confirmed to Williams that CA's accusations of copying were true, Williams immediately set out to survey the damage. Without ever looking at the ADAPTER code himself, Williams learned from Arney exactly which sections of code Arney had taken from ADAPTER.

Upon advice of counsel, Williams initiated OSCAR's rewrite. The project's goal was to save as much of OSCAR 3.4 as legitimately could be used, and to excise those portions which had been copied from ADAPTER. Arney was entirely excluded from the process, and his copy of the ADAPTER code was locked away. Williams put eight other programmers on the project, none of whom had been involved in any way in the development of OSCAR 3.4. Williams provided the programmers with a description of the ZEKE operating system services so that they could rewrite the appropriate code. The rewrite project took about six months to complete and was finished in mid-November 1989. The resulting program was entitled OSCAR 3.5.

From that point on, Altai shipped only OSCAR 3.5 to its new customers. Altai also shipped OSCAR 3.5 as a "free upgrade" to all customers that had previously purchased OSCAR 3.4. While Altai and Williams acted responsibly to correct what Arney had wrought, the damage was done. CA's lawsuit remained.

Discussion

CA contends that the district court applied an erroneous method for determining whether there exists substantial similarity between computer programs, and thus, erred in determining that OSCAR 3.5 did not infringe the copyrights held on the different versions of its CA–SCHEDULER program. CA asserts that the test applied by the district court failed to account sufficiently for a computer program's non-literal elements.

I. Copyright Infringement

In any suit for copyright infringement, the plaintiff must establish its ownership of a valid copyright, and that the defendant copied the copyrighted work. The plaintiff may prove defendant's copying either by direct evidence or, as is most often the case, by showing that (1) the defendant had access to the plaintiff's copyrighted work and (2) that defendant's work is substantially similar to the plaintiff's copyrightable material.

For the purpose of analysis, the district court assumed that Altai had access to the ADAPTER code when creating OSCAR 3.5. See *Computer Associates*, 775 F.Supp., at 558. Thus, in determining whether Altai had unlawfully copied protected aspects of CA's ADAPTER, the district court narrowed its focus of inquiry to ascertaining whether Altai's OSCAR 3.5 was substantially similar to ADAPTER. Because we approve Judge Pratt's conclusions regarding substantial similarity, our analysis will proceed along the same assumption.

As a general matter, and to varying degrees, copyright protection extends beyond a literary work's strictly textual form to its non-literal components. As we have said, "[i]t is of course essential to any protection of literary property ... that the right cannot be limited literally to the text, else a plagiarist would escape by immaterial variations". Nichols v. Universal Pictures Corp., 45 F.2d 119, 121 (2d Cir.1930)(L. Hand, J.), *cert. denied*, 282 U.S. 902 (1931). Thus, where "the fundamental essence or structure of one work is duplicated in another", 3 Nimmer, [Nimmer on Copyright] § 13.03[A][1], at 13–24, courts have found copyright infringement. This black letter proposition is the springboard for our discussion.

A. Copyright Protection for the Non-literal Elements of Computer Programs

It is now well settled that the literal elements of computer programs, i.e., their source and object codes, are the subject of copyright protection. See *Whelan*, 797 F.2d at 1233. Here, as noted earlier, Altai admits having copied approximately 30% of the OSCAR 3.4 program from CA's ADAPTER source code, and does not challenge the district court's related finding of infringement.

In this case, the hotly contested issues surround OSCAR 3.5. As recounted above, OSCAR 3.5 is the product of Altai's carefully orchestrated rewrite of OSCAR 3.4. After the purge, none of the ADAPTER source code remained in the 3.5 version; thus, Altai made sure that the literal elements of its revamped OSCAR program were no longer substantially similar to the literal elements of CA's ADAPTER.

According to CA, the district court erroneously concluded that Altai's OSCAR 3.5 was not substantially similar to its own ADAPTER program. CA argues that this occurred because the district court "committed legal error in analyzing [its] claims of copyright infringement by failing to find that copyright protects expression contained in the non-literal elements of computer software". We disagree.

CA argues that, despite Altai's rewrite of the OSCAR code, the resulting program remained substantially similar to the *structure* of its ADAPTER program. As discussed above, a program's structure includes its non-literal components such as general flow charts as well as the more specific organization of inter-modular relationships, parameter lists, and macros. In addition to these aspects, CA contends that OSCAR 3.5 is also substantially similar to ADAPTER with respect to the list of services that both ADAPTER and OSCAR obtain from their respective operating systems. We must decide whether and to what extent these elements of computer programs are protected by copyright law.

The statutory terrain in this area has been well explored. See Lotus Dev. Corp. v. Paperback Software Int'l, 740 F.Supp. 37, 47–51 (D.Mass. 1990); see also *Whelan*, 797 F.2d at 1240–42; Englund, at 885–90; Spivack, at 731–37. The Copyright Act affords protection to "original works of authorship fixed in any tangible medium of expression". § 102(a). This broad category of protected "works" includes "literary works", *id.*, which are defined by the act as

> works, other than audiovisual works, expressed in words, numbers, or other verbal or numerical symbols or indicia, regardless of the nature of the material objects, such as books, periodicals, manuscripts, phonorecords, film tapes, disks, or cards, in which they are embodied.

Section 101. While computer programs are not specifically listed as part of the above statutory definition, the legislative history leaves no doubt that Congress intended them to be considered literary works. See H.R. Rep. No. 1476, 94th Cong., 2d Sess. 54 (hereinafter "House Report"); *Whelan*, 797 F.2d at 1234; Apple Computer, Inc. v. Franklin Computer Corp., 714 F.2d 1240, 1247 (3d Cir.1983), *cert. dismissed*, 464 U.S. 1033 (1984).

The syllogism that follows from the foregoing premises is a powerful one: if the non-literal structures of literary works are protected by copyright; and if computer programs are literary works, as we are told by the legislature; then the non-literal structures of computer programs are protected by copyright. See *Whelan*, 797 F.2d at 1234 ("By analogy to other literary works, it would thus appear that the copyrights of computer programs can be infringed even absent copying of the literal elements of the program."). We have no reservation in joining the company of those courts that have already ascribed to this logic. [Citations omitted.] However, that conclusion does not end our analysis. We must determine the scope of copyright protection that extends to a computer program's non-literal structure.

As a caveat, we note that our decision here does not control infringement actions regarding categorically distinct works, such as certain types of screen displays. These items represent products of computer programs, rather than the programs themselves, and fall under the copyright rubric of audiovisual works. If a computer audiovisual display is copyrighted separately as an audiovisual work, apart from the literary work that generates it (i.e., the program), the display may be protectable regardless of the underlying program's copyright status. Of course, the copyright protection that these displays enjoy extends only so far as their expression is protectable. In this case, however, we are concerned not with a program's display, but the program itself, and then with only its non-literal components. In considering the copyrightability of these components, we must refer to venerable doctrines of copyright law.

1. Idea vs. Expression Dichotomy

It is a fundamental principle of copyright law that a copyright does not protect an idea, but only the expression of the idea. This axiom of common law has been incorporated into the governing statute. See § 102(b). See also House Report, at 5670 ("Copyright does not preclude others from using ideas or information revealed by the author's work.").

Congress made no special exception for computer programs. To the contrary, the legislative history explicitly states that copyright protects computer programs only "to the extent that they incorporate authorship in programmer's expression of original ideas, as distinguished from the ideas themselves". *Id.* at 5667; see also *id.* at 5670 ("Section 102(b) is intended ... to make clear that the expression adopted by the programmer is the copyrightable element in a computer program, and that the actual processes or methods embodied in the program are not within the scope of copyright law.").

Similarly, the National Commission on New Technological Uses of Copyrighted Works ("CONTU") established by Congress to survey the issues generated by the interrelationship of advancing technology and copyright law, see Pub. L. 93–573, § 201, 88 Stat. 1873 (1974), recommended, inter alia, that the 1976 Copyright Act "be amended ... to make it explicit that computer programs, to the extent that they embody the author's original creation, are proper subject matter for copyright". See National Commission on New Technological Uses of Copyrighted Works, Final Report 1 (1979)(hereinafter "CONTU Report"). To that end, Congress adopted CONTU's suggestions and amended the Copyright Act by adding, among other things, a provision to § 101 which defined the term "computer program". See Pub. L. No. 96–517, § 10(a), 94 Stat. 3028 (1980). CONTU also "concluded that the idea-expression distinction should be used to determine which aspects of computer programs are copyrightable". *Lotus Dev. Corp.*, 740 F.Supp., at 54 (citing CONTU Report, at 44).

Drawing the line between idea and expression is a tricky business. Judge Learned Hand noted that "[n]obody has ever been able to fix that boundary, and nobody ever can". *Nichols*, 45 F.2d at 121. Thirty years later his convictions remained firm. "Obviously, no principle can be stated as to when an imitator has gone beyond copying the 'idea,' and has borrowed its 'expression,' " Judge Hand concluded. "Decisions must therefore inevitably be ad hoc". Peter Pan Fabrics, Inc. v. Martin Weiner Corp., 274 F.2d 487, 489 (2d Cir.1960).

The essentially utilitarian nature of a computer program further complicates the task of distilling its idea from its expression. In order to describe both computational processes and abstract ideas, its content "combines creative and technical expression". See Spivack, at 755. The variations of expression found in purely creative compositions, as opposed to those contained in utilitarian works, are not directed towards practical application. For example, a narration of Humpty Dumpty's demise, which would clearly be a creative composition, does not serve the same ends as, say, a recipe for scrambled eggs—which is a more process oriented text. Thus, compared to aesthetic works, computer programs hover even more closely to the elusive boundary line described in § 102(b).

The doctrinal starting point in analyses of utilitarian works is the seminal case of Baker v. Selden, 101 U.S. 99 (1879). In *Baker*, the Supreme Court faced the question of "whether the exclusive property in a system of bookkeeping can be claimed, under the law of copyright, by means of a book in which that system is explained[.]" *Id.* at 101. The Supreme Court found nothing copyrightable in Selden's bookkeeping system, and rejected his infringement claim regarding the ledger sheets.

To the extent that an accounting text and a computer program are both "a set of statements or instructions ... to bring about a certain result", § 101, they are roughly analogous. In the former case, the processes are ultimately conducted by human agency; in the latter, by electronic means. In either case, as already stated, the processes themselves are not protectable. But the holding in *Baker* goes farther. The Court concluded that those aspects of a work, which "must necessarily be used as incident to" the idea, system or process that the work describes, are also not copyrightable. 101 U.S., at 104. Selden's ledger sheets, therefore, enjoyed no copyright protection because they were "necessary incidents to" the system of accounting that he described. *Id.* at 103. From this reasoning, we conclude that those elements of a computer program that are necessarily incidental to its function are similarly unprotectable.

While Baker v. Selden provides a sound analytical foundation, it offers scant guidance on how to separate idea or process from expression, and moreover, on how to further distinguish protectable expression from that expression which "must necessarily be used as incident to" the work's underlying concept.

2. Substantial Similarity Test for Computer Program Structure: Abstraction—Filtration—Comparison

As discussed herein, we think that district courts would be well-advised to undertake a three-step procedure, based on the abstractions test utilized by the district court, in order to determine whether the non-literal elements of two or more computer programs are substantially similar. This approach breaks no new ground; rather, it draws on such familiar copyright doctrines as merger, scenes a faire, and public domain. In taking this approach, however, we are cognizant that computer technology is a dynamic field which can quickly outpace judicial decisionmaking. Thus, in cases where the technology in question does not allow for a literal application of the procedure we outline below, our opinion should not be read to foreclose the district courts of our circuit from utilizing a modified version.

In ascertaining substantial similarity under this approach, a court would first break down the allegedly infringed program into its constituent structural parts. Then, by examining each of these parts for such things as incorporated ideas, expression that is necessarily incidental to those ideas, and elements that are taken from the public domain, a court would then be able to sift out all non-protectable material. Left with a kernel, or possibly kernels, of creative expression after following this process of elimination, the court's last step would be to compare this material with the structure of an allegedly infringing program. The result of this comparison will determine whether the protectable elements of the programs at issue are substantially similar so as to warrant a finding of infringement. It will be helpful to elaborate a bit further.

Step One: Abstraction

As the district court appreciated, see *Computer Associates*, 775 F.Supp., at 560, the theoretic framework for analyzing substantial similarity expounded by Learned Hand in the *Nichols* case is helpful in the present context. In *Nichols*, we enunciated what has now become known as the "abstractions" test for separating idea from expression:

> Upon any work ... a great number of patterns of increasing generality will fit equally well, as more and more of the incident is left out. The last may perhaps be no more than the most general statement of what the [work] is about, and at times might consist only of its title; but there is a point in this series of abstractions where they are no longer protected, since otherwise the [author] could prevent the use of his "ideas", to which, apart from their expression, his property is never extended.

Nichols, 45 F.2d at 121.

While the abstractions test was originally applied in relation to literary works such as novels and plays, it is adaptable to computer programs. [T]he abstractions test "implicitly recognizes that any given work may consist of a mixture of numerous ideas and expressions". 3 Nimmer § 13.03[F] at 13–62.34–63.

As applied to computer programs, the abstractions test will comprise the first step in the examination for substantial similarity. Initially, in a manner that resembles reverse engineering on a theoretical plane, a court should dissect the allegedly copied program's structure and isolate each level of abstraction contained within it. This process begins with the code and ends with an articulation of the program's ultimate function. Along the way, it is necessary essentially to retrace and map each of the designer's steps—in the opposite order in which they were taken during the program's creation.

Step Two: Filtration

Once the program's abstraction levels have been discovered, the substantial similarity inquiry moves from the conceptual to the concrete. Professor Nimmer suggests, and we endorse, a "successive filtering method" for separating protectable expression from non-protectable material.

See generally 3 Nimmer § 13.03[F]. This process entails examining the structural components at each level of abstraction to determine whether their particular inclusion at that level was "idea" or was dictated by considerations of efficiency, so as to be necessarily incidental to that idea; required by factors external to the program itself; or taken from the public domain and hence is nonprotectable expression. See also Kretschmer, at 844–45 (arguing that program features dictated by market externalities or efficiency concerns are unprotectable). The structure of any given program may reflect some, all, or none of these considerations. Each case requires its own fact specific investigation.

Strictly speaking, this filtration serves "the purpose of defining the scope of plaintiff's copyright". Brown Bag Software v. Symantec Corp., No. 89–16239, slip op. 3719, 3738 (9th Cir. April 7, 1992)(endorsing "analytic dissection" of computer programs in order to isolate protectable expression). By applying well developed doctrines of copyright law, it may ultimately leave behind a "core of protectable material". 3 Nimmer § 13.03[F][5], at 13–72. Further explication of this second step may be helpful.

(a) Elements Dictated by Efficiency

The portion of Baker v. Selden, discussed earlier, which denies copyright protection to expression necessarily incidental to the idea being expressed, appears to be the cornerstone for what has developed into the doctrine of merger. See Morrissey v. Procter & Gamble Co., 379 F.2d 675, 678–79 (1st Cir.1967)(relying on *Baker* for the proposition that expression embodying the rules of a sweepstakes contest was inseparable from the idea of the contest itself, and therefore were not protectable by copyright). The doctrine's underlying principle is that "[w]hen there is essentially only one way to express an idea, the idea and its expression are inseparable and copyright is no bar to copying that expression". Concrete Machinery Co. v. Classic Lawn Ornaments, Inc., 843 F.2d 600, 606 (1st Cir.1988). Under these circumstances, the expression is said to have "merged" with the idea itself. In order not to confer a monopoly of the idea upon the copyright owner, such expression should not be protected.

CONTU recognized the applicability of the merger doctrine to computer programs. In its report to Congress it stated that:

> [C]opyrighted language may be copied without infringing when there is but a limited number of ways to express a given idea.... In the computer context, this means that when specific instructions, even though previously copyrighted, are the only and essential means of accomplishing a given task, their later use by another will not amount to infringement.

CONTU Report at 20. While this statement directly concerns only the application of merger to program code, that is, the textual aspect of the program, it reasonably suggests that the doctrine fits comfortably within the general context of computer programs.

Furthermore, when one considers the fact that programmers generally strive to create programs "that meet the user's needs in the most efficient manner", Menell, at 1052, the applicability of the merger doctrine to computer programs becomes compelling. In the context of computer program design, the concept of efficiency is akin to deriving the most concise logical proof or formulating the most succinct mathematical computation. Thus, the more efficient a set of modules are, the more closely they approximate the idea or process embodied in that particular aspect of the program's structure.

While, hypothetically, there might be a myriad of ways in which a programmer may effectuate certain functions within a program,—i.e., express the idea embodied in a given subroutine—efficiency concerns may so narrow the practical range of choice as to make only one or two forms of expression workable options. Of course, not all program structure is informed by efficiency concerns. See Menell, at 1052 (besides efficiency, simplicity related to user accommodation has become a programming priority). It follows that in order to determine whether the merger doctrine precludes copyright protection to an aspect of a program's structure that is so oriented, a court must inquire "whether the use of *this particular set* of modules is necessary efficiently to implement that part of the program's process" being implemented. Englund, at 902. If the answer is yes, then the expression represented by the programmer's choice of a specific module or group of modules has merged with their underlying idea and is unprotected. *Id.* at 902–03.

Another justification for linking structural economy with the application of the merger doctrine stems from a program's essentially utilitarian nature and the competitive forces that exist in the software marketplace. See Kretschmer, at 842. Working in tandem, these factors give rise to a problem of proof which merger helps to eliminate.

Efficiency is an industry-wide goal. Since, as we have already noted, there may be only a limited number of efficient implementations for any given program task, it is quite possible that multiple programmers, working independently, will design the identical method employed in the allegedly infringed work. Of course, if this is the case, there is no copyright infringement.

Under these circumstances, the fact that two programs contain the same efficient structure may as likely lead to an inference of independent creation as it does to one of copying. Thus, since evidence of similarly efficient structure is not particularly probative of copying, it should be disregarded in the overall substantial similarity analysis. See 3 Nimmer § 13.03[F][2], at 13–65.

We conclude that application of the merger doctrine in this setting is an effective way to eliminate non-protectable expression contained in computer programs.

(b) Elements Dictated By External Factors

We have stated that where "it is virtually impossible to write about a particular historical era or fictional theme without employing certain 'stock' or standard literary devices", such expression is not copyrightable. Hoehling v. Universal City Studios, Inc., 618 F.2d 972, 979 (2d Cir.), *cert. denied*, 449 U.S. 841 (1980). For example, the Hoehling case was an infringement suit stemming from several works on the Hindenberg disaster. There we concluded that similarities in representations of German beer halls, scenes depicting German greetings such as "Heil Hitler", or the singing of certain German songs would not lead to a finding of infringement because they were "indispensable, or at least standard, in the treatment of" life in Nazi Germany. *Id.* (quoting Alexander v. Haley, 460 F.Supp. 40, 45 (S.D.N.Y.1978)). This is known as the scenes a faire doctrine, and like "merger", it has its analogous application to computer programs.

Professor Nimmer points out that "in many instances it is virtually impossible to write a program to perform particular functions in a specific computing environment without employing standard techniques". 3 Nimmer § 13.03[F][3], at 13–65. This is a result of the fact that a programmer's freedom of design choice is often circumscribed by extrinsic considerations such as (1) the mechanical specifications of the computer on which a particular program is intended to run; (2) compatibility requirements of other programs with which a program is designed to operate in conjunction; (3) computer manufacturers' design standards; (4) demands of the industry being serviced; and (5) widely accepted programming practices within the computer industry. *Id.* at 13–66–71.

Courts have already considered some of these factors in denying copyright protection to various elements of computer programs. In the Plains Cotton case, the Fifth Circuit refused to reverse the district court's denial of a preliminary injunction against an alleged program infringer because, in part, "many of the similarities between the ... programs [were] dictated by the externalities of the cotton market". Plains Cotton Co-op v. Goodpasture Computer Service, Inc., 807 F.2d 1256, 1262 (5th Cir.), *cert. denied*, 484 U.S. 821 (1987).

In Manufacturers Technologies [Inc. v. Cams, Inc., 706 F.Supp. 984 (D.Conn.1989)], the district court noted that the program's method of screen navigation "is influenced by the type of hardware that the software is designed to be used on". [*Id.*] at 995. Because, in part, "the functioning of the hardware package impact[ed] and constrain[ed] the type of navigational tools used in plaintiff's screen displays", the court denied copyright protection to that aspect of the program.

Finally, the district court in Q–Co Industries, [Inc. v. Hoffman], rested its holding on what, perhaps, most closely approximates a traditional scenes a faire rationale. There, the court denied copyright protection to four program modules employed in a teleprompter program. This decision was ultimately based upon the court's finding that "the same modules would be an inherent part of any prompting program". 625 F.Supp. 608, 616 (S.D.N.Y.1985).

Building upon this existing case law, we conclude that a court must also examine the structural content of an allegedly infringed program for elements that might have been dictated by external factors.

(c) Elements taken From the Public Domain

Closely related to the non-protectability of scenes a faire, is material found in the public domain. Such material is free for the taking and cannot be appropriated by a single author even though it is included in a copyrighted work. We see no reason to make an exception to this rule for elements of a computer program that have entered the public domain by virtue of freely accessible program exchanges and the like. Thus, a court must also filter out this material from the allegedly infringed program before it makes the final inquiry in its substantial similarity analysis.

Step Three: Comparison

The third and final step of the test for substantial similarity that we believe appropriate for non-literal program components entails a comparison. Once a court has sifted out all elements of the allegedly infringed program which are "ideas" or are dictated by efficiency or external factors, or taken from the public domain, there may remain a core of protectable expression. In terms of a work's copyright value, this is the golden nugget. At this point, the court's substantial similarity inquiry focuses on whether the defendant copied any aspect of this protected expression, as well as an assessment of the copied portion's relative importance with respect to the plaintiff's overall program. See 3 Nimmer § 13.03[F][5].

3.   Policy Considerations

We are satisfied that the three step approach we have just outlined not only comports with, but advances the constitutional policies underlying the Copyright Act. Since any method that tries to distinguish idea from expression ultimately impacts on the scope of copyright protection afforded to a particular type of work, "the line [it draws] must be a pragmatic one, which also keeps in consideration 'the preservation of the balance between competition and protection.'" *Apple Computer*, 714 F.2d at 1253 (citation omitted).

CA and some amici argue against the type of approach that we have set forth on the grounds that it will be a disincentive for future computer program research and development. At bottom, they claim that if programmers are not guaranteed broad copyright protection for their work, they will not invest the extensive time, energy and funds required to design and improve program structures. While they have a point, their argument cannot carry the day. The interest of the copyright law is not in simply conferring a monopoly on industrious persons, but in advancing the public welfare through rewarding artistic creativity, in a manner that permits the free use and development of non-protectable ideas and processes.

Recently, the Supreme Court has emphatically reiterated that "[t]he primary objective of copyright is not to reward the *labor* of authors...."

Feist Publications, Inc. v. Rural Telephone Service Co., 111 S.Ct. 1282, 1290 (1991)(emphasis added). While the *Feist* decision deals primarily with the copyrightability of purely factual compilations, its underlying tenets apply to much of the work involved in computer programming. *Feist* put to rest the "sweat of the brow" doctrine in copyright law. *Id*. at 1295. The Court flatly rejected this justification for extending copyright protection, noting that it "eschewed the most fundamental axiom of copyright law— that no one may copyright facts or ideas". *Id*. [at 1291].

Feist teaches that substantial effort alone cannot confer copyright status on an otherwise uncopyrightable work. As we have discussed, despite the fact that significant labor and expense often goes into computer program flow-charting and debugging, that process does not always result in inherently protectable expression. In view of the Supreme Court's recent holding, however, we must reject the legal basis of CA's disincentive argument.

Furthermore, we are unpersuaded that the test we approve today will lead to the dire consequences for the computer program industry that plaintiff and some amici predict. To the contrary, serious students of the industry have been highly critical of the sweeping scope of copyright protection in that it "enables first comers to 'lock up' basic programming techniques as implemented in programs to perform particular tasks". Menell, at 1087.

To be frank, the exact contours of copyright protection for non-literal program structure are not completely clear. We trust that as future cases are decided, those limits will become better defined. Indeed, it may well be that the Copyright Act serves as a relatively weak barrier against public access to the theoretical interstices behind a program's source and object codes. This results from the hybrid nature of a computer program, which, while it is literary expression, is also a highly functional, utilitarian component in the larger process of computing.

Generally, we think that copyright registration—with its indiscriminating availability—is not ideally suited to deal with the highly dynamic technology of computer science. Thus far, many of the decisions in this area reflect the courts' attempt to fit the proverbial square peg in a round hole. The district court, see *Computer Associates*, 775 F.Supp., at 560, and at least one commentator have suggested that patent registration, with its exacting up-front novelty and non-obviousness requirements, might be the more appropriate rubric of protection for intellectual property of this kind. See Randell M. Whitmeyer, Comment, A Plea for Due Processes: Defining the Proper Scope of Patent Protection for Computer Software, 85 Nw. U.L.Rev. 1103, 1123–25 (1991). In any event, now that more than 12 years have passed since CONTU issued its final report, the resolution of this specific issue could benefit from further legislative investigation—perhaps a CONTU II.

In the meantime, Congress has made clear that computer programs are literary works entitled to copyright protection. Of course, we shall abide by these instructions, but in so doing we must not impair the overall integrity of copyright law. While incentive based arguments in favor of broad copyright protection are perhaps attractive from a pure policy perspective, see *Lotus Dev. Corp.*, 740 F.Supp., at 58, ultimately, they have a corrosive effect on certain fundamental tenets of copyright doctrine. If the test we have outlined results in narrowing the scope of protection, as we expect it will, that result flows from applying, in accordance with Congressional intent, long-standing principles of copyright law to computer programs. Of course, our decision is also informed by our concern that these fundamental principles remain undistorted.

B.   The District Court Decision

We turn now to our review of the district court's decision in this particular case. At the outset, we must address CA's claim that the district court erred by relying too heavily on the court appointed expert's "personal opinions on the factual and legal issues before the court".

1.   Use of Expert Evidence in Determining Substantial Similarity Between Computer Programs

Pursuant to Fed.R.Evid. 706, and with the consent of both Altai and CA, Judge Pratt appointed and relied upon Dr. Randall Davis of the Massachusetts Institute of Technology as the court's own expert witness on the issue of substantial similarity. Dr. Davis submitted a comprehensive written report that analyzed the various aspects of the computer programs at issue and evaluated the parties' expert evidence. At trial, Dr. Davis was extensively cross-examined by both CA and Altai.

The well-established general rule in this circuit has been to limit the use of expert opinion in determining whether works at issue are substantially similar. As a threshold matter, expert testimony may be used to assist the fact finder in ascertaining whether the defendant had copied any part of the plaintiff's work. See Arnstein v. Porter, 154 F.2d 464, 468 (2d Cir.1946). To this end, "the two works are to be compared in their entirety ... [and] in making such comparison resort may properly be made to expert analysis...." 3 Nimmer § 13.03[E][2], at 13–62.16.

However, once some amount of copying has been established, it remains solely for the trier of fact to determine whether the copying was "illicit", that is to say, whether the "defendant took from plaintiff's works so much of what is pleasing to [lay observers] who comprise the audience for whom such [works are] composed, that defendant wrongfully appropriated something which belongs to the plaintiff". *Arnstein*, 154 F.2d at 473. Since the test for illicit copying is based upon the response of ordinary lay observers, expert testimony is thus "irrelevant" and not permitted. *Id.* at 468, 473. We have subsequently described this method of inquiry as "merely an alternative way of formulating the issue of substantial similarity". Ideal Toy Corp. v. Fab–Lu Ltd. (Inc.), 360 F.2d 1021, 1023 n.2 (2d Cir.1966).

Historically, *Arnstein*'s ordinary observer standard had its roots in "an attempt to apply the 'reasonable person' doctrine as found in other areas of the law to copyright''. 3 Nimmer § 13.03 [E][2], at 13–62.10–11. That approach may well have served its purpose when the material under scrutiny was limited to art forms readily comprehensible and generally familiar to the average lay person. However, in considering the extension of the rule to the present case, we are reminded of Holmes' admonition that, "[t]he life of the law has not been logic: it has been experience''. O.W. Holmes, Jr., THE COMMON LAW 1 (1881).

Thus, in deciding the limits to which expert opinion may be employed in ascertaining the substantial similarity of computer programs, we cannot disregard the highly complicated and technical subject matter at the heart of these claims. Rather, we recognize the reality that computer programs are likely to be somewhat impenetrable by lay observers—whether they be judges or juries—and, thus, seem to fall outside the category of works contemplated by those who engineered the *Arnstein* test. As Judge Pratt correctly observed:

> In the context of computer programs, many of the familiar tests of similarity prove to be inadequate, for they were developed historically in the context of artistic and literary, rather than utilitarian, works.

Computer Associates, 775 F.Supp., at 558.

In making its finding on substantial similarity with respect to computer programs, we believe that the trier of fact need not be limited by the strictures of its own lay perspective. Rather, we leave it to the discretion of the district court to decide to what extent, if any, expert opinion, regarding the highly technical nature of computer programs, is warranted in a given case.

In so holding, we do not intend to disturb the traditional role of lay observers in judging substantial similarity in copyright cases that involve the aesthetic arts, such as music, visual works or literature.

In this case, Dr. Davis' opinion was instrumental in dismantling the intricacies of computer science so that the court could formulate and apply an appropriate rule of law. While Dr. Davis' report and testimony undoubtedly shed valuable light on the subject matter of the litigation, Judge Pratt remained, in the final analysis, the trier of fact. The district court's use of the expert's assistance, in the context of this case, was entirely appropriate.

2. Evidentiary Analysis

The district court had to determine whether Altai's OSCAR 3.5 program was substantially similar to CA's ADAPTER. We note that Judge Pratt's method of analysis effectively served as a road map for our own, with one exception—Judge Pratt filtered out the non-copyrightable aspects of OSCAR 3.5 rather than those found in ADAPTER, the allegedly infringed program. We think that our approach—i.e., filtering out the unprotected aspects of an allegedly infringed program and then comparing the end product to the structure of the suspect program—is preferable, and therefore believe that district courts should proceed in this manner in future cases.

We opt for this strategy because, in some cases, the defendant's program structure might contain protectable expression and/or other elements that are not found in the plaintiff's program. Since it is extraneous to the allegedly copied work, this material would have no bearing on any potential substantial similarity between the two programs. Thus, its filtration would be wasteful and unnecessarily time consuming. Furthermore, by focusing the analysis on the infringing rather than on the infringed material, a court may mistakenly place too little emphasis on a quantitatively small misappropriation which is, in reality, a qualitatively vital aspect of the plaintiff's protectable expression.

The fact that the district court's analysis proceeded in the reverse order, however, had no material impact on the outcome of this case. Since Judge Pratt determined that OSCAR effectively contained no protectable expression whatsoever, the most serious charge that can be levelled against him is that he was overly thorough in his examination.

The district court took the first step in the analysis set forth in this opinion when it separated the program by levels of abstraction. The district court stated:

> As applied to computer software programs, this abstractions test would progress in order of "increasing generality" from object code, to source code, to parameter lists, to services required, to general outline. In discussing the particular similarities, therefore, we shall focus on these levels.

Computer Associates, 775 F.Supp., at 560. While the facts of a different case might require that a district court draw a more particularized blueprint of a program's overall structure, this description is a workable one for the case at hand.

Moving to the district court's evaluation of OSCAR 3.5's structural components, we agree with Judge Pratt's systematic exclusion of non-protectable expression. With respect to code, the district court observed that after the rewrite of OSCAR 3.4 to OSCAR 3.5, "there remained virtually no lines of code that were identical to ADAPTER". *Id.* at 561. Accordingly, the court found that the code "present[ed] no similarity at all". *Id.* at 562.

Next, Judge Pratt addressed the issue of similarity between the two programs' parameter lists and macros. He concluded that, viewing the conflicting evidence most favorably to CA, it demonstrated that "only a few of the lists and macros were similar to protected elements in ADAPTER; the others were either in the public domain or dictated by the functional demands of the program". *Id.* As discussed above, functional elements and elements taken from the public domain do not qualify for copyright protection. With respect to the few remaining parameter lists and macros, the district court could reasonably conclude that they did not warrant a finding of infringement given their relative contribution to the overall program. In any event, the district court reasonably found that, for lack of persuasive evidence, CA failed to meet its burden of proof on whether the macros and parameter lists at issue were substantially similar. See *Computer Associates*, 775 F.Supp., at 562.

The district court also found that the overlap exhibited between the list of services required for both ADAPTER and OSCAR 3.5 was "determined by the demands of the operating system and of the applications program to which it [was] to be linked through ADAPTER or OSCAR". *Id*. In other words, this aspect of the program's structure was dictated by the nature of other programs with which it was designed to interact and, thus, is not protected by copyright.

Finally, in his infringement analysis, Judge Pratt accorded no weight to the similarities between the two programs' organizational charts, "because [the charts were] so simple and obvious to anyone exposed to the operation of the program[s]". *Id*. CA argues that the district court's action in this regard "is not consistent with copyright law"—that "obvious" expression is protected, and that the district court erroneously failed to realize this. However, to say that elements of a work are "obvious", in the manner in which the district court used the word, is to say that they "follow naturally from the work's theme rather than from the author's creativity". 3 Nimmer § 13.03[F][3], at 13–65. This is but one formulation of the scenes a faire doctrine, which we have already endorsed as a means of weeding out unprotectable expression.

Since we accept Judge Pratt's factual conclusions and the results of his legal analysis, we affirm his dismissal of CA's copyright infringement claim based upon OSCAR 3.5. We emphasize that, like all copyright infringement cases, those that involve computer programs are highly fact specific. The amount of protection due structural elements, in any given case, will vary according to the protectable expression found to exist within the program at issue.

Conclusion

In adopting the above three step analysis for substantial similarity between the non-literal elements of computer programs we seek to insure two things: (1) that programmers may receive appropriate copyright protection for innovative utilitarian works containing expression; and (2) that non-protectable technical expression remains in the public domain for others to use freely as building blocks in their own work. At first blush, it may seem counterintuitive that someone who has benefited to some degree from illicitly obtained material can emerge from an infringement suit relatively unscathed. However, so long as the appropriated material consists of non-protectable expression, "[t]his result is neither unfair nor unfortunate. It is the means by which copyright advances the progress of science and art". *Feist*, 111 S.Ct., at 1290.

Accordingly, we affirm the judgment of the district court in all respects.

Apple Computer, Inc. v. Microsoft Corp.

United States Court of Appeals, Ninth Circuit, 1994.
35 F.3d 1435, cert. denied, ___ U.S. ___, 115 S.Ct. 1176, 130 L.Ed.2d 1129.

■ RYMER, CIRCUIT JUDGE.

Lisa and Macintosh are Apple computers. Each has a graphical user interface ("GUI") which Apple Computer, Inc. registered for copyright as an audiovisual work. Both GUIs were developed as a user-friendly way for ordinary mortals to communicate with the Apple computer; the Lisa Desktop and the Macintosh Finder[a] are based on a desktop metaphor with windows, icons and pull-down menus which can be manipulated on the screen with a hand-held device called a mouse. When Microsoft Corporation released Windows 1.0, having a similar GUI, Apple complained. As a result, the two agreed to a license giving Microsoft the right to use and sublicense derivative works generated by Windows 1.0 in present and future products. Microsoft released Windows 2.03 and later, Windows 3.0; its licensee, Hewlett–Packard Company (HP), introduced NewWave 1.0 and later, New-Wave 3.0, which run in conjunction with Windows to make IBM-compatible computers easier to use. Apple believed that these versions exceed the license, make Windows more "Mac-like", and infringe its copyright. This action followed.

In a series of published rulings,[b] the district court construed the agreement to license visual displays in the Windows 1.0 interface, not the interface itself; determined that all visual displays in Windows 2.03 and 3.0 were in Windows 1.0 except for the use of overlapping windows[c] and some changes in the appearance and manipulation of icons; dissected the Macintosh, Windows and NewWave interfaces based on a list of similarities submitted by Apple to decide which are protectable; and applied the limiting doctrines of originality, functionality, standardization, scenes a faire and merger to find no copying of protectable elements in Windows 2.03 or 3.0, and to limit the scope of copyright protection to a handful of individual elements in NewWave.[d] The court then held that those elements in NewWave would be compared with their equivalent Apple elements for substantial similarity, and that the NewWave and Windows 2.03 and 3.0

---

[a] The Macintosh Finder is registered as a derivative work of the Lisa Desktop. Although the district court dismissed the Finder as a work in suit, the Macintosh interface has been referred to interchangeably with the Lisa during the course of this litigation.

[b] Apple Computer, Inc. v. Microsoft Corp., 709 F.Supp. 925 (N.D.Cal.1989)(*Apple I*); Apple Computer, Inc. v. Microsoft Corp., 717 F.Supp. 1428 (N.D.Cal.1989)(*Apple II*); Apple Computer, Inc. v. Microsoft Corp., 759 F.Supp. 1444 (N.D.Cal.1991)(*Apple III*); Apple Computer, Inc. v. Microsoft Corp., 779 F.Supp. 133 (N.D.Cal.1991)(*Apple IV*); Apple Computer, Inc. v. Microsoft Corp., 799 F.Supp. 1006 (N.D.Cal.1992)(*Apple V*); Apple Computer, Inc. v. Microsoft Corp., 821 F.Supp. 616 (N.D.Cal.1993)(*Apple VI*). The first two published opinions were rendered by Hon. William S. Schwarzer; after his appointment as Director of the Federal Judicial Center, this matter was reassigned to the calendar of Hon. Vaughn R. Walker.

Our treatment of facts throughout is truncated because the district court's is so extensive.

[c] Windows 1.0 had a tiled windowing system in which the windows were connected together in a fixed pattern such that all open windows were simultaneously visible. An overlapping system allows windows to be stacked on top of one another and moved around the screen individually.

[d] These items relate to the "zooming rectangle" animation associated with the opening or closing of an icon into a window, the "dimming" of a folder icon that has been opened into a window, and the use of a trash can icon to depict the discard function. Each appears in both versions 1.0 and 3.0 of New-Wave, but none is in any version of Windows.

works as a whole would be compared with Apple's works for virtual identity. When Apple declined to oppose motions for summary judgment of noninfringement for lack of virtual identity, however, judgments in favor of Microsoft and HP were entered.

Apple asks us to reverse because of two fundamental errors in the district court's reasoning. First, Apple argues that the court should not have allowed the license for Windows 1.0 to serve as a partial defense. Second, Apple contends that the court went astray by dissecting Apple's works so as to eliminate unprotectable and licensed elements from comparison with Windows 2.03, 3.0 and NewWave as a whole, incorrectly leading it to adopt a standard of virtual identity instead of substantial similarity. We disagree.

The district court's approach was on target. In so holding, we readily acknowledge how much more complex and difficult its task was than ours. The district court had to grapple with graphical user interfaces in the first instance—and for the first time, with a claim of copying a computer program's artistic look as an audiovisual work instead of program codes registered as a literary work. In this case there is also the unusual, added complexity of a license that arguably covers some or most of the allegedly infringing works. The district court therefore had to cut new paths as it went along; we have the luxury of looking at the case at the end of the trip. From this vantage point, it is clear that treatment of Apple's GUIs, whose visual displays are licensed to a great degree and which are a tool for the user to access various functions of a computer in an aesthetically and ergonomically pleasing way, follows naturally from a long line of copyright decisions which recognizes that works cannot be substantially similar where analytic dissection demonstrates that similarities in expression are either authorized, or arise from the use of common ideas or their logical extensions.

We therefore hold:

(1) Because there was an agreement by which Apple licensed the right to make certain derivative works, the district court properly started with the license to determine what Microsoft was permitted to copy. Infringement cannot be founded on a licensed similarity. We read Microsoft's license as the district court did, to cover visual displays—not the Windows 1.0 interface itself. That being so, the court correctly decided first to identify which visual displays in Windows 2.03, 3.0 and NewWave are licensed and which are not.

(2) The district court then properly proceeded to distinguish ideas from expression, and to "dissect" unlicensed elements in order to determine whether the remaining similarities lack originality, flow naturally from basic ideas, or are one of the few ways in which a particular idea can be expressed given the constraints of the computer environment. Dissection is not inappropriate even though GUIs are thought of as the "look and feel" of a computer, because copyright protection extends only to protectable elements of expression.

(3) Having found that the similarities in Windows 2.03 and 3.0 consist only of unprotectable or licensed elements, and that the similarities be-

tween protectable elements in Apple's works and NewWave are de minimis, the district court did not err by concluding that, to the extent there is creative expression left in how the works are put together, as a whole they can receive only limited protection. When the range of protectable and unauthorized expression is narrow, the appropriate standard for illicit copying is virtual identity. For these reasons, the GUIs in Windows 2.03, 3.0 and NewWave cannot be compared for substantial similarity with the Macintosh interface as a whole. Instead, as the district court held, the works must be compared for virtual identity.[e]

Apple makes a number of arguments challenging the district court's copyright analysis. It contends that the district court deprived its works of meaningful protection by dissecting them into individual elements and viewing each element in isolation. Because the Macintosh GUI is a dynamic audiovisual work, Apple argues that the "total concept and feel" of its works—that is, the selection and arrangement of related images and their animation—must be compared with that of the Windows and NewWave GUIs for substantial similarity. Apple further asserts that in this case, the court had no occasion to dissect its works into discrete elements because Microsoft and HP virtually mimicked the composition, organization, arrangement and dynamics of the Macintosh interface, as shown by striking similarities in the animation of overlapping windows and the design, layout and animation of icons. Apple also argues that even if dissection were appropriate, the district court should not have eliminated from jury consideration those elements that are either licensed or unprotected by copyright. Though stated somewhat differently, all of these contentions boil down to the same thing: Apple wants an overall comparison of its works to the accused works for substantial similarity rather than virtual identity.

The fact that Apple licensed the right to copy almost all of its visual displays fundamentally affects the outcome of its infringement claims. Authorized copying accounts for more than 90% of the allegedly infringing features in Windows 2.03 and 3.0, and two-thirds of the features in NewWave. More than that, the 1985 Agreement and negotiations leading up to Microsoft's license left Apple no right to complain that selection and arrangement of licensed elements make the interface as a whole look more "Mac-like" than Windows 1.0.

Thus, we do not start at ground zero in resolving Apple's claims of infringement. Rather, considering the license and the limited number of ways that the basic ideas of the Apple GUI can be expressed differently, we conclude that only "thin" protection, against virtually identical copying, is appropriate. Apple's appeal, which depends on comparing its interface as a whole for substantial similarity, must therefore fail.

To prevail, Apple must show ownership of a valid copyright in the Macintosh GUI and that Microsoft and HP copied unlicensed, protected elements of its copyrighted audiovisual works. Brown Bag Software v.

[e] Since Apple contests only the legal standard of virtual identity, we do not consider whether summary judgment was appropriately entered on the merits under that standard.

Symantec Corp., 960 F.2d 1465, 1472 (9th Cir.), *cert. denied*, 113 S.Ct. 198 (1992). Copying may be shown by circumstantial evidence of access and substantial similarity of both the general ideas and expression between the copyrighted work and the allegedly infringing work. *Id.*

We have traditionally determined whether copying sufficient to constitute infringement has taken place under a two-part test having "extrinsic" and "intrinsic" components. As originally adopted in Sid & Marty Krofft Television Productions, Inc. v. McDonald's Corp., 562 F.2d 1157, 1164 (9th Cir.1977), the extrinsic prong was a test for similarity of ideas based on external criteria; analytic dissection and expert testimony could be used, if helpful. The intrinsic prong was a test for similarity of expression from the standpoint of the ordinary reasonable observer, with no expert assistance. *Id.* As it has evolved, however, the extrinsic test now objectively considers whether there are substantial similarities in both ideas and expression, whereas the intrinsic test continues to measure expression subjectively. *Brown Bag*, 960 F.2d at 1475; Shaw v. Lindheim, 919 F.2d 1353, 1357 (9th Cir.1990). Because only those elements of a work that are protectable and used without the author's permission can be compared when it comes to the ultimate question of illicit copying, we use analytic dissection to determine the scope of copyright protection before works are considered "as a whole". See, e.g., *Brown Bag*, 960 F.2d at 1475–76 (explaining that purpose of analytic dissection is to define scope of copyright protection); Pasillas v. McDonald's Corp., 927 F.2d 440, 443 (9th Cir.1991)(copyright holder cannot rely on standard elements to show substantial similarity of expression); Harper House, Inc. v. Thomas Nelson, Inc., 889 F.2d 197, 207–08 (9th Cir.1989)(trier of fact cannot base infringement decision on unprotectable aspects of plaintiff's work).

Although this litigation has raised difficult and interesting issues about the scope of copyright protection for a graphical user interface, resolving this appeal is a matter of applying well-settled principles. In this, as in other cases, the steps we find helpful to follow are these:

(1) The plaintiff must identify the source(s) of the alleged similarity between his work and the defendant's work.

(2) Using analytic dissection, and, if necessary, expert testimony, the court must determine whether any of the allegedly similar features are protected by copyright. Where, as in this case, a license agreement is involved, the court must also determine which features the defendant was authorized to copy. Once the scope of the license is determined, unprotectable ideas must be separated from potentially protectable expression; to that expression, the court must then apply the relevant limiting doctrines in the context of the particular medium involved, through the eyes of the ordinary consumer of that product.

(3) Having dissected the alleged similarities and considered the range of possible expression, the court must define the scope of the plaintiff's copyright—that is, decide whether the work is entitled to "broad" or "thin" protection. Depending on the degree of protection, the court must set the appropriate standard for a subjective comparison of the works to

determine whether, as a whole, they are sufficiently similar to support a finding of illicit copying.

A

Like the plaintiff in *Brown Bag*, in this case, Apple identified the sources of alleged similarity by submitting a list of particular features in its works which are similar to features found in Windows 2.03, 3.0 and NewWave. Apple's suggestion that its arm was twisted to provide this list of similarities and that it was somehow inappropriate for the district court to ask for a list and to rely on it, instead of considering the works as a whole, is misplaced. The court had the benefit of numerous videotapes and demonstrations of the GUIs "as a whole". The district court was nevertheless obliged to identify similarities, determine their source, and decide which elements are protectable. It was thus well within the court's case management discretion to ask for a list from Apple.

B

It is not easy to distinguish expression from ideas, particularly in a new medium. However, it must be done, as the district court did in this case. Baker v. Selden, 101 U.S. 99 (1879). As we recognized long ago in the case of competing jeweled bee pins, similarities derived from the use of common ideas cannot be protected; otherwise, the first to come up with an idea will corner the market. Herbert Rosenthal Jewelry Corp. v. Kalpakian, 446 F.2d 738, 742 (9th Cir.1971). Apple cannot get patent-like protection for the idea of a graphical user interface, or the idea of a desktop metaphor which concededly came from Xerox. It can, and did, put those ideas together creatively with animation, overlapping windows, and well-designed icons; but it licensed the visual displays which resulted.

The district court found that there are five other basic ideas embodied in the desktop metaphor: use of windows to display multiple images on the computer screen and to facilitate user interaction with the information contained in the windows; iconic representation of familiar objects from the office environment; manipulation of icons to convey instructions and to control operation of the computer; use of menus to store information or computer functions in a place that is convenient to reach, but saves screen space for other images; and opening and closing of objects as a means of retrieving, transferring and storing information. *Apple V*, 799 F.Supp., at 1026. No copyright protection inheres in these ideas. Therefore, substantial similarity of expression in unlicensed elements cannot be based on the fact that the Lisa, the Finder, Windows 2.03, 3.0 and NewWave all have windows, icons representing familiar objects from the office environment that describe functions being performed and that can be moved around the screen to tell the computer what to do, menus which give easy access to information or functions without using space on the screen, or objects that open and close.

Well-recognized precepts guide the process of analytic dissection. First, when an idea and its expression are indistinguishable, or "merged", the expression will only be protected against nearly identical copying. *Krofft*, 562 F.2d at 1167–68; *Kalpakian*, 446 F.2d at 742. For example, in this case, the idea of an icon in a desktop metaphor representing a document stored in a computer program can only be expressed in so many ways. An iconic image shaped like a page is an obvious choice.

The doctrine of scenes a faire is closely related. As we explained in Frybarger v. International Business Machines Corp., 812 F.2d 525 (9th Cir.1987), when similar features in a videogame are "as a practical matter indispensable, or at least standard, in the treatment of a given ideal", they are treated like ideas and are therefore not protected by copyright. *Id.* at 530 (quoting Atari, Inc. v. North Am. Philips Consumer Elecs. Corp., 672 F.2d 607, 616 (7th Cir.), *cert. denied*, 459 U.S. 880 (1982)). Furthermore, as *Frybarger* holds, "the mere indispensable expression of these ideas, based on the technical requirements of the videogame medium, may be protected only against virtually identical copying". *Id.*; see also *Data East*, 862 F.2d 204 at 209 (9th Cir.1988)(visual displays of karate match conducted by two combatants, one of whom wears red shorts and the other white as in the sport, and who use the same moves, are supervised by a referee and are scored alike as in the sport, are inherent in the sport of karate itself and as such are unprotectable). In this case, for example, use of overlapping windows inheres in the idea of windows. A programmer has only two options for displaying more than one window at a time: either a tiled system, or an overlapping system. As demonstrated by Microsoft's scenes a faire video, overlapping windows have been the clear preference in graphic interfaces. Accordingly, protectable substantial similarity cannot be based on the mere use of overlapping windows, although, of course, Apple's particular expression may be protected.

Apple suggests that scenes a faire should not limit the scope of its audiovisual copyright, or at least that the interactive character of GUIs and their functional purpose should not outweigh their artistry. While user participation may not negate copyrightability of an audiovisual work, the district court did not deny protection to any aspect of Apple's works on this basis. In any event, unlike purely artistic works such as novels and plays, graphical user interfaces generated by computer programs are partly artistic and partly functional. They are a tool to facilitate communication between the user and the computer; GUIs do graphically what a character-based interface, which requires a user to type in alphanumeric commands, does manually. Thus, the delete function is engaged by moving an icon on top of a trash can instead of hitting a "delete" key. In Apple's GUI, the ability to move icons to any part of the screen exemplifies an essentially functional process, indispensable to the idea of manipulating icons by a mouse.

To the extent that GUIs are artistic, there is no dispute that creativity in user interfaces is constrained by the power and speed of the computer. See Manufacturers Technologies, Inc. v. Cams, Inc., 706 F.Supp. 984, 994–95 (D.Conn.1989)(denying protection to formatting style of plaintiff's screen displays because of constraints on viable options available to programmers). For example, hardware constraints limit the number of ways to depict visually the movement of a window on the screen; because many computers do not have enough power to show the entire contents of the window as it is being moved, the illusion of movement must be shown by using the outline of a window or some similar feature. Design alternatives are further limited by the GUI's purpose of making interaction between the user and the computer more "user-friendly". These, and similar environmental and ergonomic factors which limit the range of possible expression in GUIs, properly inform the scope of copyright protection.

Originality is another doctrine which limits the scope of protection. As the Supreme Court recently made clear, protection extends only to those components of a work that are original to the author, although original selection and arrangement of otherwise uncopyrightable components may be protectable. Feist Publications, Inc. v. Rural Tel. Serv. Co., 499 U.S. 340, 348–51 (1991). Apple's argument that components should not be tested for originality because its interface as a whole meets the test is therefore misplaced.

In sum, the district court's analytic dissection was appropriately conducted under the extrinsic portion of our test for whether sufficient copying to constitute infringement has taken place. We are not persuaded to the contrary by Apple's arguments that the district court shouldn't have dissected at all, or dissected too much; that it "filtered out" unprotectable and licensed elements instead of viewing the Macintosh interface as a whole; and that it should have recognized protectability of arrangements and the "total concept and feel" of the works under a substantial similarity standard.

First, graphical user interface audiovisual works are subject to the same process of analytical dissection as are other works. We have dissected videogames, which are audiovisual works and therefore closely analogous, see, e.g., *Data East*, 862 F.2d at 208–09 (performing analytic dissection of similarities to determine whether similarities resulted from unprotectable expression); *Frybarger*, 812 F.2d at 529–30 (district court correctly concluded that similar features in videogames were unprotectable ideas and that no reasonable jury could find expressive elements substantially similar), and we have dissected nonliteral elements of computer programs, which are somewhat analogous, see, e.g., *Brown Bag*, 960 F.2d at 1475–77 (rejecting argument similar to Apple's about propriety of analytic dissection of computer program components such as screens, menus and keystrokes); Johnson Controls, Inc. v. Phoenix Control Sys., Inc., 886 F.2d 1173, 1176 (9th Cir.1989)(noting special master's detailed analysis of similarities). Other courts perform the same analysis, although articulated differently. See, e.g., Computer Assocs. Int'l, Inc. v. Altai, Inc., 982 F.2d 693, 706–11 (2d Cir.1992)(adopting "abstraction-filtration-comparison" test for analyzing nonliteral structure of computer program, relying in part on our own approach); Gates Rubber Co. v. Bando Chem. Indus., 9 F.3d 823, 834, 841 (10th Cir.1993)(adopting *Altai* test, but suggesting that comparison of works as a whole may be appropriate as preliminary step before filtering out unprotected elements); Engineering Dynamics, Inc. v. Structural Software, Inc., 26 F.3d 1335, 1342–43 (5th Cir.1994)(adopting *Gates Rubber/Altai* test to analyze scope of copyright protection for user interface, input formats and output reports); Lotus Dev. Corp. v. Borland Int'l, Inc., 788 F.Supp. 78, 90, 93 (D.Mass.1992)(describing similar three-part test); cf. Whelan Assocs. v. Jaslow Dental Lab., Inc., 797 F.2d 1222, 1236 (3d Cir.1986)(defining idea of utilitarian work as its purpose or function, and everything not necessary to that purpose as expression), *cert. denied*, 479 U.S. 1031 (1987).

Nor did the district court's dissection run afoul of the enjoinder in such cases as *Johnson Controls*, 886 F.2d at 1176, *Krofft*, 562 F.2d at 1167, and Roth [Greeting Cards v. United Card Co., 429 F.2d 1106, 1110 (9th Cir.1970)], to consider the "total concept and feel" of a work. Here, the court did not inappropriately dissect dissimilarities, and so did nothing to distract from subjectively comparing the works as a whole. See Aliotti v. R. Dakin & Co., 831 F.2d 898, 901 (9th Cir.1987) (indicating that as the concern of *Krofft*).

As we made clear in *Aliotti*, the party claiming infringement may place "no reliance upon any similarity in expression resulting from" unprotectable elements. *Id.* (emphasis added)(similarities between competing stuffed dinosaur toys on account of posture and body design, and being cuddly, stem from the physiognomy of dinosaurs or from the nature of stuffed animals and are thus unprotectable). Otherwise, there would be no point to the extrinsic test, or to distinguishing ideas from expression. In this case, it would also effectively rescind the 1985 Agreement. This does not mean that at the end of the day, when the works are considered under the intrinsic test, they should not be compared as a whole. See McCulloch v. Albert E. Price, Inc., 823 F.2d 316, 321 (9th Cir.1987) (contrasting artistic work at issue, where decorative plates were substantially similar in more than the one unprotectable element (text), with factual works which have many unprotectable elements and very little protectable expression). Nor does it mean that infringement cannot be based on original selection and arrangement of unprotected elements. However, the unprotectable elements have to be identified, or filtered, before the works can be considered as a whole. See *Harper House*, 889 F.2d at 207–08 (reversing because "total impact and effect" test of jury instruction did not distinguish between protectable and unprotectable material, thereby improperly making it possible for jury to find copying based on unprotected material instead of selection and arrangement); see also *Pasillas*, 927 F.2d at 443 (copyright holder could not rely on unprotectable elements to show substantial similarity of expression); *Frybarger*, 812 F.2d at 529 (to extent that similarities between works were confined to ideas and general concepts, they were noninfringing).

C

The district court's conclusion that the works as a whole are entitled only to limited protection and should be compared for virtual identity follows from its analytic dissection. By virtue of the licensing agreement,

Microsoft and HP were entitled to use the vast majority of features that Apple claims were copied. Of those that remain, the district court found no unauthorized, protectable similarities of expression in Windows 2.03 and 3.0, and only a handful in NewWave. Thus, any claim of infringement that Apple may have against Microsoft must rest on the copying of Apple's unique selection and arrangement of all of these features. Under *Harper House* and *Frybarger*, there can be no infringement unless the works are virtually identical.

Apple, however, contends that its audiovisual work with animation and icon design cannot be analogized to factual works such as game strategy books, see Landsberg v. Scrabble Crossword Game Players, Inc., 736 F.2d 485, 488 (9th Cir.)("[S]imilarity of expression may have to amount to verbatim reproduction or very close paraphrasing before a factual work will be deemed infringed."), *cert. denied*, 469 U.S. 1037 (1984), accounting systems, see *Selden*, 101 U.S., at 104 (copyright in book describing new accounting system not infringed when defendant copied ledger sheets used in system), or organizers, see *Harper House*, 889 F.2d at 205 (as compilations consisting largely of uncopyrightable elements, plaintiff's organizers entitled only to protection against "bodily appropriation of expression"), which are afforded only "thin" protection because the range of possible expression is narrow. See *Feist*, 499 U.S., at 349. Rather, it submits that the broader protection accorded artistic works is more appropriate. See, e.g., *McCulloch*, 823 F.2d at 321 (artistic work like a decorative plate receives broader protection because of endless variations of expression available to artist).

Which end of the continuum a particular work falls on is a call that must be made case by case. We are satisfied that this case is closer to *Frybarger* than to *McCulloch*. See also Atari Games Corp. v. Oman, 979 F.2d 242, 245 (D.C.Cir.1992)(analogizing audiovisual work like a videogame to compilation of facts). Accordingly, since Apple did not contest summary judgment under the virtual identity standard on the merits, judgment was properly entered.

We therefore hold that the district court properly identified the sources of similarity in Windows and NewWave, determined which were licensed, distinguished ideas from expression, and decided the scope of Apple's copyright by dissecting the unauthorized expression and filtering out unprotectable elements. Having correctly found that almost all the similarities spring either from the license or from basic ideas and their obvious expression, it correctly concluded that illicit copying could occur only if the works as a whole are virtually identical.

Michael Stillman v. Leo Burnett Co.

United States District Court, N.D. Illinois, 1989.
720 F.Supp. 1353.

■ DUFF, DISTRICT JUDGE.

Plaintiff Michael Stillman has sued defendants Leo Burnett Company, Inc. ("Burnett") and United Airlines, Inc. ("United") for copyright infringement under the Copyright Act, 17 U.S.C. § 501. Stillman alleges that the defendants copied a "silent" television commercial he had created for Eastern Airlines, Inc. ("Eastern"), and then misrepresented that they had created their commercial through lucky inspiration. The defendants have moved to dismiss. For the reasons set forth below, the motion will be denied.

Facts

For the purposes of this motion, the court accepts as true the allegations of the complaint, the facts contained within the complaint's exhibits, and the videotapes (with accompanying storyboards) of the two commercials.[a] Stillman is a creative advertising consultant, and the creator and producer of television commercials. In late 1981, he created a commercial for Eastern's Canadian airline passenger market, which aired on Canadian television during 1982 and 1983.

The commercial employed silence as a way of attracting viewer attention to the screen. Of the nine screens in the commercial, the first eight were black with white reverse-type writing. The writing faded in and out from screen to screen—with the exception of the Eastern name and logo, which remained on the screen—and read as follows:

Screen 1:

A SILENT COMMERCIAL FOR EASTERN SUPER 7'S

Screen 2:

MIAMI EASTERN SUPER 7'S

Screen 3:

7 NIGHTS 8 DAYS CHOICE HOTEL
EASTERN SUPER 7'S

Screen 4:

SCHEDULED ROUND TRIP FLIGHTS
EASTERN SUPER 7'S

Screen 5:

RENTAL CAR UNLIMITED
MILEAGE (AND MORE)
EASTERN SUPER 7'S

Screen 6:

ONLY $370 PER PERSON
DOUBLE OCCUPANCY
EASTERN SUPER 7'S

---

[a] In an earlier ruling, this court converted the defendants' motion to dismiss to one for summary judgment.

Screen 7:

WHY SO QUIET?
EASTERN SUPER 7'S

Screen 8:

BECAUSE THE COMPETITION IS SLEEPING
EASTERN SUPER 7'S

The last screen suddenly broke into color and sound, showing a picture of a sunset and containing a voice-over explaining the point of the silent commercial. The commercial was hugely successful and profitable for Eastern, and was widely discussed in Canadian and American advertising industry circles.

In 1986, after Eastern (inexplicably) decided not to use the silent commercial for its American market, Stillman, who owned the right to it, wrote two letters to United's president suggesting that United engage Stillman to produce silent commercials for United's American market. With the letters, he enclosed copies of the Eastern storyboard, and some ideas about how the silent commercial could be used for United.

United never hired Stillman, but in 1987 it did air a "silent" commercial on American television. This commercial, like the Eastern commercial, contained nine screens, the first eight of which were black with white reverse-type writing fading in and out from screen to screen and reading as follows:

Screen 1:

This is a silent commercial

Screen 2:

The money we saved on sound

Screen 3:

Helps keep our air fares this low:

Screen 4:

United's Chicago $89 from New York
UNITED AIRLINES

Screen 5:

United's Miami $89 from New York
UNITED AIRLINES

Screen 6:

United's Los Angeles $99
from New York
UNITED AIRLINES

Screen 7:

United's San Francisco $99
from New York
UNITED AIRLINES

Screen 8:

Call Now 212–867–3000 718–803–2200
201–624–1500 or your travel agent

Fares shown are each way with round trip—Restrictions apply. Seats are limited.

The last screen broke into color, showing an airplane taking off over the word "Roarrrrr", but maintaining silence.

The creator and producer of United's silent commercial was Leo Burnett. At the time Leo Burnett created the commercial, it was aware of Stillman's silent commercial for Eastern. Nevertheless, in interviews following the airing of the United commercial, Leo Burnett represented that it had created the silent commercial and that the creation resulted from "lucky inspiration".

In 1988, Stillman applied for and received a Certificate of Registration for his silent commercial from the United States Register of Copyrights. Shortly thereafter, he filed this lawsuit.

Discussion

Courts frequently have said that a copyright claim contains only two elements: (1) the plaintiff's ownership of a valid copyright in a work; and (2) the defendant's copying of this work in creating another one. See, e.g., Atari, Inc. v. North American Philips Consumer Electronics Corp., 672 F.2d 607, 614 (7th Cir.1982). In *Atari*, the Seventh Circuit elaborated on the second element. According to the Court of Appeals, a plaintiff can establish copying by showing (1) that the defendant had access to the plaintiff's work, and (2) that the two works are substantially similar. 672 F.2d at 614. Further, the Court of Appeals stated, a plaintiff establishes substantial similarity by showing (1) that "the defendant copied from the plaintiff's work and (2) [that] the copying, if proven, went so far as to constitute an improper appropriation". *Id.*

At first blush, this framework appears circular: To prove copying, the plaintiff must prove substantial similarity; and to prove substantial similarity, he must prove copying. See Nash v. CBS, Inc., 704 F.Supp. 823, 826 (N.D.Ill.1989). The confusion lies in the different meaning of the word "copying" in copyright law.

The copyright laws serve to promote the "progress of science and useful arts" by protecting the labors of those who create original works and thereby ensuring the profitability of their endeavors and their willingness to bring novel ideas to the public. Too much protection, however, would undermine the goal: If authors, by publishing their works, could remove the ideas incorporated in them from the public domain, then they could stifle, rather than advance, the development and exploitation of new ideas. To skate the thin line between too much and too little protection, the copyright laws have come to distinguish between the expression of ideas on the one hand, and the ideas themselves on the other. Authors may protect the former; the latter remain freely available for other authors to develop and exploit. See § 102(b).

Copying, as an element of a copyright claim, refers to the ultimate legal issue of whether the defendant violated the copyright laws by reproducing protectible expression from the plaintiff's work. Copying as a prong of substantial similarity, by contrast, is limited to the purely factual issue of whether the defendant used the plaintiff's work as a starting point for his own. See Arnstein v. Porter, 154 F.2d 464 (2d Cir.1946). Thus, a defendant who has copied from a plaintiff's work as a factual matter—that is, by employing the plaintiff's ideas, procedures or techniques—may not have copied as a legal matter; the difference between the two lies in the second prong of the substantial similarity inquiry—i.e., unlawful appropriation. If a defendant has not copied something protected by the copyright laws—specifically, the plaintiff's expression of his ideas—then his copying will not subject him to liability. Sid & Marty Krofft Television v. McDonald's Corp., 562 F.2d 1157, 1163–64 (9th Cir.1977). Thus, when the Seventh Circuit stated in *Atari* that, in effect, a plaintiff must establish copying in order to prove copying, what it must have meant was that the plaintiff must establish at least permissible copying as a prerequisite to proving illicit copying.

Yet, with this inexactitude in the *Atari* framework resolved, others emerge. If a defendant must prove copying in order to prove substantial similarity, why must he then prove access in order to establish an infringement? After all, copying, even in the permissible sense, clearly requires that the defendant have had access to—indeed, have relied upon—the plaintiff's work in creating the new one. Moreover, although it is clear why a plaintiff must show improper appropriation in order to prove a copyright violation, it is difficult to see why such appropriation stands as a prong of substantial similarity, rather than as a separate element of the copyright cause of action. Substantial similarity, in the context of the *Atari* framework (672 F.2d at 614), is merely one of two elements—the other being access—that must be proved in order to permit an inference that the defendant usurped material from the plaintiff's work; this inference arises, however, upon proof of substantial similarity between even nonprotectible elements of the two works, without any need to prove that what was taken amounted to an unlawful appropriation of the plaintiff's expression. See *Arnstein*, 154 F.2d at 469.

These difficulties arise out of the dual usages of another term—substantial similarity. As just noted, substantial similarity can refer to the likeness between two works sufficient to give rise to an inference, when supported by evidence of access, that the defendant took ideas from the plaintiff's work. Substantial similarity, however, is also used as a term of art relating to the unlawful nature of the similarities between two works. See Roth Greeting Cards v. United Card Co., 429 F.2d 1106, 1110 (9th Cir.1970); Nimmer on Copyright § 13.03[A] at 13–22.1 (1988)(similarity is not "substantial" if what was copied was nonprotectible).

Atari creates obfuscation because it refers to substantial similarity in its former usage, but then sets forth the test necessary to establish the latter. Proof of both copying and unlawful appropriation are necessary to establish substantial similarity when that term is used as a term of art; a copy that does not unlawfully appropriate protectible expression cannot be substantially similar in the sense required to establish a violation. See *Atari*, 672 F.2d at 614. They are not necessary, however, when substantial similarity is used in the sense of a factual predicate for an inference of copying. On the contrary, when the phrase is used in this sense, it is not copying which is necessary to establish substantial similarity, but rather substantial similarity which is necessary to prove copying.

This discussion suggests that some clarification of the *Atari* logic is needed. To prevail on a copyright claim, a plaintiff must prove (1) a valid copyright, and (2) illicit copying. To prove illicit copying, he must establish both (1) copying, and (2) unlawful appropriation. To establish copying, a plaintiff must show (1) access, and (2) substantial similarity between the works "when compared in their entirety including both protectible and unprotectible material". 3 Nimmer on Copyright § 13.03[e] at 13–55 (1988). Finally, to show unlawful appropriation (i.e., substantial similarity as a matter of law), the plaintiff must demonstrate that the defendant's copying extended to the plaintiff's protectible expression.

The defendants have conceded, for the purposes of this motion, both the validity of the plaintiff's copyright and their permissible copying of the Eastern commercial. Their only argument at this stage is that, even assuming such copying, they are entitled to judgment because the United silent commercial did not copy any protectible material from the Eastern commercial. This argument requires a further analysis of how a plaintiff establishes the copying of protectible expression.

As noted above, the copying/unlawful appropriation dichotomy simply reflects the fact that the copyright laws do not protect ideas, procedures, and concepts, but only the expressions of ideas. Copying occurs when a defendant usurps the former; unlawful appropriation, however, requires the purloining of expression as well. In *Krofft*, the Ninth Circuit, building on Arnstein v. Porter, *supra*, articulated a bifurcated test for proving copying and unlawful appropriation.

The first test, the so-called extrinsic test, permits a plaintiff to prove copying by showing, through analytic dissection and (if necessary) expert testimony, that the similarities between the two works—when viewed in terms of their protectible and nonprotectible elements—are so substantial as to warrant a finding that the defendant usurped, at least, the plaintiff's ideas. 562 F.2d at 1164. The second, or intrinsic, test addresses the indeterminate boundary between ideas and their expression. Because the infringement of expression occurs when "the ordinary observer, unless he set out to detect the disparities [in two works], would be disposed to overlook them, and regard [the works'] aesthetic appeal as the same", Peter Pan Fabrics, Inc. v. Martin Weiner Corp., 274 F.2d 487, 489 (2d Cir.1960)(Hand, J.), the intrinsic test precludes reference to objective criteria and expert testimony, and requires instead an inquiry into whether an ordinary observer experiencing the two works would conclude that "the accused work has captured the 'total concept and feel' of the copyrighted work". *Atari*, 672 F.2d at 614 (quoting Roth Greeting Cards v. United Card Co., 429 F.2d 1106, 1110 (9th Cir.1970)); *Krofft*, 562 F.2d at 1164; Arnstein v. Porter, 154 F.2d at 468.

Krofft further explained that summary judgment is rarely appropriate under the intrinsic test, since laymen are as qualified as judges to determine the reactions of an ordinary observer. 562 F.2d at 1166. If an ordinary observer could conclude that the defendant copied the plaintiff's expression (by using the plaintiff's work to create another work evoking a similar response in an ordinary observer), then, *Krofft* instructed (and *Atari* purported to follow, 672 F.2d at 614), the case should go to the jury.

Under *Krofft*'s extrinsic-intrinsic tests, this court could not grant the defendants' motion for summary judgment. As the defendants acknowledge, under the extrinsic test a question of fact exists as to whether they copied Stillman's work: the commercials both use silence as the means of attracting viewer attention to the screen; they both begin with a screen stating that they are silent commercials; they both contain eight screens with black background and white lettering; they both break into color in the final screen; and they both tie their silence into the low fares of their respective airlines. Further, under the intrinsic test, a reasonable jury could find similarity of expression in the two commercials. Although the commercials have a different pace, a different message, and a different final frame, these differences do not so undermine the similarities as to render implausible a jury finding that the United commercial exudes the same total concept and feel as does the Eastern commercial. See *Atari*, 672 F.2d at 618 (focus of ordinary observer test is on similarities rather than differences).

The intrinsic-extrinsic analysis, however, does not fully encompass the infringement inquiry. See *Krofft*, 562 F.2d at 1167. The intrinsic test, by focusing on the response of the ordinary observer, follows the accepted view that ordinarily a plaintiff can establish copying of expression even in the absence of identical copying. *Id*. Yet, because this test eschews analytic dissection, it fails to account for the possibility that the similarity of expression may fall within the category of what is known as nonprotectible expression. Specifically, when the expression is indistinguishable from the idea, the copyright laws prohibit only identical copying because to protect more would be to grant a monopoly over the idea. In the same vein, when the similarity between two works arises exclusively from the use of the same process or technique it cannot form the basis for a copyright claim. See Baker v. Selden, 101 U.S. (11 Otto) 99, 101 (1879). Finally, "similarity of expression, whether literal or non-literal, which necessarily results from the fact that the common idea is only capable of expression in more or less stereotyped form will preclude a finding of actionable similarity". 3 Nimmer on Copyright § 13.03[A] at 13–21–13–33 (1988). Stated in terms of the intrinsic test, a non-identical work that would evoke a similar response in an ordinary observer as does another work does not violate the latter's copyright if the similar response arises solely from the similarities of the nonprotectible elements of the two works.

The defendants insist that a comparison of the United commercial with the Eastern commercial reveals that all they copied are the nonprotectible elements of Stillman's work. They first contend that the idea of using a silent commercial to attract viewer attention to the screen is indistinguishable from the expression of that idea through the use of silence, so that their use of silence per se cannot give rise to liability. They next assert that the use of black screens with white lettering and of color screens at the end are all audio-visual techniques which similarly cannot render them liable absent identical copying. Lastly, they urge that their copying of Stillman's use of a first screen stating that the commercial is silent is necessary to the expression of a silent commercial (i.e., to inform the viewers that their sets are not broken), and thus cannot form the basis for a copyright claim. Since any similarity in the total concept and feel of the two commercials results from these nonprotectible elements, and since the two commercials are not identical, the defendants conclude that no illicit copying has occurred.

The defendants are correct insofar as they argue that, in order to determine whether all of the similarities between two works result from the copying of nonprotectible expression, the court may undertake an analytic dissection of the two works. The extrinsic and intrinsic tests both involve findings of fact, but the issue of protectibility/nonprotectibility is an issue of law. Thus, before a court may send a copyright case to the jury, it must satisfy itself that, even assuming copying of an idea and its expression, at least some of what the defendant copied falls into the area of protectible expression.[b]

The defendants, however, misapply this inquiry in the instant case. Although a plaintiff can protect neither his ideas nor his use of procedures and techniques to express these ideas, he can protect the creative arrangement and interaction of the techniques composing the expression. As *Krofft* noted in countenancing limited analytic dissection for the purpose of ensuring some copying of protectible expression, "it is the *combination* of many different elements which may command copyright protection because of its particular subjective quality". 562 F.2d at 1169 (original emphasis).

---

[b] In Olson v. National Broadcasting Co., 855 F.2d 1446 (9th Cir.1988), the Ninth Circuit (without saying so) appears to have incorporated this requirement—that, if copying occurred, it extended to protectible expression—into the extrinsic test. In *Olson*, the Court affirmed a j.n.o.v. for the defendants under the extrinsic test after analytically dissecting the two works and determining that all of their similarities resulted from similarities in nonprotectible elements of the plaintiff's work. See *id.* at 1450–53. This approach, however, loses sight of the function of the extrinsic test, which is to determine not whether illicit copying occurred, but rather whether any copying occurred. Since the Court does not appear to have questioned the jury's determination that the defendants copied from the plaintiff, see *id.* at 1448, *Krofft* should have led the *Olson* Court to find the extrinsic test satisfied, and to confine itself to reviewing the jury's verdict under the intrinsic test and, if necessary, under the idea-expression unity limitation on this test, see *id.* at 1453.

When this combination of elements is used in a way that is not "indispensable, or at least standard in the treatment of a given topic", *Atari*, 672 F.2d at 616, no idea-expression unity exists, and the requirement of near-identical similarity does not come into play.

Standing on their own, Stillman's use of an initial screen announcing that the commercial was a silent commercial, eight black screens with white lettering, and a color screen at the end, do not amount to protectible expression. Yet, the synergy of these nonprotectible elements in the Eastern commercial creates a whole that is greater than the sum of its parts. Each of the nonprotectible elements of the commercial may have been quite indispensable to a silent commercial, but Stillman's actual arrangement of these elements in the creation of his commercial was in no sense dictated by the idea of a silent commercial, and therefore renders the idea-expression unity limitation inapplicable here. Should a jury find that the defendants copied the Eastern commercial in making the United commercial, and that in doing so they created a commercial that evokes a similar response in ordinary observers, this court could not say that the defendants' copying fell exclusively within the realm of the nonprotectible. Accordingly, the defendants' motion for summary judgment must be denied.

NOTES

1. *Tests for infringement.* Arnstein v. Porter[2] is the seminal copyright infringement decision in the Second Circuit. In that case, the court held that a copyright infringement plaintiff must prove a) copying; and b) improper appropriation. The first element, copying, could be proved by the defendant's direct admission or by circumstantial evidence such as evidence of access and similarities between the two works that are sufficient to prove copying. The *Arnstein* court also held that expert testimony could be resorted to by the trier of fact to aid in this analysis. Absent evidence of access, the existing similarities must be so striking "as to preclude the possibility that the plaintiff and defendant independently arrived at the same result."[3] Once copying is established, the plaintiff must then prove improper appropriation. Satisfaction of this element is determined by the "ordinary lay hearer," and thus analytic dissection and "expert testimony are irrelevant."[4] How does this test compare with the tests invoked in *Nichols* and *Altai*? How would you compare the tests for infringement in the Second, Ninth, and Seventh Circuits? Are they markedly different or fairly consistent? Which test is best?

The court in *Apple* endorsed the "virtual identity" standard for infringement with respect to works with a narrow range of protectable and unauthorized expression. Most courts, however, invoke a more lenient standard which requires the defendant's work to be "substantially similar" to the plaintiff's if it is to be considered infringing. Why shouldn't the

---

[2] 154 F.2d 464 (2d Cir.1946).   [4] Id.

[3] Id. at 468.

standard for copyright infringement for all types of works be virtual identity rather than substantial similarity? Would paraphrasing a work render it virtually identical to the original work? Should paraphrasing be considered infringement?

2. *Protected vs. unprotected material.* Part of the difficulty with the area of copyright infringement is that one of the main issues, namely, the extent to which unprotected subject matter should be considered in copyright determinations, arises in conjunction with the following three separate inquiries: (1) Should unprotected subject matter contained in a plaintiff's work be considered in the initial determination of the copyrightability of the plaintiff's work? ; (2) Should unprotected subject matter be considered in the copying prong (generally the first prong) of an infringement inquiry?; and (3) Should unprotected subject matter be considered in the unlawful appropriation prong (generally the second prong) of an infringement inquiry? Note that this Assignment is concerned with the second and third inquiries, whereas Assignment 7 addresses the first inquiry. Of course, to the extent a defendant's alleged infringement stems from copying elements from the plaintiff's work that are not within the scope of the plaintiff's copyright, all three inquiries are related.

3. *Substantial similarity.* The dual meaning of substantial similarity is discussed in *Stillman.* The court in that case clarifies that substantial similarity can be used in a factual or evidentiary sense, which provides circumstantial evidence of copying when combined with evidence of access. In addition, substantial similarity also can be used to refer to the similarities existing between two works that render the defendant's work an unlawful appropriation of the plaintiff's work in the legal sense. In the view of the late Professor Latman, the type of substantial similarities used to establish copying in a factual sense is simply intended to prove that independent creation is unlikely and therefore such similarities "may or may not be substantial." He suggested that since these similarities are "offered as probative of the act of copying," the test for this type of similarity should be renamed "probative similarity."[5] In fact, the Second Circuit expressly adopted Professor Latman's terminology in Laureyssens v. Idea Group, Inc.[6]

4. *Unlawful appropriation.* Should the unlawful appropriation prong of the substantial similarity test consider only the similarity of protected expression, or should it also consider whether the "concept and feel" of the works at issue are similar? In Nash v. CBS, Inc.,[7] the district court in the Northern District of Illinois expressly rejected the idea that the ordinary observer test should take into account unprotected elements by comparing the works in question in their entirety, based on their "total concept and

[5] Latman, "Probative Similarity" As Proof of Copying: Toward Dispelling Some Myths in Copyright Infringement, 90 Colum. L. Rev. 1187, 1214 (1990).

[6] 964 F.2d 131, 140 (2d. Cir.1992). *Laureyssens* originally was decided a month be-

fore *Altai*, but was amended two days after the *Altai* decision.

[7] 704 F.Supp. 823, 826 (N.D.Ill.1989), aff'd, 899 F.2d 1537 (7th Cir.1990).

feel." Is *Stillman*, which was decided by the same court later that same year, consistent with this view? Can *Stillman* and *Apple* be reconciled? To what extent does the *Altai* court allow for protection of a unique arrangement of unprotectable material?

5. *Computer programs.* *Altai* observes that the case dealt with the extent to which the "non-literal" aspects of a computer program are copyrightable, and that this was a case "of first impression" in the Second Circuit. The first generation of computer cases typically dealt with whether the literal aspects of a computer program, such as the source or object code, are subject to copyright protection.[8] Currently there is no doubt that these literal aspects are protected. The second generation of computer cases deals with the non-literal aspects of computer programs. Litigation on this point has revolved around the structure, sequence, and organization of the source and object code; the structure of a program's command system; and the presentation of information on the screen (i.e., the user interface).[9] Are there any arguments against extending broad copyright protection to user interfaces? Can the three-step approach in *Altai* be applied to screen displays and user interfaces? What about a computer menu command hierarchy? The patentability of computer programs is treated in Assignment 16.

In a portion of *Altai* that does not appear in the text, the court also reversed the district court's determination that CA's trade secret misappropriation claim was preempted by § 301 of the 1976 Copyright Act and held that "with regard to OSCAR 3.5, CA has a viable trade secret claim against *Altai* that must be considered by the district court on remand."[10] The court further noted that if on remand "the district court finds that CA was injured by *Altai's* unlawful use of CA's trade secrets in creating OSCAR 3.5, CA is entitled to an award of damages for trade secret misappropriation, as well as consideration by the district court of CA's request for injunctive relief on its trade secret claim."[11] What is the impact of this determination from the standpoint of providing relief for program developers?

In MAI Systems Corp. v. Peak Computer, Inc.,[12] the Ninth Circuit held that a computer servicing company performing maintenance duties infringed the copyright in plaintiff's software by its unlicensed transfer of the computer programs from a permanent storage device such as a floppy disk

---

[8] See, e.g., Apple Computer, Inc. v. Franklin Computer Corp., 714 F.2d 1240, 1243 (3d Cir.1983), cert. dismissed, 464 U.S. 1033, 104 S.Ct. 690, 79 L.Ed.2d 158 (1984); Midway Mfg. Co. v. Strohon, 564 F.Supp. 741, 750 (N.D.Ill.1983).

[9] Lotus Dev. Corp. v. Paperback Software Int'l, 740 F.Supp. 37, 46 (D.Mass.1990)(holding that the user interface for the Lotus 1–2–3 spreadsheet program as a whole is copyrightable). This opinion also contains a good summary of the case law extending copyright

protection to the non-literal components of computer programs. See id. at 55.

[10] 982 F.2d at 719.

[11] 982 F.2d at 721. Ultimately, the Second Circuit determined that the trade secret claim was barred by the Texas statute of limitations. See Computer Associates International, Inc. v. Altai, Inc., 61 F.3d 6 (2d Cir.1995).

[12] 991 F.2d 511 (9th Cir.1993).

to the computer's random access memory ("RAM"). According to the court, the defendant's loading the software into the RAM so that it is able to view the system error log and diagnose the computer's problem shows that the representation created in the RAM is sufficiently "fixed" for purposes of establishing copyright infringement.[13]

6. *Visual art.* Note that § 501 of the copyright statute, which deals with infringement, specifically provides that a violation of the author's rights under the Visual Artists Rights Act ("VARA") constitutes infringement (VARA is discussed in Assignment 9). Although none of the major cases reproduced in this Assignment treat visual art, one of the more interesting infringement cases dealing with visual art is Steinberg v. Columbia Pictures Industries, Inc.[14] That case was an action by artist Saul Steinberg against the producers and advertisers of the movie "Moscow on the Hudson," stemming from their use of an illustration created to advertise the movie that allegedly infringed the plaintiff's famous picture. The plaintiff's picture, which had appeared on the cover of The New Yorker, depicted the world as viewed by a "typical" New Yorker. It showed minute details of a street in New York City, with a background consisting of the Hudson River, followed by tiny letters designating various major cities in the United States as well as other countries to the west (the idea being that the world pretty much revolves around New York City). The defendants' picture was similar, except that it had the Atlantic Ocean and locations in Europe as the background. What special difficulties are raised in cases involving infringements of visual art?

7. *Expert testimony.* In the traditional, bifurcated approach to infringement, expert testimony is allowed to be considered in the copying prong of the inquiry, but disallowed in the unlawful appropriation prong. Why do you suppose the traditional bifurcated approach is wary of expert testimony in the unlawful appropriation prong of the infringement test? As *Altai* illustrates, the newer trend in the computer cases is for the trier of fact to make the ultimate infringement determination, and to allow itself to be informed by expert opinion in making this decision. Courts and commentators have suggested that with respect to technically complex material, this new approach makes a good deal more sense because it is unrealistic to expect the trier of fact to be exposed to expert opinion in the copying, or extrinsic, prong of the infringement analysis, and then to forget that testimony in its unlawful appropriation analysis.[15] Does this issue have any relevance to the Principal Problem?

---

[13] Id. at 518. See also Advanced Computer Services of Michigan, Inc. v. MAI Systems Corp., 845 F.Supp. 356, 30 U.S.P.Q.2d 1443 (E.D.Va.1994); Triad Systems Corp. v. Southeastern Express Co., 31 U.S.P.Q.2d 1239 (N.D.Cal.1994), affirmed in part, reversed in part 64 F.3d 1330 (9th cir.1995).

[14] 663 F.Supp. 706 (S.D.N.Y.1987).

[15] See, e.g., Whelan Assoc., Inc. v. Jaslow Dental Lab., Inc., 797 F.2d 1222, 1233 (3d Cir.1986), cert. denied, 479 U.S. 1031, 107 S.Ct. 877, 93 L.Ed.2d 831 (1987)("join[s] the growing number of courts which do not apply the ordinary observer test in copyright cases involving exceptionally difficult materials, like computer programs, but instead adopt[s] a single substantial similarity inquiry according to which both lay and expert testimony would be admissible"); Note, The Role of the Expert Witness in Music Copyright Infringe-

8.   *Subconscious infringement.* In Bright Tunes Music Corp. v. Harrisongs Music, Ltd.,[16] the district court ruled, and the Second Circuit affirmed, that George Harrison had committed subconscious infringement when he wrote his hit song, *My Sweet Lord*, around 1970. The song that was allegedly infringed, *He's So Fine*, had been on top of the billboard charts for several weeks in both the United States and England. Although the district court did not believe that Harrison deliberately used the music of *He's So Fine* in composing his song, the unquestionable access and the virtual identity of the songs compelled a finding of subconscious infringement. The Second Circuit rejected Harrison's argument that the number of years between the time when the plaintiff's song was on the radio and the time when Harrison composed his song should preclude a finding of access, in light of the song's popularity and Harrison's admission that he remembered hearing the song. Harrison also argued before the Second Circuit that, as a policy matter, the doctrine of subconscious copying should not be recognized because it "brings the law of copyright improperly close to patent law, which imposes a requirement of novelty."[17] Do you agree? Are there any other problems with allowing good faith to establish a defense to infringement? If good faith is not relevant to the ultimate infringement determination, to what should it pertain?

9.   *Interim infringement (reverse engineering).* In Sega v. Accolade,[18] the court considered the legality of defendant's "reverse engineering" of plaintiff Sega's video game programs to discover the compatibility requirements for their own equipment. This process entailed the defendant Accolade's transformation of the "machine-readable object code contained in commercially available copies of [plaintiff's] game cartridges into human-readable source code using a process called 'disassembly' or 'decompilation.'"[19] From the disassembled code, the defendant discovered the interface specifications of the plaintiff's console. The defendant then created a development manual containing functional descriptions of these interface requirements. Subsequently, the defendant created its own games, relying on the information concerning the interface specifications contained in the development manual. Interestingly, the interface used the message "PRODUCED BY OR UNDER LICENSE FROM SEGA ENTERPRISES LTD." To achieve compatability, the defendant copied this portion of Sega's code into its own game programs with the result that they displayed the Sega trademark.

---

ment Cases, 57 Fordham L. Rev. 127, 138–39 (1988)(criticizing application of test for infringement in *Krofft* that allows the factfinder to consider expert testimony in the first prong of the substantial similarity analysis but then requires it to disregard this testimony in the second prong in the context of music infringement cases). See also Brown Bag Software v. Symantec Corp., 960 F.2d 1465, 1474 n.3 (9th Cir.), cert. denied, 506 U.S. 869, 113 S.Ct. 198, 121 L.Ed.2d 141 (1992)(noting that the law in the Ninth Circuit "appears to be moving toward the test . . . in which lay and expert testimony are uniformly admissible").

[16] 420 F.Supp. 177 (S.D.N.Y.1976), aff'd sub nom. ABKCO Music, Inc. v. Harrisongs Music, Ltd., 722 F.2d 988 (2d Cir.1983).

[17] 722 F.2d at 998.

[18] 977 F.2d 1510 (9th Cir.1992).

[19] Id. at 1514.

Sega held that such intermediate copying of a computer object code can constitute copyright infringement, and the court distinguished *Altai* on the ground that the "legality of the intermediate copying" was not "at issue."[20] Still, *Sega* ultimately concluded that the defendant's activity constituted fair use (see Assignment 12) since disassembly was the only means through which Accolade could gain access to the unprotected aspects of the program and it had a legitimate reason for such access.[21] *Sega* thus raises the issues of whether intermediate copying in and of itself is lawful, and whether some instances of such copying can be excused as fair use.

The facts of *Sega* also suggest the further issue of the "clean room" defense. That is, whether there should be infringement when a programmer other than the intermediate copier writes a new program using the intermediate copier's specifications, but never sees the original code. In *Altai*, in deciding whether OSCAR 3.5 infringed the plaintiff's copyright, should it have mattered that the defendant infringed the plaintiff's copyright in creating the prior version, OSCAR 3.4, even though the defendants took precautions not to use the plaintiff's work in the new version and none of the programmers who had been hired to create OSCAR 3.5 had been involved with the prior version?

10. *Defense summary judgments. Arnstein* also held that summary judgment could not be granted when there is the "slightest doubt" with respect to the facts, but this aspect of the case has been repudiated in the Second Circuit.[22] In the copyright context specifically, the Second Circuit has held that summary judgment for the defense may be warranted on the issue of improper appropriation if no reasonable jury could find that the works in question are substantially similar.[23] In Shaw v. Lindheim,[24] a case involving literary works, the court held that if a plaintiff satisfies the extrinsic test by showing that reasonable minds might find a substantial similarity between the objective elements of expression in the plaintiff's and defendant's respective works, the defendant is not entitled to summary judgment based on the court's subjective determination that no reasonable person could conclude the works were substantially similar in their overall concept and feel. Otherwise, a court would be granting the defendant summary judgment based exclusively "on a purely subjective determination of similarity" as a matter of law. Does *Stillman* follow the rule of *Shaw* regarding summary judgment?

BIBLIOGRAPHY

Recent articles discussing the tests for copyright infringement include: Bisceglia, Summary Judgment on Substantial Similarity in Copyright Ac-

---

[20] Id. at 1518–19.

[21] Id. at 1520. The court also concluded that Sega's use of the trademark security code to gain access to the plaintiff's console did not constitute trademark infringement. Id. at 1528–32.

[22] See, e.g., Beal v. Lindsay, 468 F.2d 287, 291 (2d Cir.1972).

[23] See, e.g., Denker v. Uhry, 820 F.Supp. 722, 728 (S.D.N.Y.1992), aff'd, 996 F.2d 301 (2d Cir.1993), and Second Circuit cases cited at p. 728 of the district court opinion.

[24] 919 F.2d 1353 (9th Cir.1990).

tions, 16 Hastings Comm. & Ent. L.J. 51 (1993); Kurtz, Speaking to the Ghost: Idea and Expression in Copyright, 47 U. Miami L. Rev. 1221 (1993); Lape, The Metaphysics of the Law: Bringing Substantial Similarity Down to Earth, 98 Dick. L. Rev. 181 (1993); Fruehwald, Copyright Infringement of Musical Compositions: A Systematic Approach, 26 Akron L. Rev. 15 (1992); Latman, "Probative Similarity" as Proof of Copying: Toward Dispelling Some Myths in Copyright Infringement, 90 Colum. L. Rev. 1187 (1990); Samuels, The Idea–Expression Dichotomy in Copyright Law, 56 Tenn. L. Rev. 321 (1989).

Articles specifically dealing with infringement in the context of computer programs include: Nimmer & Krauthaus, Software Copyright: Sliding Scales and Abstracted Expression, 32 Hous. L. Rev. 317 (1995); Karjala, Copyright Protection of Computer Software, Reverse Engineering, and Professor Miller, 19 U. Dayton L. Rev. 975 (1994); Samuelson, The Nature of Copyright Analysis for Computer Programs: Copyright Law Professors' Brief Amicus Curiae in "Lotus v. Borland", 16 Hastings Comm. & Ent. L.J. 657 (1994); Brown, "Analytical Dissection" of Copyrighted Computer Software—Complicating the Simple and Confounding the Complex, 25 Ariz. St. L.J. 801 (1993); Miller, Copyright Protection for Computer Programs, Databases, and Computer–Generated Works: Is Anything New Since Contu?, 106 Harv. L. Rev. 977 (1993); Rosen, Virtual Reality: Copyrightable Subject Matter and the Scope of Judicial Protection, 33 Jurimetrics J. 35 (1992); Samuelson, Computer Programs, User Interfaces, and Section 102(b) of the Copyright Act of 1976: A Critique of Lotus v. Paperback, 6:2 High Tech. L.J. 209 (1991); Hobbs, Methods of Determining Substantial Similarity in Copyright Cases Involving Computer Programs, 67 U. Det. L. Rev. 393 (1990); Menell, An Analysis of the Scope of Copyright Protection for Application Programs, 41 Stan. L. Rev. 1045 (1989); Samuelson & Glushko, Comparing the Views of Lawyers and User Interface Designers on the Software Copyright "Look and Feel" Lawsuits, 30 Jurimetrics J. 121 (1989); Nimmer, Bernacchi, & Frischling, A Structured Approach to Analyzing the Substantial Similarity of Computer Software in Copyright Infringement Cases, 20 Ariz. St. L.J. 625 (1988); Samuelson, Reflections on the State of American Software Copyright Law and the Perils of Teaching It, 13 Colum.-VLA J.L. & Arts 61 (1988). See also Symposium: A Manifesto Concerning the Legal Protection of Computer Programs, 94 Colum. L. Rev. 2308 (1994); Symposium: Copyright Protection and Reverse Engineering of Software, 19 U. Dayton L. Rev. 837 (1994); Symposium: Copyright Protection: Has Look & Feel Crashed?, 11 Cardozo Arts & Ent. L.J. 721 (1993); Computer Law Symposium: Software Protection in the Nineties, 15 Hastings Comm. & Ent. L.J. 557 (1993); LaST Frontier Conference Report, Computer Software and Copyright Protection, 30 Jurimetrics J. 15 (1989).

THE INTEREST IN PUBLIC ACCESS

1. INTRODUCTION

As discussed in the previous chapter, copyright law embodies the concept of ownership by enabling the copyright proprietor to exercise exclusively certain rights with respect to the protected work. In certain situations, however, copyright law recognizes the need to sanction unauthorized uses of copyrighted property. One of the most important such exemption is the fair use doctrine, which is the subject of the following Assignment. In addition to the fair use doctrine, the 1976 Copyright Act details a series of exempted activities that do not constitute copyright infringement and a series of limitations upon the scope of exclusive rights to copyrighted works. These exemptions and limitations are codified at Sections 107–120. Although many of these statutory sections are rather technical and complex, they must be read carefully to appreciate fully the delicate balance struck by copyright law respecting the oftentimes diametrically opposed interests of creators and the public in the copyrighted work.

A critical issue in copyright law is how to balance the tension between the copyright proprietor's desire to restrict access to the copyrighted work to those willing to pay for such access and the public's interest in using the protected work. This Assignment and the following Assignment explore this issue in two separate contexts. Assignment 12 explores this inquiry in the context of the fair use doctrine, and this Assignment explores it in the context of defining the copyright owner's exclusive right to publicly perform her work which is codified in § 106(4) of the statute. To fully explore the exemptions related to public performances, it is worth spending a moment considering what a public performance is. This is defined by § 101 of the statute, which provides that "[t]o perform or display a work 'publicly' means—(1) to perform or display it at a place open to the public or at any place where a substantial number of persons outside of a normal circle of a family and its social acquaintances is gathered; or (2) to transmit or otherwise communicate a performance or display of the work to a place specified by clause (1) or to the public, by means of any device or process, whether the members of the public capable of receiving the performance or display receive it in the same place or in separate places and at the same time or at different times."[1] The first clause of this definition has been called the "public place" clause and the second clause,

[1] § 101.

the "transmit" clause.[2]

To appreciate the compromise position that the copyright statute has adopted regarding public access in the context of unauthorized performances, two sets of inquiries must be pursued. First, since § 106(4) only allows the copyright proprietor the exclusive right to perform the work *publicly*, it is necessary to grapple with the statute's definition of a public performance. Second, since § 110 of the statute also exempts certain public performances and displays from copyright infringement, it is important to confront these statutory exemptions. This section of the statute, particularly § 110(5), has been the subject of some especially interesting cases. The following Principal Problem requires a consideration of both of these inquiries.

2.   PRINCIPAL PROBLEM

Plaintiff, Masada Hotel Corp. owns about 500 hotels across the country. Masada is the creator of a unique system for viewing videos that currently is operational in almost all of its hotels across the country. Plaintiff's system is comprised of a computer program, a sophisticated electronic switch, and a bank of video cassette players ("VCPs"), all of which are contained in a centralized equipment room within the hotel. The VCPs are connected by wiring to the guest rooms. Each VCP contains a video tape. When a guest requests a particular movie, a computer program directs an electric switch so that the VCP containing that movie is switched to the guest's room, and the video begins. Guests can select a particular movie from a menu of titles appearing on the screen of their television. Once a guest chooses a particular movie, that movie is eliminated from the television screen menus in all other guest rooms during the period of time in which the movie is being watched by the viewer. While the movie is being shown, the viewer cannot interrupt, rewind, or fast-forward the video. At the completion of the movie, it becomes available immediately for all the other guests of the hotel.

At the time of a guest's check-in to the hotel, the hotel clerk uses a front-desk terminal connected to the system's computer program to activate movie transmission to the occupied room. A guest can request that the clerk prevent the transmission of adult movies and even the transmission of the entire service. The plaintiff's system is more advantageous than existing closed-circuit hotel video systems with invariable movie times because there are a larger number of videos that can be shown and guests can watch the movies according to their own schedules. Additionally, the system eliminates the potential inconvenience and embarrassment to guests necessitated by in-house hotel video rental programs.

Each of the plaintiff's hotels also contains a coffee shop with about 2500 square feet, and a public area of about 1800 square feet. The radio is

[2] See Columbia Pictures Industries, Inc. v. Professional Real Estate Investors, Inc., 866 F.2d 278 (9th Cir.1989).

operated in each of the plaintiff's coffee shops throughout the day. Each coffee shop contains a single receiver that is located in a small room that is not accessible to the public. Two speakers, which are recessed in the ceiling, are connected to the receiver by thirty feet of hidden wiring. Masada believes that its activity does not constitute copyright infringement because it falls within the "homestyle" exemption contained in § 110(5) of the 1976 Copyright Act.

Masada is seeking a declaratory judgment that its viewing video system does not infringe the copyrights held by various defendant movie companies. At issue here is whether the plaintiff's system constitutes a public performance under the 1976 Copyright Act. In addition, Masada is suing for declaratory relief that its radio usage policy in its coffee shops does not violate the copyright laws. Thus, Masada also has named as a defendant ASCAP (American Society of Composers, Authors, and Publishers), a performing rights organization that collectively licenses the rights to public performances of its members' copyrighted musical compositions.

You are the presiding judge. Before determining how you should rule with respect to each issue in this case, consider the following materials.

3.   MATERIALS FOR SOLUTION OF PRINCIPAL PROBLEM

A.   STATUTORY MATERIALS: §§ 108–119, 801–803, 1001–1010 & 1101

B.   CASES:

Columbia Pictures Industries, Inc. v. Redd Horne, Inc.

United States Court of Appeals, Third Circuit, 1984.
749 F.2d 154.

■ RE, CHIEF JUDGE.

In this copyright infringement case, defendants appeal from an order of the United States District Court for the Western District of Pennsylvania which granted the plaintiffs' motion for summary judgment, and enjoined defendants from exhibiting plaintiffs' copyrighted motion pictures. Columbia Pictures Indus., Inc., v. Redd Horne Inc., 568 F.Supp. 494 (W.D.Pa.1983).

Facts

Maxwell's Video Showcase, Ltd., operates two stores in Erie, Pennsylvania. At these two facilities, Maxwell's sells and rents video cassette recorders and prerecorded video cassettes, and sells blank video cassette cartridges. These activities are not the subject of the plaintiffs' complaint. The copyright infringement issue in this case arises from defendants' *exhibition* of video cassettes of the plaintiffs' films, or what defendants euphemistically refer to as their "showcasing" or "in-store rental" concept.

Each store contains a small showroom area in the front of the store, and a "showcase" or exhibition area in the rear. The front showroom contains video equipment and materials for sale or rent, as well as dispensing machines for popcorn and carbonated beverages. Movies posters are also displayed in this front area. In the rear "showcase" area, patrons may view any of an assortment of video cassettes in small, private booths with space for two to four people. There are a total of eighty-five booths in the two stores. Each booth or room is approximately four feet by six feet and is carpeted on the floor and walls. In the front there is a nineteen inch color television and an upholstered bench in the back.

The procedure followed by a patron wishing to utilize one of the viewing booths or rooms is the same at both facilities. The customer selects a film from a catalogue which contains the titles of available films. The fee charged by Maxwell's depends on the number of people in the viewing room, and the time of day. The price is $5.00 for one or two people before 6 p.m., and $6.00 for two people after 6 p.m. There is at all times a $1.00 surcharge of the third and fourth person. The fee also entitles patrons to help themselves to popcorn and soft drinks before entering their assigned rooms. Closing the door of the viewing room activates a signal in the counter area at the front of the store. An employee of Maxwell's then places the cassette of the motion picture chosen by the viewer into one of the video cassette machines in the front of the store and the picture is transmitted to the patron's viewing room. The viewer may adjust the light in the room, as well as the volume, brightness, and color levels on the television set.

Access to each room is limited to the individuals who rent it as a group. Although no restriction is placed on the composition of a group, strangers are not grouped in order to fill a particular room to capacity. Maxwell's is open to any member of the public who wishes to utilize its facilities or services.

Maxwell's advertises on Erie radio stations and on the theatre pages of the local newspapers. Typically, each advertisement features one or more motion pictures, and emphasizes Maxwell's selection of films, low prices, and free refreshments. The advertisements do not state that these motion pictures are video cassette copies. At the entrance to the two Maxwell's facilities, there are also advertisements for individual films, which resemble movie posters.

Infringement of Plaintiffs' Copyright

It may be stated at the outset that this is not a case of unauthorized taping or video cassette piracy. The defendants obtained the video cassette copies of plaintiffs' copyrighted motion pictures by purchasing them from either the plaintiffs or their authorized distributors. The sale or rental of these cassettes to individuals for home viewing is also not an issue. Plaintiffs do not contend that in-home use infringes their copyright.

The plaintiffs' complaint is based on their contention that the exhibition or showing of the video cassettes in the private booths on defendants' premises constitutes an unauthorized public performance in violation of plaintiffs' exclusive rights under the federal copyright laws.

It is acknowledged that it is the role of the Congress, not the courts, to formulate new principles of copyright law when the legislature has determined that technological innovations have made them necessary. A defendant, however, is not immune from liability for copyright infringement simply because the technologies are of recent origin or are being applied to innovative uses. Although this case involves a novel application of relatively recent technological developments, it can nonetheless be readily analyzed and resolved within the existing statutory framework.

Section 106 of the Copyright Act confers upon the copyright holder certain exclusive rights. [Section 106(4)] provides that "in the case of literary, musical, dramatic, and choreographic works, pantomimes, *and motion pictures and other audiovisual works*, [the copyright owner has the exclusive right] *to perform the copyrighted work publicly*" (emphasis added).

It is undisputed that the defendants were licensed to exercise the right of distribution. Id. § 106(3). A copyright owner, however, may dispose of a copy of his work while retaining all underlying copyrights which are not expressly or impliedly disposed of with that copy. Id. § 202. Thus, it is clear that the plaintiffs have retained their interest in the other four enumerated rights. Since the rights granted by section 106 are separate and distinct, and are severable from one another, the grant of one does not waive any of the other exclusive rights. Thus, plaintiffs' sales of video cassette copies of their copyrighted motion pictures did not result in a waiver of any of the other exclusive rights enumerated in section 106, such as the exclusive right to perform their motion pictures publicly. In essence, therefore, the fundamental question is whether the defendants' activities constitute a public performance of the plaintiffs' motion pictures. We agree with the conclusion of the district court that these activities constitute a public performance, and are an infringement.

"To perform a work means . . . in the case of a motion picture or other audiovisual work, to show its images in any sequence or to make the sounds accompanying it audible." § 101 (1982). Clearly, playing a video cassette results in a sequential showing of a motion picture's images and in making the sounds accompanying it audible. Thus, Maxwell's activities constitute a performance under section 101.

The remaining question is whether these performances are public. Section 101 also states that to perform a work "publicly" means "[t]o perform . . . it at a place open to the public or at any place where a substantial number of persons outside of a normal circle of a family and its social acquaintances is gathered." Id. The statute is written in the disjunctive, and thus two categories of places can satisfy the definition of "to perform a work publicly." The first category is self-evident; it is "a place open to the public." The second category, commonly referred to as a semi-public place, is determined by the size and composition of the audience.

The legislative history indicates that this second category was added to expand the concept of public performance by including those places that, although not open to the public at large, are accessible to a significant number of people. See H.R. Rep. No. 1476, 94th Cong., 2d Sess. 64, reprinted in, 1976 U.S. Code Cong. & Ad. News 5659, 5677–78 (hereinafter cited as House Report). Clearly, if a place is public, the size and composition of the audience are irrelevant. However, if the place is not public, the size and composition of the audience will be determinative.

We find it unnecessary to examine the second part of the statutory definition because we agree with the district court's conclusion that Maxwell's was open to the public. On the composition of the audience, the district court noted that "the showcasing operation is not distinguishable in any significant manner from the exhibition of films at a conventional movie theater." 568 F.Supp., at 500. Any member of the public can view a motion picture by paying the appropriate fee. The services provided by Maxwell's are essentially the same as a movie theatre, with the additional feature of privacy. The relevant "place" within the meaning of section 101 is each of Maxwell's two stores, not each individual booth within each store. Simply because the cassettes can be viewed in private does not mitigate the essential fact that Maxwell's is unquestionably open to the public.

The conclusion that Maxwell's activities constitute public performances is fully supported by subsection (2) of the statutory definition of public performance:

> (2) to transmit or otherwise communicate a performance . . . of the work to a place specified by clause (1) or to the public, by means of any device or process, whether the members of the public capable of receiving the performance . . . receive it in the same place or in separate places and at the same time or at different times.

Section 101 (1982). As explained in the House Report which accompanies the Copyright Revision Act of 1976, "a performance made available by transmission to the public at large is 'public' even through the recipients are not gathered in a single place. . . . The same principles apply whenever the potential recipients of the transmission represent a limited segment of the public, such as the occupants of hotel rooms. . . ." House Report, *supra,* at 64–65. Thus, the transmission of a performance to members of the public, even in private settings such as hotel rooms or Maxwell's viewing rooms, constitutes a public performance. As the statutory language and legislative history clearly indicate, the fact that members of the public view the performance at different times does not alter this legal consequence.

Professor Nimmer's examination of this definition is particularly pertinent: "*if the same copy* . . . of a given work is repeatedly played (i.e., 'performed') by different members of the public, albeit at different times, this constitutes a 'public' performance." 2 M. Nimmer, § 8.14[C][3], at 8–142 (emphasis in original). Indeed, Professor Nimmer would seem to have envisaged Maxwell's when he wrote:

> one may anticipate the possibility of theaters in which patrons occupy separate screening rooms, for greater privacy, and in order not to have to await a given hour for commencement of a given film. These too should obviously be regarded as public performances with the underlying rationale of the Copyright Act.

Id. at 8–142. Although Maxwell's has only one copy of each film, it shows each copy repeatedly to different members of the public. This constitutes a public performance.

The First Sale Doctrine

The defendants also contend that their activities are protected by the first sale doctrine. The first sale doctrine is codified in section 109(a) of Title 17. This section provides:

> Notwithstanding the provisions of section 106(3), the owner of a particular copy or phonorecord lawfully made under this title, or any person authorized by such owner, is entitled, without the authority of the copyright owner, to sell or otherwise dispose of the possession of that copy or phonorecord.

Section 109(a)(1982). Section 109(a) is an extension of the principle that ownership of the material object is distinct from ownership of the copyright in this material. See § 202 (1982). The first sale doctrine prevents the copyright owner from controlling the future transfer of a particular copy once its material ownership has been transferred. The transfer of the video cassettes to the defendants, however, did not result in the forfeiture or waiver of all of the exclusive rights found in section 106. The copyright owner's exclusive right "to perform the copyrighted work publicly" has not been affected; only its distribution right as to the transferred copy has been circumscribed.

In essence, the defendants' "first sale" argument is merely another aspect of their argument that their activities are not public performances. For the defendants' argument to succeed, we would have to adopt their characterization of the "showcasing" transaction or activity as an "in-store rental." The facts do not permit such a finding or conclusion. The record clearly demonstrates that showcasing a video cassette at Maxwell's is a significantly different transaction than leasing a tape for home use. Maxwell's never disposed of the tapes in its showcasing operations, nor did the tapes ever leave the store. At all times, Maxwell's maintained physical dominion and control over the tapes. Its employees actually played the cassettes on its machines. The charges or fees received for viewing the cassettes at Maxwell's facilities are analytically indistinguishable from admission to any public theater. Plainly, in their showcasing operation, the appellants do not sell, rent, or otherwise dispose of the video cassette. On the facts presented, Maxwell's "showcasing" operation is a public performance, which, as a matter of law, constitutes a copyright infringement.

Conclusion

In view of the foregoing, it is the holding of this Court that the defendants' activities constituted an unauthorized, and, therefore, an unlawful public performance of the plaintiffs' copyrighted motion pictures.

The judgment of the district court, therefore, will be affirmed.

Broadcast Music, Inc. v. Claire's Boutiques, Inc.

United States District Court, N.D. Illinois, 1990.
754 F.Supp. 1324.

■ ROVNER, DISTRICT JUDGE.

I. Introduction

This case raises an issue concerning the scope of the "single receiving apparatus" exemption from the Copyright Act's grant to copyright owners of the exclusive right to publicly perform their works. It is brought by Broadcast Music, Inc. ("BMI"), which holds copyrights to musical compositions, against Claire's Boutiques, Inc. ("Claire's"), which owns and operates 749 retail stores. Pending are cross-motions for summary judgment. For the reasons described below, BMI's motion is denied and Claire's motion is granted.

II. Facts

The essential facts relevant to the pending motions are undisputed. Claire's owns and operates 719 individual retail stores under the name Claire's Boutiques and 30 stores under the name Arcadia. The Claire's Boutiques stores sell women's accessories, and the Arcadia stores sell stationery, games, and novelty items.

The Claire's Boutiques stores range in size from 458 square feet to 2000 square feet, with an average size of 861 square feet. Ninety-one of the stores are greater than 1055 square feet, and 628 are less than 1055 square feet. The Arcadia stores range in size from 748 square feet to 3300 square feet, with an average size of 2022 square feet. Twenty-seven of the stores are greater than 1055 square feet, and three are less than 1055 square feet.

During fiscal year 1990, Claire's had net sales of $168,674,000 and earned $13,402,000 in net income. The Claire's Boutiques stores averaged $264,681 in net sales and $20,986 in net profits. The Arcadia stores, which Claire's acquired in October, 1989, averaged $126,381 in net sales and $15,870 in profits during the last quarter of fiscal year 1990, which included the Christmas season.

With the exception of approximately 65 stores,[a] Claire's stores receive radio broadcasts which are normally played in the stores during all hours they are open.[b] The equipment in each store includes a 5-watt stereo receiver, an indoor antenna, two speakers, and speaker wire. The same equipment is also used in Claire's warehouse, which is approximately 10,000 square feet in size.

The receiver used by Claire's is a Radio Shack Optimus STA-20 AM/FM receiver. It does not have built-in speakers, and it has jacks that allow the connection of only two speakers. The speakers are Realistic

---

[a] Those 65 stores opened after August 1990, and Claire's has decided not to play radio broadcasts in those stores pending the result of this litigation.

[b] Because there are a number of stores in the Chicago area, it is likely that at least some play the same radio station simultaneously.

Minimus 7 speakers, also sold by Radio Shack. They measure six inches by six inches by eight inches. They are designed to be set on a flat surface or hung from a wall or ceiling. Claire's utilizes 18–gauge speaker wire to connect the speakers to the receiver. Claire's pays $103.96 for each receiver, $39.95 for each speaker, and $2.24 for each indoor antenna. These prices reflect volume discounts of 20 to 25 percent. The record does not indicate the amount Claire's spends on the speaker wire.

Altogether, Claire's owns and operates at least 669 receivers and 1,338 speakers. It orders 20 to 50 receivers per order and up to 300 speakers at a time. It maintains the equipment as a stock item, and a new receiver is shipped when a new store is built or when a receiver breaks and a new one is ordered from Claire's by the individual store. During the last four years, Claire's has spent a total of a little over $100,000 on stereo equipment.

The selling area in most stores is separated from a storage area by a partition wall. In those stores, the receiver is kept on a shelf in the storage area. In some stores, there is a closet rather than a storage area, and the receiver is kept on a shelf in the closet. In yet other stores, in which remodelling has not been completed, the receiver is kept behind the cash register counter. The parties have not contended that there is any material difference between the three arrangements, and have focused their attention on the first and most common arrangement.

The stores have decorative dropped ceilings with a grid composed of lights running just below the dropped ceiling. The speakers are attached to the upper ceiling, and they hang down to a point approximately six inches above the light grid. They are installed by general contractors when the stores are built.

A speaker wire runs from each of the receiver's two speaker jacks up the partition wall and through a hole in the partition wall. One wire is connected to a speaker which hangs from the ceiling in the rear corner of the selling area. This speaker is located at an average distance of five to fifteen feet from the receiver. The other wire runs above the dropped ceiling and is connected to a speaker which hangs from the ceiling at an average distance of twenty to thirty-five feet from the receiver. The speaker wire is concealed as much as possible.

BMI is a performing rights society recognized by the Copyright Act, 17 U.S.C.A. § 116(e)(3). It licenses public performance of copyrighted musical compositions, including about 50 percent of all compositions performed over the radio in this country. For an annual fee, BMI offers a license to music users to perform the compositions in its repertoire.

Prior to their acquisition by Claire's, the Arcadia stores subscribed to a commercial background music service. Claire's discontinued the subscription approximately six months after the acquisition. Twenty-four Claire's Boutiques stores also had a trial subscription to a commercial background music service. Claire's ended the trial subscription because its employees preferred listening to the radio.

It is BMI's position that Claire's violates the Copyright Act by playing radio broadcasts in its stores because Claire's is not licensed by BMI. BMI has offered to provide Claire's with a license which would encompass all public performances of BMI music by Claire's at an annual cost of $240 for the first location and $45 to $65 for each additional location. The total cost of the license for all the stores involved in the pending motions would be $40,385, which amounts to an average of $53.92 per store. Claire's has offered to purchase a license encompassing all stores which have a size in excess of 1055 square feet, on the condition that BMI not seek to license the remaining stores. BMI has rejected this offer.

In this action, BMI and various artists who it represents have brought suit for copyright infringement based on specific songs which were broadcast into Claire's stores over the receiver and speakers owned by Claire's. The only dispute raised by the pending motions is whether Claire's is statutorily exempt from the licensing requirements of the Copyright Act pursuant to § 110(5).

III.   Analysis

A.   Background

The Copyright Act gives a copyright holder certain exclusive rights in her copyrighted works. These include the exclusive rights of public performance of musical works. See § 106. Unlicensed performances which do not conflict with the exclusive rights granted by the Act do not infringe on the holder's rights.

In *Aiken*, the Court was faced with the issue of whether the use of a radio in a fast-food establishment infringed on the exclusive rights of the owners of the copyrighted songs broadcast on the radio. The restaurant utilized a receiver with outlets to four speakers mounted in the ceiling. The Court noted that "the broadcast of a copyrighted musical composition by a commercial radio station [is] a public performance of that composition for profit—and thus an infringement of the copyright if not licensed." Twentieth Century Music Corp. v. Aiken, 422 U.S. 151, 158 (1975). However, the Court's precedents indicated that one who listens to the broadcast through the use of a radio receiver does not perform the composition. Id. at 161, citing Fortnightly Corp. v. United Artists, 392 U.S. 390 (1968) and Teleprompter Corp. v. CBS, 415 U.S. 394 (1974). The Court then stated:

> To hold in this case that the respondent *Aiken* "performed" the petitioners' copyrighted works would thus require us to overrule two very recent decisions of this Court. But such a holding would more than offend the principles of stare decisis; it would result in a regime of copyright law that would be both wholly unenforceable and highly inequitable.

Id. 422 U.S. at 162. The Court stated that such a holding would be unenforceable because of the large number of business establishments with radio or television sets, and inequitable because it would authorize "the sale of an untold number of licenses for what is basically a single public rendition of a copyrighted work." Id. at 162–63.

In 1976, Congress created an explicit exemption modelled after the Supreme Court's holding in *Aiken*. This exemption provides:

[C]ommunication of a transmission embodying a performance or display of a work by the public reception of the transmission on a single receiving apparatus of a kind commonly used in private homes [does not constitute a copyright infringement], unless—

(A) a direct charge is made to see or hear the transmission; or

(B) the transmission thus received is further transmitted to the public.

Section 110(5).[c] This provision is discussed in the Report of the House Committee on the Judiciary:

[I]ts purpose is to exempt from copyright liability anyone who merely turns on, in a public place, an ordinary radio or television receiving apparatus of a kind commonly sold to members of the public for private use.

The basic rationale of this clause is that the secondary use of the transmission by turning on an ordinary receiver in public is so remote and minimal that no further liability should be imposed....

It is the intent of the conferees that a small commercial establishment of the type involved in [*Aiken*], which merely augmented a home-type receiver and which was not of sufficient size to justify, as a practical matter, a subscription to a commercial background music service, would be exempt. However, where the public communication was by means of something other than a home-type receiving apparatus, or where the establishment actually makes a further transmission to the public, the exemption would not apply....

Under the particular fact situation in the *Aiken* case, assuming a small commercial establishment and the use of a home receiver with four ordinary loudspeakers grouped within a relatively narrow circumference from the set, it is intended that the performances would be exempt under clause (5). However, the Committee considers this fact situation to represent the outer limit of the exemption, and believes that the line should be drawn at that point. Thus, the clause would exempt small commercial establishments whose proprietors merely bring onto their premises standard radio or television equipment and turn it on for their customers' enjoyment, but it would impose liability where the proprietor has a commercial "sound system" installed or converts a standard home receiving apparatus (by augmenting it with sophisticated or extensive amplification equipment) into the equivalent of a commercial sound system. Factors to consider would include the size, physical arrangement, and noise level of the areas within the establishment where the transmissions are made audible or visible, and the extent to which the receiving apparatus is altered or augmented for the purpose of improving the aural or visual quality of the performance for individual members of the public using those areas.

---

[c] Although this provision supported the *Aiken* result, it changed the rationale; in contrast to the Supreme Court's conclusion that no "performance" had occurred, under the new statute a performance does occur but does not require a license. See 2 Nimmer on Copyright § 8.18[B] (1990).

H.R. Rep. No. 94–1476, 94th Cong. 2d Sess. 87 (1976), reprinted in 1976 U.S. Code Cong. & Admin. News 5659, 5701 and 17 U.S.C.A. p. 145, 148–149 (1977).

At issue in this case is whether Claire's falls within the § 110(5) exemption. The burden of proof lies on Claire's to show that it falls within the exemption. BMI does not contend that Claire's makes a direct charge to see or hear the radio broadcasts, see § 110(5)(A). Accordingly, the statute provides three elements which Claire's must prove to establish that the exemption applies: (1) it uses a single receiving apparatus; (2) the receiving apparatus is of a kind commonly used in private homes; and (3) Claire's does not further transmit to the public the transmissions it receives. A central issue in this case, apparently one of first impression, is whether this analysis should focus on each individual store or on the corporation as a whole. If the individual stores would not be exempt, it is unnecessary to consider this larger issue. Accordingly, the Court shall first examine the application of the statute to the individual stores.

B. Individual Stores

1. Single Receiving Apparatus

There is no dispute that each store, considered individually, operates only one radio receiver. Accordingly, the first element of the exemption is satisfied.

2. Kind Commonly Used in Private Homes

A number of courts have examined various models and configurations of receivers and speakers in order to determine whether the sound systems are of a kind commonly used in private homes. Although by its terms the statute requires only that the "receiving apparatus" be of a kind used in private homes, courts have examined the entire sound systems, including the speakers and speaker wiring, in making this determination. See, e.g., Hickory Grove Music v. Andrews, 749 F.Supp. 1031 (D.Mont.1990). The factors which courts generally examine include (1) whether the receiver and other equipment itself is generally sold for commercial or private use; (2) the number of speakers which the receiver can accommodate; (3) the number of speakers actually used; (4) the manner in which the speakers are installed; (5) whether the speaker wires are concealed; (6) the distance of the speakers from the receiver; and (7) whether the receiver is integrated with a public announcement system or telephone lines.[d] Although courts

---

[d] See National Football League v. McBee & Bruno's, Inc., 792 F.2d 726, 731 (8th Cir.1986)(system not home-type where it used satellite dish to receive signals); Hickory Grove, 749 F.Supp. at 1038 (system not home-type where receiver was connected by concealed wiring to five recessed ceiling speakers at a distance of up to 45 feet and where speakers were originally installed to support public address system); Broadcast Music, Inc. v. Jeep Sales & Service Co., 747 F.Supp. 1190, 1193, (E.D.Va.1990)(system not home-type where it included four recessed ceiling speakers and four public address horns mounted on light poles); Crabshaw Music v. K-Bob's of El Paso, Inc., 744 F.Supp. 763, 767 (W.D.Tex.1990)(system not home-type where it included a commercial

have not generally clarified the relative weight or the relationship of these various factors, this Court finds such a discussion to be necessary.

BMI argues that the systems in this case contain certain features which are similar to those in cases where the systems have been found not to be of a type commonly used in private homes, and BMI emphasizes Claire's use of ceiling speakers and concealed wiring. Claire's responds that its equipment is less sophisticated than that in the vast majority of the cases relied on by BMI. Both of the parties' arguments are correct, but neither is determinative. In order to resolve this issue, the Court shall look in turn at each of the factors enumerated above.

1. The equipment itself. The Court finds that the components themselves are of a type commonly used in private homes. The receiver delivers only 5 watts of power, far less than many receivers sold for private use. It sells for a price lower than many receivers sold for private use. Even a cursory review of newspaper advertisements reveals many more sophisticated receivers designed for home use. Similarly, the speakers are small and are clearly designed for private home use, and the speaker wire is the type recommended by the speakers' manual.

2. Number of speakers receiver can accommodate. The receiver in this case contains jacks for only two speakers. Home-type receivers typically accommodate two or four speakers. In this respect, the receivers used by Claire's stores are home-type receivers.

3. Number of speakers used. Two speakers are in fact used in each store, and this factor weighs in favor of finding that it is a home-type

type tuner wired into a public address system, commercial quality microphones, and eleven commercial speakers installed throughout restaurant); Gnossos Music v. DiPompo, 13 U.S.P.Q.2d (BNA) 1539 (D.Me.1989)(system not home-type where it consisted of portable radio/cassette player in restaurant lobby, connected by concealed wiring to eight to ten recessed commercial-quality speakers in dining rooms and lobby); Merrill v. Bill Miller's Bar–B–Q Enterprises, Inc., 688 F.Supp. 1172, 1175 (W.D.Tex.1988)(system not home-type, even though individual components were home-type, where receiver was connected by 40 feet of hidden wiring to eight unfinished, ceiling mounted speakers spaced 30 feet apart); Merrill v. County Stores, Inc., 669 F.Supp. 1164, 1170 (D.N.H.1987)(system was not home-type where it could be interrupted for paging purposes, it was integrated into telephone network, and it included 14 or 15 recessed ceiling speakers covering 13,000 square feet of floor area); International Korwin Corp. v. Kowalczyk, 665 F.Supp. 652, 655, 657 (N.D.Ill.1987)(system not home-type where receiver had paging capabilities, three sets of speaker terminals, and capacity for driving 40 speakers, and was attached to eight remote ceiling speakers with concealed wiring), aff'd, 855 F.2d 375 (7th Cir.1988); Rodgers v. Eighty Four Lumber Co., 617 F.Supp. 1021, 1023 (W.D.Pa.1985)(system not home-type where separate receiver and amplifier were used, where system contained public address system, where there were 2 to 5 speakers inside the store and 1 to 3 speakers outside the store, and where most speakers were located 150 feet from the receiver); Springsteen v. Plaza Roller Dome, Inc., 602 F.Supp. 1113, 1118 (M.D.N.C.1985)(system not commercial, even though receiver was wired to six speakers mounted on light poles over 7500 square foot area of miniature golf course, because of inferior noise level and audibility); Lamminations Music v. P & X Markets, Inc., 1985 Copyright L. Dec. (CCH) para. 25,790 (N.D.Cal.1985)(system not home-type where it included "receiving equipment and [six to ten] ceiling-mounted speakers akin to a commercial background music system" and speakers were "not arranged within a narrow circumference from the receivers").

system. Indeed, the legislative history indicates that a system which includes four speakers may qualify for this exemption.[e]

4. *Manner in which speakers are installed.* The speakers in this case are concealed in a dropped ceiling. Many courts have treated ceiling-mounted speakers as indicative that a system is not of home-type. This court agrees that the use of ceiling-mounted speakers weighs against application of the exemption, but it cautions that this factor is not determinative. Where all other factors point to a home-style system, the fact that one hangs the speakers from a ceiling rather than setting them on the floor or shelf or mounting them on a wall should not change the result. First, it is not difficult to mount speakers in a ceiling, and private consumers increasingly utilize sophisticated home entertainment arrangements, including speakers recessed in a wall or ceiling. Second, where all other factors point in favor of a finding that the system is home-type, making the result change if the business installs the speakers in a ceiling can hardly fulfill the intent of Congress. If, as BMI states, Congress intended to protect small commercial establishments, making the copyright exemption turn on the use of ceiling-mounted speakers would be an odd choice for a yardstick.[f]

5. *Use of concealed wiring.* This factor is closely related to the use of ceiling-mounted speakers, and the analysis is similar. In virtually all of the precedents, the use of concealed wiring has been noted where the speakers were mounted in the ceiling. The Court again finds that this factor is somewhat relevant but not determinative. As Claire's points out, it is rather naive to suggest that speaker wires in private homes are generally short and exposed. Concealing the speaker wires—as well as recessing the speakers in a ceiling—serves more of an aesthetic purpose and has little relevance to the sophistication of the sound system.

6. *Distance of speakers.* In cases involving ceiling-mounted speakers attached by concealed wiring, courts have often noted the distance of the speakers from the receiver.[g] The Court finds that this factor should be considered but is relatively insignificant. Congress did intend to exempt small business establishments, and it could be argued that if the distance between the receivers and the speakers is large, the business is not likely to be the type of small establishment Congress had in mind. However, this factor is addressed by the other factors relevant to the home-type analysis; home-type components are unlikely to suffice to provide sound for a large commercial establishment. Furthermore, the area covered by a home-type sound system is not likely to be significantly affected simply by placing the speakers at a large distance from the receiver—speakers do not become louder simply by being placed further from the receiver. Finally, the Court takes judicial notice that many speakers are sold to private consumers for

[e] See H.R. Rep. No. 94–1476, *supra* [slip op.] at 8–9.

[f] Thus in *Aiken*, the result of which Congress intended to preserve, the store utilized four ceiling-mounted speakers.

[g] The House report noted that in *Aiken*, the speakers were located within a relatively small circumference.

the express purpose of listening to the radio in a room other than that in which the receiver is located.

In this case, the speakers are located up to 15 and 35 feet from the receiver. The Court finds this to be within the range of equipment commonly used in private homes.

7. Integration with other systems. The receivers used by Claire's are not integrated with public address systems or telephone lines. They play only unaltered radio broadcasts. Accordingly, this factor weighs in favor of Claire's.

To summarize, all of the factors weigh in favor of Claire's with the exception of the use of concealed wiring and ceiling-mounted speakers. As noted above, the Court does not view these two factors as sufficient in themselves to change the result. Much more significant are the nature of the components themselves and any fundamental modifications to the equipment which alter the very nature of the performance. The Court finds that the Claire's stores, examined on an individual basis, use a sound system of a type commonly used in private homes.

3.   Further Transmission

The Court next examines whether the transmissions received by each Claire's store are further transmitted to the public.[h] There are two related theories pursuant to which Claire's may be considered to engage in a further transmission of the radio broadcasts it receives: first, that further transmission occurs whenever the broadcast is relayed from a receiver to external speakers through speaker wire; and second, that further transmission occurs when the speakers are not located in the same room as the receiver.

Although there is some support for each of these theories in the case law,[i] the Court cannot accept either of them. First, to read "further transmission" as including the mere transmission over the speaker wires themselves is to read this element right out of the statute. Every radio

---

[h] The Copyright Act defines "transmit" as follows: "to 'transmit' a performance . . . is to communicate it by any device or process whereby images or sounds are received beyond the place from which they are sent." Section 101. Although the Act does not define "further transmission," it does define "secondary transmission" as "the further transmitting of a primary transmission simultaneously with the primary transmission . . . ." Section 111(f).

[i] See *Hickory Grove*, 749 F.Supp. at 1038 (further transmission occurred where radio broadcasts were sent to other rooms, public could hear them, and music was recognizable); Gnossos, 1989 Copyright L. Dec. para. 26,483 (further transmission occurred where radio broadcasts were sent to separate rooms); *Bill Miller's*, 688 F.Supp. at 1176 ("the radio broadcasts . . . were 'further transmitted' to the public because the broadcasts were initially received in a room or area without speakers and were sent to a separate room with speakers via some 40 feet of wiring"); [International Korwin Corp. v. Kowalczyk (Tadeusz), 665 F.Supp. 652 at 657 (N.D.Ill.1987)(use of speakers in separate rooms constituted further transmission); Lamminations, 1985 Copyright L. Dec. para. 25,790 ("By the very nature of the radio-over-loudspeaker installations, the performances of plaintiffs' songs were 'further transmitted' from the receivers to the loudspeakers.").

requires wiring—whether external or internal—to reach the speakers which make the sound. To describe this as a further transmission means that every sound system utilizes a further transmission.[j] If Congress had intended this result, it would not have created the § 110(5) exemption in the first place. Furthermore, the store in *Aiken*, which Congress intended to be encompassed by the exemption, involved the use of speaker wires to reach concealed ceiling speakers.

Second, it would be arbitrary and pointless to make resolution of this element dependent on the length of the speaker wire involved. The length of the wire does not alter the nature of the transmission. A system which utilizes excessive lengths of speaker wire is likely to include other features which make it not the type of system commonly used in private homes; the "further transmission" element should not be distorted to substitute for the home-type equipment element.

Third, the mere fact that the speaker wire is run through or around a wall does not alter the type of transmission. Again, the use of speaker wire either is or is not a further transmission; the analysis of this element should not depend on the manner in which the wire is routed, just as it should not depend on the wire's length. Perhaps if the receiver feeds a number of speakers, each of which is in a different room, the exemption should not apply—although again, that configuration seems more appropriately addressed in terms of the home-type element. Under BMI's logic, however, a system which is otherwise exempt would become non-exempt merely if the receiver were placed in a closet and the other aspects of the system remained the same. Congress cannot have intended the application of the exemption to turn on such an insignificant distinction. Furthermore, as noted above, speakers are often sold for private use in rooms separate from receivers. Surely Congress did not intend that such a private system would come within its idea of "further transmission."

In view of the nature and purpose of the exemption, "further transmission" can only mean something more substantial, such as a re-broadcast of a transmission or the use of cable to service multiple receivers. It cannot encompass the mere use of the speaker wire which enables a home-type receiver to drive its speakers.

4. Size of Establishment

The three factors discussed above exhaust the elements listed in the statute. However, a number of courts have proceeded—without considering the appropriateness of this endeavor—to draw additional elements from the legislative history. They have thus examined the size of the business itself, looking to such factors as the physical size of the area covered by the performance, the number of customers served, and the revenues.[k] These

---

[j] This would also imply that the original transmissions can never be heard, because they would consist merely of the radio waves before they are made audible.

[k] See Sailor Music v. Gap Stores, Inc., 668 F.2d 84, 86 (2d Cir.1981)(store with area of 2769 square feet was of sufficient size to justify subscription to commercial music ser-

factors stem from the House Report's statements that the exemption is intended to apply to "small commercial establishments" which may not be large enough to "justify ... a subscription to a commercial background music service," that the *Aiken* facts represent the "outer limit," and that the "size, physical arrangement, and noise level" of the establishment are relevant. Both parties agree in this case that the Court should look beyond the face of the statute to the factors noted in the House Report, but they disagree as to precisely which factors apply and how they are relevant. BMI focuses on the revenues and profits of the stores, and Claire's focuses on their physical size.

The Court must first address whether factors other than those specified in the statute should be considered at all. Although precedents concerning principles of statutory interpretation often send confusing signals, the Seventh Circuit in Matter of Sinclair, 870 F.2d 1340 (7th Cir.1989), has provided a thorough and sensible guide to the question of when a court may look to factors beyond the text of a statute in interpreting that statute. The court in that case resolved the superficial inconsistency between two common maxims of statutory interpretation: that courts should not look to legislative history to interpret an unambiguous statute, and that statutes should be interpreted in order to best effectuate their intent. As the court in *Sinclair* explained, the latter principle allows courts to examine even apparently unambiguous statutes in light of their legislative history in order to decode the terms used in the statute—to determine whether the words used had a different meaning to an insider than they do to the general public, or that the words have gaps which leave elaboration to the

vice and therefore not exempt), *cert. denied,* 456 U.S. 945 (1982); Hickory Grove, 749 F.Supp. at 1038–39 (only small commercial establishments qualify; relevant are square footage, capacity, and revenues; 880 square feet open to public is too large); Gnossos, 1989 Copyright L. Dec. para. 26,483 (not small commercial establishment where 1,824 square feet was open to public and dining rooms accommodated 172 people); Crabshaw [Music v. K–Bob's of El Paso, Inc., 744 F.Supp. 763, at 767 (W.D.Tex.1990)] (in finding store not exempt, court noted size was 7000 square feet and gross annual revenues were $800,000 and $900,000); *Bill Miller's,* 688 F.Supp. at 1176 [Merrill v. Bill Miller's Bar-B-Q Enterprises, 688 F.Supp. 1172 (W.D.Tex.1988)] (chain of restaurants not exempt where each restaurant covered 1000 to 1500 square feet and grossed over $500,000 annually and where restaurants had previously subscribed to music service); *County Stores,* 669 F.Supp. at 1170 [Merrill v. County Stores, 669 F.Supp. 1164 (D.Ct. New Hampshire, 1987)] (store not exempt where annual sales were $2.5 million and size was 13,000 square feet); Rodgers [v. Eighty Four Lumber Co.], 617 F.Supp. 1021 at 1023 (W.D.Pa.1985)(stores with public areas in excess of 10,000 square feet not exempt); Springsteen [v. Plaza Roller Dome, Inc.], 602 F.Supp. 1113 at 1119 [(M.D.N.C.1985)] (miniature golf course which covered 7500 square feet was not of sufficient size to justify subscription to music service where it was open only six months per year and rarely generated revenues over $1000 per month); Lamminations, 1985 Copyright L. Dec. para. 25,790 (businesses were of sufficient size to warrant use of commercial background music system where they covered 10,000 to 14,500 square feet and where two of them already used such services). See also *Kowalczyk,* 665 F.Supp. at 655, 658 (business was not small commercial establishment where it covered 2,640 square feet and had annual net profits of $35,000 to $136,000). (*Kowalczyk* was affirmed by the Seventh Circuit, which summarized the district court's opinion but did not rule on the appropriate elements to be considered. International Korwin Corp. v. Kowalczyk, 855 F.2d 375, 378 (7th Cir.1988).)

executive and judicial branches. 870 F.2d, at 1342. However, although the legislative history may thus help a court discover the statute's meaning, it may not be used to change it. Id. at 1344.

In this case, to examine statistics concerning square footage or revenues and elevate them to an importance equal or even greater than the factors enumerated in the text of § 110(5) itself is to violate this principle, drawing on legislative history to formulate "rules competing with those found in the U.S. Code." The text of the § 110(5) includes nothing at all about the size of a business, the area that it covers, or the revenue that it generates. Certainly the legislative history may be useful in terms of interpreting such factors as "further transmission" and "single receiving apparatus of a kind commonly used in private homes." It may not, however, be used to supply additional elements beyond those specified in the statute.

It certainly is apparent from the legislative history that Congress' intent in enacting § 110(5) was to exempt small commercial establishments. It is equally clear from the text of § 110(5) that Congress chose to effectuate this intent by drawing a distinction based on the type of sound equipment utilized and the nature of the transmission. It did not choose to protect small businesses by drawing distinctions based on square footage or revenues. Furthermore, it is hardly irrational for Congress to determine that its intent could indeed be realized by the manner it adopted; Congress could reasonably believe that only small commercial establishments would be able to make effective use of a single home-type receiving apparatus, and that the elements it specified would preclude larger establishments from benefitting from the exemption.

Claire's has suggested that the square footage of individual stores is of paramount importance. It notes that the store in *Aiken*, which Congress described as the "outer limit," had a total of 1055 square feet and selling space of 620 square feet, and urges that any store smaller than that should be exempt. Claire's has also offered to license those stores larger than the one in *Aiken* if BMI would not seek to license the remaining stores. As noted above, a number of courts have found the physical size of an establishment relevant, and some have even relied on it exclusively. To do so, however, is to bring into the analysis an element of arbitrariness which Congress did not include in the statute and which the Court cannot believe Congress ever intended to adopt. Surely Congress would not have wanted the exemption determined by a matter of a few square feet, and it chose more relevant criteria concerning the nature of the sound system. It is rather pedestrian to suggest that in describing *Aiken* as the outer limit, Congress could only have thought in terms of square feet. In fact, the Supreme Court in *Aiken* never even stated the physical size of the restaurant, and the size is not specified in the House Report, much less in the statute itself. The Court finds that the square feet covered by an establishment is, at best, a very minor factor in determining the applicability of the exemption.[1]

The Court finds an examination of a store's revenues and profits to be of minimal importance for the same reasons. Neither the Supreme Court nor Congress specified the amount of revenues or profits achieved by the restaurant in *Aiken*. Congress could easily have drawn a distinction based on financial criteria, and it chose to write no such distinction into the statute. Rather, it chose another manner to control the size of the establishments entitled to the exemption, and that was to rely on the type of equipment and transmission utilized.

It is equally unhelpful to discuss as a separate factor whether a business is capable of subscribing to a commercial background music service. Congress has already chosen a method for making this determination, and that method is specified in § 110(5). If courts were to look beyond the text, and place determinative emphasis on whether a given establishment could afford a commercial service, then the exemption would effectively disappear. Licensing organizations and background music providers could simply choose to extend to every small business a low enough rate to remove them from the exemption.[m]

As the statute stands, it provides no basis for concluding that the exemption is to be applied according to the size and profitability of a business. If BMI or other licensors desire another result, their remedy lies with Congress itself, which has the power to rest the exemption on such factors but has not done so.

5. Summary

The Court finds that the stores in this case, considered individually, qualify for the exemption in § 110(5). Each store uses a single receiver; each store uses equipment of a type commonly found in private homes, and no store engages in further transmission of the broadcasts it receives. The fact that some of the stores may be slightly larger than 1055 square feet or take in more revenue or profits than did the restaurant in *Aiken* does not remove them from the scope of the exemption.

C. Chain as a Whole

Having determined that the stores considered individually qualify for the exemption, the Court turns to the issue of whether the chain of stores

---

[1] Consider two distinct hypothetical establishments which utilize the basic equipment involved in this case. One, an ice cream parlor smaller in size than the restaurant in *Aiken*, has the stereo equipment prominently displayed and played at a high volume, easily audible throughout the entire seating area. The other is a cafe, much larger than the restaurant in *Aiken*, which has the stereo equipment set on a small table in a back corner, facing toward the seating area. Other factors being the same, surely Congress cannot have intended these establishments to be treated differently, and if Congress did so intend, surely it would have included physical size as an express factor in the text of the statute.

[m] If a business's revenues or ability to afford a commercial background service were of predominant importance, a large conglomerate corporation which merely placed a portable radio in a small snack shop would presumably not be exempt. Again, in light of the language of § 110(5), it is apparent that Congress did not intend such a result.

should be examined in its entirety. If the chain must be examined as a whole, it apparently is not exempt. It operates more than a single receiver—it operates at least 669—and would thus fail to satisfy the first criterion. Furthermore, a sound system of 669 speakers and 1338 speakers is not the type of system commonly found in private homes, so the chain would not satisfy the second criterion.

In support of its argument that the analysis should focus on the chain as a whole, BMI states that only one license is necessary to cover all of the stores. BMI would base the license fee, however, on the number of stores which play radio broadcasts. Furthermore, the manner in which BMI elects to structure its license agreements should not affect the scope of the exemption; the single license is not inherent in the nature of the performance but rather is determined by BMI. The exemption depends not on the type of license agreement involved, but rather on the equipment used by the allegedly infringing store.

BMI also argues that the Copyright Act defines "publicly" performing a work as being unaffected by whether "the members of the public capable of receiving the performance or display receive it in the same place or in separate places and at the same time or at different times." § 101. This definition makes it clear that the mere fact that the Claire's stores perform radio broadcasts in a number of different places does not preclude the performance from being public.[n] It does not, however, provide guidance in determining whether the entire chain is the appropriate focus for a § 110(5) inquiry.

Although this precise issue has apparently not been litigated before, there are a number of cases in which courts have examined the applicability of § 110(5) to stores which were members of chains. In each of those instances, the court has centered its analysis primarily, if not exclusively, on the individual store or stores rather than on the chain as a whole. See Sailor Music [v. Gap Stores], 668 F.2d 84, at 85–86 (2d. Cir.1981)(focusing on size of individual store); *Bill Miller's*, 688 F.Supp., at 1174–76 (examining type of components used by each store and size and revenues of each store, and noting also the revenues of the entire chain); *Rodgers* 617 F.Supp. at 1023 (focusing on size of, and type of components used by, each store); Lamminations, 1985 Copyright L. Dec. para. 25,790 (focusing on size of each store and type of components used by each store).

An examination of the text of § 110(5) provides little guidance—it defines the exemption in terms of the nature of the performance rather than the nature of the business. Although the statute does specify the elements which are relevant in determining whether a performance is exempt, it does not specify what entity should be examined—an individual store or its corporate owner. Thus, unlike the issue of the relevant elements of the exemption, it is appropriate to examine the legislative

---

[n] See, e.g., Buck v. Jewell–La Salle Realty Co., 283 U.S. 191 (1931)(hotel transmission of radio broadcasts to speakers in individual guests' rooms was a performance within the scope of the Copyright Act).

history for guidance as to whether the chain as a whole should be considered. Most helpful is the statement in the House Report that Congress intended to reaffirm that the exemption would apply to *Aiken*. In *Aiken*, the store involved was part of a chain. Twentieth Century Music Corp. v. Aiken, 356 F.Supp. 271, 272 (W.D.Pa.1973). If the *Aiken* case were to arise under current law, and if the court were to analyze the chain as a whole, the chain would not be exempt because it does not use a single receiving apparatus of a kind commonly used in private homes. Indeed, if chains are to be examined as a whole, no chain in which more than one store utilized a radio receiver would be exempt. Congress cannot have intended this result if it also intended to reaffirm the result in *Aiken*. The Court can only conclude, therefore, that Congress intended the exemption to be analyzed in terms of individual stores.° Again, BMI's arguments to the contrary are best directed toward Congress itself.

IV.   Conclusion

The Claire's stores must be considered on an individual basis rather than in the aggregate. Because each store operates only a single receiving apparatus of a type commonly used in private homes, and does not further transmit the radio broadcasts it receives, the stores are exempt from liability for copyright infringement pursuant to § 110(5).

NOTES

1. *Distinctions.* In Columbia Pictures Industries v. Professional Real Estate Investors,[3] the court affirmed a grant of summary judgment in favor of the defendant hotel in a copyright infringement suit by movie companies against the defendant based on the hotel's practice of providing videodiscs for rent to its guests for viewing in their rooms. Can a meaningful distinction be made between the hotel rooms in Professional Real Estate and the viewing booths in *Redd Horne* for purposes of applying the "public place" clause of the statutory definition of public performance? What if the

---

° BMI might argue that because the Court has determined that legislative history is relevant on this issue, the Court should rely on the House Report's reference to the size of the business and hold that the chain as a whole must be examined. The Court cannot accept this argument. In order to give effect to Congress' intent to affirm the result in *Aiken*, the only way in which courts could apply § 110(5) to chain stores would be to draw arbitrary lines based, for instance, on the number of stores in the chain. Such an exercise is not appropriate for the judiciary, and there is no indication that Congress intended to create such an exercise for the courts. If Congress had intended such lines to be drawn, it could easily have drawn them. Furthermore, there is no inherent difference

in the nature of the performance if 10 individually-owned stores, which all play an otherwise exempt radio broadcast, subsequently are combined in a chain. Of course, if the receivers operated collectively—for instance if Claire's received a radio broadcast at a central location and then re-transmitted it to the various individual stores—then the exemption would presumably not apply. However, in order to deny the exemption in that case, there would be no need to rule that the focus should shift to the chain as a whole; the text of § 110(5) would itself apply to deny the exemption, for there would be a "further transmission."

[3] 866 F.2d 278 (9th Cir.1989).

booths in *Redd Horne* contained equipment which allowed the patrons to operate the video cassettes themselves, rather than having to rely on an employee of the store to start the video? The court in *Redd Horne* states that "the transmission of a performance to members of the public, even in private settings such as hotel rooms or Maxwell's viewing rooms, constitutes a public performance" (see Infringement Section of case). Is this statement inconsistent with the court's holding in *Professional Real Estate*?

2. *Prisons.* Is a prison more like a hotel room or like the situation in *Redd Horne*? What factors should be considered in determining the status of prisons? What other institutions raise a similar set of issues?

3. *First sale. Redd Horne* rejects the defendants' reliance on the first sale doctrine, claiming that resort to this doctrine is "merely another aspect of their argument that their activities are not public performances." The first sale doctrine, which is codified at § 109(a), provides that notwithstanding the distribution right guaranteed by § 106(3), "the owner of a particular copy or phonorecord lawfully made under this title, or any person authorized by such owner, is entitled, without the authority of the copyright owner, to sell or otherwise dispose of the possession of that copy or phonorecord."[4] Thus, once a lawfully made copy of a copyrighted work is sold, the copyright holder has no control over subsequent sales or dispositions of that particular copy. What policies do you suppose support this doctrine? What is the significance of the phrase "lawfully made under this title"?[5] Should the first sale doctrine apply to works that are made in another country pursuant to a license from the United States copyright proprietor? See Assignment 5. Since the first sale doctrine only applies to copies of a copyrighted work, some have argued that it is becoming rapidly obsolete in an environment in which the contents of copyrighted works are being electronically disseminated more frequently through electronic means such as the Information Superhighway.[6]

First sale hypo. Suppose Company #1 imports electronic printed circuit boards from a video game manufactured abroad by Company #2 into this country and installs the boards into its own video game units for public, commercial use in its video arcades. Company #1 argues that once Company #2 sold these boards abroad, the first sale doctrine applies and implies a transfer of the performance right as well. Should Company #2 be precluded from claiming that Company #1's activity constitutes an unauthorized public performance by virtue of the first sale doctrine?

---

[4] § 109(a).

[5] The legislative history states that defendants should bear the burden of proving whether a particular copy was lawfully made or acquired. See H.R. Rep. No. 1476, 94th Cong., 2d Sess. 80–81, reprinted in 1976 U.S.C.C.A.N. 5659, 5694–95.

[6] See Litman, The Exclusive Right to Read, 13 Cardozo Arts & Ent. L.J. 29 (1994);

Litman, Copyright and Information Policy, 55 Law & Contemp. Probs. 185, 188–89, 208 (1992)(recommending the development of new alternatives such as "compulsory licenses for secondary uses of electronically disseminated works" to effectuate more complete access to copyrighted works).

What if, instead of Company #1 importing and using Company #2's boards, Company #1 lawfully buys Company #2's computer program and uses it to generate its own boards?

4. *The Record Rental Amendment Act and the Computer Software Rental Amendments Act.* Section 109(b) embodies the Record Rental Amendment Act of 1984, and the Computer Software Amendments Act of 1990. The Record Rental Amendment Act was passed to interfere with the practice of record shops encouraging unauthorized recordings of copyrighted music by renting records and selling blank cassette tapes. As such, it is an exception to the first sale doctrine because it restricts the use and disposition of individual phonorecords by precluding the rental, lease, or lending of such works for direct or indirect commercial advantage. What is the scope of this prohibition?

Despite the enactment of the Record Rental Amendment Act, home taping still is prevalent because people simply use other sources rather than rely on rentals from commercial outlets. As you will see in the next Assignment, making a home recording of a television show is a fair use. See Sony Corp. of America v. Universal City Studios, Inc.,[7] reprinted in Assignment 12. Should the same be true of home tapings of phonorecords?[8]

In 1992, Congress enacted the Audio Home Recording Act,[9] which requires the inclusion of the Serial Copy Management System ("SCMS") in digital audio tape recorders ("DATs"). DATs are superior to compact discs ("CDs") because they contain both a recording and a playback medium, and they allow a recording to be made which rivals that of CDs in terms of tonal quality. As one commentator has observed, "[i]f DAT were introduced in its present form any CD, itself a perfect copy of the original sound carrier, would become a master from which additional perfect copies could be made in every home with a DAT recorder."[10] The SCMS allows DATs to make direct, digital-to-digital copies of CDs and other pre-recorded cassettes, but precludes digital-to-digital copies of these copies. In other words, the Act sanctions an unlimited number of first-generation digital-to-digital copies of music, but outlaws second-generation copies of these works. Thus, this Act forges an interesting compromise respecting the appropriate degree of public access to phonorecords, CDs, and other objects in which sounds are fixed. The Act also requires a royalty payment of 3% of the transfer price on any digital audio recording medium imported, distributed or manufactured in the United States.[11] A digital audio recording medium is

---

[7] 464 U.S. 417, 104 S.Ct. 774, 78 L.Ed.2d 574 (1984).

[8] See generally Nimmer, Copyright Liability for Audio Home Recording: Dispelling the "Betamax" Myth, 68 Va. L. Rev. 1505, 1534 (1982)(observing that "audio home recording of copyrighted works has never been protected by any special exemption, express or implied, from the scope of the copyright laws" and is "not defensible under the 'fair use' doctrine"; advocating the imposition of royalty payments on the sales of recording equipment).

[9] §§ 1001–1010.

[10] Horowitz, The Record Rental Amendment of 1984: A Case Study in the Effort to Adapt Copyright Law to New Technology, 12 Colum.-VLA J.L. & Arts 31, 68–70 (1987).

[11] § 1004(b).

defined to exclude a material object embodying a sound recording when it is first distributed.[12] Thus, this royalty essentially applies to blank tapes. In addition, a 2% royalty is required on the importation, manufacture, and distribution in the United States of every digital audio recording device.[13] The Librarian of Congress arranges the distribution of royalties to the interested copyright parties.

Subsequent to the Record Rental Amendment Act, the Copyright Act was amended to provide yet another exemption to the first sale doctrine. Pursuant to the Computer Software Rental Amendments Act of 1990, the renting of computer software without the permission of the copyright owner for purposes of "direct or indirect commercial advantage" consti-tutes copyright infringement. See § 109(b). The objective of this amend-ment is similar to that of the Record Rental Amendment Act of 1984—to bolster the rights of copyright proprietors by making unauthorized home duplication more difficult, thus fostering sales of the protected work. Why should commercial rentals of records and computer software be treated differently from videos? What exceptions are provided by the Computer Software Rental Amendments Act of 1990? The copyrights of owners of computer programs also are limited by § 117 of the statute which allows the owner of a copy of a computer program to make another copy of the program if such copy "is created as an essential step in the utilization of the computer program in conjunction with a machine and . . . is used in no other manner" or "is for archival purposes only."

Discussion question. Should the exemptions from the first sale doctrine provided in § 109(b) be extended to library books? Specifically, should authors be compensated from public funds when their works are lent from libraries? This type of system is called a public lending right and it is operational in about twelve countries. How would such a system fare in this country?

5. *Display.* Section 109(c) of the Copyright Act provides another limita-tion on a copyright owner's exclusive rights. That subsection states that the owner of a lawfully made copy of a copyrighted work can publicly display that copy, without the copyright owner's permission, "either directly or by the projection of no more than one image at a time, to viewers present at the place where the copy is located."[14] Does this provision strike a reason-able balance between the competing interests of copyright owners and copy owners?

Some commentators also have advocated the adoption of a right of private display for visual artists which would become operative upon the resale of the work.[15] Functionally, this right is equivalent to a resale royalty provision, which also is known as *droit de suite*. Under *droit de suite*, visual

---

[12] § 1001(4)(B).

[13] § 1004(a).

[14] § 109(c).

[15] See Goetzl & Sutton, Copyright and the Visual Artist's Display Right: A New Doctrinal Analysis, 9 Colum.-VLA J.L. & Arts 15, 50, 53 (1984)(advocating the adoption of a compulsory license to effectuate this private right of display).

artists have a right to a percentage of the resale sales price of their works. Currently, California is the only state with such a statute,[16] and the Register of Copyrights recently recommended against the adoption of resale royalties at this time.[17]

6. *Sound recordings and digital sampling.* Pursuant to GATT, it is now unlawful for anyone to, without the consent of the performer involved, fix the sounds or sounds and images of a live musical performance. It is also unlawful to reproduce, transmit, or distribute a copy or phonorecord of such a performance from an unauthorized fixation. Section 1101 makes anyone who does these prohibited activities subject to the civil remedies for copyright infringement, and criminal sanctions for such actions can be invoked pursuant to 18 U.S.C.A. § 2319A. These measures give musicians added protection from unauthorized fixation and trafficking in their performances.

Section 114 of the Copyright Act defines the scope of exclusive rights in sound recordings. Note that the statutory definition of sound recordings provides that they "are works that result from the fixation of a series of musical, spoken, or other sounds ... regardless of the nature of the material objects, such as disks, tapes, or other phonorecords, in which they are embodied."[18] Section 114 of the statute states that the exclusive rights of the owner of a copyright in a sound recording are limited to the rights of reproduction, distribution, and preparation of derivative works under § 106, but do not include the exclusive rights to display the work and to perform it publicly (except for performances of sound recordings by means of a digital audio transmission under § 106(b)).

Section 114 also provides that with respect to the rights of reproduction and preparation of derivative works, the copyright owner has the exclusive right to duplicate the recording in forms that directly or indirectly recapture "the actual sounds fixed in the recording," but her rights "do not extend to the making or duplication of another sound recording that consists entirely of an independent fixation of other sounds, even though such sounds imitate or simulate those in the copyrighted sound recording."[19] Why does the statute adopt this "actual reproduction" standard for infringement for sound recordings, thereby differentiating sound recordings from other types of copyrighted works that are infringed when the unauthorized reproduction or derivative work is "substantially similar"? Is the need for public access greater with respect to sound recordings than for other types of copyrighted works?

In light of the foregoing, consider the legality of digital sampling. Digital sampling is a technique that involves the following steps: the recordation of a sound, its analysis, decomposition, storage of the tonal qualities in a computer, possible electronic alteration, and playback. According to one commentator: "Digital sound sampling has been used as a

---

[16] Cal. Civ. Code § 986 (West Supp. 1993).

[17] Copyright Office Report Executive Summary, Droit de Suite: The Artist's Re-

sale Royalty, 16 Colum.-VLA J.L. & Arts 381 (1992).

[18] § 101.

[19] § 114.

technique to isolate distinctive vocal and instrumental sounds. Once isolated, these sounds may be recorded and analyzed. In fact, the process allows the digital sampler to create a new song. The digital sampler can then play back a song comprised of another artist's sounds but never actually executed by the original musician."[20] The use of digital sampling in the music industry is extremely prevalent, in terms of sampling both live performances as well as sound recordings. Still, its legality has been specifically addressed by only a few courts.[21] What copyright issues are necessary to resolve in determining the legality of digital sampling?

7. *Compulsory licensing.* The 1976 Copyright Act contains five provisions for compulsory licensing. Section 111(c) provides for compulsory licenses for secondary transmissions by cable systems; § 115 mandates compulsory licenses for making and distributing phonorecords; § 803(a)(4) provides for compulsory licenses for jukeboxes in some circumstances; § 118 specifies compulsory licenses for public broadcasters; and § 119 requires compulsory licenses for satellite retransmissions to the public for private home viewing. The responsibility for adjusting the statutory royalty rates is vested in a copyright arbitration royalty panel pursuant to the Copyright Royalty Tribunal Reform Act of 1993 (prior to this amendment, the Copyright Royalty Tribunal (CRT) had this responsibility). In the case of compulsory licenses for public broadcasting, an arbitration panel also may set the initial rate. See § 801.

In theory, three schemes of compulsory licensing are possible: 1) a fixed mechanical license fee specified by the copyright statute; 2) a license fee that is subject to review and adjustment by an official body; and 3) a license fee that is the product of negotiation between the copyright owner and the user, backed up with arbitration. The first method was the one adopted by the 1909 Copyright Act for the compulsory license for making and distributing phonorecords. The 1976 Copyright Act essentially adopted the second method for the compulsory licenses established by that statute. Nevertheless, the jukebox license was subsequently revised through § 116A (currently § 116 in light of the repeal of the original § 116 pursuant to the Copyright Royalty Tribunal Reform Act of 1993) to incorporate the third method as a result of our adherence to the Berne Convention (see Assignment 6). The jukebox license contained in the original § 116 violated Berne, which safeguards to the copyright owner without qualification the right to control public performances. By providing for negotiation, the

---

[20] Houle, Digital Audio Sampling, Copyright Law and The American Music Industry: Piracy or Just a Bad "Rap", 7 Loy. L. Rev. 879, 880 (1992).

[21] See Tin Pan Apple, Inc. v. Miller Brewing Co., 30 U.S.P.Q.2d 1791 (1994)("It is common ground that if defendants did sample plaintiff's copyrighted sound recordings, they infringed that copyright, whatever

may be said of the composition copyright."); Jarvis v. A & M Records, 827 F.Supp. 282 (D.N.J.1993)(denying defendants' motion for summary judgment in a copyright infringement action involving digital sampling); Grand Upright Music Ltd. v. Warner Bros. Records, Inc., 780 F.Supp. 182 (S.D.N.Y. 1991)(indicating that unauthorized digital sampling violates the copyright law).

current § 116 is more in keeping with the spirit of Berne.[22] Note that none of the other compulsory licenses contained in the 1976 Act apparently violate the Berne Convention, since that treaty does allow for some types of compulsory licenses.[23] What effect do compulsory licenses have on the price the copyright holder obtains for the work? What are the policies favoring and disfavoring compulsory licenses?

8. *Application of § 110(5).* Courts have taken different approaches both with respect to which factors should be considered, and how the relevant factors should be applied. What factors do you think should be considered in a § 110(5) analysis? Should the applicability of this provision be determined by focusing on the details of the stereo system or might there not be a test that determines whether the music is being used in a manner that interferes with the copyright holder's primary market? Is *Claire's Boutiques'* application of the "further transmit" requirement logical? How persuasive is the conclusion reached in *Claire's Boutiques* that § 110(5) should be applied only to individual stores rather than chains? Note that this issue also is raised in the Principal Problem.

9. *ASCAP and BMI.* ASCAP (American Society of Composers, Authors, and Publishers) and BMI (Broadcast Music, Inc.) illustrate the principle that there are strength in numbers. The idea underlying these organizations is that a centralized body is better able to represent the interests of its individual members with respect to recouping royalty fees for public performances of music.[24] Taken together, ASCAP and BMI control ninety-five percent of the United States' market for performance rights to musical compositions. ASCAP represents more than 40,000 composers and publishers and controls a repertoire of about 3 million compositions and BMI represents more than 100,000 members and controls about 1.5 million compositions.[25]

As the cases demonstrate, ASCAP and BMI are vigilant about protecting their members' interests. In this regard, consider the following article by Mike Royko, which is reprinted with the permission of the Chicago Sun Times.

[22] But see § 803(a)(4)(providing for compulsory licenses if a negotiated license under § 116 is terminated or expires and is not replaced).

[23] See Martin, The Berne Convention and the U.S. Compulsory License for Jukeboxes: Why the Song Could Not Remain the Same, 37 J. Copyright Soc'y 262, 300–01 (1990).

[24] These organizations license only "non-dramatic" or small performing rights, as opposed to "dramatic" or grand rights. Dramatic rights typically are licensed by agents who act in the interest of the copyright proprietors. See Scorese, Performing Broadway Music: The Demon Grand Rights Traps, 13 Colum.-VLA J.L. & Arts 261, 267 (1989).

[25] See Avery, The Struggle Over Performing Rights to Music: BMI and ASCAP vs. Cable Television, 14 Hastings Comm. & Ent. L.J. 47, 51 (1991). The Copyright Clearance Center, which was established in 1977, performs essentially the same function as ASCAP and BMI in the context of photocopying copyrighted materials that are registered with the Center. The Center, as agent for publishers, grants blanket advance permission to photocopy the registered materials for a fee and remits these fees to the copyright owners.

Chicago Sun Times
February 17, 1984

ASCAP 'hit' gives geezers the blues

IF YOU HAPPEN to walk into Lois and Pete's Tavern on a weekend night, you'll probably hear some old geezer squeezing an accordion and singing "The Beer Barrel Polka." If he is in more of a hip mood, it might be "Poor Butterfly."

On a real lively night, there might be another geezer flailing at a piano, another geezer whacking a set of drums, and maybe even a tuba or a guitar going.

And when she's in the mood, Lois Szalacha, the owner and bartender, might belt out an old Tin Pan Alley song in her gravelly, whiskey voice.

When the song ends, the people at the bar and tables—mostly little white-haired ladies and bald, wrinkled gents—will give a wheezing cheer. If their pension checks just came, they might even buy the accordion player a drink.

It's not exactly Rick's Cafe or George's, but the regulars enjoy it. Most of them are of pension age and live within walking distance of the tavern, which is at 2916 W. Irving Park Rd.

SO ARE THE MUSICIANS. They play just for the fun of it and an occasional free beer.

"It started right after I opened the place," said Lois, who at 59 is one of the kids in the crowd. "A guy named Carmen came in and saw I had an old accordion. I used to play. He took it home, got it tuned and came in the next weekend and started playing.

"So I started buying old instruments. The piano, drums, a guitar—and some of the customers who knew how to play would get up and do some songs.

"It got to be so much fun that some people even went to the field house at Horner Park and took lessons. We got a trumpet player that way and even a guy who plays the tuba. They aren't real great, and sometimes you can't be sure what song they're playing, but it's something for them to do and it's fun."

Naturally, a city inspector showed up one day and told Lois she needed a city music license, which costs $214 a year. She grumbled but paid. In the tavern business you're used to buying licenses: city liquor, $1,338 a year; state licenses, $150; even a $25 potato chip license.

THEN ONE EVENING a couple of strangers came in. They sat at a table, listened to the music, took some notes and left.

A few weeks later, a letter came. It was from the American Society of Composers, Authors and Publisher [ASCAP] and it said that Lois had to send them $240 a year for a license to perform songs copyrighted by their members.

Lois showed the letter to her customers and said: "Can you beat that? They say we got to pay to sing songs."

The customers pondered the letter. Then they reached a legal opinion. As the accordian player put it: "They can't mean us. We're just amateurs and most of us don't even know all the words. Forget it."

So Lois forgot it.

But ASCAP didn't. Notices kept coming in the mail. Lois would show them to the old-timers and they'd say: "Ya' can't make amateurs pay to play some music."

"SO I STARTED JUST throwing their stuff in the garbage can. It went on for years. I didn't even read most of it. I don't know anything about legal stuff."

So she didn't even know that ASCAP went into federal court last June and sued her for copyright infringement, asking for $10,000 in damages.

She was served with notice of the suit, but she tossed that away, too. "I thought it was just more of their nonsense."

So she didn't even show up in court and a federal judge socked her for $3,000 in damages and gave ASCAP permission to grab the money from her bank account.

That's when she discovered what had happened—when she went to her bank and found that her $1,200 in savings was frozen. So she called a lawyer, who told her to pay up and forget it—his legal fees would be more than she could save by fighting it.

"SO NOW I CAN'T even pay my bills. It's so stupid. This is just a little neighborhood tavern with a few old people trying to have a little fun. And they make a federal case out of it."

The court record shows that the songs that the ASCAP snoops heard performed included "Poor Butterfly," "Tea for Two," "Pennies from Heaven," "With a Song in My Heart," "Where or When," and others.

And the plaintiffs were Warner Bros. Studio and heirs to the estates of composers like Vincent Youmans, Richard Rodgers and Lorenz Hart.

"Can you imagine" Lois says, "a Polish saloon keeper like me being sued by Rodgers and Hart?."

Will Lois pay? "Hell no," she says. "Now their fee is up to $324 a year. I'm already paying the city for a music license. Do they think I'm running some nightclub with Frank Sinatra singing? If I get 15 or 20 people in here on a Saturday, it's a big night. I'd rather close up and go to work somewhere as a barmaid. I'd earn more."

SHE MAY HAVE to do that because ASCAP says it won't give in.

"Payment is required wherever there is a public performance," a spokesman said. "They are paying for drinks, so she is making money."

To which Lois says: "Let that guy try to live on what I make."

Lois has one other tactic that she is considering. "Maybe we'll do nothing but Polish songs. Let those snoops write down *those* titles."

---

10. *The scope of § 110.* The following hypotheticals are intended to illustrate the scope of some of the other exemptions in § 110.

a. Suppose a college student, in order to satisfy the requirements for a theater arts course she is taking, performs a number of songs sung by Madonna as part of a presentation about the singer. Is this copyright infringement? *§ 110(1) – NO*

b. Is it copyright infringement for your client to sing "Bridge Over Troubled Waters" at a Saturday night rock mass? *§ 110(3) ambiguous but probably NO*

c. Suppose you hire a woman to entertain your daughter's friends at her 6th birthday party. The woman sings copyrighted songs, plays them on her guitar, and charges $100 for her services. Is this copyright infringement? Does it make a difference if the entertainer donates the money to UNICEF? Does it make a difference if the birthday girl's mom does the entertaining instead?

[handwritten note in margin: 110(4)(b) not public]

d. Is it copyright infringement for a shop that sells both exercise apparel and records to blast an audio cassette of the soundtrack of the movie "Flashdance" from speakers outside of the store?

BIBLIOGRAPHY

The following is a sampling of some of the pertinent literature on the topics covered in the foregoing problem and materials: McKuin, Home Audio Taping of Copyrighted Works and the Audio Home Recording Act of 1992: A Critical Analysis, 16 Hastings Comm. & Ent. L.J. 311 (1994); The Computer Software Rental Amendments Act of 1990: The Nonprofit Library Lending Exemption to the "Rental Right," 41 J. Copyright Soc'y 231 (1994); Cochran, Why Can't I Watch This Video Here? : Copyright Confusion and Performances of Videocassettes & Videodiscs in Libraries, 15 Hastings Comm. & Ent. L.J. 837 (1993); Jensen, Is the Library Without Walls on a Collision Course with the 1976 Copyright Act?, 85 Law Libr. J. 619 (1993); Jehoram, The Neighboring Rights of Performing Artists, Phonogram Producers and Broadcasting Organizations, 15 Colum.-VLA J.L. & Arts 75 (1990); Kernochan, The Distribution Right in the United States of America: Review and Reflections, 42 Vand. L. Rev. 1407 (1989); Scorese, Performing Broadway Music: The Demon Grand Rights Traps, 13 Colum.-VLA J.L. & Arts 261 (1989); Horowitz, The Record Rental Amendment of 1984: A Case Study in the Effort to Adapt Copyright Law to New Technology, 12 Colum.-VLA J.L. & Arts 31 (1987); Korman & Koenigsberg, Performing Rights in Music and Performing Rights Societies, 33 J. Copyright Soc'y 332 (1987); Nevins, Antenna Dilemma: The Exemption from Copyright Liability for Public Performance Using Technology Common in the Home, 11 Colum.-VLA J.L. & Arts 403 (1987); Shipley, Copyright Law and Your Neighborhood Bar and Grill: Recent Developments in Performances and the Section 110(5) Exemption, 29 Ariz. L. Rev. 475 (1987); Kernochan, Music Performing Rights Organizations in the United States of America: Special Characteristics, Restraints, and Public Attitudes, 10 Colum.-VLA J.L. & Arts 333 (1986); Colby, The First Sale Doctrine: The Defense That Never Was?, 32 J. Copyright Soc'y 77 (1984); D'Onofrio, In Support of Performance Rights in Sound Recordings, 29 UCLA L. Rev. 168 (1981); Korman, Performance Rights in Music Under Sections 110 and 118 of the 1976 Copyright Act, 22 N.Y.L. Sch. L. Rev. 521 (1977).

ASSIGNMENT 12

THE FAIR USE DOCTRINE

1. INTRODUCTION

The fair use doctrine has been called "the most troublesome" in all of copyright law.[1] In essence, the fair use doctrine of copyright law explicitly recognizes that some unauthorized uses of copyrighted property ought to be tolerated. In explaining the fair use doctrine, one court has observed that it "offers a means of balancing the exclusive rights of a copyright holder with the public's interest in dissemination of information affecting areas of universal concern, such as art, science and industry."[2] Thus, the doctrine seeks to achieve a balance between the optimal use by society of resources and the optimal level of creativity. You will recall that although the reward to creators is a secondary goal of copyright law's overall goal of promoting the progress of science and useful arts, such rewards are essential to effectuating copyright law's major objective of enhancing society's progress. Clearly an absence of monetary protections would result in diminished creativity. Therefore, the fair use doctrine is one way in which the copyright law attempts to strike a balance between the competing interests of the individual creator and that of society.

The fair use doctrine also is supported by an economically-based policy justification. Specifically, it allows parties to avoid market exchange. Typically, copyright infringements will be enjoined unless the doctrine of fair use, or some other use exempted by the copyright law, applies in a given situation. Thus, aside from the application of the fair use doctrine, the lawful right to use copyrighted property typically can be secured only through market exchanges. The fair use doctrine thus can be viewed as a mechanism for allowing parties the lawful right to use copyrighted works in certain instances where they would not otherwise be able to obtain such lawful rights.

The fair use doctrine is used as an affirmative defense and the doctrine is applied once it is established that the defendant's work is, in fact, substantially similar to the plaintiff's. The doctrine is codified in § 107 of the 1976 Copyright Act, although the doctrine was already well-established by the judiciary at the time the 1976 statute was enacted. The fair use doctrine is extraordinarily flexible, and its application typically turns on the particular facts in issue. Section 107 does provide some guidance, however,

---

[1] Dellar v. Samuel Goldwyn, Inc., 104 F.2d 661, 662 (2d Cir.1939).

[2] Wainwright Sec. Inc. v. Wall St. Transcript Corp., 558 F.2d 91, 94 (2d Cir.1977), cert. denied, 434 U.S. 1014, 98 S.Ct. 730, 54 L.Ed.2d 759 (1978) (enjoining defendants from publishing abstracts of plaintiff's financial research reports).

in that it sets forth the following four factors for determining whether a particular use is a fair use.

> 1. The purpose and character of the use, including whether such use is of a commercial nature or is for nonprofit educational purposes.

> 2. The nature of the copyrighted work.

> 3. The amount and substantiality of the portion used in relation to the copyrighted work as a whole.

> 4. The effect of the use upon the potential market for or value of the copyrighted work.[3]

All of these factors were widely used under the previously existing common law as well. Courts typically balance these four factors in determining whether a particular use of a work constitutes a fair use, although, as you shall see, there are other factors that often come into play in a fair use analysis. In fact, the legislative history to § 107 emphasizes that these factors are not to be considered definitive or determinative. The problem with such an ad hoc approach is that it is difficult to obtain much guidance from the existing fair use cases. This dilemma is illustrated by the two fair use cases decided by the Supreme Court in the 1980's, Sony Corp. of America v. Universal City Studios, Inc.,[4] and Harper & Row, Publishers, Inc. v. Nation Enterprises,[5] both of which are reprinted below.

2. PRINCIPAL PROBLEM

Your law firm represents Kira Davis, the promoter of the famous boxer, Bobby "Boxem" Carter. Last week, Carter was in a boxing match with a formidable opponent, James "Knockemdead" Smith. The fight aired only on cable television, and Davis owns the copyright to that broadcast. Davis sent WJN, a local broadcasting station in a major city, a telegram prior to the fight warning the station against broadcasting any part of the fight. Still, WJN picked up 22 seconds of the fight (15 action and 7 still-frame) from the cable broadcast and used this footage in its evening news broadcast. The entire fight was 13 rounds, and each round consisted of three minutes.

Davis is furious, particularly since she had warned WJN against such broadcasting. In addition, Davis has sold the delayed broadcast rights to the fight to NBC for four million dollars. NBC is quite upset and is threatening to rescind its agreement with Davis. The attorney for WJN has informed your firm that WJN's actions are totally within the bounds of the fair use doctrine.

You have the job of advising the senior partner on the case whether WJN should be protected by the fair use doctrine. The senior partner also wants you to verify whether Davis has standing to sue WJN. Before reaching an opinion, consider the following materials.

---

[3] § 107.

[4] 464 U.S. 417, 104 S.Ct. 774, 78 L.Ed.2d 574 (1984).

[5] 471 U.S. 539, 105 S.Ct. 2218, 85 L.Ed.2d 588 (1985).

3. MATERIALS FOR SOLUTION OF PRINCIPAL PROBLEM

A. STATUTORY MATERIALS: § 107

B. CASES:

Sony Corp. of America v. Universal City Studios, Inc.

Supreme Court of the United States, 1984.
464 U.S. 417, 104 S.Ct. 774, 78 L.Ed.2d 574.

■ JUSTICE STEVENS delivered the opinion of the Court.

Petitioners manufacture and sell home video tape recorders. Respondents own the copyrights on some of the television programs that are broadcast on the public airwaves. Some members of the general public use video tape recorders sold by petitioners to record some of these broadcasts, as well as a large number of other broadcasts. The question presented is whether the sale of petitioners' copying equipment to the general public violates any of the rights conferred upon respondents by the Copyright Act.

Respondents commenced this copyright infringement action against petitioners in the United States District Court for the Central District of California in 1976. Respondents alleged that some individuals had used Betamax video tape recorders (VTR's) to record some of respondents' copyrighted works which had been exhibited on commercially sponsored television and contended that these individuals had thereby infringed respondents' copyrights. Respondents further maintained that petitioners were liable for the copyright infringement allegedly committed by Betamax consumers because of petitioners' marketing of the Betamax VTR's. Respondents sought no relief against any Betamax consumer. Instead, they sought money damages and an equitable accounting of profits from petitioners, as well as an injunction against the manufacture and marketing of Betamax VTR's.

After a lengthy trial, the District Court denied respondents all the relief they sought and entered judgment for petitioners. 480 F.Supp. 429 (1979). The United States Court of Appeals for the Ninth Circuit reversed the District Court's judgment on respondents' copyright claim. 659 F.2d 963 (1981). We granted certiorari. 457 U.S. 1116 (1982). We now reverse.

An explanation of our rejection of respondents' unprecedented attempt to impose copyright liability upon the distributors of copying equipment requires a quite detailed recitation of the findings of the District Court. In summary, those findings reveal that the average member of the public uses a VTR principally to record a program he cannot view as it is being televised and then to watch it once at a later time. This practice, known as "time-shifting," enlarges the television viewing audience. For that reason, a significant amount of television programming may be used in this manner without objection from the owners of the copyrights on the programs. For the same reason, even the two respondents in this case, who do assert objections to time-shifting in this litigation, were unable to prove that the practice has impaired the commercial value of their copyrights or has created any likelihood of future harm. Given these findings, there is no basis in the Copyright Act upon which respondents can hold petitioners liable for distributing VTR's to the general public. The Court of Appeals' holding that respondents are entitled to enjoin the distribution of VTR's, to collect royalties on the sale of such equipment, or to obtain other relief, if affirmed, would enlarge the scope of respondents' statutory monopolies to encompass control over an article of commerce that is not the subject of copyright protection. Such an expansion of the copyright privilege is beyond the limits of the grants authorized by Congress.

I

The two respondents in this action, Universal City Studios, Inc., and Walt Disney Productions, produce and hold the copyrights on a substantial number of motion pictures and other audiovisual works. In the current marketplace, they can exploit their rights in these works in a number of ways: by authorizing theatrical exhibitions, by licensing limited showings on cable and network television, by selling syndication rights for repeated airings on local television stations, and by marketing programs on prerecorded videotapes or videodiscs. Some works are suitable for exploitation through all of these avenues, while the market for other works is more limited.

The respondents and Sony both conducted surveys of the way the Betamax machine was used by several hundred owners during a sample period in 1978. Although there were some differences in the surveys, they both showed that the primary use of the machine for most owners was "time-shifting." Both surveys also showed, however, that a substantial number of interviewees had accumulated libraries of tapes. Sony's survey indicated that over 80% of the interviewees watched at least as much regular television as they had before owning a Betamax. Respondents offered no evidence of decreased television viewing by Betamax owners.

Sony introduced considerable evidence describing television programs that could be copied without objection from any copyright holder, with special emphasis on sports, religious, and educational programming. For example, their survey indicated that 7.3% of all Betamax use is to record sports events, and representatives of professional baseball, football, basketball, and hockey testified that they had no objection to the recording of their televised events for home use.

Respondents offered opinion evidence concerning the future impact of the unrestricted sale of VTR's on the commercial value of their copyrights. The District Court found, however, that they had failed to prove any likelihood of future harm from the use of VTR's for time-shifting. 480 F.Supp., at 469.

The District Court concluded that noncommercial home use recording of material broadcast over the public airwaves was a fair use of copyrighted works and did not constitute copyright infringement. The Court of Appeals reversed the District Court's judgment on respondents' copyright claim. It did not set aside any of the District Court's findings of fact. Rather, it concluded as a matter of law that the home use of a VTR was not a fair use because it was not a "productive use."[a] It therefore held that it was unnecessary for plaintiffs to prove any harm to the potential market for the copyrighted works, but then observed that it seemed clear that the cumulative effect of mass reproduction made possible by VTR's would tend to diminish the potential market for respondents' works. 659 F.2d, at 974.

* * *

III

The Copyright Act does not expressly render anyone liable for infringement committed by another. In contrast, the Patent Act expressly brands anyone who "actively induces infringement of a patent" as an infringer, 35 U.S.C. § 271(b), and further imposes liability on certain individuals labeled "contributory" infringers, § 271(c). The absence of such express language in the copyright statute does not preclude the imposition of liability for copyright infringements on certain parties who have not themselves engaged in the infringing activity.[b] For vicarious liability is imposed in virtually all areas of the law, and the concept of contributory infringement is merely a species of the broader problem of identifying the circumstances in which it is just to hold one individual accountable for the actions of another.

Such circumstances were plainly present in Kalem Co. v. Harper Brothers, 222 U.S. 55 (1911), the copyright decision of this Court on which respondents place their principal reliance. In *Kalem*, the Court held that the producer of an unauthorized film dramatization of the copyrighted book Ben Hur was liable for his sale of the motion picture to jobbers, who in turn arranged for the commercial exhibition of the film. Justice Holmes, writing for the Court, explained:

> "The defendant not only expected but invoked by advertisement the use of its films for dramatic reproduction of the story. That was the most conspicuous purpose for which they could be used, and the one for which especially they were made. If the defendant did not contribute to the infringement it is impossible to do so except by taking part in the final act. It is liable on principles recognized in every part of the law." *Id.* at 62–63.

The use for which the item sold in *Kalem* had been "especially" made was, of course, to display the performance that had already been recorded upon it. The producer had personally appropriated the copyright owner's protected work and, as the owner of the tangible medium of expression

---

[a] "Without a 'productive use,' i.e. when copyrighted material is reproduced for its intrinsic use, the mass copying of the sort involved in this case precludes an application of fair use." 659 F.2d, at 971–972.

[b] As the District Court correctly observed, however, "the lines between direct infringement, contributory infringement and vicarious liability are not clearly drawn...." 480 F.Supp., at 457–458. The lack of clarity in this area may, in part, be attributable to the fact that an infringer is not merely one who uses a work without authorization by the copyright owner, but also one who authorizes the use of a copyrighted work without actual authority from the copyright owner.

upon which the protected work was recorded, authorized that use by his sale of the film to jobbers. But that use of the film was not his to authorize: the copyright owner possessed the exclusive right to authorize public performances of his work. Further, the producer personally advertised the unauthorized public performances, dispelling any possible doubt as to the use of the film which he had authorized.

Respondents argue that *Kalem* stands for the proposition that supplying the "means" to accomplish an infringing activity and encouraging that activity through advertisement are sufficient to establish liability for copyright infringement. This argument rests on a gross generalization that cannot withstand scrutiny. The producer in *Kalem* did not merely provide the "means" to accomplish an infringing activity; the producer supplied the work itself, albeit in a new medium of expression. Sony in the instant case does not supply Betamax consumers with respondents' works; respondents do. Sony supplies a piece of equipment that is generally capable of copying the entire range of programs that may be televised: those that are uncopyrighted, those that are copyrighted but may be copied without objection from the copyright holder, and those that the copyright holder would prefer not to have copied. The Betamax can be used to make authorized or unauthorized uses of copyrighted works, but the range of its potential use is much broader than the particular infringing use of the film Ben Hur involved in *Kalem*. *Kalem* does not support respondents' novel theory of liability.

Justice Holmes stated that the producer had "contributed" to the infringement of the copyright, and the label "contributory infringement" has been applied in a number of lower court copyright cases involving an ongoing relationship between the direct infringer and the contributory infringer at the time the infringing conduct occurred. In such cases, as in other situations in which the imposition of vicarious liability is manifestly just, the "contributory" infringer was in a position to control the use of copyrighted works by others and had authorized the use without permission from the copyright owner.[c] This case, however, plainly does not fall in that category. The only contact between Sony and the users of the Betamax that is disclosed by this record occurred at the moment of sale. The District Court expressly found that "no employee of Sony ... had either direct involvement with the allegedly infringing activity or direct contact with purchasers of Betamax who recorded copyrighted works off-the-air." 480 F.Supp., at 460. And it further found that "there was no evidence that any

[c] The so-called "dance hall cases," Famous Music Corp. v. Bay State Harness Horse Racing & Breeding Assn., Inc., 554 F.2d 1213 (C.A.1 1977)(racetrack retained infringer to supply music to paying customers); KECA Music, Inc. v. Dingus McGee's Co., 432 F.Supp. 72 (W.D.Mo.1977) (cocktail lounge hired musicians to supply music to paying customers); Dreamland Ball Room, Inc. v. Shapiro, Bernstein & Co., 36 F.2d 354 (C.A.7 1929)(dance hall hired orchestra to supply music to paying customers), are often contrasted with the so-called landlord-tenant cases, in which landlords who leased premises to a direct infringer for a fixed rental and did not participate directly in any infringing activity were found not to be liable for contributory infringement. E.g., Deutsch v. Arnold, 98 F.2d 686 (C.A.2 1938).

of the copies made by the other individual witnesses in this suit were influenced or encouraged by [Sony's] advertisements." *Ibid.*

If vicarious liability is to be imposed on Sony in this case, it must rest on the fact that it has sold equipment with constructive knowledge of the fact that its customers may use that equipment to make unauthorized copies of copyrighted material. There is no precedent in the law of copyright for the imposition of vicarious liability on such a theory. The closest analogy is provided by the patent law cases to which it is appropriate to refer because of the historic kinship between patent law and copyright law.[d]

In the Patent Act both the concept of infringement and the concept of contributory infringement are expressly defined by statute.[e] The prohibition against contributory infringement is confined to the knowing sale of a component especially made for use in connection with a particular patent. There is no suggestion in the statute that one patentee may object to the sale of a product that might be used in connection with other patents. Moreover, the Act expressly provides that the sale of a "staple article or commodity of commerce suitable for substantial noninfringing use" is not contributory infringement. 35 U.S.C. § 271(c).

When a charge of contributory infringement is predicated entirely on the sale of an article of commerce that is used by the purchaser to infringe a patent, the public interest in access to that article of commerce is necessarily implicated. A finding of contributory infringement does not, of course, remove the article from the market altogether; it does, however, give the patentee effective control over the sale of that item. Indeed, a finding of contributory infringement is normally the functional equivalent

---

[d] E.g., United States v. Paramount Pictures, Inc., 334 U.S., at 158; Fox Film Corp. v. Doyal, 286 U.S., at 131; Wheaton v. Peters, 8 Pet. 591, 657–658 (1834). The two areas of the law, naturally, are not identical twins, and we exercise the caution which we have expressed in the past in applying doctrine formulated in one area to the other. See generally Mazer v. Stein, 347 U.S. 201, 217–218 (1954); Bobbs–Merrill Co. v. Straus, 210 U.S., at 345.

We have consistently rejected the proposition that a similar kinship exists between copyright law and trademark law, and in the process of doing so have recognized the basic similarities between copyrights and patents. The Trade–Mark Cases, 100 U.S. 82, 91–92 (1879); see also United Drug Co. v. Theodore Rectanus Co., 248 U.S. 90, 97 (1918)(trademark right "has little or no analogy" to copyright or patent). Given the fundamental differences between copyright law and trademark law, in this copyright case we do not look to the standard for contributory in-

fringement set forth in Inwood Laboratories, Inc. v. Ives Laboratories, Inc., 456 U.S. 844, 854–855 (1982), which was crafted for application in trademark cases. There we observed that a manufacturer or distributor could be held liable to the owner of a trademark if it intentionally induced a merchant down the chain of distribution to pass off its product as that of the trademark owner's or if it continued to supply a product which could readily be passed off to a particular merchant whom it knew was mislabeling the product with the trademark owner's mark. If *Inwood*'s narrow standard for contributory trademark infringement governed here, respondents' claim of contributory infringement would merit little discussion. Sony certainly does not "intentionally [induce]" its customers to make infringing uses of respondents' copyrights, nor does it supply its products to identified individuals known by it to be engaging in continuing infringement of respondents' copyrights, see *id.*, at 855.

[e] 35 U.S.C. § 271.

of holding that the disputed article is within the monopoly granted to the patentee.[f]

For that reason, in contributory infringement cases arising under the patent laws the Court has always recognized the critical importance of not allowing the patentee to extend his monopoly beyond the limits of his specific grant. These cases deny the patentee any right to control the distribution of unpatented articles unless they are "unsuited for any commercial noninfringing use." Dawson Chemical Co. v. Rohm & Haas Co., 448 U.S. 176, 198 (1980).

We recognize there are substantial differences between the patent and copyright laws. But in both areas the contributory infringement doctrine is grounded on the recognition that adequate protection of a monopoly may require the courts to look beyond actual duplication of a device or publication to the products or activities that make such duplication possible. The staple article of commerce doctrine must strike a balance between a copyright holder's legitimate demand for effective—not merely symbolic—protection of the statutory monopoly, and the rights of others freely to engage in substantially unrelated areas of commerce. Accordingly, the sale of copying equipment, like the sale of other articles of commerce, does not constitute contributory infringement if the product is widely used for legitimate, unobjectionable purposes. Indeed, it need merely be capable of substantial noninfringing uses.

IV

The question is thus whether the Betamax is capable of commercially significant noninfringing uses. In order to resolve that question, we need not explore all the different potential uses of the machine and determine whether or not they would constitute infringement. Rather, we need only consider whether on the basis of the facts as found by the District Court a significant number of them would be noninfringing. Moreover, in order to resolve this case we need not give precise content to the question of how much use is commercially significant. For one potential use of the Betamax plainly satisfies this standard, however it is understood: private, noncommercial time-shifting in the home. It does so both (A) because respondents have no right to prevent other copyright holders from authorizing it for their programs, and (B) because the District Court's factual findings reveal that even the unauthorized home time-shifting of respondents' programs is legitimate fair use.

* * *

[f] It seems extraordinary to suggest that the Copyright Act confers upon all copyright owners collectively, much less the two respondents in this case, the exclusive right to distribute VTR's simply because they may be used to infringe copyrights. That, however, is the logical implication of their claim. The request for an injunction below indicates that respondents seek, in effect, to declare VTR's contraband. Their suggestion in this Court that a continuing royalty pursuant to a judicially created compulsory license would be an acceptable remedy merely indicates that respondents, for their part, would be willing to license their claimed monopoly interest in VTR's to Sony in return for a royalty.

B. Unauthorized Time–Shifting

Even unauthorized uses of a copyrighted work are not necessarily infringing. An unlicensed use of the copyright is not an infringement unless it conflicts with one of the specific exclusive rights conferred by the copyright statute. Moreover, the definition of exclusive rights in § 106 of the present Act is prefaced by the words "subject to sections 107 through 118." Those sections describe a variety of uses of copyrighted material that "are not infringements of copyright" "notwithstanding the provisions of section 106." The most pertinent in this case is § 107, the legislative endorsement of the doctrine of "fair use."[g]

That section identifies various factors that enable a court to apply an "equitable rule of reason" analysis to particular claims of infringement.[h] Although not conclusive, the first factor requires that "the commercial or nonprofit character of an activity" be weighed in any fair use decision.[i] If the Betamax were used to make copies for a commercial or profit-making

---

[g] The Copyright Act of 1909, 35 Stat. 1075, did not have a "fair use" provision. Although that Act's compendium of exclusive rights "to print, reprint, publish, copy, and vend the copyrighted work" was broad enough to encompass virtually all potential interactions with a copyrighted work, the statute was never so construed. The courts simply refused to read the statute literally in every situation. When Congress amended the statute in 1976, it indicated that it "intended to restate the present judicial doctrine of fair use, not to change, narrow, or enlarge it in any way." H. R. Rep. No. 94–1476, p.66 (1976).

[h] The House Report expressly stated that the fair use doctrine is an "equitable rule of reason" in its explanation of the fair use section:

"Although the courts have considered and ruled upon the fair use doctrine over and over again, no real definition of the concept has ever emerged. Indeed, since the doctrine is an equitable rule of reason, no generally applicable definition is possible, and each case raising the question must be decided on its own facts. . . .

* * *

The bill endorses the purpose and general scope of the judicial doctrine of fair use, but there is no disposition to freeze the doctrine in the statute, especially during a period of rapid technological change. Beyond a very broad statutory explanation of what fair use is and some of the criteria applicable to it, the courts

must be free to adapt the doctrine to particular situations on a case-by-case basis."

H. R. Rep. No. 94–1476, *supra*, at 65–66.

The Senate Committee similarly eschewed a rigid, bright-line approach to fair use. The Senate Report endorsed the view "that off-the-air recording for convenience" could be considered "fair use" under some circumstances, although it then made it clear that it did not intend to suggest that off-the-air recording for convenience should be deemed fair use under any circumstances imaginable. S. Rep. No. 94–473, p. 65–66 (1975). The latter qualifying statement is quoted by the dissent, and if read in isolation, would indicate that the Committee intended to condemn all off-the-air recording for convenience. Read in context, however, it is quite clear that that was the farthest thing from the Committee's intention.

[i] "The Committee has amended the first of the criteria to be considered—'the purpose and character of the use'—to state explicitly that this factor includes a consideration of 'whether such use is of a commercial nature or is for non-profit educational purposes.' This amendment is not intended to be interpreted as any sort of not-for-profit limitation on educational uses of copyrighted works. It is an express recognition that, as under the present law, the commercial or non-profit character of an activity, while not conclusive with respect to fair use, can and should be weighed along with other factors in fair use decisions." H. R. Rep. No. 94–1476, *supra*, at 66.

purpose, such use would presumptively be unfair. The contrary presumption is appropriate here, however, because the District Court's findings plainly establish that time-shifting for private home use must be characterized as a noncommercial, nonprofit activity. Moreover, when one considers the nature of a televised copyrighted audiovisual work, see § 107(2), and that time-shifting merely enables a viewer to see such a work which he had been invited to witness in its entirety free of charge, the fact that the entire work is reproduced, see § 107(3), does not have its ordinary effect of militating against a finding of fair use.

This is not, however, the end of the inquiry because Congress has also directed us to consider "the effect of the use upon the potential market for or value of the copyrighted work." § 107(4). The purpose of copyright is to create incentives for creative effort. Even copying for noncommercial purposes may impair the copyright holder's ability to obtain the rewards that Congress intended him to have. But a use that has no demonstrable effect upon the potential market for, or the value of, the copyrighted work need not be prohibited in order to protect the author's incentive to create. The prohibition of such noncommercial uses would merely inhibit access to ideas without any countervailing benefit.

Thus, although every commercial use of copyrighted material is presumptively an unfair exploitation of the monopoly privilege that belongs to the owner of the copyright, noncommercial uses are a different matter. A challenge to a noncommercial use of a copyrighted work requires proof either that the particular use is harmful, or that if it should become widespread, it would adversely affect the potential market for the copyrighted work. Actual present harm need not be shown; such a requirement would leave the copyright holder with no defense against predictable damage. Nor is it necessary to show with certainty that future harm will result. What is necessary is a showing by a preponderance of the evidence that some meaningful likelihood of future harm exists. If the intended use is for commercial gain, that likelihood may be presumed. But if it is for a noncommercial purpose, the likelihood must be demonstrated.

In this case, respondents failed to carry their burden with regard to home time-shifting. There was no need for the District Court to say much about past harm. "Plaintiffs have admitted that no actual harm to their copyrights has occurred to date." *Id.* at 451.

On the question of potential future harm from time-shifting, the District Court offered a more detailed analysis of the evidence. It rejected respondents' "fear that persons 'watching' the original telecast of a program will not be measured in the live audience and the ratings and revenues will decrease," by observing that current measurement technology allows the Betamax audience to be reflected. *Id.* at 466.[j] It rejected

---

j "There was testimony at trial, however, that Nielsen Ratings has already developed the ability to measure when a Betamax in a sample home is recording the program. Thus, the Betamax owner will be measured as a part of the live audience. The later diary can augment that measurement with information about subsequent viewing." *Id.* at 466.

respondents' prediction "that live television or movie audiences will decrease as more people watch Betamax tapes as an alternative," with the observation that "[there] is no factual basis for [the underlying] assumption." *Ibid*. It rejected respondents' "fear that time-shifting will reduce audiences for telecast reruns", and concluded instead that "given current market practices, this should aid plaintiffs rather than harm them." *Ibid*. And it declared that respondents' suggestion that "theater or film rental exhibition of a program will suffer because of time-shift recording of that program" "lacks merit." *Id*. at 467.[k]

After completing that review, the District Court restated its overall conclusion several times, in several different ways. "Harm from time-shifting is speculative and, at best, minimal." *Ibid*. "The audience benefits from the time-shifting capability have already been discussed. It is not implausible that benefits could also accrue to plaintiffs, broadcasters, and advertisers, as the Betamax makes it possible for more persons to view their broadcasts." *Ibid*. "No likelihood of harm was shown at trial, and plaintiffs admitted that there had been no actual harm to date." *Id*. at 468–469. "Television production by plaintiffs today is more profitable than it has ever been, and, in five weeks of trial, there was no concrete evidence to suggest that the Betamax will change the studios' financial picture." *Ibid*.

The District Court's conclusions are buttressed by the fact that to the extent time-shifting expands public access to freely broadcast television programs, it yields societal benefits. In Community Television of Southern California v. Gottfried, 459 U.S. 498, 508, n.12 (1983), we acknowledged the public interest in making television broadcasting more available. Concededly, that interest is not unlimited. But it supports an interpretation of the concept of "fair use" that requires the copyright holder to demonstrate some likelihood of harm before he may condemn a private act of time-shifting as a violation of federal law.

When these factors are all weighed in the "equitable rule of reason" balance, we must conclude that this record amply supports the District Court's conclusion that home time-shifting is fair use. In light of the findings of the District Court regarding the state of the empirical data, it is

In a separate section, the District Court rejected plaintiffs' suggestion that the commercial attractiveness of television broadcasts would be diminished because Betamax owners would use the pause button or fast-forward control to avoid viewing advertisements:

"It must be remembered, however, that to omit commercials, Betamax owners must view the program, including the commercials, while recording. To avoid commercials during playback, the viewer must fast-forward and, for the most part, guess as to when the commercial has passed. For most recordings, either practice may be too tedious. As defendants' survey showed, 92% of the programs were recorded with commercials and only 25% of the owners fast-forward through them. Advertisers will have to make the same kinds of judgments they do now about whether persons viewing televised programs actually watch the advertisements which interrupt them." *Id*. at 468.

[k] "This suggestion lacks merit. By definition, time-shift recording entails viewing and erasing, so the program will no longer be on tape when the later theater run begins." J. Blackmun dissenting, 417 U.S., at 467.

clear that the Court of Appeals erred in holding that the statute as presently written bars such conduct.[1]

In summary, the record and findings of the District Court lead us to two conclusions. First, Sony demonstrated a significant likelihood that substantial numbers of copyright holders who license their works for broadcast on free television would not object to having their broadcasts time-shifted by private viewers. And second, respondents failed to demonstrate that time-shifting would cause any likelihood of nonminimal harm to the potential market for, or the value of, their copyrighted works. The Betamax is, therefore, capable of substantial noninfringing uses. Sony's sale of such equipment to the general public does not constitute contributory infringement of respondents' copyrights.

V

One may search the Copyright Act in vain for any sign that the elected representatives of the millions of people who watch television every day have made it unlawful to copy a program for later viewing at home, or have enacted a flat prohibition against the sale of machines that make such copying possible.

It may well be that Congress will take a fresh look at this new technology, just as it so often has examined other innovations in the past.

---

[1] The Court of Appeals chose not to engage in any "equitable rule of reason" analysis in this case. Instead, it assumed that the category of "fair use" is rigidly circumscribed by a requirement that every such use must be "productive." It therefore concluded that copying a television program merely to enable the viewer to receive information or entertainment that he would otherwise miss because of a personal scheduling conflict could never be fair use. That understanding of "fair use" was erroneous.

Congress has plainly instructed us that fair use analysis calls for a sensitive balancing of interests. The distinction between "productive" and "unproductive" uses may be helpful in calibrating the balance, but it cannot be wholly determinative. Although copying to promote a scholarly endeavor certainly has a stronger claim to fair use than copying to avoid interrupting a poker game, the question is not simply two-dimensional. For one thing, it is not true that all copyrights are fungible. Some copyrights govern material with broad potential secondary markets. Such material may well have a broader claim to protection because of the greater potential for commercial harm. Copying a news broadcast may have a stronger claim to fair use than copying a motion picture. And, of course, not all uses are fungible. Copying

for commercial gain has a much weaker claim to fair use than copying for personal enrichment. But the notion of social "productivity" cannot be a complete answer to this analysis. A teacher who copies to prepare lecture notes is clearly productive. But so is a teacher who copies for the sake of broadening his personal understanding of his specialty. Or a legislator who copies for the sake of broadening her understanding of what her constituents are watching; or a constituent who copies a news program to help make a decision on how to vote.

Making a copy of a copyrighted work for the convenience of a blind person is expressly identified by the House Committee Report as an example of fair use, with no suggestion that anything more than a purpose to entertain or to inform need motivate the copying. In a hospital setting, using a VTR to enable a patient to see programs he would otherwise miss has no productive purpose other than contributing to the psychological well-being of the patient. Virtually any time-shifting that increases viewer access to television programming may result in a comparable benefit. The statutory language does not identify any dichotomy between productive and nonproductive time-shifting, but does require consideration of the economic consequences of copying.

But it is not our job to apply laws that have not yet been written. Applying the copyright statute, as it now reads, to the facts as they have been developed in this case, the judgment of the Court of Appeals must be reversed.

It is so ordered.

■ JUSTICE BLACKMUN, with whom JUSTICE MARSHALL, JUSTICE POWELL, and JUSTICE REHNQUIST join, dissenting.

* * *

IV

Fair Use

Congress in the 1976 Act simply incorporated a list of factors "to be considered." No particular weight, however, was assigned to any of these, and the list was not intended to be exclusive.

A

The monopoly created by copyright thus rewards the individual author in order to benefit the public. There are situations, nevertheless, in which strict enforcement of this monopoly would inhibit the very "Progress of Science and useful Arts" that copyright is intended to promote. An obvious example is the researcher or scholar whose own work depends on the ability to refer to and to quote the work of prior scholars. Obviously, no author could create a new work if he were first required to repeat the research of every author who had gone before him. The scholar, like the ordinary user, of course could be left to bargain with each copyright owner for permission to quote from or refer to prior works. But there is a crucial difference between the scholar and the ordinary user. When the ordinary user decides that the owner's price is too high, and forgoes use of the work, only the individual is the loser. When the scholar forgoes the use of a prior work, not only does his own work suffer, but the public is deprived of his contribution to knowledge. The scholar's work, in other words, produces external benefits from which everyone profits. In such a case, the fair use doctrine acts as a form of subsidy—albeit at the first author's expense—to permit the second author to make limited use of the first author's work for the public good.

A similar subsidy may be appropriate in a range of areas other than pure scholarship. The situations in which fair use is most commonly recognized are listed in § 107 itself. [O]ther examples may be found in the case law. Each of these uses, however, reflects a common theme: each is a productive use, resulting in some added benefit to the public beyond that produced by the first author's work. The fair use doctrine, in other words, permits works to be used for "socially laudable purposes." See Copyright Office, Briefing Papers on Current Issues, reprinted in 1975 House Hearings 2051, 2055. I am aware of no case in which the reproduction of a copyrighted work for the sole benefit of the user has been held to be fair use.

I do not suggest, of course, that every productive use is a fair use. A finding of fair use still must depend on the facts of the individual case, and on whether, under the circumstances, it is reasonable to expect the user to bargain with the copyright owner for use of the work. But when a user reproduces an entire work and uses it for its original purpose, with no added benefit to the public, the doctrine of fair use usually does not apply. There is then no need whatsoever to provide the ordinary user with a fair use subsidy at the author's expense.

The making of a videotape recording for home viewing is an ordinary rather than a productive use of the Studios' copyrighted works. The District Court found that "Betamax owners use the copy for the same purpose as the original. They add nothing of their own." 480 F.Supp., at 453. Although applying the fair use doctrine to home VTR recording, as Sony argues, may increase public access to material broadcast free over the public airwaves, I think Sony's argument misconceives the nature of copyright. Copyright gives the author a right to limit or even to cut off access to his work. A VTR recording creates no public benefit sufficient to justify limiting this right. Nor is this right extinguished by the copyright owner's choice to make the work available over the airwaves. Section 106 of the 1976 Act grants the copyright owner the exclusive right to control the performance and the reproduction of his work, and the fact that he has licensed a single television performance is really irrelevant to the existence of his right to control its reproduction. Although a television broadcast may be free to the viewer, this fact is equally irrelevant; a book borrowed from the public library may not be copied any more freely than a book that is purchased.

It may be tempting, as, in my view, the Court today is tempted, to stretch the doctrine of fair use so as to permit unfettered use of this new technology in order to increase access to television programming. But such an extension risks eroding the very basis of copyright law, by depriving authors of control over their works and consequently of their incentive to create. Even in the context of highly productive educational uses, Congress has avoided this temptation; in passing the 1976 Act, Congress made it clear that off-the-air videotaping was to be permitted only in very limited situations. See 1976 House Report 71; 1975 Senate Report 64. And, the Senate Report adds, "[the] committee does not intend to suggest . . . that off-the-air recording for convenience would under any circumstances, be considered 'fair use.'" *Id.* at 66. I cannot disregard these admonitions.

B

Courts should move with caution, however, in depriving authors of protection from unproductive "ordinary" uses. "[A] particular use which may seem to have little or no economic impact on the author's rights today can assume tremendous importance in times to come." Register's Supplementary Report 14. Although such a use may seem harmless when viewed in isolation, "[isolated] instances of minor infringements, when multiplied many times, become in the aggregate a major inroad on copyright that must be prevented." 1975 Senate Report 65.

I therefore conclude that, at least when the proposed use is an unproductive one, a copyright owner need prove only a potential for harm to the market for or the value of the copyrighted work. See 3 M. Nimmer, Copyright § 13.05[E][4][c], p. 13–84 (1983). Proof of actual harm, or even probable harm, may be impossible in an area where the effect of a new technology is speculative. Infringement thus would be found if the copyright owner demonstrates a reasonable possibility that harm will result from the proposed use. When the use is one that creates no benefit to the public at large, copyright protection should not be denied on the basis that a new technology that may result in harm has not yet done so.

The Studios have identified a number of ways in which VTR recording could damage their copyrights. VTR recording could reduce their ability to market their works in movie theaters and through the rental or sale of prerecorded videotapes or videodiscs; it also could reduce their rerun audience, and consequently the license fees available to them for repeated showings. Moreover, advertisers may be willing to pay for only "live" viewing audiences, if they believe VTR viewers will delete commercials or if rating services are unable to measure VTR use; if this is the case, VTR recording could reduce the license fees the Studios are able to charge even for first-run showings. Library-building may raise the potential for each of the types of harm identified by the Studios, and time-shifting may raise the potential for substantial harm as well.[a]

Although the District Court found no likelihood of harm from VTR use, 480 F.Supp., at 468, I conclude that it applied an incorrect substantive standard and misallocated the burden of proof. The District Court's reluctance to engage in prediction in this area is understandable, but, in my view, the court was mistaken in concluding that the Studios should bear the risk created by this uncertainty. The Studios have demonstrated a potential for harm, which has not been, and could not be, refuted at this early stage of technological development.

The District Court's analysis of harm, moreover, failed to consider the effect of VTR recording on "the potential market for or the value of the copyrighted work," as required by § 107(4). The requirement that a putatively infringing use of a copyrighted work, to be "fair," must not impair a "potential" market for the work has two implications. First, an infringer cannot prevail merely by demonstrating that the copyright holder suffered no net harm from the infringer's action. Indeed, even a showing

---

[a] A VTR owner who has taped a favorite movie for repeated viewing will be less likely to rent or buy a tape containing the same movie, watch a televised rerun, or pay to see the movie at a theater. Although time-shifting may not replace theater or rerun viewing or the purchase of prerecorded tapes or discs, it may well replace rental usage; a VTR user who has recorded a first-run movie for later viewing will have no need to rent a copy when he wants to see it. Both library-builders and time-shifters may avoid commercials; the library-builder may use the pause control to record without them, and all users may fast-forward through commercials on playback.

that the infringement has resulted in a net benefit to the copyright holder will not suffice. Rather, the infringer must demonstrate that he had not impaired the copyright holder's ability to demand compensation from (or to deny access to) any group who would otherwise be willing to pay to see or hear the copyrighted work. Second, the fact that a given market for a copyrighted work would not be available to the copyright holder were it not for the infringer's activities does not permit the infringer to exploit that market without compensating the copyright holder.

In this case, the Studios and their amici demonstrate that the advent of the VTR technology created a potential market for their copyrighted programs. That market consists of those persons who find it impossible or inconvenient to watch the programs at the time they are broadcast, and who wish to watch them at other times. These persons are willing to pay for the privilege of watching copyrighted work at their convenience, as is evidenced by the fact that they are willing to pay for VTR's and tapes; undoubtedly, most also would be willing to pay some kind of royalty to copyright holders. The Studios correctly argue that they have been deprived of the ability to exploit this sizable market.

It is thus apparent from the record and from the findings of the District Court that time-shifting does have a substantial adverse effect upon the "potential market for" the Studios' copyrighted works. Accordingly, even under the formulation of the fair use doctrine advanced by Sony, time-shifting cannot be deemed a fair use.

* * *

VI

The court has adopted an approach very different from the one I have outlined. There is no indication that the fair use doctrine has any application for purely personal consumption on the scale involved in this case, and the Court's application of it here deprives fair use of the major cohesive force that has guided evolution of the doctrine in the past.

[T]he Court purports to apply to time-shifting the four factors explicitly stated in the statute. The Court confidently describes time-shifting as a noncommercial, nonprofit activity. It is clear, however, that personal use of programs that have been copied without permission is not what § 107(1) protects. The intent of the section is to encourage users to engage in activities the primary benefit of which accrues to others. Time-shifting involves no such humanitarian impulse. Purely consumptive uses are certainly not what the fair use doctrine was designed to protect, and the awkwardness of applying the statutory language to time-shifting only makes clearer that fair use was designed to protect only uses that are productive.

The next two statutory factors are all but ignored by the Court—though certainly not because they have no applicability. The second factor—"the nature of the copyrighted work"—strongly supports the view that time-shifting is an infringing use. The rationale guiding application of this factor is that certain types of works, typically those involving "more of diligence than of originality or inventiveness," New York Times Co. v. Roxbury Data Interface, Inc., 434 F.Supp. 217, 221 (NJ 1977), require less copyright protection than other original works. Thus, for example, informational works, such as news reports, that readily lend themselves to productive use by other, are less protected than creative works of entertainment. Sony's own surveys indicate that entertainment shows account for more than 80% of the programs recorded by Betamax owners.

The third statutory factor—"the amount and substantiality of the portion used"—is even more devastating to the Court's interpretation. It is undisputed that virtually all VTR owners record entire works, see 480 F.Supp., at 454, thereby creating an exact substitute for the copyrighted original. Fair use is intended to allow individuals engaged in productive uses to copy small portions of original works that will facilitate their own productive endeavors. Time-shifting bears no resemblance to such activity, and the complete duplication that it involves might alone be sufficient to preclude a finding of fair use. It is little wonder that the Court has chosen to ignore this statutory factor.[b]

The fourth factor requires an evaluation of "the effect of the use upon the potential market for or value of the copyrighted work." This is the factor upon which the Court focuses, but once again, the Court has misread the statute. As mentioned above, the statute requires a court to consider the effect of the use on the potential market for the copyrighted work. The Court has struggled mightily to show that VTR use has not reduced the value of the Studios' copyrighted works in their present markets. Even if true, that showing only begins the proper inquiry. The development of the VTR has created a new market for the works produced by the Studios. That market consists of those persons who desire to view television programs at times other than when they are broadcast, and who therefore purchase VTR recorders to enable them to time-shift.[c] Because time-shifting of the Studios' copyrighted works involves the copying of them, however, the Studios are entitled to share in the benefits of that new market. Those benefits currently go to Sony through Betamax sales. Respondents therefore can show harm from VTR use simply by showing that the value of their copyrights would increase if they were compensated for the copies that are used in the new market. The existence of this effect is self-evident.

[b] The Court's one oblique acknowledgement of this third factor, *ante,* at [IV(B)], and n.[h], seems to suggest that the fact that time-shifting involves copying complete works is not very significant because the viewers already have been asked to watch the initial broadcast free. This suggestion misses the point. As has been noted, a book borrowed from a public library may not be copied any more freely than one that has been purchased. An invitation to view a showing is completely different from an invitation to copy a copyrighted work.

[c] The Court implicitly has recognized that this market is very significant. The central concern underlying the Court's entire opinion is that there is a large audience who would like very much to be able to view programs at times other than when they are broadcast. The Court simply misses the implication of its own concerns.

Campbell v. Acuff–Rose Music, Inc.

Supreme Court of the United States, 1994.
___ U.S. ___, 114 S.Ct. 1164, 127 L.Ed.2d 500.

■ JUSTICE SOUTER delivered the opinion of the Court.

Fair Use

We are called upon to decide whether 2 Live Crew's commercial parody of Roy Orbison's song, "Oh, Pretty Woman," may be a fair use within the meaning of the Copyright Act of 1976, 17 U.S.C. § 107. Although the District Court granted summary judgment for 2 Live Crew, the Court of Appeals reversed, holding the defense of fair use barred by the song's commercial character and excessive borrowing. Because we hold that a parody's commercial character is only one element to be weighed in a fair use enquiry, and that insufficient consideration was given to the nature of parody in weighing the degree of copying, we reverse and remand.

* * *

The first factor in a fair use enquiry ... draws on Justice Story's formulation, "the nature and objects of the selections made." Folsom v. Marsh, 9 F.Cas. 342, 348 (No. 4,901)(CCD Mass.1841). The enquiry here may be guided by the examples given in the preamble to § 107, looking to whether the use is for criticism, or comment, or news reporting, and the like. The central purpose of this investigation is to see, in Justice Story's words, whether the new work merely "supersedes the objects" of the original creation, Folsom v. Marsh, *supra*, at 348, or instead adds something new, with a further purpose or different character, altering the first with new expression, meaning, or message; it asks, in other words, whether and to what extent the new work is "transformative." Leval, Toward a Fair Use Standard, 103 Harv. L. Rev. 1105 (1990). Although such transformative use is not absolutely necessary for a finding of fair use, Sony Corp. of America, v. Universal City Studios, Inc., 464 U.S. 417, 455, n.40 (1984),[a] the goal of copyright, to promote science and the arts, is generally furthered by the creation of transformative works. Such works thus lie at the heart of the fair use doctrine's guarantee of breathing space within the confines of copyright, see, e.g., *Sony, supra*, at 478–480 (Blackmun, J., dissenting), and the more transformative the new work, the less will be the significance of other factors, like commercialism, that may weigh against a finding of fair use.

This Court has only once before even considered whether parody may be fair use, and that time issued no opinion because of the Court's equal division. Benny v. Loew's Inc., 239 F.2d 532 (C.A.9 1956), aff'd sub nom. Columbia Broadcasting System, Inc. v. Loew's Inc., 356 U.S. 43 (1958). Suffice it to say now that parody has an obvious claim to transformative value, as Acuff–Rose itself does not deny. Like less ostensibly humorous forms of criticism, it can provide social benefit, by shedding light on an earlier work, and, in the process, creating a new one. We thus line up with

[a] The obvious statutory exception to this focus on transformative uses is the straight reproduction of multiple copies for classroom distribution.

the courts that have held that parody, like other comment or criticism, may claim fair use under § 107.

The fact that parody can claim legitimacy for some appropriation does not, of course, tell either parodist or judge much about where to draw the line. Like a book review quoting the copyrighted material criticized, parody may or may not be fair use, and petitioner's suggestion that any parodic use is presumptively fair has no more justification in law or fact than the equally hopeful claim that any use for news reporting should be presumed fair, see *Harper & Row*, 471 U.S. 539, at 561 (1985). . . . The threshold question when fair use is raised in defense of parody is whether a parodic character may reasonably be perceived.[b]

While we might not assign a high rank to the parodic element here, we think it fair to say that 2 Live Crew's song reasonably could be perceived as commenting on the original or criticizing it, to some degree.

The Court of Appeals, however, immediately cut short the enquiry into 2 Live Crew's fair use claim by confining its treatment of the first factor essentially to one relevant fact, the commercial nature of the use. The court then inflated the significance of this fact by applying a presumption ostensibly culled from *Sony*, that "every commercial use of copyrighted material is presumptively . . . unfair. . . ." *Sony*, 464 U.S., at 451. In giving virtually dispositive weight to the commercial nature of the parody, the Court of Appeals erred.

The language of the statute makes clear that the commercial or nonprofit educational purpose of a work is only one element of the first factor enquiry into its purpose and character. As we explained in *Harper & Row*, Congress resisted attempts to narrow the ambit of this traditional enquiry by adopting categories of presumptively fair use, and it urged courts to preserve the breadth of their traditionally ample view of the universe of relevant evidence. 471 U.S., at 561, H.R.Rep. No. 94–1476, p.66 (1976)(hereinafter House Report). Accordingly, the mere fact that a use is educational and not for profit does not insulate it from a finding of infringement, any more than the commercial character of a use bars a finding of fairness. If, indeed, commerciality carried presumptive force against a finding of fairness, the presumption would swallow nearly all of the illustrative uses listed in the preamble paragraph of § 107, including news reporting, comment, criticism, teaching, scholarship, and research, since these activities "are generally conducted for profit in this country." *Harper & Row, supra*, at 592 (Brennan, J., dissenting). Congress could not have intended such a rule.

Sony itself called for no hard evidentiary presumption. There, we emphasized the need for a "sensitive balancing of interests," 464 U.S., at 455, n.40, noted that Congress had "eschewed a rigid, bright-line approach

---

[b] The only further judgment, indeed, that a court may pass on a work goes to an assessment of whether the parodic element is slight or great, and the copying small or extensive in relation to the parodic element, for a work with slight parodic element and extensive copying will be more likely to merely "supersede the objects" of the original.

to fair use," *id.* at 449, n.31, and stated that the commercial or nonprofit educational character of a work is "not conclusive," *id.* at 448–449, but rather a fact to be "weighed along with others in fair use decisions." *Id.* at 449, n.32 (quoting House Report, p.66). The Court of Appeals's elevation of one sentence from *Sony* to a per se rule thus runs as much counter to *Sony* itself as to the long common-law tradition of fair use adjudication. Rather, as we explained in *Harper & Row*, *Sony* stands for the proposition that the "fact that a publication was commercial as opposed to nonprofit is a separate factor that tends to weigh against a finding of fair use." 471 U.S., at 562. But that is all, and the fact that even the force of that tendency will vary with the context is a further reason against elevating commerciality to hard presumptive significance.

Harper & Row v. Nation Enterprises

Supreme Court of the United States, 1985.
471 U.S. 539, 105 S.Ct. 2218, 85 L.Ed.2d 588.

■ JUSTICE O'CONNOR delivered the opinion of the Court.

Not Fair Use

This case requires us to consider to what extent the "fair use" provision of the Copyright Revision Act of 1976 (hereinafter the Copyright Act), sanctions the unauthorized use of quotations from a public figure's unpublished manuscript. In March 1979, an undisclosed source provided The Nation Magazine with the unpublished manuscript of "A Time to Heal: The Autobiography of Gerald R. Ford." Working directly from the purloined manuscript, an editor of The Nation produced a short piece entitled "The Ford Memoirs—Behind the Nixon Pardon." The piece was timed to "scoop" an article scheduled shortly to appear in Time Magazine. Time had agreed to purchase the exclusive right to print prepublication excerpts from the copyright holders, Harper & Row, Publishers, Inc. (hereinafter Harper & Row), and Reader's Digest Association, Inc. (hereinafter Reader's Digest). As a result of The Nation article, Time canceled its agreement. Petitioners brought a successful copyright action against The Nation. On appeal, the Second Circuit reversed the lower court's finding of infringement, holding that The Nation's act was sanctioned as a "fair use" of the copyrighted material. We granted certiorari, 467 U.S. 1214 (1984), and we now reverse.

I

In February 1977, shortly after leaving the White House, former President Gerald R. Ford contracted with petitioners Harper & Row and Reader's Digest, to publish his as yet unwritten memoirs. The memoirs were to contain "significant hitherto unpublished material" concerning the Watergate crisis, Mr. Ford's pardon of former President Nixon and "Mr. Ford's reflections on this period of history, and the morality and personalities involved." In addition to the right to publish the Ford memoirs in book form, the agreement gave petitioners the exclusive right to license prepublication excerpts, known in the trade as "first serial rights." Two years later, as the memoirs were nearing completion, petitioners negotiated a prepublication licensing agreement with Time, a weekly news magazine. Time agreed to pay $25,000, $12,500 in advance and an additional $12,500 at publication, in exchange for the right to excerpt 7,500 words from Mr. Ford's account of the Nixon pardon. The issue featuring the excerpts was timed to appear approximately one week before shipment of the full length book version to bookstores. Exclusivity was an important consideration; Harper & Row instituted procedures designed to maintain the confidentiality of the manuscript, and Time retained the right to renegotiate the second payment should the material appear in print prior to its release of the excerpts.

Two to three weeks before the Time article's scheduled release, an unidentified person secretly brought a copy of the Ford manuscript to Victor Navasky, editor of The Nation, a political commentary magazine. Mr. Navasky knew that his possession of the manuscript was not authorized and that the manuscript must be returned quickly to his "source" to avoid discovery. 557 F.Supp. 1067, 1069 (S.D.N.Y.1983). He hastily put together what he believed was "a real hot news story" composed of quotes, paraphrases, and facts drawn exclusively from the manuscript. *Ibid.* Mr. Navasky attempted no independent commentary, research or criticism, in part because of the need for speed if he was to "make news" by "[publishing] in advance of publication of the Ford book." The 2,250–word article appeared on April 3, 1979. As a result of The Nation's article, Time canceled its piece and refused to pay the remaining $12,500.

Petitioners brought suit in the District Court for the Southern District of New York, alleging conversion, tortious interference with contract, and violations of the Copyright Act. After a 6–day bench trial, the District Judge found that "A Time to Heal" was protected by copyright at the time of The Nation publication and that respondents' use of the copyrighted material constituted an infringement under the Copyright Act. The District Court rejected respondents' argument that The Nation's piece was a "fair use" sanctioned by § 107. The court awarded actual damages of $12,500.

A divided panel of the Court of Appeals for the Second Circuit reversed. 723 F.2d 195 (1983). The Court of Appeals was especially influenced by the "politically significant" nature of the subject matter and its conviction that it is not "the purpose of the Copyright Act to impede that harvest of knowledge so necessary to a democratic state" or "chill the activities of the press by forbidding a circumscribed use of copyrighted words." *Id.* at 197, 209.

II

The Nation has admitted to lifting verbatim quotes of the author's original language totaling between 300 and 400 words and constituting some 13% of The Nation article. In using generous verbatim excerpts of Mr. Ford's unpublished manuscript to lend authenticity to its account of the forthcoming memoirs, The Nation effectively arrogated to itself the right of first publication, an important marketable subsidiary right. For the reasons set forth below, we find that this use of the copyrighted manuscript, even stripped to the verbatim quotes conceded by The Nation to be copyrightable expression, was not a fair use within the meaning of the Copyright Act.

III

A

Perhaps because the fair use doctrine was predicated on the author's implied consent to "reasonable and customary" use when he released his work for public consumption, fair use traditionally was not recognized as a defense to charges of copying from an author's as yet unpublished works. Under common-law copyright, "the property of the author ... in his intellectual creation [was] absolute until he voluntarily [parted] with the same." American Tobacco Co. v. Werckmeister, 207 U.S. 284, 299 (1907); 2 Nimmer § 8.23, at 8–273. This absolute rule, however, was tempered in practice by the equitable nature of the fair use doctrine. In a given case, factors such as implied consent through de facto publication on performance or dissemination of a work may tip the balance of equities in favor of prepublication use. But it has never been seriously disputed that "the fact that the plaintiff's work is unpublished ... is a factor tending to negate the defense of fair use." *Ibid*. Publication of an author's expression before he has authorized its dissemination seriously infringes the author's right to decide when and whether it will be made public, a factor not present in fair use of published works. Respondents contend, however, that Congress, in including first publication among the rights enumerated in § 106, which are expressly subject to fair use under § 107, intended that fair use would apply in pari materia to published and unpublished works. The Copyright Act does not support this proposition.

The Copyright Act represents the culmination of a major legislative reexamination of copyright doctrine. Among its other innovations, it eliminated publication "as a dividing line between common law and statutory protection," H. R. Rep. No. 94–1476, at 129 (1976) extending statutory protection to all works from the time of their creation. It also recognized for the first time a distinct statutory right of first publication, which had previously been an element of the common-law protections afforded unpublished works.

Though the right of first publication, like the other rights enumerated in § 106, is expressly made subject to the fair use provision of § 107, fair use analysis must always be tailored to the individual case. The right of first publication implicates a threshold decision by the author whether and in what form to release his work. First publication is inherently different from other § 106 rights in that only one person can be the first publisher; as the contract with Time illustrates, the commercial value of the right lies primarily in exclusivity. Because the potential damage to the author from judicially enforced "sharing" of the first publication right with unauthorized users of his manuscript is substantial, the balance of equities in evaluating such a claim of fair use inevitably shifts.

The Senate Report confirms that Congress intended the unpublished nature of the work to figure prominently in fair use analysis. In discussing fair use of photocopied materials in the classroom the Committee Report states:

> "A key, though not necessarily determinative, factor in fair use is whether or not the work is available to the potential user. If the work is 'out of print' and unavailable for purchase through normal channels, the user may have more justification for reproducing it.... The applicability of the fair use doctrine to unpublished works is narrowly limited since, although the work is unavailable, this is the result of a deliberate choice on the part of the copyright owner. Under ordinary circumstances, the copyright owner's 'right of first publication' would outweigh any needs of reproduction for classroom purposes." S. Rep. No. 94–473 at 64 (1975).

Although the Committee selected photocopying of classroom materials to illustrate fair use, it emphasized that "the same general standards of fair use are applicable to all kinds of uses of copyrighted material." *Id.* at 65.

Even if the legislative history were entirely silent, we would be bound to conclude from Congress' characterization of § 107 as a "restatement" that its effect was to preserve existing law concerning fair use of unpublished works as of other types of protected works and not to "change, narrow, or enlarge it." House Report, at 66. We conclude that the unpublished nature of a work is "[a] key, though not necessarily determinative, factor" tending to negate a defense of fair use. Senate Report, at 64.

We also find unpersuasive respondents' argument that fair use may be made of a soon-to-be-published manuscript on the ground that the author has demonstrated he has no interest in nonpublication. The author's control of first public distribution implicates not only his personal interest in creative control but his property interest in exploitation of prepublication rights, which are valuable in themselves and serve as a valuable adjunct to publicity and marketing. Under ordinary circumstances, the author's right to control the first public appearance of his undisseminated expression will outweigh a claim of fair use.

B

Respondents, however, contend that First Amendment values require a different rule under the circumstances of this case. The thrust of the decision below is that "[the] scope of [fair use] is undoubtedly wider when the information conveyed relates to matters of high public concern." Consumers Union of the United States, Inc. v. General Signal Corp., 724 F.2d 1044, 1050 (C.A.2 1983)(construing 723 F.2d 195 (1983)(case below) as allowing advertiser to quote Consumer Reports), *cert. denied*, 469 U.S. 823 (1984). Respondents advance the substantial public import of the subject matter of the Ford memoirs as grounds for excusing a use that would ordinarily not pass muster as a fair use—the piracy of verbatim quotations for the purpose of "scooping" the authorized first serialization. Respondents explain their copying of Mr. Ford's expression as essential to reporting the news story it claims the book itself represents. In respondents' view, not only the facts contained in Mr. Ford's memoirs, but "the precise manner in which [he] expressed himself [were] as newsworthy as what he had to say." Respondents argue that the public's interest in learning this news as fast as possible outweighs the right of the author to control its first publication.

The Second Circuit noted, correctly, that copyright's idea/expression dichotomy "[strikes] a definitional balance between the First Amendment and the Copyright Act by permitting free communication of facts while still protecting an author's expression." 723 F.2d, at 203. No author may copyright his ideas or the facts he narrates. § 102(b). As this Court long ago observed: "[The] news element—the information respecting current events contained in the literary production—is not the creation of the writer, but is a report of matters that ordinarily are publici juris; it is the history of the day." International News Service v. Associated Press, 248 U.S. 215, 234 (1918). But copyright assures those who write and publish factual narratives such as "A Time to Heal" that they may at least enjoy the right to market the original expression contained therein as just compensation for their investment. Cf. Zacchini v. Scripps–Howard Broadcasting Co., 433 U.S. 562, 575 (1977).

Respondents' theory, however, would expand fair use to effectively destroy any expectation of copyright protection in the work of a public figure. Absent such protection, there would be little incentive to create or profit in financing such memoirs, and the public would be denied an important source of significant historical information. The promise of copyright would be an empty one if it could be avoided merely by dubbing the infringement a fair use "news report" of the book.

Nor do respondents assert any actual necessity for circumventing the copyright scheme with respect to the types of works and users at issue here.[a] Where an author and publisher have invested extensive resources in creating an original work and are poised to release it to the public, no legitimate aim is served by pre-empting the right of first publication. The fact that the words the author has chosen to clothe his narrative may of themselves be "newsworthy" is not an independent justification for unauthorized copying of the author's expression prior to publication. To paraphrase another recent Second Circuit decision:

> "The fair use doctrine is not a license for corporate theft, empowering a court to ignore a copyright whenever it determines the underlying work contains material of possible public importance." Iowa State University Research Foundation, Inc. v. American Broadcasting Cos., Inc., 621 F.2d 57, 61 (1980)(citations omitted).

In our haste to disseminate news, it should not be forgotten that the Framers intended copyright itself to be the engine of free expression. By

---

[a] It bears noting that Congress in the Copyright Act recognized a public interest warranting specific exemptions in a number of areas not within traditional fair use, see, e.g., § 115 (compulsory license for records); § 105 (no copyright in Government works). No such exemption limits copyright in personal narratives written by public servants after they leave Government service.

establishing a marketable right to the use of one's expression, copyright supplies the economic incentive to create and disseminate ideas.

It is fundamentally at odds with the scheme of copyright to accord lesser rights in those works that are of greatest importance to the public. Such a notion ignores the major premise of copyright and injures author and public alike.

In view of the First Amendment protections already embodied in the Copyright Act's distinction between copyrightable expression and uncopyrightable facts and ideas, and the latitude for scholarship and comment traditionally afforded by fair use, we see no warrant for expanding the doctrine of fair use to create what amounts to a public figure exception to copyright. Whether verbatim copying from a public figure's manuscript in a given case is or is not fair must be judged according to the traditional equities of fair use.

IV

Purpose of the Use. The Second Circuit correctly identified news reporting as the general purpose of The Nation's use. News reporting is one of the examples enumerated in § 107 to "give some idea of the sort of activities the courts might regard as fair use under the circumstances." Senate Report, at 61. This listing was not intended to be exhaustive, see *ibid.*; § 101 (definition of "including" and "such as"), or to single out any particular use as presumptively a "fair" use. The drafters resisted pressures from special interest groups to create presumptive categories of fair use, but structured the provision as an affirmative defense requiring a case-by-case analysis. The fact that an article arguably is "news" and therefore a productive use is simply one factor in a fair use analysis.

We agree with the Second Circuit that the trial court erred in fixing on whether the information contained in the memoirs was actually new to the public. The Nation has every right to seek to be the first to publish information. But The Nation went beyond simply reporting uncopyrightable information and actively sought to exploit the headline value of its infringement, making a "news event" out of its unauthorized first publication of a noted figure's copyrighted expression.

The fact that a publication was commercial as opposed to nonprofit is a separate factor that tends to weigh against a finding of fair use. In arguing that the purpose of news reporting is not purely commercial, The Nation misses the point entirely. The crux of the profit/nonprofit distinction is not whether the sole motive of the use is monetary gain but whether the user stands to profit from exploitation of the copyrighted material without paying the customary price.

In evaluating character and purpose we cannot ignore The Nation's stated purpose of scooping the forthcoming hardcover and Time abstracts. The Nation's use had not merely the incidental effect but the intended purpose of supplanting the copyright holder's commercially valuable right of first publication. Also relevant to the "character" of the use is "the propriety of the defendant's conduct." 3 Nimmer § 13.05[A], at 13–72. "Fair use presupposes 'good faith' and 'fair dealing.'" Time Inc. v. Bernard Geis Associates, 293 F.Supp. 130, 146 (S.D.N.Y.1968), quoting Schulman, Fair Use and the Revision of the Copyright Act, 53 Iowa L. Rev. 832 (1968). The trial court found that The Nation knowingly exploited a purloined manuscript. Unlike the typical claim of fair use, The Nation cannot offer up even the fiction of consent as justification. Like its competitor newsweekly, it was free to bid for the right of abstracting excerpts from "A Time to Heal."

Nature of the Copyrighted Work. Second, the Act directs attention to the nature of the copyrighted work. "A Time to Heal" may be characterized as an unpublished historical narrative or autobiography. The law generally recognizes a greater need to disseminate factual works than works of fiction or fantasy.

Some of the briefer quotes from the memoirs are arguably necessary adequately to convey the facts; for example, Mr. Ford's characterization of the White House tapes as the "smoking gun" is perhaps so integral to the idea expressed as to be inseparable from it. Cf. 1 Nimmer § 1.10[C]. But The Nation did not stop at isolated phrases and instead excerpted subjective descriptions and portraits of public figures whose power lies in the author's individualized expression. Such use, focusing on the most expressive elements of the work, exceeds that necessary to disseminate the facts.

The fact that a work is unpublished is a critical element of its "nature." Our prior discussion establishes that the scope of fair use is narrower with respect to unpublished works. While even substantial quotations might qualify as fair use in a review of a published work or a news account of a speech that had been delivered to the public or disseminated to the press, see House Report, at 65, the author's right to control the first public appearance of his expression weighs against such use of the work before its release. The right of first publication encompasses not only the choice whether to publish at all, but also the choices of when, where, and in what form first to publish a work.

In the case of Mr. Ford's manuscript, the copyright holders' interest in confidentiality is irrefutable; the copyright holders had entered into a contractual undertaking to "keep the manuscript confidential" and required that all those to whom the manuscript was shown also "sign an agreement to keep the manuscript confidential." While the copyright holders' contract with Time required Time to submit its proposed article seven days before publication, The Nation's clandestine publication afforded no such opportunity for creative or quality control. It was hastily patched together and contained "a number of inaccuracies." (testimony of Victor Navasky). A use that so clearly infringes the copyright holder's interests in confidentiality and creative control is difficult to characterize as "fair."

Amount and Substantiality of the Portion Used. Next, the Act directs us to examine the amount and substantiality of the portion used in relation to the copyrighted work as a whole. In absolute terms, the words actually quoted were an insubstantial portion of "A Time to Heal." The District Court, however, found that "[The] Nation took what was essentially the heart of the book." 557 F.Supp., at 1072. We believe the Court of Appeals erred in overruling the District Judge's evaluation of the qualitative nature of the taking. A Time editor described the chapters on the pardon as "the most interesting and moving parts of the entire manuscript." The portions actually quoted were selected by Mr. Navasky as among the most powerful passages in those chapters. He testified that he used verbatim excerpts because simply reciting the information could not adequately convey the "absolute certainty with which [Ford] expressed himself," or show that "this comes from President Ford," or carry the "definitive quality" of the original. In short, he quoted these passages precisely because they qualitatively embodied Ford's distinctive expression.

As the statutory language indicates, a taking may not be excused merely because it is insubstantial with respect to the infringing work. As Judge Learned Hand cogently remarked, "no plagiarist can excuse the wrong by showing how much of his work he did not pirate." Sheldon v. Metro–Goldwyn Pictures Corp., 81 F.2d 49, 56 (CA2), *cert. denied*, 298 U.S. 669 (1936). Conversely, the fact that a substantial portion of the infringing work was copied verbatim is evidence of the qualitative value of the copied material, both to the originator and to the plagiarist who seeks to profit from marketing someone else's copyrighted expression.

Stripped to the verbatim quotes, the direct takings from the unpublished manuscript constitute at least 13% of the infringing article. The Nation article is structured around the quoted excerpts which serve as its dramatic focal points. In view of the expressive value of the excerpts and their key role in the infringing work, we cannot agree with the Second Circuit that the "magazine took a meager, indeed an infinitesimal amount of Ford's original language." 723 F.2d, at 209.

Effect on the Market. Finally, the Act focuses on "the effect of the use upon the potential market for or value of the copyrighted work." This last factor is undoubtedly the single most important element of fair use.[b] See 3 Nimmer § 13.05[A], at 13–76, and cases cited therein. "Fair use, when properly applied, is limited to copying by others which does not materially impair the marketability of the work which is copied." 1 Nimmer § 1.10[D], at 1–87. The trial court found not merely a potential but an actual effect on the market. Time's cancellation of its projected serialization and its refusal to pay the $12,500 were the direct effect of the

---

[b] Economists who have addressed the issue believe the fair use exception should come into play only in those situations in which the market fails or the price the copyright holder would ask is near zero. See, e.g., T. Brennan, Harper & Row v. The Nation, Copyrightability and Fair Use, Dept. of Justice Economic Policy Office Discussion Paper 13–17 (1984); Gordon, Fair Use as Market Failure: A Structural and Economic Analysis of the Betamax Case and its Predecessors, 82 Colum. L. Rev. 1600, 1615 (1982). As the facts here demonstrate, there is a fully functioning market that encourages the creation and dissemination of memoirs of public figures. In the economists' view, permitting "fair use" to displace normal copyright channels disrupts the copyright market without a commensurate public benefit.

infringement. The Court of Appeals rejected this fact-finding as clearly erroneous, noting that the record did not establish a causal relation between Time's nonperformance and respondents' unauthorized publication of Mr. Ford's expression as opposed to the facts taken from the memoirs. We disagree. Rarely will a case of copyright infringement present such clear-cut evidence of actual damage. Petitioners assured Time that there would be no other authorized publication of any portion of the unpublished manuscript prior to April 23, 1979. Any publication of material from chapters 1 and 3 would permit Time to renegotiate its final payment. Time cited The Nation's article, which contained verbatim quotes from the unpublished manuscript, as a reason for its nonperformance. [O]nce a copyright holder establishes with reasonable probability the existence of a causal connection between the infringement and a loss of revenue, the burden properly shifts to the infringer to show that this damage would have occurred had there been no taking of copyrighted expression. See 3 Nimmer § 14.02, at 14–7–14–8.1. Petitioners established a prima facie case of actual damage that respondents failed to rebut.

More important, to negate fair use one need only show that if the challenged use "should become widespread, it would adversely affect the *potential* market for the copyrighted work." Sony Corp. of America v. Universal City Studios, Inc., 464 U.S., at 451 (emphasis added); *id.* at 484, and n.36 (collecting cases)(dissenting opinion). This inquiry must take account not only of harm to the original but also of harm to the market for derivative works. "If the defendant's work adversely affects the value of any of the rights in the copyrighted work (in this case the adaptation [and serialization] right) the use is not fair." 3 Nimmer § 13.05[B], at 13–77–13–78.

It is undisputed that the factual material in the balance of The Nation's article, besides the verbatim quotes at issue here, was drawn exclusively from the chapters on the pardon. The excerpts were employed as featured episodes in a story about the Nixon pardon—precisely the use petitioners had licensed to Time. The borrowing of these verbatim quotes from the unpublished manuscript lent The Nation's piece a special air of authenticity—as Navasky expressed it, the reader would know it was Ford speaking and not The Nation. Thus it directly competed for a share of the market for prepublication excerpts. The Senate Report states:

> "With certain special exceptions ... a use that supplants any part of the normal market for a copyrighted work would ordinarily be considered an infringement." Senate Report, at 65.

Placed in a broader perspective, a fair use doctrine that permits extensive prepublication quotations from an unreleased manuscript without the copyright owner's consent poses substantial potential for damage to the marketability of first serialization rights in general.

V

In sum, the traditional doctrine of fair use, as embodied in the Copyright Act, does not sanction the use made by The Nation of these copyrighted materials. Any copyright infringer may claim to benefit the public by increasing public access to the copyrighted work. See Pacific & Southern Co. v. Duncan, 744 F.2d 1490 at 1499–1500 (11th Cir.1984). But Congress has not designed, and we see no warrant for judicially imposing, a "compulsory license" permitting unfettered access to the unpublished copyrighted expression of public figures.

[T]he judgment of the Court of Appeals is reversed, and the case is remanded for further proceedings consistent with this opinion.

It is so ordered.

■ [The dissenting opinion of JUSTICE BRENNAN, joined by JUSTICE WHITE and JUSTICE MARSHALL, is omitted.]

New Era Publications International, ApS v. Carol Publishing Group

United States Court of Appeals, Second Circuit, 1990.
904 F.2d 152.

■ FEINBERG, CIRCUIT JUDGE.

Defendant Carol Publishing Group appeals from a February 13, 1990 judgment of the United States District Court for the Southern District of New York, permanently enjoining it from publishing a biography in its present form, on grounds of copyright infringement. In an opinion reported at 729 F.Supp. 992, the district court held that the biography's quotations from its subject's writings—all of which had been published—did not constitute "fair use." We disagree.

Background

The biography at issue in this appeal is entitled A Piece of Blue Sky: Scientology, Dianetics and L. Ron Hubbard Exposed, and was written by Jonathan Caven–Atack. (We will refer to A Piece of Blue Sky as "the book" and to Caven–Atack as "the author.") The subject of the book is L. Ron Hubbard, the controversial founder of the Church of Scientology (the Church), who died in 1986.

The author joined the Church when he was 19 and was a member for almost nine years. In 1983, however, according to the author, his faith in the Church was shaken by what he saw as the Church's repressive practices toward dissident members. The author subsequently resigned from the Church, but undertook a thorough investigation into the Church and Hubbard. During the course of this inquiry, the author became convinced that the Church was a dangerous cult, and that Hubbard was a vindictive and profoundly disturbed man.

The author's investigation culminated in the book, which, in its present manuscript form, is 527 double-spaced pages in length. As its title makes plain, the book is an unfavorable biography of Hubbard and a strong attack on Scientology; the author's purpose is to expose what he believes is the pernicious nature of the Church and the deceit that is the foundation of its teachings. The book paints a highly unflattering portrait of Hubbard as a thoroughgoing charlatan who lied relentlessly about his accomplishments. The author's attitude toward his subject can be gauged by his descriptions of Hubbard as "an arrogant, amoral egomaniac," "a paranoid, power hungry, petty sadist," and—perhaps ironically in light of the claims in this case—"an outright plagiarist."[a] The book quotes widely from Hubbard's works, using passages from Hubbard's writings both in the body of the text and at the beginning of many chapters. The author had a rich vein of material to mine, because Hubbard wrote prolifically on a wide variety of subjects, including science fiction, philosophy and religion. We are informed that Hubbard published nearly 600 fiction and non-fiction works during his life-time, 111 of which are in print.

Plaintiff-appellee/cross-appellant New Era Publications International, ApS is the exclusive licensee of Hubbard's works. After learning that appellant Carol Publishing Group intended to publish the book, appellee sued appellant in the district court. (Although appellee named the author as a defendant, it did not serve him with a summons and complaint, and he has never entered an appearance.) Appellee claimed that the book copied "substantial portions" of certain of Hubbard's works in violation of its exclusive copyright rights under § 106, and accused appellant of willful copyright infringement under §§ 106 and 501. In particular, appellee argued that 121 passages of the book were drawn from 48 of Hubbard's works. The complaint sought, among other things, an injunction to stop publication of the book. Appellee subsequently moved for a temporary restraining order and a preliminary injunction; by stipulation, the proceedings for a permanent and for a preliminary injunction were later merged.

The district court granted a permanent injunction ... against publication of the book in its present form, noting that "[the] book is still in manuscript form, so deletion of the infringing passages will be relatively simple and inexpensive." *Id.* at 1001. The district court thereafter entered judgment, listing 103 infringing passages taken from 43 works, all published.

Appellant now appeals from the judgment granting an injunction.

Discussion

Appellant asserts that, contrary to the district court's view, all four fair use factors referred to in § 107 weigh in its favor, while appellee argues to the contrary. [F]air use is a mixed question of law and fact, *Id.* at 560, and thus the district court's conclusion on this point is open to full review on appeal. See Puma Indus. Consulting, Inc. v. Daal Assocs., Inc., 808 F.2d 982, 986 (2d Cir.1987). And, "[where] the district court has found facts sufficient to evaluate each of the statutory factors, an appellate court 'need not remand for further factfinding,'" but may resolve the issue of fair use

---

[a] We note here what should be obvious but nevertheless bears stating. We express no view of our own as to Hubbard, his teachings or the Church. The unflattering characterizations are those of the author of the book.

as a matter of law. *Harper & Row*, 471 U.S., 539 at 560 (1985)(quoting *Pacific & Southern Co. v. Duncan*, 744 F.2d 1490, 1495 n.8 (11th Cir.1984), *cert. denied*, 471 U.S. 1004, (1985)).

We have quite recently applied the doctrine of fair use in two opinions of this court. See *Salinger v. Random House, Inc.*, 811 F.2d 90 (2d Cir.), *cert. denied*, 484 U.S. 890, (1987); *New Era Publications Int'l, ApS v. Henry Holt & Co.*, 873 F.2d 576 (2d Cir.), petition for reh'g denied, 884 F.2d 659 (2d Cir.1989), *cert. denied*, 493 U.S. 1094 (1990). Our task is to apply as best we can the teachings of the governing precedents as we understand them. In doing so, on the facts before us and under the appropriate wide-ranging standard of review, we conclude that all four factors listed in § 107 favor appellant, and that appellant's use was fair.

A. Factor One: Purpose and Character of the Use

As noted above, the book is an unfavorable biography. Section 107 provides that use of copyrighted materials for "purposes such as criticism, ... scholarship, or research, is not an infringement of copyright." Our cases establish that biographies in general, and critical biographies in particular, fit "comfortably within" these statutory categories "of uses illustrative of uses that can be fair." *Salinger*, 811 F.2d, at 96; see also *New Era*, 873 F.2d, at 583.

Citing *Harper & Row*, 471 U.S., at 561, appellee argues that there is no rule that if an allegedly infringing work is a biography, factor one necessarily operates in the biographer's favor in evaluating whether there has been a "fair use." Nevertheless, "[if] a book falls into one of these categories [i.e., criticism, scholarship or research], assessment of the first fair use factor should be at an end." *New Era*, 884 F.2d, at 661 (Miner, J., concurring in the denial of rehearing in banc). True, the Supreme Court in *Harper & Row* did not end its analysis of factor one once it had determined that the allegedly infringing use (news reporting) was listed in § 107 as an example of fair use. See 471 U.S., at 561–63. However, what the Court went on to consider was the infringer's knowing exploitation of the copyrighted material—obtained in an underhanded manner—for an undeserved economic profit. See *id*. at 562–63. The present case, by contrast, does not involve "an attempt to rush to the market just ahead of the copyright holder's imminent publication, as occurred in *Harper & Row*." *Salinger*, 811 F.2d, at 96. Instead, the author uses Hubbard's works for the entirely legitimate purpose of making his point that Hubbard was a charlatan and the Church a dangerous cult. To be sure, the author and appellant want to make a profit in publishing the book. But the author's use of material "to enrich" his biography is protected fair use, "not withstanding that he and his publisher anticipate profits." *Id*.

Appellee also contends that the book's use of Hubbard's works does not serve any fair use purpose, but was rather unnecessary appropriation of Hubbard's literary expression. We do not agree with this characterization. The author uses the quotations in part to convey the facts contained therein, and not for their expression. More importantly, even passages used for their expression are intended to convey the author's perception of Hubbard's hypocrisy and pomposity, qualities that may best (or only) be revealed through direct quotation. Appellee points particularly to the 17 topic quotations that begin many of the chapters; while a few of these may arguably come close to the line separating critical study from appropriation, most do not. Indeed, even this borderline use appears to serve the author's purpose by juxtaposing the grandiose expression of the quotations with the banal (to the author) material contained in the body of the chapter. Moreover, the topic quotations sometimes serve to explain or to summarize matters discussed in the chapter.

We hold that factor one favors appellant.

B. Factor Two: Nature of the Copyrighted Work

The district court found that all of the works from which the author quoted had been published. 729 F.Supp., at 998. Whether or not a work is published is critical to its nature under factor two, because "the scope of fair use is narrower with respect to unpublished works." *Harper & Row*, 471 U.S., at 564. See also *New Era*, 873 F.2d, at 858, *Salinger*, 811 F.2d, at 96. Thus, "even substantial quotations might qualify as fair use in a review of a published work." *Harper & Row*, 471 U.S., at 564.

Furthermore, the scope of fair use is greater with respect to factual than non-factual works. See *id.* at 563. While there is no bright-line test for distinguishing between these two categories, we have referred to the former as works that are "essentially factual in nature," Maxtone–Graham v. Burtchaell, 803 F.2d 1253, 1263 (2d Cir.1986), *cert. denied*, 481 U.S. 1059 (1987), or "primarily informational rather than creative." Consumers Union of United States, Inc. v. General Signal Corp., 724 F.2d 1044, 1049 (2d Cir.1983), *cert. denied*, 469 U.S. 823, (1984). We have some hesitation in trying to characterize Hubbard's diverse body of writings as solely "factual" or "non-factual," but on balance, we believe that the quoted works—which deal with Hubbard's life, his views on religion, human relations, the Church, etc.—are more properly viewed as factual or informational.

Appellee emphasizes, however, that there is no per se rule under *Harper & Row*, *New Era* and *Salinger* that factor two favors an alleged infringer whenever the works quoted from are published, as appellant appears to suggest. Appellee is, of course, correct that there is no rule that one may copy with absolute impunity from a published work, regardless of the amount taken. Otherwise, the copyright law would be a nullity. Nevertheless, Hubbard's works have been published, and "[biographies], of course, are fundamentally personal histories and it is both reasonable and customary for biographers to refer to and utilize earlier works dealing with the subject of the work and occasionally to quote directly from such works." *Maxtone–Graham*, 803 F.2d, at 1263 (quoting Rosemont Enterprises, Inc. v. Random House, Inc., 366 F.2d 303, 307 (2d Cir.1966), *cert. denied*, 385 U.S. 1009 (1967)).

Appellee also contends that *Harper & Row* did not endorse greater copying from published works, arguing that in *Salinger*, we interpreted

Harper & Row to mean only that the likelihood "that copying will be found to be a fair use is diminished when the copyrighted material is unpublished, not that a greater quantity of copying of published works is permitted." Appellee fails to persuade us, however, that the plain language of the Supreme Court in *Harper & Row*—i.e., "even substantial quotations might qualify as fair use in a review of a published work," 471 U.S., at 564—should be disregarded. Furthermore, even assuming that appellee's characterization of *Salinger*'s gloss on this passage is correct, appellee advances no persuasive reason why a court should be less, rather than more, likely to find fair use when, as here, the copyrighted material has been published.

In addition, appellee argues that *Harper & Row* intended to allow liberal quotation only for the purpose of literary criticism or review of published works, and that the book does not purport to analyze the literary worth of Hubbard's works. But, we regard appellee's attempt to limit *Harper & Row* to literary criticism as entirely too literal-minded, particularly in the face of our cases holding that biographies are considered works of criticism, scholarship or research within the meaning of § 107. See, e.g., *Salinger*, 811 F.2d, at 96.

Appellee further asserts that many of the quoted passages are more creative or expressive than factual, and that *Maxtone–Graham* is not relevant here because that case involved "standard social science source materials"—i.e., quotations drawn from published interviews. We agree, as already indicated, that there is no easy distinction between works that are "factual" on the one hand, and "creative" or "expressive" on the other, because "[creation] of a nonfiction work, even a compilation of pure fact, entails originality." *Maxtone–Graham*, 803 F.2d, at 1262–63 (quoting *Harper & Row*, 471 U.S., at 547). Thus, reasonable people can disagree over how to classify Hubbard's works. Nevertheless, although some of the quoted passages can accurately be described as expressive—e.g., Hubbard's poetry—our review of the record persuades us that most simply cannot be so characterized.

We conclude that factor two favors appellant.

C.   Factor Three: Volume of Quotation

Factor three addresses the amount and substantiality of the portion used in relation to the copyrighted work, not to the allegedly infringing work. *Harper & Row*, 471 U.S., at 564–65. "There are no absolute rules as to how much of a copyrighted work may be copied and still be considered a fair use." *Maxtone–Graham*, 803 F.2d, at 1263. This factor has both a quantitative and a qualitative component, so that courts have found that use was not fair where the quoted material formed a substantial percentage of the copyrighted work, see, e.g., *Salinger*, 811 F.2d, at 98 (factor three favors copyright holder where one-third of 17 letters and 10% of 42 letters used) or where the quoted material was "essentially the heart of" the copyrighted work. *Harper & Row*, 471 U.S., at 565 (quoting the district court opinion in that case, 557 F.Supp. 1067, 1072 (D.C.N.Y.1983)).

Here, the book uses overall a small percentage of Hubbard's works. Appellant calculates that the book quotes only a minuscule amount of 25 of the 48 works that appellee claimed were infringed, 5–6% of 12 other works and 8% or more of 11 works, each of the 11 being only a few pages in length. (Appellee has accepted these figures "for purposes of discussion," although it adds that they may understate the true amount taken.) In the context of quotation from published works, where a greater amount of copying is allowed, see *Harper & Row*, 471 U.S., at 564, this is not so much as to be unfair. Cf. *Maxtone–Graham*, 803 F.2d, at 1263 (inclusion of 4.3% of published copyrighted work "is not incompatible with a finding of fair use"); Iowa State Univ. Research Found., Inc. v. American Broadcasting Co., 621 F.2d 57, 61–62 (2d Cir.1980)(fair use defense not available where broadcast was made containing 8% of a videotape that apparently had never been broadcast before).

Nor is the use qualitatively unfair. Appellee asserts that "key portions" of Hubbard's works are taken "[in] many cases." But the district court found that the quotations in the book's text—which amount to the bulk of the allegedly infringing passages—do not take essentially the heart of Hubbard's works. 729 F.Supp., at 1000. And our review of the remaining 17 passages, which are "set off by themselves at the beginning of a part or chapter" and "set the tone for the sections they precede," *id.* at 996, persuades us that they too do not take essentially the heart of Hubbard's works.

Appellee also argues that factor three weighs in its favor because the quotations are an important ingredient of the book, pointing out that 2.7% of the book is made up of quotations from Hubbard's works. Appellee asserts that, because of the length of Hubbard's works and because so many of his writings were quoted from, it would be of little value to focus on the amount of infringing material in relation to the copyrighted works, and cites various cases—e.g., *Harper & Row*, 471 U.S., at 566; *Salinger*, 811 F.2d, at 98–99; Meeropol v. Nizer, 560 F.2d 1061, 1070–71 (2d Cir.1977), *cert. denied*, 434 U.S. 1013 (1978)—in which courts discussed the amount used in relation to the infringing work, not the infringed work.

We do not agree with appellee's argument. Section 107 plainly commands us to consider "the amount and substantiality of the portion used in relation to *the copyrighted work* as a whole" (emphasis added), and contains no exception for lengthy works or quotations from multiple works. Furthermore, to the extent that courts have looked to the infringing work, the use here is not as significant as the use alleged in those cases. In *Salinger*, for example, the quoted materials "[to] a large extent . . . [made] the book worth reading." 811 F.2d, at 99; see also *Harper & Row*, 471 U.S., at 565–66 (quotes constituted 13% of the infringing work and played a "key role" in it); *Meeropol*, 560 F.2d, at 1070–71 (quoted material figured prominently in the promotional work for the book). By contrast, the use of the quotes here is primarily a means for illustrating the alleged gap between the official version of Hubbard's life and accomplishments, and what the author contends are the true facts. For that purpose, some conjuring up of the copyrighted work is necessary.

We find that factor three favors appellant.

D.   Factor Four: Effect on the Market

Factor four of § 107 concerns the "effect of the use upon the potential market for or value of the copyrighted work." According to the Supreme Court, this "is undoubtedly the single most important element of fair use." *Harper & Row*, 471 U.S., at 566. In evaluating this factor, courts do not focus solely on the market for the work itself, but also on the "harm to the market for derivative works." *Id.* at 568.

Appellee argues strenuously that factor four favors it, asserting that it intends to publish an authorized biography of Hubbard that will include excerpts from all of his works, including material as yet unpublished, and that the book will discourage potential readers of the authorized biography by conveying the flavor of Hubbard's writings. Appellee also contends that New Era leaves us no choice but to rule in its favor on factor four; according to appellee, that case held that publication of a similar unfavorable biography would impair the market for, and compete with, its planned biography of Hubbard.

We do not find either argument persuasive. As to the first, we found it "unthinkable" in *Maxtone–Graham* that potential customers for plaintiff's copyrighted book containing a "series of sympathetic interviews on abortion and adoption" would fail to purchase plaintiff's book because a small portion of it was used in an essay sharply critical of abortion. 803 F.2d, at 1264. Similarly, we are skeptical here that potential customers for the authorized favorable biography of Hubbard in the future will be deterred from buying because the author's unfavorable biography quotes from Hubbard's works. Indeed, it is not "beyond the realm of possibility that" the book "might stimulate further interest" in the authorized biography. *Id.*

Furthermore, even assuming that the book discourages potential purchasers of the authorized biography, this is not necessarily actionable under the copyright laws. Such potential buyers might be put off because the book persuaded them (as it clearly hopes to) that Hubbard was a charlatan, but the copyright laws do not protect against that sort of injury. Harm to the market for a copyrighted work or its derivatives caused by a "devastating critique" that "diminished sales by convincing the public that the original work was of poor quality" is not "within the scope of copyright protection." *Consumers Union*, 724 F.2d, at 1051. This is so because the critique and the copyrighted work serve "fundamentally different functions, by virtue" of, among other things, "their opposing viewpoints." *Maxtone–Graham*, 803 F.2d, at 1264. "Where the copy does not compete in any way with the original," copyright's central concern—"that creation will be discouraged if demand can be undercut by copiers"—is absent. *Consumers Union*, 724 F.2d, at 1051. Here, the purpose of the book is diametrically opposed to that of the authorized biography; the former seeks to unmask

Hubbard and the Church, while the latter presumably will be designed to promote public interest in Hubbard and the Church. Thus, even if the book ultimately harms sales of the authorized biography, this would not result from unfair infringement forbidden by the copyright laws, but rather from a convincing work that effectively criticizes Hubbard, the very type of work that the Copyright Act was designed to protect and encourage.

We conclude that factor four favors appellant.

E. Other Factors

The factors enumerated in § 107 "are not meant to be exclusive," *Harper & Row*, 471 U.S., at 560, and we have looked to such additional considerations as "bad faith by the user of copyrighted material [that] suggests unfairness," *Maxtone–Graham*, 803 F.2d, at 1264, or "prejudice suffered by [the alleged infringer] as the result of [the copyright holder's] unreasonable and inexcusable delay in bringing the action." *New Era*, 873 F.2d, at 584. Although appellee argues that the book's use of passages from Hubbard's works was "predatory" rather than fair, we simply do not agree with this characterization, and find that there are no additional factors suggesting unfairness.

Conclusion

We hold that each of the four factors of § 107 favors appellant, and that the book's use of quotations from Hubbard's published works was protected fair use.

Hustler Magazine, Inc. v. Moral Majority, Inc.

United States Court of Appeals, Ninth Circuit, 1986.
796 F.2d 1148.

■ PREGERSON, CIRCUIT JUDGE.

Hustler Magazine, Inc. published a parody featuring Reverend Jerry Falwell. Moral Majority, Inc. and Old Time Gospel Hour mailed hundreds of thousands of copies of the parody as part of a solicitation drive. Falwell also solicited contributions while displaying the parody on the Old Time Gospel Hour, a television show. Hustler Magazine, Inc. sued Moral Majority, Inc., Old Time Gospel Hour, and Falwell for copyright infringement. The district court granted the Defendants' summary judgment motion, holding that their copying constituted "fair use." Hustler appeals. We affirm.

Background

In the November 1983 and March 1984 issues of Hustler Magazine, appellant Hustler Magazine, Inc. ("Hustler") published a parody of Campari liquor advertisements. Campari advertisements consist of interviews with famous people about the first time they drank Campari. The advertisements use double entendres to give the reader the impression that the "first time" refers to the celebrity's first sexual experience.

The Hustler Magazine parody featured Reverend Jerry Falwell, a nationally known fundamentalist minister, describing his "first time" as being incest with his mother in an outhouse, and saying that he always gets "sloshed" before giving his sermons. At the bottom of the page in small print is the disclaimer "AD PARODY—NOT TO BE TAKEN SERIOUS-LY."

On November 15, 1983, Moral Majority, Inc., a conservative political lobbying group, sent out two mailings signed by Falwell. One was directed to approximately 500,000 "rank-and-file" members. It described the parody without including a copy of the actual parody, and asked for a contribution to help Falwell "defend his mother's memory" in court.[a] This first mailing is not involved in the suit. The second mailing was directed to about 26,900 "major donors" and included a copy of the parody with eight of the most offensive words blackened out. It also requested donations to help finance Falwell's suit against Hustler.

Three days later, Old Time Gospel Hour, a corporate sponsor of religious television and radio broadcasts, mailed a solicitation including a copy of the parody to approximately 750,000 supporters of its programs. This letter was also signed by Falwell, but focused on the need to keep Falwell's religious television stations open in order to combat people like Larry Flynt, Hustler's publisher. Within 30 days of the mailings, the Moral Majority received approximately $45,000 from the "major donors" letter and the Old Time Gospel Hour received approximately $672,000 from its letter. A Moral Majority executive admitted that the intent behind including copies of the parody was to raise money.

Finally, on December 4, 1983 and December 11, 1983, Falwell displayed the parody during nation-wide television broadcasts of his weekly sermon on the Old Time Gospel Hour. The amount of contributions generated from this broadcast is not in the record.

On August 8, 1984, Hustler sued Moral Majority, Inc., Jerry Falwell, and the Old Time Gospel Hour (the "Defendants") for infringing its copyright. In March 1985, the parties filed cross motions for summary judgment. The Defendants raised the defense of fair use. The district court held that Hustler had made out a prima facie case of infringement, but granted summary judgment for the Defendants. The court held that the mailings and television displays were permissible under the fair use doctrine.

Hustler timely appealed and this court has jurisdiction.

Discussion

A.   The Purpose and Character of the Defendants' Uses

The first factor listed in section 107 requires us to consider the character of the use and to weigh the commercial or nonprofit purpose of

---

[a] In an action separate from the instant case, Falwell sued Hustler, Inc., its publisher Larry Flynt, and Flynt Distributing Company in state court in Virginia for libel, invasion of privacy and the intentional infliction of emotional distress. The jury held for Falwell only on the emotional distress claim. Hustler is appealing the verdict.

the use. "The crux of the profit/non-profit distinction is not whether the sole motive of the use is monetary gain but whether the user stands to profit from exploitation of the copyrighted material without paying the customary price." Harper & Row, Publishers, Inc. v. Nation Enterprises, 471 U.S. 539 (1985).

The parties disagree about the purpose and character of the use. Falwell contends that he sent the parody to his followers to give them information to rebut the statements it contained, and that the appeal for money was ancillary. Hustler contends, however, that the advertisement was clearly a parody so there was nothing to rebut and thus the letters were purely fundraisers.

There is ample evidence that the Defendants distributed copies of the parody as an integral part of a financial appeal. All of the letters and television displays involved outright appeals for donations to the Moral Majority to support Falwell's lawsuit against Hustler[b] or to the Old Time Gospel Hour to support his radio and television network.[c]

Moreover, the chief executive officers of Moral Majority and Old Time Gospel Hour admitted that the parody was copied and sent as part of a "market approach" to fundraising. Falwell's displaying of the parodies on his television show was also motivated by financial purposes. In addition, the Defendants raised almost one million dollars and therefore clearly profited from their use of the parody without paying any price. Because the Defendants used the parody for a profit-making purpose, their use is presumptively unfair.

Even assuming that the use had a purely commercial purpose, the presumption of unfairness can be rebutted by the characteristics of the use. When the use has both commercial and non-profit characteristics, the court may consider "whether the alleged infringing use was primarily for public benefit or for private commercial gain." MCA, Inc. v. Wilson, 677 F.2d 180, 182 (2d Cir.1981).

[b] For example, the November 15, 1983 appeal to Moral Majority "major donors" reads in part:

> As you know, legal matters are time consuming and expensive. There are lawyer's fees and court costs to consider, not to mention the personal time and energy I must devote in these next trying weeks and months.

. . .

> Will you help me defend my family and myself against the smears and slander of this major pornographic magazine—will you send a gift of $500 so that we may take up this important legal-battle?

[c] Old Time Gospel Hour letter dated November 18, 1983 reads in part:

> I was ready to cut another 50–100 stations—when someone showed me a full-page liquor advertisement which appeared in the November issue of Hustler Magazine—a pornographic tabloid.

> When I saw it—I decided that, in a society containing people like Larry Flynt, the Old Time Gospel Hour must remain on the air—on every station.

. . .

> I am not a quitter. That is why I have established the Old Time Gospel Hour SURVIVAL FUND.

> [P]lease help me with this SURVIVAL FUND. Your gift of $150 can make a great difference.

In the instant case, Defendants concede that their use was in part to raise money. They contend, however, that they also used the copies to rebut the personal attack upon Falwell and make a political comment about pornography. There was no attempt to palm off the parody as that of the Defendants. In fact, the very opposite is true. Falwell was not selling the parody, but was instead using the parody to make a statement about pornography and Larry Flynt, the publisher of Hustler.[d]

Section 107 expressly permits fair use for the purposes of criticism and comment. § 107. Hustler contends, however, that Falwell copied more than was necessary for his response. Hustler points to the fact that Falwell mailed a similar letter of criticism to Moral Majority "rank and file" members without enclosing a copy of the parody. However, an individual in rebutting a copyrighted work containing derogatory information about himself may copy such parts of the work as are necessary to permit understandable comment.[e] Falwell did not use more than was reasonably necessary to make an understandable comment when he copied the entire parody from the magazine. Therefore, the public interest in allowing an individual to defend himself against such derogatory personal attacks serves to rebut the presumption of unfairness.

B.   The Nature of the Copyrighted Work

The scope of fair use is greater when "informational" as opposed to more "creative" works are involved. There is no dispute that the parody was more creative than informational. The district court discounted the significance of the work's creative nature, however, because the Defendants did not use the parody for its creative value.

[d] The November 15, 1983 appeal to Moral Majority "major donors" reads in part:

Sane and moral Americans all across our nation are outraged by how much these pornographers are getting away with these days. And pornography is no longer a thing restricted to back-alley bookshops and sordid movie houses.

Now pornography has thrust its ugly head into our everyday lives and is multiplying like a filthy plague. Flynt's magazine, for example, advertises pornographic telephone services where, for a fee, men or women will engage in an obscene phone call with you!

.   .   .

Cable pornography with its "X" rated and triple "X" rated films can bleed over into a regular cable system right into your own living room.

.   .   .

And there, in my opinion, is clear proof that the billion dollar sex industry, of which Larry Flynt is a self-declared leader, is preying on innocent, impressionable children to feed the lusts of depraved adults.

For those porno peddlers it appears that lust and greed have replaced decency and morality.

[e] The legislative history to section 107 states:

When a copyrighted work contains unfair, inaccurate, or derogatory information concerning an individual or institution, the individual or institution may copy and reproduce such parts of the work as are necessary to permit understandable comment on the statements made in the work.

House Report, at 73, U.S.Code Cong. & Admin.News 1976, p. 5687.

There is nothing in the statute, case law, or legislative history to support the district court's approach. In fact, by copying all or substantially all of the copyrighted work, "the distinction of function vanishes since whatever the intent of the copier, a verbatim reproduction will of necessity serve the function of the plaintiff's work as well as that of the Defendant's." 3 Nimmer on Copyright § 13.05[D][1]. Accordingly, the creative nature of the parody means that the scope of fair use in this case is less than the scope of fair use for informational works.

C. The Amount and Substantiality of the Portion Used

In the instant case, the Defendants copied the entire parody covering up only eight of the most offensive words. Defendants argue that they did not copy an entire work, but only one page from a 154–page magazine. Although each component of a composite work is capable of individual copyright protection and need not bear a separate copyright notice, § 404, courts have not always evaluated a component of a copyrighted composite work as an "entire work." Rather courts consider the relationship of the copied component to the composite work to determine whether to analyze the work as an "entire work."

The Fifth Circuit is one of two circuits to have expressly discussed this issue. In Triangle Publications [v. Knight–Ridder Newspapers, Inc., 626 F.2d 1171 (5th Cir.1980)], the court held that Knight–Ridder had not copied an entire work by reproducing the cover of TV Guide Magazine for comparative advertising purposes. *Id.* at 1177 & n.15. The court noted that Knight–Ridder did not copy the essence of the magazine the television schedules and articles. *Id.*

The Eleventh Circuit evaluated this issue in a slightly different context. In Pacific and Southern Co. [v. Duncan], 744 F.2d 1490 (11th. Cir.1984), a company videotaped a television station's news broadcasts and sold copies of the relevant portions. The television station sued the company for selling a tape of a story from one of its broadcasts. The court held that the feature, as a coherent narrative, stands alone as a copyrighted work. *Id.* at 1497. Therefore, the company had copied an entire work. The court distinguished the case from *Triangle Publications* because the program segment was copyrighted separately and was stored separately from the rest of the broadcast. *Id.* at 1497 n.10.

Thus to determine whether the parody should be treated as an "entire work," we consider the relationship of the copied parody to the periodical as a whole. Unlike the cover of TV Guide in *Triangle Publications*, the inside pages of a magazine are not on public display. Moreover, the parody in this case, like the story in *Pacific and Southern Co.*, represents the "essence" of Hustler Magazine. In addition, like the story in *Pacific and Southern Co.*, and unlike the magazine cover in *Triangle Publications*, the parody is not an interwoven component of the magazine, but can stand totally alone. A creative work does not deserve less copyright protection just because it is part of a composite work. Therefore, in this case, we view the Defendants as having copied an entire work.

Hustler argues that "this court has long maintained the view that wholesale copying of copyrighted material precludes application of the fair use doctrine." Marcus [v. Rowley, 695 F.2d 1171, 1176 (9th Cir.1983)].

The Supreme Court's opinion in Sony Corp. [of America v. Universal City Studios, Inc., 464 U.S. 417 (1984)], however, casts doubt on our previous pronouncements concerning wholesale copying as an absolute preclusion to fair use. In *Sony Corp.*, the Supreme Court held that "time-shifting" television programs by taping whole programs with a video tape recorder did not have its "ordinary effect of militating against a finding of fair use." *Id.* at 450.

Sony Corp. teaches us that the copying of an entire work does not preclude fair use per se. However, "a subsequent user does not require such complete copying if he is truly pursuing a different functional milieu." 3 Nimmer on Copyright § 13.05 [D]. Consequently, although wholesale copying does not preclude fair use per se, the amount of copying that the Defendants did in this case still militates against a finding of fair use.

D. Effect Upon Potential Market or Value

Finally, we must consider "the effect of the use upon the potential market for or value of the copyrighted work." § 107(4). In the instant case, the parties disagree over whether the Defendants copied the parody for commercial or noncommercial uses. In determining whether the use has harmed the work's value on market, courts have focused on whether the infringing use: (1) "tends to diminish or prejudice the potential sale of [the] work", Meeropol v. Nizer, 560 F.2d 1061, 1070 (2d Cir.1977); or (2) tends to interfere with the marketability of the work, Elsmere Music, Inc. v. National Broadcasting Co., 482 F.Supp. 741, 747 (S.D.N.Y., 1980), aff'd. 623 F.2d 252 (2d Cir.1980); or (3) fulfills the demand for the original work, Wainwright Securities Inc. v. Wall Street Transcript Corp., 558 F.2d 91, 96 (2d Cir.1977), *cert. denied*, 434 U.S. 1014 (1978).

The parody was first published September 27 and was off the news-stands before the defendants' first mailings in November. Thus, the republication did not diminish the initial sales. We agree with the district court that the effect on the marketability of back issues of the entire magazine is de minimis because it is only one page of a publication which would be purchased for "its other attractions."

Nor have the Defendants' mailings effected any potential market, even though the parody could be licensed independently of the magazine.[f] Although the Defendants used the parody for a commercial purpose in the sense that they profited from copying it, they did not actually sell the copies to willing buyers. Instead the Defendants used the copies to generate moral outrage against their "enemies" and thus stimulate monetary support for their political cause. Moreover, as the district court noted, Moral

---

[f] The fact that Hustler does not actively market the parody for other purposes is irrelevant because Section 107 looks to the "potential market" in analyzing the effects of the alleged infringement. See *Pacific and Southern Co.*, 744 F.2d at 1496.

Majority or Old Time Gospel Hour members would probably not be counted among Hustler's readers. Therefore, Hustler's creative incentives are not decreased because the Defendants are profiting from an activity that Hustler could not have taken advantage of. See *Pacific and Southern Co.*, 744 F.2d, at 1496. "Where the copy does not compete in any way with the original, . . . concern [about copiers undercutting demand and discouraging creativity] is absent." *Consumers Union*, 724 F.2d, at 1051.

The Defendants' use could not have diminished any potential sales, interfered with the marketability of the parody or fulfilled the demand for

the original work. Therefore, even viewing the Defendants' copying as a commercial use, Defendants have rebutted any presumption of unfair exploitation of Hustler's copyright monopoly.

Affirmed.

■ POOLE, dissenting.

The majority concedes that Moral Majority, Inc., Old Time Gospel Hour, and Jerry Falwell distributed or displayed Hustler Magazine's copyrighted ad parody in an effort to raise money for themselves. Despite this commercial purpose, the majority concludes that their copying constituted "fair use." I disagree.

A.   The First Factor: the Purpose and Character of the Defendants' Use

The opinion acknowledges that the parody was distributed by the defendants as an integral part of a financial appeal. Thus, the use is presumptively unfair. The defendants attempt to rebut this presumption by claiming that their primary reason for sending the copies was to refute the personal attack upon Falwell and to make a political comment about pornography.

Assuming that the defendants were also motivated by such purposes, their actions in publishing the entire parody went beyond the limited boundaries of the fair use defense. As conceded by the majority, the defendants could copy only so much of the work as was necessary to permit understandable comment. There is no reason why Falwell needed to copy the entire parody to rebut the personal attack or to comment on what the "pornographers" were publishing. A summary of the parody, such as that contained in the factual summary of the proposed opinion, would have sufficed. Quite clearly, the only reason for copying the entire parody would be to increase the chances that the parody would arouse such moral indignation that the members would be more likely to send in financial contributions to help support Falwell's lawsuit against Hustler or to support his radio and television network. Accordingly, the majority's conclusion that Falwell did not copy more of the parody than was reasonably necessary to make an understandable comment confuses Falwell's true purpose in copying the entire work.

Moreover, I disagree with the legal conclusion by the majority that "the public interest in allowing an individual to defend himself against ... derogatory personal attacks serves to rebut the presumption of unfairness." Opinion at [(A)]. Such a sweeping generalization finds no support in either the case law or the purposes underlying the fair use defense. On the contrary, it is clear that the public's interest in reading an author's work is not alone sufficient to override the protections granted under the federal copyright laws. [The fair use doctrine] is not a license for assertedly religious or "moral" theft. Accordingly, Falwell's alleged purpose of defending himself against the personal attack made by Hustler in its ad parody, if that were indeed his purpose, might certainly constitute some factor in the fair use analysis, but it does not excuse the infringement of Hustler's copyright. Falwell's claim, however, is belied by the manifestly financial gain which he hastened to secure.

As previously noted, Falwell went beyond simply criticizing and commenting on the ad parody and actively sought to exploit the emotional impact of the work to raise money. This commercial use of the copyrighted work is a separate factor that weighs against a finding of fair use. The fact that Falwell also had other motives in publishing the parody does not prevent the operation of this factor. The defendants published Hustler's parody in the hope of milking the possible indignation it would arouse for their own personal monetary benefit. This purpose weighs strongly against a conclusion that the defendants' use of the parody was a fair use.

B.   The Fourth Factor: Effect Upon Potential Market or Value

The majority also incorrectly analyzes the fourth factor listed in section 107. This factor is concerned with whether if the challenged use "should become widespread, it would adversely affect the potential market for the copyrighted work." *Sony Corp.*, 464 U.S., at 451.

If Falwell's actions were to become widespread such that individuals were sending out copies of the ad parody to the public in order to solicit money to support campaigns against "the pornographers" such as Larry Flynt, then quite clearly the future potential market for the parody would be diminished.[a] This is because the act of distributing copies of the entire copyrighted work to the public would fulfill the demand of the original. Wainwright Securities Inc. v. Wall Street Transcript Corp., 558 F.2d 91, 96 (2d Cir.1977), *cert. denied*, 434 U.S. 1014 (1978). "Isolated instances of minor infringements, when multiplied many times, become in the aggregate a major inroad on copyright that must be prevented." *Harper & Row*, 105 S.Ct., at 2235 (quoting S.Rep. No. 94–473, p. 65 (1975)).

[a] I have problems with the district court's conclusion, accepted by the majority opinion, that Moral Majority or Old Time Gospel Hour members would probably not be counted among Hustler's readers. If such a showing was made or Hustler stipulated to this fact, then such a conclusion can be accepted. Otherwise, I do not think a court can take judicial notice of such a matter. Furthermore, Hustler's future licensing rights with regard to the parody may be impaired nonetheless since these Moral Majority or Old Time Gospel Hour members may count themselves readers of a different publication which could contain this parody, e.g., a compilation of parodies of public figures which contains this parody, albeit probably a toned down version. Or the members, if they had not already seen the entire parody, may have become curious enough about its contents as to break down and purchase the back copy of Hustler magazine or a future copy wherein the magazine had republished the parody. Or, perhaps the fact that the parody was included in that back copy might tempt some persons to use that fact as a justification for looking into the other contents of the magazine—in order to comprehend how shocking was the setting in which the parody appeared.

Excerpts From Gordon, Fair Use as Market Failure: A Structural and Economic Analysis of the Betamax Case and Its Predecessors

82 Columbia L. Rev. 1600 (1982).
Copyright ©1982 by Wendy J. Gordon. Reprinted by permission. Footnotes omitted.

* * *

II. The Three Part Test for Determining Fair Use

Fair use should be awarded to the defendant in a copyright infringement action when (1) market failure is present; (2) transfer of the use to defendant is socially desirable; and (3) an award of fair use would not cause substantial injury to the incentives of the plaintiff copyright owner. The first element of this test ensures that market bypass will not be approved without good cause. The second element of the test ensures that the transfer of a license to use from the copyright holder to the unauthorized user effects a net gain in social value. The third element ensures that the grant of fair use will not undermine the incentive-creating purpose of the copyright law. The test will now be explored in detail.

A. The First Element of the Test: Market Failure

Because courts in the copyright area ordinarily assume that reliance on the market will serve social purposes, an economic judgment that transfer of a use to defendant will bring a net social benefit should not alone be sufficient to negate the tort of infringement. If the work is socially more valuable in the buyer's hands, then the economic model has suggested that he will be able to raise sufficient funds to purchase permission from the owner. In other words, to propose that fair use be imposed whenever the "social value ... outweighs any detriment to the artist," would be to propose depriving copyright owners of their right in the property precisely when they encounter those users who could afford to pay for it. Though a transfer to such user might be socially desirable, there is no need to compel it through fair use. Such transfer will in theory occur voluntarily, through purchase. Further, if the parties could arrive at mutually agreeable terms for a transfer, such an agreement would be a more reliable indicator of the transfer's value-maximizing quality than would a court's distant judgment.

An economic justification for depriving a copyright owner of his market entitlement exists only when the possibility of consensual bargain has broken down in some way. Only where the desired transfer of resource use is unlikely to take place spontaneously, or where special circumstances such as market flaws impair the market's ordinary ability to serve as a measure of how resources should be allocated, is there an economic need for allowing nonconsensual transfer. Thus, one of the necessary preconditions for premising fair use on economic grounds is that market failure must be present....

B.   The Second Element of the Test: Balancing Injury and Benefit

If market failure is present, the court should determine if the use is more valuable in the defendant's hands or in the hands of the copyright owner. One way of accomplishing that goal is to simulate the market inquiry. If, when the "market failure" were cured, the price that the owner would demand is lower than the price that the user would offer, a transfer to the user will increase social value.

A court may have difficulty in determining what price would have been offered or demanded. For example, as will be shown, fair use is often found where defendant's use of the work is noncommercial and yields "external benefits," that is, benefits to society that go uncompensated. In the presence of such market failure, the price that the defendant user would offer for use of the work will often understate the real social value of his use. The courts in fair use cases frequently make intuitive estimates of social value.

* * *

C.   The Third Element of the Test: The Substantial Injury Hurdle

The third and final part of the test is designed to maintain the appropriate balance between the incentive and dissemination interests discussed earlier. Fair use should be denied whenever a substantial injury appears that will impair incentives.

1.   Complete Market Failure

When no incentive purpose would be served by giving plaintiff protection, and where no disincentive would be created by allowing defendant free use, logic suggests that the courts should then allow fair use. Assume, for example, that prohibitively high transaction costs obtain in a particular area of use, so that copyright owners and potential users find that the costs of locating and bargaining with each other exceed whatever profit they might expect to gain from the transaction. Under such circumstances, no transactions will occur. Therefore, enforcement of market entitlements would not benefit the copyright owner, and would certainly harm the potential copyright user who is denied access, as well as those who might benefit from the use. Given the presence of a complete market failure here, judicial refusal to enforce the owner's right of control may be the only way to allow use of the work. And since a refusal to enforce in these circumstances would not deprive the owner of any revenues he would otherwise receive, there is no injury to incentives that might militate against a grant of fair use.

2.   Intermediate Cases of Market Failure

In cases of complete market failure, fair use appears to be justified upon satisfaction of the first two parts of the fair use test, i.e., identification of market failure and determination that there is a net social benefit from allowing defendant's use. There may also be intermediate cases of market failure, however, where the market cannot be relied upon to generate all desirable exchanges, but where some such transactions would be possible. In such instances, giving fair use to a class of users would enable some persons who would otherwise purchase the use to obtain that use for free. Thus fair use could cause some injury to relevant incentives because, for some users, fair use would substitute for purchase. The first two parts of the test would no longer serve to accommodate the competing interests.

In instances of intermediate market failure, both enforcement (a finding of infringement) and nonenforcement (a finding of fair use) have dangers. The danger from enforcement is that desirable transfers may be prevented. The danger from giving fair use is that incentives may be undermined. To resolve the conflict, the defendant seeking fair use treatment should be required to surmount an additional hurdle: fair use should be denied if it would leave the plaintiff copyright owner facing substantial injury to his incentives.

*   *   *

The substantial injury hurdle serves several functions. First, it preserves the incentive system at the core of copyright. Second, it reflects a recognition that judgments the courts make about whether a defendant's use is value maximizing are rough approximations. The substantial injury hurdle provides some additional protection for copyright owners against the possibility of a bad estimation. Third, awarding copyright owners a veto whenever their injury is substantial gives some guarantee that the fair use system will not put them at an intolerable disadvantage. Even if authors are viewed solely as instruments of social good, their demoralization as individuals will decrease the production of valuable works. The substantial injury hurdle can also help courts avoid the danger of making otherwise curable market failures permanent through the grant of fair use. . . .

Injury is relevant to both the second and third parts of the fair use test, but different types of injury are relevant to each part. On the question of balancing plaintiff's harm against defendant's benefit, courts should look to the injury caused to the copyright owner by the specific use made by defendant. The narrow inquiry reveals whether transferring the use to the defendant gives rise to a net social benefit. In order to prevent substantial injury to incentives, however, the court should also inquire into the extent of the losses likely to follow in the market as a whole from a grant of fair use, both from this defendant and from other similarly situated persons. . . . Thus, the inquiry into substantial injury should include consideration of cumulative harm.

This inquiry should also include harm that has not yet occurred but is likely to occur. Both the loss of revenues anticipated under the market structure prevailing at the time of suit, and the loss of those revenues that would be generated under whatever market structure would follow upon a grant of infringement, should be relevant. For example, transaction costs to obtain permission to use certain materials might be prohibitively high at one point in time, yet in some circumstances a clearinghouse system might be set up to simplify the process of purchasing permission and thus allow a market to function. To award fair use without regard to the possibility of imminent change in the market structure might be to make permanent an otherwise curable market failure and thus potentially to insulate a new and valuable use from the stimulus of consumer demand.

Whether a market failure is curable, and whether such a cure would follow upon a finding of infringement and generate substantial revenues, are difficult factual questions. They must, however, be faced; the courts should limit their grants of fair use to those occasions in which the market cannot be relied upon to allow socially beneficial uses to occur. This point is particularly important for new technologies.... When a new use for copyrighted works becomes available to the public, market mechanisms may take time to develop. At early stages of use, the transaction costs that would be involved for a user to purchase permission to use, or for the copyright owner to seek enforcement against nonpaying users, might well exceed whatever gain the parties might otherwise expect from the transaction. A custom therefore may develop under which users proceed without permission.

* * *

The risk from granting fair use without reference to such probable injury should be obvious. New technologies will make certain copyrighted works more valuable, as, for example, the invention of cinema increased the value of those books suitable for adaptation to the screen. If copyright protection is denied because of an otherwise curable market failure, then the additional revenues that would have flowed from the new technological use will not appear. If the authors' revenues fail to reflect the additional value that new technology gives to such works, then insufficient resources may be drawn into their creation. To argue that copyright owners need receive no compensation for additional uses of their works would overlook the possibility that such compensation may change the patterns of production in a desirable way. Stimulation of such response is, after all, a basic goal of copyright law.

* * *

NOTES

1. *Impact on the potential market.* Professor Nimmer suggests this is the most critical factor and that, in applying it, we should look to whether the two works fulfill the same function in terms of actual or potential consumer demand. How did the majority in *Sony* apply this factor? Is the *Sony* Court's analysis regarding market impact sound? Who should have the burden of proof on this issue?

In analyzing the necessary adverse impact upon the potential market, what type of impact is significant? Do *Sony* and *Harper* differ on this point? What view of market impact does the court in *Hustler* adopt and how does its view affect the outcome of the decision? Is there a greater impact on the potential market in *New Era* or the Principal Problem?

2. *Purpose and character of the use: commercial vs. non-commercial uses.* In *Sony,* the Court observed that "the commercial or nonprofit character of an activity [is to] be weighed in any fair use decision," and that a commercial use renders the defendant's activity "presumptively" unfair (see Section IV(B)). The Court qualifies this statement substantially in *Acuff-Rose,* wherein it expressly states that commercialization does not preclude fair use. What is the relevance of commercialization? How is the term "commercial" defined in *Sony* and *Harper*? Which of these definitions does the court in *Hustler* adopt? Does the *Hustler* court's choice of a definition for commercial use influence the outcome of the case? Why wasn't the defendant's commercial use in *Hustler* fatal to a finding of fair use? Does the majority opinion in *Hustler* give any indication of how much importance should be ascribed to a commercial use?

3. *Purpose and character of the use: productivity.* According to the majority opinion in *Sony,* whether the defendant makes a productive use of the plaintiff's work is not especially significant (see footnote 1 in Section IV(B) of the case), but this requirement is of critical importance to the dissent's view of fair use. In *Acuff-Rose,* the Court emphasizes the importance of transformative value. Is a transformative use the same as a productive use?

What test should be applied for determining what is a productive use? Would you categorize the defendants' uses in *Hustler* and *New Era* as productive?

4. *Nature of the copyrighted work: relevance of publication.* Prior to the 1976 Act, unpublished works were protected only by common law copyright. Now copyright protection is extended to unpublished works as well, and this represents a significant change wrought by the new statute. What does the Court in *Harper* mean when it says that "the scope of fair use is narrower with respect to unpublished works" (see Section IV of the case)? How does the court *New Era* interpret this statement? Should the scope of fair use be narrower regarding unpublished works? Should it ever be permissible to use unpublished material? Should it matter whether the alleged infringer directly quotes or paraphrases the unpublished material? In 1992, Congress added the following final sentence to § 107: "The fact that a work is unpublished shall not itself bar a finding of fair use if such finding is made upon consideration of all the above factors." The Committee Report to this amendment suggests reaffirmance of *Harper's* rule that the unpublished nature of a work is a "key" but not "necessarily determinative" factor prohibiting fair use.[6]

5. *Nature of the copyrighted work: fact vs. fiction.* The fair use doctrine recognizes that there is a greater need to disseminate factual works. This is discussed by the dissent in *Sony,* who believed that the entertainment component of the programs weakened the fair use claim. In *Harper,* the Court recognized that a factual work was at issue, but essentially discount-

[6] See H.R. Rep. No. 836, 102d Cong., 2d Sess. 5 (1992).

ed the importance of this criterion in this particular case because direct quotation from such works should only be allowed when necessary to convey facts adequately. The Nation's use "focus[ed] on the most expressive elements of the work, [and] exceed[ed] that necessary to disseminate the facts" (see Section IV of the case). How often would it be necessary to use direct quotation to convey facts? Note that in both *Sony* and *Harper*, application of the fact vs. fiction distinction would have suggested opposite results. How do the courts in *Hustler* and *New Era* apply the fact vs. fiction distinction? What is the relevance of this distinction to the Principal Problem?

6. *Amount of copying.* In *Hustler*, the court treats the parody as an entire work and states that the defendant's copying of the entire work "militates against a finding of fair use." Nonetheless, it can be argued that after *Sony*, this factor retains little, if any, force. In both *Sony* and *Hustler*, entire works were copied but the courts still found fair use. Basically, application of this factor is difficult because it is amorphous. How much is too much? Do we consider quantity or quality? How shall quality be judged? Also, do we compare the amount taken with the size of the defendant's work or the plaintiff's work? What is the real importance of the third fair use factor?

Although *Hustler* involves a parody, the situation there is somewhat atypical in that the parody was the copyrighted work that was allegedly infringed. In many cases, however, the defendant's work is allegedly a parody of the plaintiff's work. In the legislative notes accompanying § 107, Congress specified parodies as an example "of the sort of activities the courts might regard as fair use,"[7] but refused to endorse a per se rule protecting parodies. In general, parodies are given a broad scope of protection because they foster creativity, but the fair use doctrine still must be applied to parodies. In *Acuff-Rose*, the Supreme Court observed that "[t]he threshold question when fair use is raised in defense of parody is whether a parodic character may reasonably be perceived." How should the third fair use factor be applied in the context of parodies?

7. *Propriety and custom.* The fair use doctrine recognizes the importance of other equitable factors such as defendant's relative good faith. How important was this factor in the major cases? How can good faith and fair dealing be defined?

Can the Nation's conduct in *Harper* be equated with that of a parodist who uses a copyrighted work after being expressly denied permission by the copyright owner? Does a defendant's use of a copyrighted work subsequent to being denied permission always indicate bad faith? How does this bear on WJN's conduct in the Principal Problem?

8. *Reciprocity of protection.* In footnote a of the court's opinion in *Hustler*, the court mentions another action brought by Falwell against Hustler for libel, invasion of privacy and intentional infliction of emotional distress. In an unreported opinion, the district court dismissed Falwell's invasion of privacy claim, and allowed the jury to decide the remaining two counts. The

---

[7] § 107, historical and revision notes.

jury ruled in favor of Falwell on the emotional distress claim and in favor of Hustler on the libel claim. This ruling was affirmed by the Fourth Circuit.[8] The Supreme Court, however, reversed the appellate court's affirmance of the intentional infliction of emotional distress claim, holding that "public figures and public officials may not recover for the tort of intentional infliction of emotional distress by reason of publications such as the one here at issue without showing in addition that the publication contains a false statement of fact which was made with 'actual malice,' i.e., with knowledge that the statement was false or with reckless disregard as to whether or not it was true."[9] For purposes of the case, the Court accepted the jury's apparent finding that no reasonable person would believe that the parody was truthful or intended to be truthful.[10] Thus, Falwell cannot control Hustler's right to use his personage in the parody. How does this bear upon Hustler's right to stop Falwell?

9. *Striking the balance.* One recent case has noted the relative lack of guidance with respect to the operation of the balancing process required by fair use. In Rubin v. Brooks/Cole Publishing Co.,[11] the district court concluded that the defendant's productive use of plaintiff's work and its previously published scientific nature favored a finding of fair use, but the amount taken and the impact on the plaintiff's market weighed "slightly" in the other direction. Thus, the court struck an equitable balance by finding fair use with respect to the defendant's past conduct (thus failing to award the plaintiff any damages), but ordering injunctive relief prospectively.[12] In contrast, in a footnote in *Acuff-Rose* which is not reprinted in the text, the Court observed that because the application of the fair use doctrine "often requires close questions of judgment as to the extent of permissible borrowing ... courts may also wish to bear in mind that the goals of the copyright law ... are not always best served by automatically granting injunctive relief when parodists are found to have gone beyond the bounds of fair use."[13] See also Assignment 13 treating remedies for copyright infringement.

10. *Other defenses.* Although the fair use doctrine is by far the most notable defense to copyright infringement, other defenses also can be invoked where appropriate. Equitable defenses such as laches, estoppel, and unclean hands often are raised in copyright infringement actions. Laches is proven when a defendant establishes that the plaintiff *inexcusably or unreasonably* delayed in bringing suit and the defendant was prejudiced by this delay.[14] Estoppel requires the plaintiff to aid the defendant in committing the allegedly infringing acts, or to induce or cause their performance

---

[8] Falwell v. Flynt, 797 F.2d 1270 (4th Cir.1986).

[9] Hustler Magazine v. Falwell, 485 U.S. 46, 56, 108 S.Ct. 876, 882, 99 L.Ed.2d 41 (1988).

[10] *Id.* at 57.

[11] 836 F.Supp. 909 (D.Mass.1993).

[12] *Id.* at 922.

[13] Campbell v. Acuff–Rose Music, Inc., ___ U.S. ___, ___ n. 10, 114 S.Ct. 1164, 1171 n. 10, 127 L.Ed.2d 500 (1994).

[14] See, e.g., Jackson v. Axton, 25 F.3d 884 (9th Cir.1994); Lotus Development Corp. v. Borland International Inc., 831 F.Supp. 223, 237 (D.Mass.1993).

by the defendant.[15] Unclean hands requires that the plaintiff either participated in the infringing acts or committed fraud or some other "transgression" which resulted "in harm or prejudice to the defendant."[16]

Perhaps the most controversial defense in recent years is copyright misuse, which has been explicitly rejected by several courts as a viable defense in copyright infringement litigation.[17] Other courts assumed that copyright misuse only can be established when a violation of antitrust law has been shown.[18] The Fourth Circuit, however, breathed new life into the copyright misuse defense in 1990 in Lasercomb v. Reynolds.[19] The defendant in that case, a steel rule die manufacturer, alleged that the plaintiff misused its copyright by including in its standard licensing agreement clauses preventing the licensee from creating any computer-assisted die-making software.[20] Reversing the district court's rejection of the misuse defense, the court endorsed a broad version of the defense: "The question is not whether the copyright is being used in a manner violative of antitrust law ..., but whether the copyright is being used in a manner violative of the public policy embodied in the grant of a copyright."[21]

BIBLIOGRAPHY

The fair use doctrine has been the subject of extensive commentary. The following represents some of the more recent works on the subject: Yonover, The "Dissing" of Da Vinci: The Imaginary Case of Leonardo v. Duchamp: Moral Rights, Parody, and Fair Use, 29 Val. U. L. Rev. 935 (1995); Lape, Transforming Fair Use: The Productive Use Factor in Fair Use Doctrine, 58 Alb. L. Rev. 677 (1995); Durdik, Reverse Engineering as a Fair Use Defense to Software Copyright Infringement, 34 Jurimetrics J. 451 (1994); Leval, "Campbell v. Acuff–Rose": Justice Souter's Rescue of Fair Use, 13 Cardozo Arts & Ent. L.J. 19 (1994); Zissu, Fair Use: From "Harper & Row" to "Acuff Rose," 42 J. Copyright Soc'y 7 (1994); Anderson & Brown, The Economics Behind Copyright Fair Use: A Principled and Predictable Body of Law, 24 Loy. U. Chi. L.J. 143 (1993); Miller, Fair Use, Biographers, and Unpublished Works: Life After H.R. 4412, 40 J. Copyright Soc'y 349 (1993); McLean, All's Not Fair in Art and War: A Look at the Fair Use Defense After "Rogers v. Koons," 59 Brook. L. Rev. 373 (1993); Patry & Perlmutter, Fair Use Misconstrued: Profit, Presumptions, and Parody, 11 Cardozo Arts & Ent. L.J. 667 (1993); Samuelson, Fair Use for Computer Programs and Other Copyrightable Works in Digital Form: The Implications of "Sony," "Galoob" and "Sega," 1 J. Intell. Prop. L. 49 (1993); LeFevre, The Tell–Tale "Heart": Determining "Fair" Use of Unpublished Texts, 55 Law & Contemp. Probs. 153 (1992); Litman,

---

[15] Coleman v. ESPN, Inc., 764 F.Supp. 290, 295 (S.D.N.Y.1991).

[16] Id. at 296.

[17] Id. at 295.

[18] See, e.g., Bellsouth Advertising & Publishing Corp. v. Donnelley Info. Publishing., 933 F.2d 952, 960–61 (11th Cir.1991)(apparently requiring an antitrust violation to sustain copyright misuse defense).

[19] 911 F.2d 970 (4th Cir.1990).

[20] Id. at 972.

[21] Id. at 978 (holding that the anticompetitive clauses in plaintiff's standard licensing agreement constitute copyright misuse).

Copyright and Information Policy, 55 Law & Contemp. Probs. 185 (1992); Lupovitz, Beyond "Betamax" and Broadcast: Home Recording from Pay Television and the Fair Use Doctrine, 2 Ent., Media & Intell. Prop. L.F. 69 (1992); Patterson, Understanding Fair Use, 55 Law & Contemp. Probs. 249 (1992); Darr, Testing an Economic Theory of Copyright: Historical Materials and Fair Use, 32 B.C. L. Rev. 1027 (1991); Hall, Bare–Faced Mess: Fair Use and the First Amendment, 70 Or. L. Rev. 211 (1991); Leval, Commentary: Toward a Fair Use Standard, 103 Harv. L. Rev. 1105 (1990); Oakes, Copyrights and Copyremedies: Unfair Use and Injunctions, 18 Hofstra L. Rev. 983 (1990); Weinreb, Fair's Fair: A Comment on the Fair Use Doctrine, 103 Harv. L. Rev. 1137 (1990); Leval, Fair Use or Foul?, 36 J. Copyright Soc'y 167 (1989); Miner, Exploiting Stolen Text: Fair Use or Foul Play?, 37 J. Copyright Soc'y 1 (1989); Newman, Not the End of History: The Second Circuit Struggles with Fair Use, 37 J. Copyright Soc'y 12 (1989); Dratler, Distilling the Witches' Brew of Fair Use in Copyright Law, 43 U. Miami L. Rev. 233 (1988); Fisher, Reconstructing the Fair Use Doctrine, 101 Harv. L. Rev. 1659 (1988); Patterson, Free Speech, Copyright, and Fair Use, 40 Vand. L. Rev. 1 (1987); Francione, Facing the Nation: The Infringement and Fair Use of Factual Works, 134 U. Pa. L. Rev. 519 (1986); Kernochan, Protection of Unpublished Works in the United States Before and After the "Nation" Case, 33 J. Copyright Soc'y 322 (1986); Patry, Fair Use After "Sony" and "Harper & Row," 8 Com. & L. 21 (1986); Raskind, A Functional Interpretation of Fair Use, 31 J. Copyright Soc'y 601 (1984); Gordon, Fair Use as Market Failure: A Structural and Economic Analysis of the "Betamax" Case and Its Predecessors, 82 Colum. L. Rev. 1600 (1982).

ASSIGNMENT 13

Remedies

1. Introduction

As the materials below demonstrate, a variety of remedies for copyright infringement are available. With respect to damages, the remedial provisions of the 1976 Act allow a copyright proprietor who establishes infringement the choice of recovering either 1) statutory damages, or 2) actual damages and any of the infringer's profits not factored into the actual damage award.[1] The limitations upon these awards and the manner in which they are calculated are explored in the materials which follow. In addition, a court may impound the infringing materials and order their destruction or other disposition.[2] Courts also have the discretion to award costs and attorney's fees to the prevailing party.[3] Although most copyright infringement actions are civil in nature, § 506 of the Act provides for criminal liability for "[a]ny person who infringes a copyright willfully and for purposes of commercial advantage or private financial gain."[4] The government rarely prosecutes an infringer under the criminal provision, but when it is invoked, it usually is in connection with massive sound-recording or film piracy infringements.[5]

The 1976 Act also provides courts with the discretion to issue both temporary (preliminary) and final (permanent) injunctive relief.[6] A copyright plaintiff thus may attempt to obtain preliminary injunctive relief that will be effective during the course of litigation. Typically, such preliminary relief will be granted where a plaintiff establishes a likelihood of success on the merits and a showing of irreparable harm, which is presumed when a plaintiff establishes a *prima facie* case of copyright infringement.[7] The case law indicates that preliminary injunctions are generally issued liberally in copyright litigation.[8] A successful copyright plaintiff also may be entitled to

---

[1] § 504.

[2] § 503.

[3] § 505.

[4] § 506(a). See also the Piracy and Counterfeiting Amendments Act of 1984, 18 U.S.C.A. §§ 2318–2319A. Sections 506(b) and 509 also provide for the seizure and forfeiture of infringing goods when a person is convicted of criminal copyright infringement.

[5] See 3 Melville B. Nimmer & David Nimmer, Nimmer on Copyright, 15.01[C] (1993).

[6] § 502 (a).

[7] Bourne Co. v. Tower Records, Inc., 976 F.2d 99, 101 (2d Cir.1992).

[8] See, e.g., MAI Systems Corp. v. Peak Computer, Inc., 1992 WL 159803 (C.D.Cal. 1992); E.F. Johnson Co. v. Uniden Corp., 623 F.Supp. 1485, 1490–91 (D.Minn.1985). See generally Brown, Civil Remedies for Intellectual Property Invasions: Themes and Variations, 55 Law & Contemp. Probs. 45, 46–49 (1992).

permanent injunctive relief where there is a threat of continuing violations on the part of the defendant. Of course, injunctive relief is not an effective remedy against infringements that occurred prior to the institution of the lawsuit.

2. PRINCIPAL PROBLEM

Review the Principal Problem in Assignment 12. Assume that the court finds that WJN is liable for copyright infringement. Now Davis consults you with respect to the available remedies. In advising Davis, be sure to include your opinion on whether Davis would be entitled to prospective injunctive relief; statutory damages; actual damages and WJN's profits; and costs and attorney's fees.

3. MATERIALS FOR SOLUTION OF PRINCIPAL PROBLEM

A. STATUTORY MATERIALS: §§ 412 & 501–511

B. CASES:

Universal City Studios, Inc. v. Ahmed

United States District Court, E.D. Pennsylvania, 1993.
29 U.S.P.Q.2D (BNA) 1775.

■ HUTTON, JUDGE.

I. Factual Background

In their complaint, the plaintiffs allege that the defendants infringed the plaintiffs' copyright to the motion picture Jurassic Park by selling or holding for sale pirated videocassettes of the film. On June 18, 1993, this Court granted the plaintiffs' motion for preliminary injunctive relief and entered an Order permitting the plaintiffs to seize the counterfeit videocassettes and other merchandise from the defendants.

The Court scheduled a Return Hearing for June 28, 1993. At the Return Hearing, defendants agreed to the entry of a permanent injunction prohibiting them from ever selling any merchandise bearing the copyrights and/or trademarks of plaintiffs in and to Jurassic Park.

II. Discussion

Motion for Default Judgment

The plaintiffs have moved the Court to enter a default judgment against the defendants because they failed to plead or otherwise defend the action. Rule 55 of the Federal Rules of Civil Procedure grants the Court the power to enter default judgments in such circumstances. Rule 55 also provides that, "if, in order to enable the court to enter judgment . . . , it is necessary to determine the amount of damages, . . . the court may conduct such hearings as it deems necessary and proper." Fed.R.Civ.P. 55(b)(2).

The plaintiffs do not simply seek to have judgment entered against the defendants, they also seek to recover statutory damages and attorney's fees. However, the present record before the Court does not provide an adequate factual basis to support the award of statutory damages. Under 17 U.S.C. § 504, the plaintiffs may recover statutory damages—

> for all infringements involved in the action, with respect to any one work, for which any one infringer is liable individually, or for which two or more infringers are liable jointly and severally, in a sum of not less than $500 or more than $20,000 as the court considers just.

Section 504(c)(1). In cases of "wilful" infringement, the court may increase the damages award beyond the $20,000 limit set forth in § 504(c)(1).[a]

It is well established that the Court need not conduct an evidentiary hearing prior to awarding a plaintiff statutory damages pursuant to a default judgment. However, in the absence of an evidentiary hearing, a plaintiff must present sufficiently "detailed affidavits" to permit the court to apply the appropriate factors in awarding statutory damages. [Citations omitted.]

Because the plaintiffs have sought an amount in excess of that set forth in 504(c)(1), the first question the Court must address is whether the plaintiffs can sustain the burden of proving that the infringement was wilful. § 504(c)(2). The term "wilfully" is not defined in the Copyright Act. Courts that have considered the question have defined "wilfulness" as requiring plaintiffs to show that the infringer acted with "actual knowledge or reckless disregard for whether its conduct infringed upon the plaintiff's copyright." Original Appalachian Artworks, Inc. v. J.F. Reichert, Inc., 658 F.Supp. 458, 464 (E.D.Pa.1987). The defendants' knowledge need not be proven directly, but may be inferred from the defendant's conduct.

On the record currently before the Court, the plaintiffs sustain their burden of proving that the defendants wilfully infringed the plaintiffs' copyright to Jurassic Park. Jurassic Park was released in theaters in the Philadelphia metropolitan area on June 10, 1993. At the time the tapes were seized, the motion picture was not yet legally available on videocassettes. This is customary and it is common knowledge that films are not released on videocassette until many months or years after the film has appeared in movie theaters. Yet, between June 15, 1993 and June 17, 1993, less than one week after the film's release in movie theaters, the defendants were observed selling videocassettes of Jurassic Park. From this, it can be inferred that the defendants knew they were infringing the plaintiffs' copyright, or at the very least, they exhibited reckless disregard. Thus, the court may, in its discretion, award up to $100,000 for the infringement of the plaintiffs' copyright.

The court has broad discretion in determining the appropriate measure of statutory damages within the range permitted by the statute. The

---

[a] Although the plaintiffs assert in their Memorandum of Law that the court may award a maximum of $50,000, the statute was amended in 1989 to permit the court to award up to $100,000 in cases of wilful infringement. § 504(c)(2).

following three factors are relevant in determining the appropriate measure of statutory damages under § 504: (1) expenses saved and profits reaped by defendants in connection with the infringement; (2) revenues lost by the plaintiffs; and (3) whether the infringement was wilful and knowing, or whether it was accidental and innocent. The factors, however, are not of equal weight. As one court within this circuit has stated:

> "in weighing these factors, most courts that have pondered the issue do not attach great weight to profits gained or to income lost, because these amounts are difficult to monetize.... Courts thus have focused largely on the element of intent, and the per infringement award tends understandably to escalate, in direct proportion to the blameworthiness of the infringing conduct."

Original Appalachian, 658 F.Supp., at 465 (quotation omitted). Although statutory damages "should bear some relation to actual damages", Association of American Med. Colleges v. Mikaelian, 1986 W.L. 332 (E.D.Pa.1986), the court may award statutory damages even if there is no evidence whatsoever before the court as to the defendant's profits, the defendant's costs avoided, or the plaintiff's lost profits. See H.R. Rep. No. 1476, 94th Cong., 2d Sess. 161. This is because statutory damages are designed not solely to compensate the copyright owner for losses incurred, but also to deter future infringement. F.W. Woolworth Co. v. Contemporary Arts, 344 U.S. 228, 233 (1952).

The plaintiffs have provided absolutely no evidence as to the defendants' profits or costs avoided, or the plaintiffs' lost profits as a result of the infringements. The plaintiffs' attorney attempted to calculate lost profits in the plaintiffs' memorandum of law, but this is not evidence.[b] Although evidence as to the defendants' profits or costs avoided such as licensing fees and/or the plaintiffs' lost profits would be relevant to the court's consideration, there is a sufficient evidentiary basis to conclude that statutory damages in some amount would be appropriate.

Thus, if there was only one defendant in the present case, there would be an adequate factual basis to award statutory damages without the need for a hearing or additional affidavits. However, the current record does not permit the court to award damages where, as here, there are numerous defendants.

Moreover, as a matter of law, the plaintiffs are not entitled to the measure of damages that they seek. The plaintiffs seek one $50,000 statutory damages award against each defendant for each copyright violation, that is, for each tape that each defendant sold or held for sale. The

[b] Moreover, without further factual support, plaintiffs' counsel's estimate is not persuasive. He asserts that the average price of a movie ticket is $7.50. He further asserts that "each [counterfeit] film could be viewed on a daily basis by 25 (or more) people times 365 ..., that is $60,937.50 in direct losses for each one copy of the film in a year." Because Jurassic Park is almost two hours in length, it is difficult to understand how 25 or more people could view the film in a single day, unless the counterfeiter or the purchaser of the counterfeit film is publicly exhibiting it. There is no factual basis from which to draw such an inference.

express language of § 504(c) and the case law interpreting § 504 clearly preclude such a recovery.

In Walt Disney Co. v. Powell, the United States Court of Appeals for the District of Columbia Circuit reversed the district court's statutory damages award because the district court "mistakenly focused on the number of infringements rather than the number of works infringed." 897 F.2d 565, 569 (D.C.Cir.1990). Rather, according to the court, "only one penalty lies for multiple infringements of one work." *Id.* (citing H.R. Rep. No. 1476, 94th Cong., 2d Sess. 161 ("A single infringer of a single work is liable for a single amount . . . no matter how many acts of infringement are involved in the action and regardless of whether the acts were separate, isolated, or occurred in a related series. . . .")). Thus, the law is clear that no matter how many times a defendant infringed the plaintiffs' copyright to Jurassic Parks, the plaintiffs are entitled to only one statutory damages award.

Notably absent from the plaintiffs' memorandum of law is any reference to *Powell* or the House Report to § 504. Rather, the plaintiffs cite two cases, BMG Music v. Perez, 952 F.2d 318 (9th Cir.1991), and Flyte Tyme Tunes v. Miszkiewicz, 715 F.Supp. 919 (E.D.Wis.1989), to support their assertion that they are entitled to recover for each any every tape sold or held for sale.[c]

Perez and *Miszkiewicz* simply do not stand for the proposition for which they are cited. In both cases the courts did enter multiple statutory damages awards. However, in both cases, unlike the present case, more than one copyright was infringed. See *Perez*, 952 F.2d, at 319 (plaintiffs alleged that the defendant purchased plaintiffs' copyrighted sound recordings and sold them in violation of the Copyright Act); *Miszkiewicz*, 715 F.Supp., at 919 (plaintiffs sought damages based on defendant's unauthorized public performance of copyrighted musical compositions). In the present case, the express language of § 504, the legislative history [and] *Powell* delineate the applicable rule of law; this rule of law does not permit the plaintiffs to recover for each tape sold or held for sale because only one copyright was infringed.

For the foregoing reasons, the Court denies the plaintiffs' Motion for Default Judgment. The plaintiffs are granted leave to renew their motion in a manner consistent with this opinion.

An appropriate Order follows.

Deltak, Inc. v. Advanced Systems, Inc.

United States Court of Appeals, Seventh Circuit, 1985.
767 F.2d 357.

■ CUDAHY, CIRCUIT JUDGE.

Plaintiff Deltak, Inc., brought this copyright infringement action against defendant Advanced Systems, Inc. ("ASI"). In an Order of Febru-

---

[c] It is noteworthy that with respect to both *Perez* and *Miszkiewicz*, counsel for the plaintiffs failed to provide an accurate case name and failed to provide an accurate citation. In contrast, every other citation in the plaintiffs' memorandum of law is accurate as to the case name, and as to the book and page where the case can be found.

ary 5, 1982, the district court entered summary judgment for Deltak on the issue of ASI's liability for copyright infringement. On August 16 and 17, 1983, a bench trial was held on the issue of damages. The district court filed a searching opinion on October 20, 1983, finding that Deltak had failed to prove either its lost profits or ASI's additional revenues, and awarding no damages. 574 F.Supp. 400 (N.D.Ill.1983). Deltak now appeals the damages determination. ASI takes no appeal on liability. Although we accept a number of aspects of the district court's analysis, we vacate and remand on the issue of damages.

I

Deltak and ASI are among the largest firms in the business of selling textbooks and audio and videotapes used to teach data processing and other computer related skills. Each firm's materials are, according to the district court, highly substitutable for those of the other. During the relevant period, 1980–81, Deltak's marketing materials included a package entitled the Career Development System (the "CDS"). The complete CDS kit (the "Kit") included a videotape, a book titled In–House Education Guide, a manual of forms and a "Task List." The Task List "is a large glossy pamphlet.... On the left-hand side of each page of the Task List is a list of data-processing tasks that a company might want to teach its programmers, and on the right-hand side a list of the specific teaching materials that Deltak sells for each task." 574 F.Supp., at 402.

It is the left-hand list that ASI copied. ASI paid two consultants $3,000 to create the infringing document, which combined Deltak's CDS task designations with a list of ASI's teaching materials.

The consultants duplicated the left-hand side of the CDS Task List, using the identical language in which Deltak had described the tasks and arranging the task descriptions in the same order as Deltak; but on the right-hand side of each page, instead of listing the Deltak materials suitable to perform each task the authors of the infringing document listed ASI teaching materials. 574 F.Supp., at 402. The infringing document was developed in response to requests from ASI customers who wanted a way to key tasks on the Deltak List to ASI's materials. ASI intended that its salespeople and marketing representatives would show the document to customers to enable them to pick ASI materials with which to train their programmers in Deltak specified tasks. ASI produced either 42 or 50 copies of the document, compare 574 F.Supp., at 402 with *id*. at 404, and, in August, 1980, distributed 15 of them without charge to customers of Deltak, each of which was also an actual or potential customer of ASI.

This suit was brought in December of 1980 under the Copyright Act of 1976, alleging copyright infringement. After suit was brought, ASI began retrieving the copies, and by February, 1981, none of the infringing documents remained in the possession of customers. In May, 1981, the district court granted a preliminary injunction, and it later granted summary judgment to Deltak on the issue of liability. ASI does not contest this ruling that it infringed Deltak's copyright.

II

Section 504(a) of the Copyright Act allows recovery of damages in accordance with two distinct approaches. "Statutory damages" are available under section 504(c), but only if the copyright is timely registered. § 412. Neither statutory damages, which the district court would "have [had] no hesitation in awarding", 574 F.Supp., at 403, nor attorney's fees pursuant to section 505, are available here because, as the parties agree, Deltak did not so register its copyright.

Section 504(a) also provides that the copyright owner may recover his or her "actual damages and any additional profits of the infringer, as provided by subsection (b)." At trial, Deltak presented testimony regarding both these theories of damage recovery under section 504(b). However, the district court was unable to determine what portion of the gross revenues were due to the infringement and what portion were due to other factors such as lawful marketing methods. 574 F.Supp., at 411–12. Deltak has, for reasons not clear to this court, elected not to appeal this portion of the district court's judgment.

Deltak does, however, appeal the district court's judgment that it suffered no actual damages as a result of the infringement. It does not contend that its actual damages should be measured by any lost profits on sales of teaching materials to the customers lost because of the infringement. Instead, Deltak contends, as it did below, that its damages should be computed by multiplying $4925, which the district court "accepted" as a reasonable estimate of the profit per CDS Kit realized by Deltak, or $5000, the list price of the Kit, by fifty, the number of copies of the infringing document that were made by ASI. (For purposes of this appeal we are accepting 50 as the number of documents produced.)

There are three factual premises on which actual damages could be so awarded. First, it could be that, but for the infringement, Deltak would have sold fifty more copies to various customers (other than ASI). Second, ASI might have purchased (and hence Deltak sold) fifty copies so as not to have infringed. Third, when ASI reproduced the fifty infringing copies, it was manufacturing assets and thereby damaging Deltak to the extent of the value of use of the assets in terms of acquisition costs saved by ASI.

The trial court found that the first premise could not support recovery, 574 F.Supp., at 404, and Deltak does not appeal on this basis. The copies created by ASI could only have prevented sales by Deltak to those customers who received them. The fifteen distributed copies were all given to customers who already had a copy of the Deltak Task List. These customers had permission from Deltak to make copies of the List for the use of employees at their plant locations. There was no evidence that even one of these customers would have purchased an additional copy of the List from Deltak instead of making one itself. Given the evidence of the steep purchase price of the List, there are strong grounds for inferring that the customer would not have purchased an additional copy of it.

Deltak's argument on appeal is primarily directed toward the third premise, but also challenges the trial court's denial of the second premise. We will first consider this third argument concerning the value of use of manufactured assets. Deltak argues that by making fifty copies of the infringing work, each valued at $5000 (list price) or $4925 (profit to Deltak), ASI gained $250,000 in marketing tools without payment. The district court did find that the copied list "had some potential value to ASI as a marketing tool." 574 F.Supp., at 404. The value of the infringer's use is a permissible basis for estimating actual damages. Sid & Marty Krofft Television Productions, Inc. v. McDonald's Corp., 562 F.2d 1157, 1174 (9th Cir.1977). Value of use was accepted as such by the district court, 574 F.Supp., at 404, and on appeal ASI concurs. ("Actual damages" are not defined either in the Copyright Act or in the accompanying legislative reports. 3 M. Nimmer, Nimmer on Copyright § 14.02 at 14–6 (1984).)

However, we see no reason that damages calculated on the value of use method should vary with the number of copies the infringer produced, at least where that number differs from the number of copies used by the infringer. Here ASI ran off fifty copies of the list, but distributed only fifteen to customers of Deltak. Presumably, if ASI had run off two thousand copies, and kept all but the distributed fifteen in a locked warehouse, Deltak could claim $10,000,000, even though the effect would be no different from the actual infringement before us. We believe this is a sufficient reductio ad absurdum of Deltak's assertion that ASI profited by the value of use of all fifty copies, but it does not preclude consideration of the value to ASI of the fifteen copies distributed to customers. Cf. Alfred Bell & Co. v. Catalda Fine Arts, Inc., 86 F.Supp. 399, 411–13 (S.D.N.Y.1949)(copyright owner allowed recovery of profits only on infringing prints actually sold, not on infringing prints manufactured but not sold; infringer's costs allocated similarly), aff'd as modified on other grounds, 191 F.2d 99 (2d Cir.1951).

The primary value of these marketing tools, when in the hands of customers, was to increase sales by ASI to the customers by inducing them to switch their purchases from Deltak to ASI. However, as discussed above, the district court found that there was insufficient evidence on which it could base a finding that any of ASI's sales during the infringement period were due to the infringing copies. Since Deltak does not appeal this finding, we are constrained to hold that the value of use to Deltak of the fifteen distributed infringing copies was, in this primary sense, zero.

But the value of use of a marketing tool is not, of course, identical to the profits it generates. After all, not all marketing and advertising campaigns are successful, and even the unsuccessful ones cost money to undertake. We presume it is rather rare for the costs of a campaign to vary (after the fact) in proportion to its success. Here, the distributed copies were essential components of the (as it turned out unsuccessful) campaign undertaken by ASI. If ASI had cared to undertake its campaign in a legal manner, it could have purchased copies of the Deltak task list. Each of the copies ASI distributed had a value of use to it equal to the acquisition cost saved by infringement instead of purchase, which ASI was then free to put to other uses. See Aitken, Hazen, Hoffman, Miller, P.C. v. Empire Construction Co., 542 F.Supp. 252, 262–63 (D.Neb.1982)(awarding fair market value as actual damages for infringement of copyright in architectural plans); see also Nucor Corp. v. Tennessee Forging Steel Service, Inc., 513 F.2d 151, 152–53 (8th Cir.1975)(infringers of plaintiff's common law copyright in architectural plans were liable for fair market value of plans); Atlantic Monthly Co. v. Post Pub. Co., 27 F.2d 556, 560 (D.Mass.1928)(awarding saved acquisition cost as profit made by copyright infringer). This is simply an application of the general principle that value of use "amounts to a determination of what a willing buyer would have been reasonably required to pay to a willing seller for plaintiff['s] work." *Sid & Marty Krofft Television Productions*, 562 F.2d, at 1174.

The district court did not directly consider the saved acquisition cost of the distributed copies as the value of use of the infringement to ASI. The district court did, however, consider the problem from the other side of the counter, as it were. The district court considered Deltak's argument that it lost sales of fifty units to ASI. The value of use in terms of saved acquisition costs is equal (except for Deltak's marginal production costs) to Deltak's lost profits from the avoided sales. The district court rejected recovery on this, the second factual premise mentioned above.

> [T]he particular scenario in which ASI goes hat in hand to Deltak to buy 50 copies—or one copy—of the Task List is quite fantastic even on the counter-factual hypothesis (fundamental to this approach to estimating damages) that ASI had a pure heart.... [It is] very unlikely that even a pure-hearted ASI would have been willing to tip its competitive hand to Deltak in this fashion.

504 F.Supp., at 404.

Now it may be that ASI's competitive motivations explain why it did not purchase one or more copies of the Task List from Deltak. But the conclusion that in the counterfactual situation in which ASI does not infringe it would not have purchased any copies of the Task List from Deltak is sheer speculation. The district court cited no evidence in support of its statement, and our review of the record discloses no evidence that if ASI had not infringed it would have given up the whole marketing campaign rather than purchase any copies from Deltak. Since substantial liberality is shown to plaintiffs in infringement actions in their proof of damages (though not in their proof of infringement), this absence of evidence should cut against the infringer not against the owner. After all, we do know that ASI was willing to pay $3000 to have the infringing document produced and that it chose to undertake the infringing course with attendant risk of liability for damages rather than give up the marketing campaign.

The owner of a copyright is not allowed to recover its own lost sales and the infringer's profits if that results in double-counting of the same economic transaction, usually a sale to a third-party customer. See § 504(b). Similarly, Deltak cannot recover its lost sales to ASI and the value of use to ASI of the infringement, even though they are both measures of actual damages, since that would double count the same counterfactual transaction. Normally the owner recovers the larger of the two amounts, or all of one and so much of the other as is not included in the one. Here, however we will not take that course. We retain lingering doubts about whether, if ASI went hat in hand to Deltak to buy fifteen copies of the Task List, Deltak would have sold any to ASI. These doubts incline us to refrain from holding the district court's finding that Deltak did not lose any sales to ASI to be clearly erroneous. Application of the value of use measure of damages, however, even when based on saved acquisition cost, does not require us to hold this finding clearly erroneous, because it is based on actual savings, not on counterfactual lost sales.[a] Therefore we will apply the value of use measure of damages.

It is clear that ASI received the value of use of the fifteen copies it distributed. Deltak contends that the value of use of each of these copies was $5000, the list price of the Kit. However the value of use approach requires a determination of the fair market value of the infringed document, and, while list price is evidence of fair market value, it is not conclusive. Deltak argues that by "accepting" $4925 as a reasonable estimate of its profit per Kit, and by "not quarreling" with $5000 as the price of the Kit, the district court made a finding of fact that the value of use of each kit was $5000.

We are not persuaded. The district court's remarks[b] came at the beginning of its rejection of the lost sales measure of damages. Since it was convinced that there were no lost sales, it did not have to consider what any lost sales were worth. We believe the district court was merely accepting these figures for purposes of argument. The parties had stipu-

---

[a] It is for this reason that ASI's claim that it would never have negotiated to buy 15 copies at $5000, and thus there are no lost sales, is irrelevant. Further, a defendant infringer "cannot expect to pay the same price in damages as it might have paid after freely negotiated bargaining, or there would be no reason scrupulously to obey the copyright law." Iowa State University Research Foundation, Inc. v. American Broadcasting Cos., 475 F.Supp. 78, 83 (S.D.N.Y.1979).

[b] The district court's remarks are as follows:

> Deltak presented evidence that the price of the kit (for this is the unusual type of advertising that the seller actually sells to his customers), consisting of the Task List and certain other items, is $5,000 and that Deltak's cost of producing one more such kit is $75. I accept $4,925 as a reasonable estimate of the profit per kit

for a small increase in production. Deltak wants me to multiply the number by 50, the number of copies of the infringing document that ASI made. But the only possible factual premise for such a measure of damages would be that Deltak would have sold 50 more copies of the CDS at $5,000 apiece had it not been for the infringement. That premise was not proved at trial and is almost certainly false. I will not quarrel with the figure of $5,000 for the sale price, though there was much evidence that Deltak's average realized revenue for the sale of CDS kits was far less.

574 F.Supp. at 404. The court then went on to determine that Deltak would not have made any sales at all but for the infringement.

lated the list price to be $5000, so the court could hardly quarrel with that price and, as Deltak had presented evidence that the marginal production cost of the Kit was $75, $4925 might be a reasonable estimate of the profit per sale if the sales were at list price. But the district court did not apply the saved acquisition cost measure of value of use, and so had no need to distinguish between list price and average sales price or fair market value. The court did recognize that "there was much evidence that Deltak's average realized revenue from the sale of CDS kits was far less" than the $5000 list price. 574 F.Supp., at 404. Among this evidence was some which tended to show that of the 187 sales of Kits for which a price was recorded in Deltak's records and which were not "bundled" in a package with other products, the average price was $1900.

Since we do not believe the district court's "acceptance" was a finding of fair market value, and discern no other finding of fair market value, we must remand for further proceedings on the issue of the fair market value of the fifteen Lists. The burden of persuasion both as to showing a fair market value less than the stipulated list price and as to showing a market value for the List separate from the Kit (or a proper allocation of values) falls, of course, on ASI. The $3000 ASI paid to its consultants to fabricate the document would be deductible from any award of saved acquisition costs.

The order of the district court is VACATED, and the case REMANDED for further proceedings not inconsistent with this opinion.

Abend v. MCA, Inc.

United States Court of Appeals, Ninth Circuit, 1988.
863 F.2d 1465, aff'd, 495 U.S. 207, 110 S.Ct. 1750, 109 L.Ed.2d 184 (1990).

■ PREGERSON, CIRCUIT JUDGE.

[The facts of the case are recounted in the Supreme Court's opinion reprinted in Assignment 9.]

* * *

Neither the equities, precedent, nor Congressional intent justify us in changing the balance between owners of renewal copyrights in underlying works and owners of the copyright in derivative works when Congress has refrained from doing so. We therefore hold that defendants' continued exploitation of the "Rear Window" film without Abend's consent violates Abend's renewal copyright in the underlying story "It Had to Be Murder," unless the defendants can establish any affirmative defenses.[a]

Our holding does not mean, however, that the equities of this case have no bearing on its outcome. We are mindful that this case presents compelling equitable considerations which should be taken into account by the district court in fashioning an appropriate remedy in the event defen-

[a] For the reasons discussed in the next section, we hold that defendants cannot char-acterize their use of the underlying story as a "fair use" to avoid liability for infringement.

dants fail to establish any equitable defenses. Defendants invested substantial money, effort, and talent in creating the "Rear Window" film. Clearly the tremendous success of that venture initially and upon re-release is attributable in significant measure to, inter alia, the outstanding performances of its stars—Grace Kelly and James Stewart—and the brilliant directing of Alfred Hitchcock. The district court must recognize this contribution in determining Abend's remedy.

The district court may choose from several available remedies for the infringement. Abend seeks first an injunction against the continued exploitation of the "Rear Window" film. § 502(a) provides that the court "may . . . grant temporary and final injunctions on such terms as it may deem reasonable to prevent or restrain infringement of a copyright." Defendants argue that a finding of infringement presumptively entitles the plaintiff to an injunction, citing Professor Nimmer. See 3 M. Nimmer, Nimmer on Copyright § 14.06[B] at 14–55 to 14–56.2 (1988). However, Professor Nimmer also states that "where great public injury would be worked by an injunction, the courts might . . . award damages or a continuing royalty instead of an injunction in such special circumstances." *Id.* at 14–56.2.

We believe such special circumstances exist here. The "Rear Window" film resulted from the collaborative efforts of many talented individuals other than Cornell Woolrich, the author of the underlying story. The success of the movie resulted in large part from factors completely unrelated to the underlying story, "It Had To Be Murder." It would cause a great injustice for the owners of the film if the court enjoined them from further exhibition of the movie. An injunction would also effectively foreclose defendants from enjoying legitimate profits derived from exploitation of the "new matter" comprising the derivative work, which is given express copyright protection by section 7 of the 1909 Act. Since defendants could not possibly separate out the "new matter" from the underlying work, their right to enjoy the renewal copyright in the derivative work would be rendered meaningless by the grant of an injunction. We also note that an injunction could cause public injury by denying the public the opportunity to view a classic film for many years to come.

This is not the first time we have recognized that an injunction may be an inappropriate remedy for copyright infringement. In Universal City Studios v. Sony Corp. of Amer., 659 F.2d 963, 976 (9th Cir.1981), rev'd on other grounds, 464 U.S. 417 (1984), we stated that Professor Nimmer's suggestion of damages or a continuing royalty would constitute an acceptable resolution for infringement caused by in-home taping of television programs by VCR—"time-shifting."

As the district court pointed out in the *Sony* case, an injunction is a "harsh and drastic" discretionary remedy, never an absolute right. Universal City Studios v. Sony Corp. of Amer., 480 F.Supp. 429, 463, 464 (C.D.Cal.1979), rev'd on other grounds, 659 F.2d 963 (9th Cir.1981), aff'd 464 U.S. 417 (1984). Abend argues nonetheless that defendants' attempts to interfere with his production of new derivative works can only be remedied by an injunction. We disagree. Abend has not shown irreparable injury which would justify imposing the severe remedy of an injunction on defendants. Abend can be compensated adequately for the infringement by monetary compensation. § 504(b) provides that the copyright owner can recover actual damages and "any profits of the infringement that are *attributable to the infringement* and are not taken into account in computing the actual damages." (Emphasis added.)

The district court is capable of calculating damages caused to the fair market value of plaintiff's story by the re-release of the film. Any impairment of Abend's ability to produce new derivative works based on the story would be reflected in the calculation of the damage to the fair market value of the story. In Cream Records, Inc. v. Jos. Schlitz Brewing Co., 754 F.2d 826, 827 (9th Cir.1985), for example, the plaintiff presented evidence that defendants' unauthorized use of part of plaintiff's song in a commercial had "destroyed the value of the copyrighted work" to other advertisers. We held that the plaintiff could recover this lost value as damages. *Id.* at 827–28.

In addition to actual damages suffered, Abend would be entitled to profits attributable to the infringement. § 504(b). Defendants' fear that Abend could receive 100% of their profits is unfounded. Abend can receive only the profits attributable to the infringement. *Id.*; *Frank Music Corp.*, 772 F.2d 505, 518 (9th Cir.1985)("When an infringer's profits are attributable to factors in addition to use of [its] work, an apportionment of profits is proper."). Should the court find infringement because defendants have failed to establish any affirmative defenses, on remand it must apportion damages.

While apportioning profits is not always an easy task in these cases, neither is it a new or unusual one. In the landmark case of Sheldon v. Metro–Goldwyn–Mayer Pictures Corp., 106 F.2d 45 (2d Cir.1939), aff'd, 309 U.S. 390 (1940), Judge Learned Hand held that profits should be apportioned between the plaintiff and defendants, after finding that defendants' movie "Letty Lynton" infringed plaintiff's play "Dishonored Lady." *Sheldon*, 309 U.S., at 396. Judge Hand recognized that "no real standard" can govern this apportionment, but he "resolved to avoid the one certainly unjust course of giving the plaintiffs everything, because the defendants cannot with certainty compute their own share." *Sheldon*, 106 F.2d, at 51. The court then set plaintiffs' share of the profits at 20%, to "favor the plaintiffs in every reasonable chance of error." *Id.*

We likewise recognize that courts cannot be expected to determine with "mathematical exactness" an apportionment of profits. We require only a "reasonable and just apportionment." *Frank Music Corp.*, 772 F.2d, at 518. In *Frank*, the defendants infringed plaintiff's copyright in the play "Kismet?" by including parts of songs and six minutes of music from the play, and by using similar characters and setting in Act IV of a musical revue entitled "Hallelujah Hollywood." *Id.* at 510. We remanded to the district court for apportionment of profits using a reasonable formula.

We also required apportionment in *Cream Records*, 754 F.2d, at 828. In *Cream*, the plaintiff, owner of the copyright in "The Theme From Shaft," sought to recover all profits earned from a commercial produced by the defendants which infringed plaintiffs copyright by using a ten note ostinato from the song. *Id.* We held that "[i]n cases such as this where an infringer's profits are not entirely due to the infringement, and the evidence suggests some division which may rationally be used as a springboard, it is the duty of the court to make some apportionment." *Id.* at 828–29.

Because factors other than Woolrich's story clearly contributed to "Rear Window's" success, should the district court find that the defendants have failed to establish any affirmative defense to the infringement, the district court should award Abend actual damages and apportion profits between Abend and the defendants.

Fogerty v. Fantasy, Inc.

Supreme Court of the United States, 1994.
—— U.S. ——, 114 S.Ct. 1023, 127 L.Ed.2d 455.

■ Chief Justice Rehnquist delivered the opinion of the Court.

The Copyright Act of 1976, 17 U.S.C. § 505, provides in relevant part that in any copyright infringement action "the court may ... award a reasonable attorney's fee to the prevailing party as part of the costs." The question presented in this case is what standards should inform a court's decision to award attorney's fees to a prevailing defendant in a copyright infringement action—a question that has produced conflicting views in the Courts of Appeals.

Petitioner John Fogerty is a successful musician, who, in the late 1960's, was the lead singer and songwriter of a popular music group known as "Creedence Clearwater Revival."[a] In 1970, he wrote a song entitled "Run Through the Jungle" and sold the exclusive publishing rights to predecessors-in-interest of respondent Fantasy, Inc., who later obtained the copyright by assignment. The music group disbanded in 1972 and Fogerty subsequently published under another recording label. In 1985, he published and registered a copyright to a song entitled "The Old Man Down the Road", which was released on an album distributed by Warner Brothers Records, Inc. Respondent Fantasy, Inc., sued Fogerty, Warner Brothers, and affiliated companies,[b] in District Court, alleging that "The Old Man Down the Road" was merely "Run Through the Jungle" with new words. The copyright infringement claim went to trial and a jury returned a verdict in favor of Fogerty.

[a] Creedence Clearwater Revival (CCR), recently inducted into the Rock and Roll Hall of Fame, has been recognized as one of the greatest American rock and roll groups of all time. With Fogerty as its leader, CCR developed a distinctive style of music, dubbed "swamp rock" by the media due to its southern country and blues feel.

[b] Pursuant to an agreement between Fogerty and the Warner defendants, Fogerty indemnified and reimbursed the Warner defendants for their attorney's fees and costs incurred in defending the copyright infringement action.

After his successful defense of the action, Fogerty moved for reasonable attorney's fees pursuant to § 505. The District Court denied the motion, finding that Fantasy's infringement suit was not brought frivolously or in bad faith as required by circuit precedent for an award of attorney's fees to a successful defendant. The Court of Appeals affirmed, 984 F.2d 1524 (C.A.9 1993), and declined to abandon the existing Ninth Circuit standard for awarding attorney's fees which treats successful plaintiffs and successful defendants differently. Under that standard, commonly termed the "dual" standard, prevailing plaintiffs are generally awarded attorney's fees as a matter of course, while prevailing defendants must show that the original suit was frivolous or brought in bad faith.[c] In contrast, some courts of appeals follow the so-called "evenhanded" approach in which no distinction is made between prevailing plaintiffs and prevailing defendants. The Court of Appeals for the Third Circuit, for example, has ruled that "we do not require bad faith, nor do we mandate an allowance of fees as a concomitant of prevailing in every case, but we do favor an evenhanded approach." Lieb v. Topstone Industries, Inc., 788 F.2d 151, 156 (C.A.3 1986).

We granted certiorari, 113 S.Ct. 2992 (1993), to address an important area of federal law and to resolve the conflict between the Ninth Circuit's "dual" standard for awarding attorney's fees under § 505, and the so-called "evenhanded" approach exemplified by the Third Circuit.[d] We reverse.

Respondent advances three arguments in support of the dual standard followed by the Court of Appeals for the Ninth Circuit in this case. First, it contends that the language of § 505, when read in the light of our decisions construing similar fee-shifting language, supports the rule. Second, it asserts that treating prevailing plaintiffs and defendants differently comports with the "objectives" and "equitable considerations" underlying the Copyright Act as a whole. Finally, respondent contends that the legislative history of § 505 indicates that Congress ratified the dual standard which it claims was "uniformly" followed by the lower courts under identical

---

[c] By predicating an award of attorney's fees to prevailing defendants on a showing of bad faith or frivolousness on the part of plaintiffs, the "dual" standard makes it more difficult for prevailing defendants to secure awards of attorney's fees than prevailing plaintiffs. The Ninth Circuit has explained that prevailing plaintiffs, on the other hand, should generally receive such awards absent special circumstances such as "the presence of a complex or novel issue of law that the defendant litigates vigorously and in good faith...." McCulloch v. Albert E. Price, Inc., 823 F.2d 316, 323 (C.A.9 1987). In the instant case, the Court of Appeals explained: "The purpose of [the dual standard] rule is to avoid chilling a copyright holder's incentive to sue on colorable claims, and thereby to give full effect to the broad protection for copyrights intended by the Copyright Act." 984 F.2d, at 1532.

[d] In addition to the Ninth Circuit, the Second, Seventh, and District of Columbia Circuits have adopted a "dual" standard of awarding attorney's fees whereby a greater burden is placed upon prevailing defendants than prevailing plaintiffs. On the other hand, the Fourth and Eleventh Circuits have been identified as following an "evenhanded" approach similar to that of the Third Circuit. [Citations omitted.]

language in the 1909 Copyright Act. We address each of these arguments in turn.

The statutory language—"the court may also award a reasonable attorney's fee to the prevailing party as part of the costs"—gives no hint that successful plaintiffs are to be treated differently than successful defendants. But respondent contends that our decision in Christiansburg Garment Co. v. EEOC, 434 U.S. 412 (1978), in which we construed virtually identical language, supports a differentiation in treatment between plaintiffs and defendants.

Christiansburg construed the language of Title VII of the Civil Rights Act of 1964, which in relevant part provided that the court "in its discretion, may allow the prevailing party . . . a reasonable attorney's fee as part of the costs. . . ." § 2000e–5(k). We had earlier held, interpreting the cognate provision of Title II of that Act, 42 U.S.C. § 2000a–3(b), that a prevailing plaintiff "should ordinarily recover an attorney's fee unless some special circumstances would render such an award unjust." Newman v. Piggie Park Enterprises, Inc., 390 U.S. 400, 402 (1968). This decision was based on what we found to be the important policy objectives of the Civil Rights statutes, and the intent of Congress to achieve such objectives through the use of plaintiffs as "private attorneys general." *Ibid.* In *Christiansburg, supra,* we determined that the same policy considerations were not at work in the case of a prevailing civil rights defendant. We noted that a Title VII plaintiff, like a Title II plaintiff in *Piggie Park,* is "the chosen instrument of Congress to vindicate 'a policy that Congress considered of the highest priority.'" 434 U.S., at 418. We also relied on the admittedly sparse legislative history to indicate that different standards were to be applied to successful plaintiffs than to successful defendants.

Respondent points to our language in Flight Attendants v. Zipes, 491 U.S. 754, 758, n.2 (1989), that "fee-shifting statutes' similar language is a 'strong indication' that they are to be interpreted alike." But here we think this normal indication is overborne by the factors relied upon in our *Christiansburg* opinion which are absent in the case of the Copyright Act.[e] The legislative history of § 505 provides no support for treating prevailing plaintiffs and defendants differently with respect to the recovery of attorney's fees. The attorney's fees provision § 505 of the 1976 Act was carried forward verbatim from the 1909 Act with very little discussion. The relevant House Report provides simply:

"Under section 505 the awarding of costs and attorney's fees are left to the court's discretion, and the section also makes clear that neither costs nor attorney's fees can be awarded to or against 'the United States or an officer thereof.'" H. R. Rep. No. 94–1476, p. 163 (1976).[f]

[e] Additionally, we note that Congress, in enacting § 505 of the 1976 Copyright Act, could not have been aware of the *Christiansburg* dual standard as *Christiansburg* was not decided until 1978.

[f] The 1976 Copyright did change, however, the standard for awarding costs to the prevailing party. The 1909 Act provided a mandatory rule that "full costs *shall* be allowed." § 116 (1976 ed.)(emphasis added). The 1976 Act changed the rule from a man-

The goals and objectives of the two Acts are likewise not completely similar. Oftentimes, in the civil rights context, impecunious "private attorney general" plaintiffs can ill afford to litigate their claims against defendants with more resources. Congress sought to redress this balance in part, and to provide incentives for the bringing of meritorious lawsuits, by treating successful plaintiffs more favorably than successful defendants in terms of the award of attorney's fees. The primary objective of the Copyright Act is to encourage the production of original literary, artistic, and musical expression for the good of the public. In the copyright context, it has been noted that "entities which sue for copyright infringement as plaintiffs can run the gamut from corporate behemoths to starving artists; the same is true of prospective copyright infringement defendants." Cohen v. Virginia Electric & Power Co., 617 F.Supp. 619, 622–623 (E.D.Va.1985), aff'd on other grounds, 788 F.2d 247 (C.A.4 1986).

We thus conclude that respondent's argument based on our fee-shifting decisions under the Civil Rights Act must fail.[g]

Respondent next argues that the policies and objectives of § 505 and of the Copyright Act in general are best served by the "dual approach" to the award of attorney's fees.[h] The most common reason advanced in support of the dual approach is that, by awarding attorney's fees to prevailing plaintiffs as a matter of course, it encourages litigation of meritorious claims of copyright infringement. Indeed, respondent relies heavily on this argument. We think the argument is flawed because it expresses a one-sided view of the purposes of the Copyright Act. While it is true that one of the goals of the Copyright Act is to discourage infringement, it is by no means the only goal of that Act. In the first place, it is by no means always the case that the plaintiff in an infringement action is the only holder of a copyright; often times, defendants hold copyrights too, as exemplified in the case at hand.

More importantly, the policies served by the Copyright Act are more complex, more measured, than simply maximizing the number of meritorious suits for copyright infringement. We have often recognized the monopoly privileges that Congress has authorized, while "intended to motivate the

---

datory one to one of discretion. As the 1909 Act indicates, Congress clearly knows how to use mandatory language when it so desires. That Congress did not amend the neutral language of the 1909 rule respecting attorney's fees lends further support to the plain language of § 505—district courts are to use their discretion in awarding attorney's fees and costs to the prevailing party.

[g] We note that the federal fee-shifting statutes in the patent and trademark fields, which are more closely related to that of copyright, support a party-neutral approach. Those statutes contain language similar to that of § 505, with the added proviso that fees are only to be awarded in "exceptional

cases." § 285 (patent). Consistent with the party-neutral language, courts have generally awarded attorney's fees in an evenhanded manner based on the same criteria.

[h] Respondent points to four important interests allegedly advanced by the dual standard: (1) it promotes the vigorous enforcement of the Copyright Act; (2) it distinguishes between the wrongdoers and the blameless; (3) it enhances the predictability and certainty in copyrights by providing a relatively certain benchmark for the award of attorney's fees; and (4) it affords copyright defendants sufficient incentives to litigate their defenses.

creative activity of authors and inventors by the provision of a special reward", are limited in nature and must ultimately serve the public good. Sony Corp. of America v. Universal City Studios, Inc., 464 U.S. 417, 429 (1984).

Because copyright law ultimately serves the purpose of enriching the general public through access to creative works, it is peculiarly important that the boundaries of copyright law be demarcated as clearly as possible. To that end, defendants who seek to advance a variety of meritorious copyright defenses should be encouraged to litigate them to the same extent that plaintiffs are encouraged to litigate meritorious claims of infringement. In the case before us, the successful defense of "The Old Man Down the Road" increased public exposure to a musical work that could, as a result, lead to further creative pieces. Thus a successful defense of a copyright infringement action may further the policies of the Copyright Act every bit as much as a successful prosecution of an infringement claim by the holder of a copyright.

Respondent finally urges that the legislative history supports the dual standard, relying on the principle of ratification. See, Lorillard v. Pons, 434 U.S. 575, 580 (1978)("Congress is presumed to be aware of an administrative or judicial interpretation of a statute and to adopt that interpretation when it re-enacts a statute without change ..."). Respondent surveys the great number of lower court cases interpreting the identical provision in the 1909 Act, § 116 (1976 ed.), and asserts that "it was firmly established" that prevailing defendants should be awarded attorney's fees only where the plaintiff's claim was frivolous or brought with a vexatious purpose. Furthermore, respondent claims that Congress was aware of this construction of former § 116 because of two Copyright Studies submitted to Congress when studying revisions to the Act. W. Strauss, Damage Provisions of the Copyright Law, Study No. 22 (hereinafter Strauss Study), and R. Brown, Operation of the Damage Provisions of the Copyright Law: An Exploratory Study, Study No. 23 (hereinafter Brown Study), Studies Prepared for Subcommittee on Patents, Trademarks, and Copyrights, 86th Cong., 2d Sess. (H. Judiciary Comm. Print 1960).

[T]he Strauss and Brown Copyright Studies deal only briefly with the provision for the award of attorney's fees. In the Strauss Study, the limited discussion begins with a quote to A. Weil, American Copyright Law 530–531 (1917) for an explanation of the "discretionary awarding of attorney's fees." The study then notes that the pending bills contemplate no change in the attorney's fees provision and concludes with the simple statement "the cases indicate that this discretion has been judiciously exercised by the courts." *Ibid.*[i] This limited discussion of attorney's fees surely does not constitute an endorsement of a dual standard.

---

[i] In a footnote, the Strauss Study lists several cases exemplifying the courts' use of discretion. None of these cases explicitly require a dual standard of awarding attorney's fees, but instead offer various reasons for awarding or not awarding attorney's fees to the prevailing party.

The Brown Study was intended as a supplement to the Strauss Study and, inter alia, provides information from a survey distributed to practitioners about the practical workings of the 1909 Copyright Act.[j] It also does not endorse a standard of treating prevailing plaintiffs and defendants differently. At one point, the study notes that "courts do not usually make an allowance at all if an unsuccessful plaintiff's claim was not 'synthetic, capricious or otherwise unreasonable,' or if the losing defendant raised real issues of fact or law." Brown Study 85.

Our review of the prior case law itself leads us to conclude that there was no settled "dual standard" interpretation of former § 116 about which Congress could have been aware. We note initially that at least one reported case stated no reason in awarding attorney's fees to successful defendants. See, e.g., Marks v. Leo Feist, Inc., 8 F.2d 460, 461 (C.A.2 1925)(noting that the Copyright Act gave courts "absolute discretion", the court awarded attorney's fees to prevailing defendant after plaintiff voluntarily dismissed suit). More importantly, while it appears that the majority of lower courts exercised their discretion in awarding attorney's fees to prevailing defendants based on a finding of frivolousness or bad faith, not all courts expressly described the test in those terms.[k] In fact, only one pre-1976 case expressly endorsed a dual standard. Breffort v. I Had a Ball Co., 271 F.Supp. 623 (S.D.N.Y.1967). This is hardly the sort of uniform construction which Congress might have endorsed.

In summary, neither of the two studies presented to Congress, nor the cases referred to by the studies, support respondent's view that there was a settled construction in favor of the "dual standard" under § 116 of the 1909 Copyright Act.

---

[j] To this extent, the Brown Study focuses more on the effect that the prospect of an award of attorney's fees has on decisions to litigate or to settle cases. Based on its interview sources, the study concluded that the likelihood of getting a fee award is so problematic that "it is not a factor" that goes into the decision to settle or litigate. Brown Study 85.

[k] See, e.g., Schroeder v. William Morrow & Co., 421 F.Supp. 372, 378 (N.D.Ill.1976)(refusing to award prevailing defendant an attorney's fee because plaintiff's action was "prosecuted in good faith and with a reasonable likelihood of success"), rev'd on other grounds, 566 F.2d 3 (C.A.7 1977); Kinelow Publishing Co. v. Photography In Business, Inc., 270 F.Supp. 851, 855 (S.D.N.Y.1967)(denying fee award to prevailing defendant because plaintiff's claims, while "lacking in merit," were not "unreasonable or capricious"); Burnett v. Lambino, 206 F.Supp. 517, 518–519 (S.D.N.Y.1962)(granting fee award to prevailing defendant where "asserted claim of infringement was so demonstrably lacking in merit that bringing it was clearly unreasonable"); Cloth v. Hyman, 146 F.Supp. 185, 193 (S.D.N.Y.1956)(noting that it is proper to award fees when a copyright action is brought in bad faith, with a motive to "vex and harass the defendant," or where plaintiff's claim utterly lacks merit); Loews, Inc. v. Columbia Broadcasting System, Inc., 131 F.Supp. 165, 186 (S.D.Cal.1955)(denying prevailing defendant fee award where question presented in the case "was a nice one," and there are "no authorities squarely in point to guide the litigants or their counsel"), aff'd, 239 F.2d 532 (C.A.9 1956), aff'd, 356 U.S. 43 (1958); Krafft v. Cohen, 38 F.Supp. 1022, 1023 (E.D.Pa.1941)(denying fee award to prevailing defendant where claim brought "in good faith," and evidence demonstrated appropriation); Lewys v. O'Neill, 49 F.2d 603, at 618 (S.D.N.Y.1931) (awarding fees to prevailing defendant because plaintiff's case was "wholly synthetic").

We thus reject each of respondent's three arguments in support of the dual standard. We now turn to petitioner's argument that § 505 was intended to adopt the "British Rule." Petitioner argues that, consistent with the neutral language of § 505, both prevailing plaintiffs and defendants should be awarded attorney's fees as a matter of course, absent exceptional circumstances. For two reasons we reject this argument for the British Rule.

First, just as the plain language of § 505 supports petitioner's claim for disapproving the dual standard, it cuts against him in arguing for the British Rule. The statute says that "the court may also award a reasonable attorney's fee to the prevailing party as part of the costs." The word "may" clearly connotes discretion. The automatic awarding of attorney's fees to the prevailing party would pretermit the exercise of that discretion.

Second, we are mindful that Congress legislates against the strong background of the American Rule. Unlike Britain where counsel fees are regularly awarded to the prevailing party, it is the general rule in this country that unless Congress provides otherwise, parties are to bear their own attorney's fees. Alyeska Pipeline Co. v. Wilderness Society, 421 U.S. 240, 247–262 (1975)(tracing the origins and development of the American Rule). While § 505 is one situation in which Congress has modified the American Rule to allow an award of attorney's fees in the court's discretion, we find it impossible to believe that Congress, without more, intended to adopt the British Rule. Such a bold departure from traditional practice would have surely drawn more explicit statutory language and legislative comment. Cf., Isbrandtsen Co. v. Johnson, 343 U.S. 779, 783 (1952)("Statutes which invade the common law ... are to be read with a presumption favoring the retention of long-established and familiar principles, except when a statutory purpose to the contrary is evident"). Not surprisingly, no court has held that § 505 (or its predecessor statute) adopted the British Rule.

Thus we reject both the "dual standard" adopted by several of the Courts of Appeals, and petitioner's claim that § 505 enacted the British Rule for automatic recovery of attorney's fees by the prevailing party. Prevailing plaintiffs and prevailing defendants are to be treated alike, but attorney's fees are to be awarded to prevailing parties only as a matter of the court's discretion. "There is no precise rule or formula for making these determinations", but instead equitable discretion should be exercised "in light of the considerations we have identified." Hensley v. Eckerhart, 461 U.S. 424, 436–437 (1983).[1] Because the Court of Appeals erroneously

---

[1] Some courts following the evenhanded standard have suggested several nonexclusive factors to guide courts' discretion. For example, the Third Circuit has listed several nonexclusive factors that courts should consider in making awards of attorney's fees to any prevailing party. These factors include "frivolousness, motivation, objective unreasonableness (both in the factual and in the legal components of the case) and the need in particular circumstances to advance considerations of compensation and deterrence." Lieb v. Topstone Industries, Inc., 788 F.2d 151, 156 (C.A.3 1986). We agree that such factors may be used to guide courts' discretion, so long as such factors are faithful to the pur-

held petitioner, the prevailing defendant, to a more stringent standard than that applicable to a prevailing plaintiff, its judgment is reversed and the case is remanded for further proceedings consistent with this opinion.

It is so ordered.

N O T E S

1. *Statutory damages.* What advice would you give to Davis if she wanted to elect statutory damages? In addition to those factors mentioned by the court in *Ahmed,* can you think of any other factors that are relevant to calculating a statutory damage award? How would a court calculate the defendant's profits and savings and the plaintiff's lost revenues under the facts of the Principal Problem?

Where an infringer proves that she was not aware of and had no reason to believe that her acts constituted infringement, a statutory damages award can be reduced to an amount not less than $200. Conversely, a court can increase awards involving willful conduct on the part of the defendant to a sum of up to $100,000. Do you think Davis would be able to get increased statutory damages on the grounds that WJN acted willfully? Aside from a showing of willfulness, can you think of any other factors that are relevant to a court's decision to increase the amount of statutory damages?

Suppose CBS, rather than WJN, had broadcast 22 seconds of the fight. Should CBS' broadcast be regarded as a single infringement, notwithstanding the involvement of each local broadcasting station?

2. *Actual damages and infringer's profits.* If a plaintiff elects to recover actual instead of statutory damages, the statute provides that the plaintiff also can recover "any profits of the infringer that are attributable to the infringement and are not taken into account in computing the actual damages."[9] The theory behind allowing both actual damages and the infringer's profits is "that some types of infringement inflict more harm to the copyright owner than the benefit reaped by the infringer, for example, where the infringer's minimal use forecloses a broader market ... or where the copyright owner's provable profit margin is greater than the infringer's."[10] A double recovery, however, is strictly prohibited. Further, the statute provides that "[i]n establishing the infringer's profits, the copyright owner is required to present proof only of the infringer's gross revenue, and the infringer is required to prove his or her deductible expenses and

poses of the Copyright Act and are applied to prevailing plaintiffs and defendants in an evenhanded manner.

[9] § 504(b).

[10] Pfanenstiel Architects, Inc. v. Chouteau Petroleum Co., 978 F.2d 430, 432 (8th Cir.1992). This measure of recovery also in-

sures "that infringers are not able to retain some benefit flowing from their wrongful conduct that is not fully taken into account in the award of actual damages." U.S. Payphone, Inc. v. Executives Unlimited of Durham, Inc., 781 F.Supp. 412, 413 (M.D.N.C. 1991).

the elements of profit attributable to factors other than the copyrighted work."[11] Some courts, however, preclude a deduction of the defendant's overhead from its gross revenue in cases involving willful infringements.[12] When an infringer's profits are attributable to many factors other than its infringement, apportionment can become a difficult task. The defendant maintains the burden of proving the contribution to profits of these additional elements.[13]

The statute neither defines "actual damages" nor mandates a formula for their computation. In calculating actual damages, the primary measure of recovery is the diminishment of the market value of the plaintiff's work as a result of the infringement. In some instances, the determination of this market value is relatively uncomplicated. For example, in Cream Records v. Jos. Schlitz Brewing Co.,[14] in which a brewing company infringed a copyrighted song by using it in a television commercial, the evidence disclosed that the market value of a one-year license to use the music in question was eighty thousand dollars. Frequently, however, cases present no clear-cut evidence, and courts must rely on more indirect means of computing actual damages.

One common approach is to award a plaintiff the profits he would have received but for the defendant's infringement. Because the types of property subject to copyright protection vary considerably, courts have employed several different methods of computing a plaintiff's lost profits. When the infringed property is one of several similar items that a plaintiff produces, some courts have measured the plaintiff's lost profits by the difference between sales of the infringed item and the average sales of all of the plaintiff's other products.[15] Another means of computing a plaintiff's lost profits entails calculating the average revenue the plaintiff earned for a period of time prior to the infringement, and then subtracting from this

---

[11] § 504(b).

[12] See, e.g., Saxon v. Blann, 968 F.2d 676, 681 (8th Cir.1992). See also Allen–Myland, Inc. v. International Business Machines Corp., 770 F.Supp. 1014, 1024–25 (E.D.Pa.1991)(discussing pertinent authority on this point and examining the concept of "willfulness" in the statutory damage context as a basis for defining "willfulness" in the context of determining whether overhead should be deducted from a defendant's profits).

[13] See Walker v. Forbes, Inc., 28 F.3d 409 (4th Cir.1994)(noting that the "Copyright Act draws the line between under and overdeterrence by establishing the damages provided."); Frank Music Corp. v. Metro–Goldwyn–Mayer, Inc., 772 F.2d 505, 518 (9th Cir.1985)(in case under 1909 Act involving infringement of six minutes of music in a 100 minute musical revue, appellate court re-

manded to the district court to reconsider its apportionment of profits and to fully explain its methodology). Mathematical exactness is unnecessary, but "a reasonable and just apportionment of profits is required." Id. at 518. Frank Music also allowed for the apportionment of both the direct profits from the revue as well as indirect profits from the hotel and casino sponsoring the revue. The Ninth Circuit also reviewed the district court's post-remand decision regarding profits (see 886 F.2d 1545 (9th Cir.1989)).

[14] 754 F.2d 826, 827 (9th Cir.1985).

[15] See Stevens Linen Assocs. v. Mastercraft Corp., 656 F.2d 11, 15 (2d Cir.1981)(woven upholstery fabrics at issue); Big Seven Music Corp. v. Lennon, 554 F.2d 504, 509–12 (2d Cir.1977)(comparing sales of infringed album by John Lennon with sales of his other contemporary albums).

amount the revenue actually earned during the period of infringement.[16] A court also can measure the plaintiff's lost profits by measuring the defendant's sales during the infringement period to customers that had purchased from both the plaintiff and the defendant.[17] What would be the best measure of Davis' lost profits under the facts of the Principal Problem?

As *Deltak* suggests, sometimes other methods of ascertaining actual damages are more appropriate than a lost profits calculation. *Deltak* computes actual damages based on the value of use *to the infringer*, with the value of such use determined by what a willing buyer would be required to pay to a willing seller. Courts also may consider any value the plaintiff and defendant placed on the infringed work in prior negotiations.[18] In addition, courts can focus on the value of the property to the plaintiff.[19] Would any of these measures be applicable to the Principal Problem? Do you think the approach taken by the court in *Deltak* is sound?

Many types of copyrighted property not only have an immediate value but also are capable of generating future royalties. In making a damage determination, courts also must consider this contingent income as part of the overall award.

3. *Injunctive relief and the public interest.* As Abend v. MCA, Inc. suggests, a court's decision to grant injunctive relief must balance the public's interest in enjoying the protected work (or derivative works based on the protected work) against the property interest of the copyright owner. The Supreme Court in *Stewart* affirmed the merits of the Ninth Circuit's decision with respect to the infringement issue (see Assignment 9), but the Court explicitly noted that certiorari was not granted on the issue of relief and it did not discuss the lower court's decision in that regard.[20]

The public interest component can take on added significance when the defendant is a government entity. In 1990, the Copyright Remedy Clarification Act was passed, which expressly eliminated state immunity for copyright infringement. The Act now provides that states are not immune from suit and that all remedies, both at law and in equity, are available against a state or instrumentality of a state to the same extent as are available against any other "public or private entity."[21] Prior to the enactment of this amendment to the 1976 Act, several courts had held that the 1976 Act

[16] See Taylor v. Meirick, 712 F.2d 1112, 1119–21 (7th Cir.1983).

[17] See Stevens Linen Assocs. v. Mastercraft Corp., 656 F.2d 11, 15 (2d Cir.1981).

[18] See Szekely v. Eagle Lion Films, 242 F.2d 266, 268–69 (2d Cir.1957)(holding that the agreed compensation was an appropriate amount on which to base a damage award for common-law copyright infringement action brought by a screenplay writer who retained all rights and title to a manuscript).

[19] See Universal Pictures Co. v. Harold Lloyd Corp., 162 F.2d 354, 369–70 (9th Cir.1947)(observing that the owner of personal property, including literary property, may testify as to its value, and upholding the use of expert testimony to value copyrighted property).

[20] See Stewart v. Abend, 495 U.S. 207, 216, 110 S.Ct. 1750, 1757, 109 L.Ed.2d 184 (1990).

[21] See §§ 501(a) & 511. The patent scheme is similar. See the Patent and Plant Variety Protection Remedy Clarification Act, Pub. L. No. 102–560, 106 Stat. 4230 (1992), codified at 35 U.S.C.A. § 296, discussed in Assignment 24.

failed to waive the states' Eleventh Amendment immunity for being sued in federal court for damages.[22] Since federal courts have exclusive jurisdiction over copyrighted matters,[23] the immunity of state entities from copyright damage actions in federal court resulted in prospective injunctive relief against individual state officials as the only available remedy against state government defendants.[24] As an exclusive alternative, this remedy clearly was unsatisfactory since an award of prospective, injunctive relief in federal court against individual state officials required copyright owners to identify and sue the state officials before any significant damage occurred. The government's use could be complete by the time a lawsuit was brought, thus significantly diminishing the value of the copyrighted work.

With respect to infringements by the federal government, 28 U.S.C. § 1498(b) provides that a copyright owner has the exclusive remedy of suing the federal government in the Claims Court for damages.[25] Both the legislative history and judicial interpretations of this provision reveal that its theoretical basis derives from the Fifth Amendment's just compensation clause.[26] Research shows that both federal and state governmental entities frequently use copyrighted property without the owner's permission.[27] From a remedial standpoint, should a distinction be drawn between federal and state governmental entities? What about between governmental entities in general and private defendants?

4. *Attorney's fees.* Strictly speaking, *Fogerty* would not be relevant to the Principal Problem if Davis were to be the prevailing party. Still, does the Court provide any guidance regarding the question of when an award of attorney's fees is appropriate? In the Principal Problem, should either Davis or WJN (assuming the court found the broadcast was fair use) be able to recover attorney's fees? How do you think courts actually compute awards of attorney's fees?

5. *Prejudgment interest.* Some precedent exists for the award of prejudgment interest in copyright litigation, although the statute does not specifically provide for it. The theory underlying an award of interest is that such is necessary to fulfill the restitutionary nature of the monetary awards

---

[22] Richard Anderson Photography v. Brown, 852 F.2d 114, 120 (4th Cir.1988), cert. denied, 489 U.S. 1033, 109 S.Ct. 1171, 103 L.Ed.2d 229 (1989); BV Engineering v. University of California, Los Angeles, 858 F.2d 1394, 1400 (9th Cir.1988).

[23] See 28 U.S.C. § 1338(a)(providing federal district courts with original and exclusive jurisdiction over civil actions arising under federal copyright laws) and § 301 (preempting all "equivalent" state laws).

[24] The Supreme Court relaxed the application of the Eleventh Amendment immunity doctrine with respect to actions seeking pro-spective, injunctive relief against a state official for violations of federal constitutional law. Ex parte Young, 209 U.S. 123, 28 S.Ct. 441, 52 L.Ed. 714 (1908).

[25] See also § 502(a)(providing that injunctive relief is "subject to the provisions of section 1498 of Title 28").

[26] 28 U.S.C. § 1498(a) provides analogous relief to the owners of patented property for unlicensed uses by the federal government. See Assignment 23.

[27] See Kwall, Governmental Use of Copyrighted Property: The Sovereign's Prerogative, 67 Tex. L. Rev. 685 (1989).

under copyright law.[28] Some courts, however, have taken the position that prejudgment interest is unnecessary to deter copyright infringement given the other remedies available under the 1976 Act.[29]

BIBLIOGRAPHY

Saunders, Criminal Copyright Infringement and the Copyright Felony Act, 71 Denv. U. L. Rev. 671 (1994); Brown, Civil Remedies for Intellectual Property Invasions: Themes and Variations, 55 Law & Contemp. Probs. 45 (1992); Jaszi, 505 and All That—The Defendant's Dilemma, 55 Law & Contemp. Probs. 107 (1992); Woodin, Copyrights and State Liability, 76 Iowa L. Rev. 701 (1991); Owens, Impoundment Procedures Under the Copyright Act: The Constitutional Infirmities, 14 Hofstra L. Rev. 211 (1985).

[28] See Frank Music Corp. v. Metro–Goldwyn–Mayer, Inc., 886 F.2d 1545, 1552 (9th Cir.1989), cert. denied, 494 U.S. 1017, 110 S.Ct. 1321, 108 L.Ed.2d 496 (1990) (awarding prejudgment interest on the apportioned share of defendant's profits under the 1909 Act: "For the restitutionary purpose of this remedy to be served fully, the defendant generally should be required to turn over to the plaintiff not only the profits made from the use of his property, but also the interest on these profits, which can well exceed the profits themselves."); Allen–Myland, Inc. v. International Business Machines Corp., 770 F.Supp. 1014, 1029 (E.D.Pa.1991)(instructing special master to award prejudgment interest on damages in action involving infringement of computer microcode).

[29] See In Design v. K–Mart Apparel Corp., 13 F.3d 559, 569 (6th Cir.1994) (affirming district court's denial of prejudgment interest given the plaintiff's sizable damage award and its "lack of any initiative ... to shorten this litigation"); Robert R. Jones Assocs. v. Nino Homes, 858 F.2d 274, 282 (6th Cir.1988) (vacating district court's award of prejudgment interest under the 1976 Act).

PREEMPTION OF STATE LAWS: THE RIGHT OF PUBLICITY AND MISAPPROPRIATION

1. INTRODUCTION

Parallel to the federal development of intellectual property law, states have created a variety of rights in intellectual property that are generally referred to under the rubric of unfair trade practice laws. Some of these state laws were explored in Assignment 3. In this Assignment, we will revisit the doctrine of misappropriation and introduce the right of publicity for the purpose of illustrating the operation of § 301 of the 1976 Act, which addresses preemption of state laws by the federal copyright statute.

Misappropriation owes its origins to state unfair competition laws aimed at preventing the practice of "passing off": supplying consumers who demand the goods of one manufacturer with products produced by a different manufacturer; or marketing goods with trademarks, logos, symbols and labels similar to those of a competitor. States were concerned with these practices because they harmed both consumers and producers. Consumers wound up with purchases that disappointed their expectations, and producers found their extensive investments in quality, advertising, and goodwill undermined. By creating a right of action against the sale of goods with confusingly similar markings (a right that was discussed more extensively in Assignment 3), the states managed to deal with the consumers' interest rather well. The producers' interest was, however, only partially addressed because passing off claims reached only the investment captured in the product's specific marks and trade dress. To protect producers' other investments in their products against those who would reap where they had not sown, courts developed rights "against a defendant's competing use of a valuable product or idea created by the plaintiff through investment of time, effort, money and expertise."[1] Misappropriation is, in short, the intellectual property version of unjust enrichment.

The right of publicity discussed in the *Baltimore Orioles*, *Midler*, and *Presley* opinions reprinted infra is similar to misappropriation in many respects. It too protects against attempts to utilize another's investment— this time investment in a person's individual characteristics: name, like-

---

[1] See Mayer v. Josiah Wedgwood & Sons, Ltd., 601 F.Supp. 1523, 1534 (S.D.N.Y.1985). Misappropriation also is discussed in the Re- statement (Third) Of Unfair Competition § 38 (1993).

ness, and other recognizable attributes. The right of publicity is sometimes confused with the right of privacy because both are aimed at controlling the extent to which one party can use the details of the life of another. But the claims can be fundamentally different: right-of-privacy plaintiffs want to be left out of the limelight—they do not want features of their lives exploited at all. In contrast, the question in many right-of-publicity cases is *who* has the right to enjoy the values inhering in these features, the plaintiff or members of the public at large (the defendant being one example).[2]

The observation at the end of the previous paragraph, that the defendant in these state law cases stands as a proxy for the public's interest in the free availability of personal attributes, leads directly to the subject of this Assignment, for it suggests the possibility that there may be a conflict between federal intellectual property law and these state-based rights. After all, the Constitution gave to *Congress* the authority to create intellectual property law. The Copyright Clause can therefore be read as excluding the states from undertaking any activity in this field, especially activity that would tend to privatize material that would otherwise fall into the public domain. This is a sort of "dormant Copyright Clause" argument, akin to the dormant Commerce Clause doctrine familiar to general constitutional lawyers.

More often encountered are arguments to the effect that when Congress enacts copyright and patent legislation, it creates a dividing line between subject matter whose protection is in the public interest and subject matter whose lack of protection is in the public interest. If the second category of subject matter is supposed to be in the public domain, then any state's attempt to prevent free use of such subject matter must be viewed as preempted.

Although the dividing-line theory is appealing, it is equally plausible to assume that copyright and patent law were not meant to be the sole forms of protection for intellectual property rights, that states should have a role in protecting industries of local importance, and that it makes sense to offer more expansive protection—copyrights and patents—for major contributions, and less expansive state law protection for more minor contributions. The Supreme Court has vacillated somewhat on the appropriate scope of federal preemption. Two major cases, Sears, Roebuck & Co v. Stiffel Co.,[3] and Compco Co. v. Day–Brite Lighting, Inc.,[4] tend to support the position that a state may not prohibit the copying of something that

---

[2] Many right of publicity cases, however, do involve an objection on the part of the plaintiff to the exploitation itself. See, e.g., Waits v. Frito–Lay Inc., 978 F.2d 1093 (9th Cir.1992), cert. denied, 506 U.S. 1080, 113 S.Ct. 1047, 122 L.Ed.2d 355 (1993), discussed in note 6, infra following the major cases. See also Kwall, The Right of Publicity v. The First Amendment: A Property and Liability Rule Analysis, 70 Ind. L.J. 47 (1994).

The Right of Publicity is the subject of Restatement (Third) Of Unfair Competition §§ 46–49 (1993).

[3] 376 U.S. 225, 84 S.Ct. 784, 11 L.Ed.2d 661 (1964).

[4] 376 U.S. 234, 84 S.Ct. 779, 11 L.Ed.2d 669 (1964).

federal law has left unpatented or uncopyrighted. This approach, however, arguably was undermined by the Court's subsequent decision in Goldstein v. California,[5] which essentially allowed state law protection for material that "had not previously been protected under the federal copyright statute" on the theory that states should retain some control over protection of creative works of essentially local interest.[6]

Sears, Compco, and *Goldstein* were decided prior to the enactment of Section 301 of the Copyright Act which expressly sets out a test for determining whether a particular state law is preempted by the 1976 Act. The test under Section 301 has two parts. The first part of the preemption test focuses on the nature of the work protected by the state law. Specifically, preemption will not occur if the state law does not pertain to "works of authorship that are fixed in a tangible medium of expression and come within the subject matter of copyright."[7] The states, in other words, are free to regulate all works that are not protected by the copyright law because of their nature or form of expression. If a particular work is capable of copyright protection but is not fixed in a tangible medium of expression, protection may be obtained under state common law copyright. See Note 9 of Assignment 7 for a discussion of fixation.

The second part of the preemption test emphasizes the nature of the rights that the state law attempts to safeguard. If the state seeks to protect rights that are "not equivalent to any of the exclusive rights within the general scope of copyright," the state's law will not be preempted by section 301.[8] The application of the equivalency prong of the preemption test thus requires a determination whether a particular state law creates rights that are "equivalent" to any of the five rights protected by section 106 of the 1976 Act. Note that preemption of a state law will occur only if both parts of the test in section 301 are satisfied. Therefore, if a state law grants "equivalent rights" to a work that does not come within the scope of federal copyright law, no preemption will result. Similarly, a state may protect federally copyrightable works as long as such protection does not encompass rights equivalent to 1976 Act protections.

Section 301 has not, however, obviated all preemption problems in copyright law. Although Congress purported to enact an unambiguous

[5] 412 U.S. 546, 93 S.Ct. 2303, 37 L.Ed.2d 163 (1973).

[6] Id. at 568 (*Goldstein* validated a California statute protecting sound recordings, which were not then copyrightable subject matter). For a good discussion of these three decisions, see Abrams, Copyright, Misappropriation, and Preemption: Constitutional and Statutory Limits of State Law Protection, 1983 Sup. Ct. Rev. 509.

The Supreme Court took an approach similar to *Goldstein* in Kewanee Oil Co. v. Bicron Corp., 416 U.S. 470, 94 S.Ct. 1879, 40 L.Ed.2d 315 (1974), where the Court enforced state trade secrecy laws with respect to an invention falling within the class of patentable subject matter. In patent law, the preemption issue remains unresolved. *Kewanee* recently was drawn into question by Bonito Boats, Inc. v. Thunder Craft Boats, Inc., 489 U.S. 141, 109 S.Ct. 971, 103 L.Ed.2d 118 (1989), which held preempted a Florida statute protecting boat hull designs (a matter of special concern to coastal states like Florida). See Assignment 25.

[7] § 301(a).

[8] Id.

statutory mandate concerning the issue of preemption, the following cases and materials demonstrate that it can be exceedingly difficult to apply this provision. For example, what approach should be taken with respect to subject matter that the Act has specifically excluded from protection: should it be treated the same as subject matter that is simply omitted from statutory consideration, or should the express exclusion of certain categories of works be read as placing them irretrievably in the public domain? Similarly, what about rights specifically denied to particular categories of works: can the states substitute their own judgment or are they expressly excluded from acting? The issue of preemption under § 301 has been litigated in the context of general state based actions such as fraud, breach of contract,[9] conversion[10] and tortious interference with business relationships,[11] as well as state law actions that specifically cover intellectual property (i.e., unfair competition,[12] misappropriation,[13] and the right of publicity[14]). This Assignment illustrates the difficulties surrounding the

[9] See, e.g., National Car Rental System, Inc. v. Computer Associates International Inc., 991 F.2d 426 (8th Cir.), cert. denied, ___ U.S. ___, 114 S.Ct. 176, 126 L.Ed.2d 136 (1993)(breach of contract action not preempted); Relational Design & Technology Inc. v. Data Team Corp., 23 U.S.P.Q.2d (BNA) 1074 (D.Kan.1992)(fraud and breach of contract actions not preempted); National Car Rental System Inc. v. Computer Associates International Inc., 22 U.S.P.Q.2d (BNA) 1375 (D.Minn.1992)(breach of contract action preempted); Nobel v. Bangor Hydro–Electric Co., 584 A.2d 57 (Me.1990)(breach of contract action not preempted).

[10] See, e.g., Strauss v. The Hearst Corp., 8 U.S.P.Q.2d (BNA) 1832 (S.D.N.Y.1988) (conversion action preempted); Mayer v. Josiah Wedgwood & Sons, Ltd., 601 F.Supp. 1523 (S.D.N.Y.1985)(conversion action preempted).

[11] Cf. Cassway v. Chelsea Historic Properties I, 26 U.S.P.Q.2d (BNA) 1791 (E.D.Pa.)(tortious interference with contractual relationships claim not preempted) with Aqua Bay Concepts Inc. v. Grosse Point Board of Realtors, 24 U.S.P.Q.2d (BNA) 1372 (E.D.Mich.1992)(tortious interference with contractual relationship claim preempted).

[12] See, e.g., Wilson v. Mr. Tee's, 855 F.Supp. 679, 684–85 (D.N.J.1994)(unfair competition actions involving passing off, as opposed to "imitation," are not preempted); Nester's Map & Guide Corp. v. Hagstrom, 796 F.Supp. 729 (E.D.N.Y.1992)(no preemption where public confusion under state unfair competition claim arose not only from defendant's copying of plaintiff's taxi driver's guide but also from defendant's misleading the public into buying defendant's guide instead of plaintiff's); Nash v. CBS, Inc., 704 F.Supp. 823, 833 (N.D.Ill.1989), aff'd on other grounds, 899 F.2d 1537 (7th Cir. 1990)(court held that likelihood of consumer confusion under the state Uniform Deceptive Trade Practices Act, in and of itself, is not a "qualitatively different" element to avoid preemption, but under an "objectives" analysis this state cause of action would not be preempted); Patsy Aiken Designs, Inc. v. Baby Togs, Inc., 701 F.Supp. 108, 111–112 (E.D.N.C.1988)(in unfair competition action based on defendant's copying of plaintiff's clothing designs, court held that preemption was appropriate where plaintiff simply alleged that defendant's copying caused consumer confusion; court also noted that no preemption would result if plaintiff had shown "palming off" since that action also requires an attempt to confuse consumers by misrepresentation); Motown Record Corporation v. Hormel & Co., 657 F.Supp. 1236 (C.D.Cal.1987)(unfair competition action based on defendant's unauthorized use in a commercial of plaintiff's copyrighted song and image of the singing group that had recorded the song not "qualitatively different" from copyright infringement).

[13] See Mayer v. Josiah Wedgwood & Sons, Ltd., 601 F.Supp. 1523 (S.D.N.Y.1985).

[14] See Baltimore Orioles, Inc. v. Major League Baseball Players Association and Midler v. Ford Motor Co., reprinted infra.

application of § 301 when a plaintiff attempts to bring a misappropriation or right of publicity action involving copyrighted property. An understanding of the materials that follow will require you to master not only the copyright preemption issue, but also the important state-created rights discussed herein.

2. PRINCIPAL PROBLEM

Your clients, Nisa, Shanna and Rachel Meller, own a company called Twinkle Toes which specializes in ballet costumes and other types of dancewear. Last March, they attended a live ballet in which the famous American dancer and choreographer Ilana Kaye was the featured performer. Ilana has a policy of allowing people to videotape her performances as long as they get her permission in advance. The Mellers wrote to Ilana for permission to videotape the March performance, but they never received a response. Still they videotaped one of Ilana's solo numbers with a home-type video camera so that they could enjoy her performance at home in the future. Two months later, Ilana was struck by a car and killed. Her death caused quite a stir in the arts community.

Your clients were tremendously saddened by her death and wanted to pay her a tribute. Therefore, they made several commercials for their costumes and dancewear that feature parts of the video they taped from Ilana's March performance, which turned out to be Ilana's last live performance. The commercials do not mention Ilana's name and do not state that she is endorsing any of Twinkle Toes' products. Instead, as the announcer praises the products of Twinkle Toes, the viewer is exposed to several short segments from the video that show Ilana dancing, interspersed with other unrelated scenes such as little girls getting on their ballet costumes and standing in the various ballet positions.

Ilana left a will bequeathing everything she owned to her two sons, and they are furious with your clients. They have just instituted a lawsuit against the Mellers based on copyright infringement, misappropriation, and violation of Ilana's right of publicity. Your clients now are very nervous and want your opinion on whether any of these actions could be successful. Before advising them, consider the following materials. Are there any additional facts that you may need before you can reach a conclusion respecting the probable success of any of these claims?

3. MATERIALS FOR SOLUTION OF PRINCIPAL PROBLEM

A. STATUTORY MATERIALS: §§ 106, 301, & 1101

B. CASES:

Baltimore Orioles, Inc. v. Major League Baseball Players Association

United States Court of Appeals, Seventh Circuit, 1986.
805 F.2d 663, cert. denied, 480 U.S. 941, 107 S.Ct. 1593, 94 L.Ed.2d 782 (1987)11958583;0214;87040989.

■ ESCHBACH, SENIOR CIRCUIT JUDGE.

The primary issue involved in this appeal is whether major league baseball clubs own exclusive rights to the televised performances of major league baseball players during major league baseball games.

I

This appeal arises out of a long-standing dispute between the Major League Baseball Clubs ("Clubs") and the Major League Baseball Players Association ("Players") regarding the ownership of the broadcast rights to the Players' performances during major league baseball games. After decades of negotiation concerning the allocation of revenues from telecasts of the games, the Players in May of 1982 sent letters to the Clubs, and to television and cable companies with which the Clubs had contracted, asserting that the telecasts were being made without the Players' consent and that they misappropriated the Players' property rights in their performances. The mailing of these letters led the parties to move their dispute from the bargaining table to the courtroom.

On June 14, 1982, the Clubs filed an action (entitled Baltimore Orioles, Inc. v. Major League Baseball Players Association) in the United States District Court for the Northern District of Illinois, in which they sought a declaratory judgment that the Clubs possessed an exclusive right to broadcast the games and owned exclusive rights to the telecasts.

The parties moved for summary judgment on Counts I and II of the Baltimore Orioles complaint, which concerned the Clubs' copyright and master-servant claims. On May 23, 1985, the district court granted the Clubs summary judgment on these two counts. See Baltimore Orioles, Inc. v. Major League Baseball Players Association, Copyright L. Dec. (CCH) ¶ 25,822 (N.D.Ill.1985). On June 14, 1985, the Players filed a notice of appeal from the grant of summary judgment for the Clubs in the Baltimore Orioles action.

II

* * *

B. Copyright Claim

The Clubs sought a declaratory judgment "that the telecasts of Major League Baseball games constitute copyrighted 'works made for hire' in which defendant and Major League Baseball players have no rights whatsoever." The district court found that the Clubs, not the Players, owned a copyright in the telecasts as works made for hire and that the Clubs' copyright in the telecasts preempted the Players' rights of publicity in their performances. See *Baltimore Orioles*, 1985 Copyright L. Dec. at 19,732. Accordingly, it granted summary judgment and entered final judgment for the Clubs on this claim.

* * *

[The court affirmed the district court's ruling that the Clubs own the copyright in the telecasts as works for hire.]

2. Preemption under 17 U.S.C. § 301(a)

Although the Clubs own the copyright to the telecasts of major league baseball games, the Players claim that broadcasts of these games made without their express consent violate their rights to publicity in their performances. For the reasons stated below, we hold that the Clubs' copyright in the telecasts of major league baseball games preempts the Players' rights of publicity in their game-time performances.

> Section 301(a) provides that all legal or equitable rights that are equivalent to any of the exclusive rights within the general scope of copyright as specified by section 106 in works of authorship that are fixed in a tangible medium of expression and come within the subject matter of copyright as specified by sections 102 and 103, whether created before or after that date and whether published or unpublished, are governed exclusively by this title. Thereafter, no person is entitled to any such right or equivalent right in any such work under the common law or statutes of any State.

§ 301(a).[a] This provision sets forth two conditions that both must be satisfied for preemption of a right under state law: First, the work in which the right is asserted must be fixed in tangible form and come within the subject matter of copyright as specified in § 102; Second, the right must be equivalent to any of the rights specified in § 106.

a. Section 102 test

The works in which the Players claim rights are the telecasts of major league baseball games. As established above, the telecasts are fixed in tangible form because they are recorded simultaneously with their transmission and are audiovisual works which come within the subject matter of copyright. The first condition for preemption is, therefore, satisfied.

The Players argue, however, that the works in which they claim rights are their performances, rather than the telecasts of the games in which

---

[a] Section 301(a) has been termed "the most fundamental change in the copyright system 'since its inception'." Shipley, *Publicity Never Dies; It Just Fades Away: The Right of Publicity and Federal Preemption*, 66 Cornell L. Rev. 673, 701 (1981)(quoting U.S. Copyright Office, General Guide to the Copyright Act of 1976 2:1 (1977)). Before the Copyright Act of 1976 became effective, there had been a dual system of federal statutory and state common-law copyright protection in effect in the United States since the first copyright statute in 1970. See House Report [No. 1476, 94th Cong., 2d. Sess. 52] at 129, reprinted in 1976 U.S. Code Cong. & Ad. News at 5745. Under that system, federal copyright protection was available only for published works. See Nimmer, [Nimmer on Copyright §§ 4.01–.02, (1985)]. In addition to federal copyright protection, common-law copyrights were available under state law for unpublished works, see Wheaton v. Peters, 33 U.S. (8 Peters) 591, 657 (1834), and for published works that were not afforded federal copyright protection, see Goldstein v. California, 412 U.S. 546, 569 (1973). The 1976 Act dramatically altered this dual system of copyright protection in two ways. First, as discussed above, § 102(a) extended federal copyright protection to all works fixed in any tangible medium of expression, including simultaneously recorded "live" works, whether they are published or unpublished. More importantly, however, § 301 expressly preempted rights under state law that are equivalent to any of the bundle of rights encompassed by a federal copyright.

they play, and that performances per se are not fixed in tangible form.[b] They contend that, since the works in which they assert rights are not fixed in tangible form, their rights of publicity in their performances are not subject to preemption. We disagree. Under § 101, "[a] work is 'fixed' in a tangible medium of expression when its embodiment in a copy ..., by or under the authority of the author, is sufficiently permanent and stable to permit it to be perceived, reproduced, or otherwise communicated for a period of more than transitory duration." The Players' performances are embodied in a copy, viz, the videotape of the telecast, from which the performances can be perceived, reproduced, and otherwise communicated indefinitely. Hence, their performances are fixed in tangible form, and any property rights in the performances that are equivalent to any of the rights encompassed in a copyright are preempted.

It is, of course, true that unrecorded performances per se are not fixed in tangible form. Among the many such works not fixed in tangible form are "choreography that has never been filmed or notated, an extemporaneous speech, 'original works of authorship' communicated solely through conversations or live broadcasts, and a dramatic sketch or musical composition improvised or developed from memory and without being recorded or written down." House Report at 131, reprinted in 1976 U.S. Code Cong. & Ad. News at 5747. Because such works are not fixed in tangible form, rights in such works are not subject to preemption under § 301(a). Indeed, § 301(b), which represents the obverse of § 301(a), expressly allows the states to confer common law copyright protection upon such works, and protection has been afforded to unfixed works by some states. See, e.g., Cal. Civil Code § 980 (protecting "any original work of authorship that is not fixed in any tangible medium of expression"); cf. Estate of Hemingway v. Random House, Inc., 244 N.E.2d 250 (1968)(common law copyright might be recognized in contents of an unrecorded conversation). Nonetheless, once a performance is reduced to tangible form, there is no distinction between the performance and the recording of the performance for the purpose of preemption under § 301(a). Thus, if a baseball game were not broadcast or were telecast without being recorded, the Players' performances similarly would not be fixed in tangible form and their rights of publicity would not be subject to preemption. See Nimmer § 1.08[C] (using the example of a live broadcast of a baseball game). By virtue of being videotaped, however, the Players' performances are fixed in tangible form,

---

[b] To support their argument that their performances cannot be copyrighted, the Players refer to the "Sound Recording Performance Rights Amendment," S. 1552 and H.R. 997, 96th Cong., 1st Sess. (1979), an unsuccessful attempt to amend the Copyright Act to grant certain performance rights to sound recording artists. Nevertheless, that a Congress, for a reason that we cannot discern, has not enacted an amendment has little or no bearing on the construction of a statute enacted by an earlier Congress. In this case, the failure to enact the "Sound Recording Performance Rights Amendment" does not establish that the contributions of recording artists (and, by analogy, the performances of the Players) cannot presently be copyrighted. If anything, it suggests merely that recording artist[s] are not entitled to royalties from the compulsory licensing of sound recordings.

and any rights of publicity in their performances that are equivalent to the rights contained in the copyright of the telecast are preempted.[c]

The Players also contend that to be a "work of authorship that . . . [is] fixed in a tangible medium of expression" within the scope of § 301(a), a work must be copyrightable. They assert that the works in which they claim rights, namely their performances, are not copyrightable because they lack sufficient creativity. They consequently conclude that because the works in which they claim rights are not works within the meaning of § 301(a), their rights of publicity are not subject to preemption. There is a short answer to this argument. Congress contemplated that "[a]s long as a work fits within one of the general subject matter categories of section 102 and 103, . . . [section 301(a)] prevents the States from protecting it even if it fails to achieve Federal copyright because it is too minimal or lacking in originality to qualify." House Report at 131, reprinted in 1976 U.S. Code Cong. & Ad. News at 5747.[d] Hence, § 301(a) preempts all equivalent state-law rights claimed in any work within the subject matter of copyright whether or not the work embodies any creativity. Regardless of the creativity of the Players' performances, the works in which they assert rights are copyrightable works which come within the scope of § 301(a) because of the

---

[c] An example illustrates this point. Take the case of Zacchini v. Scripps–Howard Broadcasting Co., 433 U.S. 562 (1977), in which Hugo Zacchini sued a television station for violating his right of publicity by broadcasting the entirety of his human cannonball act. *Zacchini* was decided before § 301(a) became effective, but let us suppose that the same case arises again today. Assuming that Zacchini did not videotape or otherwise record his performance, his human cannonball act would not be fixed in tangible form and could not be copyrighted. Nonetheless, because the work in which he asserts rights would not be fixed in a tangible medium of expression, his right of publicity in his performance would not be subject to preemption. Thus, if a television station were to broadcast his act, he still could sue successfully for violation of his right of publicity in his performance. Merely that the television station might videotape its telecast would not grant the station a copyright in the broadcast of Zacchini's performance or preempt Zacchini's right of publicity. To be "fixed" in tangible form, a work must be recorded "by or under the authority of the author", here Zacchini. See § 101 (definition of "fixed"). Because Zacchini did not consent to the telecast, the broadcast could not be "fixed" for the purpose of copyrightability and Zacchini's right of publicity would not be subject to preemption.

Assume, however, that Zacchini, after the fashion of championship prize fights, transmitted his live act over closed-circuit television and simultaneously recorded it for later broadcast over a cable television network, and that the satellite signal for the closed-circuit show was intercepted and re-broadcast by a television station. Zacchini sues the station for violation of his copyright and his right to publicity. He would prevail on the copyright infringement claim only. See *McBee & Bruno's, Inc.*, 792 F.2d 726 at 732 (8th Cir.1986); *WGN Continental Broadcasting Co.*, 693 F.2d 622 at 624 (7th Cir.1982). Nevertheless, because his act was videotaped, the work in which he asserts rights would be fixed in tangible form and thus copyrightable. Assuming arguendo that a right of publicity is equivalent to one of the right as encompassed in a copyright—a subject that we soon shall take up—his right of publicity in his performance would be preempted. See Shipley, Publicity Never Dies; It Just Fades Away: The Right of Publicity and Federal Preemption, 66 Cornell L. Rev. 673, 710–11 (1981).

[d] The reason that § 301(a) preempts rights claimed in works that lack sufficient creativity to be copyrightable is to prevent the states from granting protection to works which Congress has concluded should be in the public domain.

creative contributions of the individuals responsible for recording the Players' performances. Therefore, the Players' rights of publicity in their performances are preempted if they are equivalent to any of the bundle of rights encompassed in a copyright.[e]

b. Section 106 test

A right under state law is "equivalent" to one of the rights within the general scope of copyright if it is violated by the exercise of any of the rights set forth in § 106.[f] See Allied Artists Pictures Corp. v. Rhodes, 679 F.2d 656, 662–63 (6th Cir.1982), aff'g in pertinent part, 496 F.Supp. 408, 443–44 (S.D.Ohio 1980)(right is equivalent if it creates or destroys right contained in copyright). Thus, a right is equivalent to one of the rights comprised by a copyright if it "is infringed by the mere act of reproduction, performance, distribution or display." Nimmer § 1.01[B][1].

In particular, the right to "perform" an audiovisual work means the right "to show its images in any sequence or to make the sounds accompanying it audible." § 101 (definition of "perform"). Thus, the right to perform an audiovisual work encompasses the right to broadcast it. See House Report at 63, reprinted in 1976 U.S. Code Cong. & Ad. News at 5676–77 ("[A] broadcasting system is performing when it transmits . . . [a] performance . . .; a local broadcaster is performing when it transmits the network broadcast; a cable television system is performing when it retransmits the broadcast to its subscribers. . . ."). Hence, a right in a work that is conferred by state law is equivalent to the right to perform a telecast of

---

[e] The Players' rights of publicity in their performances are preempted only if they would be violated by the exercise of the Clubs' copyright in the telecasts. A player's right of publicity in his name or likeness would not be preempted if a company, without the consent of the player, used the player's name to advertise its product, cf. Cepeda v. Swift & Co., 415 F.2d 1205, 1206 (8th Cir.1969), placed the player's photograph on a baseball trading card, cf. Fleer Corp. v. Topps Chewing Gum, Inc., 658 F.2d 139, 148–49 (3d Cir.1981), cert. denied, 455 U.S. 1019 (1982); Haelan Laboratories, Inc. v. Topps Chewing Gum, Inc., 202 F.2d 866, 868 (2d Cir.1953), cert. denied, 346 U.S. 816 (1953), or marketed a game based upon the player's career statistics, cf. Uhlaender v. Henricksen, 316 F.Supp. 1277, 1282 (D.Minn. 1970).

[f] From the time it was first proposed in 1963 as part of a general revision of copyright law until it reached the floor of the House of Representatives in 1976, the language that became § 301 contained a list of causes of action that were not "equivalent" to a copyright. That list originally consisted of breach-es of trust, invasion of privacy, and deceptive trade practices including passing off and false representations, but later came to include such actions as misappropriation, breaches of contract, trespass, conversion, and defamation. Nevertheless, in response to objections by the Department of Justice, see Copyright L. Rep. (CCH) ¶ 7305 (setting forth complete text of letters), this provision was deleted in a last-minute amendment on the House floor. Because the House's debate concerning the effect of the amendment is ambiguous, if not contradictory, and because the Senate concurred without discussion in the House's version of § 301, almost any interpretation of the concept of equivalent rights can be inferred from the legislative history. Therefore, in determining whether a particular right is equivalent to a copyright, we place little weight on the deletion of the list of nonequivalent rights. For an excellent discussion of the legislative history of § 301, see Abrams, Copyright, Misappropriation, and Preemption: Constitutional and Statutory Limits of State Law Protection, 1983 Sup.Ct.Rev. 509, 537–48. See also Nimmer, § 1.01 B[1].

that work if the state-law right is infringed merely by broadcasting the work.

In this case, the Players claim a right of publicity in their performances. As a number of courts have held, a right of publicity in a performance is violated by a televised broadcast of the performance. See Ettore v. Philco Television Broadcasting Corp., 229 F.2d 481 (3d Cir.1956), *cert. denied*, 351 U.S. 926 (1956)(broadcast of boxing match); Sharkey v. National Broadcasting Co., 93 F.Supp. 986 (S.D.N.Y.1950)(same); Lombardo v. Doyle, Dane & Bernbach, Inc., 396 N.Y.S.2d 661 (1977)(broadcast of commercial depicting bandleader's performance); Zacchini v. Scripps–Howard Broadcasting Co., 376 N.E.2d 582 (1978), on remand from 433 U.S. 562 (1977)(broadcast of human cannonball act). Indeed, from the start of this litigation, the Players consistently have maintained that their rights of publicity permit them to control telecasts of their performances, and that televised broadcasts of their performances made without their consent violate their rights of publicity in their performances. Because the exercise of the Clubs' right to broadcast telecasts of the games infringes the Players' rights of publicity in their performances, the Players' rights of publicity are equivalent to at least one of the rights encompassed by copyright, viz., the right to perform an audiovisual work. Since the works in which the Players claim rights are fixed in tangible form and come within the subject matter of copyright, the Players' rights of publicity in their performances are preempted.

The Players argue that their rights of publicity in their performances are not equivalent to the rights contained in a copyright because rights of publicity and copyrights serve different interests.[g] In their view, the pur-

---

[g] The Players cite to four opinions to support their assertion that § 301(a) does not preempt the right of publicity. See Factors Etc., Inc. v. Pro Arts, Inc., 652 F.2d 278, 289 (2d Cir.1981)(Mansfield, J., dissenting), *cert. denied*, 456 U.S. 927 (1982); Bi–Rite Enterprises, Inc. v. Button Master, 555 F.Supp. 1188 (S.D.N.Y.1983); Apigram Publishing Co. v. Factors Etc., Inc., No. C 78–525, slip op. (N.D. Ohio July 30, 1980); Lugosi v. Universal Pictures, 603 P.2d 425, 448 (1979) (Bird, C.J., dissenting). Each opinion is premised upon an erroneous analysis of preemption. The *Factors* dissent, the *Bi–Rite* court, and the *Lugosi* dissent assert without discussion that the right of publicity is not preempted because the work that it protects—a public figure's persona—cannot be fixed in a tangible medium of expression. We disagree. Because a performance is fixed in tangible form when it is recorded, a right of publicity in a performance that has been reduced to tangible form is subject to preemption.

The *Apigram* court stated without extended discussion or citation to authority that the right of publicity is not preempted because it requires additional elements other than the reproduction, performance, distribution or display of a copyrighted work. We disagree. Congress intended that "[t]he evolving common law rights of 'privacy', 'publicity', and trade secrets and the general law of defamation and fraud, would remain unaffected [by § 301(a)] so long as the causes of action contain *elements* such as an invasion of privacy or a breach of trust or confidentiality, that are *different in kind from copyright infringement.*" House Report at 132, reprinted in 1976 U.S. Code Cong. & Ad. News at 5748 (emphasis added). Thus, a right is equivalent to a copyright if (1) it is infringed by the mere act of reproduction, performance, distribution, or display, or (2) it requires additional elements to make out a cause of action, but the additional elements do not differ in kind from those necessary for copyright infringement. See Harper & Row Publishers, Inc. v. Nation Enterprises, 723

pose of federal copyright law is to secure a benefit to the public, but the purpose of state statutory or common law concerning rights of publicity is to protect individual pecuniary interests. We disagree.

The purpose of federal copyright protection is to benefit the public by encouraging works in which it is interested. To induce individuals to undertake the personal sacrifices necessary to create such works, federal copyright law extends to the authors of such works a limited monopoly to reap the rewards of their endeavors. Contrary to the Players' contention, the interest underlying the recognition of the right of publicity also is the promotion of performances that appeal to the public. The reason that state law protects individual pecuniary interests is to provide an incentive to performers to invest the time and resources required to develop such performances. In Zacchini v. Scripps–Howard Broadcasting Co., 433 U.S. 562 (1977), the principal case on which the Players rely for their assertion that different interests underlie copyright and the right to publicity,[h] the Supreme Court recognized that the interest behind federal copyright protection is the advancement of the public welfare through the encouragement of individual effort by personal gain, *id*. at 576, and that a state's interest in affording a cause of action for violation of the right to publicity "is closely analogous to the goals of patent and copyright law." *Id*. at 573. Because the right of publicity does not differ in kind from copyright, the Players' rights of publicity in their performances cannot escape preemption.

In this litigation, the Players have attempted to obtain ex post what they did not negotiate ex ante. That is to say, they seek a judicial declaration that they possess a right—the right to control the telecasts of major league baseball games—that they could not procure in bargaining with the Clubs. The Players' aim is to share in the increasingly lucrative revenues derived from the sale of television rights for over-the-air broad-

F.2d 195, 201 (2d Cir.1983), aff'g in pertinent part, 501 F.Supp. 848, 852 (S.D.N.Y.1980), rev'd on other grounds, 471 U.S. 539 (1985); cf. Crow v. Wainwright, 720 F.2d 1224, 1226 (11th Cir.1983)(publication with scienter not qualitatively different), *cert. denied*, 469 U.S. 819 (1984); Mayer v. Josiah Wedgwood & Sons, Ltd., 601 F.Supp. 1523, 1535 (S.D.N.Y.1985)(reproduction with intent, knowledge, or commercial immorality not different in kind)(discussing cases); Rand McNally & Co. v. Fleet Management Systems, Inc., 591 F.Supp. 726, 739 (N.D.Ill.1983)(publication with commercial immorality not qualitatively different). Contrary to the belief of the *Apigram* court, the right of publicity does not require an invasion of personal privacy to make out a cause of action. It is true that the rights of publicity and of privacy evolved from similar origins; however, whereas the right of privacy pro-

tects against intrusions on seclusion, public disclosure of private facts, and casting an individual in a false light in the public eye, the right of publicity protects against the unauthorized exploitation of names, likenesses, personalities, and performances that have acquired value for the very reason that they are known to the public. Because the right of publicity does not require a qualitatively different additional element, it is equivalent to a copyright and is preempted to the extent that it is claimed in a tangible work within the subject matter of copyright.

[h] We note that, in an opinion that the Players cite as support for their assertion, California Supreme Court Chief Justice Bird acknowledged that federal copyright protection and recognition of the right of publicity serve similar purposes. See Lugosi v. Universal Pictures, 603 P.2d 425, 441–42 (1979)(Bird, C.J. dissenting).

casts by local stations and national networks and for distribution by subscription and pay cable services. Contrary to the Players' contention, the effect of this decision is not to grant the Clubs perpetual rights to the Players' performances. The Players remain free to attain their objective by bargaining with the Clubs for a contractual declaration that the Players own a joint or an exclusive interest in the copyright of the telecasts.[i]

* * *

For the reasons stated above, the district court's judgment is AFFIRMED with respect to the Club's copyright claim. . . .

Midler v. Ford Motor Co.

United States Court of Appeals, Ninth Circuit, 1988.
849 F.2d 460.

■ NOONAN, CIRCUIT JUDGE.

This case centers on the protectibility of the voice of a celebrated chanteuse from commercial exploitation without her consent. Ford Motor Company and its advertising agency, Young & Rubicam, Inc., in 1985 advertised the Ford Lincoln Mercury with a series of nineteen 30 or 60 second television commercials in what the agency called "The Yuppie Campaign", The aim was to make an emotional connection with Yuppies, bringing back memories of when they were in college. Different popular songs of the seventies were sung on each commercial. The agency tried to get "the original people", that is, the singers who had popularized the songs, to sing them. Failing in that endeavor in ten cases the agency had the songs sung by "sound alikes." Bette Midler, the plaintiff and appellant here, was done by a sound alike.

Midler is a nationally known actress and singer. She won a Grammy as early as 1973 as the Best New Artist of that year. Records made by her since then have gone Platinum and Gold. She was nominated in 1979 for an Academy award for Best Female Actress in The Rose, in which she portrayed a pop singer. Newsweek in its June 30, 1986 issue described her as an "outrageously original singer/comedian", Time hailed her in its March 2, 1987 issue as "a legend" and "the most dynamic and poignant singer-actress of her time."

When Young & Rubicam was preparing the Yuppie Campaign it presented the commercial to its client by playing an edited version of Midler singing "Do You Want To Dance", taken from the 1973 Midler album, "The Divine Miss M." After the client accepted the idea and form of the commercial, the agency contacted Midler's manager, Jerry Edelstein.

---

[i] The Players also are at liberty to attempt to negotiate a contractual limitation excluding performances before broadcast audiences from their scope of employment. Cf. Brinkley v. Casablancas, 438 N.Y.S.2d 1004 (1981)(model who consented to be photographed for certain posters and to filming of modeling session for broadcasts on cable television held to possess cause for action for violation of her right of publicity when additional unauthorized posters were made from photographs taken at the modeling session).

The conversation went as follows: "Hello, I am Craig Hazen from Young and Rubicam. I am calling you to find out if Bette Midler would be interested in doing ...?" Edelstein: "Is it a commercial?" "Yes." "We are not interested."

Undeterred, Young & Rubicam sought out Ula Hedwig whom it knew to have been one of "the Harlettes" a backup singer for Midler for ten years. Hedwig was told by Young & Rubicam that "they wanted someone who could sound like Bette Midler's recording of [Do You Want To Dance.]" She was asked to make a "demo" tape of the song if she was interested. She made an a capella demo and got the job.

At the direction of Young & Rubicam, Hedwig then made a record for the commercial. The Midler record of "Do You Want To Dance" was first played to her. She was told to "sound as much as possible like the Bette Midler record", leaving out only a few "aahs" unsuitable for the commercial. Hedwig imitated Midler to the best of her ability.

After the commercial was aired Midler was told by "a number of people" that it "sounded exactly" like her record of "Do You Want To Dance." Hedwig was told by "many personal friends" that they thought it was Midler singing the commercial. Ken Fritz, a personal manager in the entertainment business not associated with Midler, declares by affidavit that he heard the commercial on more than one occasion and thought Midler was doing the singing.

Neither the name nor the picture of Midler was used in the commercial; Young & Rubicam had a license from the copyright holder to use the song. At issue in this case is only the protection of Midler's voice. The district court described the defendants' conduct as that "of the average thief." They decided, "If we can't buy it, we'll take it." The court nonetheless believed there was no legal principle preventing imitation of Midler's voice and so gave summary judgment for the defendants. Midler appeals.

The First Amendment protects much of what the media do in the reproduction of likenesses or sounds. A primary value is freedom of speech and press. Time, Inc. v. Hill, 385 U.S. 374, 388 (1967). The purpose of the media's use of a person's identity is central. If the purpose is "informative or cultural" the use is immune; "if it serves no such function but merely exploits the individual portrayed, immunity will not be granted." Felcher and Rubin, "Privacy, Publicity and the Portrayal of Real People by the Media", 88 Yale L.J. 1577, 1596 (1979). Moreover, federal copyright law preempts much of the area. "Mere imitation of a recorded performance would not constitute a copyright infringement even where one performer deliberately sets out to simulate another's performance as exactly as possible." Notes of Committee on the Judiciary, 17 U.S.C.A. § 114(b). It is in the context of these First Amendment and federal copyright distinctions that we address the present appeal.

Nancy Sinatra once sued Goodyear Tire and Rubber Company on the basis of an advertising campaign by Young & Rubicam featuring "These Boots Are Made For Walkin'", a song closely identified with her; the female singers of the commercial were alleged to have imitated her voice and style and to have dressed and looked like her. The basis of Nancy Sinatra's complaint was unfair competition; she claimed that the song and the arrangement had acquired "a secondary meaning" which, under California law, was protectible. This court noted that the defendants "had paid a very substantial sum to the copyright proprietor to obtain the license for the use of the song and all of its arrangements." To give Sinatra damages for their use of the song would clash with federal copyright law. Summary judgment for the defendants was affirmed. Sinatra v. Goodyear Tire & Rubber Co., 435 F.2d 711, 717–718 (9th Cir.1970), *cert. denied*, 402 U.S. 906 (1971). If Midler were claiming a secondary meaning to "Do You Want To Dance" or seeking to prevent the defendants from using that song, she would fail like Sinatra. But that is not this case. Midler does not seek damages for Ford's use of "Do You Want To Dance", and thus her claim is not preempted by federal copyright law. Copyright protects "original works of authorship fixed in any tangible medium of expression." § 102(a). A voice is not copyrightable. The sounds are not "fixed." What is put forward as protectible here is more personal than any work of authorship.

Bert Lahr once sued Adell Chemical Co. for selling Lestoil by means of a commercial in which an imitation of Lahr's voice accompanied a cartoon of a duck. Lahr alleged that his style of vocal delivery was distinctive in pitch, accent, inflection, and sounds. The First Circuit held that Lahr had stated a cause of action for unfair competition, that it could be found "that defendant's conduct saturated plaintiff's audience, curtailing his market." Lahr v. Adell Chemical Co., 300 F.2d 256, 259 (1st Cir.1962). That case is more like this one. But we do not find unfair competition here. One-minute commercials of the sort the defendants put on would not have saturated Midler's audience and curtailed her market. Midler did not do television commercials. The defendants were not in competition with her.

California Civil Code section 3344 is also of no aid to Midler. The statute affords damages to a person injured by another who uses the person's "name, voice, signature, photograph or likeness, in any manner." The defendants did not use Midler's name or anything else whose use is prohibited by the statute. The voice they used was Hedwig's, not hers. The term "likeness" refers to a visual image not a vocal imitation. The statute, however, does not preclude Midler from pursuing any cause of action she may have at common law; the statute itself implies that such common law causes of action do exist because it says its remedies are merely "cumulative." *Id.* § 3344(g).

The companion statute protecting the use of a deceased person's name, voice, signature, photograph or likeness states that the rights it recognizes are "property rights." *Id.* § 990(b). By analogy the common law rights are also property rights. Appropriation of such common law rights is a tort in California. Motschenbacher v. R.J. Reynolds Tobacco Co., 498 F.2d 821 (9th Cir.1974). In that case what the defendants used in their television commercial for Winston cigarettes was a photograph of a famous professional racing driver's racing car. The number of the car was changed and a winglike device known as a "spoiler" was attached to the car; the car's features of white pinpointing, an oval medallion, and solid red coloring were retained. The driver, Lothar Motschenbacher, was in the car but his features were not visible. Some persons, viewing the commercial, correctly inferred that the car was his and that he was in the car and was therefore endorsing the product. The defendants were held to have invaded a "proprietary interest" of Motschenbacher in his own identity. *Id.* at 825.

Midler's case is different from Motschenbacher's. He and his car were physically used by the tobacco company's ad; he made part of his living out of giving commercial endorsements. But, as Judge Koelsch expressed it in *Motschenbacher*, California will recognize an injury from "an appropriation of the attributes of one's identity." *Id.* at 824. It was irrelevant that Motschenbacher could not be identified in the ad. The ad suggested that it was he. The ad did so by emphasizing signs or symbols associated with him. In the same way the defendants here used an imitation to convey the impression that Midler was singing for them.

Why did the defendants ask Midler to sing if her voice was not of value to them? Why did they studiously acquire the services of a sound-alike and instruct her to imitate Midler if Midler's voice was not of value to them? What they sought was an attribute of Midler's identity. Its value was what the market would have paid for Midler to have sung the commercial in person.

A voice is more distinctive and more personal than the automobile accouterments protected in *Motschenbacher*. A voice is as distinctive and personal as a face. The human voice is one of the most palpable ways identity is manifested. We are all aware that a friend is at once known by a few words on the phone. At a philosophical level it has been observed that with the sound of a voice, "the other stands before me." D. Ihde, Listening and Voice, 77 (1976). A fortiori, these observations hold true of singing, especially singing by a singer of renown. The singer manifests herself in the song. To impersonate her voice is to pirate her identity.

We need not and do not go so far as to hold that every imitation of a voice to advertise merchandise is actionable. We hold only that when a distinctive voice of a professional singer is widely known and is deliberately imitated in order to sell a product, the sellers have appropriated what is not theirs and have committed a tort in California. Midler has made a showing, sufficient to defeat summary judgment, that the defendants here for their own profit in selling their product did appropriate part of her identity.

Reversed and remanded for trial.

State, Ex Rel. The Elvis Presley International Memorial Foundation v. Crowell

Court of Appeals, Tennessee, 1987.
733 S.W.2d 89.

■ KOCH, JUDGE.

This appeal involves a dispute between two not-for-profit corporations concerning their respective rights to use Elvis Presley's name as part of their corporate names. The case began when one corporation filed an unfair competition action in the Chancery Court for Davidson County to dissolve the other corporation and to prevent it from using Elvis Presley's name. Elvis Presley's estate intervened on behalf of the defendant corporation. It asserted that it had given the defendant corporation permission to use Elvis Presley's name and that it had not given similar permission to the plaintiff corporation.

The trial court determined that Elvis Presley's right to control his name and image descended to his estate at his death and that the Presley estate had the right to control the commercial exploitation of Elvis Presley's name and image. Thus, the trial court granted the defendant corporation's motion for summary judgment and dismissed the complaint.

The plaintiff corporation has appealed. Its primary assertion is that there is no descendible right of publicity in Tennessee and that Elvis Presley's name and image entered into the public domain when he died. It also asserts that the trial court should not have granted a summary judgment because there are disputed factual issues and that the trial court should not have permitted the corporation representing Elvis Presley's estate to intervene. We concur with the trial court's determination that Elvis Presley's right of publicity is descendible under Tennessee law. However, for the reasons stated herein, we vacate the summary judgment and remand the case for further proceedings.

I

Elvis Presley's career is without parallel in the entertainment industry. From his first hit record in 1954 until his death in 1977, he scaled the heights of fame and success that only a few have attained. His twenty-three year career as a recording star, concert entertainer and motion picture idol brought him international recognition and a devoted following in all parts of the nation and the world.

Elvis Presley was aware of this recognition and sought to capitalize on it during his lifetime. He and his business advisors entered into agreements granting exclusive commercial licenses throughout the world to use his name and likeness in connection with the marketing and sale of numerous consumer items. As early as 1956, Elvis Presley's name and likeness could be found on bubble gum cards, clothing, jewelry and numerous other items. The sale of Elvis Presley memorabilia has been described as the greatest barrage of merchandise ever aimed at the teenage set.[a] It earned millions of dollars for Elvis Presley, his licensees and business associates.

Elvis Presley's death on August 16, 1977 did not decrease his popularity. If anything it preserved it. Now Elvis Presley is an entertainment legend, somewhat larger than life, whose memory is carefully preserved by his fans, the media and his estate.

---

[a] R. Cranor, Elvis Collectibles 4 (1983).

The demand for Elvis Presley merchandise was likewise not diminished by his death. The older memorabilia are now collector's items. New consumer items have been authorized and are now being sold. Elvis Presley Enterprises, Inc., a corporation formed by the Presley estate, has licensed seventy-six products bearing his name and likeness and still controls numerous trademark registrations and copyrights. Graceland, Elvis Presley's home in Memphis, is now a museum that attracts approximately 500,000 paying visitors a year. Elvis Presley Enterprises, Inc. also sells the right to use portions of Elvis Presley's filmed or televised performances. These marketing activities presently bring in approximately fifty million dollars each year and provide the Presley estate with approximately $4.6 million in annual revenue. The commercial exploitation of Elvis Presley's name and likeness continues to be a profitable enterprise. It is against this backdrop that this dispute between these two corporations arose.

A group of Elvis Presley fans approached Shelby County officials sometime in 1979 concerning the formation of a group to support a new trauma center that was part of the Memphis and Shelby County hospital system. This group, calling themselves the Elvis Presley International Memorial Foundation, sought a charter as a Tennessee not-for-profit corporation in October, 1980. The Secretary of State denied their application on November 12, 1980 stating that "the name Elvis Presley cannot be used in the charter."

Lawyers representing the group of fans and the Presley estate met to discuss the group's use of Elvis Presley's name following the Secretary of State's rejection of the charter application. In December, 1980, the Presley estate and its trademark counsel formally declined to give the group the unrestricted right to use Elvis Presley's name and likeness. However, the Presley estate offered the group a royalty-free license to use Elvis Presley's name and likeness if the group agreed to abide by eight conditions limiting the group's activities. The group declined the offer of a royalty-free license.

The Presley estate incorporated Elvis Presley Enterprises, Inc. on February 24, 1981. Two days later on February 26, 1981, the Secretary of State, reversing its original decision, granted the fan group's renewed application and issued a corporate charter to the Elvis Presley International Memorial Foundation (International Foundation). The International Foundation raises funds by charging membership fees and dues and by sponsoring an annual banquet in Memphis. It uses its funds to support the trauma center of the new City of Memphis Hospital which was named after Elvis Presley and to provide an annual award of merit.

The Presley estate and Elvis Presley Enterprises, Inc. incorporated the Elvis Presley Memorial Foundation, Inc. (Foundation) as a Tennessee not-for-profit corporation on May 14, 1985. The Foundation is soliciting funds from the public to construct a fountain in the shopping center across the street from Elvis Presley's home.

The International Foundation's heretofore amicable relationship with the Presley estate and Elvis Presley Enterprises, Inc. deteriorated after the formation of the Foundation. On July 17, 1985, the International Foundation filed this action seeking to dissolve the Foundation and to enjoin it using a deceptively similar name.

II

* * *

[In this part of the opinion, the court affirmed the trial court's determination that Elvis Presley Enterprises should be allowed to intervene as a defendant.]

III

Elvis Presley's Right of Publicity

We are dealing in this case with an individual's right to capitalize upon the commercial exploitation of his name and likeness and to prevent others from doing so without his consent. This right, now commonly referred to as the right of publicity, is still evolving and is only now beginning to step out of the shadow of its more well known cousin, the right of privacy.

The confusion between the right of privacy and the right of publicity has caused one court to characterize the state of the law as a "haystack in a hurricane." Ettore v. Philco Television Broadcasting Corp., 229 F.2d 481, 485 (3d Cir.1956). This confusion will not retard our recognition of the right of publicity because Tennessee's common law tradition, far from being static, continues to grow and to accommodate the emerging needs of modern society.

A

The right of privacy owes its origin to Samuel Warren's and Louis Brandeis' now famous 1890 law review article. Warren & Brandeis, The Right to Privacy, 4 Harv. L. Rev. 193 (1890). The authors were concerned with the media's intrusion into the affairs of private citizens and wrote this article to vindicate each individual's "right to be left alone." The privacy interest they sought to protect was far different from a celebrity's interest in controlling and exploiting the economic value of his name and likeness.

Writing in 1890, Warren and Brandeis could not have foreseen today's commercial exploitation of celebrities. They did not anticipate the changes that would be brought about by the growth of the advertising, motion picture, television and radio industries. American culture outgrew their concept of the right of privacy and soon began to push the common law to recognize and protect new and different rights and interests.

It would be difficult for any court today, especially one sitting in Music City U.S.A. practically in the shadow of the Grand Ole Opry, to be unaware of the manner in which celebrities exploit the public's recognition of their name and image. The stores selling Elvis Presley tee shirts, Hank Williams, Jr. bandannas or Barbara Mandrell satin jackets are not selling clothing as much as they are selling the celebrities themselves. We are asked to buy the shortening that makes Loretta Lynn's pie crusts flakier or to buy the same insurance that Tennessee Ernie Ford has or to eat the sausage that Jimmy Dean makes.

There are few every day activities that have not been touched by celebrity merchandising. This, of course, should come as no surprise. Celebrity endorsements are extremely valuable in the promotion of goods and services. Carson v. Here's Johnny Portable Toilets, Inc., 698 F.2d 831, 834 (6th Cir.1983). They increase audience appeal and thus make the commodity or service more sellable. Uhlaender v. Henricksen, 316 F.Supp. 1277, 1278 (D.Minn.1970). These endorsements are of great economic value to celebrities and are now economic reality.

The first decision to recognize the right of publicity as a right independent from the right of privacy was Haelan Laboratories, Inc. v. Topps Chewing Gum, Inc., 202 F.2d 866 (2d Cir.)., *cert. denied*, 346 U.S. 816 (1953). The United States Court of Appeals for the Second Circuit stated:

> This right might be called a "right of publicity." For it is common knowledge that many prominent persons (especially actors and ball-players), far from having their feelings bruised through public exposure of their likenesses, would feel sorely deprived if they no longer received money for authorizing advertisements, popularizing their countenances, displayed in newspapers, magazines, busses, trains and subways. This right of publicity would usually yield them no money unless it could be made the subject of an exclusive grant which barred any other advertiser from using their pictures. Haelan Laboratories, Inc. v. Topps Chewing Gum, Inc., 202 F.2d 866, 868 (2d Cir.1953).

The concept of an independent right of publicity did not achieve immediate recognition. Dean Prosser, in his authoritative discussions of the right of privacy, continued to include the right of publicity as one of the four distinct interests protected by the right of privacy. W. Prosser, Handbook of the Law of Torts § 97, at 637 & 639 (2d ed. 1955). In his later writings, Prosser characterized the right of publicity as

> an exclusive right in the individual plaintiff to a species of trade name, his own, and a kind of trade mark in his likeness. It seems quite pointless to dispute over whether such a right is to be classified as "property"; it is at least clearly proprietary in nature.

See also W. Keeton, Prosser and Keeton on the Law of Torts § 117, at 854 (5th ed. 1984).

The Restatement (Second) of Torts adopted Prosser's analytic conception of the scope of the right of privacy. Restatement (Second) of Torts § 652A (1976) embodies his four right of privacy categories. However, the American Law Institute recognized that the nexus between the right of publicity and the other three categories is tenuous. Restatement (Second) of Torts § 652A(2) comm.b (1976). Based upon this difference, the Restatement (Second) of Torts § 6521 (1976) recognizes that the right of publicity may be descendible even if the other categories are not.

The legal experts have consistently called for the recognition of the right of publicity as a separate and independent right.[b] In 1977, the United States Supreme Court recognized that the right of publicity was distinct from the right of privacy. Zacchini v. Scripps–Howard Broadcasting Co., 433 U.S. 562, 571–74 (1977). Now, courts in other jurisdictions uniformly hold that the right of publicity should be considered as a free standing right independent from the right of privacy. Baltimore Orioles, Inc. v. Major League Baseball Players Association, 805 F.2d 663, 677–78 n.26 (7th Cir.1986), petition for cert. filed, 55 U.S.L.W. 3545 (U.S. Jan. 27, 1987); Carson v. Here's Johnny Portable Toilets, Inc., 698 F.2d 831, 834 (6th Cir.1983); Martin Luther King, Jr. Center for Social Change, Inc. v. American Heritage Products, Inc., 694 F.2d 674, 674–75 (11th Cir.1983); Estate of Elvis Presley v. Russen, 513 F.Supp. 1339, 1353 (D.N.J.1981); Martin Luther King, Jr. Center for Social Change, Inc. v. American Heritage Products, Inc., 296 S.E.2d 697, 703 (1982); and House v. Sports Films & Talents, Inc., 351 N.W.2d 684, 685 (Minn.App.1984).

B

The status of Elvis Presley's right of publicity since his death has been the subject of four proceedings in the Federal courts. The conflicting decisions in these cases mirror the difficulty other courts have experienced in dealing with the right of publicity.[c]

The first case originated in Tennessee and involved the sale of pewter statutes of Elvis Presley without the exclusive licensee's permission. The United States District Court recognized Elvis Presley's independent right of publicity and held that it had descended to the Presley estate under Tennessee law. Memphis Development Foundation v. Factors, Etc. Inc., 441 F.Supp. 1323, 1330 (W.D.Tenn.1977). The United States Court of Appeals for the Sixth Circuit reversed. Apparently without considering Tennessee law, the court held that Tennessee courts would find that the right of publicity would not survive a celebrity's death. Memphis Development Foundation v. Factors, Etc., Inc., 616 F.2d 956, 958 (6th Cir.1980), *cert. denied*, 449 U.S. 953 (1980).

The second and third cases originated in New York and were originally decided under New York law. On two successive days, Judge Charles H. Tenney recognized Elvis Presley's right of publicity and held that it descended at death like any other intangible property right. Factors Etc. Inc. v. Creative Card Co., 444 F.Supp. 279, 284 (S.D.N.Y.1977) and Factors Etc., Inc. v. Pro Arts, Inc., 444 F.Supp. 288, 290 (S.D.N.Y.1977). Pro Arts, Inc. appealed, and the United States Court of Appeals for the Second

[b] Halpern, The Right of Publicity: Commercial Exploitation of the Associative Value of Personality, 39 Vand. L. Rev. 1199, 1249 (1986); Kwall, Is Independence Day Dawning for the Right of Publicity?, 17 U.C.D. L. Rev. 191, 254 (1983); Hoffman, The Right of Publicity–Heirs' Right, Advertisers Windfall, or Courts' Nightmare?, 31 DePaul L. Rev. 1, 44 (1981); Gordon, Right of Property in Name, Likeness, Personality and History, 55 Nw. L. Rev. 553, 611 (1960); and Nimmer, The Right of Publicity, 19 Law & Contemp. Probs. 203, 216 (1954).

[c] Halpern, The Right of Publicity: Commercial Exploitation of the Associative Value of Personality, 39 Vand. L. Rev. 1199, 1223–29 (1986).

Circuit, applying New York law, agreed that Elvis Presley's right of publicity survived his death and remanded the case. Factors Etc., Inc. v. Pro Arts, Inc., 579 F.2d 215, 221 (2d Cir.1978), *cert. denied*, 440 U.S. 908 (1979).

The dispute between Factors, Etc., Inc. and Pro Arts, Inc. did not end. On remand, Judge Tenney permanently enjoined Pro Arts from making any commercial use of Elvis Presley's name and likeness. Pro Arts, Inc. again appealed to the United States Court of Appeals for the Second Circuit. This time Pro Arts insisted that the controversy was governed by Tennessee law and that the United States Court of Appeals for the Sixth Circuit's opinion in Memphis Development Foundation v. Factors, Etc., Inc. should control.

The United States Court of Appeals for the Second Circuit agreed that Tennessee law controlled the case. While it expressly disagreed with the Sixth Circuit's holding in Memphis Development Foundation v. Factors, Etc., Inc. it concluded that it was required to accept the Sixth Circuit's decision as controlling authority. Factors Etc., Inc. v. Pro Arts, Inc., 652 F.2d 278, 282–83 (2d Cir.1981), *cert. denied*, 456 U.S. 927 (1982).[d]

The fourth case originated in New Jersey and involved an Elvis Presley impersonator. Applying New Jersey law, the United States District Court recognized Elvis Presley's right of publicity and held that it would be descendible under New Jersey law. Estate of Elvis Presley v. Russen, 513 F.Supp. 1339, 1354–55 (D.N.J.1981).

The courts in each of these cases recognized the existence of Elvis Presley's right of publicity. All the courts, except one, also recognized that this right was descendible upon Elvis Presley's death. The reasoning employed by the United States Court of Appeals for the Sixth Circuit to deny the descendibility of Elvis Presley's right of publicity has not been widely followed. The United States Court of Appeals for the Second Circuit specifically disagreed with it. Factors Etc., Inc. v. Pro Arts, Inc., 652 F.2d 278, 282 (2d Cir.1981). It has also been consistently criticized in the legal literature.[e]

---

[d] The United States Court of Appeals for the Second Circuit continued to acquiesce in its decision after conflicting unreported decisions by Tennessee trial courts were brought to its attention. Factors Etc., Inc. v. Pro Arts, Inc., 701 F.2d 11, 12 (2d Cir.1983).

[e] Halpern, The Right of Publicity: Commercial Exploitation of the Associative Value of Personality, 39 Vand. L. Rev. 1199, 1225 (1986); McLane, The Right of Publicity: Dispelling Survivability, Preemption and First Amendment Myths Threatening to Eviscerate a Recognized State Right, 20 Cal. W. L. Rev. 415, 420–22 (1984); Kwall, Is Independence Day Dawning for the Right of Publicity?, 17 U.C.D. L. Rev. 191, 212–14 (1983)

["ignored the most compelling rationale for a descendible right of publicity"]; Hoffman, The Right of Publicity–Heirs' Right, Advertisers' Windfall, or Courts' Nightmare?, 31 DePaul L. Rev. 1, 37–3d (1981) ["display[s] a lack of understanding of the underlying social interests involved in recognizing and protecting the right of publicity"]; Felcher & Rubin, The Descendibility of the Right of Publicity: Is There Commercial Life After Death?, 89 Yale L. J. 1125, 1132 (1980) ["harsh"]; Comment, Inheritability of the Right of Publicity Upon the Death of the Famous, 33 Vand. L. Rev. 1251, 1261 (1980) ["unpersuasive" and "unconvincing"]; and Comment, Torts–Right of Publicity–Descendibility of a Celebrity's Right to Benefit from Fame, 47 Tenn. L.

C

The appellate courts of this State have had little experience with the right of publicity. The Tennessee Supreme Court has never recognized it as part of our common law or has never undertaken to define its scope. However, the recognition of individual property rights is deeply embedded in our jurisprudence. These rights are recognized in Article I, Section 8 of the Tennessee Constitution and have been called "absolute" by the Tennessee Supreme Court. Stratton Claimants v. Morris Claimants, 15 S.W. 87, 90 (1891). This Court has noted that the right of property "has taken deep root in this country and there is now no substantial dissent from it." Davis v. Mitchell, 178 S.W.2d 889, 910 (1943).

The concept of the right of property is multi-faceted. It has been described as a bundle of rights or legally protected interests. These rights or interests include: (1) the right of possession, enjoyment and use; (2) the unrestricted right of disposition; and (3) the power of testimonial disposition.

In its broadest sense, property includes all rights that have value. See R. Brown, The Law of Personal Property § 1.7, at 11 (3d ed. 1975). It embodies all the interests a person has in land and chattels that are capable of being possessed and controlled to the exclusion of others. Watkins v. Wyatt, 68 Tenn. (9 Baxt). 250, 255 (1877) and Townsend v. Townsend, 7 Tenn. (Peck) 1, 17 (1821). Chattels include intangible personal property such as choses in action or other enforceable rights of possession.

Our courts have recognized that a person's "business", a corporate name, a trade name and the good will of a business are species of intangible personal property. M. M. Newcomer Co. v. Newcomer's New Store, 217 S.W. 822, 825 (1919) [trade name]; Sanford–Day Iron Works v. Enterprise Foundry & Machine Co., 198 S.W. 258, 259 (1917) ["one's business"]; Bradford & Carson v. Montgomery Furniture Co., 92 S.W. 1104, 1106 (1905) [good will]; and Robinson v. Robinson, Inc., 9 Tenn.App. 103, 109 (1928) [corporate name].

Tennessee's common law thus embodies an expansive view of property. Unquestionably, a celebrity's right of publicity has value. It can be possessed and used. It can be assigned, and it can be the subject of a contract. Thus, there is ample basis for this Court to conclude that it is a species of intangible personal property.

D

Today there is little dispute that a celebrity's right of publicity has economic value. Courts now agree that while a celebrity is alive, the right of publicity takes on many of the attributes of personal property. It can be possessed and controlled to the exclusion of others. Its economic benefits can be realized and enjoyed. It can also be the subject of a contract and can be assigned to others.

Rev. 886, 898–99 (1980) ["ignored social policy of preventing unjust enrichment"].

What remains to be decided by the courts in Tennessee is whether a celebrity's right of publicity is descendible at death under Tennessee law. Only the law of this State controls this question. The only reported opinion holding that Tennessee law does not recognize a postmortem right of publicity is Memphis Development Foundation v. Factors, Etc., Inc., 616 F.2d 956 (6th Cir.), *cert. denied*, 449 U.S. 953 (1980). We have carefully reviewed this opinion and have determined that it is based upon an incorrect construction of Tennessee law and is inconsistent with the better reasoned decisions in this field.

The United States Court of Appeals for the Sixth Circuit appears to believe that there is something inherently wrong with recognizing that the right of publicity is descendible. Memphis Development Foundation v. Factors, Etc., Inc. 616 F.2d at 959–60 (6th Cir.1980). We do not share this subjective policy bias. Like the Supreme Court of Georgia, we recognize that the "trend since the early common law has been to recognize survivability, notwithstanding the legal problems which may thereby arise." Martin Luther King , Jr., Center for Social Change, Inc. v. American Heritage Products, Inc., 296 S.E.2d 697, 705 (1982).

We have also concluded that recognizing that the right of publicity is descendible promotes several important policies that are deeply ingrained in Tennessee's jurisprudence. First, it is consistent with our recognition that an individual's right of testamentary distribution is an essential right. If a celebrity's right of publicity is treated as an intangible property right in life, it is no less a property right at death. See Price v. Hal Roach Studios, Inc., 400 F.Supp. 836, 844 (S.D.N.Y.1975).

Second, it recognizes one of the basic principles of Anglo–American jurisprudence that "one may not reap where another has sown nor gather where another has strewn." M. M. Newcomer Co. v. Newcomer's New Store, 217 S.W. 822, 825 (1919). This unjust enrichment principle argues against granting a windfall to an advertiser who has no colorable claim to a celebrity's interest in the right of publicity.

Third, recognizing that the right of publicity is descendible is consistent with a celebrity's expectation that he is creating a valuable capital asset that will benefit his heirs and assigns after his death. See Kwall, Is Independence Day Dawning for the Right of Publicity?, 17 U.C.D. L. Rev. 191, 212–13 (1983). It is now common for celebrities to include their interest in the exploitation of their right of publicity in their estate.[f] While a celebrity's expectation that his heirs will benefit from his right of publicity might not, by itself, provide a basis to recognize that the right of publicity is descendible, it does recognize the effort and financial commitment celebrities make in their careers. This investment deserves no less recognition and protection than investments celebrities might make in the stock market or in other tangible assets.

---

[f] Hicks v. Casablanca Records, 464 F.Supp. 426, 429–30 (S.D.N.Y.1978) and Price v. Hal Roach Studios, Inc., 400 F.Supp. 836, 838–39 (S.D.N.Y.1975).

Fourth, concluding that the right of publicity is descendible recognizes the value of the contract rights of persons who have acquired the right to use a celebrity's name and likeness. The value of this interest stems from its duration and its exclusivity. If a celebrity's name and likeness were to enter the public domain at death, the value of any existing contract made while the celebrity was alive would be greatly diminished.

Fifth, recognizing that the right of publicity can be descendible will further the public's interest in being free from deception with regard to the sponsorship, approval or certification of goods and services. Falsely claiming that a living celebrity endorses a product or service violates Tenn. Code Ann. § 47–18–104(b)(2), (3) and (5). It should likewise be discouraged after a celebrity has died.

Finally, recognizing that the right of publicity can be descendible is consistent with the policy against unfair competition through the use of deceptively similar corporate names.

The legal literature has consistently argued that the right of publicity should be descendible. A majority of the courts considering this question agree. Acme Circus Operating Co. v. Kuperstock. 711 F.2d 1538, 1543–44 (11th Cir.1983); Martin Luther King, Jr. Center for Social Change Inc. v. American Heritage Products, Inc., 694, F.2d 674 (11th Cir.1983); Factors, Etc., Inc. v. Pro Arts, Inc., 579 F.2d 215, 222 (2d Cir.1978), *cert. denied*, 440 U.S. 908 (1979); Price v. Hal Roach Studios, Inc., 400 F.Supp. 836, 844 (S.D.N.Y.1975); Lugosi v. Universal Pictures., 603 P2d 425, 431 (1979); and Martin Luther King, Jr. Center for Social Change, Inc. v. American Heritage Products, Inc., 296 S.E.2d 697, 705 (1982). We find this authority convincing and consistent with Tennessee's common law and, therefore, conclude that Elvis Presley's right of publicity survived his death and remains enforceable by his estate and those holding licenses from the estate.[g]

E

While Tennessee's courts are capable of defining the parameters of the right of publicity on a case by case basis, the General Assembly also has the prerogative to define the scope of this right. The General Assembly undertook to do so in 1984 when it enacted Tenn. Code Ann. § 47–25–1101 et seq. which is known as "The Personal Rights Protection Act of 1984." Tenn. Code Ann. § 47–25–1103(a) recognizes that an individual has "a property right in the use of his name, photograph or likeness in any medium in any manner." Tenn. Code Ann. § 47–25–1.0.(b) provides that this right is descendible. Tenn. Code Ann. § 47–25–1104(a) & (b)(1) provide that the right is exclusive in the individual or his heirs and assigns until it

---

[g] There is some dispute concerning whether the right of publicity must be exercised while a celebrity is alive in order to render it descendible. We need not decide this question in this case. There is no dispute in this record that Elvis Presley commercially exploited his right of publicity while he was alive.

is terminated. Tenn. Code Ann. § 47–25–1104(b)(2) provides that the right is terminated if it is not used after the individual's death.

Our decision concerning the descendibility of Elvis Presley's right of publicity is not based upon Tenn. Code Ann. § 47–25–1101 et seq. but rather upon our recognition of the existence of the common law right of publicity. We note, however, that nothing in Tenn. Code Ann. § 47–25–1101 et seq. should be construed to limit vested rights of publicity that were in existence prior to the effective date of the act. To do so would be contrary to Article I, Section 20 of the Tennessee Constitution. A statute cannot be applied retroactively to impair the value of a contract right in existence when the statute was enacted.

* * *

[In the final part of the opinion, the court vacated the lower court's grant of summary judgment to the defendant on its countercomplaint because genuine issues of material fact exist regarding plaintiff's laches defense to defendant's countercomplaint.]

NOTES

1. *Preemption: subject matter of copyright.* The legislative history is clear that as long as a particular work is within the subject matter of copyright, this preemption condition is satisfied even if the work is not sufficiently original to qualify for copyright protection or if it has entered the public domain. For example, in Mayer v. Josiah Wedgwood & Sons, Ltd.,[15] an artist's misappropriation action against a china manufacturer for marketing a Christmas ornament allegedly containing a snowflake by the plaintiff, the plaintiff's snowflake had entered the public domain because it was published without a copyright notice. Still, the court granted the defendant's motion for summary judgment on the ground that the plaintiff's cause of action was preempted by the copyright statute. *Mayer* also suggests that because copyright law does not protect ideas, a state law offering protection to ideas would not be preempted.[16] Should Congress's decision in § 102(b) to expressly exclude ideas from the scope of copyright protection (see Note 7 in Assignment 7) be considered differently from the Copyright Act's complete omission of certain other protections? Can an argument be made that states should be prohibited from protecting subject matter specifically excluded by Congress since Congress thus showed its intent that such material should remain in the public domain? See also Note 4 infra on conflict preemption. Does this issue have any relevance to the Principal Problem? Should a cause of action based on breach of an oral contract regarding copyrighted material be preempted?

2. *Preemption: equivalency.* The 1976 Act does not define the term "equivalent," but the legislative history indicates that a state cause of action will not be preempted if it contains elements that are "different in

---

[15] 601 F.Supp. 1523 (S.D.N.Y.1985).   [16] See id. at 1532 n.16.

kind" from copyright infringement.[17] As the reading suggests, in applying this standard several courts have followed the late Professor Nimmer's suggestion that an "equivalent" right "is one which is infringed by the mere act of reproduction, performance, distribution or display."[18] Essentially, this approach requires an analysis of the state law in question to determine what acts will constitute an infringement. If the exercise of one or more of the five rights protected by federal copyright law is all that is necessary to constitute an infringement of the state law, preemption will occur.[19] If, however, other elements also are required to infringe the state law, no preemption will result. In note g of the *Baltimore Orioles* decision, the court stated that if the additional elements required by the state law "do not differ in kind from those necessary for copyright infringement," preemption will result. With respect to the right of publicity specifically, the court concluded that "[b]ecause the right of publicity does not require a qualitatively different additional element, it is equivalent to a copyright and is preempted to the extent that it is claimed in a tangible work within the subject matter of copyright." Other courts have invoked a test for preemption that focused on whether the extra element of the state law rendered the state action qualitatively different from the copyright law.[20] What does the term "qualitatively different" mean? Should a state law claim of unfair competition involving the copying of material protected by the copyright statute be preempted?

As *Baltimore Orioles* illustrates, a second approach to the "equivalency" dilemma focuses on the interests protected by the state law at issue. Specifically, a state law will be preempted if its *only* objective is to protect the creator's economic interest in his work. Can you think of any instances in which an "objectives" test would save a state law from preemption that would otherwise be vulnerable under Professor Nimmer's pure "elements" test? Which test for preemption is more workable?

3. *Preemption and misappropriation.* As originally drafted, § 301(b)(3) provided specific examples of "nonequivalent" rights that the states could continue to protect under common law or statute.[21] The stipulated rights were "breaches of contract, breaches of trust, invasion of privacy, defamation, and deceptive trade practices such as passing off and false representation,"[22] but the legislative history clearly states that the list was intended to be illustrative rather than exhaustive.[23] The version of the bill that was enacted did not contain any such examples, although this absence was not a result of a rejection of the foregoing examples but rather of a controversy

---

[17] See H.R. Rep. No. 1476, 94th Cong., 2d Sess. 109, 132, reprinted in 1976 U.S.C.C.A.N. 5659, 5748.

[18] 1 M. Nimmer, Nimmer on Copyright § 1.01[B], at 1–11, 1–12 (1984).

[19] See id.

[20] See, e.g., Mayer v. Josiah Wedgwood & Sons, Ltd., 601 F.Supp. 1523, 1535 (S.D.N.Y. 1985).

[21] See H.R. Rep. No. 1476, at 109, 1976 U.S.C.C.A.N. at 5747–48.

[22] H.R. Rep. No. 4347, 89th Cong., 2d Sess. (1966).

[23] H.R. Rep. No. 1476, at 131–32, 1976 U.S.C.C.A.N. at 5747–48.

generated by the subsequent inclusion of "misappropriation" in the House version of the bill. The court in Mayer v. Josiah Wedgwood & Sons, Ltd. summarized a bit of the legislative history in the House Report:

> "Noting that " 'misappropriation' is not *necessarily* synonymous with copyright infringement," ... the House Report used as an example of an unpreempted misappropriation action—International News Serv. v. Associated Press, 248 U.S. 215, 39 S.Ct. 68, 63 L.Ed. 211 (1918)("INS"). In INS, defendant was found to have taken the facts reported in plaintiff's transmissions of "hot news" and used them in its own competing news service. The other example advanced was of sanctions imposed on one who improperly invades another's computerized data base and gains access to the data. Both these examples involve subject matter other than copyright, specifically the facts and data as opposed to their expression. Thus, the House Report states that "a cause of action labelled as 'misappropriation' is not preempted if it is in fact based neither on a right within the general scope of copyright ... not on a right equivalent thereto." (citation omitted). It is thus not surprising that the House Report considered misappropriation to survive preemption. The tort it had in mind was not equivalent to copyright infringement." [24]

Apparently, however, the Department of Justice vigorously objected to the inclusion of "misappropriation" in the enumerated examples of non-preempted rights, and after a series of ambiguous exchanges the bill was passed in an amended version that deleted all of the proposed examples.[25] Can you think of an instance in which a cause of action based on misappropriation of a work of authorship fixed in a tangible medium of expression within the subject matter of copyright would escape preemption? Review Board of Trade of the City of Chicago v. Dow Jones & Co., Inc., reprinted in Part B of Assignment 3. Should that cause of action have been preempted?

In *Mayer*, the court ultimately held that "the alleged misappropriation" of the plaintiff's "time, talent and effort is by the reproduction of the product of her time, talent and effort.... That is precisely the type of misconduct the copyright laws are designed to guard against."[26] Is this the situation in the Principal Problem? What would be the result in the Principal Problem if the choreographic work was never fixed?

4. *Conflict preemption.* Those portions of a state law that conflict with the protections granted by the 1976 Act also will be preempted. This type of preemption, called "conflict preemption," derives from a basis independent of § 301. Here, the appropriate inquiry is whether compliance with both the federal and state law is physically impossible or if the state law poses

---

[24] 601 F.Supp. 1523, 1534 (S.D.N.Y. 1985).

[25] For a history of this aspect of the statute, see 1 M. Nimmer, § 1.01[B], at 1–14.3 to–16. See also Abrams, Copyright, Misappropriation, and Preemption: Constitu-tional and Statutory Limits of State Law Protection, 1983 Sup. Ct. Rev. 509, 537–550 for a good discussion of the legislative history of § 301.

[26] Mayer v. Wedgwood & Sons, Ltd., 601 F.Supp. 1523, 1535 (S.D.N.Y.1985).

an obstacle to fulfilling the goals of Congress. For example, in Association of American Medical Colleges v. Carey,[27] the court relied on conflict preemption to conclude that a state law that required disclosure of medical school admission test questions and answers was preempted because it denied the plaintiff who owned the copyright to the tests benefits safeguarded by the copyright statute. Similarly, in Vault Corp. v. Quaid Softward Limited,[28] the court held preempted the state License Enforcement Act which "permit[ed] a software producer to prohibit the adaptation of its licensed computer program by decompilation or disassembly" because this statute "conflict[ed] with the rights of computer program owners under § 117 and clearly 'touches upon an area' of federal copyright law."[29]

5. *Right of publicity: manner of protection, descendibility and duration.* The *Crowell* case mentions many of the judicial decisions treating the right of publicity and recognizing the descendibility of the right. About half of the states have recognized the right of publicity, and in at least 15 of these states, legislation exists that governs this area either partially or completely.[30] Many of these statutes also recognize that the right against commercial exploitation of an individual's name or likeness is descendible.[31] As *Crowell* indicates, in other jurisdictions the right of publicity is descendible as a matter of common law.[32] In contrast, in Ohio, the right of publicity is not descendible as a matter of common law.[33] Some jurisdictions make the

[27] 728 F.Supp. 873, 879 (N.D.N.Y.1990).

[28] 847 F.2d 255 (5th Cir.1988).

[29] Id. at 270.

[30] See, e.g., Cal. Civ. Code §§ 990 & 3344 (West Supp. 1994); Fla. Stat. Ann. § 540.08 (West 1990); Ind. Code § 32-13 (1994); Ky. Rev. Stat. Ann. § 391.170 (Michie/Bobbs-Merrill 1984); Mass. Ann. Laws ch. 214, § 3A (Law. Co-op. 1989); Neb. Rev. Stat. § 20-202 (1991); Nev. Rev. Stat. Ann. §§ 597.770-.810 (Michie 1994); Okla. Stat. Ann. tit. 12, §§ 1448-1449, tit. 21, §§ 839.1-.2 (West 1993); R.I. Gen. Laws § 9-1-28 (1985); Tenn. Code Ann. §§ 47-25-1101 to -1108 (1989 & Supp. 1993); Tex. Prop. Code Ann. §§ 26.001-.015 (West Supp. 1994); Utah Code Ann. §§ 45-3-1 to -6 (1993); Va. Code Ann. § 8.01-40 (Michie 1992); Wis. Stat. Ann. § 895.50 (West 1988 & Supp. 1993). In addition, the New York privacy statute addresses some aspects of the right of publicity. N.Y. Civ. Rights Law §§ 50-51 (McKinney 1992 & Supp. 1994).

[31] In California, Nevada, and Texas, statutory protection is granted for fifty years following a person's death. Kentucky also provides for fifty years of protection following death, but only for public figures. Florida allows protection for forty years after a person's death. The Virginia statute allows for twenty years of protection following death. The Tennessee statute discussed in *Crowell* provides for an initial ten year period following the individual's death. The right is then terminated by proof of non-use for a period of two years. Oklahoma and Indiana apparently grant protection for 100 years following a person's death.

[32] See also Nature's Way Products, Inc. v. Nature-Pharma, Inc., 736 F.Supp. 245, 252 (D.Utah 1990)(observing that the Utah Supreme Court would hold that "the common law right of publicity survives the death of the subject person in cases where he or she transferred or otherwise exploited such rights while alive"). As the court in *Crowell* indicates in footnote g, some courts only hold the right of publicity to be descendible if the deceased commercially exploited the right while alive. For a general discussion of the descendibility issue and the various positions taken by courts, see Kwall, Is Independence Day Dawning for the Right of Publicity?, 17 U.C. Davis L. Rev. 191, 207-228 (1983).

[33] See Reeves v. United Artists, 572 F.Supp. 1231 (N.D.Ohio 1983).

unauthorized appropriation of protected attributes actionable under its statutory right of privacy.[34] In New York, for example, the courts have held that the state's privacy law which does protect against the unauthorized use of a person's name or likeness for purposes of trade precludes a cause of action under state common law right of publicity.[35] Moreover, relatives of a deceased are precluded from suing under that statute since the right of privacy is held to be personal in nature.[36] The Virginia privacy statute specifically provides relief to the relatives of a decedent whose name or likeness is appropriated for commercial purposes,[37] while the Wisconsin privacy statute specifically limits the ability to recover for the unauthorized commercial use of protected attributes to "living" people.[38] Thus, the manner in which the right of publicity is protected and the descendibility and durational issues are subject to a complete lack of uniformity, which can be problematic for lawyers attempting to advise clients interested in the extent of protection afforded on a national basis. This situation is most difficult when the clients are relatives of a deceased individual whose publicity rights have been appropriated.

6. *Right of publicity: rationales, attributes, and scope of protection.* What are the rationales that support protection for the right of publicity? Does everyone have a right of publicity or only celebrities? The *Midler* case concluded that the distinctive and widely recognized voice of a professional singer is an attribute appropriately protected under the right of publicity. Following the Ninth Circuit's decision in *Midler*, a trial was held in the federal district court. Although the judge dismissed Ford from the case based on insufficient evidence of actual participation, the jury awarded the singer $400,000 against Young & Rubicam. In instructing the jury, the district court judge stated that a finding of misappropriation of Midler's property rights in her voice should be sustained if the jury found that her voice was widely known and deliberately imitated by the defendant to sell a product.[39] The conclusion that the right of publicity provides protection against the unauthorized imitation of a celebrity's voice when such "is a sufficient indicia of a celebrity's identity" subsequently was reaffirmed by

---

[34] Nebraska, Virginia, New York and Wisconsin take this approach.

[35] See, e.g., Stephano v. News Group Publications, Inc., 64 N.Y.2d 174, 485 N.Y.S.2d 220, 474 N.E.2d 580 (Ct.App.1984)(interpreting N.Y. Civ. Rights Law §§ 50 & 51).

[36] See Pirone v. MacMillan, Inc., 894 F.2d 579 (2d Cir.1990)(daughters of Babe Ruth could not bring action under state privacy law). There has been some discussion of codifying the right of publicity in New York. For a discussion of this movement, see Burnett, The Property Right of Publicity and The First Amendment: Popular Culture and

the Commercial Persona, 3 Hofstra Prop. L.J. 171, 186 (1990).

[37] Va. Code Ann. § 8.01–40 (Michie 1992). The Nebraska privacy statute also allows an action for the unauthorized exploitation of a person's name or likeness which is part of its privacy statute to survive that person's death. See Neb. Rev. Stat. §§ 20–202, 20–208 (1991).

[38] Wis. Stat. Ann. § 895.50 (2)(b)(West 1988 & Supp. 1993).

[39] See "Do You Want to Dance" Around the Law? Learn the Latest Steps From the Ninth Circuit in "Midler v. Ford Motor Co.", 23 Loy. L.A. L. Rev. 602, 644 (1990).

the Ninth Circuit in Waits v. Frito–Lay Inc.[40] That case involved a radio commercial for Doritos which featured a vocal performance that imitated singer Tom Waits' distinctive singing voice. Should state law publicity actions based on the appropriation of an individual's voice be preempted under § 301 of the Copyright Act? Why or why not? How is § 114(b) of the 1976 Act related to this inquiry?

What standard can be used to determine which attributes are properly protected under the right of publicity? In Carson v. Here's Johnny Portable Toilets, Inc.,[41] the Sixth Circuit held that a portable toilet manufacturer violated Johnny Carson's right of publicity when it used the phrase "Here's Johnny" in conjunction with the slogan, "The World's Foremost Commodian."[42] In so holding, the court observed that "a celebrity's legal right of publicity is invaded whenever his identity is intentionally appropriated for commercial purposes."[43] Other courts have approved equally expansive applications of the right of publicity by holding that it protects aspects of an individual's identity such as a nickname,[44] professional statistical information,[45] and a distinctive racing car.[46] Recently, the Ninth Circuit held that Vanna White had a common law right of publicity action against a company that used in an advertisement, without her consent, a robot attired to resemble White and posed next to a game board recognizable as the Wheel of Fortune game show set.[47] Can this case be distinguished from *Midler* and from *Carson?* What is the danger of too expansive an interpretation of the right of publicity?

7. *Right of publicity and the First Amendment.* In Zacchini v. Scripps–Howard Broadcasting Co.,[48] the Supreme Court explicitly considered the interplay between the right of publicity and the First Amendment. *Zacchini* involved a television station's broadcast of the plaintiff's entire human cannonball act, without consent, on its nighttime newscast. The Court in *Zacchini* observed that had the television station "merely reported that the petitioner was performing at the fair and described or commented on his act, with or without showing his picture on television, we would have a

---

[40] 978 F.2d 1093, 1098 (9th Cir.1992), cert. denied, 506 U.S. 1080, 113 S.Ct. 1047, 122 L.Ed.2d 355 (1993).

[41] 698 F.2d 831 (6th Cir.1983).

[42] Id. at 837.

[43] Id.

[44] Hirsch v. S.C. Johnson & Son, 90 Wis.2d 379, 280 N.W.2d 129 (1979)(prominent athlete had right of publicity in his nickname "Crazylegs" and could bring an action against manufacturer for commercial misappropriation of his nickname on a shaving gel).

[45] Uhlaender v. Henricksen, 316 F.Supp. 1277 (D.Minn.1970)(baseball table game manufacturer violated baseball players'

rights of publicity by the unauthorized appropriation of their names and playing statistics for commercial use).

[46] Motschenbacher v. R.J. Reynolds Tobacco Co., 498 F.2d 821 (9th Cir.1974)(in case involving television commercial featuring the unique and distinctive decorations of plaintiff's racing car, court held that California law protected an individual's proprietary interest in his identity).

[47] White v. Samsung Electronics America, Inc., 971 F.2d 1395 (9th Cir.1992), cert. denied, ___ U.S. ___, 113 S.Ct. 2443, 124 L.Ed.2d 660 (1993).

[48] 433 U.S. 562, 97 S.Ct. 2849, 53 L.Ed.2d 965 (1977).

very different case.''[49] But the defendant's filming and display of the plaintiff's circus act went way beyond the reporting of a newsworthy event. As such, the defendant's use was not in keeping with a purely informational purpose, and this situation resulted in a great degree of unjust enrichment. Of course, the challenge remains of determining where "the line in particular situations is to be drawn between media reports that are protected and those that are not.''[50]

What if the defendant in the problem, instead of using the tape for commercial purposes, merely used statistics about Ilana Kaye in a board game about 20th century dance? What if the same statistics were used in a book? State statutes that circumscribe the right of publicity when it conflicts with the First Amendment exist in several states such as California, Florida, Indiana, Nebraska, Nevada, Oklahoma, Tennessee, Texas, and Wisconsin.[51] Although the statutes in California, Nevada and Tennessee provide that it should be a question of fact whether a defendant's use of a plaintiff's protected attribute was sufficiently directly connected with commercial sponsorship so as to constitute a prohibited use, in general the statutory formulations tend to be insufficiently flexible to solve the problem. How should the potential for conflict between the right of publicity and the First Amendment be addressed?

BIBLIOGRAPHY

The following articles represent some of the recent literature on the preemption issue, some of which also treat the right of publicity specifically: Rice, Public Goods, Private Contract and Public Policy: Federal Preemption of Software License Prohibitions Against Reverse Engineering, 53 U. Pitt. L. Rev. 543 (1992); Rabinowitz and Godin, Copyright Preemption: New York State's Erroneous Interpretation, 39 J. Copyright Soc'y 243 (1992); Heald, Federal Intellectual Property Law and the Economics of Preemption, 76 Iowa L. Rev. 959 (1991); Singer, The Right of Publicity: Star Vehicle or Shooting Star?, 10 Cardozo Arts & Ent. L.J. 1 (1991); Kemp, Preemption of State Law by Copyright Law, 9 Computer L.J. 374 (1989); Shipley, Three Strikes and They're Out at the Old Ball Game: Preemption of Performers' Rights of Publicity Under the Copyright Act of 1976, 20 Ariz. St. L.J. 369 (1988); Dabney, State Law Protection of Intellectual Creations: Privacy and Preemption, 38 Syracuse L. Rev. 653 (1987); Shipley and Hay, Protecting Research: Copyright, Common-law Alternatives, and Federal Preemption, 63 N.C. L. Rev. 125 (1984); Abrams, Copyright, Misappropriation, and Preemption: Constitutional and Statutory Limits of State Law, 1983 Sup. Ct. Rev. 509 (1983); Shipley, Publicity

[49] Id. at 569.

[50] Id. at 574–75.

[51] See, e.g., Cal. Civ. Code § 3344(d)-(f) (West 1994); Fla. Stat. Ann. § 540.08(3)(a) (West 1990); Ind. Code § 32–13 (1994); Neb. Rev. Stat. §§ 20–202(1) (1991); Nev. Rev. Stat. Ann. § 597.790(2)(a)-(e) (Michie 1994); Okla. Stat. Ann. tit. 12 § 1449 (D)-(E) (West 1993); Tenn. Code Ann. § 47–25–1107 (1989 & Supp. 1993); Tex. Prop. Code Ann. § 26.012 (West Supp. 1994); and Wis. Stat. § 895.50(3)(West 1988 & Supp. 1993).

Never Dies, It Just Fades Away: The Right of Publicity and Federal Preemption, 66 Cornell L. Rev. 673 (1981).

The following articles treat the right of publicity generally: Barnett, First Amendment Limits on the Right of Publicity, 30 Tort & Ins. L.J. 635 (1995); Halpern, The Right of Publicity: Maturation of an Independent Right Protecting the Associative Value of Personality, 46 Hastings L.J. 853 (1995); McCarthy, The Human Persona as Commercial Property: The Right of Publicity, 19 Colum.-VLA J.L. & Arts 129 (1995); Grady, A Positive Economic Theory of the Right of Publicity, 1 UCLA Ent. L. Rev. 97 (1994); Kwall, The Right of Publicity v. The First Amendment: A Property and Liability Rule Analysis, 70 Ind. L.J. 47 (1994); Coombe, Authorizing the Celebrity: Publicity Rights, Postmodern Politics, and Unauthorized Genders, 10 Cardozo Arts & Ent. L.J. 365 (1992); Armstrong, The Reification of Celebrity: Persona as Property, 51 La. L. Rev. 443 (1991); Bloom, Preventing the Misappropriation of Identity: Beyond the Right of Publicity, 13 Hastings Comm. & Ent. L.J. 489 (1991); Halpern, The Right of Publicity: Commercial Exploration of the Associative Value of Personality, 39 Vand. L. Rev. 1199, 1247 (1986); Kwall, Is Independence Day Dawning for the Right of Publicity?, 17 U.C. Davis L. Rev. 191 (1983).

The following articles treat the doctrine of misappropriation generally: Karjala, Misappropriation as a Third Intellectual Property Paradigm, 94 Colum. L. Rev. 2594 (1994); Sease, Misappropriation is Seventy–Five Years Old; Should We Bury It or Revive It?, 70 N.D. L. Rev. 781 (1994); Karjala, Copyright and Misappropriation, 17 U. Dayton L. Rev. 885 (1992); Raskind, The Misappropriation Doctrine as a Competitive Norm of Intellectual Property Law, 75 Minn. L. Rev. 875 (1991).

ASSIGNMENT 15

PATENT PROTECTION: INTRODUCTION

Article I, Section 8, Clause 8 of the United States Constitution, although usually referred to as the "Copyright Clause," nonetheless expressly creates the constitutional basis for patent law. The Patent Act of 1952, 35 U.S.C. §§ 1–376, has been in effect since 1953. It protects three types of discoveries: utility inventions, designs, and asexually reproduced plants.[1] Of the three, utility patents have the most economic significance and they are the main focus of this casebook.

In many ways, a patent is the most desirable form of federal intellectual property protection; it establishes a right to prevent *all* others from making the patented product or process or using it, selling it, or offering it for sale.[2] Patentees can, in other words, bar unauthorized utilization of their inventions without the need to prove copying (as required by copyright law) or consumer confusion (as required by trademark law). At the same time, however, the term of patent protection is the shortest of the three federal regimes. For most patents filed on January 1, 1995 or later, the term of protection is 20 years from the date the patent application is filed. For patents filed prior to ~~January 1, 1995~~ but which were in force on that date, the term is 17 years from the date of issuance or 20 years from the date of application, whichever is longer.[3] Moreover, patents are more difficult to secure than either copyrights or trademarks. A higher level of ingenuity is required to merit protection and a more rigorous examination is conducted before issuance. As we will see, utility inventions are examined to determine that they are useful, original, and new. They must, in addition, be nonobvious—significant advances over earlier technologies.[4] Designs must be not only new, original, and ornamental, they too must be

6/8/95

---

[1] §§ 101, 102, 161, 171 (all citations in the Patent Unit are to 35 U.S.C. unless otherwise noted). Sexually reproduced plants also receive patent-like protection, albeit under the agricultural statutes, Plant Variety Protection Act, 7 U.S.C. § 2402.

[2] § 271(a). Patent law also creates the right to prevent others from inducing domestic infringements, § 271(b); the right to prevent domestic contributory infringements, § 271(c); the right to prevent others from selling components for assembly of the patented invention abroad, § 271(f); and the right to prevent others from importing into the United States articles manufactured with a patented process, § 271(g), see Assignment 24.

[3] § 154. Special limitations on remedies apply during the extended term of such patents, § 154(c). The term of design patents is 14 years from the date the patent issues, § 173. There are complicated provisions for patent applications that were pending when the law changed from 17 years from filing to 20 years from issuance.

[4] §§ 101–103.

552

nonobvious.[5] To receive plant patent protection, a plant must be a distinct new variety.[6]

Before embarking on an exploration of this fairly complex statutory regime, explicit consideration should be devoted to policy. This is especially true because the current statute adopts an approach to protecting intellectual property that is rather different from that taken by most industrialized countries. With the emergence of a global marketplace, the United States will, in most observers' views, be under considerable pressure to enact conforming legislation. Thus, the student is well advised to concentrate principally on underlying policy considerations.

To those who have studied copyright law, these policies will not be very surprising. The Patent Act emanates from the assumption that a period of exclusivity is needed to induce the optimum level of innovation. This assumption is based mainly on economic considerations. Inventive activities are costly. Often, expensive experimentation is required before a new idea works. Finding a commercial method for exploiting the idea also requires money, as does developing distribution channels. Sometimes, consumers need considerable education to understand both why they need and how to use the new development. Innovators must factor these costs into the price at which they sell or license. But since copyists do not incur these expenses, they could—absent patent protection—undercut the inventor in the marketplace and prevent her from recouping her costs or earning a profit. Other inventors will not be so keen to invest their efforts in developing new ideas if they know they will suffer the same fate.

At the same time, however, exclusivity is costly to society. A new invention is, of course, the output of the inventor's mind, but in some sense, it is also input. New ideas are the building blocks on which future developments depend. If they are exclusively owned, it will be difficult for others to push the frontiers of knowledge even further. Equally important, exclusivity permits the patentee to set prices that are in excess of marginal cost. Some people who would purchase the invention were it competitively priced will forgo use rather than pay this higher price. In such cases, everyone loses: the patentee does not make a sale; the non-purchaser does not enjoy the benefit of the new technology. Thus, much of patent law is, like copyright, an attempt to balance the private benefits of exclusivity against these social costs.

Given that copyright and patent law have the same basic goals, why are two regimes necessary? One answer is that while patents are occasionally granted on subject matter similar in character to the sorts of things protected by copyright (computer programs are an example), they mostly protect material that is quite different—so different that innovators require a distinct protective regime.

For example, an author usually cannot, as a practical matter, simultaneously distribute her work and keep it secret. But some inventions are

---

[5] §§ 171, 103.   [6] § 161.

"noninforming:" they can be sold *and* hidden. A new method for brewing coffee, for instance, cannot be discovered by one who observes only the brew, consequently the brewer can sell a product (brewed coffee) without endangering her secret (the brewing technique). Indeed, even some products that are informing in some respects may not reveal all of the technicalities involved in their discovery, use, or construction. Since secrecy is a genuine choice for many inventors, patent law has, in addition to the objectives set out above, the goal of inducing inventors to reveal their discoveries.

Conversely, inventors sometimes face a problem authors do not. Even the impecunious author can manage to find scraps of paper on which to scribble her insights. But such is not the case for all inventors. Some inventions are complex products that are extremely expensive to build; others are processes that cannot be effectuated without costly equipment. In the absence of adequate funding, innovations of this type remain inchoate. But, fixation—the existence of a "hard copy" of the innovation— is extremely important when rights are negotiated. Even without formal federal protection, an author can negotiate the sale of her work to a publisher, for the fixed copy acts as a record of what was created. Its transfer is a basis for implying a contract that, if the work is found valuable enough to publish, the author will be paid. In contrast, it is notoriously difficult to negotiate the sale of inchoate ideas. No investor or manufacturer will agree to buy the idea without knowing what it is—after all, it may be valueless or already commercialized. But once the inventor explains the idea, there is nothing to stop the listener from simply using it without compensating the inventor.

Patent law solves this paradox, known as "Arrow's disclosure paradox" (after Kenneth Arrow, a noted economist), by creating a public registry. The public documents filed in this registry—"patents"—function like the fixed copy of a work of authorship, for they describe to the world the metes and bounds of the registered invention. Inventors can then engage in transactions without worrying that they will be unable to demonstrate that they have transferred valuable information. The registry also ameliorates the secrecy problem. Because patents are public documents, they reveal to the public what the inventor has done, how the invention was constructed, and how it operates. Others will therefore not inadvertently duplicate the work and can, instead, build upon it. When the patent term expires, anyone can learn enough about the invention to use it effectively.

This Introduction examines a typical patent and describes the application process. As noted, this process is rigorous. It is also costly, both to the applicant and to the government. Since applicants often seek protection in many countries, the per-invention cost of worldwide protection is high. It is therefore not surprising that there are many international treaties concerning patent rights. The ones of greatest significance to the United States are described below.

1. A SAMPLE PATENT

STATUTORY MATERIAL: §§ 111–116

US005203579A

United States Patent [19]

Lipschitz

[11] Patent Number: **5,203,579**

[45] Date of Patent: **Apr. 20, 1993**

[54] **SHOP E Z CART**

[76] Inventor: Sarah Lipschitz, 2021 84 St., Apt. 5D, Brooklyn, N.Y. 11214

[21] Appl. No.: **770,363**

[22] Filed: **Oct. 3, 1991**

[51] Int. Cl.^{5} B62B 3/00
[52] U.S. Cl. 280/33.991; 248/129; 280/DIG. 4
[58] Field of Search .... 280/33.991, 33.992, 280/33.995, 33.997, 35, DIG. 4, 659, 47.34–47.35, DIG. 3; 248/95, 97, 98, 128, 129; 224/273

[56] **References Cited**

U.S. PATENT DOCUMENTS

2,762,669	9/1956	Watson	280/33.991
4,097,056	6/1978	Castellano	280/47.35
4,560,096	12/1985	Lucas et al.	280/33.992
4,601,479	7/1986	Reinbold et al.	280/47.35
4,678,195	7/1987	Trabiano	280/33.992

FOREIGN PATENT DOCUMENTS

0070674 3/1991 Japan 280/33.992

Primary Examiner—Richard M. Camby
Attorney, Agent, or Firm—John P. Halvonik

[57] **ABSTRACT**

The invention is a clothes shopping cart that is designed to hold a substantial number of clothing and accessory items for a shopper in department and clothing stores. The cart moves about easily and provides the shopper with the ability to load up the cart with goods as a shopper wheels the cart about through the department store aisles. The clothing shopping cart is designed for ease of parking in conjunction with other carts. The cart uses a U shaped base and a storage space that is oriented to allow the carts to nest with each other. The cart is constructed to permit a substantial number or items to be placed in the cart prior to purchase while allowing for an adequate amount of room between the cart and aisles of the ordinary department store, so that a plurality of cars can move in and about the department store.

3 Claims, 3 Drawing Sheets

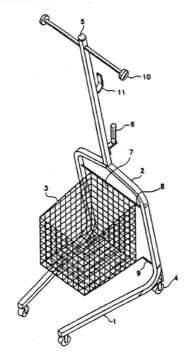

5,203,579

1

SHOP E Z CART

BACKGROUND OF THE INVENTION

1. Field of the Invention

The invention relates to the field of shopping carts and, in particular, to a cart with a U shaped support structure and V shaped base legs that allows other shopping carts to nest with it. The handle of the cart is T shaped to allow one to place clothing and other items upon the handle for storage.

2. Description of the Prior Art

While there are other shopping carts, none that applicant is aware of has the unique construction of her particular shopping cart.

SUMMARY OF THE INVENTION

The invention comprises a shopping cart of unique construction comprising a support structure of inverted U shape bent in two planes. The upper plane represents the support for the storage basket suspended from the curved portion of the U shape. The lower plane defines the orientation of the ends of the U which serve as base legs for the rollers, wheels, etc. The cart may be used within department stores so that clothing and accessory items may be placed on the cart and stored prior to purchase. The upright handle of the cart has a T shaped construction and may be used to hold clothing, etc picked up in the store.

An object of the invention is to provide a shopping cart that readily nests in conjunction with other carts.

Another objective is to provide a shopping cart that allows one to store a considerable amount of clothing with a minimum of space.

Yet another objective is to provide a shopping cart that can readily move about crowded aisles.

Other advantages of the invention should be readily apparent to those skilled in the art once the invention has been described.

DESCRIPTION OF THE DRAWINGS

FIG. 1 shows overall construction of the Cart
FIG. 2A shows front view of cart
FIG. 2B shows side view of cart
FIG. 2C shows above view of the legs showing angled orientation
FIG. 3 shows the carts nested

DESCRIPTION OF THE PREFERRED EMBODIMENT

The shop EZ Cart is substantially as shown in FIG. 1. The base is of a U shaped construction with the ends 1 of the U serving as a wheeled support base that lies in a plane parallel to the floor. The support legs should have four rollers 4 or other wheeled means on the two ends for ease of movement, preferably 2 rollers per leg. The curved central portion 2 of the U is bent upward (i.e.: the U is inverted when the cart is in ordinary position) in a plane that is perpendicular to the first plane.

The plane with the legs is about parallel to the floor upon which the cart will move and toward that end rollers, casters, etc. designated 4 are mounted on the bottom surface of the legs. Two of each caster are preferably on each end.

The construction of the base should preferably be of metal rods, tubes, etc. that are typically used in the shopping cart industry.

The actual storage container 3 is preferably a wire basket suspended from the curved portion of the U. As the curved portion lies above the floor, the middle of

2

the U shape is actually the highest point of the base above the ground. The basket is suspended from the U shaped portion of the base, preferably near the highest standing parts of the base so that the basket rests above the plane of the floor.

The basket is preferably a wire basket of the kind that are commonly used in shopping carts. The basket is open at the top and the back wall 7 of the basket (that part of the basket that is closest to being directly below the curved part of the U) pivots upward so that other carts can nest with the subsequent baskets fitting inside the basket of the previous carts. The back wall of the basket forms a plane about perpendicular to the plane of the base and parallel to the plane of the upper part of the U. The basket is supported on the U shape by supports 8,9 in connection with the back wall. The upper part of the back wall should be pivotally connected to the upper support 8.

Goods are placed in the cart in the usually manner by depositing them into the open upper part, the back wall remains in place during use. The back wall pivots upward only when the carts are nested.

The storability of the cart is enhanced by the orientation of the container with the pivoting back wall. The baskets of the successive carts are stacked adjacent will nest the basket portion of the next cart.

The bottom ends (legs) of the cart are slightly tapered inward so that they are converging. Thus the ends would form a V shape if they were extended all the way forward (which they are not). As it is, the angled ends enhance nesting because they allow successive, adjacent cart legs to fit within the space between the ends of the first cart.

The T shaped upper portion 5 should have rubberized ends 10 and these should be larger in diameter to prevent hangers from sliding off the upper handle. The upper portion is preferably of rounded construction and should allow hangers with clothing to hang from it. The rubber ends prevent hangers from falling off and will not snag clothing. Additional hooks 11 may be placed on the handle portion of the T to allow clothing, etc. to be stored.

A rubberized handle 6 may be placed in close connection with the upper part of the U to allow one to guide and push the vehicle.

I claim:

1. A shopping cart for the temporary storing of clothing comprising: base portion of substantially U shaped construction having two ends and a curved central portion connecting said ends, said U shape laying along two planes, said ends lying in a first plane and said curved portion lying in a second plane perpendicular to said first plane, said ends having roller means for movement, storage compartment in connection with said curved portion, said storage compartment having bottom wall, back and front walls and two side walls, said back wall located below said second portion of said U shape and about co-planar with said second plane, said back wall capable of pivoting upward so as to allow a plurality of said carts to nest alongside one another, said ends being slightly angled so as to facilitate nesting with other said carts, said cart having a handle portion in connection with said curved portion at about near the center of said curved portion, said handle having a T-shaped portion near said top end.

2. The apparatus of claim 1 wherein said handle means has a gripping portion.

3. The apparatus of claim 2 wherein each of said ends have two roller means for movement of said cart.

* * * * *

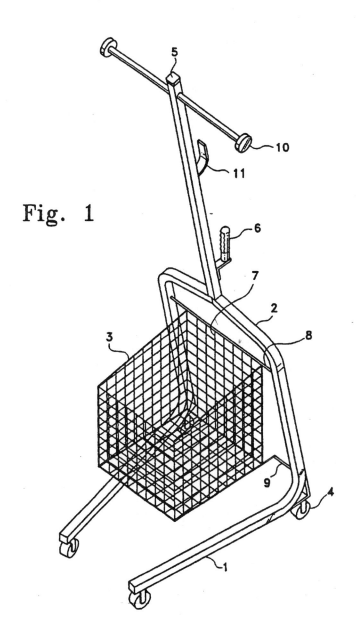

Fig. 1

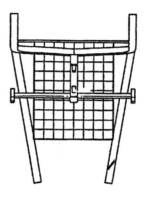

Fig. 2A

Fig. 2B

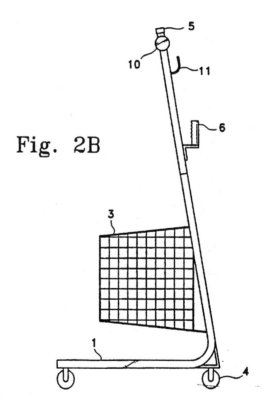

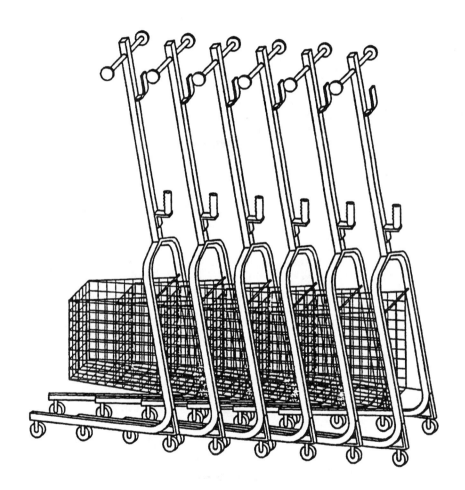

Fig. 3

It is clear from its very first page that Patent 5,203,579 ameliorates many of the unique problems presented by the sort of innovations that patent law protects. It starts with two important dates: April 20, 1993, the date of issuance, and October 3, 1991, the date the application was filed. Since patents issued (or applied for) prior to 1995 and in force (or pending) on June 8, 1995, generally expire 17 years from the date of issuance or 20 years from the date of application, depending on which term is longer, § 154, these dates apprise the public of the time when this invention will be in the public domain, free for all to use. In this case, 20 years from filing would mean the patent expires on October 3, 2011; 17 years from issuance means expiration occurs on April 20, 2010. Since the 20–year term is longer, the actual expiration date is October 3, 2011.[7] (In the future, this calculation will be easier: a patent applied for after June 8, 1995 will remain in force for 20 years from the date of the application).

The patent also provides the name of the inventor, Sarah Lipschitz, as well as her address. Had she assigned her rights to another, the assignee's name and address would also be recorded here. Members of the public who wish to use this invention before October 3, 2011 now know with whom to deal. Should they have any questions about, say, mechanical details of this cart, they know just who possesses the technical knowledge they need.

But what is the invention? An abstract is provided. As with abstracts in technical journals, this is a quick overview of what Ms. Lipschitz has constructed: a shopping cart for clothing (as opposed to groceries) that moves through crowded aisles easily and nests conveniently. Drawings are included if they are needed to insure understanding of the invention, § 113. For anyone interested in utilizing this invention, more information will be required: indeed, it is supplied—in the body of the document.

What would people reading patents wish to know? Surely, anyone interested in utilizing this cart will want to know if the patent is valid. There is no point, after all, in paying royalties to Ms. Lipschitz or waiting until the year 2011 if the patent is not enforceable. Thus, the patent contains whatever information Ms. Lipschitz possessed on the questions of usefulness, originality, novelty, and nonobviousness. The Background and Summary sections describe the problem she faced (building a nesting cart that carries clothing conveniently), the literature in the field, and explain why these older inventions were deficient. The patent also lists the "references"—documents on previous inventions—that Ms. Lipschitz showed the patent examiner, along with the examiner's own "Field of Search" in the materials on file in the Patent and Trademark Office (PTO).

Next, readers will want details on the invention. These are found in the main body of the patent, the "specification"—"a written description of the invention and of the manner and process of making and using it, in such full, clear, concise, and exact terms as to enable any person skilled in the art to which it pertains . . . to make and use the same, and shall set forth the best mode contemplated by the inventor of carrying out his

---

[7] There are a few exceptions to this term. Sections 155–156 extend the term of protection for substances that cannot be sold until they receive clearance from the Federal Food and Drug Administration (FDA) and are triggered by extensive delays between the time that clearance is sought and obtained. The term of a design patent is 14 years, § 173. Note also that special rules on remedies apply to patents subject to the interim term provision.

invention."[8] This language is said to contain three separate requirements: enablement, best mode, and description. Together, they form the quid pro quo of patent protection: in exchange for revealing information that might otherwise be kept secret, the government grants a legal right to exclude all others from using the information for 20 years.

Enablement. The enablement requirement, which is found in the phrase that begins "to enable any person," § 112, is in some sense the most important. It requires the inventor to reveal all the information that the public will need to gain the full benefit of the invention after the patent expires, including information on how to construct and use the invention. Of course, the patentee is not required to write a primer on her field. Rather, the statute permits her to assume readers possess basic knowledge in the art to which the invention pertains. Ms. Lipschitz, for example, can use words like "rollers," "casters," and "U shaped construction" because people skilled in mechanical engineering already know these terms. Furthermore, courts construing this provision understand what anyone who has ever tried to assemble a bicycle knows: directions are never unambiguous and some experimentation will be necessary to convert what is on paper into a working version of the invention. However, if the amount of experimentation is "unduly extensive,"[9] or if the patentee has not provided enough information about the elements needed to construct the invention,[10] she will be regarding as not having fulfilled her duty and the patent will not be valid.

Best mode. The best mode requirement, found in the phrase beginning "and shall set forth," § 112, also focuses on the period after the patent expires. It aims at assuring effective competition. That is, while the enablement requirement will allow others to compete with the patentee (because they can build working versions of the invention), they may not be able to compete effectively if they do not know the most efficient way to utilize the invention. This provision deals with this problem by requiring

---

[8] § 112.

[9] See, e.g., Amgen, Inc. v. Chugai Pharmaceutical Co., Ltd., 927 F.2d 1200, 1213–14 (Fed.Cir.1991). In this case, the patent contained a broad claim for all possible DNA sequences capable of producing the protein that instructs bone marrow cells to increase production of red blood cells. The patentee had only isolated one such sequence—the DNA sequence encoding erythropoietin. Since the number of sequences that might encode erythropoietin or its analogs was in the millions, and the patentee had no way of specifying which ones would increase red blood cell production, the court held that "unduly extensive" experimentation would be required to find biologically active sequences. The broad claim was invalidated on enablement grounds.

[10] See, e.g., White Consolidated Industries, Inc. v. Vega Servo–Control, Inc., 713 F.2d 788 (Fed.Cir.1983). The invention was a system for controlling machine tools with a computer. The specification described one of the programs needed to run the computer as "The language TRANSLATOR used in the RUN mode may be a known translator capable of converting, in a single pass, a part program in programming language into a part program in machine language form, as for example, SPLIT." At the time, SPLIT was widely available for purchase, but it was held as a trade secret. Since its features were not disclosed, users could not create the program themselves, nor could they tell what other programs were sufficiently like SPLIT to substitute for it. Accordingly, the court held the patent invalid for lack of enablement.

the patentee to reveal the patentee's own—subjective—judgment as to the "preferred embodiment" of the invention. Compliance with the provision is determined by whether, from an objective point of view, that "preferred embodiment" has been well enough disclosed to enable a person with ordinary skill in the art.[11] Note that the best mode requirement works better in theory than in practice. It reveals what the patentee knew when the patent was filed.[12] By the time the patent expires, the patentee or her assignee will have enjoyed 20 years of experience with the invention. Although she will, presumably, have learned much more about utilizing it efficiently, there is no requirement that the patent be continuously updated.[13]

Description. The description of the invention is, of course, also helpful in conveying to the public exactly what it is that has been invented. However, its primary focus is actually somewhat different from that of the enablement and best mode provisions. Since the description requirement is tied to the application process, it will be discussed below. At this point, it is enough to say that the phrase beginning "a written description," § 112, establishes a requirement that the inventor demonstrate that she is "in possession of the invention," meaning that on the date the application was filed, she fully understood what it was she had invented.[14]

Finally, having learned that the patent is valid and that the invention is useful, the reader will need to know what constitutes infringement. That is, the patent contains all sorts of information, including data on earlier technologies and details of construction that are not part of the invention itself.[15] Readers should not have to guess which bits of information are regarded by the patentee as proprietary. The storehouse of knowledge grows faster if information that the inventor does not consider part of the invention enters the public domain immediately and unequivocally. Accordingly, § 112 sets out a "peripheral claiming" regime that requires that "[t]he specification [] conclude with one or more claims particularly pointing out and distinctly claiming the subject matter which the applicant

---

[11] See, e.g., Wahl Instruments, Inc. v. Acvious, Inc., 950 F.2d 1575, 1579 (Fed.Cir. 1991)(the purpose of the requirement is "to restrain inventors from applying for a patent while at the same time concealing from the public preferred embodiments of their inventions which they have in fact conceived."); Chemcast Corp. v. Arco Industries Corp., 913 F.2d 923 (Fed.Cir.1990)(requiring that, in certain cases, patentee reveal not only the generic properties of material used in the invention, but also its trade name and supplier).

[12] See, e.g., Spectra–Physics, Inc. v. Coherent, Inc., 827 F.2d 1524, 1535 (Fed.Cir. 1987).

[13] There have, however, been a few lower court decisions requiring applicants who file continuations (described infra) to reveal what they consider the best mode when the continuation is filed, see, e.g., Transco Prods. v. Performance Contracting, Inc., 821 F.Supp. 537 (N.D.Ill.1993) reversed & vacated 38 F.3d 551 (Fed.Cir.1994). But no court has ever required updating after the patent has issued.

[14] See, e.g., Fiers v. Revel, 984 F.2d 1164 (Fed.Cir.1993)(description of DNA must give its structure, not merely a potential method for isolating it); Vas–Cath Inc. v. Mahurkar, 935 F.2d 1555, 1563 (Fed.Cir.1991).

[15] Indeed, patents sometimes contain information that, standing on its own, would be inventive enough to qualify for a patent, had the patentee recognized its significance.

regards as his invention"—that is, that the patentee state precisely how to recognize the borders (periphery) of the claimed invention.[16]

In the shopping cart patent, this requirement is met with the language that begins "I claim:".[17] A few features of the claim are worth examining. First, note the format: three claims, one independent (Claim 1)[18] and two dependent (Claims 2 and 3).[19] The first claim broadly covers any shopping cart that contains a base with U-shaped construction of the specified type, with a pivoting back wall that makes nesting possible, and a T-shaped handle. This claim affords Ms. Lipschitz the most protection because many different shopping carts are likely to infringe it. However, it is also the most risky, for the claim is so general, there is a real possibility that someone else may have previously invented a cart fitting this description. The earlier invention may not have been presented to the examiner and it will probably not have been known to Ms. Lipschitz either. However, if someone finds out about it, that person could go to court to have Claim 1 declared invalid for lack of novelty or for being obvious. There is no "blue penciling" of patent claims: if this claim is invalidated, it is struck in its entirety, even if a court could have edited the claim to transform it into a patentable claim of more modest dimensions.

Claims 2 and 3 are therefore important adjuncts to Claim 1. They describe these more modest inventions. They are called "dependent" claims because they incorporate "independent" Claim 1 by reference, and then contain language to limit it. Claim 2 is limited to shopping carts of the Claim 1 type, that contain a handle that includes a grip. Claim 3 is even narrower: it is limited to Claim 1 shopping carts with the handle-gripping feature, which also have rollers. If the prior art does not contain these other features, Claims 2 and 3 will survive even if Claim 1 is struck. Some shopping carts will escape infringement, but Ms. Lipschitz will surely be happier with half a loaf than no loaf at all.

A second notable feature of this patent is the rather stilted language used to describe the cart. Remember, claims are significant not only because they define the invention, but also because they announce the boundaries of the public domain. Users of the patent system will pounce on the word choices made and on the punctuation utilized in an attempt to wrest as many inventive features as possible out of the patentee's hands. As a result, patent attorneys and agents have developed a formalized vocabulary with settled meaning. To give just one example, notice that Ms. Lipschitz's claim uses the word "comprising."[20] "Consisting of" may sound like a synonym, but it is not. Patent attorneys call "consisting of" a "close-ended phrase:" it implies that *only* shopping carts with exactly the features

---

[16] To understand peripheral claiming, it is helpful to know its opposite: core claiming. In a core claiming system, the patent lays out the central insight of the invention, leaving it to the public to determine which extensions of that insight also infringe. In peripheral claiming, it is the metes and bounds of the invention that are delineated.

[17] See Lipschitz Patent, p.2, col.2, line 45.

[18] Id. at line 46.

[19] Id. at lines 64 and 66.

[20] Id. at line 47.

specified will infringe; shopping carts sporting features *in addition to* the ones described by Ms. Lipschitz will not infringe. In contrast, "comprising" is open-ended. Shopping carts with more features will infringe these claims, so long as they do, in fact, contain the features Ms. Lipschitz described. "Consisting of" is used to distinguish an invention from prior art that is somewhat similar. "Comprising" is used when the invention is so novel that there is no other art in the field that needs to be avoided.

Finally, notice that Ms. Lipschitz did not use the word "wheel" in describing the feature of Claim 3 that imparts mobility. Instead, she referred to "roller means for movement."[21] Claim 3 is drafted in what is called "means plus function form." This format is extremely useful to patentees because it extends the reach of their claims to embodiments that they cannot foresee at the time the patent issues. In this case, for example, Ms. Lipschitz's central insight is a movable shopping cart for clothing. It is irrelevant *how* motion is imparted because the method of creating movement is not the thing she has invented. Accordingly, anyone who uses a moving cart (with a handle with a grip) should be considered an infringer of Claim 3: it does not matter whether they use wheels similar to those in the diagram, casters, soda cans, hair curlers, roller blades, or some other wheel-like thing. By substituting "roller means for movement" for "wheel," Ms. Lipschitz creates a claim that clearly covers all of these devices, and even includes means for movement that have yet to be invented. Means plus function claiming is specifically permitted by § 112 of the Act. However, Assignment 22 will show that means plus function claims are interpreted more restrictively than claims that avoid this format.

2.   THE APPLICATION PROCESS

STATUTORY MATERIALS: §§ 131–141

Ms. Lipschitz filed her application on Oct. 3, 1991. It issued on April 20, 1993: what happened in the intervening 18 months? Patent applications are prosecuted by a small group of lawyers and patent agents who have passed a special examination administered by the PTO. Their practice is largely controlled by the Patent Rules of Practice, 37 C.F.R., and by the Manual of Patent Examining Procedure, which is published by the PTO. This is a highly specialized bar because, as noted above, language is critical and courts will not modify claims in order to save them. Drafting and prosecution are learned by apprenticeship to experienced drafters and are well beyond the scope of this casebook.

In any event, the patent usually begins as an application in a form very similar to that of the issued patent.[22] It is submitted to the PTO in the name of the actual inventor or inventors, each of whom swears she believes

---

[21] Id. at line 67.

[22] Under a recent amendment to § 111, applicants can file provisional applications that conform only to §§ 112 ¶ 1 and 113. If a full application is filed within 12 months, then the provisional application's date can be used for priority purposes, see Assignment 21. The patent term will, however, run from the date the full application is filed.

herself to be the first inventor, §§ 111, 115, & 116. Note that this marks an important difference between patent and copyright law: the patent is always awarded initially to the inventor, even if the invention was made for hire.[23] Inventions made pursuant to an employment relationship can be assigned to the employer. Indeed, many employers make the obligation to assign a part of the employment contract.[24] However, even in such circumstances, the employer will not be considered an inventor (or a joint inventor).[25]

The completed application, if accompanied by the required fee, is immediately awarded a filing date, § 111.[26] It is then classified according to the technical art to which the invention belongs, assigned to an examining group, and ultimately given to an examiner experienced in that area. The examiner will review the application and in all likelihood find some problems with it. Correspondence and/or personal interviews will follow, and the application will usually be amended. A record of each draft and the exchanges between examiner and attorney are kept for posterity in what is called the prosecution history or (for mysterious reasons) the "file wrapper." The file wrapper becomes part of the public record if the patent issues and is frequently consulted in infringement actions to interpret the claims. If the patent does not issue, neither the wrapper nor the application is made public, § 122. Instead, the applicant is permitted to keep her invention as a trade secret.

There are several kinds of objections that the examiner can make. Possibly, the examiner will find that the application claims an invention that is the subject of another party's application or the subject of a patent currently in force. In that case, an interference will be declared, § 135, and

[23] Compare § 201 of the Copyright Act, Assignment 9, supra. In addition to creating a special rule of authorship for works made for hire, the Copyright Act also varies the substantive rules regarding such works. For example, there are no termination rights for such works, 17 U.S.C. § 203, nor are there moral rights in them, 17 U.S.C. § 106A. In contrast, all patents are equal, regardless of the circumstances in which the underlying inventions were created. Thus, patents belonging to employers by assignment are accorded the same rights as patents retained by the initial inventor(s).

[24] If the inventor becomes incapacitated or dies, or a recalcitrant inventor attempts to defeat the assignee's expectations by refusing to apply for a patent, the statute permits the legal representative or party to whom the invention is assigned to prosecute the application. The patent will, however, be granted to the actual inventor, § 118.

[25] This is not to say that the sort of employment problems that crop up in copy-

right and were treated in Assignment 9 do not exist in patent law as well. An employee who was hired for the specific purpose of solving a particular problem will generally find that the employment contract will be read as implying a duty to assign to the employer any patent rights created, see, e.g., Aero Bolt & Screw Co. v. Iaia, 180 Cal.App.2d 728, 5 Cal.Rptr. 53 (1960). Inventions made by employees hired for other purposes, but developed through the use of the employer's facilities, may be subject to a shop right—a right of the employer to a nonexclusive, royalty-free, nontransferable license to make and use the invention, cf. United States v. Dubilier Condenser Corp., 289 U.S. 178, 53 S.Ct. 554, 77 L.Ed. 1114 (1933). See generally, Coolley, Recent Changes in Employee Ownership Laws, 41 Bus. Law. 57 (1985)(reviewing state statutes regulating these relationships).

[26] The fee schedule is set out in § 41.

both applicants (or the applicant and the patentee) will be given notice to appear before the Board of Patent Appeals and Interferences (BPAI), a legislative court administered within the PTO. The BPAI will then determine all issues of patentability and will also decide which of the parties has the right to the patent under the priority provision of the statute, § 102(g). The priority rule will be discussed in detail in Assignment 21. Oversimplified, the person who invents first receives the patent. Thus, an interference requires the parties to prove their dates of invention, with the burden of proof placed on the party who filed the later application. As with other civil litigation, settlements are permitted. However, because the settlement, like all agreements among competitors, implicates antitrust policy, it must be in writing and filed with the PTO, § 135(c).

Often, the Examiner will reject the application for failure to comply with the substantive provisions of the Act, such as for inadequacies in the specification or because the invention is not novel or nonobvious under the requirements of §§ 102 and 103. If the application is rejected, the Examiner must give the applicant notice and reasons for the rejection. The applicant is then permitted to amend her application and have it reexamined, § 132.

Sometimes, the applicant finds that her application requires a more fundamental change. If the application is found to cover more than one independent and distinct invention, the examiner has authority to require the applicant to prepare separate applications for each invention, § 121. It is here where the description requirement of § 112 becomes important. Although the applicant could start from scratch by filing a new application, she would have to relinquish the filing date of the first application. But the filing date is valuable. For example, it determines who bears the burden of proof in an interference. The applicant would therefore prefer to keep the original filing date, which she can do by filing what are called "divisional applications." These applications will retain the filing date of the first—"parent"—application, so long as the applicant can show from the description contained in the parent application that she was in possession of the invention disclosed in the divisionals on the earlier date, § 120.

Finally, during the time that the application is pending in the PTO, the applicant may come to understand her initial insight better and discover it has other patentable features. Again, while she could file a brand new application, she would prefer to get the benefit of the filing date of the first application. A continuation-in-part ("CIP") application contains all of the information in the parent application and then adds new material. The matters disclosed in the parent's description will get the benefit of the earlier date, § 120, and the new material will be assigned the filing date of the CIP application itself.[27]

---

[27] Continuations of continuations are also possible, without limit. Indeed, patentees have been known to drag the application process out for decades. When the term of protection began on issuance, this procedure led to the problem of the "submarine:" an application that lurked in the PTO, undetected by an industry that expanded in reliance on free access to the invention and was pro-

Applicants dissatisfied with the decisions of the PTO have several levels of appeal. Parties to an interference can appeal the decision of the BPAI to the Court of Appeals for the Federal Circuit (CAFC), the appellate court that hears appeals in all patent cases tried in federal courts, § 141. Alternatively, the applicant can seek review of the BPAI by suing the Commissioner of Patents in the United States District Court for the District of Columbia. Appeal from this court is to the CAFC, § 146. A similar avenue for appeal is open after an application has been examined and rejected twice: the applicant can appeal to the BPAI, § 134, and can seek review of that decision in the CAFC or bring a de novo action in district court, §§ 141, 145.

Of course, not all errors are the PTO's. After the patent issues, the patentee may, for example, find that she has omitted to claim part of her discovery, submitted a defective drawing, or failed to join an inventor. Errors committed without deceptive intent can be corrected through reissue, § 251, a procedure conducted along the same lines as the initial examination. Reissue is available at any time, except that the scope of the claims can be enlarged only within two years of the initial grant. Reissued patents have the same effect as initial patents with regard to claims contained in both. However, those who had begun to practice the inventions claimed only in the second patent enjoy "intervening rights"—the right to continue usages that began before the reissue took place, § 252.

In addition, a patentee occasionally discovers that the subject matter of an issued patent is covered by a patent that she already holds. There are two types of so-called "double patenting." "Same-invention type double patenting" occurs when the claims in the second patent turn out to cover exactly the same invention as that claimed in the first patent. "Obviousness type double patenting" occurs when the second set of claims are obvious variations on the first patent's claims.[28] In the case of same-invention double patenting, the second patent is invalid for, essentially, lack of novelty. In case of obviousness type double patenting, however, the only problem is that the term of protection will be too long if both patents remain in force.[29] If double patenting occurred without deceptive intent, this problem can usually be cured by simply disclaiming the part of the term that extends beyond the period of the first patent, § 253.[30]

Students are often puzzled by the parties' incentives during prosecution. At first blush, it would appear to be good strategy to reveal to the examiner as little as possible about the prior art. That way, the invention

foundly undermined when the patent finally surfaced.

[28] See, e.g., Gerber Garment Technology, Inc. v. Lectra Systems, Inc., 916 F.2d 683 (Fed.Cir.1990)(double patenting occurred when divisional application overlapped with parent application); In re Vogel, 422 F.2d 438 (C.C.P.A.1970)(method of packaging meat and beef obvious in light of previous patent for a method of packaging pork).

[29] For example, if the first patent issued in 1980 and the second patent issued in 1990, the latter patent would not expire until 2010, and the term for both combined would be 30 years (1980–2010).

[30] In the example above, the disclaimer would produce the result that both patents expired in 2000.

will be more likely to appear to meet the requirements of the Act. However, there are several features of the system that make this a poor way to proceed. First, an applicant bears a duty of candor—a duty to reveal to the PTO all of the information she possesses that is material to the question of patentability. If this duty is breached, the patent that issues will be unenforceable *in its entirety*—as to claims to which the hidden information pertained and as to all other claims in the patent as well.[31] Second, invalidity is always a valid defense. Unlike the case with trademarks, there is no time after which patents become incontestable.[32] Moreover, parties threatened with enforcement actions can ask for a declaratory judgment that the patent is invalid.[33] Validity determinations are made on the basis of all material presented in court, not just the art previously examined by the PTO. Although at this point the patent will be presumed valid, § 282, courts, as a practical matter, tend to give greater scrutiny to material that has not been passed on by the PTO. Finally, any party, including the Commissioner of Patents, can ask the PTO to reexamine the patent to determine the patentability of the invention in light of prior art, §§ 301–307. Thus, the victory obtained through breach of the duty to conduct examination equitably will be a hollow one.

3. THE INTERNATIONAL STAGE

STATUTORY MATERIALS: §§ 104, 119, 351–376, & Paris Convention, Arts. 2 and 4

A patent largely creates rights only within the nation that issued it. Inventors who wish to exploit their inventions globally will therefore desire protection in several countries. The International Convention for the Protection of Industrial Property (the Paris Convention), and the General Agreement on Tariffs and Trade (the GATT) provide this assurance as to countries that have signed this treaty. In addition, patentees seek to minimize the cost of obtaining global protection. The Patent Cooperation Treaty (PCT) is helpful.

a. *The Paris Convention.* This Convention was promulgated in 1883, adopted by the United States in 1887, and implemented through domestic legislation in 1903. It is recognized by well over 100 countries.[34] As it

---

[31] The leading case is J.P. Stevens & Co. v. Lex Tex, Ltd., 747 F.2d 1553 (Fed.Cir. 1984). However, the standards enunciated there may somewhat overstate the parties' obligations as of more recent cases in which the court has emphasized the importance of proving intent, see, e.g., In re Harita, 847 F.2d 801 (Fed.Cir.1988); FMC Corp. v. Manitowoc Co., Inc., 835 F.2d 1411 (Fed.Cir.1987). The PTO from time to time promulgates its own standard of disclosure, 37 C.F.R. § 1.56. Attorneys are, of course, subject to disciplinary action. See generally, Amberg, Evolution And Future Of New Rule 56 And The Duty Of Candor, The PTO's New Duty of Disclosure Rules May Be a Trap for Unwary Practitioners, 20 AIPLA Q.J. 163 (1992).

[32] 15 U.S.C. § 1065. See Assignment 2, Part B, Note 9.

[33] See, e.g., International Harvester Co. v. Deere & Co., 623 F.2d 1207 (7th Cir.1980).

[34] A list of signatories is included in the Manual of Patent Examining Procedure § 201.13.

pertains to patent law, this Convention has two crucial features. First, under Art. 2 of the Convention:

> "[n]ationals of any country of the Union shall ... enjoy in all the other countries of the Union the advantages that their respective laws now grant, or may hereafter grant, to nationals...."

This "national treatment" provision assures inventors that the patents they acquire in a foreign country will be treated exactly the same as the patents acquired by nationals of that country. That way, all exploiters of patentable property compete in each country on a level playing field— French patentees do not enjoy special advantages in France any more than American patentees enjoy unique privileges in the United States. Note, however, that French patentees cannot enjoy in the United States privileges granted by France but not by the United States (and vice versa). Rather, within the borders of every country, patent holders are treated alike. The obligations undertaken by the United States through its adherence to the Convention are executed in § 119 of the Patent Act.

Second, Art. 4 of the Convention provides that:

> "Any filing that is equivalent to a national filing under the domestic legislation of any country of the Union ... shall be recognized as giving rise to [a] right of priority."

The priority right is defined as 12 months for patents. Implemented in §§ 119 and 365 of the Patent Act, this provision means that when someone who has filed an application in one signatory files a second application in another country, the filing date assigned to the latter application is the date of the first-filed application—as long as no more than 12 months have elapsed between filings.[35] For example, imagine an applicant files first in France on January 12, 1991. As long as she files her U.S. application by January 12, 1992, the U.S. filing date for most purposes will be considered January 12, 1991.

This ability to, essentially, predate a filing is extremely important to foreign applicants. An applicant is always entitled to claim that her invention was reduced to practice on the filing date for purposes of determining (among other things) priority, novelty, and nonobviousness. Filing dates are also used to assign burdens of proof in interferences. Since (except as to signatories to certain treaties) U.S. law forbids the use of foreign activities to establish the date on which the invention was reduced to practice, § 104(a), the ability of foreigners to rely on the date of their home-country filing can make the difference between winning a patent (or defeating the patent of another) and becoming a licensee, an infringer, or a nonparticipant in the market for the invention.[36]

---

[35] The new provisional application process of § 111(b) may also trigger this requirement.

[36] This does not apply include the signatories to the General Agreement on Tariffs and Trade (GATT) and the North American Free Trade Agreement (NAFTA), see § 104(a)(3).

The 12–month grace period permitted between filings is in the nature of a compromise. On the one hand, it gives applicants time to determine whether it is worth spending the resources to seek foreign protection, hire international counsel, obtain translations of their applications, and conform their applications to the requirements of each signatory's law. On the other hand, it gives signatories some assurance that patent applications will be made promptly so that their nationals will quickly gain the benefit of the invention.[37]

It is also important to note the things that the Paris Convention does *not* do. It does not demand precisely equivalent treatment of foreign and domestic *applicants* (as opposed to patentees). Instead, each country is permitted to enact provisions aimed at further encouraging importation of new technologies.[38] Nor does the Convention create an international patent, good in all signatory nations. Rather, each nation separately examines each application and entertains challenges to validity in accordance with domestic law. Finally, the Paris Convention does not create a unified international patent law. Indeed, signatories' laws differ in fundamental ways. In the United States, for example, the first person to invent an invention is generally awarded the patent, even if others filed applications earlier. In most other countries, the first to file is always the first in right.

b. *The General Agreement on Tariffs and Trade.* Unlike the other international agreements discussed in this Introduction, the GATT was not originally designed to deal with intellectual property. Instead, it is, as its name suggests, a general agreement designed to increase international commerce by reducing tariffs and other barriers to trade. When this Agreement went into force in 1948 with the United States as an original signatory, the parties to GATT focused on commerce in products like corn, chickens, lamps, and steel; it was only in 1986, during the so-called Uruguay Round of GATT trade negotiations, that intellectual property was introduced into the discussion. After a slow start in which the propriety of treating intellectual products as equivalent to grain and manufactured goods was questioned, the Uruguay Round ended with an agreement on Trade–Related Aspects of Intellectual Property Rights, (TRIPS). GATT is administered by the World Trade Organization (WTO).

Under TRIPS, the signatory countries agreed to a set of basic principles. The first two mirror the Paris Convention: signatories to TRIPS

---

[37] Signatories are permitted to go even further to encourage applicants to file their foreign applications within 12 months of the domestic application. As will be seen in Assignment 20, § 102(d) of the Patent Act punishes delay by barring a patent on applications filed outside the 12–month period, if the foreign patent issues before the U.S. patent issues.

[38] For example, certain foreign applicants cannot rely on activities in their home country to demonstrate invention, § 104(a); foreign patents are effective references only with respect to material in the claims, not in the remainder of the specification, Reeves Bros. v. United States Laminating Corp., 282 F.Supp. 118 (E.D.N.Y.1968); in some instances, foreign disclosures must be more complete than U.S. disclosures, In re Gosteli, 872 F.2d 1008 (Fed.Cir.1989), and issued foreign patents are not effective as references against co-pending applications from the date of application, In re Hilmer, 424 F.2d 1108 (C.C.P.A.1970).

agree to accord national treatment to foreign patent applicants and to accord priority according to the applicant's national filing date.[39] The third extends the core principle of the GATT to intellectual property: it requires member countries to accord to other member nations most-favored-nation (MFN) treatment.[40] This means that any time one member of the GATT enters into an agreement related to intellectual property with any other member, the advantages of the agreement are generalized to apply to all other signatories.

The fourth significant feature of TRIPS is that it establishes a set of universal minimum standards governing the use of intellectual products. With respect to patent law, these standards include a prohibition against excluding from protection any particular field of technology,[41] a prohibition against discriminating among applications according to the place where invention occurred,[42] a requirement that applicants disclose their inventions "in a manner sufficiently clear and complete for the invention to be carried out by a person skilled in the art,[43] a right in patentees to prevent third parties from "making, using, offering for sale, selling, or importing "the patented invention",[44] and a period of protection that extends for at least 20 years from the date the application is filed.[45] Signatories retain the right to permit certain unauthorized uses of the patented invention, but only within narrow limits.[46]

c. *The Patent Cooperation Treaty.* The PCT is, like the intellectual property related aspects of the GATT, a relatively recent development. Promulgated in 1970 and implemented (in stages) by the United States starting in 1975, see §§ 351–376,[47] the PCT is aimed at saving resources for both applicants and national patent offices through the elimination of duplicative examinations. An applicant can file an "international application" designating the countries in which patent protection is desired. Each

---

[39] Final Act Embodying the Results of the Uruguay Round of Multilateral Trade Negotiations and Marrakesh Agreement Establishing the World Trade Organization, signed at Marrakesh (Morocco), April 15, 1994, Annex 1C, Agreement on Trade–Related Aspects of Intellectual Property Rights, Arts. 3(1) and 4A(1), reprinted in The Results of the Uruguay Round of Multilateral Trade Negotiations—The Legal Texts (GATT Secretariat ed. 1994)[hereinafter, the TRIPS Agreement].

[40] Id., Art. 4.

[41] Id., Art. 27(1). There are, however, some exceptions, including "diagnostic, therapeutic and surgical methods for the treatment of humans and animals," and "plants and animals other than microorganisms" Art. 27(3)(a).

[42] Id. This prohibition required a change in U.S. patent law, which, as we saw, generally does discriminate according to where an invention occurs, § 104. Thus, § 104 does not apply to signatories of GATT (or, for that matter, to Canada or Mexico, which negotiated for exemptions under the North American Free Trade Agreement (NAFTA)).

[43] Id., at Art. 29(1).

[44] TRIPS Agreement, Art. 28(1).

[45] Id., at Art. 33. This too required a change in U.S. law, which formerly extended protection for 17 years from the date of issuance, which may or may not be longer, depending on the length of the examination procedure, see § 154. (It is because of this GATT-driven change that the calculation of Lipschitz's patent term was so complicated).

[46] Id., at Arts. 30 and 31.

[47] The signatories of the PCT are listed in the Manual of Patent Examining Procedure § 1870.

signatory establishes a Receiving Office—generally the same agency that examines domestic applications—to receive applications, check their compliance with formalities, and forward copies to an International Searching Authority (ISA) and to the International Bureau (IB), which acts as a central repository. Several designated countries' patent offices, including the United States' PTO, act as ISAs; the World Intellectual Property Organization (WIPO) in Geneva, Switzerland currently serves as IB.

The ISA receiving an application conducts an international search aimed at discovering prior art that may be relevant in determining whether the invention is new and nonobvious. It transmits its Search Report to the IB and to the applicant. The applicant then has a number of options. She can have the IB transmit the application (which can be amended in light of the Search Report), along with the Report to the countries she designated, each of which will then determine patentability according to its own domestic law. Alternatively, the applicant can ask the IB to forward the application to an International Preliminary Examining Authority (once again, certain signatories' patent offices), which conducts an International Preliminary Examination, in a format similar to an examination within the PTO. This Examination results in a written opinion as to whether each claim is novel, involves an inventive step, and is industrially applicable. The International Preliminary Examination Report is forwarded to the IB, to the applicant, and to the patent offices of the designated countries. The Preliminary Examination Report is nonbinding; once it is received, domestic patent offices will determine patentability under domestic law.

The PCT has certain advantages. The applicant can file a single application in her own country's Receiving Office, in the applicant's own language. Although translation into designated countries' languages may ultimately be necessary to obtain actual patents, the expense need not be incurred until after the Search Report and (if the applicant so desires) the International Preliminary Examination Report have provided the applicant with reason to believe that the invention is patentable. Although countries are free to differ with the opinion of the International Preliminary Examining Authority, its report will certainly save local patent offices time and money. Furthermore, at least one patent office will certainly agree with its conclusions—namely, the one that conducted the examination. Thus, the typical U.S. applicant will use the U.S. PTO as Receiving Office, ISA, and International Preliminary Examining Authority. She will conduct all her business in English, and have a good idea of what is patentable before she needs to hire translators and approach foreign offices. Simultaneously, she will have come close to finishing with the PTO's own examination of her application.

There are, however, certain disadvantages to a PCT application, particularly for Americans. First, the PCT application must be drafted somewhat differently from purely domestic applications. There is a standardized format that must be utilized and, in keeping with the law of many signatories, there is a "unity of invention" requirement which forces inventors to split up applications in a manner not required by current U.S.

law. Second, and again in accordance with most countries' patent laws, the IB publishes all applications 18 months after they are filed. In contrast, U.S. applications have enjoyed confidentiality until they issue, § 122. However, these disadvantages are not serious for most potential users of the system. They would file abroad anyway, where they would meet the same requirements.

Like the Paris Convention, the PCT does not go as far as many would like. The validity of a patent depends on the laws of each country where protection is sought; since patentability standards differ, the cost of obtaining world-wide protection is high and there remains the chance that some inventions will be patented by one party in one country and by a different party in other countries. To fully integrate world economies, countries must agree to enact patent law that is, in all major respects, identical. The countries of Europe have pioneered such an effort in the European Patent Convention (EPC), which established a European Patent Office and a substantive patent law which must be accepted by each EPC signatory. However, what the European Patent Office issues is not a Convention-wide patent. Rather, it is essentially a bundle of individual national patents, which can be challenged separately in each nation's domestic courts.[48]

Further and more widespread harmonization is currently on the international agenda, see Wegner, Patent Harmonization (1993). But true harmonization will require countries to compromise on some very fundamental issues—first to file versus first to invent and preissuance disclosure are two. Further, countries will be called upon to abandon law that is particularly well adapted to their own cultural traditions. It remains to be seen whether the international community believes the benefits of harmonization will outweigh these costs.[49]

[48] See generally, Vandebeek, Realizing the European Common Market by Unifying Intellectual Property Law: Deadline 1992, 1990 B.Y.U. L. Rev. 1605.

[49] See generally, Fryer, Patent Law Harmonization Treaty Decision is Not Far Off— What Course Should the U.S. Take?, 30 IDEA: J.L. & Tech. 309 (1990).

SUBJECT MATTER

1. INTRODUCTION

Sections 100 and 101 of the Patent Act together define the scope of patentable subject matter. Section 101, the more general provision, announces that patents are available for any "new and useful process, machine, manufacture, or composition of matter, or any useful improvement thereof." "New" and "useful" denote standards of inventiveness; they are discussed in Assignments 18 and 17. This Assignment is concerned only with the kinds of innovations that are eligible for patent protection: machines, manufactures, compositions of matter, processes, and improvements thereof.

Machines, manufactures, and compositions of matter are generally easy to recognize. They are things such as steam engines, pencils, and aspirin. "Process" requires slightly more exposition. One definition was provided in an early, much-cited case, Cochrane v. Deener:[1]

> "A process is a mode of treatment of certain materials to produce a given result. It is an act, or a series of acts, performed upon the subject matter to be transformed and reduced to a different state of thing."

As the Principal Cases below demonstrate, this definition works well when transformations are physically observable; electronic transformations of the sort occurring in a computer are more difficult to analyze.

"Process" also has a second definition, provided by § 100: "The term 'process' means process, art or method, and includes a new use of a known process, machine, manufacture, composition of matter, or material." This provision is an important addition to patent law, for it enables the law to motivate the search for new ways to use old materials. Although an inventor cannot obtain a patent on the actual material (it is not "new"), a process patent can be obtained on the new way to use it. A process patent may not be as valuable as a product patent because it is difficult to monitor its use. Nonetheless, it is better to have this limited right, than no legal ability to capture any of the benefits of inventing the new use.

This "better-than nothing" approach applies to improvements as well. Improving an existing technology does not create a right to a patent on the entire technology, only to a patent on the improvement itself. Thus, if the the underlying technology is in the public domain, only those who wish to practice the improved version need the patentee's permission. If the underlying technology is also patented, then those who wish to practice the

---

[1] 94 U.S. 780, 788, 24 L.Ed. 139 (1876).

improved version will need permission from two sources: the party who holds the patent on the basic invention and the party who holds the patent on the improvement. By the same token, each of the patentees will need the other party's permission ("cross licenses") to use the improvement.

But the real problem posed by §§ 100 and 101 lies not in what they do say so much as in what they omit. Compare these provisions with the definition of copyrightable subject matter in § 102 of the Copyright Act. In addition to providing a list of material that is copyrightable, the Copyright Act adds a definition of that which is not copyrightable. That is, § 102(b) expressly notes that copyright is not available for ideas, concepts, principles, and discoveries. At first blush, the express exclusions of the Copyright Act makes it appear that patent law is intended to cover ideas and principles. Indeed, the materials on the copyrightability of computer programs assumed that patent law picks up precisely where copyright leaves off.

On further thought, however, it is evident why this assumption could not be true. Copyright excludes ideas and principles because creating exclusive rights in them would make it too difficult for others to make their own contributions to the storehouse of knowledge. The same concern necessarily animates patent law, for if the basic building blocks of science could be privately owned, innovation would certainly be slowed. As Assignment 7 made clear, copyright protects the public domain by drawing (with some difficulty) a line between ideas and expression. The analogue in patent law is the line between an idea and its embodiment: "While a scientific truth, or the mathematical expression of it, is not a patentable invention, a novel and useful structure created with the aid of knowledge of scientific truth may be."[2]

2.   PRINCIPAL PROBLEM

Gamma Biotech, Inc. is one of the new biotechnology companies that is trying to strike it rich on the tremendous commercial potential of proteins, which can be used for everything from pharmaceuticals to detergent. It has come to us for advice on the patentability of a protein that it has recently identified as a possible cure for brain cancer. This protein (like all proteins) is made by body cells under the direction of genes. In this case, the cells in question were first obtained by Dr. Alpha, who treated a certain Brenda Walsh for a fast-growing brain tumor. Dr. Alpha removed Walsh's tumor and then grew its cell line in his laboratory. He gave a sample of these cells to his friend, Professor Beta, who isolated and sequenced the genetic material and then published her findings. Gamma used this article to find the particular protein it believes can cure brain cancer.

Gamma has several questions for us. First, it wants to know whether it can patent a protein, which is, after all, a naturally-occurring chemical.

[2] MacKay Radio & Telegraph Co. v. Radio Corp. of America, 306 U.S. 86, 94, 59 S.Ct. 427, 431, 83 L.Ed. 506 (1939).

Next, it wants us to predict whether Beta will be successful at patenting the genes she isolated and whether Alpha will manage to patent the cell line he grew.

Of course, to really understand what is going on here, you need to know a little biology. The nuclei of a plant or animal's cells contain chemicals that store the information necessary for the organism to function. These chemicals, called chromosomes, are made of double strands of deoxyribonucleic acid (DNA). The backbone of these strands is, in turn, made of combinations of four chemicals called adenine (A), guanine (G), cytosine (C) and thymine (T) arranged linearly. The strands are held together because pairs of these chemicals are complementary: the A's on one strand bond to the T's on the other. Similarly, the G's and C's bond. The order (or sequence) of these chemicals in the linear arrangement on the strands determines the structure of the proteins that the DNA programs the cells to create. Or, as biochemists would say, a particular piece of DNA "codes for," or "encodes," a particular protein.

Since DNA creates valuable proteins, and since the structure of these proteins depends on the structure of the DNA that created them, it would be very nice to isolate DNA from cell lines that demonstrate interesting behavior, like the fast-growing cell line that Dr. Alpha started from Brenda Walsh's tumor. The DNA strands are, unfortunately, very long. Much of them have (so far as can be determined) no value at all. The 3% that is valuable codes for many different proteins. Accordingly, to get at interesting proteins, it is necessary to break the DNA up, get rid of the garbage, and then find the pieces of the sequence—the genes—that code for specific proteins.

One way to do that is to use standard, well known techniques to isolate an intermediate chemical, called messenger ribonucleic acid (mRNA), which a gene uses to convey its information to other processes within a cell. mRNA, which is single stranded, is also made from four chemicals with complementary aspects. Three are just like DNA—G, C, and A, but in mRNA, T is replaced by Uracil (U). The order of these chemicals on each mRNA backbone is determined by the sequence of the specific gene that uses it. mRNA, though closer to the interesting protein than DNA, is, however, not quite close enough. That is because mRNA is not stable. However, there are techniques that can be used to convert mRNA into stable double-stranded DNA-like chemicals.

These techniques were used by Beta when she studied the Walsh cell line that her friend, Alpha, gave her. She isolated mRNA from the Walsh cell line and used standard laboratory techniques to eliminate the useless parts. Next, she exploited the fact that the G's on an mRNA will bind to C's and the A's will bind to U's and T's to make each strand of mRNA generate a complementary strand. The results were double-stranded molecules very, very similar to the genes of interest. In fact, they are identical to the original DNA in Walsh's body, except that they lack the noncoding parts. Called cDNA, these strands can be maintained for long periods of time and propagated.

Beta used her supply of cDNAs to isolate particular genes. Using standard techniques, she figured out the sequence of the chemicals and then published her results. Gamma saw the publication and requested supplies of her genes. Using well-known techniques, it caused the genes to generate the proteins they encode for, and found the one it suspects will cure cancer.

So, to return to the initial question: can Alpha patent the cell line isolated generated from the tumor in Brenda Walsh's head? Can Beta patent the cDNA she generated from the cell line and sequenced? Can Gamma patent the protein generated from the cDNA?

3. MATERIALS FOR SOLUTION OF PRINCIPAL PROBLEM

A. STATUTORY MATERIAL: § 101

B. CASES:

Diamond v. Chakrabarty

Supreme Court of the United States, 1980.
447 U.S. 303, 100 S.Ct. 2204, 65 L.Ed.2d 144.

■ MR. CHIEF JUSTICE BURGER delivered the opinion of the Court.

We granted certiorari to determine whether a live, human-made micro-organism is patentable subject matter under 35 U.S.C.A. § 101.

I

In 1972, respondent Chakrabarty, a microbiologist, filed a patent application, assigned to the General Electric Co. The application asserted 36 claims related to Chakrabarty's invention of "a bacterium from the genus Pseudomonas containing therein at least two stable energy-generating plasmids, each of said plasmids providing a separate hydrocarbon degradative pathway." This human-made, genetically engineered bacterium is capable of breaking down multiple components of crude oil. Because of this property, which is possessed by no naturally occurring bacteria, Chakrabarty's invention is believed to have significant value for the treatment of oil spills.

Chakrabarty's patent claims were of three types: first, process claims for the method of producing the bacteria; second, claims for an inoculum comprised of a carrier material floating on water, such as straw, and the new bacteria; and third, claims to the bacteria themselves. The patent examiner allowed the claims falling into the first two categories, but rejected claims for the bacteria. His decision rested on two grounds: (1) that micro-organisms are "products of nature," and (2) that as living things they are not patentable subject matter under 35 U.S.C. § 101.

Chakrabarty appealed the rejection of these claims to the Patent Office Board of Appeals, and the Board affirmed the Examiner on the second ground. Relying on the legislative history of the 1930 Plant Patent Act, in which Congress extended patent protection to certain asexually reproduced plants, the Board concluded that § 101 was not intended to cover living things such as these laboratory created micro-organisms.

The Court of Customs and Patent Appeals, by a divided vote, reversed.
* * *

II

The Constitution grants Congress broad power to legislate to "promote the Progress of Science and useful Arts, by securing for limited Times to Authors and Inventors the exclusive Right to their respective Writings and Discoveries." Art. I, § 8, cl. 8. The patent laws promote this progress by offering inventors exclusive rights for a limited period as an incentive for their inventiveness and research efforts. The authority of Congress is exercised in the hope that "[t]he productive effort thereby fostered will have a positive effect on society through the introduction of new products and processes of manufacture into the economy, and the emanations by way of increased employment and better lives for our citizens." Kewanee Oil Co. v. Bicron Corp., 416 U.S.470, 480 (1974).

The question before us in this case is a narrow one of statutory interpretation requiring us to construe 35 U.S.C. § 101, which provides:

"Whoever invents or discovers any new and useful process, machine, manufacture, or composition of matter, or any new and useful improvement thereof, may obtain a patent therefor, subject to the conditions and requirements of this title."

Specifically, we must determine whether respondent's micro-organism constitutes a "manufacture" or "composition of matter" within the meaning of the statute.

III

In cases of statutory construction we begin, of course, with the language of the statute. And "unless otherwise defined, words will be interpreted as taking their ordinary, contemporary common meaning." We have also cautioned that courts "should not read into the patent laws limitations and conditions which the legislature has not expressed."

Guided by these canons of construction, this Court has read the term "manufacture" in § 101 in accordance with its dictionary definition to mean "the production of articles for use from raw or prepared materials by giving to these materials new forms, qualities, properties, or combinations, whether by hand-labor or by machinery." American Fruit Growers, Inc. v. Brogdex Co., 283 U.S. 1, 11 (1931). Similarly, "composition of matter" has been construed consistent with its common usage to include "all compositions of two or more substances and ... all composite articles, whether they be the results of chemical union, or of mechanical mixture, or whether they be gases, fluids, powders or solids." Shell Development Co. v. Watson, 149 F.Supp. 279, 280 (D.D.C.1957). In choosing such expansive terms as "manufacture" and "composition of matter," modified by the comprehensive "any," Congress plainly contemplated that the patent laws would be given wide scope.

The relevant legislative history also supports a broad construction. The Patent Act of 1793, authored by Thomas Jefferson, defined statutory subject matter as "any new and useful art, machine, manufacture, or composition of matter, or any new or useful improvement [thereof]." Act of Feb. 21, 1793, § 1, 1 Stat. 319. The Act embodied Jefferson's philosophy that "ingenuity should receive a liberal encouragement." 5 Writings of Thomas Jefferson 75–76 (Washington ed. 1871). Subsequent patent statutes in 1836, 1870, and 1874 employed this same broad language. In 1952, when the patent laws were recodified, Congress replaced the word "art" with "process," but otherwise left Jefferson's language intact. The Committee Reports accompanying the 1952 Act inform us that Congress intended statutory subject matter to "include anything under the sun that is made by man." S. Rep. No. 1979, 82d Cong., 2d Sess., 5 (1952); HR Rep. No. 1923, 82d Cong., 2d Sess., 6 (1952).

This is not to suggest that § 101 has no limits or that it embraces every discovery. The laws of nature, physical phenomena, and abstract ideas have been held not patentable. Thus, a new mineral discovered in the earth or a new plant found in the wild is not patentable subject matter. Likewise, Einstein could not patent his celebrated law that $E = mc^2$; nor could Newton have patented the law of gravity. Such discoveries are "manifestations of . . . nature, free to all men and reserved exclusively to none." Funk Brothers Seed Co. v. Kalo Inoculant Co., 333 U.S. 127, 130 (1948).

Judged in this light, respondent's micro-organism plainly qualifies as patentable subject matter. His claim is not to a hitherto unknown natural phenomenon, but to a nonnaturally occurring manufacture or composition of matter—a product of human ingenuity "having a distinctive name, character [and] use." The point is underscored dramatically by comparison of the invention here with that in *Funk*. There, the patentee had discovered that there existed in nature certain species of root-nodule bacteria which did not exert a mutually inhibitive effect on each other. He used that discovery to produce a mixed culture capable of inoculating the seeds of leguminous plants. Concluding that the patentee had discovered "only some of the handiwork of nature," the Court ruled the product nonpatentable:

> "Each of the species of root-nodule bacteria contained in the package infects the same group of leguminous plants which it always infected. No species acquires a different use. The combination of species produces no new bacteria, no change in the six species of bacteria, and no enlargement of the range of their utility. Each species has the same effect it always had. The bacteria perform in their natural way. Their use in combination does not improve in any way their natural functioning. They serve the ends nature originally provided and act quite independently of any effort of the patentee."

Here, by contrast, the patentee has produced a new bacterium with markedly different characteristics from any found in nature and one having the potential for significant utility. His discovery is not nature's handiwork, but his own; accordingly it is patentable subject matter under § 101.

IV

Two contrary arguments are advanced, neither of which we find persuasive.

(A)

The petitioner's first argument rests on the enactment of the 1930 Plant Patent Act, which afforded patent protection to certain asexually reproduced plants, and the 1970 Plant Variety Protection Act, which authorized protection for certain sexually reproduced plants but excluded bacteria from its protection. In the petitioner's view, the passage of these Acts evidences congressional understanding that the terms "manufacture" or "composition of matter" do not include living things; if they did, the petitioner argues, neither Act would have been necessary.

We reject this argument. Prior to 1930, two factors were thought to remove plants from patent protection. The first was the belief that plants, even those artificially bred, were products of nature for purposes of the patent law. This position appears to have derived from the decision of the patent office in Ex parte Latimer, 1889 Dec.Com.Pat. 123, in which a patent claim for fiber found in the needle of the *Pinus australis* was rejected. The Commissioner reasoned that a contrary result would permit "patents [to] be obtained upon the trees of the forest and the plants of the earth, which of course would be unreasonable and impossible." The *Latimer* case, it seems, came to "se[t] forth the general stand taken in these matters" that plants were natural products not subject to patent protection. Thorne, Relation of Patent Law to Natural Products, 6 J. Pat.Off.Soc. 23, 24 (1923). The second obstacle to patent protection for plants was the fact that plants were thought not amenable to the "written description" requirement of the patent law. See 35 U.S.C. § 112. Because new plants may differ from old only in color or perfume, differentiation by written description was often impossible.

In enacting the Plant Patent Act, Congress addressed both of these concerns. It explained at length its belief that the work of the plant breeder "in aid of nature" was patentable invention. And it relaxed the written description requirement in favor of "a description ... as complete as is reasonably possible." 35 U.S.C. § 162. No Committee or Member of Congress, however, expressed the broader view, now urged by the petitioner, that the terms "manufacture" or "composition of matter" exclude living things. The sole support for that position in the legislative history of the 1930 Act is found in the conclusory statement of Secretary of Agriculture Hyde, in a letter to the Chairmen of the House and Senate Committees considering the 1930 Act, that "the patent laws ... at the present time are understood to cover only inventions or discoveries in the field of inanimate nature." Secretary Hyde's opinion, however, is not entitled to controlling weight. His views were solicited on the administration of the new law and not on the scope of patentable subject matter—an area beyond his competence. Moreover, there is language in the House and Senate Committee Reports suggesting that to the extent Congress considered the matter it found the Secretary's dichotomy unpersuasive. The Reports observe:

> "There is a clear and logical distinction *between the discovery of a new variety of plant and of certain inanimate things*, such, for example, as a new and useful natural mineral. The mineral is created wholly by nature unassisted by man.... On the other hand, a plant discovery resulting from cultivation is unique, isolated, and is not repeated by nature, nor can it be reproduced by nature unaided by man...." (emphasis added).

Congress thus recognized that the relevant distinction was not between living and inanimate things, but between products of nature, whether living or not, and human-made inventions. Here, respondent's microorganism is the result of human ingenuity and research. Hence, the passage of the Plant Patent Act affords the Government no support.

Nor does the passage of the 1970 Plant Variety Protection Act support the Government's position. As the Government acknowledges, sexually reproduced plants were not included under the 1930 Act because new varieties could not be reproduced true-to-type through seedlings. By 1970, however, it was generally recognized that true-to-type reproduction was possible and that plant patent protection was therefore appropriate. The 1970 Act extended that protection. There is nothing in its language or history to suggest that it was enacted because § 101 did not include living things.

In particular, we find nothing in the exclusion of bacteria from plant variety protection to support the petitioner's position. The legislative history gives no reason for this exclusion. As the Court of Customs and Patent Appeals suggested, it may simply reflect congressional agreement with the result reached by that court in deciding In re Arzberger, 112 F.2d 834 (1940), which held that bacteria were not plants for the purposes of the 1930 Act. Or it may reflect the fact that prior to 1970 the Patent Office had issued patents for bacteria under § 101. In any event, absent some clear indication that Congress "focused on [the] issues ... directly related to the one presently before the Court," there is no basis for reading into its actions an intent to modify the plain meaning of the words found in § 101.

(B)

The petitioner's second argument is that micro-organisms cannot qualify as patentable subject matter until Congress expressly authorizes such protection. His position rests on the fact that genetic technology was unforeseen when Congress enacted § 101. From this it is argued that resolution of the patentability of inventions such as respondent's should be left to Congress. The legislative process, the petitioner argues, is best equipped to weigh the competing economic, social, and scientific considerations involved, and to determine whether living organisms produced by genetic engineering should receive patent protection. In support of this position, the petitioner relies on our recent holding in Parker v. Flook, 437 U.S. 584 (1978), and the statement that the judiciary "must proceed cautiously when ... asked to extend patent rights into areas wholly unforeseen by Congress." Id. at 596.

It is, of course, correct that Congress, not the courts, must define the limits of patentability; but it is equally true that once Congress has spoken it is "the province and duty of the judicial department to say what the law is." Marbury v. Madison, 1 Cranch 137, 177 (1803). Congress has performed its constitutional role in defining patentable subject matter in § 101; we perform ours in construing the language Congress has employed. In so doing, our obligation is to take statutes as we find them, guided, if ambiguity appears, by the legislative history and statutory purpose. Here, we perceive no ambiguity. The subject-matter provisions of the patent law have been cast in broad terms to fulfill the constitutional and statutory goal of promoting "the Progress of Science and the useful Arts" with all that means for the social and economic benefits envisioned by Jefferson. Broad general language is not necessarily ambiguous when congressional objectives require broad terms.

Nothing in *Flook* is to the contrary. That case applied our prior precedents to determine that a "claim for an improved method of calculation, even when tied to a specific end use, is unpatentable subject matter under § 101." The Court carefully scrutinized the claim at issue to determine whether it was precluded from patent protection under "the principles underlying the prohibition against patents for 'ideas' or phenomena of nature." We have done that here. *Flook* did not announce a new principle that inventions in areas not contemplated by Congress when the patent laws were enacted are unpatentable per se.

To read that concept into *Flook* would frustrate the purposes of the patent law. This Court frequently has observed that a statute is not to be confined to the "particular application[s] ... contemplated by the legislators." This is especially true in the field of patent law. A rule that unanticipated inventions are without protection would conflict with the core concept of the patent law that anticipation undermines patentability. Mr. Justice Douglas reminded that the inventions most benefiting mankind are those that "push back the frontiers of chemistry, physics, and the like." Great A. & P. Tea Co. v. Supermarket Corp., 340 U.S. 147, 154 (1950)(concurring opinion). Congress employed broad general language in drafting § 101 precisely because such inventions are often unforeseeable.

To buttress his argument, the petitioner, with the support of amicus, points to grave risks that may be generated by research endeavors such as respondent's. The briefs present a gruesome parade of horribles. Scientists, among them Nobel laureates, are quoted suggesting that genetic research may pose a serious threat to the human race, or, at the very least, that the dangers are far too substantial to permit such research to proceed apace at this time. We are told that genetic research and related technological developments may spread pollution and disease, that it may result in a loss of genetic diversity, and that its practice may tend to depreciate the value of human life. These arguments are forcefully, even passionately, presented; they remind us that, at times, human ingenuity seems unable to control fully the forces it creates—that with Hamlet, it is sometimes better "to bear those ills we have than fly to others that we know not of."

It is argued that this Court should weigh these potential hazards in considering whether respondent's invention is patentable subject matter under § 101. We disagree. The grant or denial of patents on micro-organisms is not likely to put an end to genetic research or to its attendant risks. The large amount of research that has already occurred when no researcher had sure knowledge that patent protection would be available suggests that legislative or judicial fiat as to patentability will not deter the scientific mind from probing into the unknown any more than Canute could command the tides. Whether respondent's claims are patentable may determine whether research efforts are accelerated by the hope of reward or slowed by want of incentives, but that is all.

What is more important is that we are without competence to entertain these arguments—either to brush them aside as fantasies generated by fear of the unknown, or to act on them. The choice we are urged to make is a matter of high policy for resolution within the legislative process after the kind of investigation, examination, and study that legislative bodies can provide and courts cannot. That process involves the balancing of competing values and interests, which in our democratic system is the business of elected representatives. Whatever their validity, the contentions now pressed on us should be addressed to the political branches of the Government, the Congress and the Executive, and not to the courts.

We have emphasized in the recent past that "[o]ur individual appraisal of the wisdom or unwisdom of a particular [legislative] course ... is to be put aside in the process of interpreting a statute." Our task, rather, is the narrow one of determining what Congress meant by the words it used in the statute; once that is done our powers are exhausted. Congress is free to amend § 101 so as to exclude from patent protection organisms produced by genetic engineering. Cf. 42 U.S.C. § 2181(a), exempting from patent protection inventions "useful solely in the utilization of special nuclear material or atomic energy in an atomic weapon." Or it may chose to craft a statute specifically designed for such living things. But, until Congress takes such action, this Court must construe the language of § 101 as it is. The language of that section fairly embraces respondent's invention.

Accordingly, the judgment of the Court of Customs and Patent Appeals is

Affirmed.

■ [The dissenting opinion of JUSTICE BRENNAN, joined by JUSTICES WHITE and MARSHALL, is omitted.]

In Re Alappat

United States Court of Appeals, Federal Circuit, 1994.
33 F.3d 1526.

■ RICH, CIRCUIT JUDGE.

Kuriappan P. Alappat, Edward E. Averill, and James G. Larsen (collectively Alappat) appeal the April 22, 1992, reconsideration decision of the

Board of Patent Appeals and Interferences (Board) of the United States Patent and Trademark Office (PTO), Ex Parte Alappat, 23 U.S.P.Q.2d 1340 (BPAI, 1992), which sustained the Examiner's rejection of claims 15–19 of application Serial No. 07/149,792 ('792 application) as being unpatentable under 35 U.S.C. § 101 (1988).

THE MERITS

Our conclusion is that the appealed decision should be reversed because the appealed claims are directed to a "machine" which is one of the categories named in 35 U.S.C. § 101, as the first panel of the Board held.

A. Alappat's Invention

Alappat's invention relates generally to a means for creating a smooth waveform display in a digital oscilloscope. In short, and in lay terms, the invention is a [computer that achieves] an improvement in an oscilloscope comparable to a TV having a clearer picture.[a]

[a] [The court's more detailed description of the invention is as follows:

"The screen of an oscilloscope is the front of a cathode-ray tube (CRT), which is like a TV picture tube, whose screen, when in operation, presents an array (or raster) of pixels arranged at intersections of vertical columns and horizontal rows, a pixel being a spot on the screen which may be illuminated by directing an electron beam to that spot, as in TV. Each column in the array represents a different time period, and each row represents a different magnitude. An input signal to the oscilloscope is sampled and digitized to provide a waveform data sequence (vector list), wherein each successive element of the sequence represents the magnitude of the waveform at a successively later time. The waveform data sequence is then processed to provide a bit map, which is a stored data array indicating which pixels are to be illuminated. The waveform ultimately displayed is formed by a group of vectors, wherein each vector has a straight line trajectory between two points on the screen at elevations representing the magnitudes of two successive input signal samples and at horizontal positions representing the timing of the two samples.

"Because a CRT screen contains a finite number of pixels, rapidly rising and falling portions of a waveform can appear discontinuous or jagged due to differences in the elevation of horizontally contiguous pixels included in the waveform. In addition, the presence of 'noise' in an input signal can cause portions of the waveform to oscillate between contiguous pixel rows when the magnitude of the input signal lies between values represented by the elevations of the two rows. Moreover, the vertical resolution of the display may be limited by the number of rows of pixels on the screen. The noticeability and appearance of these effects is known as aliasing.

"To overcome these effects, Alappat's invention employs an anti-aliasing system wherein each vector making up the waveform is represented by modulating the illumination intensity of pixels having center points bounding the trajectory of the vector. The intensity at which each of the pixels is illuminated depends upon the distance of the center point of each pixel from the trajectory of the vector. Pixels lying squarely on the waveform trace receive maximum illumination, whereas pixels lying along an edge of the trace receive illumination decreasing in intensity proportional to the increase in the distance of the center point of the pixel from the vector trajectory. Employing this anti-aliasing technique eliminates any apparent discontinuity, jaggedness, or oscillation in the wave-

The Examiner's final rejection of claims 15–19[b] was under 35 U.S.C. § 101 "because the claimed invention is nonstatutory subject matter," and the original three-member Board panel reversed this rejection. That Board panel held that, although claim 15 recites a mathematical algorithm, the claim as a whole is directed to a machine and thus to statutory subject matter named in § 101.

In its reconsideration decision, the five-member majority of the expanded, eight-member Board panel "modified" the decision of the original panel and affirmed the Examiner's § 101 rejection.

* * * * *

(a)

The plain and unambiguous meaning of § 101 is that any new and useful process, machine, manufacture, or composition of matter, or any new and useful improvement thereof, may be patented if it meets the requirements for patentability set forth in Title 35, such as those found in §§ 102, 103, and 112. The use of the expansive term "any" in § 101 represents Congress's intent not to place any restrictions on the subject matter for which a patent may be obtained beyond those specifically recited in § 101 and the other parts of Title 35. Indeed, the Supreme Court has acknowledged that Congress intended § 101 to extend to "anything under the sun that is made by man." Diamond v. Chakrabarty, 447 U.S. 303, 309 (1980), quoting S.Rep. No.1979, 82nd Cong., 2nd Sess., 5 (1952); H.R.Rep. No.1923, 82nd Cong., 2nd Sess., 6 (1952). Thus, it is improper to read into § 101 limitations as to the subject matter that may be patented where the legislative history does not indicate that Congress clearly intended such limitations. See Chakrabarty, 447 U.S. at 308 ("We have also cautioned that courts 'should not read into the patent laws limitations and conditions which the legislature has not expressed.'"), quoting United States v. Dubilier Condenser Corp., 289 U.S. 178, 199 (1933).

Despite the apparent sweep of § 101, the Supreme Court has held that certain categories of subject matter are not entitled to patent protection. In Diamond v. Diehr, 450 U.S. 175 (1981), its most recent case addressing § 101, the Supreme Court explained that there are three categories of

---

form, thus giving the visual appearance of a smooth continuous waveform."—eds.]

[b] [In an earlier portion of the opinion, the court noted:

"Claim 15, the only independent claim in issue, reads: A rasterizer for converting vector list data representing sample magnitudes of an input waveform into anti-aliased pixel illumination intensity data to be displayed on a display means comprising: (a) means for determining the vertical distance between the endpoints of each of the vectors in the data list; (b) means for determining the elevation of a row of pixels that is spanned by the vector; (c) means for normalizing the vertical distance and elevation; and (d) means for outputting illumination intensity data as a predetermined function of the normalized vertical distance and elevation.

"Each of claims 16–19 depends directly from claim 15 and more specifically defines an element of the rasterizer claimed therein."—eds.]

subject matter for which one may not obtain patent protection, namely "laws of nature, natural phenomena, and abstract ideas." Diehr, 450 U.S. at 185.[c] Of relevance to this case, the Supreme Court also has held that certain mathematical subject matter is not, standing alone, entitled to patent protection. See Diehr, 450 U.S. 175; Parker v. Flook, 437 U.S. 584 (1978); Gottschalk v. Benson, 409 U.S. 63 (1972). A close analysis of Diehr, Flook, and Benson reveals that the Supreme Court never intended to create an overly broad, fourth category of subject matter excluded from § 101. Rather, at the core of the Court's analysis in each of these cases lies an attempt by the Court to explain a rather straightforward concept, namely, that certain types of mathematical subject matter, standing alone, represent nothing more than abstract ideas until reduced to some type of practical application, and thus that subject matter is not, in and of itself, entitled to patent protection.

Diehr also demands that the focus in any statutory subject matter analysis be on the claim as a whole. Indeed, the Supreme Court stated in Diehr: " [W]hen a claim containing a mathematical formula, [mathematical equation, mathematical algorithm, or the like], implements or applies that formula, [equation, algorithm, or the like], in a structure or process which, when considered as a whole, is performing a function which the patent laws were designed to protect (e.g., transforming or reducing an article to a different state or thing), then the claim satisfies the requirements of § 101. Diehr, 450 U.S. at 192. It is thus not necessary to determine whether a claim contains, as merely a part of the whole, any mathematical subject matter which standing alone would not be entitled to patent protection. Indeed, because the dispositive inquiry is whether the claim as a whole is directed to statutory subject matter, it is irrelevant that a claim may contain, as part of the whole, subject matter which would not be patentable by itself. "A claim drawn to subject matter otherwise statutory does not become nonstatutory simply because it uses a mathematical formula, [mathematical equation, mathematical algorithm], computer program or digital computer." Diehr, 450 U.S. at 187.

---

[c] Laws of nature and natural phenomena are in essence "manifestations of . . . nature [i.e., not 'new'], free to all men and reserved exclusively to none," see Chakrabarty 447 U.S. at 309, quoting Funk Bros. Seed Co. v. Kalo Inoculant Co., 333 U.S. 127, 130 (1948), whereas abstract ideas constitute disembodied concepts or truths which are not "useful" from a practical standpoint standing alone, i.e., they are not "useful" until reduced to some practical application. Of course, a process, machine, manufacture, or composition of matter employing a law of nature, natural phenomenon, or abstract idea may be patentable even though the law of nature, natural phenomenon, or abstract idea employed would not, by itself, be entitled to such protection. See e.g. Parker v. Flook, 437 U.S. 584, 590 (1978)("a process is not unpatentable simply because it contains a law of nature or a mathematical algorithm."); Funk Bros. Seed, 333 U.S. at 130 ("He who discovers a hitherto unknown phenomenon of nature has no claim to a monopoly of it which the law recognizes. If there is to be invention from such a discovery, it must come from the application of the law to a new and useful end."); MacKay Radio & Telegraph Co. v. Radio Corp. of America, 306 U.S. 86, 94 (1939)("While a scientific truth, or the mathematical expression of it, is not a patentable invention, a novel and useful structure created with the aid of knowledge of scientific truth may be.").

(b)

Given the foregoing, the proper inquiry in dealing with the so called mathematical subject matter exception to § 101 alleged herein is to see whether the claimed subject matter as a whole is a disembodied mathematical concept, whether categorized as a mathematical formula, mathematical equation, mathematical algorithm, or the like, which in essence represents nothing more than a "law of nature," "natural phenomenon," or "abstract idea." If so, Diehr precludes the patenting of that subject matter. That is not the case here.

Although many, or arguably even all, of the means elements recited in claim 15 represent circuitry elements that perform mathematical calculations, which is essentially true of all digital electrical circuits, the claimed invention as a whole is directed to a combination of interrelated elements which combine to form a machine for converting discrete waveform data samples into anti-aliased pixel illumination intensity data to be displayed on a display means. This is not a disembodied mathematical concept which may be characterized as an "abstract idea," but rather a specific machine to produce a useful, concrete, and tangible result.

The fact that the four claimed means elements function to transform one set of data to another through what may be viewed as a series of mathematical calculations does not alone justify a holding that the claim as a whole is directed to nonstatutory subject matter. See In re Iwahashi, 888 F.2d 1370, 1375 (Fed.Cir.1989), 12 U.S.P.Q.2d at 1911. Indeed, claim 15 as written is not "so abstract and sweeping" that it would "wholly pre-empt" the use of any apparatus employing the combination of mathematical calculations recited therein. See Benson, 409 U.S. at 68–72. Rather, claim 15 is limited to the use of a particularly claimed combination of elements performing the particularly claimed combination of calculations to transform, i.e., rasterize, digitized waveforms (data) into anti-aliased, pixel illumination data to produce a smooth waveform.

Furthermore, the claim preamble's recitation that the subject matter for which Alappat seeks patent protection is a rasterizer for creating a smooth waveform is not a mere field-of-use label having no significance. Indeed, the preamble specifically recites that the claimed rasterizer converts waveform data into output illumination data for a display, and the means elements recited in the body of the claim make reference not only to the inputted waveform data recited in the preamble but also to the output illumination data also recited in the preamble. Claim 15 thus defines a combination of elements constituting a machine for producing an anti-aliased waveform.

The reconsideration Board majority also erred in its reasoning that claim 15 is unpatentable merely because it "reads on a general purpose digital computer 'means' to perform the various steps under program control." Alappat, 23 U.S.P.Q.2d at 1345. The Board majority stated that it would "not presume that a stored program digital computer is not within the § 112 ¶ 6 range of equivalents of the structure disclosed in the specification." Alappat, 23 U.S.P.Q.2d at 1345. Alappat admits that claim

15 would read on a general purpose computer programmed to carry out the claimed invention, but argues that this alone also does not justify holding claim 15 unpatentable as directed to nonstatutory subject matter. We agree. We have held that such programming creates a new machine, because a general purpose computer in effect becomes a special purpose computer once it is programmed to perform particular functions pursuant to instructions from program software. In re Freeman, 573 F.2d 1237, 1247 n. 11, 197 U.S.P.Q. 464, 472 n. 11 (CCPA 1978).

Under the Board majority's reasoning, a programmed general purpose computer could never be viewed as patentable subject matter under § 101. This reasoning is without basis in the law. The Supreme Court has never held that a programmed computer may never be entitled to patent protection. Indeed, the Benson court specifically stated that its decision therein did not preclude "a patent for any program servicing a computer." Benson, 409 U.S. at 71. Consequently, a computer operating pursuant to software may represent patentable subject matter, provided, of course, that the claimed subject matter meets all of the other requirements of Title 35. In any case, a computer, like a rasterizer, is apparatus not mathematics.

CONCLUSION

For the foregoing reasons, the appealed decision of the Board affirming the examiner's rejection is

REVERSED.

■ ARCHER, CHIEF JUDGE, with whom NIES, CIRCUIT JUDGE, joins, concurring in part and dissenting in part.

A

I disagree with the majority's conclusion that Alappat's "rasterizer," which is all that is claimed in the claims at issue, constitutes an invention or discovery within 35 U.S.C. § 101. I would affirm the board's decision sustaining the examiner's rejection of claims 15–19 to the rasterizer under 35 U.S.C. § 101 because Alappat has not shown that he invented or discovered a machine within § 101.

Alappat has arranged known circuit elements to accomplish nothing other than the solving of a particular mathematical equation represented in the mind of the reader of his patent application. Losing sight of the forest for the structure of the trees, the majority today holds that any claim reciting a precise arrangement of structure satisfies 35 U.S.C. § 101. As I shall demonstrate, the rationale that leads to this conclusion and the majority's holding that Alappat's rasterizer represents the invention of a machine are illogical, inconsistent with precedent and with sound principles of patent law, and will have untold consequences.

B

The Patent Clause of the Constitution empowers the Congress to "promote the Progress of . . . useful Arts, by securing for limited Times to

... Inventors the exclusive right to their ... Discoveries." U.S. Const. art. I, § 8, cl. 8.

Congress has implemented this limited grant of power in 35 U.S.C. § 101 by enumerating certain subject matter, the invention or discovery of which may entitle one to a patent: "Whoever invents or discovers any new and useful process, machine, manufacture, or composition of matter, or any new and useful improvement thereof, may obtain a patent therefor, subject to the conditions and requirements of this title." 35 U.S.C. § 101 (1988). The terms used in § 101 have been used for over two hundred years—since the beginnings of American patent law—to define the extent of the subject matter of patentable invention. See In re Chatfield, 545 F.2d 152, 159, 191 U.S.P.Q. 730, 736–37 (CCPA 1976)(Rich, J., dissenting); 1 D. Chisum, Patents § 1.01 (1993).

Coexistent with the usage of these terms has been the rule that a person cannot obtain a patent for the discovery of an abstract idea, principle or force, law of nature, or natural phenomenon, but rather must invent or discover a practical "application" to a useful end. Diamond v. Diehr, 450 U.S. 175, 185, 187–88, 209 U.S.P.Q. 1, 7–9 (1981)(citing, for example, Rubber–Tip Pencil Co. v. Howard, 87 U.S. (20 Wall.) 498, 507 (1874)); Parker v. Flook, 437 U.S. 584, 589, 591, 198 U.S.P.Q. 193, 197–98 (1978).

Thus patent law rewards persons for inventing technologically useful applications, instead of for philosophizing unapplied research and theory. Brenner v. Manson, 383 U.S. 519, 534–35, 148 U.S.P.Q. 689, 695 (1966) ("Unless and until a process is refined and developed to this point—where specific benefit exists in currently available form—there is insufficient justification for" the reward of a patent.); Graham v. John Deere Co., 383 U.S. 1, 5, 148 U.S.P.Q. 459, 462 (1966)("the federal patent power ... is limited to the promotion of advances in the 'useful arts' "); In re Meyer, 688 F.2d 789, 795, 215 U.S.P.Q. 193, 197 (CCPA 1982)(quoting O'Reilly v. Morse, 56 U.S. (15 How.) 62, 132–33 (1853)(Grier, J., concurring)); 1 D. Chisum, Patents § 1.01, at 1–5 & n. 9 (1993)("[I]n enacting patent legislation, Congress is confined to the promotion of the 'useful arts,' not 'science' (i.e., knowledge) in general.... The general purpose of the statutory classes of subject matter is to limit patent protection to the field of applied technology, what the United States constitution calls 'the useful arts.' ").

Additionally, unapplied research, abstract ideas, and theory continue to be the "basic tools of scientific and technological work," which persons are free to trade in and to build upon in the pursuit of among other things useful inventions. Flook, 437 U.S. at 589, 198 U.S.P.Q. at 197 (quotations omitted). Even after a patent has been awarded for a new, useful, and nonobvious practical application of an idea, others may learn from the underlying ideas, theories, and principles to legitimately "design around" the patentee's useful application. See Slimfold Mfg. Co. v. Kinkead Indus., Inc., 932 F.2d 1453, 1457, 18 U.S.P.Q.2d 1842, 1845–46 (Fed.Cir.1991).

The requirement of the patent law that an invention or discovery reside in the application of an abstract idea, law of nature, principle, or natural phenomenon is embodied in the language of 35 U.S.C. § 101. A patent can be awarded to one who "invents or discovers" something within the enumerated classes of subject matter—"process," "machine," "manufacture," "composition of matter." These terms may not be read in a strict literal sense entirely divorced from the context of the patent law. Rather they must be read as incorporating the longstanding and well-established limitation that the claimed invention or discovery must reside in a practical application.

In addition to the basic principles embodied in the language of § 101, the section has a pragmatic aspect. That subject matter must be new (§ 102) and nonobvious (§ 103) in order to be patentable is of course a separate requirement for patentability, and does not determine whether the applicant's purported invention or discovery is within § 101. Diehr, 450 U.S. at 190, 209 U.S.P.Q. at 10. Section 101 must be satisfied before any of the other provisions apply, and in this way § 101 lays the predicate for the other provisions of the patent law. See Flook, 437 U.S. at 593, 198 U.S.P.Q. at 199 (The determination of "what type of discovery is sought to be patented must precede the determination of whether that discovery is, in fact, new or obvious."); Diehr, 450 U.S. at 189, 209 U.S.P.Q. at 9 ("[s]pecific conditions for patentability follow" § 101). When considering that the patent law does not allow patents merely for the discovery of ideas, principles, and laws of nature, ask whether, were it not so, the other provisions of the patent law could be applied at all. If Einstein could have obtained a patent for his discovery that the energy of an object at rest equals its mass times the speed of light squared, how would his discovery be meaningfully judged for nonobviousness, the sine qua non of patentable invention? 35 U.S.C. § 103. When is the abstract idea "reduced to practice" as opposed to being "conceived"? See id. § 102(g). What conduct amounts to the "infringement" of another's idea? See id. § 271.

Consider for example the discovery or creation of music, a new song. Music of course is not patentable subject matter; a composer cannot obtain exclusive patent rights for the original creation of a musical composition. But now suppose the new melody is recorded on a compact disc. In such case, the particular musical composition will define an arrangement of minute pits in the surface of the compact disc material, and therefore will define its specific structure. See D. Macaulay, The Way Things Work 248–49 (Houghton Mifflin 1988). Alternatively suppose the music is recorded on the rolls of a player piano or a music box.

Through the expedient of putting his music on known structure, can a composer now claim as his invention the structure of a compact disc or player piano roll containing the melody he discovered and obtain a patent therefor? The answer must be no. The composer admittedly has invented or discovered nothing but music. The discovery of music does not become patentable subject matter simply because there is an arbitrary claim to some structure.

And if a claim to a compact disc or piano roll containing a newly discovered song were regarded as a "manufacture" and within § 101 simply because of the specific physical structure of the compact disc, the "practical effect" would be the granting of a patent for a discovery in music. Where the music is new, the precise structure of the disc or roll would be novel under § 102. Because the patent law cannot examine music for "nonobviousness," the Patent and Trademark Office could not make a showing of obviousness under § 103. The result would well be the award of a patent for the discovery of music. The majority's simplistic approach of looking only to whether the claim reads on structure and ignoring the claimed invention or discovery for which a patent is sought will result in the awarding of patents for discoveries well beyond the scope of the patent law.

Patent cases involving the distinction between idea or principle may involve subtle distinctions. Flook, 437 U.S. at 589, 198 U.S.P.Q. at 197. Section 101 embodies the very soul of the intangible nature of invention. Without particular claimed subject matter in mind, it is impossible to generalize with bright line rules the dividing line between what is in substance the invention or discovery of a useful application within § 101 versus merely the discovery of an abstract idea or law of nature or principle outside § 101. Each case presenting a question under § 101 must be decided individually based upon the particular subject matter at issue. See In re Grams, 888 F.2d 835, 839, 12 U.S.P.Q.2d 1824, 1828 (Fed.Cir.1989)(Section 101 analysis "depends on the claims as a whole and the circumstances of each case."). There are however answers in every § 101 case. But they are found by applying precedent and principles of patent law to the particular claimed subject matter at issue.

Every case involving a § 101 issue must begin with this question: What, if anything, is it that the applicant for a patent "invented or discovered"? In re Abele, 684 F.2d 902, 907, 214 U.S.P.Q. 682, 687 (CCPA 1982), quoted in In re Grams, 888 F.2d 835, 839, 12 U.S.P.Q.2d 1824, 1827 (Fed.Cir.1989); see Kneass v. Schuylkill Bank, 14 F.Cas. 746, 748 (C.C.Pa. 1820)(No. 7875)(Washington, J.). To resolve this inquiry, the patent or patent application must be reviewed and the subject matter claimed as the invention or discovery "must be considered as a whole." Diehr, 450 U.S. at 188, 209 U.S.P.Q. at 9; Flook, 437 U.S. at 594, 198 U.S.P.Q. at 199; In re Walter, 618 F.2d 758, 205 U.S.P.Q. 397, 405 (CCPA 1980)(Inquiry under section 101 depends on "the relationship which the truth or principle bears to the substance of the invention as claimed.").

In considering claimed subject matter for eligibility under § 101, "it must be determined whether a scientific principle, law of nature, idea, or mental process, which may be represented by a mathematical algorithm, is included in the subject matter" claimed as the invention or discovery. In re Meyer, 688 F.2d 789, 795, 215 U.S.P.Q. 193, 198 (CCPA 1982). When the claimed invention or discovery includes "a mathematical formula (or scientific principle or phenomenon of nature), an inquiry must be made into whether the claim is seeking patent protection for that formula in the abstract," Diehr, 450 U.S. at 191, 209 U.S.P.Q. at 10, or whether the "claim containing a mathematical formula implements or applies that formula in a structure or process which, when considered as a whole, is performing a function which the patent laws were designed to protect," id. at 192, 209 U.S.P.Q. at 10.

Thus the dispositive issue is not whether the claim recites on its face something more physical than just abstract mathematics. If it were, Benson and Flook would have come out the other way and Diehr would have been a very short opinion. The dispositive issue is whether the invention or discovery for which an award of patent is sought is more than just a discovery in abstract mathematics. Where the invention or discovery is only of mathematics, the invention or discovery is not the "kind" of discovery the patent law was designed to protect and even the most narrowly drawn claim must fail. Diehr, 450 U.S. at 192 n. 14, 209 U.S.P.Q. at 10 n. 14. To come within the purview of § 101 and the patent law, a mathematical formula or operation must be "applied in an invention of a type set forth in 35 U.S.C. § 101." Meyer, 688 F.2d at 795, 215 U.S.P.Q. at 198.

So what did Alappat invent or discover? Alappat's specification clearly distinguishes between an "oscilloscope" and a "rasterizer," and Alappat claims his invention in claims 15–19 to be only the "rasterizer."

The "rasterizer" as claimed is an arrangement of circuitry elements for converting data into other data according to a particular mathematical operation. The rasterizer begins with vector "data"—two numbers. "[I]t does not matter how they are ascertained." Brief for Alappat at 39. The two numbers, as they might to any algebra student, "represent" endpoints of a line.

The claimed "rasterizer" ends with other specific "data"—an array of numbers, as the original and reconsideration panels of the board both expressly agreed. See Diehr, 450 U.S. at 186, 209 U.S.P.Q. at 8 ("The claims [in Flook]were drawn to a method for computing an 'alarm limit.' An 'alarm limit' is simply a number...."); Abele, 684 F.2d at 909, 214 U.S.P.Q. at 688 (the "claim presents no more than the calculation of a number and display of the result"); Walter, 618 F.2d at 768, 205 U.S.P.Q. at 407 ("if the end-product of a claimed invention is a pure number, as in Benson and Flook, the invention is nonstatutory"). The end-data of the "rasterizer" are a predetermined and claimed mathematic function of the two input numbers.

Alappat admits that each of the circuitry elements of the claimed "rasterizer" is old. He says they are merely "form." Thus, they are only a convenient and basic way of electrically representing the mathematical operations to be performed, that is, converting vector data into matrix or raster data. In Alappat's view, it is the new mathematic operation that is the "substance" of the claimed invention or discovery. Claim 15 as a whole thus claims old circuitry elements in an arrangement defined by a mathematical operation, which only performs the very mathematical operation that defines it. Rather than claiming the mathematics itself, which of course Alappat cannot do, Alappat claims the mathematically defined structure. But as a whole, there is no "application" apart from the mathematical operation that is asserted to be the invention or discovery.

What is going on here is a charade. Alappat asks the following: An input to ... a circuit or processing function is converted into a different thing at the output (otherwise why have the circuit or function in the first place?). If the process is new, useful, and nonobvious, does it really matter whether the implementation is in the form of analog components, digital components, programs for a computer, or a combination thereof? Isn't such a differentiation exalting form over substance? ... [Br. for Alappat at 48.]

The questions are properly answered thusly: "No," in Alappat's claimed "rasterizer" it really does not matter how the mathematics is implemented, and "Yes," assigning § 101 significance to the disclosed structure would be exalting form over substance. So where the claimed structure does not matter and the invention or discovery is only of a "new, useful, and nonobvious" process for solving a mathematical formula, Benson, Flook, Diehr, and years of precedent command that the patent law shall not exalt form over substance, but rather recognize that the substance is outside § 101.

The subject matter of claim 15, as in Flook, "has no substance apart from the calculations involved. The calculations are the beginning and end of the claim[ ]." Walter, 618 F.2d at 769, 205 U.S.P.Q. at 409. Also as in Flook, the oscilloscope disclosed in Alappat's specification presents a general technological environment for the claimed "rasterizer," insignificant in relation to it. Claim 15 is not even limited to the environment of an oscilloscope. See Abele, 684 F.2d at 909, 214 U.S.P.Q. at 688. The claimed rasterizer mathematical function presumably has application in conjunction with any current or future device that prints in an x-y coordinate grid, such as oscilloscopes, computer monitors, televisions, laser printers, mechanical printing devices, etc.

This is not to say that digital circuitry cannot be an element in an otherwise statutory machine. Under Diehr, it can. But Alappat expressly recognizes the distinction between a "machine," even giving some examples, and the "digital processing" one of its components might perform: In today's technological environment virtually every machine, from cars to washing machines to instruments [e.g., oscilloscopes], uses digital processing, either with specific digital circuitry and/or a microprocessor executing a program. [Brief for Alappat at 47.]

Getting back to the music analogy, Alappat is like a composer who claims his song on a compact disc, and then argues that the compact disc is equivalent to a player piano or a music box with the song on a roll or even sheet music because they all represent the same song. The composer is thus clearly asking for (and getting from the majority) a patent for the discovery of a song and a patent covering every physical manifestation of the song.

■ NEWMAN, CIRCUIT JUDGE, concurring [omitted].

■ MAYER, CIRCUIT JUDGE, with whom MICHEL, CIRCUIT JUDGE, joins, dissenting [omitted].

■ PLAGER, CIRCUIT JUDGE, concurring [omitted].

In Re Grams

United States Court of Appeals, Federal Circuit, 1989.
888 F.2d 835.

■ ARCHER, CIRCUIT JUDGE.

Applicants Ralph A. Grams and Dennis C. Lezotte (Grams) appeal from the decision of the Board of Patent Appeals and Interferences (Board) affirming the examiner's rejection of claims 1 and 3–16, which constitute all the claims remaining in Application S.N. 625,247, filed June 27, 1984. The claims were rejected under 35 U.S.C. § 101 as being directed to nonstatutory subject matter because they in essence claim either a mathematical algorithm or a method of doing business. We affirm.

BACKGROUND

The invention provides a method of testing a complex system to determine whether the system condition is normal or abnormal and, if it is abnormal, to determine the cause of the abnormality. As disclosed in the specification, the invention is applicable to any complex system, whether it be electrical, mechanical, chemical, biological, or combinations thereof. The system comprises a plurality of constituent subsystems or parts, some characteristic of which is represented by a set of correlated parameters susceptible of measurement and representative of the overall system. The disclosed invention involves considering the entire set of parameters, diagnosing the existence of an abnormality, and identifying which particular parameters of the set are responsible for the abnormality.

The claims limit the disclosed invention to the diagnosis of an individual.[a] Step [a] requires the performance of clinical laboratory tests on an

[a] [The court gave as an example Claim 1, on which the other claims depend:

"1. A method of diagnosing an abnormal condition in an individual, the individual being characterized by a plurality of correlated parameters of a set of such parameters that is representative of the individual's condition, the parameters comprising data resulting from a plurality of clinical laboratory tests which measure the levels of chemical and biological constituents of the individual [sic] and each parameter having a reference range of values, *the method comprising* [a] performing said plurality of clinical laboratory tests on the individual to measure the values of the set of parameters; [b] producing from the set of measured parameter values and the reference ranges of values a first quantity representative of the condition of the individual; [c] comparing the first quantity to a first predetermined value to determine whether the individual's condition is abnormal; [d] upon determining from said comparing that the individual's condition is abnormal, successively testing a plurality of different combinations of the constituents of the individual by eliminating parameters from the set to form subsets corresponding to said combinations, producing for each subset a second quantity, and comparing said second quantity with a second predetermined value to detect a non-significant deviation from a normal condition; and [e] identifying as a result of said testing a complementary subset of parameters corresponding to a combination of constituents responsible for the abnormal condition, said complementary subset comprising the parameters eliminated from the set so as to produce a subset having said non-significant deviation from a normal condition. (Emphasis and bracketed letters added.)" —eds.]

individual to obtain data for the parameters (e.g., sodium content). The remaining steps, [b]-[e], analyze that data to ascertain the existence and identity of an abnormality, and possible causes thereof. In that regard, steps [b]-[e] are in essence a mathematical algorithm, in that they represent "[a] procedure for solving a given type of mathematical problem." Gottschalk v. Benson, 409 U.S. 63, 65 (1972).[b]

Applicants do not dispute that claim 1 includes a mathematical algorithm. However, they contend that the mere recital of an algorithm does not automatically render a claim nonstatutory. They are correct in that regard, but the inclusion of a mathematical algorithm in a claim can render it nonstatutory if the claim in essence covers only the algorithm. The Board held that was the case here.

ISSUE

Whether the algorithm-containing claims at issue are drawn to statutory subject matter.

OPINION

Section 101 of Title 35 states:

Whoever invents or discovers *any new and useful process*, machine, manufacture, or composition of matter, or *any* new and useful improvement thereof, may obtain a patent therefor, subject to the conditions and requirements of this title.

(Emphasis added.) Intuitively, one might conclude that the statute's "any ... process" would include the diagnostic method claimed by applicants. Indeed, even without physical step [a] present in the claims, application of the algorithm in steps [b]-[e] seems to be a type of "process"....

[In this portion of the opinion, the Court reviews the Supreme Court cases on computer programs, concluding:]

On the other hand, "the mere presence of a mathematical exercise, as a step or steps in a process involving nonmathematical steps, should not slam the door of the Patent and Trademark Office upon an applicant[.]" Thus, if there are physical steps included in the claim in addition to the algorithm, the claim might be eligible for patent protection. As stated in In re Walter, 618 F.2d 758 (CCPA 1980):

Once a mathematical algorithm has been found, the claim *as a whole* must be further analyzed. If it appears that the mathematical algorithm is implemented in a specific manner to define structural relationships between the physical elements of the claim (in apparatus claims) or to refine or limit claim steps (in process claims), the claim being otherwise statutory, the claim passes muster under § 101.

(Emphasis in original; footnote omitted).

[b] It is of no moment that the algorithm is not expressed in terms of a mathematical formula. Words used in a claim operating on data to solve a problem can serve the same purpose as a formula.

The *Walter* test, of deciding whether the algorithm "define[s] structural relationships" or "refine[s] or limit[s] claim steps" in an otherwise statutory claim, "was not intended to be the exclusive test for determining the presence of statutory subject matter." In re Meyer, 688 F.2d 789, 796 (CCPA 1982). Thus, though satisfaction of the *Walter* test necessarily depicts statutory subject matter, failure to meet that test does not necessarily doom the claim. As stated in In re Abele, 684 F.2d 902, 907 (CCPA 1982), "Walter should be read as requiring *no more than* that the algorithm be 'applied in any manner to physical elements or process steps[.]' " (Emphasis added.) That statement is followed by this proviso:

> provided that its application is circumscribed by more than a field of use limitation or non-essential post-solution activity. Thus, if the claim would be "otherwise statutory," albeit inoperative or less useful without the algorithm, the claim likewise presents statutory subject matter when the algorithm is included.[c]

In all instances, this critical question must be answered: "What did applicants invent?" And in answering this inquiry:

> [e]ach invention must be evaluated as claimed: yet semantogenic considerations preclude a determination based solely on words appearing in the claims. In the final analysis under § 101, the claimed invention, as a whole, must be evaluated for what it is.
>
> Hence, the analysis requires careful interpretation of each claim in light of its supporting disclosure.

Abele, 684 F.2d at 907.

Though that analysis can be difficult, it is facilitated somewhat if, as here, the only physical step involves merely gathering data for the algorithm. As stated in In re Christensen, 478 F.2d 1392, 1394 (CCPA 1973):

> Given that the method of solving a mathematical equation may not be the subject of patent protection, it follows that the addition of the old and necessary antecedent steps of establishing values for the variables in the equation cannot convert the unpatentable method to patentable subject matter.

The reason for this was explained in In re Sarkar, 588 F.2d at 1335:

> No mathematical equation can be used, as a practical matter, without establishing and substituting values for the variables expressed therein. Substitution of values dictated by the formula has thus been viewed as a form of mathematical step. If the steps of gathering and substituting values were alone sufficient, every mathematical equation, formula, or algorithm having any practical use would be per se subject to patenting as a

---

[c] We do not read the last sentence of this quote as declaring patentable any claim that is statutory without the algorithm. We read it consistently with the previous sentence, and with *Walter*, as requiring (to meet the *Walter* test) not only that the physical steps in the claim (without the algorithm) constitute a statutory process but, also, that the algor- ithm operates on a claimed physical step. *Accord In re Meyer*, 688 F.2d 789, 795 (CCPA 1982)("the decisive question is whether that mental process is applied to physical elements or process steps in an otherwise statutory process, machine, manufacture, or composition of matter").

"process" under § 101. Consideration of whether the substitution of specific values is enough to convert the disembodied ideas present in the formula into an embodiment of those ideas, or into an application of the formula, is foreclosed by the current state of the law.

See also In re Richman, 563 F.2d 1026, 1030 (CCPA 1977) ("[N]otwithstanding that the antecedent steps are novel and unobvious, they merely determine values for the variables used in the mathematical formulae used in making the calculations. [They] do not suffice to render the claimed methods, considered as a whole, statutory subject matter."). Accord In re Meyer, 688 F.2d 789, 794 (CCPA 1982)("[data-gathering] step[s] cannot make an otherwise nonstatutory claim statutory" (citing with approval *In re Richman*)).

Whether section 101 precludes patentability in every case where the physical step of obtaining data for the algorithm is the only other significant element in mathematical algorithm-containing claims is a question we need not answer. Analysis in that area depends on the claims as a whole and the circumstances of each case. Rather, we address only the claims and other circumstances involved here.

The sole physical process step in Grams' claim 1 is step [a], *i.e.*, performing clinical tests on individuals to obtain data. The specification does not bulge with disclosure on those tests. To the contrary, it focuses on the algorithm itself, although it briefly refers to, without describing, the clinical tests that provide data. Thus, it states: "The [computer] program was written to analyze the results of up to eighteen clinical laboratory tests produced by a standard chemical analyzer that measures the levels of the chemical biological components listed...." The specification also states that "[t]he invention is applicable to any complex system, whether it be electrical, mechanical, chemical or biological, or combinations thereof." From the specification and the claim, it is clear to us that applicants are, in essence, claiming the mathematical algorithm, which they cannot do under *Gottschalk v. Benson*. The presence of a physical step in the claim to derive data for the algorithm will not render the claim statutory.

Because we affirm the Board's holding that the applicants' claims are unpatentable under section 101 as being drawn to a nonstatutory mathematical algorithm, we need not address the issue of whether they are also unpatentable as a method of doing business.

NOTES

1. *Ideas vs. embodiments.* The difficulty in drawing a line between an idea, or a principle of nature, and its embodiment became evident early in patent law's history. In particular, consider two early cases, O'Reilly v. Morse,[4] involving the patent on the telegraph, and Dolbear v. American Bell Telephone Co. ("the Telephone Cases").[5] Commentators have long had

[4] 56 U.S. (15 How.) 62, 14 L.Ed. 601 (1854).

[5] 126 U.S. 1, 8 S.Ct. 778, 31 L.Ed. 863 (1888).

difficulty explaining how the Supreme Court could have invalidated the eighth claim in Samuel F.B. Morse's patent on the telegraph on the ground that it claimed a principle rather than an embodiment, yet uphold the fifth claim of Alexander Graham Bell's patent on the telephone. Morse's claim read as follows:

> "Eighth. I do not propose to limit myself to the specific machinery ... described in the foregoing specification and claims; the essence of my invention being the use of the motive power of the electric or galvanic current, which I call electro-magnetism, however developed, for making or printing intelligible characters (letters or signs), at any distances ..."

Bell claimed:

> "The method of, and apparatus for, transmitting vocal or other sounds telegraphically, as herein described, by causing electrical undulations, similar in form to the vibrations of the air accompanying the said vocal or other sounds, substantially as set forth."

As to *Morse,* the Supreme Court said:

> "If this claim can be maintained, it matters not by what process or machinery the result is accomplished. For aught that we now know some future inventor, in the onward march of science, may discover a mode of writing or printing at a distance by means of the electric or galvanic current, without using any part of the process or combination set forth in the plaintiff's specification.... But yet if it is covered by this patent the inventor could not use it, nor the public have the benefit of it without the permission of this patentee."[6]

In contrast, in *The Telephone Cases,* the Court held:

> "The patent for the art does not necessarily involve a patent for the particular means employed for using it. Indeed, the mention of any means ... is only necessary to show that the art can be used. ..."[7]

Admittedly, Bell drafted his claim so that it would appear limited to "undulations." In contrast, Morse made very clear that his claim was meant to be broad. Yet in actual fact, both claims are equally drawn to principles, in Morse's case, the principle of using the wave properties of electromagnetism to transmit signs; in Bell's, the principle of using its oscillations to transmit sound. And so, the Supreme Court's concern that Morse was tying up basic building blocks of knowledge and extending the reach of his claim to those who were not utilizing his insight is equally applicable to Bell.

To be sure, *The Telephone Cases* tried to distinguish *Morse:*

> "In the present case the claim is not for the use of a current of electricity in its natural state as it comes from the battery, but for putting a continuous current in a closed circuit into a certain specified

---

[6] 56 U.S. (15 How.) at 113.   [7] 126 U.S. at 533.

condition suited to the transmission of vocal and other sounds, and using it in that condition for that purpose."[8]

However, the argument is somewhat less than convincing.[9]

Rather than indulge in similar talmudic distinctions, the lower courts invented a series of "rules of thumb" to help draw the line between principles and the embodiments. Among the inventions considered unpatentable were business systems,[10] printed matter,[11] functions-of-machines,[12] mental steps,[13] and methods dependent on human reactions.[14] Although

[8] Id. at 534.

[9] See, e.g., D. Chisum, Patents § 1.03[2].

[10] In In re Wait, 73 F.2d 982 (C.C.P.A. 1934), for example, the applicant claimed a process for the exchange of stocks and commodities that obviated the need for a broker. The court rejected the claims as drawn to non-statutory subject matter, holding:

> The process, when analyzed carefully, appears to comprise, in its essence, nothing more than the advertising of, or giving publicity to, offers of purchase or sale by one party, the acceptance thereof by another, and the making of a record of the transaction followed by a withdrawal of the offer. Surely these are, and always have been, essential steps in all dealings of this nature, and even conceding, without holding, that some methods of doing business might present patentable novelty, we think such novelty is lacking here.

73 F.2d at 983. See also, e.g., Hotel Security Checking Co. v. Lorraine Co., 160 F. 467 (2d Cir.1908).

[11] See, e.g., Ex parte Gwinn, 112 U.S.P.Q. (BNA) 439 (P.Bd.App. 1955).

[12] Wyeth v. Stone, 30 F.Cas. 723 (No. 18,107)(C.C.D. Mass.1840) is a good example. The patentee had invented a new machine to cut ice. His patent read: "It is claimed, as new, to cut ice of a uniform size, by means of an apparatus worked by any other power than human." Justice Story (riding Circuit) invalidated the claim, stating:

> It is a claim for an art or principle in the abstract, and not for any particular method of machinery, by which ice is to be cut. No man can have a right to cut ice by all means or methods, or by all or any sort of apparatus, although he is not the inventor of any or all such means, methods, or apparatus. A claim broader

than the actual invention of the patentee is, for that very reason, upon the principles of the common law, utterly void ...

30 F.Cas. at 730. Later courts distinguished between claims drawn to particular machines and claims drawn to the "function of the machine," see, e.g., Corning v. Burden, 56 U.S. (15 How.) 252, 14 L.Ed. 683 (1853).

[13] Halliburton Oil Well Cementing Co. v. Walker, 146 F.2d 817 (9th Cir.1944), is most often cited. There, the court invalidated Walker's patent on a method for determining the location of an obstruction in a well, noting:

> In substance, Walker's method here claimed consists in setting down three knowns in a simple equation and from them determining or computing an unknown. The three knowns are: (a) the distance from the well head to the tubing catcher (for example); (b) the length of time it takes an echo to return from that obstruction; and (c) the length of time it takes an echo to return from the fluid surface. From these three knowns can then be determined the distance of the fluid surface from the well head.
>
> * * *
>
> It must be remembered that this is purely a method patent. No apparatus is claimed. Given an apparatus for initiating an impulse wave in a well and a means for differentiating between and for recording echoes returned from obstruction in it, anybody with a rudimentary knowledge of arithmetic will be able to do what Walker claims a monopoly of doing. If his method were patentable it seems to us that the patentee would have a monopoly much broader than would the patentee of a particular apparatus....

146 F.2d at 821–22.

[14] See, e.g., Ex parte Turner, 1894 Comm'n Dec. 36.

later courts rightly rejected these doctrines as too simplistic,[15] the Principal Cases indicate that the line drawing has not become any easier.

2. *Computer Programs.* Because the mental-steps doctrine considered any series of steps that *could* be performed in a person's head unpatentable, it was clear from the dawn of the computer era that programs would pose problems to patent law. But surprisingly, the first Court to consider programs put its objection in more general terms. Thus, in Gottschalk v. Benson,[16] the issue was whether a computerized method for converting numerals expressed as binary-coded decimals into pure binary numerals was a patentable process. The Court held it was not. Justice Douglas explained:

> "It is conceded that one may not patent an idea. But in practical effect that would be the result if the formula for converting BCD to pure binary were patented in this case. The mathematical formula involved here has no substantial practical application except in connection with a digital computer, which means that if the judgment below is affirmed, the patent would wholly pre-empt the mathematical formula and in practical effect would be a patent on the algorithm itself."[17]

The next patentees to reach the Supreme Court took a different tack. Instead of applying for patents on mathematical manipulations, these applicants tried to conform their claims to the process paradigm described by Cochrane v. Deener. In Parker v. Flook,[18] the claims were drawn to a physical reaction: the catalytic conversion of hydrocarbons. The process used a computer program to continuously monitor a set of variables, compare changes in the variables, and signal abnormalities so that the reaction could be stopped. Flook was careful to stress the chemical changes occurring in the course of using his program rather than focus on the operation of the program itself. Nonetheless, the Court held the claim unpatentable, saying that a "conventional, post-solution application" that was well known in the art could not turn a rule of nature into patentable subject matter.

Several justices dissented. They agreed that care needed to be taken to guard against patenting principles, however, they thought that the use of a principle in one step of a broader process should not render the whole process unpatentable. To them, the problem in *Flook* was not the subject matter of the claim, but the invention's lack of novelty.

---

[15] See, e.g., Application of Tarczy–Hornoch, 397 F.2d 856 (C.C.P.A.1968)(overruling the function-of-machine doctrine). Cf. Cincinnati Traction Co. v. Pope, 210 Fed. 443 (C.C.A.6 1913)(casting some doubt on the printed-matter doctrine and the business-method doctrine).

[16] 409 U.S. 63, 93 S.Ct. 253, 34 L.Ed.2d 273 (1972).

[17] Id. at 71–72. Justice Douglas defined "algorithm" as "[a] procedure for solving a given type of mathematical problem," id. at 65.

[18] 437 U.S. 584, 98 S.Ct. 2522, 57 L.Ed.2d 451 (1978).

The tide did eventually turn in the direction urged by the dissenters. The Court of Claims and Patent Appeals (CCPA)[19] had not interpreted *Benson* as prohibiting patents on every invention containing algorithms. Rather, it focused on *Benson*'s preemption language and began developing the tests discussed in *Grams* and *Alappat* to determine when a patent application wholly preempted the algorithm used and when it merely utilized an algorithm to accomplish a particular task.[20] When the Supreme Court invalidated the patent involved in *Flook*, substantial doubt was cast on all the patents that were issued under the CCPA test, but these concerns were partially resolved in Diamond v. Diehr.[21] The invention at issue there was a process for curing rubber in a mold. The essentials of the process were commonly used in the industry, but it was not efficient as it was difficult to calculate when the rubber should be released from the mold. Diehr's solution coupled a standard device for measuring temperature to a computer programmed to use the well-known Arrhenius rate equation to continuously calculate the curing time from the temperature and signal when the curing process was finished. The Court found that:

> "[The] 'Arrhenius' equation is not patentable in isolation, but when a process for curing rubber is devised which incorporates in it a more efficient solution of the equation, that process is at the very least not barred at the threshold by § 101."[22]

By laying to rest the idea that all works reciting algorithms are per se unpatentable, *Diehr* opened the door to patent protection for the emerging computer industry. However, the striking similarity between the processes at issue in *Flook* and *Diehr*, coupled with *Diehr*'s failure to cite the CCPA cases with approval, left unanswered the question of how to draw the elusive line between ideas and embodiments. As the Principal Cases demonstrate, the CCPA's view has lead to two lines of cases. Both assume that *Benson* remains good law, so that algorithms can be patented only if they are limited by specific embodiments. In In re Alappat, the limiting embodiment is the machine that executes the program. In In re Grams, the embodiment is the physical process that the program mediates. The entire process is patentable, but only if it involves more than "mere" post-solution activity (the problem in *Flook*) or the gathering of data (the problem in *Grams*). Thus, where *Grams* permits patent protection for computer processes, *Alappat* protects computer products.

Is this the ideal resolution of the computer program problem? Remember, the real concern is protecting the public domain—making sure that patentees do not tie up every application of a principle of nature, including applications they have not invented. At least two other methods for achieving that result are possible, both of which are less abstract than the

---

[19] At the time that this first generation of computer cases was litigated, the CCPA was the court that reviewed decisions of the PTO. It has since been replaced by the CAFC, see Assignment 19, Note 2.

[20] See, e.g., In re Bergy, 563 F.2d 1031 (C.C.P.A.1977), vacated sub nom. Parker v. Bergy, 438 U.S. 902 (1978).

[21] 450 U.S. 175, 101 S.Ct. 1048, 67 L.Ed.2d 155 (1981).

[22] Id. at 188.

inquiry required by the subject-matter cases. First, applications could be rejected for failure to meet the specification requirements. As the introductory assignment explained, § 112 requires the patentee to give enough information in his specification to enable persons with skill in the art to practice the invention. Since as-yet-undiscovered applications will not be enabled, overbroad claiming will run afoul of § 112. Second, instead of limiting the patentee during issuance, when future applications are difficult to predict, limitations could be imposed at the infringement stage. At that point, it is clear what other uses can be made of the principle the patentee claims to have invented. If he did not enable that application, the use should not be considered infringement.

Finally, it may be time to reconsider *Benson*. Was Justice Douglas correct in assuming that algorithms always recite rules of nature? Just because many principles of nature are represented mathematically, does it follow that every mathematical representation is a principle of nature? Mathematical notation is just a form of language; it is sometimes used to express thoughts that could be expressed, albeit at greater length, in English.[23] Furthermore, some rules of nature are too complicated to use without modification. In such cases, the inventive feature of the program is the way it simplifies the actual rule of nature without losing its relevance. In a concurring opinion to yet another computer program case, Judge Rader had the following to say about the patentability of a program that analyzes electrocardiographic signals in order to determine certain characteristics of heart function in the hours immediately after a heart attack:

> "[W]hile many ... steps involve the mathematical manipulation of data, the claims do not describe a law of nature or a natural phenomenon. Furthermore the claims do not disclose mere abstract ideas, but a practical and potentially life-saving process. Regardless of whether performed by computer, these steps comprise a 'process' within the meaning of § 101." [24]

Conversely, limiting algorithms to physical applications may not do enough to constrain them. In particular, *Alappat* may prove to be a time-bomb. First, *Alappat* wrote his claims in "means plus function" form, which allows him to assert that other machines that perform the same functions are infringing, even if they use somewhat different means. Second, the patentee's right of action is not confined to literal infringement. As with copyright's substantial similarity test and trademark's confusing similarity test, patentees can assert rights against those who use "equivalents" of their inventions. The bottom line is that the scope accorded *Alappat* could be so broad, virtually all computers operating his program will be considered infringing. Indeed, this is exactly the problem that led the examiner and the Board of Patent Appeals and Interferences to reject the claims in the first place. Presumably, the CAFC's rejection of this position means that it thinks the means-plus-function claims can be read

---

[23] See, e.g., In re Meyer, 688 F.2d 789 (C.C.P.A.1982).

[24] Arrhythmia Research Technology, Inc. v. Corazonix Corp., 958 F.2d 1053, 1060 (Fed. Cir.1992).

narrowly and the doctrine of equivalents can be contained. Assignment 22 will reassess this issue.

In any event, the Patent and Trademark Office released these procedures for examiners to follow when evaluating computer-implemented inventions. The original guidelines provided, in part, as follows:

1. Determine what the applicant has invented by reviewing the written description and the claims.

* * *

(c) Considering each claim as a whole, classify the invention defined by each claim as to its statutory category (i.e., process, machine, manufacture or composition of matter). Rely on the following presumptions in making this classification.

(i) A computer or other programmable apparatus whose actions are directed by a computer program or other form of "software" is a statutory "machine."

(ii) A computer-readable memory that can be used to direct a computer to function in a particular manner when used by the computer is a statutory "article of manufacture".

(iii) A series of specific operational steps to be performed on or with the aid of a computer is a statutory "process."

A claim that clearly defines a computer-implemented process but is not cast as an element of a computer-readable memory or as implemented on a computer should be classified as a statutory "process." If an applicant responds to an action of the Office based on this classification by asserting that subject matter claimed in this format is a machine or an article of manufacture, reject the claim under 35 U.S.C. § 112, second paragraph, for failing to recite at least one physical element in the claims that would otherwise place the invention in either of these two "product" categories. The Examiner should also object to the specification under 37 CFR 1.71(b) if such an assertion is made, as the complete invention contemplated by the applicant has not been cast precisely as being an invention within one of the statutory categories.

A claim that defines an invention as any of the following subject matter should be classified as non-statutory:

— a compilation or arrangement of data, independent of any physical element;

— a known machine-readable storage medium that is encoded with data representing creative or artistic expression (e.g., a work of music, art or literature);

— a "data structure" independent of any physical element (i.e., not as implemented on a physical component of a computer such as a computer-readable memory to render that component capable of causing a computer to operate in a particular manner); or

— a process that does nothing more than manipulate abstract ideas or concepts (e.g., a process consisting solely of the steps one would follow in solving a mathematical problem).

Claims in this form are indistinguishable from abstract ideas, laws of nature and natural phenomena and may not be patented. Non-statutory claims should be handled in the manner described in section (2)(c) below.

2(a)

* * *

Claims must be defined using the English language. See, 37 CFR 1.52(a). A computer programming language is not the English language, despite the fact that English words may be used in that language. Thus, an applicant may not use computer program code, in either source or object format, to define the metes and bounds of a claim. A claim which attempts to define elements of an invention using computer program code, rather than the functional steps which are to be performed, should be rejected under § 112, second paragraph, and should be objected to under 37 CFR 1.52(a).

* * *

(c) A claim as a whole that defines non-statutory subject matter is deficient under § 101, and under § 112, second paragraph. Determining the scope of a claim as a whole requires a clear understanding of what the applicant regards as the invention. The review performed in step 1 should be used to gain this understanding.

* * *

An invention is not statutory if it falls within any of the non-statutory claim categories outlined in section (1)(c) above. Also, in rare situations, a claim classified as a statutory machine or article of manufacture may define non-statutory subject matter. Non-statutory subject matter (i.e., abstract ideas, laws of nature and natural phenomena) does not become statutory merely through a different form of claim presentation.

Such a claim will (a) define the "invention" not through characteristics of the machine or article of manufacture claimed but exclusively in terms of a non-statutory process that is to be performed on or using that machine or article of manufacture, and (b) encompass any product in the stated class (e.g., computer, computer-readable memory) configured in any manner to perform that process.

Does the analysis used in *In re Grams* survive? As this casebook went to press, these guidelines were being replaced.

3. *Business methods.* In the course of coming to grips with computer programs, the courts seem to have changed the rule regarding business methods. As we saw, one of the old rules of thumb held business methods unpatentable. Although use of thumbs to decide abstract issues is questionable, no one seriously doubted that business methods are not among the technologies at which patent law is directed. Nonetheless, now that processes utilizing programs are considered patentable, business methods that utilize programs have been successfully patented. In Paine, Webber, Jackson & Curtis, Inc. v. Merrill Lynch, Pierce, Fenner & Smith, Inc.,[25] for example, the court upheld the patent on a "Cash Management Account" that used a computer to track clients' deposits in a brokerage securities account, a money market fund, and a Visa charge/checking account.

4. *Biologicals.* To a large extent, the patent problem facing biology mirrors the saga of computer programs. Cell lines and DNA (whether naturally occurring or artificially produced) are not only commercial products, they are also the tools of basic biological research. Indeed patents on biological products present obstacles to biologists. They may hinder innovation and ensnare inventors who use the product in ways not enabled by the patentee. In addition, as with the computer cases, applicants for patents on the "new" biologicals had to deal with some old "rules of thumb."

a. *Material derived from living organisms.* An early case here is Funk Brothers Seed Co. v. Kalo Inoculant Co.,[26] discussed in *Chakrabarty*. The invention was a culture of nitrogen-fixing bacteria used to innoculate plant seeds. Many strains of bacteria were prepared in a laboratory and combined in order to make a product useful to a broad range of plants. The Supreme Court held the preparation not patentable on the ground that each bacterium is a "manifestation of laws of nature, free to all men and reserved exclusively to none."[27]

Funk's apparent unwillingness to extend patent protection to artificially-enhanced naturally occurring materials was, however, short lived. In 1947, after years of unsuccessful efforts, researchers of Merck & Co. isolated the active substance that gave cow liver its therapeutic benefits to anemia patients. A patent issued on the successful product, termed vitamin B_{12}. In Merck & Co. v. Olin Mathieson Chemical Corp.,[28] the Fourth Circuit upheld the validity of the patent over a challenge that the product was naturally occurring. In the course of the opinion, the court rejected the argument that vitamin B_{12} was not patentable subject matter because it was merely a purification of living materials:

> "The fact ... that a new and useful product is the result of processes of extraction, concentration and purification of natural materials does not defeat its patentability.
>
> · · ·
>
> "The compositions of the patent here ... never existed before; there was nothing comparable to them. If we regard them as a purification of the active principle in natural fermentates, the natural fermentates are quite useless, while the patented compositions are of great medicinal and commercial value. The step from complete uselessness to great and

[25] 564 F.Supp. 1358 (D.Del.1983).

[26] 333 U.S. 127, 130, 68 S.Ct. 440, 441, 92 L.Ed. 588 (1948).

[27] Id. at 130.

[28] 253 F.2d 156 (4th Cir.1958).

perfected utility is a long one. That step is no mere advance in the degree of purity of a known product."[29]

Of course, prior to *Chakrabarty, Funk* could also have been read as prohibiting the patenting of living things. Since *Chakrabarty,* however, the PTO has taken the position that all non-human living things that are artificially produced are patentable.[30]

b. *Medicine.* The seminal case is Morton v. New York Eye Infirmary,[31] which invalidated the patent on ether as used to anesthesize surgical patients. This was probably the single most important discovery in the science of surgery, for no matter how successful a procedure, there was always danger that an unanesthesized patient would die of shock. In finding the patent invalid, the *Morton* court cited several grounds: ether was known, the effect of inhaling it was known, and the invention was dependent on human reaction. Furthermore, at the time of *Morton,* the Patent Act did not provide for process patents in the manner of § 101. Nonetheless, there is a strong suspicion that the real ground for *Morton* was the notion that life-saving procedures should not be privately owned. Indeed, one of the first significant medical substances to be patented was the scarlet fever vaccine, and the decision to patent it was greeted with substantial criticism on precisely this ground. Interestingly, the inventors, George and Gladys Dick, tried to defended their action on humanitarian grounds, claiming that the patent enabled them to control quality.[32] And although numerous decisions have upheld patents on medicines since *Morton,*[33] the debate over the propriety of patents in the field has not abated.[34]

c. *The property analogy.* Another manifestation of the concern over granting exclusive rights in biological materials is evident in the debate over whether the law should consider body parts as property. Some people argue that recognizing such rights would be a species of slavery.[35] Another

---

[29] 253 F.2d at 163. In support, the court quoted from Judge Learned Hand's opinion in Parke–Davis & Co. v. H K Mulford Co., 189 Fed. 95 (S.D.N.Y.1911), aff'd, 196 F. 496 (2d Cir.1912), upholding a patent on "Adrenalin," a substance isolated and purified from suprarenal glands of living animals.

[30] See, e.g., Ex parte Allen, 2 U.S.P.Q.2d (BNA) 1425 (Bd.Pat.App. & Int. 1987)(upholding a patent on a polyploid pacific oyster); U.S. Pat. No. 4,736,866 (patent on the so-called "Harvard mouse").

[31] 17 F.Cas. 879 (C.C.S.D.N.Y. 1862).

[32] See Charles Weiner, Patenting and Academic Research: Historical Case Studies, in Owning Scientific and Technical Information (V. Weil and J. Snapper, eds.)(Rutgers Univ. Press 1989).

[33] See, e.g., Ex parte Scherer, 103 U.S.P.Q. (BNA) 107 (P.T.O. Bd. App.1954); Dick v. Lederle Antitoxin Laboratories, 43 F.2d 628 (S.D.N.Y.1930). See generally, Gregory Burch, Ethical Considerations in the Patenting of Medical Processes, 65 Tex. L. Rev. 1139 (1987).

[34] See, e.g., Bruce Nussbaum, Good Intentions: How Big Business and the Medical Establishment are Corrupting the Fight Against AIDS, Alzheimer's, Cancer, and More (Penguin Books 1990).

[35] Cf. Davis v. Davis, 842 S.W.2d 588 (Tenn.1992)(rejecting the notion that frozen embryos are property), cert. denied sub nom. Stowe v. Davis, 507 U.S. 911, 113 S.Ct. 1259, 122 L.Ed.2d 657 (1993). See generally, Note, Patents on People and the U.S. Constitution: Creating Slaves or Enslaving, 16 Hastings Const. L.Q. 221 (1989).

rationale for rejecting the property analogy is that ownership of rights to body parts will impede research.

Consider, for example, Moore v. University of California.[36] John Moore had had his spleen removed at UCLA Medical Center as part of his treatment for hairy-cell leukemia. Doctors required him to return to the Center from his home in Seattle on a number of occasions so they could take further samples of blood, blood serum, skin, bone marrow aspirate, and sperm. Unbeknownst to him, these samples were used not for treatment, but to grow a cell line of his T-lymphocytes, which was later patented and subject to lucrative licensing agreements. Moore sued on, among other things, a theory of tortious conversion, asserting that the samples and cell line were his property. In rejecting his claim, the court stated:

> "The extension of conversion law into this area will hinder research by restricting access to the necessary raw materials. Thousands of human cell lines already exist in tissue repositories, such as the American Type Culture Collection and those operated by the National Institutes of Health and the American Cancer Society. These repositories respond to tens of thousands of requests for samples annually. Since the patent office requires the holders of patents on cell lines to make samples available to anyone, many patent holders place their cell lines in repositories to avoid the administrative burden of responding to requests. At present, human cell lines are routinely copied and distributed to other researchers for experimental purposes, usually free of charge. This exchange of scientific materials, which still is relatively free and efficient, will surely be compromised if each cell sample becomes the potential subject matter of a lawsuit.

> "To expand liability by extending conversion law into this area would have a broad impact. The House Committee on Science and Technology of the United States Congress found that '49 percent of the researchers at medical institutions surveyed used human tissues or cells in their research.' Many receive grants from the National Institute of Health for this work. In addition, 'there are nearly 350 commercial biotechnology firms in the United States actively engaged in biotechnology research and commercial product development and approximately 25 to 30 percent appear to be engaged in research to develop a human therapeutic or diagnostic reagent.... Most, but not all, of the human therapeutic products are derived from human tissues and cells, or human cell lines or cloned genes.' "

5. *Non-utility patents*. The focus of this case book is on utility patents, but it is important to recognize that the law provides patent, or patent-like, protection to two other kinds of subject matter, plants and designs.

a. *Plants*. Plants are protected under two different statutes. The Plant Patent Act, §§ 161–164 of the Patent Act, creates rights in new and distinct plants that are asexually reproduced, while the Plant Variety Protection Act (PVPA), 7 U.S.C.A. §§ 2321–2583, creates rights in sexually

---

[36] 51 Cal.3d 120, 271 Cal.Rptr. 146, 793 P.2d 479 (1990)(en banc).

reproduced plants. The PVPA is wholly administered by the Department of Agriculture, which assists the Commissioner of Patents with administering the Plant Patent Act. These statutes differ from standard patent law by substituting for the specification requirement of § 112, a requirement that the patentee place a sample of the protected plant on deposit, where it can be studied by others. The PVPA also differs from patent law in that it contains research and farmer's crop exemptions and a compulsory license provision. After *Chakrabarty,* there is a question whether the limitations of the PVPA can be avoided by applying for utility patents instead. The answer, so far, is yes.[37]

b. *Designs.* Sections 171–173 of the Patent Act create patent rights in new, original, and ornamental designs for articles of manufacture. The terms "new" and "original" have essentially the same meaning as they have for utility patents. Applications are scrutinized for nonobviousness and also to make sure that the design is ornamental rather than primarily functional. Infringement is determined in a manner rather similar to the way that copyright infringement is analyzed. However, the term of protection is shorter (14 years).

Design patents are sometimes thought of as protecting designs that are so inseparable from function that they cannot be protected by copyright, see Assignment 8. While it is nice to think that patent law takes up exactly where copyright leaves off, this notion is true to only a limited extent. First, § 171 specifies that a design must be "ornamental." Designs that are dictated purely by functional considerations are not any more eligible for patent protection than they are for copyright protection. Thus, purely functional designs—for instance, boat hulls, dashboards, and refrigerator panels—receive no protection under U.S. patent law *or* copyright law. The tendency has been to try to acquire trademark rights in some feature of a successful design, but this is a problem too as it creates a term of protection that is far too long. In the view of many commentators, the absence of effective protection has put American designers and consumer product manufacturers in a competitively uncomfortable position.

Second, even for designs that fit within the legislative scheme, the general consensus is that the design statute does not work particularly well. The extensiveness of the examination system is a problem because a patent may not issue until after the popularity of the design has peaked. Moreover, decisions on what is nonobvious and what is an infringement tend to be very subjective. Congress has from time to time considered new design legislation, but has never acted.[38]

BIBLIOGRAPHY

On the patenting of biologicals, see Landau, Multicellular Vertebrate Mammals as "Patentable Subject Matter" Under 35 U.S.C.A. § 101: Pro-

---

[37] Ex parte Hibberd, 227 U.S.P.Q.2d (BNA) 443 (Pat.Off.Bd.App. 1985).

[38] See William T. Fryer, Industrial Design Protection in the United States of America–Present Situation and Plans for Revision,

70 J.Pat.Off.Soc. 821 (1988); J.H. Reichman, Design Protection and the New Technologies: The United States Experience in a Transnational Perspective, 19 U.Balt.L.Rev. 6 (1991).

motion of Science and the Useful Arts or an Open Invitation for Abuse?, 97 Dick. L. Rev. 203 (1993); Note, Protecting Plant–Derived Drugs: Patents and Beyond, 10 Cardozo Arts & Ent. L.J. 169 (1991); Seibold, Can Chakrabarty Survive the "Harvard Mouse"?, 2 U. Fla. J.L. & Pub. Pol'y 81 (1988/89); Merges, Intellectual Property in Higher Life Forms: The Patent System and Controversial Technologies, 47 Md. L. Rev. 1051 (1988); Czarnetzky, Altering Nature's Blueprints For Profit: Patenting Multicellular Animals, 74 Va.L.Rev. 1327 (1988); Eisenberg, Proprietary Rights and the Norms of Science in Biotechnology Research, 97 Yale L.J. 177 (1987); Bozicevic, Distinguishing 'Products of Nature' From Products Derived From Nature, 69 J.Pat. Off.Soc'y 415 (1987); Beier, Crespi & Straus, Biotechnology and Patent Protection: An International Review 56 (1985); Linck, Patentable Subject Matter Under Section 101—Are Plants Included?, 67 J.Pat.Off. Soc'y 489 (1985); Schroeder, Patenting Microorganisms: Working the Bugs Out of the International Depositary Authority, 14 Cal.W.Int'l.J. 49 (1984); Meyer, Problems and Issues in Depositing Microorganisms for Patent Purposes, 65 J.Pat.Off.Soc'y 455 (1983); Note, Building a Better Bacterium: Genetic Engineering and the Patent Law after Diamond v. Chakrabarty, 81 Colum. L. Rev. 159 (1981); Wegner, Patenting Nature's Secrets—Microorganisms, 7 Int'l Rev. Indus. Prop. & Copyright L. 235 (1976). Some international aspects of this problem are also discussed in Oddi, The International Patent System and Third World Development: Reality or Myth? 1987 Duke L.J. 831 (1987).

On the patenting of computer products, see: Donner, Two Decades of Gottschalk v. Benson: Putting the "rithm" Back into the Patenting of Mathematical Algorithms, 5 Software L.J. 419 (1992); Samuelson, Benson Revisited: The Case Against Patent Protection for Algorithms and Other Computer Program–Related Inventions, 39 Emory L.J. 1025 (1990); Ratner & Nigon, The Patentability of Computer Programs: The PTO Guidelines, In re Grams and In re Iwahashi, 6 Comput. L. 21 (1989); Barrett, United States Patent and Trademark Office, Patentable Subject Matter: Mathematical Algorithms and Computer Programs, 1106 Off.Gaz.Pat.Office 5 (Sept. 5, 1989); Chisum, The Patentability of Algorithms, 47 U.Pitt. L.Rev. 959 (1986); H. Hanneman, The Patentability of Computer Software (1985); Davidson, Protecting Computer Software: A Comprehensive Analysis, 23 Jurimetrics J. 337 (1983); Stout, Protection of Programming in the Aftermath of Diamond v. Diehr, 4 Computer L.J. 207 (1983); Gemignani, Should Algorithms Be Patentable?, 22 Jurimetrics J. 326 (1982); Novick & Wallenstein, Comment, The Algorithm and Computer Software Patentability: A Scientific View of a Legal Problem, 7 Rutgers J. Computers Tech. & L. 313, 316–17 (1980).

On design patents, see: Brown, Design Protection: An Overview, 34 UCLA L.Rev. 1341 (1987).

*

UTILITY

1. INTRODUCTION

In one sense, it is clear why the Patent Act would require an invention to be "useful," § 101. A patent is the quid pro quo for providing a social benefit; a useless invention provides no benefit, and so does not deserve a patent. In another sense, however, this requirement is somewhat mystifying. Since no one would waste time and money protecting an invention that has no use, there appears to be little reason to demand an inquiry into usefulness. Besides, what would it matter if a patent were granted on a useless invention? If the invention has no use, no one will use it and thus no one will pay the costs associated with exclusivity.

One explanation that has been offered for the utility requirement harkens back to trademark law. That is, the public may believe the United States to be certifying as wholesome those products that carry the federal government's own mark. Indeed, the term "patent medicine" derives from the practice of using a remedy's patent to imply therapeutic benefit.[1] Thus, it is not surprising that in some early cases, the utility requirement was used to deny patents to unwholesome—or immoral—products.[2] But imposing a requirement that the invention be nondeleterious—a requirement of "beneficial utility"—is problematic. The PTO does not have the expertise to test products for efficacy, safety, or morality. Nor would we want the PTO making decisions in conflict with those of agencies such as the Food and Drug Administration (FDA) and the Environmental Protection Agency (EPA), which have express authority over some of these issues. Moreover, wholesomeness is often contextual. A product that is considered immoral in one era may become indispensible to a new generation.

This leaves two other justifications for utility. One is that it serves as an adjunct to the specification requirement of § 112 in that it assures that the invention does what is claimed in the specification.[3] In fact, the PTO generally assumes that an invention has both "general utility," the capaci-

---

[1] Cf. Bd. of Pharmacy v. Sherman, 74 N.J.Super. 417, 181 A.2d 418 (1962); Merges, Intellectual Property in Higher Life Forms: The Patent System and Controversial Technologies, 47 Md.L.Rev. 1051 (1988). Even in this modern, technologically sophisticated era, patents are used in advertising everything from mattresses (Sealy Posturepedics) to makeup (Lancome).

[2] See, e.g., Rickard v. Du Bon, 103 Fed. 868 (2d Cir.1900)(process for flecking tobacco leafs); Meyer v. Buckley Mfg, 15 F.Supp. 640 (N.D.Ill.1936)(gambling machine). The same inclination can be observed in the Lanham Act, see 15 U.S.C. § 1052(a).

[3] See, e.g., Cusano v. Kotler, 159 F.2d 159 (3d Cir.1947)(shuffleboard); Chicago Patent Corp. v. Genco, 124 F.2d 725 (7th Cir.1941)(pinball).

ty to do *something*,[4] and "specific utility," the potential to work as claimed.[5] However, if the Office has specific reasons to believe otherwise—as it does, for example, in the case of perpetual motion machines, which necessarily violate the laws of thermodynamics—then the applicant can be required to furnish a working model. For most inventions, the burden is on the PTO to prove that the invention does not have utility.[6] For drug cases, however, the burden is on the applicant.[7] Another dimension of utility associates it with problems akin to those addressed by the subject matter requirement. That is, the requirement that an invention have an end-use insures that the invention has *a* use—that it is more than just a principle of nature. Thus, the hurdle imposed by utility acts as another way to remove from the scope of patentability discoveries that are fundamental building blocks of science.

2. PRINCIPAL PROBLEM

Return to the facts of the Principal Problem in Assignment 16: Does Beta's cDNA sequence meet the requirement of utility?

3. MATERIALS FOR SOLUTION OF PRINCIPAL PROBLEM

A. STATUTORY MATERIAL: § 101

B. CASES:

Brenner v. Manson

Supreme Court of the United States, 1966.
383 U.S. 519, 86 S.Ct. 1033, 16 L.Ed.2d 69.

■ MR. JUSTICE FORTAS delivered the opinion of the Court.

[4] See, e.g., In re Eltgroth, 419 F.2d 918, 922 (C.C.P.A.1970) ("Undoubtedly, the alleged utility of control of the aging process in living organisms and the significant beneficial results flowing therefrom is adequate [to satisfy the utility requirement.] Yet, there is a conspicuous absence of proof thereof ... [W]e find the instant record too speculative to satisfy the requirement of 35 U.S.C. § 101."); In re Woody, 331 F.2d 636, 639–40 (C.C.P.A.1964)(claims to a method of forming underground caverns in salt formations with a nuclear explosion properly rejected as unenabled under § 112 and inoperative under § 101 because the method had never been carried out).

This form of utility is sometimes called operability, see e.g. Chisum, Patents § 4.04.

[5] See, e.g., Ex parte McKay, 200 U.S.P.Q. (BNA) 324 (PTO Bd. App.1975)(patent on method for extracting oxygen from extraterrestrial materials upheld as potentially useful, even though "practical considerations would dictate against its commercial exploitation on earth").

[6] See, e.g., Newman v. Quigg, 877 F.2d 1575 (Fed.Cir.1989)(upholding a finding that experiments by the National Bureau of Standards demonstrated that an "Energy Generation System Having Higher Energy Output Than Input" was not workable).

[7] Even here, all that is required is enough evidence for people in the field to conclude the invention will work. Thus, tests on animals or in vitro are sometimes enough to support a claim of therapeutic effect in humans, see, e.g., In re Brana, 51 F.3d 1560 (Fed.Cir.1995); Cross v. Iizuka, 753 F.2d 1040 (Fed.Cir.1985); Nelson v. Bowler, 626 F.2d 853 (C.C.P.A.1980). See also Proposed Utility Examinations guidelines, 60 Fed.Reg. 97 (Jan. 3., 1995).

In January 1960, respondent Manson, a chemist engaged in steroid research, filed an application to patent [an allegedly novel process for making certain known steroids;] precisely the same process described by Ringold and Rosenkranz [in an application filed on December 17, 1956]. He asserted that it was he who had discovered the process, and that he had done so before December 17, 1956. Accordingly, he requested that an "interference" be declared in order to try out the issue of priority between his claim and that of Ringold and Rosenkranz.

A Patent Office examiner denied Manson's application, and the denial was affirmed by the Board of Appeals within the Patent Office. The ground for rejection was the failure "to disclose any utility for" the chemical compound produced by the process. Letter of Examiner, dated May 24, 1960. This omission was not cured, in the opinion of the Patent Office, by Manson's reference to an article in the November 1956 issue of the Journal of Organic Chemistry, 21 J.Org.Chem. 1333–1335, which revealed that steroids of a class which included the compound in question were undergoing screening for possible tumor-inhibiting effects in mice, and that a homologue[a] adjacent to Manson's steroid had proven effective in that role. Said the Board of Appeals, "It is our view that the statutory requirement of usefulness of a product cannot be presumed merely because it happens to be closely related to another compound which is known to be useful."

The Court of Customs and Patent Appeals (hereinafter CCPA) reversed, Chief Judge Worley dissenting. 52 C.C.P.A. (Pat.) 739, 745, 333 F.2d 234, 237–238. The court held that Manson was entitled to a declaration of interference since "where a claimed process produces a known product it is not necessary to show utility for the product," so long as the product "is not alleged to be detrimental to the public interest." Certiorari was granted, 380 U.S. 971, 85 S.Ct. 1334, 14 L.Ed.2d 267, to resolve this running dispute over what constitutes "utility" in chemical process claims. . . .

II

Our starting point is the proposition, neither disputed nor disputable, that one may patent only that which is "useful." In Graham v. John Deere Co., 383 U.S. 1, at 5–10, 86 S.Ct. 684, at 687–690, we have reviewed the history of the requisites of patentability, and it need not be repeated here. Suffice it to say that the concept of utility has maintained a central place in all of our patent legislation, beginning with the first patent law in 1790 and culminating in the present law's provision that

> "Whoever invents or discovers any new and useful process, machine, manufacture, or composition of matter, or any new and useful improve-

---

[a] "A homologous series is a family of chemically related compounds, the composition of which varies from member to member by CH_2 (one atom of carbon and two atoms of hydrogen) . . . . Chemists knowing the proper-ties of one member of a series would in general know what to expect in adjacent members." Application of Henze, 181 F.2d 196, 200–201, 37 C.C.P.A. (Pat.) 1009, 1014.

ment thereof, may obtain a patent therefor, subject to the conditions and requirements of this title." [§ 101]

As is so often the case, however, a simple, everyday word can be pregnant with ambiguity when applied to the facts of life. That this is so is demonstrated by the present conflict between the Patent Office and the CCPA over how the test is to be applied to a chemical process which yields an already known product whose utility—other than as a possible object of scientific inquiry—has not yet been evidenced. It was not long ago that agency and court seemed of one mind on the question. In Application of Bremner, 182 F.2d 216, 217, 37 C.C.P.A. (Pat.) 1032, 1034 [1950], the court affirmed rejection by the Patent Office of both process and product claims. It noted that "no use for the products claimed to be developed by the processes had been shown in the specification." It held that "It was never intended that a patent be granted upon a product, or a process producing a product, unless such product be useful." Nor was this new doctrine in the court. See Thomas v. Michael, 166 F.2d 944, 946–947, 35 C.C.P.A. (Pat.) 1036, 1038–1039.

The Patent Office has remained steadfast in this view. The CCPA, however, has moved sharply away from Bremner. The trend began in Application of Nelson, 280 F.2d 172, 47 C.C.P.A. (Pat.) 1031. There, the court reversed the Patent Office's rejection of a claim on a process yielding chemical intermediates "useful to chemists doing research on steroids," despite the absence of evidence that any of the steroids thus ultimately produced were themselves "useful." The trend has accelerated, culminating in the present case where the court held it sufficient that a process produces the result intended and is not "detrimental to the public interest." 333 F.2d at 238, 52 C.C.P.A. (Pat.), at 745.

Respondent does not—at least in the first instance—rest upon the extreme proposition, advanced by the court below, that a novel chemical process is patentable so long as it yields the intended product and so long as the product is not itself "detrimental." Nor does he commit the outcome of his claim to the slightly more conventional proposition that any process is "useful" within the meaning of § 101 if it produces a compound whose potential usefulness is under investigation by serious scientific researchers, although he urges this position, too, as an alternative basis for affirming the decision of the CCPA. Rather, he begins with the much more orthodox argument that . . . supporting affidavits . . . reveal that an adjacent homologue of the steroid yielded by his process has been demonstrated to have tumor-inhibiting effects in mice, and that this discloses the requisite utility. We do not accept any of these theories as an adequate basis for overriding the determination of the Patent Office that the "utility" requirement has not been met.

Even on the assumption that the process would be patentable were respondent to show that the steroid produced had a tumor-inhibiting effect in mice, we would not overrule the Patent Office finding that respondent has not made such a showing. The Patent Office held that, despite the reference to the adjacent homologue, respondent's papers did not disclose a sufficient likelihood that the steroid yielded by his process would have similar tumor-inhibiting characteristics. Indeed, respondent himself recognized that the presumption that adjacent homologues have the same utility has been challenged in the steroid field because of "a greater known unpredictability of compounds in that field." In these circumstances and in this technical area, we would not overturn the finding of the Primary Examiner, affirmed by the Board of Appeals and not challenged by the CCPA.

The second and third points of respondent's argument present issues of much importance. Is a chemical process "useful" within the meaning of § 101 either (1) because it works—i.e., produces the intended product? or (2) because the compound yielded belongs to a class of compounds now the subject of serious scientific investigation? These contentions present the basic problem for our adjudication. Since we find no specific assistance in the legislative materials underlying § 101, we are remitted to an analysis of the problem in light of the general intent of Congress, the purposes of the patent system, and the implications of a decision one way or the other.

In support of his plea that we attenuate the requirement of "utility," respondent relies upon Justice Story's well-known statement that a "useful" invention is one "which may be applied to a beneficial use in society, in contradistinction to an invention injurious to the morals, health, or good order of society, or frivolous and insignificant"—and upon the assertion that to do so would encourage inventors of new processes to publicize the event for the benefit of the entire scientific community, thus widening the search for uses and increasing the fund of scientific knowledge. Justice Story's language sheds little light on our subject. Narrowly read, it does no more than compel us to decide whether the invention in question is "frivolous and insignificant"[b]—a query no easier of application than the one built into the statute. Read more broadly, so as to allow the patenting of any invention not positively harmful to society, it places such a special meaning on the word "useful" that we cannot accept it in the absence of evidence that Congress so intended. There are, after all, many things in this world which may not be considered "useful" but which, nevertheless are totally without a capacity for harm.

It is true, of course, that one of the purposes of the patent system is to encourage dissemination of information concerning discoveries and inventions. And it may be that inability to patent a process to some extent discourages disclosure and leads to greater secrecy than would otherwise be the case. The inventor of the process, or the corporate organization by which he is employed, has some incentive to keep the invention secret while

[b] Note on the Patent Laws, 3 Wheat.App. 13, 24. See also Justice Story's decisions on circuit in Lowell v. Lewis, 15 Fed.Cas. 1018 (No. 8568)(C.C.D.Mass.), and Bedford v. Hunt, 3 Fed.Cas. 37 (No. 1217)(C.C.D.Mass.).

uses for the product are searched out. However, in light of the highly developed art of drafting patent claims so that they disclose as little useful information as possible—while broadening the scope of the claim as widely as possible—the argument based upon the virtue of disclosure must be warily evaluated. Moreover, the pressure for secrecy is easily exaggerated, for if the inventor of a process cannot himself ascertain a "use" for that which his process yields, he has every incentive to make his invention known to those able to do so. Finally, how likely is disclosure of a patented process to spur research by others into the uses to which the product may be put? To the extent that the patentee has power to enforce his patent, there is little incentive for others to undertake a search for uses.

Whatever weight is attached to the value of encouraging disclosure and of inhibiting secrecy, we believe a more compelling consideration is that a process patent in the chemical field, which has not been developed and pointed to the degree of specific utility, creates a monopoly of knowledge which should be granted only if clearly commanded by the statute. Until the process claim has been reduced to production of a product shown to be useful, the metes and bounds of that monopoly are not capable of precise delineation. It may engross a vast, unknown, and perhaps unknowable area. Such a patent may confer power to block off whole areas of scientific development, without compensating benefit to the public. The basic quid pro quo contemplated by the Constitution and the Congress for granting a patent monopoly is the benefit derived by the public from an invention with substantial utility. Unless and until a process is refined and developed to this point—where specific benefit exists in currently available form—there is insufficient justification for permitting an applicant to engross what may prove to be a broad field.

These arguments for and against the patentability of a process which either has no known use or is useful only in the sense that it may be an object of scientific research would apply equally to the patenting of the product produced by the process. Respondent appears to concede that with respect to a product, as opposed to a process, Congress has struck the balance on the side of nonpatentability unless "utility" is shown. Indeed, the decisions of the CCPA are in accord with the view that a product may not be patented absent a showing of utility greater than any adduced in the present case. We find absolutely no warrant for the proposition that although Congress intended that no patent be granted on a chemical compound whose sole "utility" consists of its potential role as an object of use-testing, a different set of rules was meant to apply to the process which yielded the unpatentable product. That proposition seems to us little more than an attempt to evade the impact of the rules which concededly govern patentability of the product itself.

This is not to say that we mean to disparage the importance of contributions to the fund of scientific information short of the invention of something "useful," or that we are blind to the prospect that what now seems without "use" may tomorrow command the grateful attention of the public. But a patent is not a hunting license. It is not a reward for the search, but compensation for its successful conclusion. "(A) patent system must be related to the world of commerce rather than to the realm of philosophy. * * *"c

The judgment of the CCPA is reversed.

■ JUSTICE HARLAN, concurring in part and dissenting in part.

[After explaining why most of the majority's arguments "have almost no force," Justice Harlan went on to say:]

More to the point, I think, are the Court's remaining, prudential arguments against patentability; namely, that disclosure induced by allowing a patent is partly undercut by patent-application drafting techniques, that disclosure may occur without granting a patent, and that a patent will discourage others from inventing uses for the product. How far opaque drafting may lessen the public benefits resulting from the issuance of a patent is not shown by any evidence in this case but, more important, the argument operates against all patents and gives no reason for singling out the class involved here. The thought that these inventions may be more likely than most to be disclosed even if patents are not allowed may have more force; but while empirical study of the industry might reveal that chemical researchers would behave in this fashion, the abstractly logical choice for them seems to me to maintain secrecy until a product use can be discovered. As to discouraging the search by others for product uses, there is no doubt this risk exists but the price paid for any patent is that research on other uses or improvements may be hampered because the original patentee will reap much of the reward. From the standpoint of the public interest the Constitution seems to have resolved that choice in favor of patentability.

What I find most troubling about the result reached by the Court is the impact it may have on chemical research. Chemistry is a highly interrelated field and a tangible benefit for society may be the outcome of a number of different discoveries, one discovery building upon the next. To encourage one chemist or research facility to invent and disseminate new processes and products may be vital to progress, although the product or process be without "utility" as the Court defines the term, because that discovery permits someone else to take a further but perhaps less difficult step leading to a commercially useful item. In my view, our awareness in this age of the importance of achieving and publicizing basic research should lead this Court to resolve uncertainties in its favor and uphold the respondent's position in this case.

■ [JUSTICE DOUGLAS dissented in part, for substantially the reasons given by JUSTICE HARLAN.]

c Application of Ruschig, 343 F.2d 965, 970, 52 C.C.P.A. (Pat.) 1238, 1245 (Rich, J.).

Introduction of Legislation for a Moratorium on the Patenting of Genetically Engineered Animals

HON. BENJAMIN L. CARDIN OF MARYLAND
138 Cong.Rec. E1117–02.

Tuesday, April 28, 1992

Mr. Speaker, today I am introducing a bill to provide for a 5–year moratorium on the granting of patents on invertebrate or vertebrate animals, including those that have been genetically engineered. The availability of patents encourages the creation of genetically engineered animals, in most cases, animals whose genetic compositions have been manipulated by genetic engineering techniques to contain foreign genes from other animals, including humans. The resulting animals have combinations of genes and traits not found in nature. We have little experience in assessing the economic, ethical, and environmental consequences of the creation, release, and patenting of such creatures. The moratorium provided for in this bill would simply give the Congress the time to fully access, consider, and respond to the issues raised by the patenting of such animals.

At the outset, I want to make it clear this legislation is not intended to halt the promising field of biotechnology. The various techniques of biotechnology, when used responsibly have enormous potential to benefit society in a number of areas, including the creation of important new pharmaceutical and agricultural products. However, with the new benefits of biotechnology come risks. Genetic engineering allows scientists to take human genetic traits and insert them into the permanent genetic code of animals. Biotechnology is also becoming increasingly adept at mixing and matching the genetic traits of animals, insects, and plants to create new and different species. To suddenly and unconditionally grant patents for any and all of these genetic creations without a strict Federal review process would be irresponsible and impudent.

The bill I am introducing, which was introduced in the Senate on June 13, 1991, by Senator MARK HATFIELD of Oregon, will provide Congress the time to examine the risks of animal patenting. Specifically, the bill provides that no animal shall be patented until the commercialization and release of such an animal has been subjected to a Federal review process established to impose "environmental, health and safety, economic and ethical standards."

If patents are to be issued, we must ensure the patenting of genetically engineered animals will not cause economic harm to the Nation's farmers and researchers. In economic terms the Patent Office decision provides Government authority for the genetic manipulation, and ownership of all animal species. The use, enjoyment, and protection of animals, long a public right and responsibility, could be turned over to the public sector. In years to come there could be increasing competition for corporate control and ownership of the gene pool of animal species. The most immediate economic effect of this policy could be felt in agriculture, where the major chemical biotechnology, and pharmaceutical companies could conceivably position themselves to take over animal husbandry. The Patent Office has confirmed farmers will have to pay patent fees every time they breed a patented animal or sell part of their herds which contain such patented animals. This will also be true for researchers using patented laboratory animals. The economic consequences of animal patenting on small farmers and research institutions need to be carefully examined.

Unlike most intellectual property issues, the patenting of animals also creates a wide array of ethical concerns. The patent policy creates the need to establish reasonable limits to man's right to manipulate and refashion the biotic community to meet his industrial requirements. This includes the necessity of carefully examining the ethics of transferring of human genetic traits into animals. The potential for patenting and owning animals with human traits bring up an important public policy need to decide on how many, and what kind of, human genetic traits should be engineered into animals. Currently, thousands of animals have been created with human genes engineered into their permanent genetic code. There is a real urgency in regulating these transfers prior to further creation, patenting, and dissemination of these animals with human genes.

It is important to note that the patent decision, by encouraging genetic manipulation, could indirectly cause suffering to genetically engineered animals and extend that suffering through generations of the offspring of those altered animals.

Moreover, it is important to remember that even patenting laws have an influence on the way we think. Will future generations follow the ethics of this patent policy and view life as mere chemical manufacture and invention with no greater value or meaning than industrial products?

The patenting of animals could also indirectly cause environmental harm. The effect of species alteration could impact the delicate balance of the environment. The creation of new species and the effect of their release into their environment cannot be easily predicted, and should be carefully considered. Animals which are larger and have increased reproductivity could alter the depletion patterns of the ecosystem. Also, if the creation of new improved species leads to the popularization of that animal, valuable native gene pools could be lost. For example, salmon are currently being created with cattle genes to increase growth. When released into the environment these fish have the potential to invade new habitats and displace existing populations. If the genetically engineered salmon turn out to over populate or consume too much, they could cause irremediable damage to the environment. In addition, they could mate with native salmon and pollute the native gene pool forever. We must remember biological pollution cannot be recalled.

Despite the potential threat created by the release of genetically engineered animals, no Federal regulatory regime exists on the release of such animals. As long as this significant regulatory void exists, it is irresponsible to stimulate the creation of transgenic animals with the patent law. Moreover, this moratorium will provide the time and the incentive for industry, the public sector, and Congress to fashion appropriate safeguards.

The patenting of animals also brings up an important question about the role of Congress in extending patents into new areas of technology. In 1980 the Supreme Court opened the door to the patenting of animals with a 5 to 4 decision in *Diamond versus Chakrabarty*, which allowed the patenting of a genetically engineered microbe. In 1987, the Patent and Trademark Office (PTO), using a broad interpretation of the Chakrabarty case, announced it would consider applications for patents on genetically altered animals. One year later, in April 1988, PTO approved the first animal patent for the transgenic nonhuman mammals genetically engineered to contain a cancer causing gene (U.S. Patent No. 4,736,866). Presently, over 160 patent applications on animals are pending at the PTO.

It has been an established legal precedent for some time that Congress, not the PTO, makes decisions on extending patent coverage into the controversial areas. It is the duty of Congress, not the PTO, to determine whether living organisms, like plants and animals, are patentable. In the past, Congress actively participated in these types of decisions. For example, in 1930 Congress enacted the Plant Patent Act and, then, in 1970 enacted the Plant Variety Protection Act. In contrast, in 1987 with regard to the patenting of animals the PTO, not Congress, decided nonhuman animals constituted patentable subject matter.

As a result, one patent has been issued, the number of patent applications continues to grow, and no concrete progress has been made to ensure society will be able to deal with the unique ramifications of patenting genetically engineered animals. The economic, ethical, and environmental questions on animal patenting have been raised at a series of hearing conducted by the Intellectual Property and Administration of Justice Subcommittee. It is now imperative that Congress become more involved in this issue. A moratorium would provide the time necessary to conduct this vital public policy debate and to take regulatory steps needed to reap the benefits of this promising new technology, and avoid its risks.

NOTES

1. *Metes and bounds.* In *Brenner,* was Justice Fortas correct in thinking that without a specific use, "the metes and bounds of [the] monopoly are not capable of precise delineation?" The application was for a patent on a process; as with any other patented process, the boundaries are clearly confined to use of the process, § 271(a). Of course, uses not known to the inventor at the time of issuance would also be included, but this is true of every patent. The principal uses of the laser, for example, were found well after its inventor applied for patent protection, yet the inventor enjoys rights over all of these later-discovered applications.[8] If rights over uses not contemplated by the inventor are considered excessive, is not the remedy to

---

[8] See, e.g., Gould v. General Photonics Corp., 534 F.Supp. 399 (N.D.Cal.1982).

confine *all* patents to the uses described in the specification? Why limit only those patentees who cannot articulate any use at the time of application? Furthermore, it is the *claiming* provision, not the *utility* provision, of the statute that is meant to delineate the metes and bounds of the invention.

2. *Patents as hunting licenses.* Justice Fortas is certainly right in thinking that the patentee in *Brenner* "flunked" the test of finding a use for the steroid he learned to synthesize. But should the Court have assumed that denying a patent will free—or encourage—others to seek a use for this steroid? What would be the reward? The inventor of the use could not patent the steroid. Unless the applicant kept the steroid secret, it became part of the public domain when the patent was rejected.[9] Although the use itself might be the subject of a process patent, the difficulty of monitoring usage makes process patents much less valuable than product patents. In contrast, granting the patent in the *Brenner* case would certainly have given the patentee incentive to encourage others to conduct research. Although the patentee would be forced to share royalties with the person who found a use, *some* profit is better than none at all.

3. *Use patents.* Commentators have proposed a solution to both the windfall problem identified in Note 1 and the incentive problem discussed in Note 2. They would divide utility patents into two categories and issue how-to-make patents to those, like the applicant in *Brenner,* who discover a method for synthesizing a new compound and how-to-use patents to those who discover new applications. How-to-make patents would be infringed only when the product is manufactured in the manner claimed by the patentee; how-to-use patents would be infringed only when the product is used in the specified manner. In this way, synthetic chemists would receive some reward for their efforts, but the incentive to find new uses would be preserved.[10]

4. *Rights to inventions made with federal assistance.* For many years, patent rights to inventions made under federal research grants were allocated by the federal agency responsible for the grants, with each agency having its own policy. Some agencies took the position that the public should hold the patents to government-funded inventions because it had paid for their development. Other agencies permitted the individual researchers to own rights to their inventions, but only if they agreed to grant the United States royalty-free licenses. However, there was long a suspicion that the commercial potential of government-sponsored inventions was underdeveloped. One explanation offered was similar to that discussed

---

[9] Indeed, the rush to patent c-DNA sequences derives from the fear that nothing associated with the work will be patentable if the sequences fall into the public domain, see, e.g., Robin Herman, The Great Gene Gold Rush: U.S. Rankles Other Countries With Preemptive Strike in the Race to Patent Human Genes, The Washington Post, June 16, 1992, Health, p. z11 (describing National Institute of Health patent policy as an attempt to keep options open).

[10] For an example of such a proposal, see Paul H. Egger, Uses, New Uses and Chemical Patents–A Proposal, 51 J. Pat Off. Soc. 768, 784–87 (1969).

above: without strong private patent protection, no one has the incentive to make the effort to get the invention from the lab bench to the consumer.[11]

In the Patent and Trademark Law Amendment Act of 1980, Congress included provisions that allow federally-funded researchers to retain full control over the patent rights to their inventions, unless the funding agency finds that exceptional circumstances mandate that the government retain these rights. To counteract the argument that the public would then pay twice for new inventions (once in funding their development, a second time through the high prices patents make possible), Congress limited the ability to acquire patent rights to nonprofit organizations, such as universities, and to small business firms. In that way, any overpayment by the public subsidizes activities that are in the public interest. To counteract the fear that such patents would block further developments, the agencies funding the research were given so-called "march-in rights"—rights to grant licenses in the event that the patentee fails to use the patent to "hunt" for uses for the invention. See §§ 200–211 of the Patent Act.

5. *"Utility . . . as a possible object of scientific inquiry"*. Note that *Brenner* distinguishes between utility to researchers and utility to end-users, implying that only the latter qualifies as a specific utility under § 101. This distinction is even clearer in the case *Brenner* relied upon, *Application of Bremner,* which held that a chemical intermediate lacked utility. Intermediates have a transitory existence, and so are, indeed, of little use to consumers. However, they are of considerable interest to chemists, who use the structure of intermediates to understand, among other things, the mechanism and timing of reactions.

What accounts for this distinction, which is found nowhere in the Patent Act? Perhaps the idea is that discoveries of interest only to scholars are similar in effect to principles of nature, that tying up the tools of inventiveness will block research or raise its costs to prohibitive levels. This would account for the hostility to patent protection in cases like *Brenner* and *Bremner;* it would also account for congressional reluctance to continue granting patents on genetically-altered animals of use to researchers. Is this a cogent analysis? If these research tools are valued and needed, it would appear desirable for the patent system to encourage their development. Could the cost issue be treated better by developing a research (i.e. experimental use) defense to patent infringement? This solution would be similar to copyright's fair use defense.

6. *The Luddite perspective examined.* The excerpt on animal patents illustrates that the fight to deny patents to socially dysfuncuct products has not abated, even if it has shifted ground from arguments over subject matter to arguments over utility. Would research on animals actually stop if patent protection is denied? If a field has enough potential, academic research—which has its own reward system—will certainly continue. In-

---

[11] See Jerome S. Gabig, Jr., Federal Research Grants: Who Owns the Intellectual Property, 9 Harv. J.L. & Pub. Pol. 639 (1986).

dustrial research may also continue, with researchers counting on state-based trade secrecy protection as the vehicle for capturing financial reward. Is this a better state of affairs? As Justice Fortas noted, patents do encourage (or facilitate) publication of research results. Even if the public does not like the work, it can at least monitor the research for side effects and can take steps to assert direct control over further developments.

BIBLIOGRAPHY

On the utility requirement in general, see Sibley, Practical Utility: Evolution Suspended, 32 Idea 203 (1992); Mirabel, "Practical Utility" is a Useless Concept, 36 Am.U.L.Rev. 811 (1987); Cooper, Patent Problem for Chemical Researchers—The Utility Requirement After Brenner v. Manson, 18 Idea 23 (1976); Comment, The Patentability of Chemical Intermediates, 56 Cal.L.Rev. 497 (1968); Velvel, A Critique of Brenner v. Manson, 49 J.Pat.Off.Soc'y 5 (1967); Meyer, Utility Requirement in the Statute, 49 J.Pat.Off.Soc'y 533 (1967).

On the significance of patents to the research community, see, e.g., F.M. Scherer, The Economic Effects of Compulsory Licensing (N.Y.U. 1977); Kitch, The Nature and Function of the Patent System, 20 J.L. & Econ. 265 (1977); National Academy of Sciences, The Role of Patents in Research (1962); Roberts, Genome Patent Fight Erupts, 254 Science 184 (1991).

The controversy over patenting animals has raged through both academic and popular literature. For an example of a patent on an animal, see U.S. Pat. 4,736,866 (the "Harvard mouse"). For a sample of the lay literature, see, Free For All—You Gave Short Shrift To Our Side, The Washington Post, December 3, 1988, p. a23; Gladwell, Genetically Altered Livestock: Who Owns Their Offspring? ; Debate Rages Between Scientists, Farmers, The Washington Post, October 9, 1988, p.a1; May, Role As 'Cancer Detective' Seen For Patented Mouse, Los Angeles Times, April 13, 1988, p.1, col.1; Gorner and Kotulak, Cattle–Cloning Labs Transform the Barnyard, Chicago Tribune, April 10, 1990, p.1; Cowen, Bioethics and the Matter of Life, Christian Science Monitor, January 24, 1989, p.13. For articles in the legal literature, see, e.g., Symposium on Biomedical Technology and Health Care: Social and Conceptual Transformations: Patenting Animals and Other Living Things, 65 S. Cal. L. Rev. 597 (1991); The Randolph W. Thrower Symposium: Genetics and the Law, 39 Emory L.J. 875 (1990); Note, Biotechnology and Animal Rights: When Someone Builds a Better Mouse, 32 Ariz. L. Rev. 691 (1990); Note, Patents On People and the U.S. Constitution: Creating Slaves or Enslaving Science, 16 Hastings Const. L.Q. 221 (1989).

Many of the arguments on the effects of patents on farmers echo the debate that raged when plants came under patent protection through the Plant Variety Protection Act and the Plant Patent Act, see, Buttel and Belsky, Biotechnology, Plant Breeding, and Intellectual Property: Social and Ethical Dimensions, in Owning Scientific and Technical Information 110 (V. Weil and J.W. Snapper, eds. 1989); Griliches, Hybrid Corn: An

Exploration in the Economics of Technological Change, 4 Econometrica 501 (1957).

Finally, articles on patenting genes include: Margolis, Patenting Human Genes: Sheer Lunacy or Sound Legal Protection?, 9 No. 10 Health Span 14 (1992); Eisenberg, Genes, Patents, and Product Development, 257 Sci. 903 (1992); Adler, Genome Research: Fulfilling the Public's Expectations for Knowledge and Commercialization, 257 Sci. 908 (1992); Eisenberg, Genetics and the Law: Patenting the Human Genome, 39 Emory 721 (1990).

NOVELTY

1. INTRODUCTION

A. SECTION 102

Among other things, § 102 refines the requirement, set out in § 101, that the invention be "new." Unfortunately, this section does several other things as well. Indeed, it is one of the most confusingly drafted provisions in the United States Code, laying out four distinct concepts in no discernable order. These are: novelty (newness),[1] statutory bar,[2] priority,[3] and originality.[4] Equally confusing is the fact that the novelty provisions of § 102 are not the only place in the Patent Act where "new" is interpreted. Section 103 provides further elaboration on the concept. It requires that the invention must be more than an obvious improvement over the technology that preceded it.

Because novelty is more closely related to the question of nonobviousness than it is to the other concepts in § 102, the next group of Assignments will depart from the order followed by the Patent Act. Immediately after this Assignment on novelty, § 103 will be examined. Originality will be discussed in Assignment 19, Note 6, and then the statutory bars (Assignment 20) and priority (Assignment 21) will be covered.

B. NOVELTY

In some ways, the requirement that the invention be new is easy to justify. An old invention—or as patent lawyers say, an invention that is "anticipated by the prior art"—is a discovery that, in some sense, already exists in the storehouse of knowledge. People who work in the field know of it (or can find it), can use it, and can bring it to the public's attention. There is no need to encourage someone to invent this invention, and therefore there is no need to incur the costs associated with exclusivity. Moreover, if an invention is old, there may be people who are already relying on its free availability. Subsequent issuance of a patent covering the invention would frustrate these users' expectations.

The things considered relevant to the novelty inquiry go by a variety of names. The ones most often seen are: "prior art," "references," and "disclosures." What counts as a reference (prior art/disclosure) is enumerated in the provisions of § 102 that describe activity occurring "before the

---

[1] §§ 102(a), (e), and the first sentence of (g).

[2] §§ 102(b), (c), and (d).

[3] § 102(g).

[4] § 102(f).

invention ... by the applicant." Under § 102(a), this includes knowledge or use of the invention by others in the United States, or publication or patenting anywhere in the world. Under § 102(e), this includes disclosures contained in an application for a U.S. patent—so long as the application eventually results in a patent. Finally, under the first sentence of § 102(g), this includes inventions by another person in the United States—so long as that person has not abandoned, suppressed, or concealed the invention. These provisions are not mutually exclusive. An invention can, all at the same time, be made by another (who does not abandon it), it can be disseminated within the United States, it can be described in print, and it can be disclosed in a pending application. However, if even only one of these events occurs, the applicant cannot receive a patent.

Despite the ease with which the novelty requirement can be justified, two mysteries remain. First, it is worth thinking about why patent law and copyright law take such different positions on novelty. Copyright requires only that the work be original; it is not disqualifying that a work is similar to another copyrighted work or to material already in the public domain. In contrast, originality, while a requirement of patent law,[5] is not sufficient. Once an invention runs afoul of the novelty requirement, its inventor is deprived of all rights, irrespective of the effort put into the work or the absence of public knowledge about the earlier technology.

What accounts for this difference? One possibility is that absolute rights are more necessary to reap the rewards of inventorship than authorship. In some sense, all works within the ambit of copyright are unique. After all, the proverbial monkeys with typewriters never have managed to duplicate Shakespeare. Moreover, a work acquires some of its value from the fact that it was written by a particular person. For example, no matter how accurate the historian, a study of the Ford presidency will never fully substitute for Gerald Ford's own account. Therefore, Ford's copyright will have value no matter how many other books are written about, say, the pardon of Richard Nixon. In contrast, inventions are fungible. The purchaser of the lightbulb cares only that it works; there is no value in using the specific bulb invented by Thomas Edison. Thus, if two inventors receive patents on the same invention, they will be in essentially perfect competition. Absent collusion, they will drive the price down to marginal cost and neither will capture the benefits patent law seeks to provide. Patent exclusivity must, in short, be just that: a right to exclude *all* others, even other independent inventors.[6]

First Amendment values may also account for part of the difference between copyright and patent law's positions on novelty. Because copyright is thought to further the interest in free expression,[7] denying copyright to

---

[5] As noted above, the originality requirement is set out in § 102(f), and is discussed in Assignment 19 at Note 6.

[6] It is worth noting, however, that in many countries, independent inventors are not left out in the cold. They can acquire a *limited* right to use their inventions for their own use, but no right to grant licenses to others. This alternative is discussed in Note 2(b), infra.

[7] See, e.g., Assignment 7.

an independent author may raise constitutional concerns.[8] Although inventors have, from time to time, asserted First Amendment rights to conduct and publish research, these rights are not as well developed as they are in the copyright context.[9]

Finally, some commentators offer a "search model" that claims that the novelty requirement (or lack thereof) can be explained by examining the ratio between the cost of searching prior art to learn a particular innovation and the cost of developing that same innovation from scratch. When this ratio is low, the law encourages people to conduct a meticulous review of earlier work before they set out on expensive independent efforts. When this ratio is high, however, prior-art searches do not make economic sense, and so the law does not encourage them. In most of the patent industries, the literature is well indexed, there are abstracting services, and periodic articles that survey the field. Because this literature is conducive to efficient search, the novelty provisions require it. In many of the fields where copyright is pertinent—art, music, and poetry, for example—there is no systematic indexing or abstracting.[10] Since searching would be onerous, if not impossible, it is better if creators started fresh rather than do research. Accordingly, copyright law does not strip these creators of their rights when the works they produce turn out to be similar to material already in existence.[11]

The second mystery surrounding novelty involves the choices Congress made in § 102. Not all bits of prior knowledge render an invention "not new." As the principal cases demonstrate, some kinds of prior knowledge are not deemed anticipatory. Consider the extent to which the "search model" discussed in the previous paragraph helps decide which kinds of knowledge count for novelty purposes.

2. PRINCIPAL PROBLEM

Here is an oldie but goodie from our firm's case files. See if you think it was handled properly. Our clients were Larry Nichols and Moleculon Corporation, inventor and assignee of U.S. Letters Patent No. 3,655,201 (the '201). They told us the following: It seems Nichols has been interested in puzzles since he was a youngster in the early 50's, when his mother gave him a number puzzle consisting of a two-dimensional square frame in which 15 numbered and interlocking (smaller) squares were fitted. A space, which could theoretically hold another square, was left free so that the 15

---

[8] Cf. Dreyfuss, A *Wiseguy*'s Approach to Information Products: Muscling Copyright and Patent Into a Unitary Theory of Intellectual Property, 1992 S.Ct. Rev. 195.

[9] See, e.g., United States v. The Progressive, Inc., 467 F.Supp. 990 (W.D.Wis.1979); Robertson, The Scientists' Right to Research: A Constitutional Analysis, 51 S.Cal.L.Rev. 1203 (1978). See generally, Francione, Experimentation and the Marketplace Theory of the First Amendment, 136 U. Pa. L. Rev. 417 (1987).

[10] Full text data bases may ultimately make searching for, say an iambic pentameter poem on the grace of a giraffe as easy as searching chemical abstracts for articles on ethyl alcohol, but such capacity is not available yet.

[11] Cf. Merges, Patent Law and Policy 192–195 (1992).

existing squares could be moved about. The objective of the puzzle was to arrange the numbered squares in a variety of ways without removing them from the frame. Nichols had always felt a three-dimensional version of the puzzle was possible, and on a summer evening in 1957, the idea occurred to him for an assembly of eight cubes stacked in a 2x2x2 arrangement, with each of the six faces of the composite cube distinguished by a different color. He recognized that the smaller cubes could be rotated in sets of four around one of three mutually perpendicular axes and placed in a variety of arrangements.

Nichols very quickly realized that magnets could be used to hold the cubes in assembled form yet allow them rotational movement, but he had considerable difficulty translating his idea into a workable model. He played with the problem for many years, including the time when he was a graduate student in organic chemistry at Harvard. During that period, 1959–1962, he and a few close friends made many paper models that used a variety of construction techniques, such as tongue-in-groove and tab-and-slot arrangements. None of these worked in a truly satisfactory manner.

In 1962, Nichols received his Ph.D. and went to work for the Moleculon Research Corporation. In 1968, he happened on some small, strong magnets in a retail store and, using Moleculon's machine shop, he undertook to make a wood block model of his puzzle. Working after hours, he drilled holes in the internal faces of eight small wooden blocks, inserted the magnets, properly oriented them, and glued them in. He painted each face a different color and—low an behold—the puzzle worked. Nichols kept his creation in his office. In late 1968, Moleculon's principal shareholder and operating officer, Dr. Harold Obermayer, entered the office, saw the model on Nichols' desk, and began to play with it. Obermayer asked if he could buy a copy; Nichols told him it was not available commercially but allowed him to take the model home to play with.

Obermayer so enjoyed the puzzle that he offered to put Moleculon's efforts into its commercialization. On January 2, 1969, Nichols signed a written agreement assigning all his rights in the puzzle to Moleculon in return for a share of any proceeds. Moleculon assumed all expenses of commercializing the puzzle, initiated contacts with Parker Brothers, Ideal Corp., and other manufacturers of children's games, and hired an attorney to help Nichols prepare a patent application. Although none of Moleculon's contacts resulted in any kind of marketing agreement, the patent application was filed on January 12, 1970, and a patent issued on April 11, 1972, naming Larry D. Nichols as inventor and Moleculon Corp. as assignee and claiming rights to both the puzzle and its solution.[12]

[12] A representative claim to the puzzle reads as follows:

"A puzzle comprising at least eight pieces, visually distinguishable indicia on at least one face of each piece with the eight pieces together having at least two visually distinct indicia, means associat-ed with each of the remaining faces only of each of the pieces releasably maintaining the pieces in assembled relationship forming a composite structure, said maintaining means enabling three inter-affiliated groups of four contiguous pieces each to be rotated respectively

In February, 1981, Obermayer became aware of a puzzle manufactured by the Ideal Corp. called Rubik's Cube, a 3x3x3 cube of rotating blocks painted six different colors. Obermayer immediately contacted Ideal to call its attention to the '201 patent. Ideal's attorney invited Obermayer to a meeting at which the attorney explained that Ideal did not get the idea of the cube from Nichol's patent. Rather, one of its marketing agents on a trip to Eastern Europe saw some Hungarian children playing with a traditional folk puzzle of this type. The agent brought a copy to corporate headquarters, where the decision was made to rush it to market. It hit the stores in June, 1980 and was snapped up by puzzle lovers everywhere.

According to the attorney, Ideal never attempted to patent the puzzle. The patenting decision was made after Ideal's patent department found a patent ("Gustafson") issued in March 1963 describing a ball-shaped puzzle with an outer shell that rotated around an inner shell. The outer shell was divided into eight pieces, each painted with a bit of the map of the world; when purchased, the puzzle looked like a globe. Any four contiguous pieces could be rotated together around their center—for example, the northern hemisphere could be rotated around the North Pole so that Europe appeared above South America, or the western hemisphere could be rotated to make the U.S. level with Australia. If several rotations were made consecutively, the world could be entirely jumbled. Bringing it back into shape required the same type of reiterative solution used in Rubik's cube (that is, the solver places one piece in the right place, then must undo that solution to make room to position the next piece, resolve the puzzle for that piece, and then undo the solution to position the next piece . . .).

Moleculon engaged us to sue Ideal for patent infringement. Of course, our first concern was whether the patent would hold up if challenged in litigation. What do you think?

about three mutually perpendicular aces, the two distinct indicia being so located on the respective pieces that the groups can be rotated to effect the display of at least two distinct indicia of the composite structure."

A representative claim to the puzzle's solution reads:

"A method for restoring a preselected pattern from sets of pieces which pieces have constantly exposed and constantly nonexposed surfaces, the exposed surfaces adapted to be combined to form the preselected pattern, which sets when in random engagement fail to display said preselected pattern which comprises:

a. engaging eight cube pieces as a composite cube;

b. rotating a first set of cube pieces comprising four cubes about a first axis;

c. rotating a second set of four cubes about a second axis; and

d. repeating steps (b) and (c) until the preselected pattern is achieved."

3. MATERIALS FOR SOLUTION OF PRINCIPAL PROBLEM

A. STATUTORY MATERIAL: §§ 102 (a), (e), (g), & § 104

B. CASES:

Gayler v. Wilder

Supreme Court of the United States, 1850.
51 U.S. (10 How.) 477, 13 L.Ed. 504.

■ MR. CHIEF JUSTICE TANEY delivered the opinion of the Court.

[A patent was granted on June 1, 1843 to one Daniel Fitzgerald claiming "an improvement, new and useful, in the construction of iron chests, or safes, intended to resist the action of fire, and for the safe-keeping and preserving books and papers, and other valuables, from the destruction by fire."]

The remaining question is upon the validity of the patent an which the suit was brought.

It appears that James Conner, who carried on the business of a stereotype founder in the city of New York, made a safe for his own use between the years 1829 and 1832, for the protection of his papers against fire; and continued to use it until 1838, when it passed into other hands. It was kept in his counting-room and known to the persons engaged in the foundery; and after it passed out of his hands, he used others of a different construction.

It does not appear what became of this safe afterwards. And there is nothing in the testimony from which it can be inferred that its mode of construction was known to the person into whose possession it fell, or that any value was attached to it as a place of security for papers against fire; or that it was ever used for that purpose.

Upon these facts the court instructed the jury, "that if Connor had not made his discovery public, but had used it simply for his own private purpose, and it had been finally forgotten or abandoned, such a discovery and use would be no obstacle to the taking out of a patent by Fitzgerald or those claiming under him, if he be an original, though not the first, inventor or discoverer."

The instruction assumes that the jury might find from the evidence that Conner's safe was substantially the same with that of Fitzgerald, and also prior in time. And if the fact was so, the question then was whether the patentee was "the original and first inventor or discoverer," within the meaning of the act of Congress.

The act of 1836, ch. 357, § 6[a] authorizes a patent where the party has discovered or invented a new and useful improvement, "not known or used by others before his discovery or invention." And the 15th section provides

---

[a] [This is the predecessor to § 102(a)—eds.]

that, if it appears on the trial of an action brought for the infringement of a patent that the patentee "was not the original and first inventor or discoverer of the thing patented," the verdict shall be for the defendant.

Upon a literal construction of these particular words, the patentee in this case certainly was not the original and first inventor or discoverer, if the Conner safe was the same with his, and preceded his discovery. But we do not think that this construction would carry into effect the intention of the legislature. It is not by detached words and phrases that a statute ought to be expounded. The whole act must be taken together, and a fair interpretation given to it, neither extending nor restricting it beyond the legitimate import of its language, and its obvious policy and object. And in the 15th section, after making the provision above mentioned, there is a further provision, that, if it shall appear that the patentee at the time of his application for the patent believed himself to be the first inventor, the patent shall not be void on account of the invention or discovery having been known or used in any foreign country, it not appearing that it had been before patented or described in any printed publication.

In the case thus provided for, the party who invents is not strictly speaking the first and original inventor. The law assumes that the improvement may have been known and used before his discovery. Yet his patent is valid if he discovered it by the efforts of his own genius, and believed himself to be the original inventor. The clause in question qualifies the words before used, and shows that by knowledge and use the legislature meant knowledge and use existing in a manner accessible to the public. If the foreign invention had been printed or patented, it was already given to the world and open to the people of this country, as well as of others, upon reasonable inquiry. They would therefore derive no advantage from the invention here. It would confer no benefit upon the community, and the inventor therefore is not considered to be entitled to the reward. But if the foreign discovery is not patented, nor described in any printed publication, it might be known and used in remote places for ages, and the people of this country be unable to profit by it. The means of obtaining knowledge would not be within their reach; and, as far as their interest is concerned, it would be the same thing as if the improvement had never been discovered. It is the inventor here that brings is to them, and places it in their possession. And as he does this by the effort of his own genius, the law regards him as the first and original inventor, and protects his patent, although the improvement had in fact been invented before, and used by others.

So, too, as to the lost arts. It is well known that centuries ago discoveries were made in certain arts the fruits of which have come down to us, but the means by which the work was accomplished are at this day unknown. The knowledge has been lost for ages. Yet it would hardly be doubted, if any one now discovered an art thus lost, and it was a useful improvement, that, upon a fair construction of the act of Congress, he would be entitled to a patent. Yet he would not literally be the first and original inventor. But he would be the first to confer on the public the benefit of the invention. He would discover what is unknown, and communicate knowledge which the public had not the means of obtaining without his invention.

Upon the same principle and upon the same rule of construction, we think that Fitzgerald must be regarded as the first and original inventor of the safe in question. The case as to this point admits, that, although Conner's safe had been kept and used for years, yet no test had been applied to it, and its capacity for resisting heat was not known; there was no evidence to show that any particular value was attached to it after it passed from his possession, or that it was ever afterwards used as a place of security for papers; and it appeared that he himself did not attempt to make another like the one he is supposed to have invented, but used a different one. And upon this state of the evidence the court put it to the jury to say, whether this safe had been finally forgotten or abandoned before Fitzgerald's invention, and whether he was the original inventor of the safe for which he obtained the patent; directing them, if they found these two facts, that their verdict must be for the plaintiff. We think there is no error in this instruction. For if the Conner safe had passed away from the memory of Conner himself, and of those who had seen it, and the safe itself had disappeared, the knowledge of the improvement was as completely lost as if it had never been discovered. The public could derive no benefit from it until it was discovered by another inventor. And if Fitzgerald made his discovery by his own efforts, without any knowledge of Conner's, he invented an improvement that was then new, and at that time unknown; and it was not the less new and unknown because Conner's safe was recalled to his memory by the success of Fitzgerald's.

We do not understand the Circuit Court to have said that the omission of Conner to try the value of his safe by proper tests would deprive it of its priority; nor his omission to bring it into public use. He might have omitted both, and also abandoned its use, and been ignorant of the extent of its value; yet, if it was the same with Fitzgerald's, the latter would not upon such grounds be entitled to a patent, provided Conner's safe and its mode of construction were still in the memory of Conner before they were recalled by Fitzgerald's patent.

The circumstances above mentioned, referred to in the opinion of the Circuit Court, appeared to have been introduced as evidence tending to prove that the Conner safe might have been finally forgotten, and upon which this hypothetical instruction was given. Whether this evidence was sufficient for that purpose or not, was a question for the jury, and the court left it to them. And if the jury found the fact to be so, and that Fitzgerald again discovered it, we regard him as standing upon the same ground with the discoverer of a lost art, or an unpatented and unpublished foreign invention, and like him entitled to a patent. For there was no existing and living knowledge of this improvement, or of its former use, at the time he made the discovery. And whatever benefit any individual may derive from it in the safety of his papers, he owes entirely to the genius and exertions of Fitzgerald.

Upon the whole, therefore, we think there is no error in the opinion of the Circuit Court, and the judgment is therefore affirmed.

■ MR. JUSTICE MCLEAN, dissenting [omitted].

Coffin v. Ogden

Supreme Court of the United States, 1873.
85 U.S. (18 Wall) 120, 21 L.Ed. 821.

■ MR. JUSTICE SWAYNE stated the case, recited the evidence, and delivered the opinion of the Court.

The appellant was the complainant in the court below, and filed this bill to enjoin the defendants from infringing the patent upon which the bill is founded. The patent is for a door lock with a latch reversible, so that the lock can be applied to doors opening either to the right or the left hand. It was granted originally on the 11th of June, 1861, to Charles R. Miller, assignee of William S. Kirkham, [reissued and reassigned, ultimately to the complainant]. The answer alleges that the thing patented, or a material and substantial part thereof, had been, prior to the supposed invention thereof by Kirkham, known and used by divers persons in the United States, and that among them were Barthol Erbe, residing at Birmingham, near Pittsburg, and Andrew Patterson, Henry Masta, and Bernard Brossi, residing at Pittsburg, and that all these persons had such knowledge at Pittsburg. The appellees insist that Erbe was the prior inventor, and that this priority is fatal to the patent. This proposition, in its aspects of fact and of law, is the only one which we have found it necessary to consider.

Kirkham made his invention in March, 1861. This is clearly shown by the testimony, and there is no controversy between the parties on the subject.

It is equally clear that Erbe made his invention not later than January 1st, 1861. This was not controverted by the counsel for the appellant; but it was insisted that the facts touching that invention were not such as to make it available to the appellees, as against the later invention of Kirkham and the patent founded upon it. This renders it necessary to examine carefully the testimony upon the subject.

Erbe's deposition was taken at Pittsburg upon interrogatories agreed upon by the parties and sent out from New York. He made the lock marked H. E. (It is the exhibit of the appellees, so marked). He made the first lock like it in the latter part of the year 1860. He made three such before he made the exhibit lock. The first he gave to Jones, Wallingford & Co. The second he sent to Washington, when he applied for a patent. The third he made for a friend of Jones. He thinks the lock he gave to Jones, Wallingford & Co. was applied to a door, but is not certain.

Brossi. In 1860 he was engaged in lockmaking for the Jones and Nimmick Manufacturing Company. He had known Erbe about seventeen years. In 1860 Erbe was foreman in the lock shop of Jones, Wallingford & Co., at Pittsburg. In that year, and before the 1st of January, 1861, he went to Erbe's house. Erbe there showed him a lock, and how it worked, so that it could be used right or left. He says: "He (Erbe) showed me the follower made in two pieces. One piece you take out when you take the knob away. The other part—the main part of the follower—slides forward in the case of the lock with the latch, so you can take the square part of the latch and turn it around left or right, whichever way a person wants to." He had then been a lockmaker eight years. He examined the lock carefully.

Masta. In 1860 he was a patternmaker for Jones, Wallingford & Co. Had known Erbe fourteen or fifteen years. Erbe showed him his improvement in reversible locks New Year's day, 1861. He examined the lock with the case open. "There is not a particle of difference between the exhibit and the original lock. It is all the same." He identifies the time by the facts that he commenced building a house in 1861, and that year is marked on the water conductor under the roof. [*Patterson* was deposed to similar effect.]

The case arose while the Patent Act of 1836 was in force, and must be decided under its provisions. The sixth section of that act requires that to entitle the applicant to a patent, his invention or discovery must be one "not known or used by others before his invention or discovery thereof." The fifteenth section allowed a party sued for infringement to prove, among other defences, that the patentee "was not the original and first inventor of the thing patented, or of a substantial and material part thereof claimed to be new."

The whole act is to be taken together and construed in the light of the context. The meaning of these sections must be sought in the import of their language, and in the object and policy of the legislature in enacting them. The invention or discovery relied upon as a defence, must have been complete, and capable of producing the result sought to be accomplished; and this must be shown by the defendant. The burden of proof rests upon him, and every reasonable doubt should be resolved against him. If the thing were embryotic or inchoate; if it rested in speculation or experiment; if the process pursued for its development had failed to reach the point of consummation, it cannot avail to defeat a patent founded upon a discovery or invention which was completed, while in the other case there was only progress, however near that progress may have approximated to the end in view. The law requires not conjecture, but certainty. If the question relate to a machine, the conception must have been clothed in substantial forms which demonstrate at once its practical efficacy and utility. The prior knowledge and use by a single person is sufficient. The number is immaterial. Until his work is done, the inventor has given nothing to the public. In Gayler v. Wilder the views of this court upon the subject were thus expressed: "We do not understand the Circuit Court to have said that the omission of Conner to try his safe by the proper tests would deprive it of its priority; nor his omission to bring in into public use. He might have omitted both, and also abandoned its use and been ignorant of the extent of its value; yet if it was the same with Fitzgerald's, the latter would not, upon such grounds, be entitled to a patent; provided Conner's safe and its mode of construction were still in the memory of Conner before they were recalled by Fitzgerald's patent." Whether the proposition expressed by the proviso in the last sentence is a sound one, it is not necessary in this case to consider.

Here it is abundantly proved that the lock originally made by Erbe "was complete and capable of working." The priority of Erbe's invention is clearly shown. It was known at the time to at least five persons, including Jones, and probably to many others in the shop where Erbe worked; and the lock was put in use, being applied to a door, as proved by Brossi. It was thus tested and shown to be successful. These facts bring the case made by the appellees within the severest legal tests which can be applied to them. The defence relied upon is fully made out.

Scripps Clinic & Research Foundation v. Genentech, Inc.

United States Court of Appeals, Federal Circuit, 1991.
927 F.2d 1565, 18 U.S.P.Q.2d (BNA) 1001, 18 U.S.P.Q.2d (BNA) 1896.

■ PAULINE NEWMAN, CIRCUIT JUDGE.

The Invention

Factor VIII:C, called the clotting or procoagulant factor, is found in all mammals. It has been the subject of extensive scientific research, over many years. At the time the claimed invention was made, it was known that human Factor VIII:C is a complex protein produced by the Factor VIII:C gene and secreted into the blood stream. It occurs in normal blood plasma (plasma is the fluid fraction of blood) at a concentration of about 200 nanograms per milliliter. The total protein content of plasma is about 70 milligrams (0.070 gram) per milliliter; since a nanogram is one billionth of a gram, the total protein in plasma is 350,000 times greater than the Factor VIII:C protein in plasma. Most of the problems faced by researchers attempting to isolate Factor VIII:C were due to the amount and nature of the other proteins in the plasma.

It was known that in normal blood Factor VIII:C exists in complex association with another protein, named the "von Willebrand factor" or Factor VIII:RP (RP means "related protein").

Before the invention here at issue was made, scientists had succeeded in concentrating the Factor VIII: C in plasma. This concentrate has been used to replace transfusions of whole blood in the treatment of hemophilia. The process was expensive and, because of the large volume of whole blood needed as starting material, the possibility of contamination and disease from impurities in the source blood, the large amount of extraneous plasma proteins in the concentrate, and the large volume of concentrate that still had to be administered to the patient, there has been a continuing search for improvement. The record reflects the difficulties, over decades of research, in isolating and studying Factor VIII:C. Scripps reports that Genentech's scientists had been working in the field and had not isolated human Factor VIII:C in sufficient purity and amount to conduct successful characterization experiments.

At the Scripps Clinic & Research Foundation, Dr. Zimmerman and Dr. Fulcher were studying Factor VIII:C from human and porcine blood. These scientists succeeded in isolating and, for the first time, characterizing Factor VIII:C, by a process of chromatographic absorption of the Factor VIII:C complex using monoclonal antibodies specific to Factor VIII:RP, followed by separation of the Factor VIII:C.[a] Monoclonal antibodies are produced by the cloned copies of a single hybridoma cell. A hybridoma is a hybrid cell that is immortal: that is, it does not die as do normal cells, but continues to reproduce clones that in turn produce a specific antibody. As described in the R'011 patent, the hybridoma was made by fusing a mouse spleen cell that produced the desired antibody to Factor VIII:RP, with a mouse cancer cell, which contributed the immortality. The patent describes the method of assay for clones producing antibodies to VIII:RP, their isolation, and preparation of the monoclonal antibodies for use as the immunoadsorbent.

The claimed process whereby the Factor VIII:C/VIII:RP complex is separated from the other materials in blood, followed by separation of the VIII:C from the VIII:RP, is described in the R'011 patent and was summarized by Scripps as follows:

> The first step involves the application of a solution containing Factor VIII complex (Factor VIII:C/Factor VIII:RP) to a column packed with agarose beads. Attached to the beads is a monoclonal antibody to Factor VIII:RP. The monoclonal antibody binds and immobilizes the Factor VIII:RP part of the Factor VIII complex while the non-Factor VIII materials simply pass through the column. A calcium salt solution is then applied to break the bond between the Factor VIII:C and the Factor VIII:RP. The Factor VIII:C is eluted from the column while the Factor VIII:RP remains bound to the antibody.

The procedure produces purified but dilute Factor VIII:C:

> After this first step the Factor VIII:C is highly purified, but dilute. A second step to concentrate the Factor VIII:C solution may then be performed. This involves absorbing the Factor VIII:C on an aminohexylagarose column. The Factor VIII:C on the aminohexyl column is then eluted with a very small amount of calcium salt solution, resulting in a highly concentrated solution of highly purified Factor VIII:C.

Anticipation

The district court held, on cross-motions for summary judgment, that "it had been proved by clear and convincing evidence" that claims 24, 26,

---

[a] Drs. Zimmerman and Fulcher characterized the Factor VIII:C using a technique described as SDS-gel ("SDS" stands for sodium dodecyl sulfate) electrophoresis and production of a precipitating heterologous antibody. This work was reported in Fulcher and Zimmerman, Proc. Nat'l Acad. Sci. USA, "Characterization of the Human Factor VIII Procoagulant Protein with a Heterologous Precipitating Antibody", Vol. 79, pp. 1648–52, March, 1982. It is not disputed that this is the first time that human Factor VIII:C was sufficiently pure to be characterized scientifically, and that the Zimmerman/Fulcher characterization is now the generally recognized "fingerprint" of Factor VIII:C.

and 27 were invalid for anticipation, ... based on subject matter described in a 1979 dissertation by Robert B. Harris entitled "Isolation and Characterization of Low Molecular Weight, Non–Aggregated Antihemophilic Factor from Fresh Human Plasma."

A

Invalidity for anticipation requires that all of the elements and limitations of the claim are found within a single prior art reference. Carella v. Starlight Archery and Pro Line Co., 804 F.2d 135, 138, 231 U.S.P.Q. 644, 646 (Fed.Cir.1986); RCA Corp. v. Applied Digital Data Systems, Inc., 730 F.2d 1440, 1444, 221 U.S.P.Q. 385, 388 (Fed.Cir.1984). There must be no difference between the claimed invention and the reference disclosure, as viewed by a person of ordinary skill in the field of the invention.

It is sometimes appropriate to consider extrinsic evidence to explain the disclosure of a reference. Such factual elaboration is necessarily of limited scope and probative value, for a finding of anticipation requires that all aspects of the claimed invention were already described in a single reference: a finding that is not supportable if it is necessary to prove facts beyond those disclosed in the reference in order to meet the claim limitations. The role of extrinsic evidence is to educate the decision-maker to what the reference meant to persons of ordinary skill in the field of the invention, not to fill gaps in the reference. See Studiengesellschaft Kohle, mbH v. Dart Industries, Inc., 726 F.2d 724, 727, 220 U.S.P.Q. 841, 842 (Fed.Cir.1984)(although additional references may serve to reveal what a reference would have meant to a person of ordinary skill, it is error to build "anticipation" on a combination of these references). If it is necessary to reach beyond the boundaries of a single reference to provide missing disclosure of the claimed invention, the proper ground is not § 102 anticipation, but § 103 obviousness. Indeed, a publication on the Harris dissertation was included in the prior art statement filed by Scripps and was a cited reference under § 103.

B

In the summary judgment proceedings the parties filed three successive declarations of Dr. Harris, each explaining his dissertation. In the first declaration, filed by Miles, Inc., Harris stated that he isolated "a low molecular weight antihemophilic factor." In his second ("supplemental") declaration, filed by Scripps, Harris described this factor as not a naturally occurring substance, and of low specific activity:

6. The material I identified as low molecular weight antihemophilic factor (LMW–AHF) was not a naturally occurring substance. The material of my dissertation is the result of reacting plasma with a reducing agent called dithiothreitol (DTT) prior to purification. The reduced plasma is run through an initial purification step, and is then chemically reacted with radioactively labeled iodoacetamide (14C–IAA). This reduced and alkylated material was the LMW–AHF reported in my dissertation. After further purification, I obtained a maximum specific activity of 59.1 [units]/mg.

In the third Harris declaration, filed by Miles, Harris stated that his dissertation

> accurately reports on my work in which I was able to, and did, obtain a human VIII:C preparation having a potency of 193 [units]/ml and being substantially free of VIII:RP, the ratio of VIII:C to VIII:RP being greater than 100,000 times the ratio in plasma.

The third Harris declaration was cited by the district court in support of its finding of anticipation.

The parties debate whether Harris' statement in his second declaration that his product was chemically changed from naturally occurring VIII:C, is contradicted by the statement in his third declaration that he obtained a human VIII:C preparation. Scripps also points out that neither the potency value nor the ratio of VIII:C to VIII:RP described in the third Harris declaration appears in the Harris dissertation. Nor does the gel pattern evidence on which the district court found that:

> Harris also based his identification of his preparation upon sodium dodecyl sulfate polyacrylamide gel electrophoresis (SDS–PAGE) tests [the same tests used by Dr. Fulcher]. While Harris' gel patterns do not match the gel pattern found by Dr. Fulcher, there is no evidence that if he had VIII:C, it would necessarily have the gel pattern found by Dr. Fulcher.

Scripps, 707 F.Supp. 1547, 1551 n. 6 (N.D.Cal.1989), 11 U.S.P.Q.2d 1187, 1190 n. 6. Further, this finding that human Factor VIII:C, if obtained by Harris, would not necessarily have the "fingerprint" gel pattern of Dr. Fulcher, was not simply an adverse factual inference, improper on summary judgment; it was a finding of scientific fact contrary to the evidence. This finding also appears to be inconsistent with the court's finding that Dr. Harris had obtained purified Factor VIII:C because he based his identification on the same tests and gel patterns taught by Zimmerman and Fulcher. Also contradicting the court's conclusion was Scripps' evidence that the human Factor VIII:C SDS-gels of the inventors, the defendants, and non-parties to the litigation were the same, and that Dr. Harris' gel patterns were different.

To the extent that apparent inconsistencies among the three Harris declarations raise questions of credibility and weight, whether of witness or of interpretation of scientific data, they were improperly resolved on summary judgment.

Scripps also raised the question of whether the Harris dissertation was enabling and placed the purported anticipatory teaching of purified Factor VIII:C in possession of the public. Scripps pointed out that data in Harris' third declaration, on which the court relied, do not appear in his dissertation or in any other reference. See Akzo N.V. v. United States Int'l Trade Comm'n, 808 F.2d 1471, 1479, 1 U.S.P.Q.2d 1241, 1245 (Fed.Cir.1986), cert. denied, 482 U.S. 909, 107 S.Ct. 2490, 96 L.Ed.2d 382 (1987) (anticipatory reference must be enabling); In re Brown, 329 F.2d 1006, 1011, 141 U.S.P.Q. 245, 249 (CCPA 1964). The need to consider this issue, on disputed factual premises, also negates the propriety of the grant of summary judgment based on anticipation.

The grant of partial summary judgment of invalidity of claims 24, 26, and 27 for anticipation by the Harris dissertation is reversed. The issue is not amenable to summary disposition, and is remanded for trial.

N O T E S

1. *The § 102(a) inquiry.* The principal cases all deal with anticipation under § 102(a): that is, the argument that the patent should not issue because one of the activities enumerated in § 102(a) had occurred before the applicant invented the invention. Note that although the section does not specifically require that the prior activity be "public," all of the cases construing this provision do impute into it a requirement of some level of publicity. For example, the safe in *Gayler* differed from the lock in *Ogden* in that its special characteristic—fireproofness—was hidden and could not be discerned or copied by mere inspection, whereas anyone viewing the *Ogden* lock could see it was reversible.

A consideration of the rationale underlying the novelty provision makes the reason for requiring some publicity clear. After all, if the prior activity does not inform the public of the invention, then the applicant *is* the one who is disseminating something new. Since the applicant provided the benefit patent law is aimed at producing, she should be entitled to receive the reward of a patent. Furthermore, awarding a patent to the applicant would not require people who were enjoying the invention for free to suddenly pay royalties. After all, no one could figure out how to practice the invention from the safe in *Gayler*: First it was hidden and then it was lost. Analysis of § 102(a) cases therefore focuses on three issues: first, whether the contents of the reference in fact put the invention into the hands of the public; second, whether the reference is accessible to the public; third, whether the date of reference actually precedes the date of the applicant's invention.

a. *Contents.* What must a reference teach in order to be considered anticipatory?

(i) Enablement. Because the novelty requirement is intended to prevent the patenting of inventions that are already available to the public, the first content requirement is straight forward: a reference will anticipate only if it contains enough information to allow the public to practice the invention. Thus, one reason why the Harris dissertation in *Scripps* was not anticipatory is because it was not enabling. Starting from Harris's manuscript, much more research is required to achieve the *Scripps* development.[13] It is precisely the promise of a patent that encourages this kind of work.

This statement of the justification for enablement highlights an important nuance in the way that patent law is construed. If the concept of "public" retained its ordinary meaning in the discussion of enablement,

---

[13] See, e.g., Seymour v. Osborne, 78 U.S. (11 Wall.) 516, 20 L.Ed. 33 (1870); Pfizer, Inc. v. Int'l Rectifier Corp., 545 F.Supp. 486 (C.D.Cal.1980).

there would be few inventions that would be unpatentable. For instance, most disclosures are of a technical nature and could not, realistically speaking, enable the ordinary person to practice the invention. But, realistically speaking, what the ordinary person can do is not very relevant. Only people who are trained in the field to which the invention pertains will read disclosures such as the Harris dissertation. Accordingly, it is the person *with ordinary skill in the art to which the invention pertains* who counts for § 102(a) purposes, and indeed, for most of patent law. Thus, the focus in *Scripps* is not on what Harris teaches the public at large, but on what Harris teaches the ordinary biochemist.

(ii) The every element test. Another way to look at the relationship between Harris and Scripps is to note that there are elements in the Scripps invention that are not described in the Harris dissertation. Since inventiveness is required to supply these missing elements, patent protection is warranted. Thus, the "every element" test: anticipation under § 102(a) requires that the reference disclose *every* element of the applicant's invention.

The test for anticipation is sometimes expressed as: "That which infringes, if later, would anticipate, if earlier."[14] To see why anticipation is tied to infringement, focus on the party who invented the reference that is said to anticipate. (In the case of *Scripps,* this would be Harris.) Do we want to consider that person an infringer of the applicant's patent (i.e.: do we want Harris to be considered an infringer of Scripps' patent)? If the inventor of the reference had all the same insights as the patent applicant, we certainly would not want to do so. After all, the inventor of the reference may have relied on the continued free availability of his discovery by committing time and effort into commercializing it. Since that is exactly

---

[14] Knapp v. Morss, 150 U.S. 221, 228, 14 S.Ct. 81, 84, 37 L.Ed. 1059 (1893). For an example of how this works, consider a reference describing an alloy of titanium containing 0.25% nickel. Someone applies for a patent on the later discovered invention of titanium alloys containing anywhere between 0.1% and 0.5% nickel. Should the reference be considered anticipatory? The answer is, yes. The person who invented the 0.25% nickel alloy should not suddenly discover herself an infringer for using what she invented. Yet she would be one if a patent were granted on the application since 0.25 falls within the range claimed.Cf. Titanium Metals Corp. v. Banner, 778 F.2d 775 (Fed. Cir.1985).

Note, however, that a reference disclosing alloys in a range from 0.1%–0.25% nickel would not necessarily anticipate an application for an alloy containing precisely 0.25% nickel. If the 0.25% alloy had surprisingly different characteristics, its identification may be considered a nonobvious improvement over prior art, see, e.g., In re Meyer, 599 F.2d 1026 (C.C.P.A.1979).

The results here could also be explained on the search cost model described in the Introduction. Under this approach, the issue is whether the law should encourage metallurgists interested in inventing new alloys of titanium to read this reference and explore its significance. Consider the reference discussed in the first paragraph (the .25% nickel alloy). Since reading about its existence should alert metallurgists to the possibility of other alloys with slightly different amounts of nickel, the law should regard the .25% nickel reference as anticipatory. But since the range reference in the second paragraph would not tell metallurgists about a surprisingly different characteristic of the .25% nickel alloy, there is no point in requiring them to read that reference first, and so that reference would not be regarded as anticipatory.

the sort of activity society wants, this reliance interest deserves protection. Thus, if the inventor of the reference would be considered an infringer of the patent were it to issue, the patent should be denied: that which would infringe is deemed to anticipate. (Of course, in the actual *Scripps* case, Harris may not have had all of the applicants' insights. If that is the case, he had no reliance interest in the free availability of Scripps' invention, and so we do not mind if he is considered an infringer of the Scripps patent.)

(iii) Inherency. Reconsider the facts of the Principal Problem. What if someone back in the early 1950's had invented a mechanical joint that effected a coupling similar to that found in Nichols' cube, and even utilized a color scheme similar to Nichols' to keep the sides of the coupling aligned: should the joint be considered anticipatory? On the one hand, nothing about the joint suggests it would make a fun puzzle; its intended function was never to amuse. On the other hand, the joint does contain every element of the cube and enables the construction of the puzzle. Anyone with the idea of a three dimensional puzzle had only to look at this joint to fully effectuate the idea. If the goal is to encourage research in prior art, then § 102(a) prior art should be—and is—considered to encompass information of this type, information "inherent" in other works.[15]

b.   *Accessibility.* A reference is able to teach the public the invention only if the public (the relevant public) is aware of its existence (or can make itself aware at reasonable cost). There are several dimensions to this issue.

(i) Geography. Section § 102(a) makes knowledge or use of the invention anticipatory only when it occurs in the United States. In contrast, any publication or patent is anticipatory, including those that are disseminated exclusively abroad.

What accounts for the difference in the way foreign events are treated? Here is a place where the search model discussed in the Introduction is especially useful. Because literature searches of both domestic and foreign journals, books, and patents are relatively inexpensive, the statute encourages them. Searching for "knowledge" (that is, unwritten knowledge) and "use" is, however, relatively expensive, especially if it involves activities occurring in far away places, among different cultures, and in different languages. Accordingly, the statute makes a distinction here and does not bar patents because of foreign knowledge or use of the invention but does prevent the patenting of things domestically known or used. Alternatively, one could say that because foreign uses and knowledge are hard to find, the public—the American public, that is—does not actually enjoy the benefit of the invention until the applicant re-invents it in the United States.

A more protectionist explanation for this difference is, however, available. Note that § 102(a) is bolstered in an important way by § 104(a).

---

[15] See, e.g., Jones v. Hardy, 727 F.2d 1524 (Fed.Cir.1984). It is, however, important to distinguish elements that are an inherent part of a work and elements that are accidentally present. Tilghman v. Proctor, 102 U.S. 707, 26 L.Ed. 279 (1881), holds that an accidental and unrecognized element of the invention will not be considered in determining novelty.

Section 104(a) bars an applicant from establishing a date of invention through activity occurring abroad (unless a treaty declares otherwise).[16] That is, just as *challengers* to the patent cannot rely on foreign knowledge and use by virtue of § 102(a), *applicants* are barred from relying on foreign activities to establish invention by virtue of § 104(a). The net effect is to enhance the significance (for patent purposes) of work done in the United States, primarily by Americans, and to diminish the importance of work done abroad, primarily by foreigners.[17] As international communication improves and the global market becomes the principal arena for patent exploitation, this parochialism becomes less tenable.[18] Indeed, § 104 once included all foreign countries. The North American Free Trade Agreement (NAFTA) and the General Agreement on Tariffs and Trade (GATT) required the United States to amend it so that signatories of these treaties are treated as equivalent to the United States for purposes of establishing the date of invention. Many commentators believe that if world-wide harmonization of the patent laws is to be achieved, the United States will be required to eliminate this distinction entirely.[19]

(ii) Dissemination. The search model also suggests why it is that not every domestic use will be considered public enough to be anticipatory. This is because some instances of use will be so hard to find, that searching will not be cost effective. It is this problem which may account for the difference between *Gayler* and *Ogden*. Both inventions were in "use," but only one was disseminated enough to make search expedient—that is, enough to assure public availability. The lock, after all, was seen by several artisans, any one of whom could duplicate the invention and make it available to others; the applicant added nothing to the fund of knowledge. But the safe was never inspected. When its inventor stopped using it, its inventive feature was lost; the new inventor enriched the storehouse of knowledge, and that contribution merits a patent. Alternatively, since no one saw the safe and relied on its status in the public domain, no one's interests would be frustrated by awarding the patent. In contrast, for all anyone knew, Brossi, Masta, or Patterson could have invested in efforts to commercialize the lock the moment they saw it.

Is it always the case that "patents" and "publications" will have achieved the level of dissemination required to effectively give the invention to the public? Especially since the advent of desktop publishing, it is possible to "publish" an article without disseminating it widely. For example, some dissertations are printed up and distributed only within the

---

[16] The provision itself mentions NAFTA and GATT. The Paris Convention for the Protection of Industrial Property creates another important exception. It permits inventors to use as their date of invention the date on which they filed a patent application in another signatory country, so long as the U.S. application is filed within 12 months of the foreign filing, see Patent Act § 119. See generally, Section 3 of Assignment 15.

[17] See also In re Hilmer, 359 F.2d 859 (C.C.P.A.1966)(Hilmer I) and In re Hilmer, 424 F.2d 1108 (C.C.P.A.1970)(Hilmer II), discussed in Note infra.

[18] Cf., e.g., Monaco v. Hoffman, 189 F.Supp. 474 (D.D.C.1960).

[19] See, e.g., Wegner, Patent Law Simplification and the Geneva Patent Convention, 14 A.I.P.L.A. Q.J. 154 (1986).

degree-candidate's department. Only one copy may be retained by the University. Should the information in such a "publication" be considered to meet the publicity gloss of § 102(a)? Most courts decide that question by asking whether a researcher with ordinary skill in the art could have found the publication. Is it, for example, indexed or abstracted? If not, despite technical compliance with the "publication" requirement, such a work will not be considered anticipatory.[20]

Conversely, there are some documents that do not quite meet the stature of being a "patent" or "publication" that nonetheless have achieved the level of publicity necessary to find anticipation. For example, some countries have alternatives to patent protection that allow the inventor to avoid a rigorous examination if he is willing to accept less protection for a shorter term. The certificates issued under these regimes are available to the public just as patents are, but they go by names such as "inventor's certificates" or "petit patents." Should they be considered "patents" or "publications" for purposes of § 102(a)? Since they too encourage people to disclose new inventions and facilitate public dissemination, the answer is that they are considered "patents" for the purpose of § 102(a).[21]

(iii) Operability. There is another distinction between *Gayler* and *Ogden* that helps account for the difference in result. In *Ogden*, the latch was actually placed upon a door, where the operability of its special feature could be readily determined. In *Gayler*, however, because the allegedly fireproof safe was never exposed to fire, its inventive characteristic was never put to the test. Although § 102(a) does not expressly require proof that the prior art reference was operable, courts have construed it to impute such a requirement. Patents are considered operable because they must have met the requirement of utility in order to have issued. Printed publications are, in most technical fields, a good proxy for operability because articles are generally subjected to peer review prior to publication. Given the gloss of *Gayler*, inventions that are "used" in this country are also likely to have been operable. That leaves the category of "known," which has—interestingly—been interpreted as requiring some level of actual use.[22]

(iv) Field of knowledge. How far afield must the inventor cast the search net? In the inherency example, it was assumed that a mechanical joint could anticipate a child's puzzle, even though puzzle-makers are not

---

[20] See, e.g., Blandford v. Masco Industries, Inc., 799 F.Supp. 666, 25 U.S.P.Q.2d (BNA) 1074 (N.D.Tex.1992); Jockmus v. Leviton, 28 F.2d 812 (2d Cir.1928)(L. Hand, J.).

[21] See, e.g., Reeves Bros. v. United States Laminating Corp., 282 F.Supp. 118 (E.D.N.Y. 1968). Of course, the other elements of anticipation, including enablement, must be met; the fact that a disclosure meets these requirements to the satisfaction of a foreign patent examiner does not necessarily mean it meets the requirements of U.S. patent law, see, e.g.,

United States v. Adams, 383 U.S. 39, 86 S.Ct. 708, 15 L.Ed.2d 572 (1966).

But see In re Carlson, 983 F.2d 1032, 25 U.S.P.Q.2d (BNA) 1207 (Fed.Cir.1992)(holding a German "Geschmackmuster," a design registration, qualifies as a foreign patent under § 102(a) despite the fact that disclosure is available only in the city where the registered design is deposited).

[22] See D. Chisum, Patents § 3.05[3]; Westinghouse Machine Co. v. General Elec. Co., 207 F. 75 (2d Cir.1913).

likely to be acquainted with work in the mechanical arts. However, the novelty provisions are in fact interpreted to charge the inventor with knowledge of the entire universe of prior art, including art in fields very different from their own specialities.[23] Does this make sense under the search model? Searching the entire domain of knowledge sounds extremely expensive. On the other hand, it is worth remembering that every element of the claimed invention must appear in the reference. It is not very likely that an entire invention will be duplicated in a field quite distant from the one to which the invention pertains.

c. *Dating invention.* The final question under the anticipation sections involves dating. That is, the *"effective date"* of the reference—the date the public received the benefit of the prior art—must precede the *"critical date"*—in the case of § 102(a), the date on which the applicant invented the invention. In *Scripps,* for example, the Harris dissertation cannot function as prior art unless it was published (or at least indexed) before the date Scripps claims for the invention.

What should count as the *critical date*? In most cases, invention is not a sudden, one time event. As in the Principal Problem, the inventor has an idea that she ponders and experiments with for some time before it is fully realized. Should the conception of the idea be the critical date? The date on which the working model is finished? The date of first commercialization?

The practice in the PTO is that the critical date is assumed to be the date on which the applicant files a complete application disclosing the invention.[24] If the examiner cannot cite to prior art dating from an earlier time, the invention will be considered novel. If, however, the examiner finds a suitable reference, the inquiry goes to the next stage. To be anticipatory, a reference must predate the date of *invention* not *filing.* Thus, the applicant is permitted to establish that she invented the invention on an earlier date. The usual procedure is to "swear behind": to file an affidavit under Patent Office Rule 131 claiming "completion of the invention in this country" on a date that—hopefully—precedes the reference.[25] "Completion" is defined by the PTO as "reduction to practice" or "conception coupled with due diligence" from the date of the reference to reduction to practice. These technical terms, "reduction to practice" and "due diligence," are also utilized in determining priority. Accordingly, they will be discussed in Assignment 21.

Note that Rule 131 carries out the mandate of § 104(a) by, indeed, barring inventors from relying on activity occurring outside the United States unless international treaties require otherwise.

What should count as the *effective date* of a reference? As with the other elements of novelty, it is the date on which an ordinary artisan in the

[23] D. Chisum, at § 3.02[3].

[24] See, e.g., Bates v. Coe, 98 U.S. 31, 25 L.Ed. 68 (1878).

[25] 37 C.F.R. § 1.131.

field has effective access to the disclosure. For a patent, this is the date of issuance; for a book or journal article, it is the date of publication.[26] For publications that receive only modest circulation, it may be the date of indexing.[27]

2. *§§ 102(e) and (g).* This Assignment focuses on § 102(a) because most cases involving novelty raise § 102(a) issues. However, the other novelty provisions deserve some attention.

a. *§ 102(e).* Consider this modification to the Principal Problem: what if a puzzlemaker had acquired a U.S. patent on a very different kind of three dimensional puzzle but in the course of describing the state of the art at the time of the invention, disclosed a puzzle much like Nichols'? If the patent issued before Nichols' invention, he would clearly lose under § 102(a). However, what if the patent had been *applied for* before Nichols invented his cube, but did not issue until *after* Nichols' critical date? It could be argued that Nichols should still receive his patent. Because the PTO keeps applications secret,[28] the invention was simply not available in the United States on the date he invented the puzzle. On the other hand, if the PTO conducted its business rapidly, it *could* have been available—why should Nichols get a patent just because the PTO operates slowly?

In Alexander Milburn Co. v. Davis–Bournonville Co.,[29] the Supreme Court responded to this concern by interpreting "patent" to cover applications that eventually result in issued patents. The current Act codifies this holding in § 102(e), which prevents the patenting of an invention described in a U.S. patent application filed before the invention's critical date. Thus, whereas § 102(a) deals with public prior art, § 102(e) provides that in one particular circumstance, secret prior art will also be anticipatory. That circumstance is a disclosure in the patent pipeline at the time of the second invention.

Note, however, that a patent must eventually issue in order for § 102(e) to operate (the statute refers to "a *patent* granted on an application ...."). This is because a rejected applicant may choose to keep the invention as a trade secret. If so, the new applicant (Nichols in our example) would be the one who made the invention public and that is a contribution that entitles him to a patent.

Finally, what if the puzzle had been described in a *Hungarian* patent application? Clearly, if the patent had issued before Nichols' invention, § 102(a) would have prevented Nichols from acquiring a patent. Why should delays in the Hungarian patent office be any more helpful to Nichols than delays in the PTO? Despite the logic of this position, *Davis-Bournonville* has not been extended to this situation, and § 102(e) is expressly

---

[26] See, e.g., In re Schlittler, 234 F.2d 882 (C.C.P.A.1956).

[27] Compare In re Hall, 781 F.2d 897 (Fed.Cir.1986), with In re Cronyn, 890 F.2d 1158 (Fed.Cir.1989).

[28] § 122.

[29] 270 U.S. 390, 46 S.Ct. 324, 70 L.Ed. 651 (1926).

limited to U.S. patent applications.[30] Perhaps this is another example of the protectionist slant of U.S. law. On the other hand, it is possible that courts are reluctant to extend the reach of a provision that deems secret art anticipatory, for it is information that no amount of searching could have revealed to the second inventor. Furthermore, no one could have relied on this invention being freely available. Indeed, efforts to extend § 102(e) in other purely domestic circumstances—such as manuscripts in the publication pipeline—have also, generally, failed.[31]

b. *§ 102(g)*. This provision deems anticipatory *any* invention made in the United States that has not been abandoned, suppressed, or concealed. Thus, § 102(g)—like § 102(e)—allows certain secret art to block the award of a patent. Indeed, at first blush, this provision appears to eviscerate § 102(a), or at least the gloss that assures that knowledge and/or use of the invention has enough publicity to enable an ordinary artisan to search for it easily. After all, *some* non-abandoned inventions may be extremely difficult to find. Indeed, some may be practiced in a manner intended to keep others from learning of them.

But closer inspection reveals that § 102(g) does not entirely eviscerate § 102(a). To see the difference, ask why should a patent ever be blocked by genuinely secret art. Certainly, it is not easy to explain this with the search model. The answer here lies in focusing on the first inventor, who has not "abandoned, suppressed or concealed" the invention, and therefore must by implication be busy using it (albeit, so secretly, it does not qualify as § 102(a) art). If the second applicant's patent issues, that person is suddenly an infringer. Yet she did nothing wrong: there is no requirement that inventors obtain patents.[32] Trade secrecy law is not preempted by the Patent Act,[33] and the first inventor may have been expecting to capture her rewards through secrecy. Alternatively, she may have tried hard, but unsuccessfully, to disseminate the invention more broadly or even patent it. Section 102(g) protects such an inventor's reliance interest in the continued free availability of her invention. Thus, § 102(g) differs from § 102(a) in that it requires proof of continued use by the inventor.[34] In contrast,

---

[30] See In re Hilmer, 359 F.2d 859 (C.C.P.A.1966)(Hilmer I) and In re Hilmer, 424 F.2d 1108 (C.C.P.A.1970)(Hilmer II).

[31] See, e.g., In re Schlittler, 234 F.2d 882 (C.C.P.A.1956); Protein Foundation, Inc. v. Brenner, 260 F.Supp. 519 (D.D.C. 1966)(§ 102(b)); Ex parte Osmond, Smith, and Waite, 191 U.S.P.Q. (BNA) 334 (Pat.Off. Bd.App. 1976)

[32] See, e.g., Checkpoint Systems, Inc. v. U.S. ITC, 54 F.3d 756 (Fed.Cir.1995).

[33] See Assignment 25.

[34] See, e.g., E.I. du Pont de Nemours & Co. v. Phillips Petroleum Co., 849 F.2d 1430, 1437 (Fed.Cir.)("the requirement of proving

no abandonment, suppression, or concealment does mollify somewhat the 'secret' nature of § 102(g) prior art"), cert. denied, 488 U.S. 986, 109 S.Ct. 542, 102 L.Ed.2d 572 (1988); Dunlop Holdings v. Ram Golf Corp., 524 F.2d 33 (7th Cir.1975).

But see Gillman v. Stern, 114 F.2d 28 (2d Cir.1940)(L. Hand, J.), holding that a machine is not anticipated under § 102(g) by sales of its output, so long as the sales are "noninforming"—they do not reveal how the machine itself was made. The decision frustrated the reliance interests of the first inventor, who was indeed using his machine. It has been criticized on the ground that Judge Hand considered the first inventor's failure to acquire a patent on the machine an aban-

§ 102(a) requires publicity, but not a continuation of use by the inventor— or by anyone else. Furthermore, § 102(g) requires proof positive that the invention is operable (otherwise, how could its inventor be using it?). Section 102(a) has been interpreted to require some suggestion of operability but not actual proof.

This focus on the first inventor does, unfortunately, have the effect of frustrating the second inventor's interests. Although that inventor may have searched prior art diligently and invested in development in reliance on the fact that the invention was not known, she is nonetheless barred from obtaining a patent. Is there a better way to deal with this problem? In some countries, secret art is never anticipatory. Accordingly, the second inventor's expectations are fulfilled with a patent. However, the first inventor is also protected: she enjoys a "prior user right," which is the right to use the invention without paying royalties, limited to the uses being made at the time of the second invention.[35]

BIBLIOGRAPHY

Comment, In re Cronyn: Can Student Theses Bar Patent Applications?, 18 J.C. & U.L. 105 (1991); Vick, Publish and Perish: The Printed Publication as a Bar to Patentability, 18 AIPLA Q.J. 235 (1990); Scotchmer and Green, Novelty and Disclosure in Patent Law, 21 Rand J. Econ. 21 (1990); Gates, Trade Secret Software: Is it Prior Art?, 6 Computer Lawyer 11 (1989); Wegner, Patent Law Simplification and the Geneva Patent Convention, 14 AIPLA Q.J. 154 (1986); Burke, The "Noninforming Public Use" Concept and Its Application to Patent–Trade Secret Conflicts, 45 Ala. L. Rev. 1060 (1981); Robbins, The Rights of a First Inventor–Trade Secret User As Against Those of the Second Inventor–Patentee (Part I), 61 J.Pat.Off.Soc. 574 (1979); Jorda, The Rights of a First Inventor–Trade Secret User As Against Those of the Second Inventor–Patentee (Part II), 61 J.Pat.Off.Soc. 593 (1979).

donment, although abandonment under § 102(g) is interpreted as abandonment of the *invention*, not the right to acquire a patent. See, e.g., Robbins, The Rights of a First Inventor–Trade Secret User As Against Those of the Second Inventor–Patentee (Part I), 61 J.Pat.Off.Soc. 574 (1979); Jorda, The Rights of a First Inventor–Trade Secret User As Against Those of the Second Inventor– Patentee (Part II), 61 J.Pat.Off.Soc. 593 (1979).

[35] See, e.g., Fryer, Patent Law Harmonization Treaty Decision is Not Far Off—What Course Should The U.S. Take? : A Review of the Current Situation and Alternatives Available, 30 IDEA 309 (1990).

NONOBVIOUSNESS AND ORIGINALITY

1. INTRODUCTION

When the patent law was recodified in 1952, nonobviousness was set out as a statutory requirement for the first time. The new provision, § 103, did not, however, mark a major change in the law, for the courts had long imposed as a matter of common law a requirement of "invention" closely akin to what is now called nonobviousness.[1]

A moment's thought reveals why an intellectual property system that requires novelty might also impose a condition of nonobviousness. The novelty provision is intended to secure to the public domain inventions that were effectively available to the public prior to the intervention of the applicant. However, the test for novelty is rather limited. After all, every element of the invention must be revealed in a single prior disclosure.[2] This limitation means that some innovations that are arguably available to the public escape the novelty requirement. These are the inventions that, while not revealed in a single source, are either effectively disclosed in a series of references or represent minor changes in existing technology. Since it is not unreasonable (or, in the search model, overly costly) to expect ordinary artisans to pull together the things they learn, and even to make modest advances, it is apparent why patents should not issue on inventions that are obvious.

Understanding the need to augment the novelty requirement does not, unfortunately, provide an easy test for determining which advances are so available to the public they should not be patentable. Prior to the 1952 Act, the courts experimented with a variety of formulations. In Hotchkiss v. Greenwood,[3] the Supreme Court held unpatentable inventions that could have been constructed with the "skill ... possessed by an ordinary mechanic acquainted with the business." Some courts enunciated a series of negative tests of invention. For example, changes in form, proportions, or degree and aggregations of old elements were held unpatentable.[4] Other

---

[1] See, e.g., Edmund Kitch, Graham v. John Deere Co: New Standards for Patents, 1966 S.Ct. Rev. 303.

[2] See Note 2(a)(ii) of Assignment 18.

[3] 52 U.S. (11 How.) 248, 13 L.Ed. 683 (1850).

[4] See, e.g., Carbice Corp. v. Am. Patents Dev. Corp., 283 U.S. 420, 51 S.Ct. 496, 75 L.Ed. 1153 (1931); Dunbar v. Myers, 94 U.S. (4 Otto) 187, 24 L.Ed. 34 (1876).

courts looked to external signs of inventiveness, such as commercial success and the failure of others, especially in the face of long-felt need.[5]

The trend of using inventiveness to enhance the standard of patentability culminated in two cases heavily influenced by Justice William O. Douglas, who was always highly skeptical of patents. Writing for the Court in Cuno Engineering Corp. v. Automatic Devices Corp.,[6] he held that in order to be patentable, a "new device, however useful it may be, must reveal [a] flash of creative genius, not merely the skill of the calling."[7] *Cuno Engineering* was followed by Great Atlantic & Pacific Tea Co. v. Supermarket Equipment Corp.,[8] which involved the patent on the familiar three-sided frame that is used to push groceries along the counter toward the check-out clerk. The majority opinion, authored by Justice Jackson, considered the device to be a combination of known elements. According to the Court, "[t]he conjunction or concert of known elements must contribute something; only when the whole in some way exceeds the sum of its parts is the accumulation of old devices patentable."[9] No patent was available for this device because "two and two have been added together, and still they make only four."[10] Concurring, Justice Douglas added:

> "Every patent is the grant of a privilege of exacting tolls from the public. The Framers plainly did not want those monopolies freely granted. The invention, to justify a patent, had to serve the ends of science—to push back the frontiers of chemistry, physics, and the like; to make a distinctive contribution to scientific knowledge. That is why through the years the opinions of the Court commonly have taken 'inventive genius' as the test. It is not enough that an article is new and useful. The Constitution never sanctioned the patenting of gadgets. Patents serve a higher end—the advancement of science."[11]

Given that genuine advances in science are usually in the nature of unpatentable discoveries of nature,[12] that geniuses are born rather infrequently, that most inventions combine known elements, and that two plus two invariably equals four, *Cuno Engineering* and *Great A & P* together created chaos in the law of patentability. Decisions of lower courts became difficult to reconcile and patentees sometimes found themselves sued in more than one circuit. More important, as validity became increasingly difficult to predict, patents lost value. The Supreme Court simply retreated from the fray; from 1950, when *Great A & P* was decided, until 1966, it did not review any patent cases on this issue.

[5] See, e.g., Smith v. Goodyear Dental Vulcanite Co., 93 U.S. (3 Otto) 486, 23 L.Ed. 952 (1876).

[6] 314 U.S. 84, 62 S.Ct. 37, 86 L.Ed. 58 (1941).

[7] Id. at 90–92.

[8] 340 U.S. 147, 71 S.Ct. 127, 95 L.Ed. 162 (1950).

[9] Id. at 152.

[10] Id.

[11] Id. at 154–155 (footnotes omitted)(Douglas, J., concurring).

[12] See Assignment 16.

The field was therefore left to Congress, which responded with the formulation now found in § 103(a). Harkening back to *Hotchkiss*, the statute renders unpatentable inventions that "would have been obvious at the time the invention was made to a person having ordinary skill in the art." Patentability could no longer be negated by "the manner in which the invention was made," § 103(c).

2. PRINCIPAL PROBLEMS

(i) PROBLEM A

Return to the facts of the Principal Problem of Assignment 18: is Nichols' cube nonobvious?

(ii) PROBLEM B

Return to the facts of the Principal Problem of Assignment 16: is the protein manufactured by Gamma nonobvious even though Dr. Beta has determined the DNA sequence that encoded it?

(iii) PROBLEM C

ref #1 Drug X

A group of public-interest researchers called the Coalition to Fight Terminal Diseases (CFTD) has come to us for advice. Drug X is currently the only drug on the market effective in treating a certain terminal contagious disease. The Alpha Company patented this drug in 1989. Pleased with its profits, Alpha has done no further research with it. CFTD has. It discovered a more purified version of Drug X which has fewer side effects and more therapeutic potential. CFTD has asked us for advice on whether it can patent its purified version.

To really understand what is going on here, you need to know a little chemistry. What CFTD discovered was that Drug X (like many drugs) actually exists in two structural forms, a so-called "(R)" form [here, (R)-X] and an "(S)" form [(S)-X]. These have identical chemical constitutions (the same atoms appear in the same order), but the structures are mirror images of each other, much like left and right hands. These mirror-image structures are called "enantiomers" and it is well known in pharmacological circles that despite being structurally identical, enantiomers do not usually have the same biological activity. Commonly, only one of the two provides therapeutic benefit; the other may be inactive or cause undesirable side effects.

ref #2 article

Clinical experience showed that although X was useful in controlling the progression of disease, treatment had to be terminated at the end stage because of side effects. This is where CFTD stepped in. First, after determining that Alpha was selling X as a mixture of the two enantiomeric forms, it set out to purify the product so that the biologically beneficial enantiomer could be administered alone. A 1965 article in the Journal of the Australian Chemical Society on "Differential Solubility of Enantiomers" listed a group of solvents in which R-and S-enantiomers generally tend to have different solubilities. When none of the solvents listed in the article worked for X, CFTD scientists instead tried solvents that were known to dissolve the same sorts of things as the ones on the list. After several months' experimentation, one solvent was found that provided some separation. Further isolation was achieved by following a 1984 article in the New Zealand Journal of Solid State Chemistry on "Isolation through Adsorption," which described techniques for purifying chemical compounds by pouring them down columns packed with solids to which they adsorb (i.e. cling). CFTD researchers again spent many months finding just the right solid. Using a combination of these two techniques, 99% separation was achieved, and each enantiomer was further purified with standard purification methods.

(R)-X and (S)-X were then tested using procedures suggested by the FDA for a period of two years. In early 1993, (R)-X was identified as the therapeutic enantiomer. Use of (R)-X alone caused no new side effects, reduced the known side effects, and effectively controlled the disease. (S)-X was found to cause the side effects that require termination of treatment. CFTD published its research results immediately and has had an extraordinary number of requests for treatment doses of (R)-X.

As noted, CFTD has come to us for advice. Although its primary mission is to cure this terrible disease, it needs money to pursue its objectives and would like to secure a patent on both (R)-X itself and on its method of purification. What is your view on the patentability of any of the discoveries made by CFTD?

3. MATERIALS FOR SOLUTION OF PRINCIPAL PROBLEMS

A. STATUTORY MATERIAL: §§ 103 & 102(f)

B. CASES:

Graham v. John Deere Co.

Supreme Court of the United States, 1966.
383 U.S. 1, 86 S.Ct. 684, 15 L.Ed.2d 545.

■ MR. JUSTICE CLARK delivered the opinion of the Court.

After a lapse of 15 years, the Court again focuses its attention on the patentability of inventions under the standard of Art. I, § 8, cl. 8, of the Constitution and under the conditions prescribed by the laws of the United States. Since our last expression on patent validity, Great A. & P. Tea Co. v. Supermarket Equipment Corp., 340 U.S. 147, 71 S.Ct. 127, 95 L.Ed. 162 (1950), the Congress has for the first time expressly added a third statutory dimension to the two requirements of novelty and utility that had been the sole statutory test since the Patent Act of 1793. This is the test of obviousness, i.e., whether "the subject matter sought to be patented and the prior art are such that the subject matter as a whole would have been obvious at the time the invention was made to a person having ordinary skill in the art to which said subject matter pertains. Patentability shall not be negatived by the manner in which the invention was made." § 103 of the Patent Act of 1952, 35 U.S.C. § 103 (1964 ed.).

The questions, involved in each of the companion cases before us, are what effect the 1952 Act had upon traditional statutory and judicial tests of patentability and what definitive tests are now required. We have concluded that the 1952 Act was intended to codify judicial precedents embracing the principle long ago announced by this Court in Hotchkiss v. Greenwood, 11 How. 248, 13 L.Ed. 683 (1851), and that, while the clear language of § 103 places emphasis on an inquiry into obviousness, the general level of innovation necessary to sustain patentability remains the same.

I

The Cases

(a). No. 11, Graham v. John Deere Co., an infringement suit by petitioners, presents a conflict between two Circuits over the validity of a single patent on a "Clamp for vibrating Shank Plows." The invention, a combination of old mechanical elements, involves a device designed to absorb shock from plow shanks as they plow through rocky soil and thus to prevent damage to the plow. In 1955, the Fifth Circuit had held the patent valid under its rule that when a combination produces an 'old result in a cheaper and otherwise more advantageous way,' it is patentable. Jeoffroy Mfg., Inc. v. Graham, 219 F.2d 511, cert. denied, 350 U.S. 826, 76 S.Ct. 55, 100 L.Ed. 738. In 1964, the Eighth Circuit held, in the case at bar, that there was no new result in the patented combination and that the patent was, therefore, not valid. 333 F.2d 529, reversing D.C., 216 F.Supp. 272. We granted certiorari, 379 U.S. 956, 85 S.Ct. 652, 13 L.Ed.2d 553. Although we have determined that neither Circuit applied the correct test, we conclude that the patent is invalid under § 103 and, therefore, we affirm the judgment of the Eighth Circuit.

[(b). Omitted is a discussion of Calmar, Inc. v. Cook Chemical Co., and No. 43, Colgate–Palmolive Co. v. Cook Chemical Co., involving the invention of a finger-operated sprayer with a "hold down" cap that enables containers to be shipped without spillage.—eds.]

II

At the outset it must be remembered that the federal patent power stems from a specific constitutional provision which authorizes the Congress "To promote the Progress of * * * useful Arts, by securing for limited Times to * * * Inventors the exclusive Right to their * * * Discoveries." Art. I, § 8, cl. 8. The clause is both a grant of power and a limitation. This qualified authority, unlike the power often exercised in the sixteenth and seventeenth centuries by the English Crown, is limited to the promotion of advances in the "useful arts." It was written against the backdrop of the practices—eventually curtailed by the Statute of Monopolies—of the Crown in granting monopolies to court favorites in goods or businesses which had long before been enjoyed by the public. See Meinhardt, Inventions, Patents and Monopoly, pp. 30–35 (London, 1946). The

Congress in the exercise of the patent power may not overreach the restraints imposed by the stated constitutional purpose. Nor may it enlarge the patent monopoly without regard to the innovation, advancement or social benefit gained thereby. Moreover, Congress may not authorize the issuance of patents whose effects are to remove existent knowledge from the public domain, or to restrict free access to materials already available.

Congress quickly responded to the bidding of the Constitution by enacting the Patent Act of 1790 during the second session of the First Congress. It created an agency in the Department of State headed by the Secretary of State, the Secretary of the Department of War and the Attorney General, any two of whom could issue a patent for a period not exceeding 14 years to any petitioner that "hath * * * invented or discovered any useful art, manufacture, * * * or device, or any improvement therein not before known or used" if the board found that "the invention or discovery (was) sufficiently useful and important * * *." 1 Stat. 110. This group, whose members administered the patent system along with their other public duties, was known by its own designation as "Commissioners for the Promotion of Useful Arts."

Thomas Jefferson, who as Secretary of State was a member of the group, was its moving spirit and might well be called the "first administrator of our patent system." See Federico, Operation of the Patent Act of 1790, 18 J.Pat.Off.Soc. 237, 238 (1936). He was not only an administrator of the patent system under the 1790 Act, but was also the author of the 1793 Patent Act. In addition, Jefferson was himself an inventor of great note. His unpatented improvements on plows, to mention but one line of his inventions, won acclaim and recognition on both sides of the Atlantic. Because of his active interest and influence in the early development of the patent system, Jefferson's views on the general nature of the limited patent monopoly under the Constitution, as well as his conclusions as to conditions for patentability under the statutory scheme, are worthy of note.

Jefferson, like other Americans, had an instinctive aversion to monopolies. It was a monopoly on tea that sparked the Revolution and Jefferson certainly did not favor an equivalent form of monopoly under the new government. His abhorrence of monopoly extended initially to patents as well. From France, he wrote to Madison (July 1788) urging a Bill of Rights provision restricting monopoly, and as against the argument that limited monopoly might serve to incite "ingenuity," he argued forcefully that "the benefit even of limited monopolies is too doubtful to be opposed to that of their general suppression," V Writings of Thomas Jefferson, at 47 (Ford ed., 1895).

His views ripened, however, and in another letter to Madison (Aug. 1789) after the drafting of the Bill of Rights, Jefferson stated that he would have been pleased by an express provision in this form: "Art. 9. Monopolies may be allowed to persons for their own productions in literature, & their own inventions in the arts, for a term not exceeding—years, but for no longer term & no other purpose." Id., at 113. And he later wrote: "Certainly an inventor ought to be allowed a right to the benefit of his invention for some certain time. * * * Nobody wishes more than I do that ingenuity should receive a liberal encouragement." Letter to Oliver Evans (May 1807), V Writings of Thomas Jefferson, at 75–76 (Washington ed.).

The patent monopoly was not designed to secure to the inventor his natural right in his discoveries. Rather, it was a reward, an inducement, to bring forth new knowledge. The grant of an exclusive right to an invention was the creation of society—at odds with the inherent free nature of disclosed ideas—and was not to be freely given. Only inventions and discoveries which furthered human knowledge, and were new and useful, justified the special inducement of a limited private monopoly. Jefferson did not believe in granting patents for small details, obvious improvements, or frivolous devices. His writings evidence his insistence upon a high level of patentability.

As a member of the patent board for several years, Jefferson saw clearly the difficulty in "drawing a line between the things which are worth to the public the embarrassment of an exclusive patent, and those which are not." The board on which he served sought to draw such a line and formulated several rules which are preserved in Jefferson's correspondence. Despite the board's efforts, Jefferson saw "with what slow progress a system of general rules could be matured." Apparently Congress agreed with Jefferson and the board that the courts should develop additional conditions for patentability. Although the Patent Act was amended, revised or codified some 50 times between 1790 and 1950, Congress steered clear of a statutory set of requirements other than the bare novelty and utility tests reformulated in Jefferson's draft of the 1793 Patent Act.

III

The difficulty of formulating conditions for patentability was heightened by the generality of the constitutional grant and the statutes implementing it, together with the underlying policy of the patent system that "the things which are worth to the public the embarrassment of an exclusive patent," as Jefferson put it, must outweigh the restrictive effect of the limited patent monopoly. The inherent problem was to develop some means of weeding out those inventions which would not be disclosed or devised but for the inducement of a patent.

This Court formulated a general condition of patentability in 1851 in Hotchkiss v. Greenwood, 11 How. 248, 13 L.Ed. 683. The patent involved a mere substitution of materials—porcelain or clay for wood or metal in doorknobs—and the Court condemned it, holding:

> "(U)nless more ingenuity and skill * * * were required * * * than were possessed by an ordinary mechanic acquainted with the business, there was an absence of that degree of skill and ingenuity which constitute essential elements of every invention. In other words, the improvement is the work of the skilful mechanic, not that of the inventor." At p. 267.

The Hotchkiss test laid the cornerstone of the judicial evolution suggested by Jefferson and left to the courts by Congress. The language in the case, and in those which followed, gave birth to "invention" as a word of legal art signifying patentable inventions. The Hotchkiss formulation, however, lies not in any label, but in its functional approach to questions of patentability. In practice, Hotchkiss has required a comparison between the subject matter of the patent, or patent application, and the background skill of the calling. It has been from this comparison that patentability was in each case determined.

IV

The 1952 Patent Act

The Act sets out the conditions of patentability in three sections. An analysis of the structure of these three sections indicates that patentability is dependent upon three explicit conditions: novelty and utility as articulated and defined in § 101 and § 102, and nonobviousness, the new statutory formulation, as set out in § 103. The first two sections, which trace closely the 1874 codification, express the 'new and useful' tests which have always existed in the statutory scheme and, for our purposes here, need no clarification. The pivotal section around which the present controversy centers is § 103.

It is undisputed that this section was, for the first time, a statutory expression of an additional requirement for patentability, originally expressed in Hotchkiss. It also seems apparent that Congress intended by the last sentence of § 103 to abolish the test it believed this Court announced in the controversial phrase "flash of creative genius," used in Cuno Engineering Corp. v. Automatic Devices Corp., 314 U.S. 84, 62 S.Ct. 37, 86 L.Ed. 58 (1941).

It is contended, however, by some of the parties and by several of the amici that the first sentence of § 103 was intended to sweep away judicial precedents and to lower the level of patentability. Others contend that the Congress intended to codify the essential purpose reflected in existing judicial precedents—the rejection of insignificant variations and innovations of a commonplace sort—and also to focus inquiries under § 103 upon nonobviousness, rather than upon "invention," as a means of achieving more stability and predictability in determining patentability and validity.

The Reviser's Note to this section, with apparent reference to Hotchkiss, recognizes that judicial requirements as to "lack of patentable novelty (have) been followed since at least as early as 1850." The note indicates that the section was inserted because it "may have some stabilizing effect, and also to serve as a basis for the addition at a later time of some criteria which may be worked out." To this same effect are the reports of both Houses, supra, which state that the first sentence of the section "paraphrases language which has often been used in decisions of the courts, and the section is added to the statute for uniformity and definiteness."

We believe that this legislative history, as well as other sources, shows that the revision was not intended by Congress to change the general level of patentable invention. We conclude that the section was intended merely as a codification of judicial precedents embracing the Hotchkiss condition, with congressional directions that inquiries into the obviousness of the subject matter sought to be patented are a prerequisite to patentability.

V

Approached in this light, the § 103 additional condition, when followed realistically, will permit a more practical test of patentability. The emphasis on non-obviousness is one of inquiry, not quality, and, as such, comports with the constitutional strictures.

While the ultimate question of patent validity is one of law, Great A. & P. Tea Co. v. Supermarket Equipment Corp., supra, 340 U.S. at 155, 71 S.Ct. at 131, the § 103 condition, which is but one of three conditions, each of which must be satisfied, lends itself to several basic factual inquiries. Under § 103, the scope and content of the prior art are to be determined; differences between the prior art and the claims at issue are to be ascertained; and the level of ordinary skill in the pertinent art resolved. Against this background, the obviousness or nonobviousness of the subject matter is determined. Such secondary considerations as commercial success, long felt but unsolved needs, failure of others, etc., might be utilized to give light to the circumstances surrounding the origin of the subject matter sought to be patented. As indicia of obviousness or nonobviousness, these inquiries may have relevancy. See Note, Subtests of "Nonobviousness": A Nontechnical Approach to Patent Validity, 112 U.Pa.L.Rev. 1169 (1964).

This is not to say, however, that there will not be difficulties in applying the nonobviousness test. What is obvious is not a question upon which there is likely to be uniformity of thought in every given factual context. The difficulties, however, are comparable to those encountered daily by the courts in such frames of reference as negligence and scienter, and should be amenable to a case-by-case development. We believe that strict observance of the requirements laid down here will result in that uniformity and definiteness which Congress called for in the 1952 Act.

VI

We now turn to the application of the conditions found necessary for patentability to the cases involved here:

This patent, No. 2,627,798 (hereinafter called the '798 patent) relates to a spring clamp which permits plow shanks to be pushed upward when they hit obstructions in the soil, and then springs the shanks back into normal position when the obstruction is passed over.

Background of the Patent

Chisel plows, as they are called, were developed for plowing in areas where the ground is relatively free from rocks or stones. Originally, the shanks were rigidly attached to the plow frames. When such plows were used in the rocky, glacial soils of some of the Northern States, they were found to have serious defects. As the chisels hit buried rocks, a vibratory motion was set up and tremendous forces were transmitted to the shank near its connection to the frame. The shanks would break. Graham, one of the petitioners, sought to meet that problem, and in 1950 obtained a patent, U.S. No. 2,493,811 (hereinafter '811), on a spring clamp where solved some of the difficulties. Graham and his companies manufactured and sold the '811 clamps. In 1950, Graham modified the '811 structure and filed for a patent. That patent, the one in issue, was granted in 1953. This suit against competing plow manufacturers resulted from charges by petitioners that several of respondents' devices infringed the '798 patent.

The Prior Art

We confine our discussion to the prior patent of Graham, '811, [which was] among the references asserted by respondents. The Graham '811 and '798 patent devices are similar in all elements, save two: (1) the stirrup and the bolted connection of the shank to the hinge plate do not appear in '811; and (2) the position of the shank is reversed, being placed in patent '811 above the hinge plate, sandwiched between it and the upper plate. The shank is held in place by the spring rod which is hooked against the bottom of the hinge plate passing through a slot in the shank. Other differences are of no consequence to our examination. In practice the '811 patent arrangement permitted the shank to wobble or fishtail because it was not rigidly fixed to the hinge plate; moreover, as the hinge plate was below the shank, the latter caused wear on the upper plate, a member difficult to repair or replace.

Graham's '798 patent application contained 12 claims. All were rejected as not distinguished from the Graham '811 patent. The inverted position of the shank was specifically rejected as was the bolting of the shank to the hinge plate. The Patent Office examiner found these to be 'matters of design well within the expected skill of the art and devoid of invention.' Graham withdrew the original claims and substituted the two new ones which are substantially those in issue here. His contention was that wear was reduced in patent '798 between the shank and the heel or rear of the upper plate. He also emphasized several new features, the relevant one here being that the bolt used to connect the hinge plate and shank maintained the upper face of the shank in continuing and constant contact with the underface of the hinge plate.

Graham did not urge before the Patent Office the greater "flexing" qualities of the '798 patent arrangement which he so heavily relied on in the courts. The sole element in patent '798 which petitioners argue before us is the interchanging of the shank and hinge plate and the consequences flowing from this arrangement. The contention is that this arrangement—which petitioners claim is not disclosed in the prior art—permits the shank to flex under stress for its entire length. As we have sketched (see sketch, "Graham '798 Patent" in Appendix), when the chisel hits an obstruction the resultant force (A) pushes the rear of the shank upward and the shank pivots against the rear of the hinge plate at (C). The natural tendency is for that portion of the shank between the pivot point and the bolted connection (i.e., between C and D) to bow downward and away from the hinge plate.

The maximum distance (B) that the shank moves away from the plate is slight—for emphasis, greatly exaggerated in the sketches. This is so because of the strength of the shank and the short—nine inches or so—length of that portion of the shank between (C) and (D). On the contrary, in patent '811 (see sketch, "Graham '811 Patent" in Appendix), the pivot point is the upper plate at point (c); and while the tendency for the shank to bow between points (c) and (d) is the same as in '798, the shank is restricted because of the underlying hinge plate and cannot flex as freely. In practical effect, the shank flexes only between points (a) and (c), and not along the entire length of the shank, as in '798. Petitioners say that this

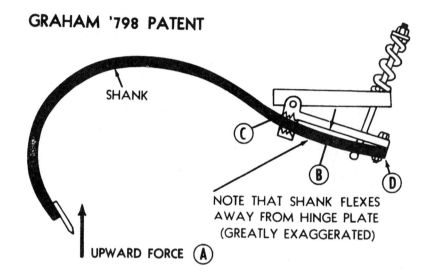

GRAHAM '798 PATENT

SHANK

NOTE THAT SHANK FLEXES
AWAY FROM HINGE PLATE
(GREATLY EXAGGERATED)

UPWARD FORCE (A)

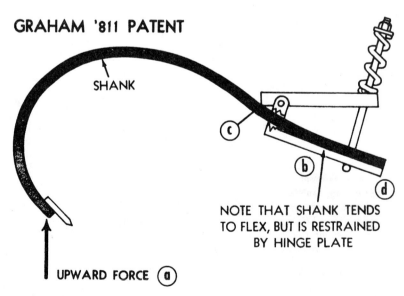

GRAHAM '811 PATENT

SHANK

Prior Art

NOTE THAT SHANK TENDS
TO FLEX, BUT IS RESTRAINED
BY HINGE PLATE

UPWARD FORCE (a)

difference in flex, though small, effectively absorbs the tremendous forces of the shock of obstructions whereas prior art arrangements failed.

The Obviousness of the Differences

We cannot agree with petitioners. We assume that the prior art does not disclose such an arrangement as petitioners claim in patent '798. Still we do not believe that the argument on which petitioners' contention is bottomed supports the validity of the patent. The tendency of the shank to flex is the same in all cases. If free-flexing, as petitioners now argue, is the crucial difference above the prior art, then it appears evident that the desired result would be obtainable by not boxing the shank within the confines of the hinge. The only other effective place available in the arrangement was to attach it below the hinge plate and run it through a stirrup or bracket that would not disturb its flexing qualities. Certainly a person having ordinary skill in the prior art, given the fact that the flex in the shank could be utilized more effectively if allowed to run the entire length of the shank, would immediately see that the thing to do was what Graham did, i.e., invert the shank and the hinge plate.

Sakraida v. Ag Pro, Inc.

Supreme Court of the United States, 1976.
425 U.S. 273, 96 S.Ct. 1532, 47 L.Ed.2d 784.

■ MR. JUSTICE BRENNAN delivered the opinion of the Court.

Respondent Ag Pro, Inc., filed this action against petitioner Sakraida on October 8, 1968, in the District Court for the Western District of Texas for infringement of United States Letters Patent 3,223,070, entitled "Dairy Establishment," covering a water flush system to remove cow manure from the floor of a dairy barn. The patent was issued December 14, 1965, to Gribble and Bennett, who later assigned it to respondent.

Systems using flowing water to clean animal wastes from barn floors have been familiar on dairy farms since ancient times.[a] The District Court

[a] Among the labors of Hercules is the following: "Heracles now set out to perform his fifth Labour, and this time his task was to cleanse the stables of Augeas in a single day. Augeas was a rich king of Elis, who had three thousand cattle. At night the cattle always stood in a great court surrounded with walls, close to the king's palace, and as it was quite ten years since the servants had cleaned it out, there was enough refuse in the court to build up a high mountain. Heracles went to Augeas and asked if he would give him the tenth part of his flocks if he thoroughly cleansed his stables in a single day. The king looked upon this as such an absolutely impossible feat that he would not have minded promising his kingdom as a reward for it, so he laughed and said, 'Set to work, we shall not quarrel about the wages,' and he further promised distinctly to give Heracles what he asked, and this he did in the presence of Phyleus, his eldest son, who happened to be there. The next morning Heracles set to work, but even his strong arms would have

found, and respondent concedes, that none of the 13 elements of the Dairy Establishment combination is new, and many of those elements, including storage of the water in tanks or pools, appear in at least six prior patented systems. The prior art involved spot delivery of water from tanks or pools to the barn floor by means of high pressure hoses or pipes. That system required supplemental hand labor, using tractor blades, shovels, and brooms, and cleaning by these methods took several hours. The only claimed inventive feature of the Dairy Establishment combination of old elements is the provision for abrupt release of the water from the tanks or pools directly onto the barn floor, which causes the flow of a sheet of water that washes all animal waste into drains within minutes and requires no supplemental hand labor. As an expert witness for respondent testified concerning the effect of Dairy Establishment's combination: "(W)ater at the bottom has more friction than this water on the top and it keeps moving ahead and as this water keeps moving ahead we get a rolling action of this water which produced the cleaning action.... You do not get this in a hose.... (U)nless that water is continuously directed toward the cleaning area the cleaning action almost ceases instantaneously...."

[The District Court found the patent invalid on the ground that "(T)o those skilled in the art, the use of the old elements in combination was not an invention by the obvious-nonobvious standard. Even though the dairy barn in question attains the posture of a successful venture, more than that is needed for invention." The Court of Appeals reversed, concluding that "although the (respondent's) flush system does not embrace a complicated technical improvement, it does achieve a synergistic result through a novel combination."]

We cannot agree that the combination of these old elements to produce an abrupt release of water directly on the barn floor from storage tanks or pools can properly be characterized as synergistic, that is, "result(ing) in an effect greater than the sum of the several effects taken separately." Anderson's–Black Rock v. Pavement Salvage Co., 396 U.S. 57, 61, 90 S.Ct. 305, 308, 24 L.Ed.2d 258, 261 (1969). Rather, this patent simply arranges old elements with each performing the same function it had been known to perform, although perhaps producing a more striking result than in previous combinations. Such combinations are not patentable under standards appropriate for a combination patent. Exploitation of the principle of gravity adds nothing to the sum of useful knowledge where there is no change in the respective functions of the elements of the combination; this particular use of the assembly of old elements would be obvious to any person skilled in the art of mechanical application.

failed to accomplish the task if they had not been aided by his mother-wit. He compelled a mighty torrent to work for him, but you would hardly guess how he did it. First he opened great gates on two opposite sides of the court, and then he went to the stream, and when he had blocked up its regular course with great stones, he conducted it to the court that required to be cleansed, so that the water streamed in at one end and streamed out at the other, carrying away all the dirt with it. Before evening the stream had done its work and was restored to its usual course." C. Witt, Classic Mythology 119–120 (1883).

Though doubtless a matter of great convenience, producing a desired result in a cheaper and faster way, and enjoying commercial success, Dairy Establishment "did not produce a 'new or different function' ... within the test of validity of combination patents." Anderson's-Black Rock v. Pavement Co., supra, 396 U.S., at 60, 90 S.Ct., at 308, 24 L.Ed.2d, at 261. These desirable benefits "without invention will not make patentability." Great A. & P. Tea Co. v. Supermarket Corp., 340 U.S., at 153, 71 S.Ct., at 130, 95 L.Ed., at 167.

Stratoflex, Inc. v. Aeroquip Corp.

United States Court of Appeals, Federal Circuit, 1983.
713 F.2d 1530.

■ MARKEY, CHIEF JUDGE.

II.　Background

A.　The Technology

Stratoflex and Aeroquip manufacture electrically conductive polytetrafluoroethylene (PTFE)[a] tubing used in the aircraft and missile industry to convey pressurized fuel, lubricants, and other fluids.

PTFE has replaced organic and synthetic rubbers and plastic in fuel hoses because it has a number of superior characteristics. Though pure PTFE is dielectric (non-conductive), it can be made with fillers to make it conductive, though the "filled" tubing is more susceptible to leakage when voids form between the PTFE and filler particles.

B.　The Invention

The Slade invention relates to a composite PTFE tubing, formed of an inner layer of electrically conductive PTFE having particles such as carbon black uniformly distributed in it and an outer layer of essentially pure nonconductive PTFE. Claim 1 [is] representative:

> 1.　A tubular extrudate formed of attached concentric tubular extrusions, the inner tubular extrusion comprising associated particles of unsintered tetrafluoroethylene polymer and pulverulent, inert, electrically conductive particles, and the outer tubular extrusion comprising associated particles of unsintered tetrafluoroethylene polymer.

The particles in the inner layer of the claimed tubing dissipate electrostatic charges built up on the inner surface of the tubing, conducting them lengthwise of the tubing to grounded metal fittings at the ends of a hose assembly of which the tubing is part, to prevent arcing or discharging through the tubing wall to the surrounding metal braid. Arcing causes "pin holes" through which fuel can leak. The outer layer is coextruded or bonded around the inner layer to contain any fuel leaking through the

---

[a] The parties refer to polytetrafluoroethylene also as "Teflon," a registered trade-mark of the E.I. Dupont de Nemours Company.

inner layer. The composite tubing has excellent conductivity, while retaining the desirable characteristics of PTFE tubing.

C.   Events Leading to the '087 Patent

Pure PTFE tubing had been used successfully in aircraft engines since at least 1956. In 1959, with the introduction of hydrocarbon jet fuels, leaks were noticed. Aeroquip assigned two staff engineers, Abbey and Upham, to determine the cause. They found the problem to be the arcing of electrostatic charges through the wall of the pure dielectric PTFE tubing to create "pin holes" as described above.

Abbey and Upham found the "pin hole" phenomenon exhibited by all three types of PTFE (White–Titeflex; Pink/Red–Aeroquip; Black–Goodrich) used in aircraft engines. The black tubing appeared superior because the carbon black it contained gave it an intermittent conductivity. The carbon black took the form of discontinuous strings and arcing across the spaces between string ends conveyed charges to the ends of the tubing. Electrical erosion of the strings, however, widened the spaces, destroying conductivity and leading to the "pin hole" phenomenon. Abbey and Upham concluded that susceptibility of PTFE tubing to "pin holing" was proportional to its conductivity, and that carbon black increased the conductivity of PTFE tubing.

In early 1960, having determined the cause of leaking, Aeroquip approached Raybestos–Manhattan (Raybestos), a PTFE hose manufacturer, for a solution. Aeroquip later purchased the hose section of Raybestos, obtaining the Slade patent by mesne assignment.

Raybestos assigned the project to the inventor, Winton Slade, who prepared several samples of conductive PTFE tubing (powdered lead, copper, chemically etched, and carbon black) and sent them for testing to Aeroquip in the summer of 1960. In the Fall, Aeroquip ordered a small production quantity of carbon black tubing. That tubing was not a composite and the carbon black was not uniformly distributed in it.

Slade conceived of the composite tube of the invention as early as August 5, 1960 and reduced it to practice in November of 1961. He filed a patent application on May 22, 1962, with claims directed to the composite tubing and also to various processes for making it. [After an interference that led to agreements to grant Titeflex royalty-free licenses,] Slade's original application issued with its product claims as the '087 patent on October 1, 1969.

D.   Stratoflex Actions

From 1962 to 1970, Stratoflex purchased PTFE tubing containing carbon black from B.F. Goodrich. When Goodrich ceased production, Stratoflex purchased conductive PTFE tubing made by Titeflex under its license. Stratoflex then began manufacturing and selling its own "124" and "127" composite tubing having an inner layer with conductive carbon black uniformly dispersed throughout, and an outer layer that is essentially nonconductive, though that outer layer includes a small amount of carbon black to color the tubing and to aid extrusion.

On December 8, 1978, Aeroquip charged that Stratoflex's unauthorized manufacture and sale of "124" and "127" tubing infringed its rights under the '087 patent.

E.   Trial and Opinion

Trial was held on December 15, 16, 18, 19 and 22, 1980. Stratoflex alleged that the '087 patent was invalid. On August 16, 1982, Judge Boyle issued judgment and an accompanying opinion [holding the patent invalid under § 103].

Obviousness

The declaration that claim[] 1 of the '087 patent [is] invalid was based on a conclusion that the inventions set forth in those claims would have been obvious under 35 U.S.C. § 103, in the light of facts found in the course of following the guidelines set forth in Graham v. John Deere Co., 383 U.S. 1, 17, 86 S.Ct. 684, 693, 15 L.Ed.2d 545 (1966).

Scope and Content of the Prior Art

Aeroquip contends that the scope of the relevant prior art excludes rubber hose because PTFE is a unique material, possessing properties that differ significantly from rubber, and that, because the claims are limited to PTFE, the rubber hose art could at most be peripherally relevant as background information.

The scope of the prior art has been defined as that "reasonably pertinent to the particular problem with which the inventor was involved." In re Wood, 599 F.2d 1032, 1036, 202 U.S.P.Q. 171, 174 (Cust. & Pat.App. 1979), see Weather Engineering Corp. of America v. United States, 614 F.2d 281, 222 Ct.Cl. 322, 204 U.S.P.Q. 41 (Ct.Cl.1980). The problem confronting Slade was preventing electrostatic buildup in PTFE tubing caused by hydrocarbon fuel flow while precluding leakage of fuel. None of the unique properties of PTFE would change the nature of that problem. Nor would anything of record indicate that one skilled in the art would not include the rubber hose art in his search for a solution to that problem.

Indeed, Slade himself referred to a standard textbook on conductive carbon black in rubber when he began his search for a solution. Judge Boyle correctly found Slade's act an acknowledgement by the problem solver of what he considered relevant prior art.

The examiner cited two prior art references in the rubber hose art, one disclosing the problem of electrostatic buildup caused by fuel flow. The Abbey–Upham report, though concerned with PTFE, included a conductivity comparison with carbon black filled rubber hose, and its bibliography listed several articles on electrostatic buildup in rubber. The record reflects that PTFE and rubber are used by the same hose manufacturers to make hoses and that the same and similar problems have been experienced with both. There is no basis for finding that a solution found for a problem experienced with one material would not be looked to when facing a problem with the other. The finding that the rubber hose art is relevant and thus within the scope of the art was not clearly erroneous.

The content of the prior art included the Abbey–Upham Report and several patents relating to conductive and composite rubber hose and to PTFE tubing.

The Abbey–Upham Report, as above indicated, discloses the cause of PTFE tubing "pin holes" as the arcing of electrostatic charges laterally through the non-conductive PTFE tubing wall to the surrounding metal braid, that carbon black increases conductivity of PTFE, and that susceptibility of PTFE tubing to "pinholing" is directly proportional to its conductivity. Judge Boyle correctly found the report to have disclosed the basic concepts underlying the claimed invention, but not that of forming PTFE tubing as a composite having a conductive inner layer and a nonconductive outer layer.

United States Patent No. 2,341,360 ('360 patent) teaches composite tubing having carbon black in one layer to make it electrically conductive for dissipation of static electricity.

U.S. Patent No. 2,781,288 ('288 patent) teaches a composite rubber hose with each layer arranged to take advantage of its particular properties. It suggests carbon black as a filler, but not as a conductor.

Aeroquip's attack on the content-of-the-prior-art findings is limited to its argument that rubber hose should be excluded. That argument having been found wanting, the findings on the content of the prior art cannot be viewed as clearly erroneous.

Consideration of the scope and content of the prior art tilts the scales of decision toward a conclusion of obviousness. Thus the Abbey–Upham report teaches use of carbon black to increase conductivity of PTFE tubing to reduce the chance of electrostatic buildup on the tubing wall. It would appear to have been obvious to one skilled in the art to place the conductive material in the wall where the electrostatic buildup occurs (here the inner wall subjected to electrostatic buildup by fuel flow) as suggested by the '360 patent. It would appear to have been obvious from the '288 patent to form a composite tubing with layers arranged to take advantage of their physical and chemical properties. On this record, consideration of the prior art as a whole, and in the absence of evidence that any special problem in following its teachings was created by the unique properties of PTFE, it would appear to have been obvious to place a conductive PTFE layer inside an essentially non-conductive outer PTFE layer to prevent fuel seepage associated with the conductive layer.

Differences Between the Claimed Invention and the Prior Art

Aeroquip concedes that pure PTFE had been known to be dielectric, that carbon black was known to be conductive, and that PTFE had been made into tubing containing at least a small amount of carbon black. It alleges that the prior art does not show the composite tubing set forth in the claims, specifically a composite PTFE tubing with its inner layer formed of uniformly distributed carbon black and PTFE, to provide conductivity sufficient to dissipate electrostatic buildup, and an outer layer of relatively pure PTFE that prevents fuel leakage. It is true that no single reference shows all elements of the claims, but the holding here is one of invalidity for obviousness, not for anticipation. The question, therefore, is whether the invention set forth in claims 1, as a whole, would have been obvious to one of ordinary skill in the art when made, in view of the teachings of the prior art as a whole.

Though findings on the "differences" from the prior art are suggested by Graham v. John Deere, supra, the question under 35 U.S.C. § 103 is not whether the differences themselves would have been obvious. Consideration of differences, like each of the findings set forth in Graham, is but an aid in reaching the ultimate determination of whether the claimed invention as a whole would have been obvious.

Judge Boyle found that the differences between the claimed invention and the prior art were use of PTFE in concentric tubes and the "salt and pepper" process of forming the inner layer. The first difference would indicate a mere change of material.

With respect to use of a different material, the problem (leakage) and the cause ("pin holes" from electrostatic charges) were known with respect to that material (PTFE). A solution for the electrostatic charge problems, i.e., dissipation of charges lengthwise of the tubing, was known. Nothing in the first difference found would indicate that it would have been nonobvious to transfer that solution from tubing formed of other materials to tubing formed of PTFE. As above indicated, no special problem needed to be or was overcome in substituting a different material (PTFE) for the materials (rubber and plastics) of the prior art.

Aeroquip challenges the finding that the Abbey–Upham report does not teach away from use of carbon black in PTFE tubing, citing this language in the report: "The possibility of establishing continuous longitudinal strings of carbon particles during extrusion, especially in view of the relatively small percentage of carbon black used in Teflon hose seemed remote."

In the sentence following that cited to us by Aeroquip, the Abbey–Upham report describes uneven spacing between carbon black particles as a possible cause of intermittent conductivity. Far from "teaching away," therefore, the report may be viewed as pointing in the direction of uniform dispersion of such particles, as set forth in claim 7, to produce less intermittent conductivity.

The findings that the differences here were use of a different material and uniform dispersion of carbon black particles were not clearly erroneous. Those differences do not tilt the scales toward a conclusion of nonobviousness of the invention as a whole in light of all prior art teachings summarized above.

Level of Ordinary Skill

The district court found the level of ordinary skill to be that of a chemical engineer or equivalent, having substantial experience in the extrusion arts. Aeroquip says that was too high, suggesting that of an engineer or technician in the PTFE art, as described by its expert, Townsend Beaman. The suggestion is but another effort to limit the prior art to PTFE tubing and avoid inclusion of the art of making fuel hoses of other materials.

The level of ordinary skill may be determined from several factors. Orthopedic Equipment Company v. United States, 702 F.2d 1005, 217 USPQ 193 (Fed.Cir.1983) see Jacobson Brothers Inc. v. United States, 512 F.2d 1065, 206 Ct.Cl. 518 (Ct.Cl.1975). Slade had the level of skill set by the district court. Stratoflex witness Linger was a mechanical engineer with years of experience in the rubber and PTFE hose art. Mr. Beaman was patent counsel for Aeroquip. Judge Boyle correctly viewed Beaman as an observer of, not a worker in, the relevant art.

The statute, 35 U.S.C. § 103, requires that a claim be declared invalid only when the invention set forth in that claim can be said to have been obvious "to one of ordinary skill in the art." As an aid in determining obviousness, that requirement precludes consideration of whether the invention would have been obvious (as a whole and just before it was made) to the rare genius in the art, or to a judge or other layman after learning all about the invention.

Aeroquip has not shown the finding on the level of ordinary skill in the art to have been erroneous here.

Secondary Considerations

It is jurisprudentially inappropriate to disregard any relevant evidence on any issue in any case, patent cases included. Thus evidence rising out of the so-called "secondary considerations" must always when present be considered en route to a determination of obviousness. Indeed, evidence of secondary considerations may often be the most probative and cogent evidence in the record. It may often establish that an invention appearing to have been obvious in light of the prior art was not. It is to be considered as part of all the evidence, not just when the decisionmaker remains in doubt after reviewing the art.

Judge Boyle made findings on secondary considerations, but said she did not include them in her analysis because she believed the claimed inventions were plainly obvious and "those matters without invention will not make patentability" and should be considered only in a close case. That was error.

Enroute to a conclusion on obviousness, a court must not stop until all pieces of evidence on that issue have been fully considered and each has been given its appropriate weight. Along the way, some pieces will weigh more heavily than others, but decision should be held in abeyance, and doubt maintained, until all the evidence has had its say. The relevant evidence on the obviousness-nonobviousness issue, as the Court said in Graham, supra, and as other courts had earlier emphasized, includes evidence on what has now been called "secondary considerations." It is error to exclude that evidence from consideration.

The evidence and findings on secondary considerations being present in the record, the interests of judicial economy dictate its consideration and evaluation on this appeal. The result being unchanged, a remand for reconsideration of the evidence would in this case constitute a waste of resources for the courts and the parties.

A nexus is required between the merits of the claimed invention and the evidence offered, if that evidence is to be given substantial weight enroute to conclusion on the obviousness issue. Solder Removal Co. v. USITC, 582 F.2d 628, 637, 65 CCPA 120, 199 U.S.P.Q. 129, 137 (CCPA 1978) and cases cited therein.

Aeroquip says commercial success is shown because: the "entire industry" makes the tubing claimed in the '087 patent; only Stratoflex is not licensed. We are not persuaded.

Recognition and acceptance of the patent by competitors who take licenses under it to avail themselves of the merits of the invention is evidence of nonobviousness. Here, however, Aeroquip does not delineate the make-up of the "entire industry." The record reflects only two manufacturers, Titeflex and Resistoflex, in addition to the parties. Titeflex has a royalty-free license, resulting from the interference settling agreement described above. Resistoflex has a license that includes several other patents and the right to use the trademark "HI-PAC" for complete hose assemblies. Aeroquip has shown neither a nexus between the merits of the invention and the licenses of record, nor that those licenses arose out of recognition and acceptance of the patent.

The military specifications were promulgated after the claimed invention was known. Thus the invention did not meet a longfelt but unfilled need expressed in the specifications. Moreover, the record does not support Aeroquip's assertion that the specifications can be met only by tubing covered by the claims of the '087 patent. The nexus required to establish commercial success is therefore not present with respect to the military specifications.

Nor is there evidence that others skilled in the art tried and failed to find a solution for the problem. Aeroquip cites Abbey and Upham, but their effort was limited to investigation of the problem and its cause, and was not directed to its solution.

Upon full consideration of the evidence respecting the secondary considerations in this case, and of Aeroquip's arguments, we are persuaded that nonobviousness is not established by that evidence. Judge Boyle's error in refusing to include that evidence in her analysis was therefore in this case harmless.

"Synergism" and "Combination Patents"

Judge Boyle said "synergism" is "a symbolic reminder of what constitutes nonobviousness when a combination patent is at issue," and that under "either standard (Graham analysis or synergism) the combination . . . simply lacks the unique essence of authentic contribution to the Teflon art which is the heart of invention."

A requirement for "synergism" or a "synergistic effect" is nowhere found in the statute, 35 U.S.C. When present, for example in a chemical case, synergism may point toward nonobviousness, but its absence has no place in evaluating the evidence on obviousness. The more objective findings suggested in Graham, supra, are drawn from the language of the statute and are fully adequate guides for evaluating the evidence relating to compliance with 35 U.S.C. § 103. Bowser, Inc. v. United States, 388 F.2d 346, 181 Ct.Cl. 834, 156 U.S.P.Q. 406 (Ct.Cl.1967). Judge Boyle treated synergism as an alternative consideration. Hence the error of its analytical inclusion is harmless in view of Judge Boyle's employment of the Graham aids.

The reference to a "combination patent" is equally without support in the statute. There is no warrant for judicial classification of patents, whether into "combination" patents and some other unnamed and undefined class or otherwise. Nor is there warrant for differing treatment or consideration of patents based on a judicially devised label. Reference to "combination" patents is, moreover, meaningless. Virtually all patents are "combination patents," if by that label one intends to describe patents having claims to inventions formed of a combination of elements. It is difficult to visualize, at least in the mechanical-structural arts, a "non-combination" invention, i.e., an invention consisting of a single element. Such inventions, if they exist, are rare indeed. Again, however, Judge Boyle's inclusion in her analysis of a reference to the '087 patent as a "combination" patent was harmless in view of her application of Graham guidelines.

Similarly, Judge Boyle's reference to "the heart of invention" was here a harmless fall-back to the fruitless search for an inherently amorphous concept that was rendered unnecessary by the statute, 35 U.S.C. The Graham analysis here applied properly looked to patentability, not to "invention." [W]e affirm the judgment declaring claim 1 invalid for obviousness.

In Re Dillon

United States Court of Appeals, Federal Circuit, 1990. *(en banc)*
919 F.2d 688.

■ LOURIE, CIRCUIT JUDGE.

Diane M. Dillon, assignor to Union Oil Company of California, appeals the November 25, 1987, decision of the Board of Patent Appeals and Interferences (Board) of the United States Patent and Trademark Office

(PTO), Appeal No. 87–0944, rejecting claims 2–14, 16–22, and 24–37, all the remaining claims of patent application Serial No. 671,570 entitled "Hydrocarbon Fuel Composition." We affirm the rejection of all of the claims.[a]

The Invention

Dillon's patent application describes and claims her discovery that the inclusion of certain tetra-orthoester compounds in hydrocarbon fuel compositions will reduce the emission of solid particulates (i.e., soot) during combustion of the fuel. In this appeal Dillon asserts the patentability of claims to hydrocarbon fuel compositions containing these tetra-orthoesters, and to the method of reducing particulate emissions during combustion by combining these esters with the fuel before combustion.

The tetra-orthoesters are a known class of chemical compounds. It is undisputed that their combination with hydrocarbon fuel, for any purpose, is not shown in the prior art, and that their use to reduce particulate emissions from combustion of hydrocarbon fuel is not shown or suggested in the prior art.

The Rejection

The Board held all of the claims to be unpatentable on the ground of obviousness, 35 U.S.C. § 103, in view of certain primary and secondary references. As primary references the Board relied on two Sweeney U.S. patents, 4,390,417 ('417) and 4,395,267 ('267). Sweeney '417 describes hydrocarbon fuel compositions containing specified chemical compounds, viz., ketals, acetals, and tri-orthoesters, used for "dewatering" the fuels, particularly diesel oil. Sweeney '267 describes three-component compositions of hydrocarbon fuels heavier than gasoline, immiscible alcohols, and tri-orthoesters, wherein the tri-orthoesters serve as cosolvents to prevent phase separation between fuel and alcohol. The Board explicitly found that the Sweeney patents do not teach the use of the tetra-orthoesters recited in appellant's claims.

The Board cited Elliott U.S. Patent 3,903,006 and certain other patents, including Howk U.S. Patent 2,840,613, as secondary references. Elliott describes tri-orthoesters and tetra-orthoesters for use as water scavengers in hydraulic (non-hydrocarbon) fluids. The Board stated that the Elliott reference shows equivalence between tetra-orthoesters and tri-orthoesters, and that "it is clear from the combined teachings of these references . . . that [Dillon's tetra-orthoesters] would operate to remove water from non-aqueous liquids by the same mechanism as the orthoesters of Sweeney."

The Board stated that there was a "reasonable expectation" that the tri- and tetra-orthoester fuel compositions would have similar properties,

---

[a] A panel of this court heard this appeal and reversed the Board on December 29, 1989. 892 F.2d 1554, 13 U.S.P.Q.2d 1337. The PTO petitioned for rehearing and suggested rehearing in banc on February 12, 1990. Rehearing in banc was ordered on May 21, 1990, and the judgment which was entered on December 29, 1989, was vacated, the accompanying opinion being withdrawn.

based on "close structural and chemical similarity" between the tri- and tetra-orthoesters and the fact that both the prior art and Dillon use these compounds as "fuel additives." The Commissioner argues on appeal that the claimed compositions and method "would have been prima facie obvious from combined teachings of the references." On this reasoning, the Board held that unless Dillon showed some unexpected advantage or superiority of her claimed tetra-orthoester fuel compositions as compared with tri-orthoester fuel compositions, Dillon's new compositions as well as her claimed method of reducing particulate emissions are unpatentable for obviousness. It found that no such showing was made.

The Issue

The issue before this court is whether the Board erred in rejecting as obvious under 35 U.S.C. § 103 claims to Dillon's new compositions and to the new method of reducing particulate emissions, when the additives in the new compositions are structurally similar to additives in known compositions, having a different use, but the new method of reducing particulate emissions is neither taught nor suggested by the prior art.

The Broad Composition Claims

The Board found that the claims to compositions of a hydrocarbon fuel and a tetra-orthoester were prima facie obvious over Sweeney '417 and '267 in view of Elliott and Howk. We agree. Appellant argues that none of these references discloses or suggests the new use which she has discovered. That is, of course, true, but the composition claims are not limited to this new use; i.e., they are not physically or structurally distinguishable over the prior art compositions except with respect to the orthoester component. We believe that the PTO has established, through its combination of references, that there is a sufficiently close relationship between the tri-orthoesters and tetra-orthoesters (see the cited Elliott and Howk references) in the fuel oil art to create an expectation that hydrocarbon fuel compositions containing the tetra-esters would have similar properties, including water scavenging, to like compositions containing the tri-esters, and to provide the motivation to make such new compositions. Howk teaches use of both tri-and tetra-orthoesters in a similar type of chemical reaction. Elliott teaches their equivalence for a particular practical use. Our case law well establishes that such a fact situation gives rise to a prima facie case of obviousness.

Appellant cites In re Wright, 848 F.2d 1216, 1219, 6 U.S.P.Q.2d 1959, 1961 (Fed.Cir.1988), for the proposition that a prima facie case of obviousness requires that the prior art suggest the claimed compositions' properties and the problem the applicant attempts to solve. The earlier panel opinion in this case, In re Dillon, 892 F.2d 1554, 13 U.S.P.Q.2d 1337 (now withdrawn), in fact stated "a prima facie case of obviousness is not deemed made unless both (1) the new compound or composition is structurally similar to the reference compound or composition and (2) there is some suggestion or expectation in the prior art that the new compound or composition will have the same or a similar utility as that discovered by the applicant." Id. at 1560, 13 U.S.P.Q.2d at 1341 (emphasis added).

This court, in reconsidering this case in banc, reaffirms that structural similarity between claimed and prior art subject matter, proved by combining references or otherwise, where the prior art gives reason or motivation to make the claimed compositions, creates a prima facie case of obviousness, and that the burden (and opportunity) then falls on an applicant to rebut that prima facie case. Such rebuttal or argument can consist of a comparison of test data showing that the claimed compositions possess unexpectedly improved properties or properties that the prior art does not have (In re Albrecht, 514 F.2d 1389, 1396, 185 U.S.P.Q. 585, 590 (CCPA 1975)); that the prior art is so deficient that there is no motivation to make what might otherwise appear to be obvious changes (Albrecht, 514 F.2d at 1396, 185 U.S.P.Q. at 590; In re Stemniski, 444 F.2d 581, 58 CCPA 1410, 170 U.S.P.Q. 343 (CCPA 1971); In re Ruschig, 343 F.2d 965, 52 CCPA 1238, 145 U.S.P.Q. 274 (CCPA 1965)), or any other argument or presentation of evidence that is pertinent. There is no question that all evidence of the properties of the claimed compositions and the prior art must be considered in determining the ultimate question of patentability, but it is also clear that the discovery that a claimed composition possesses a property not disclosed for the prior art subject matter, does not by itself defeat a prima facie case. Shetty, 566 F.2d at 86, 195 U.S.P.Q. at 756. Each situation must be considered on its own facts, but it is not necessary in order to establish a prima facie case of obviousness that both a structural similarity between a claimed and prior art compound (or a key component of a composition) be shown and that there be a suggestion in or expectation from the prior art that the claimed compound or composition will have the same or a similar utility as one newly discovered by applicant. To the extent that Wright suggests or holds to the contrary, it is hereby overruled. In particular, the statement that a prima facie obviousness rejection is not supported if no reference shows or suggests the newly-discovered properties and results of a claimed structure is not the law.

Under the facts we have here, as described above, we have concluded that a prima facie case has been established. The art provided the motivation to make the claimed compositions in the expectation that they would have similar properties. Appellant had the opportunity to rebut the prima facie case. She did not present any showing of data to the effect that her compositions had properties not possessed by the prior art compositions or that they possessed them to an unexpectedly greater degree. She attempted to refute the significance of the teachings of the prior art references. She did not succeed and we do not believe the PTO was in error in its decision.

Appellant points out that none of the references relates to the problem she confronted, citing In re Wright, and that the combination of references is based on hindsight. It is clear, however, that appellant's claims have to be considered as she has drafted them, i.e., as compositions consisting of a fuel and a tetra-orthoester, and that Sweeney '417 and '267 describe the combination of a liquid fuel with a related compound, a tri-orthoester.

While Sweeney does not suggest appellant's use, her composition claims are not limited to that use; the claims merely recite compositions analogous to those in the Sweeney patents, and appellant has made no showing overcoming the prima facie presumption of similar properties for those analogous compositions. The mention in the appealed claims that the amount of orthoester must be sufficient to reduce particulate emissions is not a distinguishing limitation of the claims, unless that amount is different from the prior art and critical to the use of the claimed composition. See In re Reni, 419 F.2d 922, 925, 57 CCPA 857, 164 U.S.P.Q. 245, 247 (CCPA 1970). That is not the case here. The amount of ester recited in the dependent claims can be from 0.05–49%, a very broad range; a preferred range is .05–9%, compared with a percentage in Sweeney '417 approximately equimolar to the amounts of water in the fuel which the ester is intended to remove (.01–5%).

Appellant attacks the Elliott patent as non-analogous art, being in the field of hydraulic fluids rather than fuel combustion. We agree with the PTO that the field of relevant prior art need not be drawn so narrowly. As this court stated in In re Deminski, 796 F.2d 436, 442, 230 U.S.P.Q. 313, 315 (Fed.Cir.1986)(quoting In re Wood, 599 F.2d 1032, 1036, 202 U.S.P.Q. 171, 174 (CCPA 1979)): [t]he determination that a reference is from a nonanalogous art is therefore two-fold. First, we decide if the reference is within the field of the inventor's endeavor. If it is not, we proceed to determine whether the reference is reasonably pertinent to the particular problem with which the inventor was involved. Following that test, one concerned with the field of fuel oils clearly is chargeable with knowledge of Sweeney '417, which discloses fuel compositions with tri-orthoesters for dewatering purposes, and chargeable with knowledge of other references to tri-orthoesters, including for use as dewatering agents for fluids, albeit other fluids. These references are "within the field of the inventor's endeavor." Moreover, the statement of equivalency between tri-and tetra-orthoesters in Elliott is not challenged. We therefore conclude that Elliott is not excludable from consideration as non-analogous art. It is evidence that supports the Board's holding that the prior art makes the claimed compositions obvious, a conclusion that appellant did not overcome.

Appellant urges that the Board erred in not considering the unexpected results produced by her invention and in not considering the claimed invention as a whole. The Board found, on the other hand, that no showing was made of unexpected results for the claimed compositions compared with the compositions of Sweeney. We agree. Clearly, in determining patentability the Board was obligated to consider all the evidence of the properties of the claimed invention as a whole, compared with those of the prior art. However, after the PTO made a showing that the prior art compositions suggested the claimed compositions, the burden was on the applicant to overcome the presumption of obviousness that was created, and that was not done. For example, she produced no evidence that her compositions possessed properties not possessed by the prior art compositions. Nor did she show that the prior art compositions and use were so lacking in significance that there was no motivation for others to make obvious variants. There was no attempt to argue the relative importance of the claimed compositions compared with the prior art. See In re May, 574 F.2d 1082, 1092–95, 197 U.S.P.Q. 601, 609–11 (CCPA 1978).

Appellant's patent application in fact included data showing that the prior art compositions containing tri-orthoesters had equivalent activity in reducing particulate emissions (she apparently was once claiming such compositions with either tri-orthoesters or tetra-orthoesters). She asserts that the examiner used her own showing of equivalence against her in violation of the rule of In re Ruff, 256 F.2d 590, 596, 45 CCPA 1037, 118 U.S.P.Q. 340, 346 (CCPA 1958). While we caution against such a practice, it is clear to us that references by the PTO to the comparative data in the patent application were not employed as evidence of equivalence between the tri- and tetra-orthoesters; the PTO was simply pointing out that the applicant did not or apparently could not make a showing of superiority for the claimed tetra-ester compositions over the prior art tri-ester compositions.

■ ARCHER, CIRCUIT JUDGE, with whom MARKEY and MICHEL, CIRCUIT JUDGES, join, joining-in-part [omitted].

■ NEWMAN, CIRCUIT JUDGE, with whom COWEN AND MAYER, JJ. join, dissenting.

[After an extensive review of precedent, the dissent concluded:]

The Merits

Applying the guidance of precedent to Dillon's invention: the compositions are new, and their property and use of reducing particulate emissions is not taught or suggested in the prior art. There is no objective teaching in the prior art that would have led one of ordinary skill to make this product in order to solve the problem that was confronting Dillon: to reduce soot from combustion of hydrocarbon fuels. There is no reasonable basis in the prior art for expecting that Dillon's new compositions would have the particulate-reducing property that she discovered. As shown in Part I, ante, structure, properties and use must be considered in determining whether a prima facie case under section 103 has been made.

The Sweeney references show the water-sequestration property of tri-orthoesters in hydrocarbon fuels, and the Elliott reference shows the water-sequestration property of tri- and tetra-orthoesters in hydraulic fluids (which are not hydrocarbons and not fuels). There is no suggestion in the prior art that would have led one of ordinary skill to make Dillon's new compositions in the expectation that they would reduce particulate emissions from combustion. No reference suggests any relationship between the properties of water-sequestration and soot-reduction. All this is undisputed.

Dillon raises the question of whether the Sweeney and Elliott references are properly combinable, arguing that they are not in analogous arts. This question need not be decided, for even when combined these references offer no suggestion of the property of reducing particulate emissions from combustion. In re Naber, 494 F.2d 1405, 1407, 181 U.S.P.Q. 639, 641 (CCPA 1974)("even if one of ordinary skill in the art were moved to combine the references, there would be no recognition that the problem of combustible deposits had been solved'').

The board stated that it is inherent in Dillon's compositions that they would reduce particulate emissions, that Dillon "merely recited a newly discovered function inherently possessed" by the prior art. Arguments based on "inherent" properties can not stand when there is no supporting teaching in the prior art. Inherency and obviousness are distinct concepts. In re Spormann, 363 F.2d 444, 448, 53 CCPA 1375, 150 U.S.P.Q. 449, 452 (CCPA 1966):

> [T]he inherency of an advantage and its obviousness are entirely different questions. That which may be inherent is not necessarily known. Obviousness cannot be predicated on what is unknown.

When the PTO asserts that there is an explicit or implicit teaching or suggestion in the prior art, the PTO must produce supporting references. In re Yates, 663 F.2d 1054, 1057, 211 U.S.P.Q. 1149, 1151 (CCPA 1981).

The applicant's newly discovered properties must be considered in determining whether a prima facie case of unpatentability is made, along with all the other evidence. Neither structure nor properties can be ignored; they are essential to consideration of the invention as a whole. But Dillon's own discovery of the soot-reducing property of the tri-orthoester fuel composition is not evidence against her in determining whether the prior art makes a case of prima facie obviousness. In re Wertheim, 541 F.2d 257, 269, 191 U.S.P.Q. 90, 102 (CCPA 1976)(applicant's own disclosures can not be used to support a rejection of the claims "absent some admission that matter disclosed in the specification is in the prior art"); In re Ruff, 256 F.2d at 598, 118 U.S.P.Q. at 347 ("The mere statement of this proposition reveals its fallaciousness").

In view of the complete absence of any suggestion in the prior art that Dillon's new compositions would have her newly discovered and unobvious property and use of soot reduction, I would reverse the rejection of the composition and the use claims.

The Commissioner raised the policy argument that Dillon is simply removing from the public an obvious variant of Sweeney's and Elliott's compositions, one that might be useful to scavenge water in fuels. In Ruschig the court had considered the argument, and remarked that the provision of adequate patent protection for the applicant's new compounds, not previously in existence and having a new and unobvious use, was favored over the "mere possibility that someone might wish to use some of them for some such [other] purpose." 343 F.2d at 979, 145 U.S.P.Q. at 286. This practical wisdom has been tested by long experience. It accords with judicial recognition that: Although there is a vast amount of knowledge about general relationships in the chemical arts, chemistry is still largely empirical, and there is often great difficulty in predicting precisely how a given compound will behave. In re Carleton, 599 F.2d 1021, 1026, 202 U.S.P.Q. 165, 170 (CCPA 1979).

Granting Dillon a patent on her invention takes away nothing that the public already has; and the public receives not only the knowledge of Dillon's discovery, for abandoned patent applications are maintained in secrecy, but Dillon is not deprived of an incentive to discover and to commercialize this new product for this new use.

In Re Bell

United States Court of Appeals, Federal Circuit, 1993.
991 F.2d 781.

■ LOURIE, J.

Applicants Graeme I. Bell, Leslie B. Rall, and James P. Merryweather (Bell) appeal from the March 10, 1992 decision of the U.S. Patent and Trademark Office (PTO) Board of Patent Appeals and Interferences, Appeal No. 91–1124, affirming the examiner's final rejection of claims 25–46 of application Serial No. 065,673, entitled "Preproinsulin–Like Growth Factors I and II," as unpatentable on the ground of obviousness under 35 U.S.C. Section 103 (1988). Because the Board erred in concluding that the claimed nucleic acid molecules would have been obvious in light of the cited prior art, we reverse.

BACKGROUND

The claims of the application at issue are directed to nucleic acid molecules (DNA and RNA)[a] containing human sequences which code for human insulin-like growth factors I and II (IGF), single chain serum proteins that play a role in the mediation of somatic cell growth following the administration of growth hormones.[b]

[a] A basic familiarity with recombinant DNA technology is presumed. For a general discussion, see In re O'Farrell, 853 F.2d 894, 895–99, 7 U.S.P.Q.2d 1673, 1674–77 (Fed.Cir. 1988).

[b] Claim 25 is conceded to be representative of the claims at issue:

A composition comprising nucleic acid molecules containing a human sequence encoding insulin-like growth factor (hIGF) substantially free of nucleic acid molecules not containing said hIGF sequence, wherein said hIGF sequence is selected from the group consisting of:

(a) 5 "-GGA CCG GAG ACG CUC UGC GGG GCU GAG CUG GUG GAU GCU CUU CAG UUC GUG UGU GGA GAC AGG GGC UUU UAU UUC AAC AAG CCC ACA GGG UAU GGC UCC AGC AGU CGG AGG GCG CCU CAG ACA GGU AUC GUG GAU GAG UGC UGC UUC CGG AGC UGU GAU CUA AGG AGG CUG GAG AUG UAU UGC GCA CCC CUC AAG CCU GCC AAG UCA GCU–3", wherein U can also be T;

(b) 5 "-GCU UAC CGC CCC AGU GAG ACC CUG UGC GGC GGG GAG CUG GUG GAC ACC CUC CAG UUC GUC UGU GGG GAC CGC GGC UUC UAC UUC AGC AGG CCC GCA AGC CGU GUG AGC CGU CGC AGC CGU GGC AUC GUU GAG GAG UGC UGU UUC CGC AGC UGU GAC CUG GCC CUC CUG GAG ACG UAC UGU GCU ACC CCC GCC AAG UCC GAG–3", wherein U can also be T;

(c) nucleic acid sequences complementary to (a) or (b); and

(d) fragments of (a), (b) or (c) that are at least 18 bases in length and which will selectively hybridize to human genomic DNA encoding hIGF.

The relevant prior art consists of two publications by Rinderknecht disclosing amino acid sequences for IGF–I and -II and U.S. Patent 4,394,-443 to Weissman et al., entitled "Method for Cloning Genes." Weissman describes a general method for isolating a gene for which at least a short amino acid sequence of the encoded protein is known. The method involves preparing a nucleotide probe corresponding to the known amino acid sequence and using that probe to isolate the gene of interest. It teaches that it is advantageous to design a probe based on amino acids specified by unique codons.[c] The Weissman patent specifically describes the isolation of a gene which codes for human histocompatibility antigen, a protein unre-lated to IGF. It describes the design of the probe employed, stating that it was based on amino acids specified by unique codons.

The examiner rejected the claims as obvious over the combined teach-ings of Rinderknecht and Weissman. She determined that it would have been obvious, "albeit tedious," from the teachings of Weissman to prepare probes based on the Rinderknecht amino acid sequences to obtain the claimed nucleic acid molecules. According to the examiner, "it is clear from [Weissman] that the ordinary artisan knows how to find the nucleic acid when the amino acid sequence is known" and that "the claimed sequences and hosts would have been readily determinable by and obvious to those of ordinary skill in the art at the time the invention was made."

The Board affirmed the examiner's rejection, holding that the examin-er had established a prima facie case of obviousness for the claimed sequences "despite the lack of conventional indicia of obviousness, e.g., structural similarity between the DNA which codes for IGF–I and the amino acid sequence of the polypeptide which constitues [sic] IGF–I." Slip op. at 6. The Board reasoned that "although a protein and its DNA are not structurally similar, they are correspondently linked via the genetic code."Id. at 4 n.1. In view of Weissman, the Board concluded that there was no evidence "that one skilled in the art, knowing the amino acid sequences of the desired proteins, would not have been able to predictably clone the desired DNA sequences without undue experimentation."Id. at 8.

The issue before us is whether the Board correctly determined that the amino acid sequence of a protein in conjunction with a reference indicating a general method of cloning renders the gene prima facie obvious.

DISCUSSION

We review an obviousness determination by the Board de novo. In re Vaeck, 947 F.2d 488, 493, 20 U.S.P.Q.2d 1438, 1442 (Fed.Cir.1991). Bell argues that the PTO has not shown how the prior art references, either

---

[c] A sequence of three nucleotides, called a codon, codes for each of the twenty natural amino acids. Since there are twenty amino acids and sixty-four possible codons, most amino acids are specified by more than one codon. This is referred to as "degeneracy" in the genetic code. The term "unique" refers to an amino acid coded for by a single codon. See Amgen Inc. v. Chugai Pharmaceutical Co., 927 F.2d 1200, 1207–08 n.4, 18 U.S.P.Q.2d 1016, 1022 n.4 (Fed.Cir.), cert. denied, 112 S.Ct. 169 (1991).

alone or in combination, teach or suggest the claimed invention, and thus that it has failed to establish a prima facie case of obviousness.

We agree. The PTO bears the burden of establishing a case of prima facie obviousness. In re Fine, 837 F.2d 1071, 1074, 5 U.S.P.Q.2d 1596, 1598 (Fed.Cir.1988). "A prima facie case of obviousness is established when the teachings from the prior art itself would appear to have suggested the claimed subject matter to a person of ordinary skill in the art."In re Rinehart, 531 F.2d 1048, 1051, 189 U.S.P.Q. 143, 147 (CCPA 1976).

The Board supported the examiner's view that the "correspondent link" between a gene and its encoded protein via the genetic code renders the gene obvious when the amino acid sequence is known. In effect, this amounts to a rejection based on the Rinderknecht references alone. Implicit in that conclusion is the proposition that, just as closely related homologs, analogs, and isomers in chemistry may create a prima facie case, see In re Dillon, 919 F.2d 688, 696, 16 U.S.P.Q.2d 1897, 1904 (Fed.Cir.1990)(in banc), cert. denied, 111 S.Ct. 1682 (1991), the established relationship in the genetic code between a nucleic acid and the protein it encodes also makes a gene prima facie obvious over its correspondent protein.

We do not accept this proposition. It may be true that, knowing the structure of the protein, one can use the genetic code to hypothesize possible structures for the corresponding gene and that one thus has the potential for obtaining that gene. However, because of the degeneracy of the genetic code, there are a vast number of nucleotide sequences that might code for a specific protein. In the case of IGF, Bell has argued without contradiction that the Rinderknecht amino acid sequences could be coded for by more than 10^{36} different nucleotide sequences, only a few of which are the human sequences that Bell now claims. Therefore, given the nearly infinite number of possibilities suggested by the prior art, and the failure of the cited prior art to suggest which of those possibilities is the human sequence, the claimed sequences would not have been obvious.

Bell does not claim all of the 10^{36} nucleic acids that might potentially code for IGF. Neither does Bell claim all nucleic acids coding for a protein having the biological activity of IGF. Rather, Bell claims only the human nucleic acid sequences coding for IGF. Absent anything in the cited prior art suggesting which of the 10^{36} possible sequences suggested by Rinderknecht corresponds to the IGF gene, the PTO has not met its burden of establishing that the prior art would have suggested the claimed sequences.

This is not to say that a gene is never rendered obvious when the amino acid sequence of its coded protein is known. Bell concedes that in a case in which a known amino acid sequence is specified exclusively by unique codons, the gene might have been obvious. Such a case is not before us.[d] Here, where Rinderknecht suggests a vast number of possible nucleic acid sequences, we conclude that the claimed human sequences would not have been obvious.

---

[d] We also express no opinion concerning the reverse proposition, that knowledge of the structure of a DNA, e.g., a cDNA, might make a coded protein obvious.

Combining Rinderknecht with Weissman does not fill the gap. Obviousness "cannot be established by combining the teachings of the prior art to produce the claimed invention, absent some teaching or suggestion supporting the combination." In re Fine, 837 F.2d at 1075, 5 U.S.P.Q.2d at 1598 (citing ACS Hosp. Sys. v. Montefiore Hosp., 732 F.2d 1572, 1577, 221 U.S.P.Q. 929, 933 (Fed.Cir.1984)). What a reference teaches and whether it teaches toward or away from the claimed invention are questions of fact. See Raytheon Co. v. Roper Corp., 724 F.2d 951, 960–61, 220 U.S.P.Q. 592, 599–600 (Fed.Cir.1983), cert. denied, 469 U.S. 835 [225 U.S.P.Q. 232] (1984).

While Weissman discloses a general method for isolating genes, he appears to teach away from the claimed invention by emphasizing the importance of unique codons for the amino acids. Weissman suggests that it is generally advantageous to design a probe based on an amino acid sequence specified by unique codons, and also teaches that it is "counterproductive" to use a primer having more than 14–16 nucleotides unless the known amino acid sequence has 4–5 amino acids coded for by unique codons. Bell, in contrast, used a probe having 23 nucleotides based on a sequence of eight amino acids, none of which were unique. Weissman therefore tends to teach away from the claimed sequences since Rinderknecht shows that IGF–I has only a single amino acid with a unique codon and IGF–II has none.

The PTO, in urging us to affirm the Board, points to the suggestion in Weissman that the disclosed method can "easily" be applied to isolate genes for an array of proteins including peptide hormones. The PTO thus argues that in view of Weissman, a gene is rendered obvious once the amino acid sequence of its translated protein is known. We decline to afford that broad a scope to the teachings of Weissman. While "a reference must be considered not only for what it expressly teaches, but also for what it fairly suggests," In re Burckel, 592 F.2d 1175, 1179, 201 U.S.P.Q. 67, 70 (CCPA 1979), we cannot say that Weissman "fairly suggests" that its teachings should be combined with those of Rinderknecht, since it nowhere suggests how to apply its teachings to amino acid sequences without unique codons.

We conclude that the Board clearly erred in determining that Weissman teaches toward, rather than away from, the claimed sequences. Therefore, the requisite teaching or suggestion to combine the teachings of the cited prior art references is absent, see In re Fine, 837 F.2d 1075, 5 U.S.P.Q.2d at 1599 , and the PTO has not established that the claimed sequences would have been obvious over the combination of Rinderknecht and Weissman.

NOTES

1. *The § 103(a) inquiry.* In theory, the inquiry here is quite similar to the examination for novelty. References are found and dated to determine whether effective dates precede the critical date, the adequacy of dissemination is determined, and the contents of the art are scrutinized. Although § 103 does not list the activities that come within its scope, it is universally assumed that the same art that is pertinent to nonobviousness is also the art that is relevant to novelty. This includes § 102(a) art—information known or used in the United States as well as both domestic and foreign patents and printed publications. It also includes 102(e) art—information contained in patent applications, so long as the patent eventually issues. And, it includes 102(g) art—inventions made in this country that have not been abandoned, suppressed, or concealed.[13] As with novelty, the critical date is the date on which the invention is reduced to practice; the effective date is the date on which the reference is accessible to the public.

At this point, however, the analyses diverge, for while novelty is defined quite rigidly, the nonobviousness inquiry is far more open ended. This creates two difficult issues for the courts.

a. *Policy considerations*. First, there is a pure policy question here: how large a contribution must an inventor make to merit a patent? Justice Douglas thought the advance ought to be of major scientific significance; although the Graham Court read § 103 as adopting the less formidable *Hotchkiss* formulation, it was not willing to say that Congress had lowered the standard of patentability. This creates problems for inventions that are not deeply insightful, yet require considerable funds and efforts to make. As In re Dillon and In re Bell demonstrate, this is particularly a concern in chemical and biochemical cases. In both fields, theory is well enough advanced to predict the advantages of yet-unsynthesized structures. However, bringing these structures into being requires very costly research. Absent a legal right—a patent right—to recapture the expense, it is not clear that the work will be done.

b. *Practical application*. Agreeing on the level of contribution required does not eliminate the practical problem of implementation. Although the § 103 inquiry requires comparisons between sophisticated technologies, it is conducted by judges with no more training in technical matters than any law student, and by lay jurors, some of whom know more but most of whom know a great deal less than students know. As the Principal Cases indicate, there has been much experimentation here as courts have searched for ways to formulate a clear test for nonobviousness.

(i) Teaching away. Some cases are made easy by the fact that the prior art "teaches away" from the invention in the sense that it discourages doing what the inventor has done. Such was claimed for certain of the references in *Stratoflex* and *Bell*. Indeed, on the same day that the Supreme Court invalidated the plow patent in Graham, it decided United States v.

---

[13] See, e.g., Hazeltine Research, Inc. v. Brenner, 382 U.S. 252, 86 S.Ct. 335, 15 L.Ed.2d 304 (1965); In re Bartfeld, 925 F.2d 1450 (Fed.Cir.1991)(§ 102(e)); Hybritech Inc. v. Monoclonal Antibodies, Inc., 802 F.2d 1367 (Fed.Cir.1986)(§ 102(g)). In addition, as Note 6, infra, makes clear, information de-

Adams,[14] which upheld the patent on a battery utilizing plain water as the electrolyte. Although wet batteries were well known and every element of the invention could be found in other batteries, the Court found that long-accepted theories in the art should have deterred anyone from trying to put together the battery at issue in the case. "[K]nown disadvantages in old devices which would naturally discourage the search for new inventions may be taken into account in determining obviousness."[15] Accordingly, the patent in Adams was upheld.

Similarly, prior work may obscure the problem the inventor needs to resolve. In Eibel Process Co. v. Minnesota & Ontario Paper Co.,[16] for example, the invention was in the field of paper making. At the time, paper was made by pouring wet stock onto a conveyer belt ("wire") which moved it through a drying environment. The industry had tried to speed up operations by moving the wire quickly, but if it moved too fast, the product turned out to be uneven. The inventor found a solution: he changed the pitch of the container from which the stock was poured. The Court held the invention nonobvious, stating that "[t]he invention was not the mere use of a high or substantial pitch to remedy a known source of trouble. It was the discovery of the source not before known and the application of the remedy for which Eibel was entitled to be rewarded in his patent."[17] The industry had not understood that the stock needed to be moving at a speed close to that of the wire when it hit the wire; Eibel's discovery of the problem merited a patent even though the solution was trivial once the problem was understood.

(ii) Combination patents. As *Ag Pro* demonstrates, "combinations" were at one time split out for separate consideration. Because combination inventions are clearly made up of known elements, they were considered likely to be obvious. Thus, a special showing of synergy (or as the case puts it, synergistic results) was required. In theory, synergy should have been as easy to spot as teaching away. In practice, however, such was not the case.

One difficulty with the formulation was that there was considerable controversy over what should be considered a combination. At some level of particularity, every advance is a combination because innovation is largely a process of analogizing to earlier work, borrowing relevant bits and pieces from several sources.[18] Furthermore, close inspection of any invention will reveal how it works: two things never add up to more than the sum of their parts. For this reason, *Stratoflex* ultimately rejected the combination-patent idea as well as the search for synergy.

---

rived from another under § 102(f) is included as prior art for § 103 purposes.

[14] 383 U.S. 39, 86 S.Ct. 708, 15 L.Ed.2d 572 (1966).

[15] Id. at 52.

[16] 261 U.S. 45, 43 S.Ct. 322, 67 L.Ed. 523 (1923).

[17] Id. at 68.

[18] For vivid examples of how inventions build upon each other, see H. Petroski, The Evolution of Useful Things (Alfred A. Knopf 1992).

(iii) Secondary considerations. The so-called secondary considerations are factors external to the invention itself that demonstrate its inventiveness. They include long-felt need for a solution to the problem the invention addresses, the failure of others to find such a solution, the commercial success of the invention in the marketplace, and acquiescence—the willingness of others to accept the patent as valid and take a license or forgo use of the invention. Their use represents another attempt to find an objective test for nonobviousness, although they too have met with considerable controversy.

On the one hand, it does seem that these are signs that the invention is a significant advance. If need for the innovation existed for a long time, it can be assumed that others would have invented it had this been easy to do. Since the need persisted until this applicant came along, he must have made the kind of breakthrough necessary to earn a patent. Similarly, if others tried to invent and failed, but the applicant tried and succeeded, her contribution must not have been obvious. By the same token, there are many entrepreneurs ready to earn an easy dollar. If the invention is a great commercial success, one of them would have brought it to market sooner if it was obvious to make. Finally, acquiescence is an indication that the people who *do* know the technology agree that the advance merits a patent.

On the other hand, these factors may be present for reasons other than the intrinsic creativity of the invention. Developments in other fields may make easy something that was formerly difficult. Suddenly, long-felt need will be met and failure will be overcome by a commercially successful new product. Furthermore, if the inventor charges licensees less than the cost of challenging the patent, there will be acquiescence rather than litigation. As *Stratoflex* makes clear, the CAFC's response here is to recognize both the value and the danger of relying on these factors. It requires the lower courts to look at secondary considerations in every case, but also to consider whether there is a nexus between the invention and the factor. Absent a showing that the factor is present because of inventiveness, the consideration will not be taken into account in determining nonobviousness. While this resolution may not be theoretically satisfying, it does focus the lower courts on issues that can be measured without a high level of technological skill.

(iv) Suggestions in the prior art. The CAFC has also attempted to objectify the analysis under § 103 by prohibiting courts from combining elements of different references unless they can point to suggestions within the references that the combination would achieve the advantages found in the invention.[19]

2. *The Court of Appeals for the Federal Circuit.* Interestingly, the CAFC was itself a response to the § 103 problem. In the early 1970's, Congress had created a commission to make recommendations for improving the

---

[19] See, e.g., Interconnect Planning Corp. v. Feil, 774 F.2d 1132 (Fed.Cir.1985); Lindemann Maschinenfabrik GMBH v. American Hoist & Derrick Co., 730 F.2d 1452 (Fed.Cir. 1984).

administration of federal justice. The Hruska Commission that was formed identified patent law as one of the areas in which the delivery of justice could be improved. It suggested that Congress create a specialized court with the technical expertise and experience necessary to decide difficult technological issues expediently.[20] The CAFC was established in 1982 to hear patent appeals from the district courts in all of the federal circuits. It was no surprise to the patent bar that *Stratoflex* appeared so soon after the court was established, for the judges of the new court took the resolution of the nonobviousness problem as their premier challenge.[21]

The CAFC has two important advantages over the regional circuits that previously decided patent appeals. First, it can require all the district courts to use the same objective tests of nonobviousness. Second, because every patent appeal winds up in this court, there is no longer an incentive to shop for a forum with a higher or lower standard of nonobviousness. Cases like *Graham*, where the same patent was upheld on one circuit and invalidated on another, can no longer occur. The law on nonobviousness may not be theoretically perfect, but it is at least administered equitably.[22]

3. *Does § 103 render the § 102 inquiry superfluous?* Since § 103 looks at the same art as § 102, but lacks its rigidity of application, it is easy to fall into the trap of thinking that § 103 renders § 102 superfluous, for anything that is not new also appears to be obvious. Close attention to the details of the nonobviousness inquiry makes the independent significance of § 102 clearer.

(i) Inherency. Note 1(a)(iii) in Assignment 18 explained that information inherent in a reference counts for novelty purposes, even if use of the information is not specifically indicated. But as Judge Newman's dissent in *Dillon* makes clear, inherency is not sufficient for nonobviousness. In order for a reference to be utilized, the element of interest must be expressly pointed out. In terms of the search-model discussed in the Introduction to Assignment 18, it is easy to understand why this should be true. It would be too costly to require inventors to research all prior art with enough insight to appreciate every scrap of information inherent in it, and then combine all of this learning to produce the invention. But it is cost-effective to look for an *entirely* effectuated invention in earlier work. Accordingly, inherency is a feature of § 102(a) jurisprudence, but it is not used in the § 103 analysis.

(ii) Field of reference. Note 1(b)(iv) in Assignment 18 discussed the fact that every field is considered fair game when novelty is the issue. But such is not the case in § 103. The information that is relevant to the nonobviousness query must be information in the same field of the invention, information found in "analogous arts," (i.e. arts where people working in

[20] See Commission on Revision of the Federal Court Appellate System, Structure and Internal Procedures: Recommendations for Change, reprinted in 67 F.R.D. 195 (1975).

[21] See, e.g., Markey, The Phoenix Court, 10 AIPLA Q.J. 227 (1982).

[22] See, e.g., Dreyfuss, The Federal Circuit: A Case Study in Specialized Courts, 64 N.Y.U. L. Rev. 1 (1989).

the field of the invention would look if confronted with the kind of problem the applicant faced),[23] or references from other fields that in some way suggest they would helpful in solving this inventor's problem.[24]

4. *Process patents*. It is important to remember that the applicant in *Dillon* sought a product patent, a patent on a fuel additive. The application was rejected because the additive was, essentially, old news. But Dillon was using the additive to do something different from what the prior art additives did. While they scavenged water, hers reduced soot. Would she have had more success applying for a *process* patent on a method for using her additive to reduce soot? Section 100(b) of the Patent Act defines processes to include new methods for using known compositions of matter. Since Dillon had developed a new method (soot reduction) for using an old composition (the additive), her application would appear to exemplify exactly the situation § 100(b) was designed to address. Awarding Dillon a patent would compensate for the inventive work she did without removing a known product from the public domain.

Until 1985, Dillon's process application would probably have met with success. However, in that year, the CAFC decided In re Durden,[25] which raised the standard for patenting processes. *Durden* rejected a patent on a method claim whose only inventive feature was that a starting material (i.e. one of the ingredients) was new. The court reasoned that since the method itself was known in the prior art, the invention was obvious. Given *Durden*, Dillon's process claim would be problematic because she is using an old method (adding an additive to fuel); only her starting material is new, and under *Durden*, that is not enough.

Durden was greeted with much criticism in the patent bar,[26] especially in that part of the bar concerned with biotechnology patents. Process patents are sometimes important to this industry for the same reasons they are important to Dillon: to create a financial return on researching new uses for known materials. However, the industry also needs process protection for another reason. Some of the commercially significant research in biotechnology involves the isolation and characterization of naturally occurring genes and the use of these genes to manufacture known proteins. Although the genes themselves are often patented, competitors can take them out of the country, where their use will not infringe the patent. The proteins produced are then re-imported into this country. Since the proteins were known and were not patentable, there is still no infringement. However, importation into the United States of a product manufactured by a process patented in the United States *is* an infringement, § 271(g). Hence, the special need for process patents. If the genetic researcher can

---

[23] See, e.g., Union Carbide Corp. v. American Can Co., 724 F.2d 1567 (Fed.Cir. 1984); In re Wood, 599 F.2d 1032 (C.C.P.A. 1979).

[24] See, e.g., In re Grabiak, 769 F.2d 729, 732 (Fed.Cir.1985).

[25] 763 F.2d 1406 (Fed.Cir.1985).

[26] See, e.g., Wegner, Much Ado About Durden, 71 J.Pat.Off.Soc., 785 (1985) ; Wegner, Biotechnology Process Patents: Judicial or Legislative Remedy, 73 J.Pat.Off.Soc. 24 (1991).

get a patent on the *process* for using the gene, she is protected. She can sue the importer of the protein under § 271(g) for importing a product (the protein) that is manufactured by a process patented in the United States.

At the behest of the biochemistry industry, Congress recently amended § 103 and § 103(b) was added.[27] The new subsection creates a special rule for any biotechnological process on which a patent application is filed simultaneously with an application for a patent on a composition of matter that is either a starting material in the process or the end product of the process. Section 103(b) provides that if this composition of matter is found to be novel and nonobvious, then the process will also be considered nonobvious. There is an important proviso: both process and product must, at the time they were invented, have been owned by the same person or subject to an obligation of assignment to the same person.

Because § 103(b) applies only to biological processes (which are defined in the provision), the change does not help in cases like *Dillon*. However, even before Congress amended § 103, the CAFC refined its position on the nonobviousness of processes. In In re Pleuddemann,[28] it attempted to distinguish between claims for *making* a new product and claims for *using* a new product, so that making a new product with an old process is now more likely to be patentable. In addition, in a part of *Dillon* that was not reproduced above, the court noted that *Durden* does not mean that every new-material process claim must be rejected; each case is to be decided on its own facts. This leaves some room to use process patents as a method to induce people to invest in the kind of work conducted by Dillon.[29]

5. *Presumption of Validity.* In an omitted section of *Stratoflex,* the CAFC discussed § 282 of the Act, which creates a presumption that a patent is valid. As we have seen, similar presumptions exist in both copyright and trademark law. In both systems, the presumption has the effect of requiring the challenger to disprove validity, cf. Assignments 6 and 3. In the Principal Case, however, the district court had held that the presumption of patent validity applied only with respect to material that had been reviewed by the PTO; since material introduced for the first time by Stratoflex had never been scrutinized, the patentee, Aeroflex, bore the burden of showing that its invention was nonobvious over this art. The CAFC reversed:

> "Introduction of more pertinent prior art than that considered by the examiner does not ... 'weaken' or 'destroy' the presumption. Nor does such introduction 'shift' the burden of persuasion. The presumption continues its procedural burden-assigning role throughout the trial."[30]

Given that patent applications are much more rigorously examined than copyright and trademark applications, does it make sense to treat the presumptions in the same way in all three areas?

---

[27] The paragraphs of § 103 were also, for the first time, separately designated with letters.

[28] 910 F.2d 823 (Fed.Cir.1990).

[29] See also Moleculon Research Corp. v. CBS, Inc., 793 F.2d 1261, 1268 (Fed.Cir. 1986).

[30] *Stratoflex,* 713 F.2d at 1534.

6. *Originality (derivation).* As in copyright, patent protection is available only to the original creator of the work. The clearest statement of this requirement is found in § 102(f), which bars a patent if the subject matter was not invented by the applicant. See also § 111, which requires that the application be made by the inventor, and §§ 115–116, requiring applicants to swear that they believe themselves to be the original and first inventors of the subject matter of the application. Because the applicant who runs afoul of these provisions can be said to have "derived" the invention from another, patent attorneys usually speak of "derivation" rather than "originality."

Despite the clear bar on inventions derived from others, there are rather few cases decided on pure originality grounds. As in copyright, proof is hard to come by. People rarely copy the works of others in public. It is often much easier to simply consider the first inventor's work as part of the prior art, and then reject the second inventor's application on the ground that the invention is obvious or not novel.

For example, consider the case in which A invents a widget in the United States and shows it to B, who then applies for a patent. Derivation requires a showing that the invention was conceived by the first inventor (here, A) and the complete conception was communicated to the applicant (B).[31] It is often easier to simply show that the invention was used by another (namely, A) in the United States (§ 102(a)) or invented in this country by another who did not abandon, suppress, or conceal it (§ 102(g)). If B did not brazenly apply for a patent on A's precise invention but instead made some minor changes, the application could be rejected on § 103 grounds.

Why, then, is § 102(f) broken out as a separate section? To answer that question, it is necessary to remember that not *all* prior inventions enter the prior art for novelty and nonobviousness purposes. Section 102(a) art is limited to inventions that are somewhat public. Moreover, foreign information is not anticipatory unless it is found in a patent or in a printed publication. Section 102(g) has similar limitations. Thus, an invention known only to, let us say, one other American or to a foreigner may not be effective anticipation. However, the applicant will nonetheless be barred from receiving a patent if, instead of inventing the invention herself, this other American—or the foreigner—told her about it.[32]

What if, in these hypotheticals, the information that the first inventor communicated to the applicant was not enough to construct the invention, but it was enough to render the invention obvious? From the discussion so far, it would appear that § 103 is not applicable because, by hypothesis, the information did not qualify as prior art under the novelty provisions. However, the applicant has clearly not made the type of contribution that patent law rewards. The application should certainly be rejected, and it will

---

[31] See, e.g., Johnson & Johnson v. W.L. Gore Assoc., 436 F.Supp. 704, 711 (D.C.Del. 1977).

[32] Section 102(f) is also not affected by § 104's bar on using foreign inventive activities.

be: on "§ 102(f)/103" grounds.[33] Since information communicated to an inventor can render the invention obvious, it is said that § 102(f) art is prior art for § 103 purposes.

7. *The last sentence of § 103(c): common ownership.* Prior to 1984, the combination of § 103 with §§ 102(f) or (g) sometimes worked considerable mischief in large research organizations. Imagine, for example, that a scientist is assigned to develop a new product. After working on the project for a while, he comes up with a key insight. However, before he can bring the invention to the point where it can be practiced, priorities within the firm change, and the scientist is assigned to another task. Some years later, interest is rekindled. But since the first scientist is busy, a second scientist takes over the project. The second scientist combines the earlier insight with her own findings and completes the project. What happens when the firm tries to get a patent? The first researcher's work may be deemed to render the invention obvious on the basis of § 102(f)/103, or possibly § 102(g)/103.[34]

This state of affairs was highly inefficient as it led firms to institute procedures to prohibit their employees from sharing information. Finding this practice a waste of expensive talent, Congress enacted the second paragraph of § 103(c), which prevents the work of one inventor from being considered in reviewing the patent application of another when both did the work that is the subject of the application for the same company or when their work was subject to an obligation of assignment to the same entity.[35]

BIBLIOGRAPHY

Wegner, Biotechnology Process Patents: Judicial or Legislative Remedy, 73 J.Pat.Off.Soc'y 24 (1991); Dreyfuss, The Federal Circuit: A Case Study in Specialized Courts, 64 N.Y.U. L. Rev. 1 (1989); Wegner, Much Ado About Durden, 71 J.Pat.Off.Soc'y 785 (1989); Litman, Obvious Process Rejections Under 35 USC 103, 71 J.Pat.Off.Soc'y 775 (1989); Merges, Economic Perspectives on Innovation: Patent Standards and Commercial Success, 76 Cal. L. Rev. 803 (1988); Note: Patent Law: Obviousness, Secondary Considerations, and the Nexus Requirement, 1986 Ann. Surv. Am. L. 117; Mintz & Racine, Anticipation and Obviousness in the Federal Circuit, 13 AIPLA Q.J.L. 195 (1985); Comment, The Use of Derived Information as Prior Art Under Section 102 of the Patent Act, 79 Nw. U.L.Rev. 423 (1984); Stiefel, Section 102(f) as a Basis for Section 103 Art— Myth or Reality, 61 J.Pat.Off.Soc'y 734 (1979); Kitch, Graham v. John Deere Co: New Standards for Patents, 1966 S.Ct. Rev. 303.

[33] See, e.g., In re Bass, 474 F.2d 1276 (C.C.P.A.1973).

[34] See, e.g., Kimberly–Clark Corp. v. Johnson and Johnson, 745 F.2d 1437 (Fed. Cir.1984). Section 102(g) is in the picture because it too permits invalidation based on secret art. That is, in the hypothetical, the work of the first researcher could be considered an invention invented by another in the United States. Even if not communicated to the second researcher, it could be disqualifying.

[35] At the same time, § 116, was modified so that successive researchers will sometimes be considered joint inventors.

STATUTORY BARS

1. INTRODUCTION

Unlike the novelty and nonobviousness provisions of §§ 102(a), (e), (g), and § 103, which are directed to events preceding invention, the statutory bars focus on events preceding the filing of a patent application. These provisions augment § 101 by adding new conditions for acquiring a patent. They enumerate activities that are regarded as so antithetical to the policies underlying patent law that their existence will bar a patent even if the invention is otherwise innovative enough to deserve one. Consequently, they are sometimes referred to as "loss of right" provisions.

The statutory bars are enumerated in those provisions of § 102 that describe activity occurring *before*—in most cases, more than a year before—the application was filed: under § 102(b), public use or sale of the invention in the United States more than a year before filing, or publication or patenting anywhere in the world more than a year before filing; under § 102(c), abandonment; under § 102(d), the issuance of an applicant's foreign patent before the issuance of a U.S. patent—if the foreign patent was applied for more than a year before the U.S. filing.

The statutory bars can be thought of as statutes of limitation. The patent system is aimed at encouraging more than merely invention: it is also intended to promote dissemination. The costs of exclusivity are balanced out only if the social benefits provided by the invention are in fact captured through its widespread use. Thus, the inventor who keeps the invention to herself should not always be eligible to receive a patent. Furthermore, patents are time-bound: they last no more than 20 years. The inventor who enjoys exclusive benefits of the invention before applying for a patent should be penalized for, in effect, trying to extend the term of protection beyond the limit set by Congress.

Because the policies underlying the statutory bars are so strong, it is somewhat surprising that some of the subsections provide for a one-year grace period—that is, public use, sale, publication, and patenting bar a patent only if they occurred *more* than a year before the application is filed. In many countries, these events would bar a patent even if they occurred the day before filing.[1] The United States, however, recognizes that in many areas, the PTO is not the most efficient vehicle for disseminating inventions. For example, academic researchers rely much more on research conferences than patents to learn and exchange information; industrial

---

[1] See, e.g., European Patent Convention, art. 54(1)(1977).

innovators use trade fairs. If these avenues could not be pursued until the application is filed, dissemination will be delayed rather than encouraged. Accordingly, so long as these activities do not go on for too long (defined as a year), the patent will not be barred.[2]

2. PRINCIPAL PROBLEM

Reconsider the Problem at issue in Assignment 18. Do any of the activities described raise a statutory bar?

3. MATERIALS FOR SOLUTION OF PRINCIPAL PROBLEM

A. STATUTORY MATERIALS: §§ 102(b), (c), & (d)

B. CASES:

Egbert v. Lippmann

Supreme Court of the United States, 1881.
104 U.S.(14 Otto) 333, 26 L.Ed. 755.

■ MR. JUSTICE WOODS delivered the opinion of the Court.

This suit was brought for an alleged infringement of the complainant's reissued letters-patent, No. 5216, dated Jan. 7, 1873, for an improvement in corset-springs. The original letters bear date July 17, 1866, and were issued to Samuel H. Barnes. The reissue was made to the complainant, under her then name, Frances Lee Barnes, executrix of the original patentee.

The bill alleges that Barnes was the original and first inventor of the improvement covered by the reissued letters-patent, and that it had not, at the time of his application for the original letters, been for more than two years in public use or on sale, with his consent or allowance.[a] The answer takes issue on this averment. We have, therefore, to consider whether the defense that the patented invention had, with the consent of the inventor, been publicly used for more than two years prior to his application for the original letters, is sustained by the testimony in the record.

The evidence on which the defendants rely to establish a prior public use of the invention consists mainly of the testimony of the complainant.

She testifies that Barnes invented the improvement covered by his patent between January and May, 1855; that between the dates named the witness and her friend Miss Cugier were complaining of the breaking of their corset-steels. Barnes, who was present, and was an intimate friend of the witness, said he thought he could make her a pair that would not

[2] There are also countries that attempt to compromise these positions by providing a grace period, but only for narrow categories of dissemination, see, e.g., Toshiko Takenaka, The Substantial Identity Rule Under the Japanese Standard, 9 UCLA Pac. Basin L.J. 220, 224–25 (1991).

[a] [At that time, the Patent Act rendered a patent invalid if the invention was in public use, with the consent and allowance of the inventor, for more than two years prior to the application—eds.]

break. At their next interview he presented her with a pair of corset-steels which he himself had made. The witness wore these steels a long time. In 1858 Barnes made and presented to her another pair, which she also wore a long time. When the corsets in which these steels were used wore out, the witness ripped them open and took out the steels and put them in new corsets. This was done several times.

It is admitted, and, in fact, is asserted, by complainant, that these steels embodied the invention afterwards patented by Barnes and covered by the reissued letters-patent on which this suit is brought.

Joseph H. Sturgis, another witness for complainant, testifies that in 1863 Barnes spoke to him about two inventions made by himself, one of which was a corset-steel, and that he went to the house of Barnes to see them. Before this time, and after the transactions testified to by the complainant, Barnes and she had intermarried. Barnes said his wife had a pair of steels made according to his invention in the corsets which she was then wearing, and if she would take them off he would show them to witness. Mrs. Barnes went out, and returned with a pair of corsets and a pair of scissors, and ripped the corsets open and took out the steels. Barnes then explained to witness how they were made and used.

This is the evidence presented by the record, on which the defendants rely to establish the public use of the invention by the patentee's consent and allowance. The question for our decision is, whether this testimony shows a public use within the meaning of the statute.

We observe, in the first place, that to constitute the public use of an invention it is not necessary that more than one of the patented articles should be publicly used. The use of a great number may tend to strengthen the proof, but one well-defined case of such use is just as effectual to annul the patent as many. McClurg v. Kingsland, 1 How. 202; Consolidated Fruit–Jar Co. v. Wright, 94 U.S. 92; Pitts v. Hall, 2 Blatchf. 229. For instance, if the inventor of a mower, a printing-press, or a railway-car makes and sells only one of the articles invented by him, and allows the vendee to use it for two years, without restriction or limitation, the use is just as public as if he had sold and allowed the use of a great number.

We remark, secondly, that, whether the use of an invention is public or private does not necessarily depend upon the number of persons to whom its use is known. If an inventor, having made his device, gives or sells it to another, to be used by the donee or vendee, without limitation or restriction, or injunction of secrecy, and it is so used, such use is public, even though the use and knowledge of the use may be confined to one person.

We say, thirdly, that some inventions are by their very character only capable of being used where they cannot be seen or observed by the public eye. An invention may consist of a lever or spring, hidden in the running gear of a watch, or of a rachet, shaft, or cog-wheel covered from view in the recesses of a machine for spinning or weaving. Nevertheless, if its inventor sells a machine of which his invention forms a part, and allows it to be used without restriction of any kind, the use is a public one. So, on the other hand, a use necessarily open to public view, if made in good faith solely to test the qualities of the invention, and for the purpose of experiment, is not a public use within the meaning of the statute. Elizabeth v. American Nicholson Pavement Company, 97 U.S. 126; Shaw v. Cooper, 7 Pet. 292.

Tested by these principles, we think the evidence of the complainant herself shows that for more than two years before the application for the original letters there was, by the consent and allowance of Barnes, a public use of the invention, covered by them. He made and gave to her two pairs of corset-steels, constructed according to his device, one in 1855 and one in 1858. They were presented to her for use. He imposed no obligation of secrecy, nor any condition or restriction whatever. They were not presented for the purpose of experiment, nor to test their qualities. No such claim is set up in her testimony. The invention was at the time complete, and there is no evidence that it was afterwards changed or improved. The donee of the steels used them for years for the purpose and in the manner designed by the inventor. They were not capable of any other use. She might have exhibited them to any person, or made other steels of the same kind, and used or sold them without violating any condition or restriction imposed on her by the inventor.

According to the testimony of the complainant, the invention was completed and put into use in 1855. The inventor slept on his rights for eleven years. Letters-patent were not applied for till March, 1866. In the mean time, the invention had found its way into general, and almost universal, use. A great part of the record is taken up with the testimony of the manufacturers and venders of corset-steels, showing that before he applied for letters the principle of his device was almost universally used in the manufacture of corset-steels. It is fair to presume that having learned from this general use that there was some value in his invention, he attempted to resume, by his application, what by his acts he had clearly dedicated to the public.

"An abandonment of an invention to the public may be evinced by the conduct of the inventor at any time, even within the two years named in the law. The effect of the law is that no such consequence will necessarily follow from the invention being in public use or on sale, with the inventor's consent and allowance, at any time within the two years before his application; but that, if the invention is in public use or on sale prior to that time, it will be conclusive evidence of abandonment, and the patent will be void." Elizabeth v. Pavement Company, supra.

We are of opinion that the defense of two years' public use, by the consent and allowance of the inventor, before he made application for letters-patent, is satisfactorily established by the evidence.

■ MR. JUSTICE MILLER dissenting [omitted.]

Metallizing Engineering Co. v. Kenyon Bearing & Auto Parts Co.

United States Court of Appeals, Second Circuit, 1946.
153 F.2d 516.

■ L. HAND, CIRCUIT JUDGE.

The defendants appeal from the usual decree holding valid and infringed all but three of the claims of a reissued patent, issued to the plaintiff's assignor, Meduna; the original patent issued on May 25, 1943, upon an application filed on August 6, 1942. The patent is for the process of 'so conditioning a metal surface that the same is, as a rule, capable of bonding thereto applied spray metal to a higher degree than is normally procurable with hitherto known practices.'

claim

The only question which we find necessary to decide is as to Meduna's public use of the patented process more than one year before August 6, 1942. The district judge made findings. The kernel of them is the following: "the inventor's main purpose in his use of the process prior to August 6, 1941, and especially in respect to all jobs for owners not known to him, was commercial." Upon this finding he concluded as matter of law that the use was not public but secret, and for that reason that its predominantly commercial character did prevent it from invalidating the patent. For the last he relied upon our decisions in Peerless Roll Leaf Co. v. Griffin & Sons, 29 F.2d 646, and Gillman v. Stern, 114 F.2d 28. We think that his analysis of Peerless Roll Leaf Co. v. Griffin & Sons, was altogether correct, and that he had no alternative but to follow that decision; on the other hand, we now think that we were then wrong and that the decision must be overruled for reasons we shall state. Gillman v. Stern, supra, was, however, rightly decided.

B-Lo

So far as we can find, the first case which dealt with the effect of prior use by the patentee was Pennock v. Dialogue, 2 Pet. 1, 4, 7 L.Ed. 327, in which the invention had been completed in 1811, and the patent granted in 1818 for a process of making hose by which the sections were joined together in such a way that the joints resisted pressure as well as the other parts. It did not appear that the joints in any way disclosed the process; but the patentee, between the discovery of the invention and the grant of the patent, had sold 13,000 feet of hose; and as to this the judge charged: "If the public, with the knowledge and tacit consent of the inventor, be permitted to use the invention, without opposition, it is a fraud on the public afterwards to take out a patent." The Supreme Court affirmed a judgment for the defendant, on the ground that the invention had been "known or used before the application." "If an inventor should be permitted to hold back from the knowledge of the public the secrets of his invention; if he should * * * make and sell his invention publicly, and thus gather the whole profits, * * * it would materially retard the progress of science and the useful arts" to allow him fourteen years of legal monopoly "when the danger of competition should force him to secure the exclusive right" 2 Pet. at page 19, 7 L.Ed. 327. In Shaw v. Cooper, 7 Pet. 292, 8 L.Ed. 689, the public use was not by the inventor, but he had neglected to prevent it after he had learned of it, and this defeated the patent. "Whatever may be the intention of the inventor, if he suffers his invention to go into public use, through any means whatsoever, without an immediate assertion of his right, he is not entitled to a patent" 7 Pet. at page 323, 8 L.Ed. 689.

In the lower courts we may begin with the often cited decision in Macbeth–Evans Glass Co. v. General Electric Co., 6 Cir., 246 F. 695, which concerned a process patent for making illuminating glass. The patentee had kept the process as secret as possible, but for ten years had sold the glass, although this did not, so far as appears, disclose the process. The court held the patent invalid for two reasons, as we understand them: the first was that the delay either indicated an intention to abandon, or was of itself a forfeiture, because of the inconsistency of a practical monopoly by means of secrecy and of a later legal monopoly by means of a patent. So far, it was not an interpretation of 'prior use' in the statute; but, beginning on page 702 of 246 F. 695 Judge Warrington seems to have been construing that phrase and to hold that the sales were such a use.

Coming now to our own decisions (the opinions in all of which I wrote), the first was Grasselli Chemical Co. v. National Aniline & Chemical Co., 2 Cir., 26 F.2d 305, in which the patent was for a process which had been kept secret, but the product had been sold upon the market for more than two years. We held that, although the process could not have been discovered from the product, the sales constituted a 'prior use,' relying upon Egbert v. Lippmann, 104 U.S. 333. There was nothing in this inconsistent with what we are now holding. But in Peerless Roll Leaf Co. v. Griffin & Sons, supra, 2 Cir., 29 F.2d 646, where the patent was for a machine, which had been kept secret, but whose output had been freely sold on the market, we sustained the patent on the ground that "the sale of the product was irrelevant, since no knowledge could possibly be acquired of the machine in that way. In this respect the machine differs from a process * * * or from any other invention necessarily contained in a product" 29 F.2d at page 649. So far as we can now find, there is nothing to support this distinction in the authorities, and we shall try to show that we misapprehended the theory on which the prior use by an inventor forfeits his right to a patent. In Gillman v. Stern, supra, 2 Cir., 114 F.2d 28, it was not the inventor, but a third person who used the machine secretly and sold the product openly, and there was therefore no question either of abandonment or forfeiture by the inventor. The only issue was whether a prior use which did not disclose the invention to the art was within the statute; and it is well settled that it is not. As in the case of any other anticipation, the issue of invention must then be determined by how much the inventor has contributed any new information to the art. Gayler v. Wilder, 10 How. 477, 496, 497, 13 L.Ed. 504; Tilghman v. Proctor, 102 U.S. 707, 711, 26 L.Ed. 279.

From the foregoing it appears that in Peerless Roll Leaf Co. v. Griffin & Sons, supra, 2 Cir., 29 F.2d 646, we confused two separate doctrines: (1) The effect upon his right to a patent of the inventor's competitive exploitation of his machine or of his process; (2) the contribution which a prior use by another person makes to the art. Both do indeed come within the phrase, "prior use"; but the first is a defence for quite different reasons from the second. It had its origin—at least in this country—in the passage we have quoted from Pennock v. Dialogue, supra, 2 Pet. 1, 7 L.Ed. 327; i.e., that it is a condition upon an inventor's right to a patent that he shall not exploit his discovery competitively after it is ready for patenting; he must content himself with either secrecy, or legal monopoly. It is true that for the limited period of two years he was allowed to do so, possibly in order to give him time to prepare an application; and even that has been recently cut down by half. But if he goes beyond that period of probation, he forfeits his right regardless of how little the public may have learned about the invention; just as he can forfeit it by too long concealment, even without exploiting the invention at all. Woodbridge v. United States, 263 U.S. 50, 44 S.Ct. 45, 68 L.Ed. 159; Macbeth–Evans Glass Co. v. General Electric Co., supra, 6 Cir., 246 F. 695. Such a forfeiture has nothing to do with abandonment, which presupposes a deliberate, though not necessarily an express, surrender of any right to a patent. Although the evidence of both may at times overlap, each comes from a quite different legal source: one, from the fact that by renouncing the right the inventor irrevocably surrenders it; the other, from the fiat of Congress that it is part of the consideration for a patent that the public shall as soon as possible begin to enjoy the disclosure.

■ Judgment reversed; complaint dismissed.

UMC Electronics Co. v. United States

United States Court of Appeals, Federal Circuit, 1987.
816 F.2d 647.

■ Nies, Circuit Judge.

UMC Electronics Company brought this action, pursuant to 28 U.S.C. § 1498(a), to recover compensation for use of its patented invention by the United States.

I

Background

The claimed invention is an aviation counting accelerometer (ACA), a device for sensing and for recording the number of times an aircraft has been subjected to predetermined levels of acceleration. The sensor component is mounted on the aircraft in a direction to measure acceleration loading and is connected electrically to the recorder component. Records produced by an ACA can indicate an aircraft's remaining useful life and show the need for structural inspection, overhaul, or rotation to less demanding service.

The patent application which became the patent in this suit ('513) was filed on August 1, 1968. Under 35 U.S.C. § 102(b) the commercial exploitation and the state of development of the invention one year before the filing of the application for the subject invention are critical to resolution of the on-sale issue.

Prior to the late 1960's when UMC first entered this field, the U.S. Navy had procured ACA's from Maxson Electronics Company and from Giannini Controls Corporation. The Navy was dissatisfied with these ACA's because they sometimes recorded data that defied common sense, failed to count accelerations, or counted accelerations that never occurred. In 1966 the Navy contacted Preston Weaver, an employee of UMC, told him of the problems with existing ACA's and informed him of the Navy's interest in buying improved devices. Weaver designed an accelerometer, model UMC–A, and in late 1966, UMC was awarded a contract to supply the Navy with approximately 1600 units.

In early 1967, UMC concluded that its model UMC–A would not meet the Navy's performance specification required by its contract. Like the Maxson and Giannini ACA's, the UMC–A accelerometer utilized, as part of its sensor, an electromechanical transducer to mechanically generate signals that indicate levels of acceleration. Like the Maxson and Giannini devices, the UMC–A device sometimes counted and sometimes did not count the same acceleration load. The problem lay in the inherent frequency of the mass-spring system in the transducer. The devices could not distinguish between acceleration due to inflight maneuvers, which determines actual stress, and acceleration from other sources, e.g., windgusts or weapons release.

To prevent UMC from losing the ACA contract, Weaver began work to improve the sensor portion of an ACA and conceived his invention which uses an analog transducer in the sensor. An analog transducer electrically generates a varying signal (in contrast to the mechanically produced signal of prior devices) which can be filtered electronically to selectively remove the effects of superimposed vibrations. The Claims Court found that in April–May of 1967 Weaver built and tested an engineering prototype of his ACA containing a commercial analog transducer, a filter, a timing circuit and a voltage sensor that measured one load level. UMC sought to modify the existing contract for ACA's to substitute an analog transducer for the electro-mechanical transducer specified in the contract, but was unsuccessful in negotiating a modification.

In late May, 1967, the Navy issued new specifications and in July, 1967, requested proposals from contractors to deliver ACA's built to the new specification (Mil–A–22145B). Technically, the request for proposals called separately for a certain number of sensor components of an ACA system and a certain number of recorders, the two units being compatible in combination. UMC responded to the request on July 27, 1967, the final date for making a proposal, with an offer to supply $1,668,743 worth of its improved ACA (hereinafter model UMC–B). UMC represented as part of its proposal that the sensor portion "has been constructed and tested in conjunction with voltage sensing and time controlled circuitry." In response to a Navy inquiry, on August 2, 1967, after the critical date, UMC submitted a technical proposal which described the model UMC–B in detail and included test results and schematic drawings. On August 9, 1967, UMC gave a demonstration of its device to the Navy at the UMC facility.

In early 1968 the Navy canceled the request to which the above submission of UMC was directed, and in July 1968, it issued another. The latter request eventually led to a contract with Systron–Donner Corporation, which company has been providing the Navy with ACA's utilizing analog transducers since 1970.

In June, 1980, UMC filed the instant action against the United States seeking compensation (after attempting for a number of years to obtain compensation directly from the Navy) by reason of the Navy's alleged use of its invention in the Systron–Donner ACA's. The Claims Court upheld the validity of the patent claims, which were challenged by the government on a number of grounds, but found that the Systron–Donner ACA's did not fall within the scope of the claims. Both parties appeal: UMC asking for reversal of the Claims Court's finding of no infringement; the government seeking to have the claims in suit held invalid. Since we conclude that the Claims Court erred as a matter of law in holding that the claims of the '513 patent were not invalid under section 102(b), we need discuss only that issue in detail.

II

[The court reviews the Claims Court decision, which concluded that since the product was not reduced to practice—no physical embodiment had been built—it could not have been "on sale" within the meaning of § 102(b).]

III

[In the next part of the opinion, the court determines that on the date that UMC purportedly offered the invention to the government, it did not have a complete physical embodiment of the invention.]

Per the government, UMC's substantial attempted commercial exploitation of the claimed invention contravenes the policies of the on-sale bar despite the absence of a complete embodiment and, thus, raises an on-sale bar under section 102(b). For this proposition the government relies on the decision of this court in Barmag Barmer Maschinenfabrik AG v. Murata Mach., Ltd., 731 F.2d 831, 221 U.S.P.Q. 561 (Fed.Cir.1984) ... On the other hand, UMC maintains that, as a matter of law, there is no on-sale bar unless the claimed invention had been reduced to practice before the critical date, and urges that we here reject the contrary suggestion in Barmag. Thus, we address first the issue whether reduction to practice of the claimed invention before the critical date is required to invoke the on-sale bar, and conclude, for reasons that follow, that reduction to practice is not always a requirement of the on-sale bar.[a] This leads to the issue whether there is an on-sale bar in this case. On the undisputed facts, we hold that the invention of the '513 patent was on sale within the meaning of section 102(b).

IV

Whether a reduction to practice is a requirement of the on-sale bar of 35 U.S.C. § 102(b) requires a review of our precedent. However, the issue

[a] The public use bar of section 102(b) implicates different considerations and nothing said here should be construed to encompass that part of the statute.

has been directly addressed by this court or its predecessors in only two cases, Barmag and General Electric Co. v. United States, 654 F.2d 55, 60–61, 211 U.S.P.Q. 867, 872–73 (Ct.Cl.1981)(en banc), although the issue has surfaced in others. In General Electric Co. v. United States, 654 F.2d at 61–64, 211 U.S.P.Q. at 873–75, the Court of Claims, one of this court's predecessors, analyzed an on-sale bar issue by focusing on the policies underlying the bar to determine whether application of the bar would further those policies. Those policies were stated to be:

First, there is a policy against removing inventions from the public which the public has justifiably come to believe are freely available to all as a consequence of prolonged sales activity. Next, there is a policy favoring prompt and widespread disclosure of new inventions to the public. The inventor is forced to file promptly or risk possible forfeiture of his invention [patent] rights due to prior sales. A third policy is to prevent the inventor from commercially exploiting the exclusivity of his invention substantially beyond the statutorily authorized 17–year period. The on-sale bar forces the inventor to choose between seeking patent protection promptly following sales activity or taking his chances with his competitors without the benefit of patent protection. The fourth and final identifiable policy is to give the inventor a reasonable amount of time following sales activity (set by statute as 1 year) to determine whether a patent is a worthwhile investment. This benefits the public because it tends to minimize the filing of inventions [sic] of only marginal public interest. 654 F.2d at 61, 211 U.S.P.Q. at 873 (citations omitted). On the facts of that case, the court held that the policies were violated and that there was a reduction to practice before the critical date. 654 F.2d at 62, 211 U.S.P.Q. at 874. The latter holding obviated the need to agree or disagree with a detailed analysis of the trial judge, who had concluded that reduction to practice was not "indispensable in every case."

In a number of decisions the factual findings leading to the conclusion that there was no on-sale bar appear to be based on the assumption that reduction to practice is required, even though "reduction to practice" is not mentioned in the decision. [The court reviews In re Dybel, 524 F.2d 1393, 187 U.S.P.Q. 593 (CCPA 1975), Shatterproof Glass Corp. v. Libbey–Owens Ford Co., 758 F.2d 613, 622–23, 225 U.S.P.Q. 634, 638–40 (Fed.Cir.), cert. dismissed, 474 U.S. 976, 106 S.Ct. 340, 88 L.Ed.2d 326 (1985), and Great Northern Corp. v. Davis Core & Pad Co., 782 F.2d 159, 164–65, 228 U.S.P.Q. 356, 358 (Fed.Cir.1986), concluding that it had "not squarely address the issue of whether reduction to practice is an indispensable requirement of the on-sale bar."]

The regional circuits that have considered the question have given lip service to a requirement of reduction to practice as part of the on-sale bar. However, when faced with a specific factual situation which appeared to fall within the intent of the statutory bar but did not technically satisfy the requirements for reduction to practice, these courts have stepped back from a rigid application of that requirement. In such cases, in an attempt to shoehorn the reduction to practice concept into the on-sale bar analysis, the courts looked to see whether the invention was "sufficiently" reduced to practice for purposes of the bar. See, e.g., Dart Indus., Inc. v. E.I. DuPont DeNemours & Co., 489 F.2d 1359, 1365, 179 U.S.P.Q. 392, 396 (7th Cir.1973). In this case, the government appears to urge such a position.

Adoption of a "sufficiently" reduced-to-practice requirement is in fact an abandonment of reduction to practice as that term is used in other contexts. This court observed in Barmag, 731 F.2d at 838 n. 6, 221 U.S.P.Q. at 567 n. 6, that our case law does not support a variegated definition of reduction to practice. At this point, we point out that "reduction to practice" is a term of art which developed in connection with interference practice to determine priority of invention between rival claimants. In that context Judge Rich has said: "There are no degrees of reduction to practice; either one has or has not occurred." Wolter v. Belicka, 409 F.2d 255, 262, 161 U.S.P.Q. 335, 340 (CCPA 1969)(Rich, J., dissenting). It can only cause confusion in interference law, with its special technical considerations, and in operation of the on-sale bar, which is guided by entirely different policies, to adopt modifiers in connection with "reduction to practice," whatever the context.

Moreover, since reduction to practice is a term of art under this court's precedent, any specific ruling in one context on whether there is or is not a "reduction to practice" necessarily carries over into the other. For example, a holding here, like the trial court's, that there can be a reduction to practice without an embodiment containing all elements of the claim would have a major unintended impact on interference law. Conversely, by invoking reduction to practice as developed in interference law, an inventor might be able to escape the on-sale bar simply through deft claim draftsmanship.

In view of all of the above considerations, we conclude that reduction to practice of the claimed invention has not been and should not be made an absolute requirement of the on-sale bar.

We hasten to add, however, that we do not intend to sanction attacks on patents on the ground that the inventor or another offered for sale, before the critical date, the mere concept of the invention. Nor should inventors be forced to rush into the Patent and Trademark Office prematurely. On the other hand, we reject UMC's position that as a matter of law no on-sale bar is possible unless the claimed invention has been reduced to practice in the interference sense.

We do not reject "reduction to practice" as an important analytical tool in an on-sale analysis. A holding that there has or has not been a reduction to practice of the claimed invention before the critical date may well determine whether the claimed invention was in fact the subject of the sale or offer to sell or whether a sale was primarily for an experimental purpose. Thus, we simply say here that the on-sale bar does not necessarily turn on whether there was or was not a reduction to practice of the claimed invention. All of the circumstances surrounding the sale or offer to sell, including the stage of development of the invention and the nature of the invention, must be considered and weighed against the policies underlying section 102(b).

The above conclusion does not lend itself to formulation into a set of precise requirements. However, we point out certain critical considerations in the on-sale determination and the respective burdens of proof which have already been established in our precedent. Thus, without question, the challenger has the burden of proving that there was a definite sale or offer to sell more than one year before the application for the subject patent, and that the subject matter of the sale or offer to sell fully anticipated the claimed invention or would have rendered the claimed invention obvious by its addition to the prior art. Cf. D.L. Auld, 714 F.2d at 1150, 219 U.S.P.Q. at 17 (102(b) only). If these facts are established, the patent owner is called upon to come forward with an explanation of the circumstances surrounding what would otherwise appear to be commercialization outside the grace period. See Smith & Griggs Mfg. Co. v. Sprague, 123 U.S. 249, 8 S.Ct. 122, 31 L.Ed. 141 (1887); D.L. Auld, 714 F.2d at 1150, 219 U.S.P.Q. at 17; In re Dybel, 524 F.2d at 1400, 187 U.S.P.Q. at 598, and cases cited therein. The possibilities of such circumstances cannot possibly be enumerated. If the inventor had merely a conception or was working towards development of that conception, it can be said there is not yet any "invention" which could be placed on sale. A sale made because the purchaser was participating in experimental testing creates no on-sale bar. See, e.g., Great Northern, 782 F.2d at 165, 228 U.S.P.Q. at 358.

V

The issue of whether an invention is on sale is a question of law. Barmag, 731 F.2d at 836–37, 221 U.S.P.Q. at 565–66. Because the Claims Court's factual findings are not disputed, and the issue may be resolved by application of the proper rule of law to those findings, we need not remand.

UMC made a definite offer to sell its later patented UMC–B accelerometer to the Navy more than one year prior to the date of the application for the patent in suit. In its bid, UMC specified a price of $404.00 for each sensor component of the ACA and $271.00 for the compatible recorder component. The total contract price was in excess of $1.6 million. This written offer which revealed use of the analog transducer in the ACA was supplied on July 27, 1967. UMC admits that the offer it made was for profit, not to conduct experiments.

UMC's activities evidence, at least prima facie, an attempt to commercialize the invention of the '513 patent by bidding on a large government contract more than one year prior to the filing of the underlying application and thereby to expand the grace period in contravention of the policies underlying the statute.

Countering the prima facie case, UMC offers only the purely technical objection that no complete embodiment of the invention existed at the time of the sale. In this case, that circumstance is unavailing when we look at the realities of the development of this invention. While UMC asserts that its improved ACA required further "development," as evidenced by its seeking a waiver of the liquidated damages provision in the RFP, that fact might weigh in UMC's favor if UMC had sought by convincing evidence to prove that the primary purpose of the sale was for experimental work. However, the contract was not a research and development contract, and UMC admits that the offer it made was for profit, not to conduct experimental work.

We do not attempt here to formulate a standard for determining when something less than a complete embodiment of the invention will suffice under the on-sale bar. However, the development of the subject invention was far beyond a mere conception. Much of the invention was embodied in tangible form. The prior art devices embodied each element of the claimed invention, save one, and that portion was available and had been sufficiently tested to demonstrate to the satisfaction of the inventor that the invention as ultimately claimed would work for its intended purpose. Thus, we conclude from the unchallenged facts with respect to the commercial activities of UMC, coupled with the extent to which the invention was developed, the substantial embodiment of the invention, the testing which was sufficient to satisfy the inventor that his later claimed invention would work, and the nature of the inventor's contribution to the art, that the claimed invention was on sale within the meaning of section 102(b).

Accordingly, we hold all claims of the '513 patent invalid.

■ SMITH, J., dissenting [omitted.]

TP Laboratories, Inc. v. Professional Positioners, Inc.

United States Court of Appeals, Federal Circuit, 1984.
724 F.2d 965.

■ NIES, CIRCUIT JUDGE.

I

Appellant-plaintiff, TP Laboratories, Inc., makes and sells orthodontic supplies and appliances to the dental profession. TP Laboratories is a separate business from the professional practice of the Kesling and Rocke Orthodontic Group (K & R), a group of four orthodontists, Doctors Harold D. Kesling, Robert A. Rocke, Peter C. Kesling and David L. Kesling, but the firms are closely connected. The record before us shows that Dr. Harold Kesling, now deceased, (Kesling), who is the inventor named in the patent in suit, was an officer and one of the owners of TP Laboratories. Dr. Peter Kesling is president. The two businesses share a small building and employ the same office manager.

Kesling conceived and made the first prototype of the invention of the patent in suit in 1956. It was not, however, until February 19, 1962, that Kesling filed a patent application on his invention for which the '820 patent was granted on April 20, 1965. On November 1, 1965, the patent was assigned to TP Laboratories.

The subject matter of the '820 patent is a molded tooth positioning appliance which is to be worn several hours a day by a person undergoing orthodontal treatment. The general type of device is not new. The improvement by Kesling lies in placing wires in the device which fit in the embrasure area between the teeth and keep the appliance in position without the necessity of the patient exerting constant jaw pressure. The wires are referred to as "seating devices," "seating springs," "precision seating springs," "springs," or "metal adjuncts." Because of the shape, as seen below, the invention is also referred to as a tooth positioner with "C's".

The use of tooth positioners with C's in the treatment of three K & R patients during the period 1958–61 led to the issues under 35 U.S.C. § 102(b). It is undisputed that these three devices fell within the language of the '820 claims and no modification of design was made as a consequence of these uses. The evidence which established these uses was found in the patient records of K & R and the underlying facts are not in dispute. Appellant characterizes these uses as secret and/or experimental; appellees urge that they are, as found by the district court, public uses within the meaning of the statute.

The first use of the claimed invention on a patient occurred on August 25, 1958. Orthodontal treatment of this patient (Furst) spanned the time period between February 1958 and April 1964. Use of the device terminated after approximately two months. During discovery, the device itself was produced, having been retained by K & R in the patient's model box. This patient's manibular model from the model box was inscribed "experimental wires." Over the six year period of treatment, this patient was also fitted with other devices, retainers as well as positioners not embraced by the '820 claims.

Another patient (Rumely–Brady) who had begun treatment in August 1958 was supplied with a tooth positioner equipped with C's on November 10, 1959. Entry on the record card of this patient indicates "results fair" on December 18, 1959; "results better" on February 5, 1960, and "results good" on August 1, 1960. Nevertheless, use of the device was discontinued on January 16, 1961, in favor of retainers, because certain spacing irregularities were not being corrected. The same positioner with C's was again prescribed on May 5, 1961, and was used in conjunction with various other devices until at least March of 1962. The patient missed a later scheduled appointment which is the last entry on her card.

A positioner with C's was prescribed for a third patient (Spiers–Elliott) on November 1, 1960. Its use apparently was discontinued about three months later, a different device being mailed to the patient on February 2, 1961. During the treatment of this patient, which spanned the period of time between January 21, 1960, and November 24, 1961, three different positioners were prescribed, only one of which was embraced by the '820 claims.

The initial use in each of the above cases occurred prior to the critical date of February 19, 1961. During the years 1958–60, K & R placed 606 tooth positioners, of which only the three described above were within the claims of '820. In 1961, after the critical date, 28 tooth positioners with C's were prescribed by K & R out of a total of 151.

The above devices were made for the K & R patients by TP, including C's handmade by Kesling. There is no evidence that K & R charged patients specifically for any positioner. With two of the three patients, K & R followed its regular practice of setting a fixed total fee for professional services, which included necessary appliances. One patient (Furst), whose father was a dentist, received free treatment as a professional courtesy.

Sales of the patented device to other orthodontists began in 1966, that is, only after TP's acquisition of the patent. Appellees, Huge and Allessee, had no knowledge of the invention even though employed at TP prior to 1961.

II

A

"The general purpose behind all the [§ 102(b)] bars is to require inventors to assert with due diligence their right to a patent through the prompt filing ... of a patent application." 2 D. Chisum, Patents § 601 (1981 & Supp.1983).

More specifically, courts have discerned a number of factors which must be weighed in applying the statutory bar of § 102(b). Operating against the inventor are the policies of 1) protecting the public in its use of the invention where such use began prior to the filing of the application, 2) encouraging prompt disclosure of new and useful information, 3) discouraging attempts to extend the length of the period of protection by not allowing the inventor to reap the benefits for more than one year prior to the filing of the application. In contrast to these considerations, the public interest is also deemed to be served by allowing an inventor time to perfect his invention, by public testing, if desired, and prepare a patent application.

The district court's consideration of the issue of public use proceeded according to the following two-step analysis: the first step in analyzing PRO's 35 U.S.C. § 102(b) assertion is to determine whether a public use occurred. If a public use is found, then the Court must ascertain whether the use was not a public use under the statute because it was experimental.

As to the first step, the district court reasoned: The evidence in this case clearly establishes use by at least three patients more than one year prior to the application date. Furthermore, these users were "under no limitation, restriction or obligation of secrecy to the inventor." Randolph v. Allis–Chalmers Manufacturing Co., 264 F.2d [533] at 535 [120 U.S.P.Q. at 513]. [T]he claimed invention was not kept secret. It was open to public observation without restriction which is sufficient to constitute "public use."

On the second issue as perceived by the district court, the court placed a heavy burden of proof on the patent owner to prove that the inventor's use had been experimental and expressly found that TP did not carry that "burden." First, the evidence presented does not establish that the patentee was conducting a bona fide experiment. On the contrary, the record shows that the uses were random and poorly monitored. The only records kept by Dr. H. Kesling were the patient records. Furthermore, while the issue of experimentation is in effect a matter of the inventor's intent, in the present case the evidence indicates that his intent was not experimentation. In experimenting on a prior "invention," Dr. H. Kesling kept accurate records of the results of his experiments. In the present case, the records are scanty at best. [Finally,] [t]he delay here was unreasonable because the device proved satisfactory immediately. At least as early as 1960 Dr. Kesling learned that the invention was workable. At that point his time began to run under 35 U.S.C. § 102(b).

We disagree with this analysis and the shift in the burden of proof which led the district court to an erroneous result.

B

It is not public knowledge of his invention that precludes the inventor from obtaining a patent for it, but a public use or sale of it.

The above quotation is from City of Elizabeth v. American Nicholson Pavement Co., 97 U.S. 126, 136, 24 L.Ed. 1000 (1877), which is the starting place for analysis of any case involving experimental use. There, a toll road, built according to the invention of the patent in suit, was in daily use for a period of 6 years before the inventor filed for a patent. In upholding the validity of the patent, the Supreme Court spoke with clarity but through the years the guidelines set forth therein have been obfuscated. Returning to the original, we quote the following passages which are particularly pertinent to our analysis here:

> That the use of the pavement in question was public in one sense cannot be disputed. But can it be said that the invention was in public use? The use of an invention by the inventor himself, or of any other person under his direction, by way of experiment, and in order to bring the invention to perfection, has never been regarded as such a use. Curtis, Patents, sect. 381; Shaw v. Cooper, 7 Pet. 292 [8 L.Ed. 689]. Now, the nature of a street pavement is such that it cannot be experimented upon satisfactorily except on a highway, which is always public. When the subject of invention is a machine, it may be tested and tried in a building, either with or without closed doors. In either case, such use is not a public use, within the meaning of the statute, so long as the inventor is engaged, in good faith, in testing its operation. He may see cause to alter it and improve it, or not. His experiments will reveal the fact whether any and what alterations may be necessary. If durability is one of the qualities to be attained, a long period, perhaps years, may be necessary to enable the inventor to discover whether his purpose is accomplished. And though, during all that period, he may not find that any changes are necessary, yet he may be justly said to be using his machine only by way of experiment; and no one would say that such a use, pursued with a bona fide intent of testing the qualities of the machine, would be a public use, within the meaning of the statute. So long as he does not voluntarily allow others to make it and use it, and so long as it is not on sale for general use, he keeps the invention under his

own control, and does not lose his title to a patent. It would not be necessary, in such a case, that the machine should be put up and used only in the inventor's own shop or premises. He may have it put up and used in the premises of another, and the use may inure to the benefit of the owner of the establishment. Still, if used under the surveillance of the inventor, and for the purpose of enabling him to test the machine, and ascertain whether it will answer the purpose intended, and make such alterations and improvements as experience demonstrates to be necessary, it will still be a mere experimental use, and not a public use, within the meaning of the statute. Whilst the supposed machine is in such experimental use, the public may be incidentally deriving a benefit from it. If it be a grist-mill, or a carding-machine, customers from the surrounding country may enjoy the use of it by having their grain made into flour, or their wool into rolls, and still it will not be in public use, within the meaning of the law. But if the inventor allows his machine to be used by other persons generally, either with or without compensation, or if it is, with his consent, put on sale for such use, then it will be in public use and on public sale, within the meaning of the law. 97 U.S. at 134–35.

In the decision on appeal, the trial court looked for proof of an exception to the public use bar. However, in Elizabeth, the Supreme Court did not refer to "experimental use" as an "exception" to the bar otherwise created by a public use. More precisely, the Court reasoned that, if a use is experimental, even though not secret, "public use" is negated. This difference between "exception" and "negation" is not merely semantic. Under the precedent of this court, the statutory presumption of validity provided in 35 U.S.C. § 282 places the burden of proof upon the party attacking the validity of the patent, and that burden of persuasion does not shift at any time to the patent owner. It is constant and remains throughout the suit on the challenger. As stated in Richdel, Inc. v. Sunspool Corp., 714 F.2d 1573, 1579, 219 U.S.P.Q. 8, 11–12 (Fed.Cir.1983): 35 USC 282 permanently places the burden of proving facts necessary to a conclusion of invalidity on the party asserting such invalidity. Stratoflex, Inc. v. Aeroquip Corp., 713 F.2d 1530, 218 U.S.P.Q. 871 (Fed.Cir.1983); Solder Removal, supra, 582 F.2d [628] at 633, 199 U.S.P.Q. at 133.

Under this analysis, it is incorrect to impose on the patent owner, as the trial court in this case did, the burden of proving that a "public use" was "experimental." These are not two separable issues. It is incorrect to ask: "Was it public use?" and then, "Was it experimental?" Rather, the court is faced with a single issue: Was it public use under § 102(b)?

Thus, the court should have looked at all of the evidence put forth by both parties and should have decided whether the entirety of the evidence led to the conclusion that there had been "public use." This does not mean, of course, that the challenger has the burden of proving that the use is not experimental. Nor does it mean that the patent owner is relieved of explanation. It means that if a prima facie case is made of public use, the patent owner must be able to point to or must come forward with convincing evidence to counter that showing. See Strong v. General Electric Co., 434 F.2d 1042, 1044, 168 U.S.P.Q. 8, 9 (5th Cir.1970). The length of the test period is merely a piece of evidence to add to the evidentiary scale.

The same is true with respect to whether payment is made for the device, whether a user agreed to use secretly, whether records were kept of progress, whether persons other than the inventor conducted the asserted experiments, how many tests were conducted, how long the testing period was in relationship to tests of other similar devices. In other words, a decision on whether there has been a "public use" can only be made upon consideration of the entire surrounding circumstances.

While various objective indicia may be considered in determining whether the use is experimental, the expression by an inventor of his subjective intent to experiment, particularly after institution of litigation, is generally of minimal value.

C

Applying the principles set forth above to this case, that non-secret uses of the device were made prior to the critical date is not in itself dispositive of the issue of whether activity barring a patent under 35 U.S.C. § 102(b) occurred. Minnesota Mining & Manufacturing Co. v. Johnson & Johnson, 179 U.S.P.Q. 216, 220 (N.D.Ill.1973). The fact that the device was not hidden from view may make the use not secret but non-secret use is not ipso facto "public use" activity. City of Elizabeth v. American Nicholson Pavement Co., 97 U.S. at 136. Nor, it must be added, is all secret use ipso facto not "public use" within the meaning of the statute, if the inventor is making commercial use of the invention under circumstances which preserve its secrecy.

Turning to the instant case, we note first that disclosure of the seating device to patients could not be avoided in any testing. In some circumstances, no doubt it would be significant that no pledge of confidentiality was obtained from the user. In the circumstances of use by orthodontal patients, we attach no importance to the fact that the doctor did not ask a patient to swear to secrecy. As in City of Elizabeth, testing of the device had to be public to some extent and it is beyond reasonable probability that a patient would show the device to others who would understand the function of the C's or would want to duplicate the device. One is all that is needed and, if lost or broken, the patient would expect it to be replaced by the treating dentist.

In any event, a pledge of confidentiality is indicative of the inventor's continued control which here is established inherently by the dentist-patient relationship of the parties. Nothing in the inventor's use of the device on his patients (or the transfer to them) is inconsistent with experimentation. Similarly, the routine checking of patients by one of the other K & R orthodontists does not indicate the inventor's lack of control or abandonment to the public.

Secondly, the finding is clearly erroneous that the invention "proved satisfactory immediately," or "by April of 1959." In this connection, it is noted that the '820 patent itself describes a utility of the patented device for correcting orthodontal irregularities as "urging teeth into preselected positions." The patient records discussed above indicate that treatment to correct such orthodontal irregularities can range from two to six years. Moreover, while results appeared to be good within six months use by one patient, the variable of patient cooperation cannot be checked by one patient alone. Use on three patients is not an obviously excessive number. In other words, the test for success of the improvement was not whether it could be used at all, but whether it could be said to work better on patients than a positioner without C's. Again, as in City of Elizabeth, the test of necessity had to run for a considerable time and on several patients before the inventor could know whether "it was what he claimed it to be" and would "answer the purpose intended."

A factor in favor of the patentee is that during this critical time the inventor had readily available all of the facilities of TP to commercially exploit the device. Yet, no positioners with C's were offered competing orthodontists despite the fact this was one facet of the inventor's total business activity. Further, the inventor made no extra charge for fitting the three patients with the improved positioners although that in itself is not critical. The facts here indicate the inventor was testing the device, not the market. No commercial exploitation having been made to even a small degree prior to filing the patent application, the underlying policy of prohibiting an extension of the term is clearly not offended in this respect.

Indeed, none of the policies which underlie the public use bar and which, in effect, define it have been shown to be violated. At most, the record shows that the uses were not secret, but when the evidence as to the facts of use by the inventor is considered as a whole, we conclude that appellees failed to prove that the inventor made a public use of the subject invention within the meaning of 35 U.S.C. § 102(b). The patent may not be held invalid on this ground.

NOTES

1. *The § 102(b) inquiry.* The principal cases deal mainly with the statutory bar of § 102(b)—that is, with the argument that the patent should not issue because one of the activities enumerated in this provision occurred more than a year before the applicant filed for a patent. The analysis looks at the same three issues examined in the novelty section: contents, accessibility, and dates. However, each of these prongs is evaluated quite differently, for the policies underlying novelty and bar differ in important respects.

   a.   *Contents.* What must a reference teach in order to act as a bar? For novelty, where the issue was whether the inventor had made a new contribution to the storehouse of knowledge, the analysis looked at whether the public was able to practice the invention from the information in the prior art—enablement. Here, however, the focus is on the inventor and whether she waited too long. For that purpose, the prior art does not necessarily have to reveal every element of the claimed invention. Consider first the case in which the inventor was herself responsible for the prior art. She does not need enabling information to know that she ought to be applying for the patent—she already has the ability to practice the invention. Accordingly, enablement is not necessary in cases like *Egbert,* where the inventor created the prior art.

Now consider the situation where the prior art belonged to another. If it fully reveals the invention, once again the inventor should know that the time to apply for a patent has arrived (or, will arrive within the year). What if the contents do not reveal the entire invention? This issue was considered in In re Foster.[3] The application on the invention, a rubber-like polymer, had been filed on August 21, 1956. The examiner found a reference partly revealing this polymer dated August 1954 (which, as we saw in Assignment 18, precedes the date the PTO takes as the date of invention). Since the invention would, per § 103, have been considered obvious in light of this reference, the applicant needed to establish an earlier date of invention. A Rule 131 affidavit was filed establishing an invention date of December 16, 1952. Since invention now predated this disclosure, the patent could not be denied on the ground that the invention was obvious when made. Still, the court viewed the claim as rather stale. Citing § 102(b), it stated:

> "[S]ince the purpose of the statute has always been to require filing of the application within the prescribed period after the time the public came into possession of the invention, we cannot see that it makes any difference how it came into such possession, whether by a public use, a sale, a single patent or publication, or by combinations of one or more of the foregoing. In considering this principle, we assume, of course, that by these means the invention has become obvious to that segment of the 'public' having ordinary skill in the art. Once this has happened, the purpose of the law is to give the inventor only a year within which to file and this would seem to be liberal treatment."[4]

Foster-type rejections—so called "§ 102(b)/103" rejections—have been affirmed as valid by the CAFC with regard to prior art of the type involved in *Foster.*[5] Section 102(b)/103 has not, however, been used in connection with any types of prior art other than patents and printed publications.[6] To put this another way, *Foster*'s version of the statutory bar applies to applications on inventions that are obvious from patents and publications more than year before the filing date.

---

[3] 343 F.2d 980 (C.C.P.A.1965).

[4] Id. at 988.

[5] Indeed, in a portion of the UMC opinion not reproduced in text, the court claimed that another reason to reject reduction to practice as a criterion for "on sale" is that if reduction were required, there could not be § 102(b)/103 rejections: an invention that is barred as obvious from a combination of references is not an invention that has ever been built.

[6] D. Chisum, Patents, § 5.03[2], citing In re Ownby, 471 F.2d 1233, 1236 (C.C.P.A.), cert. denied, 412 U.S. 950, 93 S.Ct. 3013, 37 L.Ed.2d 1002 (1973). Further, there appears to be no such thing as a § 102(e)/102(b) rejection (for inventions revealed in an application pending more than a year before this inventor's application was filed), or a § 102(g)/102(b) rejection (for inventions revealed in a discovery by another in the United States more than a year before the application, and not abandoned.)

b. *Accessibility*. As in § 102(a), this provision also distinguishes between activities occurring in the United States and abroad. Use or sale will bar a patent only if it took place in the United States, whereas patents and printed publications are effective as bars no matter where in the world they occurred. At this point, however, the similarity between these provisions ends, for despite the fact that only § 102(b) uses the word "public," *less publicity is required to raise a statutory bar than to run afoul of the novelty provisions.* As *UMC* makes clear, since the question for loss of right is what the *applicant* knew and enjoyed, it makes no difference that the *public* may never have seen an embodiment of the invention. Thus, the modesty of Ms. Barnes was quite irrelevant to the question whether her use barred Egbert's patent.

At the same time, however, it is important to note that there is a surviving doctrine of "noninforming public uses" that do not create statutory bars. For example, in Gillman v. Stern,[7] the patent on a new quilt-puffing machine was issued despite the fact that the output of a similar machine was sold by a third party for longer than the statutory period, the theory being that the quilts that were sold did not reveal the machine itself. Similarly, in W.L. Gore & Assoc. v. Garlock,[8] a patent issued on a method for stretching teflon to make the thread from which Gortex is manufactured, despite the fact that a tape using the thread, and a machine for making the tape, had been sold by someone other than the patentee for too long. Once again, the court reasoned that the thread and the machine had not revealed the process for making the thread. These cases are difficult to square with the general trend in § 102(b) cases to ignore enablement as a criterion for barring a patent. Furthermore, the results in these cases frustrate the interests of the people who were selling the noninforming products. If the second inventor's patent is not barred by § 102(b), they become infringers. This issue is explored further in Note 2, below.

c. *Dating invention*. Notice that the critical date is different for 102(b) than for novelty. For novelty, the critical date is the date of invention; for § 102(b), it is one year preceding the date of application. The effective date of a patent or publication remains the same. The result is to put a limit on the use of Rule 131 affidavits. An inventor can "swear behind" a reference, but if the effective date of the reference is more than a year before the filing, swearing behind will not help: the patent will be barred by § 102(b).

2. *Third-party art*. Since § 102(b) is mainly intended to encourage inventors to apply for patents and to punish them for enjoying exclusive benefits in the invention for more than the statutory term, application of § 102(b) to prior articles, patents, and activities *of the inventor* makes sense, as does the lower level of dissemination and enablement required. However, under this approach, it seems curious to apply § 102(b) to the actions of parties other than the inventor. Commercial use of an invention by another does not implicate the applicant; he did not try to extend his rights beyond the

---

[7] 114 F.2d 28 (2d Cir.1940)(analyzed as a § 102(g) case).

[8] 721 F.2d 1540 (Fed.Cir.1983).

term chosen by Congress, nor did he sit on his rights. If the other party's use is not publicly accessible, the applicant may not even have known that the grace period had begun.[9]

As is clear from *Metallizing Engineering*, Learned Hand would have drafted a much better statute. He would have distinguished between uses by the inventor and uses by third parties. He also would have drawn a distinction between informing and noninforming uses. In Hand's view, any use by the applicant, whether informing or not, should bar the issuance of the patent. Since the inventor knows what he invented and also what he is using the invention for, he needs no further information to realize that the time has come to file for the patent. Besides, why should the public's lack of knowledge save an inventor who is trying to extend the statutory term?

But third party uses can be a different matter. If the inventor knows a third party has begun to disseminate the information, he can rush right off to the PTO. As long as he applies within a year of this use, his patent will be granted. However, if the third party's use is noninforming, as in the case with the quilt and the Gortex thread described in Note 1(b), there is nothing to warn the first inventor. Therefore, he is in no way deficient for delaying his application and, in Hand's view, there is no reason to bar his patent.

From the public's point of view, the Hand approach also seems right. Although the principal thrust of § 102(b) is directed at the inventor, § 102(b) also protects the public domain, that is, the public's right to rely on the free availability of inventions that are known to the public (for more than a year) and not claimed. Informing public uses will always trigger this interest. Utilization of an invention for more than a year in a manner that enables others to learn how it works essentially "gives" the public the invention—puts it into the domain of public knowledge. But noninforming public uses do not do this: even if the invention is widely disseminated, no one can reverse engineer it or rely on its free availability. Thus, noninforming public uses do not jeopardize the public domain interest protected by § 102(b). Since, as the previous paragraph showed, third party uses also do not jeopardize the interest in regulating the inventor, Hand's formulation has a great deal to recommend it. Do you see any disadvantages? (Look at all of this from the point of view of the third-party himself).

3. *Market vs. development testing.* TP Labs and its germinal case, *Elizabeth Paving,* create the so-called experimental use exception to § 102(b). Both involved experiments intended to perfect the product that was the subject of the patent application. Innovative firms also engage in another type of experimentation: market testing. This research looks at how the product will be used by end-users and is intended to improve its user-friendliness, determine the proper positioning and pricing of the product in the market, and develop advertising strategies that will help consumers

---

[9] For an especially egregious decision, see Lorenz v. Colgate–Palmolive–Peet Co., 167 F.2d 423 (3d Cir.1948), holding an applicant barred by the activity of a party who stole the invention from him.

understand how the product will benefit them. Should this form of testing receive the benefit of the exception?

On the one hand, the objective of the patent laws is to produce products people can use. This testing is as important to useability as development testing. Furthermore, the law is intended to provide the inventor with approximately 20 years in which to earn a profit. This testing puts the inventor (or her successors in interest) in a position to begin to earn that profit on the day the patent issues. On the other hand, such testing has little to do with the inventive concept; it does not advance science or technology. Thus, it is no surprise that the courts have refused to give market research the benefit of the experimental use exception.[10]

4. *Pre-market clearance.* Some products are subject to federal or state requirements that manufacturers receive clearance before their products are put on the market. In the case of drugs, for example, the Federal Food and Drug Administration requires tests demonstrating safety and efficacy. Complying with these requirements can take a long time, yet § 102(b) appears to require an early filing. The result is that the owners of patents in areas requiring clearance may have less than the statutory period in which to recoup their costs. In the drug field, Congress has from time to time enacted private bills to extend rights on drugs that were subject to long delays in the FDA.[11] The Patent Act also contains provisions for extending or restoring patent terms in the case of certain products subject to regulatory review, see §§ 155–56.[12]

5. *Sections 102(c) and (d).* The other statutory bars are not the subject of significant amounts of litigation.

a. *Section 102(c).* A much-cited case on abandonment is Macbeth–Evans Glass Co. v. General Electric Co.,[13] which is described in *Metallizing Engineering*. The invention was a "method ... for making glass for illuminating purposes such as in electric and other shades and globes." The applicant, Macbeth, had perfected the method in 1903 and began selling the glass immediately, keeping the method of manufacture secret. However, in May 1910, one of his employees quit. This employee then sold his knowledge to what later became GE. On May 9, 1913, Macbeth applied for a patent. The court held that Macbeth's actions in using the invention without benefit of a patent manifested an intent to forgo the right to a patent—to effectuate an abandonment to the public domain. According to the court, patent rights and trade secret rights are inconsistent in that the former rewards the inventor for revealing the invention to the public, while the latter hides the invention from the public. One can choose one or the

---

[10] See, e.g., In re Smith, 714 F.2d 1127 (Fed.Cir.1983)(market testing of carpet deodorizer).

[11] See, e.g., S. Rep. 102–414, 102d Cong., 2d Sess. 1992 (Report on S 526, 1165, and 1506, to extend the patent term of the drugs Ethiofos and Ansaid, and the food additive, Olestra, respectively.)

[12] As a result of the legislation conforming U.S. patent law to the GATT, § 154 was amended to include a new term-extension provision.

[13] 246 Fed. 695 (6th Cir.1917).

other, not both. The court also noted the term-expanding effect of what Macbeth had tried to do.

Two questions are raised by § 102(c). First, why is it so rarely used? The answer is that current understanding of the publicity requirement of § 102(b) makes subsection (c) largely superfluous. Almost any action that gives rise to an inference of abandonment also triggers § 102(b).[14] The only exceptions are acts of abandonment that occur within a year of filing. Because there is no grace period under subsection (c), patents in such cases would be barred under (c), but not (b). However, abandonment is usually an inference based on action.[15] Unless the action goes on for some time— probably longer than a year, the inference cannot be drawn. Thus, the only pure abandonment cases are ones in which the inventor expressly states an intent to donate the invention to the public and changes his mind within the year—not a common occurrence.

The second question is what is the difference between abandonment in § 102(g) and § 102(c)? Section 102(c) is concerned with abandoning the *right to a patent*, for instance, keeping it as a trade secret (Macbeth is an example). Section 102(g) is about abandoning the *invention*, for example, putting it in the bottom drawer of a desk.

b. *Section 102(d)*. Section 102(d) is aimed at encouraging foreign inventors to patent their inventions in the United States. It is difficult to apply for protection in several countries simultaneously. Each country examines applications under its own law, charges a fee, and many will review only applications written in the official language of the country. Compliance is costly, and the applicant may not want to incur these costs until commercial value is assured. At the same time, the United States created patent law in order to encourage dissemination of advances to its own citizens. Inventors who disseminate only abroad are ignoring this interest and may even put the United States in a competitively inferior position.

Section 102(d) attempts to find a comfortable middle position between forcing people to invest in a U.S. patent before they are ready and allowing them to impose on Americans the costs of delay. It bars a patent on an invention for which a patent was applied for abroad under the authority of the U.S. applicant, but only if the foreign application is filed more than a year before the U.S. application is filed and only in the event that the foreign patent issues before the U.S. patent issues. In other words, two things are required to trigger § 102(d): first, a foreign filing more than a year before the U.S. filing; second, foreign issuance before U.S. issuance.

Why is § 102(d) used infrequently? Delays in foreign patent offices are as rampant as delays in the PTO. Unless the foreign application is filed a very long time before the U.S. application, it is not likely to issue before the

---

[14] For example, if *Macbeth-Evans* arose today, it would probably be analyzed under § 102(b). As Notes 1(b) and 2 made clear, the fact that the glass does not enable the process for making it is not likely to be relevant, especially since the sale was by the inventor rather than a third-party.

[15] Cf. Part B of Assignment 4.

PTO is ready to issue the U.S. patent. Furthermore, the bar is easy to avoid. All one has to do is file in the U.S. within a year of the foreign filing. Finally, § 102(d) is generally interpreted as requiring that the U.S. and foreign applications claim identical inventions.[16] The occasional applicant who misses the filing date may be able to avoid subsection (d) by carefully drafting the U.S. claims so they are not identical to the foreign claims.

BIBLIOGRAPHY

Carstens and Nard, Conception and the "On Sale" Bar, 34 Wm. & Mary L.Rev. 393 (1993); Vick, Publish and Perish: The Printed Publication as a Bar to Patentability, 18 AIPLA Q.J. 235 (1990); Rooklidge, Application of the On–Sale Bar to Activities Performed Before Reduction to Practice, 72 J.Pat.Off. Soc'y 543 (1990); West & Linck, The Law of "Public Use" and "On Sale": Past, Present and Future, 72 J.Pat.Off. Soc'y 114 (1990); Eisenberg, Patents and the Progress of Science: Exclusive Rights and Experimental Use, 56 U.Chi.L.Rev. 1017, 1024 (1989); Pitlick, "On Sale" Activities of an Independent Third Party Inventor, Or—Whose Widget Is It?, 64 J.Pat.Off. Soc'y 138, 140–41 (1982); David, The University–Academic Connection in Research: Corporate Purposes and Social Responsibilities, 84 J.Pat.Off. Soc'y 209, 211 (1982); G.T. Welch, Patent Law's Ephemeral Experimental Use Doctrine, 11 Tol.L.Rev. 865–92 (1980); Chisum, Foreign Activity: Its Effect On Patentability Under United States Law, 11 Int'l Rev.Indus.Prop. & Copyright L. 26 (1980); Wells & Riggins, Public Use and Sale as a Bar to Obtaining a Patent and Its Application to Government Activities, 18 Am.U.L.Rev. 43, 51–57 (1968); Pigott, The Concepts of Public Use and Sale, 49 J.Pat.Off. Soc'y 399, 411–26 (1967); Vassil, Public Use; The Inventor's Dilemma, 36 Geo.Wash.L.Rev. 297 (1958).

---

[16] See, e.g., General Electric Co. v. Alexander, 280 Fed. 852 (2d Cir.1922)(decided under the predecessor of sec. 102(d)).

PRIORITY

1. INTRODUCTION

A patent is a genuinely exclusive right: only one patent will be awarded for any given invention. Since it is sometimes the case that more than one entity independently invents the same invention, the patent system needs a priority rule to determine which inventor is entitled to the patent. The primary function of § 102(g) is to set out this rule. It establishes a modified "first to invent" system under which the first party to invent the invention receives the patent, unless that entity engages in certain disqualifying acts.

What are the disqualifying acts? Abandonment, suppression or concealment are the simple cases: as between someone who quickly brings his invention to the PTO for dissemination and someone who allows it to languish on a back burner, the law prefers the party who is eager. But the statute also creates a more intricate form of disqualification, a form that takes into account the complex nature of invention. This test breaks the inventive act into three steps: conception (i.e. thinking up the new idea), diligence (i.e. industrious experimentation), and reduction to practice (i.e. creating a physical rendition that works). Of these steps, conception is the most valued. Accordingly, the first inventor to conceive the invention is the one who generally wins the patent race. But the statute recognizes that the public cannot do very much with raw ideas; benefits flow mainly from the working rendition. Accordingly, if the first to conceive does not reduce to practice first, the statute looks into the cause of the delay. If it is lack of diligence, defined as failure to work on the concept from just before the second inventor conceived it, then the first to conceive is disqualified, and the second inventor—the first to reduce to practice—gets the patent.

This is a complicated rule. Hopefully, it will become clearer after the Problem and Cases are analyzed. To begin, it is helpful to think about why simpler rules were rejected. The statute could create an absolute first-to-invent rule. But as the previous paragraph indicates, awarding strictly according to the time of conception would divest the system of the ability to motivate inventors to translate their ideas into viable applications. Thus, the statute needs to include a role for reduction to practice.

Of course, reduction could have the starring role. There would be much more motivation to reduce quickly if reduction were the sole criterion of priority. Indeed, almost the entire patent world uses a simple variant of a reduction-based rule by awarding the patent to the first to file the patent application.[1] The United States's unique position is usually explained by reference to the high respect paid here to the small inventor, who is regarded as a principal source of American ingenuity. Since the small inventor could never outcompete a major research corporation in preparing the patent application, it has always been considered inequitable to have the race turn solely on reduction to practice or on its substitute, filing.

Moreover, there may be such a thing as inventing too soon. Some ideas may be difficult to bring to fruition when first conceived, but become easier to utilize after collateral developments are made. In such instances, it would waste resources to "encourage" the inventor to make a working model quickly—a phenomenon economists call "dissipation of rents." On this theory, a priority test based exclusively on reduction to practice can be viewed as unwise.[2] The result is a test that takes both conception and reduction to practice into account and links them through a requirement of diligence.

But why is diligence required only from the time that the second inventor enters the picture—why not require diligence from the time of conception? Again, the reason may have to do with rent dissipation: there is no point in requiring the first inventor to incur the costs of diligence if a later collateral development makes his work superfluous. Of course, the statute could demand diligence from the time that working hard becomes cost-effective, but that rule would be difficult to administer since it would require resolution of complex factual questions. Requiring diligence from the time another inventor enters the race is, however, a good proxy for cost-effective diligence. The entry of others into a field is some indication that others consider the area ripe for development. Hence, the complicated priority rule of § 102(g).

Priority disputes are resolved within the PTO under its interferences procedure, which is described in Note 5, infra.

2.   PRINCIPAL PROBLEM

In 1975, M. Palin, an amateur train buff living in Massachusetts, discovered a device that, when mounted on the last car in a train, stabilizes

concept 1

---

[1] England, for example, uses such a system, see Patents Act, 1977, ch. 37, s. 5(1)(Eng.).

[2] See, e.g., Barzel, Optimal Timing of Innovations, 50 Rev. Econ. & Stat. 348 (1968). The gasoline-powered internal combustion engine, which was conceived in 1879 and awarded a patent in 1895, may be an example of an invention that was delayed in order to take advantage of collateral developments, see Electric Vehicle Co. v. C.A. Duerr & Co., 172 Fed. 923, 935 (S.D.N.Y.1909)("Selden did not overstep the law. He did delay. He was not in a hurry. He could not get any one to back him, and doubtless appreciated that, if he was ahead of the times, it was wise not to let his patent get ahead, too. If he had gotten his grant in 1880, without a moneyed backer, the patent might and probably would have expired, or nearly so, before any one saw its possibilities; and, if the business world had seen them within 17 years, that term would then so nearly have expired that Selden would never have been able to get to final hearing before it ran out. At best, an accounting and not an injunction would have been his lot. The difference he may well have considered as a lawyer, and personally I believe he did think of it.").

its motion. Traditionally, railroads use cabooses for this purpose, but cabooses weigh a great deal and their shape makes them unsuitable for carrying any sort of load. Experimenting on a miniature train set of his own construction, Palin quickly realized that his device made the use of cabooses unnecessary. But since he liked their look, he decided not to notify any railroad companies of his new discovery.

Concept 2

By the late 1980s, railroads found themselves locked in such keen competition with trucking companies that it became imperative to search for more economical ways of running trains. On February 1, 1991, Edward (Ned) Kelly, an individual who, at varying times in his checkered and highly successful career had worked with various railway companies, formulated the idea of a device that, when mounted on the end of a train instead of the caboose, would stabilize the train enough so that it would be unnecessary to use a caboose. A week later, Kelly drew his girlfriend a diagram of the invention to explain why he spent all his time playing around in the basement workroom of his Virginia home. He worked on the invention off and on, but on the first weekend in June, he married his friend and went on a long honeymoon. When he returned, he realized he didn't know enough about making machines to construct his device. On January 2, 1992, he hired a machinist who manufactured the device immediately. Kelly quickly engaged an attorney to prepare a patent application, but the lawyer was not convinced the device worked or was worth the cost of patenting. She spent several months urging Kelly to try it out, and then some more time was spent convincing a railway to overcome their past, very bad, experiences with Kelly and work with him. A small railroad finally cooperated, and the device was tried on February 1, 1993 by mounting it to the end of a caboose. With some substantial fiddling, it worked as predicted on its second run, and the patent application was filed the next day.

≈ 1 yr delay

RTP 2

Concept 3

Meanwhile, work on similar fronts was afoot at other locations. During the summer of 1991, Professor Dina Wontchablow, a mechanical engineering professor at Kitchen University, in Kitchen, Texas had the idea for something she called the "Stabilitator." However, she was in the middle of another project, one that she needed to finish in order to apply for tenure. On June 15, 1991, she made an entry in her laboratory notebook explaining, from the theoretical perspective, how the idea would work, and went back to her other research. Even after her tenure was granted in October, 1991 she put off working on the Stabilitator, first to take a well-earned vacation, and second, because Kitchen U. gives tenured professors support to hire a masters degree student, and Wontchablow thought someone would really enjoy this subject. In the spring semester beginning January 10, 1992, someone did sign up to work under her supervision, and Wontchablow's assessment proved correct. The graduate student succeeded in building a prototype by the end of the semester. Over the summer, the model was tested by a railroad owned by an alumna of Kitchen University, and the patent application was prepared by a patent law professor at Kitchen University Law School and filed on January 2, 1993.

Then there is Watty Piper, owner of a single-engine train company that specializes in carrying donated toys from Knoxville to Appalachian mountain children. Piper's caboose was old and malfunctioned in a storm on January 5, 1992. While struggling with the caboose during the storm, Piper envisioned a stabilizing device that would perform much better. He worked like a man possessed, muttering "I think I can, I think I can" as he slaved away in his machine shop. By March he had substituted his new device for the old caboose. As the good little children of Appalachia soon knew, it worked just fine, and Piper immediately contacted a patent attorney. The attorney did not take Piper very seriously, and put off work on the application until June. He finally got around to working on it that fall, and, after asking Piper to conduct some additional tests, and working through several drafts of the application, managed to file it on March 1, 1993.

All three applications were presented to the same examiner, who immediately declared an interference. A story about the interference was published in the June, 1993 Railroad Engineering News, M. Palin's favorite magazine. Seeing that cabooses would soon be a thing of the past anyway, Palin decided that he might as well benefit from his discovery. He filed a patent application on his invention that same July.

QUESTION: To whom should the patent be awarded?

3.   MATERIALS FOR SOLUTION OF PRINCIPAL PROBLEM

A.   STATUTORY MATERIAL: § 102(g)

B.   CASES:

Townsend v. Smith

Court of Customs and Patent Appeals, 1929.
36 F.2d 292.

■ GRAHAM, PRESIDING JUDGE.

Harry P. Townsend, the appellant, presented his application to the Patent Office on January 13, 1922, praying that a patent might be issued to him on improvements in machines for cutting multiple threads on wood screws. On December 8, 1924, an interference proceeding was instituted and declared between his application and a patent issued to one Henry L. Smith, the appellee, No. 1,452,986, granted April 24, 1923, for a similar invention.

The sole question at issue in this case is the question of priority as between the appellant and appellee. Townsend claims to have conceived the idea of his invention on or about June 1, 1921. The Examiner of Interferences found that he had done so, while the Board of Examiners in Chief and the Commissioner of Patents, respectively, held that he had not proved such conception by such clear and convincing evidence as is required in such cases.

As both applications were co-pending at the time of the inadvertent issuance of the patent to appellee, and as but a short time intervened between the respective dates of application, the burden upon the appellant to prove prior conception is slight, and it is sufficient if he establish his case by a mere preponderance of the evidence. Having this rule, which we consider to be a reasonable one, in mind, we have examined the record carefully to ascertain what the facts are in this regard.

Townsend testifies that, while building wood screw threaders for the Ewing Bolt & Screw Company, on or about June 1, 1921, there was trouble with one of his screw threading machines. Townsend was an experienced builder of such machines, and understood them thoroughly at that time. He states that one of the gears had been cut with the wrong number of teeth, with the result that the threading tool, on the moment of initiating each cut on the screw blank, did not start in the same spot that it formerly did, and made a new mark each time the tool passed over the screw. He conceived the idea at the time, and mentioned it to the workmen around him, that this was the way to make a double threaded screw. At that time he was well acquainted with the Caldwell invention of double threaded wood screws. He says he explained it to two workmen, Pond and Clark, but that these men did not recollect it, except Clark recollected that some of the gears were cut wrong. He changed the machine at that time, putting on another gear, after which it cut single threaded screws, as it should have. He states that he thought nothing more about it until October 21, 1921, when he visited Smith and Caldwell at Providence, in answer to a letter informing him that they were interested in a machine for cutting a double threaded screw. He then promised them he would change one of his single threaded wood screw machines, which he was building for a Japanese order, and make it into a double threaded screw machine; that he did this on or about the 10th or 11th of November, 1921, and wrote to Swift November 14th to come and see the machine. On the same day he wrote out the details of his invention for his attorney, for the purpose of making application for a patent. On November 21st the machine was demonstrated, and was afterwards changed back to a single thread machine and shipped to Japan on November 30, 1921.

It is said by the Board of Examiners in Chief and the Commissioner that this testimony lacks corroboration of any kind. Townsend testifies that he did not know that a man by the name of Oscar J. Reeves had witnessed his occurrence of June 1st until about six weeks before the time of the hearing in May, 1925, but that Reeves, at that time, told him he had been present. The Board of Examiners in Chief and the Commissioner both reject the testimony of Reeves on the ground that it is not in harmony with Townsend's testimony, and is not to be relied upon as corroborative. Reeves is not related to either of the parties, and has no interest in the result of the proceeding. He testifies he was not well, and, in order to put in the time, on frequent occasions visited Townsend's shop where he was much interested in the operation of automatic machinery; that some time before June 17, 1921, which date he fixes by the fact that a short time thereafter he purchased a car and went to the country for his health, staying all summer, he was in Townsend's shop, and Townsend and his helpers were having trouble with a screw threading machine; that they had a wrong set of gearing in the machine which caused it to cut a double thread screw instead of a single thread; that Townsend made adjustments on the machine, and explained each adjustment to those about the machine; that he said at that time the trouble was caused by a wrong set of gears in the machine; that he explained to the men the changes he would have to make on the machine before it was ready for shipment, and so adjusted it that it worked before the witness left, making a single threaded screw after adjustment. Reeves testified, on being shown the drawings, that the adjustments were made on gears No. 42 and No. 43, which are the gears involved in the issue before us. On cross-examination he stated that double threaded screws were made with the machine, at that time, before the gears were changed, and that some of these were distributed among the bystanders.

It is said that, because Reeves goes further in this matter than Townsend, and states that double threaded screws were actually made and distributed at that time, that he must be in error; that his testimony is in conflict with that of Townsend in this respect; and that therefore it should be rejected as corroboration.

The rule is well settled in this jurisdiction as to what is required to constitute a conception and disclosure of an invention. It is well stated in Mergenthaler v. Scudder, 11 App.D.C. 264. A complete conception as defined in an issue of priority of invention is a matter of fact, and must be clearly established by proof. The conception of the invention consists in the complete performance of the mental part of the inventive art. All that remains to be accomplished in order to perfect the act or instrument belongs to the department of construction, not invention. It is therefore the formation in the mind of the inventor of a definite and permanent idea of the complete and operative invention as it is thereafter to be applied in practice that constitutes an available conception within the meaning of the patent laws. A priority of conception is established when the invention is made sufficiently plain to enable those skilled in the art to understand it.

Does the alleged conception and disclosure of Townsend, in June, meet these requirements? We are inclined to the belief that it does. It will be remembered that Townsend, accidentally, it is true, had before him, at the time he claims to have conceived the invention, a machine which was actually cutting the threads upon the screw blank in the same manner as the final invention. The only thing required to change the single thread screw machine to a double thread screw machine was the change in gears, which was already an accomplished fact by the error that had occurred. There can be no doubt that Townsend, and those about him, understood perfectly, at that time, just how such a machine could be constructed. This is not such a case as arises when an alleged inventor mentally conceives of some invention and makes an oral disclosure to another, which disclosure may or may not be complete. Here the parties had a complete working model, and there was nothing left to the imagination. The demonstration and disclosure were complete. We can see no reason for discarding the testimony of Reeves on the theory that he testifies screws were made and distributed, while Townsend does not. Townsend did not deny that this happened, nor did any one else. The fact that Reeves went further than Townsend in this regard is not a sufficient fact upon which we should conclude that he committed perjury or was totally mistaken in all that he said.

Another circumstance which leads us to believe Townsend's story has foundation is the fact that, when he was finally called upon to construct a machine on the Swift and Caldwell order, Townsend disclosed fully to those men just how he proposed to make the machine. He went to his shop, according to the testimony of Clark, and informed him that he wanted to set up one of the machines in the shop to cut a double thread; that thereupon the witness Clark and Townsend, "simply took the machine we had, cut a new cam, changed the gears, and cut a double thread on our regular machine." This was but a few days after his interview with Swift and Caldwell, and at this time the idea was so well developed in Townsend's mind that there were no preliminary difficulties in the preparation of the double threaded screw machine. In Townsend's explanation to Swift, according to the testimony of the witness, John W. Caldwell, Townsend was definite and clear as to the method of converting one of his own machines for this purpose.

For these reasons we conclude that the Examiner of Interference correctly held that Townsend had established conception of this invention in June, 1921. It is agreed that Townsend reduced to practice on November 14, 1921, when he prepared and operated his machine. It is held by all the tribunals in the Patent Office that appellee, Smith, conceived the invention on the 19th or 20th of October, 1921. Appellee does not insist upon any earlier date. Whether this was the exact date of conception we are not now called upon to say, in view of our conclusion in the matter generally. After Smith's conception, no question is raised as to his diligence. He made the necessary drawings and started construction of his machine. According to the preliminary statement in this interference, the appellee, Smith, completed a fully operative machine and operated the same on or about December 12, 1921. This, appellee concedes in his argument, he must rely upon as his date for formal reduction to practice. His preliminary statement is his pleading and he is bound by it. Lindmark v. De Ferranti, 34 App.D.C. 445; Browne v. Dyson, 39 App.D.C. 415. Appellant, Townsend, filed his application for a patent in the Patent Office on January 13, 1922. The Smith application was made on January 3, 1922. No question arises in the case as to the diligence of either Townsend or Smith after October, 1921, when they were each requested to prepare plans for double threaded screw machines by the Commercial Service Company. From that time forward each party moved with all the diligence required by the law.

From what has been said it appears that the appellant, Townsend, was the first to conceive and the first to reduce to practice. This being so, and there being no abandonment or negligence since reduction to practice, Townsend is entitled to priority. It has been argued that after Townsend's conception in June, 1921, he did nothing until October 21, 1921, and that this should be considered such failure to act promptly as to deprive him of the benefit of a claim of priority of conception. We do not understand this to be the law. Where an inventor has established priority of conception, disclosure and reduction to practice, in the absence of any clearly proved abandonment, his right to a patent has not become forfeited either to the public or to his rival. It has been held that a lapse of two years between a reduction to practice and the filing of an application, does not, in itself, constitute an abandonment. Rolfe v. Hoffman, 26 App.D.C. 336.

Griffith v. Kanamaru

United States Court of Appeals, Federal Circuit, 1987.
816 F.2d 624.

■ NICHOLS, SENIOR CIRCUIT JUDGE.

Background

This patent interference case involves the application of Griffith, an Associate Professor in the Department of Biochemistry at Cornell University Medical College, for a patent on an aminocarnitine compound, useful in the treatment of diabetes, and a patent issued for the same invention to Kanamaru, an employee of Takeda Chemical Industries.

Griffith had established conception by June 30, 1981, and reduction to practice on January 11, 1984. Kanamaru filed for a United States patent on November 17, 1982. The board found, however, that Griffith failed to establish reasonable diligence [and decided that he] failed to establish a prima facie case for priority against Kanamaru's filing date. This result was based on the board's conclusion that Griffith's explanation for inactivity between June 15, 1983, and September 13, 1983, failed to provide a legally sufficient excuse to satisfy the "reasonable diligence" requirement of 35 U.S.C. § 102(g). Griffith appeals on the issue of reasonable diligence.

Analysis

I

Griffith must establish a prima facie case of reasonable diligence, as well as dates of conception and reduction to practice, to avoid summary judgment on the issue of priority. As a preliminary matter we note that, although the board focused on the June 1983 to September 1983 lapse in work, and Griffith's reasons for this lapse, Griffith is burdened with establishing a prima facie case of reasonable diligence from immediately before Kanamaru's filing date of November 17, 1982, until Griffith's reduction to practice on January 11, 1984. 35 U.S.C. § 102(g); 37 C.F.R. § 1.617(a).

On appeal, Griffith presents two grounds intended to justify his inactivity on the aminocarnitine project between June 15, 1983, and September 13, 1983. The first is that, notwithstanding Cornell University's extraordinary endowment, it is reasonable, and as a policy matter desirable, for Cornell to require Griffith and other research scientists to obtain funding from outside the university. The second reason Griffith presents is that he reasonably waited for Ms. Debora Jenkins to matriculate in the Fall of 1983 to assist with the project. He had promised her she should have that task which she needed to qualify for her degree. We reject these arguments and conclude that Griffith has failed to establish grounds to excuse his inactivity prior to reduction to practice.

II

The reasonable diligence standard balances the interest in rewarding and encouraging invention with the public's interest in the earliest possible disclosure of innovation. 6 C. Gholz, I. Kayton, D. Conlin & R. Schwaab, Patent Practice 24–9 (1985) citing Hull v. Davenport, 90 F.2d 103, 105, 24 CCPA 1194, 1196, 33 U.S.P.Q. 506, 508 (1937). Griffith must account for the entire period from just before Kanamaru's filing date until his reduction to practice. 3 D. Chisum, Patents § 10.07 at 10–120 (1986). As one of our predecessor courts has noted: Public policy favors the early disclosure of inventions. This underlies the requirement for "reasonable diligence" in reducing an invention to practice, not unlike the requirement that, to avoid a holding of suppression or concealment, there be no unreasonable delay in filing an application once there has been a reduction to practice.

The board in this case was, but not properly, asked to pass judgment on the reasonableness of Cornell's policy regarding outside funding of research. The correct inquiry is rather whether it is reasonable for Cornell to require the public to wait for the innovation, given the well settled policy in favor of early disclosure. As the board notes, Chief Judge Markey has called early public disclosure the "linchpin of the patent system." Horwath v. Lee, 564 F.2d 948, 950, 195 U.S.P.Q. 701, 703 (CCPA 1977). A review of caselaw on excuses for inactivity in reduction to practice reveals a common thread that courts may consider the reasonable everyday problems and limitations encountered by an inventor. See, e.g., Bey v. Kollonitsch, 806 F.2d 1024, 231 U.S.P.Q. 967 (Fed.Cir.1986)(delay in filing excused where attorney worked on a group of related applications and other applications contributed substantially to the preparation of Bey's application); Reed v. Tornqvist, 436 F.2d 501, 168 U.S.P.Q. 462 (CCPA 1971)(concluding it is not unreasonable for inventor to delay completing a patent application until after returning from a three week vacation in Sweden, extended by illness of inventor's father); Keizer v. Bradley, 270 F.2d 396, 47 CCPA 709, 123 U.S.P.Q. 215 (1959)(delay excused where inventor, after producing a component for a color television, delayed filing to produce an appropriate receiver for testing the component); Courson v. O'Connor, 227 F. 890, 894 (7th Cir.1915)("exercise of reasonable diligence * * * does not require an inventor to devote his entire time thereto, or to abandon his ordinary means of livelihood"); De Wallace v. Scott, 15 App.D.C. 157 (1899)(where applicant made bona fide attempts to perfect his invention, applicant's poor health, responsibility to feed his family, and daily job demands excused his delay in reducing his invention to practice); Texas Co. v. Globe Oil &

Refining Co., 112 F.Supp. 455, 98 U.S.P.Q. 312 (N.D.Ill.1953)(delay in filing application excused because of confusion relating to war).

Griffith argues that the admitted inactivity of three months between June 15, 1983, and September 13, 1983, which he attributes to Cornell's "reasonable" policy requiring outside funding and to Griffith's "reasonable" decision to delay until a graduate student arrived, falls within legal precedent excusing inactivity in the diligence context. We disagree. We first note that, in regard to waiting for a graduate student, Griffith does not even suggest that he faced a genuine shortage of personnel. He does not suggest that Ms. Jenkins was the only person capable of carrying on with the aminocarnitine experiment. We can see no application of precedent to suggest that the convenience of the timing of the semester schedule justifies a three-month delay for the purpose of reasonable diligence. Neither do we believe that this excuse, absent even a suggestion by Griffith that Jenkins was uniquely qualified to do his research, is reasonable.

Griffith's second contention that it was reasonable for Cornell to require outside funding, therefore causing a delay in order to apply for such funds, is also insufficient to excuse his inactivity. The crux of Griffith's argument is that outside funding is desirable as a form of peer review, or monitoring of the worthiness of a given project. He also suggests that, as a policy matter, universities should not be treated as businesses, which ultimately would detract from scholarly inquiry. Griffith states that these considerations, if accepted as valid, would fit within the scope of the caselaw excusing inactivity for "reasonable" delays in reduction to practice and filing.

These contentions on delay do not fit within the texture and scope of the precedent cited by the parties or discussed in this opinion. Griffith argues this case is controlled by the outcome of Litchfield v. Eigen, 535 F.2d 72, 190 U.S.P.Q. 113 (CCPA 1976). We disagree. In Litchfield, Judge Rich held that the inventors failed to establish due diligence because of their inactivity between April 1964 and September 1965. Id. at 76–77, 190 U.S.P.Q. at 116. The court based this conclusion on the finding that the inventors possessed the capacity to test the invention and chose instead to test other compounds. Id. Judge Rich did not reach the issue of the alleged budgetary limitations imposed by the sponsor and stated that the inventors failed to show any evidence of such financial limitations and that, therefore, the court could not consider this contention. Id.

Griffith's excuses sound more in the nature of commercial development, not accepted as an excuse for delay, than the "hardship" cases most commonly found and discussed supra. Delays in reduction to practice caused by an inventor's efforts to refine an invention to the most marketable and profitable form have not been accepted as sufficient excuses for inactivity. D. Chisum, Patents § 10.07[2] at 10–122 & n. 4 (1986)(citations omitted).

Cornell University has made a clear decision against funding Griffith's project in order to avoid the risks and distractions, albeit different in each case, that would result from directly financing these inventions. Griffith has placed in the record, and relies on, an able article by President Bok of Harvard, Business and the Academy, Harvard Magazine, May–June 1981, 31, App. at 81. Bok is explaining the policy issues respecting academic funding of scientific research, for the benefit of Harvard's alumni who must, of course, make up by their contributions the University's annual deficit. While much academic research could produce a profit, pursuit of such profit may be business inappropriate for a university though it would be right and proper for a commercial organization. For example, it might produce conflicts between the roles of scientists as inventors and developers against their roles as members of the university faculty. However large the university's endowment may be, it may be better to enlist private funding and let this source of funds develop the commercial utilization of any invention as perhaps, the beneficial owner. If there is a patent, the source of funds may end up assignee of the patent. It seems also implicit in this policy choice that faculty members may not be allowed single-minded pursuit of reduction to practice whenever they conceive some idea of value, and at times the rights of other inventors may obtain a priority that a single-minded pursuit would have averted. Bok says diligent reduction to practice, to satisfy the patent laws, may interfere with a faculty member's other duties. Bok is asking the approval of his alumni, not of the courts. The management of great universities is one thing, at least, the courts have not taken over and do not deem themselves qualified to undertake. Bok does not ask that the patent laws or other intellectual property law be skewed or slanted to enable the university to have its cake and eat it too, i.e., to act in a noncommercial manner and yet preserve the pecuniary rewards of commercial exploitation for itself.

If, as we are asked to assume, Cornell also follows the policy Bok has so well articulated, it seems evident that Cornell has consciously chosen to assume the risk that priority in the invention might be lost to an outside inventor, yet, having chosen a noncommercial policy, it asks us to save it the property that would have inured to it if it had acted in single-minded pursuit of gain.

III

The record reveals that from the relevant period of November 17, 1982 (Kanamaru's filing date), to September 13, 1983 (when Griffith renewed his efforts towards reduction to practice), Griffith interrupted and often put aside the aminocarnitine project to work on other experiments. Between June 1982 and June 1983 Griffith admits that, at the request of the chairman of his department, he was primarily engaged in an unrelated research project on mitochondrial glutathione metabolism. Griffith also put aside the aminocarnitine experiment to work on a grant proposal on an unrelated project. Griffith's statement in the record that his unrelated grant application, if granted, might "support" a future grant request directed to the aminocarnitine project does not overcome the conclusion that he preferred one project over another and was not "continuously" or "reasonably" diligent. Griffith made only minimal efforts to secure funding directly for the aminocarnitine project.

The conclusion we reach from the record is that the aminocarnitine project was second and often third priority in laboratory research as well as the solicitation of funds. We agree that Griffith failed to establish a prima facie case of reasonable diligence or a legally sufficient excuse for inactivity to establish priority over Kanamaru.

Paulik v. Rizkalla

United States Court of Appeals, Federal Circuit, 1985.
760 F.2d 1270.

■ PAULINE NEWMAN, CIRCUIT JUDGE.

This appeal is from the decision of the United States Patent and Trademark Office Board of Patent Interferences (Board), awarding priority of invention to the senior party[a] Nabil Rizkalla and Charles N. Winnick (Rizkalla), on the ground that the junior party and de facto first inventors Frank E. Paulik and Robert G. Schultz (Paulik) had suppressed or concealed the invention within the meaning of 35 U.S.C. § 102(g). We vacate this decision and remand to the Board.

I

Rizkalla's patent application has the effective filing date of March 10, 1975. Paulik's patent application was filed on June 30, 1975. The interference count is for a catalytic process for producing alkylidene diesters. Paulik presented deposition testimony and exhibits in support of his claim to priority; Rizkalla chose to rely solely on his filing date.

The Board held and Rizkalla does not dispute that Paulik reduced the invention of the count to practice in November 1970 and again in April 1971. On about November 20, 1970 Paulik submitted a "Preliminary Disclosure of Invention" to the Patent Department of his assignee, the Monsanto Company. The disclosure was assigned a priority designation of "B", which Paulik states meant that the case would "be taken up in the ordinary course for review and filing."

Despite occasional prodding from the inventors, and periodic review by the patent staff and by company management, this disclosure had a lower priority than other patent work. Evidence of the demands of other projects on related technology was offered to justify the patent staff's delay in acting on this invention, along with evidence that the inventors and assignee continued to be interested in the technology and that the invention disclosure was retained in active status.

In January or February of 1975 the assignee's patent solicitor started to work toward the filing of the patent application; drafts of the application were prepared, and additional laboratory experiments were requested by the patent solicitor and were duly carried out by an inventor. The Board

---

[a] [Note that in interference practice, the first party to file is called the "senior party," irrespective of the order of invention. The second to file, the junior party, bears the burden of proof—eds.]

held that "even if Paulik demonstrated continuous activity from prior to the Rizkalla effective filing date to his filing date ... such would have no bearing on the question of priority in this case", and cited 35 U.S.C. § 102(g) as authority for the statement that "[w]hile diligence during the above noted period may be relied upon by one alleging prior conception and subsequent reduction to practice, it is of no significance in the case of the party who is not the last to reduce to practice." The Board thus denied Paulik the opportunity to antedate Rizkalla, for the reason that Paulik was not only the first to conceive but he was also the first to reduce to practice.

The Board then held that Paulik's four-year delay from reduction to practice to his filing date was prima facie suppression or concealment under the first clause of § 102(g), that since Paulik had reduced the invention to practice in 1971 and 1972 he was barred by the second clause of section 102(g) from proving reasonable diligence leading to his 1975 filing, and that in any event the intervening activities were insufficient to excuse the delay. The Board refused to consider Paulik's evidence of renewed patent-related activity.

II

The Board's decision converted the case law's estoppel against reliance on Paulik's early work for priority purposes, into a forfeiture encompassing Paulik's later work, even if the later work commenced before the earliest activity of Rizkalla. According to this decision, once the inference of suppression or concealment is established, this inference cannot be overcome by the junior party to an interference. There is no statutory or judicial precedent that requires this result, and there is sound reason to reject it.

United States patent law embraces the principle that the patent right is granted to the first inventor rather than the first to file a patent application.[b] The law does not inquire as to the fits and starts by which an invention is made. The historic jurisprudence from which 35 U.S.C. § 102(g) flowed reminds us that "the mere lapse of time" will not prevent the inventor from receiving a patent. Mason v. Hepburn, 13 App.D.C. 86, 91, 1898 C.D. 510, 513 (1898). The sole exception to this principle resides in § 102(g) and the exigencies of the priority contest.

There is no impediment in the law to holding that a long period of inactivity need not be a fatal forfeiture, if the first inventor resumes work on the invention before the second inventor enters the field. We deem this result to be a fairer implementation of national patent policy, while in full accord with the letter and spirit of § 102(g).

The Board misapplied the rule that the first inventor does not have to show activity following reduction to practice to mean that the first inventor

[b] As observed by the Industrial Research Institute, a first-to-invent system "respects the value of the individual in American tradition and avoids inequities which can result from a 'race to the Patent Office'." Final Report of the Advisory Committee on Industrial Innovation, U.S. Dept. of Commerce, Sept. 1979, p. 174.

will not be allowed to show such activity. Such a showing may serve either of two purposes: to rebut an inference of abandonment, suppression, or concealment; or as evidence of renewed activity with respect to the invention. Otherwise, if an inventor were to set an invention aside for "too long" and later resume work and diligently develop and seek to patent it, according to the Board he would always be worse off than if he never did the early work, even as against a much later entrant.

Such a restrictive rule would merely add to the burden of those charged with the nation's technological growth. Invention is not a neat process. The value of early work may not be recognized or, for many reasons, it may not become practically useful, until months or years later. Following the Board's decision, any "too long" delay would constitute a forfeiture fatal in a priority contest, even if terminated by extensive and productive work done long before the newcomer entered the field.

We do not suggest that the first inventor should be entitled to rely for priority purposes on his early reduction to practice if the intervening inactivity lasts "too long," as that principle has evolved in a century of judicial analysis. Precedent did not deal with the facts at bar. There is no authority that would estop Paulik from relying on his resumed activities in order to pre-date Rizkalla's earliest date. We hold that such resumed activity must be considered as evidence of priority of invention. Should Paulik demonstrate that he had renewed activity on the invention and that he proceeded diligently to filing his patent application, starting before the earliest date to which Rizkalla is entitled—all in accordance with established principles of interference practice—we hold that Paulik is not prejudiced by the fact that he had reduced the invention to practice some years earlier.

III

This appeal presents a question not previously treated by this court or, indeed, in the historical jurisprudence on suppression or concealment. We take this opportunity to clarify an apparent misperception of certain opinions of our predecessor court which the Board has cited in support of its holding.

There is over a hundred years of judicial precedent on the issue of suppression or concealment due to prolonged delay in filing. From the earliest decisions, a distinction has been drawn between deliberate suppression or concealment of an invention, and the legal inference of suppression or concealment based on "too long" a delay in filing the patent application. Both types of situations were considered by the courts before the 1952 Patent Act, and both are encompassed in 35 U.S.C. § 102(g). The result is consistent over this entire period—loss of the first inventor's priority as against an intervening second inventor—and has consistently been based on equitable principles and public policy as applied to the facts of each case.

The earliest decisions dealt primarily with deliberate concealment. In 1858, the Supreme Court in Kendall v. Winsor, 62 U.S. (21 How.) 322, 328, 16 L.Ed. 165 (1858) held that an inventor who "designedly, and with the view of applying it indefinitely and exclusively for his own profit, withholds his invention from the public" impedes "the progress of science and the useful arts."

In Mason v. Hepburn, supra, the classical case on inferred as contrasted with deliberate suppression or concealment, Hepburn was granted a patent in September 1894. Spurred by this news Mason filed his patent application in December 1894. In an interference, Mason demonstrated that he had built a working model in 1887 but showed no activity during the seven years thereafter. The court held that although Mason may have negligently rather than willfully concealed his invention, the "indifference, supineness, or wilful act" of a first inventor is the basis for "the equity" that favors the second inventor when that person made and disclosed the invention during the prolonged inactivity of the first inventor. 13 App.D.C. at 96, 1898 C.D. at 517.

The legislative history of section 102(g) makes clear that its purpose was not to change the law. As described in H.R.Rep. No. 1923, 82d Cong., 2d Sess. 17–18 (1951), section 102(g) "retains the present rules of [the case] law governing the determination of priority of invention." The pre–1952 cases all dealt with situations whereby a later inventor made the same invention during a period of either prolonged inactivity or deliberate concealment by the first inventor, after knowledge of which (usually, but not always, by the issuance of a patent to the second inventor) the first inventor was "spurred" into asserting patent rights, unsuccessfully.

The decisions after the 1952 Act followed a similar pattern, as the courts considered whether to extinguish a first inventor's priority under section 102(g). The cases show either intentional concealment or an unduly long delay after the first inventor's reduction to practice. Some cases excused the delay, and some did not. A few examples will illustrate the application of the statute:

In Gallagher v. Smith, 206 F.2d 939, 41 C.C.P.A. 734, 99 U.S.P.Q. 132 (1953), a seven-year delay (from 1938 to 1945) was excused in the absence of evidence of actual concealment or suppression, as against a later applicant who had a reduction to practice in 1943. Note that the applicant who had delayed was nonetheless the first to file.

Young v. Dworkin, 489 F.2d 1277, 180 U.S.P.Q. 388 (CCPA 1974), held that a 27–month delay amounted to suppression. Young had refrained from filing a patent application until he had acquired the machines to practice his invention commercially. Focusing on the character of Young's activity between his reduction to practice and filing date, the court found that during Young's prolonged period of inactivity Dworkin conceived the invention and filed his patent application. In concurrence, Judge Rich observed that "it is not the time elapsed that is the controlling factor but the total conduct of the first inventor," adding "[i]t may also be a relative matter, taking into account what the later inventor is doing too." 489 F.2d at 1285, 180 U.S.P.Q. at 395.

In Peeler v. Miller, 535 F.2d 647, 190 U.S.P.Q. 117 (CCPA 1976), relied on by the Board, Miller was inactive during the four-year period following his reduction to practice, and the proffered excuse (that work of higher priority was done in other areas) was found inadequate. As noted by the Board, there are many similarities with the case at bar. The difference, however, is significant: Peeler had entered the field and filed his patent application while Miller remained dormant; Rizkalla entered the field, according to the record before us, after Paulik had renewed activity on the invention.

IV

The decisions applying section 102(g) balanced the law and policy favoring the first person to make an invention, against equitable considerations when more than one person had made the same invention: in each case where the court deprived the de facto first inventor of the right to the patent, the second inventor had entered the field during a period of either inactivity or deliberate concealment by the first inventor. Often the first inventor had been spurred to file a patent application by news of the second inventor's activities. Although "spurring" is not necessary to a finding of suppression or concealment, see Young v. Dworkin, 489 F.2d at 1281, 180 U.S.P.Q. at 391–92 and citations therein, the courts' frequent references to spurring indicate their concern with this equitable factor.

This result furthers the basic purpose of the patent system. The exclusive right, constitutionally derived, was for the national purpose of advancing the useful arts—the process today called technological innovation. As implemented by the patent statute, the grant of the right to exclude carries the obligation to disclose the workings of the invention, thereby adding to the store of knowledge without diminishing the patent-supported incentive to innovate.

But the obligation to disclose is not the principal reason for a patent system; indeed, it is a rare invention that cannot be deciphered more readily from its commercial embodiment than from the printed patent. The reason for the patent system is to encourage innovation and its fruits: new jobs and new industries, new consumer goods and trade benefits. We must keep this purpose in plain view as we consider the consequences of interpretations of the patent law such as in the Board's decision.

A foreseeable consequence of the Board's ruling is to discourage inventors and their supporters from working on projects that had been "too long" set aside, because of the impossibility of relying, in a priority contest, on either their original work or their renewed work. This curious result is neither fair nor in the public interest. We do not see that the public interest is served by placing so severe a sanction on failure to file premature patent applications on immature inventions of unknown value. In reversing the Board's decision we do not hold that such inventions are necessarily entitled to the benefits of their earliest dates in a priority contest; we hold only that they are not barred from entitlement to their dates of renewed activity.

■ RICH, CIRCUIT JUDGE, concurring. [omitted]

■ MARKEY, CHIEF JUDGE, additional views.

I agree with the opinions of Judges Newman and Rich. I write only to explicate the importance, as I see it, of those opinions to the functioning of the patent system and the effect of our decision on inventors whether self-employed, employed by small businesses, or employed by large corporations.

The patent system does not operate in a vacuum. Patent applications are expensive. Nothing in the law precludes a pause in a series of steps taken to make an invention publicly known. The risk that another may file during a pause period is sufficient to discourage suppressors and concealers. For this court effectively to require that applications be filed on every shadow of a shade of an idea immediately upon its conception, or risk loss of the opportunity to patent (and potentially the right to make, use, or sell the invention), would impose a new and onerous rule. To render a restart after a pause meaningless does not contribute to a smooth working of the patent system. That result is neither required by statute nor intended by Congress. The rich corporation might well be able to flood the Patent Office with rushed applications and with refilings of those applications, avoiding all pauses on the way to filing a patent application. Less affluent businesses and individual inventors, however, would find it extremely difficult, if not impossible, to participate in a patent system so conducted.

On the other hand, I can see no harm to the patent system in a determination that a period of inactivity can be cured by a resumption of activity before the filing date of another and a requirement that the question of priority be then fought out on the basis of the date of renewed activity on the one side and whatever may be the earliest date established on the other side.

■ FRIEDMAN, CIRCUIT JUDGE (with whom Davis, Kashiwa, Bennett and Jack R. Miller, Circuit Judges, join), dissenting. [omitted]

NOTES

1. *Conception.* Conception is a mental activity. It "occurs when 'the inventive idea is crystallized in all of its essential attributes and becomes so clearly defined in the mind of the inventor as to be capable of being converted to reality and reduced to practice by the inventor or by ones skilled in the art.' "[3] This does not mean that the invention must be operable. If that were the case, conception and reduction would be the same thing. Rather, the mental formulation must be complete enough so that only routine experimentation is needed to make the invention operable.[4]

---

[3] Burroughs Wellcome Co. v. Barr Laboratories, Inc., 828 F.Supp. 1200, 29 U.S.P.Q.2d (BNA) 1721, 1725 (E.D.N.C. 1993), quoting Techitrol, Inc. v. United States, 440 F.2d 1362, 1369–70 (Ct.Cl.1971).

[4] It can be helpful to think of a spectrum of experimentation. Small amounts of experimentation are consistent with conception, see, e.g., Summers v. Vogel, 332 F.2d 810 (C.C.P.A.1964); if serious levels of research

Nor is it necessary for the inventor to appreciate that what he thought of is new or advantageous,[5] though at some point he will need to recite a use to meet the utility requirement, see Assignment 17.

It is important to understand that despite the mental nature of the activity of conception, something physical is required to prove conception. As with other representations concerning invention, once the time of conception is put into issue, corroboration will be required. The requirement is readily understood because it is very easy to tell a good—self-serving—story. However, the corroboration requirement may represent a formidible barrier to small inventors. Large research and development firms require their researchers to record faithfully all of their work on the pages of dated and numbered laboratory notebooks, which are never torn out and regularly countersigned. But inventors of the type encountered in the Principal Problem are unlikely to be this sophisticated. The CAFC has adopted a rule of reason approach that looks to individual circumstances, but nonetheless requires some independent evidence of the facts that need to be proved in an interference.[6]

2. *Reduction to practice: constructive vs. actual.* There are two ways to demonstrate that an invention has been reduced to practice. First, the applicant can do what Townsend did in the Principal Case: construct an embodiment of the invention and test it to establish its capacity to perform successfully for its intended purpose.[7] Alternatively, the applicant can rely on her filing date. Since the invention must have specific utility to meet the "useful" standard of § 101, and since the application must provide a disclosure that enables others to use it, it can safely be assumed that once an application is made, the invention is reduced to practice. For obvious reasons, the first method (building an embodiment) is called "actual reduction to practice;" the second (relying on the filing date), "constructive reduction to practice." Applicants who rely on constructive reduction need never build a working model of their inventions unless requested to do so by the Commissioner, § 114.

Why do you suppose Kanamaru relied on constructive reduction to practice in the Griffith case? Since at the time of the case, § 104 prevented a foreign applicants from relying on inventive activities undertaken abroad, these applicants were "stuck" with their filing dates. However, under § 119, the statute executing the Paris Convention, applicants from signatory countries can, for purposes of establishing the date of invention, rely on the date the application is filed *abroad*, so long as the U.S. filing is within one year.

are required, then the mental formulation will be considered more in the nature of a hope than a concept see, e.g., Fredkin v. Irasek, 397 F.2d 342 (C.C.P.A.1968), cert. denied, 393 U.S. 980, 89 S.Ct. 450, 21 L.Ed.2d 441 (1968).

[5] See, e.g., MacMillan v. Moffett, 432 F.2d 1237 (C.C.P.A.1970).

[6] See, e.g., Coleman v. Dines, 754 F.2d 353 (Fed.Cir.1985).

[7] See, e.g., Newkirk v. Lulejian, 825 F.2d 1581, 1582 (Fed.Cir.1987); Kimberly–Clark Corp. v. Johnson & Johnson, 745 F.2d 1437, 1445 (Fed.Cir.1984).

3. *Diligence*. Notice that the diligence cases are mainly about excuses—excuses for failing to work continuously on the invention from just before the time that the other party conceived the invention. Even very short delays must be accounted for. In In re Mulder,[8] for example, the first-to-invent had only two days to account for, but he lost nonetheless.

What counts as an excuse? As the Principal Cases indicate, commercial considerations will not do; neither will doubts about the value of the enterprise.[9] But the demands of the inventor's day job,[10] poverty,[11] and illness,[12] will be accepted as excusing lack of diligence. Curiously, in the case of constructive reductions to practice, the patent attorney's other workload also counts.[13] As usual, corroboration is required.[14]

What about personal excuses? Illness is clearly acceptable. What about marriage, child birth, or childcare duties?

4. *Abandonment*. Mason v. Hepburn[15] is the germinal case. Mason had built a working model of a gun clip in 1887 and hid it away, revealing it only after he had heard that Hepburn had obtained a patent on the same invention in 1894. The interference wound up in court and Hepburn, the second inventor, won. The court reasoned that as between Hepburn and Mason, Hepburn was the more deserving as it was he who had brought the invention to the public. Mason did not care about the public; he was merely spurred by Hepburn. The first sentence of § 102(g) captures this equitable notion that as between two inventors, the one who abandoned it should not later obtain the patent on it. But the codification is not complete. Section 102(g) says nothing about spurring, and as Paulik v. Rizkalla makes clear, this had given rise to doubt as to its significance in certain contexts.[16]

5. *Interference practice*. Section 135 of the Patent Act controls priority practice. It gives the Commissioner of Patents the authority to declare an interference whenever an application claims the same thing as is claimed in a pending application or in an unexpired patent. The Board of Patent Appeals and Interferences decides priority (as well as issues of patentability) in an inter partes proceeding between the affected parties. In the proceeding, the senior party (first to file) enjoys the presumption of having invented first. Junior parties bear the burden of demonstrating their earlier dates of invention.[17]

It is important to consider the parties' motivations in an interference. Each party's main objective is to prove it should be the one to receive the

---

[8] 716 F.2d 1542 (Fed.Cir.1983).

[9] Christie v. Seybold, 55 Fed. 69 (6th Cir.1893) is an oft-cited case.

[10] See, e.g., Courson v. O'Connor, 227 Fed. 890 (C.C.A.7 1915).

[11] See Christie, supra.

[12] See, e.g., De Wallace v. Scott, 15 App. D.C. 157 (1899).

[13] See, e.g., Courson, supra.

[14] See, e.g., Gould v. Schawlow, 363 F.2d 908 (C.C.P.A.1966).

[15] 13 App. D.C. 86, 1898 C.D. 510 (1898).

[16] See, e.g., the discussion of Young v. Dworkin, 489 F.2d 1277 (C.C.P.A.1974), recounted in Paulik.

[17] For an example of such a case, see Hahn v. Wong, 892 F.2d 1028 (Fed.Cir.1989).

patent. But once it becomes clear that the other side will win, the next-best result is usually to convince the PTO that the invention is not patentable by anyone, for example, by demonstrating that the party likely to win learned enough from another to render the invention obvious, § 102(f)/103. That way, the losers avoid becoming infringers. But there is sometimes another alternative. As with other lawsuits, parties can settle interferences privately, agreeing, for example, that one applicant will be awarded the patent and the others will receive licenses on favorable terms,[18] or that all the applicants will apply together as joint inventors.[19] Such settlements save PTO resources, but they can work against the public interest. They eliminate the incentive to bring to the PTO's attention information on which to reject all the applications. They are also wonderful vehicles for dividing up markets and engaging in other forms of anticompetitive conduct. Accordingly, agreements to settle interferences must be placed on public record in the PTO, § 135(c).

Many commentators wonder whether settlements will be a feature of interference practice in the future. The reason for the concern relates to the change in the way the patent term is calculated. Prior to 1995, patents ran for 17 years from the time of issuance. For applications made after June 8, 1995, patents will usually run for 20 years from the time of application.[20] Since a patent cannot be enforced until it issues, the effect of interferences post–1995 will be to "eat up" the patent term: the longer the interference, the shorter will be the time when anyone need pay royalties to the patentee. Accordingly, a party who believes he will lose in an interference may have a substantial interest in prolonging the proceeding. To prevent the patent from being undermined by lengthy interferences, § 154 has been amended to extend for up to five years the term of a patent whose issuance is delayed by an interference, § 154(b).

6. *First to file.* Reconsider the point made in the Introduction: the United States is one of only two countries in the world with a priority rule that turns on who invented first. (The other country is the Philippines). Every

[18] Stratoflex v. Aeroquip was such a case, see Assignment 19.

[19] A well-known recent example of an interference settled this way concerned patent rights to the method for testing the blood supply for the AIDS virus. Dr. Luc Montagnier of Paris' Pasteur Institute and Dr. Robert Gallo of the National Cancer Institute, two pioneers in AIDS research, had worked cooperatively in the past, but each applied for a patent on the test claiming to be the true inventor. Jonas Salk (developer of the polio vaccine) stepped in to mediate on the theory that the dispute was "unhealthy" to science. He persuaded the parties to seek the patent jointly and to use 80% of the royalties to create a new center for AIDS-related research, see Yalta of AIDS: Ending a Bitter Feud, 129 TIME, April 13, 1987, at p. 57(1). But see Cohen, Pasteur Wants More HIV Blood Test Royalties, 255 Science 792, Feb. 14, 1992 (reporting on a demand by the Pasteur Institute for a restructuring of the agreement in light of evidence that Gallo's work was based on samples "remarkably similar" to samples that Montagnier had sent him.).

[20] There are transition rules in effect for patent applications pending at the time of the change. In addition, patents in force at that time will endure for 17 years from issuance or 20 years from application, which ever is longer, but subject to special remedies limitations, § 154(c).

other nation awards the patent to the first to file.[21] The advantages to first-to-file are obvious. There is no interference practice, no need to prove the dates of conception and reduction to practice, no need for corroboration, no need to excuse delay. Moreover, this rule provides more motivation to make the invention useable than the diligence requirement of § 102(g). U.S. applicants can always hope no one else will be able to prove a conception date falling in the period of inactivity, and—if that fails—that the delay will be excused. In other countries, inventors know that all is lost if they don't file first.

What prevents the U.S. from changing § 102(g) to conform to the law of other nations? At first blush, the change may seem to be constitutionally impermissible. After all, Congress's power is limited to the protection of "inventors," not "filers." But the first-to-file is an "inventor," she's just not necessarily the *first* inventor. That is, changing the priority rule does not entail a change in the originality requirement of § 102(f): if the applicant did not invent the invention, she cannot acquire a patent.

Another version of the constitutionality claim derives from language in Graham v. John Deere stating that Congress cannot use its patent power to remove inventions from the public domain, see Assignment 19. The argument here is that if the first to invent does not apply for a patent, the invention falls into the hands of the public, and the first to file cannot take it back. However, if this argument were true, then the *current* law would also be in trouble. Remember, §§ 102(a), (e), and (g) do not impose a requirement of *absolute* novelty. There are many kinds of references that are not considered anticipatory even though they fully reveal the invention.

If the obstacle to changing the law is not constitutional, then it must be based on policy. As noted in the Introduction, one policy justification for the current system is that first-to-invent is more responsive to small inventors. But isn't the effort to protect these inventors misguided? The evidence is that most interferences are won by the first party to file because that party enjoys a presumption in its favor that is difficult to overcome.[22] Moreover, the Notes on conception and reduction to practice attest to the many disadvantages under which small inventors operate now.

The theoretical explanation offered in the Introduction, that it is better if things are not invented too soon, is also inadequate to justify retention of the current system. First, it does not square with the diligence cases, which do not excuse waiting for collateral developments. Second, the common

---

[21] See generally, Macedo, First-to-File: Is American Adoption of the International Standard in Patent Law Worth the Price, 18 AIPLA Q.J. 193 (1990), citing, Law of June 20, 1947, Concerning the Issuance of Patents, [1947] Laws and Resolutions of the Republic of the Philippines 153. See also WIPO Doc. HL/CE/III/4 at 3 (Nov. 27, 1987), and noting that Canadian patent law, which was a first-to-invent system, see Christiani v. Rice, [1930] Can. S.Ct. 443, 456, has recently changed to a first-to-file system.

[22] See News & Comments, 34 Pat. Trademark & Copyright J. (BNA) 403, (Aug. 20, 1987)(quoting Richard Witte, chairman of the ABA–PTC Committee No. 108 on Patent System Policy Planning)(citing a figure of 75% for the percent of interferences won by the senior applicant).

intuition is that all-out efforts do produce superior results. Thus, the invent-too-soon rationale is not likely to have held sway with Congress when it voted on the Patent Act.

A more plausible explanation for the status quo is that U.S. patent attorneys are nervous about moving to first-to-file. Currently, they can save a late filing with proof of conception and diligence, using their own work load as an excuse; under first-to-file, a day's delay could mean that the client loses the patent right. Since malpractice litigation is not as well developed in other countries as it is here, the loss of a patent in this manner could be more costly to U.S. lawyers than it is to their foreign counterparts. However, as world markets become more important to U.S. companies, this objection is weakening. U.S. patent attorneys currently prepare their clients' foreign applications knowing that priority will be determined by filing date; all they need do is treat the U.S. application the same way.

Finally, there is one credible argument for first-to-invent: applications are likely to be less informative if applicants are forced to move more quickly. Is that reason enough to continue to put up with the labyrinth of § 102(g)?

7. *Provisional applications.* In 1995, § 111 of the Patent Act was amended to permit the filing of provisional applications. Provisionals must include only the information required by § 112 ¶ 1 and by § 113. If an application that meets all the filing requirements is filed within 12 months, the date of the provisional will be used for priority purposes. However, the patent term will begin to run from the date of the filing of the full application. Will this provision help or hurt small inventors?

BIBLIOGRAPHY

Macedo, First-to-File: Is American Adoption of the International Standard in Patent Law Worth the Price, 18 AIPLA Q.J. 193 (1990); Gholz, A Critique of Recent Opinions of the Federal Circuit in Patent Interferences, 71 J. Pat. & Trademark Off. Soc'y 439 (1989); Rollins, Ties Go to the Runner, 69 J. Pat. & Trademark Off. Soc'y 407 (1987); Dunner, First to File: Should Our Interference System be Abolished?, 68 J. Pat. & Trademark Off. Soc'y 561 (1986); Gholz, Old Rule Interferences After the Promulgation of the New Rules, 68 J. Pat. & Trademark Off. Soc'y 335 (1986); Armitage, Reform of the Law on Interference: A New Role for an Ancient Institution in the Context of a First–To–File System, 64 J. Pat. Off. Soc'y 663 (1982); Note, The Constitutionality of the First-to-File System, 11 IDEA 241 (1967).

THE SCOPE OF THE PATENT HOLDER'S RIGHTS: INFRINGEMENT AND CONTRIBUTORY INFRINGEMENT

1. INTRODUCTION

The Patent Act does not provide the patentee with affirmative rights to sell or license her invention. Rather, the Act gives to the patentee only the right to exclude others: a cause of action against those who make, use, sell, or offer for sale the patented invention in the United States. In addition to this action for infringement, the patentee can also recover from anyone who induces or contributes to infringement by others in the United States, imports into the United States products made abroad using a patented process, or distributes components for the assembly of a patented product abroad.

Since the patent holder is the only one who can exploit the invention free of the risk of being sued for infringement, ownership of a patent does, as a practical matter, represent a potentially significant income stream. If the invention is unique in the sense that there is nothing available that is roughly comparable to it, the patentee is something of a monopolist. In the absence of competitors, she has the power to control the price at which the invention is available to others. As a result, that price may be higher than the competitive price would be and the quantity available for sale may be lower than the competitive quantity would be. In effect, the value the public attaches to the invention (as measured by the difference between the marginal cost of the product and the price at which the public is willing to purchase the invention) is converted into profit for the patentee.

In many ways, this is exactly how the statute should work: the supracompetitive profit that the patentee earns compensates her for the investment she made and the risks she took in conceiving the inventive idea and bringing it to fruition. It is the opportunity for such reward that motivates others to undertake similar risks and investments in the future. Courts, therefore, are careful to interpret the scope of the patent broadly enough to insure that the patent does, in fact, cut off the ability of others to market inventions similar to the patented invention and drive the price the patentee can charge down to competitive levels.

There are, however, ways in which a patent monopoly is troublesome—indeed, as troublesome as any other monopoly. Output is restricted and prices are high; the patentee may be able to use control over the invention to restrain trade in other areas. Sometimes everyone loses: a deadweight social loss is produced when the patentee does not make a sale to a potential user who sets a value on the invention that is lower than the price the patentee is charging, but higher than the price at which the invention would be sold if the market were competitive. Furthermore, invention often occurs sequentially: technology expands more rapidly if one person's insight can be used as a building block for future developments by another. The patentee's right to exclude interferes with this development because the patentee is not likely to grant others permission to develop superceding inventions.

Because of these competing considerations, courts entertaining infringement actions must draw fine lines between undercompensating the patentee and shortchanging the public. Copyrights present some of these same problems, but §§ 107–120 of the Copyright Act, which limit exclusive rights, provide considerable guidance. There is nothing comparable in the Patent Act, and so courts must fall back on common law and other statutory regimes. This Assignment focuses on the patentee and demonstrates how infringement is defined to assure an adequate return. The next Assignment focuses on the public-interest side of the issue and describes the devices that have been developed to cabin the manner in which the patent is exploited. It is, however, important to appreciate that the division in these two Assignments is somewhat arbitrary. When deciding a case, a court will always consider both the private and public perspective.

2. PRINCIPAL PROBLEM

This Problem requires us to give more advice to the Coalition to Fight Diseases (CFTD), who was the client in Problem C of Assignment 19 that figured out a new way to treat a disease using a purified version of a known drug, X. CFTD "forgot" to stress something the first time around: it seems X, the drug it purified, is patented. CFTD wants to know whether it will commit patent infringement if it distributes its purified versions of X.

Now that I have a better idea of the whole story, let me recount it from the top. In 1989, the Alpha Company obtained U.S. Patent 1,ZZZ,ZZZ. It consists of two claims: Claim 1 is on "Chemical X" whose structure is depicted in the patent (but omitted here). Claim 2 is on the process for using X to treat a certain terminal contagious disease. In 1991, the Food and Drug Administration (FDA) approved the use of X for the treatment of this disease. The FDA's approval is limited: because X produces side effects that grow increasingly severe with use and debilitation, it is unsuitable to, and therefore not approved for, the end stage of illness. X is currently the only known treatment for this disease. Accordingly, Alpha has been able to establish a price for each dose of X that is well above the marginal cost of production.

It was out of concern for the victims of this disease, that a group of public-interest researchers organized our client, CFTD. CFTD knew that many chemicals to which the body is responsive are actually mixtures of two substances of identical chemical constitution and essentially identical structural form. The two substances, called "enantiomers," are mirror images of each other—much like left and right hands. Despite their identical constitutions and structures, it is often the case that each enantiomer will work differently in the body: one may have no effect or a deleterious effect, and the other a beneficial effect. For example, one enantiomer may treat disease while the other causes severe side effects.

CFTD suspected that X is, in fact, this sort of mixture. Initially, it asked Alpha for permission to work with X, but Alpha refused. CFTD then got samples of X through a physician's prescription. Using this sample, CFTD managed to separate X into its enantiomers, (R)-X and (S)-X, and to identify R-(X) as the biologically beneficial enantiomer. It then figured out how to manufacture (R)-X in commercial amounts and now it is ready for distribution. As I said, it is interested in knowing whether distribution of R-(X) in the future will be considered infringement.

3. MATERIALS FOR SOLUTION OF PRINCIPAL PROBLEM

A. STATUTORY MATERIAL: § 271

B: CASES:

Fromson v. Advance Offset Plate, Inc.

United States Court of Appeals, Federal Circuit, 1983.
720 F.2d 1565.

■ MARKEY, CHIEF JUDGE.

Appeal from four judgments of the U.S. District Court for the District of Massachusetts holding that claims 1, 4, 6, 7, 12 and 16 of U.S. Patent 3,181,461 issued to Fromson are not infringed. We vacate and remand.

BACKGROUND

A. The Technology

The Fromson patent involves a process for making a photographic printing plate for use in the art of lithography. The art involves creation on a printing surface of certain areas that are hydrophilic (water attracting) and organophobic (ink repelling) and other areas that are organophilic (ink attracting) and hydrophobic (water repelling).

At the time of the Fromson invention, the state of the art was depicted generally by U.S. Patent 2,714,006, issued on July 26, 1955 to Jewett and Case (Jewett). Jewett teaches the preparation of a presensitized lithographic plate. [These plates are made out of aluminum sheets that are treated with diazo coatings to make them them light-sensitive. Using stencils, appropriate areas are then exposed to light, washed with water and wiped with image developer or printer's developing ink. The resulting plates have ink- and water-attracting and repelling portions that recreate the stencil's image when the plates are used for printing.]

B. The Fromson Patent

In the 1950's, Fromson was in the business of selling metals and began, through Ano–Coil Corporation, to manufacture and sell anodized aluminum. In anodization, aluminum is coated with oxide while it is the anode in an electrolytic bath wherein it is subjected to an electric current, whence the term "anodized." The anodized aluminum was used in articles such as television antennas, furniture tubing, and nameplates.

Fromson, with no background in lithography, conceived of using anodized aluminum as a replacement for non-anodized aluminum in the plate taught by Jewett. His invention according to the Fromson patent improves the Jewett plate in a number of ways. It enables use in preparation of the plate of light-sensitive compounds other than diazo compounds. It enables the coating to absorb nitrogen-containing materials released by the light-sensitive compounds when exposed to light. Also, as the district court found, the Fromson plate enjoys improved corrosion resistance and a longer press life.

Fromson filed his application for patent in May, 1963, and the patent issued in May, 1965, containing eleven product and five process claims. Claim 1 is representative of the product claims:

> 1. A sensitized photographic printing plate comprising an aluminum sheet having a surface which has been treated to form an aluminum oxide coating on said surface, a water-insoluble, hydrophilic, organophobic layer on said sheet resulting from the reaction of the aluminum oxide coating and an alkali metal silicate applied to said coating, and a light-sensitive coating over said layer [e.g., diazo resin] having one solubility in relation to a solvent in a state before exposure to light and another solubility in relation to said solvent in another state after exposure to light, said light-sensitive material being soluble in said solvent in one of said states and being insoluble in said solvent and in water, hydrophobic and organophilic in its other state.

C. The Advance Plate

After issuance of his patent, Fromson's invention enjoyed extensive commercial success and was the subject of licensing agreements with several companies. Fromson sued Advance Offset Plate, Inc. ("Advance"), charging it with infringement and of product claims 1, 4, 6 and 7, and process claims 12 and 16.

Though preparation of the Advance plate involves treatment of anodized aluminum with an aqueous solution of alkali metal silicate to yield a water-insoluble, hydrophilic layer, as set forth in the claims, Advance den[ies] infringement on the sole ground that there is no "reaction" between the aluminum oxide and sodium silicate. It is undisputed that Advance do[es] what the claims say, i.e., appl[ies] a water solution of an alkali metal silicate to an oxide coated aluminum sheet to produce a layer, but it is argued that the layer does not result from a "reaction" as we are asked by Advance to define that term.

Issue

Whether the district court erred in finding no infringement of claims 1, 4, 6, 7, 12, and 16.

Opinion

The issue of infringement raises at least two questions: (1) what is patented, and (2) has what is patented been made, used or sold by another. SSIH Equipment S.A. v. USITC, 718 F.2d 365, 376, 218 U.S.P.Q. 678, 688 (Fed.Cir.1983). The first is a question of law; the second a question of fact. Id.; Kalman v. Kimberly–Clark Corp., 713 F.2d 760, 771, 218 U.S.P.Q. 781, 788, 789 (Fed.Cir.1983). The present decision of the district court turned on the first question, which we review as a matter of law.

A.   Contentions of the Parties

Advance contend[s] that "the Court was totally convinced, based on the evidence presented, that Fromson was indeed referring to and claiming a 'reaction product' formed by the reaction of an aluminum oxide with sodium silicate, i.e., an aluminosilicate compound." Fromson argues that "reaction" in the claims should be interpreted to cover the claimed treatment of an oxide coated aluminum sheet with an aqueous solution of alkali metal silicate to form a water insoluble, hydrophilic, organophobic layer on the sheet, and that whether the layer is an aluminosilicate compound is irrelevant, there being no reference to any such compound in the asserted claims. We agree.

B.   Claim Construction—The Specification

In Autogiro Co. of America v. United States, 384 F.2d 391, 397, 155 U.S.P.Q. 697, 702 (Ct.Cl.1967), our predecessor court recognized that patentees are not confined to normal dictionary meanings: The dictionary does not always keep abreast of the inventor. It cannot. Things are not made for the sake of words but words for things. To overcome this lag, patent law allows the inventor to be his own lexicographer. (Citations omitted.) A patentee's verbal license "augments the difficulty of understanding the claims", and to understand their meaning, they must be construed "in connection with the other parts of the patent instrument and with the circumstances surrounding the inception of the patent application." Id. Accord, General Electric Co. v. United States, 572 F.2d 745, 751–53, 198 U.S.P.Q. 65, 70–73 (Ct.Cl.1978).

This appeal hinges on construction of "reaction." The specification discloses a new and improved method of forming plates for use in lithography. Fromson discovered that the treatment of anodized aluminum with an aqueous solution of water soluble alkali metal silicate produces a water insoluble, hydrophilic, organophobic layer on the aluminum, a layer having exceptional lithography-related properties. Fromson's invention included the formation of the layer, not its exact structure. Though Fromson referred to the disclosed treatment as involving a "reaction", he also referred to it in the specification as an "application" and as "adsorption."

Not all references to "reaction" were accompanied by a reference to formation of an aluminosilicate.

Fromson did theorize that his new, improved layer was an aluminosilicate believed "to be in the nature of a commercial zeolite", having "properties of a molecular sieve", but expressed that theory as merely a "belief." There is no basis or warrant for incorporating that belief as a limitation in the claims. It is undisputed that inclusion of Fromson's theory and belief was unnecessary to meet the enablement requirement of 35 U.S.C. § 112 (that a patentee describe how to make and use the invention). Moreover, it is axiomatic that an inventor need not comprehend the scientific principles on which the practical effectiveness of his invention rests. See, e.g., Diamond Rubber Co. v. Consolidated Rubber Co., 220 U.S. 428, 435–36, 31 S.Ct. 444, 447–48, 55 L.Ed. 527 (1911).

C. Claim Construction—The Claims

Significant evidence of the scope of a particular claim can be found on review of other claims. General Electric v. United States, supra, 572 F.2d at 752, 198 U.S.P.Q. at 70. Here, claim 5 (not asserted) limits the layer described in claim 1 to "an aluminosilicate structure in the nature of a zeolite molecular sieve", i.e., to Fromson's theory of what is formed. In Kalman v. Kimberly–Clark Corp., supra, 713 F.2d at 770, 218 U.S.P.Q. at 788, this court said "where some claims are broad and others narrow, the narrow claim limitations cannot be read into the broad whether to avoid invalidity or to escape infringement." Accord, Environmental Designs, Ltd. v. Union Oil Co. of California, 713 F.2d 693, 699, 218 U.S.P.Q. 865, 871 (Fed.Cir.1983); Caterpillar Tractor Co. v. Berco, S.P.A., 714 F.2d 1110, 1115, 219 U.S.P.Q. 185, 188 (Fed.Cir.1983). The aluminosilicate limitation of narrow claim 5 cannot, therefore, be read into broader claim 1.

D. Claim Construction—Prosecution History

The district court noted some of Fromson's arguments during prosecution of his application, in which he stressed the importance of "reacting" anodized aluminum with alkali metal silicate. However, whether the interaction of these two materials was a "reaction" or something else was immaterial to consideration of the prior art. It does not appear, moreover, that Fromson used "reacting" in his arguments any differently than he had in the specification and claims, i.e., to describe what he believed the interaction was between oxide coated aluminum and an aqueous solution of alkali metal silicate. Thus, Fromson's arguments focused on the fact of an interaction and production of a new layer with particular properties, not on the specific nature of the interaction or on any chemical structure of the layer.

That Fromson speculated, on one page of a response to a rejection, that the reaction layer is "believed to be in the nature of a commercial zeolite" is of no moment, in view of the total absence from the other thirteen pages in that response of any reference to formation of an aluminosilicate or zeolite, and in view of his clear labeling of the zeolite statement as a "belief." Instead, Fromson referred in those thirteen pages to an aluminum oxide-sodium silicate reaction surface or layer, indicating that he did not know, and did not care, what the "reaction" or the structure of the resulting product might be.

E.   Claim Construction—Other Considerations

That "reaction" in the claims need not be confined to production of an aluminosilicate is consistent with the dictionary definition. That in Webster's New Collegiate Dictionary (1974) includes both "chemical transformation or change", and "interaction of chemical entities", which are consistent with the definitions appearing in Hackh's Chemical Dictionary (1969) and the American Heritage Dictionary (1970).

When an oxide coated aluminum surface is contacted with an aqueous solution of water soluble alkali metal silicate, chemical change occurs in at least two ways. First, ions or other chemical units in solution have somehow interacted to form a solid structure. Second, the water insoluble solid structure, whatever may be its precise nature (e.g., silica or aluminosilicate), is not identical to the water soluble alkali metal silicate and oxidized aluminum that interacted to produce it. Moreover, there is clearly present an "interaction of chemical entities."

The foregoing is fully consistent with long-standing use of "reaction" in the lithography art. Claims are normally construed as they would be by those of ordinary skill in the art. See e.g., Schenck v. Nortron Corp., 713 F.2d 782, 785, 218 U.S.P.Q. 698, 701–02 (Fed.Cir.1983). Jewett interchangeably uses terms such as "treating", "treatment", and "react", to describe a lithographic plate producing process. Jewett's claims use "reacting", "treatment", and "reaction product." Jewett makes no attempt to define the structure of the layer there disclosed (as an aluminosilicate compound or otherwise), although it does mention the hydrophilic layer as being chemically bonded to the aluminum surface. Jewett refers to the layer as "silicate treatment", as "silicate or silicon containing" film, or as "an inorganic material such as silicate." It is not unreasonable to conclude that one of ordinary skill in the lithography art would interpret "react" in Fromson to mean the same thing it appears to mean in Jewett, i.e., the treatment of a metal substrate with an aqueous solution to yield a layer, regardless of the chemical structure of the layer or the proper label for the phenomena that produced it.

CONCLUSION

We hold, therefore, that the district court erred as a matter of law in interpreting the claims as limited to the product of a chemical reaction producing a new chemical compound in the restrictive sense of those terms.

Graver Tank & Manufacturing Co. v. Linde Air Products Co.

Supreme Court of the United States, 1950.
339 U.S. 605, 70 S.Ct. 854, 94 L.Ed. 1097.

■ MR. JUSTICE JACKSON delivered the opinion of the Court.

Linde Air Products Co., owner of the Jones patent for an electric welding process and for fluxes to be used therewith, brought an action for infringement against Lincoln and the two Graver companies. The trial court held four flux claims valid and infringed and certain other flux claims and all process claims invalid. The Court of Appeals affirmed findings of validity and infringement as to the four flux claims but reversed the trial court and held valid the process claims and the remaining contested flux claims. We granted certiorari and reversed the judgment of the Court of Appeals insofar as it reversed that of the trial court, and reinstated the District Court decree. Rehearing was granted, limited to the question of infringement of the four valid flux claims and to the applicability of the doctrine of equivalents to findings of fact in this case.

At the outset it should be noted that the single issue before us is whether the trial court's holding that the four flux claims have been infringed will be sustained. Any issue as to the validity of these claims was unanimously determined by the previous decision in this Court and attack on their validity cannot be renewed now by reason of limitation on grant of rehearing. The disclosure, the claims, and the prior art have been adequately described in our former opinion and in the opinions of the courts below.

In determining whether an accused device or composition infringes a valid patent, resort must be had in the first instance to the words of the claim. If accused matter falls clearly within the claim, infringement is made out and that is the end of it.

But courts have also recognized that to permit imitation of a patented invention which does not copy every literal detail would be to convert the protection of the patent grant into a hollow and useless thing. Such a limitation would leave room for—indeed encourage—the unscrupulous copyist to make unimportant and insubstantial changes and substitutions in the patent which, though adding nothing, would be enough to take the copied matter outside the claim, and hence outside the reach of law. One who seeks to pirate an invention, like one who seeks to pirate a copyrighted book or play, may be expected to introduce minor variations to conceal and shelter the piracy. Outright and forthright duplication is a dull and very rare type of infringement. To prohibit no other would place the inventor at the mercy of verbalism and would be subordinating substance to form. It would deprive him of the benefit of his invention and would foster concealment rather than disclosure of inventions, which is one of the primary purposes of the patent system.

The doctrine of equivalents evolved in response to this experience. The essence of the doctrine is that one may not practice a fraud on a patent. Originating almost a century ago in the case of Winans v. Denmead, 15 How. 330, 14 L.Ed. 717, it has been consistently applied by this Court and the lower federal courts, and continues today ready and available for utilization when the proper circumstances for its application arise. "To temper unsparing logic and prevent an infringer from stealing the benefit of the invention" a patentee may invoke this doctrine to proceed against the producer of a device "if it performs substantially the same function in substantially the same way to obtain the same result." Sanitary Refrigerator Co. v. Winters, 280 U.S. 30, 42, 50 S.Ct. 9, 13, 74 L.Ed. 147. The theory on which it is founded is that "if two devices do the same work in substantially the same way, and accomplish substantially the same result, they are the same, even though they differ in name, form or shape." Union Paper–Bag Machine Co. v. Murphy, 97 U.S. 120, 125, 24 L.Ed. 935. The doctrine operates not only in favor of the patentee of a pioneer or primary invention, but also for the patentee of a secondary invention consisting of a combination of old ingredients which produce new and useful results, Imhaeuser v. Buerk, 101 U.S. 647, 655, 25 L.Ed. 945, although the area of equivalence may vary under the circumstances. See Continental Paper Bag Co. v. Eastern Paper Bag Co., 210 U.S. 405, 414–415, 28 S.Ct. 748, 749, 52 L.Ed. 1122, and cases cited; Seymour v. Osborne, 11 Wall. 516, 556, 20 L.Ed. 33; Gould v. Rees, 15 Wall. 187, 192, 21 L.Ed. 39. The wholesome realism of this doctrine is not always applied in favor of a patentee but is sometimes used against him. Thus, where a device is so far changed in principle from a patented article that it performs the same or a similar function in a substantially different way, but nevertheless falls within the literal words of the claim, the doctrine of equivalents may be used to restrict the claim and defeat the patentee's action for infringement. Westinghouse v. Boyden Power–Brake Co., 170 U.S. 537, 568, 18 S.Ct. 707, 722, 42 L.Ed. 1136.

What constitutes equivalency must be determined against the context of the patent, the prior art, and the particular circumstances of the case. Equivalence, in the patent law, is not the prisoner of a formula and is not an absolute to be considered in a vacuum. It does not require complete identity for every purpose and in every respect. In determining equivalents, things equal to the same thing may not be equal to each other and, by the same token, things for most purposes different may sometimes be equivalents. Consideration must be given to the purpose for which an ingredient is used in a patent, the qualities it has when combined with the other ingredients, and the function which it is intended to perform. An important factor is whether persons reasonably skilled in the art would have known of the interchangeability of an ingredient not contained in the patent with one that was.

In the case before us, we have two electric welding compositions or fluxes: the patented composition, Unionmelt Grade 20, and the accused composition, Lincolnweld 660. The patent under which Unionmelt is made claims essentially a combination of alkaline earth metal silicate and calcium fluoride; Unionmelt actually contains, however, silicates of calcium and magnesium, two alkaline earth metal silicates. Lincolnweld's composition is similar to Unionmelt's, except that it substitutes silicates of calcium and manganese—the latter not an alkaline earth metal—for silicates of calcium and magnesium. In all other respects, the two compositions are alike. The mechanical methods in which these compositions are employed are similar. They are identical in operation and produce the same kind and quality of weld.

The question which thus emerges is whether the substitution of the manganese which is not an alkaline earth metal for the magnesium which is, under the circumstances of this case, and in view of the technology and the prior art, is a change of such substance as to make the doctrine of equivalents inapplicable; or conversely, whether under the circumstances the change was so insubstantial that the trial court's invocation of the doctrine of equivalents was justified.

Issue

Without attempting to be all-inclusive, we note the following evidence in the record: Chemists familiar with the two fluxes testified that manganese and magnesium were similar in many of their reactions (R. 287, 669). There is testimony by a metallurgist that alkaline earth metals are often found in manganese ores in their natural state and that they serve the same purpose in the fluxes (R. 831–832); and a chemist testified that 'in the sense of the patent' manganese could be included as an alkaline earth metal (R. 297). Much of this testimony was corroborated by reference to recognized texts on inorganic chemistry (R. 332). Particularly important, in addition, were the disclosures of the prior art, also contained in the record. The Miller patent, No. 1,754,566, which preceded the patent in suit, taught the use of manganese silicate in welding fluxes (R. 969, 971). Manganese was similarly disclosed in the Armor patent, No. 1,467,825, which also described a welding composition (R. 1346). And the record contains no evidence of any kind to show that Lincolnweld was developed as the result of independent research or experiments.

prior art

The trial judge found on the evidence before him that the Lincolnweld flux and the composition of the patent in suit are substantially identical in operation and in result. He found also that Lincolnweld is in all respects equivalent to Unionmelt for welding purposes. And he concluded that "for all practical purposes, manganese silicate can be efficiently and effectively substituted for calcium and magnesium silicates as the major constituent of the welding composition." These conclusions are adequately supported by the record; certainly they are not clearly erroneous.

Affirmed.

■ MR. JUSTICE MINTON took no part in the consideration or decision of this case.

■ MR. JUSTICE BLACK, with whom MR. JUSTICE DOUGLAS concurs, dissenting.

I heartily agree with the Court that "fraud" is bad, "piracy" is evil, and "stealing" is reprehensible. But in this case, where petitioners are not charged with any such malevolence, these lofty principles do not justify the Court's sterilization of Acts of Congress and prior decisions, none of which are even mentioned in today's opinion.

What is not specifically claimed is dedicated to the public. See, e.g., Miller v. Brass Co., 104 U.S. 350, 352, 26 L.Ed. 783. For the function of claims under R.S. § 4888, as we have frequently reiterated, is to exclude from the patent monopoly field all that is not specifically claimed, whatever may appear in the specifications. See, e.g., Marconi Wireless Co. v. United States, 320 U.S. 1, 23, 63 S.Ct. 1393, 1403, 87 L.Ed. 1731, and cases there cited. Today the Court tacitly rejects those cases. It departs from the underlying principle which, as the Court pointed out in White v. Dunbar, 119 U.S. 47, 51, 7 S.Ct. 72, 74, 30 L.Ed. 303, forbids treating a patent claim "like a nose of wax, which may be turned and twisted in any direction, by merely referring to the specification, so as to make it include something more than, or something different from, what its words express. * * * The claim is a statutory requirement, prescribed for the very purpose of making the patentee define precisely what his invention is; and it is unjust to the public, as well as an evasion of the law, to construe it in a manner different from the plain import of its terms." Giving this patentee the benefit of a grant that it did not precisely claim is no less "unjust to the public" and no less an evasion of R.S. § 4888 merely because done in the name of the "doctrine of equivalents."

In seeking to justify its emasculation of R.S. § 4888 by parading potential hardships which literal enforcement might conceivably impose on patentees who had for some reason failed to claim complete protection for their discoveries, the Court fails even to mention the program for alleviation of such hardships which Congress itself has provided. 35 U.S.C. § 64, 35 U.S.C.A. § 64, authorizes reissue of patents where a patent is "wholly or partly inoperative" due to certain errors arising from "inadvertence, accident, or mistake" of the patentee. And while the section does not expressly permit a patentee to expand his claim, this Court has reluctantly interpreted it to justify doing so. Miller v. Brass Co., 104 U.S. 350, 353–354, 26 L.Ed. 783. That interpretation, however, was accompanied by a warning that "Reissues for the enlargement of claims should be the exception and not the rule." 104 U.S. at page 355, 26 L.Ed. 783. And Congress was careful to hedge the privilege of reissue by exacting conditions It also entrusted the Patent Office, not the courts, with initial authority to determine whether expansion of a claim was justified, and barred suits for retroactive infringement based on such expansion. Like the Court's opinion, this congressional plan adequately protects patentees from "fraud," "piracy," and "stealing." Unlike the Court's opinion, it also protects business men from retroactive infringement suits and judicial expansion of a monopoly sphere beyond that which a patent expressly authorizes.

■ MR. JUSTICE DOUGLAS, dissenting [omitted].

Hughes Aircraft Co. v. United States

United States Court of Appeals, Federal Circuit, 1983.
717 F.2d 1351.

■ MARKEY, CHIEF JUDGE.

Hughes Aircraft Company (Hughes) appeals that part of a judgment of the United States Claims Court finding non-infringement of U.S. patent No. 3,758,051 (the Williams patent) by the government's "store and execute" (S/E) spacecraft.

Background

Throughout the late 1950's and early 1960's, the Department of Defense and the National Aeronautics and Space Administration (NASA) engaged in an intense effort to build a synchronous communications satellite with an orbital period equalling the rotational period of the earth. The goal was a satellite moving in a west-to-east orbit with a radius of 22,750 nautical miles and having a linear velocity of 10,090 feet per second, so that it could "hover" above a fixed point on earth.

Despite huge expenditures, the government never solved the technical problem of attitude control. That problem is described as the need to orient the satellite in space, without exceeding weight limitations, while insuring that (1) its directional antennas were always pointed toward the earth, and (2) that it would obtain a reliable, adequate fuel supply from the sun.

Working for Hughes, Williams solved the problem. He created a practical system for attitude control of a spin-stabilized satellite. In the Williams system, signals sent by a ground crew control the satellite by causing a jet on the satellite to pulse at a selected satellite position in successive spin cycles, thereby "precessing" the satellite in a selected direction. Williams taught how a jet valve on the satellite's periphery could discharge gas in brief, successive pulses on command. He taught that an on-board V-beam sun sensor (vertical slit and canted slit) could collect raw data from the sun and transmit it to earth, enabling a ground crew to determine the satellite's existing and desired orientations.

When, using conventional radio signals, the ground crew pulses the attitude jet, torque is applied to the satellite and its spin axis is "precessed" parallel to the earth's axis, causing the beam of the satellite's antenna to point to the earth continuously during the 24–hour period of each orbit, and insuring that the satellite's solar cells receive maximum light from the sun.

Hughes disclosed the invention to NASA, [the parties entered a contract, and on July 26, 1963, SYNCOM II, the world's first synchronous communications satellite, was launched and placed in orbit. Meanwhile, Williams had filed the parent application. After several interactions with the Examiner, including the cancellation of some claims and the filing of a continuation drafted to avoid the art disclosed by another satellite ("Mc-Lean"), this ultimately resulted in the patent at issue here.]

On November 13, 1973, Hughes filed this action in the Court of Claims under 28 U.S.C. § 1498, seeking reasonable and entire compensation for the unauthorized manufacture or use by the United States of the claimed invention in the government's SKYNET II, NATO II, DSCS II, IMP (H and J), SOLRAD (9 and 10), and PIONEER (10 and 11) spacecraft. The government disputed validity and denied infringement. [After a trial court decision in the Government's favor, Hughes appealed.]

OPINION

Infringement

(A) Literal Infringement

The trial judge correctly found, and it is here undisputed, that there are only two distinctions in the structure of the claimed Williams satellite from that of the S/E spacecraft: (1) the SKYNET II, NATO II, and DSCS II spacecraft do not include Williams' means for providing to the ground crew an indication of ISA position, having substituted computer-retention of that information; and (2) in all S/E systems, Williams' means for receiving synchronized control signals for immediate execution are substituted for by an on-board computer for receiving control signals and storing them for later execution. Because the claims speak of means for "providing an indication" of ISA position "to a location external" to the satellite, and to means for receiving from the external location firing signals "synchronized with said indication", there can be no literal infringement. At trial, Hughes conceded the absence of literal infringement and predicated its case for infringement on the doctrine of equivalents.

(B) Doctrine of Equivalents and Doctrine of File Wrapper Estoppel

The doctrine of equivalents comes into play only when actual literal infringement is not present. Under the doctrine of equivalents, an accused product that does not literally infringe a structural claim may yet be found an infringement "if it performs substantially the same function in substantially the same way to obtain the same result" as the claimed product or process. Graver Tank & Mfg. Co. v. Linde Air Products Co., 339 U.S. 605, 608, 70 S.Ct. 854, 856, 94 L.Ed. 1097 (1950)(quoting from Sanitary Refrigerator Co. v. Winters, 280 U.S. 30, 42, 50 S.Ct. 9, 13, 74 L.Ed. 147). The doctrine is judicially devised to do equity. "Courts have also recognized that to permit imitation of a patented invention which does not copy every literal detail would be to convert the protection of the patent grant into a hollow and useless thing," id. 339 U.S. at 607, 70 S.Ct. at 856, and again, "The essence of the doctrine is that one may not practice a fraud on a patent," id. at 608, 70 S.Ct. at 856.

Hughes, having the burden of proving infringement by a preponderance of the evidence, Roberts Dairy Co. v. United States, 530 F.2d 1342, 1357, 182 U.S.P.Q. 218, 227 (Trial Div., Ct.Cl.1974), aff'd 198 U.S.P.Q. 383 (Ct.Cl.1976), characterizes as "inconsequential" the differences in operation of the claimed invention and the accused S/E spacecraft. It asserts that the Williams satellite and S/E spacecraft are "obvious and exact equivalents." Hughes argues that: (1) though sun pulses are not sent to the ground by the SKYNET II, NATO II, or DSCS II spacecraft, they are retained in the on-board computer and used in the spacecraft for the same purpose as in Williams' "real-time" satellite, i.e., as reference points to fire the precession jet; (2) respecting immediate and delayed firing, the Williams satellite and all S/E spacecraft require "synchronization of jet firing with spin position"; and (3) "[i]f there were doubt as to whether the S/E spacecraft are obvious and exact equivalents of Williams, the S/E spacecraft nevertheless fall within the broad range of equivalents to which the pioneer Williams patent is entitled."

Addressing the last argument first, we agree with the trial judge that Williams' invention is not of such "pioneer" status as to entitle the invention to the very broad range of equivalents to which pioneer inventions are normally entitled. McLean, not Williams, was the first to disclose the basic operational concept in which a pulsed jet is used to precess the spin axis of a spin-stabilized body. That does not mean, as discussed below, that the Williams invention is entitled to no range of equivalents. Nor is the Williams invention entitled only to that very narrow range of equivalents applicable to improvement patents in a crowded art.

Having chosen specific words of limitation to avoid the McLean disclosure, Hughes is estopped by the prosecution history of the application ("file wrapper estoppel"), from obtaining a claim interpretation so broad as to encompass the McLean structure, or to encompass all structures in which a pulsed jet is used to precess the spin axis of a spin-stabilized body. The doctrine of prosecution history estoppel precludes a patent owner from obtaining a claim construction that would resurrect subject matter surrendered during prosecution of his patent application. The estoppel applies to claim amendments to overcome rejections based on prior art, Dwyer v. United States, 357 F.2d 978, 984, 149 U.S.P.Q. 133, 138 (Ct.Cl.1966), and to arguments submitted to obtain the patent, Coleco Industries, Inc. v. ITC, 573 F.2d 1247, 1257, 197 U.S.P.Q. 472, 480 (Cust. & Pat.App.1978). Williams did not, of course, surrender subject matter related to employment of an on-board computer to accomplish in a differently timed manner what is accomplished by his disclosed structure.

An applicant for patent is required to disclose the best mode then known to him for practicing his invention. 35 U.S.C. § 112. He is not required to predict all future developments which enable the practice of his invention in substantially the same way.

The trial judge correctly stated that Hughes is estopped from asserting that the elements of its claims "are unnecessary to avoid the art." The relevant consideration, however, is not whether the claims avoid the art but whether the accused S/E spacecraft are equivalents of the inventions set forth in the claims interpreted in light of the prior art. The government is not claiming that its S/E spacecraft are built and operated in accord with the prior art, or that it is merely following the teachings of McLean. If it had followed those teachings in constructing its S/E spacecraft, there is no question that the range of equivalents to which Williams' claimed invention is entitled could not be broad enough to encompass such spacecraft.

Some courts have expressed the view that virtually any amendment of the claims creates a "file wrapper estoppel" effective to bar all resort to the doctrine of equivalents, and to confine patentee "strictly to the letter of the limited claims granted," Nationwide Chemical Corp. v. Wright, 584 F.2d 714, 718–19 (5th Cir.1978); Ekco Products Co. v. Chicago Metallic Manufacturing Co., 347 F.2d 453, 455 (7th Cir.1965). We, as has the Supreme Court, reject that view as a wooden application of estoppel, negating entirely the doctrine of equivalents and limiting determination of the infringement issue to consideration of literal infringement alone. That view, as above indicated, fails to recognize that the doctrine of equivalents is unnecessary when literal infringement is present and is contrary to the guidance provided by the Supreme Court in Graver, supra.

Amendment of claims is a common practice in prosecution of patent applications. No reason or warrant exists for limiting application of the doctrine of equivalents to those comparatively few claims allowed exactly as originally filed and never amended. Amendments may be of different types and may serve different functions. Depending on the nature and purpose of an amendment, it may have a limiting effect within a spectrum ranging from great to small to zero. The effect may or may not be fatal to application of a range of equivalents broad enough to encompass a particular accused product. It is not fatal to application of the doctrine itself.

Application of the Doctrine of Equivalents

The issue, as above indicated, is whether the accused S/E spacecraft infringe the claims under the doctrine of equivalents. That question turns on whether the S/E spacecraft employ substantially the same means which "perform substantially the same function" as that performed by the claimed invention, and do so "in substantially the same way" the claimed invention does, and "obtain the same result" as that obtained by the claimed invention.

There are striking overall similarities between Williams' claimed satellite and the S/E spacecraft: (1) each is spin-stabilized; (2) each contains a jet on the periphery, connected by a valve to a tank containing fluid for expulsion substantially parallel to the spin axis; (3) each employs sun sensors to sense ISA position; (4) each requires knowledge of orientation relative to a fixed external coordinate system; (5) each contains radio equipment for communicating with the ground; (6) each transmits spin rate and sun angle information to a ground crew; and (7) in each, jet firing is synchronized with ISA position to effect controlled precession and thus to achieve a desired orientation. Only elements (1) and (2) are found in McLean. Clearly, the S/E spacecraft are much closer to Williams' satellite than they are to McLean's space vehicle. It is clear also that, in constructing its S/E spacecraft, the government followed the teachings of Williams much more than it did those of McLean. In following Williams' teachings, the government merely employed a modern day computer to do indirectly what Williams taught it to do directly.

That an appropriate range of equivalents of the claims extends beyond devices that send the ISA position indication to ground is consistent with Williams' patent specification: As an example of one means of controlling the starting time and duration of pulses to the jet control valves ... in such a way as to result in thrust during the correct portion of each spin revolution, cam-controlled contacts or switches may be used. In the operation of the S/E spacecraft, the information that is transmitted to the ground crew, to enable them to determine and provide thrust during "the correct portion of each spin revolution", is the modern-day equivalent of sending the ISA position indication to the ground for that same purpose in Williams. Put another way, retention of the ISA position in an on-board computer, while transmitting sufficient information to enable the ground crew to use that computer-retained information to control the satellite, is the modern-day equivalent of providing an indication of ISA to ground as taught by Williams.

The S/E spacecraft and the Williams claimed satellite each have on-board means for transmitting to ground the sun angle and spin rate. In each, the ground crew determines: (1) present orientation; (2) desired orientation; and (3) where in the spin cycle and how many times the jet must be pulsed to change (1) to (2). Each system, furthermore, provides for receipt of command signals to cause firing of the precession jet. The S/E spacecraft uses sun pulses retained on-board as reference points to fire the jet. Williams uses sun pulses sent to ground as reference points to fire the jet. The difference between operation by retention and operation by sending is achieved by relocating the function, making no change in the function performed, or in the basic manner of operation, or in the result obtained.

Conclusion on Equivalents

The S/E spacecraft and the claimed Williams satellite reflect the precise circumstance envisaged in Graver, supra, for they perform the same function (receipt of and response to command signals from an external location to accomplish precession), in substantially the same way (jet firings synchronized, albeit later and internally, with ISA position) to obtain substantially the same result (controlled precession of spin axis in a predetermined direction to orient a hovering satellite). At the same time, neither resembles as closely the self-guiding space vehicle of McLean or its purely automatic operation.

Accordingly, we hold that Hughes has proven that the government's S/E spacecraft infringe Williams' claims 1, 2, and 3 under the doctrine of equivalents.

■ DAVIS, CIRCUIT JUDGE, concurring in part and dissenting in part. [omitted]

Aro Manufacturing Co. v. Convertible Top Replacement Co., Inc.

Supreme Court of the United States, 1961.
365 U.S. 336, 81 S.Ct. 599, 5 L.Ed.2d 592.

■ MR. JUSTICE WHITTAKER delivered the opinion of the Court.

On April 17, 1956, respondent, Convertible Top Replacement Co., Inc., acquired a "Territorial Grant" (coextensive with "the Commonwealth of Massachusetts") of all rights in Letters Patent No. 2,569,724, commonly known as the Mackie–Duluk patent, and 10 days later commenced this action against petitioners, Aro Manufacturing Co., Inc., and several of its officers, to enjoin the alleged infringement and contributory infringement of the patent and for an accounting of profits.

The patent—one for a "Convertible Folding Top with Automatic Seal at Rear Quarter"—covers the combination, in an automobile body, of a flexible top fabric, supporting structures, and a mechanism for sealing the fabric against the side of the automobile body in order to keep out the rain. Tops embodying the patent have been installed by several automobile manufacturers in various models of convertibles. The components of the patented combination, other than the fabric, normally are usable for the lifetime of the car, but the fabric has a much shorter life. It usually so suffers from wear and tear, or so deteriorates in appearance, as to become "spent," and normally is replaced, after about three years of use. The consequent demand for replacement fabrics has given rise to a substantial industry, in which petitioner, Aro Manufacturing Co., is a national leader. It manufactures and sells replacement fabrics designed to fit the models of convertibles equipped with tops embodying the combination covered by the patent in suit.

Validity of the patent is not challenged in this Court. The principal, and we think the determinative, question presented here is whether the owner of a combination patent, comprised entirely of unpatented elements, has a patent monopoly on the manufacture, sale or use of the several unpatented components of the patented combination. More specifically, and limited to the particular case here, does the car owner infringe (and the supplier contributorily infringe) the combination patent when he replaces the spent fabric without the patentee's consent?

Since the patentees never claimed the fabric or its shape as their invention, and the claims made in the patent are the sole measure of the grant, the fabric is no more than an unpatented element of the combination which was claimed as the invention, and the patent did not confer a monopoly over the fabric or its shape.

It follows that petitioners' manufacture and sale of the fabric is not a direct infringement under 35 U.S.C. § 271(a), 35 U.S.C.A. § 271(a).... But the question remains whether petitioners' manufacture and sale of the fabric constitute a contributory infringement of the patent under 35 U.S.C. § 271(c), 35 U.S.C.A. § 271(c). It is admitted that petitioners know that the purchasers intend to use the fabric for replacement purposes on automobile convertible tops which are covered by the claims of respondent's combination patent, and such manufacture and sale with that knowledge might well constitute contributory infringement under § 271(c), if, but only if, such a replacement by the purchaser himself would in itself constitute a direct infringement under § 271(a), for it is settled that if there is no direct infringement of a patent there can be no contributory infringement.

This Court's decisions specifically dealing with whether the replacement of an unpatented part, in a patented combination, that has worn out, been broken or otherwise spent, is permissible "repair" or infringing "reconstruction," have steadfastly refused to extend the patent monopoly beyond the terms of the grant. Wilson v. Simpson, 9 How. 109, 13 L.Ed. 66—doubtless the leading case in this Court that deals with the distinction—concerned a patented planing machine which included, as elements, certain cutting knives which normally wore out in a few months' use. The purchaser was held to have the right to replace those knives without the patentee's consent. The Court held that, although there is no right to "rebuild" a patented combination, the entity "exists" notwithstanding the fact that destruction or impairment of one of its elements renders it inoperable; and that, accordingly, replacement of that worn-out essential part is permissible restoration of the machine to the original use for which it was bought. 9 How. at page 123. The Court explained that it is "the use of the whole" of the combination which a purchaser buys, and that repair or replacement of the worn-out, damaged or destroyed part is but an exercise of the right "to give duration to that which he owns, or has a right to use as a whole." Ibid.

The distilled essence of the Wilson case was stated by Judge Learned Hand in United States v. Aluminum Co. of America, 2 Cir., 148 F.2d 416, 425: "The (patent) monopolist cannot prevent those to whom he sells from * * * reconditioning articles worn by use, unless they in fact make a new article."

Respondent has strenuously urged, as an additional relevant factor, the "essentialness" of the fabric element to the combination constituting the invention. It argues that the particular shape of the fabric was the advance in the art—the very "heart" of the invention—which brought the combination up to the inventive level, and, therefore, concludes that its patent should be held to grant it a monopoly on the fabric. The rule for which respondent contends is: That when an element of a patented machine or combination is relatively durable—even though not so durable as the entire patented device which the owner purchased—relatively expensive, relatively difficult to replace, and is an "essential" or "distinguishing" part of the patented combination, any replacement of that element, when it wears out or is otherwise spent, constitutes infringing "reconstruction," and, therefore, a new license must be obtained from, and another royalty paid to, the patentee for that privilege.

We cannot agree. For if anything is settled in the patent law, it is that the combination patent covers only the totality of the elements in the claim and that no element, separately viewed, is within the grant.

In order to call the monopoly, conferred by the patent grant, into play for a second time, it must, indeed, be a second creation of the patented entity.... Mere replacement of individual unpatented parts, one at a time, whether of the same part repeatedly or different parts successively, is no more than the lawful right of the owner to repair his property. Measured by this test, the replacement of the fabric involved in this case must be characterized as permissible "repair," not "reconstruction." Reversed.

■ MR. JUSTICE BLACK, concurring (omitted).

■ MR. JUSTICE BRENNAN, concurring in the result.

I agree that the replacement of the top was "repair" and not "reconstruction," but I cannot agree that the test suggested by my Brother Whittaker for determination of that question is the correct one. My Brother

Harlan's dissent cogently states the reasons why I also think that is too narrow a standard of what constitutes impermissible "reconstruction." For there are circumstances in which the replacement of a single unpatented component of a patented combination short of a second creation of the patented entity may constitute "reconstruction." ... Appropriately to be considered are the life of the part replaced in relation to the useful life of the whole combination, the importance of the replaced element to the inventive concept, the cost of the component relative to the cost of the combination, the common sense understanding and intention of the patent owner and the buyer of the combination as to its perishable components, whether the purchased component replaces a worn-out part or is brought for some other purpose, and other pertinent factors.

... The life of the top was approximately three years in contrast to the several times longer life of the other components of the combination. The top was replaceable at a cost of from $30 to $70 depending on the fabric; in contrast the cost of other elements of the combination was approximately $400. These considerations of themselves suggest that the replacement was mere "repair" of the worn component and not "reconstruction" of the patented combination. Surely they support the inference that all concerned knew that the fabric of the top would become weather-beaten or unable to perform its protective function long before those other components, not so exposed and more durable as well, wore out. Its perishable nature coupled with its fractional cost as compared to the whole combination and its ready replaceability all point to the conclusion reached here. And particularly persuasive, I think, that this replacement was mere "repair," is the role of the top relative to other components in the inventive concept. Patentable novelty inhered not merely in the shape of the fabric; the record shows that a wiping arm which pressed the material in such way as to create a seal at the belt line of the vehicle played a significantly important role in the inventive concept. The claim for the combination is that it made possible an automatic top, made the top weathertight and prevented unauthorized access to the vehicle. The wiper arm, rather than the shape of the material alone, accomplished the inventive purposes of providing a top which was weathertight and prevented unauthorized access. The shape of the fabric was thus not the essence of the device and in all the circumstances it seems reasonable and sensible to treat the replacement of the top as "repair."

I, therefore, think that the judgment of the Court of Appeals must be reversed, except, however, as to the relief granted respondent in respect of the replacements made on Ford cars before July 21, 1955.

■ MR. JUSTICE HARLAN, whom MR. JUSTICE FRANKFURTER and MR. JUSTICE STEWART join, dissenting (omitted).

The parties to the above case paid another visit to the Supreme Court three years later. In Aro Manufacturing Co. v. Convertible Top Replacement Co.,[1] the issue was whether Aro was liable for contributory infringement for selling replacement tops to owners of 1952–1954 Fords. It was undisputed that Ford had failed to take a license under the patent for cars manufactured in those years, making Ford's manufacture and sale of the tops direct infringement. The Court held:

"... [W]ith Ford lacking authority to make and sell, it could by its sale of the cars confer on the purchasers no implied license to use, and their use of the patented structures was thus 'without authority' and infringing under § 271(a). Not only does that provision explicitly regard an unauthorized user of a patented invention as an infringer, but it has often and clearly been held that unauthorized use without more, constitutes infringement. Birdsell v. Shaliol, 112 U.S. 485; Union Tool Co. v. Wilson, 259 U.S. 107, 114. . . .

"If the owner's *use* infringed, so also did his *repair* of the top-structure, as by replacing the worn-out fabric component. Where use infringes, repair does also, for it perpetuates the infringing use." [Footnotes omitted]

In a later portion of the opinion, the Court held that to prove its case, the plaintiff would have to show that Aro knew "that the combination for which [its] component was especially designed was both patented and infringing."

Paper Converting Machine Co. v. Magna–Graphics Corp.

United States Court of Appeals, Federal Circuit, 1984.
745 F.2d 11.

NICHOLS, SENIOR CIRCUIT JUDGE.[a]

This appeal is from a judgment of the United States District Court for the Eastern District of Wisconsin (Reynolds, C.J.), 576 F.Supp. 967, entered on December 1, 1983, and awarding plaintiff Paper Converting Machine Company (Paper Converting) $893,064 as compensation for defendant Magna–Graphics Corporation's (Magna–Graphics) willful infringement of United States Patent No. Re. 28,353. We affirm-in-part and vacate-in-part.

I

Although the technology involved here is complex, the end product is one familiar to most Americans. The patented invention relates to a machine used to manufacture rolls of densely wound ("hard-wound") industrial toilet tissue and paper toweling. The machine, commonly known as an automatic rewinder, unwinds a paper web continuously under high tension at speeds up to 2,000 feet per minute from a large-diameter paper

---

[1] 377 U.S. 476 (1964).

[a] Note that at the time this case was decided, § 271 did not provide patent holders with the right to prevent others from offering to sell the patented invention.

roll—known as the parent roll or bedroll—and simultaneously rewinds it onto paperboard cores to form individual consumer products.

Before the advent of automatic rewinders, toilet tissue and paper towel producers used "stop-start" rewinders. With these machines, the entire rewinding operation had to cease after a retail-sized "log" was finished so that a worker could place a new mandrel (the shaft for carrying the paperboard core) in the path of the paper web. In an effort to increase production, automatic rewinders were introduced in the early 1950's. These machines automatically moved a new mandrel into the path of the paper web while the machine was still winding the paper web onto another mandrel, and could operate at a steady pace at speeds up to about 1,200 feet per minute.

In 1962, Nystrand, Bradley, and Spencer invented the first successful "sequential" automatic rewinder, a machine which not only overcame previous speed limitations, but also could handle two-ply tissue. This rewinder simultaneously cut the paper web and impaled it on pins against the parent roll. Then, after a new mandrel was automatically moved into place, a "pusher" would move the paper web away from the parent roll and against a glue-covered paperboard core to begin winding a new paper log.

On April 20, 1965, United States Patent No. 3,179,348 (the '348 patent) issued, giving to Paper Converting (to whom rights in the invention had been assigned) patent protection for machines incorporating the sequential rewinding approach.

III

A

In early 1980 Fort Howard became interested in purchasing a new high-speed rewinder line. Both Paper Converting and Magna–Graphics offered bids. Because Magna–Graphics offered to provide an entire rewinder line for about 10 percent less than did Paper Converting, it won the contract. Delivery would have been before the '353 patent expired. Magna–Graphics began to build the contracted for machinery, but before it completed the rewinder, on February 26, 1981, the federal district court in Wisconsin determined that a similar Magna–Graphics' rewinder built for and sold to Scott infringed the '353 patent. The court enjoined Magna–Graphics from any future infringing activity. Because at the time of the federal injunction the rewinder intended for Fort Howard was only 80 percent complete, Magna–Graphics sought a legal way to fulfill its contract with Fort Howard rather than abandon its machine. First, [it tried to build a rewinder that did not infringe the patent, but counsel could not determine whether the new design would be infringing.]

Magna–Graphics thereafter continued to construct the Fort Howard machine, all the while staying in close consultation with its counsel. After finishing substantially all of the machine, Magna–Graphics tested it to ensure that its moving parts would function as intended at a rate of 1,600 feet of paper per minute. Although Magna–Graphics normally fully tested machines at its plant before shipment, to avoid infringement in this instance, Magna–Graphics ran its tests in two stages over a period of several weeks in July and August of 1981.

In the first stage of its test, Magna–Graphics checked the bedroll to determine whether the pushers actuated properly. During this stage of tests, no cutoff blades or pins were installed. In the second stage of the test, Magna–Graphics checked the cutoff roll to determine whether the cutting blade actuated as intended. During this phase of the testing, no pins or pusher pads were installed. At no time during the tests were the pins, pushers, and blade installed and operated together.

To further its scheme to avoid patent infringement, Magna–Graphics negotiated special shipment and assembly details with Fort Howard. Under the advice of counsel, Fort Howard and Magna–Graphics agreed that the rewinder's cutoff and transfer mechanism would not be finally assembled until April 22, 1982, two days after the expiration of the '353 patent. With this agreement in hand, Magna–Graphics shipped the basic rewinder machine to Fort Howard on September 17, 1981, and separately shipped the cutoff roll and bedroll on October 23, 1981. The rewinder machine was not assembled or installed at the Fort Howard plant until April 26, 1982.

B

With this case we are once again confronted with a situation which tests the temporal limits of the American patent grant. See Roche Products, Inc. v. Bolar Pharmaceutical Co., 733 F.2d 858, 221 U.S.P.Q. 937 (Fed.Cir.1984). We must decide here the extent to which a competitor of a patentee can manufacture and test during the life of a patent a machine intended solely for post-patent use. Magna–Graphics asserts that no law prohibits it from soliciting orders for, substantially manufacturing, testing, or even delivering machinery which, if completely assembled during the patent term, would infringe. We notice, but Magna–Graphics adds that it is totally irrelevant, that Paper Converting has lost, during the term of its patent, a contract for the patented machine which it would have received but for the competitor's acts.

The disjunctive language of the patent grant gives a patentee the "right to exclude others from making, using or selling" a patented invention during the 17 years of the patent's existence. 35 U.S.C. § 154. See also 35 U.S.C. § 271. Congress has never deemed it necessary to define any of this triad of excludable activities, however, leaving instead the meaning of "make," "use," and "sell" for judicial interpretation. See Roche Products, Inc. v. Bolar Pharmaceutical Co., supra.

It is undisputed that Magna–Graphics intended to finesse Paper Converting out of the sale of a machine on which Paper Converting held a valid patent during the life of that patent. Given the amount of testing performed here, coupled with the sale and delivery during the patent-term of a "completed" machine (completed by being ready for assembly and with no useful noninfringing purpose), we are not persuaded that the district court committed clear error in finding that the Magna–Graphics' machine infringed the '353 patent.

To reach a contrary result would emasculate the congressional intent to prevent the making of a patented item during the patent's full term of 17 years. If without fear of liability a competitor can assemble a patented item past the point of testing, the last year of the patent becomes worthless whenever it deals with a long lead-time article. Nothing would prohibit the unscrupulous competitor from aggressively marketing its own product and constructing it to all but the final screws and bolts, as Magna–Graphics did here. We rejected any reduction to the patent-term in Roche; we cannot allow the inconsistency in the patent law which would exist if we permitted it here. Magna–Graphics built and tested a patented machine, albeit in a less than preferred fashion.

V

The judgment of the district court awarding damages and prejudgment interest for Paper Converting's lost profits on two automatic rewinder lines is affirmed.

■ Nies, Circuit Judge, dissenting-in-part [omitted].

NOTES

1. *Literal infringement.* Literal infringement involves a two-part analysis. First, the claims are interpreted. Second, each claim is examined to see if it "reads on" (that is, describes) the so-called "accused device" (or, of course, the accused process). The patentee is not required to show copying: even an independent inventor who never heard of the patent or the patentee will be considered an infringer if he practices the invention described in any one of the claims.

a. *Claim interpretation.* As *Fromson* demonstrates, the claims, no matter how carefully drawn, can turn out to be ambiguous. After all, the patentee wrote her application when her discovery was in its infancy: she may not have completely understood what she was observing, and may not have had a literature from which to draw a vocabulary. By the time an infringement action is brought, her wording may not resonate with current understandings in the field, and so the claims may be difficult to interpret.

Courts considering ambiguous claims will often rely on expert testimony. Experts in the field can testify on what the wording means to the person with ordinary skill in the art; experts in drafting patents can describe how similar wording is used in other applications. But by far the most important evidence is what the patentee said, did, and wrote in her patent application, because this is what tells the public what she meant to keep and what she meant to release to the public domain. Thus, if other claims in the patent shed light on the meaning of particular language, that evidence will be regarded as significant. The prosecution history will also be examined with care, first to see whether words in claims that were cancelled reflect on the meaning of the claims that were allowed, and second, to determine whether the applicant said anything to the examiner that revealed her meaning. Furthermore, if the prosecution history reveals that the examiner regarded some aspect of the claims in the application as unpatentable, and the applicant in response relinquished that claim, the patentee will be estopped from later arguing for an interpretation of the allowed claims that will give her rights over the relinquished technology. The public is entitled to rely on the fact that a claim was cancelled.

b. *Comparing the claims to the accused device.* Recall the test for novelty: "That which infringes, if later, would anticipate, if earlier."[2] *Fromson* and *Hughes* demonstrate that this test does work. In both cases, the court decided infringement by determining whether the accused device possessed every element of the claimed invention. This is the exact obverse of the novelty test, which looked to see whether every element in the claimed invention was described in the reference.

2. *Infringement under the doctrine of equivalents.* As described in *Graver Tank,* infringement under the doctrine of equivalents is determined by comparing the accused device (or process) to the patented invention to see if it "performs substantially the same function in substantially the same way to obtain the same result." In some ways, this "function/way/result" test mirrors the "substantial similarity" test for copyright infringement and the "confusing similarity" test for trademark infringement, see Assignments 10 and 3. For that reason, many regard the doctrine of equivalents as justified in a manner that mirrors the policies of copyright and trademark law. A cause of action to prevent express infringement is thought not sufficient protection for the right holder because it would be too easy to make a trivial variation and capture a part of the market. Thus, some leeway is created by permitting the patentee to show that the accused device is an obvious variation on the patented invention.

Some commentators, however, offer a different explanation for this doctrine. Looking back at older case law, they explain the doctrine as concerned with mistakes—that is, as allowing the patentee to stretch the claims to cover things he should have claimed, but inadvertently omitted. These commentators argue that the patent reward is an important part of the system for encouraging innovation. Inventive activities would be chilled if inventors knew that simple errors might bar them from receiving their expected returns.

A related justification for the doctrine of equivalents can be called the "quasi-mistake" approach. It recognizes the dynamic quality of innovation. Under this view, patentees cannot be expected to claim every variation on their invention because some variations only become possible because of developments other fields. *Hughes* is an example: the developments in the computer field that made an onboard processor possible mostly occurred after the *Hughes* patent issued. If the patentee is to capture the rewards of

---

[2] Knapp v. Morss, 150 U.S. 221, 228, 14 S.Ct. 81, 84, 37 L.Ed. 1059 (1893). See Assignment 18.

inventing, the variations made possible through later developments ought to be considered infringing.

Do any of these explanations make sense? The defect in the copyright/trademark analogy is that the extensive patent application process gives the patent holder ample opportunity to identify the exact inventive concept and claim all the obvious changes that could be made in it. Thus, there is little need to give the patentee extra leeway at the infringement stage. As to the mistake ideas: is not a mistake the worst case for the doctrine? After all, the burden of error must fall somewhere; putting it on the patentee encourages accurate claiming.

Besides, the statute has its own solutions for these problems. As to leeway, the last paragraph of § 112 allows the patentee to claim inventions of more than one element ("combinations") by expressing "a means ... for performing a specified function." An illustration of this "means plus function" claiming can be found in the Lipschitz patent of Assignment 15. It allows the patentee to extend the reach of her patent to *literally* cover other embodiments of the inventive concept, including some that could not have been foreseen at the time the claims were drafted. For mistake, the reissue provision of §§ 251–252 gives patentees a two-year window in which to correct for error. This provision has an important advantage over common law, for it also protects the public. It gives those who practiced the invention in reliance on the original patent "intervening rights," meaning the right to continue any activity that began before the reissue.

3. *The reverse doctrine of equivalents.* Note that Graver Tank also envisioned the possibility that an invention could be literally described by a claim, but be so far removed from the patented invention that it should not be considered infringing. Boyden Power–Brake Co. v. Westinghouse[3] is an example. The patentee had shown that a train could be made to brake much faster if an auxiliary air supply is released against the wheels. The actual device that was patented did not, however, release air nearly fast enough to make much of a difference to railroad safety. The accused device got the air to the wheel effectively. Although this device was literally described by the patent, the Supreme Court found that it was really utilizing a very different insight, and so did not infringe under the reverse doctrine of equivalents.

The reverse doctrine is infrequently used. Some economists argue that it should be utilized more because it solves a persistent problem in patent law: providing enough incentive to make important improvements. Current law may provide an improver with a patent right of his own, but the right is of limited value because the improver cannot use his improvement without a license from the patentee who has rights to the underlying invention. Although in theory, the patentee should be willing to license the improver because the improvement makes his own invention more desirable, in practice parties have trouble achieving the optimal result. With a robust reverse doctrine of equivalents, improvers know that if they make a

[3] 170 U.S. 537, 18 S.Ct. 707, 42 L.Ed. 1136 (1897).

sufficiently important improvement, they may be "out from under" the patent. Thus, they have a greater incentive to be inventive.

4. *Brakes on the doctrine of equivalents.* Many devices perform the same function in the same way to achieve the same result. If *Graver Tank* were applied broadly, it would stifle inventiveness for the reasons set out in Note 3. Moreover, widespread, unchecked use of the doctrine has the effect of making it difficult for third parties to know when their activity will be deemed to infringe a patent. Out of concern that use of the doctrine of equivalents has gone to far, the CAFC has begun to emphasize its limits.

a. *Nonobviousness.* One of the oldest limits on the doctrine of equivalents is that the patentee cannot use it to stretch the patent to encompass activity that would have been considered obvious (or non-novel) at the time he made his invention. That is, the doctrine cannot be used to acquire exclusive rights over inventions that could not have been patented in the first place. In Wilson Sporting Goods Co. v. David Geoffrey & Assoc.,[4] Judge Rich attempted to make this analysis easier. He suggested contructing a hypothetical claim that would cover the accused product. Then, ask whether that claim could have been patented at the time the application on the patent in issue was pending.

b. *Prosecution history estoppel.* Note 1(a) described use of prosecution history estoppel to prevent patentees from interpreting claims in a manner that would resurrect rights to inventions that were expressly relinquished. It is used in a similar way when the doctrine of equivalents is raised, for the patentee is also precluded from using this doctrine to capture technology that was described in claims that were relinquished during prosecution.

c. *The every-element test.* Lately, the CAFC has stressed the fact that the every-element test applies as much to infringement under the doctrine of equivalents as it does to literal infringement. In Pennwalt Corp. v. Durand–Wayland, Inc.,[5] for example, the court required that the accused device contain an equivalent to each and every element of the patented invention. In that case, both inventions sorted fruit by color and weight. The patented invention had discrete electrical components and the progress of the fruit through the sorter could be continuously observed on monitoring equipment. The accused device was computerized. Although it probably could have been easily programmed to monitor the fruit's progress, this was not a feature users cared about, so it was not so programmed. The court held that there was no infringement under the doctrine of equivalents because the accused device did not have an equivalent to the patented invention's progress tracker.

The "all-elements" test, as the CAFC calls it, works better in theory than in practice. Courts following *Pennwalt* have had difficulty applying it because the differences between the accused invention and the patented

---

[4] 904 F.2d 677 (Fed.Cir.1990).

[5] 833 F.2d 931 (Fed.Cir.1987), cert. denied, 485 U.S. 961, 108 S.Ct. 1226, 99 L.Ed.2d 426 (1988).

invention that make literal infringement unavailable, also tend to obscure the element by element comparison.[6]

d. *Insubstantiality*. In a recent en banc opinion, Hilton Davis Chemical Co. v. Warner–Jenkinson Company, Inc.,[7] the Federal Circuit stressed that "the doctrine [of equivalents] applies if, and only if, the differences between the claimed and accused products or processes are insubstantial." Thus, even if an invention meets the function/way/result test, it will not be considered to infringe if it represents a substantially different product or process from the patented one. The court indicated that the factors to be considered in determining insubstantiality include: 1) whether persons with skill in the art actually knew of the equivalence of the claimed and accused inventions, 2) whether a person with skill could have known of the equivalence, and 3) whether the defendant had intended to copy (which could imply that it was only interested in making trivial changes), or had intended to design around (which could imply that it had attempted to make significant changes), or had inadvertently arrived at the same invention through independent research.

e. *Other factors*. An emphasis on insubstantiality certainly accords well with the first explanation for the doctrine described in Note 2, but will it make the law on infringement more tractable? *Hilton Davis* produced three separate dissents that represented 5 of the judges on the Federal Circuit. (The majority comprised 7 judges). Concerned that the court had offered insufficient guidelines to cabin use of the doctrine, each dissent suggested that other factors should inform a doctrine of equivalents analysis. Judge Lourie, for example, would also have looked to the behavior of the patentee and the infringer. As to the patentee, he argued that those who "impair the ability of the public to reasonably understand from the claims what is patented" and those who fail to seek reissue when it is available, should be less entitled to use the doctrine than others. As to the infringer, he would would have made only those who proceeded in bad faith to free ride on the patentee (i.e. copyists) vulnerable to infringement under the doctrine. All of the dissenters also felt that the doctrine should be in the hands of the court rather than the jury, see Note 5, infra.

5. *The role of the jury.* In recent years, the Federal Circuit has begun to pay serious attention to the allocation of authority as between judge and jury. In Markman v. Westview Instruments, Inc.,[8] the court held that claim interpretation is a question of law. Therefore, even in jury-tried cases, questions such as the one at issue in *Fromson* are henceforth to be decided by the judge. Once the meaning of the patented claim is determined by the court, it will be explained to the jury, which will then decide whether the claim as interpreted has been infringed.

Hilton Davis also involved an allocation question. Prior to the decision, it had been argued that the doctrine of equivalents was equitable in nature.

---

[6] See, e.g., Corning Glass Works v. Sumitomo Electric U.S.A., Inc., 868 F.2d 1251 (Fed.Cir.1989).

[7] 62 F.3d 1512 (Fed.Cir.1995)(en banc), cert. granted __ U.S. __, 116 S.Ct. 1014, __ L.Ed.2d __ (1996).

[8] 52 F.3d 967 (Fed.Cir.1995)(en banc).

Since the Seventh Amendment protects the right to trial by jury only for actions at law, doctrine of equivalents claims were, under this approach, for the court alone. The *Hilton Davis* majority rejected this analysis, reasoning that doctrine of equivalents claims sound at law, not in equity. According to the majority, the doctrine is merely another way to determine whether the accused and patented inventions are the same.[9]

The dissenters in *Hilton Davis* disagreed strongly with this result. Judge Plager, for example, claimed that giving this issue to the court would have been the "bold and clean solution" to the doctrine of equivalents problem.[10] Judges are less swayed by sentiment than juries and are better able to apply accurately the Federal Circuit's admonishments on determining when variations are insubstantial. Moreover, since a judge's reasoned decision is more easily reviewed than a jury's verdict, the Federal Circuit could have played a larger role in supervising the doctrine's use.

6. *Pioneer patents.* One of the reasons that the doctrine of equivalents has become controversial is that it is often invoked in connection with "pioneer patents," that is, patents on the inventions that give birth to entirely new industries.[11] That it should be invoked in this context is not surprising. Of all inventions, pioneers should receive the largest opportunity for reward because they open new and fruitful directions for research, act as a basis for many other inventions, and, in the end, confer the greatest public benefit. Moreover, inventors who have a choice between working on something known and safe or working on something new and risky will choose the safer course—unless the rewards are structured to compensate for the extra risk. A generous doctrine of equivalents provides the additional motivation needed to work in the riskier area. Besides, it is when fields are new that "quasi-mistakes" are most likely to arise.

Despite the cogency of these arguments, the view that pioneers should be given broad scope has recently been attacked. In Merges & Nelson, On the Complex Economics of Patent Scope,[12] the authors argue that it is most important for the public to have free access to those inventions that give rise to entirely new fields. If these inventions are privately owned, the patentees could, essentially, deny others permission to enter the field. As a result, progress will be slowed. In contrast, if there is competition to utilize the breakthrough insight, development of the new field is likely to occur rapidly. Besides, a broad scope is not necessary to assure an adequate return on investment, because the pioneer inventor has, in addition to the right to sue for literal patent infringement, significant first-mover advantages. That is, as the first on the market, he has a period of exclusivity in which to earn supracompetitive profits, create a loyal customer base, and establish a trademark.

---

[9] Hilton Davis, 62 F.3d at 1527–28.

[10] Id. at 1543 (Plager, J., dissenting).

[11] See, e.g., Hilton Davis Chemical Co. v. Warner–Jenkinson Company, Inc., 62 F.3d 1512, 1539 (Fed.Cir.1995)(Lourie, J., dissenting), cert. granted __ U.S. __, 116 S.Ct. 1014, __ L.Ed.2d __ (1996).

[12] 90 Colum.L.Rev. 839 (1990).

There is another, more subtle reason to give pioneer patents a strict interpretation. Reconsider Assignment 16 on patentable subject matter. There, we saw how difficult it is to draw a line between principles and embodiments. At that time, we saw this line-drawing as critical because we considered it important to make sure that principles remain in the public domain, where they can function as the spring boards for new inventions. In a sense, the issue concerning pioneers is a reprise of that discussion. Indeed, the cases mentioned in that Assignment all involved pioneer inventions (the telephone, the telegraph, the earliest computer programs and biotechnologies), and the Courts' concern was that if the patents were upheld, research would be stifled. But if pioneer patents are given a more strict interpretation, the Courts' concerns would be substantially mitigated. Thus, it would not be so important to draw the difficult line between idea and embodiment absolutely accurately.

7. *The doctrine of equivalents and means plus function claiming.* Especially when used with the doctrine of equivalents, means plus function claiming can get out of hand and expand the scope of the patent to embodiments that the inventor did not enable. The last paragraph of § 112 can, however, be read to limit the utility of this provision. It requires that means-plus-function claims "be construed to cover the corresponding structure ... described in the specification and equivalents thereof." According to the CAFC, this language requires that means plus function claims be interpreted with reference to the specification as well as to the language of the claims. Thus, although the specification is usually used as an *example*—one particular embodiment of the claims, in means-plus-function cases, the court now considers the specification a *limit* on the claims. The accused product must duplicate every structure in the specification, or use an equivalent of that exact structure.[13]

Because the CAFC's interpretation of § 112 uses the word "equivalent," it is sometimes conflated with the doctrine of equivalents, but the two are different. *Graver Tank*'s doctrine of equivalents expands the scope of the claims; the requirement of structural equivalents shrinks the scope of claims.

8. *Extraterritoriality.* A U.S. patent is territorial in the sense that it provides for exclusivity only within the United States. If an inventor wants similar protection in another country, he must apply for patent protection there. Such protection is generally available to Americans only if the country in question has entered into a treaty with the United States in which each country agrees to provide the other's citizens with the opportunity to acquire patent rights. As noted in the Introduction, the United States has entered into such treaties. It has also signed the Patent Cooperation Treaty, which facilitates the process for applying for foreign patents.

In addition to seeking protection for their inventions abroad, patentees sometimes claim that foreign activities affect *domestic* patent rights. In

---

[13] See, e.g., Intellicall, Inc. v. Phonometrics, Inc., 952 F.2d 1384 (Fed.Cir.1992).

Deepsouth Packing Co. v. Laitram Corp.,[14] for example, the patent covered machinery for shrimp deveining. The alleged infringer was selling the machines in a disassembled form for export, with simple instructions allowing the foreign purchaser to put them together with about an hour's worth of work. The Supreme Court held that no infringement of the U.S. patent had occurred, partly because it considered the invention a combination, and thought that combinations could not be infringed until all elements are assembled; in part because it thought the patentee was trying to give extraterritorial application to the patent. The second part of the Court's reasoning was legislatively overruled in § 271(f). Recognizing the significance of foreign sales to the overall reward the patentee earns, Congress redefined conduct of the type at issue in *Deepsouth Packing* as infringing. Did the CAFC effectively overrule the first part of the Court's reasoning in *Paper Converting*?

At the time of *Deepsouth Packing*, patentees had a second concern with foreign activities. Since U.S. process patents were only considered infringed by activity based in the United States, patented processes could be utilized abroad with impunity. The products made by the processes could then be imported into the United States, where they could be priced to undercut sales by domestic, royalty-paying producers. As a result, the income stream to the patentee was diminished and the rewards of innovation reduced. Section 271(g) brought an end to this practice by considering products made with patented processes to be infringing, even when manufacture occurs abroad. Section 103(b) was aimed at curing another extraterritoriality problem, see Assignment 19, note 4.

9. *Nonobviousness revisited*. To what extent do cases like *Paper Converting* and *Aro* need to be revised now that the Court of Appeals for the Federal Circuit has declared that all inventions are combinations?[15] What should be the test for determining whether an invention is in use?

BIBLIOGRAPHY

Merges & Nelson, On the Complex Economics of Patent Scope, 90 Colum.L.Rev. 839 (1990); Adelman & Francione, The Doctrine of Equivalents in Patent Law: Questions Pennwalt Did Not Answer, 137 U.Pa. L.Rev. 673 (1989); Noonan, Understanding Patent Scope, 65 Or. L. Rev. 717 (1986); Farley, Infringement Questions Stemming From the Repair or Reconstruction of Patented Combinations, 68 J. Pat. & Trademark Off. Soc'y 149 (1986); Kitch, The Nature and Function of the Patent System, 20 J.L. & Econ. 265 (1977).

[14] 406 U.S. 518, 92 S.Ct. 1700, 32 L.Ed.2d 273, 173 U.S.P.Q. (BNA) 769 (1972).

[15] In addition to *Stratoflex,* discussed in Assignment 19, see Chore–Time Equip. Inc.

v. Cumberland Corp., 713 F.2d 774, 781 (Fed. Cir.1983).

THE INTEREST IN PUBLIC ACCESS

1. INTRODUCTION

The previous Assignment was principally aimed at demonstrating how infringement is defined to assure patentees an adequate return on investment. However, as with copyright and trademark, a mechanism is also needed to balance the competing interests of society so as to achieve optimal levels of creativity and usage. For patentable material, this adjustment is particularly critical because the patent right prohibits even independent inventors from exploiting their work. As we saw above, one way to protect the public interest lies in the definition of patent scope. In addition, *Aro*'s discussion of the right to repair began an investigation into judicially-created exceptions to the patent right. This Assignment examines other common law approaches to restraining the patentee, such as the right to experiment, see Roche Products, Inc. v. Bolar Pharmaceutical Co., infra, patent misuse, see Dawson Chemical Co. v. Rohm & Haas Co., infra, and the first sale doctrine, see Adams v. Burke, infra. As Note 1 indicates, the antitrust laws can also be used to control the manner in which patentees exploit their unique positions in the marketplace.

2. PRINCIPAL PROBLEM

CFTD, the client of Assignments 19 and 22 is back in our office. Having just learned that it will probably be guilty of infringement if it distributes a purified component of patented Drug X, CFTD is now (somewhat belated) concerned about its past activities.

Here is what happened. CFTD was interested in Drug X, which is the only known treatment for a certain terminal disease, but which cannot be used in its end stages because of side effects. CFTD had the idea that purifying X could eliminate the material causing the side effects. It began its investigation by asking Alpha Co., the holder of the patent on X, for permission to use it. When Alpha refused, CFTD asked Dr. Beta to write it a prescription for X. Through ordinary market channels, CFTD used the prescription to purchase pills containing X. Ignoring the label on the bottle, "FOR MEDICINAL USE ONLY," CFTD scientists used a standard series of techniques to purify X from the tableting and coating materials used in fabrication. They quickly ascertaining that X is indeed made up of components. After CFTD identified the components as (R)-X and (S)-X, the scientists developed a method for separation, tested each, and found that only (R)-X actually treats the disease; (S)-X causes the side effects that require termination of treatment.

CFTD's foremost concern is to find out whether any of its activities infringed Alpha's patent. Nevertheless it is also planning for the future. (R)-X really is a better treatment for the disease. Accordingly, CFTD is asking other lawyers at our firm to seek FDA approval for (R)-X and to apply for similar regulatory approval in foreign countries.

Finally, CFTD notes that (R)-X is the only available therapy for the approximately 15,000 patients who, at any point in time, are in the end stage of disease. It has asked our associates to explore the possibility of applying for an exclusive right under the Orphan Drug Act, 21 U.S.C. §§ 360aa-dd, which is partially reproduced below. What CFTD needs from us is an assessment of whether these activities will infringe Alpha's patent on X.

21 U.S.C. § 360bb. Designation of drugs for rare diseases or conditions

(a) Request by sponsor; preconditions; definition

(1) The manufacturer or the sponsor of a drug may request the Secretary to designate the drug as a drug for a rare disease or condition. . . .

(2) For purposes of paragraph (1), the term "rare disease or condition" means any disease or condition which (A) affects less than 200,000 persons in the United States, or (B) affects more than 200,000 in the United States and for which there is no reasonable expectation that the cost of developing and making available in the United States a drug for such disease or condition will be recovered from sales in the United States of such drug . . .

§ 360cc. Protection for drugs for rare diseases or conditions

(a) Exclusive approval, certification, or license

Except as provided in subsection (b) of this section, if the Secretary—

(1) approves an application filed pursuant to § 355 of this title, or

(2) issues a certification under § 357 of this title, or

(3) issues a license under § 262 of Title 42

for a drug designated under § 360bb of this title for a rare disease or condition, the Secretary may not approve another application under § 355 of this title, issue another certification under § 262 of Title 42 for such drug for such disease or condition for a person who is not the holder of such approved application, of such certification, or of such license until the expiration of seven years from the date of the approval of the approved application, the issuance of the certification, or the issuance of the license. . . .

3. MATERIALS FOR SOLUTION OF PRINCIPAL PROBLEM

A. STATUTORY MATERIAL: § 271

B. CASES:

Special Equipment Co. v. Coe

Supreme Court of the United States, 1945.
324 U.S. 370, 65 S.Ct. 741, 89 L.Ed. 1006.

■ MR. CHIEF JUSTICE STONE delivered the opinion of the Court.

This is a suit in equity, brought in the District Court of the District of Columbia, under R.S. § 4915, 35 U.S.C.A. § 63, to compel respondent, the Commissioner of Patents, to issue a patent upon an application for a subcombination of the elements of a machine for which the inventor had previously filed a patent application. The district court gave judgment for respondent. The Court of Appeals for the District affirmed, 144 F.2d 497, 498, and we granted certiorari, 323 U.S. 697, 65 S.Ct. 120. The question is whether the Court of Appeals correctly rested its decision upon the ground that petitioner did not intend to make or use the invention and that the purpose of seeking the patent was to exploit and protect the combination invention embodied in the complete machine, of which the subcombination is a part. . . .

The patent application for the complete machine discloses a highly ingenius device, which is said to have achieved a great advance in the art by increasing the speed and skill with which pears are prepared for canning, and to result in a great saving of manpower. The . . . application for the subcombination specifies and claims the [complete] apparatus [which cleaves, cores, and pares pears], but without the splitting knife. In the operation of the device thus claimed the pears are pre-split by hand. [The Commissioner rejected this application].

The District Court sustained the Commissioner [and the Court of Appeals affirmed] for [among other reasons] that . . . [i]t thought that the grant of a patent which the patentee has no intention of exploiting as a distinct invention "for the purpose of blocking the development of machines which might be constructed by others," is inconsistent with the constitutional requirement that the patent grant must "promote the Progress of Science and useful Arts."

Section 4886 of the Revised Statutes, 35 U.S.C.A. § 31, authorizes "any person who has invented * * * any new and useful * * * machine" to "obtain a patent." The patent grant is not of a right to the patentee to use the invention, for that he already possesses. It is a grant of the right to exclude others from using it.

It by no means follows that such a grant is an inconsistent or inappropriate exercise of the constitutional authority of Congress. . . . Congress, in the choice of means of promoting the useful arts by patent grants, could have provided that the grant should be conditioned upon the use of the patented invention, as in fact it did provide by the Act of 1832 (4 Stat. 577) authorizing the issue of patents to aliens conditioned upon the use of the invention, which provision was later repealed (5 Stat. 117, 125). But Congress was aware that an unpatented invention could be suppressed and the public thus deprived of all knowledge or benefit of it. It could have concluded that the useful arts would be best promoted by compliance with the conditions of the statutes which it did enact, which require that patents be granted only for a limited term upon an application fully disclosing the invention and the manner of making and using it. It thus gave to the inventor limited opportunity to gather material rewards for his invention and secured to the public the benefits of full knowledge of the invention and the right to use it upon the expiration of the patent.

[The Court goes on to find that the assumption that the patentee would suppress the second patent was not warranted by the record].

Reversed.

■ MR. JUSTICE DOUGLAS, with whom MR. JUSTICE BLACK and MR. JUSTICE MURPHY concur, dissenting.

It is a mistake ... to conceive of a patent as but another form of private property. The patent is a privilege "conditioned by a public purpose." Mercoid Corp. v. Mid–Continent Inv. Co., 320 U.S. 661, 666, 64 S.Ct. 268, 271, 88 L.Ed. 376. The public purpose is "to promote the Progress of Science and useful Arts." The exclusive right of the inventor is but the means to that end. That was early recognized by this Court ... See Pennock v. Dialogue, 2 Pet. 1, 19, 27 U.S. 1, 19, 7 L.Ed. 327; Kendall v. Winsor, 21 How. 322, 327, 328, 62 U.S. 322, 327, 328, 16 L.Ed. 165; Seymour v. Osborne, 11 Wall. 516, 533, 534, 78 U.S. 516, 533, 534, 20 L.Ed. 33. But the Paper Bag case [Continental Paper Bag Co. v. Eastern Paper Bag Co., 210 U.S. 405, 28 S.Ct. 748, 52 L.Ed. 1122 (1908)] marked a radical departure from that theory. It treated the "exclusive" right of the inventor as something akin to an "absolute" right. It subordinated the public purpose of the grant to the self-interest of the patentee.

The result is that suppression of patents has become commonplace. Patents are multiplied to protect an economic barony or empire, not to put new discoveries to use for the common good. "It is common practice to make an invention and to secure a patent to block off a competitor's progress. By studying his ware and developing an improvement upon it, a concern may 'fence in' its rival; by a series of such moves, it may pin the trade enemy within a technology which rapidly becomes obsolete. As often as not such maneuvers retard, rather than promote, the progress of the useful arts...." Hamilton, Patents and Free Enterprise (1941), p. 161. The use of a new patent is suppressed so as to preclude experimentation which might result in further invention by competitors. A whole technology is blocked off. The result is a clog to our economic machine and a barrier to an economy of abundance.

It is difficult to see how ... suppression of patents can be reconciled with the provision of the statute which authorizes a grant of the "exclusive right to make, use, and vend the invention or discovery." Rev.Stat. § 4884, 35 U.S.C. § 40, 35 U.S.C.A. § 40. How may the words "to make, use, and vend" be read to mean "not to make, not to use, and not to vend?" Take the case of an invention or discovery which unlocks the doors of science and reveals the secrets of a dread disease. Is it possible that a patentee could be permitted to suppress that invention for seventeen years (the term of the letters patent) and withhold from humanity the benefits of the cure? But there is no difference in principle between that case and any case where a patent is suppressed because of some immediate advantage to the patentee.

■ MR. JUSTICE RUTLEDGE, dissenting (omitted).

Adams v. Burke

Supreme Court of the United States, 1873.
84 U.S. (17 Wall.) 453, 21 L.Ed. 700.

■ MR. JUSTICE MILLER delivered the opinion of the court.

On the 26th day of May, 1863, letters-patent were granted to Merrill & Horner, for a certain improvement in coffinlids, giving to them the exclusive right of making, using, and vending to others to be used, the said improvement. On the 13th day of March, 1865, Merrill & Horner, the patentees, by an assignment duly executed and recorded, assigned to Lockhart & Seelye, of Cambridge, in Middlesex County, Massachusetts, all the right, title, and interest which the said patentees had in the invention described in the said letters-patent, for, to, and in a circle whose radius is ten miles, having the city of Boston as a centre. They subsequently assigned the patent, or what right they retained in it, to one Adams.

Adams now filed a bill in the court below, against a certain Burke, an undertaker, who used in the town of Natick (a town about seventeen miles from Boston, and therefore outside of the circle above mentioned) coffins with lids of the kind patented, alleging him to be an infringer of their patent, and praying for an injunction, discovery, profits, and other relief suitable against an infringer.

We have repeatedly held that where a person had purchased a patented machine of the patentee or his assignee, this purchase carried with it the right to the use of that machine so long as it was capable of use, and that the expiration and renewal of the patent, whether in favor of the original patentee or of his assignee, did not affect this right. The true ground on which these decisions rest is that the sale by a person who has the full right to make, sell, and use such a machine carries with it the right to the use of that machine to the full extent to which it can be used in point of time.

The right to manufacture, the right to sell, and the right to use are each substantive rights, and may be granted or conferred separately by the patentee.

But, in the essential nature of things, when the patentee, or the person having his rights, sells a machine or instrument whose sole value is in its use, he receives the consideration for its use and he parts with the right to restrict that use. The article, in the language of the court, passes without the limit of the monopoly. That is to say, the patentee or his assignee having in the act of sale received all the royalty or consideration which he claims for the use of his invention in that particular machine or instrument, it is open to the use of the purchaser without further restriction on account of the monopoly of the patentees.

It seems to us that, although the right of Lockhart & Seelye to manufacture, to sell, and to use these coffin-lids was limited to the circle of ten miles around Boston, that a purchaser from them of a single coffin acquired the right to use that coffin for the purpose for which all coffins are used. That so far as the use of it was concerned, the patentee had received his consideration, and it was no longer within the monopoly of the patent. It would be to engraft a limitation upon the right of use not contemplated by the statute nor within the reason of the contract to say that it could only be used within the ten-miles circle.

A careful examination of the plea satisfies us that the defendant, who, as an undertaker, purchased each of these coffins and used it in burying the body which he was employed to bury, acquired the right to this use of it freed from any claim of the patentee, though purchased within the ten-mile circle and used without it.

The decree of the Circuit Court dismissing the plaintiff's bill is, therefore, AFFIRMED.

■ MR. JUSTICE BRADLEY (with whom concurred JUSTICES SWAYNE and STRONG), dissenting (omitted).

Roche Products, Inc. v. Bolar Pharmaceutical Co., Inc.

United States Court of Appeals, Federal Circuit, 1984.
733 F.2d 858.

■ NICHOLS, SENIOR CIRCUIT JUDGE.

I

At stake in this case is the length of time a pharmaceutical company which has a patent on the active ingredient in a drug can have exclusive access to the American market for that drug. Plaintiff-appellant Roche Products, Inc. (Roche), a large research-oriented pharmaceutical company, wanted the United States district court to enjoin Bolar Pharmaceutical Co., Inc. (Bolar), a manufacturer of generic drugs, from taking, during the life of a patent, the statutory and regulatory steps necessary to market, after the patent expired, a drug equivalent to a patented brand name drug. Roche argued that the use of a patented drug for federally mandated premarketing tests is a use in violation of the patent laws. [The patent covers flurazepam hydrochloride (flurazepam hcl), the active ingredient in Roche's successful brand name prescription sleeping pill "Dalmane."]

II

The district court correctly recognized that the issue in this case is narrow: does the limited use of a patented drug for testing and investigation strictly related to FDA drug approval requirements during the last 6 months of the term of the patent constitute a use which, unless licensed, the patent statute makes actionable? The district court held that it does not. This was an error of law.

III

A

When Congress enacted the current revision of the Patent Laws of the United States, the Patent Act of 1952, ch. 950, 66 Stat. 792 (codified at 35 U.S.C.), a statutory definition of patent infringement existed for the first time since § 5 of the Patent Act of 1793 was repealed in 1836. Title 35 U.S.C. § 271(a) incorporates the disjunctive language of the statutory patent grant which gives a patentee the "right to exclude others from making, using, or selling" a patented invention, 35 U.S.C. § 154....

It is beyond argument that performance of only one of the three enumerated activities is patent infringement. It is well-established, in particular, that the use of a patented invention, without either manufacture or sale, is actionable. See Aro Manufacturing Co. v. Convertible Top Replacement Co., 377 U.S. 476, 484, 84 S.Ct. 1526, 1531, 12 L.Ed.2d 457, 141 U.S.P.Q. 681, 685 (1964); Coakwell v. United States, 372 F.2d 508, 510, 178 Ct.Cl. 654, 153 U.S.P.Q. 307, 308 (1967). Thus, the patentee does not need to have any evidence of damage or lost sales to bring an infringement action.

Because Congress has never defined use, its meaning has become a matter of judicial interpretation. Although few cases discuss the question of whether a particular use constitutes an infringing use of a patented invention, they nevertheless convincingly lead to the conclusion that the word "use" in § 271(a) has never been taken to its utmost possible scope.

Bolar argues that its intended use of flurazepam hcl is excepted from the use prohibition. It claims two grounds for exception: the first ground is based on a liberal interpretation of the traditional experimental use exception; the second ground is that public policy favors generic drugs and thus mandates the creation of a new exception in order to allow FDA required drug testing. We discuss these arguments seriatim.

B

The so-called experimental use defense to liability for infringement generally is recognized as originating in an opinion written by Supreme Court Justice Story while on circuit in Massachusetts. In Whittemore v. Cutter, 29 Fed.Cas. 1120, 1121, (C.C.D.Mass.1813)(No. 17,600), Justice Story sought to justify a trial judge's instruction to a jury that an infringer must have an intent to use a patented invention for profit, stating:

[I]t could never have been the intention of the legislature to punish a man who constructed such a machine merely for philosophical experiments, or for the purpose of ascertaining the sufficiency of the machine to produce its described effects.

Despite skepticism, see, e.g., Byam v. Bullard, 4 Fed.Cas. 934 (C.C.D.Mass.1852)(No. 2,262)(opinion by Justice Curtis), Justice Story's seminal statement evolved until, by 1861, the law was "well-settled that an experiment with a patented article for the sole purpose of gratifying a philosophical taste, or curiosity, or for mere amusement is not an infringement of the rights of the patentee." Peppenhausen v. Falke, 19 Fed.Cas. 1048, 1049 (C.C.S.D.N.Y.1861)(No. 11,279). (For a detailed history and analysis of the experimental use exception, see Bee, Experimental Use as an Act of Patent Infringement, 39 J.Pat.Off.Soc'y 357 (1957).) Professor Robinson firmly entrenched the experimental use exception into the patent law when he wrote his famous treatise, W. Robinson, The Law of Patents for Useful Inventions § 898 (1890):

§ 898. No Act an Infringement unless it Affects the Pecuniary Interests of the Owner of the Patented Invention.

[T]he interest to be promoted by the wrongful employment of the invention must be hostile to the interest of the patentee. The interest of the patentee is represented by the emoluments which he does or might receive from the practice of the invention by himself or others. These, though not always taking the shape of money, are of a pecuniary character, and their value is capable of estimation like other property. Hence acts of infringement must attack the right of the patentee to these emoluments, and either turn them aside into other channels or prevent them from accruing in favor of any one. An unauthorized sale of the invention is always such an act. But the manufacture or the use of the invention may be intended only for other purposes, and produce no pecuniary result. Thus where it is made or used as an experiment, whether for the gratification of scientific tastes, or for curiosity, or for amusement, the interests of the patentee are not antagonized, the sole effect being of an intellectual character in the promotion of the employer's knowledge or the relaxation afforded to his mind. But if the products of the experiment are sold, or used for the convenience of the experimentor, or if the experiments are conducted with a view to the adaptation of the invention to the experimentor's business, the acts of making or of use are violations of the rights of the inventor and infringements of his patent. In reference to such employments of a patented invention the law is diligent to protect the patentee, and even experimental uses will be sometimes enjoined though no injury may have resulted admitting of positive redress. [Emphasis supplied, footnotes omitted].

Bolar concedes, as it must, that its intended use of flurazepam hcl does not fall within the "traditional limits" of the experimental use exception as established in these cases or those of other circuits. Its concession here is fatal. Despite Bolar's argument that its tests are "true scientific inquiries" to which a literal interpretation of the experimental use exception logically should extend, we hold the experimental use exception to be truly narrow, and we will not expand it under the present circumstances.

Bolar's intended "experimental" use is solely for business reasons and not for amusement, to satisfy idle curiosity, or for strictly philosophical inquiry. Bolar's intended use of flurazepam hcl to derive FDA required test data is thus an infringement of the '053 patent. Bolar may intend to perform "experiments," but unlicensed experiments conducted with a view to the adaption of the patented invention to the experimentor's business is a violation of the rights of the patentee to exclude others from using his patented invention. It is obvious here that it is a misnomer to call the intended use de minimis. It is no trifle in its economic effect on the parties even if the quantity used is small. It is no dilettante affair such as Justice Story envisioned. We cannot construe the experimental use rule so broadly as to allow a violation of the patent laws in the guise of "scientific inquiry," when that inquiry has definite, cognizable, and not insubstantial commercial purposes.

C

Bolar argues that even if no established doctrine exists with which it can escape liability for patent infringement, public policy requires that we create a new exception to the use prohibition. Parties and amici seem to think, in particular, that we must resolve a conflict between the Federal Food, Drug, and Cosmetic Act (FDCA), 21 U.S.C. §§ 301–392 (1982), and the Patent Act of 1952, or at least the Acts' respective policies and purposes. We decline the opportunity here, however, to engage in legislative activity proper only for the Congress.

The new drug approval procedure which existed between 1938 and 1962 was relatively innocuous and had little impact on the development of pioneer prescription new drugs. Section 505 of the FDCA, ch. 675, 52 Stat. 1052 (1938), required the manufacturer of a pioneer new drug to submit to the FDA a New Drug Application (NDA) containing information concerning the safety of the drug. If the FDA did not disapprove the new drug within 60 days after it received the NDA, marketing could begin.

The provisions of the Drug Amendments of 1962, Pub.L. No. 87–781, 76 Stat. 780, caused a substantial increase in the time required for development and approval of a pioneer new drug. Beginning in 1962, the amended Section 505 (codified at 21 U.S.C. § 355 (1982)) required an NDA to contain proof of efficacy (effectiveness) as well as safety, and required the FDA affirmatively to approve the NDA rather than just to permit marketing by inaction. A recent study indicated that it now can take on average from 7 to 10 years for a pharmaceutical company to satisfy the current regulatory requirements. National Academy of Engineering, The Competitive Status of the U.S. Pharmaceutical Industry 79–80 (1983).

Because most FDA-required testing is done after a patent issues, the remaining effective life of patent protection assertedly may be as low as 7 years. Id., citing Statement of William M. Wardell to the Subcommittee on Investigations and Oversight of the Committee on Science and Technology, U.S. House of Representatives, Feb. 14, 1982, at 14. Litigation such as this is one example of how research-oriented pharmaceutical companies have sought to regain some of the earning time lost to regulatory entanglements. They gain for themselves, it is asserted, a de facto monopoly of upwards of 2 years by enjoining FDA-required testing of a generic drug until the patent on the drug's active ingredient expires.

Bolar argues that the patent laws are intended to grant to inventors only a limited 17–year property right to their inventions so that the public can enjoy the benefits of competition as soon as possible, consistent with the need to encourage invention. The FDCA, Bolar contends, was only intended to assure safe and effective drugs for the public, and not to extend a pharmaceutical company's monopoly for an indefinite and substantial period of time while the FDA considers whether to grant a pre-marketing clearance. Because the FDCA affected prevailing law, namely the Patent Act, Bolar argues that we should apply the patent laws to drugs differently.

No matter how persuasive the policy arguments are ... this court is not the proper forum in which to debate them. Where Congress has the clear power to enact legislation, our role is only to interpret and apply that legislation. "[I]t is not our job to apply laws that have not yet been written." Sony Corp. of America v. Universal City Studios, Inc., 464 U.S. 417, 456, 104 S.Ct. 774, 796, 78 L.Ed.2d 574, 220 U.S.P.Q. 665, 684 (1984). We will not rewrite the patent laws here.

V

Conclusion

The decision of the district court holding the '053 patent not infringed is reversed. The case is remanded with instructions to fashion an appropriate remedy. Each party to bear its own costs.

After *Bolar*, Congress amended the Patent Act to provide an extension of the patent term for certain subject matter that cannot be sold without the approval of the Federal Food and Drug Administration, see § 156. The same enactment created § 271(e)(1), permitting certain uses of patented products to generate information required under federal laws regulating drugs. In Eli Lilly & Co. v. Medtronic, Inc.,[1] the Supreme Court held that this exemption also applies to medical devices requiring FDA approval.

Dawson Chemical Co. v. Rohm & Haas Co.

Supreme Court of the United States, 1980.
448 U.S. 176, 100 S.Ct. 2601, 65 L.Ed.2d 696.

■ MR. JUSTICE BLACKMUN delivered the opinion of the Court.

This case presents an important question of statutory interpretation arising under the patent laws. The issue before us is whether the owner of

---

[1] 496 U.S. 661, 110 S.Ct. 2683 (1990).

a patent on a chemical process is guilty of patent misuse, and therefore is barred from seeking relief against contributory infringement of its patent rights, if it exploits the patent only in conjunction with the sale of an unpatented article that constitutes a material part of the invention and is not suited for commercial use outside the scope of the patent claims. The answer will determine whether respondent, the owner of a process patent on a chemical herbicide, may maintain an action for contributory infringement against other manufacturers of the chemical used in the process. To resolve this issue, we must construe the various provisions of 35 U.S.C. § 271, which Congress enacted in 1952 to codify certain aspects of the doctrines of contributory infringement and patent misuse that previously had been developed by the judiciary.

I

[Respondent, Rohm & Haas, is a manufacturer of chemicals and the holder of a patent ("the Wilson patent") on a method for using propanil (3,4–dichloropropionanilide) to kill weeds. Propanil was known before its herbicidal action was recognized. Accordingly, the chemical itself is not protected by a patent].

A

Petitioners, too, are chemical manufacturers. They have manufactured and sold propanil for application to rice crops since before Rohm & Haas received its patent. They market the chemical in containers on which are printed directions for application in accordance with the method claimed in the Wilson patent. Petitioners did not cease manufacture and sale of propanil after that patent issued, despite knowledge that farmers purchasing their products would infringe on the patented method by applying the propanil to their crops. Accordingly, Rohm & Haas filed this suit, in the United States District Court for the Southern District of Texas, seeking injunctive relief against petitioners on the ground that their manufacture and sale of propanil interfered with its patent rights.

The complaint alleged not only that petitioners contributed to infringement by farmers who purchased and used petitioners' propanil, but also that they actually induced such infringement by instructing farmers how to apply the herbicide. See 35 U.S.C. §§ 271(b) and (c). Petitioners responded to the suit by requesting licenses to practice the patented method. When Rohm & Haas refused to grant such licenses, however, petitioners raised a defense of patent misuse and counterclaimed for alleged antitrust violations by respondent.

B

For present purposes certain material facts are not in dispute. First, the validity of the Wilson patent is not in question at this stage in the litigation. We therefore must assume that respondent is the lawful owner of the sole and exclusive right to use, or to license others to use, propanil as a herbicide on rice fields in accordance with the methods claimed in the

Wilson patent. Second, petitioners do not dispute that their manufacture and sale of propanil together with instructions for use as a herbicide constitute contributory infringement of the Rohm & Haas patent. Tr. of Oral Arg. 14. Accordingly, they admit that propanil constitutes "a material part of [respondent's] invention," that it is "especially made or especially adapted for use in an infringement of [the] patent," and that it is "not a staple article or commodity of commerce suitable for substantial noninfringing use," all within the language of 35 U.S.C. § 271(c).

As a result of these concessions, our chief focus of inquiry must be the scope of the doctrine of patent misuse in light of the limitations placed upon that doctrine by § 271(d). On this subject, as well, our task is guided by certain stipulations and concessions. The parties agree that Rohm & Haas makes and sells propanil; that it has refused to license petitioners or any others to do the same; that it has not granted express licenses either to retailers or to end users of the product; and that farmers who buy propanil from Rohm & Haas may use it, without fear of being sued for direct infringement, by virtue of an "implied license" they obtain when Rohm & Haas relinquishes its monopoly by selling the propanil. See App. 35–39....

The parties disagree over whether respondent has engaged in any additional conduct that amounts to patent misuse. Petitioners assert that there has been misuse because respondent has "tied" the sale of patent rights to the purchase of propanil, an unpatented and indeed unpatentable article, and because it has refused to grant licenses to other producers of the chemical compound. They argue that § 271(d) does not permit any sort of tying arrangement, and that resort to such a practice excludes respondent from the category of patentees "otherwise entitled to relief" within the meaning of § 271(d). Rohm & Haas, understandably, vigorously resists this characterization of its conduct. It argues that its acts have been only those that § 271(d), by express mandate, excepts from characterization as patent misuse. It further asserts that if this conduct results in an extension of the patent right to a control over an unpatented commodity, in this instance the extension has been given express statutory sanction.

II

[In this part of the opinion, the Court conducts an extensive review of cases involving contributory infringement and patent misuse. It concludes as follows:]

First, we agree with the Court of Appeals that the concepts of contributory infringement and patent misuse "rest on antithetical underpinnings." 599 F.2d, at 697. The traditional remedy against contributory infringement is the injunction. And an inevitable concomitant of the right to enjoin another from contributory infringement is the capacity to suppress competition in an unpatented article of commerce. See, e. g., Thomson–Houston Electric Co. v. Kelsey Electric R. Specialty Co., 72 F. 1016, 1018–1019 (C.C.Conn.1896). Proponents of contributory infringement defend this result on the grounds that it is necessary for the protection of the patent right, and that the market for the unpatented article flows from the patentee's invention. They also observe that in many instances the article is "unpatented" only because of the technical rules of patent claiming, which require the placement of an invention in its context. Yet suppression of competition in unpatented goods is precisely what the opponents of patent misuse decry.[a] If both the patent misuse and contributory infringement doctrines are to coexist, then, each must have some separate sphere of operation with which the other does not interfere.

Second, we find that the majority of cases in which the patent misuse doctrine was developed involved undoing the damage thought to have been done by [Henry v]. A. B. Dick [Co., 224 U.S. 1 (1912)].[b] The desire to extend patent protection to control of staple articles of commerce died slowly, and the ghost of the expansive contributory infringement era continued to haunt the courts. As a result, among the historical precedents in this Court, only the Leeds & Catlin [Co. v. Victor Talking Machine Co, 213 U.S. 325 (1909)][c] and Mercoid [Corp. v. Mid–Continent Investment Co., 320 U.S. 661 (1944) and Mercoid Corp. v. Minneapolis–Honeywell Regulator Co., 320 U.S. 680 (1944)][d] cases bear significant factual similarity to the present controversy. Those cases involved questions of control over unpatented articles that were essential to the patented inventions, and that were unsuited for any commercial noninfringing use. In this case, we face similar questions in connection with a chemical, propanil, the herbicidal properties of which are essential to the advance on prior art disclosed by respondent's patented process. Like the record disc in Leeds & Catlin or the stoker switch in the Mercoid cases, and unlike the dry ice in Carbice [Corp. v. American Patents Development Corp., 283 U.S. 27 (1931)][e] or the bituminous emulsion in Leitch [Mfg. Co. v. Barber Co., 302 U.S. 458 (1938)][f], propanil is a nonstaple commodity which has no use except through practice of the patented method. Accordingly, had the present case arisen prior to Mercoid, we believe it fair to say that it would have fallen

[a] Even in the classic contributory infringement case of Wallace v. Holmes, 29 F.Cas. 74 (No. 17,100) (CC Conn.1871), the patentee's effort to control the market for the novel burner that embodied his invention arguably constituted patent misuse. If the patentee were permitted to prevent competitors from making and selling that element, the argument would run, he would have the power to erect a monopoly over the production and sale of the burner, an unpatented element, even though his patent right was limited to control over use of the burner in the claimed combination.

[b] [Holding that it was not misuse for the patentee of a printing press to require purchasers to buy all paper and ink supplies from the patentee—eds].

[c] [Upholding an injunction against contributory infringement on a finding that it was not misuse for the patentees to bar others from manufacturing unpatented phonograph discs especially designed to be used in connection with a patented disc-and-stylus combination—eds].

[d] [Substantially modifying A.B. Dick; holding that any attempt to control the market for unpatented goods constitutes misuse, even if the goods have no use outside a patented invention—eds].

[e] [Finding it misuse for the patentee to authorize use of a patented design for a refrigeration package only to those who purchased dry ice refrigerant from a party designated by the patentee—eds].

[f] [Finding misuse in an attempt to exploit a process patent for the curing of cement through sale of bituminous emulsion, an unpatented staple—eds].

close to the wavering line between legitimate protection against contributory infringement and illegitimate patent misuse.

III

A

The critical inquiry in this case is how the enactment of § 271 affected the doctrines of contributory infringement and patent misuse. Viewed against the backdrop of judicial precedent, we believe that the language and structure of the statute lend significant support to Rohm & Haas' contention that, because § 271 (d) immunizes its conduct from the charge of patent misuse, it should not be barred from seeking relief. The approach that Congress took toward the codification of contributory infringement and patent misuse reveals a compromise between those two doctrines and their competing policies that permits patentees to exercise control over nonstaple articles used in their inventions.

Section 271(c) identifies the basic dividing line between contributory infringement and patent misuse. It adopts a restrictive definition of contributory infringement that distinguishes between staple and nonstaple articles of commerce. It also defines the class of nonstaple items narrowly. In essence, this provision places materials like the dry ice of the Carbice case outside the scope of the contributory infringement doctrine. As a result, it is no longer necessary to resort to the doctrine of patent misuse in order to deny patentees control over staple goods used in their inventions.

The limitations on contributory infringement written into § 271(c) are counterbalanced by limitations on patent misuse in § 271(d). Three species of conduct by patentees are expressly excluded from characterization as misuse. First, the patentee may "deriv[e] revenue" from acts that "would constitute contributory infringement" if "performed by another without his consent." This provision clearly signifies that a patentee may make and sell nonstaple goods used in connection with his invention. Second, the patentee may "licens[e] or authoriz[e] another to perform acts" which without such authorization would constitute contributory infringement. This provision's use in the disjunctive of the term "authoriz[e]" suggests that more than explicit licensing agreements is contemplated. Finally, the patentee may "enforce his patent rights against ... contributory infringement." This provision plainly means that the patentee may bring suit without fear that his doing so will be regarded as an unlawful attempt to suppress competition. The statute explicitly states that a patentee may do "one or more" of these permitted acts, and it does not state that he must do any of them.

In our view, the provisions of § 271(d) effectively confer upon the patentee, as a lawful adjunct of his patent rights, a limited power to exclude others from competition in nonstaple goods. A patentee may sell a nonstaple article himself while enjoining others from marketing that same good without his authorization. By doing so, he is able to eliminate competitors and thereby to control the market for that product. Moreover, his power to demand royalties from others for the privilege of selling the nonstaple item itself implies that the patentee may control the market for the nonstaple good; otherwise, his "right" to sell licenses for the marketing of the nonstaple good would be meaningless, since no one would be willing to pay him for a superfluous authorization. See Note, 70 Yale L.J. 649, 659 (1961).

Rohm & Haas' conduct is not dissimilar in either nature or effect from the conduct that is thus clearly embraced within § 271(d). It sells propanil; it authorizes others to use propanil; and it sues contributory infringers. These are all protected activities. Rohm & Haas does not license others to sell propanil, but nothing on the face of the statute requires it to do so. To be sure, the sum effect of Rohm & Haas' actions is to suppress competition in the market for an unpatented commodity. But as we have observed, in this its conduct is no different from that which the statute expressly protects.

The one aspect of Rohm & Haas' behavior that is not expressly covered by § 271(d) is its linkage of two protected activities—sale of propanil and authorization to practice the patented process—together in a single transaction. Petitioners vigorously argue that this linkage, which they characterize pejoratively as "tying," supplies the otherwise missing element of misuse. They fail, however, to identify any way in which this "tying" of two expressly protected activities results in any extension of control over unpatented materials beyond what § 271(d) already allows. Nevertheless, the language of § 271(d) does not explicitly resolve the question when linkage of this variety becomes patent misuse. In order to judge whether this method of exploiting the patent lies within or without the protection afforded by § 271(d), we must turn to the legislative history.

B

[In this section, the Court conducts a review of the legislative history of § 271]

C

[T]he materials that we have culled are exemplary, and they amply demonstrate the intended scope of the statute. It is the consistent theme of the legislative history that the statute was designed to accomplish a good deal more than mere clarification. It significantly changed existing law, and the change moved in the direction of expanding the statutory protection enjoyed by patentees. The responsible congressional Committees were told again and again that contributory infringement would wither away if the misuse rationale of the Mercoid decisions remained as a barrier to enforcement of the patentee's rights. They were told that this was an undesirable result that would deprive many patent holders of effective protection for their patent rights. They were told that Congress could strike a sensible compromise between the competing doctrines of contributory infringement and patent misuse if it eliminated the result of the Mercoid decisions yet preserved the result in Carbice. And they were told that the proposed legislation would achieve this effect by restricting contributory infringement to the sphere of nonstaple goods while exempting the control of such goods from the scope of patent misuse. These signals cannot be ignored. They fully support the conclusion that, by enacting §§ 271(c) and (d), Congress granted to patent holders a statutory right to control nonstaple goods that are capable only of infringing use in a patented invention, and that are essential to that invention's advance over prior art.

We find nothing in this legislative history to support the assertion that respondent's behavior falls outside the scope of § 271(d). To the contrary, respondent has done nothing that would extend its right of control over unpatented goods beyond the line that Congress drew.

[P]etitioners argue that respondent's unwillingness to offer similar licenses to its would-be competitors in the manufacture of propanil legally distinguishes this case and sets it outside § 271(d). To this argument, there are at least three responses. First, as we have noted, § 271(d) permits such licensing but does not require it. Accordingly, petitioners' suggestion would import into the statute a requirement that simply is not there. Second, petitioners have failed to adduce any evidence from the legislative history that the offering of a license to the alleged contributory infringer was a critical factor in inducing Congress to retreat from the result of the Mercoid decisions. Indeed, the Leeds & Catlin decision, which did not involve such an offer to license, was placed before Congress as an example of the kind of contributory infringement action the statute would allow. Third, petitioners' argument runs contrary to the long-settled view that the essence of a patent grant is the right to exclude others from profiting by the patented invention. 35 U.S.C. § 154; see Continental Paper Bag Co. v. Eastern Paper Bag Co., 210 U.S. 405, 424–425, 28 S.Ct. 748, 753–754, 52 L.Ed. 1122 (1908); Zenith Radio Corp. v. Hazeltine Research, Inc., 395 U.S. 100, 135, 89 S.Ct. 1562, 1582, 23 L.Ed.2d 129 (1969). If petitioners' argument were accepted, it would force patentees either to grant licenses or to forfeit their statutory protection against contributory infringement. Compulsory licensing is a rarity in our patent system,[g] and we decline to manufacture such a requirement out of § 271(d).

V

Under the construction of § 271(d) that petitioners advance, the rewards available to those willing to undergo the time, expense, and interim frustration of such practical research would provide at best a dubious incentive. Others could await the results of the testing and then jump on the profit bandwagon by demanding licenses to sell the unpatented, nonstaple chemical used in the newly developed process. Refusal to accede to such a demand, if accompanied by any attempt to profit from the invention

---

[g] Compulsory licensing of patents often has been proposed, but it has never been enacted on a broad scale. See, e. g., Compulsory Licensing of Patents under some Non–American Systems, Study of the Subcommittee on Patents, Trademarks, and Copyrights of the Senate Committee on the Judiciary, 85th Cong., 2d Sess., 1, 2 (Comm. Print 1959). Although compulsory licensing provisions were considered for possible incorporation into the 1952 revision of the patent laws, they were dropped before the final bill was circulated. See House Committee on the Judiciary, Proposed Revision and Amendment of the Patent Laws: Preliminary Draft, 81st Cong., 2d Sess., 91 (Comm. Print 1950).

through sale of the unpatented chemical, would risk forfeiture of any patent protection whatsoever on a finding of patent misuse. As a result, noninventors would be almost assured of an opportunity to share in the spoils, even though they had contributed nothing to the discovery. The incentive to await the discoveries of others might well prove sweeter than the incentive to take the initiative oneself.

■ MR. JUSTICE WHITE, with whom MR. JUSTICE BRENNAN, MR. JUSTICE MARSHALL, and MR. JUSTICE STEVENS join, dissenting. [omitted]

In 1988, Congress further clarified the reach of the misuse doctrine by amending the Act to include §§ 271(d)(4) and (5).

NOTES

1. *The antitrust connection.* The Introduction mentioned that antitrust law provides a further check on the patentee. In Walker Process Equipment, Inc. v. Food Machinery & Chemical Corp.,[2] the Supreme Court held that if inequitable conduct in the Patent Office (then called fraud) renders the patent unenforceable, attempts to monopolize the subject matter (i.e. enforce the patent) may amount to a violation of the Sherman Act.[3] In addition, patent licensing arrangements are sometimes challenged for violating antitrust statutes. For instance, in Transparent-Wrap Machine Co. v. Stokes & Smith Co.,[4] the Supreme Court condemned a grant-back provision—that is, an arrangement requiring a licensee to grant to the patentee any rights acquired in improvements to the licensed invention; in Zenith Radio Corp. v. Hazeline Research Inc.,[5] package licensing (an agreement requiring licensees to pay for an entire package of patents, including ones the licensee did not need) was similarly found to violate the antitrust laws. In Hartford-Empire Co. v. United States,[6] the Sherman Act was deemed violated by a binding agreement between a group of competitors to pool their patent rights.

Since the exclusive right of a patent is by its nature anticompetitive, the relationship between antitrust policy and patent law is necessarily fraught with difficulty. During times when competition is deemed more important than providing incentives to innovation, the business practices of patent holders come under considerable scrutiny. In the 1970's, for example, the Justice Department announced that nine specific licensing practices (the "Nine No–Nos") would be regarded as per se unlawful under the

[2] 382 U.S. 172, 86 S.Ct. 347, 15 L.Ed.2d 247 (1965).

[3] 15 U.S.C. §§ 15–16.

[4] 329 U.S. 637, 67 S.Ct. 610, 91 L.Ed. 563 (1947).

[5] 395 U.S. 100, 89 S.Ct. 1562, 23 L.Ed.2d 129 (1969).

[6] 323 U.S. 386, 65 S.Ct. 373, 89 L.Ed. 322 (1945).

antitrust laws.[7]

Recently, however, innovation has received renewed appreciation. Furthermore, strong arguments are now made that arrangements such as the No–Nos are not always anticompetitive. First, so long as patentees and licensees have equal bargaining power and engage in arms' length negotiations, the agreements that they reach are likely to be coincident with the public interest. After all, the licensee will pay no more for the patented invention than it is worth; the licensing provisions simply determine the form of payment. Second, certain concessions do no more than meter the use of the patented invention, thereby allowing the licensee to pay exactly what the patented invention is worth to that licensee. In *Dawson,* for example, tying sales of propanil to the right to practice the invention enabled the patentee to charge each farmer an amount commensurate with the use that farmer made of the weed-killing process. In the absence of tying, everyone would have had to pay the same price for a license. Farmers with small properties (and hence, few weeds), unable to afford the license at the single (supracompetitive) price, would have been foreclosed from using the process. In other words, tying can be socially beneficial: it eliminates the deadweight social loss discussed in the Introduction to the previous Assignment. For these reasons, the Justice Department has announced that its No–Nos will henceforth be judged under a rule of reason.[8]

Given the Justice Department's view, should the doctrine of misuse be reconsidered? As Dawson v. Rohm & Haas demonstrated, this doctrine is also intended to curb anticompetitive conduct. However, it takes a different approach from antitrust law. First, whereas antitrust law generally limits only those competitors who have a dominant market position, application of the doctrine of patent misuse does not require a showing that the patentee has any special place in the industry. Thus, a patentee could be found guilty of misuse even if many other products compete with the patented invention. Second, where antitrust law imposes monetary liability on a losing defendant, the misuse doctrine renders her patent unenforceable until the misuse is "purged"—i.e. until the patentee stops engaging in the activity that amounted to misuse.

2. *Other limits on contract terms.* The term of the patent is also an important limit on the patentee, and several cases have considered the extent to which a patentee can contractually obligate a licensee to continue

[7] Remarks by Bruce Wilson, Department of Justice Luncheon Speech, Law on Licensing Practice: Myth or Reality (Jan. 21, 1975). These included tie-ins (which were in issue in Dawson), tie-outs (requirements that the licensee refrain from selling other products), resale restrictions, minimum price restraints, package licensing, grant-backs, royalties schedules not dependent on sales of the patented invention, restrictions on the sales of products made from the patented process, and restraints on the patentees's ability to grant licenses.

[8] See R. Andewelt, Deputy Director of Operations, Antitrust Div., U.S. Dep't of Justice, The Antitrust Division's Perspective on Intellectual Property and Licensing—The Past, The Present, and the Future, Remarks to the American Bar Association, 30 Pat., Trademark, and Copyright J. 321 (1985); Vertical Restraints Guidelines, 50 Fed. Reg. 6263, 6271 (1985).

paying royalties after the patent has expired or been found unenforceable by a court. In Brulotte v. Thys,[9] the Supreme Court held it misuse of a patent to make a contract binding a licensee to royalty payments extending beyond the patent's term. According to the Court, the patentee was using the patent as leverage to extract monopoly profits from an invention for a longer period than the patentee was entitled to protection, thereby attempting to secure a right denied by federal law. Similarly, in Lear v. Adkins,[10] the Court held unenforceable a contract provision requiring a licensee to pay royalties even if the patent was invalidated. The Court reasoned that any doctrine that effectively estops a licensee from challenging the validity of a patent is void on public policy grounds:

> "Licensees may often be the only individuals with enough economic incentive to challenge the patentability of an inventor's discovery. If they are muzzled, the public may continually be required to pay tribute to would-be monopolists without need or justification. We think it plain that the technical requirements of contract doctrine must give way before the demands of the public interest . . ."[11]

Because both of these cases involve a clash between state (contract) law and federal (patent) law, both can be analyzed as preemption cases. Under such an analysis, do either survive Kewanee Oil Co. v. Bicron Corp., reprinted in Assignment 25? Is the Justice Department's current analysis of licensing practices (see Note 1) pertinent here?

3. *Patent law's influence on copyright.* Should the doctrine of misuse be imported into copyright law? Despite the declining viability of misuse defenses in patent law, litigants have begun to assert claims of misuse in copyright cases, see, e.g., Bellsouth Advertising & Publishing Corp. v. Donnelley Information Publishing, Inc.,[12] Lasercomb America, Inc. v. Reynolds,[13] and United Telephone Co. v. Johnson Publishing Co.[14]

4. *Copyright law's influence on patent law.* Should patent law incorporate the compulsory license approach taken by copyright, see Assignments 11 and 12? As the *Dawson* Court noted (and as is implied in *Coe*), the United States has consistently taken the position that there should be no compulsory licensing of patents. However, many countries think differently. One type of provision found in the law of several nations is a compulsory license that can be invoked in the event that the patentee refuses to engage in the activities required to fully disseminate the invention. For example, in Britain, the state is permitted to compel licensing if a patented invention is not commercialized "to the fullest extent that is reasonably practical" for three years.[15] German patent law provides for a compulsory license if the patentee is not willing to grant a license to someone who offers "reasonable

---

[9] 379 U.S. 29, 85 S.Ct. 176, 13 L.Ed.2d 99 (1964).

[10] 395 U.S. 653, 89 S.Ct. 1902, 23 L.Ed.2d 610 (1969).

[11] Id. at 670–71, 89 S.Ct. at 1911.

[12] 933 F.2d 952 (11th Cir.1991).

[13] 911 F.2d 970 (4th Cir.1990).

[14] 855 F.2d 604 (8th Cir.1988).

[15] Patents Act, 1977, c. 37 § 48.

compensation.''[16] Although there has been little litigation under this provision in recent years, German practitioners claim it has a significant *in terrorem* effect on patentees.

Even in the United States, patents are sometimes subject to government control. Royalty-free licenses are occasionally used as a remedy in antitrust litigation, see, e.g., United States v. General Electric Co.[17] Compulsory licenses have been created by statute when important national interests are at stake, see, e.g., the Clean Air Act, 42 U.S.C. § 7608. Furthermore, the government retains so-called march-in rights to inventions created with government funding. When the rights holder to such an invention fails to take steps to commercialize it within a reasonable time, the federal agency that provided the source of the funds may step in and grant licenses to parties who are willing to bring the invention into public use.[18]

28 U.S.C. § 1498, the provision at issue in the *Hughes Aircraft* case of the previous Assignment, is also interesting. It permits the United States to use a patented invention without authorization but gives the patentee a right to "reasonable and entire compensation." Thus, it essentially operates as a limited exercise of the power of eminent domain in favor of federal employees and contractors. Should more be done to assure public access to important innovations? The United States could utilize its condemnation authority more broadly to give other members of the public rights to utilize inventions of national significance.

There are at least two other alternatives for promoting public access. Courts could be more sparing about granting injunctive relief in private cases when important public interests are involved, see Assignment 24. A second possibility would be to give states greater leeway to use patented works. Prior to 1992, the Eleventh Amendment blocked states from being sued for infringement.[19] However, in 1992, Congress amended the Patent Act to make states liable, see § 296 and Assignment 13.

BIBLIOGRAPHY

Some articles in this area include: Eisenberg, Patents and the Progress of Science: Exclusive Rights and Experimental Use, 56 U.Chi.L.Rev. 1017 (1989); Dreyfuss, Dethroning Lear: Licensee Estoppel and the Incentive to Innovate, 72 Va. L. Rev. 677 (1986); Hantman, Experimental Use as an Exception to Patent Infringement, 67 J. Pat. & Trademark Off. Soc'y 617 (1985); Kaplow, Extension of Monopoly Power Through Leverage, 85 Colum. L. Rev. 515 (1985); Kaplow, The Patent–Antitrust Intersection: A Reappraisal, 97 Harv. L. Rev. 1813 (1984); Lourie, Patent Term Restora-

---

[16] German Patent Act § 24 (Law of December 16, 1980, as amended Dec. 9, 1986).

[17] 115 F.Supp. 835 (D.N.J.1953). See also Charles Pfizer & Co. v. Federal Trade Comm'n, 401 F.2d 574 (6th Cir.1968)(requiring licensing at a reasonable royalty), cert.

denied, 394 U.S. 920, 89 S.Ct. 1195, 22 L.Ed.2d 453 (1969).

[18] § 203.

[19] See Chew v. California, 893 F.2d 331 (Fed.Cir.), cert. denied, 498 U.S. 810, 111 S.Ct. 44, 112 L.Ed.2d 20 (1990).

tion, 66 J. Pat. Off. Soc'y 526 (1984); National Institute on Industrial and Intellectual Property Symposium, 53 Antitrust L.J. 485 (1984)(discussing the patent/antitrust interface); Oddi, Contributory Infringement/ Patent Misuse: Metaphysics and Metamorphosis, 44 U. Pitt. L. Rev. 73 (1982); Baxter, Legal Restrictions on Exploitation of the Patent Monopoly: An Economic Analysis, 76 Yale L.J. 267 (1966). Two extremely helpful books are R. Bork, The Antitrust Paradox 372 (1978); W. Bowman, Patent and Antitrust Law 55 (1973). The antitrust casebook, L. Schwartz, J. Flynn and H. First, Free Enterprise and Economic Organization: Antitrust (6th ed. 1983), contains a large section on the conflict between patent and antitrust laws.

ASSIGNMENT 24

REMEDIES

1. INTRODUCTION

Because patents are intended to create financial incentives to invest in innovation, it should be no surprise that the Patent Act provides a right to monetary compensation for unauthorized utilization of patented inventions, § 284. As the following materials make clear, however, it is not always easy to determine the amount of compensation the patentee deserves. Should the patentee be compensated for sales she was not, in fact, in a position to make? How should profits on such sales be determined? Should the patentee be compensated for losing the opportunity to sell materials that are used in conjunction with the patented product? It is easier by far to issue an injunction. And since a patent is the right to prevent others from dealing in the invention, injunctive relief is a key remedial device, § 283. A preliminary injunction prevents the alleged infringer from competing during the course of the litigation; a permanent injunction gives back to the patentee her exclusive market position for the remaining term of the patent.

Injunctions, however, pose problems of their own. First, an injunction cannot compensate for infringements that occurred before the suit was commenced. More important, injunctive relief can impose high social costs. If the patentee cannot fully meet consumer demand, there will be social loss over and above the deadweight loss usually associated with patents: some consumers who would buy the invention even at a supracompetitive price are forced to forgo purchase. For certain patented products, like medicine, this loss may be substantial. Furthermore, the investment that the infringer sunk into production may be lost. If, for example, the production line that makes the patented product cannot be put to other use, it will have to stand idle or be dismantled. The workers on the production line may lose their jobs. Since an injunction is an equitable remedy, courts must balance the interests of the patentee in injunctive relief against the social costs entailed. The calculus may be different depending on whether the patentee is asking for preliminary or permanent relief.

One way to avoid all of these problems is to provide strong disincentives to infringement. If all that the Act did was give patentees the right to prevent future infringements and to receive a monetary award equivalent to what the infringer would have paid if she had received authorization, there would be many situations were there would be little reason *not to* infringe: the infringer would be no worse off than if she had bargained for a license. Because of difficulties of proof, she may even be better off. To create the right incentives, the Patent Act gives the court power to award up to treble damages and to shift the costs of litigation on to the losing side. §§ 284, 285.

2. PRINCIPAL PROBLEM

In 1944, Irwin Sea conceived of a camera that automatically produced a fully developed picture moments after the shutter clicked. Sea worked on his conception for a quarter of a century, founding a new company— Bolaroid—in the process. In 1974, Bolaroid produced the Quantro, the first instant camera with genuine consumer appeal. Patented in 1975, it went on the market in 1976 at a price of $60. The Quantro was an immediate success: it sold 500,000 units in the first year, along with other camera paraphernalia, such as the film the Quantro required, camera cases, lenses, lens cleaner, straps, tripods, and such.

Prior to Quantro's success, Zodak had been the largest producer of cameras for the amateur market in the United States. It first heard of Bolaroid in the early 1970's. Quickly recognizing the appeal of instant photography, it too entered the field, introducing its first instant camera, the EX, in 1980. The EX was not as good as the Quantro in terms of convenience of use or picture quality. However, Zodak did not want to lose market share. Accordingly, it took a very low profit on the EX, pricing it at $20 less than the Quantro. Because of this price differential, and because Zodak's name was much better known that Bolaroid's, Zodak ended 1980 with close to half the instant camera market, both companies selling about 300,000 units.

Zodak was not, however, pleased. Unable to manufacture an instant camera as good as Bolaroid's, it changed its strategy. It decided to portray instant photography as a gimmick, fun at carnivals and birthday parties, but unsuitable for any real photographic needs. In 1983, it came out with the Candle which produced fairly terrible pictures. The Candle sold in stores for $15. (This price represented Zodak's cost, although it did make money on Candle film, camera cases, etc.). The Candle could also be obtained from a certain cereal company for 50 labels and a $2.95 handling charge.

Needless to say, the Candle posed a real problem to Bolaroid. Because Zodak was so well identified with photography, the Candle capped consumers' expectations as to both price and quality. Bolaroid was forced to shelve its plans to create an instant camera for professional photographers and instead devote its resources to competing with the Candle. In 1985, it produced the One–Hop, which it sold (at a very low profit margin) for $28.00. This proved to be the most popular instant camera ever, selling 600,000 units in its first year and doubling that amount in the next year.

By 1987, new problems in this field emerged. The art of film development changed and developers were able to offer one-day, then 3–hour, and then 1–hour developing services. At the same time, the market for Quantros, One–Hops, EXs and Candles became saturated. Both Zodak and Bolaroid cut back on production.

Starting from the early 1980s, Bolaroid and Zodak were in negotiations over the question whether Zodak was infringing Bolaroid's patents. In 1988, these negotiations broke down completely. Bolaroid then sued Zodak in federal court, claiming that each and every Zodak camera infringed Bolaroid's Quantro patents. Zodak was initially unworried about the litigation. It had hired a well known patent attorney back in 1980, when it first marketed an instant camera. The attorney had found differences between Zodak's cameras and Bolaroid's claims. Although he thought that these differences were rather minor, he considered them strong enough to support a nonfrivolous argument that Zodak's cameras were noninfringing. Besides, the attorney reasoned that Zodak had the resources to appeal any adverse trial court decision to a court of appeals. At the time, the regional circuits rarely sustained holdings of patent validity.

Things did not work out as planned. As you know, the CAFC was established in 1982 and began to uphold many more patents than the regional circuits had done. After years of procedural machinations, the trial court in Bolaroid v. Zodak decided the Quantro patents were valid and infringed by both the Candle and the EX. The CAFC affirmed and returned the case to the district court to decide remedial issues:

First, should Zodak be enjoined from producing instant cameras and film? Hundreds of workers owe their jobs to the Zodak's instant photography line; Zodak has invested many thousands of dollars in the machinery that produces the cameras and films. Moreover, owners of Zodak cameras will not be able to use their cameras if film is unavailable. Second, how should Bolaroid be compensated for past infringements? Third, should Zodak be liable for treble damages or attorney's fees?

3. MATERIALS FOR SOLUTION OF PRINCIPAL PROBLEM

A. STATUTORY MATERIAL: §§ 281–287

B. CASES:

Rite-Hite Corporation v. Kelley Company, Inc.

United States Court of Appeals, Federal Circuit, 1995.
56 F.3d 1538.

[This case was decided by the Federal Circuit sitting in an en banc court of twelve judges. It produced a fractured result: six judges joined an opinion authored by Judge Lourie. As to one issue, they were joined by Judge Newman, writing for herself and one other judge. On a second issue,

Judge Nies, writing for herself and three others, agreed with the result Judge Lourie reached, but not with his reasoning. Excepts from all three opinions are reproduced below.]

■ [LOURIE, CIRCUIT JUDGE:]

BACKGROUND

On March 22, 1983, Rite–Hite sued Kelley, alleging that Kelley's "Truk Stop" vehicle restraint infringed Rite–Hite's U.S. Patent 4,373,847 ("the '847 patent"). The '847 patent, issued February 15, 1983, is directed to a device for securing a vehicle to a loading dock to prevent the vehicle from separating from the dock during loading or unloading. Any such separation would create a gap between the vehicle and dock and create a danger for a forklift operator.

[After the district court's decision on liability was affirmed by the CAFC and a permanent injunction issued], the damage issues were tried to the [district] court. Rite–Hite sought damages calculated as lost profits for two types of vehicle restraints that it made and sold: the "Manual Dok–Lok" model 55 (MDL–55), which incorporated the invention covered by the '847 patent, and the "Automatic Dok–Lok" model 100 (ADL–100), which was not covered by the patent in suit. The ADL–100 was the first vehicle restraint Rite–Hite put on the market and it was covered by one or more patents other than the patent in suit. The Kelley Truk Stop restraint was designed to compete primarily with Rite–Hite's ADL–100. Both employed an electric motor and functioned automatically, and each sold for $1,000–$1,500 at the wholesale level, in contrast to the MDL–55, which sold for one-third to one-half the price of the motorized devices. Rite–Hite does not assert that Kelley's Truk Stop restraint infringed the patents covering the ADL–100.

Of the 3,825 infringing Truk Stop devices sold by Kelley, the district court found that, "but for" Kelley's infringement, Rite–Hite would have made 80 more sales of its MDL–55; 3,243 more sales of its ADL–100; and 1,692 more sales of dock levelers, a bridging platform sold with the restraints and used to bridge the edges of a vehicle and dock. The court awarded Rite–Hite as a manufacturer the wholesale profits that it lost on lost sales of the ADL–100 restraints, MDL–55 restraints, and restraint-leveler packages. It also awarded to Rite–Hite as a retailer reasonable royalty damages on lost ADL–100, MDL–55, and restraint-leveler sales caused by Kelley's infringing sales.[a] Finally, prejudgment interest, calculated without compounding, was awarded. Kelley's infringement was found to be not willful.

On appeal, Kelley contends that the district court erred as a matter of law in its determination of damages. Kelley does not contest the award of

---

[a] [Rite–Hite was a retailer of its own devices. It also distributed product through independent sales organizations (ISOs). The question whether the ISOs had standing to join in this suit is omitted from the opinions as reproduced above. It is discussed in Note 8, infra—eds.]

damages for lost sales of the MDL–55 restraints; however, Kelley argues that the patent statute does not provide for damages based on Rite–Hite's lost profits on ADL–100 restraints because the ADL–100s are not covered by the patent in suit; lost profits on unpatented dock levelers are not attributable to demand for the '847 invention and, therefore, are not recoverable losses; and the court erred in calculating a reasonable royalty based as a percentage of ADL–100 and dock leveler profits.

We affirm the damage award with respect to Rite–Hite's lost profits as a manufacturer on its ADL–100 restraint sales, affirm the court's computation of a reasonable royalty rate, [and] vacate the damage award based on the dock levelers.

DISCUSSION

A

I. Lost Profits on the ADL–100 Restraints

[This portion of the opinion was joined by Judges Lourie, Rich, Michel, Plager, Clevenger, Schall, Newman, and Rader]

The district court's decision to award lost profits damages pursuant to 35 U.S.C. § 284 turned primarily upon the quality of Rite–Hite's proof of actual lost profits. The court found that, "but for" Kelley's infringing Truk Stop competition, Rite–Hite would have sold 3,243 additional ADL–100 restraints and 80 additional MDL–55 restraints. The court reasoned that awarding lost profits fulfilled the patent statute's goal of affording complete compensation for infringement and compensated Rite–Hite for the ADL–100 sales that Kelley "anticipated taking from Rite–Hite when it marketed the Truk Stop against the ADL–100." Rite–Hite, 774 F.Supp. 1514, 1540 (E.D. Wis. 1991). The court stated, "[t]he rule applied here therefore does not extend Rite–Hite's patent rights excessively, because Kelley could reasonably have foreseen that its infringement of the '847 patent would make it liable for lost ADL–100 sales in addition to lost MDL–55 sales." Id. The court further reasoned that its decision would avoid what it referred to as the "whip-saw" problem, whereby an infringer could avoid paying lost profits damages altogether by developing a device using a first patented technology to compete with a device that uses a second patented technology and developing a device using the second patented technology to compete with a device that uses the first patented technology.

Kelley maintains that Rite–Hite's lost sales of the ADL–100 restraints do not constitute an injury that is legally compensable by means of lost profits. It has uniformly been the law, Kelley argues, that to recover damages in the form of lost profits a patentee must prove that, "but for" the infringement, it would have sold a product covered by the patent in suit to the customers who bought from the infringer. Under the circumstances of this case, in Kelley's view, the patent statute provides only for damages calculated as a reasonable royalty. Rite–Hite, on the other hand, argues that the only restriction on an award of actual lost profits damages for patent infringement is proof of causation-in-fact. A patentee, in its view, is entitled to all the profits it would have made on any of its products "but for" the infringement. Each party argues that a judgment in favor of the other would frustrate the purposes of the patent statute. Whether the lost profits at issue are legally compensable is a question of law, which we review de novo.

The statute [35 U.S.C. § 284] mandates that a claimant receive damages "adequate" to compensate for infringement. Section 284 further instructs that a damage award shall be "in no event less than a reasonable royalty"; the purpose of this alternative is not to direct the form of compensation, but to set a floor below which damage awards may not fall. Thus, the language of the statute is expansive rather than limiting. It affirmatively states that damages must be adequate, while providing only a lower limit and no other limitation.

The Supreme Court spoke to the question of patent damages in General Motors Corp. v. Devex Corp., 461 U.S. 648, 654 (1983) stating that, in enacting § 284, Congress sought to "ensure that the patent owner would in fact receive full compensation for 'any damages' [the patentee] suffered as a result of the infringement." Thus, while the statutory text states tersely that the patentee receive "adequate" damages, the Supreme Court has interpreted this to mean that "adequate" damages should approximate those damages that will fully compensate the patentee for infringement. Further, the Court has cautioned against imposing limitations on patent infringement damages, stating: "When Congress wished to limit an element of recovery in a patent infringement action, it said so explicitly." General Motors, 461 U.S. at 653 (refusing to impose limitation on court's authority to award interest).

In Aro Mfg. Co. v. Convertible Top Replacement Co., 377 U.S. 476 (1964), the Court discussed the statutory standard for measuring patent infringement damages, explaining: The question to be asked in determining damages is "how much had the Patent Holder and Licensee suffered by the infringement. And that question [is] primarily: had the Infringer not infringed, what would the Patentee Holder–Licensee have made?" 377 U.S. at 507, (plurality opinion)(citations omitted). This surely states a "but for" test. In accordance with the Court's guidance, we have held that the general rule for determining actual damages to a patentee that is itself producing the patented item is to determine the sales and profits lost to the patentee because of the infringement. To recover lost profits damages, the patentee must show a reasonable probability that, "but for" the infringement, it would have made the sales that were made by the infringer. King Instrument Corp. v. Otari Corp., 767 F.2d 853, 863, (Fed.Cir.1985), cert. denied, 475 U.S. 1016 (1986).

Panduit Corp. v. Stahlin Bros. Fibre Works, Inc., 575 F.2d 1152 (6th Cir.1978), articulated a four-factor test that has since been accepted as a useful, but non-exclusive, way for a patentee to prove entitlement to lost profits damages. State Indus., Inc. v. Mor–Flo Indus., Inc., 883 F.2d 1573, 1577 (Fed.Cir.1989), cert. denied, 493 U.S. 1022 (1990). The Panduit test requires that a patentee establish: (1) demand for the patented product;

(2) absence of acceptable non-infringing substitutes; (3) manufacturing and marketing capability to exploit the demand; and (4) the amount of the profit it would have made. Panduit, 575 F.2d at 1156. A showing under Panduit permits a court to reasonably infer that the lost profits claimed were in fact caused by the infringing sales, thus establishing a patentee's prima facie case with respect to "but for" causation. A patentee need not negate every possibility that the purchaser might not have purchased a product other than its own, absent the infringement. Id. The patentee need only show that there was a reasonable probability that the sales would have been made "but for" the infringement. Id. When the patentee establishes the reasonableness of this inference, e.g., by satisfying the Panduit test, it has sustained the burden of proving entitlement to lost profits due to the infringing sales. Id. at 1141. The burden then shifts to the infringer to show that the inference is unreasonable for some or all of the lost sales. Id.

Applying Panduit, the district court found that Rite–Hite had established "but for" causation. In the court's view, this was sufficient to prove entitlement to lost profits damages on the ADL–100. Kelley does not challenge that Rite–Hite meets the Panduit test and therefore has proven "but for" causation; rather, Kelley argues that damages for the ADL–100, even if in fact caused by the infringement, are not legally compensable because the ADL–100 is not covered by the patent in suit.

Preliminarily, we wish to affirm that the "test" for compensability of damages under § 284 is not solely a "but for" test in the sense that an infringer must compensate a patentee for any and all damages that proceed from the act of patent infringement. Notwithstanding the broad language of § 284, judicial relief cannot redress every conceivable harm that can be traced to an alleged wrongdoing. For example, remote consequences, such as a heart attack of the inventor or loss in value of shares of common stock of a patentee corporation caused indirectly by infringement are not compensable. Thus, along with establishing that a particular injury suffered by a patentee is a "but for" consequence of infringement, there may also be a background question whether the asserted injury is of the type for which the patentee may be compensated.

We believe that under § 284 of the patent statute, the balance between full compensation, which is the meaning that the Supreme Court has attributed to the statute, and the reasonable limits of liability encompassed by general principles of law can best be viewed in terms of reasonable, objective foreseeability. If a particular injury was or should have been reasonably foreseeable by an infringing competitor in the relevant market, broadly defined, that injury is generally compensable absent a persuasive reason to the contrary. Here, the court determined that Rite–Hite's lost sales of the ADL–100, a product that directly competed with the infringing product, were reasonably foreseeable. We agree with that conclusion. Being responsible for lost sales of a competitive product is surely foreseeable; such losses constitute the full compensation set forth by Congress, as interpreted by the Supreme Court, while staying well within the traditional meaning of proximate cause. Such lost sales should therefore clearly be compensable.

Recovery for lost sales of a device not covered by the patent in suit is not of course expressly provided for by the patent statute. Express language is not required, however. Statutes speak in general terms rather than specifically expressing every detail. Under the patent statute, damages should be awarded "where necessary to afford the plaintiff full compensation for the infringement." General Motors, 461 U.S. at 654. Thus, to refuse to award reasonably foreseeable damages necessary to make Rite–Hite whole would be inconsistent with the meaning of § 284.

Kelley asserts that to allow recovery for the ADL–100 would contravene the policy reason for which patents are granted: "[T]o promote the progress of . . . the useful arts." U.S. Const., art. I, § 8, cl. 8. Because an inventor is only entitled to exclusivity to the extent he or she has invented and disclosed a novel, nonobvious, and useful device, Kelley argues, a patent may never be used to restrict competition in the sale of products not covered by the patent in suit. In support, Kelley cites antitrust case law condemning the use of a patent as a means to obtain a "monopoly" on unpatented material. See, e.g., Ethyl Gasoline Corp. v. United States, 309 U.S. 436, 459 (1940)("The patent monopoly of one invention may no more be enlarged for the exploitation of a monopoly of another than for the exploitation of an unpatented article, or for the exploitation or promotion of a business not embraced within the patent.").

These cases are inapposite to the issue raised here. The present case does not involve expanding the limits of the patent grant in violation of the antitrust laws; it simply asks, once infringement of a valid patent is found, what compensable injuries result from that infringement, i.e., how may the patentee be made whole. Rite–Hite is not attempting to exclude its competitors from making, using, or selling a product not within the scope of its patent. The Truk Stop restraint was found to infringe the '847 patent, and Rite–Hite is simply seeking adequate compensation for that infringement; this is not an antitrust issue.

Kelley further asserts that, as a policy matter, inventors should be encouraged by the law to practice their inventions. This is not a meaningful or persuasive argument, at least in this context. A patent is granted in exchange for a patentee's disclosure of an invention, not for the patentee's use of the invention. There is no requirement in this country that a patentee make, use, or sell its patented invention. See Continental Paper Bag Co. v. Eastern Paper Bag Co., 210 U.S. 405, 424–30 (1908)(irrespective of a patentee's own use of its patented invention, it may enforce its rights under the patent). If a patentee's failure to practice a patented invention frustrates an important public need for the invention, a court need not enjoin infringement of the patent. See 35 U.S.C. § 283 (1988)(courts may grant injunctions in accordance with the principles of equity). Accordingly, courts have in rare instances exercised their discretion to deny injunctive relief in order to protect the public interest. See, e.g., Hybritech, Inc. v. Abbott Lab., 4 U.S.P.Q.2d 1001 (C.D.Cal.1987)(public interest required that injunction not stop supply of medical test kits that the patentee itself was not marketing), aff'd, 849 F.2d 1446 (Fed.Cir.1988); Vitamin Technologists, Inc. v. Wisconsin Alumni Research Found., 64 U.S.P.Q. 285 (9th Cir.1945)(public interest warranted refusal of injunction on irradiation of oleomargarine); City of Milwaukee v. Activated Sludge, Inc., 21 U.S.P.Q. 69 (7th Cir.1934)(injunction refused against city operation of sewage disposal plant because of public health danger). Whether a patentee sells its patented invention is not crucial in determining lost profits damages. Normally, if the patentee is not selling a product, by definition there can be no lost profits. However, in this case, Rite–Hite did sell its own patented products, the MDL–55 and the ADL–100 restraints.

Kelley has thus not provided, nor do we find, any justification in the statute, precedent, policy, or logic to limit the compensability of lost sales of a patentee's device that directly competes with the infringing device if it is proven that those lost sales were caused in fact by the infringement. Such lost sales are reasonably foreseeable and the award of damages is necessary to provide adequate compensation for infringement under 35 U.S.C. § 284. Thus, Rite–Hite's ADL–100 lost sales are legally compensable and we affirm the award of lost profits on the 3,283 sales lost to Rite–Hite's wholesale business in ADL–100 restraints.

II. Damages on the Dock Levelers

[This portion of the opinion was joined by Judges Lourie, Rich, Michel, Plager, Clevenger, and Schall]

Based on the "entire market value rule," the district court awarded lost profits on 1,692 dock levelers that it found Rite–Hite would have sold with the ADL–100 and MDL–55 restraints. Kelley argues that this award must be set aside because Rite–Hite failed to establish that the dock levelers were eligible to be included in the damage computation under the entire market value rule. We agree.

When a patentee seeks damages on unpatented components sold with a patented apparatus, courts have applied a formulation known as the "entire market value rule" to determine whether such components should be included in the damage computation, whether for reasonable royalty purposes,[b] see Leesona Corp. v. United States, 599 F.2d 958, 974 (Ct.Cl.), cert. denied, 444 U.S. 991 (1979), or for lost profits purposes, see Paper Converting Machine Co. v. Magna–Graphics Corp., 745 F.2d 11, 23 (Fed. Cir.1984). Early cases invoking the entire market value rule required that for a patentee owning an "improvement patent" to recover damages calculated on sales of a larger machine incorporating that improvement, the patentee was required to show that the entire value of the whole machine, as a marketable article, was "properly and legally attributable" to the patented feature. Subsequently, our predecessor court held that damages for component parts used with a patented apparatus were recoverable under the entire market value rule if the patented apparatus "was of such

[b] This issue of royalty base is not to be confused with the relevance of anticipated collateral sales to the determination of a rea-sonable royalty rate. See Deere & Co. v. International Harvester Co., 710 F.2d 1551, 1559 (Fed.Cir.1983).

paramount importance that it substantially created the value of the component parts." Marconi Wireless Telegraph Co. v. United States, 53 U.S.P.Q. 246, 250 (Ct. Cl.1942), aff'd in part and vacated in part, 320 U.S. 1 (1943). We have held that the entire market value rule permits recovery of damages based on the value of a patentee's entire apparatus containing several features when the patent-related feature is the "basis for customer demand." State Indus., 883 F.2d at 1580.

The entire market value rule has typically been applied to include in the compensation base unpatented components of a device when the unpatented and patented components are physically part of the same machine. See, e.g., Western Elec. Co. v. Stewart–Warner Corp., 631 F.2d 333 (4th Cir.1980), cert. denied, 450 U.S. 971 (1981). The rule has been extended to allow inclusion of physically separate unpatented components normally sold with the patented components. See, e.g., Paper Converting, 745 F.2d at 23. However, in such cases, the unpatented and patented components together were considered to be components of a single assembly or parts of a complete machine, or they together constituted a functional unit.

In Paper Converting, this court articulated the entire market value rule in terms of the objectively reasonable probability that a patentee would have made the relevant sales. See 745 F.2d at 23. Furthermore, we may have appeared to expand the rule when we emphasized the financial and marketing dependence of the unpatented component on the patented component. See id. In Paper Converting, however, the rule was applied to allow recovery of profits on the unpatented components only because all the components together were considered to be parts of a single assembly. The references to "financial and marketing dependence" and "reasonable probability" were made in the context of the facts of the case and did not separate the rule from its traditional moorings.

Specifically, recovery was sought for the lost profits on sales of an entire machine for the high speed manufacture of paper rolls comprising several physically separate components, only one of which incorporated the invention. The machine was comprised of the patented "rewinder" component and several auxiliary components, including an "unwind stand" that supported a large roll of supply paper to the rewinder, a "core loader" that supplied paperboard cores to the rewinder, an "embosser" that embossed the paper and provided a special textured surface, and a "tail sealer" that sealed the paper's trailing end to the finished roll. Although we noted that the auxiliary components had "separate usage" in that they each separately performed a part of an entire rewinding operation, the components together constituted one functional unit, including the patented component, to produce rolls of paper. The auxiliary components derived their market value from the patented rewinder because they had no useful purpose independent of the patented rewinder.

Similarly, our subsequent cases have applied the entire market value rule only in situations in which the patented and unpatented components were analogous to a single functioning unit. See, e.g., Kalman v. Berlyn Corp., 914 F.2d 1473, 1485 (Fed.Cir.1990)(affirming award of damages for filter screens used with a patented filtering device); Kori Corp. v. Wilco Marsh Buggies & Draglines, Inc., 761 F.2d 649, 656 (Fed.Cir.)(affirming an award of damages for unpatented uppers of an improved amphibious vehicle having a patented pontoon structure), cert. denied, 474 U.S. 902 (1985).

Thus, the facts of past cases clearly imply a limitation on damages, when recovery is sought on sales of unpatented components sold with patented components, to the effect that the unpatented components must function together with the patented component in some manner so as to produce a desired end product or result. All the components together must be analogous to components of a single assembly or be parts of a complete machine, or they must constitute a functional unit. Our precedent has not extended liability to include items that have essentially no functional relationship to the patented invention and that may have been sold with an infringing device only as a matter of convenience or business advantage. We are not persuaded that we should extend that liability. Damages on such items would constitute more than what is "adequate to compensate for the infringement."

The facts of this case do not meet this requirement. The dock levelers operated to bridge the gap between a loading dock and a truck. The patented vehicle restraint operated to secure the rear of the truck to the loading dock. Although the two devices may have been used together, they did not function together to achieve one result and each could effectively have been used independently of each other. The parties had established positions in marketing dock levelers long prior to developing the vehicle restraints. Rite–Hite and Kelley were pioneers in that industry and for many years were primary competitors. Although following Rite–Hite's introduction of its restraints onto the market, customers frequently solicited package bids for the simultaneous installation of restraints and dock levelers, they did so because such bids facilitated contracting and construction scheduling, and because both Rite–Hite and Kelley encouraged this linkage by offering combination discounts. The dock levelers were thus sold by Kelley with the restraints only for marketing reasons, not because they essentially functioned together. We distinguish our conclusion to permit damages based on lost sales of the unpatented (not covered by the patent in suit) ADL–100 devices, but not on lost sales of the unpatented dock levelers, by emphasizing that the Kelley Truk Stops were devices competitive with the ADL–100s, whereas the dock levelers were merely items sold together with the restraints for convenience and business advantage. It is a clear purpose of the patent law to redress competitive damages resulting from infringement of the patent, but there is no basis for extending that recovery to include damages for items that are neither competitive with nor function with the patented invention.

III. [Deleted: see Note 8]

IV. Computation of Reasonable Royalty

[This portion of the opinion was joined by Judges Lourie, Rich, Michel, Plager, Clevenger and Schall]

The district court found that Rite–Hite as a manufacturer was entitled to an award of a reasonable royalty on 502 infringing restraint or restraint-leveler sales for which it had not proved that it contacted the Kelley customer prior to the infringing Kelley sale. Rite–Hite, 774 F.Supp. at 1534. The court awarded a royalty equal to approximately fifty percent of Rite–Hite's estimated lost profits per unit sold to retailers. Id. at 1535. Further, the court found that Rite–Hite as a retailer was entitled to a reasonable royalty amounting to approximately one-third its estimated lost distribution income per infringing sale. Kelley challenges the amount of the royalty as grossly excessive and legally in error.

A patentee is entitled to no less than a reasonable royalty on an infringer's sales for which the patentee has not established entitlement to lost profits. 35 U.S.C. § 284 (1988). The royalty may be based upon an established royalty, if there is one, or if not, upon the supposed result of hypothetical negotiations between the plaintiff and defendant.[c] The hypothetical negotiation requires the court to envision the terms of a licensing agreement reached as the result of a supposed meeting between the patentee and the infringer at the time infringement began.

The district court here conducted the hypothetical negotiation analysis. It determined that Rite–Hite would have been willing to grant a competitor a license to use the '847 invention only if it received a royalty of no less than one-half of the per unit profits that it was foregoing. In so determining, the court considered that the '847 patent was a "pioneer" patent with manifest commercial success; that Rite–Hite had consistently followed a policy of exploiting its own patents, rather than licensing to competitors; and that Rite–Hite would have had to forego a large profit by granting a license to Kelley because Kelley was a strong competitor and Rite–Hite anticipated being able to sell a large number of restraints and related products. It was thus not unreasonable for the district court to find that an unwilling patentee would only license for one-half its expected lost profits and that such an amount was a reasonable royalty. The fact that the award was not based on the infringer's profits did not make it an unreasonable award.

■ NIES, CIRCUIT JUDGE, with whom ARCHER, CHIEF JUDGE, SMITH, SENIOR CIRCUIT JUDGE, and MAYER, CIRCUIT JUDGE join, dissenting-in-part.

SUMMARY

The majority uses the provision in 35 U.S.C. § 284 for "damages" as a tool to expand the property rights granted by a patent. I dissent.

---

[c] The hypothetical negotiation is often referred to as a "willing licensor/ willing licensee" negotiation. However, this is an inaccurate, and even absurd, characterization when, as here, the patentee does not wish to grant a license. See Hanson v. Alpine Valley Ski Area, Inc., 718 F.2d 1075, 1081 (The willing licensee/licensor concept is "employed by the court as a means of arriving at reasonable compensation and its validity does not depend on the actual willingness of the parties to the lawsuit to engage in such negotiations[; t]here is, of course, no actual willingness on either side.").

I would hold that the diversion of ADL–100 sales is not an injury to patentee's property rights granted by the '847 patent. To constitute legal injury for which lost profits may be awarded, the infringer must interfere with the patentee's property right to an exclusive market in goods embodying the invention of the patent in suit. The patentee's property rights do not extend to its market in other goods unprotected by the litigated patent. Rite–Hite was compensated for the lost profits for 80 sales associated with the MDL–55, the only product it sells embodying the '847 invention. That is the totality of any possible entitlement to lost profits. Under 35 U.S.C. § 284, therefore, Rite–Hite is entitled to "damages" calculated as a reasonable royalty on the remainder of Kelley's infringing restraints.

I also disagree that the calculations of a reasonable royalty may be based on a percentage of Rite–Hite's lost profits. Under 35 U.S.C. § 284, a reasonable royalty must be attributed to Kelley's "use of the invention." A royalty must be based on the value of the patented hook, not on other features in the infringing device, e.g., the motors, which form no part of the patented invention used by Kelley.

LOST PROFITS

The Insufficiency of "But–For" as the Sole Test

The term "damages" in the patent statute must be interpreted in light of the familiar common law principles of legal or proximate cause associated generally with that term. In rejecting a "but-for" standard for determining "damages" in the Clayton Act, the Supreme Court observed: "[A] number of judge-made rules circumscribed the availability of damages recoveries in both tort and contract litigation—doctrines such as foreseeability and proximate cause, directness of injury, certainty of damages, and privity of contract...." Associated Gen. Contractors, Inc. v. California State Council of Carpenters, 459 U.S. 519, 532–33 (1983) (citations omitted).

Under this Supreme Court precedent, the law is clear that proximate cause is applied as a legal limitation on "damages" in connection with the statutory torts which the Court has considered. A "but-for" test tells us nothing about whether the injury is legally one which is compensable. As above stated, the lack of proximate causation will preclude recovery for certain losses even though a "but-for" standard of injury in fact is satisfied.

Property Rights Granted by Patent

An inventor is entitled to a patent by meeting the statutory requirements respecting disclosure of the invention. Prior commercialization of the invention has never been a requirement in our law to obtain a patent. An inventor is merely required to teach others his invention in his patent application. Thus, when faced with the question of whether a patentee was entitled to enjoin an infringer despite the patentee's failure to use its invention, the Supreme Court held for the patentee. Congress provided a right to exclusive use and to deny that privilege would destroy that right. An injunction preserves the patentee's exclusive right to market embodiments of the patented invention.

These clearly established principles, however, do not lead to the conclusion that the patentee's failure to commercialize plays no role in determining damages. That the quid pro quo for obtaining a patent is disclosure of the invention does not dictate the answer to the question of the legal scope of damages. The patent system was not designed merely to build up a library of information by disclosure, valuable though that is, but to get new products into the marketplace during the period of exclusivity so that the public receives full benefits from the grant. The Congress of the fledgling country did not act so quickly in enacting the Patent Act of 1790 merely to further intellectual pursuits.

Thus, a patentee may withhold from the public the benefit of use of its invention during the patent term, and the public has no way to withdraw the grant for nonuse. Like the owner of a farm, a patentee may let his property lay fallow. But it is anomalous to hold that Congress, by providing an incentive for the patentee to enter the market, intended the patentee to be rewarded the same for letting his property lay fallow during the term of the patent as for making the investment necessary to commercializing a new product or licensing others to do so, in order that the public benefits from the invention.

Precedent Respecting the Apportionment of Profits and the Entire Market Value Rule

The patentee's willingness and ability to supply the patented invention during the period of infringement is the thread that runs through all precedent of this court respecting "lost profits" awards. See Kori Corp. v. Wilco Marsh Buggies & Draglines, Inc., 761 F.2d 649, 653 (Fed.Cir.), cert. denied, 474 U.S. 902 (1985)(Patentee "is entitled to be compensated [for its lost profits] on the basis of its ability to exploit the patent ")(emphasis added). While the majority does not specifically overturn any of our precedent, the basic premises expressed therein are eviscerated.

"Foreseeability" is not the Test for Patent Damages

In the majority's view, the consideration of patent rights ends upon a finding of infringement. The separate question of damages under its test does not depend on patent rights but only on foreseeable competitive injury. This position cannot be squared with the premise that compensation is due only for injury to patent rights. Thus, the majority's foreseeability standard contains a false premise, namely, that the "relevant market" can be "broadly defined" to include all competitive truck restraints made by the patentee. The relevant market for determining damages is confined to the market for the invention in which the patentee holds exclusive property rights.

The majority goes on to find the award of damages for lost sales of ADL–100s a foreseeable injury for infringement of the '847 patent. This is a remarkable finding. The facts are that Rite–Hite began marketing its ADL–100 motorized restraint in 1980. Kelley put out its Truk Stop restraint in June 1982. There is no dispute in this case that Kelley "designed around" the protection afforded by any patent related to the ADL–100 with which

Kelley's Truk Stop restraint was intended to compete. Two years later, the '847 patent in suit issued on the later-developed alternative hook technology used in the MDL–55. Kelley would have to have had prescient vision to foresee that it would be held an infringer of the unknown claims of the subsequently issued '847 patent and that its lawful competition with the ADL–100 would be transformed into a compensable injury.

The ADL–100 Patents

If nothing else, the patent term limit provision of 35 U.S.C. § 154 is skewed by protecting the profits on goods made under one patent for infringement of another. Under the majority's decision, the 17–year terms of the ADL–100 patents are meaningless. Rite–Hite is entitled to the add-on years provided by the later '847 patent after the terms of the ADL–100 patents expire. Congress has provided the term and the basis for protection of ADL–100 restraints. An award of damages on ADL–100s based on infringement of the '847 patent expands the term of protection as well as the basis for protection. Moreover, the majority would award damages for losses connected to the ADL–100 even if the patents on that device are invalid (albeit under a slight variation of a "but-for" test). If Rite–Hite had asserted infringement of the ADL–100 patents, it would receive no lost profits based on invalid ADL–100 patents but, nevertheless, is held entitled to lost profits on ADL–100s based on the '847 patent. This construction of the statute seems patently absurd.

No one argues that Rite–Hite is violating the antitrust laws. However, an award of damages for infringement of one patent based on losses of sales of a product not within the protected market violates antitrust policies. Under those policies, Rite–Hite is not entitled to tribute for infringement of one patent for losses in connection with a competitive product protected, if at all, only by other patents. This court has no license to elevate patent rights in the guise of damages over antitrust policies which preclude enlargement of the exclusive market provided by the '847 patent to promote and exploit the business of a patentee in goods not embraced within the patent.

LEVELER SALES

I agree with the majority that under the entire market value rule, Rite–Hite is not entitled to lost profits on dock levelers, sold in conjunction with patented or unpatented restraints. However, I disagree with the majority's reasoning. The entire market value rule is based on a realistic evaluation of the commercial magnetism of the patented invention, not on whether components in a machine—or auxiliary goods—function together. I will not lengthen this already lengthy opinion but merely note that the majority proffers strained interpretations of the cited precedent. I would deny the award because the sales of levelers were not attributable to consumer demand for the invention of the '847 patent.

CALCULATION OF A REASONABLE ROYALTY

The district court awarded damages in the form of a reasonable royalty for 502 infringing sales based on lost profits on Rite–Hite's restraints and restraint leveler packages. This "reasonable royalty," which totals $1,045.00 per infringing restraint, is more than the price of Rite–Hite's patented MDL–55, more than 75 percent of the average net sale price of Kelley's Truk–Stop, and 33 times greater than Kelley's net profit on its entire machine. If lost profits on ADL–100's were not recoverable as such, the court said it would have raised the amount of the reasonable royalty to include all of Rite–Hite's anticipated profits on ADL–100 units and packages. Rite–Hite, 774 F.Supp. at 1540 n. 22.

In determining a reasonable royalty, the district court started with basically wrong ideas even if ADL–100s and levelers were protected by the '847 patent. The court erroneously believed Kelley had to pay a reasonable royalty on ADL–100 sales if lost profits were not awarded. Id. This is a fundamental misunderstanding. Rite–Hite is entitled to a reasonable royalty on Kelley's sales of infringing devices. Rite–Hite would be entitled to a reasonable royalty on those sales even if it made no sales of a competing product. Further, where a patentee is not entitled to lost profit damages, lost profits may not, in effect, be awarded by merely labelling the basis of the award a reasonable royalty. See SmithKline Diagnostics, Inc. v. Helena Labs. Corp., 926 F.2d 1161, 1165, 1168 (Fed.Cir.1991)(rejecting SKD's proposed use of its lost profits figure as a "reasonable royalty").

■ NEWMAN, CIRCUIT JUDGE, with whom CIRCUIT JUDGE RADER joins, concurring in part and dissenting in part.

The court today takes an important step toward preserving damages as an effective remedy for patent infringement. Patent infringement is a commercial tort, and the remedy should compensate for the actual financial injury that was caused by the tort. Thus I concur in the majority's result with respect to entitlement to damages for lost sales of the ADL–100.

Yet the court draws a new bright line, adverse to patentees and the businesses built on patents, declining to make the injured claimants whole. The majority now restricts en banc the patentee's previously existing, already limited right to prove damages for lost sales of collateral items—the so-called "convoyed" sales. Such remedy is now eliminated entirely unless the convoyed item is "functionally" inseparable from the patented item. The court thus propounds a legally ambivalent and economically unsound policy, authorizing damages for the lost sales of the ADL–100 but not those dock levelers that were required to be bid and sold as a package with the MDL–55 and the ADL–100.

I.   THE LOST PROFITS FOR THE ADL–100

I agree that lost profits on the lost sales of the MDL–55 and the ADL–100 are the proper measure of compensatory damages for Kelley's infringement of Rite–Hite's '847 patent. The considerations with respect to the ADL–100 are those of general damages: directness, foreseeability, duty.

Patent damages must be viewed with a practical eye in order to implement the policy of damages law. It is not the usual situation that an infringing device takes sales from a patentee's line of more than one product, not all of which were made under the patent that is infringed. However, this does not change the application of 35 U.S.C. § 284. It may be simply differences in inventorship, or the timing of the discoveries, that places inventions in different patents of the same patent owner. Such a situation is not unusual. An example may be the case at bar, wherein Rite–Hite disclosed and claimed the infringed restraint in a later-filed patent having a different inventive entity than the patent on the ADL–100. Examples abound in the chemical field, where inventors may create related chemical compounds, obtain patents as the research progresses, and commercialize one of them. Should the infringer divert sales from another member of this series, according to Kelley, the only damages available would be a royalty at a sufficiently low rate to provide a profit to the infringer. The patent law is not prisoner of such irrational economics.

II. THE LOST CONVOYED SALES OF DOCK LEVELERS

A. Principles of Damages Law

The basic principle of damages law is that the injured party shall be made whole. On the facts on which the district court awarded damages for certain lost sales of dock levelers, the relationships were direct, causation was proved, the scope of recovery was narrow, and the circumstances were unusual. Reversing the district court, the majority holds that if the patented and convoyed items also have a separate market, there can never be recovery for the lost sales of the convoyed items. I do not believe that such a rule is necessary, or correct, in patent cases.

The majority adopts the rule for patent cases that lost "convoyed" sales can not be recompensed, whatever the directness of the injury and whatever the weight of the proof, unless the thing convoyed is a "functional" part of the thing patented. Heretofore, the question of recovery for lost sales of collateral items was a matter of fact and proof, the court looking at the closeness of the relationship between the items and the quality of the proof, cognizant of the policy of setting reasonable limits to liability.

A wrongdoer is, simply put, responsible for the direct, foreseeable consequences of the wrong. Indeed, in General Motors Corp. v. Devex Corp., 461 U.S. 648, 655 (1983), the Court referred to "Congress' overriding purpose of affording patent owners complete compensation," the Court observing that: When Congress wished to limit an element of recovery in a patent infringement action, it said so explicitly. 461 U.S. at 653. Thus the Court reiterated that limitations to recovery for patent infringement are not to be inferred.

B. The "Package" Sales of Dock Levelers and Truck Restraints

These dock leveler sales were as direct a target of the infringement as were the ADL–100 sales, and the quality of the proofs was equally high. The evidence shows the same transaction-by-transaction losses of sales to

Kelley for the dock levelers as for the ADL–100 truck restraints, indeed in the same bid and sale packages. Precedent previously recognized that compensation may be appropriate when the items are sold together, whether or not they also have separate markets.

Recovery of damages for lost "convoyed" sales has always required a high standard of proof, lest remote and speculative claims be opportunistically pressed. However, it is not correct to hold that recovery is never possible unless the relationship of the patented and convoyed products is such that the only and necessary use is as a "single functioning unit." Indeed, even the majority's new requirement is met in this case. These specific dock levelers were not sold separately because the customer or Kelley required that they be sold together; and it is undisputed that they are used together.

The correct question is not whether the infringing truck restraint was part of a larger combination whereby the truck restraint could not function without the dock leveler, or whether the truck restraint or the dock leveler also had an independent market and use. The correct rule was stated in Leesona Corp. v. United States, 599 F.2d 958, 974 (Ct.Cl.), cert. denied, 444 U.S. 991 (1979), that it is not the physical joinder or separation of the contested items that determines their inclusion in or exclusion from the compensation base, so much as their financial and marketing dependence on the patented item under standard marketing procedures for the goods in question.

Radio Steel & Mfg. Co. v. MTD Products, Inc.

United States Court of Appeals, Federal Circuit, 1986.
788 F.2d 1554.

■ FRIEDMAN, CIRCUIT JUDGE.

I

The case involves U.S. Patent No. 3,282,600, owned by Radio Steel & Mfg. Co. (Radio Steel). The patent covers an improved wheelbarrow. The complaint alleged that MTD Products, Inc. (MTD), had manufactured and sold wheelbarrows that infringed the patent. After trial, the district court held that the patent was valid but not infringed. Radio Steel & Mfg. Co. v. MTD Products, Inc., 566 F.Supp. 609 (N.D.Ohio 1983). In a previous appeal, 731 F.2d 840 (Fed.Cir.), cert. denied, 469 U.S. 831, 105 S.Ct. 119, 83 L.Ed.2d 62 (1984), we affirmed the district court's holding of patent validity, reversed its holding of noninfringement, and remanded the case for an accounting.

Following a trial in the accounting phase of the case, the district court awarded Radio Steel damages of $588,719.93 plus postjudgment interest and costs. The court found that "[t]he overwhelming majority of MTD's sales of the infringing wheelbarrows was to three retail store chains: White Stores, Montgomery Ward, and K–Mart." It determined that Radio Steel was entitled to recover lost profits on MTD's sales to K–Mart and the

White Stores, which it calculated at $296,937.21. On MTD's sales to stores other than those two, the court ruled that Radio Steel was entitled to a reasonable royalty of ten percent, which amounted to $155,634.81.

The district court's combined damage award of $588,719.93 included prejudgment interest. The court rejected MTD's contention that Radio Steel was not entitled to prejudgment interest because it had allowed patent notices to remain on its wheelbarrows after the patent had expired.

The court held that MTD's infringement was not willful and therefore declined to enhance the damages or to award attorney fees.

II

In its appeal, MTD contends that (A) the award of lost profits was improper, (B) the ten percent royalty rate was excessive, and (C) Radio Steel's failure to remove patent markings from its wheelbarrows after the patent had expired barred the award to it of prejudgment interest.

A. Lost Profits. In awarding lost profits, the district court applied the standard announced in Panduit Corp. v. Stahlin Bros. Fibre Works, Inc., 575 F.2d 1152 (6th Cir.1978), which we implicitly approved in Central Soya Co., Inc. v. George Hormel & Co., 723 F.2d 1573 (Fed.Cir.1983). Under Panduit, to receive lost profits a patent owner must prove: (1) demand for the patented product, (2) absence of acceptable noninfringing substitutes, (3) his manufacturing and marketing capability to exploit the demand, and (4) the amount of the profit he would have made. Panduit, supra at 1156. The district court found that Radio Steel had proved the four elements of Panduit with respect to sales MTD made to K–Mart and the White Stores.

On appeal, MTD challenges only the district court's finding that there were no acceptable noninfringing substitutes. That was a finding of fact that we can reverse only if it is clearly erroneous. MTD has not shown that the finding has that fatal flaw.

The district court found that the patented wheelbarrow has several attributes which demonstrate an absence of substitutes. The patented wheelbarrow could be shipped unassembled, thereby allowing more compact shipping with lower shipping costs. The wheelbarrows could be easily assembled at the stores.... The absence of the "shin scraper" brace along the rear of the legs, which was necessary in other wheelbarrows to achieve structural regidity [sic], also added to the popularity of the patented wheelbarrow.... Although other noninfringing contractor-type wheelbarrows exist in the market, such wheelbarrows are not acceptable substitutes for the patented product.

MTD contends, however, that wheelbarrows for many years past ... perform the same function of transporting a load contained in a bowl or tray on one wheel propelled by an operator holding the handles on which the bowl or tray is mounted and propelling the assembly on the single wheel. All wheelbarrows which have been on the market produce this result and are available acceptable substitutes. Some of these wheelbarrows ... have two-piece handles which facilitate packaging of the parts of the wheelbarrow, and these too are available acceptable non-infringing wheel-barrows.

This argument is another formulation of the contention, rejected twice by the district court and once by this court, that the patent simply was a combination of old elements. It ignores the district court's earlier ruling in the liability phase that "[i]t is the totality of all the elements and their interaction with each other which is the inventor's contribution to the art of wheelbarrow making." 566 F.Supp. at 619. It also ignores the statement in our prior opinion that "as the district court held, the '600 patent 'descri[bed] . . . a new and improved complete wheelbarrow.'" 731 F.2d at 845. The various wheelbarrows to which MTD refers incorporate only some, but not all, of the elements of the patent. They do not establish that the district court's finding that these were not acceptable noninfringing substitutes is clearly erroneous.

B. *Reasonable Royalty.* The district court's determination that ten percent was a reasonable royalty on MTD's sales to stores other than K–Mart or White Stores reflected the court's own independent judgment and was not based upon the court's acceptance of the evidence of either party. Indeed, the court rejected the reasonable royalty figures of both parties.

The district court rejected MTD's estimate of two percent, stating that it did not find that figure to be a reasonable royalty. It observed that Radio Steel lost sales not only of the patented wheelbarrows, but also of collateral items that are normally attendant to the sales of wheelbarrows, such as garden carts and lawn mowers. The court also noted that MTD made substantial sales to White Stores, Montgomery Ward, and K–Mart of noninfringing wheelbarrows with the sale of the infringing wheelbarrows.

The court rejected Radio Steel's figure of twenty-one percent, indicating its view that that amount, which is two-thirds of Radio Steel's incremental profit, was too high a royalty for a patent that would expire in three years. The court also expressed concern that Radio Steel's twenty-one percent figure would allow the company to collect unreasonably high royalties from MTD's sales to Montgomery Ward, with whom Radio Steel had been unable to establish a regular and consistent merchandising arrangement. The court concluded that [c]onsidering the age of the patent, the patent's novelty and contribution to the industry, Radio Steel's unwillingness to license, the profit margin on the wheelbarrows, the availability of wheelbarrows from other manufacturers, and the collateral sale benefits, the Court finds 10% to be a reasonable royalty on MTD's sale of wheelbarrows to other than K–Mart and the White Stores.

MTD challenges the ten percent royalty on two grounds.

1. MTD asserts that ten percent is unreasonably high because it far exceeds the profit MTD actually made on the infringing wheelbarrows. It relies on testimony by its treasurer that the profit MTD made on the sale of infringing wheelbarrows was low, and that in one year it had a loss on those sales.

The determination of a reasonably royalty, however, is based not on the infringer's profit, but on the royalty to which a willing licensor and a willing licensee would have agreed at the time the infringement began. Panduit, 575 F.2d at 1158. Moreover, the district court could well have discounted MTD's profit figures because the treasurer also testified that the infringing wheelbarrows might have been utilized as loss-leaders at various times during the period of infringement.

MTD contends that ten percent is not commensurate with the "patent's novelty and contribution" to the industry. MTD contends that the patent's "contribution, if any, consisted of forming channels on the ends of the cross-brace member as demonstrated at the trial on liability." MTD continues: [Radio Steel] did not invent the wheel, nor the bowl or tray, nor the supporting legs, nor the handles and certainly not two-piece handles which are useful in the packaging of the wheelbarrow parts. Wheelbarrows are extremely old and any contribution to the world's knowledge of wheelbarrows must of necessity be of a minute scale. The cost of forming channels on the ends of the cross-brace member, is to be compared to the cost of the wheel, the bowl or tray, the legs, and the handles. The value of each of the parts is commensurate with the cost. The importance of each of these parts is to be considered. The wheel is important; the bowl or tray is important; the legs are important; and the handles (one piece or two pieces) are important.

This is but another phrasing of the argument, which we have rejected in our discussion of lost profits, that the patent is only a combination of old elements and that their aggregation constituted a "minuscule" and "meager" contribution to the art.

The record fully supports the district court's selection of a ten percent reasonable royalty. MTD's treasurer testified that at the time of infringement, MTD expected to make a net profit of about six percent on its sale of infringing wheelbarrows. Radio Steel's vice president of finance testified that its net profit from its sales of patented wheelbarrows was ten plus-or-minus two percent. On this record we have no basis for rejecting the district court's selection of ten percent as a reasonable royalty rate. Deere & Co. v. International Harvester Co., 710 F.2d 1551 (Fed.Cir.1983).

C. Prejudgment Interest. MTD contends that Radio Steel was equitably barred from receiving prejudgment interest because it failed to remove its patent notice from its wheelbarrows for one-and-one-half years after the patent expired. The district court rejected this contention because "MTD has not shown it suffered from such actions of Radio Steel, and the Court fails to see the relevance of such actions to the infringement in question." We agree with that ruling.

MTD argues that General Motors Corp. v. Devex Corp., 461 U.S. 648, 103 S.Ct. 2058, 76 L.Ed.2d 211 (1983), indicated that prejudgment interest may be denied to a prevailing patentee in an infringement suit under certain circumstances. The only example the Supreme Court gave was a case in which a patentee unduly delays the prosecution of an infringement suit. Id. at 657, 103 S.Ct. at 2063. The actual holding in General Motors was that "prejudgment interest should be awarded under § 284 absent some justification for withholding such an award." Id. The justification to which the Supreme Court referred must have some relationship to the award of prejudgment interest, which award the Court held "is necessary [in the typical case] to ensure that the patent owner is placed in as good a position as he would have been in had the infringer entered into a reasonable royalty agreement." Id. at 655, 103 S.Ct. at 2062 (footnote omitted).

MTD has not shown why Radio Steel's failure to remove the patent markings from its wheelbarrows for a brief period after the patent had expired warrants denying Radio Steel the prejudgment interest that is necessary to restore the patentee to the position in which it would have been had there been a reasonable royalty agreement. See Arcadia Machine & Tool, Inc. v. Sturm, Ruger & Co., Inc., 786 F.2d 1124 (Fed.Cir.1986). Radio Steel's nonremoval of the markings is irrelevant because Radio Steel was awarded damages for infringement only during the term of the patent. The award of prejudgment interest to Radio Steel does not reward it for any wrongful activity on its part during the time relevant to this suit.

III

In its cross-appeal, Radio Steel contends that the district court should have found that the infringement was willful and therefore should have awarded enhanced damages under 35 U.S.C. § 284 (1982) and attorney fees under 35 U.S.C. § 285 (1982).

The district court found that in August 1980, MTD offered at a trade show a prototype of a wheelbarrow that Radio Steel considered to infringe the patent. Radio Steel notified MTD of the potential infringement. Upon receiving the notice from Radio Steel, MTD obtained an opinion from outside patent counsel who, upon examining the patent, informed MTD that he believed the patent was invalid, but suggested design modifications that would avoid infringement. MTD's patent counsel did not obtain the prosecution history of Radio Steel's patent prior to rendering his opinion.

The district court concluded that the infringement was not willful. It stated that MTD did contact outside patent counsel for a determination of infringement and took affirmative steps to avoid infringement. When MTD received a second notice from Radio Steel stating that Radio [Steel] believed the modified wheelbarrow infringed the patent, MTD was acting under the good faith belief that its wheelbarrow did not infringe the patent.

Radio Steel contends that under our decisions MTD was not entitled to rely upon the opinion of its patent counsel given under the circumstances that here existed.

The record shows that MTD's patent counsel gave his opinion on validity and infringement at a meeting held shortly after Radio Steel gave the notice of infringement to MTD. At that meeting, counsel examined the patent, an accused MTD wheelbarrow, and some MTD drawings. Counsel, however, did not review the prior art or the prosecution history of the patent. Counsel concluded that the accused wheelbarrow literally infringed the Radio Steel patent but that the patent was invalid. He suggested a design modification to avoid literal infringement. The opinion he gave at the meeting was not reduced to writing.

Radio Steel argues that under Central Soya Co., Inc. v. George A. Hormel & Co., 723 F.2d 1573 (Fed.Cir.1983) and Underwater Devices, Inc. v. Morrison–Knudsen Co., 717 F.2d 1380 (Fed.Cir.1983), "an infringer may not in good faith, justifiably rely on the opinion of counsel and proceed in the face of a known patent unless counsel's advice is 'competent', 'authoritative', or 'contains sufficient internal indicia of credibility to remove any doubt that (the infringer) in fact received a competent opinion.' "

As we have indicated, however, the various factors we have discussed in those cases are just that: factors the district court is to consider in determining willfulness. In making that determination, it "is necessary to look at 'the totality of the circumstances presented in the case.' " Central Soya, 723 F.2d at 1577.

In those cases we referred to the facts relating to opinions by patent counsel to explain why the factual finding in each case of willful infringement was not clearly erroneous. Underwater Devices, supra at 1390. We have never suggested that unless the opinion of counsel met all of those requirements, the district court is required to find that the infringement was willful.

In this case, the district court found that MTD, after being notified of possible infringement on its part, obtained a validity and infringement opinion from an outside patent attorney. Based on that opinion, MTD made the design modifications its patent attorney suggested, to avoid possible infringement of the patent. The district court held that "MTD was acting under the good faith belief that its wheelbarrow did not infringe the patent."

This is not a case in which an outside patent attorney initially was reluctant to give an oral opinion based on the facts before him, but was pressured or coerced into doing so by his client, or in which the client previously had received a number of carefully prepared written opinions but in the particular case had acted on the basis of an oral, almost off-the-cuff opinion. In those situations the opinion of counsel might not suffice to establish nonwillfulness. In the present case, however, the district court considered the factors on both sides and concluded that MTD's infringement was not willful. We cannot reverse that determination as clearly erroneous.

Roche Products, Inc. v. Bolar Pharmaceutical Co., Inc.

United States Court of Appeals, Federal Circuit, 1984.
733 F.2d 858.

■ NICHOLS, SENIOR CIRCUIT JUDGE.

[The facts are as set out in the excerpt of this opinion reproduced in Assignment 23. After finding that Roche's valid patent on the sleeping medication Dalmane was infringed, the court went on to consider the issue of remedies:]

IV

The district court refused to grant a permanent injunction against Bolar because it believed the law did not require that it find infringement of the '053 patent. Since we hold that there is infringement, Roche is entitled to a remedy. We are not in a position, however, to decide the form of that remedy.

Roche requested us, at first, to remand this case to the district court with instructions to enter a permanent injunction against infringement by Bolar. [In addition], Roche requests . . . an order to confiscate and destroy the data which Bolar has generated during its infringing activity, citing, Pfizer, Inc. v. International Rectifier Corp., 217 U.S.P.Q. 157 (C.D.Cal. 1982) (granting an injunction of that nature to remedy infringement done in contempt of a court order).

Statute provides the basis for Roche's request for injunctive relief, 35 U.S.C. § 283: The several courts having jurisdiction of cases under this title may grant injunctions in accordance with the principles of equity to prevent the violation of any right secured by patent, on such terms as the court deems reasonable.

Section 283, by its terms, clearly makes the issuance of an injunction discretionary: the court "may grant" relief "in accordance with the principles of equity." The trial court thus has considerable discretion in determining whether the facts of a situation require it to issue an injunction. The scope of relief, therefore, is not for us to decide at the first instance, nor is this the time or place for a discourse on the "principles of equity."

Whether an injunction should issue in this case, and of what form it should take, certainly depends on the equities of the case. Bolar, Roche, and amici Pharmaceutical Manufacturers Association and Generic Pharmaceutical Industry Association, each detail the "catastrophic" effect our decision for either party will have on the American public health system. It is true that it "is a principle of general application that courts, and especially courts of equity, may appropriately withhold their aid where the plaintiff is using the right asserted contrary to the public interest," Morton Salt Co. v. Suppiger Co., 314 U.S. 488, 492, 62 S.Ct. 402, 405, 86 L.Ed. 363 (1942), reh'g denied, 315 U.S. 826, 62 S.Ct. 620, 86 L.Ed. 1222 (1942). Since "the standards of the public interest, not the requirements of private litigation, measure the propriety and need for injunctive relief in these cases," Hecht Co. v. Bowles, 321 U.S. 321, 331, 64 S.Ct. 587, 592, 88 L.Ed. 754 (1944), rev'g Brown v. Hecht Co., 137 F.2d 689 (D.C.Cir.1943), we remand this case to the district court for further proceedings to consider what this interest is and what measures it calls for.

There are other aspects here that might make a tribunal reluctant to select, within the scope of its discretion, relief along the harsher side of the possible scale. The case clearly was regarded by both sides as a test. The good faith with which Bolar acted is undisputed, at least before us. Bolar says it did nothing clandestine, but notified Roche what it was going to do at all times before doing it, so Roche could act promptly to defend what it believed to be its rights. The case may be unlike Pfizer, Inc., supra, in that Bolar scrupulously obeyed all court orders while they were in effect, or so it says, whereas in Pfizer, Inc., the infringer acted in defiance of court decrees. The destruction of material in Pfizer, Inc., was ordered after everything milder had proved useless. If other measures can be made sufficient, one might well be reluctant to order destruction of the records of research and tests that may embody information that would contribute to the health and happiness of the human race. All this is, of course, for the district judge to consider so far as he finds the factual predicates established.

The actual infringing acts are said to have all occurred in the relatively brief period between vacation of the lower court's restraining order and the expiration of the patent. Counsel for Roche was candid in explaining that he pushed so hard for the harsh relief he did because he thought any money damages would have to be nominal. The correctness of this belief has not been briefed or argued, and we hesitate to state a firm position, but tentatively, at least, we are skeptical. It is clear that the economic injury to Roche is, or is threatened to be, substantial, even though the amount of material used in the tests was small. If the patent law precludes substantial damages, there exists a strange gap in the panoply (in its proper meaning, a suit of armor) of protection the patent statutes place around an aggrieved and injured patentee. The district judge, before getting into the issue of equitable relief, must determine if he can deal with the case by adequate money damages. If he can, the predicate for equitable relief of a harsh, or even a mild, character is gone.

Counsel are equally mistaken in their apparent belief that once infringement is established and adjudicated, an injunction must follow. In Hecht Co. v. Bowles, supra, the statute, unlike the one we have here, was seemingly mandatory by its language that once a violation was shown, an injunction must follow, and the D.C. Circuit had so held. But the circumstances made an injunction somewhat repugnant. Hecht Co., an unquestionably legitimate and long-established District of Columbia retailer, had got tangled up in the price control regulations of World War II, and its employees had in good faith unwittingly committed some violations. The situation was ironic in that the Hecht Co. had been a leader in extending the patriotic cooperation of the retail trade in application of the unpopular but necessary retail price controls, and had itself offered its own operation for study as illustrating the problems and how they could be solved.

After discovering some loopholes in the statute, in light of the legislative history, Justice Douglas continued at 329, 64 S.Ct. at 591–592: We are dealing here with the requirements of equity practice with a background of several hundred years of history. Only the other day we stated that "An appeal to the equity jurisdiction conferred on federal district courts is an appeal to the sound discretion which guides the determinations of courts of equity." Meredith v. Winter Haven, 320 U.S. 228, 235 [64 S.Ct. 7, 11, 88 L.Ed. 9]. The historic injunctive process was designed to deter, not to punish. The essence of equity jurisdiction has been the power of the Chancellor to do equity and to mould each decree to the necessities of the particular case. Flexibility rather than rigidity has distinguished it. The qualities of mercy and practicality have made equity the instrument for nice adjustment and reconciliation between the public interest and private needs as well as between competing private claims. We do not believe that such a major departure from that long tradition as is here proposed should be lightly implied. While two justices declined to join in the opinion, none expressed themselves in favor of affirming the D.C. Circuit. In short, if Congress wants the federal courts to issue injunctions without regard to historic equity principles, it is going to have to say so in explicit and even shameless language rarely if ever to be expected from a body itself made up very largely of American lawyers, having, probably, as much respect for traditional equity principles as do the courts. If an injunction was not mandatory in Hecht Co. v. Bowles, the more permissive statutory language here makes it a fortiori that an injunction is not mandatory now.

V

Conclusion

The decision of the district court holding the '053 patent not infringed is reversed. The case is remanded with instructions to fashion an appropriate remedy. Each party to bear its own costs.

NOTES

1. *Monetary relief.* Prior to 1946, patent actions were regarded as sounding entirely in equity: the injunction is clearly an equitable remedy and monetary relief was conceptualized as an accounting for the profits that the defendant had earned through unauthorized use of the patented invention. At the time, courts encountered considerable difficulties with the accounting phase of the case because there was no accurate way to apportion the defendant's earnings between profit made on account of the invention, profits made on account of the defendant's own efforts (e.g. in marketing), and costs of production.[1] In 1946, Congress amended the statute to drop the reference to infringer's profits.[2] However, it was unclear whether Congress meant to restrict the patentee to an award of damages for his own lost profits or to give patentees a right to choose between compensation and

---

[1] See, e.g., Westinghouse Elec. & Mfg. Co. v. Wagner Elec. & Mfg. Co., 225 U.S. 604, 32 S.Ct. 691, 56 L.Ed. 1222 (1912); Elizabeth v. American Nicolson Pavement Co., 97 U.S. (7 Otto) 126, 24 L.Ed. 1000 (1877).

[2] Act of August 1, 1946, Ch. 726, § 1, 60 Stat. 778.

an accounting. Some courts used defendant's profits as evidence of plaintiff's loss.[3] When the Patent Act was recodified in 1952, the entire monetary relief issue was reconsidered. Section 284 now indicates that the basic damage award is meant to compensate the patentee for the losses caused by the infringement. Compensation can be determined from the patentee's lost profits, or by establishing a royalty rate which is then applied to the sales price of the infringing articles.

a. *Lost profits.* As *Rite–Hite* demonstrates, one of the problems in a lost profit calculation is determining what is "lost." Are sales "lost" when the patentee is not, in fact, competing with the defendant in the marketplace for the patented invention? Which of the *Rite–Hite* decisions on the ADL–100 restraint issue is the most defensible? The decisions of Judges Lourie and Newman create a remedy rule that maximizes the patentee's expected return, thus offering the greatest incentive to innovate. It also seems to mesh best with the rule in Special Equipment Co. v. Coe, Assignment 23, supra, which allows patentees to refrain from exploiting the patented invention. Here, for example, the patentee apparently felt it would maximize its return by incorporating the patented invention into the cheaper restraint, while selling unpatented versions of the automatic restraint. Kelley interfered with that decision by marketing an automatic restraint that incorporated the patented invention. Accordingly, Judge Lourie's faction forced Kelley to pay for the business that Rite–Hite lost on both the patented and unpatented restraints.

In contrast, Judge Nies's rule, which would allow patentees to recover only in markets that it is exploiting, would reduce the patentee's flexibility and diminish the incentive to innovate. At the same time, however, it has the benefit of giving patentees strong incentives to bring their products to market. Here, for example, customers clearly wanted an automatic restraint that incorporated the patentee's invention. If the patentee had known that forgoing that market meant forgoing profits on automatic restraints, it probably would have chosen to sell an automatic version of the patented invention itself. Thus, this rule furthers the goal of fulfilling consumer demand for patented technologies.[4]

The discussion of the ADL–100 issue treats the question whether *substitute* technologies should be included in the base from which lost profits are calculated. A second question, the "entire market value rule" question, asks whether *complementary* products, which are generally sold at the same time as the patented item, should be included in the base. Courts—and panels of the CAFC—have long disagreed on when such sales—called "collateral" or "convoyed" sales—should be included in the base. Indeed, *Rite–Hite* was probably accepted for en banc review mainly to consider this issue, which was raised by the dock levelers.

---

[3] For a discussion of both the pre- and post–1946 case law, see Judge Nies's full opinion in *Rite–Hite*.

[4] Or does it? Would it not be better to permit Rite–Hite to collect damages but refuse to issue it an injunction? That way, consumer demand is satisfied (by Kelley), while Rite–Hite enjoys the tribute that its inventiveness earned.

As a matter of patent policy, which opinion is best on this issue? Judge Newman tries to put the patentee in exactly the position it would have been in had the infringement not occurred. She, thus, once again would offer the largest reward, and so create the greatest incentive to innovate. However, it can be very difficult to determine what customers would have bought under other circumstances. In ordinary contract cases, such speculative injuries are rarely considered compensable. Of course, patentees could reduce the speculative nature of the inquiry by requiring customers for the patented item to purchase complementary products. But that requirement—tying the patented item to other products—could be considered a violation of the antitrust laws, see Assignment 23. Moreover, read broadly, the entire market value rule can compensate patentees for their marketing schemes rather than their inventiveness.

Because of these problems, the remainder of the court would not go as far as Judge Newman advocates. Judge Nies does not fully explain her position on this issue.[5] She would, apparently, repudiate the entire market value rule and limit patentees to lost profits on the patented invention. In contrast, Judge Lourie tries to find a happy medium. He would compensate patentees when the patented invention and the related item form a single "functional unit."

It remains to be seen whether the "functional unit" approach will work, but the prospects seem dim. First, why was the dock leveler and the restraint not considered part of a single functional unit? Second, this rule encourages patentees to engage in tying. Not, of course, through market tie-ins that would run afoul of the antitrust laws, but so-called "technological tying." That is, patentees may well try to design the commercial embodiments of their patented inventions in a manner that forms a "functional unit" with other products. Third, the Lourie decision may be unstable because its two main parts are not completely consistent with one another. It is easy to *say* that products that substitute for the patented invention are included in the base on which profits are calculated, but that complementary products are not. What, however, is the overarching theory of this decision? If the idea is to return the patentee to the position it would have been in if the infringement had not occurred, or to compensate the patentee for all foreseeable injuries, then the patentee should be compensated for lost dock leveler sales as well as lost ADL–100 sales. If the idea is to compensate the patentee only for losing sales of the patented invention, then neither the ADL–100 nor the dock leveler sales should count. This opinion offers no real theory for splitting the difference. Finally, consider how royalties were determined in *Rite–Hite* and *Radio Steel:* do collateral sales sneak in through the back door? See Note 1(b), infra.

Even after the base for calculating profits is determined, several difficult questions remain, for the patentee must establish what he would have earned if the infringement had not occurred. This is where the four-

---

[5] Although most of Judge Nies's opinion was heavily edited, the dock leveler portion of it was reproduced in full.

part test of Panduit Corp. v. Stahlin Bros. Fibre Works, Inc., discussed in both *Rite–Hite* and *Radio Steel,* comes in. Pre-infringement data can be used to make the showing required, but these must be adjusted for changes in the market for the patented item. And although courts do sometimes look at the defendant's profits in making this determination,[6] these data must also be corrected to account for sales attributable to the defendant's reputation, marketing scheme, production technique, and such.

b. *Royalties.* Courts can avoid the problem of computing the actual amount of lost profits by using the royalty method of awarding damages. If the patentee is engaged in a licensing program, the royalty rate will be the one established in similar contracts. If there are no licenses, the court will impute a royalty based on similar transactions in the industry, the infringer's anticipated profits, the utility of the invention as compared to unpatented alternatives, and on whether the invention was a "pioneer" in its field.

Note that in *Radio Steel,* the court also enhanced the royalty rate to compensate the patentee for sales lost on related items. *Radio Steel* was decided before *Rite–Hite:* given the strict test that the *Rite–Hite* court articulated for deciding whether to include complementary products in the *base* used to calculate damages, is this decision still good law—does it make sense to include these items when determining the royalty *rate*? Did the *Rite–Hite* plurality in effect do the same thing?

2. *Willful infringement.* Although § 284 does not specify the circumstances for trebling damages, courts usually make this discretionary award only when the infringement was willful. In Bott v. Four Star Corp.,[7] for example, the Federal Circuit instructed the district courts to consider the totality of the circumstances, including: (1) whether the infringer deliberately copied the ideas or design of another; (2) whether the infringer, when he knew of the other's patent protection, investigated the scope of the patent and formed a good faith belief that it was invalid or that it was not infringed, and (3) the infringer's behavior as a party to the litigation.

3. *Attorney's fees.* Section 285 permits an award of attorney's fees to the prevailing party in "exceptional circumstances." When it is the patentee who prevails, fees are usually awarded only in cases where infringement is willful or where the infringer has litigated in bad faith.[8] When the patentee loses, this award is usually based on inequitable conduct in the PTO or bad

---

[6] See, e.g., Velo–Bind, Inc. v. Minnesota Mining & Mfg. Co., 647 F.2d 965 (9th Cir.), cert. denied, 454 U.S. 1093, 102 S.Ct. 658, 70 L.Ed.2d 631 (1981).

[7] 807 F.2d 1567 (Fed.Cir.1986).

[8] See, e.g., Kloster Speedsteel AB v. Crucible Inc., 793 F.2d 1565 (Fed.Cir.1986). Although willfulness is also a ground for awarding up to treble damages, it is not necessarily the case that these two awards go hand in hand, see, e.g., Paper Converting Machine Co. v. Magna–Graphics Corp., 785 F.2d 1013 (Fed.Cir.1986), which is excerpted in Assignment 22. There, the court awarded treble damages because it considered the attempt to separate the toilet paper-rolling invention into two parts a willful infringement. However, it did not believe the behavior amounted to the exceptional circumstances required for an award of attorney fees.

faith litigation.[9] Of course, as with all federal suits, patent litigation is subject to the Federal Rules of Civil Procedure, including Rule 11.

4. *Prejudgment interest.* Interest is allowed on all monetary judgments awarded in civil suits in federal court, 28 U.S.C. § 1961. Prior to 1983, there was considerable controversy as to whether a prevailing patentee could collect interest on damages accrued prior to reduction of the claim to judgment. The question was answered in General Motors Corp. v. Devex Corp.,[10] where the Court reasoned that § 284 gave the court flexibility to award damages "adequate to compensate for the infringement." If the case dragged on for a long time, the patentee should be compensated for lost earnings on the lost profits. *Devex* was a good example of the injury caused by protracted litigation. By the time the Supreme Court decided the case, it had been sub judice for 36 years; the trial court awarded damages equal to a reasonable royalty of $8,813,945.50 and prejudgment interest amounting to $11,022,854.97.

5. *Injunctive relief.* There are two types of injunctions: preliminary and permanent. In cases outside the patent area, preliminary relief is granted when the moving party proves a likelihood of success on the merits and irreparable injury. Prior to the establishment of the CAFC, however, it was often harder to get preliminary relief in patent litigation. Courts reasoned that since patentees could be made whole with a monetary award, there was little point in enjoining the defendant preliminarily and force the public to suffer a diminution in output of the patented product before infringement was proven. Accordingly, they required the patentee to prove that the patent was unquestionably valid and that the infringement was clear.[11]

Initially, the CAFC saw no reason to treat patentees this way. Because patent litigation often took many years, infringers could make large inroads into the patentee's business, establish customer loyalty, and enjoy a favorable marketing position when the patent expired. Furthermore, the goals of patent law and copyright are similar, and courts in copyright cases are fairly generous about granting preliminary relief on the presumption that the injury flowing from unauthorized usages of a protected work is irreparable. Early CAFC cases suggested that the patentees should be treated just like holders of other intellectual property.[12] Recent cases, however, show some evidence of retreat from this position. In Illinois Tool Works, Inc. v. Grip–Pak, Inc.,[13] the CAFC indicated that the presumption of irreparable

---

[9] See, e.g., Cambridge Prods., Ltd. v. Penn Nutrients, Inc., 962 F.2d 1048 (Fed.Cir. 1992). Not all inequitable conduct results in an award of attorney fees. For example, in J.P. Stevens Co. v. Lex Tex Ltd., Inc., 747 F.2d 1553 (Fed.Cir.1984), the court found that the applicant's failure to reveal material references did not amount to the sort of behavior justifying an award of attorney fees.

[10] 461 U.S. 648, 103 S.Ct. 2058, 76 L.Ed.2d 211 (1983).

[11] See, e.g., D. Chisum, Patents, § 20.04 (1987).

[12] See, e.g., Atlas Powder Co. v. Ireco Chems., 773 F.2d 1230 (Fed.Cir.1985); Smith Int'l v. Hughes Tool Co., 718 F.2d 1573 (Fed. Cir.), cert. denied, 464 U.S. 996, 104 S.Ct. 493, 78 L.Ed.2d 687 (1983).

[13] 906 F.2d 679 (Fed.Cir.1990).

injury is rebuttable, and in Chrysler Motors Corp. v. Auto Body Panels,[14] the Federal Circuit reinstated the requirement that patentees make a strong showing of validity.

While it is impossible to know exactly what the CAFC is thinking, it is likely that the court has become more sensitive to the public-interest side of the injunction issue. As noted in *Bolar,* injunctions—both preliminary and permanent—are a matter of equity, and the equities can favor the public's interest in accessing the invention. Allowing the infringer to meet demand while at the same time compensating the patentee furthers both public and private goals, creating a kind of ad hoc compulsory license. Does the fact that Congress has always rejected compulsory licensing in patent law mean that courts should be *more* or *less* willing to deny injunctive relief?

6. *Exclusion orders.* In addition to enjoining domestic usages of the patented invention, patentees can prevent importation of infringing articles under 19 U.S.C. § 1337(a), which makes unlawful:

> (1)(B) The importation into the United States, the sale for importation, or the sale within the United States after importation ... of articles that—
>
>> (i) infringe a valid and enforceable United States patent ...; or
>>
>> (ii) are made, produced, processed, or mined under, or by means of, a process covered by claims of a valid and enforceable United States patent.

This statute has an important exception:

> (2) Subparagraph [] (B) of paragraph (1) appl[ies] only if an industry in the United States, relating to the articles protected by the patent ... exists or is in the process of being established.
>
> (3) For purposes of paragraph (2), an industry in the United States shall be considered to exist if there is in the United States, with respect to the articles protected by the patent ... concerned—
>
>> (A) significant investment in plant and equipment;
>>
>> (B) significant employment of labor or capital; or
>>
>> (C) substantial investment in its exploitation, including engineering, research and development, or licensing.

The statute covers copyrighted and trademarked works as well as semiconductor chips (mask works).

7. *Time limitations.* Damages cannot be recovered for infringements that occurred before the infringer had notice of the patent. Marking patented articles with the word "patent" (or the abbreviation "pat.") followed by the number of the patent serves as constructive notice. If no goods are sold, if the patent is for a process, or if the patentee chooses not to mark her goods, then the patentee must prove actual notice, § 287. In addition, no recovery

---

[14] 908 F.2d 951 (Fed.Cir.1990).

can be had for infringements that are more than six years old at the time of filing, § 286.

Finally, the defenses of laches and estoppel can also bar relief. Laches occurs when a patentee unreasonably delays filing suit after he knows or should have known of the infringement. It blocks relief for past infringements, but not an injunction to prevent future infringement. In contrast, estoppel, which occurs when an infringer reasonably relies on the patentee's representation that he will not enforce the patent, prevents the patentee from receiving all relief.

8. *Standing.* In an omitted portion of *Rite–Hite,* the court discussed whether independent sales organizations that sold the '847 and the ADL–100 through licensing agreements with Rite–Hite had standing to pursue their own actions against Kelley. Judge Lourie's plurality opinion, which, on this issue, was joined by Judges Archer, Smith, Nies and Mayer, said no. In their view, the only licensees who have sufficient interest in the patent to sue are those holding an exclusive right to practice the invention. Nonexclusive licensees (including those with exclusive licenses to particular territories) have received only a promise by the patentee to forebear from suing them for infringement. Judges Newman and Rader thought these organizations' injuries were directly and foreseeably caused by the infringement, giving them the right to sue along with Rite–Hite.

BIBLIOGRAPHY

Miller, Recent Developments Regarding the Awarding of Multiple Damages and Attorney Fees in Patent Cases, 27 IDEA 227 (1987); Metcalf, Preliminary Injunctions and Their Availability: How to Defend Against the Early Injunction, 15 AIPLA L.Q. 104 (1987); Schwartz, Injunctive Relief in Patent Cases, 50 Alb. L. Rev. 565 (1986); Foster, The Preliminary Injunction—A "New" and Potent Weapon in Patent Litigation, 68 J. Pat. & T. Off. Soc'y 401 (1986); Chisum, Remedies for Patent Infringement, 13 AIPLA L.Q. 380 (1985); Hulbert & Consalvi, De–Vexing Prejudgment Interest Awards in Patent Cases—At What Point Interest?, 67 J.Pat.Off. Soc'y 103 (1985); Sobel, Examining the Extra Burden Imposed on a Patentee Who Seeks a Preliminary Injunction, 32 Amer. U. L. Rev. 985 (1983).

PREEMPTION OF STATE LAWS: TRADE SECRETS, COVENANTS NOT TO COMPETE, AND LEGAL HYBRIDS

1. INTRODUCTION

This Assignment treats two issues. It begins with a discussion of state laws that touch on the protection of patentable subject matter and ends with an investigation of the question whether all (or some) of these state laws should be considered preempted by federal patent law.

State laws protecting invention can be divided into two major categories: trade secrecy laws and contractual provisions that bar entry into competition. There is also a smaller set of laws sometimes referred to as "hybrid" provisions. These mix copyright and patent concepts to tailor protection to the needs of particular industries.

For trade secrecy, the common law was first summarized in the first Restatement of Torts, §§ 757–761, it was not addressed by the second Restatement of Torts, but is now a part of the Restatement of Unfair Competition Law, which was published in 1995.[1] In addition, in 1979, the National Conference of Commissioners on Uniform State Laws promulgated a Uniform Trade Secrets Act, which has been adopted by a majority of the states. Although the Restatement of Torts differed in some details from the Uniform Act, the new Restatement of Unfair Competition Law is intended to be "applicable to actions under the Uniform Trade Secrets Act as well as to actions at common law."[2] Both create rights of action against those who acquire by improper means information that is valuable because it is not generally known, and then use that information for their own economic benefit. Plaintiffs must have made all reasonable efforts to keep the information confidential, such as revealing it only on a need-to-know basis and warning recipients of its confidential nature. "Improper means" covers a wide array of behavior, ranging from industrial espionage, bribery, and trespass, to breaches of duties of confidentiality.

Improper means does not, however, include reverse engineering—that is, taking a product apart to see how it works. That is considered "fair

---

[1] American Law Institute, Rest. 3d Unfair Competition Law (1995)(your editors have no explanation for why this Restatement is called "3d" when it is, in fact, the first independent Restatement of this area of the law and the second restatement over-all).

[2] Id. at § 39, Comment b.

means." Since there is no time limit to trade secrecy protection, reverse engineering is the principal way in which a trade secret enters the public domain. Although the distinction between, say, breaking into a factory (improper) and breaking into the product (proper) may seem artificial, trade secrecy law is a rather efficient way to protect innovators against ruinous competition. Because reverse engineering generally takes time (time to decide the product is worth figuring out as well as time to actually do the engineering and bring the product to market), the first inventor enjoys a period of exclusivity in which to recapture the costs of invention, build a reputation, and establish a base of loyal customers. Furthermore, the copyist is not quite a free rider because reverse engineering is generally expensive. Thus, after the secret is discovered, the parties compete on a fairly level playing field. Finally, inventiveness often correlates with difficulty of reverse engineering, with the result that the more inventive the product, the longer its inventor enjoys the so-called "first mover advantage," and the more profit she earns.

Because improper means covers a broad range of activity, it might be thought that trade secrecy law would fulfill all the interests that states have in creating their own branch of intellectual property law. There are, however, at least three problems with trade secrecy protection. First, consider the problem of monitoring. Much of what is protected by trade secrecy law is industrial know-how: information about how to do things better. Since it is not possible to peer into rival factories to check whether competitors are using stolen secret processes, enforcement is often suboptimal. Second, some products are very easy to figure out. If it is too easy to reverse engineer the product, the innovator will not have the lead time needed to recoup costs. Third, trade secret holders are often reluctant to enforce their rights. Because trade secrecy litigation requires the plaintiff to tell the court enough about the secret to determine whether it has been taken by improper means (rather than reverse engineered) and whether it is being utilized, lawsuits can carry an unacceptably high risk of disclosure.

To avoid these problems, inventors sometimes rely on covenants not to compete. These are contracts between the innovator and those to whom the secret must be told—usually, employees or investors—in which the latter promise not to enter into specified businesses for a specific period of time and within a particular geographic area. Because these contracts spell out overt behavior that must be avoided, they can be enforced without the inventor knowing whether a secret has indeed been stolen and without any need to disclose to the court what the secret is.

Covenants not to compete are, of course, limited in that they can be enforced only against people who have entered into agreements with the inventor. However, the typical defendant in a trade secret action is someone who has had contact with the inventor—most often, an ex-employee. Thus, in a high percent of the cases, covenants not to compete mirror the protection offered by trade secrecy, but without the attendant risks.

That leaves the small group of cases where trade secrecy protection is inadequate, and it is also not feasible to enter into contracts with everyone who is in a position to learn the secret information (e.g., by reverse engineering). It is here that hybrid laws become important. Invariably creatures of statute, their main virtue is that they closely match the details of the protective regime to the needs of particular industries. *Bonito Boats*, infra, furnishes an example of one such provision.

Should these state-based rights be preempted? The Patent Act does not contain a provision equivalent to § 301 of the Copyright Act, so there is no legislative direction. As the cases below demonstrate, the Supreme Court has vacillated between the extremes, resting for the moment on middle ground that is difficult to fully define.

2. PRINCIPAL PROBLEM

Our client is MAI Systems, a computer "boutique" situated in California. It designs, manufactures, and builds computers to customer specifications. This equipment is sold outright to customers. In addition, MAI designs the programs (operating systems and application programs) that run on its computers. These are not sold—rather, they are licensed to customers and loaded into the computers before they are shipped. Finally, MAI offers its customers service contracts that cover routine maintenance and emergency repairs on all computers and programs. Since virtually all new customers purchase MAI service contracts, MAI routinely loads the diagnostic program it uses for servicing right into the memory of all computers shipped. However, the documentation sent to customers reveals neither the presence of this program nor the method of accessing it.

In recent years, our client has become concerned by an upstart company, Peak Computers. Organized in 1990, Peak advertises itself as offering maintenance that rivals that of large companies, but at much lower prices. At first, Peak did not do very well. However, in 1991, Eric Francis left his job as customer service manager at MAI and joined Peak. He was rapidly followed by many MAI customers. Indeed, in the years since Francis's departure, Peak has acquired hundreds of customers, over 70% of which bought their equipment from MAI.

MAI suspects that Peak owes its recent success to more than just Eric Francis' business acumen. Rather, it believes that Francis is using MAI-generated information. That is, in MAI's view, the only one in a really good position to diagnose malfunctions in a computer system is its designer. Therefore, the only way that Peak can charge less than MAI and still earn a profit is by utilizing MAI diagnostic equipment—the material that is loaded on the computer at shipment. MAI believes this usage is actionable: the software is not sold, it is only licensed, and Peak is not a licensee.

MAI further claims that the two most difficult aspects of the service business lie in finding customers and accurately pricing the service contracts sold to them. The latter problem is due to the fact that different customers have different needs and vary in their ability to use computers and programs without messing them up. Since profit margins are low, improperly priced service contracts can spell disaster. MAI suspects that

Peak is so successful because when Francis left MAI, he took with him MAI's Customer Database, which lists the names and addresses of all MAI customers and describes each customer's business, computation needs, and repair record. Because MAI has always known the value of the Database, it has long required all employees with access to it to sign confidentiality agreements.

As the computer market becomes saturated, the servicing portion of MAI's business has become more important to its profitability. It has asked us to seek an injunction that will shut Peak down. California has adopted the Uniform Trade Secrets Act, Cal. Civ. Code §§ 3426–3426.10 (West Supp. 1993). Please advise on which aspects of Peak's operations are, indeed, actionable and on the relief you believe MAI can reasonably expect to receive.

3. MATERIALS FOR SOLUTION OF PRINCIPAL PROBLEM

A. STATUTORY MATERIAL:

Uniform Trade Secrets Act (found in the Statutory Supplement), & § 301 of the Copyright Act

B: CASES:

Dionne v. Southeast Foam Converting & Packaging, Inc.

Supreme Court of Virginia, 1990.
240 Va. 297, 397 S.E.2d 110.

■ POFF, SENIOR JUSTICE.

Robert Dionne, while employed by a corrugated box manufacturer, had developed several new products for use in packaging commodities shipped in commerce. In 1983, Robert created and incorporated Sefco as a family company producing foam products for that purpose. In the company's parking lot one day, he found a board of expanded polystyrene (EPS) which had been crushed beneath the wheels of a truck. Upon examination of the board, brittle in its original form, Robert discovered that the compressed material had become resilient, pliable, and shock-absorbing. Recognizing the potential demand for such a material for packing inside cartons in which furniture and other commodities are transported, he and members of his family began conducting experiments on means and methods of compressing EPS for use in the "inner packaging industry."

Encouraged by what he learned, Robert prepared and forwarded to a patent attorney a description of the process, the product, and its function. A search of the patent records revealed that patents had been issued for 17 foam products made of EPS compressed in different ways for different uses. One of the patents, that for an egg carton, had expired in 1980.

Relying upon the attorney's opinion that Sefco's product did not satisfy the novelty requirement of the patent law, the Dionne family began to focus upon new techniques in the manufacturing process. Two of Robert's sons, Pierre, who had become a full-time Sefco salesman in 1984, and Paul, engaged Mike Harris, a machine shop operator, to build a number of machines designed to facilitate the process and improve the quality of the end product. The brothers required Harris to sign a "non-disclosure" agreement in which he covenanted not to reveal any information about the machines, the manufacturing process, or the product. Employing the new Harris machines and larger hydraulic presses acquired from another source, Sefco made its first sale of compressed EPS to furniture manufacturers in September 1985. The product was sold under the trade name "Durofoam" or "Dur-o-foam."

Robert became terminally ill in 1987, and his wife, Pauline, and their three sons, Paul, Pierre, and Jacques, assumed control and operation of the family business. Robert died in May 1987, and Paul and Pierre renewed their efforts, begun earlier that year, to investigate the possibility of further refinements in the manufacturing process. With the use of a new press designed to create uniform products in mass quantities, they conducted experiments to determine the effects of different levels of pressure applied to blocks of EPS for different periods of time.

Based upon the results of these experiments, Sefco applied for a patent in June 1987. The application identified the product as "Durafoam" and the inventor as Robert Dionne. In a letter she addressed to the patent attorney, Pauline Dionne, who had acquired title to Sefco at Robert's death, asked the attorney "to include Pierre and Paul as co-inventors" because, she wrote, "they discovered a new and improved process of treating EPS for resiliency and enhanced cushioning qualities."

The research conducted by the family prompted an application for another patent. As explained by Paul, "at about the time we were developing Durafoam we were developing the angle packaging material." This product, he said, was "a paper backing material laminated to the Durafoam" and cut into shapes needed to "wrap around corners or . . . edges of tables, dressers, and nightstands." In January 1988, Pierre applied (in his own name as inventor) for a design patent on this product.

Thereafter, a bitter family quarrel developed. In efforts to restore harmony, the parties agreed that Pierre would assign 90% of his interest in the patent pending on the angle-packaging product to Sefco; that Pauline would give each of the three brothers a 10% share of Sefco; and that all Sefco owners would sign a "Confidential Information Agreement" similar to those Sefco consistently had required all its employees, suppliers, customers, contractors, and other plant visitors to execute. In pertinent part, the agreement Pierre signed provided that "[i]n consideration of being employed by SEFCO [the subscriber] shall not during, or at any time after the termination of my employment with the Company, use for myself or others, or disclose or divulge to others any trade secrets, confidential information, or any other data of the Company in violation of this agreement." Consummation of these agreements failed to resolve the family dispute, and Pierre's employment was terminated in June 1988.

Witnesses representing several of Sefco's suppliers and customers testified that Pierre had advised them that he planned to commence a new business manufacturing a foam material for use in the inner packaging industry. The new product, he explained, would be named "Flexfoam", and, while it would be similar in quality to Durafoam, it would be manufactured in a "more cost effective" way.

All these witnesses agreed that Durafoam is a product unique in its market area. Even the witness called by Pierre testified, on cross examination, that he knew of no company other than Sefco that had produced a marketable product with the functional qualities of Durafoam.

When the Dionne family learned of Pierre's plans, Sefco filed its bill of complaint [in a court of equity]. In a letter opinion, the chancellor held that "the manufacture of Durafoam is a trade secret" within the definition of the Uniform Trade Secrets Act, Code § 59.1–336 through–343, and that Pierre's conduct constituted a misappropriation within the meaning of the Act.[a] Applying Code § 59.1–337(A) which provides that "[a]ctual or threatened misappropriation may be enjoined", the chancellor entered the injunction Pierre challenges on appeal.

Pierre contends that this two-fold holding is twice flawed. First, pointing to the issuance and expiration of the egg-carton patent as an example, he argues that what is involved is merely an "adaptation of previously known technology to a new product line in a different market" and this, he says, is not a trade secret. That term is defined in the Act, adopted by the General Assembly by Acts 1986, c. 210, in the following language:

> "Trade secret" means information, including but not limited to, a formula, pattern, compilation, program, device, method, technique, or process, that:
>
> (1) Derives independent economic value, actual or potential, from not being generally known to, and not being readily ascertainable by proper means by, other persons who can obtain economic value from its disclosure or use, and
>
> (2) Is the subject of efforts that are reasonable under the circumstances to maintain its secrecy.

Pierre's first contention misapprehends the nature of a trade secret. The crucial characteristic of a trade secret is secrecy rather than novelty. See generally, Developments in the Law—Competitive Torts, 77 Harv. L.Rev. 888, 949–50 (1964). The secrecy need not be absolute; the owner of a trade secret may, without losing protection, disclose it to a licensee, an employee, or a stranger, if the disclosure is made in confidence, express or implied. Kewanee Oil Co. v. Bicron Corp., 416 U.S. 470, 475, 94 S.Ct. 1879, 1883, 40 L.Ed.2d 315 (1974). Although the subject of a trade secret may be

[handwritten in margin: validity argument]

---

[a] The chancellor also ruled that the confidentiality agreement Pierre signed was legally enforceable and that Pierre had breached that agreement. In the view we take of the issues, we need not consider Pierre's attack on those rulings.

novel in the sense that it is something generally unknown in the trade or business, "[n]ovelty, in the patent law sense, is not required for a trade secret." Id. at 476, 94 S.Ct. at 1883. Indeed, a trade secret "may be a device or process which is clearly anticipated in the prior art or one which is merely a mechanical improvement that a good mechanic can make." Restatement of Torts § 757 comment b (1939).

Summarizing the evidence, the chancellor made a series of factual findings keyed to the several elements of the statutory definition quoted above. Specifically, he found that "the plaintiff has used reasonable security measures designed to maintain the confidentiality of Durafoam"; that "Durafoam has a value and it is generally unknown in the sales area of the plaintiff"; that "[t]he plaintiff has an investment of time, money and effort expended in research and the development of equipment and/or machinery to produce Durafoam"; that "the plaintiff has a competitive advantage in manufacturing and selling Durafoam"; and that "Durafoam is a unique product in said sales area, producing over 80% of the Plaintiff's business."

We hold that the evidence fully supports these findings and that they completely satisfy the statutory definition of the term trade secret. Consequently, we reject Pierre's first contention.

In his second argument, Pierre insists that he cannot be found guilty of misappropriating something which he "personally developed or substantially contributed to developing while employed at SEFCO." We must reject this argument as well.

ownership argument

Pierre relies upon the court's opinion in Structural Dyn. Res. Corp. v. Engineering Mech. R. Corp., 401 F.Supp. 1102 (E.D.Mich.1975). There, the court was asked to decide, among other things, whether employees who had appropriated to their own use trade secrets claimed by their former employer were guilty of an actionable breach of trust. In the course of its opinion, the court weighed competing societal interests. As the court reasoned, the public has an interest in motivating innovation and creativity by placing qualified limits on disclosure of trade secrets, and the public has an interest in preserving the job mobility of workers who have acquired knowledge and skills useful in producing improved consumer products at lower cost. In a common-law analysis, the court struck the balance in favor of the employees on the ground that they personally had created the subjects of the trade secrets.

Pierre's reliance upon this opinion is wholly misplaced. Absent a statute, the weighing process conducted there is a proper judicial function. However, "it is the responsibility of the legislature, not the judiciary, to formulate public policy, to strike the appropriate balance between competing interests, and to devise standards for implementation." Wood v. Board of Supervisors of Halifax Cty., 236 Va. 104, 115, 372 S.E.2d 611, 618 (1988).

By adopting the Uniform Trade Secrets Act, the General Assembly has struck the public-policy balance to be applied by courts in this Commonwealth. In determining whether Pierre is guilty of misappropriation of trade secrets, we look to the words the lawmakers used. Insofar as pertinent here, the act provides: Misappropriation means:

. . . . .

2. Disclosure or use of a trade secret of another without express or implied consent by a person who

. . . . .

b. At the time of disclosure or use, knew or had reason to know that his knowledge of the trade secret was

. . . . .

(2) Acquired under circumstances giving rise to a duty to maintain its secrecy or limit its use....

Code § 59.1–336(2)(b)(2).

Upon consideration of the testimony and other evidence before him, the chancellor had every reason to conclude, as he did, that the Durafoam process was Sefco's trade secret and that Pierre "knew or had reason to know that his knowledge of the trade secret was ... [a]cquired under circumstances giving rise to a duty to maintain its secrecy or limit its use." No member of the Dionne family ever revealed the details of the Durafoam process to anyone except the patent attorney. Unauthorized persons were excluded from the plant. All employees, suppliers, customers, and contractors were required to sign agreements to treat any information they may have acquired as confidential. Each member of the Dionne family, Pierre included, signed such a paper. And it was Pierre himself who prepared and filed an application on behalf of Sefco to convert the trade secret into a patent and then urged Sefco to dispatch "cease and desist" letters to all potential competitors. We agree with the chancellor's conclusions.

Code § 59.1–337(A) provides:

Actual or threatened misappropriation may be enjoined. Upon application to the court, an injunction shall be terminated when the trade secret has ceased to exist, but the injunction may be continued for an additional reasonable period of time in order to eliminate commercial advantage that otherwise would be derived from the misappropriation.

Referring to this section of the act, Sefco acknowledges on brief that, when the Durafoam process ceases to be a trade secret, "[Pierre] may petition the Court to modify its earlier order and limit the injunction to only such time as would be a reasonable period of time to eliminate the commercial advantage that has been gained as a result of his misappropriation." For such purposes, the decree entered against Pierre expressly provides that the injunction shall continue "until the further order of this Court."

The Gillette Company v. Williams

United States District Court for the District of Connecticut, 1973.
360 F.Supp. 1171.

■ ZAMPANO, DISTRICT JUDGE.

[Peter Williams was hired by Gillette–England in 1961, having trained as a physicist and worked as a scientist at Imperial Chemical Industries for

13 years. He was hired as group leader in a lab devoted to research in the "wet shave" field (i.e. involving safety razors). Before he began to work, he signed a non-disclosure agreement standard for all Gillette–England employees who are on the monthly payroll. It enjoined him, both during and after his employ, from disclosing or using confidential and secret information. After a few months, he was transferred to a new job that put him in more intimate contact with important confidential wet shave data. At that time, he was required to sign a Special Agreement that provided, in pertinent part, that:

> 3. [Williams] hereby covenants with [Gillette–England] and as separate covenants with [The Gillette Corporation, U.S].:
>
> (a) that for two years following termination of his employment with [Gillette–England] he will not without the consent in writing of [Gillette–England] be employed by or act as officer of or advisor to any firm or Company engaged in the manufacture of safety razors or blades therefor in the United States of America or for sale therein.

In return, Gillette agreed to pay Williams one-half his final Gillette salary for the duration of the two-year period if during that time he wished to accept employment proscribed by the agreement to which Gillette objected.

Williams continued to rise within Gillette and to be exposed to increasingly important data. In 1972, however, he left for a position with Gillette's chief competitor, the Warner–Lambert Company, Schick Safety Razor Division ("Schick"). Within a week, Gillette began sending him letters and notices. One indicated that his employment was terminated, a second reminded him of the covenants he had signed, and the remainder were formal objections to his employment at Schick. When Williams failed to resign, this suit for damages and injunctive relief was filed].

1.   Reasonableness of the Covenant

The Court recognizes that the post-employment restrictive covenant is a contract in restraint of trade and, as such, is the subject of special judicial scrutiny. It seems clear that the plaintiff has established the reasonableness of the post-employment restrictive covenant. The highly competitive, specialized and secret nature of Gillette's wet shave business justifies its extraction of such agreements from certain employees to protect its legitimate business interests.

By his own admissions, Williams had access to and acquired knowledge of many trade secrets concerning the wet shave business during certain years of his employment. At the time the parties entered into the contract containing the restrictive covenant, it was reasonable to assume that a key employee, as Williams was, might be familiar with valuable confidential information if he subsequently left Gillette's employment to work for a competitor. Recognizing that it would be virtually impossible to avoid or detect his divulging such information to a competitor, Gillette understandably required Williams to sign the agreement as a condition of employment in order to protect its competitive position in the market.

Williams received an added consideration for signing the restrictive covenant; the two-year limitations period was more than reasonable considering the nature of Gillette's business; the territorial scope of the provision was necessary to protect Gillette's international market position; and there was no financial oppression in the event Williams had to accept a position outside the wet shave field at a lesser salary.

2. Access to and Possession of Confidential Information

The most strongly contested issue between the parties concerns Williams' access to or possession of Gillette's confidential information during the period 1968 to 1972. In lengthy, comprehensive briefs, each party, with remarkable ingenuity, excerpts language from the leading English and American cases to support their respective positions. Fine lines are drawn between "access to" and "possession of" confidential information by Williams at the time he entered Schick's employ.

The primary concern of the Court, however, is the context in which each of the cited cases arose. A careful review of the leading authorities reveals that there is a distinction between actions seeking enforcement of an employee's agreement not to compete, such as the one pending before this Court, and a tort claim for a trade secret misappropriation. It must also be emphasized that the specific contract terms in this case were designed to protect the plaintiff from a former employee's using or divulging "any matter concerning the confidential affairs or secrets of [Gillette–England or the plaintiff] or any confidential information relating thereto...." and furthermore, from a former employee within the United States working "directly or indirectly ... in research or development work on or the manufacture of safety razors or blades."

On the present state of the record, the scales balancing the factual presentation of evidence tip slightly in favor of the plaintiff; the defendant certainly may have the opportunity to reverse the balance or bring them into equilibrium.

Accordingly, the defendant's motion to dismiss the plaintiff's application for a preliminary injunction is denied.

Kewanee Oil Co. v. Bicron Corp.

Supreme Court of the United States, 1974.
416 U.S. 470, 94 S.Ct. 1879, 40 L.Ed.2d 315.

■ MR. CHIEF JUSTICE BURGER delivered the opinion of the Court.

We granted certiorari to resolve a question on which there is a conflict in the courts of appeals: whether state trade secret protection is preempted by operation of the federal patent law.

I

Harshaw Chemical Co., an unincorporated division of petitioner, is a leading manufacturer of a type of synthetic crystal which is useful in the detection of ionizing radiation. In 1949 Harshaw commenced research into the growth of this type crystal and was able to produce one less than two inches in diameter. By 1966, as the result of expenditures in excess of $1 million, Harshaw was able to grow a 17–inch crystal, something no one else had done previously. Harshaw had developed many processes, procedures, and manufacturing techniques in the purification of raw materials and the growth and encapsulation of the crystals which enabled it to accomplish this feat. Some of these processes Harshaw considers to be trade secrets.

The individual respondents former employees of Harshaw who formed or later joined respondent Bicron. While at Harshaw the individual respondents executed, as a condition of employment, at least one agreement each, requiring them not to disclose confidential information or trade secrets obtained as employees of Harshaw. Bicron was formed in August 1969 to compete with Harshaw in the production of the crystals, and by April 1970, had grown a 17–inch crystal.

Petitioner brought this diversity action in United States District Court for the Northern District of Ohio seeking injunctive relief and damages for the misappropriation of trade secrets. The District Court, applying Ohio trade secret law, granted a permanent injunction against the disclosure or use by respondents of 20 of the 40 claimed trade secrets until such time as the trade secrets had been released to the public, had otherwise generally become available to the public, or had been obtained by respondents from sources having the legal right to convey the information. [The Sixth Circuit reversed, finding Ohio's trade secret law to be in conflict with the patent laws of the United States].

II

Ohio has adopted the widely relied-upon definition of a trade secret found at Restatement of Torts § 757, comment b (1939). According to the Restatement,

> (a) trade secret may consist of any formula, pattern, device or compilation of information which is used in one's business, and which gives him an opportunity to obtain an advantage over competitors who do not know or use it. It may be a formula for a chemical compound, a process of manufacturing, treating or preserving materials, a pattern for a machine or other device, or a list of customers.

The subject of a trade secret must be secret, and must not be of public knowledge or of a general knowledge in the trade or business. This necessary element of secrecy is not lost, however, if the holder of the trade secret reveals the trade secret to another "in confidence, and under an implied obligation not to use or disclose it." Cincinnati Bell Foundry Co. v. Dodds, 10 Ohio Dec.Reprint 154, 156, 19 Weekly Law Bull. 84 (Super.Ct.1887).

The protection accorded the trade secret holder is against the disclosure or unauthorized use of the trade secret by those to whom the secret has been confided under the express or implied restriction of nondisclosure or nonuse. The law also protects the holder of a trade secret against disclosure or use when the knowledge is gained, not by the owner's volition, but by some "improper means," Restatement of Torts § 757(a), which may include theft, wiretapping, or even aerial reconnaissance. A trade secret law, however, does not offer protection against discovery by fair and honest means, such as by independent invention, accidental disclosure, or by so-called reverse engineering, that is by starting with the known product and working backward to divine the process which aided in its development or manufacture.

III

The first issue we deal with is whether the States are forbidden to act at all in the area of protection of the kinds of intellectual property which may make up the subject matter of trade secrets.

Article I, § 8, cl. 8, of the Constitution grants to the Congress the power

> (t)o promote the Progress of Science and useful Arts, by securing for limited Times to Authors and Inventors the exclusive Right to their respective Writings and Discoveries . . .

In the 1972 Term, in Goldstein v. California, 412 U.S. 546, 93 S.Ct. 2303, 37 L.Ed.2d 163 (1973), we held that the cl. 8 grant of power to Congress was not exclusive and that, at least in the case of writings, the States were not prohibited from encouraging and protecting the efforts of those within their borders by appropriate legislation. The States could, therefore, protect against the unauthorized rerecording for sale of performances fixed on records or tapes, even though those performances qualified as "writings" in the constitutional sense and Congress was empowered to legislate regarding such performances and could pre-empt the area if it chose to do so. This determination was premised on the great diversity of interests in our Nation—the essentially non-uniform character of the appreciation of intellectual achievements in the various States. Evidence for this came from patents granted by the States in the 18th century. 412 U.S., at 557, 93 S.Ct., at 2310.

Just as the States may exercise regulatory power over writings so may the States regulate with respect to discoveries. States may hold diverse viewpoints in protecting intellectual property to invention as they do in protecting the intellectual property relating to the subject matter of copyright. The only limitation on the States is that in regulating the area of patents and copyrights they do not conflict with the operation of the laws in this area passed by Congress, and it is to that more difficult question we now turn.

IV

The patent law does not explicitly endorse or forbid the operation of trade secret law. However, as we have noted, if the scheme of protection developed by Ohio respecting trade secrets "clashes with the objectives of the federal patent laws," Sears, Roebuck & Co. v. Stiffel Co., 376 U.S. 225, 231, 84 S.Ct. 784, 789, 11 L.Ed.2d 661 (1964), then the state law must fall. To determine whether the Ohio law "clashes" with the federal law it is helpful to examine the objectives of both the patent and trade secret laws.

The stated objective of the Constitution in granting the power to Congress to legislate in the area of intellectual property is to "promote the Progress of Science and useful Arts." The patent laws promote this progress by offering a right of exclusion for a limited period as an incentive to inventors to risk the often enormous costs in terms of time, research, and development. The productive effort thereby fostered will have a positive effect on society through the introduction of new products and processes of manufacture into the economy, and the emanations by way of increased employment and better lives for our citizens. In return for the right of exclusion—this "reward for inventions," Universal Oil Products Co. v. Globe Oil & Refining Co., 322 U.S. 471, 484, 64 S.Ct. 1110, 1116, 88 L.Ed. 1399 (1944)—the patent laws impose upon the inventor a requirement of disclosure. To insure adequate and full disclosure so that upon the expiration of the 17–year period "the knowledge of the invention enures to the people, who are thus enabled without restriction to practice it and profit by its use," United States v. Dubilier Condenser Corp., 289 U.S. 178, 187, 53 S.Ct. 554, 77 L.Ed. 1114 (1933), the patent laws require that the patent application shall include a full and clear description of the invention and "of the manner and process of making and using it" so that any person skilled in the art may make and use the invention. 35 U.S.C. § 112. When a patent is granted and the information contained in it is circulated to the general public and those especially skilled in the trade, such additions to the general store of knowledge are of such importance to the public weal that the Federal Government is willing to pay the high price of 17 years of exclusive use for its disclosure, which disclosure, it is assumed, will stimulate ideas and the eventual development of further significant advances in the art. The Court has also articulated another policy of the patent law: that which is in the public domain cannot be removed therefrom by action of the States.

The maintenance of standards of commercial ethics and the encouragement of invention are the broadly stated policies behind trade secret law. "The necessity of good faith and honest, fair dealing, is the very life and spirit of the commercial world." National Tube Co. v. Eastern Tube Co., 3 Ohio Cir.Cr.R., N.S. at 462.

In Wexler v. Greenberg, 399 Pa. 569, 578–579, 160 A.2d 430, 434–435 (1960), the Pennsylvania Supreme Court noted the importance of trade secret protection to the subsidization of research and development and to increased economic efficiency within large companies through the dispersion of responsibilities for creative developments.

Having now in mind the objectives of both the patent and trade secret law, we turn to an examination of the interaction of these systems of protection of intellectual property—one established by the Congress and the other by a State—to determine whether and under what circumstances the latter might constitute "too great an encroachment on the federal patent system to be tolerated." Sears, Roebuck & Co. v. Stiffel Co., 376 U.S., at 232, 84 S.Ct., at 789.

As we noted earlier, trade secret law protects items which would not be proper subjects for consideration for patent protection under 35 U.S.C. § 101. As in the case of the recordings in Goldstein v. California, Congress, with respect to nonpatentable subject matter, "has drawn no balance; rather, it has left the area unattended, and no reason exists why the State should not be free to act." Goldstein v. California, supra, 412 U.S., at 570, 93 S.Ct. at 2316 (footnote omitted).

Since no patent is available for a discovery, however useful, novel, and nonobvious, unless it falls within one of the express categories of patentable subject matter of 35 U.S.C. § 101, the holder of such a discovery would have no reason to apply for a patent whether trade secret protection existed or not. Abolition of trade secret protection would, therefore, not result in increased disclosure to the public of discoveries in the area of nonpatentable subject matter. Also, it is hard to see how the public would be benefited by disclosure of customer lists or advertising campaigns; in fact, keeping such items secret encourages businesses to initiate new and individualized plans of operation, and constructive competition results. This, in turn, leads to a greater variety of business methods than would otherwise be the case if privately developed marketing and other data were passed illicitly among firms involved in the same enterprise.

The question remains whether those items which are proper subjects for consideration for a patent may also have available the alternative protection accorded by trade secret law. Certainly the patent policy of encouraging invention is not disturbed by the existence of another form of incentive to invention. In this respect the two systems are not and never would be in conflict. Similarly, the policy that matter once in the public domain must remain in the public domain is not incompatible with the existence of trade secret protection. By definition a trade secret has not been placed in the public domain.

The more difficult objective of the patent law to reconcile with trade secret law is that of disclosure, the quid pro quo of the right to exclude. We are helped in this stage of the analysis by Judge Henry Friendly's opinion in Painton & Co. v. Bourns, Inc., 442 F.2d 216 (C.A.2 1971). There the Court of Appeals thought it useful, in determining whether inventors will refrain because of the existence of trade secret law from applying for patents, thereby depriving the public from learning of the invention, to distinguish between three categories of trade secrets:

> (1) the trade secret believed by its owner to constitute a validly patentable invention; (2) the trade secret known to its owner not to be so patentable; and (3) the trade secret whose valid patentability is considered dubious.

Id., at 224. Trade secret protection in each of these categories would run against breaches of confidence—the employee and licensee situations—and theft and other forms of industrial espionage.

As to the trade secret known not to meet the standards of patentability, very little in the way of disclosure would be accomplished by abolishing trade secret protection. With trade secrets of nonpatentable subject matter, the patent alternative would not reasonably be available to the inventor. "There can be no public interest in stimulating developers of such (unpatentable) knowhow to flood an overburdened Patent Office with applications (for) what they do not consider patentable." Ibid. The mere filing of applications doomed to be turned down by the Patent Office will bring forth no new public knowledge or enlightenment, since under federal statute and regulation patent applications and abandoned patent applications are held by the Patent Office in confidence and are not open to public inspection. 35 U.S.C. § 122; 37 CFR § 1.14(b).

Even as the extension of trade secret protection to patentable subject matter that the owner knows will not meet the standards of patentability will not conflict with the patent policy of disclosure, it will have a decidedly beneficial effect on society. Trade secret law will encourage invention in areas where patent law does not reach, and will prompt the independent innovator to proceed with the discovery and exploitation of his invention. Competition is fostered and the public is not deprived of the use of valuable, if not quite patentable, invention.

Even if trade secret protection against the faithless employee were abolished, inventive and exploitive effort in the area of patentable subject matter that did not meet the standards of patentability would continue, although at a reduced level. Alternatively with the effort that remained, however, would come an increase in the amount of self-help that innovative companies would employ. Knowledge would be widely dispersed among the employees of those still active in research. Security precautions necessarily would be increased, and salaries and fringe benefits of those few officers or employees who had to know the whole of the secret invention would be fixed in an amount thought sufficient to assure their loyalty. Smaller companies would be placed at a distinct economic disadvantage, since the costs of this kind of self-help could be great, and the cost to the public of the use of this invention would be increased. The innovative entrepreneur with limited resources would tend to confine his research efforts to himself and those few he felt he could trust without the ultimate assurance of legal protection against breaches of confidence. As a result, organized scientific and technological research could become fragmented, and society, as a whole, would suffer.

Another problem that would arise if state trade secret protection were precluded is in the area of licensing others to exploit secret processes. The holder of a trade secret would not likely share his secret with a manufacturer who cannot be placed under binding legal obligation to pay a license fee or to protect the secret. The result would be to hoard rather than disseminate knowledge. Instead, then, of licensing others to use his invention and making the most efficient use of existing manufacturing and marketing structures within the industry, the trade secret holder would tend either to limit his utilization of the invention, thereby depriving the public of the maximum benefit of its use, or engage in the time-consuming and economically wasteful enterprise of constructing duplicative manufacturing and marketing mechanisms for the exploitation of the invention. The detrimental misallocation of resources and economic waste that would thus take place if trade secret protection were abolished with respect to employees or licensees cannot be justified by reference to any policy that the federal patent law seeks to advance.

Nothing in the patent law requires that States refrain from action to prevent industrial espionage. In addition to the increased costs for protection from burglary, wire-tapping, bribery, and the other means used to misappropriate trade secrets, there is the inevitable cost to the basic decency of society when one firm steals from another. A most fundamental human right, that of privacy, is threatened when industrial espionage is condoned or is made profitable; the state interest in denying profit to such illegal ventures is unchallengeable.

The next category of patentable subject matter to deal with is the invention whose holder has a legitimate doubt as to its patentability. The risk of eventual patent invalidity by the courts and the costs associated with that risk may well impel some with a good-faith doubt as to patentability not to take the trouble to seek to obtain and defend patent protection for their discoveries, regardless of the existence of trade secret protection. Trade secret protection would assist those inventors in the more efficient exploitation of their discoveries and not conflict with the patent law. In most cases of genuine doubt as to patent validity the potential rewards of patent protection are so far superior to those accruing to holders of trade secrets, that the holders of such inventions will seek patent protection, ignoring the trade secret route. For those inventors "on the line" as to whether to seek patent protection, the abolition of trade secret protection might encourage some to apply for a patent who otherwise would not have done so. Some of the nonpatentable discoveries will be thrown out by the Patent Office, but in the meantime society will have been deprived of use of those discoveries through trade secret-protected licensing. Some of the [nonpatentable discoveries] may not be thrown out. This Court has noted the difference between the standards used by the Patent Office and the courts to determine patentability. Graham v. John Deere Co., 383 U.S. 1, 18, 86 S.Ct. 684, 694, 15 L.Ed.2d 545 (1966). In Lear, Inc. v. Adkins, 395 U.S. 653, 89 S.Ct. 1902, 23 L.Ed.2d 610 (1969), the Court thought that an invalid patent was so serious a threat to the free use of ideas already in the public domain that the Court permitted licensees of the patent holder to challenge the validity of the patent. Better had the invalid patent never issued. More of those patents would likely issue if trade secret law were abolished. Eliminating trade secret law for the doubtfully patentable invention is thus likely to have deleterious effects on society and patent policy which we cannot say are balanced out by the speculative gain which might result from the encouragement of some inventors with doubtfully patentable inventions which deserve patent protection to come forward and apply for patents. There is no conflict, then, between trade secret law and the patent law policy of disclosure, at least insofar as the first two categories of patentable subject matter are concerned.

The final category of patentable subject matter to deal with is the clearly patentable invention, i.e., that invention which the owner believes to meet the standards of patentability. It is here that the federal interest in disclosure is at its peak; these inventions, novel, useful and nonobvious, are "the things which are worth to the public the embarrassment of an exclusive patent." Graham v. John Deere Co., supra, at 9, 86 S.Ct., at 689 (quoting Thomas Jefferson). The interest of the public is that the bargain of 17 years of exclusive use in return for disclosure be accepted. If a State, through a system of protection, were to cause a substantial risk that holders of patentable inventions would not seek patents, but rather would rely on the state protection, we would be compelled to hold that such a system could not constitutionally continue to exist. In the case of trade secret law no reasonable risk of deterrence from patent application by those who can reasonably expect to be granted patents exists.

Trade secret law provides far weaker protection in many respects than the patent law. While trade secret law does not forbid the discovery of the trade secret by fair and honest means, e.g., independent creation or reverse engineering, patent law operates "against the world," forbidding any use of the invention for whatever purpose for a significant length of time. The holder of a trade secret also takes a substantial risk that the secret will be passed on to his competitors, by theft or by breach of a confidential relationship, in a manner not easily susceptible of discovery or proof. Where patent law acts as a barrier, trade secret law functions relatively as a sieve. The possibility that an inventor who believes his invention meets the standards of patentability will sit back, rely on trade secret law, and after one year of use forfeit any right to patent protection, 35 U.S.C. § 102(b), is remote indeed.

Nor does society face much risk that scientific or technological progress will be impeded by the rare inventor with a patentable invention who chooses trade secret protection over patent protection. The ripeness-of-time concept of invention, developed from the study of the many independent multiple discoveries in history, predicts that if a particular individual had not made a particular discovery others would have, and in probably a relatively short period of time. If something is to be discovered at all very likely it will be discovered by more than one person. Singletons and Multiples in Science (1961), in R. Merton, The Sociology of Science 343 (1973). Even were an inventor to keep his discovery completely to himself, something that neither the patent nor trade secret laws forbid, there is a high probability that it will be soon independently developed. If the invention, though still a trade secret, is put into public use, the competition is alerted to the existence of the inventor's solution to the problem and may be encouraged to make an extra effort to independently find the solution thus known to be possible. The inventor faces pressures not only from private industry, but from the skilled scientists who work in our universities and our other great publicly supported centers of learning and research.

Trade secret law and patent law have co-existed in this country for over one hundred years. Each has its particular role to play, and the operation of one does not take away from the need for the other. Trade secret law encourages the development and exploitation of those items of lesser or different invention than might be accorded protection under the patent laws, but which items still have an important part to play in the technological and scientific advancement of the Nation. Trade secret law promotes the sharing of knowledge, and the efficient operation of industry; it permits the individual inventor to reap the rewards of his labor by contracting with a company large enough to develop and exploit it. Congress, by its silence over these many years, has seen the wisdom of allowing the States to enforce trade secret protection. Until Congress takes affirmative action to the contrary, States should be free to grant protection to trade secrets.

■ MR. JUSTICE MARSHALL, concurring in the result.

Unlike the Court, I do not believe that the possibility that an inventor with a patentable invention will rely on state trade secret law rather than apply for a patent is "remote indeed." State trade secret law provides substantial protection to the inventor who intends to use or sell the invention himself rather than license it to others, protection which in its unlimited duration is clearly superior to the 17–year monopoly afforded by the patent laws. I have no doubt that the existence of trade secret protection provides in some instances a substantial disincentive to entrance into the patent system, and thus deprives society of the benefits of public disclosure of the invention which it is the policy of the patent laws to encourage. This case may well be such an instance.

But my view of sound policy in this area does not dispose of this case. Rather, the question presented in this case is whether Congress, in enacting the patent laws, intended merely to offer inventors a limited monopoly in exchange for disclosure of their invention, or instead to exert pressure on inventors to enter into this exchange by withdrawing any alternative possibility of legal protection for their inventions. I am persuaded that the former is the case.

■ MR. JUSTICE DOUGLAS, with whom MR. JUSTICE BRENNAN concurs, dissenting [omitted].

Bonito Boats, Inc. v. Thunder Craft Boats, Inc.

Supreme Court of the United States, 1989.
489 U.S. 141, 109 S.Ct. 971, 103 L.Ed.2d 118.

■ JUSTICE O'CONNOR delivered the opinion of the Court.

We must decide today what limits the operation of the federal patent system places on the States' ability to offer substantial protection to utilitarian and design ideas which the patent laws leave otherwise unprotected.

I

In September 1976, petitioner Bonito Boats, Inc. (Bonito), a Florida corporation, developed a hull design for a fiberglass recreational boat which it marketed under the trade name Bonito Boat Model 5VBR. App. 5. Designing the boat hull required substantial effort on the part of Bonito. A set of engineering drawings was prepared, from which a hardwood model was created. The hardwood model was then sprayed with fiberglass to create a mold, which then served to produce the finished fiberglass boats for sale. The 5VBR was placed on the market sometime in September 1976. There is no indication in the record that a patent application was ever filed for protection of the utilitarian or design aspects of the hull, or for the process by which the hull was manufactured. The 5VBR was favorably received by the boating public, and "a broad interstate market" developed for its sale. Ibid.

In May 1983, after the Bonito 5VBR had been available to the public for over six years, the Florida Legislature enacted Fla.Stat. § 559.94 (1987). The statute makes "[i]t ... unlawful for any person to use the direct molding process to duplicate for the purpose of sale any manufactured vessel hull or component part of a vessel made by another without the written permission of that other person." § 559.94(2). The statute also makes it unlawful for a person to "knowingly sell a vessel hull or component part of a vessel duplicated in violation of subsection (2)." § 559.94(3). Damages, injunctive relief, and attorney's fees are made available to "[a]ny person who suffers injury or damage as the result of a violation" of the statute. § 559.94(4). The statute was made applicable to vessel hulls or component parts duplicated through the use of direct molding after July 1, 1983. § 559.94(5).

On December 21, 1984, Bonito filed this action in the Circuit Court of Orange County, Florida. [The trial court dismissed the complaint as based on a statute preempted by federal patent law. The Florida Supreme Court affirmed].

II

Article I, § 8, cl. 8, of the Constitution gives Congress the power "[t]o promote the Progress of Science and useful Arts, by securing for limited Times to Authors and Inventors the exclusive Right to their respective Writings and Discoveries." The Patent Clause itself reflects a balance between the need to encourage innovation and the avoidance of monopolies which stifle competition without any concomitant advance in the "Progress of Science and useful Arts." As we have noted in the past, the Clause contains both a grant of power and certain limitations upon the exercise of that power. Congress may not create patent monopolies of unlimited duration, nor may it "authorize the issuance of patents whose effects are to remove existent knowledge from the public domain, or to restrict free access to materials already available." Graham v. John Deere Co. of Kansas City, 383 U.S. 1, 6, 86 S.Ct. 684, 688, 15 L.Ed.2d 545 (1966).

From their inception, the federal patent laws have embodied a careful balance between the need to promote innovation and the recognition that imitation and refinement through imitation are both necessary to invention itself and the very lifeblood of a competitive economy.

[In the next part, the Court reviews the principal requirements for obtaining a patent].

The applicant whose invention satisfies the requirements of novelty, nonobviousness, and utility, and who is willing to reveal to the public the substance of his discovery and "the best mode . . . of carrying out his invention," 35 U.S.C. § 112, is granted "the right to exclude others from making, using, or selling the invention throughout the United States," for a period of 17 years. 35 U.S.C. § 154. The federal patent system thus embodies a carefully crafted bargain for encouraging the creation and disclosure of new, useful, and nonobvious advances in technology and design in return for the exclusive right to practice the invention for a period of years.

The attractiveness of such a bargain, and its effectiveness in inducing creative effort and disclosure of the results of that effort, depend almost entirely on a backdrop of free competition in the exploitation of unpatented designs and innovations. The novelty and nonobviousness requirements of patentability embody a congressional understanding, implicit in the Patent Clause itself, that free exploitation of ideas will be the rule, to which the protection of a federal patent is the exception. Moreover, the ultimate goal of the patent system is to bring new designs and technologies into the public domain through disclosure. State law protection for techniques and designs whose disclosure has already been induced by market rewards may conflict with the very purpose of the patent laws by decreasing the range of ideas available as the building blocks of further innovation. The offer of federal protection from competitive exploitation of intellectual property would be rendered meaningless in a world where substantially similar state law protections were readily available. To a limited extent, the federal patent laws must determine not only what is protected, but also what is free for all to use.

Thus our past decisions have made clear that state regulation of intellectual property must yield to the extent that it clashes with the balance struck by Congress in our patent laws. The tension between the desire to freely exploit the full potential of our inventive resources and the need to create an incentive to deploy those resources is constant. Where it is clear how the patent laws strike that balance in a particular circumstance, that is not a judgment the States may second-guess. We have long held that after the expiration of a federal patent, the subject matter of the patent passes to the free use of the public as a matter of federal law.

In our decisions in Sears, Roebuck & Co. v. Stiffel Co., 376 U.S. 225, 84 S.Ct. 784, 11 L.Ed.2d 661 (1964), and Compco Corp. v. Day–Brite Lighting,

Inc., 376 U.S. 234, 84 S.Ct. 779, 11 L.Ed.2d 669 (1964), we found that publicly known design and utilitarian ideas which were unprotected by patent occupied much the same position as the subject matter of an expired patent. The Sears case involved a pole lamp originally designed by the plaintiff Stiffel, who had secured both design and mechanical patents on the lamp. Sears purchased unauthorized copies of the lamps, and was able to sell them at a retail price practically equivalent to the wholesale price of the original manufacturer. Stiffel brought an action against Sears in Federal District Court, alleging infringement of the two federal patents and unfair competition under Illinois law. The District Court found that Stiffel's patents were invalid due to anticipation in the prior art, but nonetheless enjoined Sears from further sales of the duplicate lamps based on a finding of consumer confusion under the Illinois law of unfair competition. The Court of Appeals affirmed, coming to the conclusion that the Illinois law of unfair competition prohibited product simulation even in the absence of evidence that the defendant took some further action to induce confusion as to source.

This Court reversed, finding that the unlimited protection against copying which the Illinois law accorded an unpatentable item whose design had been fully disclosed through public sales conflicted with the federal policy embodied in the patent laws. The Court stated: "In the present case the 'pole lamp' sold by Stiffel has been held not to be entitled to the protection of either a mechanical or a design patent. An unpatentable article, like an article on which the patent has expired, is in the public domain and may be made and sold by whoever chooses to do so. What Sears did was to copy Stiffel's design and sell lamps almost identical to those sold by Stiffel. This it had every right to do under the federal patent laws." 376 U.S., at 231, 84 S.Ct., at 789. [A similar conclusion was reached in Compco].

The pre-emptive sweep of our decisions in Sears and Compco has been the subject of heated scholarly and judicial debate. See, e.g., Symposium, Product Simulation: A Right or a Wrong?, 64 Colum.L.Rev. 1178 (1964). Read at their highest level of generality, the two decisions could be taken to stand for the proposition that the States are completely disabled from offering any form of protection to articles or processes which fall within the broad scope of patentable subject matter. Since the potentially patentable includes "anything under the sun that is made by man," Diamond v. Chakrabarty, 447 U.S. 303, 309, 100 S.Ct. 2204, 2207, 65 L.Ed.2d 144 (1980)(citation omitted), the broadest reading of Sears would prohibit the States from regulating the deceptive simulation of trade dress or the tortious appropriation of private information.

That the extrapolation of such a broad pre-emptive principle from Sears is inappropriate is clear from the balance struck in Sears itself. The Sears Court made it plain that the States "may protect businesses in the use of their trademarks, labels, or distinctive dress in the packaging of goods so as to prevent others, by imitating such markings, from misleading purchasers as to the source of the goods." Sears, supra, 376 U.S., at 232, 84

S.Ct., at 789 (footnote omitted). Trade dress is, of course, potentially the subject matter of design patents. Yet our decision in Sears clearly indicates that the States may place limited regulations on the circumstances in which such designs are used in order to prevent consumer confusion as to source. Thus, while Sears speaks in absolutist terms, its conclusion that the States may place some conditions on the use of trade dress indicates an implicit recognition that all state regulation of potentially patentable but unpatented subject matter is not ipso facto pre-empted by the federal patent laws.

What was implicit in our decision in Sears, we have made explicit in our subsequent decisions concerning the scope of federal pre-emption of state regulation of the subject matter of patent. Thus, in Kewanee Oil Co. v. Bicron Corp., 416 U.S. 470, 94 S.Ct. 1879, 40 L.Ed.2d 315 (1974), we held that state protection of trade secrets did not operate to frustrate the achievement of the congressional objectives served by the patent laws. Despite the fact that state law protection was available for ideas which clearly fell within the subject matter of patent, the Court concluded that the nature and degree of state protection did not conflict with the federal policies of encouragement of patentable invention and the prompt disclosure of such innovations.

Several factors were critical to this conclusion. First, because the public awareness of a trade secret is by definition limited, the Court noted that "the policy that matter once in the public domain must remain in the public domain is not incompatible with the existence of trade secret protection." Id., at 484, 94 S.Ct., at 1887. Second, the Kewanee Court emphasized that "[t]rade secret law provides far weaker protection in many respects than the patent law." Id., at 489–490, 94 S.Ct., at 1889–1890. This point was central to the Court's conclusion that trade secret protection did not conflict with either the encouragement or disclosure policies of the federal patent law. The public at large remained free to discover and exploit the trade secret through reverse engineering of products in the public domain or by independent creation. Thus, the possibility that trade secret protection would divert inventors from the creative effort necessary to satisfy the rigorous demands of patent protection was remote indeed. Finally, certain aspects of trade secret law operated to protect non-economic interests outside the sphere of congressional concern in the patent laws. As the Court noted, "[A] most fundamental human right, that of privacy, is threatened when industrial espionage is condoned or is made profitable." Id., at 487, 94 S.Ct., at 1889 (footnote omitted). There was no indication that Congress had considered this interest in the balance struck by the patent laws, or that state protection for it would interfere with the policies behind the patent system.

At the heart of Sears and Compco is the conclusion that the efficient operation of the federal patent system depends upon substantially free trade in publicly known, unpatented design and utilitarian conceptions. In Sears, the state law offered "the equivalent of a patent monopoly," 376 U.S., at 233, 84 S.Ct., at 789, in the functional aspects of a product which had been placed in public commerce absent the protection of a valid patent. While, as noted above, our decisions since Sears have taken a decidedly less rigid view of the scope of federal pre-emption under the patent laws, e.g., Kewanee, supra, 416 U.S., at 479–480, 94 S.Ct., at 1885–1886, we believe that the Sears Court correctly concluded that the States may not offer patent-like protection to intellectual creations which would otherwise remain unprotected as a matter of federal law. Both the novelty and the nonobviousness requirements of federal patent law are grounded in the notion that concepts within the public grasp, or those so obvious that they readily could be, are the tools of creation available to all. They provide the baseline of free competition upon which the patent system's incentive to creative effort depends. A state law that substantially interferes with the enjoyment of an unpatented utilitarian or design conception which has been freely disclosed by its author to the public at large impermissibly contravenes the ultimate goal of public disclosure and use which is the centerpiece of federal patent policy. Moreover, through the creation of patent-like rights, the States could essentially redirect inventive efforts away from the careful criteria of patentability developed by Congress over the last 200 years. We understand this to be the reasoning at the core of our decisions in Sears and Compco, and we reaffirm that reasoning today.

III

We believe that the Florida statute at issue in this case so substantially impedes the public use of the otherwise unprotected design and utilitarian ideas embodied in unpatented boat hulls as to run afoul of the teaching of our decisions in Sears and Compco. It is readily apparent that the Florida statute does not operate to prohibit "unfair competition" in the usual sense that the term is understood. The law of unfair competition has its roots in the common-law tort of deceit: its general concern is with protecting consumers from confusion as to source. While that concern may result in the creation of "quasi-property rights" in communicative symbols, the focus is on the protection of consumers, not the protection of producers as an incentive to product innovation. Judge Hand captured the distinction well in Crescent Tool Co. v. Kilborn & Bishop Co., 247 F. 299, 301 (C.A.2 1917), where he wrote: "[T]he plaintiff has the right not to lose his customers through false representations that those are his wares which in fact are not, but he may not monopolize any design or pattern, however trifling. The defendant, on the other hand, may copy plaintiff's goods slavishly down to the minutest detail: but he may not represent himself as the plaintiff in their sale."

In contrast to the operation of unfair competition law, the Florida statute is aimed directly at preventing the exploitation of the design and utilitarian conceptions embodied in the product itself. The sparse legislative history surrounding its enactment indicates that it was intended to create an inducement for the improvement of boat hull designs. See Tr. of Meeting of Transportation Committee, Florida House of Representatives, May 3, 1983, reprinted at App. 22 ("[T]here is no inducement for [a] quality boat manufacturer to improve these designs and secondly, if he does, it is immediately copied. This would prevent that and allow him recourse in circuit court"). To accomplish this goal, the Florida statute endows the original boat hull manufacturer with rights against the world, similar in scope and operation to the rights accorded a federal patentee. Like the patentee, the beneficiary of the Florida statute may prevent a competitor from "making" the product in what is evidently the most efficient manner available and from "selling" the product when it is produced in that fashion. Compare 35 U.S.C. § 154. The Florida scheme offers this protection for an unlimited number of years to all boat hulls and their component parts, without regard to their ornamental or technological merit. Protection is available for subject matter for which patent protection has been denied or has expired, as well as for designs which have been freely revealed to the consuming public by their creators.

That the Florida statute does not remove all means of reproduction and sale does not eliminate the conflict with the federal scheme. In essence, the Florida law prohibits the entire public from engaging in a form of reverse engineering of a product in the public domain. This is clearly one of the rights vested in the federal patent holder, but has never been a part of state protection under the law of unfair competition or trade secrets. The duplication of boat hulls and their component parts may be an essential part of innovation in the field of hydrodynamic design. Variations as to size and combination of various elements may lead to significant advances in the field. Reverse engineering of chemical and mechanical articles in the public domain often leads to significant advances in technology. If Florida may prohibit this particular method of study and recomposition of an unpatented article, we fail to see the principle that would prohibit a State from banning the use of chromatography in the reconstitution of unpatented chemical compounds, or the use of robotics in the duplication of machinery in the public domain.

Moreover, as we noted in Kewanee, the competitive reality of reverse engineering may act as a spur to the inventor, creating an incentive to develop inventions that meet the rigorous requirements of patentability. The Florida statute substantially reduces this competitive incentive, thus eroding the general rule of free competition upon which the attractiveness of the federal patent bargain depends. The protections of state trade secret law are most effective at the developmental stage, before a product has been marketed and the threat of reverse engineering becomes real. During this period, patentability will often be an uncertain prospect, and to a certain extent, the protection offered by trade secret law may "dovetail" with the incentives created by the federal patent monopoly. In contrast, under the Florida scheme, the would-be inventor is aware from the outset of his efforts that rights against the public are available regardless of his ability to satisfy the rigorous standards of patentability. Indeed, it appears that even the most mundane and obvious changes in the design of a boat hull will trigger the protections of the statute. See Fla.Stat. § 559.94(2)(1987)(protecting "any manufactured vessel hull or component part"). Given the substantial protection offered by the Florida scheme, we cannot dismiss as hypothetical the possibility that it will become a significant competitor to the federal patent laws, offering investors similar protection without the quid pro quo of substantial creative effort required by the federal statute. The prospect of all 50 States establishing similar protections for preferred industries without the rigorous requirements of patentability prescribed by Congress could pose a substantial threat to the patent system's ability to accomplish its mission of promoting progress in the useful arts.

[Finally], one of the fundamental purposes behind the Patent and Copyright Clauses of the Constitution was to promote national uniformity in the realm of intellectual property. Absent such a federal rule, each State could afford patent-like protection to particularly favored home industries, effectively insulating them from competition from outside the State.

Congress has considered extending various forms of limited protection to industrial design either through the copyright laws or by relaxing the restrictions on the availability of design patents. Congress explicitly refused to take this step in the copyright laws, see 17 U.S.C. § 101; H.R.Rep. No. 94–1476, p. 55 (1976), U.S.Code Cong. & Admin.News 1976, pp. 5659, 5668, and despite sustained criticism for a number of years, it has declined to alter the patent protections presently available for industrial design. It is for Congress to determine if the present system of design and utility patents is ineffectual in promoting the useful arts in the context of industrial design. By offering patent-like protection for ideas deemed un-protected under the present federal scheme, the Florida statute conflicts with the "strong federal policy favoring free competition in ideas which do not merit patent protection." Lear, Inc., 395 U.S., at 656, 89 S.Ct., at 1903. We therefore agree with the majority of the Florida Supreme Court that the Florida statute is preempted by the Supremacy Clause, and the judgment of that court is hereby affirmed.

NOTES

1. *Trade Secrets:* a. *"Tippees".* What if, in the *Gillette* case, Williams had revealed secret information to Schick and Schick had used it: could Gillette sue Schick for appropriating its trade secret? Schick, after all, is not bound by the agreement that Williams' signed. It is, instead, the recipient of a tip. Federal securities laws sometimes bar those who possess confidential information about firms from using that information to buy and sell stock. Those who receive such "inside information"—"tippees"—are sometimes also barred on the theory that their use of the information inflicts the same injury as the "tipper" creates.[3] Should the recipients of confidential know-how be treated the same as their tippers? See the Uniform Trade Secrets Act § 1(2)(ii)(B)(III)(yes); Restatement of Unfair Competition § 41 (yes, if the tippee knew of the relationship between the owner of the secret and the tipper).

[3] 15 U.S.C.§ 78j; 17 C.F.R. § 240.10b–5

b. *Use.* A trade secrecy violation requires more than simply a taking by improper means: it also requires use. There are two aspects to this requirement. First, there is a question about *how* the information is being used. Omnitech International Inc. v. The Clorox Co.[4] is an example. In that case, Clorox became interested in the insecticide business. It entered into negotiations with Omnitech, which marketed a product called "Dr. X." The two companies signed an agreement whereby Clorox received permission to use secret information to conduct various laboratory and marketing tests on Dr. X. Based, in part, on information generated in those tests, Clorox decided to buy rights to a different product. Omnitech claimed that using its secret information to make this decision amounted to a trade secret violation. The court held it did not:

> [T]o sustain a trade secrets action under the "use" prong of [the Louisiana Trade Secrets Act], a plaintiff must necessarily demonstrate that the defendant received some sort of unfair trade advantage.... Omnitech has wholly failed to demonstrate that Clorox gained any competitive edge in the insecticide market as a result of any trade secret of Omnitech.

The second prong of the use requirement concerns *what* information is being used. Just as a court in a patent infringement action must determine whether the accused product comes within the scope of the patent claims, a trade secrets court must determine whether the defendant's activity is within the scope of the plaintiff's secret information. As in patent and copyright, complete duplication is not required; obvious variations are also considered actionable.[5]

c. *Remedies.* State courts have encountered significant difficulties in formulating remedies for breach of state-based protections. Because states often conceptualize these laws as property rights, injunctive relief has been the most prevalent remedy. But how long should the injunction endure?

In Shellmar Products Co. v. Allen–Qualley Co.,[6] the court permanently enjoined the defendant from using the information it had improperly acquired. This remedy creates the maximum level of deterrence, but to many observers, it seems too long. After all, once others discover the secret, enjoining a single market participant does not help the innovator. It does, however, harm the public in that it removes an important competitor from the marketplace. Accordingly, many courts agree with a position similar to the one taken in *Dionne,* where the injunction was made to last only until the secret became public knowledge. The advantage here is that once the innovator is forced to compete, the defendant can join the market. The downside is that if the defendant is the major competitor, enjoining him may prevent the secret from ever being discovered. Thus, the public is once

---

[4] 11 F.3d 1316, 29 U.S.P.Q.2d (BNA) 1665 (5th Cir.1994).

[5] See, e.g., Forest Laboratories, Inc. v. Formulations, Inc., 299 F.Supp. 202 (E.D. Wis. 1969), rev'd in part, 452 F.2d 621 (7th Cir.1971).

[6] 87 F.2d 104 (7th Cir.1934).

again the loser. Lamb–Weston, Inc. v. McCain Foods, Ltd.[7] represents a middle ground. In that case, the court attempted to calculate the time it would have taken to acquire the information by proper means—by reverse engineering the plaintiff's product. It then enjoined the defendant for that period of time. This rule, which is endorsed by § 44 of the Restatement of Unfair Competition Law, has the advantage of restoring the innovator to the position she would have been in had the violation not occurred, while—at the same time—freeing the defendant to compete.[8] The main problem with this remedy is that detailed knowledge of a field is required in order to estimate how long it would take to properly acquire the secret. Litigating the question can therefore be protracted and the result may be unsatisfactory to all parties.

Would courts be better off awarding monetary damages rather than injunctive relief? If these damages are considered to be a form of compulsory royalty, the duration problem does not disappear, for the court must still decide how long defendant should be required to pay.[9] However, monetary relief could be thought of as compensating the plaintiff for bearing the full cost of development. If it were possible to calculate the plaintiff's costs (plus a reasonable profit) and require the defendant to share them, then the public would enjoy the benefits of competition, the innovator would enjoy a return on the investment in invention, and all market participants would compete on a level playing field.

2. *Hybrids:* a. *State hybrids. Bonito Boats* considered the validity of Florida's direct molding statute. This is one of the hybrid provisions that fills the gap between trade secrecy protection and "non-compete" agreements: it protects the innovators of products that can be easily reverse engineered against parties with whom they cannot contract.

Note that the Court held the law preempted on two grounds. First, it found that the federal intellectual property system requires that nonsecret information remain in the public domain. In that sense, the decision is similar to the preemption cases discussed in Assignment 14. However, this Court also gave a kind of Commerce Clause spin to the Copyright Clause. It interpreted the provision as promoting national uniformity, that is, as preventing states from insulating their local industries from out-of-state competition. Is this a valid interpretation of the Copyright Clause? Although the legislative history of the Commerce Clause evidences a concern with promoting interstate business, the history of the Copyright Clause does not. Rather, it appears that the Framers were mainly concerned that state-by-state intellectual property protection would be ineffectual.[10]

Interestingly, in an omitted portion of *Bonito Boats,* the Court considered (and rejected) the reasoning in a CAFC decision that upheld a similar

---

[7] 941 F.2d 970 (9th Cir.1991).

[8] See especially, Rest. 3d Unfair Competition Law § 44, Comment f.

[9] See Rest. 3d Unfair Competition Law § 45, Comment h.

[10] See Bruce W. Bugbee, Genesis of American Patent and Copyright Law 130 (Public Affairs Press, 1967).

direct molding statute from California.[11] That both statutes emanated from coastal states should not be surprising: the importance of the ship-building industry to both states led their legislators to appreciate the deficiencies in other intellectual property laws. Does *Bonito Boats,* then, overrule the copyright preemption cases that approve state legislative activity in areas of local concern, see, e.g., Goldstein v. California?[12]

b. *Federal hybrids.* Not all industries that demand special protection are of only local importance. For example, in 1984, the semiconductor chip industry persuaded Congress that it needed special protection on a national scale. Semiconductor chips (sometimes called "mask works") are purely functional products, and so their design does not qualify for copyright protection. And since most semiconductor innovations are too mundane to meet the nonobviousness test of § 103 of the Patent Act, patent protection is also unavailable. The Semiconductor Chip Act, 17 U.S.C. §§ 901–914, creates a 10–year exclusive reproduction, importation, and distribution right for original works that are not staples of the semiconductor industry. The statute contains several features that tailor it to the needs of this industry. One interesting example is § 906. Out of concern for the need to use one chip design as a building block for others, this provision exempts from infringement uses that are solely for the purpose of analysis. If the knowledge so obtained is used to design a chip that is original enough to merit its own protection, that chip will not be considered to infringe the design of the chip that was used for inspiration.

3. *Preemption: the bottom line.* What is the rule on federal preemption of state law? The two 1964 cases cited in *Bonito Boats,* Sears, Roebuck & Co. v. Stiffel Co.,[13] and Compco Corp. v. Day–Brite Lighting, Inc.,[14] often referred to jointly as "*Sears/Compco,*" had confined states to protecting consumers from confusion. Many observers regard this as too stingy to innovators. Innovators do suffer at the hands of competitors who dress their products up in a way that leads consumers to mistakenly purchase from the wrong vendor (indeed, this is the main thrust of trademark law). However, innovators are also harmed by free riders—those who copy the innovation at low cost and then compete the price down to the point where the innovator cannot recoup the costs of development. When, in 1974, the *Kewanee* Court recognized the free rider problem and approved trade secrecy law, the *Sears/Compco* approach was generally regarded as thoroughly overruled. Thus, *Bonito Boats'* favorable citation of these cases came as something of a surprise.

Does *Bonito Boats* distinguish *Kewanee* persuasively? *Bonito Boats* relies heavily on the notion that trade secrets do not remove knowledge from the public domain whereas the direct molding statute does. *Bonito Boats* does not, however, explain why innovators who cannot hide their

[11] Interpart Corp. v. Italia, 777 F.2d 678 (Fed.Cir.1985).

[12] 412 U.S. 546, 93 S.Ct. 2303, 37 L.Ed.2d 163 (1973), discussed in Assignment 14.

[13] 376 U.S. 225, 231, 84 S.Ct. 784, 789, 11 L.Ed.2d 661 (1964).

[14] 376 U.S. 234, 84 S.Ct. 779, 11 L.Ed.2d 669 (1964).

innovations from the public are in any less need of protection from free riders than those who can. Some have explained *Bonito Boats* as protecting the public's right to reverse engineer. However, Florida did not prevent the public from reverse engineering. Even under the direct molding statute, anyone could take measurements of desirable boat hulls and build new molds to those measurements. All the statute did was prevent one form of copying: duplicating a boat hull by a method similar to the one that dentists use to make an impression of teeth. That is, what Florida did was prevent inexpensive copying, not all copying. The Court derides this distinction, but isn't it precisely the *free* ride that Florida was trying to prevent? Didn't the direct molding statute strike exactly the right balance, giving the public access to the innovative ideas in a new hull without giving it the ability to undercut the innovator?

Was the Court's problem that the direct molding statute was enacted after the hull at issue was created, making it clear that no special incentives were needed to motivate its creation? Was it the perpetual nature of the protection that bothered the Court?

Finally, is *Bonito Boats* a constitutional or a statutory case? If it is the Constitution that bars protection of subpatentable inventions, is the Semiconductor Chip Act unconstitutional? Is the Orphan Drug Act discussed in Assignment 23 unconstitutional? Is Congress constitutionally disabled from enacting special legislation for the computer or biotechnology industry?

4. *Other limitations on state trade secrecy laws. Kewanee* and *Bonito Boats* discuss the problems with trade secrecy law that flow from a constitutional vision of what belongs in the public domain. However, there are other problems with maintaining secrets. For example, products containing secret ingredients can be harmful to the environment, to those who manufacture them, and to those who use them. These concerns have prompted the enactment of laws outside the copyright/patent sphere that limit the reach of state protective regimes. For instance, the Occupational Safety and Health Act,[15] requires manufacturers to reveal information about secret products in certain circumstances. Similarly, some states have enacted "right to know" legislation that compromises trade secrets in the interest of giving regulators the information they need to keep the environment and the workplace safe.[16]

Should these regulations be regarded as unconstitutional takings of property without just compensation? That issue was considered in Ruckelshaus v. Monsanto Co.,[17] which concerned the premarket clearance procedures of the Federal Insecticide, Fungicide, and Rodenticide Act (FIFRA).[18] These procedures require manufacturers to submit to the Environmental Protection Agency data supporting their claims of efficacy and environmental safety. The legislation authorizes the EPA to use the data submitted by

---

[15] 29 U.S.C. §§ 651–678

[16] See, e.g., O'Reilly, Driving a Soft Bargain: Unions, Toxic Materials, and Right to Know Legislation, 9 Harv. L. Rev. 307 (1985).

[17] 467 U.S. 986, 104 S.Ct. 2862, 81 L.Ed.2d 815 (1984).

[18] 7 U.S.C. §§ 136–136y.

one manufacturer in reviewing the applications of other manufacturers who seek to market the same product.[19] Noting that this data can cost millions of dollars to produce, Monsanto claimed that this authorization amounted to a taking. In a profoundly convoluted opinion, the Court held that Monsanto's reasonable expectations of confidentiality were completely determined by the particular statutory scheme in operation when it submitted the data. FIFRA had been changed several times; during periods when the statute failed to explicitly provide that data were submitted in confidence, use of data to review competitors' registrations did not require compensation. However, during periods when FIFRA did provide for confidentiality for trade secrets, the EPA could not reutilize these trade secrets without paying the submitter reasonable compensation.

As a policy matter, what should FIFRA provide? In terms of the competitive picture, are research data any different from other industrial information that is expensive to create and cheap to copy?

5. *Other limitations on covenants not to compete.* Virtually all states are concerned with the effects of covenants not to compete, especially when they are aimed at restraining ex-employees. Employment compensation is, after all, not only monetary: many employees (including graduating law students!) choose their jobs with an eye toward the quality of training they will receive. If they cannot use the skills thus acquired in other employment settings, this portion of their compensation has no value. Society also loses because employees who are restrained by these covenants cannot put their their skills to their most productive use.

Economists are, of course, quick to argue that the picture is not so bleak. As in *Gillette,* the employer must pay extra for the promise to forgo future employment, so the value of the wage "package" will be the same regardless of whether the employee is required to sign a noncompete agreement. Furthermore, if there is a better—and better paid—use for the employee's talent, all the employee need do is breach the covenant, take the other job, and pay the employer damages.

Despite the theoretical appeal of this analysis, significant concerns nonetheless remain. The employer and employee may not have equal bargaining power (especially in cases like *Gillette,* where the covenant is signed after the employee commits to the job). Furthermore, the employee may not fully understand the implications of the agreement. The terms of such agreements are therefore usually scrutinized for reasonableness before they are enforced. In some states, courts refuse to enforce covenants that impose conditions beyond what the employer reasonably needs to protect her investment in innovation.[20] Most states, though, will modify such agreements to bring the terms in line with what they regard as reasonable, and enforce only the revised version.[21] In addition, some states limit the

---

[19] See § 136a(c)(1)(F).

[20] See, e.g., McLeod v. Meyer, 237 Ark. 173, 372 S.W.2d 220 (1963).

[21] See, e.g., Solari Indus., Inc. v. Malady, 55 N.J. 571, 264 A.2d 53 (1970).

force of these contracts statutorily.[22]

6. *Employee rights.* Note that in all the principal cases, the assumption was that any innovation made by the employee belonged to the employer. This is because in each of these cases, the employee's duty was expressly to develop new products. In most such employment relationships, the employer's right to the employee's innovations is secured by contract. In the remainder, the employment contract is read to imply this right. Sometimes, however, an employee who was *not* hired specifically for research and development makes an invention at the place of employment and during working hours: to whom does this invention belong? In most states, the parties split the difference: the employee owns the rights to the invention, but the employer enjoys a "shop right," which is a nonexclusive license to practice the invention in his business. This arrangement is thought to compensate the employer for the use of his time and facilities, while giving the employee the benefits of her ingenuity.[23]

7. *The law of ideas.* Reconsider the facts of the *Dionne* case: what if, instead of setting up his own company to exploit his insight concerning compressed polystyrene, Robert had approached the company producing polystyrene with the idea of compressing it? If the company utilized his idea, could it be forced to compensate him for it? What would be the cause of action? Trade secrecy law would be unavailing. First, as *Clorox* indicates, competition may be a required element, and Robert is not in a position to compete. Moreover, once Robert revealed the idea to the company, it would no longer be a secret, and so there would be no "trade secret" to sell. Of course, he could have asked the company to agree to pay him before he revealed the secret—in which case he could have sued on the contract. But why would the company agree to pay for an idea sight unseen? After all, the idea could turn out to be terrible, or one it already was considering; it could be an idea that was already in the public domain, or already claimed by another. (Remember that in the actual case, there were patents on 17 different compressed foam products).

Should utilizing an undeveloped idea submitted by one who has not been specifically hired for the purpose be actionable? Great ideas sometimes do occur to people who are not positioned to exploit them. Creating a financial incentive to transmit these ideas to those who can use them is, therefore, in the public interest. However, large companies, particularly movie and television companies, receive so very many ideas, and so very many unoriginal ideas, they would be paralyzed if they were vulnerable to suit by every submitter.

Jurisdictions balance these problems by creating rights of action in favor of idea submitters in only extremely limited circumstances, usually only for the idea that is so novel, concrete, and valuable that it seems

---

[22] See, e.g., Cal. Bus. & Prof. Code § 16600 (1993).

[23] See, e.g., United States v. Dubilier Condenser Corp., 289 U.S. 178, 53 S.Ct. 554, 77 L.Ed. 1114 (1933).

unfair to ignore the submitter. In most cases, the law is based on implied contract—either implied-in-fact, from the circumstances of submission, or implied-in-law (quantum meruit), based on the unjust enrichment of the party exploiting the idea. Novelty and concreteness are the touchstones for this cause of action, but the custom of the industry, the track record of the submitter, and the circumstances surrounding the negotiations that led to the submission are all considered as well. For example, in Buchwald v. Paramount Pictures Corp.,[24] the writer Art Buchwald won compensation when Paramount filmed the movie "Coming to America" from a plot idea that he submitted. The idea was spelled out in Buchwald's treatment ("concrete"), it was a new ("novel") idea, and the submitter was someone whom Paramount should have known is usually paid for his writings. Moreover, once Paramount made the movie, the value of the idea plummeted, making it virtually useless to Buchwald.

8. *Federal preemption. Sears/Compco, Kewanee,* and *Bonito Boats* all dealt with the question whether state protection of inventions is inconsistent with federal protection. But there is another sort of preemption argument. It is that the federal regimes are preemptive of each other—that the same innovation cannot be protected by both patent and copyright law, or by both patent and trademark law.

Application of Yardley[25] considered the interaction of copyright and patent law. In that case, the Patent Office refused to grant a design patent on the Spiro Agnew wristwatch on the ground that the picture had been registered in the Copyright Office.[26] The PTO reasoned that the two statutes present creators with a choice. Once one regime is chosen, the creator is estopped from also utilizing the other regime.[27] The CCPA reversed. It saw in neither the Supreme Court's acknowledgment that the "election of protection doctrine" existed, nor in the existence of two separate protective regimes any "intent of Congress to hold that an author-inventor *must* elect between the two available modes of securing exclusive rights."[28] The Court went on to say: "If anything, the concurrent availability of both modes of securing exclusive rights aids in achieving the stated purpose of the constitutional provision."[29]

The germinal case on trademark/patent preemption is Singer Manufac-

---

[24] 13 U.S.P.Q.2d (BNA) 1497 (Cal. Super. 1990).

[25] 493 F.2d 1389 (C.C.P.A.1974).

[26] Spiro Agnew was a Vice President of the United States who distinguished himself in part by pleading nolo contendere to a criminal charge and resigning from office. The watchface was similar to the more famous Mickey Mouse watch, but showed Mr. Agnew dressed in shorts with the hands of the watch emanating from his belly button.

[27] This estoppel argument is, in fact, also made in connection with state preemption. An example is Macbeth–Evans Glass Co. v. General Electric Co., 246 Fed. 695 (6th Cir. 1917), which was discussed in Assignment 20. In that case, the court held that Macbeth's decision to practice his invention as a trade secret estopped him from later seeking a patent.

[28] *Yardley,* 493 F.2d at 1394, referring in part, to Mazer v. Stein, 347 U.S. 201, 74 S.Ct. 460, 98 L.Ed. 630 (1954).

[29] *Yardley* at 1396.

turing Co. v. June Manufacturing Co.[30] Singer controlled the patents on many aspects of the sewing machine. In the years immediately preceding the expiration of its most important patents, it tried to establish the name "Singer" and the shape of its machines as trademarks. However, when the patents expired and competitors entered the field, they nonetheless called their machines "Singer" and used similar shapes. Singer sued to enforce its marks and lost, the Supreme Court holding:

> "This coincidence between the expiration of the patents and the appearance of the word 'Singer' alone tends to create a strong implication that the company [acted] in order thereby to retain in the possession of the company the real fruits of the monopoly when the monopoly had passed away."[31]

In other words, the Singer Court thought that trademark protection for a formerly patented article would impermissibly extend the term of protection beyond the statutory term of the patent, thereby preventing the public from truly enjoying free access to the invention upon patent expiration.[32]

Recent lower court cases have, however, questioned the doctrine of trademark/patent preemption as well. For example, in Kohler Co. v. Moen Inc.,[33] Kohler opposed Moen's registration of a faucet design and faucet handle design as trademarks, claiming that trademark protection for configurations is in direct conflict with patent law as interpreted by *Bonito Boats*. The Seventh Circuit disagreed. It saw trademark law as protecting goodwill, not innovation. Since the state-preemption cases clearly left room for states to protect goodwill, Congress could certainly do so as well. To Kohler's concern that trademark protection would take functional features out of public use, the court's answer was that trademark law has its own functionality doctrine to prevent that from occurring. The court concluded by noting that several other circuits have reached the same conclusion.[34]

In dissent, Judge Cudahy argued that the thrust of the state preemption cases was that "product designs are dedicated to the public unless they are protected by a valid patent."[35] In his view, the doctrine of functionality has not gone far enough to prevent perpetual monopolies on product ideas, designs, and development. Which view is the more persuasive, the majority's or the dissent's?

BIBLIOGRAPHY

There are two standard treatises on trade secrecy: R. Milgrim, Milgrim on Trade Secrets (1989) and M. Jager, Trade Secrets Law (1988). See also

---

[30] 163 U.S. 169, 16 S.Ct. 1002, 41 L.Ed. 118 (1896).

[31] Id. at 181, 16 S.Ct. at 1006.

[32] See also Kellogg Co. v. National Biscuit Co., 305 U.S. 111, 59 S.Ct. 109, 83 L.Ed. 73 (1938)(trademark on the words "shredded wheat" was invalid following the expiration of the design patent on pillow-shaped cereal).

[33] 12 F.3d 632 (7th Cir.1993).

[34] The court cited Esercizio v. Roberts, 944 F.2d 1235 (6th Cir.1991), cert. denied, 505 U.S. 1219, 112 S.Ct. 3028, 120 L.Ed.2d 899 (1992); In re Teledyne Inds., Inc., 696 F.2d 968 (Fed.Cir.1982); Dallas Cowboys Cheerleaders, Inc. v. Pussycat Cinema, Ltd., 604 F.2d 200 (2d Cir.1979).

[35] Kohler, 12 F.3d at 646.

Karjala, Copyright and Misappropriation, 17 Dayton L.Rev. 885 (1992); Friedman, Landes, and Posner, Some Economics of Trade Secret Law, 5 J. Econ. Persp. 61 (1991); Stedman, Trade Secrets, 23 Ohio St. L.J. 4 (1962).

On covenants not to compete, see F. Gurry, Breach of Confidence (1989)(on law of the U.K.); Kitch, The Law and Economics of Rights in Valuable Information, 9 J. Leg. Stud. 683 (1980); Blake, Employee Agreements Not to Compete, 73 Harv. L. Rev. 625 (1960).

On hybrid legislation, see Reichman, Electronic Information Tools—The Outer Edge of World Intellectual Property Law, 24 I.I.C. 446 (1993); Rauch, The Realities of Our Times: The Semiconductor Chip Protection Act of 1984 and the Evolution of the Semiconductor Industry, 75 J.Pat. & Trademark Off. Soc'y 93 (1993); Reichman, Legal Hybrids Between the Patent and Copyright Paradigms, in Information Law Towards the 21st Century 325 (Willem F. Korthals Altes et al. eds., 1992); Heald, The Vices of Originality, 1991 S.Ct. Rev. 31; Reichman, Design Protection and the New Technologies: The United States Experience in a Transnational Perspective, 19 U. Balt.L.Rev. 6 (1989–90); Brown, Copyright–Like Protection for Designs, 19 Balt.L.Rev. 198 (1989–90); Samuelson, Modifying Copyrighted Software: Adjusting Copyright Doctrine to Accommodate Technology, 28 Jurimetrics 179 (1988); Menell, Tailoring Legal Protection for Computer Software, 39 Stan. L. Rev. 1329 (1987); Brown, Design Protection: An Overview, 34 U.C.L.A. L.Rev. 1341 (1987).

On protecting subpatentable and subcopyrightable works generally, see Ginsburg, No "Sweat"? Copyright and Other Protection of Works of Information After Feist v. Rural Telephone, 92 Colum. L. Rev. 338 (1992); Ginsburg, Creation and Commercial Value: Copyright Protection of Works of Information, 90 Colum.L.Rev. 1865 (1990); Gordon, An Inquiry into the Merits of Copyright: The Challenges of Consistency, Consent, and Encouragement Theory, 41 Stan. L. Rev. 1343 (1989); Dreyfuss, Information Products: A Challenge to Intellectual Property Theory, 20 J.Int'l L. & Pol. 897 (1988); Raskind, Reverse Engineering, Unfair Competition, and Fair Use, 70 Minn. L. Rev. 385 (1985); Kastenmeier & Remington, The Semiconductor Chip Act of 1984: A Swamp or Firm Ground, 70 Minn. L. Rev. 417 (1985).

On "right to know" legislation, see Lyndon, Secrecy and Innovation in Tort Law and Regulation, 23 N.Mex. L.Rev. 1 (1993); Gelfand, "Taking" Informational Property Through Discovery, 66 Wash.U.L.Q. 703 (1988); Carle, A Hazardous Mix: Discretion to Disclose and Incentives to Suppress Under OSHA's Hazardous Communication Standard, 97 Yale L. Rev. 581 (1988).

On preemption, see Dreyfuss, A Wiseguy's Approach to Information Products: Muscling Copyright and Patent Into a Unitary Theory of Intellectual Property, 1992 S.Ct. Rev. 195; Flynn, The Orphan Drug Act: An Unconstitutional Exercise of the Patent Power, 1992 Utah L. Rev. 389; Wiley, Bonito Boats: Uninformed but Mandatory Innovation Policy, 1989 S.Ct. Rev. 283; Goldstein, Kewanee Oil Co. v. Bicron Corp.: Notes on a Closing Circle, 1974 S.Ct.Rev. 92.

INDEX

References are to pages.

†